RENEWALS 458-4574

studies in jazz

Institute of Jazz Studies, Rutgers University
General Editors: *Dan Morgenstern & Edward Berger*

Brimming with vitality and jubilant over his band's universal recognition as the best in the land, Benny doffs his glasses uncharacteristically in this handsome 1937 portrait.   (Photo, Vitaphone, Inc.)

BENNY GOODMAN

Listen to His Legacy

by

D. RUSSELL CONNOR

Studies in Jazz, No. 6

THE SCARECROW PRESS, INC.

and the

INSTITUTE OF JAZZ STUDIES

Metuchen, N.J., & London   1988

Library of Congress Cataloging-in-Publication Data

Connor, D. Russell (Donald Russell)
  Benny Goodman : listen to his legacy / by D. Russell Connor.
    p.   cm. — (Studies in jazz ; no. 6)
  Includes indexes.
  ISBN 0-8108-2095-1
  1. Goodman, Benny, 1909-   —Discography. 2. Goodman, Benny,
1909-   . I. Title. II. Series.
ML156.7.G66C67   1988   87-32069
016.7899′12542—dc19

DEDICATION

With love and respect for my mother, Clara W. Schmidt. She may not have been fully in sympathy with my preoccupation with Jazz, but she has ever been supportive, tolerant and understanding, as mothers usually are.

CONTENTS

ACKNOWLEDGMENTS

Almost 13 years have elapsed since publication of ''BG—On The Record,'' generously described as, ''The most authoritative and comprehensive biography. discography ever written about a jazz musician.'' Since then major discoveries about Benny Goodman's works have been made, and he, of course, continued to record and perform. His fans throughout the world have inundated me with information and questions about his recordings and his appearances in person and via radio, television and film. It became clear that it was time to collate these data, time to publish a new testament to the supreme clarinetist in all of Jazz, and one of its most prolific practitioners.

As before I am indebted to Mr. Goodman for his cooperation and assistance. Old friends Ken Crawford, Frank Driggs, Joe Harvey, Warren Hicks, John Paul Jones, John McDonough, Virgil Thomas and Jerry Valburn once again shared their research with me. In addition, these enthusiasts have been helpful:

Bob Bierman, George Blau, Joe Boughton, Brian Boyd, Sid Bromley, Harold Callanan, Wendy Chamberlin, ''Doc'' Cheatham, Dave Chertok, Charles DeLimur, Don Eagle, Harold Ellingham, Jack Ellsworth, Ted Fagan, John Fell, Carl Friedner, Wally Fry, Eric Gee, John Gill, Dave Gloss, Dave Goldenberg, Gene Goodman, Morton Gould, Jean-Paul Guiter, Wally Heider, Rod Holcombe, Guy Houten, Cole Johnson, Ed Jones Sr., Harry Jones, Roy Kirkham, Mike Kirsling, Joe Knox, Don Koehnemann, Bo Lennartsson, Rainer Lotz, Peter Lowe, Jacques Lubin, Jim Maher, Peter Mallon, John Markham, Jerry Newhouse, Karl Pearson, Bill Piccone, Ed Polic, Mike Romano, Jim Ryan, Mort Savada, Bill Savory & Helen Ward, Mickey Sheen, Joe Showler, Sheila Stead, ''Slam'' Stewart, Mike Sutcliffe, Peter Venudor, Howard Waters, Bill Weicker, Henry Whiston, ''Bozy'' White and Art Zimmerman.

I am most appreciative of the efforts and advice put forward by Donna Connor, who acted as photographic consultant, and by Dave Custis, who assembled the several indexes.

Separate notice for their years-long contributions to my efforts is merited by Muriel Zuckerman, Loren Schoenberg and Lloyd Rauch, all formerly of Mr. Goodman's staff; Arend Buck of West Germany; Bill Harper of Canada; Phil Kidby of Great Britain; Kurt Mueller of Switzerland and Thailand; Anders Ohman of Sweden; Yasuo Segami of Japan; and Art Norton and Jack Towers of the United States.

The cooperation of Rca-France, Radio France and Radio Sweden, the National Broadcasting Company, Columbia Records, the Library of Congress, and R. J. Reynolds Industries, Inc., is noted with thanks.

My apologies to those whose names have been inadvertently omitted. My sincere gratitude is extended to all who have contributed to this work.

RUSS CONNOR
1986

EDITOR'S FOREWORD

The incredible mass of information contained in this remarkable volume could only have been assembled by one man—D. Russell Connor. Goodman's friend and confidant for over thirty years, Russ is one of the few to have penetrated the "inner circle." He brings to these pages not only the most meticulous factual research and documentation, but an insider's perspective on the complexities and contradictions that were Benny Goodman.

Unlike other volumes in this series, some of which germinated at the Institute of Jazz Studies, *Benny Goodman: Listen to His Legacy* has had a long and distinguished life of its own. It's progenitor, *BG—Off The Record,* was published in 1958 and became the model for a new and challenging genre of jazz literature: the bio-discography. In that portentous work, and its 1969 revision *BG—On The Record,* Russ (and collaborator Warren Hicks) introduced many discographical conventions that have since become standard practice. For example, the authors recognized the need for inclusion of airchecks as an essential component of a discography. The scope of this new work displays similar foresight. By detailing Goodman's participation in films, television programs, and other visually preserved performances, the author has laid the groundwork for the next generation of discographical documentation.

Casual fans and serious researchers alike will find this an indispensable source. The author has carefully chronicled the Goodman story from its beginning and has added a wealth of new material, both discographical and anecdotal. Comprehensive indexes facilitate location of specific titles and artists. Particularly fascinating are the insights into Goodman's final year, during which time he reassumed the role which catapulted him to fame—that of bandleader.

Unfortunately, the discography is now complete, in the sense that there can be no new performances (although there will undoubtedly be significant new discoveries). But thanks to the dedication of Russ Connor, the full acknowledgment of Benny Goodman's achievements has just begun.

EDWARD BERGER

INTRODUCTION

BENNY GOODMAN: A Personal Assessment

I was privileged to have enjoyed Benny Goodman's company and confidences for more than 30 years. Even longer, I listened to his broadcasts, watched him perform, collected his recordings. My reflections on half a century's fascination with the man and his music are these:

His was the most complex personality I ever encountered. He was wholly unpredictable: his reaction to a given set of circumstances in one instance often was the reverse of his response to like stimuli at another time. Not even his secretary Muriel Zuckerman, who was closer to Benny for more years than I, could anticipate him. Only after a puzzling event could we piece together assumptions to explain his behavior. Then would come realization that what he had done was perfectly logical, to his mind. Almost without exception, his actions were premeditated and purposive, rarely spontaneous.

He held his own counsel; seldom did he reveal his private thoughts, share the confidences that bind people together. He had legions of acquaintances, but few close friends. Although sometimes inexplicable enthusiasms for newcomers would admit them to his orbit briefly, he was suspicious of those who sought him out. Bitter experience had taught him that too many would abuse an association with him for personal advantage. The initiative had to be his; he would decide whether a relationship would be beneficial to him, if he believed you could be trusted. The relatively few who qualified on his terms were his confidantes for life.

For as long as I knew him, and even before, Benny lived with pain. Major surgery for unrelated physical impairments in 1940, 1964 and 1983 let him function but did little to alleviate the suffering they caused. Only his first operation was public knowledge; details of the latter two were kept secret, were unknown even to some of his relatives. He endured his afflictions stoically, for the most part refused to speak of them. He would never admit publicly that the pain they caused him was responsible for some of his outre' behavior. But I knew him to break off a conversation rudely, to leave a dinner table abruptly, to quit a stage apparently without reason, to cancel engagements in the middle of a tour, simply so he could be alone to cope with the ailment then troubling him.

Not all of this extraordinary conduct can be attributed to pain. The title, "King Of Swing," meant something more to Benny than it does to the press and the public. Deference accorded him over decades by his colleagues and fans had its effect: he was the king of his world, and he came to expect the indulgences granted to royalty. His demeanor was regal, which led even some of his sidemen to describe him as "tall." He was not, his height was about 5'10", no more; it was his commanding presence that projected the illusion. He was proud, even vain, fully conscious of his accomplishments and his talent. He was a King, he would live and die a King, and he would be treated as one.

He was a maze of contradictions. His absentmindedness, his forgetfulness, are legendary. He seemed unable to remember tune titles; when we discussed this song or that, he would hum it for me, never name it. Again and again, his introductions on stage of members of his groups were embarrassing; he would mispronounce names, fail to think of others. But if you could capture his attention truly—that was the distinction—he would detail minutely all the incidents of a day long in the past. Tales of his pennypinching are notorious, and many of them are accurate. Gene Krupa told me, at the end of the 1953 concert tour that Benny abandoned, "You know what Ben gave me, after I took over the whole thing for him? A watch, a good one, but hell I've got a hundred of 'em." Not nearly so well documented is Benny's liberality with individuals in need; I knew him to give another drummer, who had suffered a stroke, a check for $1,000, "just to help out." Because Benny was such a private person, similar kind acts and his many free performances that raised hundreds of thousands of dollars for charitable organizations and other institutions, have not had the publicity they deserve.

Dismissive of the state of his own health, Benny was alert to the well-being of those around him; I knew his concern to extend to the ailing wife of an employee, to send her to his personal physician, and to pay his fees. Deft and nimble with his clarinet, he was ham-handed with mechanical and electronic gear; he brutalized audio components, VCR's, telephone answering devices. Very well read and possessed of an extensive vocabulary, he frequently resorted to the shockingly scatological argot of the jazz musician.

He could not tell a joke successfully, but he had an incisive sense of humor. I once asked him why working so hard had not led him, like so many of his fellows, to liquor and drugs. He thought for a moment—he always thought before he spoke—then said, "I guess it's because I'm Jewish." Conservative in his own affairs, he was a political liberal, and he campaigned for the Democrat Party.

There were constants, of course. He had enormous energy, which permitted him pursuits beyond the sphere of music. He appreciated painting and sculpture, frequented galleries and museums, collected worthwhile examples of each. He enjoyed both spectator and participant sports; he was a fair golfer, a good fisherman. He read eclectically on a wide range of topics, retained what he had read. He knew good food and its preparation, kept an excellent cellar; dinner at his home might include a rack of lamb he had personally selected, accompanied by a 1964 Petrus bordeaux. He dressed well, if modestly; I once inquired if a suede trench coat I admired had come from a bespoke tailor on Savile Row; he laughed, "Nah, I got it at Barney's." In his youth, certainly, he sought feminine companionship, to understate the case. But he was always discreet; only once did I know him to speak of a romantic episode in the past. Was "Ann Graham," credited as vocalist on his 1934 recording of "It Happens To The Best Of Friends," a pseudonym, as some claimed? "No, no, Ann was with us for a while at Billy Rose's. She was a lovely gal, good looking, had great legs and could sing. I tried to date her, but got nowhere. She liked a guy in the band who played trombone, Jack Lacey."

But the main focus of his life was music; all else was subordinate to it. Beyond innate talent, he brought to it constant study, ceaseless practice, the discipline of a martinet for himself as well as for those who worked for him. He sought from it nothing less than perfection. And in my view he succeeded; he was the first among equals of the great jazz instrumentalists, and his 1937–1938 orchestra has no rival. I shall remember Benny Goodman the man, but history will judge him on his accomplishments.

Listen to his legacy.

*

BENJAMIN DAVID GOODMAN—the world over, "BG"—was born May 30, 1909, in Chicago, Illinois. Had he been given prior choice of the time and place of his birth, he could not have chosen more advantageously than Fate herself decided. For as Benny neared puberty, Jazz came to Chicago, up river from New Orleans. Thus he has lived all his life with the music he loves.

Benny began his formal musical education at age 10 in the Kehelah Jacob Synagogue, at the instance of his father. Two years later, still with the encouragement of his family, Benny furthered his study of music at Hull House; his first clarinet instructor was Johnny Sylvester, who taught both reed and brass instruments. Concurrently, Benny studied privately with classicist Franz Schoepp, who also tutored Jimmy Noone and Buster Bailey. (One of Benny's prized possessions is his first clarinet exercise book. Now bound in leather and prominently displayed on an antique music stand in his New York apartment, it has maestro Schoepp's and Benny's penciled notes in its margins.) Thirty years after his introduction to the clarinet, Benny continued his studies with the English master, Reginald Kell, in 1949. Adhering to the regimen of a lifetime, Benny probed and practiced daily.

Benny's informal musical education was even more formidable. With Chicago then the Mecca of the jazz giants, Benny availed himself of every opportunity to listen to, enjoy and absorb the work and technique of Louis Armstrong, King Oliver, Freddie Keppard, Johnny and Baby Dodds, Lil Hardin, Bessie Smith, Jimmy Noone, Bix Beiderbecke, and the New Orleans Rhythm Kings, with Leon Rapollo, Paul Mares and George Brunies. Benny worked in and around the Windy City with Jimmy McPartland, Frank Teschmacher, Bud Freeman and Dave Tough of the "Austin High Gang" (although it is questionable if any but Freeman ever actually attended Austin High), and with Muggsy Spanier and others.

Benny's first professional performance was his imitation of Ted Lewis in Chicago's Central Park Theater in 1921. In 1922 and 1923 he worked intermittently with Charles "Murph" Podalsky's various combinations. In the summer of 1923 he worked with Bix Beiderbecke for the first time, in the now legendary riverboat excursion of August 8. In fall of 1923 Benny began his first lengthy commitment at Guyon's Paradise, where Jules Herbevaux conducted. Later that year and into 1924 Benny was hired by Arnold Johnson for an engagement at the Green Mill Gardens. In fall of 1924 and into 1925, he played regularly for Art Kassel, who had a long stay in the Midway Gardens. His next regular job was with Ben Pollack.

It is at this point that our narrative begins. Those interested in a fuller account of Benny's early years are referred to his and Irving Kolodin's "The Kingdom Of Swing," published originally by Stackpole Sons, New York, in 1939, and republished by Frederick Ungar Publishing Company, New York, in 1961.

*

This work has two principal objectives. The first is to detail all commercial recordings made by Benny Goodman, both issued and unissued; and to list all extant non-commercial recordings made by him, of whatever origin. The second is to give a running account of Benny Goodman's whereabouts, his engagements, his associations and his accomplishments throughout his working life, to add form and substance to his remarkable career.

The author is confident that more than ninety-five per cent of all of Goodman's commercial recordings are catalogued herein. (In the context of this work, a "commercial recording" is a sound recording that has most, if not all, of these attributes: One that is professionally made, usually in a studio specifically equipped for the purpose, by an organization whose avowed intent was either to record, manufacture, sell or otherwise distribute sound recordings in permanent form to given segments of the public; and one made with the foreknowledge and consent of the performer, and for which the performer was compensated in some manner.) It is acknowledged that some commercial recordings by Benny Goodman between the years 1926 and 1934 may have been omitted because they have escaped the notice of the author and his hundreds of correspondents. It is likely that during those same years Goodman made some commercial recordings wherein his playing cannot be audibly identified, and for which no written evidence has been discovered that would link him to such recordings. It seems probable that some few original-issue Armed Forces Radio Service transcriptions will come to light in future. And it is certain that commercial recording companies, including Benny Goodman's Park Recording Company, have in their possession unreleased Goodman material whose full details are not displayed in this work. Although these caveats may seem substantial, the author believes that in toto they aggregate to not more than five per cent of everything Benny Goodman ever recorded commercially.

Privately-recorded Goodman performances elude assessment as to their number. Termed "air checks" generally, such (usually) non-authorized recordings of Goodman performances made by professionals and amateurs alike from radio broadcasts, film, telecasts and concert appearances, seem without limit. For example: "BG—On The Record," which pioneered the listing of air checks, contained all of Goodman's non-commercial recordings known to the author in 1969. Included in this work are 1,600-plus additional Goodman renditions for the period covered by "BG—On The Record," now found to be extant. Disclosure of this "new/old" material was spurred by the original publication; undoubtedly, this new volume will bring forth more.

To insure the authenticity of commercial recordings and air checks in this text, every effort was made to acquire, or audit, original releases, base transcriptions, tapes and acetates, and written records. Film, in original form, or via videocassette or audio track, was similarly examined. In large measure the effort was successful, and perhaps ninety-eight per cent of all listings in the text are so accredited. The reader is cautioned that all too frequently, unauthorized ("bootleg") releases, and an occasional authorized issue, misidentify their contents. Erroneous matrices, takes, dates, person-

nel, locations and related data appear in their liner notes. To the fullest extent possible, such errors of fact have been corrected in this work, by reference to, and comparison with, studio masters, studio files, original-issue records, source acetates and tapes, unissued material in Mr. Goodman's library, and other first-generation resources.

With few exceptions, the listings of commercial recordings in the text are in accord with visual and/or auditorial inspection. Listings of issued records show all elements of their labels as they appear on the original releases, including spelling, catalog, matrix and take numbers, vocal credits, and et cetera. Listings of air checks are in concord with program logs (where applicable), Mr. Goodman's itinerary, published radio and television logs and other pertinent sources. Composer credits, which appear in an Index of Tune Titles, are from ASCAP and BMI catalogs, and other data in the New York Public Library. Arranger credits are from the original manuscripts, and from related notations in Mr. Goodman's possession; they appear throughout the text.

Recordings and air checks found questionable as to Benny Goodman's participation by the author were taped and circulated among knowledgeable Goodman collector-specialists. A near-unanimous consensus was required either to accredit or discredit them. When an even division of opinion became manifest, recordings and air checks in question were played for Mr. Goodman by the author. His judgments—save in a very few instances; and these are noted in the text—were considered to be definitive. The more common of those commercial recordings erroneously attributed to Benny Goodman appear in chronological apposition in the text.

Emphasis throughout this work is on original issues, whether first released in the United States or elsewhere. This emphasis is extended to original issues of alternative versions—"takes"—of a given matrix, for in essence these renditions are separate and distinct recordings. Secondary, subsidiary releases of previously-issued matrices and takes are shown in some detail, but these listings are not exhaustive. Some such releases are knowingly excluded because of their audio qualities, some because they are no more than copies of copies that are easily obtainable, and some because they could not be verified by those who recommended them to the author. The author is satisfied that nothing new, or different, is lost by the omission of such replications.

This volume's second objective—to provide biographical material that illuminates Benny Goodman's working life beyond the bare bones of his recorded performances—is more a matter of exclusion than one of inclusion. For more than half a century, Benny Goodman's activities have been newsworthy, and the volumes written about him aggregate to a vast accumulation of fact, speculation and gossip. From these sources, and from his personal relationship with Mr. Goodman, the author has selected those items of intelligence that highlight a life in Jazz that is unequalled by any other performer, in terms of the consistently high standard of product over so long a time. Facts alone are all that are needed to assure Benny Goodman's unique niche in history, and these are what the author has employed to realize this second objective.

*

The author welcomes additional information about commercial recordings and air checks made by Benny Goodman. He may in future publish supplements to this work, when new data reach substantial proportions.

RUSS CONNOR
173 North Park Drive
Levittown, PA. 19054 U.S.A.

FORMAT

The overall format of this work is a chronological progression. Three type fonts are employed to differentiate among the three major categories of included information. The type style used in this paragraph is employed throughout the work for narrative text, descriptive matter, and the author's comments, opinions, value judgments and personal reminiscences.

This type face is employed throughout to identify commercial recordings, whether issued or unissued, as defined in the "Introduction." Each listing of commercial recordings contains several elements. These are shown next. Further explanation follows, per numbers in parentheses.

NAME OF RECORDING UNIT (1)		Date and locale of recording
Matrix—take (2)	Catalog number (3)	Solo identification (4)
	Tune title—vocalist—arranger (5)	

(1) This is the name credited on the label of the original issue; or, if the recording is unissued, it is the name credited by the studio for the recording. An identical recording may have been issued on more than one label, each crediting a different name, usually a pseudonym. All such names appear in this position; following each is an identifying abbreviation, in parentheses. This abbreviation appears after relevant catalog numbers.

(2) Most recordings were assigned a "matrix" number by the recording studio, to provide certain identification of that recording, and to differentiate it from all others. Successive recordings of the same tune title, under a given matrix, were further identified by "take" numbers. Matrix numbers are almost invariably consecutive; take numbers may be consecutive, but may almost be assigned as a matter of preference. Further discussion is in the text. Certain issued recordings that are splices of more than one take are identified by the symbol, "S".
Some recordings were not assigned matrix numbers. In such cases, a release number appearing on the issued record appears in this position. Through May 4, 1939, takes known to have been recorded that have not been issued are shown in parentheses. Beginning August 10, 1939, a different system is employed. An explanation of the change is in the text at that juncture.

(3) Numbers appearing on the labels of issued records, assigned by the issuing agency, appear in this position. If there is no issue for a given matrix and take—and if a test pressing of that matrix and take is known to be in private collections—the notation, "UNISSUED—Test Pressing," appears in place of catalog numbers. Further, if a tape of an unissued matrix and take is known to be in private collections, the notation, "UNISSUED—Tape," appears in place of catalog numbers.

(4) For all listings prior to the year 1935, a notation following the display of catalog numbers indicates whether or not there is an audible solo by Benny Goodman in that recording; and it specifies the nature of such included soli, in parentheses.
From the year 1935 forward, these notations are omitted. During this latter period, it is not necessary to demonstrate Mr. Goodman's presence for a given recording session or other whole performance conducted by him. However, when he does not participate in a given rendition during such sessions or performances, the notation, "NO BG," in parentheses following the tune title, is made to note his absence.

(5) The name of the arranger of a given tune is shown in this position, following the title of the tune and other credits, such as vocalists. Names are shown as abbreviations, in parentheses, according to an included key or special mention in the "Personnel" listing. Arranger credits are usually entered for the first extant or known performance of the tune, and for the first commercial recording of that tune.

The type face used in this paragraph is employed throughout the text for "privately-recorded"/"air check" performances, as defined in the "Introduction." The positional format of each element of privately-recorded/air check listings is the same as those for like elements of commercial recordings. In a few instances, this type face is employed to list recordings authorized by Benny Goodman, about which full details are no longer obtainable. Some air checks are the source of authorized issues of selected excerpts from such performances; these authorized issues are shown in the type face employed for commercial recordings. All other renditions in these performances are shown in this type face; unauthorized ("bootleg") issues of these renditions are noted in this type face, in parentheses, either following the tune title or at the end of each such listing. The symbol "-0-" appears in the position normally occupied by a matrix number when there has been no authorized release.

LABEL ABBREVIATIONS

Following are the abbreviations used in the text for the labels on which Benny Goodman's recordings and transcriptions are issued. Labels of U.S. origin are not further qualified. Labels issued in countries other than the U.S. are qualified in parentheses following them; consult the "Country of Origin" listing for these abbreviations. Labels whose country of origin is unknown are qualified by "(?)" following them.

AC	Aircheck	CW	Cunningham & Walsh
AF	Air Force Reserve, United States	DAN	Dan (Jap)
AFF	Affinity (UK)	DE	Decca
AFR	Armed Forces Record, United States	DEC	Decatur
AFRS	Armed Forces Radio Service, United States	DI	Diva
AFRS/T	Armed Forces Radio & Television Service, United States	DIV	Divergent (?)
AMI	Amiga (EG)	DJ	"Disc Jockey" Release
AOH	Ace of Hearts (UK)	DLT	Delta (G)
APEX	Apex (C)	DO	Domino
ARIEL	Ariel (UK)	DON	Donna Discs
ARIS	Aristo(crat)	DR	Dragon (Sd)
ASR	Alberti Special Record (WG)	DRJ	Dr. Jazz
AUR	Aurora (C)	EBW	Edison Bell Winner (UK)
BA	Banner	EL	Electrola (Hmv & CAP H, WG)
BAND	Bandstand	ELEC	Elec (Jap)
BB	Bluebird	EMA	Emanon
BBDO	Batten, Barton, Durstine & Osborne	EMB	Embassy (Au)
BBL/A	Big Band Landmarks/Archives	EMI	E M I (Hmv & CAP E, F, H, WG)
BC	Bel Canto	EPIC	Epic
BEP	Beppo (It)	ETR	Eterna (WG)
BER	Bernardo	EUR	Europa (It)
BG	B(enny) G(oodman)	EVA	Evatone
BILT	Biltmore	EX	Extreme Rarities
BIO	Biograph	FAN	Fanfare
BlA	Blue Ace	FDC	F D C (It)
BlC	Blue Coal Minstrels	FED	Federal Civil Defense, United States
BlD	Blu-Disc	FEST	Festival (Au, E, Fr)
BlL	Black Lion (WG)	FH	First Heard (A, E)
BOM	Book-Of-The-Month Club	FO	Folkways
BR	Brunswick	FONT	Fontana (UK, Jap)
BrX	Brunswick Export (SA)	FR	Franklin Mint
BRO	Broadway	FT	First Time
BRS	British Rhythm Society	GALA,	Gala International (UK)
BT	Broadcast Tributes	GAPS	Gaps (?)
CA	Cameo	GOJ	Giants Of Jazz
CAD	Cadet	GOL	Golden Era
CAM	Camden	GOTH	Gotham
C/P	Camden/Pickwick International	GR	Gramophone (HmvEu)
CAP	Capitol	GRIV	Great River Pool Co.
CBS	C B S (Eu, UK)	GS	National Guard, United States
CC	Collectors Classics	HA	Harmony
CENT	Century	HARR	Harrison
CH	Challenge	HIND	Hindsight
CHESS	Chess	HIS	Historia (WG)
CIC	Cicala (It)	HIST	Historical
CID	Compagnie Ind. du Disque (Fr)	HJCA	Hot Jazz Club Of America
CIF	Classics International Filmusic	HL	Hal
CL	Clarion	HMV	His Master's Voice (UK)
CLRL	Classics Record Library—also, BOM	HOM	Hall Of Music
CMND	Command	HOW	Hit Of The Week
CMS	Commodore Music Shop	HR	Honeysuckle Rose
CN	Connoisseur (?)	IMP	Imperial (Cz, Fr, G)
CO	Columbia	INT	International (It)
CoET	Columbia Electrical Transcription	JA	Jazztone
CoSP	Columbia Special Products	JAA	Jazz Archives
CoX	Columbia Export (SA)	JAN	Jazz Anthology (Fr)
CoTel		JAY	Jay
TRANS	Columbia Tele-Focal 12" Transcription	JAZ	Jazum
COLR	Collectors (E)	JCI	Jazz Collector's Items (Jap)
COR	Coronet (Au)	JCLS	Jazz Classics
CQ	Conqueror	JD	Jazz Document (Sd)
CR	Crown	JE	Jewel
CRL	Coral	JM	Jazz Moderne (?)

JO	Joker (It)		RE	Regal (78: U.S.; LP: Au, G)
JOY	Joyce		RED	Redwood (C)
JP	Jazz Panorama		REX	Rex (UK)
JR	Jolly Roger		RITZ	Ritz (Arg)
JS	Jazz Society (Fr, Jap, Sd)		RLM	Realm/Vista (UK)
JU	Jazz Unlimited		RO	Romeo
JUG	Jugoton (Y)		ROY	Royal (C)
KOJ	Kings Of Jazz (It)		RS	Rose
KON	Konsa (?)		RTB	R T B (Y)
KOS	King Of Swing (Fr)		RZ	Regal Zonophone (UK, Au)
LI	Lincoln		SA	Saga (E)
LON	London (E)		SB	Sunbeam
LSS	Longines Symphonette Society		SC	Soundcraft
LU	Lucky (Jap)		SE	Special Editions
LY	Lyric (Au)		SEN	Sentry
MARK	Mark '56		SG	Sounds Good/Sounds Great
MAY	Mayfair (UK)		SH	Sandy Hook
MB	Martin Block		SHRDLU	Shrdlu
MCA	M C A Records		SIG	Signal
ME	Melotone		SIL	Silvertone
MEGA	Mega		SM	Smithsonian Institution
MEL	Melodeon		SONY	Sony (Jap)
MER	Meritt		SPJ	Spook Jazz (UK)
MET	Metro (Fr, WG)		SPR	Superior (C)
MFP	Music For Pleasure (E)		ST	Strumthorpe
MGM	Metro-Goldwyn-Mayer		STO	La Storia del Jazz (It)
MIC	Microphone (C)		STS	Stash
MIR	Mirror (?)		SUP	Supertone (UK)
MM	Music Masters		SVL	Saville (UK)
MPS	M P S (WG)		SW	Swaggie (Au)
MS	Mainstream		SWD	Swedisc (Jap)
MU	Musidisc (Fr)		SWE	Swing Era
MUC	Music For Collectors (?)		SWF	Swing Fan (WG)
NARAS	National Academy Of Recording Arts And Sciences		SWH	Swing House (E)
NARC	National Association For Retarded Children		SWT	Swing Treasury
NATCHEZ	Natchez (SA)		TAX	Tax (Sd)
NBC	National Broadcasting Company Thesaurus		TB	Taystee Breadwinners
NM	Neiman Marcus		TCF	20th Century-Fox
NOST	Nostalgia Book Club		TEM	Temple
OD	Odeon		TL	Time-Life
ODY	Odyssey		TOM	The Old Masters
OFC	Only For Collectors (Arg)		TOSH	Toshiba (Jap)
OK	Okeh		TR	Top Rank (UK)
OM	Ombrads		TRIB	Tribute From Sweden
ON	Onward To Yesterday		TT	Take Two
OR	Oriole		UHCA	United Hot Clubs Of America
OS	Oscar (It)		USN	Navy Department, United States
OWI	Office Of War Information, State Department, United States		UST	Treasury Department, United States
			USW	War Department, United States
PA	Parlophone		VANG	Vanguard
PAL	Palm (Fr, E)		VC	Vogue-Coral (UK)
PANA	Panachord (UK)		VD	V-Disc
PARA	Paramount Studios		VDP	La Voce Del Padrone (HmvIt)
PAT	Pathe		VE	Velvetone
PAU	Pausa		VELP	Veronica (Sd)
PB	Playboy		VER	Verve
PE	Perfect		VET	Veterans' Administration, United States
PHIL	Philips (UK, CONT, Au, Jap)		VI	Victor
PHILCO	Philco		VJ	Vintage Jazz
PHM	Philomel		VJMS	Vintage Jazz Music Society (UK)
PHON	Phontastic (Sd)		VO	Vocalion
PIC	Pickwick (Fr)		VOA	Voice Of America, State Department, United States
POL	Polydor (Fr)		VSM	La Voix De Son Maitre (HmvFr)
POLK	Polk		WCC	Warner Communication Co.
POLY	Polygon		W-E	Western Electric
PR	Prestige		WBIB	Westinghouse—Benny In Brussels
PU	Publix		WBRO	World Broadcasting Co.
PUR	Puritone		WNEW	Radio Station WNEW
QD	Queen Disc (It)		WI	Windmill (E)
RAD	Radiola		WPRO	World Program Service
RADA	Radio Archives		WOR	W O R
RADR	Radio Rarities		WR	Winters-Rosen
RADY	Radio Yesteryear		WWF	Westinghouse—Plays World Favorites
RAR	Rarities (E)		"X"	VI "X" Vault Originals
RCA	Radio Corp. of America (as Victor-Interchangeably)		YB	Yeri-Bean (CR)
RD	Reader's Digest		ZONO	Zonophone

COUNTRY OF ORIGIN ABBREVIATIONS

Following are the abbreviations used to qualify the labels; i.e., to show in which country the label was manufactured and/or initially distributed. Thus, PaA is American Parlophone; PaE is English Parlophone; PaFr is French Parlophone; ViArg is Argentine Victor; ViC is Canadian Victor; and so on.

A	United States Of America
Arg	Argentina
Au	Australia
Aus	Austria
Bel	Belgium
Br	Brazil
C	Canada
Ch	Chile
Cont	Great Britain primarily; for distribution in Continental Europe
CR	Costa Rica
Cz	Czechoslovakia
E	Great Britain
EG	East Germany (E.G.D.R.)
Eu	European
Fin	Finland
Fr	France
G	Germany; same as WG (F.R.W.G.)
H	Holland (Netherlands)
Ind	India
Ir	Ireland
It	Italy
Jap	Japan
Mex	Mexico
Nor	Norway
NZ	New Zealand
SA	South America
Scan	Scandinavia
Sd	Sweden
Sp	Spain
Sw	Switzerland
UK	United Kingdom
WG	West Germany; same as G(F.R.W.G.)
Y	Yugoslavia

INSTRUMENTAL ABBREVIATIONS

acc	accordion
as	alto saxophone
bar	baritone saxophone
bjo	banjo
bo	bongos
b	string bass
b-clt	bass clarinet
b-sax	bass saxophone

cel	violoncello
celeste	celeste
clt	clarinet
c-mel	C-melody saxophone
cnt	cornet
d	drums
fl	flute
Fr-h	French horn
g	guitar
goofus	goofus
harp	harp
marimba	marimba
mel	mellophone
org	organ
p	piano
ss	soprano saxophone
tbn	trombone
ts	tenor saxophone
tpt	trumpet
tu	tuba
uke	ukelele
vib	vibraphone, vibraharp
viola	viola
v	violin
xyl	xylophone

MISCELLANEOUS ABBREVIATIONS

accomp	accompaniment
arr	arranger
CAS	cassette
CD	compact disc
dir	director
EP	extended play record
ET	electrical transcription
ldr	leader
LP, Lp	long playing record
mx	matrix
StLp	stereo long playing record
StT	stereo tape
StTC	stereo tape cartridge
subt	subtone
unk	unknown
voc	vocal, vocalist

THE BEN POLLACK ERA

In August 1925, at age 16, Benny Goodman joined Ben Pollack's Orchestra at the Venice Ballroom, greater Los Angeles, California, upon the earnest recommendation of fellow-Chicagoan Gil Rodin. This was the beginning of a productive—and as tenures go in the band business, enduring—association of the two Ben's that would last, with but brief interruptions, for almost exactly four years.

It also marked the emergence of Benny Goodman as a jazz musician of major stature. Benny got his first musicians' union card at age 13 in 1923, and so he had worked for several years professionally before he joined Pollack. But it was in the years with Pollack that he first played with a formally constituted orchestra with stable personnel, the band that can claim it was the first fully-instrumented white group dedicated to Jazz.

During the Pollack Era Benny gained musical maturity long before he attained his legal majority. His distinctive tone, his matchless technique, his wealth of invention, his musical competence and his proficiency on several instruments, all evolved in those years, and singled him out as a musician who had diverse talents. Before the end of his tenure with Pollack, Benny Goodman's reputation was firmly established with band leaders, recording contractors, and his fellow sidemen. It took dancing and listening America—and the rest of the world—just a little while longer to catch on.

The band came back to Chicago in late January 1926 with high hopes for major engagements in a city appreciative of Jazz. But these were soon dashed; glowing reports of its success on the West Coast had not reached the midwest public, and it proved more difficult to book an 11-man orchestra than it did smaller groups. As a result, the sidemen had to find jobs with other leaders; Benny signed on with still another Ben, Benny Kreuger, who was musical director of the stage band at the Uptown Theater. He rejoined Pollack for a two-week stint at Castle Farms, near Cincinnati, Ohio, then returned to the Uptown. Pollack was engaged for a brief period at the Venetian Room of the Southmoor Hotel in May, but evidently Benny then kept his steady job with Kreuger. In July, however, he apparently did go back with Pollack, once more in the Southmoor. In September he was once again in the Pollack fold, now in the Webster Hotel, Chicago. So strongly did the sidemen believe in each other and what they could accomplish with Pollack, that they returned to his orchestra whenever circumstances permitted.

Victor had shown some interest in recording the Pollack group when it came back to Chicago from the Venice Ballroom. It auditioned the band during its hotel stands, eventually proffered a contract, and Benny's very first recording session was set.

Benny does not remember the initial Pollack record date for Victor. His autobiography cites the December 9, 1929 session, which produced the first Pollack record that was released to the public, as his first experience in a recording studio. But trumpeter Earl Baker is adamant that Benny sat alongside him when the band first recorded for Victor in September. Baker, perhaps better known as the composer of "Darktown Shuffle" and his work with the Seattle Harmony Kings, recalls the event clearly. He said it was especially memorable because of the recording of "I'd Love To Call You My Sweetheart," which had a vocal accompaniment by Pollack, Glenn Miller and probably Al Harris (not Frank Sylvano, named in other accounts). His vivid recollection is Miller's fury with the other sidemen, who broke up completely when they listened to the playback, so bad was the trio's attempt.

THIS, then, is Benny's initial recording session:

THE WHITE TOPS (WT) September 14, 1926, Chicago
BEN POLLACK AND HIS CALIFORNIANS (BP)

WT—Benny Goodman, clt; Fud Livingston, foot org; Lou Kessler, bjo.
BP —Benny Goodman, clt; Harry Greenberg, Al Harris, Earl Baker, tpt; Glenn Miller, tbn; Gil Rodin, as; Fud Livingston, ts; Vic Briedis, p; Lou Kessler, bjo; Harry Goodman, tu; Ben Pollack, d.

BVE 36236- UNISSUED (WT)
(1,2) **Hot Stuff** - voc Ben Pollack

BVE 36237- UNISSUED (BP)
(1,2,3) **I'd Love To Call You My Sweetheart** - voc trio

BVE 36238- UNISSUED (BP)
(1,2,3) **Sunday** - voc Ben Pollack

Earl Baker offers a more tangible souvenir of Benny's early days. On more than one occasion during the fall and winter of 1926, Baker, Goodman, Miller and a few other jazzmen gathered at the Chicago apartment of Earl's mother for informal rehearsals and jam sessions. Earl recorded some of the proceedings on an Edison cylinder phonograph; eventually these were transferred onto Lp, JAA43:

EARL BAKER CYLINDERS *Fall, Winter, 1926, Chicago*

Benny Goodman, clt; Earl Baker, tpt; John Kurzenknabe, bjo.

-O- *(What Can I Say, Dear) After I Say I'm Sorry?*
-O- *(What Can I Say, Dear) After I Say I'm Sorry?-Intro only*
-O- *I Love My Baby (My Baby Loves Me)-Intro only*
-O- *I Love My Baby (My Baby Loves Me)*
-O- *Sobbin' Blues*

ADD: Glenn Miller, tbn.
-O- *Five Foot Two, Eyes of Blue*

SUBSTITUTE: Phil Barger, g, for Kurzenknabe
-O- *Then I'll Be Happy*

On a sunny summer day in the middle 1950's, Earl played his precious cylinders—they were almost his only artifacts from the beginnings of his career—in the attic of his Brigantine, New Jersey, home for an audience of one, the author. Each of the seven cylinders was wrapped in cotton wadding, boxed, and kept in the dry attic for protection against moisture. The machine was similarly protected, emerged bright and shiny from its case, ready to operate with no preliminary preparation. I sat enthralled as we listened to a Benny Goodman of a quarter-century earlier; he was clearly identifiable, for the audio quality was about the same as that of the "dime store labels" of the early 1930's.

Those who have my earlier book on Benny Goodman, "BG-On The Record," will note a far different listing in it for the Baker cylinders than the listing above. That listing reflected what I heard that day, for I took careful notes. In the years between then and the late 1970's when the transfer to tape and to Lp was made, a great deal of deterioration had taken place—this despite the years-long efforts of those who had acquired the cylinders from Baker's widow to keep them safe and to refurbish them, and after many experiments with different processes to transfer them. Too bad; there is little left to renew my memory of a golden moment.

Contemporary trade papers indicate Pollack's band was booked into the Southmoor in December, but do not specify a date. The band was in the Webster Hotel when it recorded what was to become Benny's debut on records that were released:

BEN POLLACK AND HIS CALIFORNIANS December 9, 1926, Chicago

Benny Goodman, clt; Harry Greenberg, Al Harris, poss. Earl Baker, tpt; Glenn Miller, tbn; Gil Rodin, as; Fud Livingston, ts; VICTOR YOUNG, AL BELLER, v; Vic Briedis, p; Lou Kessler, bjo; Harry Goodman, tu; Ben Pollack, d.

BVE 37218-3 VI 20394 B. **LP:** BRO 103 (no solo)
  When I First Met Mary - voc Joey Ray

BVE 37219-4 LP RcaFr FXMI 7165 (clt solo)
(1,2,3) **'Deed I Do** - voc Ben Pollack

That's *the* Victor Young on violin; he and Al Beller (Pollack's cousin) were hired because Glenn Miller, who was doing most of the arranging, wanted to emulate the sound of the commercially successful Roger Wolfe Kahn orchestra, which had a string section.

BEN POLLACK AND HIS CALIFORNIANS   **December 17, 1926, Chicago**

Personnel as December 9, with Baker definite and Briedis doubling on celeste on BVE 37260; no v on BVE 37261. The Williams' Sisters are Dorothy and Hanna, the latter heavy-weight champion Jack Dempsey's wife.

BVE 37219-6 (5)	VI 20408 A. HMV B5281, VDP R4819. **LP:** RcaFr FXMI 7283, MUC 5 OFC 40 (clt solo)
	'Deed I Do - voc Ben Pollack
BVE 37260-3	VI 20461 B. **LP:** BRO 103 (no solo)
	You're The One For Me - voc Ilomay Bailey

(VI 20461 B is the rarest of the Pollack Victor's)

BVE 37261-2	VI 20425 B, HmvAu Ea156 **LP:** RcaFr FXMI 7165, BRO 103. (clt solo)
BVE 37261-3	**LP:** "X" LX 3003, RcaFr FXMI 7165. **LP:** "X" EVA A3003, SB 136. (clt solo)
	He's The Last Word - voc Williams' Sisters

Little is known of Benny's—or Pollack's—activities in early 1927, but it has been established that Benny's first recordings under his own name, "That's A Plenty" and "Clarinetitis," were **NOT** recorded at that time. It seems beyond dispute that he waxed those sides in Chicago, while there playing a hotel date with Sam Lanin, on June 13, 1928, q.v.

About this time (early Spring of 1927), Benny cut what are among the rarest Goodmania of all: He recorded a number of clarinet passages into a Dictaphone, and these were transcribed and published by Melrose as " 'One Hundred Jazz Breaks' by Benny Goodman." Copies of the published folios are extant, but the discs have never been found.

Billboard and **Variety** variously list the Pollack crew in the Rendezvous in April and the Blackhawk in May, both Chicago. A photo in **Billboard** in June pictures BG, Greenberg, Harris, Miller, Rodin, Livingston, Briedis, Kessler, and H. Goodman together with Pollack. This lends credence to a belief that Benny was with Pollack when the next two sessions were cut. Unfortunately, none of the four sides has ever been issued.

BEN POLLACK AND HIS CALIFORNIANS   **June 24, 1927, Chicago**

Personnel as December 9, 1927 sans Baker, Young, and Beller.

BVE 39058- (1,2,3,4,5)	UNISSUED
	That's What I Think Of You - voc Ben Pollack
BVE 39059- (1,2,3,4,5)	UNISSUED
	Who Is Your "Who?" - voc Ben Pollack

BEN POLLACK AND HIS CALIFORNIANS   **July 7, 1927, Chicago**

Personnel as June 24.

BVE 39090- (1,2,3)	UNISSUED
	Honey Do - voc Ben Pollack
BVE 39091- (1,2,3)	UNISSUED
	I Ain't That Kind Of A Baby - voc Ben Pollack

Summer jobs in Chicago were scarce, so the Pollack orchestra, BG included, combined a business and vacation trip to California that lasted until Fall 1927. It then returned to Chicago and the Blackhawk with new personnel. Minus its "Californians" tag the band cut some sides for Victor, two of which have been released:

BEN POLLACK AND HIS ORCHESTRA   **December 7, 1927, Chicago**

Benny Goodman, clt & tpt; JIMMY McPARTLAND, cnt; FRANK QUARTELL, tpt; Glenn Miller, tbn; Gil Rodin, as; LARRY BINYON, ts; Vic Briedis, p; DICK MORGAN, bjo; Harry Goodman, tu; Ben Pollack, d.

BVE 41342-2	VI 21184 A. **LP:** RcaFr FXMI 7283, BRO 103, (clt solo, tpt brk)
BVE 41342-3	**LP:** "X" LX 3003, RcaFr FXMI 7165, TL STLJ05, SB 136. **EP:** "X" EVA A 3003. **ET:** AFRS Amer Pop Music #56 (clt solo, tpt brk)
	Waitin' For Katie - voc (Pollack and chorus)
BVE 41343-1	As BVE 41342-3, but omit TL (clt solo)
BVE 41343-2	As BVE 41342-2, except VI 21184 **B.** (clt solo)
	Memphis Blues

BVE 41344-(1)	UNISSUED
	California Medley

(On both takes of "Waitin' For Katie" Benny plays a two-bar tpt intro to McPartland's solo, then joins in for the three-part tpt chorus.)

Shortly after the December 7th session Benny quit Pollack to go with Isham Jones for a few months. Jones had Frankie Quartell assemble the "best musicians in Chicago" for his engagement at Fronton, part of the Rainbo Gardens. Included in the group were BG; Quartell, Earl Baker, tpt; Benny Neibaur, tbn; Bud Friedman (not Freeman), sax; Whitey Drobeck, p; -?- Rose, bjo; John Kuhn, tu; Bob Conselman, d; and Jones as leader, arranger, composer and occasional sax player. Benny and Baker both say they made no records with this band, and none is cited by discographers.

Benny recorded next for Vocalion, using as sidemen his cohorts from the Pollack band. This was to set a pattern for the next several years: Benny and key Pollack personnel will record for many different leaders and contractors, and the records will appear under numerous pseudonyms on a multitude of labels.

Note that the matrices cited are correct, despite false numbers pressed into the wax of the Vocalion issue. Issues subsequent to the original Vocalion are credited to "Benny Goodman And His Boys."

BENNIE GOODMAN'S   **January 23, 1928, Chicago**
BOYS WITH JIM AND GLENN

Benny Goodman, clt; Jimmy McPartland, cnt; Glenn Miller, tbn; Vic Briedis, p.; Dick Morgan, g; Harry Goodman, tu; Bob Conselman, d & vib.

C 1652	VO 15656 A, BR 80027 B, BR 80185. **LP:** BR BL58015, OFC 24, FestAu CFR10-437, MCA(US) 2-4018, TL STLJ05, VoE VLP2, CRL(G) 6796, MCA(G) 6796, SB 141, AFF 1018. **45:** BR set 9-7017. **EP:** BR EG71015, CRL CONT 94268 (clt solo)
C 1653	UNISSUED
	A Jazz Holiday
C 1654	VO 15656 B, BR 80027 A, HRS7 (dubbed mx P22488-1). **LP:** BR BL54010, BR BL58015, FestAu CRF10-437, CRL(F) CVM40012, VC LVA9011, LSS LW267, MCA(US) 2-4018, TL STLJ05, VoE VLP2, CRL(G) 6796, SB 141, MCA(G) 6796, AFF 1018. **45:** BR set 9-7017. **EP:** BR EB71015, CRL(G) 94109. **ET:** AFRS Amer Pop Music #s 56, 67 (clt solo)
C 1655	UNISSUED
	Wolverine Blues

In early 1928 Gil Rodin again induced Benny to join Pollack; with BG back in the fold the Pollack orchestra took its first crack at the "Big Apple," Broadway and New York City. The band opened March 6 at the Little Club, 44th Street off Broadway. Here Benny and the others met and jammed with the cream of the jazz musicians of the period, who had gravitated to New York. Here, too, Benny began to get calls from resident leaders and contractors who had become impressed with his all around proficiency, apart from his jazz talents. So it was that Benny's first New York record date was not for Pollack, but for Nat Shilkret. Benny's entree here was Fud Livingston, who had left Pollack in Chicago, lured by Shilkret's tempting $250 per week.

ALL STAR ORCHESTRA   **March 21, 1928, New York**

Benny Goodman, clt & as; Jimmy McPartland, cnt; Ray Lodwig, Fuzzy Farrar, tpt; Glenn Miller, Tommy Dorsey, tbn; Joe Venuti, Max Farley, v; Dudley Fosdick, mel; Paul Mertz, p; Carl Kress, bjo; Joe Tarto, tu; Chauncey Morehouse, d; Nat Shilkret, dir; Scrappy Lambert, voc. (Others suggested are Del Steiger, tpt, and Miff Mole, tbn.)

BVE 43384-2	VI 21605 B. **LP:** BRO 103 (clt bridge)
	I'm More Than Satisfied - voc (Scrappy Lambert)
BVE 43385-1	VI 21423 A. **LP:** SB 112 (clt solo)
BVE 43385-2	**LP:** RcaFr FXMI 7283 (clt solo)
	Oh, Baby! - voc (Scrappy Lambert)

This early version of "Oh, Baby!" compares interestingly with Goodman's 1946 effort for Columbia. Note Tommy Dorsey's presence for the first time on a date with BG. Benny's participation is confirmed by Goodman himself. Examination of literally hundreds more Shilkret records has not produced any other identifiable BG solos.

Then came Pollack's initial New York recording session. The sides were held for many years before they were released. When RCA decided to issue something from this date, it chose to put out excerpts of two takes of one tune, nothing of the other.

BEN POLLACK AND HIS CALIFORNIANS   April 6, 1928, New York

Benny Goodman, clt; Jimmy McPartland, cnt; AL HARRIS, tpt; Glenn Miller, tbn; Gil Rodin, as; BUD FREEMAN, ts; ED BERGMAN, AL BELLER, v; unknown cello; Vic Briedis, p; Dick Morgan, bjo; Harry Goodman, tu; Ben Pollack, d.

BVE 43540-2,3	**LP:** "X" LX 3003. **EP:** "X" EVA B 3003 (clt solos - ptl.)	
	Singapore Sorrows - voc (Ben Pollack)	

(Complete versions of BVE 43540-2 and -3 are extant via tests.)

BVE 43541-(1)	UNISSUED	
	Sweet Sue-Just You - voc Ben Pollack (poss. Franklyn Baur)	

Victor again prevailed on Benny, this time to accompany its prolific "pop" singer, Johnny Marvin. Importantly, the Marvin session produced Benny's first recorded alto saxophone solo. Note that the two listed below were the only sides cut this date; and that a myriad of other Johnny Marvin recordings, many with prominent clarinet solos, fail to evidence Benny Goodman on any of them.

JOHNNY MARVIN   April 19, 1928, New York

Benny Goodman, clt & as; poss. either Mannie Klein, Jimmy McPartland or Leo McConville, tpt; poss. either Matty Malneck or Joe Venuti, v; poss. either Rube Bloom or Frank Banta, p; poss. either Eddie Lang or Carl Kress, g; plus unknown d on BVE 43579.

BVE 43578-1	VI 21376 B, HMV B2789, HMVAu EA361. **LP:** RcaFr FXMI 7165, SB 112 (clt solo)	
BVE 43578-3	**LP:** RcaFr FXMI 7283 (clt solo)	
	Angel - voc Johnny Marvin	
BVE 47579-1	**LP:** RcaFr FXMI 7165 (as solo)	
BVE 43579-3	VI 21435 B, HMV B2812. **LP:** RcaFr FXMI 7283, SB 112 (as solo)	
	My Pet - voc Johnny Marvin	

There is a wide divergence of opinion among collectors as to the personnel for the Johnny Marvin sides, above. Benny is a certainty, the others reasonable possibilities.

Initial releases of "Singapore Sorrows" and "Sweet Sue-Just You" were from the following session, a re-make date.

BEN POLLACK AND HIS CALIFORNIANS   April 26, 1928, New York

Personnel as April 6.

BVE 43540-4	**LP:** "X" LX 3003, VI LEJ5, RcaFr FXMI 7165, SB 136. **EP:** "X" EVA B3003 (clt solo)	
BVE 43540-6	VI 21437 B. **LP:** RcaFr FXMI 7165. (clt solo)	
	Singapore Sorrows - voc Ben Pollack	
BVE 43541-5	VI 21437 A (no solo)	
	Sweet Sue-Just You - voc (Franklyn Baur)	

Victor provided retailers with descriptive labels for store record jackets in the '20's. The one for "The Saint Louis Blues" in the next session reads, "Contralto solo with orchestral accompaniment - extremely popular 'blue' melody - well sung, expressive and clear - good piano parts." And for the following date's "Choo-Choo Train," "Popular song for contralto with piano, guitar and saxophone accompaniment - sung in similar style." Didn't they know about our Benny?

IRENE BEASLEY   May 1, 1928, New York

Benny Goodman, clt & as; plus unknown tpt, p, g, v, cello; plus unknown tbn on BVE 43936. Possibly similar personnel to April 19.

BVE 43935-2	**LP:** RcaFr FXMI 7283 (clt accomp)	
BVE 43935-3	VI 21467 A (clt accomp)	
	The Saint Louis Blues - voc Irene Beasley	

BVE 43936-2	VI 21639 A (as accomp)	
	If I Could Just Stop Dreaming - voc Irene Beasley	
BVE 43937-2	VI 21639 B (no solo)	
	Missin' My Pal - voc Irene Beasley	
BVE 43938	UNISSUED	
	Swing Along Honey And Smile - voc Irene Beasley	

It now seems likely that Irene Beasley's VI 40173 release of "You'll Come Back To Me Someday" was not recorded on May 3, under matrix BVE 45005, with Benny Goodman as accompanist. Instead, the release is believed to have been recorded April 11, 1929, under matrix BVE 51802, with Phil Napoleon, tpt; Teddy Lessoff, Sam Freed, v; Bill Wirges, p; and Carson Robinson, g, as her accompaniment. There are no known issues from matrix BVE 45005.

IRENE BEASLEY   May 3 or 5, 1928, New York

Benny Goodman, clt; plus unknown tpt, v, p, g; aurally and logically, personnel similar to that of May 1.

BVE 45005-(1,2)	UNISSUED **You'll Come Back To Me Someday** - voc Irene Beasley	
BVE 45006-2	**LP:** RcaFr FXMI 7283, SB 112 (clt solo)	
BVE 45006-3	VI 21467 B. **LP:** HIST HLP25, STO 3123, JO 3123 (clt solo)	
	Choo-Choo Train - voc Irene Beasley	

Victor's recording sheets are dated May 5, 1928, for Beasley matrix BVE 45006. May 3, however, is stamped conspicuously into the test pressing of take 2 of that matrix. This suggests either a split date and perhaps additional unknown BG/Beasley sides, or more likely, an error in Victor's listing.

May 5 was the final day of Pollack's initial engagement at the Little Club. The band worked sporadically for the next two months—some NBC radio dates, a few theatres in the East. The band was in New York in early June, and Benny assumed leadership of some of its personnel for a record date contracted by Walter Melrose. Benny gave a "one-man-band" performance in his first New York studio date as a leader.

BENNIE GOODMAN'S BOYS   June 4, 1928, New York

Benny Goodman, clt, as, bar, cnt; Jimmy McPartland, cnt; Glenn Miller, tbn; Fud Livingston, clt, as; Vic Briedis, p; Dick Morgan, g; Harry Goodman, tu; Ben Pollack, d.

E 27638	BR 4013, BR 80029 B, BrF 500201, BrG A7839. **45:** BR set 9-7017. **EP:** BR EB71016, CRLCont 94268. **LP:** BR BL58015, FestAu CRF10-437, CrlG 6796, VoE VLP2, MCA 2-4018, McaG 6796, SB 141, AFF 1018. (clt, cnt)	
E 27638-ALT	BR 4013. **LP:** SB 112 (clt, cnt)	
	Jungle Blues	
E 27639	BR 4013, BR 80029 A. **45, EP, LP,** same as E 27638 (clt, bar)	
E 27639-ALT	BrF 500201, BrF 7839, BrG A7839. **LP:** OFC 24, SB 112 (clt, bar)	
	Room 1411	
E 27640	BR 3975, BR 80030 B, BrF 500202, BrG A7815. **45, EP, LP,** same as E 27638, plus LP's BR BL54010, CrlFr CVM40012, VC LVA9011, LSS LW267, TL STLJ05, ARIS 12017 (as, bar)	
	Blue	

[The session was scheduled to end at this juncture. Indeed, the HANAPI TRIO, a Hawaiian group, cut succeeding matrices E 27641, "Sweet Kalua Lady," and E 27642, "Lei Lani," both issued on BR 4057. Benny's group was kidding around, preparing to leave, playing a "cod Dixie" (as Jimmy McPartland termed it) version of "St. Louis Blues," with Tommy Dorsey—in the studio for a different session—joining in the fun. To everyone's astonishment the contractor shouted, "That's great! It's just what I want; you'll have

June 4, 1928, continued

June 4, 1928, continued

to record it!" So, using the chords of "St. Louis Blues," the group cut one more side.]

Add Tommy Dorsey, tbn.

E 27643   BR 3975, BR 80030 A, BrG A7815. **45:** BR set 9-7017.
                    EP: BR EB71016. **LP:** BR BL58015, FestAu
                    CRF10-437, MCA 2-4018, McaG 6796, VoE VLP2, SB
                    141, AFF 1018. (clt)
                    Shirt Tail Stomp

Discovery of an alternate take of "Jungle Blues" on BR 4013 suggests the possibility of an alternate take of "Room 1411" on BR 4013 also, as well as on the non-U.S. issues known to have it. At this writing this theoretical copy of BR 4013 has not been reported.

A final observation on this unusual session: "Room 1411" was originally titled, "Goin' To Town." It was renamed to commemorate room 1411 of the Whitby Hotel, New York, where the Pollack bandsmen, at liberty and broke, had moved in en masse on Benny.

When quizzed about various artists of the '20's with whom he logically might have recorded, Benny felt certain "I'd done some things with Gene Austin." For years the only substantiation of this hazy recollection was a Pollack session of Dec. 3, 1928, when Austin contributed a vocal to one tune. But an eventual discovery, accredited by Benny, affirms BG's memory six months' earlier:

GENE AUSTIN   June 6, 1928, New York

Benny Goodman, clt & as; plus unknown cnt, tbn, 2 v, cel, p, bjo, d.

BVE 45562-1   UNISSUED - Test Pressing (clt, as accomp)
BVE 45562-2   VI 21714 A, BB 6853. **LP:** "X" LX988, RcaFr FXMI 7165
                    (clt, as accomp)
                    St. Louis Blues - voc Gene Austin

[Austin mx BVE 45563-1 "Then Came The Dawn," issued on VI 21564 B, was also cut this session, but without BG or the tbn.]

On June 20, in New York, JACK PETTIS AND HIS PETS cut three sides for Vocalion: mx E 7394 "Dry Martini," mx E 7395 "Hot Heels," and mx E 7396 "Broadway Stomp." Many collectors are persuaded that the clarinetist on these recordings is Benny Goodman. Benny has heard them, says definitely not. The author agrees, believes Don Murray to have been the clarinetist on the Pettis date.

Here is the re-dated Goodman trio session, made while Benny was on leave from the Pollack band, in Chicago with Sam Lanin for a date in the Congress Hotel:

BENNY GOODMAN,   June 13, 1928, Chicago
Clarinet Solo with piano and drums

Benny Goodman, clt; Mel Stitzel, p; Bob Conselman, d.

C 2006   VO 15705, ME 12073, PANA 25017 B, BILT 1021, JCLS
(E 7398 A)   529. **EP:** Fest Au XP45-1150, CrlG 94109. **LP:** BR
                 BL54010, CrlF CVM40012, CrlG 6796, VC LVA9011,
                 LSS LW267, MCA 2-4018, McaG 6797, VoE VLP2, SB
                 112, AFF 1018 (clt solo)
         ✓**That's A Plenty**

C 2007   same issues, plus BrF 500202, **LP:** TL STLJ05, less LP
(E 7397 A)   LSS LW267 (clt solo)
         ✓**Clarinetitis**

The summer was a "dark" season for the big Pollack band, but BG kept busy with temporary jobs for other leaders, among them Lanin, Nat Shilkret, Meyer Davis, and Joe Moss. Examination of records made by these orchestras in mid-1928 has failed to uncover any BG clarinet.

Pollack finally got a lengthier engagement and Benny came back. The band went into Atlantic City's Million Dollar Pier July 2, and a notable event took place: Frank Teschmacher joined, subbing for an ailing Gil Rodin. He merged talents with fellow readman BG and Bud Freeman, thus affording those fortunate enough to be present with an unparalleled opportunity of hearing the three great Chicago reed men play together. As if that weren't enough, another Chicago clarinetist, "Mezz" Mezzrow, claims that he also substituted for Rodin in Atlantic City.

While the band played Million Dollar Pier Jimmy McPartland left to join vocalist Bea Palmer. Pollack wired Earl Baker in Chicago to replace him. Larry Binyon also came, taking over Bud Freeman's chair. Baker recalls that this was his introduction to Jack Teagarden, which puts Big Tea in the band as early as July 1928.

McPartland soon missed the good jazz and carefree cameraderie of the Pollack crew and returned. Baker remembers that thereupon Pollack ". . . gave me a hard time in order to get me to quit, and so relieve him of paying my train fare back to Chicago." But Earl hung on through the Atlantic City gig (which ended September 3) and a New York theater date later that month.

Glenn Miller played alongside Tea through most or all of the Million Dollar Pier stint, but immediately thereafter joined Paul Ash at the Paramount Theater, New York City. (Glenn was about to marry, had to have the steady income that Ash offered, and wanted to locate permanently in New York.) Eventually Baker left Pollack to join Ash, and McPartland—who had been in and out of the Pollack band—returned for the hot horn parts.

Harry Goodman probably switched to string bass, for the most part, in mid-1928. However, aural evidence insists he plays tuba on record, and he is so listed. Harry's first instrument, incidentally, in his and Benny's early Hull House days, was trombone. In the words of "Murph" Podalsky, Harry was a "horrible trombone player." It was Murph who influenced Harry to take up the tuba; Murph had booked a job, needed a tuba but not a trombone, and told Harry if he wanted to work he'd play tuba.

The band went into the Florentine Grill of the Park Central Hotel, New York, on September 28. Its next record session was Big Tea's first with Pollack. The band was then identified on label as "Ben Pollack and his Park Central Orchestra," a nod to the hotel that was to employ it for almost a year.

BEN POLLACK AND HIS   October 1, 1928, New York
PARK CENTRAL ORCHESTRA

Benny Goodman, clt; Jimmy McPartland, Al Harris, tpt; JACK TEAGARDEN, tbn, Gil Rodin, as; LARRY BINYON, ts & fl; Ed Bergman, Al Beller, v; BILL SCHUMANN, cello; Vic Briedis, p; Dick Morgan, bjo; Harry Goodman, tu; Ben Pollack, d.

BVE 47576-   UNISSUED
(1,2,3)   **You're Gone** - voc Franklyn Baur

BVE 47577-2   VI 21716 B, HMV B5587, HMVAu EA456 (no solo)
                 Forever - voc (Franklyn Baur)

BEN POLLACK AND HIS   October 15, 1928, New York
PARK CENTRAL ORCHESTRA

Personnel as October 1.

BVE 47742-1   VI 21743 B, HMV B 5596. **LP:** FO FP69, FO FJ2808,
                 RcaFr FXMI 7283, TOM 22, SVL 154 (clt solo)
BVE 47742-3   **LP:** "X" LX 3003, SB 136. **EP:** "X" EVA A3003 (clt
                 solo)
                 Buy, Buy For Baby (Or Baby Will Bye Bye You) - voc
                 Belle Mann

BVE 47743-1   VI 27143A, HMV B5596 **LP:** TOM 22, SVL 154 (no solo)
                 She's One Sweet Show Girl - voc Belle Mann

The next day marked Benny's first association with a now-famous pseudonym, "The Whoopee Makers." The term probably was an accurate description of the personal habits of Benny, Jimmy, Big Tea, Dick Morgan and others of the Pollack band, for these were the days of wine and honey. Note that matrix E 28357 provides an unique instance of Benny's playing a soprano saxophone:

THE WHOOPEE MAKERS (WM)   October 16, 1928, New York
HOTSY TOTSY GANG (HTG)

Personnel probably as October 1, possibly substituting IRVING MILLS, v. for either Bergman or Beller, Pollack (BP) and Mills (IM) are the vocalists who appear on the label under pseudonyms.

E 28356   VO 15763 (WM). **LP:** SB 113 (clt solo)
             Dardanella (arr Bob Haring) - voc "Jim Bracken" (BP)

E 28357   BR 4112. **LP:** OFC 20 (HTG), SB 113 (clt bridge, ss
             solo)
             I Couldn't If I Wanted To (I Wouldn't If I Could) (arr
             Don Wilkinson) - voc "Milton Irving" (IM)

E 28358 BR 4122, BrF 8064, BrG A8064. **LP:** OFC 20, SB 113 (HTG) (clt intro, as solo)
>**Since You Went Away** (arr Elliott Jacoby) - voc "Milton Irving" (IM)

Although it is well known that Benny played a number of times for Sam Lanin, Goodman collectors have come to regard as suspect reputed BG/Lanin records, because examination of so many of them have proved to be false alarms. The next session, however, seems unquestionably an authentic BG/Lanin recorded collaboration; Benny regards the solo as his.

This was BG's first effort for the Columbia label. The "W" prefix to the matrix denotes a Western Electric recording system process, for which Columbia paid WE royalties. In main the prefix is used to identify issues on the CO label; this practice varied, however.

IPANA TROUBADOURS, c. October 25, 1928, New York
S. C. Lanin, Director

Benny Goodman, clt; Jimmy McPartland, cnt; Tommy Dorsey, tbn; unk tpt, as, ts, p, bjo, tu, d, voc. The unknown logically are Pollack men.

W 147142-3 CO 1638-D, CoE 5243 (no solo)
>**Glorianna** - voc ref

W 147143-2 CO 1638-D **LP:** TOM 28, SB 112 (clt solo)
>**Do You? That's All I Want To Know** - voc ref

(Other CO matrices recorded this date show no evidence of BG.)

The next session is in dispute - the author cannot recommend it. The clt is certainly not typical BG, but some collectors think Benny played alto sax and that Jimmy Dorsey is responsible for the clt solos. Frank Signorelli, pianist on the date, is adamant that both Goodman and Dorsey were present.

GOODY AND HIS GOOD TIMERS (GGT) c. November 1928, New York
DIXIE DAISIES (DD)

Benny Goodman (?), Jimmy Dorsey, clt & as; Jimmy McPartland, cnt; Jack Teagarden, tbn; poss. Bud Freeman, ts; Matty Malneck, v; Frank Signorelli, p; Dick Morgan, bjo; Harry Goodman, tu; Ben Pollack, d; Irving Mills (IM), voc. No violin on "Cause I'm In Love."

108485-2 PE 15105 A, PAT 36924 A (GGT); CA 9004, RO 808, LI
(3503) 3033 (DD) (clt intro)
>**Cause I'm In Love** - voc "Goody Goodwin" on PE, "Erwin Magee" on PAT (IM)

108486-1 CA 9004, RO 808, LI 3033 (DD) (as solo)
108486-2 PE 15083 A, PAT 36902 A, Pat F X6279 (GGT); RO 808
(3502) (DD). **LP:** EPIC LN24045, CoE 33SX1545, VJMS 6, CN 523 (GGT) (as solo)
>**Digga Digga Do** - voc "Goody Goodwin" on PE, PAT, "voc ref" on CA (IM) (arr Elliot Jacoby)

The two listings for the upcoming "Whoopee Stomp" are genuine matrices. For some time it is was believed that each represented a different session; now it is fairly certain that these are different takes from the same session.

A very few copies of PE 15126 B, and all copies of VoE 12, have the number "3" pressed into the wax in the position appropriate to take numbers. This has misled some into thinking these issues to be alternates to mx 108515-2. There is no aural or time differentials between any issues, however. A discernible "hiss" indicates the false take 3's to have been dubbed from a genuine take 2 record.

MILLS MUSICAL CLOWNS (MMC) c. November 1928, New York
DIXIE DAISIES (DD)
THE LUMBERJACKS (L)
WHOOPEE MAKERS (WM)
BENNY GOODMAN AND HIS ORCHESTRA (BG)
BENNY GOODMAN'S WHOOPEE MAKERS
WITH JACK TEAGARDEN (BGWM)

Benny Goodman, clt; Jimmy McPartland, cnt; poss. Al Harris, tpt; Jack Teagarden, tbn; Gil Rodin, as; Larry Binyon (or poss. Bud Freeman), ts; Vic Briedis, p; Dick Morgan, bjo; Harry Goodman, tu; Ray Bauduc (or remotely poss. Ben Pollack), d.

108513-1 PE 15096 B, PAT 36915 B (MMC). **LP:** SB 141 (clt solo)
3514-A ALT TAKE: CA 9030, RO 834, LI 3059 (L), SHRDLU 7051 (BGWM). **EP:** VJMS VEP13 (WM). **LP:** RS 010B, CN 523, SB 112 (WM (clt solo)
>**Whoopee Stomp**

108514-2 PE 15111 B, PAT 36930 B (MMC). CA 9034, RO 838, LI
(3561) 3063 (DD). **LP:** SB 112 (clt solo)
>**Baby**

108515-2 PE 15126 B, PAT 36945 B (WM), CA 9035, RO 839, LI
(3562) 3064 (DD), VoE 12, SHRDLU 7051, ImpCz A6002 (BGWM), ImpFr 10221 (BG). **LP:** EPIC LN24045, CoE 33SX1545, SB 141, RS 010A, TL STLJ08 (WM) (clt solo)
>**Bugle Call Rag** - (spoken intro, Jack Teagarden)

Benny's first effort for the HARMONY label was accompaniment for a gal thought to have been Annette Hanshaw, using the pseudonyms. . .

DOT DARE (DD) PATSY YOUNG (PY) November 22, 1928, New York

Benny Goodman, clt & as; prob. Mannie Klein, tpt; prob. Joe Venuti, v; plus unknown p, cello, d.

147482-3 HA 792-H, DI 2792-G, PUR 1220-S (DD): VE 1792-V
   (PY) **LP:** SB 112, SH 246 (as solo)
>**I Wanna Be Loved By You** - voc (Annette Hanshaw?)

147483-3 same issues (clt accomp, solo)
>**Is There Anything Wrong In That?** - voc (Annette Hanshaw?)

(Other HA mxs recorded Nov. 22, 147478 through 147481, are not BG items.)

A much-disputed session on November 23 produced an early "Stardust," issued as by GOODY AND HIS GOODTIMERS and THE DETROITERS. Matrix for this recording is 3455-A (108499); issues are on PE, PAT, and subsidiary labels. Benny states unreservedly that the clarinet here is not his, but rather Jimmy Dorsey's. In light of his decision, this side can no longer be considered a Goodman item.

JIMMY McHUGH'S BOSTONIANS (JMB) November 27, 1928, New York
SUNNY CLAPP & HIS BAND O'SUNSHINE (SC)

Benny Goodman, clt; Jimmy McPartland, cnt; Jack Teagarden, tbn; Gil Rodin, as; Larry Binyon, ts; Ed Bergman, v, 147495/6 only; Vic Briedis, p; Dick Morgan, bjo; Harry Goodman, tu; Ray Bauduc, d; plus prob. Al Harris, tpt. Vocalist "Claud(e) Reese" is most likely composer, band leader-sometime singer Sunny Clapp.

147495-2 HA 795-H, VE 1795-V, DI 2795-G. **LP:** EPIC LN24045,
   CoE 33SX1545 (JMB) (clt intro)
>**Baby!** (arr Elliott Jacoby) - voc Claude Reese

147496-2 HA 899-H, VE 1899-V, DI 2899-G (SC) (no solo)
>**Remember I Love You** - voc Claud(e) Reese

147497-2 HA 836-H, VE 1836-V, DI 2836-G. **LP:** EPIC LN24045,
   CoE 33SX1545 (JMB) (clt solo)
>**The Whoopee Stomp** (arr George Terry)

Note that the matrices for the next Pollack session are out of numerical sequence with a later Pollack session. Explanation for this apparent discrepancy is Victor's practice of assigning matrix numbers in blocks, plus haphazard usage at its several studios. Dates listed have been checked carefully and are correct.

BEN POLLACK AND HIS December 3, 1928, New York
PARK CENTRAL ORCHESTRA

Personnel as October 1.

BVE 49220-3 VI 28127 B, ZonoAu EE144. **LP:** SVL 154 (no solo)
>**Then Came The Dawn** - voc Dick Robertson

BVE 49221-2 same issues plus VDP R14070, **LP:** TOM 22 (clt solo)
BVE 49221-3 RcaFr FXMI 7283 (clt solo)
>**Sentimental Baby** - voc Gene Austin

Jimmy McHugh and Dorothy Fields approached Pollack with an offer that he have his band "double" from the Park Central to the pit for their new musical, "Hello, Daddy." Pollack satisfied the residency requirements of the New York musicians' local, and accepted.

The revue opened in Philadelphia December 10 at the Market Street Theatre, with Philadelphia-local musicians. After a successful two-week tryout the show moved to Broadway December 26, and opened in the Mansfield Theatre—with the Pollack orchestra.

Ray Bauduc, Big Tea's buddy, joined Pollack just prior to the New York debut of "Hello, Daddy." One bit of jazz lore is that Pollack forsook the drums because he felt he wasn't recognized as the band's leader while he was behind the traps. Perhaps a more cogent explanation is that he realized he should no longer perform as a drummer along with his growing responsibilities as leader and business agent.

In any event, Bauduc came on. Ironically, Ray's first recording work while a member of the Pollack band was not for Pollack at all, but rather for Ben's "Bad Boys," and on a Sunday, at that.

THE LUMBERJACKS (L)　　　　　**December 23, 1928, New York**
THE DIXIE DAISIES (DD)
THE CAROLINERS (C)

Benny Goodman, clt & as; Jimmy McPartland, cnt; Jack Teagarden, tbn; Gil Rodin, as; Larry Binyon, ts; Vic Briedis, p; Dick McPartland, g; Harry Goodman, tu; Ray Bauduc, d; unknown vocalists.

3579-B　　CA 9041, RO 845, LI 3070 (L). **LP:** CN 523, SB 112 (as solo)
　　　　　Blue Little You - voc ref

3580-B　　CA 9043, RO 847, LI 3072 (DD) (no solo)
　　　　　Japanese Dream - voc ref

3581-C　　CA 9042, RO 846, LI 3071 (c). **LP:** SB 112 (clt solo)
　　　　　Hungry For Love - voc ref

On Christmas Eve day, two days before "Hello, Daddy" was to open in New York, the Pollack orchestra recorded two tunes from the show:

BEN POLLACK AND HIS　　　　**December 24, 1928, New York**
　　PARK CENTRAL ORCHESTRA

Benny Goodman, clt; Jimmy McPartland, cnt; Al Harris, tpt; Jack Teagarden, tbn; Gil Rodin, as; Larry Binyon, ts; Eddie Bergman, Al Beller, v; Bill Schumann, cel; Vic Briedis, p; Dick Morgan, g; Harry Goodman, tu; RAY BAUDUC, d.

BVE 48286-　UNISSUED (remake date, January 24, 1929)
(1,2,3)　　　**Let's Sit And Talk About You** - voc Scrappy Lambert

BVE 48287-1　**LP:** Rca Fr 741.101 (clt solo)
BVE 48287-2　VI 21858 B, VDP R14136. **LP:** TOM 22, SVL 154 (clt solo)
　　　　　Futuristic Rhythm - voc Ben Pollack

The day "Hello, Daddy" began its New York run presents a problem: Did Goodman participate in a recording session December 26 that included other members of the Pollack orchestra? He is not identifiable aurally, although there is some substance to the belief that his is the flute solo on the third side. It seems likely that this session is a continuation of the one on December 23, which would argue Benny's presence—although it is known that Teagarden is not on the upcoming sides. And note that contrary to prior listings, it is now believed that only one take each of the three sides is extant.

THE LUMBERJACKS (L)　　　　　**December 26, 1928, New York**
THE CAROLINERS (C)
THE DIXIE DAISIES (DD)

Personnel as December 23, except BG's presence is uncertain, and Teagarden is replaced by an unknown trombone. Vocalists are also not known.

3588-B　　CA 9045, RO 849, LI 3074 (L). **LP:** CN 523 (no solo)
　　　　　Let Me Be Alone With You - voc ref

3589-C　　CA 9046, RO 850, LI 3075 (C) (subt clt)
　　　　　June - voc ref

3590-B　　CA 9047, RO 851, LI 3076 (DD). **LP:** SB 112 (poss. BG flt solo)
　　　　　I'm Just Wondering Who

Capitalizing on the instant success of "Hello, Daddy," Benny and the "Pollack Band without Pollack" recorded some of the tunes from the show for various labels, under various pseudonyms. (Note that a claim of an issued take 1 of mx 108565, "Futuristic Rhythm," on PE has never been substantiated.)

MILLS MUSICAL CLOWNS (MMC)　　**December 27, 1928, New York**
THE COTTON PICKERS (CP)
THE DIXIE DAISIES (DD)

Benny Goodman, clt & as; Jimmy McPartland, cnt; Jack Teagarden, tbn; Gil Rodin, as; Larry Binyon, ts; Vic Briedis, p & celeste; Dick Morgan, bjo; Harry Goodman, tu; Ray Bauduc, d.

108565-3　　PE 15125 A, PAT 36944 A (MMC). **LP:** RS 010B, SB 114 (clt solo)
　　　　　Futuristic Rhythm - voc Mildred Roselle

108566-1　　Same issues (MMC), except no RS (as solo)
　　　　　Out Where The Blues Begin - voc Mildred Roselle

108567-1　　PE 15111 A, PAT 36930 A (MMC); CA 9048, RO 852
(3591)　　　(CP); LI 3077 (CP, DD). **EP:** VJMS VEP13. **LP:** CN 523, SB 114 (clt solo)
　　　　　Railroad Man - (voc Dick Morgan)

It seems incongruous that the very corny "Railroad Man" was bracketed with the two tunes recorded "straight" this date, until it is remembered that the record contractors, mindful of the success of the earlier "Shirt Tail Stomp," insisted on a full dollop of corn from each session by 'Ben's Bad Boys.' Note that Dick Morgan is shown as "vocalist" on "Railroad Man," for there is indeed a vocal of sorts, but that the label legends fail to list a vocal refrain.

The "Hello, Daddy" kick continues, with songwriter Jimmy McHugh credited with this session. There is a question as to whether these tunes were cut January 8 or 9; evidence favors January 8.

JIMMY McHUGH's BOSTONIANS　　**January 8, 1929, New York**

Benny Goodman, clt & as; Jimmy McPartland, cnt; prob. Al Harris, tpt; Jack Teagarden, tbn; Gil Rodin, as; Larry Binyon, ts; Vic Briedis, p; Dick Morgan, bjo; Harry Goodman, tu; Ray Bauduc, d.

147759-2　　HA 836-H, VE 1836-V, DI 2836-G. **LP:** BIO 2, SB 114 (clt solo)
　　　　　Futuristic Rhythm - voc "Marvin Young" (Irving Kaufman)

147760-2　　HA 823-H, VE 1823-V, DI 2823-G (no solo)
　　　　　Let's Sit And Talk About You - voc "Jim Andrews" (Kaufman)

147761-3　　Same issues plus Lp, SB 114 (clt solo)
　　　　　In A Great Big Way - voc "Jim Andrews" (Kaufman)

Three BG items for which there are no specific, known recording dates break up the "Hello, Daddy" monopoly. Guess is that despite the seeming out-of-sequence matrices they were recorded in early-to-middle January, 1929, and all at one session.

CAROLINERS (C)　　　　　**c. January 1929, New York**
DIXIE DAISIES (DD)
SOCIETY NIGHT CLUB ORCHESTRA (SNCO)

Personnel unknown, prob. same as January 8. BG definite.

3620-b　　CA 9087, RO 889, LI 3114 (C) (clt brdg)
　　　　　I Wonder Where Mary Is Tonight - voc ref

3621-c　　CA 9085, RO 887, LI 3112 (DD). **LP:** CN 523, SB 114 (clt solo)
　　　　　There's Something New 'Bout The Old Moon Tonight - voc ref

3622-c　　CA 9072, RO 876, LI 3101 (SNCO) (no solo)
　　　　　Mexicali Moon - voc ref

Irving Mills arranged two of the hits from "Hello, Daddy" for Brunswick; and it is believed that non-vocal "G" takes of "Futuristic Rhythm" and "Out Where The Blues Begin" were also recorded, but these have never turned up. There is also some evidence that a third tune was recorded at this session, but it too has not been found.

HOTSY TOTSY GANG January 14, 1929, New York

Personnel as January 8 except poss. no ts; Briedis doubles on celeste.

E 29064	BR 4200, BrF 8149, BrG A8149. **LP:** OFC 26, HIST 28, SB 113 (clt solo)
	Futuristic Rhythm (arr Irving Mills) - voc (Smith Ballew)
E 29065	same issues, plus LP, JO3122 (as solo)
	Out Where The Blues Begin (arr Irving Mills) - voc (Smith Ballew)
	UNISSUED
	South Breeze

The next date apparently was a continuation of THE HOTSY TOTSY GANG session, but the initial release was switched to Okeh:

LOUISVILLE RHYTHM KINGS January 16, 1929, New York

Personnel as January 8 except poss. VIC MOORE, d, for Bauduc.

401535-A	OK 41189, OdF 165642, OdG AI89242, PaG B12755 (no solo)
	Let's Sit And Talk About You - voc (Smith Ballew)

The record contractors continued to insist that Benny and his cohorts grind out the salable "Shirt Tail Stomp" brand of corn, even though the Pollack band's reputation for playing legitimate jazz was growing. Close listening reveals Dick Morgan's reference to Benny in the midst of BG's razz-ma-tazz alto solo. Note that both released takes of "Icky Blues" may not appear on all labels; those that are certain are listed in ( ). Note too, discovery of a take 3 of matrix 8477, "Shirt Tail Stomp." As of December 1985, only one copy of this take is known to exist, placing it among the very rarest of all Goodman recordings. A poor dub of it is on a bootleg LP.

JIMMY BRACKEN'S January 18, 1929, New York
TOE TICKLERS (JBTT)
DIXIE JAZZ BAND (DJB)
KENTUCKY GRASSHOPPERS (KG)

Benny Goodman, clt & as; Jimmy McPartland, cnt; Glenn Miller, tbn; Larry Binyon, ts; Vic Briedis, p; Dick Morgan, bjo & voc (DM); Harry Goodman, tu; Ray Bauduc, d. (Gil Rodin, as, evidently not present.)

8476 (1,2)	UNISSUED (Rejected)
	Tiger Rag
8477-2	DO 4274, RE 8726, APEX 8950 (JBTT). **LP:** CN 523 (clt solo)
8477-3	BA 6355-B (KG). **LP:** SB 141 (clt solo)
	Shirt Tail Stomp
8478-2,3	DO 4278-B (2), RE 8723 (2), BER 3001-B (2) (JBTT); OR 1515-b (3), CH 958-b (3), JE 5547 (3) (DJB); BA 6323 (3) (KG). **LP:** SB 114 (2,3) (as solo)
	Icky Blues - voc "Icky Morgan" on DO, BA & BER, "Tom Howard" on OR, CH (all DM)

The artist credit—"Ben's Bad Boys" - on Victor's label for the next session's efforts seems an unsubtle statement of Pollack's attitude toward Benny and other of Pollack's employees who were recording independently with increasing frequency. However, Pollack - and Victor - could not help but be impressed by the commercial success of the moonlighters' records. Therefore, another doggy version of "Shirt Tail Stomp" was cut, along with the legitimate sides.

"Shirt Tail Stomp" was witheld from public release for almost 30 years. Initial holdup may have resulted from the objections of Benny and the others, for they truly despised this kind of non-music. And possibly Pollack, a sensitive jazz musician himself, sided with them.

Liner notes for the initial issue of "Shirt Tail Stomp" list Jack Teagarden as trombonist. Collectors generally agree, however, that Glenn Miller made these sides, although he was out of the band and Big Tea was in. Personnel listed is believed correct:

BEN'S BAD BOYS January 22, 1929, New York
Ben Pollack, Director

Benny Goodman, clt; Jimmy McPartland, cnt; Glenn Miller, tbn; Vic Briedis, p; Dick Morgan, bjo; Harry Goodman, tu; Ray Bauduc and/or Ben Pollack, d. Vocal interjection on "Yellow Dog Blues" is Pollack's.

BVE 49673-1	**LP:** RcaFr FXMI 7165, SB 136 (clt solo)
BVE 49673-2	VI 21971 B, ViArg 21971 B. **LP:** RcaFr FXMI 7165, OFC 40 (clt solo)
	Wang Wang Blues
BVE 49674-1	**LP:** RcaFr FMXI 7165, SB 136 (clt solo)
BVE 49674-2	VI 21971 A, ViArg 21971 A. **EP:** "X" EVA A3003. **LP:** "X" LX 3003, OFC 40, RcaFr FXMI 7165 (clt solo)
BVE 49674-3	**LP:** RcaFr FXMI 7165, SB 136 (clt solo)
	Yellow Dog Blues - (voc interjection, Pollack)
BVE 49675-1	**LP:** CAM CAL446, RcaFXMI 7165 (clt solo)
	Shirt Tail Stomp

Nat Shilkret also recorded for Victor on January 22: "I Want To Be Bad" and "You Wouldn't Fool Me, Would You?," both released on VI 21859. There is no evidence of Benny's participation on either side.

BEN POLLACK AND HIS January 24, 1929, New York
PARK CENTRAL ORCHESTRA

Personnel as December 24, 1928. Scrappy Lambert (SL) is the vocalist.

BVE 48286-4	VI 21858 A. **LP:** SVL 154 (clt solo)
	Let's Sit And Talk About You - voc "Burt Lorin" (SL)
BVE 48302-1	VI 21857 A, HMVAu EA530 (subt clt accomp)
	Sally Of My Dreams - voc "Burt Lorin" (SL)

The next date has piqued the interest of jazz buffs for many years. Rare BING CROSBY-SAM LANIN recordings—mx 401555, "I'm Crazy Over You"; mx 401556, "Susianna"; and mx 401557, "If I Had You"—were cut the same day, in the same studio, as indisputable Goodman items. Clarinet may be heard on the Crosby efforts; but it is Jimmy Dorsey's, not Benny Goodman's.

BENNIE'S LOUISVILLE January 25, 1929, New York
RHYTHM KINGS (BLRK)
LOUISVILLE RHYTHM KINGS (LRK)
ROOF GARDEN ORCHESTRA (RG)

Benny Goodman, clt & as; Jimmy McPartland, cnt; Jack Teagarden, tbn; Gil Rodin, as; Larry Binyon, ts; Vic Briedis, p; Dick Morgan, bjo; Harry Goodman, tu; Ray Bauduc, d; Smith Ballew (SB), voc.

401558-A	PaE R340 (BLRK); PaF 22305 (LRK); OdF 221129 (RG). **LP:** IAJRC-2 (LRK) (no solo)
	Shout Hallelujah! 'Cause I'm Home - voc (SB)
401559-A	OK 41189, OdF 165642, OdG A189242, PaIT B12755 (LRK). **LP:** TOM 22 (clt solo)
	In A Great Big Way - voc trio (SB, two unknown)

Might mention that Mr. Goodman never cared for the spelling, "Bennie." For those who would write him, make it "Benny." And never "Ben"—he doesn't like that at all. He tolerated "Ben" from Gene Krupa, but from no one else.

Red Nichols, who knew Benny in the pre-Pollack Chicago days, was very active in New York in the late '20's as a pit orchestra leader and record contractor; it was inevitable that he would employ Benny for both. But did he, for the February 1 studio date, following? The author includes it because of its widespread acceptance by Goodman collectors, but does not believe the alto solo is Benny's.

RED NICHOLS AND HIS FIVE PENNIES February 1, 1929, New York

Benny Goodman (?), clt & as; Red Nichols, Mannie Klein, tpt; Miff Mole, tbn; Dudley Fosdick, mel; Art Schutt, p; Carl Kress, g; Chauncey Morehouse, d.

E 29209	BR 4243, BrE 02356, BrE 3931 (no solo)
	I Never Knew
E 29210	Same issues plus LP, SB 137 (as solo)
	Who's Sorry Now?

Varying personnels have been ascribed to the next Nichols session. The BrE label lists "Pee Wee Russell" and goes on in that vein. In his biography Benny "remembers" Big Tea, Krupa and Bud Freeman for these sides. Personnel listed here is generally accredited, BG's memory after all those years and all those records notwithstanding.

RED NICHOLS AND HIS FIVE PENNIES   **February 5, 1929, New York**

Benny Goodman, clt; Red Nichols, Mannie Klein, tpt; Miff Mole, tbn; Fud Livingston, ts; Lennie Hayton, p; Carl Kress, g; Vic Berton, d.

E 29222   BR 4363, BR 6825, BrE 01856, BrE 5019, BrF 1029, BrF
               500403, BrG A8298. **LP:** BR BL58027, DE DL34313,
               SB 137. **45:** BR Set 9-7021 (clt solo)
               Chinatown, My Chinatown

E 29223   UNISSUED
               On The Alamo

JACK PETTIS' ORCHESTRA (JP)   **February 8, 1929, New York**
JACK BINNEY AND HIS ORCHESTRA (JB)

Benny Goodman, clt; Bill Moore, tpt; Jack Teagarden, tbn; Jack Pettis, C-mel; Al Goering, p; Dick McDonough, g; Merrill Klein, tu; Dillon Ober, d.

401594-B   OK 41411, OdG 03184 B, OdF 238288, PaE R673 (JP),
               PaA 34076 (JB). **LP:** EPIC LN24045, CoE 33SX1545
               (JP), BIO 1, RITZ Q1 (clt solo)
               Freshman Hop (arr Pettis)

401595-D   OK 41411, PaE R673, OdF 238288, OdG A286016 B,
               Odlt SSA2317 (JP). **LP:** EPIC LN24045, CoE
               33SX1545 (JP), BIO 1, TL STLJ05 (clt solo)
               Sweetest Melody (arr Pettis)

401596-B   OK 41410, OdG 031814 A (JP), PaA 34076 (JB). **LP:**
               EPIC LN24045, CoE 33SX1545, BIO 1,RITZ Q1 (clt
               solo)
               Bag O' Blues (arr Goering)

Another session was set up by the contractor of the January 18 "Shirt Tail Stomp"/"Icky Blues" date. But this time Gil Rodin, the boys' business agent, was ill, so Benny took charge. He had no stomach for the demeaning pop effluvia recorded earlier, and guts enough to insist on legitimate jazz. He liked the results—but the contractor screamed, refused to pay off until the session was remade. It was, in part on March 15, with Gil Rodin once again calling the shots.

In some manner, despite the objections of the contractor, two takes each of two of the sides cut February 11 eventually got to market. Note particularly the marked difference between take 1 of "Four Or Five Times" recorded this date and take 3 of that tune from March 15. Another notable difference is the addition of a scat vocal, beloved by the cornfed contractors, to the later version of "It's Tight Like That."

Known takes for the various issues are once more in ( ).

JIMMY BRACKEN'S TOE TICKLERS (JB)   **February 11, 1929, New York**
SOUTHERN NIGHT HAWKS (SNH)
LOU CONNOR & HIS COLLEGIATES
  (LOU CONNOR'S COLLEGIATES) (LC)
KENTUCKY GRASSHOPPERS (KG)

Benny Goodman, clt & as; Jimmy McPartland, cnt; poss. Al Harris, tpt; Jack Teagarden, tbn; Larry Binyon, ts; Vic Briedis, p; Dick Morgan, bjo; Harry Goodman, tu: Ray Bauduc, d.

8541-1,2   DO 4274 (1,2), RE 8726, APEX 8950 (2), CQ 7306 (1)
(2062-1,2)   (JB), CrC 81092 (SNH), OR 1483 (2), JE 5520 (1)
               (LC), BA 6295 B (1,2) (KG). **LP:** SB 114 (1,2) (clt
               solo)
               It's Tight Like That - voc intro (Jack Teagarden)

8542-1,2   DO 4278 A (1,2), RE 8723 (1), APEX 8936, CQ 7303,
(2061-1,2)   BER 3001 A (JB), OR 1483 (1), JE 5520 (1) (LC), BA
               6295 A (1) (KG). **LP:** RS 010A (2), SB 114 (1,2) (clt
               solo)
               Four Or Five Times

8543-(1,2)   UNISSUED (Rejected)
               Makin' Friends - voc Jack Teagarden

BEN POLLACK AND HIS   **March 1, 1929, New York**
  PARK CENTRAL ORCHESTRA

Benny Goodman, clt; Jimmy McPartland, cnt; RUBY WEINSTEIN, tpt; Jack Teagarden, tbn; Gil Rodin, as; Larry Binyon, ts; Ed Bergman, Al Beller, v; Bill Schumann, cel; Vic Briedis, p; Dick Morgan, g; Harry Goodman, tu; Ray Bauduc, d; Smith Ballew (SB), voc.

BVE 50905-2   VI 21941, HMVAu EA543. **LP:** RcaFr FXMI 7283, TOM
               22, SVL 154 (clt solo)
               Louise - voc "Charles Roberts" (SB)

BVE 50906-3   Same issues plus VDP R14182, Less RcaFr (no solo)
               Wait 'Til You See "Ma Cherie" - voc "Charles
               Roberts" (SB)

Mezz Mezzrow's claim that he was with Pollack in this period has not been substantiated. The clarinet soli throughout are without question Benny Goodman's.

BEN POLLACK AND HIS   **March 5, 1929, New York**
  PARK CENTRAL ORCHESTRA

Personnel as March 1.

BVE 50912-2   VI 21944 A. **LP:** RcaFr FXMI 7283, TOM 22, OFC40, TL
               STLJ08, SVL 154 (clt solo)
BVE 50912-3   **LP:** VI LPV528, RcaFr 731.088 (clt solo)
               My Kinda Love (One Way To Paradise) - voc Ben
               Pollack

BVE 50913-2   VI 21944 B. **LP:** RcaFr FXMI 7283, TOM 22, SVL 154
               (clt solo)
               On With The Dance! - voc Ben Pollack

Here is the first of the re-make sessions stemming from the BG-led date of February 11:

JIMMY BRACKEN'S TOE TICKLERS (JBTT)   **March 15, 1929, New York**
TED WHITE'S COLLEGIANS (TWC)
KENTUCKY GRASSHOPPERS (KG)
LOU CONNOR & HIS COLLEGIATES
  (LOU CONNOR'S COLLEGIATES) (LC)
SOUTHERN NIGHT HAWKS (SNH)
FRANK ARNOLD AND HIS ORCHESTRA (FAr)
LESLIE NORMAN'S ORCHESTRA (LN)

Personnel as February 11, plus Gil Rodin, as. Al Harris, tpt, probably out.

8477-5   DO 4274, APEX 8950, RE 8726 (JBTT), OR 1544, JE
(2187-5)   5577 (TWC), BA 6355 (KG). **LP:** SB 114 (clt solo)
               Shirt Tail Stomp

8541-4   DO 4274, APEX 8950, RE 8726 (JBTT), OR 1483, JE
(2062-4)   5520 (LC), BA 6295 (KG), CrC 81092 (SNH), MIC
               22455 (FAr). **LP:** RS 010A, SB 114, TL STLJ08 (clt
               solo)
               It's Tight Like That -voc (Jack Teagarden)

8542-3   DO 4278, APEX 8936, RE 8723, CQ 7303, BER 3001 A
(2061-3)   (JBTT), OR 1483, JE 5520 (LC), BA 6295 (KG), MIC
               22441 (LN). **LP:** SB 114 (clt solo)
               Four Or Five Times - voc (Dick Morgan)

Next are (at least) three BG sessions whose dates are unknown. Dates given are approximations. Personnels are believed correct. It has been suggested that Benny also plays trumpet on "Freshman Hop."

TEN FRESHMEN (TF)   **March 1929, New York**
MILLS MUSICAL CLOWNS (MMC)
TEN BLACK DIAMONDS (TBD)

Benny Goodman, clt; Bill Moore, Phil Hart, tpt; Paul Weigan, tbn; Jack Pettis, C-mel; Al Goering, p; Clay Bryson, bjo; Merrill Klein, tu; Dillon Ober, d.

108645-2   PE 15235 A, PAT 37054 A (TF), CA 0108 B, BA 0508 B,
(9103-2)   OR 1760, RO 1125 (TBD). **LP:** RS 010B, BIO 1, SB
               107 (clt solo)
               Freshman Hop

108646-2   PE 15136 B, PAT 36955 B (MMC). **LP:** BIO 1, SB 107, VJSM 6 (clt solo)
Sweetest Melody

108647-2   PE 15235 B, PAT 37054 B (TF). **LP:** RS 010B, BIO 1, (clt solo)
Bag O' Blues

PAUL MILLS AND HIS　　　　　　　　　　**April 1929, New York**
MERRY MAKERS (PMMM)
WHOOPEE MAKERS (WM)
JACK TEAGARDEN AND THE WHOOPEE MAKERS (JTWM)
COTTON PICKERS (CP)　THE LUMBERJACKS (L)　DIXIE DAISIES (DD)
MILLS MERRY MAKERS (MMM)　BROADWAY BROADCASTERS (BB)

Personnel as March 15.

3760-C   CA 9126, RO 928, LI 3153. **LP:** CN 523 (PMMM) (no solo)
Little Rose Covered Shack - voc ref (Scrappy Lambert)

3766-C   PE 15223 B, PAT 37042 B (WM); UHCA 40 (JTWM); CA 9174, RO 976, LI 3201 (CP). **LP:** EPIC LN 24045, CoE 33SX1545, SB 141 (WM) (clt solo)
Dirty Dog - voc Jack Teagarden

3767-B   CA 9147, RO 949, LI 3714. **LP:** CN 523 (L) (no solo)
Would You Be Happy - voc ref (Scrappy Lambert)

3768-C   CA 9142, RO 944, LI 3169. **LP:** HARR LPD (DD) (no solo)
(Eyes Of Blue) You're My Waterloo - voc ref (Scrappy Lambert)

108723-2   PE 15142 A (MMM). **LP:** PHON 7608 (clt solo)
108723-3   PE 15142 A, PAT 36961 A (MMM); CA 9130, Ro 932, LI
(3773-3)   3157. **LP:** CN 523, SB 107 (BB) (clt solo)
Honey - voc "Harold Lang" on PE, "voc ref" on CA, RO, LI (Scrappy Lambert)

Notes, April 1929 listing:
This listing embraces two, perhaps three, recording sessions.
CA-RO matrix 3769-A, "My Sin," CA 9127, Cliff Roberts and his Orchestra, sometimes added to this listing, has a true PE-PAT matrix of 108747-1 which was recorded later. Clarinet accompaniment cannot clearly be credited to BG.
PE-PAT matrix 108722-2, "Coquette," PE 15146 and PAT 36965, Veo's Hotel McAlpin Orchestra, apparently recorded the same day as "Honey," does not include BG. Veo's was a hotel band, not a studio group.
Claims of an issued "A" take for "Would You Be Happy" are false.

APRIL 4, 1929, New York - On this date another re-make session stemming from Feb. 11 produced additional takes of mx 8476, "Tiger Rag," and mx 8543, "Makin' Friends," plus mx 8657, "Sweet Liza." These are not Goodman items - musicians on the date verify Jimmy Dorsey substituting for BG, and close listening bears them out. A report that Maurie Bercov, clt, replaced BG in the Pollack band in Spring, 1929, for a brief period may have meaning in JD's substitution for BG on the April 4 session.
Next is the Nichols' date Benny "remembers" in his biography. His faulty recollection is understandable, for this is the session that produced "On The Alamo" that was released. It is also Benny's first known recording date with Gene Krupa:

RED NICHOLS AND HIS FIVE PENNIES　　　**April 18, 1929, New York**

Benny Goodman, clt; Red Nichols, Leo McConville, tpt; Glenn Miller, Jack Teagarden, tbn; Babe Russin, ts; Jack Russin, p; Carl Kress, g; poss. Artie Miller, b; Gene Krupa, d.

E 29708-A   BR 4373, BR 6718, VO 4599, OK 4599, BrE 01591, BrF 500404, BrG A9206, CoAu DO1236. **LP:** AOH AH63 (clt solo)

E 29708-B   BR 80006 A. **45:** BR set 9-7008. **EP:** BR EB71018. **7" LP:** SW JCS33734. **LP:** BR BL54008, BR BL54010, BR BL54047, BR BL58008, BrE LAT8307, CRL 100, CrlFr CVM40012, CrlG LPC96016, Fest Au B12-1488, MCA 2-4018, VC LVA9011, LSS LW267, AFF 1018 (clt solo)
Indiana (arr Miller)

E 29709-A   BR 4373, BR 6718, VO 4599, OK 4599, BrE 01591, BrF 500404, BrG A9206, BR 80006 B, LuJap S28. **45:** BR set 9-7008. **EP:** BR EB71018. **7" LP:** SW JCS 33734. **LP:** BR BL54008, BR BL58008, AFF 1018, BrE LAT8307, CRL 100, CrlFr CVM40012, FestAu B12-1488, PHON 7608, VC LVA9011, LSW LW267 (clt solo)
Dinah (arr Miller)

E 29710-A   BR 4363, BrE 5019 (no solo)
On The Alamo - voc Scrappy Lambert (arr Fred Van Epps, Jr.)

E 29710-G   BR 6825, BrE 01856, BrF 1029, BrF 500403, BrG A8298. **LP:** EMA 2 (clt solo)
On The Alamo (no vocal) (arr Fred Van Epps, Jr.)

Coincidentally, Benny's next studio stint marked his first recording date with another great drummer who was also to join with him years later, Dave Tough:

LOUISIANA RHYTHM KINGS,　　　**April 23, 1929, New York**
Direction of Red Nichols

Benny Goodman, clt; Red Nichols, tpt; Miff Mole (possibly Glenn Miller), tbn; Art Schutt, p; Dave Tough, d.

E 29689   VO 15828, HRS 15, HJCA 612 A. **LP:** OFC 26, JAZ 14, SB 137 (clt solo)
Ballin' The Jack

E 29690   UNISSUED
You've Never Been Blue

E 29691   VO 15810. **LP:** IAJRC-1, HIST HLP25, STO 3123, JO 3123, SB 137 (clt solo)
I'm Walking Through Clover (I'm Happy In Love)

The only contemporary release from the next session, "Bugle Call Blues" - VI 38105, gave no hint of Benny's participation, for the prominent clarinet on it belongs to Tony Parenti, a sometime substitute for Benny in the Pollack band. Discovery of single takes of the other three performances on test pressings substantiated Parenti's contention that Benny was on the date, for his soli are easily distinguishable. Note that the Neiman-Marcus release, a very rare issue, is transcribed from the master and is of excellent audio quality. The RITZ bootlegs are poor quality, evidently dubs of dubs, ad infinitum.

JACK PETTIS AND HIS PETS　　　**May 9, 1929, New York**

Benny Goodman, Tony Parenti, clt & as; Bill Moore, Phil Hart, tpt; Tommy Dorsey, tbn; Jack Pettis, c-mel & ts; Matty Malneck, v; Al Goering, p & celeste; Clay Bryson, g; Merrill Klein, b; Dillon Ober, d.

BVE 51691-1   **LP:** RITZ Q1 (BG 1st clt solo)
(2,3)   **Companionate Blues**

BVE 51692-1   **LP:** RITZ Q1 (BG clt solo)
(2,3)   **Campus Crawl**

BVE 51693-1   **LP:** NM 40456, RITZ Q1 (BG 1st clarinet solo, as solo)
(2,3)   **Wild And Wooly Willy**

BVE 51694-2   VI 38105 B, HMV B4893, HMV B6288. **LP:** RITZ Q1 (no
(1)   BG solo)
Bugle Call Blues

Songwriter-pop singer Sammy Fain was next to engage BG:

SAMMY FAIN (THE CROONING COMPOSER)   **May 10, 1929, New York**

Benny Goodman, clt; plus prob. Mannie Klein or Phil Napoleon, tpt; Joe Venuti, v; Eddie Lang, g; Rube Bloom, p.

148508-2   HA 943-H, VE 1943-V, DI 2943-G. **LP:** SB 107 (clt solo)
        To Be In Love (Espesh'lly With You) - voc Sammy Fain

148509-1   Same issues (clt solo)
148509-2   VE 1943-V. **LP:** SB 107 (clt solo)
        What A Day! - voc Sammy Fain

148510-2   HA 961-H, VE 1961-V, DI 2961-G (clt subt & accomp)
        Why Can't You - voc Sammy Fain

Other Co matrices recorded May 10 - W 148497 and W 148502 thru 07 are by different groups and do not include Benny Goodman.

The next entry is speculative. On May 17 Gil Rodin took some of his cohorts from the Pollack band into the studios of the Independent Recording Laboratory, Inc., New York, and there they cut three tunes. But none has been issued, for all were rejected. Benny's participation is therefore problematic, although custom would indicate his presence. The same tunes were re-cut June 6, and the eventual releases are from this latter date. Benny, however, did not join in the June 6 session.

JIM BRACKEN'S TOE TICKLERS (JBTT)   **May 17, 1929, New York**
GIL RODIN & HIS BOYS (GR)

Quite likely the usual "Pollack band without Pollack," including Benny Goodman.

8761 (108932)   UNISSUED (JBTT) (Rejected)
        After You've Gone - voc Jack Kaufman

8762 (108931)   UNISSUED (JBTT) (Rejected)
        Twelfth St. Rag

8763 (108930)   UNISSUED (GR) (Rejected)
        It's So Good

Discovery of a datebook kept by band leader, record contractor, agent, promoter Ed Kirkeby added a good deal of knowledge to personnels of the '30's. It confirmed some, negated others that discographers had guessed at over the years. One supposed BG item it eliminated is the session of May 23, the SEVEN HOT AIR MEN recordings of "Gotta Feelin' For You," mx W 148617-2, and "Low Down Rhythm," mx W 148618-2, released on CO 1850-D et al. The clarinetist was Pete Pumiglio, later prominent as a member of Raymond Scott's small groups.

BEN POLLACK AND HIS   **May 27, 1929, New York**
PARK CENTRAL ORCHESTRA

Personnel as March 1. Scrappy Lambert (SL), voc.

BVE 53517-3   VI 22252 (subt clt)
        I'd Like To Be A Gypsy - voc "Burt Lorin" (SL)

BVE 53518-   UNISSUED - Test Pressing (clt solo)
(1,2,3)   **Finding The Long Way Home** - voc SL

(A test pressing of matrix BVE 53518, discovered in 1983, bears no take designation.)

Mr. Goodman does not remember any association with the next entry; actually, "Carl Fenton" was a pseudonym for Gus Haenschen, and Gus does not ring a bell with Benny. Adjacent matrices do not reveal any evidence of BG; and other records by Fenton-Haenschen also fail to produce identifiable Benny Goodman. Nevertheless, the two clt solos seem unmistakably BG's - he agrees - and the inclusion of this session is thus fully warranted. The record, incidentally, is one of the rarest of BG's Brunswick's.

CARL FENTON'S ORCHESTRA   **poss. June 19, 1929, New York**

Benny Goodman, clt; plus full orch. incl. unknown 2 tpt, tbn, as, v. p, bjo, d.

E 30035   BR 4421. **LP:** TOM 19, SB 107 (clt solo)
        What A Day! - voc (Dick Robertson)

E 30036   Same issues (clt solo)
        Maybe-Who Knows - voc (Dick Robertson)

"Hello, Daddy" closed June 15 after a lengthy run of 198 performances. Pollack continued working at the Park Central, from whence his

band broadcast over radio station WEAF, New York. All efforts to uncover airchecks of these broadcasts unfortunately have failed.

SAMMY FAIN (THE CROONING COMPOSER)   **July 16, 1929, New York**

Personnel as May 10.

148816-1   HA 993-H, VE 1993-V, DI 2993-G (subt clt solo)
        Liza (All The Clouds'll Roll Away) - voc Sammy Fain

148817-3   Same issues plus LP, SB 107 (clt solo)
        Ain't Misbehavin' - voc Sammy Fain

Next, what may be Benny's last record session as a regular member of Pollack's band. And listen carefully to the tenor sax solo on "Won't cha?"—it may be Benny's.

BEN POLLACK AND HIS   **July 25, 1929, New York**
PARK CENTRAL ORCHESTRA

Personnel as March 1, with Goodman possibly doubling on ts on BVE-53948. Scrappy Lambert (SL), voc.

BVE 53947-2   VI 22071 A, VDP R14236 **LP:** SVL 154 (no solo)
        In The Hush Of The Night - voc "Burt Lorin" (SL)

BVE 53948-2   VI 22071 B **LP:** SVL 154 (subt clt solo, poss. ts solo)
        Won'tcha? - voc "Burt Lorin" (SL)

BVE 53949-2   **LP:** "X" LX3003, RcaFr FXMI 7283, NM 40456, PHON
        LV50, SB 136. **EP:** "X" EVA B3003 (clt solo)

BVE 53949-3   VI 22074 A, VDP R14234, EIG EG1867. **LP:** RcaFr FXMI
        7283, PHON 7608, TOM 22, SVL 154 (clt solo)
        Bashful Baby - voc "Burt Lorin" (SL)

Inability to pinpoint precisely Benny's leaving Pollack's employ raised a question that long troubled Goodman collectors: Was his first motion picture Vitaphone Film #872, a Warner Bros./Vitaphone short subject featuring the Pollack band, made in New York, possibly on August 10, 1929?

The question was prompted by discovery of a 16", 33-1/3 rpm transcription, recorded "inside-out" by Rca-Victor, that contains selections from the film. Its several tunes together offer no certain evidence of the identity of the clarinetist. The author played a tape of the ET for Mr. Goodman, who simply shrugged at the brief clarinet passages. He said he recalled faintly that Pollack "made a movie" at that time, but that he had no recollection of participating in it. What was needed was the film itself, visual identification. Diligent search over 25 years failed to uncover it.

At last, in 1986, a print was located in the Library of Congress. Unfortunately, it had no accompanying sound track. A tape of the ET was painstakingly made to synchronize with the film; happily, it meshed exactly. And in the opening sequence, Benny is clearly identifiable, up front in the three-man reed section, playing baritone. Thus a quarter-century puzzle was solved, and Benny's first film, and his first electrical transcription, is confirmed:

BEN POLLACK AND HIS ORCHESTRA   **? August 10, 1929, New York**
Personnel as March 1, with Benny doubling on bar.

VA-872-4-1   ET: VITAPHONE No. 872
        California Echoes (theme) - medley:
           California, Here I Come
           Memories
           The Sweetheart Of Sigma Chi
        My Kinda Love-voc Ben Pollack, Jack Teagarden,
         ensemble
        Song Of The Islands (theme)

Out of the Park Central in July, the Pollack orchestra played a few theatre dates, then took a two-week vacation. It may have been during this vacation that Benny and brother Harry went home to Chicago, and while there recorded:

BENNIE GOODMAN'S BOYS   **August 13, 1929, Chicago**

Benny Goodman, clt; Wingy Mannone, tpt; Bud Freeman, ts; Joe Sullivan, p; Herman Foster, bjo; Harry Goodman, tu; Bob Conselman, d.

C 4035   BR 4968, BR 80028 B, BrE 1264, BrF 500318. **LP:** BR
        BL54010, BR BL58015, FestAu CFR10-437, CrlFr
        CVM40012, LSS LW267, VC LVA9011, ARIS 12016,

McaG/CrlG 6796, MCA 2-4018, VoE VLP2, SB 141, AFF 1018. **45:** BR set 9-7017. **ET:** AFRS Remember 484 (clt solo)
After A While (scat voc Mannone)

C 4036 Same issues, except: add **LP:** DE DL8398, BrE LAT8166, PHON 7608; **EP:** CrlG 94109; and delete ARIS 12016, AFRS Remember 484 (clt solo)
Muskrat Scramble

Note that ''Muskrat Scramble'' is spelled that way on the original issue, BR 4968. BrF 500318 uses ''Muscrat Scramble;'' subsequent issues use the more usual ''Muskrat Ramble.''

It is not known whether Benny recorded the next three Pollack sides. Absence of an identifiable clt solo on any side makes it impossible to resolve the question.

According to Benny's biography and other sources, he had some disagreements with Pollack and quit the band formally in August or September. Benny remembers rejoining the band briefly, after he had left it, for one week in the Fox Bushwick Theatre, Brooklyn, beginning August 26. It is also likely that in September he played for Pollack when the band substituted on the Fleischmann Radio Show for regular Rudy Vallee, who'd gone to Hollywood to film ''Vagabond Lover.'' These factors suggest BG might well have made the upcoming date.

The three records involved are fairly easy to obtain, and are inexpensive. Goodman collections having the goal of totality should include them. But beyond this date, Benny is no longer a regular member of the Pollack band; he returned for record sessions only.

BEN POLLACK AND HIS　　　　　　　**August 15, 1929, New York**
PARK CENTRAL ORCHESTRA

Personnel as March 1, with Goodman in question, and prob. MURPH STEINBERG, tpt, for McPartland. Scrappy Lambert (SL), voc.

BVE 53989-2 VI 22106 A, VDP R14253. **LP:** TOM 22, SVL 154 (no solo)
Where The Sweet Forget-Me-Nots Remember - voc ''Burt Lorin'' (SL)

BVE 53990-3 VI 22147 B, VDP R14294. **LP:** RcaFr 741.101, TOM 22, SVL 154 (clt bridge)
Song Of The Blues - voc ''Burt Lorin'' (SL)

BVE 53991-2 VI 22089 A, HMVAu EA610, VDP R14287. **LP:** TOM 22, SVL 154 (clt bridge)
True Blue Lou - voc ''Burt Lorin'' (SL)

Contrary to some discographies, the RED NICHOLS session of August 20, 1929, which produced ''I May Be Wrong'' and ''The New Yorkers,'' issued on BR 4500 et al, does not include Benny Goodman. Red's clarinetist for this date was Pee Wee Russell. Benny's next recordings with Red were:

RED NICHOLS AND HIS FIVE PENNIES　　　**September 9, 1929, New York**

Benny Goodman, clt; Red Nichols, Mickey Bloom, Tommy Thunen, tpt; Jack Teagarden, Glenn Miller, Bill Trone, tbn; Jimmy Dorsey, as; Rube Bloom, p; Tommy Fellini, bjo; Joe Tarto, tu; Dave Tough, d. Scrappy Lambert (SL), voc.

E 30538-A BR 4790, BR 6832, BRE 02505, BrF 8744, BrG A8744. **LP:** SB 137 (clt solo)

E 30539 UNISSUED
Nobody Knows (And Nobody Seems To Care) - voc (SL)

E 30540 Same issues except delete BRE 02545, and add **LP:** AOH168 (clt solo)

E 30541 UNISSUED
Smiles - voc (SL)

E 30542 UNISSUED (Rejected)
E 30543 UNISSUED
Say It With Music - probable vocal, Scrappy Lambert

(Recurring claims that alternate, non-vocal takes of ''Nobody Knows'' and ''Smiles'' exist on BR 4790; that BrG A8744, ''Smiles,'' is matrix E 30541; and that ''Say It With Music,'' matrices E 30542 and E 30543, was issued from this session, are all unsubstantiated and appear to be false.)

Out of Pollack's band, Benny joined Eddie Paul in the pit of the Paramount Theatre in New York on Glenn Miller's recommendation. While there Benny cut his first CHARLESTON CHASERS set:

THE CHARLESTON CHASERS　　　　　　**September 28, 1929, New York**

Benny Goodman, clt; Phil Napoleon, tpt; Miff Mole, tbn; Babe Russin, ts; Art Schutt, p; Joe Tarto, b; Stan King, d; Eva Taylor (ET), voc.

W 149072-2 CO 1989-D, CoE CB16, CoArg A8219. **LP:** VJM 44, TOM 6 (clt accomp)
What Wouldn't I Do For That Man! - voc (ET)

W 149073-3 Same issues plus **LP:** NOST 890/1 (clt solo)
Turn On The Heat - voc (ET)

Five and six shows a day, six days a week, with a non-jazz band soon had Benny fed up with his job at the Paramount. He quit, joined Red Nichols in New York's new Hollywood Restaurant early in October.

The next entry is a doubtful one. Clt accompaniment on two sides seems more BG's than not, so inclusion on that basis seems warranted:

COLUMBIA PHOTO PLAYERS (CPP)　　　**November 18, 1929, New York**
RUDY MARLOW AND HIS ORCHESTRA (RM)
THE CAPITOLIANS (C)

Poss. Benny Goodman, clt & as; plus full orch. incl 2 tpt, tbn, ts, 2 v, p, bjo, b, d, voc.

149434-2 CO 2048-D, CoE CB 24 (CPP) (clt accomp)
Take Everything But You - voc ref

195044 ???
495005 ???
100338-1 HA 1064-H, VE 2064-V, DI 3064-G (RM); PU 1088-P (C) (clt accomp)
Take Everything But You - no vocal

149435-3 CO 2048-D (CPP) (no solo)
Love Made A Gypsy Out Of Me - voc ref

The CO 195000 matrix series shown above was used to identify non-vocal versions of tunes destined for the Latin America trade. Catalog numbers are missing for some of these matrices, so evidently not all were issued. Interesting ones will crop up later, however.

The next day Benny recorded for the first time with Jimmy Melton, a stellar personality of the 20's and 30's. Years later BG will appear with Melton again, on Jimmy's radio program.

JAMES MELTON　　　　　　　　　**November 19, 1929, New York**

Benny Goodman, clt; plus unknown 3 v, b, p.

W 149445-3 CO 2050-D. RZAu G20674 (no solo)
Love (Your Spell Is Everywhere) - voc James Melton

W 149446-6 CO 2084-D. **LP:** SB 107 (clt solo)
The Shepherd's Serenade (Do You Hear Me Calling You) - voc James Melton

Other CO matrices recorded November 19—149439 through 149441, and W 149442 through W 149444—were cut by different groups and are thought not to include Benny Goodman.

JAMES MELTON　　　　　　　　　**December 6, 1929, New York**

Personnel as November 19.

W 149695-3 CO 2065-D. **LP:** SB 107 (clt solo)
There Will Never Be Another Mary - voc James Melton

W 149696-3 CO 2084-D, ReE MR41, RZAu G20766. **LP:** SB 107 (clt solo)
The Sacred Flame - voc James Melton

Other CO matrices recorded December 6—W 149690 through W 149694—were not by Melton and are believed not to include Benny Goodman.

Concluding Benny's recording activities for the year 1929, and with it the BEN POLLACK ERA, is a double date for Ben Selvin. This was Benny's first session for Selvin, and it serves to introduce the BEN SELVIN ERA:

OSCAR GROGAN   **December 11, 1929, New York**

Benny Goodman, clt & as; Bob Effros, Tommy Gott, tpt; Tommy Dorsey, 1 unknown, tbn; Joe Dubin, ts; Ben Selvin, 1 unknown, v; Irving Brodsky, p; Jack Hansen, b; Stan King, d.

W 149709-2   CO 2074-D (subt clt solo)
              Love Made A Gypsy Out Of Me - voc Oscar Grogan

W 149710-3   same issue (subt clt solo)
              All That I'm Asking Is Sympathy - voc Oscar Grogan

THE KNICKERBOCKERS (K)   **same session**
JOE CURRAN'S BAND (JC)
EDDIE GORDON'S BAND (EG)
RUDY MARLOW & HIS ORCHESTRA (RM)
KOLSTER DANCE ORCH. (KDO)
ROOF GARDEN ORCHESTRA (RGO)

Same personnel. Smith Ballew (SB), voc.

W 149711-3   CO 2067-D, CoE CB65 (K). **LP:** SB 108 (clt solo)
              Why Do You Suppose? - voc (SB)

W 195055   OdA ONY36007 (EG)
W 495010-1   PaA PNY24008 (JC) (clt solo)
W 495010-3   PaE R658 (RGO)
              Why Do You Suppose? - no vocal

W 149712-3   CO 2072-D (KDO). **LP:** SB 108 (clt solo)
              Do Ya' Love Me? (Just A Tiny Bit, Do Ya'?) - voc (SB)

W 195056   ???

100353-1   HA 1088-H, VE 2088-V, DI 3088-G (RM). **LP:** TOM 17
(W 495011-1)   (clt solo)
              Do Ya' Love Me? (Just A Tiny Bit, Do Ya'?) - no vocal

(Columbia's files indicate matrices W 195056 and W 495011 were cut, but do not specify releases for them. Possibilities are OdA, PaA and PaE.

There remains one piece of unfinished business for the year 1929: The author is unable to verify a claim that Benny appeared in a six-minute movie short, "Me And The Boys." Produced under British auspices by Victor Saville in RKO's New York studios, it reputedly features Benny, Jimmy McPartland, Jack Teagarden, Vic Briedis, Dick Morgan and Ray Bauduc in two selections. The first is "Mean To Me," with a vocal by Englishwoman Estelle Brody. McPartland, Tea and Morgan join her in the vocal for the second, "My Suppressed Desire." No one known to the author has ever seen this film, and Benny says he has no recollection of it.

THE BEN SELVIN ERA

The title, THE BEN POLLACK ERA, accurately describes the first three years of Benny Goodman's recording career because he worked more, and recorded more, with Pollack and members of that orchestra than with any others. An equally apt classification for the next few years is less obvious.

"The Studio Group Era" has some appeal. Indeed, Benny's regular affiliations are so temporary and tenuous for the next several years that were it not for his work with studio orchestras, assembled only for recording dates, there would be little early-Thirties' BG to deal with. THE BEN SELVIN ERA was chosen instead, for two reasons: During the first half of the decade Benny made more recordings with Ben Selvin and under his aegis than he did for any other leader, artist or contractor. The title also helps establish a trinity of Bens—Pollack, Selvin, and eventually Goodman.

A word about Selvin, musician (violin), leader, composer, contractor, record company executive. Ben Selvin has had a remarkable career in music, and an astonishing one in the field of phonograph records. Fifty-seven years ago, as this is written, he had already surpassed the output of most recording artists to this date. Witness this excerpt from **The Dance Magazine,** issue of May 1928:

> "You've seen his name hundreds of times on talking machine records, and you've had it poured at you out of loud speakers: Ben Selvin. In 1917 he had his first orchestra in the Moulin Rouge in New York, where he played for a world's record long-run engagement, until 1924: seven years straight. He and the orchestras under his baton have made over THREE THOUSAND RECORDS for different mechanical companies, and he broadcasts steadily. Lately he became head of broadcasting promotion work for one of the biggest record ng companies in the country."

When that article appeared, Selvin was 28 years of age. He would continue in the record business into his seventies, ending his career as an executive with RCA. Certainly the total number of recordings for which he is responsible, in his various capacities, is fantastic.

But the concern here is with Benny Goodman; Ben Selvin serves as a reference point and classification device. Both are needed to keep Goodman in focus, for his associations are short-lived albeit recurring, his progress erratic, his attainments diverse. These are the years of the Great Depression; still Benny chose to break off many a job because of musical or personality clashes with his bosses. Yet his acknowledged skills and talents kept him well paid while others starved. He played heavily scored popular and semi-classical music for money, but turned ever back to jazz for kicks. New York was his base, but he moved so peripatetically in the East that it is impossible to chronicle his whereabouts. But he seemed ever in the studios, mostly Columbia's and its affiliates, working for Ben Selvin.

Working with Benny for Selvin, according to Herman Wolfson (retired in Florida) were: Fuzzy Farrar, Bob Effros or Charley Margulis, lead tpt; Mannie Klein, 2nd tpt; Tommy Dorsey, tbn; Lou Martin, as; Wolfson, ts; Joe Venuti, v; Eddie Lang, g; and Rube Bloom, p. These were the men Selvin sought, says Wolfson, and more often than not they constituted his studio orchestra at this time.

Some Goodman enthusiasts champion a Selvin/Columbia session of January 14 as BG's first efforts for 1930, but there is nothing definitive on the matrices cited, 149754, 55, 56 and W 149759, 60. Choice here is a double date two days later:

RUBE BLOOM AND HIS BAYOU BOYS   January 16, 1930, New York

Benny Goodman, clt; Mannie Klein, tpt; Tommy Dorsey, tbn; Adrian Rollini, b-sax; Rube Bloom p; unknown bjo (probably Eddie Lang); Stan King, d.

W 149771-4   CO 2103-D, Coe DC57, CoAu D034. **LP:** TOM 4, NOST 890/1 (clt solo)
The Man From The South (With A Big Cigar In His Mouth) - voc Roy Evans, Rube Bloom

W 149772-2   CO 2103-D, CoE DC57, CoE CB75, CoAu D034. **LP:** TOM 4 (clt solo)
St. James Infirmary - voc Roy Evans

LEE MORSE AND HER BLUE GRASS BOYS   same date

Goodman, Klein, Dorsey, Bloom as above; plus Eddie Lang, g.

W 149773-4   CO 2101-D (clt accomp)
Until Love Comes Along - voc Lee Morse

W 149774-1   CO 2101-D, CoE DB 140. **LP:** TT 213 (clt accomp)
Blue, Turning Grey Over You - voc Lee Morse

Red Nichols was selected as pit band leader for the Gershwins' "Strike Up The Band," and among others Red hired Benny, Bill Moore, Tommy Thunen, Glenn Miller, Babe Russin and Gene Krupa for what would become a long-run engagement. The sparkling musical comedy was on the road in Philadelphia when Benny received a proposition from Gil Rodin: the Pollack band had just finished a stand at the Park Central, and its principal members had decided to form a cooperative; was Benny interested? He was, but cautiously—he contacted his roommate Jimmy Dorsey, who agreed to substitute for Benny with Red; and he got Red's agreement to take on Jimmy while Benny took a two-week leave of absence. The co-op quickly fizzled (later it worked—the Bob Crosby band was a co-op formed by ex-Pollack bandsmen), and Benny reapplied for his job with Red. But Red said no, he was happy with Jimmy, and refused to take Benny back. That left Benny without a job in this, the first year of the Great Depression. He never quite forgave Nichols for this breach of trust.

Without a permanent job Benny played a number of college dance dates with pickup groups. A notable one was for Yale University, at York Hall, New Haven, in February; his cornetist was Bix Beiderbecke. (Another possible BG-Bix collaboration was in June—the "Camel Pleasure Hour" radio series, which included in its studio orchestra Tommy Dorsey, Lennie Hayton, Art Bernstein and Gene Krupa. But Benny has no recollection of what might have been his first association with R.J. Reynolds.) Benny does recall a near-miss with Bix at this time, a prom at Princeton University, in a group with Joe Sullivan and Gene Krupa—Bix was ill, and Max Kaminsky substituted for him.

Benny was not without regular employment for long. He signed with Don Voorhees, who had some lucrative radio contracts and whose orchestra included good personnel, such as Chelsea Qualey, Frank Guarente, Bill Moore, Bill Trone, Joe Tarto, Art Schutt, Dick McDonough and Chauncey Morehouse. Voorhees, too, had a pit job for a Broadway musical, "9:15 Revue"; it opened February 11, but closed February 17. But Benny stayed on with Voorhees because of the radio work.

There is no concrete evidence of BG on CO matrices W 149985 through W 149993, and W 150056, recorded February 14, as some claim. His next studio work was with Ruth Etting, a big "name" in the '30s:

RUTH ETTING   March 4, 1930, New York

Benny Goodman, clt & as; Mannie Klein, tpt; Rube Bloom, p; Ward Ley, b; unknown v, d.

W 150062-3   CO 2146-D, CO 3085-D, CoE DB440, CoAu DO 320. **LP:** CO ML5050, PHON 7604 (as brks)
Ten Cents A Dance - voc Ruth Etting

W 150063-2   CO 2146-D, CoE DB147 (clt accomp)
Funny, Dear, What Love Can Do - voc Ruth Etting

(Other CO matrices recorded March 4 show no evidence of BG.)

IRVING MILLS AND HIS   **March 21, 1930, New York**
HOTSY TOTSY GANG

Benny Goodman, clt & as; Bill Moore, Mannie Klein (or alternately, Phil Napoleon, Sterling Bose), tpt; Tommy Dorsey or Charlie Butterfield, tbn; Jack Pettis, ts, C-mel; unknown, v; Al Goering, p; Dick McDonough, bjo; Harry Goodman, b; Gene Krupa, d.

E 32401   BR 4998, BrG A8831. **LP:** TOM 12, SB 113 (clt solo)
I Wonder What My Gal Is Doin' Now

E 32402   BR 4838, BrAu 4838, BrE 03297, BrF 500147. **EP:** CrlG 94256. **LP:** VoE VLP2, AFF 1018, TOM 12, SB 113 (clt solo)
Crazy About My Gal

E 32403   same issues (clt solo)
Railroad Man

LEE MORSE AND HER   **March 27, 1930, New York**
BLUE GRASS BOYS

Benny Goodman, clt; Mannie Klein, tpt; Tommy Dorsey, tbn; Rube Bloom, p & organ on W 150139 only; Eddie Lang, g.

W 150138-2   CO 2165-D, CoE DB147. **LP:** TT 201 (clt accomp)
Cooking Breakfast For The One I Love - voc Lee Morse

W 150139-2   CO 2165-D, CoE DB161. **LP:** TT 201(clt accomp)
Sing You Sinners - voc Lee Morse

(Other CO matrices recorded March 27 show no evidence of BG.)

CO matrices W 150153 through W 150155, recorded March 31, do not include Benny Goodman, as is sometimes claimed.

Next for Benny was another double date, coupling Rube Bloom and The Columbia Photo Players, a Ben Selvin nom-de-recording. It introduces the rare CO "X" series, green and gold-labeled issues that were marketed in Latin America. Arrangements used for them are much the same as those used for domestic releases, but vocals are omitted—the language factor—and solo instrumental work is of course different. Because of the take numbers, it is assumed that the non-vocal versions were recorded first, then the matrix was changed and the vocal version waxed. Collectors find CO "X" issues desirable because of their rarity and variations in the solos.

RUBE BLOOM AND HIS BAYOU BOYS   **April 9, 1930, New York**

Benny Goodman, clt & as; Mannie Klein, tpt; Tommy Dorsey, tbn; Babe Russin, ts; Adrian Rollini, b-sax & goofus; Rube Bloom, p; unknown bjo; Stan King, d.

W 150156-4   CO 2186-D. **LP:** TOM 4 (clt solo)
Mysterious Mose - voc Roy Evans

W 150157-3   same issues (clt solo)
Bessie Couldn't Help It - voc Roy Evans

THE COLUMBIA PHOTO PLAYERS (CPP)   **same date**
BEN SELVIN Y SU ORQUESTA (BS)

Benny Goodman, clt & as; Tommy Dorsey, tbn; plus unknown tpt, as, ts, 2 v, p, g, b, d, voc. Possibly others from BLOOM sides preceding; possibly on these and like sides, Ben Selvin should be credited as one violinist.

W 195092-1   CO 4094-X (BS) **LP:** SB 108, BIO 1 (clt solo)
Todo Para Ti (The Whole Darned Thing's For You) - no voc

W 150158-3   CO 2177-D, CoE CB103 (CPP) **LP:** BIO 1, TOM 17 (clt solo)
The Whole Darned Thing's For You - voc ref

W 195093-1   CO 4093-X (Cpp) **LP:** SB 108 (clt solo)
Aqui Estoy Para Ti (I'm In The Market For You) - no voc

W 150192-3   CO 2187-D (CPP). **LP:** TOM 17 (clt solo)
I'm In The Market For You - voc ref

(Matrices bridging W 150158 and W 150192 were not recorded April 9 and do not include Benny Goodman.)

Many Selvin personnels—and others too, in the '30's—are vague because the record companies did not retain detailed data on these sessions and thus the information is unobtainable for the most part. It should be noted that Gene Krupa did not participate in many BG-Selvin sessions, contrary to the assumption of other discographers. As Gene remembers it, he worked for Selvin at a later time than Benny, and more often with another clarinetist of some repute: Artie Shaw.

On April 10 Ben Selvin supervised CO matrices W 150195, 96 as by ROY EVANS, and W 150197, 98, 99 as by FRANK AUBURN AND HIS ORCHESTRA, among others. Some think this a BG session—they cite an intro clt solo on mx W 150198-1,2, and two clarinets in evidence on both EVANS' sides. Benny and discriminate collectors say no, however, and the opinion here is that this is not a BG date.

There is a contention that the BG/Bix date at Williams College actually occurred May 17, 1930, and not June 11, 1931, as is cited later in this work. Benny has no records that would show substantiation for either date, but rather thinks the gig was not too long before Bix died. In any event, next is Benny's first recording session with him:

HOAGY CARMICHAEL AND   **May 21, 1930, New York**
HIS ORCHESTRA

Benny Goodman, clt; Bix Beiderbecke, cnt; Bubber Miley, tpt; Tommy Dorsey, tbn; Jimmy Dorsey, Arnold Brilhart, as; Bud Freeman, ts; Joe Venuti, v; Irving Brodsky, p; Hoagy Carmichael, organ (mx BVE 59800 only); Eddie Lang, g; Harry Goodman, b or tu; Gene Krupa, d. Vocalists are Carmichael (HC), Brodsky (IB), Venuti (JV), and Carson Robison.

BVE 59800-2   VI 38139 B, VI 25494, HMV B4897, HMV B6288, HMV B8549, HMVAu 8549, HMVAu EA1200, ViArg 1A-018, HJCA 100. **LP:** VI LPT3072, ViJap 5280/2, RcaFr 731.036/7, DIV 302, JO 3570. **EP:** VI EPBT3072 (clt accomp)
Rockin' Chair - voc ref (HC, IB)

BVE 62301-1   VI 38139 A, VI 25371, ViArg 1A-108, JCLS 532. **LP:** VI LPT3072, VI LPM2323, VI LEJ-2, CAM CAL385, CamE CDN112, Rcalt LPM10042, RcaE RD27225, JCI RA5298, RcaFr 731.036/7, JO 3570. **EP:** VI EPBT3072, HMV 7EG8037 (clt solo)
Barnacle Bill, The Sailor - voc Carson Robison & chorus (HC, JV)

(The matrices above are consecutive.)

A report that Benny was on a CO session the same day, May 21, is untrue. Matrices in question are W 150499, W 150158 as by ANSON WEEKS AND HIS HOTEL MARK HOPKINS ORCH., issued on CO 2211-D. (Matrices intervening between those cited were not recorded May 21.)

RUBE BLOOM & HIS BAYOU BOYS   **May 24, 1930, New York**

Personnel as April 9 BLOOM date, plus Dick McDonough, g for unknown bjo, and Eddie Walters, uke and voc on W 150532 only. BG also featured on as.

W 150531-1   CO 2218-D (clt solo, as accomp)
W 150531-3   CO 2218-D. **LP:** TOM 4 (clt solo, as accomp)
On Revival Day (A Rhythmic Spiritual) - voc ref (Roy Evans)

W 150532-4   CO 2218-D. **LP:** TOM 4 (clt solo)
There's A Wah-Wah Gal In Agua Caliente - voc Eddie Walters

THE CHARLESTON CHASERS   **May 26, 1930, New York**

Benny Goodman, clt & as; Phil Napoleon, possibly one other, tpt; Tommy Dorsey, tbn; Art Schutt, p; Eddie Walters, uke; Ward Ley, b; Stan King, d.

W 150537-3   CO 2219-D, CO TEL TRANS 91961, CoArg A8846. **LP:** NOST 890/1, TOM 6, VJM VLP44 (clt solo)
Here Comes Emily Brown - voc Eddie Walters

W 150538-3   CO2219-D, CoArg A8846. **LP:** VJM VLP44, TOM 6 (clt accomp)
Wasn't It Nice? - voc Eddie Walters

Tele-Focal transcriptions were Columbia's initial attempt to introduce a transcription service for radio stations. They are 12" shellac discs, one-sided, that have spoken announcements before and/or following a tune; the tune is a dub of an issued record. This appears true of all Tele-Focal transcriptions.

The next listing is a possibility only, for there is insufficient clarinet on either side to permit positive identification.

RUTH ETTING   **June 2, 1930, New York**

Possibly Benny Goodman, clt & as; Mannie Klein, tpt; Rube Bloom, p; plus unknown 2 v, b.

W 150560-3	CO 2216-D (clt accomp) **I Never Dreamt (You'd Fall In Love With Me)** - voc Ruth Etting
W 150561-3	same issue (clt accomp) **Dancing With Tears In My Eyes** - voc Ruth Etting

Next was BG's first date with a great musical comedy star:

ETHEL WATERS   **June 3, 1930, New York**

Benny Goodman, clt; Mannie Klein, tpt; Tommy Dorsey, tbn; Adrian Rollini, b-sax; Ben Selvin. v Rube Bloom, p.

W 150562-3	CO 2222-D (clt accomp) **My Kind Of A Man** - voc Ethel Waters
W 150563-4	same issue. **LP:** CO KG 31571, CBSAu 220121 (clt accomp) **You Brought A New Kind Of Love To Me** - voc Ethel Waters

There is no verification on the records available to the author (W 195111 has not been located) of Benny's presence on the Selvin session of June 5; but since he does accompany Lee Morse on succeeding matrices the same day, it is logical to assume his participation:

BEN SELVIN Y SU ORQUESTA (BSY)   **June 5, 1930, New York**
BEN SELVIN AND HIS ORCHESTRA (BS)

Usual Selvin instrumentation—2 tpt, tbn, 3 reed, v, rhythm—and likely "regular" Selvin personnel, including Goodman.

W 195111	CO 4478-X (BSY) (clt ?) **With My Guitar And You** - (prob. no vocal)
W 150568-3	CO 2221-D (BS) (no solo) **With My Guitar And You** - voc ref
W 150569-2	CO 2221-D, CoTEL Trans 91941 (BS) (no solo) **Around The Corner** - voc Helen Richards and the Radiolites

LEE MORSE AND HER BLUE GRASS BOYS   **same date**

Benny Goodman, clt; Mannie Klein, tpt; Tommy Dorsey, tbn; prob. Rube Bloom, p, and Eddie Lang, g.

W 150570-1	CO 2225-D, CoE DB252. **LP:** TT 213 (clt accomp) **Swingin' In A Hammock** - voc Lee Morse
W 150571-3	CO 2225-D (clt accomp) **Seems To Me** - voc Lee Morse

Sultry-voiced Miss Morse made a Vitaphone short in June, "Lee Morse In The Music Racket." The author has not had access to it, but suggests that Benny may have participated in it also.

The very next day, June 6, is the subject of two controversies. The first does not involve Benny—he is clearly present—but does concern Bix Beiderbecke. Whether Bix is the featured cornetist on the JACK WINN/IRVING MILLS sides is unresolved. The author's opinion is that he is not, for these reasons:

The recordings under discussion were played for Mr. Goodman on four different occasions over time, and he remains adamant that Bix was not on the date. He believes that either Sterling Bose or Jimmy McPartland was the cornet soloist. In 1986, a New York radio station played the sides, telephoned Benny to ask if they included Bix. He replied that he thought they did. The author challenged him about this apparent changed opinion. His reply: "Hell, what's the difference now?"

Jack Teagarden at first disclaimed any recollection of the recordings, when they were played for him in 1958. But he then recognized his own playing, and concluded that the cornetist was Bix. Jack's opinions must be considered suspect, however; in DOWN BEAT, issue of August 20, 1959, he ascribed to Bix the cornet soli by Red Nichols on Nichols' "Nobody's Sweetheart."

Gene Krupa, percussionist on the WINN/MILLS sides, shares Benny's view that the cornetist was Sterling Bose, not Bix. Gene's memory was acute; and such was his regard for Bix that he insisted he would undoubtedly have remembered a recording date with him.

On July 7, 1973, the author played the recordings in question for Jimmy McPartland, Bill Challis and Joe Tarto at a jazz seminar at Rutgers University, New Brunswick, New Jersey, before an audience of jazz record collectors. Their reaction was immediate and unanimous: not Bix. (Jimmy added that he was not the cornetist, he believed it might be Bose or even Mannie Klein, "who could play anybody's style.") The author feels that no one then alive was more knowledgeable about Bix as person and performer than McPartland, Challis and Tarto.

In sum, no one can state with certainty the identity of the cornetist on this session:

JACK WINN AND HIS   **June 6, 1930, New York**
   DALLAS DANDIES (JW)
IRVING MILLS AND HIS HOTSY TOTSY GANG (IM)

Benny Goodman, clt; unknown cnt; poss. Ray Lodwig, tpt; Jack Teagarden, tbn; unknown as/ts; Min Leibrook, b-sax; Matty Malneck and poss. Joe Venuti, v; Jack Russin or Frank Signorelli, p; unknown g; Gene Krupa, d.

E 32948 A	VO 15860, BR X15860, ME 12051. **LP:** OFC 20, IAJRC 2, JO 3570, SB 113 (JW). **EP:** CrIG 94256 (take unknown) (clt solo)
E 32948 B	ME 12051. **LP:** SW JCS33763, JO 3570, SB 113 (JW) (clt solo) **Loved One**

(It is believed the BR X was used in export.)

E 32949 A	BR 4983, BrE 02821, BrF 500091. **LP:** SW JCS33763, JO 3570, SB 113, OFC 20 (IM) (clt solo) **Deep Harlem**
E 32950	same issues (IM) (clt solo) **Strut Miss Lizzie** - voc (Dick Robertson)

Unfortunately for this work, the second half of the June 6 controversy involves Benny Goodman's participation:

Probably under the direction of Ben Selvin, another series of matrices was cut in Columbia's studios this date. On two of the sides issued clarinet passages are hidden behind vocals; they peep out so indistinctly and briefly as to be of little value toward identification. On one side there is a clt solo, but collectors differ as to whether this is Benny's, at least BG on a good day with a good reed. More, there is an alto sax solo on another side much in Benny's style; further, there is an alto sax lead that could be Benny's . . . and so on.

In an attempt to resolve this controversy, the records were played for Benny several times. On each occasion he hesitated but finally decided that yes, it was he on the series.

Despite Benny's stamp of approval some collectors insist the clarinetist is not BG. There is, however, enough substance to include this session as a Goodman date; certainly its exclusion on an absolute basis is unwarranted.

SAM NASH AND HIS ORCHESTRA (SN)   **June 6, 1930, New York**
RAY SEELEY AND HIS ORCHESTRA (RS)
WILL PERRY AND HIS ORCH. (WP)
FRANK AUBURN & HIS ORCHESTRA (FA)
HOTEL PENNSYLVANIA MUSIC (HP)
LLOYD KEATING & HIS MUSIC (LK)
THE PARAMOUNTEERS (P)
TAMPA BLUE ORCHESTRA (TBO)
ROOF GARDEN ORCHESTRA (RGO)

Prob. Benny Goodman, clt & as; Tommy Dorsey, tbn; Jack Russin, p; plus unknown 2 tpt; ts, 2 v, bjo, d. Scrappy Lambert (SL), voc.

W 404204-A   PaA 34097 (SN); OdA 36106 (RS) (clt accomp)
(100402-1)   HA 1182-H, VE 2182-H, VE 2182-V, DI 3182-G (FA); CL
        5008-C (HP); PU 2024-P (P) **LP:** JAZ 14 (clt accomp)
        Swingin' In A Hammock - voc "Robert Wood" (HA
        series) (SL)

W 404205-B   PaA 34099 (SN); OdA 36106 (RS), PaE R743 (RGO). **LP:**
        SVL 165 (clt accomp)
(100403-1)   HA 1181-H, VE 2181-V, DI 3181-G, CL 5045-C (LK) (cit
        accomp)
        I Love You So Much - voc "Tom Frawley" (HA series)
        (SL)

W 404206-A   PaA 34098 (SN); OdA 36107 (RS); PaE 6349 (WP). **LP:**
        SB 108 (as solo)
        Can I Help It? (If I'm In Love With You) - voc ref (SL)

W 404207-A   PaA 34099 (SN); OdA 36107 (RS); PaE R754 (TBO) (as
        lead)
        You're The Sweetest Girl (This Side of Heaven) - voc
        ref (SL)

W 404208-   PaA 34093 (SN); OdA 36103 (RS)
        You (I Love But You)

W 404209-B   PaA 34094 (SN); OdA 36103 (RS) (no solo)
        My Love (I'll Be Waiting For You) - voc ref

W 404210-A   PaA 34100 (SN); OdA 36108 (RS); PaE R754 (TBO) (no
        solo)
(W 490081-A)   OdA 36109 (RS)
        Old New England Moon - voc ref (trio)

(The 100,000 matrix series seems to be a "false" series here, the music being identical—where a check has been possible—with the "true" 400,000 series.)

An inadvertent but glaring omission in "BG—On the Record" is a Sam Lanin recording session of June 9, one renowned among collectors of Jack Teagarden, but less well known to Goodman specialists. Although Benny worked for Lanin occasionally on dance dates, he seldom recorded with him: Lanin usually employed altoists Arnold Brilhart and Lyle Bowen for studio work. But Benny is unmistakably identifiable here, via a clarinet solo on the second tune.

SAM LANIN AND HIS   **June 9, 1930, New York**
  FAMOUS PLAYERS (SL)
ALBERT MASON'S ORCHESTRA (AM)
SAM LANIN'S FAMOUS PLAYERS & SINGERS (FSP)

Three tpt, tbn, 3 saxes, p/celeste, bjo, tu, d - including Benny Goodman, clt; Mannie Klein, tpt; Jack Teagarden, tbn; Art Schutt, p; Scrappy Lambert, voc.

W 404214-C   PaA PNY34104 (AM), OdA ONY36112 (SL), PaE R741
        (FSP) (clt lead)
        Live And Love Today - voc (Scrappy Lambert)

W 404215-B   PaA PNY34105 (AM), OdA ONY36112 (SL), PaE E5194
        (AM) (clt solo)
        Seems To Me - voc (Scrappy Lambert)

W 404216-B   PaA PNY34104 (AM), OdA ONY36113 (SL), PaE R742
        (FSP), PaE E5194 (AM) (clt lead)
        Rollin' Down The River - voc (Scrappy Lambert)

Co matrices W 150582-1 "I Love You So Much" and W 150583-2 "F'r Instance," CALIFORNIA RAMBLERS, CO 2231-D, recorded June 12, are sometimes credited to BG. There is an alto sax solo on the first side, but it is Pete Pumiglio's, not Benny's.

Ed Kirkeby directed a group for CO on June 20 whose records included matrix W 404229-B "Just A Little Closer," issued under several pseudonyms: EARL MARLOW'S ORCHESTRA, ED LLOYD AND HIS ORCH., WEBSTER MOORE AND HIS HIGH HATTERS, and RUDY MARLOW AND HIS ORCHESTRA. One subtone clt solo and an as solo from this side only prompted a belief that Benny participated in the session. But Kirkeby's notebook certifies the clarinetist to have been Pumiglio.

Benny never got back into Red Nichols' pit band for "Strike Up The Band"—Jimmy Dorsey remained. It is known, however, that Nichols frequently recorded with personnel different from that of his regular group. Here are two Nichols dates that feature BG rather than Dorsey, during the run of "Strike Up The Band":

RED NICHOLS AND HIS FIVE PENNIES   **July 2, 1930, New York**

Benny Goodman, clt; Red Nichols, Ruby Weinstein, Charlie Teagarden, tpt; Jack Teagarden, Glenn Miller, tbn; Sid Stoneburn, as; Babe Russin, ts; Joe Sullivan, p; Teg Brown, g; Art Miller, b; Gene Krupa, d.

E 33304-A   BR 4877, BR 6835, BrE 1019, BrF 8962, BrG A8962,
        Delt BM1166 (clt solo)
E 33304-B   BR 80004 B. **45:** BR 9-80004 (Set 9-7008). **EP:** BrE
        B71017. **LP:** BR BL58008, CrlG LPC960 16. **ET:**
        Dep't. Of State "Notes On Jazz" Series (clt solo)
        Peg O' My Heart

E 33305-A   BR 4944, BR6841, BrE 1048, BrF 8997, BrG A8997. **LP:**
        SWF 1004, SB 137 (clt solo)
        Sweet Georgia Brown

E 33306-A   BR 4877, BR 6835, BR 80004 A, BrE 1019, BrF 8962,
        BrG A 8962, Delt BM1166, DeSw F 49014. **45:** BR
        9-80004, (Set 9-7008). **EP:** BR EB71017. **LP:** BR
        BL58008, BR BL 54008, BR BL 54047, BrE LAT8307,
        FestAu B12-1488, CrlG LPC96016, AOH AH63, SW
        JC33734, MCA 2-4018. **ET:** AFRS AMER. Pop Mus.
        73 (clt solo)
        China Boy

E 33307-(A,B)   UNISSUED
        Chong, He Came From Hong Kong

RED NICHOLS AND HIS FIVE PENNES   **July 3, 1930, New York**

Personnel as July 2. Jack Teagarden and Teg Brown (JT, TB) are the unlabeled vocalists on "The Sheik of Araby."

E 33333-A   BR 4885, BR 6836, BR 80005 A, BrF 8866, BrG A8866,
        BrE 1104, BrF 500403. **45:** BR 9-80005 (Set 9-7008).
        EP: BR EB71017. **LP:** BR BL58008, BR BL54010, CrlF
        CVM40012, BR BL54047, VC LVA9011, CrlG
        LP96016, VC (SA) BL54010, LSS LW267, MCA
        2-4018, AOH168, AFF 1018, TL STLJ08 (clt solo)
        The Sheik Of Araby -voc (JT, TB)

E 33334-A   BR 4885, BR 6836, BrF 8866, BrG A8866, BrE 1204,
        BrF 500200. **LP:** TL STL-J05, MCA 2-4018, AFF 1018
        (clt solo)

E 33334-B   BR 80005 B. **45:** BR 9-80005 (Set 9-7008). **EP:** BR
        EB71017. **LP:** BR BL58008, BR BL54047, TL STLJ27
        (clt solo)
        Shim-Me-Sha-Wabble

(CO matrices W 150617 thru W 150620, recorded July 3, include Jimmy Dorsey, not, Benny Goodman.)

BEN SELVIN AND HIS ORCHESTRA   July 7, 1930, New York

Benny Goodman, clt; Mannie Klein, tpt; Tommy Dorsey, tbn; Jimmy Dorsey, as; Herman Wolfson, ts; Eddie Walters (EW), uke & voc; plus unknown tpt, p, tu, d.

W 150621-1   CO 2255-D. **LP:** SB 108 (clt solo)
W 150621-3   CO 2255-D. **LP:** SB 108 (clt solo)
              Why Have You Forgotten Waikiki? - voc ref (EW)
W 150622-2   CO 2255-D, CoE CB225. **LP:** SB 108, BIO 1, SVL 165
              (clt solo)
W 150622-3   CO225-D. **LP:** SB 108 (clt solo)
              It's Easy To Fall In Love - voc ref (EW)

LEE MORSE AND HER BLUE GRASS BOYS   July 7, 1930, New York

Benny Goodman, clt; Mannie Klein, tpt; Tommy Dorsey, tbn; Rube Bloom, p; Eddie Lang, g.

W 150623-2   CO 2248-D. **LP:** TT 201 (clt accomp)
              Little White Lies - voc Lee Morse
W 150624-3   same issues (clt accomp)
              Nobody Cares If I'm Blue - voc Lee Morse

BG accompanies pianist/vocalist Art Gillham for the first time:

ART GILLHAM   July 24, 1930, New York
(THE WHISPERING PIANIST)

Benny Goodman, clt & as; Mannie Klein, tpt; prob. Art Gillham, p; plus unknown v, g.

W 150661-2   CO 2291-D (clt accomp)
              Good Evenin' - voc Art Gillham
W 150662-1   CO 2265-D (clt accomp)
              Confessin' (That I Love You) - voc Art Gillham
W 150665-2   CO 2265-D. **LP:** SB 107 (clt solo)
              **My Heart Belongs To The Girl Who Belongs To
              Somebody Else** - voc Art Gillham
W 150666-3   CO 2291-D (clt accomp)
              I'm Drifting Back To Dreamland - voc Art Gillham

(Intervening CO matrices were not recorded July 24 and do not include Benny Goodman.)

LEE MORSE AND HER BLUE GRASS BOYS   July 25, 1930, New York

Benny Goodman, clt; Mannie Klein, tpt; Tommy Dorsey, tbn; Rube Bloom, p; Eddie Lang, g.

W 150675-1   CO 2270-D. **LP:** TT 201 (clt accomp)
              I Still Get A Thrill (Thinking Of You) - voc Lee Morse
W 150676   UNISSUED
              So Beats My Heart For You -voc Lee Morse

(Other CO matrices recorded July 25 do not include Benny Goodman.)

Although Benny was kept busy in the recording studios during Spring and Summer 1930, he was even more occupied with radio broadcasts. Among the conductors for whom he worked on the several networks were Frank Black, Al Goodman, Andre Kostelanetz, Erno Rapee, Dave Rubinoff, Donald Voorhees and Paul Whiteman. No program transcriptions of any of these broadcasts, in which Benny is in evidence, have been discovered. And although it is suggested that he recorded with some of these leaders, examination of the records they made during this period—or indeed at any time— has failed to produce any that include identifiable Goodman soli. If he is present on any, his participation is buried in the heavily scored arrangements employed by these large orchestras.

There may be an exception. When asked if he had ever made any Hit-Of-The-Week recordings, Benny laughed and said he recalled having made "some of those paper records" for Voorhees, for whom he had played most frequently. The side listed next is possibly one of them, although the clarinet lead, the only audible clarinet contribution on it, is no certain guarantee.

DON VOORHEES ORCHESTRA   prob. August 1930, New York

Poss. Benny Goodman, clt & as; Tommy Dorsey, tbn; Dick McDonough, g; Chauncey Morehouse, d; Scrappy Lambert (SL), voc; plus unknown 2 tpt, as, ts, 2 v, p, tu.

1091   HOW 1091 (clt lead)
              Go Home And Tell Your Mother - voc (SL)

Continuing research by Glenn Miller specialist Ed Polic and others into transcriptions made by Red Nichols for National Radio Advertising, Inc., uncovered some delightful "new" recordings by Benny that, somewhat uncharacteristically, he has forgotten completely. The author played them for him in October 1982, but even that failed to jog his memory. He did, however, ask that "Oh, Baby!" be replayed; that one he liked. And note that their matrix numbers dovetail neatly with other Brunswick matrices of the period, and that gaps in them suggest others remain to be discovered.

RED NICHOLS AND HIS ORCHESTRA   August 2, 1930, New York

Benny Goodman, clt & as; Red Nichols, Charlie Teagarden, Mannie Klein, tpt; Glenn Miller, tbn; poss. Sid Stoneburn, as; prob. Babe Russin, ts; Adrian Rollini, b-sax; Lou Raderman, Ed Solinsky, v; Joe Sullivan, p; Teg Brown, g; Gene Krupa, d.

XE 33545-A   **LP:** MER 18
              ("HEAT" Program A, Part 2)
              My Future Just Passed; Oh Baby! (clt solo); **My Future
              Just Passed**
XE 33548   **LP:** JAA 43
              ("HEAT" Program F, Part 1)
              St. Louis Blues (clt solo)
XE 33549   **LP:** JAA 43, BRO 100, RADR 100
              ("HEAT" Program E, Part 3)
              Call Of The Freaks (clt solo)
XE 33550-B   **LP:** MCA 1518
              ("HEAT" Program - ? -)
              The Sheik Of Araby (clt solo)

RED NICHOLS AND HIS ORCHESTRA   August 3, 1930, New York

Personnel as August 2, except: Bud Freeman, ts, replaces Russin; Joe Venuti, v, replaces either Solinsky or Raderman; Ray Bauduc, d, replaces Krupa; and add either Jack Hansen or Joe Tarto, tu, and Dick Robertson, voc.

XE 33555   **LP:** MER 18
              ("HEAT" Program A, Part 1)
              Turn On The Heat (theme); **Strike Up The Band!** - voc
              Dick Robertson; **Alexander's Ragtime Band; Strike Up
              The Band!** (clt in coda)
XE 33556-A   **LP:** MER 18
              ("HEAT" Program D, Part 3)
              Black and Blue (clt solo); **Ain't Misbehavin'** - voc Dick
              Robertson; **Black and Blue** (clt obl)
XE 33559-B   **LP:** MCA 1518
              ("HEAT" Program - ? -)
              Sweet Georgia Brown (clt obl); **I Ain't Got Nobody** (clt
              solo); **Sweet Georgia Brown**

Two "HEAT" programs dated approximately August 25, numbers I-Part 3 and H-Part 2, available on Lp's JAA 43 and MER 18 respectively, were also played for Benny. These drew a raised eyebrow, meaning, "You should know better—that's not me." His opinion is that the audible clarinet belongs to either Bud Freeman or possibly Jimmy Dorsey.

RED NICHOLS AND HIS FIVE PENNIES   **August 27, 1930, New York**

Benny Goodman, clt; Red Nichols, Charlie Teagarden, tpt; Glenn Miller, poss. Charlie Butterfield, tbn; Bud Freeman, ts; Adrian Rollini, b-sax, xyl; Joe Sullivan, p; Gene Krupa, d.

E 34109-A   BR 4925, BR 6839, BrE 1062. **LP:** VoE VLP2, SB 137
              (clt solo)
              Carolina In The Morning

E 34110   UNISSUED
              How Come You Do Me Like You Do?

E 34111-A   same issues as E 34109-A, except no VoE (clt solo)
              Who?

E 34112   BR 4944, BR 6841, BrE 1048, BrF 8997, BrG A8997.
              LP: VoE VLP 2, SB 137 (clt solo)
              By The Shalimar

    ETHEL WATERS' CO matrices W 150747-1 "You're Lucky To Me" and W 150748-2 "Memories Of You," CO 2288-D, plus Selvin's THE COLUMBIA PHOTO PLAYERS' W 150749-3 "I'm Learning A Lot About You"/W 150750-4 "One More Waltz," CO 2285-D, all recorded August 29, have found favor with BG collectors. A clarinet solo on W 150749-3 is the chief basis for the Goodman claim, but the decision of the author is that Jimmy Dorsey cut all these sides, not Benny Goodman.

    The next session presents an unique opportunity to make direct comparisons of the clarinet styles of Goodman, Dorsey, and Pee Wee Russell. Each may be heard on this celebrated Bix date.

BIX BEIDERBECKE   **September 8, 1930, New York**
   AND HIS ORCHESTRA

Benny Goodman, Jimmy Dorsey, Pee Wee Russell, clt & as; Bix Beiderbecke, cnt; Ray Lodwig, tpt; Boyce Cullen, tbn; Bud Freeman, ts; Joe Venuti, v; Irving Brodsky, p; Eddie Lang, g; Min Leibrook, b; Gene Krupa, d; Wes Vaughn (WV), voc. Label credits on BVE 63631-1 read, "Bix Beiderbecke And His Orchestra, Joe Venuti, Directing." Ray Lodwig gets directorial credit on BVE 63632-2,3.

BVE 63630-1   **LP:** (7") NATCHEZ WEP804, RcaFr 731.131, HIST 28,
                JO 3122, JO 3570, (clt solos - BG)

BVE 63630-2   VI 23018 B, VI 25370 B, HMV B8419, GrF K6238. **LP:**
                OFC 34, RcaFr 731.036/7, JO 3570 (clt solos - BG)
                Deep Down South - voc ref (WV)

BVE 63631-1   VI 23008 A, HMV B4889. **LP:** OFC 34, RcaFr 731.036/7,
(2)   JO 3570 (clt brk - Pee Wee)
                I Don't Mind Walkin' In The Rain (When I'm Walkin' In
                The Rain With You) - voc ref (WV)

(One hour lunch break - Venuti and Lang do not return.)

BVE 63632-2   VI 23008 B. **LP:** VI LPM2323, RcaE RD27225, RcaFr
(1)   731.036/7, JO 3570, JCI RA5298 (clt solo - JD; see
                note)

BVE 63632-3   VI 23008 B, VI 26415 A, HMV B8419, HMV B4889. **LP:**
                RcaFr 731.036/7, OFC 34, JO 3570 (clt solo - JD)
                I'll Be A Friend "With Pleasure" - voc ref (WV)

(Some collectors believe BG solo's on BVE 63632-2; the author does not. It is thought, however, that all three clarinetists participated on all sides, regardless of the solo assignments. The plethora of clarinetists is due to Bix's sensitivity. BG, JD and Pee Wee were all in town when this date was set, Bix had worked with each of them, and because he did not wish to offend any one of them, all were invited.)

    A possible BG item is RUTH ETTING's CO matrix W 150826-3 "If I Could Be With You (One Hour Tonight)," CO 2300-D, recorded September 18. Clarinet is subtone throughout, and thus cannot be credited fully. Other CO matrices recorded September 18 show no evidence of Goodman.

    Next for Benny was another "double-date," with the issues appearing on Columbia and Brunswick.

LEE MORSE AND HER   **September 26, 1930, New York**
   BLUE GRASS BOYS

Benny Goodman, clt; Mannie Klein, tpt; Tommy Dorsey, tbn; Eddie Lang, g; plus unknown p, v. Org replaces p on W 150843-3.

W 150842-2   CO 2308-D, CoE DB355 (clt accomp)
               Just A Little While - voc Lee Morse

W 150843-3   CO 2308-D (subt clt intro & accomp)
               When The Organ Played At Twilight - voc Lee Morse

RED NICHOLS AND HIS FIVE PENNIES   **same date**

Benny Goodman, clt; Red Nichols, Charlie Teagarden, poss. Ruby Weinstein, tpt; Jack Teagarden, Glenn Miller, poss. George Stoll, tbn; poss. Sid Stoneburn, as; Babe Russin, ts; Jack Russin, p; Art Miller, b; Gene Krupa, d. Voc chorus includes Marshall Smith, Ray Johnson, Del Porter and Dwight Snyder.

E 34626-A   UNISSUED
              On Revival Day (A Rhythmic Spiritual)-Part I

E 34627-A   BR 6026, BR 6843, BrE 1087, BrF 9008, BrG A9008.
              LP: AOH 168, MCA 1518 (clt accomp)

E 34627-B   **LP:** SB 137 (clt accomp)
              On Revival Day (A Rhythmic Spiritual)-Part I - voc Jack
              Teagarden (& chorus)

E 34628-A   same 78 rpm issues as E 34627-A. **EP:** CrlG 94269. **LP:**
              MCA 1518, AOH 168 (clt solo)

E 34628-B   **LP:** SB 137 (clt solo)
              On Revival Day (A Rhythmic Spiritual)-Part II - voc
              Jack Teagarden (& chorus)

(It should be pointed out here, as elsewhere, that bootleg issues of legitimately unissued masters are generally of unsatisfactory audio quality, and that the collector who seeks good audio quality should try to obtain test pressings or first-generation tapes of them.)

    Possible Goodman items are RUTH ETTING'S CO matrices W 150844-4 "Body And Soul," CO 2300-D, and W 150845-3 "Laughing At Life," CO 2318-D, recorded Sept. 29. As on her Sept. 18 date, there is strong subtone clt that seems more Benny's than another clarinetist's.

    Lee Morse was featured in another film short in October, "Song Service," this time for Paramount. As before, this too should be checked by film/BG collectors.

    "Reliable Red" Nichols continued to be chosen for choice Broadway show assignments; on September 29 Benny rejoined Red for pit work for the Gershwins' new musical, "Girl Crazy," starring Ginger Rogers and Ethel Merman. The pit band next waxed two tunes from the show; and note that MCA's liner notes claiming an alternate take for "I Got Rhythm" are in error.

LORING "RED" NICHOLS AND HIS   **October 23, 1930, New York**
   ORCHESTRA (RN)
THE CAPTIVATORS (C)

Benny Goodman, clt; Red Nichols, Ruby Weinstein, Charlie Teagarden, tpt; Glenn Miller, tbn; Sid Stoneburn, as; Larry Binyon, ts, fl; Ed Bergman, Ed Solinsky, v; Jack Russin, p; Art Miller, b; Gene Krupa, d; Scrappy Lambert (SL) and Dick Robertson (DR), voc.

E 34958   BR 4957, BR 6842, BrF 8963, BrG A8963 (RN). **LP:** SB
              157 (no solo)
              Embraceable You - voc (SL)

E 34959-A   BR 4957, BR 6711, BrE 1300, BrF 8963, BrG A8963,
              BrIt 4872. **LP:** AOH AH63, MCA 1518 (RN) (clt solo)
              I Got Rhythm - voc Dick Robertson

E 34960   ME 12005 (C) **LP:** SB 157 (clt solo)
              A Girl Friend Of A Boy Friend Of Mine - voc (DR)

E 34961   ME 12005, PANA 25001, PANAAu 12005, EMB E125.
              LP: BRO 110, SB 157 (C) (no solo)
              Sweet Jennie Lee! - voc (DR)

(On this Nichols date and others to come, the presence of a guitar is not ascertainable aurally, and is therefore questionable.)

    Until one tune was issued in 1966 on a Columbia Record Club "Exclusive Club Record" 12" Lp titled, "The Sound Of Jazz Genius," a Red McKenzie session of October 30 was unknown to most jazz fans. The date still presents problems: the Lp's liner notes are partially in error, and the full personnel is as yet a mystery. Further, the first tune cut on the date, later dubbed from a test pressing and "bootlegged" on Lp, features different personnel than the tune issued on CO.

Pee Wee Russell is listed as clarinetist on the CO Lp, but Benny affirmed his clarinet with a decisi "That's me!" upon listening to "Arkansas Blues" for the first time. could not identify the brief and barely audible clarinet passage on a test ssing of the other selection.

At all odds, a noteworthy addition to the Goodman "Sound Of Jazz Genius," to say nothing of the genius of Thomas "Fats" Waller.

RED McKENZIE AND HIS
MOUND CITY BLUE BLOWERS
October 30, 1930, New York

Red McKenzie, comb (kazoo); Bud Freeman, Coleman Hawkins, ts; Fats Waller, p; plus unknown g, poss. Eddie Condon; and remotely possible, Benny Goodman, clt, in the coda only.

10194-3   **LP: IAJRC-2**
     Girls Like You Were Meant For Boys Like Me

Benny Goodman, clt; Red McKenzie, comb; Fats Waller, p; plus unknown g, possibly Eddie Condon; plus unknown suitcase.

10195-3   **LP:** CO D-77 (Lp mx. XLP 79759), IAJRC-2, CBSFr
     63.366, (clt solo)
     Arkansas Blues - voc Red McKenzie

(IAJRC-2's liner notes show take 1 for mx. 10195, but this is at odds with source information.)

CO matrices 150907 through 150912, and W 404533 through W 404538, recorded October 29; and CO matrices 150913 through 150926, recorded October 31, are ascribed elsewhere to Benny Goodman. Judgment here is that these are not Goodman efforts, but rather those of the "great confuser" to the BG fan and discographer, Jimmy Dorsey.

A TED WALLACE AND HIS CAMPUS BOYS' session of November 3, formerly attributed to Goodman, has been shown by the Kirkeby appointment book not to include Benny. Matrices are W 150929-2 "Sweetheart Of All My Student Days" / W 150930-1 "The Little Things In Life," CO 2334-D. The reed men on the date were Bobby Davis and Joe Gillespie.

LORING "RED" NICHOLS
AND HIS ORCHESTRA
November 6, 1930, New York

Personnel as October 23, plus JACK TEAGARDEN, tbn.

E 35214-A   BR 4982, BR 6844, BrF A9003, BrG A9003 (clt solo)
     "Linda" - voc Harold Arlen

E 35215-A   same issues, plus **LP,** SB 137 (clt solo)
     Yours And Mine - voc (Eddy Thomas)

The next day saw the first in a series of Melotone recordings that eventually were released as by "Benny Goodman And His Orchestra." Benny recalls that most of the personnel for these dates came from Nichols's groups with whom he was playing in the pit for "Girl Crazy." It is important to note that here, as on subsequent Melotone releases in this series, Jack Teagarden is not the trombonist, although he is so credited in other discographies.

BENNY GOODMAN
AND HIS ORCHESTRA
November 7, 1930, New York
ROXY CLUB ORCH. - EmbAu only

Benny Goodman, clt & as; Tommy Dorsey, tbn; Sid Stoneburn, clt & as; Larry Binyon, ts; Eddie Lang, g; plus unknown 2 tpt, 2 v, p, b, d.

E 35341   ME 12023, PANA 12000. **LP:** SB 106 (clt accomp)
     "He's Not Worth Your Tears" - voc ref

E 35342   ME 12024. **LP:** SB 157 (no solo)
     "Linda" - voc (prob. Benny Goodman)

E 35343   ME 12023, EMB E121. **LP:** SB 157 (no solo)
     And Then Your Lips Met Mine - voc ref (prob. Scrappy
     Lambert)

E 35344   ME 12024. **LP:** SB 106 (no solo)
     Overnight - voc ref (prob. Scrappy Lambert)

(Original matrices for these difficult-to-obtain Goodman sides and other ME matrices were later turned over to Decca by Columbia. If there were any written data about them, these may also have been transferred, or perhaps

destroyed. In any event, cooperative Columbia no longer has data on these issues, and attempts to get more details on them from Decca have been unavailing. The records qualify as jazz items only because of BG's presence, and may therefore never be reissued. Thus additional information about them may not appear.)

Possible Goodman items are the CAVALIERS' CO matrices W 150949-2 "Waiting By The Silv'ry Rio Grande"/W 150950-2 "I'm Alone Because I Love You," CO 2339-D, recorded Nov. 12. Strong subtone clt solos are to be heard on both sides, but are not definitive.

Roy Bargy has said that he was not present on the Nichols date next, and a companion date on Jan. 5, 1931, as heretofore had been thought. No alternative pianist has been suggested. Also, some collectors believe only Glenn Miller, not Tommy Dorsey, is present on tbn.

RED AND HIS BIG TEN
November 18, 1930, New York

Benny Goodman, clt; Red Nichols, Ruby Weinstein, tpt; Glenn Miller, poss. Tommy Dorsey, tbn, Sid Stoneburn (occasionally, "Stoneberg"), as; Pete Pumiglio, ts; Carl Kress, g; Gene Krupa, d; unknown p.

BVE 64623-1   VI 23026 B. **LP:** TOM 35 (no solo)
     That's Where The South Begins - voc Dick Robertson

BVE 64624-3   V 23026 A, HMV B5977. **LP:** RcaFr FXMI 7283, TOM 35
     (clt solo)
     I'm Tickled Pink With A Blue-Eyed Baby - voc Dick
     Robertson

Possible Goodman items are ETHEL WATERS' CO matrices W 150966-2 "I Got Rhythm"/W 150967-5 "Three Little Words," CO 2346-D, recorded Nov. 18 also. ("I Got Rhythm" is also on LP, EPIC 22N6072; and "Three Little Words" is also on EP, CO BL31572 and LP, CO KG31571.) Intermittent clt accomp can be heard on both sides. Others present are Mannie Klein, tpt, and Eddie Lang, g, plus unknown v, p. Other CO matrices cut this date, 150960 through 150965, show no evidence of BG and so fail to substantiate BG on the Waters' issue.

Possible Goodman items are MICKIE ALPERT AND HIS ORCHESTRA's CO matrices W 150970-2 "We're Friends Again"/W 150973-2 "Hurt," CO 2344-D, and W 150971-5 "You're The One I Care For," CO 2361-D, recorded November 24. (W 150972 "On A Little Balcony In Spain" was not issued.) Subtone clarinet and an alto sax solo on "We're Friends Again" suggest BG.

LEE MORSE AND HER
BLUE GRASS BOYS
November 26, 1930, New York

Benny Goodman, clt; Mannie Klein, tpt; Tommy Dorsey, tbn; Rube Bloom, p; Eddie Lang, g.

W 150986-2   CO 2348-D. **LP:** TT 201 (clt accomp)
     You're Driving Me Crazy! - voc Lee Morse

W 150987-3   same 78 issue (clt accomp)
     He's My Secret Passion - voc Lee Morse

(Other CO matrices recorded November 26, 150980 through 150985, show no evidence of Benny Goodman.)

Two versions of "You're Driving Me Crazy" were recorded December 8. The first, by Ben Selvin, matrix W 404579 (151161), has a short clarinet solo that has found favor with some BG fans; judgment here is that it is not Benny's. The second version, by Sammy Fain, matrix 151150, shows no evidence at all of BG; nor do any of the other matrices recorded on December 8. All in all, no BG from this date.

RED NICHOLS AND HIS
FIVE PENNIES
December 10, 1930, New York
THE REDHEADS - ME, PE, RO and OR issues

Benny Goodman, clt & b-sax; Red Nichols, Wingy Mannone, Charlie Teagarden, tpt; Glenn Miller, tbn; Babe Russin, ts; Jack Russin, p; Art Miller, b; Gene Krupa, d.

E 35733-A   BR 6058, ME 12495, PE 15684, RO 1950, OR 2574,
     BrE 1120, BrF 9024, BrG A9024. **LP:** TOM 4, VOE
     VLP 2, SWF 1004, SB 137 (clt solo)
     Bug-A-Boo - voc (Wingy Mannone)

December 10, 1930, continued

December 10, 1930, continued

E 35734-A same issues, except omit TOM 4, VoE VLP2 (clt solo)
Corrine Corrina - voc (Wingy Mannone)

E 35735-A BR 6149, BrE 1180, BrF 9099, BrG A9099. **LP:** VoE VLP2, AFF 1018, SB 137 (clt solo)
How Come You Do Me Like You Do - voc (Harold Arlen)

Benny's next recorded efforts are interesting because they saw him in the studios with Nichols and Selvin on the same day, the only time this is known to have occurred; and because Nichols's band is really Ben Pollack's, and later the nucleus of Bob Crosby's!

LORING "RED" NICHOLS AND   **December 12, 1930, New York**
    HIS ORCHESTRA (RN)
THE CAPTIVATORS (C)
CLUB ALBANY ORCHESTRA (CAO)
BLUE DIAMOND ORCHESTRA (BDO)

Benny Goodman, clt & as; Red Nichols, Ruby Weinstein, tpt; Glenn Miller, tbn; Gil Rodin, as; Eddie Miller, ts; Nappy Lamare, g; Harry Goodman, b; Ray Bauduc, d; Dick Robertson (DR), Scrappy Lambert (SL), voc.

E 35738-A BR 6014, BrE 1082, BrF 9002, BrG A9002, Brit 4764 (RN), SUP 2167 (BDO). **LP:** SB 157 (clt solo)
Blue Again - voc (DR)

E 35739-A same issues except no SUP (RN) (no solo)
When Kentucky Bids The World "Good Morning" - voc Dick Robertson

E 35740 ME 12049, PANA 25015 (C), MAY G2003 (CAO). **LP:** EMA ESLI, SB 157 (clt intro)
What Good Am I Without You? - voc (SL)

E 35741 ME 12049 (C). **LP:** EMA ESLI, SB 157 (clt solo)
We're Friends Again - voc (SL)

BEN SELVIN AND HIS ORCHESTRA   **same date**

Benny Goodman, clt; Mannie Klein, tpt; Herman Wolfson, ts; Charles Magnante, acc; plus unknown tpt, v, p, bjo, tu, d.

W 151117-1 CO 2356-D, CoE CB226. **LP:** TOM 17 (clt solo)
I Miss A Little Miss (Who Misses Me In Sunny Tennessee) - voc (qtte)

W 151118-2 CO 2356-D, CoE CB225, CO TEL TRANS 91981. **LP:** TOM 17, SVL 165. **ET:** HOLLYWOOD LIGHTS HL9 (clt solo)
Cheerful Little Earful - voc Helen Rowland

LEE MORSE AND HER   **December 23, 1930, New York**
    BLUE GRASS BOYS

Benny Goodman, clt; Mannie Klein, tpt; Tommy Dorsey, tbn; Eddie Lang, g; Rube Bloom, p; plus unknown v on W 151174 only.

W 151173-3 CO 2365-D. **LP:** TT 213 (clt accomp)
The Little Things In Life - voc Lee Morse

W 151174-2 same 78 issue (clt accomp)
Tears - voc Lee Morse

Only the first of seven matrices cut on the next Selvin session offers unmistakable evidence of Benny's participation. It is likely that he was present for all, but there is no proof, neither audible nor on file. Not even the CO "X" issues, non-vocal and recorded for export, have clt solos. Benny feels it is highly unlikely that he would have been hired to record but one tune—contracts didn't work that way.

BEN SELVIN & HIS ORCHESTRA (BS)   **December 26, 1930, New York**
BEN SELVIN Y SU ORQUESTA (BSYSO)
THE MIDNIGHT MINSTRELS (MM)

Benny Goodman, clt & as; Tommy Dorsey, tbn; Charles Magnante, acc; plus unknown 2 tpt, as, ts, 2 v, p, g, b, d.

W 151177-3 CO 2366-D, CoE CB235, ReAu 29063. **LP:** SB 108 (BS) (clt solo)
Yours And Mine - voc Smith Ballew

W 195125-1 CO 4544 X (BSYSO) (no solo)
En Un Balconcito En Espana (On A Little Balcony In Spain) - no voc

W 151178-3 CO 2367-D (BS), ReE MR303 (MM) (no solo)
On A Little Balcony In Spain - voc Smith Ballew

W 195128-1 CO 4434 X (BSYSO), CoE DC 104 (BS) (no solo)
Toque Su Mandolina (Lady Play Your Mandolin) - no voc

W 151179-2 CO 2367-D, CoE CB230 (BS), CoAu 319. **ET:** HOLLYWOOD LIGHTS HL 10 (no solo)
Lady Play Your Mandolin - voc Paul Small

W 195129-1 CO 4544 X (BSYSO) (no solo)
Bailarina Espanola (Little Spanish Dancer) - no voc

W 151180-3 CO 2366-D (BS), ReAu 20963 (no solo)
Little Spanish Dancer - voc Al Shayne

CO matrices W 151181-3 and W 151182-2, recorded either Dec. 27 or Dec. 28, are not Goodman items.

A multi-pseudonymed Ed Kirkeby session of Dec. 30, previously thought to have included BG, has been proven by the Kirkeby appointment book to have had reedmen Bobby Davis and Joe Gillespie, not Benny. Matrices and titles involved are: W 404591 (100456-1) "Reaching For The Moon"; W 404592 (100457-1) "When You Fall In Love Fall In Love With Me"; W 404593 (100460-1) "He's My Secret Passion"; W 404594 (100462-1) "Lady Play Your Mandolin"; W 404595 "Where Have You Been"; issues are PaA, OdA, HA, VE and CL.

1931 found Benny continuing his diverse activities, and as busy as ever: much radio work, movie soundtrack recording for Paramount at its Astoria, Long Island studios, many dance dates in and around New York, and an astonishing number of record dates. Despite the deepening Depression, twenty-one year old Benny Goodman prospered because of his reputation as a versatile musician, an instrumentalist capable of discharging any musical demands made of him.

For the first time in his career Benny was to record in 1931 with his one-time idol and the clarinetist he had impersonated 10 years earlier in Chicago's Central Park Theatre, Ted Lewis. It happened one week after his first '31 record session with Red Nichols.

RED AND HIS BIG TEN   **January 5, 1931, New York**

Benny Goodman, clt; Red Nichols, Ruby Weinstein, tpt; Glenn Miller, poss. Tommy Dorsey, tbn; Sid Stoneburn, as; Pete Pumiglio, ts; Carl Kress, g; Gene Krupa, d; unknown p.

BVE 67760-1 VI 23033, A, VDP R14590. **LP:** RcaFR FXMI 7283, TOM 35, SVL 146 (clt solo)
At Last I'm Happy - voc Paul Small (as "Johnny Davis" on VDP)

BVE 67761-1 VI 23033 B. **LP:** TOM 35, SVL 146 (no solo)
If You Haven't Got A Girl - voc Paul Small

TED LEWIS AND HIS BAND   **January 12, 1931, New York**

Benny Goodman, clt & as; Muggsy Spanier, cnt; George Brunies, tbn; Ted Lewis, clt & as; Sam Shapiro, Sol Klein, v; Jack Aaronson, p; Tony Gerardi, g; Harry Barth, b & tu; John Lucas, d; unknown tpt, ts.

W 151196-4 CO 2378-D, CO 2721-D, CoE CB304. **LP:** BIO 8, SB 115 (subt clt accomp)
Headin' For Better Times - voc Ted Lewis & The Bachelors

W 151197-3 CO 2408-D, CoE CB281. **LP:** BIO 8, SB 115 (clt accomp)
At Last I'm Happy - voc Ted Lewis

"Thirteen" once again proves hazardous for the BG enthusiast, this time January 13. Recorded on that date were three tunes by Ruth Etting, one by Ted Lewis. Clarinet may be heard on all four, but unfortunately it is all subtone. It seems logical that Goodman would have continued with Lewis; and what clarinet is evident seems more Benny's than anyone else's.

RUTH ETTING   January 13, 1931, New York

Benny Goodman, clt; plus unknown tpt, 2 v, p, g (poss. personnel from the Lewis session following).

W 151202-3 CO 2377-D (subt clt accomp)
            Reaching For The Moon - voc Ruth Etting

W 151203-3 same issue (subt clt accomp)
            Overnight - voc Ruth Etting

W 151204-3 CO 2398-D, CoE DB440 (subt clt accomp)
            Love Is Like That (What Can You Do?) - voc Ruth Etting

TED LEWIS AND HIS BAND   same date

Personnel as Jan 12, but Brunies is absent.

W 151206-1 CO 2378-D. **LP:** BIO 8 (subt clt accomp; as solo is
            Lewis's)
            Just A Gigolo - voc Ted Lewis

(Intervening CO matrix W 151205 was not recorded January 13.)

The sides preceding are certain as to date but uncertain as to BG; the next 12 are certain as to BG, but eight are uncertain as to date. Four—those released as by Goodman and Art Kahn—were cut January 14. The balance, four with matrices numerically just before the January 14 sides, and four with matrices immediately following, cannot be pinpointed. Decca claims not to have complete data on Melotone, Brunswick and Vocalion recordings made prior to December 1931. One or the other of the dates assigned, however, likely is correct.

The fact that Benny's orchestral waxings split the matrices by vocalists Grace Johnston and Sid Garry need not mean that they intervened chronologically. Block assignment, or assignment prior to the date of recording of the matrices, may have been responsible.

In any event, the rare Melotone issues by Johnston and Garry here listed are authentic BG. Other releases by these artists, on Melotone and other labels, have failed to produce evidence of Goodman's presence.

GRACE JOHNSTON (GJ)   January 13 or 14, 1931, New York
SID GARRY (SG)

Benny Goodman, clt & as; plus unknown tpt, tbn, ts, v, p. The unknowns may be, in order, Ruby Weinstein, Tommy Dorsey, Larry Binyon, Sam Shapiro, and Art Schutt.

E 35920   ME 12104 (GJ). **LP:** SB 106 (clt solo)
          (You Gave Me) Ev'rything But Love - voc Grace
          Johnston

E 35921   ME 12065, PANA 25073 (GJ) (no solo)
          I'm One Of God's Children (Who Hasn't Got Wings) -
          voc Grace Johnston

E 35922   ME 12065, PANA 25039 (GJ) (no solo)
          Walkin' My Baby Back Home - Grace Johnston

E 35923   ME 12069, PANA 25026 (SG). **LP:** SB 106 (clt solo)
          At Last I'm Happy - voc Sid Garry

It is not known if E 35923 completes this session; but it is known that E 35924 begins Benny's orchestra's session, and that the correct date for the BG Orchestra session is January 14.

Thanks to erstwhile Decca A&R man Eugene Williams, it is also known that the recording sheets originally scheduled all of Benny's orchestra's cuts to be released as by "Benny Goodman's Orchestra." Two of these credits were scratched out, however, and "Art Kahn's Orchestra" was substituted. This was done, in Williams's opinion, because some Decca executive questioned the marketability of Goodman's name.

BENNY GOODMAN   January 14, 1931, New York
  AND HIS ORCHESTRA (BG)
ART KAHN'S ORCHESTRA (AK)
SOUTHERN SYNCOPATORS - EmbAu only

Benny Goodman, clt & as; and poss. Ruby Weinstein, Charlie Teagarden, tpt; Tommy Dorsey, tbn; Sid Stoneburn, clt & as; Larry Binyon, ts; Sam Shapiro, v (omit on E 35924); Art Schutt, p; Eddie Lang or Dick McDonough, g; Harry Goodman, b; unknown d (not Gene Krupa); Paul Small (PS), voc on Kahn releases; unknown voc on Goodman releases.

E 35924   ME 12079, PanaAu P12079 (BG). **LP:** SB 106 (clt solo)
          If You Haven't Got A Girl - voc ref

E 35156   ME 12090 (AK), EMB E124. **LP:** SB 106 (clt solo)
          I'm Happy When You're Happy - voc (PS)

(Matrices E 35924 and E 35156 are consecutive)

E 35157   ME 12090 (AK), EMB E134. **LP:** SB 106 (no solo)
          You Didn't Have To Tell Me (I Knew It All The Time) -
          voc (PS)

E 35158   ME 12079, PanaAu P12079 (BG). **LP:** SB 157 (no solo)
          Falling In Love Again - voc ref

Note the presence of a guitar in the next block of Johnston-Garry matrices, absent in their first set. This suggests that the two sets were cut on different dates, and that the second set was recorded on the same day as the Goodman-Kahn session.

GRACE JOHNSTON (JOHNSON ON   January 14, 1931, New York
  SOME LABELS) (GJ)
SID GARRY (SG)

Personnel prob. as Jan. 14 Goodman-Kahn, except omit Teagarden, Stoneburn, H. Goodman and d.

E 35159   ME 12095, PANA 25020 (GJ) (clt accomp)
          You Didn't Have To Tell Me (I Knew It All The Time) -
          voc Grace Johnson

E 35160   ME 12104, PANA 25039 (GJ). **LP:** SB 157 (no solo)
          By A Lazy Country Lane -voc Grace Johnston

E 35161   ME 12095, PANA 25020 (GJ) (clt accomp)
          Keep A Song In Your Soul - voc Grace Johnson

E 35162   ME 12069 (SG) (no solo)
          The River And Me - voc Sid Garry

Evidently BG never recorded again with Grace Johnston or Sid Garry; other of their records fail to reveal Benny's presence.

BEN SELVIN & HIS ORCHESTRA (BS)   January 15, 1931, New York
JOHNNY WALKER & HIS ORCHESTRA (JW)

Benny Goodman, clt & as; Mannie Klein, tpt; Tommy Dorsey, tbn; plus unknown tpt, as, ts, p, g, d, xyl.

W 151207-3 CO 2381-D (BS) (clt solo)
            He's Not Worth Your Tears - voc (Helen Rowland)

W 151217-3 CO 2381-D, CoE CB252 (BS). **LP:** SB 108. **ET:**
            HOLLYWOOD LIGHTS HL 11 (clt solo)
            **Would You Like To Take A Walk (Sump'n Good'll Come
            From That)** - voc (Helen Rowland)

W 151218-3 CO 2380-D (JW). **LP:** SB 108`(clt solo)
            Personally, I Love You - voc (Paul Small)

(Intervening matrices above either were not cut Jan. 15 or were cut by different groups that do not include BG.)

The next session "double-dates" Benny with Red Nichols and Lee Morse, and double-crosses the Goodman discographer and collector—Jimmy Dorsey cut two sides with Annette Hanshaw in the same studio, on the same day, using matrices immediately preceding those assigned to BG-Morse. To top it off, another of the vocalists Benny accompanied, Ruth Etting, waxed one side the same day, same studio, using the matrix immediately following those of BG-Morse—using piano accompaniment only!

This BG-JD split happened on more than one occasion. Benny delights in telling the story that when he and Jimmy roomed together, it was a question of who answered the phone that determined which of them worked in the studios that day.

LORING "RED" NICHOLS January 16, 1931, New York
AND HIS ORCHESTRA

Benny Goodman, clt; Red Nichols, Ruby Weinstein, Charlie Teagarden, tpt; Jack Teagarden, Glenn Miller, tbn; Sid Stoneburn, as; Larry Binyon, ts; Ed Solinsky, Ed Bergman, v; Jack Russin, p; poss. Teg Brown, g; Art Miller, b; Gene Krupa, d.

E 35167-A BR 6029, BR 6842, BrF 9007, BrG A9007 (no solo)
  "You Said It" - voc (Harold Arlen)

E 35168-A BR 6029, BR 6711, BrE 1300, BrF 9007, BrG A9007,
  CoAu D01236, BrIt 4872. **LP:** AOH AH63 (no solo)
  Sweet And Hot - voc (Harold Arlen)

E 35169-(A,B) UNISSUED
  Keep A Song In Your Soul - voc Jack Teagarden

LEE MORSE same date
AND HER BLUE GRASS BOYS

Benny Goodman, clt; Mannie Klein, tpt; Tommy Dorsey, tbn; Rube Bloom, p; Eddie Lang, g.

W 151225-3 CO 2388-D, CoE DB579. **LP:** TT 213 (clt accomp)
  I'm One Of God's Children (Who Hasn't Got Wings) -
  voc Lee Morse

W 151226-3 CO 2388-D (clt accomp)
  Blue Again - voc Lee Morse

Benny had just spent five consecutive days in the studios; evidently he began to lose those races to the telephone, because he does not appear again on wax until . . .

ANNETTE HANSHAW January 20, 1931, New York

Benny Goodman, clt; Mannie Klein, tpt; Tommy Dorsey, tbn; Irving Brodsky or Rube Bloom, p; Eddie Lang, g; poss. Artie Bernstein, b; unknown v on 151234 only.

151234-1 HA 1273-H, VE 2273-V, CL 5217-C, CoE DB470. **LP:** SB
  111, SH 247 (clt solo)
  I Hate Myself (For Falling In Love With You) - voc
  Annette Hanshaw

151235-2 HA 1273-H, VE 2274-V, CL 5216-C, CoE DB470. **LP:** SB
  111, SH 247 (clt solo)
  You're The One I Care For - voc Annette Hanshaw

151236-2 HA 1288-H, VE 2315-V, CL 5249-C. **LP:** SB 111, SH 247
  (clt solo) **Would You Like To Take A Walk (Sump'n
  Good'll Come From That)** - voc Annette Hanshaw

151237-(1,2,3) UNISSUED
  Walkin' My Baby Back Home - voc Annette Hanshaw

(These Hanshaw Harmonies seem among the most difficult of the HA series to obtain. And note that CoE issue uses a "W" prefix before the matrix.)

This next date is the first of two sessions on which Benny rejoined his ex-boss Ben Pollack, for recording purposes only.

BEN POLLACK & HIS ORCH. January 21, 1931, New York
JACK TEAGARDEN AND THE BEN POLLACK ORCH. - UHCA issue only

Benny Goodman, clt & as; Charlie Teagarden, Ruby Weinstein, Sterling Bose, tpt; Jack Teagarden, tbn; Gil Rodin, as; Eddie Miller, ts; Ed Bergman, Ed Solinsky, v; Bill Schumann, cello; Gil Bowers, p; Nappy Lamare, g; Harry Goodman, b; Ray Bauduc, d.

10378-2 PE 15424, OR 2193, RO 1561, BA 32074, RE 10250, JE
  6193, CQ 7772, ROY 391066. **LP:** HIST 33, SB 136
  (clt solo)
  Sing Song Girl - voc "Ted Bancroft" on PE (Ben
  Pollack)

10379-3 same issues, except omit LPs (no solo)
  (When You Fall In Love) Fall In Love With Me - voc
  "Ted Bancroft" on PE (Ben Pollack?)

(There is a question as to the identity of the vocalist on 10379-3. Some insist it is Eddie Gale—others say "Eddie Gale" is another pseudonym for Ben Pollack.)

10380-2,3 PE 15428-B (2,3), OR 2208-B (2,3), RO 1573-B (2,3),
  BA 32101 (2,3), CQ 7763-B (2,3), RE 10266 (2),
  UHCA 103 B (2), VoAu 821 (), LyAu 3375 () (no solo)
  You Didn't Have To Tell Me (I Knew It All The Time) -
  voc Jack Teagarden

(Known takes are listed in ( ). UHCA issue is a dub.)

RED NICHOLS AND HIS FIVE PENNIES January 23, 1931, New York
SUPERTONE DANCE ORCHESTRA - SUP S2186 only.

Benny Goodman, clt & as; Red Nichols, Charlie Teagarden, poss. Ruby Weinstein, tpt; Jack Teagarden, tbn; Sid Stoneburn, as; Larry Binyon, ts; Jack Russin, p; poss. Teg Brown, g; Art Miller, b; Gene Krupa, d.

E 35954-A BR 6035, BrE 1076, BrF 9000, BrG A9000, SUP S2186
  (clt accomp)
  The Peanut Vendor - voc (Paul Small)

E 35955-A same issues (clt accomp)
  Sweet Rosita - voc (Paul Small)

Purists will object to listing Nichols's instrument as a trumpet. This same objection is valid for other brass men who usually employed a cornet. For the sake of simplicity, this discography more often than not ignores the distinction.

An Ed Kirkeby-directed session of Jan. 27, that encompassed CO matrices W 404828 through W 404832, does not include BG, as had previously been suspected. Reedmen on the date, as noted in Kirkeby's appointment book, are Joe Gillespie, Elmer Feldkamp, and Tommy Bohn.

Commercial releases from Benny's next Melotone date skip the next-to-last matrix, E 35837. The matrix was used to record "Auld Lang Syne" for the National Radio Advertising Company, New York, and was destined for its "Elks Magazine Program," a commercial radio broadcast. No copies of this matrix are extant, and thus it cannot be proved that BG cut it; but it is likely that he did.

BENNY GOODMAN AND HIS ORCHESTRA February 5, 1931, New York
STANLEY COOKE & HIS ORCH. - AurC 22000 only
TIN PAN PARADERS - SUP S2185 only
BROADWAY ORCH. - EmbAu only

Benny Goodman, clt & as; and instrumentation and personnel similar to Jan. 14 Goodman-Kahn, but substituting Glenn Miller, tbn, and poss. Gene Krupa, d.

E 35834 ME 12120. **LP:** SB 157 (clt solo)
  We Can Live On Love - voc (Paul Small)

E 35835 same issues (clt solo)
  When Your Lover Has Gone - voc (Paul Small)

E 35836 ME 12100, PANA 25013, AurC 22000, SUP S2185, EMB
  E118. **LP:** SB 157 (no solo)
  99 Out Of A Hundred Wanna Be Loved - voc (Paul
  Small)

(E 35837) ??? (no public release)
  (Auld Lang Syne)

E 35838 ME 12100. **LP:** SB 106 (clt solo)
  Mine Yesterday-His Today - voc (Paul Small)

THE CAVALIERS (WALTZ ARTISTS) (C) February 6, 1931, New York
MICKIE ALPERT & HIS ORCHESTRA (MA)
BEN SELVIN & HIS ORCHESTRA (BS)

Benny Goodman, clt & as; Tommy Dorsey, tbn; Art Schutt, p; plus unknown 2 tpt, as, ts, 2 v, g, bjo, b, d, xylo.

W 151282-2 CO 2399-D (C) (subt clt solo)
  Wabash Moon - voc ref (trio)

W 151283-2 same issue (C) (subt clt solo)
  **When Your Hair Has Turned To Silver (I Will Love You
  Just The Same)** - voc ref (trio)

W 151284-1   CO 2403-D (MA) (no solo)
Sing Song Girl (Little Yella Cinderella) - voc (trio)

W 151285-1,2   CO 2400-D, CoE CB279, ReAu 21042 (BS). **LP:** SB 108 (clt solo)
99 Out Of A Hundred Wanna Be Loved - voc Helen Rowland

(Both takes of W 151285 are on CO 2400-D and SB 108; CoE CB279 take(s) are unknown; ReAu is take 2.)

W 151286-1   CO 2403-D (MA) (no solo)
I Surrender, Dear - voc Helen Rowland

W 151287-2   CO 2400-D (BS) (subt clt solo)
Love For Sale

This bio-discography usually lists "clt" as Benny's instrument in the personnel section; occasionally it shows "clt & as," rarely does it cite others. When only "clt" is shown, it should not imply that he did not play alto sax or another reed instrument; he was versed in several and played them as the band's lineup, or arrangement, dictated. The listing indicates the principal instrument he used, so far as the ear can detect or written records establish.

A subtone clarinet solo on one side is the only substantiation of BG's presence on the next session. Once again, what clarinet can be heard seems more Benny's than his contemporaries.

THE RADIOLITES   February 7, 1931, New York

Benny Goodman, clt & as; Tommy Dorsey, tbn; Dick McDonough, g; plus unknown 2 tpt, as, ts, 2 v, p, b, d.

W 151288-3   CO 2405-D, ReAu 21042 (no solo)
I'm Happy When You're Happy - voc (poss. Scrappy Lambert)

W 151289-2   same issues (subt clt solo)
Were You Sincere? - voc (poss. Scrappy Lambert)

In early 1931 Benny was in the midst of a recording contract with Melotone that marketed the releases under his name. But the arrangements were undistinguished, and the personnel really were Red Nichols's. The efforts produced cannot be identified with what we now may call, "typical Goodman style," for they did not swing.

But on February 9 (some say Feb. 19) Benny cut some sides that did swing. Two of them have swung ever since; Benny often remarks that the Glenn Miller-arranged "Basin Street" and "Beale Street" from this session were the very first things he did that truly were in the style he was trying to develop. The other two sides, less known, also feature Benny blowing especially tasty clarinet.

JOHNNY WALKER & HIS ORCHESTRA (JW)   February 9, 1931, New York
THE CHARLESTON CHASERS
Under The Direction of Bennie Goodman (CC)

Benny Goodman, clt & as; Ruby Weinstein, Charlie Teagarden, tpt; Jack Teagarden, Glenn Miller, tbn; Sid Stoneburn, as; Larry Binyon, ts & fl (fl on W 151291 only); Art Schutt, p; Dick McDonough, g; Harry Goodman, b; Gene Krupa, d.

W 151290-3   CO 2404-D (JW). **LP:** VJM VLP 44, SB 108, SB 138 (clt solo)
When Your Lover Has Gone - voc (Paul Small)

W 151291-2   same issues plus ReAu 21038 (JW) (clt solo)
Walkin' My Baby Back Home - voc (Paul Small)

W 151292-2   CO 2415-D, CO 2914-D, OK 41577, BR 7645, BILT 1098 (dub), HJCA HC89 (dub), CoAu D01202, PaE R1356, PaE DP 377, Palt B71143, CoJap J1131, LuJap 60154. **EP:** CO B821. **LP:** CO CL821, JP 1807 (dub), JR 5023 (dub), COR KLP679, CoJap PL2030, SONY 50432, TL STLJO5, VJM VLP44 (dub), SB 138 (dub) (CC) (clt solo)
Basin Street Blues - voc (Jack Teagarden) (arr Glenn Miller)

W 151293-3   same issues, except: delete PaE R1356, PaE DP377, CoJap PL2030, TL STLJ05; and add PaE R1431 (78), and FO FP69 (dub), FO FJ2808 (dub), CoJap PL5020, TL STLJ08 (LPs) (clt solo)
Beale Street Blues - voc (Jack Teagarden) (arr Miller)

(NOTES: OK 41577 shows false mxs. 17096-1, 17097-1; Special CO release CO 2914-D/CO 2845-D couples "Basin Street Blues" with W 265167, "Texas Tea Party"—some copies of this issue have overlabels reading "Special Release from Melody Ranch, 4707 State St."; many later issues credit "Benny Goodman and His Orchestra" instead of "Charleston Chasers"; and other CO mxs. recorded this date (Feb. 9), W 404836 through W 404839, feature Jimmy Dorsey, not Benny Goodman.)

ETHEL WATERS   February 10, 1931, New York

Benny Goodman, clt; Mannie Klein, tpt; Tommy Dorsey, tbn; Joe Venuti, v; Rube Bloom, p; Eddie Lang, g.

W 151298-3   CO 2409-D. **EP:** CO BL31571. **LP:** CO KG 31571, CBSAu 220121 (clt accomp)
When Your Lover Has Gone - voc Ethel Waters

W 151299-3   same issues plus **LP,** SB 111 (clt solo)
Please Don't Talk About Me When I'm Gone - voc Ethel Waters

Goodman specialists, the author among them, have long assumed that the BEN POLLACK session of February 12, 1931, included Benny Goodman. Their assumption was based on two factors: 1, there is a ricky-tick clarinet solo on the only side thought to have been released from the session, "I'm A Ding Dong Daddy (From Dumas)"; and 2, the unissued sides are titles that were re-cut by Pollack March 2, and Benny is unquestionably among the sidemen on that date.

Now it would appear that this logically derived inference is simply wrong. In 1981 a diligent search turned up two previously-unheard sides from the February 12 session, 10416-2 "I've Got Five Dollars," and 10417-2 "Sweet And Hot"; the prominent clarinet on both sides is not Benny Goodman's. Reassessment of the corny clarinet solo on "I'm A Ding Dong Daddy (From Dumas)" leads to the conclusion that almost anyone could have played it, not a note can be solely ascribed to Benny.

Thus, eliminate Lincoln's Birthday, 1931, as a Goodman date; maybe Benny was on holiday.

One more time . . . "13" proves unlucky for the BG enthusiast: On February 13 TED LEWIS AND HIS BAND waxed "Truly I Love You." CO Matrix W 151306-2, CO 2408-D. Some discographers and collectors assume the personnel for this cut to be the same as for its flip side. W 151197-3, recorded Jan. 12, a valid Goodman item. The instrumentation for "Truly I Love You" seems the same for its reverse side, and Spanier is present; but there is no hint whatsoever of Benny's presence. Decision here is that Lewis's effort on the 13th did not include BG.

That decision holds for CO matrices W 151305-2 (TED WALLACE AND HIS CAMPUS BOYS, CO 2402-D), and CO matrices W 151307-2/W 151308-2 (EMERSON GILL & HIS ORCHESTRA, CO 2416-D), also cut Feb. 13, according to Columbia's files. These sides had some slight support as Goodman items, but Ed Kirkeby's appointment book establishes Bobby Davis, Elmer Feldkamp and Tommy Bohn as the reed men.

All in all, no BG on February 13. And none on Feb. 18, when Jimmy Dorsey, not Benny Goodman, cut CO matrices 151325 through 151330.

LORING "RED" NICHOLS   February 19, 1931, New York
AND HIS ORCHESTRA
SUPERTONE DANCE ORCHESTRA—SUP S2191 only

Personnel as Nichols, January 16.

E 36108-A   BR 6068, Br 6845, BrF 9032, BrG A9032. **LP:** AOH 168 (clt solo)
Things I Never Knew Till Now - voc (Harold Arlen)

E 36109-A   Br 6070, BrF 9046, BrG A9046, SUP S2191 (clt solo)
Teardrops And Kisses - voc (Harold Arlen)

E 36110-A   BR 6070, BrF 9046, BrG A9046, SUP S2191 (clt solo)
Were You Sincere? - voc (Harold Arlen)

E 36111-A   BR 6068, Br 6845, BrF 9032, BrG A9032. **LP:** AOH 168 (clt solo)
Keep A Song In Your Soul - voc (Jack Teagarden)

LEE MORSE AND HER   **February 20, 1931, New York**
   BLUE GRASS BOYS (LM)
CHARLES LAWMAN WITH THE RONDOLIERS (CL)

Benny Goodman, clt; Mannie Klein, tpt; Tommy Dorsey, tbn; Rube Bloom, p;
Eddie Lang, g; plus unknown v's on W 151336 only.

W 151334-3   CO 2417-D (LM). **LP:** SB 111 (clt solo)
      Walkin' My Baby Back Home - voc Lee Morse

W 151335-3   same issues (LM) (clt solo)
      I've Got Five Dollars - voc Lee Morse

W 151336-2   CO 2420-D (CL) (clt accomp)
      Prairie Skies - voc Charlie Lawman with the Rondoliers

(Other CO matrices recorded Feb. 20, by ANNETTE HANSHAW - W 151331-1
"Ever Since Time Began," W 151332-2 "Walkin' My Baby Back Home," And
W 151333-2 "You're Just Too Sweet For Words Honey O' Mine"—feature
Jimmy Dorsey, not Benny Goodman.)

BEN SELVIN AND HIS ORCHESTRA   **February 27, 1931, New York**

Benny Goodman, clt & as; Mannie Klein, tpt; Tommy Dorsey, tbn; Herman
Wolfson, ts; Irving Brodsky, p; Cornell Smelser, acc; plus unknown tpt, as, 2
v, bjo, b, d, xylo. "The Sunshine Boys" are Joe and Dan Mooney.

W 151363-2   CO 2426-D. **LP:** TOM 16 (clt solo)
      You Said It - voc Helen Rowland, Paul Small

W 151364-2   CO 2426-D (subt clt)
W 151364-3   CO 2426-D (subt clt). **LP:** TOM 16 (one take)
      Learn To Croon - voc Helen Rowland, Paul Small

W 151365-2   CO 2421-D, CO 38240. **LP:** TOM 16 (clt, as solos)
      Smile, Darnya, Smile - voc The Sunshine Boys

(W 151366—see ENRIQUE MADRIGUERA, following.)

W 151367-3   CO 2421-D. **LP:** TOM 16 (clt solo)
      The One Man Band - voc The Sunshine Boys

For some reason that is not known (possibly because of prior assignment of matrix numbers), the Selvin series of Feb. 27 was interrupted to
permit Enrique Madriguera to cut vocal and non-vocal versions of two tunes.
It seemed unlikely to collectors that Benny would have recorded with this
tango and rumba maestro. so for some years this possibility remained just
that. When the domestic CO release finally was acquired, however, it produced an unmistakable BG solo. Not only that, but it gave evidence that
some of the other Selvin personnel also joined with Benny; this leads to the
supposition that this was nothing other than a full Selvin date, with
"Madriguera" used as a pseudonym. It is believed, however, that
Madriguera had a regularly constituted orchestra.

The rare CO "X" releases have so far proved elusive; they may provide additional solo BG on this interesting date.

MADRIGUERA Y SUS   **same date (February 27)**
   NOTAS MAGICAS (M)
ENRIQUE MADRIGUERA'S HAVANA CASINO ORCH. (EM)

Benny Goodman, clt & as; plus prob. other Selvin personnel preceding, incl.
Mannie Klein, tpt; Tommy Dorsey, tbn; and unidentified tpt, tbn, as, ts, v, ac,
p, tu, maracas, woodblocks, bo, d.

W 195131-   CO 4476-X (M) (   )
      Lamento Africano (African Lament)

W 151366-1   CO 2422-D, CoAu DO 392 (EM) (no solo)
W 151366-2   CO 2422-D (EM) (no solo)
      African Lament (Lamento Africano) - voc (Paul Small)

W 195132-   CO 4477-X (M) (   )
      ¡Ay Mama Ines! (Mama Inez)

W 151368-2   CO 2422-D, CoAu DO 392 (EM). **LP:** SB 109 (clt solo)
      Mama Inez (Oh! Mom-E-Nez) - voc ref (laughing effects,
        ensemble)

(It is not known if W 151366-2 was issued on CoAu DO392.)

The Feb. 27 session was not yet concluded. There remained one more
cut by CHARLIE LAWMAN, to complete an issue begun one week earlier,
on Feb. 20.

Note that the intervening CO matrices, W 151369 through W 151372,
were not recorded Feb. 27 and do not include Benny Goodman.

CHARLIE LAWMAN   **same date (February 27)**

Benny Goodman, clt; Mannie Klein, tpt; Irving Brodsky, p; Eddie Lang, g; plus
unknown v's, xylo.

W 151373-1   CO 2420-D (clt accomp)
      Wabash Moon - voc Charlie Lawman

Next for Benny was the second of two studio-only collaborations with
Ben Pollack. For many years it was assumed that only two takes of one tune
were released from this session. The other tunes cut this date—"I've Got
Five Dollars" and "Sweet And Hot"—were considered unissued, so far as
Pollack was concerned.

Basis for this assumption was the common circulation of PE 15431 and
subsidiary labels credited to "BEN POLLACK & HIS ORCH." with appropriate matrices, but each with take 10. When played, it was evident that
these sides were not by Pollack's band. They were in fact recorded at a later
date by a group directed by Ed Kirkeby.

But persistence paid off. Eventually a copy of PE 15431 was discovered
that unquestionably was cut by Benny and Pollack's men. Then another copy
was located that additionally offered an alternate take of each tune. These
very rare issues—only one or two of each set of takes is known to exist—
must be classified as major additions to recorded Goodmania. Known couplings are 6-4, 5-5.

Investigation to date has failed to locate the Pollack efforts on PE's
subsidiaries: RE 10273, RO 1576, BA 32104, OR 2213, JE 6213 and CQ
7684. Collectors are cautioned that the Kirkeby recordings are on these
issues. Beware the take 10's.

BEN POLLACK & HIS ORCH. (BP)   **March 2, 1931, New York**
DUKE WILSON & HIS TEN BLACK BERRIES (DW)

Benny Goodman, clt; Charlie Spivak, Ruby Weinstein, Sterling Bose, tpt; Jack
Teagarden, tbn; Gil Rodin, as; Eddie Miller, ts; Ed Bergman, Ed Solinsky, v;
Bill Schumann, cel; Sam Prager, p; Nappy Lamare, g; Harry Goodman, b; Ray
Bauduc, d. (No v or cel on matrix 10422)

10416-5   PE 15431 A. **LP:** BIO 1, SB 136 (BP) (clt solo)
10416-6   PE 15431 A. **LP:** SB 136 (BP) (clt solo)
      I've Got Five Dollars - voc Ben Pollack

10417-4   PE 15431 B. **LP:** EPIC LN24045, CoE 33SX1545, SB 136
       (BP) (clt solo)
10417-5   PE 15431 B. **LP:** SB 136 (BP) (clt solo)
      Sweet And Hot - voc Ben Pollack (and Jack Teagarden,
       Nappy Lamare)

(intervening matrices are not by Pollack)

10422-4   PE15617 B, RoyC 91358 B, MeC 91358 B. **LP:** IAJRC-1,
       SB 136 (DW) (clt solo)
10422-5   PE 15617 B, RO 1858 B, OR 2488 B, BA 32463 B. **EP:**
       VJMS VEP13. **LP:** BIO 2, RS 010A (DW) (clt solo)
10422-6   **LP:** BIO 2 (DW) (clt solo)
      Beale Street Blues - voc Jack Teagarden

TED LEWIS AND HIS BAND   **March 5, 1931, New York**

Benny Goodman, clt; Muggsy Spanier, cnt; George Brunies, tbn; Ted Lewis,
clt & as; Fats Waller, p; Tony Gerardi, g; Harry Barth, b; John Lucas, d. Add
Sam Shapiro, Sol Klein, v, on matrix W 151395 only.

W 151395-2   CO 2428-D. **LP:** CO DZ-77, GAPS 020, SB 115, BIO 7
       (clt solo)
      Egyptian-Ella -voc Ted Lewis

W 151396-1   CO 2428-D. **LP:** CO DZ-77, CBSFr 63366, COLR 12-7,
       SB 115 (clt colo)
      **I'm Crazy 'Bout My Baby (And My Baby's Crazy 'Bout
      Me)** - voc (Fats Waller)

TED LEWIS AND HIS BAND   **March 6, 1931, New York**

Personnel as March 5. V's on mx W 151397 only.

W 151397-3   CO 2527-D, ME 13379, PE 16109, RO 2506, OR 3132,
(17065-1)   BA 33412, CO 35684, CO 38841, BRS 1009 (dub),
                      CoAu 2756, CoE FB2820, CoE CB446, CoF DF765,
                      CoG DW4053. **EP:** CO B2101, PhilE BBE 12106,
                      PhilCont 429194BE. **LP:** CO CL6127, CBSFr 63361,
                      SB 115, BIO 7, TL STLJ15 (clt solo)
              Dallas Blues - voc (Fats Waller)

W 151398-2   CO 2527-D, OK 41579, CO 35684, CO 38840, CoFr DF
(17064-1)   765, BRS 1009 (dub), CoAu 2756, CoE FB2820, CoE
                      CB446, CoG DW4053. **EP:** CO B2101, PhilE BBE
                      12106, PhilCont 429194BE, EPIC L2N6072. **LP:** CO
                      CL6127, CBSFr 63366, SB 115, BIO 7 (clt solo)
              Royal Garden Blues - voc (Fats Waller)

(Some later issues -e.g., OK, red-label CO's—show a false matrix and take, indicated above parenthetically. There is no musical difference.)

Note that beginning with the next session two matrix series run concurrently, a change from previous PaA/HA sets. There is no musical difference in each PaA/HA combination, although a take 2 may be matched with a take ''A.'' The 150,000 series is believed to govern.

THE HARMONIANS (H)   **March 16, 1931, New York**
CHESTER LEIGHTON & HIS SOPHOMORES (CL)
JACK WHITNEY AND HIS NEW YORKERS (JW)
SAM NASH AND HIS ORCHESTRA (SN)
WALLY EDWARDS AND HIS ORCHESTRA (WE)
ED LLOYD AND HIS ORCHESTRA (EL)
ROOF GARDEN ORCHESTRA (RG)
RAY SEELEY AND HIS ORCHESTRA (RS)
ARIEL DANCE ORCHESTRA (ADO)
FRANK AUBURN AND HIS ORCHESTRA (FA)

Benny Goodman, clt & as; Mannie Klein, tpt; Tommy Dorsey, tbn; Herman Wolfson, ts; Charles Magnante, acc; plus unknown tpt, as, 2 v, p, g, tu, d. The vocalists are unknown.

W 151423-1   HA 1308-H (H); VE 2342-V, CL 5276-C (CL) (as solo,
                      subt clt)
(W 495048-) PaA 34194 (JW); OdA 36202 (WE); PaE R944 (RG); ArE
                      24729. **LP:** SB 109 (ADO)
              **If You Should Ever Need Me, You'll Always Find Me
              Here** - voc ''Lou Brady''

W 151424-1   HA 1308-H (H); VE 2340-V, CL 5274-C (CL) (no solo)
(W 495049-A) PaA 34195 (JW); OdA 36202 (WE)
              Oh, Donna Clara - voc ''Lou Brady''

W 151425-2   HA 1311-H (H); VE 2352-V, CL 5286-C (FA) (clt solo)
(W 495050-A) PaA 34196 (SN); OdA 36203 (RS); OK 41487 (EL). **LP:**
                      SB 109
              You'll Be Mine In Apple Blossom Time - voc ''Lou
              Brady''

W 151426-2   HA 1310-H (H); VE 2349-V, CL 5283-C (FA) (clt solo)
(W 495051-) PaA 34197 (SN); OdA 36203 (RS). **LP:** TOM 16, SB 109
              **I'm Crazy 'Bout My Baby (And My Baby's Crazy 'Bout
              Me)** - voc ''Lou Brady''

BENNY GOODMAN AND HIS ORCHESTRA   **March 18, 1931, New York**
SAVOY JAZZ ORCH. - EmbAu only

Benny Goodman, clt & as; Charlie Teagarden, tpt; Glenn Miller, tbn; Eddie Lang, g; Ray Bauduc, d; plus unknown tpt, as, ts, p, b.

E 36481   ME 12138, PANA 25046, **LP:** SB 106 (clt solo)
           What Have We Got To Do To-Night But Dance - voc
           (Paul Small)

E 36482   ME 12149, PANA 25031, PanaAu P12149. **LP:** SB 106
           (clt solo)
           Little Joe - voc (Dick Robertson)

E 36483   ME 12149, PanaAu P12149, EMB E135. **LP:** SB 106 (no
           solo)
           It Looks Like Love - voc (Paul Small)

E 36484   ME 12138. **LP:** SB 106 (clt solo)
           I Wanna Be Around My Baby All The Time - voc (Paul
           Small)

(Known issues of PanaAu that duplicate BG ME catalog numbers are shown above. It is possible that other PanaAu duplications were issued.)

On March 18 Kirkeby cut the original 10416 and 10417 Pollack matrices arbitrarily as re-make take 10's. Despite the fact that Benny was in the same studio on March 18 with his own band, there is no audible evidence whatsoever that he participated in the Kirkeby session.

HELEN ROWLAND   **March 20, 1931, New York**
AND PAUL SMALL (HR & PS)
THE RONDOLIERS (R)

Benny Goodman, clt & as; Mannie Klein, tpt; Tommy Dorsey, tbn; Eddie Lang, g & bjo; plus unknown p, b; and unknown v on W 151445 only.

W 151445-3   CO 2436-D (HR & PS) (clt & as accomp)
              You'll Be Mine In Apple Blossom Time - voc Helen
              Rowland, Paul Small

W 151446-3   same issue (R) (clt accomp)
              Childlins' - voc The Rondoliers

Other CO matrices recorded March 20 included W 151447-2 ''Siboney'' and W 151448-3 ''Adios,'' by ENRIQUE MADRIGUERA'S HAVANA CASINO ORCHESTRA, issued on CO 2434-D and CoAu DO389; and mxs W 15499 and W 15140 by KATE SMITH. The Madriguera releases are possible BG's, although there are no identifiable clt passages. Kate Smith used p accomp only.

CO matrices W 151461 through W 151469, and CO mx W 495054, all recorded March 26, do not include BG as suggested elsewhere.

Benny got sandwiched in the middle of the next date: The first tune recorded by Lee Morse, ''The Tune That Never Grows Old,'' W 151470-2, CO 2436-D, was tired to begin with as far as we're concerned—an unidentifiable v substitutes for BG. Benny can be heard on the second and third cuts; the fourth is unissued, so his presence there, although likely, is not certain. The fifth and sixth msx, W 151474 and W 151475, offer piano accomp only.

LEE MORSE AND HER   **March 27, 1931, New York**
BLUE GRASS BOYS (LM)
ROY EVANS (RE)

Benny Goodman, clt; Mannie Klein, tpt; Tommy Dorsey, tbn; Rube Bloom, p; Eddie Lang, g.

W 151471-3   CO 2436-D (LM) (clt accomp)
              By My Side - voc Lee Morse

W 151472-2   Co 2469-D, ReE MR410 (RE) (clt accomp)
              Roll On, Mississippi, Roll On - voc Roy Evans

W 151473-(1) UNISSUED (RE) (   )
              Hang Out The Stars In Indiana - voc Roy Evans

As noted earlier, Benny worked occasionally with Lanin groups, but rarely recorded with them. Here is one of those rare instances, unconfirmed until the very last tune:

JERRY FENWYCK & HIS ORCHESTRA (JF)   **April 3, 1931, New York**
SAM LANIN AND HIS ORCHESTRA (SL)
RAY SEELEY AND HIS ORCHESTRA (RS)
FRANK AUBURN & HIS ORCHESTRA (FA)
WALLY EDWARDS & HIS ORCHESTRA (WE)
PHIL HUGHES & HIS HIGH HATTERS (PH)
THE DEAUVILLE SYNCOPATORS (DS)
THE NEW YORK SYNCOPATORS (NYS)
GOLDEN TERRACE DANCE ORCHESTRA (GT)
LLOYD KEATING AND HIS ORCHESTRA (LK)
DAVID EDWARDS & HIS BOYS (DE)
SAM LANIN AND HIS FAMOUS PLAYERS (LFP)

Benny Goodman, clt & as; Mannie Klein, tpt; Tommy Dorsey, tbn; Herman Wolfson, ts; Irving Brodsky, p; plus unknown tpt, as, 2 v, bjo, tu, d. Vocal credits are given per HA-VE-CL; they may not appear on all issues. The 495,000 series mxs may be sans vocal. Dick Robertson or Paul Small is suggested as vocalist.

W 151483-1	HA 1314-H, VE 2373-V, CL 5307-C (JF) (no solo)
(W 495053-)	PaA 34202 (SL); OdA 36209 (RS)
W 151483-2	HA 1314-H (JF) (no solo) (other 2nd takes unknown)
	That Little Boy Of Mine - voc "Jerry Fenwyck"
W 151478-2	HA 1316-H, VE 2376-V, CL 5310-C (FA) (no solo)
(W 495055-)	PaA 34200, PaE R956 (SL); OdA 36210 (WE)
	It Looks Like Love - voc "Robert Wood"
W 151479-2	HA 1313-H, VE 2372-V, CL 5306-C (PH) (no solo)
(W 404903-)	PaA 34201 (DS); OdA 36208 (NYS); OK 41493 (GT); PaE R965 (SL)
	Whistling In The Dark - voc "Phil Hughes"
W 151480-1	HA 1315-H, VE 2377-V, CL 5311-C (FA) (clt intro)
(W 495057-)	PaA 34202, OdA 36211 (SL); PaE R965 (LK)
	Think A Little Kindly Of Me - voc "Robert Wood"
W 151481-2	HA 1314-H, VE 2371-V, CL 5305-C (JF) (no solo)
(W 495058-)	PaA 34203, OdA 36211 (LK)
	Out Of Nowhere - voc "Jerry Fenwyck"
W 151482-1	CL 5304-C (PH) (clt solo)
W 151482-2	HA 1313-H, VE 2370-V, CL 5304-C (PH); OdArg 193702 (SL). **LP:** SB 107 (clt solo)
(W 404902-A)	PaA 34199 (DS); OdA 36208 (NYS); OK 41492 (DE); PaE R1070 (LFP)
	Just A Crazy Song (Hi, Hi, Hi) - voc "Phil Hughes"

TED LEWIS AND HIS BAND   **April 13, 1931, New York**

Benny Goodman, clt & as; Muggsy Spanier, cnt; poss. Dave Klein, tpt; George Brunies, tbn; Ted Lewis, clt & as; Sam Shapiro, Sol Klein, v; Jack Aaronson, p; Tony Gerardi, g; Harry Barth, b; John Lucas, d.

W 151513-2	CO 2467-D, CO 38843, DEC 504 (dub). **LP:** CO CL6127, NOST 890/1, TL STLJO5, SB 115, BIO 7 (clt solo)
	Dip Your Brush In The Sunshine (And Keep On Painting Away) - voc Ted Lewis
W 151514-2	CO 2452-D, CoAu DO427, CoE CB351, CoF DF823. **LP:** SB 115 (clt solo)
	One More Time - voc Ted Lewis

(CO 38843 shows a false take 1 on mx W 151513; all issues are take 2. Other CO matrices recorded April 13, W 151515 & W 151516, are not by BG).

TED LEWIS AND HIS BAND   **April 15, 1931, New York**
Personnel as April 13.

W 151517-3	CO 2452-D, CoAu DO 427, CoE CB304, Colt CQ744. **LP:** EPIC LN3170, SB 115 (clt solo)
	Ho Hum! - voc Ted Lewis
W 151518-3	CO 2467-D (no solo)
	The Little Old Church In The Valley - voc Ted Lewis

(Other CO matrices recorded April 15, W 351000 through W 351004, show no evidence of BG as is sometimes claimed.)

There is very little substantive BG on the next two sessions; clarinet that may be heard is all subtone. But it is strong subtone, and the opinion here is that it is indeed Benny Goodman's.

RUTH ETTING   **April 16, 1931, New York**
Prob. Benny Goodman, clt; Mannie Klein, tpt; Irving Brodsky, p; Eddie Lang, g; unknown v.

W 151519-2	CO 2454-D, CoE DB546. **LP:** TT 211 (subt clt accomp)
	Out Of Nowhere - voc Ruth Etting
W 151520-3	CO 2454-D (subt clt intro & accomp)
	Say A Little Prayer For Me - voc Ruth Etting

CHESTER LEIGHTON & HIS   **April 22, 1931, New York**
  SOPHOMORES (CL)
FRANK AUBURN & HIS ORCHESTRA (FA)
BUDDY CAMPBELL AND HIS ORCHESTRA (BC)
BEN SELVIN AND HIS ORCHESTRA (BS)

Prob. Benny Goodman, clt & as; Mannie Klein, tpt; Tommy Dorsey, tbn; Herman Wolfson, ts; plus unknown tpt, 2 v, p, g, b, d, xylo. Smith Ballew, voc. (SB)

W 351011-2	HA 1320-H, VE 2385-V, CL 5319-C (CL) (subt clt solo)
	Now You're In My Arms - voc "Chester Leighton" (SB)
W 351012-2	HA 1321-H, VE 2386-V, CL 5320-C (FA) (no solo)
(W 404910)	OK 41495 (BC)
	Rocky Mountain Lullaby - voc "Robert Wood" (SB)
W 351013-1	same issues plus PaE R987, OdArg 193779 (BS) (no solo)
(W 404911-)	OK 41495 (BC)
	When The Moon Comes Over The Mountain - voc "Robert Wood" (trio incl. Smith Ballew)
W 351014-2	HA 1320-H, VE 2385-V, CL 5319-C (CL) (as bridge)
	Star Dust - voc "Chester Leighton" (SB)

The next session was Benny's last with Red Nichols and his Orchestra. As Benny recalls it, he was with Red until the close of "Girl Crazy." Other information suggests Benny and Red parted company before the closing, and Jimmy Dorsey took Benny's chair in the pit as well as in the studios.

LORING "RED" NICHOLS   **April 24, 1931, New York**
  AND HIS ORCHESTRA

Benny Goodman, clt & as; Red Nichols, Ruby Weinstein, Charlie Teagarden, tpt; Glenn Miller, George Stoll, tbn; Sid Stoneburn, as; Larry Binyon, ts & fl; Ed Bergman, Ed Solinsky, v; Fulton McGrath, p; poss. Teg Brown, g; Art Miller, b; Gene Krupa, d; Smith Ballew (SB), voc.

E 36728-B	BR 6191, BrE 1275 (clt solo)
	It's The Darn'dest Thing - voc (SB)
E 36729-A	BR 6191, BR 6845, BrE 1275 **LP:** IAJRC 22 (clt solo)
	Singin' The Blues - voc (SB)
E 36730	BR 6118, BrF 9055, BrG A9055 (no solo)
	Love Is Like That (What Can You Do?) - voc (SB)

BEN SELVIN AND HIS ORCHESTRA   **May 7, 1931, New York**

Benny Goodman, clt & as; Mannie Klein, tpt; plus unknown tbn, as, ts, p, g, b, d.

W 151547-3	CO 2463-D. **LP:** SB 109 (clt solo)
	Poor Kid - voc (Sid Garry)
W 151548-2	CO 2463-D, CO TEL TRANS 98741 (subt clt solo)
	Now You're In My Arms - voc Helen Rowland

ROY CARROLL & HIS   May 9, 1931, New York
  SANDS POINT ORCH. (RC)
BEN SELVIN & HIS ORCH. (BS)
BUDDY CAMPBELL & HIS ORCH. (BC)
LLOYD KEATING & HIS MUSIC (LK)
GOLDEN TERRACE DANCE ORCH. (GT)
ROOF GARDEN ORCH. (RGO)

Benny Goodman, clt & as; Mannie Klein, tpt; Tommy Dorsey, tbn, plus unknown tpt, as, ts, p, g, b, d. Unknown xylo on W 351016. Unknown v on W 351017.

W 351015-2	HA 1322-H, VE 2387-V, CL 5321-C (RC); PaE R974 (BS) (clt accomp)
(W 404912-)	OK 41499 (BC)
	(There Ought To Be A) Moonlight Saving Time - voc Paul Small
W 351016-2	same issues plus OdArg 193766 and **LP:** BIO 1, SB 109 (RC) (clt solo)
(W 404913-)	OK 41499 (BC)
	Roll On, Mississippi, Roll On - voc Paul Small

(Some copies CK 41499 show the genuine matrices, W 351015-2 and W 351016-2. It should be remembered that OK issues are **not** different takes.)

W 351017-1	HA 1323-H, VE 2388-V, CL 5322-C (LK) Palt B27458 (BS) (subt clt solo)
(W 404914-)	OK 41500 (GT)
	Wrap Your Troubles In Dreams (And Dream Your Troubles Away) - voc Paul Small
W 351018-2	same issues except no Palt plus PaE R991 (RGO) (clt accomp)
(W 404915-)	OK 41500 (GT)
	I "Wanna" Sing About You - voc Paul Small

FRANK AUBURN & HIS ORCHESTRA (FA)   May 19, 1931, New York
LLOYD KEATING & HIS MUSIC (LK)
GOLDEN TERRACE DANCE ORCHESTRA (GT)
PHIL HUGHES AND HIS HIGH HATTERS (PH)
ROOF GARDEN ORCH. (RGO)

Personnel similar to May 9. Scrappy Lambert (SL), voc.

W 351019-1	HA 1327 H, VE 2399-V, CL 5335-C (FA) (subt clt accomp)
	My Cradle Sweetheart - voc "Tom Frawley" (SL)
W 351020-2	same issues plus PaE R991 (RGO) (subt clt accomp, as accomp)
(W 404944-B)	OK 41505 (GT)
	Faithfully Yours - voc "Tom Frawley" (SL)
W 351021-1	HA 1326-H, VE 2398-V, CL 5334-C (LK) (subt clt accomp)
	Have You Forgotten? - voc "Robert Wood" (SL)
W 351022-2	same issues plus **LP:** SB 109 (subt clt accomp, as solo)
(W 404945-B)	OK 41505 (GT); OdArg 193794 (LK)
	(Yoo-hoo-hoo I'll Call To You) Under Your Window Tonight - voc "Robert Wood" (SL)
W 351023-2	HA 1333-H, VE 2406-V, CL 5342-C (PH). **LP:** SB 109 (as solo)
	Treat Me Like A Baby - voc "Phil Hughes" (SL)

Disassociated from Nichols, Benny once again worked more frequently with Don Voorhees. It is not certain, but BG probably was with Voorhees in May when the MAXWELL HOUSE ORCHESTRA, Don Voorhees Director, cut two sides for **Hit-Of-The-Week.** They are 1154 "I'm Thru With Love," and 1155 "Roll On, Mississippi, Roll On." The clt solo on 1155 is not quite BG's usual technique and tone, however, and these releases qualify as Goodman possibilities only.

ROY CARROLL & HIS   May 21, 1931, New York
  SANDS POINT ORCH. (RC)
GOLDEN TERRACE DANCE ORCHESTRA (GT)
BUDDY CAMPBELL & HIS ORCHESTRA (BC)
CHESTER LEIGHTON & HIS SOPHOMORES (CL)

Personnel similar to May 9. Dick Robertson (DR), voc.

W 351024-2	HA 1329-H, VE 2402-V, CL 5338-C (RC). **LP:** SB 109 (clt solo)
(W 404919-)	OK 41503 (BC)
	Let's Get Friendly - voc "Roy Carroll" (DR)
W 351025-2	same issues plus PaE R995, OdG A221374. **LP:** BIO 1 (GT) (clt, as solos)
(W 404918-)	OK 41503 (BC)
	One More Time - voc "Roy Carroll" (DR)
W 351026-2	HA 1328-H, VE 2401-V, CL 5337-C (CL) (as accomp, subt clt)
	Love Is Like That (What Can You Do?) - voc "Bobby Dix" (DR)
W 351027-2	same issues plus **LP:** SB 109 (clt accomp, as solo)
	Two Little, Blue Little Eyes - voc "Bobby Dix" (DR)

A RUTH ETTING-ART GILLHAM "double-date" of May 26 offers little proof that it included BG. Matrices are W 151569 "Faithfully Yours" and W 151570 "(There Ought To Be A) Moonlight Saving Time," both Etting, CO 2470-D; and W 151571 "Just A Minute To Say Goodbye" by Gillham, CO 2506-D. Opinion here: a remote possibility only.

LLOYD KEATING & HIS MUSIC (LK)   May 28, 1931, New York
BEN SELVIN & HIS ORCH. (BS)
BUDDY CAMPBELL & HIS ORCHESTRA (BC)
FRANK AUBURN AND HIS ORCHESTRA (FA)
GOLDEN TERRACE DANCE ORCHESTRA (GT)

Personnel similar to May 9, prob. incl. Joe Venuti, v and Eddie Lang, g. Dick Robertson (DR), voc.

W 351028-2	HA 1330-H, VE 2403-V, CL 5339-C (LK); PaE R987 (BS) (no solo)
(W 404951-)	OK 41507 (BC)
	You Can't Stop Me From Loving You - voc "Bobby Dix" (DR)
W 351029-2	same HA-VE-CL issues plus PaE R1035 (BS); OdG A221386 (GT) (no solo)
	Sing A Little Jingle - voc "Bobby Dix" (DR)
W 351030-2	HA 1331-H, VE 2404-V, CL 5340-C, OdArg 193723 B (FA) (subt clt)
	In The Merry Month Of Maybe - voc "Robert Wood" (DR)
W 351031-2	same issues plus OdF 238956 and **LP:** SB 109 (FA) (clt solo)
	I Found A Million Dollar Baby (In A Five And Ten Cent Store) - voc "Robert Wood" (actually, a qtte)

(Other CO matrices recorded May 28, W 151572, W 151573 and W 151574 do not include Benny Goodman.)

There is little substantive clarinet to be heard on the next session, but it is considered a probable Goodman effort.

BEN SELVIN AND HIS ORCHESTRA   June 1, 1931, New York

Prob. Benny Goodman, clt & as; Mannie Klein, tpt; poss. Joe Venuti, v; Eddie Lang, g; plus unknown tpt, tbn, as, ts, p, b, d.

W 151577-2	CO 2473-D (subt clt solo)
W 151577-3	CO 2473-D (subt clt solo)
	High And Low (I've Been Looking For You) - voc (trio)
W 151578-2	CO 2473-D (subt clt accomp)
	Dancing In The Dark - voc ref

The MAXWELL HOUSE ORCHESTRA, Don Voorhees, Director, cut two more **Hit-Of-The-Week** sides in June: 1162 ''I Found A Million Dollar Baby'' and ''Many Happy Returns Of The Day'' on 1163. There is no definitive clt on either side, and they can only be considered BG possibilities in light of Benny's association with Voorhees.

LEE MORSE AND HER BLUE GRASS BOYS　　　June 3, 1931, New York

Benny Goodman, clt; Mannie Klein, tpt; Tommy Dorsey, tbn; Eddie Lang, g; Irving Brodsky or Rube Bloom, p; unknown blues-blowing on W 151585.

W 151585-3　　CO 2474-D. **LP:** TT 213 (clt accomp)
　　　　　　Let's Get Friendly - voc Lee Morse

W 151586-2　　same issues (clt accomp)
　　　　　　I'm Thru With Love - voc Lee Morse

PHIL HUGHES AND HIS　　　　　　June 5, 1931, New York
　HIGH HATTERS (PH)
JACK WHITNEY AND HIS ORCHESTRA (JW)
BEN SELVIN & HIS ORCH. (BS)
ROY CARROLL & HIS SANDS POINT ORCH. (RC)

Benny Goodman, clt & as; Mannie Klein, tpt; Herman Wolfson, ts; Irving Brodsky, p; plus unknown tpt, tbn, 2 v, as, g, b, d. Scrappy Lambert (SL), voc. It has been suggested that Bunny Berigan is the ''unknown'' tpt.

W 351032-2　　HA 1333-H, VE 2406-V, CL 5342-C (PH); PaE R994
　　　　　　(BS). **LP:** SB 109 (clt solo)
　　　　　　Look In The Looking Glass - voc ''Phil Hughes'' (duet)

W 351033-2　　HA 1335-H, VE 2408-V, CL 5344-C (JW). **LP:** SB 109
　　　　　　(clt solo)
　　　　　　You Forgot Your Gloves - voc ''Jerry Fenwyck'' (SL)

W 351034-3　　HA 1334-H, VE 2407-V, CL 5343-C, OdArg 193722 (RC)
　　　　　　(subt clt solo)
　　　　　　Dancing In The Dark - voc ''Roy Carroll'' (SL)

W 351035-1　　same issues plus **LP:** SB 109 (as solo)
　　　　　　High And Low (I've Been Looking For You) - voc ''Roy
　　　　　　Carroll'' (SL)

W 351036-2　　HA 1335-H, VE 2408-V, CL 5344-C (JW) (no solo)
　　　　　　Falling In Love - voc ''Jerry Fenwyck'' (SL)

One year ago—June 6, 1930—was the Mills date on which, some collectors believe, Benny and Bix Beiderbecke worked together. That is still uncertain; but it is a fact that they did work together on June 11 of 1931. Unfortunately, it was not a recording session, but a dance date at Williams College, Williamstown, Mass.

Benny recalls that Bix was ill at this time; and that his malaise worsened because Bix and Tommy Dorsey rented a plane to make the gig on time, and Bix was no flight enthusiast. Benny does not remember a bit of jazz lore that says he played cornet that night in Bix's stead. But he is firm in his belief that the Williams date was the last time he and Bix were together.

CO matrices W 151604 through W 151612, recorded June 15, do not include Goodman as suggested elsewhere.

ETHEL WATERS　　　　　　　　June 16, 1931, New York

Benny Goodman, clt; Mannie Klein, tpt; Tommy Dorsey, tbn; Eddie Lang, g; Rube Bloom, p.

W 151613-2　　CO 2481-D. **LP:** CO CL2792 (clt accomp)
W 151613-3　　CO 2481-D, CoE DB579, ReAu 21179 (clt accomp)
　　　　　　You Can't Stop Me From Lovin' You - voc Ethel Waters

W 151614-2　　CO 2481-D (clt accomp)
　　　　　　Without That Gal! - voc Ethel Waters

Bix had exited; but as if to compensate, another brilliant—and essentially tragic—horn man came onto Benny's horizon. Here are BG's certain first records with Bunny Berigan:

LLOYD KEATING & HIS MUSIC (LK)　　　June 18, 1931, New York
GOLDEN TERRACE (DANCE) ORCHESTRA (GT)
BUDDY CAMPBELL & HIS ORCHESTRA (BC)
CHESTER LEIGHTON & HIS SOPHOMORES (CL)
JERRY FENWYCK & HIS ORCHESTRA (JF)

Benny Goodman, clt & as; Bunny Berigan, tpt; Tommy Dorsey, tbn; Herman Wolfson, ts; Irving Brodsky, p; Eddie Walters, uke; plus unknown tpt, as, g, b, d, tu (poss. Tommy Dorsey, doubling), xylo, 2 v. Walters (EW) and Dick Robertson (DR), voc.

W 351041-2　　HA 1339-H, VE 2414-V, CL 5350-C (LK). **LP:** SB 109 (clt
　　　　　　solo)
　　　　　　I'm Keepin' Company - voc ''Robert Wood'' (EW)

W 351042-2　　HA 1340-H, VE 2415-V, CL 5351-C (CL). **LP:** SB 110 (clt
　　　　　　solo)
　　　　　　On The Beach With You - voc ''Chester Leighton'' (EW)

W 351043-2　　HA 1342-H, VE 2417-V, CL 5353-C (CL); PaE R1015,
　　　　　　OdG A221372 (GT) (subt clt solo)
(404959-B)　　OK 41511 (BC)
　　　　　　Just One More Chance - voc ''Jerry Fenwyck'' (DR)

W 351044-2　　same issues except substitute (JF) for (CL), delete PaE
　　　　　　R1015 and add PaE R995 (as bridge)
(404973-)　　OK 41517 (GT)
　　　　　　Makin' Faces At The Man In The Moon - voc ''Jerry
　　　　　　Fenwyck'' (DR)

W 351045-2　　HA 1340-H, VE 2415-V, CL 5351-C, OdF 238956 (CL);
　　　　　　PaE R1036. **LP:** SB 110 (GT) (clt solo)
(404953-B)　　OK 41508 (GT)
　　　　　　Without That Gal! - voc ''Chester Leighton'' (DR)

W 351046-2　　HA 1343-H, VE 2419-V, CL 5355-C (LK) (clt solo)
　　　　　　Let's Drink A Drink TO THE FUTURE - voc ''Bobby Dix''
　　　　　　(DR)

W 351047-2　　HA 1339-H, VE 2414-V, CL 5350-C (LK) (no solo)
(404950-)　　OK 41507 (BC)
　　　　　　When Yuba Plays The Rumba On The Tuba - voc
　　　　　　''Robert Wood'' (EW)

W 351048-1　　HA 1341-H, VE 2416-V, CL 5352-C (JF) (subt clt solo)
　　　　　　How The Time Can Fly (Whenever I'm With You) - voc
　　　　　　''Jerry Fenwyck'' (EW)

Possible Goodman items are the Ben Selvin ''CO'' matrices W 351037 through W 351040, recorded June 19, and released on the HA-VE-CL series. Only the first of the four sides—W 351037-2 ''Many Happy Returns Of The Day,'' HA 1338-H, VE 2413-V, CL 5349-C, GEORGIA MOON-LIGHT SERENADERS: PaE R1014, GOLDEN TERRACE ORCHESTRA: and OK 41508, GOLDEN TERRACE DANCE ORCHESTRA—offers any clarinet, and it is subtone. Possible date only.

BENNY GOODMAN AND HIS ORCHESTRA　　　June 20, 1931, New York
CLIFF BRYAN AND HIS ORCHESTRA - MAY issues only
CORINTHIC ORCHESTRA - EmbAu only

Benny Goodman, clt & as; Bunny Berigan, Mannie Klein, tpt; Tommy Dorsey, tbn; Sid Stoneburn, as; Larry Binyon, ts & fl; Eddie Lang, g; Gene Krupa, d; unknown p, b, voc (poss. Smith Ballew).

E 36835　　ME 12205. **LP:** SB 106 (clt solo)
　　　　　　Slow But Sure - voc

E 36874　　ME 12208, PANA 25069, MAY 2030, EMB E145. **LP:** SB
　　　　　　106 (no solo)
　　　　　　Pardon Me Pretty Baby (Don't I Look Familiar To You) -
　　　　　　voc

E 36875　　ME 12208, PANA 25069, MAY 2030. **LP:** SB 106 (clt
　　　　　　solo)
　　　　　　What Am I Gonna Do For Lovin'? - voc

E 36876   ME 12205, PANA 25091, MAY 2033. **LP:** SB 106 (clt
                 solo)
                 You Can't Stop Me From Lovin' You - voc

(Matrices for this date are consecutive)

BEN SELVIN & HIS ORCHESTRA   **June 22, 1931, New York**

Benny Goodman, clt & as; Mannie Klein, tpt; Herman Wolfson, ts; Eddie
Walters (EW), uke and voc; plus unknown tpt, as, 2v, p, g, b, d, xylo.

W 151626-3   CO 2491-D. **LP:** TOM 16 (clt solo)
                  Sing Another Chorus Please - voc (EW)

W 151627-2   CO 2487-D. **LP:** SB 110 (clt solo)
                  Let's Drink A Drink TO THE FUTURE! - voc (qtte)

W 151628-2   CO 2487-D (subt clt accomp)
W 151628-3   CO 2487-D (subt clt accomp)
                  Just One More Chance - voc (poss. Scrappy Lambert)

Benny doesn't solo on his next date with Ted Lewis; his presence is
"confirmed," however, by two sides preceding the Lewis matrices, cut the
same day. These were the only recordings BG was ever to make with Frank
Parker, who also had a lengthy career in show business.

FRANK PARKER   **July 1, 1931, New York**

Benny Goodman, clt; plus unknown v sect, oboe, p, b (possibly personnel
from the LEWIS session following).

W 151660-2   CO 2490-D (subt clt accomp)
                  Many Happy Returns Of The Day - voc Frank Parker

W 151661-1   same issue (subt clt solo)
                  Come To Me - voc Frank Parker

TED LEWIS AND HIS BAND   **same date**

Benny Goodman, clt & as; Muggsy Spanier, cnt; George Brunies, tbn; Ted
Lewis, clt & as; Sam Shapiro, Sol Klein, v; Jack Aaronson, p; Tony Gerardi, g;
Harry Barth, b; John Lucas, d.

W 151662-3   CO 2492-D. **LP:** SB 115 (no solo)
                  I'm All Dressed Up With A Broken Heart - voc Ted
                  Lewis, trio

W 151663-3   CO 2492-D, CoE CB351 (no solo)
                  I Love You In The Same Sweet Way - voc Ted Lewis,
                  trio

The next session is in dispute. Benny's opinion, on listening to "My
Sweet Tooth . . . ," was that it was difficult to tell, but the clt solo did seem
his. Berigan enthusiasts differ as to Bunny's participation. The author feels
both BG and Bunny are good bets here.

Reminder: Separate listings are given the OK's to indicate their different matrix numbers. They are **not** different takes.

LLOYD KEATING AND (&) HIS MUSIC (LK)   **July 3, 1931, New York**
BEN SELVIN & HIS ORCH. (BS)
ROY CARROLL & HIS SANDS POINT ORCH. (RC)
JACK WHITNEY & HIS ORCHESTRA (JW)
CLOVERDALE COUNTRY CLUB ORCHESTRA (CC)
GOLDEN TERRACE (DANCE) ORCHESTRA (GT)
BUDDY CAMPBELL & HIS ORCHESTRA (BC)
PHIL HUGHES & HIS HIGH HATTERS (PH)
FRANK AUBURN & HIS ORCHESTRA (FA)

Benny Goodman, clt & as; Bunny Berigan, Mannie Klein (or poss. Jack
Purvis), tpt; Herman Wolfson, ts; Irving Brodsky, p; plus unknown tpt, tbn,
as, g, b, d; on some sides, 2 v, xylo. Dick Robertson (DR), Scrappy Lambert
(SL), voc.

W 351053-2   HA 1343-H, VE 2419-V, CL 5355-C, OdF 250022 (LK);
(404956-)   PaE R1035, OdArg 193767 (BS) (no solo)
                  OK 41510 (GT)
                  **I'm An Unemployed Sweetheart Looking For Somebody
                  To Love** - voc "Bobby Dix" (DR)

W 351054-1   HA 1345-H, VE 2421-V, CL 5357-C (RC); OdArg 193779
(404955-)   (BS) (no solo)
                  OK 41509 (BC)
                  It's The Girl - voc "Roy Carroll" (DR)

W 351055-2   HA 1354-H, VE 2430-V, CL 5366-C, OdF 250022 (JW)
                  (no solo)
                  There's No Other Girl (After Loving You) - voc "Bobby
                  Dix" (DR)

W 351056-2   HA 1350-H, VE 2426-V, CL 5362-C (LK); PaE R1015,
(404958-B)   OdG A221372 (GT). **LP:** TOM 16 (clt solo)
                  OK 41511 (BC)
                  **My Sweet Tooth Says I Wanna (But My Wisdom Tooth
                  Says No)** - voc "Robert Wood" (DR)

W 351057-2   HA 1345-H, VE 2421-V, CL 5357-C (RC) (subt clt solo)
                  (With You On My Mind, I Find) I Can't Write The Words
                  - voc "Roy Carroll" (SL)

W 351058-3   HA 1353-H, VE 2429-V, CL 5365-C (PH) (no solo)
(404983-)   OK 41520 (CC)
                  Why Dance? - voc "Phil Hughes" (SL)

W 351059-1   HA 1344-H, VE 2420-V, CL 5356-C (FA); PaE R1046,
(404957-)   OdArg 193767 (BS). **LP:** SB 110 (as solo, clt accomp)
                  OK 41510 (GT)
                  Hikin' Down The Highway - voc "Robert Wood" (SL)

W 351060-2   HA 1353-H, VE 2429-V, CL 5365-C (PH) (subt clt solo,
                  as accomp)
                  It's A Long Time Between Kisses - voc "Phil Hughes"
                  (SL)

(Other CO matrices recorded July 3—W 151664 "I'm An Unemployed Sweetheart . . . ," and W 151665 "It's The Girl," TED WALLACE AND HIS CAM-
PUS BOYS, CO 2493-D—were proved by the Kirkeby appointment book not to
include BG. Saxes on the date were Bobby Davis, Paul Mason and Elmer
Feldkamp.)

JACK WHITNEY & HIS ORCHESTRA (JW)   **July 7, 1931, New York**
CHESTER LEIGHTON & HIS SOPHOMORES (CL)
JERRY FENWYCK & HIS ORCHESTRA (JF)
BUDDY CAMPBELL & HIS ORCHESTRA (BC)
LLOYD KEATING AND HIS MUSIC (LK)
ARIEL DANCE ORCHESTRA (ADO)
BEN SELVIN & HIS ORCH. (BS)
GOLDEN TERRACE DANCE ORCHESTRA (GT)

Benny Goodman, clt & as; Mannie Klein, tpt; probably Tommy Dorsey, tbn;
Herman Wolfson, ts; plus unknown tpt, as, p, g, b, d; plus 2 v, xylo on some
sides. Dick Robertson (DR), voc.

W 351065-3   HA 1354-H, VE 2430-V, CL 5366-C. **LP:** SB 110 (JW)
                  (clt solo)
                  (If I Hadn't Been) So Sure Of You - voc "Bobby Dix"

W 351066-2   HA 1351-H, VE 2427-V, CL 5363-C, OdF 238996, OdF
(404960-B)   351070 (CL); Ariel 4765 (ADO) (no solo)
                  OK 41512 (GT)
                  I Love You In The Same Sweet Way - voc "Chester
                  Leighton"

W 351067-1   HA 1348-H, VE 2424-V, CL 5360-C (JF) (no solo)
(40496?-)   OK 41509 (BC)
                  I'm All Dressed Up With A Broken Heart - voc "Jerry
                  Fenwyck"

W 351068-2   HA 1351-H, VE 2427-V, CL 5363-C (CL) (subt clt solo)
(404961-B)   OK 41512 (GT)
                  **The Kiss That You've Forgotten (Is The Kiss I Can't
                  Forget)** - voc "Chester Leighton"

July 7, 1931, continued

July 7, 1931, continued

W 351069-2   HA 1352-H, VE 2428-V, CL 5364-C. **LP:** TOM 16 (JF)
       (clt solo)
       Nobody Loves No Baby Like My Baby Loves Me! - voc
       "Jerry Fenwyck" (DR)

W 351070-2   HA 1352-H, VE 2428-V, CL 5364-C, OdF 238996, OdF
       351070 (JF); OdArg 193728 (BS). **LP:** TOM 16 (clt
       solo)
       Do The New York - voc "Jerry Fenwyck" (DR)

W 351071   UNISSUED
       Two Heads In The Moonlight (Are Better Than One)

W 130478-1   HA 1350-H, VE 2426-V, CL 5362-C (LK) (no solo)
       Two Heads In The Moonlight (Are Better Than One) -
       voc "Robert Wood"

W 351072-1   HA 1348-H, VE 2424-V, CL 5360-C (JF) PaE R1046. **LP:**
       SB 110 (BS) (clt solo)
       Take It From Me (I'm Takin' To You) - voc "Jerry
       Fenwyck" (DR)

W 351073-2   HA 1364-H, VE 2441-V, CL 5377-C (LK) (clt accomp)
       Little Hunka Love - voc "Robert Wood" (DR)

(Other CO matrices recorded July 7—W 365025 through W 365028—feature
Jimmy Dorsey, not BG.)

LEE MORSE AND HER BLUE GRASS BOYS   July 8, 1931, New York

Benny Goodman, clt; Mannie Klein, tpt; . . . Campbell, tbn; R. Downey, p;
Eddie Lang, g.

W 151670-1   CO 2497-D. **LP:** NOST 890/1, SB 111 (clt solo)
       It's The Girl! - voc Lee Morse

W 151671-3   same issues, except delete NOST (clt solo)
       **I'm An Unemployed Sweetheart Looking For Somebody
       To Love** - voc Lee Morse

BEN SELVIN AND (&) HIS ORCHESTRA   July 14, 1931, New York

Benny Goodman, clt & as; Mannie Klein, tpt; Tommy Dorsey, tbn; Herman
Wolfson, ts; Joe Venuti, v; plus unknown tpt, as, v, g, p, b, d; plus xylo on
mx W 151683.

W 151680-3   CO 2499-D. **LP:** SB 110 (clt solo)
       Do The New York - voc male qtte, fem trio (Danford
       Sisters)

W 151681-3   CO 2499-D (subt clt solo)
       Hikin' Down The Highway - voc qtte

W 151682-1   CO 2501-D. **LP:** SB 110 (clt solo, as solo)
       **My Sweet Tooth Says I Wanna (But My Wisdom Tooth
       Says No)** - voc (fem trio)

W 151683-2   same issues (as solo)
       Nobody Loves No Baby Like My Baby Loves Me! - voc
       (fem trio)

W 710000   UNISSUED
       Beggin' For Love

(Other "CO" matrices recorded July 14—W 365027, W 365028—do not
include Benny Goodman.)

LLOYD KEATING AND HIS MUSIC   July 16, 1931, New York

Benny Goodman, clt & as; Mannie Klein, tpt; Tommy Dorsey, tbn; Herman
Wolfson, ts; plus unknown tpt, as, p, g, b, d. Scrappy Lambert (SL), voc.

W 710001-   UNISSUED
       Sweet Summer Breeze

W 710002-   UNISSUED (re-made Aug. 13, 1931 without BG)
       Little Girl

W 710003-   UNISSUED
(1,2)   **Slow But Sure**

W 351061-2   HA 1356-H, VE 2432-V, CL 5368-C (clt, as soli)
       There's A Time And Place For Everything - voc "Bobby
       Dix" (SL)

W 351062-2   HA 1364-H, VE 2441-V, CL 5377-C (no solo)
       Waiting For The Moon - voc "Robert Wood" (SL)

FRANK AUBURN & HIS ORCHESTRA (FA)   July 21, 1931, New York
BUDDY CAMPBELL & HIS ORCHESTRA (BC)
BEN SELVIN & HIS ORCH. (BS)
LLOYD KEATING AND HIS MUSIC (LK)
GOLDEN TERRACE DANCE ORCHESTRA (GT)
ARIEL DANCE ORCHESTRA (AR)
PHIL HUGHES & HIS HIGH HATTERS (PH)
THE KNICKERBOCKERS (K)

Benny Goodman, clt & as; Bob Effros, Ruby Weinstein, tpt; Tommy Dorsey,
tbn; Lou Martin, as; Herman Wolfson, ts; B. Pobersky, v; Rube Bloom, p; Carl
Kress, g; Hank Stern, b; M. Schlesinger, d & xylo; Dick Robertson (DR),
Scrappy Lambert (SL), voc.

W 351063-2   HA 1357-H, VE 2433-V, CL 5369-C (FA); PaE R1047
       (BS); Ariel 4672 (AD) (clt accomp)
(404962-B)   OK 41513 (BC)
       Me! -voc "Robert Wood" (DR)

W 351074-2   HA 1358-H, VE 2434-V, CI 5370-C (PH) (no solo)
       If You Haven't Got Love - voc "Phil Hughes" (SL)

W 351075-2   HA 1356-H, VE 2432-V, CL 5368-C (LK) (clt, as solos)
       There's No Depression In Love - voc "Bobby Dix" (SL)

W 351076-2   HA 1357-H, VE 2433-V, CL 5369-C (FA); PaE R1047
       (BS) (no solo)
       Give Me Your Affection Honey - voc "Robert Wood"
       (SL)

W 351077-2   HA 1358-H, VE 2434-V, CL 5370-C (PH); OdArg 193728
       (BS) (clt lead)
(404963-B)   OK 41513 (BC)
       I Love Louisa - voc "Phil Hughes" (SL & chorus)

W 151694-3   CO 2502-D, ReAu 21183 (K); OdG A221393 (GT) (no
       solo)
       Slow But Sure - voc (DR)

W 151695-3   CO 2502-D, CoE CB 360 (K). **LP:** BIO 1, SVL 165, SB
       110 (clt solo)
       Me! - voc (DR)

"CO" matrices W 351064-2 and W 351078-1, JERRY FENWYCK & HIS
ORCHESTRA, recorded July 23, do not include BG, as some sources
assert.

     The next date is a remote BG possibility only; there is no definitive clt
or alto on any side. But listing it permits explanation of the HA 6000 (VE
10000, CL 11000) series. These numbers were used for double-track records—one set of grooves starts at one spot on the periphery of the record,
the second set at a different spot. One track is a vocal version, the other an
instrumental, of one tune. Probably these "two for-one" records were made
because the Nation was sliding deeper into the Depression, and gimmicks
were needed to sell them competitively.

PHIL HUGHES AND HIS   July 28, 1931, New York
   HIGH HATTERS (PH)
GOLDEN TERRACE DANCE ORCHESTRA (GT)
LLOYD KEATING AND HIS MUSIC (LK)
FRANK AUBURN AND HIS ORCHESTRA (FA)

Poss. Benny Goodman, clt & as; Tommy Dorsey, tbn; Herman Wolfson, ts;
plus unknown 2 tpt, as, 2 v, p, g, b, d. Smith Ballew (SB), voc.

W 351081-1   HA 1363-H, VE 2440-V, CL 5376-C (PH); OdG A221408
       (GT) (no solo)
(404964-A)   OK 41514 (GT)
       Sweet And Lovely - voc "Phil Hughes" (SB) ("voc ref"
       on OK)

W 351082-2   same issues (clt lead)
(404965-B)   OK 41514 (GT)
                I Can't Get Mississippi Off My Mind - voc "Phil
                Hughes" (SB) ("voc ref" on OK)

W 710004-2   HA 6000-H, VE 10000-V, CL 11000-C (LK); (clt lead on
                A track)
                Tom Boy - voc "Jack Miller" (SB)

W 710005-1   same issues (no solo)
                The Birthday Of A Kiss - voc "Jack Miller" (SB)

W 710006-2   HA 6001-H, VE 10001-V, CL 11001-C (FA); (clt lead on
                A track)
                Sunny Skies - voc "Jack Miller" (SB)

Since there is almost a two-month hiatus from the last certain BG session (July 21) to the next (Sept. 15), a revue of what's been happening to our subject seems in order.

In the first seven months of 1931 Benny Goodman recorded more than 175 sides that became issued records. This does not include other BG recordings: the unissued certainties, the "probables," the "possibles," and those yet to be discovered. Were but a handful of these added to those released, Benny's year-to-date produce would equal one side per day, each and every day. A remarkable feat.

This prolific output was achieved despite Benny's otherwise full schedule. Into early May he had played six times each week in the pit for "Girl Crazy." Most of his weekends were taken up by dance dates. In between he had somehow crammed radio gigs and movie soundtrack engagements. In an era when to work at all was to contravene alarming unemployment statistics, Benny Goodman worked as often as he chose

He had earned a vacation. He'll be back in September.

CO matrices W 151737, W 151738, and W 351083 through W 351088, recorded August 18, feature Tommy Dorsey, Joe Venuti, Eddie Lang and other Selvin studio men; but not Benny Goodman.

CO matrices W 151741 "Life Is Just A Bowl of Cherries," backed by W 151742 "Guilty," CO 2523-D, recorded August 21 as by TED WALLACE AND HIS CAMPUS BOYS, were shown by the Kirkeby appointment book not to include BG. Bobby Davis, Elmer Feldkamp and Paul Mason were the reed section on that date.

The Selvin session of August 25 was long judged to be but a possible Goodman date; but over time so many collectors have come to accept it as valid that it now warrants full description. Note that the subtone clarinet solo on "Life Is Just A Bowl Of Cherries,"once the cornerstone of pro-Goodman adherents, is now thought to be by Herman Wolfson. Contrarily, the tenor saxophone solo on "What Is It?" is now suggested as Benny's.

JACK WHITNEY & HIS ORCHESTRA (JW)   August 25, 1931, New York
BUDDY CAMPBELL & HIS ORCHESTRA (BC)
LLOYD KEATING AND HIS MUSIC (LK)
CHESTER LEIGHTON & HIS SOPHOMORES (CL)
BEN SELVIN AND HIS ORCHESTRA (BS)

Poss. Benny Goodman, clt & ts; Herman Wolfson, clt & ts; plus the usual Selvin instrumentation of 2 tpt, tbn, as, v(s), p, g, b, d. Vocalist is Paul Small (PS).

W 351089-1   HA 1365-H, VE 2442-V, CL 5378-C (JW). **LP:** SVL 165
                ("J UK release) (no solo)
                This Is The Missus - voc "Bobby Dix" (PS)

W 351090-1   HA 1366-H, VE 2443-V, CL 5379-C (LK) (no solo)
(404979-)   OK 41518 (BC)
                I Apologize - voc "Robert Wood" (HA series), voc ref
                (OK) (PS)

W 351091-1   HA 1366-H, VE 2443-V, CL 5379-C (LK) (no OK release)
                (clt lead, poss ts solo)
                What Is It? - voc "Robert Wood" (PS)

W 351092-1   HA 1365-H, VE 2442-V, CI 5378-C (JW) (clt lead;
                Wolfson subt clt solo)
(404970-A)   OK 41516 (BC), PaE R1073 (BS)
                Life Is Just A Bowl Of Cherries - voc "Bobby Dix" (HA
                series), voc ref (OK) (PS)

W 351093-1   HA 1370-H, VE 2447-V, CL 5383-C (CL) (no solo)
(404971-A)   OK 41516 (BC)
                Now That You're Gone - voc "Chester Leighton" (HA
                series), voc ref (OK) (PS)

Non-Goodman recordings, in the opinion of the author, include:
CO matrices W 151773 and W 151774, September 4—unmistakably Jimmy Dorsey;
"CO" matrices W 351100, W 351101, W 710007, and W 710008—no evidence at all of BG, on this September 9 date; and
CO matrices W 151777 through W 151780, September 10—definitely Jimmy Dorsey once more.

Benny's two-month vacation from the studios did not mean he was idle. In mid-August he and Glenn Miller were hard at work putting together a pit band for "Free For All." This Oscar Hammerstein-Dick Whiting opus, produced by Frank Mandel and starring Jack Haley, opened in the Manhattan Theatre, New York, on September 8. It closed two weeks later . . . Possibly the rehearsals helped keep Benny out of the studios.

Although there definitely is no swinging clarinet on the next two sides, repeated listening, cross-checking with knowledgeable collectors, and BG's opinion strengthen the conviction that Benny had a date in 1931 with the "Moon Over The Mountain" lady, Kate Smith.

RUTH BROWN (RB)   September 15, 1931, New York
KATE SMITH The Songbird Of The South With Her Swanee Music (KS)

Benny Goodman, clt; Tommy Dorsey, tbn; plus unknown tpt, v, viola, p, g, d, xylo.

W 365031-2   HA 1371-H, VE 2448-V, (RB); CL 5384-C (KS) (clt
                accomp)
                Shine On, Harvest Moon - voc Kate Smith

W 365032-2   same issues plus CoE DB734 (KS) (clt accomp)
                I Apologize - Kate Smith

"Free For All" may have lasted only two weeks, but here's its pit band doing one tune from the show, "Not That I Care."

BENNY GOODMAN &   September 18, 1931, New York
  HIS ORCHESTRA (BG)
THE RADIOLITES (R)
MIDNIGHT MINSTRELS (MM)
SMITH BALLEW & HIS ORCH. (SB)

Benny Goodman, clt & as; Charlie Teagarden, Ruby Weinstein, tpt; Glenn Miller, tbn; Sid Stoneburn, as; Larry Binyon, ts; Irving Brodsky, p; Johnny Williams, d; plus unknown reed, g, b. Alan Moran, Jack Eaton and L. McManus are also suggested as among the personnel, but their instruments are not known. Smith Ballew (SB) is the vocalist.

W 151794-2   CO 2542-D (BG). **LP:** SB 138 (no solo)
                Not That I Care - voc (SB)

W 151795-2   same issues, plus LP, NOST 890/1 (clt solo)
                Help Yourself To Happiness - voc (SB)

W 151796-2   CO 2540-D (R), CoE CB398 (SB), RE 21298. **LP:** SB 138
                (clt accomp)
                Love Letters In The Sand - voc (SB)

W 151797-2   CO 2540-D (R), ReE MR499 (MM). **LP:** SB 138 (no
                solo)
                I Don't Know Why (I Just Do) - voc (SB)

PHIL HUGHES & HIS HIGH HATTERS (PH)   September 22, 1931, New York
BUDDY CAMPBELL AND HIS ORCHESTRA (BC)

Benny Goodman, clt & as; Bob Effros, Mannie Klein, tpt; S. Lewis, tbn; Lou Martin, as; Herman Wolfson, ts; B. Pobersky, v; Lennie Hayton, p; John Cali, g; Hank Stern, b; M. Schlesinger, d; Dick Robertson (DR), voc.

W 351104-2   HA 1373-H, VE 2451-V, CL 5387-C (PH) (no solo)
(404985-A)   OK 41521 (BC)
    Was It Wrong - voc "Phil Hughes" (DR)

W 351105-2   same issues (no OK) (PH) (clt accomp)
    When It's Sleepy Time Down South - voc "Phil Hughes" (DR)

W 236000   UNISSUED
    I'm Just A Dancing Sweetheart

W 236001   UNISSUED
    Linda

ANNETTE HANSHAW   September 22, 1931, New York

Benny Goodman, clt; Mannie Klein, tpt; Irving Brodsky, p; Eddie Lang, g; Jules Tott, b.

W 356033-(1,2)   UNISSUED
    Sweet And Lovely

W 365034-2   HA 1376-H, VE 2454-V, CL 5390-C (clt accomp)
    Guilty - voc Annette Hanshaw

W 365035-2   same issues plus **LP:** SB 111 (clt solo)
    I Don't Know Why (I Just Do) - voc Annette Hanshaw

With the abrupt closing of "Free For All," Benny was freed for all the studio dates he could handle, and he recorded almost as frequently as he had in the first seven months of 1931. Another noteworthy change was from Don Voorhees's Maxwell House Coffee radio show to Dave Rubinoff's Chase and Sanborn (coffee) Hour.

ROY CARROLL & HIS SANDS POINT ORCH. (RC)   October 2, 1931, New York
CLOVERDALE COUNTRY CLUB ORCHESTRA (CC)
BEN SELVIN AND HIS ORCHESTRA (BS)

Benny Goodman, clt & as; Bob Effros, Lou Garcia, tpt; S. Lewis, tbn; Lou Martin, as; Herman Wolfson, ts; Charles Magnante, acc; B. Pobersky, v; Irving Brodsky, p; John Cali, g; Hank Stern, b; Gus Von Hallberg, d; Scrappy Lambert, (SL), voc.

W 351106-2   HA 1379-H, VE 2457-V, CL 5393-C (RC) (no solo)
(404988-)   OK 41523 (CC)
    Good Night Sweetheart -voc "Roy Carroll" (SL)

W 351107-2   same issues plus PaE R1128 (RC), **LP:** SB 110 (clt solo)
    Waitin' For A Call From You - voc "Roy Carroll" (SL)

W 236002   UNISSUED
    You Call It Madness

W 236003   UNISSUED
    I'm Just A Dancing Sweetheart

D'ORSAY DANCE ORCH. (DD)   October 8, 1931, New York
ED PARKER AND HIS ORCHESTRA (EP)
LLOYD KEATING AND HIS MUSIC (LK)
GOLDEN TERRACE DANCE ORCHESTRA (GT)
CLOVERDALE COUNTRY CLUB ORCHESTRA (CC)
BUDDY CAMPBELL AND HIS ORCHESTRA (BC)

Personnel same as October 2, except no acc, v.

W 351108-1   HA 1380-H, VE 2458-V, CL 5394-C (DD) (no solo)
(404992-A)   OK 41525 (EP)
    It's The Darn'dest Thing - voc "Le Dandy Trio"

W 351109-1   HA 1381-H, VE 2459-V, CL 5395-C (LK) (subt clt solo)
(W 404989-)   OK 41523 (CC)
    Who Am I? - voc Wallace Trio

W 351110-2   same issues (no solo)
(W 405056-)   OK 41529 (GT)
    Call Me Darling (Call Me Sweetheart, Call Me Dear) - voc Wallace Trio

W 351111-2   HA 1380-H, VE 2458-V, CL 5394-C (DD). **LP:** TOM 16 (clt solo)
(W 404991-A)   OK 41524 (BC)
    Everyone In Town Loves Little Mary Brown - voc "Le Dandy Trio"

Further delving into Columbia's files revealed that Benny was present for a session on October 13, notwithstanding that the three issued sides from the date fail to offer clarinet soli. The files also bring forward mx W 151837, earlier believed to have been recorded October 16:

THE CAMPUS COLLEGIATES (TCC)   October 13, 1931, New York
BUDDY CAMPBELL AND HIS ORCHESTRA (BC)
THE CAVALIERS (C)
BEN SELVIN & HIS ORCHESTRA (BS)

Benny Goodman, clt & as; Mannie Klein, tpt; Lou Martin, as; Herman Wolfson, ts; Joe Venuti, v; Lennie Hayton, p; Ed Lang, g; Ward Ley, b; Gus von Hallberg, d; tbn not listed.

W 351113-2   HA 1382-H, VE 2460-V, CL 5396-C (TCC) (clt obl behind voc)
(W 405052-A)   OK 41527 (BC)
    Charlie Cadet - voc ref (qtte)

W 151837-2   CO 2555-D (C) (no solo)
    A Faded Summer Love - voc ref (trio)

W 151838-1   CO 2554-D (BS) (clt lead)
    Charlie Cadet - voc ref (qtte)

(W 351114-1,2 was also recorded October 13, but is unissued from this date.)

Here is the revised October 16 session:

JERRY FENWYCK & HIS ORCHESTRA (JF)   October 16, 1931, New York
THE MIDNIGHT MINSTRELS (MM)
CLOVERDALE COUNTRY CLUB ORCHESTRA (CC)
THE CAVALIERS (C)
BEN SELVIN & HIS ORCHESTRA (BS)

Benny Goodman, clt & as; Mannie Klein, Tommy Gott, tpt; Tommy Dorsey, tbn; Louis Martin, as; Herman Wolfson, ts; Joe Venuti, v; Cornell Smelser, acc; Rube Bloom, p; Carl Kress, g; Ward Ley, b; G. von Hallberg, d; Paul Small (PS), voc.

W 351114-3   HA 1384-H, VE 2462-V, CL 5398-C (JF), ReE MR699 (MM) (no solo)
(W 405054)   OK 41528 (CC)
    A Faded Summer Love - voc "Orlando Robertson" (PS)

W 151849-2   CO 2555-D (C) (no solo)
    Call Me Darling (Call Me Sweetheart, Call Me Dear) - voc (PS)

W 151850-3   CO 2554-D (BS). **LP:** TOM 16, SVL 165 (clt solo)
    Little Mary Brown - voc (male trio)

Next for Benny was his final date with Lee Morse:

LEE MORSE AND HER BLUE GRASS BOYS   October 19, 1931, New York

Benny Goodman, clt; Mannie Klein, tpt; Tommy Dorsey, tbn; R. Downey p; John Cali, g.

W 151852-3   CO 2564-D (clt accomp)
    Call Me Darling (Call Me Sweetheart, Call Me Dear) - voc Lee Morse

W 151853-2   same issue (no solo)
    I'm For You A Hundred Per Cent - voc Lee Morse

Here is a confirmed instance of Benny's soloing on bass clarinet:

HOTEL COMMODORE   **October 21, 1931, New York**
  DANCE ORCHESTRA (HC)
BUDDY CAMPBELL & HIS ORCHESTRA (BC)
JERRY FENWYCK & HIS ORCHESTRA (JF)

Benny Goodman, clt, b-clt, as; Mannie Klein, tpt; Tommy Dorsey, tbn; Joe Venuti, v; plus unknown as, ts, p, g, b, d, voc.

W 351115-2	HA 1385-H, VE 2463-V, CL 5399-C (HC). **LP:** SB 110 (b-clt solo)
(W 405053-A)	OK 41527 (BC) **Lucille** - voc "Robert Wood" ("voc ref" on OK)
W 236004-1	HA 6500-H, VE 10500-V, CL 11500-C (JF) (no solo) **When The Rest Of The Crowd Goes Home I Always Go Home Alone** - voc "Bobby Dix"
W 236005-2	same issues (JF) (no solo) **You Call It Madness But I Call It Love** - voc "Bobby Dix"

"CO" matrices W 351116 through W 351119, W 365036 and W 365037, recorded Oct. 22, do not include BG, according to Columbia's files.

However, October 22 did produce a great Benny Goodman session, the upcoming LANG-VENUTI efforts. If you ever need to convince a jazz fan that Benny cut some stupendous things prior to his Victor band, these are the sides to play. They may even convert the non-jazz listener, for these recordings have the unity and simplicity basic to universal appeal.

What makes them so great? First, the performers were compatible; their separate styles complemented and extended each other's extemporaneous conceptions. This is true especially of Goodman and Teagarden. Some of their best individual work over time occurred when they played together. It was beyond rapport; it was a kind of friendly competition that inspired each to rare heights of musical invention.

Second, the tunes were jazz tunes, not the insipid "pops" these men daily played in the studios, for the movies, and in the fiddle-riddled orchestras on radio. One can sense the freedom and exuberance that the happy combinations of chords imparted.

And third . . . "It just came out that way," as Benny puts it. Another day it might not. Jazz improvisation is like that. But on this day, October 22, 1931, the celestial stars and the earthbound All Stars were in perfect harmony. The Depression didn't penetrate the sound-proofed studio; the Prohibition gin must have come from a clean bathtub; and . . . "It just came out that way."

EDDIE LANG-JOE VENUTI AND   **October 22, 1931, New York**
  THEIR ALL STAR ORCHESTRA
NEW YORK STOMPERS - (MAY issues only)

Benny Goodman, clt; Charlie Teagarden, tpt; Jack Teagarden, tbn; Joe Venuti, v. Frank Signorelli, p; Eddie Lang, g; Joe Tarto or Ward Ley, b; Neil Marshall, d.

E 37269-A	VO 15864, BR X 15864, ME 12294, POLK 9095, PANA 25168, MAY G2068, BR 80078, BrE 02000, BrF 500161, UHCA 109, BrG A9915, BrG A86010, DeE F5883. **EP:** CrIG EPC94085, BrE OE9468. **LP:** BR BL58039, DE DL 4540, FO FJ2807, FO FP67, (7") SW JCS33734, TL STLJ 12 (clt solo) **Beale Street Blues** - voc Jack Teagarden
E 37270-A	same issues except delete FO FJ2807 & FO FP67; and substitute BR 80077, UHCA 108 & DeE F5884 for their counterparts above (clt solo) **After You've Gone** - voc Jack Teagarden
E 37271-A	VO 15858, ME 12277, PANA 25151, MAY G2071, BR 80077, UHCA 106, BrF 500167, BrG A9916, BrG A86011, DeE F5884. **EP:** CrIG EPC94085, BrE OE9468, FestAu XP451150. **LP:** BR BL54010, BR BL58039, DE DL8383, BrE LAT8166, BrF & BrG LPB 87014, CrlF CVM40012, DeScan BKL8166, DE DL4540, FestAu FAL-1, VC LVA9011, VC(SA) BL54010, (7") SW JCS33734 (clt solo) **Farewell Blues**

E 37272-A	same issues except delete FestAu EP & LP, BrF & BrG Lp's, BrE Lp & DE Lp DL8398; and substitute BR 80078, DeE F5883 and UHCA 107 for their counterparts above and add LP, TL STLJO8 (clt solo) **Someday Sweetheart**

(Additional LP reissues include: all matrices, MCA 2-4018, CrIEu 3442; mxs E 37269, E 37271, E 37272, LSS LW267; mx E 37271, TL STLJO5; mx E 37269, DE DL34313; mxs E 37269, E 37270, AOH 168.)

TED LEWIS AND HIS BAND   **October 26, 1931, New York**

Benny Goodman, clt; Muggsy Spanier, cnt; George Brunies, tbn; Sam Shapiro, Sol Klein, v; Jack Aaronson, p; Tony Gerardi, g; Harry Barth, b; John Lucas, d.

W 151864-4	CO 2560-D, CoAu DO665. **LP:** SB 115 (clt solo) **Old Playmate** - voc Ted Lewis

TED LEWIS AND HIS BAND   **October 27, 1931, New York**

Personnel as October 26.

W 151865-3	CO 2560-D, CoAu DO665. **LP:** SB 115 (clt solo) **An Ev'ning In Caroline** - voc Ted Lewis

Strong clarinet leads and a subtone solo combine to make Benny's presence on this next date a probability.

LLOYD KEATING AND HIS MUSIC (LK)   **November 10, 1931, New York**
D'ORSAY DANCE ORCH. (DD)
BUDDY CAMPBELL AND HIS ORCHESTRA (BC)

Benny Goodman, clt & as; Mannie Klein, tpt; Tommy Dorsey, tbn; Joe Venuti, v; Carl Kress, g; plus unknown tpt, as, ts, v, p, b, d, voc.

W 236006-2	HA 6501-H, VE 10501-V, CL 11501-C (LK) (clt ld) **An Ev'ning In Caroline-Intro. Lucille** - voc "Glenn Cross"
W 236007	UNISSUED **Why Did It Have To Be Me?**
W 351127-3	HA 1393-H, VE 2474-V, CL 5414-C (DD) (subt clt solo) **In A Dream** - voc "Le Dandy"
W 351128-2 (W 405069-)	same issues (DD) (clt ld) OK 41536 (BC) **Where The Blue Of The Night Meets The Gold Of The Day** - voc "Le Dandy"

CO matrices W 151876 through W 151878, recorded Nov. 11, give no indication that they include Benny.

Note that the recording dates are beginning to be less frequent. The reason was the omnipresent Depression—records weren't selling.

JERRY FENWYCK & HIS   **November 16, 1931, New York**
  ORCHESTRA (JF)
ED PARKER AND HIS ORCHESTRA (EP)
CLOVERDALE COUNTRY CLUB ORCHESTRA (CC)
ROY CARROLL AND HIS SANDS POINT ORCH. (RC)
BUDDY CAMPBELL AND HIS ORCHESTRA (BC)

Benny Goodman, clt & as; Bob Effros, Mannie Klein, tpt; Charlie Butterfield, tbn; Lou Martin, as; Herman Wolfson, ts; Joe Venuti, v; Rube Bloom, p; John Cali, g; Ward Ley, b; M. Schlesinger, d; Dick Robertson (DR), voc.

W 236008	UNISSUED **Why Did It Have To Be Me? Intro.: I Can't Write The Words**
W 351131-2 (W 405097-A)	HA 1394-H, VE 2475 V, CL 5415-C (JF) (subt clt accomp) OK 41537 (EP) **When I Wore My Daddy's Brown Derby (And You Wore Your Mother's Blue Gown)** - voc Dick Robertson ("voc ref" on OK)

November 16, 1931, continued

November 16, 1931, continued

W 351132-2	HA 1395-H, VE 2476-V, CL 5416-C (RC) (subt clt accomp)
(W 405066-1)	OK 41535 (CC)
	You Were My Salvation - voc "Roy Carroll" (DR) ("voc ref" on OK)
W 351133-2	same issues (RC) (subt clt ld & accomp)
(W 405068-)	OK 41536 (BC)
	Home - voc "Roy Carroll" (DR) ("voc ref" on OK)
W 351134-2	HA 1394-H, VE 2475-V, CL 5415-C, OdArg 193794 (JF). **LP:** HIST 33 (clt solo)
(W 405096-A)	OK 41537 (EP)
	Potatoes Are Cheaper Tomatoes Are Cheaper Now's The Time To Fall In Love - voc Dick Robertson ("voc ref" on OK)

CO matrices W 151881, W 151882 and W 351135, recorded Nov. 17, offer no evidence of BG's participation.

CO matrices W 351136, W 351137, and W 236009, recorded November 23, do not include Benny Goodman, according to Columbia's files.

"CO" matrices W 130614-1 "Why Did It Have To Be Me?" Intro.: I Can't Write The Words," was recorded satisfactorily on Nov. 24, after two attempts on Nov. 10 and Nov. 16. There is a strong subtone clt solo on this side that may be Benny's; but there is no further confirmation via the other releases from this session. W 130614-1's issues are all by LLOYD KEATING AND HIS MUSIC: HA 6501-H, VE 10501-V, and CL 11501-C.

Alternate takes are rare on the HA-VE-CL series. Rarer still are numerically different takes on this series that are identical musically. This happens on mx 351138, next session. The HA copy shows take 2; the VE & CL releases show take 1; careful examination convinces that there is no difference between them. Take 2 is arbitrarily listed as the correct take, on the assumption that the HA issue governs.

ROY CARROL AND (&) HIS   **November 27, 1931, New York**
   SANDS POINT ORCH. (RC)
BUDDY CAMPBELL AND HIS ORCHESTRA (BC)
BEN SELVIN AND HIS ORCHESTRA (BS)
ARIEL DANCE ORCHESTRA (A)
THE CAVALIERS (C)

Personnel as Nov. 16, except: Charles Margulis, tpt, replaces Effros, and Tommy Dorsey, tbn, replaces Butterfield. Paul Small (PS) may be a second voc.

W 351138-2	HA 1397-H, VE 2480-V, CL 5420-C, OdArg 193780 (RC), ARIEL 4829 (A). **LP:** SB 110 (clt solo)
(W 405115-A)	OK 41543 (BC)
	Bend Down, Sister - voc "Roy Carroll" (DR)
W 351139- (1,2)	UNISSUED (re-recorded Jan. 12, 1932, without BG) **One Little Quarrel**
W 151891-2	CO 2575-D, CoE CB406 (BS). **LP:** TOM 16 (clt solo)
	Bend Down, Sister - voc ref (PS?)
W 151892-2	CO 2575-D (BS), ReAu 21280. **LP:** TOM 16 (clt solo)
	Potatoes Are Cheaper—Tomatoes Are Cheaper Now's The Time To Fall in Love - voc ref (PS?)
W 151893-2	CO 2579-D (C) (no solo)
	Save The Last Dance For Me - voc ref (DR?)
W 151894	UNISSUED **I Wonder Who's Under The Moon**

Columbia was experimenting desperately with its HA 6500 (and related VE, CL) series to spur declining sales. The first release, from Oct. 21, HA 6500, ran better than 4½ minutes, but had only one tune per side. The second release, from Nov. 10/Nov. 24 HA 6501, also ran long, but each side featured a medley of two tunes. The third release, from the next session, went back to one tune—but on the one side offered an instrumental version, then a vocal version, the two separated by a "flat track" on the disk. Oddly, the instrumental version, which features the full band, has no BG solo; the vocal version, cut only by a vocalist accompanied by clt, v, and p, provides distinctive BG clt.

JERRY FENWYCK & HIS ORCHESTRA (JF)   **December 7, 1931, New York**
CLOVERDALE COUNTRY CLUB ORCHESTRA (CC)
BUDDY CAMPBELL AND HIS ORCHESTRA (BC)
LLOYD KEATING AND HIS MUSIC (LK)

Benny Goodman, clt & as; Mannie Klein, tpt; Herman Wolfson, ts; Joe Venuti, v; Carl Kress, g; plus unknown tpt, tbn, as, p, b, d, xylo. Smith Ballew (SB), voc.

W 351140-2	HA 1397-H, VE 2480-V, CL 5420-C (JF) (no solo)
(W 405108-)	OK 41539 (CC)
	By The Sycamore Tree - voc "Jerry Fenwyck" (SB)
W 351141-2	HA 1398-H, VE 2481-V, CL 5421-C. **LP:** SB 110 (JF) (clt solo)
(W 405114-A)	OK 41543 (BC)
	I Wouldn't Change You For The World - voc "Jerry Fenwyck" (SB)
W 351142-2	same issues except omit LP (JF) (no solo)
(W 405109-)	OK 41539 (CC)
	Save The Last Dance For Me - voc "Jerry Fenwyck" (SB)
W 236010-2	HA 6502-H, VE 10502-V, CL 11502-C (LK) (clt accomp)
	Ooh That Kiss - voc "Bobby Dix" (SB)

Jimmy Dorsey is the clarinetist on KATE SMITH's "CO" matrices W 365048 and W 365049, recorded December 10. But latterday access to Columbia's personnel files refutes a contention in "BG—On The Record": Benny is indeed present on a session of December 18:

JERRY FENWYCK &   **December 18, 1931, New York**
  HIS ORCHESTRA (JF)
CLOVERDALE COUNTRY CLUB ORCHESTRA (CC)
D'ORSAY DANCE ORCH. (DD)
BUDDY CAMPBELL AND HIS ORCHESTRA (BC)
BEN SELVIN & HIS ORCHESTRA (BS)

Benny Goodman, clt & as; Bob Effros, Mannie Klein, tpt; Tommy Dorsey, tbn; Lou Martin, as; Herman Wolfson, ts; Joe Venuti, v; Rube Bloom. p; Eddie Lang, g; Ward Ley, b; M. Schlesinger, d; Paul Small (PS), voc.

W 351143-2	HA 1403-H, VE 2502-V, CL 5442-C (JF) (no solo)
W (405112-)	OK 41542 (CC)
	All Of Me - voc Paul Small ("voc ref" on OK)
W 351144-2	HA 1401-H, VE 2500-V, CL 5440-C (DD) (no solo)
(W 405113-)	OK 41542 (CC)
	I Found You - voc "Le Dandy" (PS) ("voc ref" on OK)
W 351145-2	same as W 351144-2 (DD) (no solo)
(W 405118-)	OK 41545 (BC)
	You're My Everything - voc "Le Dandy" (PS) ("voc ref" on OK)
W 152048-1	CO 2585-D (BS) (clt lead)
W 152048-2	CO 2585-D (BS) (clt lead)
	All Of Me - voc ref (PS)
W 152049-3	CO 2585-D (BS) (clt lead)
	I Found You - voc ref (PS)

In terms of recordings made for sale to the public, the December 18 session was Benny's last for 1931, his most productive year ever. Despite the acclaim and popularity that will come to him in future, never again will he cut as many discs in a single 12-month period.

But in terms of music recorded to be made available to the public, December 18 may not have been Benny's final studio date for 1931. In that year and in 1932, the DL&W Coal Company sponsored a radio series titled, "The Blue Coal Minstrels." Benny is audibly present on some of the programs in that series.

Each program, slightly under 14 minutes in length, used a minstrel show as a format, with humor by the "end men," songs by a "dramatic tenor" and others, and orchestral selections. Produced by New York advertising agency Ruthrauff & Ryan, Inc., the series promoted the sponsor's "blue coal," anthracite coated with an identifying dye. Programs appropriate to this work featured announcer Glen Alden; end men "Tambo and Bones" (not otherwise identified); tenor . 'erick Vettel; "Blue Coal Mammy'' (a female vocalist, also not further identified); and the ''Blue Coal Orchestra.''

The programs were prerecorded by Columbia's transcription service in New York; 16 of these transcriptions are known to exist. Four of them (with consecutive matrix numbers) are believed to have been recorded at one session. Two of those four offer orchestral renditions that include clarinet soli by Benny Goodman. A third includes a possible alto solo by Benny, and the fourth gives no solo evidence of his participation. None of the other 12 extant ET's contains anything to indicate Benny's presence, and they are not listed herein.

Neither the recording dates nor the broadcast dates are known. The matrix numbers suggest that the programs were prerecorded either in late 1931 or in early 1932:

THE BLUE COAL MINSTRELS   Winter, 1931–1932, New York

Benny Goodman, clt & as; prob. Mannie Klein, tpt; poss. Joe Venuti, v; and unknown tbn, ts, acc, p, g/bjo, b, d. Frederick Vettel, others, voc.

W 300904-1   ET: CO ET, Program No. 15
               "Blue Coal" theme - voc chorus
               Blue In My Heart - voc "Blue Coal Mammy"
               Bend Down, Sister - voc chorus (BG clt solo)
               Sweetheart, I'm On My Way - voc Frederick Vettel
               (Miss) Annabelle Lee - voc "Bones"
               Blue Again - voc chorus (theme)

W 300905-1   ET: CO ET, Program No. 16
               "Blue Coal" theme - voc chorus
               Guilty - voc "Blue Coal Mammy"
               (Everyone In Town Loves) Little Mary Brown (BG clt
                 soli)
               You Were My Salvation - voc Frederick Vettel
               Oh, Susannah - voc "end man"
               Blue Again - voc chorus (theme)

W 300906-1   ET: CO ET, Program No. 17
               "Blue Coal" theme - voc chorus
               I Apologize - voc "Blue Coal Mammy"
               Happy Feet (poss. BG as solo)
               One Kiss, One Smile, One Tear - voc Frederick Vettel
               What A Day! - voc "end men" (prob. BG clt obl)
               Blue Again - voc chorus (theme)

W 300907-1   ET: CO ET, Program No. 18
               "Blue Coal" theme - voc chorus
               Little Cotton Dolly - voc "Blue Coal (male) Quartet"
               **The Man From The South (With A Big Cigar In His
                 Mouth)**
               If I Had To Go On Without You - voc Frederick Vettel
               She's So Nice - voc "end man"
               Blue Again - voc chorus (theme)

(Program No. 19 (matrix W 300908-1) offers no hint of Goodman's participation. Program No. 20 (matrix W 300909-1) includes an alto solo on one tune, "Nobody's Sweetheart," that might hesitantly be ascribed to Benny. But the absence of vocals by "Blue Coal Mammy" on Programs 18, 19 and 20 suggests the transcriptions may have been recorded in sets of three, and that Benny only was present for Nos. 15, 16 and 17.)

We still are not finished with the 1931 chapter of the Benny Goodman story; there remain his ventures into a burgeoning new medium, sound-on-film, the "talkies." For then Manhattan and Long Island were important centers of film and film-sound activity, and schooled musicians in the area were as much in demand for the movies as they were for phonograph records.

Benny remembers recording "a lot of tunes for the movies," but very little of the specifics. His excursions to the motion picture sound stages on Long Island call to mind fun and sun on the beach: he'd rush through whatever he had to play in order to go swimming. He has no recollection of having recorded a sound track for the Paramount Publix film, "The Tarnished Lady," reputedly Tallulah Bankhead's first sound film. The author played a portion of the sound track for him, but it did nothing to stir his memory. (But it is still a Goodman possibility.)

Although Benny does not recall working with Miss Bankhead, he does remember making a movie with "the gal with the great legs—Marlene

Dietrich," but cannot think of its title. Could it have been Paramount Publix's sensational, "The Blue Angel"? Benny just shrugs.

In all likelihood Benny was employed in 1931 by the Van Buren Company, then located in the 1600 block of Broadway, whose business was adding sound tracks to silent comedies and to cartoons. Such Chaplin classics as "The Adventurer," "Easy Street" and "The Immigrant" thus become suggested targets for research by film collectors, along with the "Aesop's Fables" and "Tom And Jerry" cartoons that Van Buren processed for release by Pathe'. But collectors should be wary: when television began to program such old films, the sound tracks were judged unsatisfactory, and they were re-recorded.

In sharp contrast to 1931's "record record" output, there are only three certain Goodman recording dates in all of 1932, and one probable movie soundtrack. His first studio date is March 15; but first, let us dispose of some dates championed by a few collectors as Goodman sessions:

Jan. 12—"CO" matrices W 351149 through W 351154, plus W 236013 and W 236014 offer nothing to substantiate BG's presence.

Jan. 29—CO matrices W 152097 through W 152099 and W 236015 do not evidence BG's participation.

Feb. 4—CO matrices W 152014, W 152105, W 351155, and W 236016 fail to reveal any indication they were made by Benny Goodman.

Benny's explanation for the dearth of his records at this point in his career is twofold. He notes that the market for phonograph records was depressed, as was the market for almost everything else in this, the first national Election Year of the Great Depression. With recording dates few and far between, Benny turned to other media to support his mother and other members of his family—to radio, and to the movies. His income was perhaps halved; nevertheless it averaged to an astonishing $200. per week, at a time when college graduates were overjoyed to accept jobs starting at $25. per week.

Benny also indicates his interests in music had begun to expand. Jazz was his first love—it has remained so all of his life—but there were other musical forms that captured his attention and challenged his skill. He frequented the jazz haunts less, the concert halls more, and in this manner partially disassociated himself from the jazz leaders and studio directors for whom he had recorded. And perhaps incidental to his broader outlook was the economic realization that the thoroughly-schooled clarinetist and saxophonist, able to read at sight and execute any score, had the better chance of overriding the deepening Depression.

Written data of the recording companies underline Benny's initial point: far fewer records were made in 1932 than in 1931. Further examination of these data reveals that a greater percentage of those that were made were recorded by the "name" orchestras, those led by men with national reputations. This gives rise to two possible additional causes for the paucity of recordings by BG in 1932. Those orchestras with set personnel didn't hire casuals such as Goodman. And if hired by those without fixed personnel, Benny's clarinet had little opportunity of being heard in the heavily-scored arrangements then used by the larger orchestras.

There is another explanation. Benny readily admits he was "difficult" in those days. He was cocksure of his ability, and no one was going to tell him how to play the clarinet. Occasionally some conductor tried . . . and that was the final bar in that working arrangement. Benny's singlemindedness stood him in good stead later, when he impressed his mode of playing on his sidemen and drove them to match his level of skill. But it hurt him in 1932—the boss can do what the employee cannot.

Whatever the reasons, there are but three known Goodman record dates in all of 1932. Two were on consecutive days:

TED LEWIS AND HIS BAND   March 15, 1932, New York

Benny Goodman, clt & as; Muggsy Spanier, cnt; George Brunies, tbn; Ted Lewis, as; Sam Shapiro, Sol Klein, v; Jack Aaronson, p; Tony Gerardi, g; Harry Barth, b; John Lucas, d; plus unknown tpt.

W 152136-1   CO 2635-D. **LP:** SB 115 (clt solo)
               My Woman! - voc Ted Lewis

W 152137-2   CO 2652-D. **LP:** BIO 8, SB 115 (clt accomp)
               In A Shanty In Old Shanty Town - voc Ted Lewis

TED LEWIS AND HIS BAND   **March 16, 1932, New York**

Personnel as March 15.

W 152140-4   CO 2652-D (clt solo) **LP:** BIO 7, SB 115
              Sweet Sue - Just You - voc Ted Lewis

W 152141-1   CO 2635-D (clt solo). **LP:** BIO 7, SB 115
              Somebody Loves You - voc Ted Lewis

(Other CO matrices recorded March 16 do not include Benny Goodman.)

In the Spring of 1932 crooner Russ Columbo asked Benny to organize a band that he could front for cafe dates and other personal appearances. Among those hired at various times were Jimmy McPartland and Bob ''Bo'' Ashford, tpt; Babe Russin, ts; Joe Sullivan and Marlon Skiles, p; brother Harry Goodman, b; and Gene Krupa, d. On occasion Benny led one of the groups backing Russ.

One Columbo engagement was at the Waldorf-Astoria in New York; neither Benny nor Gene was in that group. Another was the Woodmansten Inn gig on Pelham Parkway, New York, a summer date that both Benny and Gene played. Later were some theatre dates that Gene made but Benny did not.

That Benny contracted supporting groups for Russ, and led certain of them, brought about recurring assertions that Benny recorded with him. Benny says no, he never did. Gene, who did cut some sides with Columbo, is firm that Benny was not on any of the records he made with Columbo.

''Guilty,'' ''Sweet And Lovely,'' ''Where The Blue Of The Night,'' ''You Try Somebody Else'' and ''Living In Dreams'' are the Columbo issues most often proffered as Goodman possibilities. The author finds nothing on any of these that indicates BG's presence. Goodman collectors generally agree. Further, Victor's recording sheets name Nat Shilkret as director for a number of Columbo's studio sessions. Occasionally Columbo is credited, but BG is never mentioned.

Columbo is listed as director on June 16 for the session that produced ''Just Another Dream Of You'' and ''Living in Dreams.'' This suggests that Goodman could have been de facto leader. But the single subtone clarinet solo from this date is far removed from BG's style and sound.

In sum, there is no written or audible substantiation of Benny Goodman's presence on any issued Russ Columbo record.

Sometime in the first half of 1932 the Van Buren Co. added a sound track to Chaplin's ''One A.M.'' Benny's reaction to a tape of appropriate passages was that he likely was the clarinetist.

Victor Young's BR 20112 12″ recording (c. April 15, 1932) of ''OK, America-Parts 1 & 2,'' matrices Bx 11704-A/11720-A, has some support as a Goodman possibility. There is on it good clarinet accompaniment behind the Boswell Sisters' vocal; but the judgment here is that it's Jimmy Dorsey's, not Benny's.

Next, the only other known certain BG recording session in 1932. Collectors can attest to the limited sale of records in this Depression year, for these issues are among the rarer Selvin discs.

BEN SELVIN AND HIS ORCHESTRA (BS)   **June 9, 1932, New York**
THE CAVALIERS (C)

Benny Goodman, clt & as; Mannie Klein, tpt; Herman Wolfson, ts; Joe Venuti, v; Carl Kress, g; plus unknown tpt, tbn (poss. Tommy Dorsey), as, p, b, d.

W 152209-2   CO 2669-D. **LP:** PHON 7641, SB 110 (BS) (clt solo)
              Cabin In The Cotton -voc (Helen Rowland)

W 152210-1   CO 2669-D (BS) (subt clt intro)
              **(I've Got The Words—I've Got The Tune) Hummin' To
              Myself** - voc (Scrappy Lambert)

W 152211-1   CO 2670-D (C) (no solo)
              Masquerade - voc (Scrappy Lambert)

W 152212-2   same issue (C) (subt clt solo)
              Sylvia - voc (male trio)

On Sunday, August 14, Benny was guest soloist on the Paul Whiteman General Motors' program, National Broadcasting radio network. Backed by Whiteman, Benny played solo clarinet on ''St. Louis Blues'' and ''Beale Street Blues.'' No acetates of this radio show are known to exist.

A recently-discovered 12″ pressing, with two tracks on one side recorded at 33⅓ rpm, has to date defied efforts to establish its provenance; but Benny agrees that although he can offer no enlightenment, the clarinet solo on its second track is ''probably'' his. (The first track is by a different group, offers no hint of Benny's participation.) The arrangement, the complement,

the general ''feel'' of the recording suggest a performance date in 1932 or 1933:

THE WESTERNAIRES   **c. 1932–1933, New York**

Probably Benny Goodman, clt; and unknown personnel, including tpt, tbn, as, ts, v, p, g/bjo, b, d.

6349-2   12″ ET: W-E Wide Range Transcription, No. 478
          Puttin' On The Ritz (probable BG clt solo)

Having cited chapter and verse in support of Benny's assertion that he never recorded with crooner Russ Columbo, the author must now reverse this tactic to refute his equally positive belief that he never recorded with another, even more famous crooner, Bing Crosby.

Benny says he cannot remember ever having recorded with Bing, and that a date in the studios with Bing isn't something he'd likely forget. They knew each other well in those days, and admired each other's work. Benny recalls Bing's playing ''parlor golf'' in the apartment Benny occupied in New York—putting balls into highball glasses. Bing (later) invited Benny to appear on his radio show, but it didn't come about. Benny ''regrets not having worked with Bing.'' Bing termed Benny's Victor-era band ''immortal.'' That they could have and should have pooled their talents is obvious; but for one reason and another, says Benny, it never happened.

The author believes it did happen, on a session commonly listed as a Crosby-Dorsey Brothers date. The tone, the style, and the lilt of the clarinet on that January 26, 1933, session seem unquestionably Benny's. Most BG and Dorsey collectors now agree. Benny, upon listening to the record, just pressed his lips together and refused to commit himself.

BING CROSBY (C)   **January 26, 1933, New York**
BING CROSBY with The MILLS BROTHERS (M)

Benny Goodman, clt; Bunny Berigan, tpt; Tommy Dorsey, tbn; Al Hoffman, v; Fulton McGrath, p; Eddie Lang, g; Art Bernstein, b; Stan King, d.

B 12991-A   BR 6491, CO 4301-M, CO 4417-M, CoAu DO3506, CoC
             C6282, BrE 1531, CoE DB1964, Colnd DB30006, Colr
             IDB75. **EP:** CO B280, FONT TFR6012, FontCont
             662021TR. **LP:** CO CL6027, HA HL7094, PHILCO 435,
             CoE 33S1036, BIO 13, CorAu KLP672 (C), CO alb.
             P614370, HL 520 (clt accomp)

B 12991-B   **LP:** JASS 7 (C) (clt accomp)
             I've Got The World On A String - voc Bing Crosby

B 12992-A   BR 6525, CoAu DO1130, BrE 1469, CoE DB1971, Colnd
             DB30010 (M) (clt accomp)

B 12992-B   BR 6525, CO 4304-M, CO 4420-M, CoAu DO1130, CoC
             C6282, BrE 1469. **EP:** CO B280, FONT TFR6012, PHIL
             BBE 12142, FontCont 662021TR, PhilCont 429320BE.
             LP: CO CL6027, HA HL7094, PHILCO 435, CorAu
             KLP672, CoE 33S1036, PHON 7647, HIS 622, HL
             520, BIO 13, (M) (clt accomp)
             My Honey's Lovin' Arms - voc Bing Crosby, Mills Bros.

Benny has not been identified on any other record made in early 1933. A brief BG-like clt is on CO matrix W 152385-1, ''Was My Face Red,'' by Phil Harris and his Cocoanut Grove Orch., recorded March 3, issued on CO 2766-D. For a number of reasons it is not considered to have been Benny Goodman's. Benny's activities in the Spring of 1933 were in the main confined to radio work for conductors Dave Rubinoff, Al Goodman and Johnny Green, with an occasional movie soundtrack thrown in.

Two sound tracks, both from Paramount shorts filmed in March 1933, have caught the attention of Goodman collectors. One is intriguingly titled, ''Let's Dance,'' and it features George Burns and Gracie Allen, along with snippets of jazz tunes: ''Nobody's Sweetheart,'' ''China Boy,'' ''Dinah'' and ''After You've Gone.'' Do you remember making a sound track for Burns & Allen in 1933? Benny: ''No, not at all.'' Does that sound like you, those brief bits of clarinet underneath all the dialog? ''Hell, you can hardly hear it. Who can tell?''

The second is, ''Captain Henry's Radio Show—A Picturization Of One Of The Popular Radio Programs.'' Its large cast includes among others Annette Hanshaw, Muriel Wilson, Lanny Ross, Molasses and January and Don Voorhees and his Orchestra, all within 10 minutes' running time. Do you recall making this one? ''No, I don't; y'know, I was doing a lot of things in those days, and it's so long ago.'' How about that solo, in Annette Hanshaw's feature, ''We Just Couldn't Say Goodbye''? ''Well, that one could be. Annette Hanshaw, eh? I remember her, made some records with her. But I think that was earlier than—what, 1933?—not long after I first came to New York with Benny Pollack.''

Films are not the author's principal area of expertise; he recommends Benny's judgments to collectors. And he would add a cautionary note: Benny's opinions are based on single auditions of what are usually but snatches of clarinet work, often obscured by dialog. But his approach to such examinations is sound; he will not claim credit for material of which he is uncertain. This attitude should be adopted by collectors, who too often are prone to say, ''That's Benny!'' about a few bars of generic and indistinguishable clarinet.

On June 12 Adrian Rollini fronted a studio group that recorded four tunes for Columbia. Two were released originally on American Columbia, a third on English Parlophone, and the fourth was not issued contemporaneously. They are W 265131-2 ''Blue Prelude,'' CO 2785-D and PaE R2515; W 265132-2 ''Mississippi Basin,'' PaE R2515; W 265133-2, ''Charlie's Home,'' test pressing; and W 265134-2 ''Happy As The Day Is Long,'' CO 2785-D. The Columbia label credits ''ADRIAN AND HIS ORCH.,'' the Parlophone ''ADRIAN ROLLINI & HIS ORCHESTRA.''

Personnel for the session is listed widely as including Mannie Klein, Tommy Dorsey, Jimmy Dorsey, Art Rollini, Art Schutt, Dick McDonough, Herb Weil . . . and Benny Goodman. A number of clarinet solos are in evidence on the releases. They have been variously ascribed, some to BG, others to JD. Although a few collectors denied Benny's participation, a majority of seasoned collectors polled championed his presence.

To settle this ''to BG or not BG'' controversy, or to assign the clarinet solos correctly, if indeed both Benny and Jimmy made this date, all four sides were played for Mr. Goodman. At their conclusion his decision was an emphatic: ''Hell, that's not me, that's Jimmy—Jimmy Dorsey—I **never** played like that!''

So—scratch the June 12 Rollini session as a Goodman date.

Having just lost a Goodman session, let's gain one:

Sometime in mid-1933, possibly in July, the World Transcription Service recorded a potpourri of tunes and pressed them onto a single demonstration ET, later onto an advertising ET. On the 16″ disc are ''Love Is The Sweetest Thing '' with a vocal by Stuart Allen; two instrumentals, ''Reflections On The Water'' and ''Ragging The Scale''; and a medley, ''Shine On Your Shoes'' and ''Louisiana Hayride.''

''Love . . . ,'' ''Reflections . . . ,'' and ''Ragging . . . '' offer no hint of Benny's participation; indeed, these tunes may not have been recorded at the same time as the medley. But in the ''Shine On Your Shoes'' portion of the medley—up jumps a Goodman clarinet solo.

REESE & ABBOT ORCH.   c. July 1933, New York

Benny Goodman, clt; plus unknown full orch. Suggestions for some of the other participants are Mannie Klein, tpt; Russ Morgan, tbn; Eddie Miller, ts.

SS-5803-4   **ET:** World Broadcasting System Wide Range
               Demonstration Prog. No. 5803, Chevrolet Motor Co.
               ''Musical Moments,''   Prog. No. 98. **LP:** JAZ 1 (clt
               solo)
               Medley: Shine On Your Shoes/Louisiana Hayride

The upcoming session terminates the BEN SELVIN ERA. Although Ben Selvin continued to head Columbia's recording facilities for some years, from this juncture he seems to become a nonparticipating A&R (Artists and Repertoire) executive, and his name appears on very few Columbia labels. The author has been unable to mark BG on any of the Selvin sides recorded after July 5, 1933.

FRAN FREY AND HIS ORCH. (FF)   July 5, 1933, New York
BEN SELVIN AND HIS ORCHESTRA (BS)

Benny Goodman clt & as; Phil Jardine, Ruby Weinstein, A. Rattini, tpt; Andy Russo, tbn; Jack Mayhew, as; Larry Binyon, ts; H. Urbin, J. Bowman, J. Rosenblatt, v; F Leightner, p; Perry Botkin, g; Ward Ley, b; H. Reese, d; Irene Collins, Fran Frey, Jack Miller, voc.

W 152430-1   CO 2788-D (FF), ReAu 21798 (no solo)
               Moonstruck - voc Irene Collins and Fran Frey

W 152431-2   CO 2789-D (BS) (clt lead)
               Reflections In The Water

W 152432-2   CO 2789-D (BS). **LP:** SB 110 (as solo)
               Morning, Noon And Night - voc Jack Miller

W 152433-2   CO 2788-D (FF), ReAu 21798 (no solo)
               Learn to Croon - voc Fran Frey

(CO mx W 152434 ''I've Got To Pass Your House To Get To My House,'' Gertrude Niessen, CO 2787-D, also recorded July 5, has no BG.)

If July 5 is the last BG-Selvin date, the BEN SELVIN ERA and the second phase of Goodman's recording career ended here. But the third phase, the BENNY GOODMAN ERA, is still some 18 months away. For Benny the next year and a half can be considered an interim of marking time while the economy still languished. It was also a time of some interesting recording dates.

THE BOSWELL SISTERS   September 11, 1933, New York

Benny Goodman, clt & as; Mannie Weinstock, tpt; Charles Butterfield, tbn; Chester Hazlett, as; Harry Hoffman, v; Martha Boswell, p; Perry Botkin, g, bjo; Dick Cherwin, b; Stan King, d.

B 13990-A   BR 6650, CoAu DO1110, BrE 01592, BrG A9484. **LP:**
               BIO 3 (subt clt accomp)
               Sophisticated Lady - voc The Boswell Sisters

B 13991-A   same 78 issues plus CoE DB 1960, BrIt 4849, BrIt 4862.
               LP: BIO 16, SB 111 (clt solo)
               That's How Rhythm Was Born - voc The Boswell Sisters

(Other matrices recorded this date, B 13986 thru B 13989, by Henry King and his Orchestra, and released on VO 2561 and VO 2550, show no evidence of BG.)

Toward the end of September, John Hammond—who was to play a significant role in his future brother-in-law's success—approached Benny about waxing some all-star records. Hammond's idea was to release them initially in England, where America's jazz had attracted an audience that seemed likely to guarantee the commercial success of the issues. Benny was not convinced that this was the route to take, and he admits to having given John a cool reception. Eventually he succumbed to Hammond's enthusiasm; but several sessions intervened.

JOE VENUTI AND HIS BLUE SIX   October 2, 1933, New York

Benny Goodman, clt; Bud Freeman, ts; Adrian Rollini, b-sax; Joe Venuti, v; Joe Sullivan, p; Dick McDonough, g; Neil Marshall, d.

W 265146-2   CoE CB708, DE 18167 A, CoAu DO1201. **EP:** CoE
               SEG7663. **LP:** DE DL5383, PR 7644, EMI 39, ReAu
               1037, TL STLJ12, MFP 1069 (clt solo)
               Sweet Lorraine

W 265147-1   TEST PRESSING (clt solo)
W 265147-2   CO 2834-D, CoE CB708, DE 18167 B, CoAu DO1036,
               Colt DQ 1325. **EP:** CoE SEG7663. **LP:** as W 265146,
               except substitute MFP 1161, plus ReG 1076, omit TL
               (clt solo)
               Doin' The Uptown Lowdown

W 265148-2   CoE CB686, DE 18168 A, CoAu DO1071. **EP:** CoE
               SEG7663. **LP:** as W 265146, except substitute MFP
               1161, plus ReG 1076, omit TL (clt solo)
               The Jazz Me Blues

W 265149-1   TEST PRESSING (clt solo)
W 265149-2   COE CB686, DE 18168 B, CoAu DO1201. **EP:** CoE
               SEG7663. **LP:** as W 265146 except substitute TL
               STLJ27 (clt solo)
               In De Ruff

(''In De Ruff'' is really Melrose and Oliver's ''Sugarfoot Stomp,'' but the Blue Six are given composer credit on the CoE label and Venuti is credited on DE. And note the discovery of two new takes from this session. All take 2's are also on LP, SW 8457/8.)

It might seem that the October 2 Venuti session was the one John Hammond suggested to Benny—''all stars,'' and the initial release in England. It is not; that session is still to come.

More than two years had elapsed since Benny had accompanied Ethel Waters. Their reunion October 10 featured two good tunes, unusual instrumentation, and a different tempo and varied attacks by BG and Mannie Klein, on the two released takes of ''Heat Wave.'' Known takes are in ( ).

ETHEL WATERS   **October 10, 1933, New York**

Benny Goodman, clt & as; Charlie Margulis, Mannie Klein, tpt; Tommy Dorsey, tbn; T. Timothy, as; Herman Wolfson, ts; B. Pobersky, S. Noble, v; E. Seidel, p; Jules Tott, b. Note that Columbia's personnel files confirm Mannie Klein as "hot" tpt, eliminate this session as a Bunny Berigan date.

W 152521-1,3   CO 2826-D, CoE 1436(1). **LP:** CO CL 2792 (1), SB 111 (3), JR 4516 (clt solo)
Heat Wave - voc Ethel Waters

W 152522-2   same 78 issues. **LP:** CO CL 2792, JR 4516, CO P4-12964 (clt accomp)
Harlem On My Mind - voc Ethel Waters

To this point the author has rejected Adrian Rollini-led dates as non-BG recording sessions. Next for Benny was his first under Rollini. There will be more authentic sessions, and at least one doubtful one, ahead.

ADRIAN ROLLINI AND HIS ORCHESTRA   **October 16, 1933, New York**

Benny Goodman, clt; Bunny Berigan, tpt; Al Philburn, tbn; Art Rollini, ts; Adrian Rollini, b-sax, vb, cello; Fulton McGrath, p; Dick McDonough, g; Artie Miller, b; Herb Weil, d. voc.

14147-1   ME 12815, PE 15831, RO 2148, BA 32873, OR 2775, CQ 8249, DO 153, DeE F3796, RoyC 91615. **LP:** SB 134 (clt solo)
You've Got Ev'rything - voc (Herb Weil)

14148-1   same issues (clt solo)
And So, Good-Bye - voc (Herb Weil)

(Intervening matrices are not BG-Rollini recordings)

14152-1   ME 12829, PE 15389, OR 2784, BA 32880. **LP:** HIST ASC5829-19, SB 134 (clt solo)
Sweet Madness - voc Herbert Weil

14153-2   same issues plus DeE F3827 (clt solo)
Savage Serenade - voc Clay Bryson

Next is the first of the two sessions that became necessary to record satisfactory takes of the four "all star" sides John Hammond had persuaded Benny to make. They agreed on the personnel after some differences, and Hammond set out to sign up the musicians. (Gene Krupa recalls that he and Jack Teagarden were working for Mal Hallet in Boston at the time, and that Hammond came to Beantown to ask them to record with Benny.) The group assembled in Columbia's studios at 55 Fifth Avenue in New York on October 18.

Collectors should take note of the inclusion of two alternate-take test pressings, never before cataloged, major additions to the extant works of Benny, Jack, Gene and the other participants. The first, W 265165-1, "Ain't-Cha Glad?", is from the personal collection of John Hammond.

The second, W 265167-1, "Texas Tea Party," was a gift from Benny Goodman to the author. It was gratefully received, of course, but it did present a problem: when was it recorded? It has no date written on its label or inscribed in its wax. Columbia's files omit any mention of a recording of matrix W 265167 on October 18, only list that matrix as of the second session, October 27. Hammond's autobiography maintains that only W 265164, "I Gotta Right To Sing The Blues," and W 265165, "Ain't-Cha Glad?," were cut on October 18.

Despite that evidence, the author leans toward October 18 as the date of the first take of "Texas Tea Party," for two reasons. One, the take 1 version, following the opening clarinet/guitar duet and ensemble introduction, offers a piano solo, which the author believes is Joe Sullivan's. The issued take, made October 27, has a passage by Benny instead of a piano solo; and Sullivan, of course, was not in the October 27 personnel. Two, the test pressing's lyrics are "straight"—Teagarden makes no reference to marijuana, whereas on the issued version Jack double-entendre's "tea." The author thinks it unreasonable to believe the lyrics were altered so much during one recording session, assumes that this change occurred in the interval between the two dates.

In deference, however, to Columbia's files and Hammond's recollection, W 265167-1 is shown as coming from either October 18 or October 27.

BENNY GOODMAN   **October 18, 1933, New York**
AND HIS ORCHESTRA

Benny Goodman, clt; Charlie Teagarden, Mannie Klein, tpt; Jack Teagarden, tbn & voc; Art Karle, ts; Joe Sullivan, p; Dick McDonough, g; Art Bernstein, b; Gene Krupa, d; Art Schutt, arr.

W 265164-2   CO 2835-D, CoE CB692, CO 3168-D, CoE FB2822, HJCA HC96. **EP:** CO B1806, CoE SEG7806, CoG C41112, Colt SEDQ611, CoJap EM12. **LP:** JP 1807, JR 5023, CoJap PL5017, PaE PMC1222, ReAu/E 2041, EMI 39, SONY 50432, PR 7644, SB 138, TL STLJO8, SW 8457/8 (clt solo)
I Gotta Right To Sing The Blues - voc Jack Teagarden

W 265165-1   TEST PRESSING (clt solo)
W 265165-2   same 78 issues as 265164-2, plus CoAu DO1071, LuJap 60400. **EP:** same issues. **LP:** same issues, except: omit SONY, substitute ReAu/E 1037 for ReAu/E 2041, and add EPIC LN24046, CoE 33SX1553, MFP 1069, PHON 7647 (clt solo)
Ain't-Cha Glad? - voc Jack Teagarden

(CO 3168-D - and CO 3167-D from October 27 - are credited to "Benny Goodman All Star Recording." Note that bootleg Lp JAZ 1's "Ain't-Cha Glad?" is not from this session.)

BENNY GOODMAN   **October 18 or 27, 1933, New York**
AND HIS ORCHESTRA

Personnel as October 18, with possibly Frank Froeba, p, replacing Sullivan.

W 265167-1   TEST PRESSING (clt solo)
Texas Tea Party - voc Jack Teagarden

Even more of a mystery than the date of the Columbia test pressing of "Ain't-Cha Glad?" is the provenance of two additional versions of that tune, plus one of "I Gotta Right To Sing The Blues," that appear on a World Broadcasting System demo ET. When, and under what circumstances, was this 16" electrical transcription recorded? No one to whom the author spoke remembers how it came about, although Benny has a hazy recollection that World was trying to establish a kind of "Muzak" service, and that he recorded for World at its 57th Street studio. But then he confuses what might have happened here with the "Bill Dodge" World recordings that were made some five or six months later.

The arrangements used for the World cuts are identical to those recorded for Columbia, and the personnel is the same, even as to the questionable identity of the pianist—Sullivan or either Frank Froeba or Art Schutt. Given that the sidemen assembled for the Hammond-contracted Columbia sessions were in main regularly employed and could not get to, or remain in, New York for any length of time, it seems logical that the World recordings were made at about the same time as the Columbia's.

Hammond notes that there was a tight budget for the Goodman "all star" project, that only one session had been contemplated, and that the two dates required to complete the recordings imposed a financial burden. This condition, coupled with the limited availability of the musicians who are identical on all versions, the use of the same arrangements, and the fact that no one remembers a separate session for World, suggests that Columbia may have sold some of the material to World, and that indeed there was no separate recording session for the transcription company. But that supposition is just that, a possibility only.

In any event, it is stressed that all versions of "Ain't-Cha Glad?" and both versions of "I Gotta Right To Sing The Blues" are unique in themselves; there is no cross-matching of takes.

BENNIE GOODMAN'S   **c. October 18–27, 1933, New York**
  ORCHESTRA

Personnel as October 18, except possibly Frank Froeba or Art Schutt, p, replaces Sullivan.

SS 5873-4   **ET:** World Broadcasting System Wide Range Demonstration 5873

        Ain't-Cha Glad? - voc (Jack Teagarden) (clt solo) (take 1)

        Ain't-Cha Glad? - voc (Jack Teagarden) (clt solo) (take 2)

        I Gotta Right To Sing The Blues - voc (Jack Teagarden) (clt solo)

("Bennie Goodman's Orchestra" is written on the label; "Larry Abbott Orchestra" is inscribed in the ET's shellac. All three cuts are on Lp, JAZ 1.)

Sometime after October 18, but before October 27, Joe Sullivan left the New York area and went to California. Hammond says that Frank Froeba replaced him as pianist for the "all stars," but Gene Krupa "kind of" remembered Art Schutt as participating in the second session. Consensus is Froeba, and likely Schutt was present only in his role as arranger.

BENNY GOODMAN   **October 27, 1933, New York**
  AND HIS ORCHESTRA

Personnel as October 18, except Frank Froeba, p, replaces Sullivan. Dick McDonough (DM), is also a "vocalist" on W 265166.

W 265166-2   CO 2845-D, CoE CB712, CO 3167-D, CoE FB2823, HJCA HC104, JAY 9, PhilCont/Au B21325H, LuJap 60400.
        EP: CO B1806, CoE SEG7806, CoG C41112, ColT SEDQ611, CoJap EM12. **LP:** JP 1807, JR 5023, EPIC LN24046, CoE 33SX1553, ReAu/E 1037, PR 7644, EMI 39, SB 138, SW 8457/8, MFP 1069, PHON 7647 (clt solo)
        Dr. Heckle And Mr. Jibe - voc Jack Teagarden (and DM)

W 265167-2   same 78 issues, except omit LuJap **EP:** same issues. **LP:** same issues, except: substitute ReAu/E 2041 for ReAu/E 1037, and add SONY 50432, KON 8400.16, STS 100, TL STLJO8 (clt solo)
        Texas Tea Party - voc Jack Teagarden

Benny has been credited with taking part in various recording sessions that had Chick Bullock as leader. There is general agreement now that the next listing is the only authentic Bullock-led BG date. Collectors will find the issues credited to Bullock quite rare, those credited to Kahn fairly common.

CHICK BULLOCK (CB)   **October 30, 1933, New York**
CHICK BULLOCK AND HIS LEVEE LOUNGERS (LL)
ART KAHN'S ORCHESTRA (AK)

Benny Goodman, clt; plus probably Mannie Klein, tpt; Al Philburn, tbn; Joe Venuti or Harry Hoffman, v; Fulton McGrath, p; Dick McDonough, g; Art Bernstein, b; Stan King, d; unknown ts.

14218-1   PE 12951, BA 32862, OR 2790. (CB) **LP:** SB 133 (no solo)
        By A Waterfall - voc Chick Bullock

14219-1   same issues (clt solo)
        Honeymoon Hotel - voc Chick Bullock

14220-1   PE 15836, OR 2781 (LL). **LP:** SB 133 (clt solo)
        Ain't-Cha Glad? - voc Chick Bullock

14221-1   same issues (clt solo, accomp)
        No One Loves Me Like That Dallas Man - voc Chick Bullock

14222-1   ME 12862, PE 15841, RO 2159, BA 32882, OR 2786 (AK). **LP:** SB 133 (clt solo)
        I'd Be Telling A Lie - voc Chick Bullock

14223-1   same issues plus CQ 8279, **LP,** NOST 890/1 (clt solo, accomp)
        Annie Doesn't Live Here Anymore - voc Chick Bullock

It seems expedient at this juncture to depart from the strict chronological order in the text for two reasons: 1, the recording dates of the material to be catalogued are unknown; and 2, the material is coherent, its separate segments form an entity: The Taystee Breadwinners Program.

So titled, a weekly 15-minute radio broadcast sponsored by the "makers of Taystee Bread" commenced late in 1933, according to available information. The series continued for at least 28 weeks; it may have been extended to 39 weeks, which would be in accord with multiples of 13 weeks, standard radio contract practice.

The programs were produced, recorded and transcribed by the Columbia Electrical Transcriptions Division of Columbia Records, Inc., in New York City. Evidence suggests that at least three, and possibly four, transcriptions were produced at a given recording session.

Known programs are identical in format, interspersing comedy dialogue and sketches with musical selections. Starred were the "Happiness Boys," Billy Jones and Ernie Hare, who were announced on the programs as, "The Taystee Loafers." The orchestra was directed by Ben Selvin, and was billed as, "The Taystee Breadwinners Orchestra." Invited guests, invariably female vocalists, were featured on each program. The announcer was Louis A. Whitten.

Personnel of this studio orchestra fluctuated. Its instrumentation included one or two trumpets, trombone, one or two alto saxes, tenor saxophone, violin, piano, guitar/banjo, bass and drums, and an occasional accordion.

Benny Goodman is identifiable, via clarinet or alto saxophone soli, on some of the programs. Ben Selvin, v, and Harry DaCosta, p, are likely present on all. Other instrumentalists may include, among others: Mannie Klein, Ruby Weinstock, Sterling Bose, tpt; Tommy Dorsey, Miff Mole, Charlie Butterfield, tbn; Artie Shaw, Jimmy Dorsey, as; Art Karle, Art Rollini, Hank Ross, ts; Perry Botkin, Carl Kress, George Van Eps, g/bjo.

Where known, matrix and take numbers are shown. Missing matrix numbers cannot be extrapolated with certainty; evidently this series of matrix numbers was used for other sets of ET's. Recording dates, as stated, are unknown, but obviously would precede broadcast dates. Possible **broadcast** dates are suggested, based on very flimsy evidence.

THE TAYSTEE BREADWINNERS   **Broadcast November 14, 1933 (?)**
  Program No. 2

Personnel as in foreword.

301433   **ET:** TB—Program No. 2
        Theme - voc Jones & Hare
        When Veronica Plays The Harmonica - voc Jones & Hare
        Night On the Water - voc Hare
        Music Makes Me - voc The DeMarco Sisters
        I'm Walkin' The Chalkline, Honey- voc Jones & Hare (BG clt solo)
        Theme - voc Jones & Hare

THE TAYSTEE BREADWINNERS   **Broadcast November 28, 1933 (?)**
  Program No. 4

Personnel as in foreword.

301435-1   **ET:** TB—Program No. 4
        Theme - voc Jones & Hare
        Hi! Nellie - voc Jones & Hare
        Don't Say Goodnight - voc Hare
        Puddin' Head Jones - voc The DeMarco Sisters
        Extra - voc Jones & Hare, The DeMarco Sisters (BG as solo)
        Theme -voc Jones & Hare

THE TAYSTEE BREADWINNERS Broadcast December 26, 1933 (?)
 Program No. 8

Personnel as in foreword.

301439 **ET:** TB—Program No. 8
   Theme - voc Jones & Hare
   In A Shelter From A Shower - voc Jones & Hare (BG clt
    solo)
   Ha-Cha-Chorn-Ya Brown - voc Jones & Hare
   Lullaby In Blue - voc Audrey (Marsh ?)
   Inka Dinka Doo - voc Jones & Hare
   Theme - voc Jones & Hare

THE TAYSTEE BREADWINNERS Broadcast January 2, 1934 (?)
 Program No. 9

Personnel as in foreword.

-?- **ET:** TB—Program No. 9
   Theme - voc Jones & Hare
   Over Somebody Else's Shoulder - voc Jones & Hare
   My Voice Became A Bass - voc Hare
   This Little Piggy - voc Audrey (Marsh ?) (BG clt solo)
   Let's Go Places And Do Things - voc Jones & Hare
   Theme - voc Jones & Hare

THE TAYSTEE BREADWINNERS Broadcast January 9, 1934 (?)
 Program No. 10

Personnel as in foreword.

-?- **ET:** TB—Program No. 10
   Theme - voc Jones & Hare
   The Pity Of It All - voc Jones & Hare
   The Women Are Wild Over Me - voc Jones
   Love Locked Out - voc Audrey (Marsh ?) (BG subt clt
    solo)
   Who's Gonna Take Me Home? - voc Jones & Hare
   Theme - voc Jones & Hare

THE TAYSTEE BREADWINNERS Broadcast January 23, 1934 (?)
 Program No. 12

Personnel as in foreword.

301445-1 **ET:** TB— Program No. 12
   Theme - voc Jones & Hare
   Like Taking Candy From A Baby - voc Jones & Hare
   A Rough Idea Of My Old Kentucky Home - voc Hare
   Everything I Have Is Yours - voc Shirley Howard (BG clt
    accomp)
   Carioca - voc Jones & Hare

THE TAYSTEE BREADWINNERS Broadcast January 30, 1934 (?)
 Program No. 13

Personnel as in foreword.

-?- **ET:** TB—Program No. 13
   Theme - voc Jones & Hare
   I Hate Myself (For Being So Mean To You) - voc Jones
    & Hare
   I'm Gonna Make The Grade - voc Hare
   Paper Moon - voc Shirley Howard (BG clt solo)
   Marching Along Together - voc Jones & Hare

THE TAYSTEE BREADWINNERS Broadcast February 6, 1934 (?)
 Program No. 14

Personnel as in foreword.

-?- **ET:** TB—Program No. 14
   Theme - voc Jones & Hare
   Pretty Polly Perkins - voc Jones & Hare
   When That Old Devil's Driven Away - voc Ernie Hare
   You Oughta Be In Pictures - voc Shirley Howard
   Hallelujah! - voc Jones & Hare (BG clt solo)

THE TAYSTEE BREADWINNERS Broadcast February 20, 1934 (?)
 Program No. 16

Personnel as in foreword.

301450-1 **ET:** TB—Program No. 16
   Theme - voc Jones & Hare
   It's Springtime On Parade - voc Jones & Hare
   There Goes My Heart - voc Hare
   Why Do I Dream Those Dreams? - voc Gloria Grafton
   All Pals Together - voc Jones & Hare (BG clt obl)

A "Taystee Breadwinners" ET available to the author, Program No. 19, matrix 301456-1, with a suggested broadcast date of March 13, 1934, includes no audibly identifiable Benny Goodman. Solo opportunities in this program's final tune, "Dixie Lee," are taken by Tommy Dorsey and an unknown tenor saxophonist, who is not considered to be BG.

THE TAYSTEE BREADWINNERS Broadcast March 27, 1934 (?)
 Program No. 21

Personnel as in foreword.

301458-2 **ET:** TB—Program No. 21
   Theme - voc Jones & Hare
   Love Thy Neighbor - voc Jones & Hare
   Nothing Ever Happens To Me - voc Hare
   Two Loves - voc acc, Gypsy Nina
   . . . comedy verse, voc by Harry DaCosta
   Put On Your Old Gray Bonnet - voc Jones & Hare (BG clt
    solo)

("Put On Your Old Gray Bonnet" is also on LP, IAJRC 14.)

Benny is not audibly identifiable on the other "Taystee Breadwinner" ET's examined by the author, Programs 23, 26, 27 and 28. Indeed, a clarinet solo on "Pretty Polly Perkins," Program 27, is not Benny's; it may be Artie Shaw's.

When asked if he had any recollection of this series, Benny drew a blank. He volunteered that he remembered a series he'd done with comedians Pick and Pat, but not Jones & Hare. Unfortunately, the author has nothing to offer in audible support of Benny's memory of a long-ago radio series.

Back to the chronology, and Benny's first known recording date with Red Norvo, the beginning of a working relationship that would persist for decades. It fortuitously offers a rare example of Benny's soloing on bass clarinet.

RED NORVO November 21, 1933, New York

Benny Goodman, b-clt; Red Norvo, marimba; Dick McDonough, g; Art Bernstein, b.

B 14361-A BR 6906, BR 8236, BrE 01686, BrF 500368, BrG A9528.
   EP: EPIC EG7119. **LP:** EPIC LG3128, EPIC EE22009,
   PHIL BBL7077, PhilCont B074080L, TL STLJ14, SB
   148 (b-clt accomp)
   In A Mist

B 14362-A same issues (b-clt solo)
   Dance Of The Octopus

Composer-guitarist-vocalist, and yes, jazz singer Steve Washington joined talents with Benny the very next day. Unfortunately, this was Benny's only date with Washington, for the session produced some excellent jazz. The records are hard to obtain and merit reissue.

It was a double-date, too—and farewell to Annette Hanshaw, for this was the last time Benny recorded with her.

STEVE WASHINGTON November 22, 1933, New York
 AND HIS ORCHESTRA (SW)
ANNETTE HANSHAW (AH)

Benny Goodman, clt; plus poss. Mannie Klein or Sterling Bose, tpt; Joe Venuti or Harry Hoffman, v; Fulton McGrath, p; Dick McDonough, g; Art Bernstein, b; Stan King, d, xylo; unknown ts.

B 14363-A VO 2598 (SW). **LP:** NOST 890/1, BIO 1, SB 133 (clt
   solo)
   We Were The Best Of Friends - voc Steve Washington

B 14364-A	same issues except omit NOST (clt solo)
	Sing A Little Low-Down Tune - voc Steve Washington
B 14365-A	VO 2609 (SW). **LP:** SB 133, BIO 1 (clt solo)
	Blue River - voc Steve Washington
B 14366-A	same issues (clt solo)
	Love Me - voc Steve Washington
B 14367-1	ME 12851, PE 12959, OR 2799, EBW W71 (AH). **LP:** NOST 890/1, SB 111, SB 133, SB P511 (clt solo)
	Give Me Liberty Or Give Me Love - voc Annette Hanshaw
B 14368-1	same issues except omit NOST 809/1, SB 111 (clt accomp)
	(Little Sing-A-Lee) Sing A Little Low-Down Tune - voc Annette Hanshaw

An ADRIAN ROLLINI AND HIS ORCHESTRA recording session of November 24, 1933, matrices 14378 thru 14381, has long been in dispute. The personnel obviously includes Artie Shaw; and since Shaw and Benny were together in Al Goodman's orchestra in 1933 when it played for Will Rogers' radio series, the combination seemed possible. But repeated listening by the author, and advice from Shaw specialists, now convinces him that Benny was not present for the Rollini sides.

A different session on November 24 raises another question involving Benny. Some say he was present for only one of four sides; Benny insists he was on all four. Clarinet may be heard on one side only, but it was the second one recorded. The author is inclined to go along with Benny, but with no firm conviction. Note that all takes on all issues are -2.

The session was Benny's only date with the greatest of the blues singers, Bessie Smith. Benny's first, but Bessie's last of more than 150 issued sides; she never recorded again and died tragically in an automobile accident in 1937.

BESSIE SMITH   November 24, 1933, New York
Acc. By Buck And His Band

Benny Goodman, clt; Frankie Newton, tpt; Jack Teagarden, tbn; Chu Berry, ts; Buck Washington, p; Bobby Johnson, g; Billy Taylor, b.

W 152577-2	OK 8945, CO 37575, UHCA 47, PaAu A7548, PaE R1793, CoSd DS1538, OdG 026927, Palt B71192. **EP:** PHIL BBE12231, PhilCont 429224BE, CO G4-6. **LP:** CO GL504, CO CL856, CO ML4808, CorAu KLP615, PHIL BBL7020, PhilCont B07003L, CO KG 30788, SONY 55024, CO ALB GP33, TL STLJ28
	Do Your Duty - voc Bessie Smith (-0- clt)
W 152578-2	OK 8949, CO 37574, UHCA 49/50, OK 6893, PaAu A7613, PaE R2146, Palt B71096, CoSd DS1601. **EP:** CO G4-6. **LP:** CO GL504, CO CL856, CO ML4808, PHIL BBL7020, PhilCont B07003L, CO KG 30788, SONY 55024, CO ALB GP33, CBS 62378, TL STLJ28, CO CB16, CO P75-5470
	Gimme A Pigfoot - voc Bessie Smith (clt accomp)
W 152579-2	same issues except omit CBS, TL, CO CB, CO P75 (-0- clt)
	Take Me For A Buggy Ride - voc Bessie Smith
W 152580-2	OK 8945, CO 37575, UHCA 48, PaAu A7548, PaE R1793, CoSD DS1538, OdG 026927, Palt B71192. **EP:** CO G4-6. **LP:** CO GL504, CO CL856, CO ML 4808, PHIL BBL7020, PhilCont B07003L, CO KG 30788, SONY 55024, CO ALB GP 33, TL STLJ28
	I'm Down In The Dumps - voc Bessie Smith (-0- clt)

Billie Holiday, just 17 years old and fresh from her native Baltimore, debuted on BG's next studio date. On the same date Ethel Waters, still young at twice Billie's age, but with a decade of success behind her, grooves her final sides with Benny. In just three cuts on this date, a distillate of an evolution in jazz singing.

Audible evidence disputes John Hammond's contention that different groups cut Ethel's and Billie's efforts. Also, the date of Nov. 17 for this session on CO CL821's jacket is at odds with the recording sheets.

ETHEL WATERS With   November 27, 1933, New York
Benny Goodman's Orch. (EW)
BENNY GOODMAN & HIS ORCH. (BG)

Benny Goodman, clt; Charlie Teagarden, Shirley Clay, tpt; Jack Teagarden, tbn; Art Karle, ts; Joe Sullivan, p; Dick McDonough, g; Art Bernstein, b; Gene Krupa, d.

W 152566-1	CO 2853-D (EW). **LP:** SB 111 (clt solo)
W 152566-2	CO 2853-D, PaE R2394, PaAu A6865 (EW). **LP:** CO KG 31571, CoAu 220121, SB 111 (clt solo)
	I Just Couldn't Take It Baby - voc Ethel Waters
W 152567-1	same issues as W -152566-1, plus LP, PHON 7647 (EW) (clt solo)
W 152567-2	same issues as W -152566-2 (EW) (clt solo)
	A Hundred Years From Today - voc Ethel Waters
W 152568-3	CO 2856-D, SE 5009, CoE CB786, CoE FB2826. **EP:** CO B821. **LP:** CO CL821, CO CL1758 (Set C3L-21), CorAu KLP679, CBS(E) BPG62037, CBS 66377, CoSP P12973, SONY 50432, SONY SOPH61/2, TL STLJ03, SB 138, CoSP P3M-5869, CO KG32121, PHON 7647 (clt solo)
	Your Mother's Son-In-Law - voc Billie Holiday

Tantalizingly Goodman-like clarinet soli are on some World transcriptions probably recorded in October/November 1933. The ET's bear matrices BB 6495 through BB 6500 inclusively; their 24 selections are numbered in blocks from 165 through 180. Label artist credit is accorded the "George Wood" orchestra; if World's custom is consistent here, the credit is a pseudonym for a group whose real identity is unknown.

Six of the 24 tunes catch one's ear: "Somebody Loves Me," "Star Dust," "Thou Swell," "Rise 'n' Shine," "Heat Wave" and "My Pretty Girl." Clarinet soli on two of them, "Somebody Loves Me" and "Rise 'n' Shine" seem closest to Benny's tone and conception. But upon listening carefully to all six cuts, Benny said no, the soli weren't his. He did say that the arrangements, quite good for their time, reminded him of the charts that Vic Arden wrote in those years—" . . . in blocks, well-contained, very discrete."

The author accepts Benny's judgment, the few other Goodman collectors who have heard these sides aren't so sure. The author would note that possibly more than one clarinetist is involved; listening to those soli that are rather clearly not his, Benny may have decided that none was. In any event, a tape of the six selections noted is recommended to in-depth Goodman enthusiasts, just in case . . .

BENNY GOODMAN & HIS ORCH.   December 4, 1933, New York

Personnel as Nov. 27.

W 152574-2	CO 2856-D, CoE DB5014, CoE MC5014. **LP:** EPIC LN24046, EPIC JSN, CoE 33SX1553, SB 138 (clt solo)
	Tappin' The Barrel - voc Jack Teagarden
W 152575-(1,2)	UNISSUED **Riffin' The Scotch**
W 152576-(1)	UNISSUED **Keep On Doin' What You're Doin'**

Note that in the next session, despite the gap in numbers, the matrices are consecutive. No reason is known for this apparent policy of Columbia's in the early '30's.

Of interest too is the split in trumpet solos on "Riffin' The Scotch." Charlie Teagarden takes the solo immediately preceding the vocal, then Shirley Clay comes on for the one following the vocal. This affords the collector a chance to compare the seldom-distinguishable Clay with a trumpet player more often heard.

BENNY GOODMAN   December 18, 1933, New York
  AND HIS ORCHESTRA (ORCH.)
BROADWAY BANDITS (on RZAu only)

Personnel as Nov. 27. Deane Kincaide (DK), arr.

W 152599-1   CO 2867-D, CoE CB745, Colt DQ1178, RZAu 22040 **EP:**
              CO B821. **LP:** CO CL821, CorAu KLP679, SONY
              50432, SB 138 (clt solo)
              Keep On Doin' What You're Doin' - voc Jack Teagarden

W 152650-2   CO 2867-D, SE 5009, CoE DB5014, CoE MC5014. **EP:**
              CO B821. **LP:** CO CL821, CO CL1758 (Set C3L-21),
              FONT TFL5106, PhilCont B07550L. CorAu KLP679,
              CBS(E) BPG62037, CoSP P3M5869, SONY 50432,
              SONY SOPH61/2, CBS 66377, SB 138 (clt solo)
              Riffin' The Scotch (arr DK) - voc Billie Halliday (sic)

W 152651-1   CO 2871-D, CoE DB5016, CoE MC5016, PaAu 3812. **EP:**
              CO B821. **LP:** CO CL821, CorAu KLP679, SONY
              50432, SB 139 (clt solo)
              Love Me Or Leave Me (arr DK)

W 152652-2   same issues plus CO 35839 (clt solo)
              Why Couldn't It Be Poor Little Me (arr DK)

From the flutter-tongue tag on the first side on, there's no doubt about
the next Rollini session; it's all Benny's and not Artie Shaw's. Nor is there a
violin, which must have confused purchasers of the English Rex issue,
labeled "Joe Venuti Orchestra."

ADRIAN ROLLINI AND HIS ORCHESTRA   January 11, 1934, New York

Benny Goodman, clt; Bunny Berigan, tpt; Al Philburn, tbn; Adrian Rollini,
b-sax, xylo; Fulton McGrath, p (poss. Roy Bargy); Dick McDonough, g; Artie
Miller, b; Herb Weil, d.

14565-1   ME 12892, PE 15876, RO 2201, BA 32949. **LP:** SB 134
           (clt intro, tag)
           On The Wrong Side Of The Fence - voc (Herb Weil)

14566-2   same issues (clt accomp)
           Ol' Pappy - voc (Herb Weil)

14567-1   ME 12893, PE 15877, BA 32950, OR 2829, REX 8107.
           LP: SB 134 (clt solo)
           Who Walks In When I Walk Out - voc (Herb Weil)

14568-1   same issues except no REX 8107 (clt solo)
           Got The Jitters - voc (Clay Bryson)

If nothing else the next date proves Benny was still available for non-
jazz/vocal studio dates as late as 1934. This is his only session with the
YACHT CLUB BOYS, who evidently are responsible for the lyrics; no
composer credits appear on the records.

THE YACHT CLUB BOYS   January 16, 1934, New York
  (Adler, Kelly, Kern & Mann)

Benny Goodman, clt; plus unknown v, p, g, b.

W 152688-2   CO 2908-D, CoE DB1356, CoE FB1238 (clt accomp)
              Sing-Sing Isn't Prison Any More - voc YCB

W 152689-2   same issues (clt accomp)
              The Great American Tourist - voc YCB

W 152690-2   CO 2887-D, CoE DB1357, CoE FB1237 (clt accomp)
              We Own A Salon - voc YCB

W 152691-1   same issues, plus **LP**, NOST890/1 (clt solo)
              The Super-Special Picture Of The Year - voc YCB

For his next recording session, Benny enlisted the talent of still another
great jazz singer, Mildred (Rinker) Bailey, then complemented her wonderful vocals with the tenor saxophone of a giant of jazz, the "Hawk," Coleman Hawkins.

BENNY GOODMAN   February 2, 1934, New York
  AND HIS ORCHESTRA (ORCH.)
BROADWAY BANDITS (RZAu only)

Benny Goodman, clt; Mannie Klein, Charlie Margulis, tpt; Sonny Lee, tbn;
Coleman Hawkins, ts; Art Schutt, p; Dick McDonough, g; Art Bernstein, b;
Gene Krupa, d. Art Schutt (AS), George Bassman (GB), arr.

W 152701-3   CO 2907-D, CoE CB759, JCLS 528, JAY 10. **LP:** JP
              1812, CBS 68227, TL STLJO6, SVL 172, SB 139 (clt
              solo)
              Georgia Jubilee (arr AS)

W 152702-2   CO 2892-D. **LP:** SB 139 (clt solo)
W 152702-3   CO 2892-D, CoE CB730, TEM/SEN 4003, LuJap LX12,
              ViJap1840. **LP:** CO CL1860 (Set C3L22), SVL 172,
              CBS 68277, SB 139 (clt solo)
              Junk Man - voc (Mildred Bailey)

W 152703-2   same issues, plus **LP**, SONY 50432 (clt solo)
              Ol' Pappy (arr GB) - voc (Mildred Bailey)

W 152704-2   same issues as W 152701 plus RZAu 22040, and **LP:** CO
              CL1850 (Set C3L22), SONY 50432 (clt solo)
              Emaline - voc (Mildred Bailey)

In two or perhaps three sessions, in February and/or March, Benny cut
24 sides for The World Broadcasting System, Inc. They were originally
issued on three vertical-cut 16″ electrical transcriptions, 33⅓ rpm, four tunes
per side, and leased to radio stations.

Each ET side has a (pressing) matrix number; this is listed below in the
left-hand margin. Each tune carries its own catalog number, which consists
of a common prefix and a number in sequence. (The prefix "300" was used
by World to denote "Popular Dance Orchestra-With Vocal;" the prefix
"200" was for the same type rendition without vocal.) These tune numbers
are listed in the usual place for catalog numbers.

Labels of early World ETs frequently did not show recording groups,
but did assign names—often pseudonyms—to vocalists. It was necessary to
use a catalog, keyed to tune numbers, to identify a recording group. Here,
too, pseudonyms were used almost exclusively. But for some copies of the
Benny Goodman World recordings at least, the ET's themselves bear these
label credits: mx's BB 6451 and CBB 6452, "Bill Dodge's Orchestra"; BB
6460 and BB 6461, "Bill Dodge and his Swing Seven." To simplify matters, "Bill Dodge" is applied here.

The Dodge matrix series suggests at least two recording sessions. The
sequences of numbers need not govern, however. If they are merely pressing
matrices, then the four tunes they embrace may come from as many as four
recording sessions. It is possible that four titles were selected from four
different dates in order to "program" a single ET.

Three sets of "reissues" of the BG-World ETs are known. Of the first
set only four discs have come to light. This set was released by Western
Electric—each disc is one-sided, has two tunes, is a vertical-cut 12″ 33⅓
ET. They are shown in the text as subsidiary issues. In the 1950's all 24
tunes were released via a limited edition set of three 10″ vinyl pressing Lps.
In 1966 all 24 tunes were again bootlegged on two 12″ Lps, MELODEON
MLP7328 and MLP7329. Neither of the later issues is listed again, below.

Those are the "facts" of the ETs. No data have come to light that aid in
the identification of the Dodge personnel.

There is agreement among collectors, discographers and other jazz
afficionados about most of the Dodge lineup. Disagreement involves a second trumpet, a trombone, a tenor sax, and drums. In part this lack of
unanimity may stem from the likelihood that two or more sessions, each with
slightly different personnel, make up the Dodge ETs.

The author believes at least two sessions took place, and that their
personnels differed. Personnel listed here is based on the author's opinion,
consideration of the opinions of knowledgeable collectors, and the opinions
of Benny Goodman, Jack Teagarden, and Gene Krupa, for whom the author
played the Dodge ETs.

It should be understood that the primary issue is "**ET: WORLD**"
throughout, and these are omitted for sake of eliminating redundancy.

BILL DODGE   **February and/or March, 1934, New York**

Benny Goodman clt; Bunny Berigan, Shirley Clay, tpt; Joe Harris, tbn; unknown ts; Art Schutt, p; Dick McDonough, g; Art Bernstein, b; Gene Krupa, d; Red McKenzie (RM), voc. (BG, all tunes - clt solo)

BB 6451	300-49-	**Junk Man** - "Joe Carroll" (RM) (also W-E S2087)
	300-50-	**Dinah** - voc "Joe Carroll" (RM) (also W-E S2087)
	300-51-	**I Gotta Right To Sing The Blues** - voc "Joe Carroll" (RM)
	300-52-	**Love Is The Sweetest Thing** - voc "Joe Carroll" (RM)
CBB 6452	200-53-	**I Just Couldn't Take It Baby** (also W-E S2047)
	200-54-	**Ol' Pappy** (also W-E S2047)
	200-55-	**Old Man Harlem** (also W-E S2048)
	200-56-	**Keep On Doin' What You're Doin'** (also W-E S2048)
BB 6453	200-57-	**Nobody's Sweetheart Now**
	200-58-	**Ain't-Cha Glad?**
	200-59-	**Dr. Heckle And Mr. Jibe**
	200-60-	**Georgia Jubilee**

At this juncture the author believes the personnel changed. He suggests Mannie Klein, tpt, for Clay; Jack Jenney, tbn, for Harris; and Art Rollini, ts, for the unknown on the preceding session. Another body of opinion holds that here Stan King, or possibly Sammy Weiss, d, replaced Krupa. Krupa's opinion, upon listening to all the sides, was that he cut them all.

BB 6459	200-61-	**Texas Tea Party**
	200-62-	**Honeysuckle Rose**
	200-63-	**Holiday**
	200-64-	**Emaline**
BB 6460	200-65-	**Sweet Sue—Just You**
	200-66-	**A Hundred Years From Today**
	200-67-	**Riffin' The Scotch**
	200-68-	**Your Mother's Son-In-Law**
BB 6461	200-69-	**Basin Street Blues**
	200-70-	**Tappin' The Barrel**
	200-71-	**Love Me Or Leave Me** (also W-E S2056)
	200-72-	**I Can't Give You Anything But Love, Baby** (also W-E S2056)

Despite a number of records released with his name on them, and many dance dates on which he was contractor and leader, Benny Goodman cannot be said to have had a band in early 1934. The simple truth is that without a permanent booking of some duration, he could not afford a continuing payroll. This was the middle of the Depression, and no one took unnecessary financial gambles.

Brother Harry came back into New York with Ben Pollack's band in March, and saw things differently. He believed the time was ripe for a new, musicianly big band, and he believed Benny was the man to lead it. He discussed it with Benny for many long hours. Benny agreed it would be wonderful to have the kind of band he'd always wanted, to play his kind of music, and he thought he knew whom he could get to join up. After all, he was sick of waltz medleys, and old soldiers wanting to sit in on drums, and funny hats. And Gene and Bunny and the rest of them felt the same way. But! What about that payroll?

Oscar Levant thought he could help. Oscar, who had worked with Benny on the Hoffman Ginger Ale radio program, knew showman Billy Rose. Rose was part of a syndicate that had bought the old Manhattan Theatre at Broadway and 53rd. They were planning to open it as "Billy Rose's Music Hall," a supper club, and they needed not one but a couple of bands. Oscar would get Benny an audition.

Benny got an audition. Then he got a second one, and finally got the job. But all of that took time, and two record dates came first.

The initial session offers only subtone clarinet to argue Benny's presence, and can be rated nothing more than a possible BG date. It serves, however, to introduce another jazz singer, Lee Wiley, later Mrs. Jess Stacy.

JOHNNY GREEN AND HIS ORCHESTRA   **March 17, 1934, New York**

Poss. Benny Goodman, clt & as; Mannie Klein, tpt; Johnny Green, p; plus unknown tpt, tbn, as, ts, 2 v, g, b, d.

B 14962-A	BR 6797, BrE 01799. **LP:** SB 148 (subt clt solo)	
	Live And Love Tonight - voc Howard Phillips	
B 14963-A	BR 6855, BrE 01757. **LP:** CO KG31564, CoAlb P6 14538, PHM 1000, SB 148 (clt bridges)	
	Easy Come, Easy Go - voc Lee Wiley	
B 14964-A	same issues except omit CO LP's (no solo)	
	Repeal The Blues - voc Lee Wiley	
B 14974-A	BR 6797, BrE 01799. **LP:** SB 148 (subt clt solo)	
	Cocktails For Two - voc Howard Phillips	

(Missing matrices above were not recorded March 17, and are non-BG.)

A claim by vocalist Joey Nash that Benny recorded six Victor sides with Richard Himber and his Orchestra on March 19 is false. "No way," says Benny.

The ADRIAN ROLLINI AND HIS ORCHESTRA session of March 24, matrices 14995 thru 14999, formerly considered as at best a dubious Goodman session, is now judged a certain non-BG set. Clarinetist is Artie Shaw.

The second date is authentic, and is Benny's first recording session with a long-time friend and associate, Teddy Wilson:

BENNY GOODMAN AND HIS ORCHESTRA   **May 14, 1934, New York**

Benny Goodman, clt; Charlie Teagarden, George Thow, tpt; Jack Teagarden, tbn; Hank Ross, ts; Teddy Wilson, p; Benny Martel, g; Art Bernstein or possibly Harry Goodman, b; Ray McKinley, d.

W 152736-1	CO 2923-D, PaE R2695, OdG A272264, OdSw A272264. **LP:** JP 1812, EPIC LN24046, CoE 33SX1553, SB 139, SVL 172 (clt solo)
	I Ain't Lazy—I'm Just Dreamin' - voc Jack Teagarden
W 152737-1	same issues plus **LPs** JR 5023, NOST 890/1, TL STLJ20, (clt solo)
	As Long As I Live - voc Jack Teagarden
W 152738-1	CO 2927-D, CO 35839, CoE CB786, CoE FB2826. **EP:** CO B821. **LP:** CO CL821, JR 5023, CorAu KLP679, EPIC LN24046, CoE 33SX1553, SONY 50432, SB 139, TL STLJ08, SVL 172 (clt solo)
	Moonglow
W 152739-2	CO 2927-D, CoE DB5005, CoE MC5005, CoG DW4361, Colt CQ1416. **LP:** SB 139, NOST 890/1, SVL 172 (clt solo)
	Breakfast Ball

Benny auditioned for Rose, weeks passed, and there was no reply. Finally a call came from Rose, but it was merely a request for a second audition. Benny rounded up the boys and this time added a vocalist—lovely Helen Ward, who came over from the Waldorf-Astoria where she was singing with Enrique Madriguera's Latin band. Helen must have tipped the scales in Benny's favor, for he got the job.

Benny opened in the Music Hall June 21 (for union scale - $850./ week), opposite Jerry Arlen's society band but without Helen Ward, who had helped with the audition only. The artist credit on the releases from Benny's next recording session reflects his orchestra's location.

Personnel listed for the next session includes many of the sidemen who made the Music Hall gig. Others believed to have played the engagement are PeeWee Erwin and Eddie Wade, tpt; Babe Russin, ts; and Carl LaMagna and Irving Raymond, v. An eyewitness recalls that in addition to clarinet, Benny blew hot tenor sax (see "Take My Word," August 16) most creditably. This is significant, for with Benny playing tenor the Music Hall band's lineup becomes three trumpets, two trombones, four reeds, and four rhythm (not counting those violins, of course). This is this instrumentation that was to rocket the Goodman band to fame, and establish the standard for other swing bands. Offhand, we can't remember Benny playing or recording with this instrumentation before.

Note that the original CO issues include the legend "MUSIC HALL" in their artist credits, but later releases do not. Also, that the first BR releases had gold and black labels whereas the later ones had silver and black.

Perhaps coincidentally, the Gold Reserve Act of 1934 effectively had removed the Nation from the gold standard . . .

BENNY GOODMAN AND HIS MUSIC HALL ORCHESTRA
August 16, 1934, New York

Benny Goodman, clt; Russ Case, Jerry Neary, Sam Shapiro, tpt; Red Ballard, Jack Lacey, tbn; Hymie Schertzer, Ben Kantor, as; Art Rollini, ts; Claude Thornhill, p; George Van Eps, g; Hank Weyland, b; Sammy Weiss, d. Arrangers are Benny Carter (BC), Will Hudson (WH) and Dean Kincaide (DK).

CO 15641-1   CO 2947-D. **LP:** NOST 890/1, SB 139, SVL 172 (prob. BG ts solo)
Take My Word (arr BC)

CO 15642-1   CO 2947-D. **LP:** SB 139, SVL 172 (clt solo)
It Happens To The Best Of Friends (arr BC) - voc Ann Graham

CO 15643-1   CO 2958-D, JCLS 535 A, CoAu DO1302, CoE FB1003, CoG DW4375. **EP:** CO B821. **LP:** CO CL821, JP 1812, CorAu KLP679, SONY 50432, SB 139, SVL 172 (clt solo)
Nitwit Serenade (arr WH)

CO 15644-1   same issues except delete JCLS 535 A and add: BR 7644, CO 36109, CoC 461, CoE DB3315, LuJap S3, CoSw MZ252, LuJap LX12, CoFin DYC146, Colt DQ2641. **45:** CoE SCM5053, CoG SCMW104. **EP:** ReSp SEML34017 (clt solo)

CO 15644-2   **LP:** SB 139 (clt solo)
Bugle Call Rag (arr DK)

For many years the VoE 12 issue from the next session was a good collectors' item because it offered a take 2 of "I'm Getting Sentimental Over You," and known PE and ME issues were take 1 only. Eventually a PE release was found that had take 2, then later a ME issue was also discovered that had take 2. The PE issue has a purple and gold label instead of the usual black and gold; the ME issue a blue and silver label (as have some take 1 ME issues), in contrast to the more ordinary green and gold label. Known copies of BA, RO, and OR have take 1.

Various artist credits appear on the non-U.S. releases: VoE 12 and VoE 3 name "BENNY GOODMAN'S MODERNISTS," VoE S187, "BENNY GOODMAN AND HIS ORCHESTRA;" REX, "HOLLYWOOD DANCE ORCHESTRA;" and ImpBel, an elaborate "BENNY GOODMAN AND HIS MODERNISTS HARLEM HOT SHOTS." The reverse of the ImpBel release also says, "BENNY GOODMAN . . ." and so on, but mistakenly so; "March Winds And April Showers" is by Wingy Mannone and does not include BG.

VINCENT ROSE AND HIS ORCHESTRA (VR) THE MODERNISTS (M)
September 11, 1934, New York

Personnel as Aug. 16 except Harry Goodman, b, leaves Pollack to replace Hank Weyland.

15881-1   ME 13158, PE 16001, BA 33191, RO 2363, OR 2989 (VR). **LP:** SB 135, SVL 172 (clt solo)
Learning - voc Tony Sacco

15882-1   same issues plus CQ 8432 (VR); REX 8335 and **LP,** NOST 890/1 (clt solo)
Stars Fell On Alabama - voc Tony Sacco

15883-1   ME 13159, PE 16002, BA 33192, RO 2364, OR 2990, CQ 8526 (M); ImpG 17041, ImpBel 35002, VoE 3, VoE S187. **LP:** SB 135, SVL 172 (clt solo)
Solitude

15884-1   ME 13159, PE 16002, BA 33192, RO 2364, OR 2990 (M). **LP:** SB 135 (clt solo)

15884-2   ME 13159, PE 16002 (M); VoE 12, VoE S187. **LP:** NOST 890/1, SB 135 (clt solo)
I'm Getting Sentimental Over You - voc Tony Sacco

Although Benny had several times signed on Jack Teagarden for one of his recording dates, Jack had never reciprocated . . . until this next session.

Note that some discographers suggest a different rhythm section, namely Terry Shand, p; Art Miller, b; and Herb Quigley, d, than the one listed here.

JACK TEAGARDEN (AND HIS ORCHESTRA)
September 18, 1934, New York

Benny Goodman, clt; Charlie Teagarden, tpt; Jack Teagarden, tbn; Frank Trumbauer, C-mel; Caspar Reardon, harp; Art Tatum, p; Art Bernstein, b; Larry Gomar, d (or Shand, Miller and Quigley, as noted).

B 15938-A   BR 7652, BrE 01979, PaE R2599, BrF 500512, PolyF 580014, BrG A9843, OdG A272291, LuJap S3. **LP:** FO FJ2807, FO FP67, SB 135 (clt solo)
Junk Man

B 15939-A   BR 6993, BrE 01913, BrF 500482. **LP:** JR 5026, EPIC LN24046, CoE 33SX1553, SB 135, TL STLJO8 (clt accomp)
Stars Fell On Alabama - voc Jack Teagarden

B 15940-A   same issues (clt solo)
Your Guess Is Just As Good As Mine - voc Jack Teagarden

Musically, things were going well at the Music Hall: "The band had settled down and was beginning to sound really good," Benny remembers. But there was trouble in the front office. One version is that Rose fell out with his associates and was himself fired. Another is that Rose went on a talent scouting trip to Europe, and was voted out by new management that took over while he was gone. In any event, the power struggle caused another casualty—Benny and the band were put on notice.

Faced with the end of the Music Hall engagement, Benny needed a new venture to bolster his morale. He found it in a proposed jazz tour of Europe, as leader of a group of all-stars. Together with John Hammond, Benny began to put together a "dream" band that included Adolphus "Doc" Cheatham, Henry "Red" Allen, Bill Coleman, and Charlie Teagarden, tpt; Jack Teagarden, J.C. Higginbotham, and Will Bradley, tbn; Benny Carter and Edgar Sampson, as; Leon "Chu" Berry, ts (Big Tea plumped for his buddy, Bud Freeman); Teddy Wilson, p; Lawrence Lucie, g; Hank Weyland, b; Gene Krupa, d; Red Norvo, marimba; and Bessie Smith, voc.

Benny says that this ambitious and daring lineup—at this time whites and blacks just did not play together in public—was never assembled, so far as he can recall, and certainly was never given contracts. Benny's intention was to leave for England sometime in October. But before the personnel could be gotten together, signed and rehearsed, booking difficulties in Great Britain caused the sudden cancellation of the entire tour. The Music Hall-jazz tour one-two blow almost floored Benny.

Although cancelled, the all-star project has a curious echo; it may be commemorated in a Columbia recording session on October 16.

Research into Columbia's recording sheets uncovered an enigmatic entry for that date. They listed matrix 16132, cut October 16 in New York, right in the midst of the European tour negotiations. The tune was titled, "Stars" . . . ! Artist credit was, "BENNIE GOODMAN ORCHESTRA." Instrumentation was shown as clt, tpt, tbn, ts, p, g, b, d. No other data were listed.

"Stars" bade fair to remain a first class mystery until a test pressing turned up to confirm the session; then a second test pressing, most fortunately an alternate take, also was discovered, that further substantiated the date.

Benny opens take 1 of "Stars" with a full chorus. Then vocalist Tony Sacco takes over, backed by Teddy Wilson. Take 2 is begun by a trumpet chorus by "Doc" Cheatham. Benny and Teddy "fill" behind the vocal. In the coda of each take, a trombone has a Big Tea-like sound, thought to have been Jack Lacey's. Big-toned bass throughout both takes sounds like Art Bernstein's. Tenor sax, guitar, and drums are too hidden to warrant even a guess as to their identities.

Gene Krupa draws a blank of this date, although he remembers the circumstances of the proposed jazz tour fairly clearly. He believes he was working steadily outside New York at the time, headed enthusiastically to join up when he heard of it, then promptly reversed his field back to his job when it was cancelled.

(Chronologically, note that BG is not in Decca matrices 38844 through 38847, cut October 15 by JOHNNIE DAVIS AND HIS ORCHESTRA, as cited in other sources.)

BENNIE GOODMAN ORCHESTRA   **October 16, 1934, New York**

Benny Goodman, clt; "Doc" Cheatham, tpt; poss. Jack Lacey, tbn; unknown ts; Teddy Wilson, p; unknown g; poss. Art Bernstein, b; unknown d; Tony Sacco, voc.

16132-1	REJECTED (Test Pressing) (clt solo)	
16132-2	REJECTED (Test Pressing) (clt solo)	
	Stars - voc Tony Sacco	

(Two 16,000-series matrices were cut Oct. 16 by Leo Reisman. Although not heard, these seem unlikely to include BG. And note that poor dubs of 16132-1,2 are or LP, SB 148.)

The very next day, October 17, was Benny's final day at the Music Hall. "I really struggled, trying to keep the band together," Benny recollects, "and did book a couple of dance dates around New York." One inducement to keep going was the prospect of going on the air nationwide, sponsored by a cracker company—scouts had checked out the band in the Music Hall. But more of that later.

Another JOHNNIE DAVIS AND HIS ORCHESTRA session, cut October 22, Decca matrices 38866 through 38869, is considered by some to include BG. It does not. But Benny did work for Decca the next day, Oct. 23, with Adrian Rollini. This date too, is subject to dispute, although it does not involve Benny.

For years Bunny Berigan was credited via record labels and Lp jackets, and in discographies, with participation in the Rollini session. But the trumpet is not Bunny's at all, but rather Mannie Klein's, whose great work over the years has consistently been underrated and often confused. Other evidence indicates the second trumpet on the date was Dave Klein's, Mannie's brother—Mannie recalls his lips were giving him trouble at the time, and he needed someone to help out.

ADRIAN ROLLINI AND HIS ORCHESTRA   **October 23, 1934, New York**

Benny Goodman, clt; Mannie Klein, Dave Klein, tpt; Jack Teagarden, tbn; Art Rollini, ts; Adrian Rollini, b-sax; Fulton McGrath or Howard Smith, p; George Van Eps, g; Art Bernstein, b; Stan King, d.

38874	**LP:** SB 148 (dub of Test Pressing) (clt solo)
	It Had To Be You - voc Ella Logan
38875-A	DE 265, OdArg 284143, BrE 01942, BrG A82586, **LP:** BR BL58039, MCA 2-4018, SWF 1017, SB 148, AFF 1018 (clt solo)
	Sugar
38876-A	DE 359, DE 3862, BR 80144, OdArg 284143, BrE 01942. **EP:** DE ED843, FestAu XP45-1150. **LP:** BR BL54010, BR BL58039, DE DL8244, BrE LAT8124, VC LVA9011, CrlF CVM40012, BrF & BrG LPBM87003, DeScan BKL8124, VC(SA) BL54010, DE DL4540, DE DL34313, MCA 2-4018, CRL 3442, SB 148 (clt solo)
	Davenport Blues
38877-A	DE 359, DE 3525, BR 80144, BrE 03447. **LP:** BR BL58039, MCA 2-4018, SB 148, TL STLJ12 (clt solo)
	Somebody Loves Me
38878-A	DE 265, BrE 02510, BrG A82586. **LP:** BR BL58039, DE DL4540, MCA 2-4018, CRL 3442, SWF 1017, SB 148 (clt solo)
	Riverboat Shuffle

HARRY ROSENTHAL   **November 14, 1934, New York**
   AND HIS ORCHESTRA

Benny Goodman, clt; plus prob. Red Ballard, Jack Lacey, tbn; Toots Mondello, Hymie Schertzer, as; Art Rollini, ts; Fulton McGrath, p; George Van Eps, g; Harry Goodman, b; Sammy Weiss, d; unknown acc, v section, harp. Note that there are no trumpets on these sides.

CO 16316-1	CO 2982-D. **LP:** SB 140 (subt clt solo)
	Say When - voc Peter Cantor
CO 16317-1	same issues, plus **LP:** NOST 1005, CO P5-14320 (clt solo)
	When Love Comes Swingin' Along - voc Peter Cantor

The November 14 Rosenthal session is not well known, and seldom appears in discographies as a Goodman entry. Widespread publication as a Goodman date has been given a Rosenthal session of November 24. On that date CO matrices CO 16347-1 "You're The Top"/CO 16348-1 "All Through The Night" were recorded and issued on CO 2986-D et al. Helen Ward sings, a clarinet is prominent, and everyone was satisfied that this was an authentic Goodman item.

When **shown** CO 2986-D, Benny dismissed it with an offhand, "Yeah, I'm on that." But when the tunes were **played** for him, he exploded, "Oh, hell no, that's certainly not me—I never played like that in my life!" So scratch another counterfeit BG. Claude Thornhill directed the November 24 session, and the clarinetist was Slats Long.

Two names suggested for the personnel for the next session are in question. Some researchers contend there never was a trumpeter named "Art Sylvester," that it is a pseudonym. And Dick Clark, who certainly is a real person, says he did not join Goodman until January 1935. Clark recalls he was with Buddy Rogers and his Orchestra in Chicago in December, with Gene Krupa, and that he stayed with Rogers until the band broke up sometime that month.

BENNY GOODMAN   **November 26, 1934, New York**
   AND HIS (MUSIC HALL) ORCHESTRA

Benny Goodman, clt; Pee Wee Erwin, Jerry Neary, Art Sylvester (?), tpt; Red Ballard, Jack Lacey, tbn; Toots Mondello, Hymie Schertzer, as; Art Rollini, unknown, ts; Frank Froeba, p; George Van Eps, g; Harry Goodman, b; Sammy Weiss, d; George Bassman (GB), Jiggs Noble (JN), arr.

CO 16364-1	CO 2988-D, CoE FB1023. **LP:** SB 140, SVL 172 (clt solo)
	I'm A Hundred Percent For You (arr GB) - voc Helen Ward
CO 16365-1	CO 3011-D, JCLS 535, CoAu DO1362, PaE R2437. **LP:** NOST 890/1, SB 140, SVL 172 (clt solo)
	Cokey
CO 16366-1	CO 2988-D, CoE FB1023. **LP:** NOST 890/1, SB 140, SVL 172 (clt solo)
	Like A Bolt From The Blue (arr JN) - voc Buddy Clark
CO 16367-1	CO 3011-D, CoAu DO1362, PaE R2896, CoE DB5011. **EP:** CO B821. **LP:** CO CL821, JP1812, CorAu KLP679, SONY 50432, SB 140, SVL 172 (clt solo)
	Music Hall Rag

Many jazz commentators note that "Music Hall Rag" is more than faintly reminiscent of "The World Is Waiting For The Sunrise," but few mention the nuances of "Good-Bye," just before the vocal of "Like A Bolt From The Blue."

On the recommendation of Joe Bonine, for whom Benny had worked on the "Pick And Pat" radio program, the National Biscuit Company formally auditioned the Goodman band in November for its projected "Let's Dance" network broadcasts. Competition was keen for the three openings, but Benny won one spot by the narrow margin of a single vote. Others chosen were the Latin band of Xavier Cugat and the lush orchestra of Kel Murray (Murray Kellner). All three were signed by Dorothy McCann, a representative of the advertising agency that then had the National Biscuit account.

The program went on the air at 10:30 p.m., Eastern Standard Time, and ended at 1:30 a.m., EST, in New York, from whence the broadcast originated. It alternated sets by Goodman, Cugat, and Murray. The first program was Saturday, December 1, 1934. The last was May 25, 1935.

Happily, the December 1 broadcast was in part privately recorded. It is this initial "Let's Dance" program that begins the listing of air checks, for coincidentally it is the first known instance of any off-the-air Goodman recording. Reports that the earlier Music Hall broadcasts had been privately recorded have never been substantiated.

The author is aware that although the air checks listed herein are extensive, they are by no means exhaustive. It is likely that hundreds, possibly thousands, more privately-recorded selections by Benny Goodman exist in the hands of collectors unknown to the author and his contributing sources. The author's temerity in listing those air checks known to him—a field of discography that he pioneered—is conditioned by these judgments:

Privately-recorded air checks add another dimension to the already celebrated career of Benny Goodman. They present him in company with great musicians, vocalists, entertainers and "personalities" with whom he never recorded commercially. They fill voids in his "recorded life"; a notable example is the two recording bans of the 1940's. They give certain evidence of his band's changing personnels and the locations of his engagements. On occasion they showcase Benny and his sidemen generating excitement and spontaneity seldom captured in the recording studios. They offer unparalleled performances of tunes never recorded commercially, and some startlingly different and extended versions of those that were. They provide important rungs in Goodman's personal ladder to success that otherwise would be missing, as witness the "Let's Dance" series. They demonstrate the incredible mass of Goodman's produce over time, and they illustrate as words cannot his several "periods," and subtle shifts in technique. In short the air checks underline the enormity of Goodman's talent and add one more measure to the stature of a musician often described as "a legend in his own time."

The author believes air checks to be the new direction of collecting. Commercial recordings are finite. In this era of the tape recorder a fan interested in the music can easily, and at modest cost, acquire all of Goodman's commercial recordings via tape. Should his hobby, and his enjoyment, then terminate? The author thinks not. For air checks seem to be almost infinite in number, and thus can extend the enthusiast's "collection," and add to his gratification, as far and as long as he cares to continue. The author fully understands that by listing air checks he vitiates what is probably the foremost ambition of all discographers: totality. He realizes his listings are incomplete, but hopes that they will cause readers to call attention to air checks not listed, and so approach completeness. He admits the listings are often inexact as to personnel, dates and locations; but perhaps imperfection is a characteristic of a pioneer effort. And he is aware that harsh words will be directed to him when, on the strength of these listings, collectors acquire some of the air checks and find them unsatisfactory. Some are poorly recorded, some begin several bars too late and end several too soon, and some (recorded via a microphone) even have the recordist "singing along" with Peggy Lee . . . But despite their imperfections, and underneath the hiss and crackle and static, the music, Benny's brand, is there, and much of it is great.

An end to explanations and apologies. Herewith the first of many, the beginning of Benny Goodman's air checks.

"LET'S DANCE"   December 1, 1934, New York
  NBC Radio Network

Benny Goodman, clt; Bunny Berigan, Jerry Neary, Sammy Shapiro (?), tpt; Red Ballard, Jack Lacey, tbn; Toots Mondello, Hymie Schertzer, as; Art Rollini, poss. Ben Kantor, ts; Frank Froeba, p; George Van Eps, g; Harry Goodman, b; Stan King, d; Joe Lippman (JL), arr; Buddy Clark, Helen Ward, voc.

The Object Of My Affection (arr JL) - voc Buddy Clark (LP: SH 2031, SB 100)
With Every Breath I Take (arr JL) - voc Helen Ward (LP: SB 150)

"LET'S DANCE"   December 8, 1934, New York
  NBC Radio Network
Personnel as December 1.

Not Bad (arr JL) - voc Buddy Clark and Helen Ward (LP: SB 104)
Crazy Rhythm (arr JL) - voc Helen Ward (LP: SH 2031, SB 100)

Benny "remembers" Gene Krupa's coming into the band in February 1935; but this is too late, for Krupa is identifiable on the next air check. Gene left Buddy Rogers's band to join Benny just before this broadcast:

"LET'S DANCE"   December 22, 1934, New York
  NBC Radio Network

Personnel as December 1, except GENE KRUPA, d, replaces King.

Indiana (LP: SB 150)
Solitude - voc Helen Ward (poss. arr. George Van Eps) (LP: SB 150)

The importance of Krupa's union with Goodman cannot be overstated. Benny got in Gene, in addition to Gene's technical proficiency, rock-solid beat, feeling for jazz and showmanship, a loyal co-worker who gave everything he had to make the new band a success. Jobs for the Goodman band were few in its early days, and Gene's pay usually was the $87.50 per week he drew for the "Let's Dance" broadcasts. Gene was in it all the way, the money was enough to sustain him, and like Benny he was determined that this time Jazz was going to make it.

Upon joining Benny, one of Gene's first moves was to make ready his equipment. He discussed his kit with Billy Maher, then Benny's band boy

and later the proprietor of a New York retail outlet for musical instruments. Billy asked, what did Gene want on the face of his bass drum? Practice then was to have a pastoral scene painted on the bass, lighted by an electric bulb within. Billy suggested Gene's initials instead, for a bucolic sketch seemed inappropriate to Benny's brand of music. Gene agreed. But one look persuaded Gene that Billy's first attempt wouldn't do—it gave the impression that the band was Gene's, not Benny's.

How about adding 'BENNY GOODMAN?' Billy tried it, but the result was too crowded. "Hey, Billy, what do you think of a big 'BG' and a smaller 'GK'?" Gene asked; so Billy experimented with that combination, plus some stripes and a heraldic shield. He finally came up with a sketch they both liked. Then, using India ink, a ruler, and a brush from a child's paint set, he transferred the design onto the drum. The familiar gk/BG shield became a hallmark of the Swing Era, and was the prototype of bass drum insignia used by many fine drummers to this day.

Gene felt that this insignia prompted the public's use of "BG" for Benny Goodman, and the author concurs. And he would note yet another link between Gene and his drums, and a sobriquet still applied to Benny: As the new band gained exposure, so too did its members gain recognition; and none more than Gene, certainly its most eye-catching attraction. Capitalizing on his popularity, the Slingerland Drum Company signed him to a contract, featured him in its advertisements. One such magazine ad in 1935 billed him as—"The King of Swing"! Thus Gene held the title some months before the Nation's press awarded it to Benny.

It should be borne in mind that the band's personnel fluctuated in late 1934 and early 1935, and that our listings for the "Let's Dance" broadcasts are close approximations, not certainties. For example, union records show this lineup for a dance date in Binghamton, New York: Berigan, Neary and Freddie Goodman, tpt; Schertzer, Gil Rodin, Rollini and Kantor, reeds; the stable rhythm section, Froeba, Van Eps, H. Goodman and Krupa; mysteriously, no trombones; and puzzlingly, Sammy Shapiro, violin. Gene Goodman, Benny's brother who acted as road agent, believes that the Binghamton date was on Christmas Eve, recalls that the bus broke down, and that an all-girl orchestra filled in for them until they arrived.

Bunny's battle with the bottle necessitated substitutions in the trumpet section more than once, and on the "Let's Dance" programs his slot was taken by Mannie Klein, who was in Kel Murray's companion orchestra. Pee Wee Erwin and Charlie Spivak also sat in on occasion. As for "Art Sylvester" . . . was this an early pseudonym for trumpeter Shapiro, who would become Sammy **Spear,** musical director for Jackie Gleason's TV series?

Note that the intrusion of the closing theme, "Good-Bye," midway in the next listing indicates the end of one of the half-hour segments on the broadcast. Incidentally, "Good-Bye" originally was titled, "Blue Serenade."

"LET'S DANCE"   January 5, 1935, New York
  NBC Radio Network

Personnel as December 22, 1934. Fletcher Henderson (FH), Deane Kincaide (DK), Spud Murphy (SM), Gordon Jenkins (GJ), arr.

Let's Dance (theme) (LP: SB 150)
Love is Just Around The Corner - voc Buddy Clark (poss. arr FH) (LP: SH 2031, SB 100)
I've Got A Feeling I'm Falling - voc Helen Ward (arr FH) (LP: SB 105)
The Dixieland Band - voc Helen Ward (arr DK) (LP: SB 104)
Serenade To A Wealthy Widow (LP: SH 2031, SB 104)
Stormy Weather - voc Helen Ward (LP: SH 2031, SB 100)
Good-Bye (Blue Serenade) (theme) (arr GJ) (LP: SB 104)
Throwin' Stones At The Sun - voc Helen Ward (LP: SB 105)
Honeysuckle Rose (arr FH) (LP: SH 2031, SB 100)
Limehouse Blues (arr BC) (LP: SH 2031, SB 100)
Night And Day - voc Helen Ward (n/c) (LP: SB 104)
Between The Devil And The Deep Blue Sea - voc Helen Ward (arr FH) (LP: SB 104)
Star Dust (arr SM) (LP: SH 2031, SB 100)
Okay, Toots - voc Buddy Clark (LP: SB 153)
Like A Bolt From The Blue - voc Buddy Clark (n/c) (LP: SB 153)

"LET'S DANCE"   January 12, 1935, New York
  NBC Radio Network

Personnel as composite of December 22, 1934, and January 15, 1935, next.

You're Not The Only Oyster In The Stew - voc Helen Ward (arr JL) (LP: SB 104)
I've Got A New Deal In Love - voc Helen Ward (arr JL) (LP: SB 150, 153)
Between The Devil And The Deep Blue Sea - voc Helen Ward (LP: SB 153)

Blue Moon - voc Helen Ward (n/c) (LP: SB 153)
In A Blue And Pensive Mood - voc Helen Ward (LP: SB 153)
Three Little Words - voc Helen Ward (arr FH) (LP: SB 153)
Blame It On My Youth - voc Buddy Clark
You Didn't Know Me From Adam - voc Helen Ward

BENNY GOODMAN AND HIS ORCHESTRA   January 15, 1935, New York

Benny Goodman, clt; Pee Wee Erwin, Ralph Muzzillo, Jerry Neary, tpt; Red Ballard, Jack Lacey, tbn; Toots Mondello, Hymie Schertzer, as; Art Rollini, Dick Clark, ts; Frank Froeba, p; George Van Eps, g; Harry Goodman, b; Gene Krupa, d.

CO 16638-1   CO 3033-D, BR 7644, CO 36109, CoC 461, PaE R2437,
CoSw MZ252. **EP:** CO B821. **LP:** CO CL821, CorAu
KLP679, SONY 50432, SB 140 (clt solo)
The Dixieland Band - voc Helen Ward (arr DK)

CO 16639-1   CO 3003-D. **LP:** NOST 890/1, SB 140 (clt solo)
Blue Moon - voc Helen Ward

CO 16640-1   CO 3003-D, CoE FB1037. **LP:** SB 140 (clt solo)
Throwin' Stones At The Sun - voc Helen Ward

CO 16641-1   CO 3033-D, PaE R2896, CoE DB5011. **LP:** JP 1812,
NOST 1004, SB 140 (clt solo)
Down Home Rag

(NOST 1004 is author's preferred designation for CoSP boxed set, P3-13618.)

Three other 16,000-series matrices were cut Jan. 15—B 16642, B 16643 and 16644. The first two are by Connie Boswell and have no BG interest. The third, 16644-1, by CHICK BULLOCK AND HIS LEVEE LOUNGERS, "You Fit Into The Picture," issued on ME 13298, PE 16065 and BA 33331, intrigues some BG collectors.

Accompanying Bullock are a violin, reed section and rhythm section - no brass. The saxes have the sound of the then BG reed section; the pianist might be Froeba; but Krupa says he is not the drummer. (The author marks him as Sammy Weiss.)

Following Chick's vocal is a lengthy full-register clarinet solo, BG-like in conception, but off somewhat in tone. All this the same day and same studio as a positive Goodman session. But the decision here is no BG.

Another non-BG item, possibly from this period, is a 16″ electrical transcription—Davis & Schwegler No. DST-174—offering "Swing Out With Benny," "Amethyst Mood," "Let Me Fill My Eyes," and "Johnny's Rhythm," as by AL GOLDEN AND HIS MONARCHS OF RHYTHM. There is clarinet throughout and it is remarkably close to Benny's sound. But despite this and one title's reference to ". . . Benny," Mr. Goodman and the author concur that it is someone else.

Also possibly from this era is a Red Nichols and his Orchestra film sequence that may have Benny Goodman on camera, but not in its soundtrack. The source film has not been available, but an excerpt from it is on two commercial videotapes, Z319 "The Best Of The Big Band Era," and Z330 "Jazz Legends, 1929–1950." The image is indistinct, but because of his posture and general physical characteristics, the clarinet player is thought to be Benny. However, there is general agreement that the clarinet passages in the single rendition, "The Dixieland Band," are not Goodman's. Efforts to locate the film itself, to resolve this tantalizing mystery, are continuing.

The next authentic Goodman session produced some of the least characteristic, most unusual sides Benny ever cut—unbalanced instrumentation, offbeat scoring, unconventional tunes. Not until Eddie Sauter fed in his unorthodox charts did Benny slant so far from his customary swing idiom; and nothing in this vein, save perhaps the BG-Norvo "In A Mist" date, preceded these sides.

The date, of course, is the REGINALD FORESYTHE session, an event Krupa recalls with clarity and great relish. Gene remembers that Benny, he and the other BG sidemen admired "Reggie" Foresythe, and given a chance to record some of his compositions, they leapt at it. They were pleased with the results; the sounds are still fresh, and Gene cited "Lullaby" as a continuing favorite of his.

Another interesting aspect is that Benny splits the clarinet solo on "The Melancholy Clown" right down the middle with Mince. The first eight bars are BG's, the second eight Johnny's.

Finally for this unique set of recordings, Sol Schoenbach, now retired as director of the Music Settlement House in Phila., recounts this story of Benny's sense of practicality: The arrangement for "Dodging A Divorcee" ran almost six minutes, twice too long to fit on a 10″ 78. Benny's solution: "We'll just play it twice as fast." And they did.

THE NEW MUSIC OF   January 23, 1935, New York
REGINALD FORESYTHE

Benny Goodman, Johnny (Muenzenberger) Mince, clt; Toots Mondello, Hymie Schertzer, as; Dick Clark, ts; Sol Schoenbach, bassoon; Reginald Foresythe, p; John Kirby, b; Gene Krupa, d.

COW 16597-1   CO 3060-D, CoE FB1233. **LP:** SB 135 (clt solo - 1st
eight bars)
The Melancholy Clown

COW 16598-1   CO 3012-D, CoE FB1031, CoG DW4270. **LP:** SB 135 (no
solo)
Lullaby

COW 16599-1   CO 3060-D, CoE FB1233. **LP:** SB 135 (clt solo)
The Greener The Grass

COW 16600-2   CO 3012-D, CoE FB1031, CoG DW4270. **LP:** NOST
890/1, SB 135 (clt solo)
Dodging A Divorcee

"LET'S DANCE"   January 26, 1935, New York
NBC Radio Network

Personnel as January 15. BARRY McKINLEY, voc, replaces Buddy Clark.

I Guess I'll Have To Change My Plans - voc Helen Ward (LP: SB 100)
Sweet And Lovely - voc BARRY McKINLEY (LP: SB 150)
That's A Plenty (arr JL) (LP: SH 2031, SB 104)
Am I Blue? - voc Helen Ward (arr. FH) (LP: SB 104)
Basin Street Blues (arr FH) - voc Barry McKinley (LP: SB 150)
Blue Skies (arr FH) (LP: SB 150)

"LET'S DANCE"   February 2, 1935, New York
NBC Radio Network

Personnel as January 15. Horace Henderson (HH), arr.

I Guess I'll Have To Change My Plans - voc Helen Ward (LP: SH 2031, SB 150)
St. Louis Blues (arr JL) - voc Helen Ward (LP: SB 105)
Love Me Or Leave Me (arr FH) (LP: SB 104)
When We're Alone (Penthouse Serenade) - voc Helen Ward (arr JL) (LP: SB 105)
Margie (LP: SB 104)
The Object Of My Affection - voc Barry McKinley (LP SB 150)
Between The Devil And The Deep Blue Sea (n/c) (LP: SB 150)
Sweet and Lovely - voc Barry McKinley (LP: SB 105)
I've Got The World On A String - voc Helen Ward (LP: SB 105)
Chicago (arr HH) (LP: SH 2031, SB 100)
Someone To Watch Over Me - voc Helen Ward (LP: SB 150)
I Can't Give You Anything But Love, Baby (arr FH) (LP: SH 2031, SB 100)

Arrangement credits are according to original manuscripts and other data in Mr. Goodman's library; they may differ from those published previously. The author will list them, where known, in each commercial recording session. When the selection appears first as an air check, credit will be listed there as well. Credits for arrangements will not be repeated in air checks.

"LET'S DANCE"   February 9, 1935, New York
NBC Radio Network

Personnel as January 15, except RAY HENDRICKS, voc.

I Surrender, Dear (arr SM) (LP: SB 104)
A Needle In A Haystack - voc Helen Ward (LP: SB 104)
Blue Skies (LP: SB 104)
I'm Growing Fonder Of You - voc RAY HENDRICKS (LP: SB 105)
Can't We Be Friends? (arr FH) (n/c) (LP: SB 104)
Poor Butterfly (arr FH)
Royal Garden Blues

"LET'S DANCE"   February 16, 1935, New York
NBC Radio Network

Personnel as January 15, Jimmy Mundy (JM), arr.

Honeysuckle Rose
Madhouse (arr JM)

BENNY GOODMAN   **February 19, 1935, New York**
  AND HIS ORCHESTRA

Personnel as January 15. Fud Livingston (FL), arr.

CO 16887-1   CO 3018-D, CoF DF1732, Colt DQ 1554. **LP:** SB 140 (clt solo)
            Singing A Happy Song - voc Helen Ward (arr SM)

CO 16888-1   CO 3015-D, CoE FB1050, CoF DF1753, LuJap LX15. **LP:** SB 140 (clt solo)
            Clouds - voc Ray Hendricks (arr FL)

CO 16889-1   CO 3018-D, CoE FB1064, CoF DF1732, Colt DQ1554. **LP:** SB 140 (no solo)
            I Was Lucky - voc Helen Ward (arr SM)

CO 16890-1   CO 3015D, CoE DB5002, PaE R2895, CoG DW4367, Colt DQ2553, LuJap LX15. **LP:** SB 140 (clt solo)
            Night Wind - voc Helen Ward

Tapes of a 16″ acetate that bears the inscription "November 1934" have been circulated with the statement that it was an audition recording for the "Let's Dance" series. It is not—it is excerpted from the next listed "Let's Dance" broadcast.

"LET'S DANCE"   **February 23, 1935, New York**
  NBC Radio Network

Personnel as January 15. (Ray Hendricks was on this broadcast, but his vocals are not extant.)

Makin' Whoopee (LP: SB 105)
At The Darktown Strutters' Ball (arr SM) (n/c) (LP: SB 150)
I Was Lucky - voc Helen Ward (arr SM) (LP: SB 150)
Indiana (arr FH?) (LP: SB 100)
The Lullaby Of Broadway - voc Helen Ward (LP: SB 153)
Rose Room (LP: SB 153)

"LET'S DANCE"   **March 2, 1935, New York**
  NBC Radio Network

Personnel as January 15.

If The Moon Turns Green - voc Ray Hendricks (arr SM) (LP: SB 150)
What's The Reason? (I'm Not Pleasin' You) - voc Helen Ward (arr FH) (LP: SB 104)
Anything Goes - voc Helen Ward (LP: SB 153)
Sweet And Lovely - voc Ray Hendricks (arr FH) (LP: SB 153)

"LET'S DANCE"   **March 9, 1935, New York**
  NBC Radio Network

Personnel as January 15, but is that Bunny on "Solitude"?

Solitude - voc Helen Ward (LP: SB 100)
Good-Bye (theme) (LP: SB 150)

"RADIO CITY MATINEE"   **March 27, 1935, New York**
  NBC Radio Network

Personnel as January 15.

Anything Goes - voc Helen Ward (LP: SH 2031, SB 100)
(I Would Do) Anything For You (arr FH)
Honeysuckle Rose (n/c)
Restless - voc Helen Ward (arr SM)
You're The Top - voc Helen Ward

"LET'S DANCE"   **March 30, 1935, New York**
  NBC Radio Network

Personnel as January 15.

I Can't Believe That You're In Love With Me (to station break)
Rockin' Chair

We thus arrive, after more than eight years of Benny Goodman on record, at that point casual jazz fans assume is the start of Benny's recording career, his first "BENNY GOODMAN AND HIS ORCHESTRA" Victor session. For it is from this juncture forward that Benny's records found popular approval. The past eight years, however, are too important to the

jazz chronicler and to the collector to be dismissed as mere overture. To emphasize their significance, a brief review is in order.

In those eight years a talented teenager of 17 had become, at age 25, a giant of jazz, one of very few who may accurately be so designated. He had in that span worked with and recorded with the important white jazz musicians of that era. Before it became an accepted practice, he had hired and performed with some of the black jazz greats. He had accompanied, on record or on location, some of the brightest stars of the entertainment world: Bing Crosby, Bessie Smith, Russ Columbo, Billie Holiday, Buddy Clark, Kate Smith, Jimmy Melton, Ethel Waters, Frank Parker, Mildred Bailey, Gene Austin, Ruth Etting, Chick Bullock, Lee Morse, Johnny Marvin, the Boswell Sisters, Hoagy Carmichael, Annette Hanshaw, Oscar Levant and many, many more. He had been a featured instrumentalist with Ben Pollack, Ben Selvin, Red Nichols, Isham Jones, Ted Lewis, and Sam Lanin, among others. He had been sought after by, and had worked for, Paul Whiteman, Frank Black, Andre Kostelanetz, Erno Rapee, Al Goodman, Nat Shilkret, Don Voorhees, Arnold Brilhart, Dave Rubinoff and other of America's best known conductors.

He had, in eight years, led several of his own bands. He had had a share of a sponsored, nationwide radio program. He had made movie soundtracks and radio transcriptions. He had played for some of the Nation's finest Broadway musicals, and had been among the first to record the great tunes from these shows. He had played many of the popular radio programs. He had investigated, become enamored of, and performed classical music 20 years before that became the vogue of the jazz musician. He had risen from near-poverty to become the main support of his family . . . this through the country's worst Depression. He had become, in the view of many, the world's greatest jazz clarinetist. All of this Benny Goodman had accomplished in eight crowded years, and yet more: He had made a prodigious number of records, among them jazz classics that bid fair to endure so long as man appreciates and enjoys freedom of expression in music.

The author is frequently asked to name his choices of the "best" records Benny ever made. Through the text some personal choices are cited. But even this "list," sparse as it is, is worth little. In the first place the author is a BG enthusiast (if not, this work would never have been undertaken!) and his opinion is necessarily prejudiced; there would be too many "best" records. Too, some of his choices would be the obvious ones known widely as jazz gems; what would be added by the author's recognition? Others of his choices would have an opposite "fault"—these are the rare recordings, those not re-released on Lp, and so unavailable to the casual listener to jazz. But if the author may suggest a general guidepost to excellence in pre-1935 Goodman recordings, it is this: Pay attention to those on which Benny and Jack Teagarden both play. There was a musical rapport, a physiochemical reaction almost, between those two, a philosopher's stone that often turned banal dross into musical gold.

In turn, the author sought Mr. Goodman's choices, not of his records but of the musicians with whom he worked. He declined; he sees no validity in choosing what amount to "all-star bands." He holds the conviction that many instrumentalists cannot be compared, because their abilities lay in different directions, more suitable to one purpose than another. He has found often that on a given day one musician or combination of musicians may produce a great recording or rendition; but that on another day, for whatever reason, the same man or men might not—"some gigs come off, some just do not. We're dealing with art and talent, not science and machinery." Benny has found through the years, as have all of us but less intimately, that musicians' abilities wax and wane; he feels it "absurd" to propose a comparison between a musician who may have reached his peak a quarter-century ago and today's jazz poll winner whose talent may still be developing.

The author respects Mr. Goodman's views, but points out that they derive from a base totally different from that of the jazz historian. Benny isn't interested in history; he is interested in tomorrow. For he is, essentially, a working musician, even now. He is concerned with the men available for his next engagement; it is futile to wish for Big Tea, it is without purpose to remember how well Gene played thirty years ago. Who is available, how would he fit . . . that's what matters now. Benny's calendar is still as crowded as he cares to make it; there isn't time for retrospection.

Historians, of course, deal in retrospection. As they look back, they make judgments . . . they compare. Often these comparisons are subjective; the author has already stated his position on naming Benny's "best" records, and its relation to complete objectivity. But the author takes a slightly different position on comparing musicians:

The gulf of years that may separate two musicians disappears on the turntable and the tape recorder. What Louis did in the '20's is directly, immediately, and fairly subject to comparison to what Miles, or Art, or Dizzy did in the '60's. The story each told on record is not subject to misquotation. The sounds of the past are equally the sounds of today—all one has to do is flick a switch. It seems to the author that there is a standard of comparison for musicians more viable than that for artists in other disciplines. Personal preference will always shade absolute objectivity; but for the comparison of musicians, the basis for preference may be demonstrated with reason and fidelity unsullied by the emotion of nostalgia or the bias of faulty memory.

Thus, when the historians of the future turn to the music of this century, they will have more than mere artifacts on which to base their judgments. They will have Benny's sounds as they are for all time, not as they were in time past. It is the feeling here that Benny's work, at its best, will never suffer by comparison.

THE BENNY GOODMAN ERA

Inexorably and seemingly without volition, present discussion of the career and works of Benny Goodman turns ever to the events and personalities incident to a very few years in his past. The name Goodman automatically conjures up the names of Krupa, or James, or Hampton, or Wilson. His latest concert evokes reminiscences of the Paramount or Carnegie Hall; his radio and television appearances recall the Camel Caravan broadcasts and "Hollywood Hotel." Benny's newest album is quickly disposed of; collectors talk of Jess's out-of-character choruses on the Columbia "Sing, Sing, Sing," or Harry's seismic blast on the "Roll 'Em" air check. And thus it goes, the Conditioned Goodman Response, for such was the lasting impact of the Benny Goodman Orchestra of 1935–1938.

Because Goodman is historically inseparable from his sidemen and his engagements of those years, and because it was then that he first gained world-wide acclaim, the BENNY GOODMAN ERA begins with his initial Victor recording session, April 4, 1935. It is not equally clear when that era ends. For Benny seems almost as popular as ever, and as influential as before, each time he leaves his home in Connecticut to hit the concert tour or tour overseas in behalf of the U.S. Department of State. Although American dance music and jazz have changed since Goodman's heyday, whenever Benny blows again old fans and new converts discover anew that Swing's The Thing.

From this precise point forward, the character of appreciation of Goodman's produce subtly shifts emphasis. Prior to this time interest is almost wholly in Goodman the individual performer, the clarinet soloist in somebody's . . . anybody's, orchestra. From here on the focus enlarges to center on Benny's BAND and Benny's SMALL GROUPS, and Benny is but an integral part of those combinations. This is unfortunate, for Benny played exceptionally well in the mid- and late-'30's. That he receives relatively less individual notice is not so much due to the other voices in his orchestra, but that the total band was so overwhelming.

For it seems certain (with a nod to Gestalt psychology) that the whole of Goodman's Victor-era band was greater than the sum of its individual parts. It is beyond argument that Benny would not have become quite so towering a figure, nor would that band have been as awe-inspiring as it was, each without the other. Certain members of the band were indispensable to it, and Benny to them; united they produced something unique. Without each other the product would have been different.

GENE KRUPA certainly was one of the key components. His ability, his love of jazz, his untiring effort for and loyalty to Goodman have been noted earlier. But there was more. While with Benny, Gene raised the status of the drum to that of a necessary ingredient of a jazz band, and a solo voice that people would listen to. All the drummers who have followed owe him that debt. He was, until he died, a serious student of the many forms tympani take in diverse kinds of music, and he channeled his knowledge into dance band drumming. When with Benny his "taste," his rhythmic invention, his stable rhythmic platform was a solid rock upon which the soloists could confidently build. His enthusiasm, his drive, and his showmanship all contributed to the band's musical greatness and commercial success. Gene Krupa was a man of genuine musical integrity. He believed heart and soul in jazz. He always performed as well as he was able, and he insisted that others do the same. The Benny Goodman Orchestra would not have been the same without him; but then, neither would Jazz itself.

LIONEL HAMPTON—Many of the things said about Krupa are also true of the Hamp. Again, a man of strong jazz persuasion and conviction, a superb technician, a great showman, a loyal, earnest musician who literally sweated, and probably would have bled, to produce great music. On top of all this Lionel had - and has - a genius for impromptu composition, an ability to build whole new musical patterns from the base chords of whatever the Quartet happened to be playing. Like Benny and Gene, Lionel's place in the Hall of the Giants of Jazz is secure.

HARRY JAMES brought a new kind of rebellious jazz trumpet to the white band scene, a departure from the invariably melodic horns of Bix and Bunny, Red and Mannie, and others like them. He slashed, he ripped, he rent the melody; his forte was a dare-devil dive into new sounds and constructions . . . And most of the time he extricated himself with grace and finesse, and his solos made sense after all. His great power, endurance, and control of his horn helped build the Goodman brass into a brilliant and precise five-man section that breathed, phrased, and thought as one man. Other than Benny himself, if there was one aspect of the Goodman orchestra that remains incomparable, it was that brass section, propelled and prodded by Harry James.

TEDDY WILSON—Did Teddy really ever play "hot" piano? Many critics now concede that he did. The "cool" Teddy Wilson was an illusion created by his gentle personality, his self-effacing modesty, and by his immaculately clean playing. Benny has often said that the chief reason he enjoyed Teddy's playing so much was that he knew Teddy would play flawlessly, that he would improvise chorus after chorus without mistake.

JESS STACY, now, made mistakes. Some of them are embarassingly evident on record. But somewhere from the depths of his Irish ancestry Jess pulled those poignantly beautiful chords, and the mistakes are forgiven. The man had no peer at accompanying a vocalist—it is true that some literally hated him, because unintentionally he stole their spotlight. Beauty is the word for Jess . . . Perhaps not hot jazz, but certainly, and always, beauty.

Others, too, were essential. The corps of arrangers, headed by FLETCHER HENDERSON, literally charted the band's highroad to success. The reeds, led by HYMIE SCHERTZER, achieved a blend and coherence that gave unmistakable identity to the band. Despite Harry James, without ZIGGY ELMAN and CHRIS GRIFFIN the trumpet section would not have been quite so powerful and precise. The point is that this orchestra was something more than a music machine with replaceable parts.

If essentiality can be graduated in degrees, then there was one component of the band more necessary than all the others. For this band was first and always Benny's band, and it could not have been what it was without him. His peerless personal ability, his unflagging energy, his coldly impersonal discipline, and his unwavering dedication to a goal of matchless excellence drove his men to the very limits of their considerable abilities . . . and oftimes beyond. If ever an artist knew precisely what he wanted—and got it—that artist was Benny Goodman.

* * *

The following are some discographical notes that apply in part to the Goodman-Victor sessions that end May 4, 1939, and in part to the balance of the text.

ADDITIONAL ARRANGERS

Count Basie (CB)	Edgar Sampson (ES)
Harry James (HJ)	Claude Thornhill (CT)
William Miller (WM)	Mary Lou Williams (MLW)
Fred Norman (FN)	Henri Woode (HW)
David Rose (DR)	

Goodman's solos are no longer noted; his presence on the records following is certain, unless specifically indicated otherwise.

Personnel replacements are shown in CAPITALS.

The word "Orchestra" is occasionally abbreviated on VI labels; captions herein use the full spelling.

Almost without exception, U.S. Victor catalog numbers are duplicated without change for Canadian Victor and Argentine Victor. To conserve space, CanVi and ArgVi issues are omitted.

Personnel, recording dates, and other pertinent data for Victor recording sessions come from the original recording sheets and are presumed correct. Personnels for air checks are interpolated from Victor sessions, supplemented by aural evidence and information gotten from trade papers, newspapers, and other sources.

As noted earlier, arranger credits are from Mr. Goodman's files, in many cases from the original manuscripts.

There are several explanations offered for Victor's practice of adding an "A" to a take number. Two of them involve the simultaneous use of two turn-tables to record one tune—the undesignated turntable and the "A" (alternate?) turntable. (The third theory has to do with multiple cuts on one 16" master; this supposition has little to support it.) The author believes that one or the other of the explanations embracing two simultaneous recordings of one performance is correct. Unless the issued record shows an "A" following the take number in the wax, therefore, listings herein omit the "A" for it has no significance in regard a different, or alternate, performance.

* * *

During the first few months of 1935 Benny and the still-jelling band "woodshedded" in and around New York, striving through constant rehearsal to evolve its sound and style, and to execute with swing and precision the big arrangements that were beginning to fill out the band's book. (One series of engagements was a succession of one-nighters in Harlem's Savoy Ballroom opposite Chick Webb. This presaged a notable "Battle Of Swing" a few years later.) Finally the band cut its first sides for Victor, and they illustrate how far it had progressed since its February date for Columbia.

BENNY GOODMAN AND HIS ORCHESTRA   April 4, 1935, New York

Benny Goodman, clt; George "Pee Wee" Erwin, Ralph Muzzillo, Jerry Neary, tpt; Sterling "Red" Ballard, Jack Lacey, tbn; Toots Mondello, Hymie Schertzer, as; Art Rollini, Dick Clark, ts; Frank Froeba, p; George Van Eps, g; Harry Goodman, b; Gene Krupa, d.

BS 89516-1 (2,3)   VI 25009 A, HMVAu EA1521, C.I. #1 (7" 78 rpm). **45:** C. I. #1. **LP:** CAM 624, CamE CDN148, RcaFr 731.092
Hunkadola (arr DK)

BS 89517-1   **LP:** CAM 872, CamE 872, RcaE 1021, RcaFr 731.092
BS 89517-2   VI 25011 A, HMV BD284, HMVAu EA1477. **LP:** ViG LPM10022
I'm Livin' In A Great Big Way - voc Buddy Clark (arr FH)

BS 89518-1   **LP:** RcaG PJM 2-8064
BS 89518-2   VI 25011 B, HMVAu EA1477. **LP:** ViG LPM10025
Hooray For Love - voc Helen Ward

BS 89519-1(2)   VI 25009 B, BB 10851, HMV BD183, HMVAu EA1521. **LP:** TL STBB03, ViG LPM10025, RcaFr 741.072. **ET:** Jill's Juke Box H-46, No. 4
The Dixieland Band - voc Helen Ward (arr DK)

(From this juncture into the late 1950s, all "processed" (fake) stereo LP's are not accorded separate listing; e.g., monaural CAM CAL 624 and "stereo" CAM S624 are catalogued once, as CAM 624. It is now believed that Jack Lacey continued as trombonist with the band, and that Joe Harris usually performed as a vocalist. All takes above are also on LP, RcaBB AXM2-5505, and counterpart RcaG releases. ViG LPM10022 and ViG LPM10025 list erroneous takes for matrices BS 89517 and BS 89518. "C.I." issues are Rca pressings, advertising premiums for a shampoo.)

"LET'S DANCE"   April 6, 1935, New York
NBC Radio Network.

Personnel as April 4.

Restless (to station break)
Let's Dance (theme)
At The Darktown Strutters' Ball (to station break)
Let's Dance (theme)

"LET'S DANCE"   April 13, 1935, New York
NBC Radio Network

Personnel as April 4.

Let's Dance (theme) (LP: SH 2031, SB 100)
Get Happy (arr SM) (LP: SB 104)
It's An Old Southern Custom - voc Helen Ward (arr FH) (LP: SB 104)

As an indication of the humble beginnings of Benny Goodman and his Orchestra: on Easter Monday, they played a dance date in Whitehall, New York, for the Whitehall Elks Lodge. A union "report" for April shows the personnel to be that of the studio session of April 4, except Sammy Shapiro and Johnny Mince replace Muzzillo and Mondello, respectively.

Possibly Benny felt that the band needed beefing up, for on its next date in the studio Benny had Jack Teagarden sit in. This is Big Tea's only recording session with BG's Victor band.

BENNY GOODMAN AND HIS ORCHESTRA   April 19, 1935, New York

Benny Goodman, clt; Pee Wee Erwin, NATE KAZEBIER, Jerry Neary, tpt; JACK TEAGARDEN, Jack Lacey, tbn; Toots Mondello, Hymie Schertzer, as; Art Rollini, Dick Clark, ts; Frank Froeba, p; ALLAN REUSS, g; Harry Goodman, b; Gene Krupa, d.

BS 89566-1(2)   VI 25024 B, BB 10459, HMV B8450, HMV JF48 EIG EG3698. **EP:** RcaE RCX1065. **LP:** VI LPM2247, RcaAu L101039, Rca RDG1014
Japanese Sandman (arr FH)

BS 89567-1(2)   VI 25021 A, HMV BD182. **LP:** VI LPM6702, ViJap RA-69
You're A Heavenly Thing - voc Helen Ward (arr FH)

BS 89568-1(2)   VI 25021 B, HMV BD182. **LP:** ViG LPM10025
Restless - voc Helen Ward (arr SM)

BS 89569-1(2)   VI 25024A, BB 10799, HMV B8450, HMV JF48, EIG EG3698. **EP:** VI EPOT6703 **LP:** VI LPT6703, ViArg AYL3000-5. **ET:** AFRS "Remember," Series H54, Prog. #13/14
Always (arr HH)

(All cuts above are on LP, RcaBB AXM2-5505, RcaG P JM2-8064, RcaFr 731.092.)

The final "Let's Dance" broadcast was May 25, and before its close Benny and his band began their first hotel date. Quite unwisely, they were booked into New York's Roosevelt Hotel, for years the wintering quarters of Guy Lombardo. Accustomed to the Royal Canadians, the clientele, the management, and even the waiters didn't dig Benny. He was given notice on opening night, and the disastrous engagement came to an end three weeks later.

In early 1935 the National Broadcasting Company inaugurated its "Thesaurus" electrical transcription service. Its discs were 16" lateral cut 33⅓ rpm plastic ETs, distributed on a lease basis to subscribing radio stations. In addition to releases by Xavier Cugat, Ferde Grofe, George Hall, Harry Reser, Nathaniel Shilkret and some vocal groups, the Thesaurus catalog featured some excellent swing. ET's by the swing bands were released under the generic artist credit, RHYTHM MAKERS ORCHESTRA (some issues, THE RHYTHM MAKERS). Eventually they included the orchestras of Benny Goodman, Artie Shaw, Bunny Berigan, Les Brown, Joe Haymes, Charlie Barnet and Chick Webb. All of the ET's were recorded in New York City and pressed in Camden, New Jersey.

Originally, seven BG-RHYTHM MAKERS transcriptions were distributed. Later, selections from these BG ET's were scrambled with tunes from the ET's cut by the other participating RHYTHM MAKERS orchestras, and released on a reissue series. The original ET's have red labels with gold print; the reissues have buff labels with red print. The original Goodman transcriptions are numbered 123 through 127, plus 165 and 295; the reissues are numbered in the 1100's. In the Goodman listing below, reissue catalog numbers are shown in () following the tune titles.

For many years the date or dates of the BG-RHYTHM MAKERS sessions was a matter of speculation. Fifty-one Goodman tunes were released, and it was assumed that this volume meant more than one session had taken place. But eventually information offered by Pee Wee Erwin, and an appointment book kept by Jack Lacey, pointed to but a single recording date. Research by RCA-Victor's Brad McCuen finally confirmed that all 51 tunes were recorded at one mammoth session, June 6, 1935, from 9:30 a.m. to 5:30 p.m., with an hour off for lunch at 1:15. As a sidelight, Lacey's diary says that each tune was cut but once-there were no second takes. And for this exercise in exhaustion, each sideman received for his marathon performance the magnificent sum of $1.00 per tune.

Unfortunately, no one seems to have kept personnel records of the session. The listing herein is based on aural evidence and the opinions of Benny Goodman, Gene Krupa, and Pee Wee Erwin. Possibly most important is that Bunny Berigan did not participate; trumpet solos some fans credit to Berigan are actually by Pee Wee Erwin.

All selections are by the full orchestra; all are instrumentals. No composer or arranger credits are listed on the labels.

Here, then, the Benny Goodman RHYTHM MAKERS, another notable achievement by BG: So far as can be determined, the single most productive recording session in all of Jazz.

RHYTHM MAKERS ORCHESTRA   June 6, 1935, New York
  (THE RHYTHM MAKERS)

Benny Goodman, clt; Pee Wee Erwin, RALPH MUZZILLO, and Nate Kazebier or Jerry Neary, tpt; RED BALLARD, Jack Lacey, tbn; Toots Mondello, Hymie Schertzer, as; Art Rollini, Dick Clark, ts; Frank Froeba, p; Allan Reuss, g; Harry Goodman, b; Gene Krupa, d.

MS 92210-1   **ET:** NBC Thesaurus #123
       A. **Makin' Whoopee**
       B. **Poor Butterfly** (arr FH)
       C. **Ballade In Blue** (arr SM) (Ballad in Blue, 1153)
       D. **Beautiful Changes** (arr FH) (1179)

MS 92211-1   **ET:** NBC Thesaurus #165
       E. **I Would Do Most Anything For You** (arr FH)
       F. **Medley: Sophisticated Lady and Mood Indigo** (arr SM) (1153)
       G. **I Can't Give You Anything But Love** (arr FH) (1153)
       H. **Yes, We Have No Bananas** (arr SM)

MS 92212-1   **ET:** NBC Thesaurus #125
       A. **Rose Room** (1179)
       B. **I Never Knew** (arr FH)
       C. **Love Dropped In For Tea** (arr SM)
       D. **Farewell Blues** (arr SM) (1154)

MS 92213-1   **ET:** NBC Thesaurus #123
       E. **Pardon My Love** (poss. arr Oscar Levant)
       F. **I Was Lucky** (arr SM) (1179)
       G. **If I Could Be With You** (arr FH) (1134)
       H. **Dark Town Strutters Ball** (arr SM) (1179)

MS 92214-1   **ET:** NBC Thesaurus #165
       A. **St. Louis Blues** (arr JL or SM)
       B. **Down Home In Indiana** (Back Home In Indiana, 1172)
       C. **I Surrender Dear** (arr SM) (1153)
       D. **Bugle Call Rag** (arr DK) (1153)

MS 92215-1   **ET:** NBC Thesaurus #124
       E. **Can't We Be Friends?** (arr FH)
       F. **Life Is A Song** (arr SM)
       G. **Sweet Little You** (arr SM)
       H. **Between The Devil And The Deep Blue Sea** (arr FH) (1144)

MS 92216-1   **ET:** NBC Thesaurus #295
       A. **Royal Garden Blues**
       B. **Sweet And Lovely** (arr FH) (1183)
       C. **Three Little Words** (arr FH) (1133)
       D. **Sugar Foot Stomp** (arr FH) (1137)

MS 92217-1   **ET:** NBC Thesaurus #125
       E. **When We're Alone** (arr JL)
       F. **There Must Have Been A Devil In The Moon** (arr SM)
       G. **Jingle Bells** (arr SM)
       H. **Restless** (arr SM)

MS 92218-1   **ET:** NBC Thesaurus #124
       A. **Sometimes I'm Happy** (arr FH) (1134)
       B. **Wrappin' It Up** (arr FH) (1144)
       C. **Rosetta** (arr FH) (1136)
       D. **You Can Depend On Me** (arr SM)

MS 92219-1   **ET:** NBC Thesaurus #127
       E. **Anything Goes** (1133)
       F. **I Get A Kick Out Of You** (arr SM) (1134)
       G. **King Porter Stomp** (arr FH) (1136)
       H. **Digga Digga Doo** (arr SM) (1144)

MS 92220-1   **ET:** NBC Thesaurus #126
       A. **Down By The River** (arr DK)
       B. **Every Little Moment** (arr SM) (1183)
       C. **Star Dust** (arr SM) (1154)
       D. **Dear Old Southland** (arr HH) (1154)

MS 92221-1   **ET:** NBC Thesaurus #126
       E. **Ding Dong Daddy From Dumas** (arr SM) (1183*)
       F. **Lovely To Look At** (arr SM) (1183*)
       G. **She's A Latin From Manhattan** (arr SM) (1134)
       H. **I Know That You Know** (arr FH) (1133)

(*There are two pressing masters for reissue 1183. Master-1 includes "Ding Dong Daddy From Dumas," whereas master-2 substitutes "Lovely To Look At" in its stead.)

MS 92222-1   **ET:** NBC Thesaurus #127
       A. **Stompin' At The Savoy** (arr ES) (1183)
       B. **Down South Camp Meetin'** (arr FH) (1153)

(Excerpts from Goodman's "Rhythm Makers" ETs are on U.S. and foreign LPs. Among them are: Alamac 2423; French Almanac 180.049; Ariston 12022; BiacBrad 10544; BYG 29.085; Extreme Rarities 1001; IAJRC-1; French Jazz Society 67416; Monkey 40036; French Musidisc 30JA5151/5152; Rose unnumbered; and Sunbeam 101, 102 and 103.)

The New York Times's radio log for June 22 lists a "Radio City Party" broadcast, 9:00–9:30 p.m., via WEAF and the NBC network. Featured are Benny Goodman and his Orchestra, and his vocalists Helen Ward and Ray Hendricks. Named, too, are Joe Twerp (his real name) and a female trio, evidently vocalists. Curiously, the Times carries this identical listing for the three succeeding Saturdays, in its editions of June 29, July 6 and July 13. No acetates of any of these broadcasts are known to be extant.

Benny's sad experience in the Hotel Roosevelt did not sway him from his swing format—almost in defiance, he brought Bunny Berigan back into the band:

BENNY GOODMAN AND HIS ORCHESTRA   June 25, 1935, New York

Personnel as June 6, except BUNNY BERIGAN, tpt, and GEORGE VAN EPS, g, replace Erwin and Reuss, respectively. Muzzillo out.

BS 92520-2(1)   VI 25081 A. **EP:** RcaE RCX1064. **LP:** VI LPM2247, RcaAu L101039, Rca RDG1014, RcaFr FXMI-7083, RcaBB AXM2-5505, TL STBB03
       Get Rhythm In Your Feet (And Music In Your Soul) - voc Helen Ward (arr FH)

BS 92521-1   VI 25081 B, BB 10851, HMV B8389, EIG EG3562, ViJap A1037, ViJap JA622, **LP:** JAZ 7, RcaBB AXM2-5505
       Ballad In Blue (arr SM)

BS 92522-2(1)   VI 25136 A, VI 25860 B, BB 10680, HMV B8398, HMV B8810, HMVAu EA1620, ViC 25782, GrF K8237, HMVSw JK2214, ViJap A-1045. **EP:** VI EPOT 6703. **LP:** VI LPT6703, ViArg AYL3000-5, RcaFr FXM37273, RcaFr 741.044, RcaBel 230.233 ViJap RA-69, RcaFr PM45354, RcaBB AXM2-5505
       Blue Skies (arr FH)

BS 92523-1(2)   VI 25136 B, BB 10458, HMV B8398, HMVAu EA1620, EIG EG3562. **EP:** RcaE RCX1065. **LP:** VI LPM2247, RcaAu L101039, RcaFr 741.072, Rca RDG1014, ViJap RA-69, RcaFr PM45354, RcaBB AXM2-5505
       Dear Old Southland (arr HH)

BENNY GOODMAN AND HIS ORCHESTRA   July 1, 1935, New York

Personnel as June 25, except RALPH MUZZILLO, tpt, replaces Neary.

BS 92546-1(2)   VI 25090 B, VI 20-2408, VI 27-0060, VD 38-B, NavyVD 124-B, HMV J0261, EIG EG3894. **EP:** VI EPA515, VI EPA5004, VI EPB1239, VI SP4528, RcaE RCX1009, JUG EPRC9061. **LP:** VI LPM1239, VI LPM3175, VI DRLI-0062, RD 3-76, RD RDA76A, JO 3057, SIG 132, C/P 25231. **ET:** AFRS P-863, AFRS Jill's Juke Box 151, AFRS Jill's All-Time Juke Box 36.
       Sometimes I'm Happy (arr FH)

BS 92547-1A   VI 25090 A, VI 20-2406, VI 27-0059, VI 44-0006, VD
(2)   15-B, NavyVD 117-B, HMV B8374, ViArg 1A-0756,
            ViArg 68-0817, ViJap A-1442, ViJap DC18. **45:** VI
            447-0006. **EP:** VI EPA664, VI EPA5043, RcaBel
            85506, RcaE RCX1019, RcaNZ RPX1330, RcaFr
            A75307. **LP:** VI LPM1099, VI LSP4005(e), VI
            LPLI-2470, VI ANLI-0973, HMV DLP1112, HMV DLP
            1116, RD4-45, TL STLJO5, RcaE DHY0001, RcaE
            PL12470, RcaF 740.552, ViJap RA 5380-1/2, RcaCont
            89323, RcaG ''Golden Age of Jazz''. **ET:** AFRS Jill's
            Juke Box 151, AFRS P-865
            King Porter (arr FH)

(Mxs BS 92546-⁻ and BS 93547-1A are also on: VI 27-0027, HMV B8523, HMV JF40, GrFr ⟨8101, HMVAu EA1586. **45:** VI 420-0027, VI 420-0153, VI 447-0153. **EP:** V EPB1005, RcaAu 20036. **LP:** VI LPT1005, VI VPM6040, ViJap RA69, RcaBB AXM2-5505, RcaG PJM2-8064, RcaFr 741.044, RcaFr FXM3-7273, Rca⁼r PM45354, HIS H263, SM 6-0610.)

BS 92548-1(2)   VI 25268 B, BB 10460, HMV B8389, HMVAu EA1723,
            ViJap JA942. **EP:** VI EPOT 6703. **LP:** VI LPT6703,
            ViArg AYL3000-5, CAM 872, RcaBel 230.233, RcaFr
            PM45354, C/P 7055
            **(You Got Me In Between) The Devil And The Deep Blue
            Sea** - voc Helen Ward (arr FH)

BS 92549-1   VI 25145 B, HMVAu EA1588. **45:** VI 47-2973. **LP:** ViG
            LPM10022, BBL/A 2203, RcaFr FXM3-7273.
            Jingle Bells (arr SM)

(Mxs BS 92548-⁻ and BS 92549-1 are also on **LP:** RcaBB AXM2-5505, RcaG PNM2-8064, ViJap RA69, RcaFr 741.059. Note that liner notes for both ViG LPM10022 and RcaFr 741.059 erroneously indicate an unissued take for ''Jingle Bells''; both are take-1.)

Benny's biography, ''The Kingdom Of Swing,'' says that his first records with Teddy Wilson's band followed Teddy's cutting some trio sides for BG. This is an error—it was the other way 'round. It should be remembered that Teddy was not yet a regular member of BG's entourage; he does not join for almost a year from now.

TEDDY WILSON AND HIS ORCHESTRA   July 2, 1935, New York

Benny Goodman, clt; Roy Eldridge, tpt; Ben Webster, ts; Teddy Wilson, p; John Trueheart, g; John Kirby, b; Cozy Cole, d.

B 17766-1   BR 7501, BR 8336, CO 36205, CoArg 291363, CoC
           C6203, BrE 02063, BrFr 500600, BrG A81010. **EP:**
           PhilCont 429117BE. **LP:** PhilCont BO7625R
           I Wished On The Moon - voc Billie Holiday

B 17767-1   BR 7498, BR 8336, CO 36206, CoArg 291317, CoC
           C6204, BrE 02066, BrFr 500602, BrG A9867, CoJap
           S10008. **EP:** FONT TFE17214. **LP:** CBS CL2666, CbsH
           S65407, PhilCont BO7625R, SONY SOPM38, CoSP
           12970, CO PL5021, CO PMS54, CO ZL1106, BOM
           P4-12969, Co C-32060, CO PG36811
           What A Little Moonlight Can Do - voc Billie Holiday

B 17768-1   BR 7501, BR 8087, CO 36205, CoArg 291363, CoC
           C6203, BrE 02063, BrFr 500600, BrG A81010, RZAu
           C22605, PhilCont B21177H, BrG A81528, DeSW
           M30371. **EP:** PhilCont 429117BE. **LP:** CBS CL2666,
           CbsH S65407, SONY SOPM38, CoSP 12970, CO
           D448, Co alb. P2M-5267, CO C-32060
           Miss Brown To You - voc Billie Holiday

(Mxs B 17766-1, B 17767-1 and B 17768-1 are also on **LP:** CO CL637, CO CL6040, CoJap PL2028, COR KLL1677, COR KLP1637, PHIL BBR8061, PhilCont BO7651R, SONY SOPH61/2, SONY SOPL176, TL STLJ03. No alternate takes from this session are extant.)

Matrix B 17769-1 ''A Sunbonnet Blue (And A Yellow Straw Hat)'' was also cut by Teddy Wilson's Orchestra on July 2, but without Benny. For some unaccountable reason, he left the studio before the final side was recorded.

Benny and the band opened July 5 in Pittsburgh's Stanley Theatre. At the end of the week's engagement they returned to New York, where Benny, Teddy and Gene waxed the first Trio sides. And note, importantly, the recently discovered alternate takes of ''After You've Gone'' and ''Body And Soul,'' transferred from test pressings onto MER and RcaFr LP's.

BENNY GOODMAN TRIO   July 13, 1935, New York

Benny Goodman, clt; Teddy Wilson, p; Gene Krupa, d.

BS 92704-1   **LP:** MER 3, RcaFr PM43176
BS 92704-2   VI 25115 B, VI 40-0107, VI 27-0117, VI 20-0150, HMV
           B8381, HMVAu EA1568, HMVFin TG153, ViJap
           JA571. **45:** VI 427-0117, VI 420-0150, VI 447-0150.
           EP: VI EPAT 26, HMV 7EG8095, ViArg AGET5, RcaAu
           20024, RcaE RCX1009, JUG EPRC9061. **LP:** VI
           LPT17, VI LPV1009, VI LSP4005(e), VI ANLI-0973, VI
           CPLI-2470, HMV DLPC11, RcaE PL 12470, RcaFr
           730.629, RcaFr 740.552, RcaFr FXM3-7273, TL
           STLJ05, RcaCont 89323. **ET:** VOA World of Jazz 5,
           VOA American Jam Session 23
           After You've Gone

BS 92705-1   VI 25115 A, VI 40-0106, VI 27-0118, HMV B8381,
           HMVAu EA1568, HMVFin TG153, ViJap JA571. **45:** VI
           427-0118. **EP:** VI EPA744, HMV 7EG8095. **LP:** VI
           LPT17, VI LPM1226, HMV DLPC11, RcaFr 430-230,
           RcaFr LPM1226, TL STLJ05, Rcalt LPM10043, RD
           3-76, RD RDA76A, SM P6-11891, C/P 25361
BS 92705-2   **LP:** MER 3, RcaFr PM43176
           Body And Soul

BS 92706-1   VI 25181 B, BB 10463, HMV B8402, ViArg 68-0832,
           GrFr K7650, HMVAu EA1622, EIG EG3360, HMVIt
           GW1237, ViJap JA836, ViJap A-1447. **EP:** HMV
           7EG8095. **LP:** CAM 624, CamE CDN148, VI LPV1009,
           RcaFr 730.629, RcaAu VJL2-0327
           Who?

BS 92707-1   VI 25181 A, BB 10463, VI 27-0117, HMV B8402, VIArg
           68-0832, HMVAu EA1622, GrFr K7650, EIG EG3704,
           HMVSw JK2395, ViJap A-1293. **45:** VI 427-0117. **EP:**
           VI EPAT26, HMV 7EG8095, ViArg AGET5. **LP:** VI
           LPT17, VI LPV1032, HMV DLPC11, RcaFr 730.707,
           TL STLJ20
           Someday Sweetheart

(Mxs BS 92704-2, BS 92705-1, BS 92706-1 and BS 92707-1 are also on **LP:** RcaBB AXM2-5505, RcaG PJM2-8064, RcaFr PM43176, ViJap RA72. Note that VI EPA5004's liner notes erroneously list the Trio's version of ''After You've Gone''; it's Tommy Dorsey's.

This was the last New York was to see of Benny for some 10 months, for the band began its first extended road trip. The tour included dates at Ocean Beach Pier, Jackson, Mich.; Oletagy Park, Columbus, Ohio; Luna Pier, Lakeside, Mich.; the Modernistic Ballroom, Milwaukee, Wisc.; a three-week stand at Elitch's Gardens, Denver, Colo.; at a location in Grand Junction, Colo.; at McFadden's Ballroom, Oakland; and at Pismo Beach, Calif. Some of these engagements were mildly successful, others were not. Then on August 21 BG opened in the Palomar Ballroom in Los Angeles. After a few sets of dance tunes, Benny signalled the band to put up the big Henderson arrangements. This is what the crowd had been waiting for, this is what it had heard on the ''Let's Dance'' broadcasts, and it roared its approval.

Before the band had headed west, several changes in its personnel took place. In July Jess Stacy replaced Frank Froeba, who had chosen to stay in New York, Toots Mondello left, Bill DePew came in, and Hymie Schertzer moved over to first alto. Allan Reuss returned, supplanting George Van Eps. Joe Harris also rejoined, at first only as male vocalist. He did not regularly play 'bone until Jack Lacey left, during the Palomar engagement, on September 25.

SUSTAINING BROADCAST   *August 22, 1935,*
CBS-Don Lee Network   *Palomar, Los Angeles*

Benny Goodman, clt; Nate Kazebier, Bunny Berigan, Ralph Muzzillo, tpt; Red Ballard, Jack Lacey, tbn; Hymie Schertzer, BILL DePEW, as; Art Rollini, Dick Clark, ts; JESS STACY, p; ALLAN REUSS, g; Harry Goodman, b; Gene Krupa, d; Helen Ward, Joe Harris, voc.

Good-Bye (opening theme)
At The Darktown Strutters' Ball
East Of The Sun - voc Joe Harris
I Hate To Talk About Myself - voc Helen Ward (arr SM)
Star Dust (arr SM) (LP: SB 105)
I'm In The Mood For Love - voc Joe Harris (arr SM)
The Dixieland Band - voc Helen Ward
Ballad In Blue
What A Little Moonlight Can Do - voc Helen Ward (arr FH)
Basin Street Blues - voc Joe Harris (LP: SB 105)
Good-Bye (theme) (LP: SB 105)

(Harry Geller, tpt, is reported to have been in the band opening night, 21 August; it is not known whose place he had taken, if the report is accurate. Kazebier, Berigan and Muzzillo played most of the Palomar engagement. Note that Spud Murphy's arrangement of "Star Dust" was the version played at this time; Fletcher-Henderson's arrangement is still in the future. In addition to LP credits above, entire broadcast is on LP, GOL 15001.)

For the first time in years, Benny recorded outside New York. And this date produced what has become one of the most difficult of all alternate take original issues for the collector to acquire.

Two takes of "Madhouse," 1 and 2, were recorded at this session. Both were released on VI 25268; originally, both were released on the elaborate scroll label, and later both were issued on the round gold label. So far so good.

In addition to issuing a genuine take 1—one musically different from take 2—Victor also released a "fake" take 1. That is to say, copies of VI 25268 were pressed bearing an identifying "1" in the position that take numbers almost invariably occupy. When played, these take "1's" turn out to be identical to take 2's.

Aurally, it is easy to distinguish a genuine take 1 from take 2. In addition to tempo and solo work, a fortuitous mnemonic difference facilitates identification: on the genuine take 1 Krupa strikes a single rim shot immediately following Stacy's solo. On take 2, Gene hits two rim shots.

Visually, however, it is almost impossible to distinguish one from the other. At one time collectors thought they had the problem solved—copies of genuine take 1's seemed always to list "Hines, Mundy" as composers, and copies of take 2's seemed always to list only "Mundy." But this characteristic broke down; copies of take 2's turned up that showed both composers. What seems to hold now is that the genuine "1's" are a minute fraction larger than the fake "1's" around the printed label.

Since the subject of take numbers has arisen, it is pertinent to bring to the attention of collectors these considerations:

It most likely was in the early 1930's that take numbers began to be assigned on the basis of preference, not on the basis of sequence of recording. That is, a take "1" was the choice of an artist and recording staff as the best performance of a given tune at one recording session, **no matter if it were the second or any subsequent attempt at recording the tune.** Take "2" was assigned to the second best, and so on. Thus assignment of a take "1" to the initial performance would only take place if the initial performance was the superior one. Once a take number was committed it was not used again for that matrix; if the matrix were re-recorded at a later date, the next higher number in sequence was the "choice" performance of **that** session.

There seem several causes for the initial release of "second choice" takes or more than one take: Two or more processing plants; a mistake; an accident to the take "1" masters, a change in opinion; or a deliberate attempt to spur sales to collectors.

Generally speaking, Benny is not enthralled with the release of alternate takes. His position is that the take he originally chose represented the best performance of that tune, and secondary takes do not. He is a proud man, and even after the elapse of decades he is mindful of the takes being re-released. He doesn't care to hear those alternates.

The author feels differently. True, some alternates are imperfect, have noticeable mistakes, some of which may be Benny's. But some of them seem to swing a bit more than the original, error or not. And they have merit in that they are "new" BG, not the same things that have been issued time and again in the past.

BENNY GOODMAN   *September 27, 1935, Hollywood*
AND HIS ORCHESTRA

Personnel as August 22, except JOE HARRIS, tbn, replaces Lacey.

BS 97015-2(1) VI 25195 A. **LP:** RcaFr FXMI-7083, BBL/A 2203, JAZ 7
  Santa Claus Came In The Spring - voc Joe Harris (arr SM)

BS 97016-1(2) VI 25215 A, VI 20-2409, VI 27-0000, ViArg 1A-0754, HMVAu EA1643, ViJap A-1058, ViJap JA672. **45:** VI 427-0000, VI 420-0150, VI 447-0150. **EP:** VI EPATI, VI EPA5072, VI EPOT6703, VI EPB1099, RcaAu 20024, RcaE RCX1033, RcaBel 85.507, RcaNZ RPX 1358. **LP:** VI LPT1, VI LPM1099, VI LPT6703, VI LSP4005(e), VI WPT1, VI ANLI-0973, VI CPLI-2470, ViArg AYL3000-5, RcaE PL12470, RcaFr 740.552, RD "The Great Band Era," RD 3-25, VI VPM6063, RcaCont, 89323, TL STBB03. **ET:** AFRS P-863
  Good-Bye (arr GJ)

BS 97017-1 VI 25268 A. **LP:** RcaBB AXM2-5505, RcaG PJM2-8064, JAZ 7

BS 97017-2 VI 25268 A, VI 20-2406, ViArg 68-0817, ViJap JA942, BB 10461, HMV B8431, HMV J090, HMVAu EA1723, EIG EG3704. **EP:** VI EPA5042, VI EPOT6703, RcaAu 20172, RcaE RCX1026, RcaNZ RPX 1352. **LP:** VI LPT6703, ViJap RA69, ViArg AYL3000-5, RcaFr 741.084, RcaFr PM45354, TL STBB03. **ET:** AFRS Jill's Juke Box 151, AFRS P-865
  Madhouse (arr JM)

(Mxs BS 97015-2, BS 97016-1 and BS 90717-2 are also on **LP:** RcaBB AXM2-5505, RcaG PJM2-8064.)

Bunny Berigan left the band the end of September, returned to his home in Fox Lake, Wisconsin. Jazz lore has it that upon leaving he mailed his trumpet to CBS's Mark Warnow in New York as a sign that he was available; and that Warnow immediately wired Bunny that he was hired. But according to Bunny's son-in-law, Bob Davis, and Harry Geller, who took Bunny's chair with Benny, Bunny posted the horn for a less devious, more practical reason: knowing himself well, he feared the horn would somehow disappear during his hegira east. Whatever, it's our loss that this great jazz talent departed the band before it reached the pinnacle of national acclaim it would achieve before year's end.

Benny finished at the Palomar October 1, his original one-month engagement having been almost doubled because of the band's success. After a week at the Paramount Theatre in Los Angeles and a few dates in Texas, the band turned east to Chicago, where it opened the Joseph Urban Room of the Congress Hotel on November 6.

In retrospect it sometimes is forgotten that Benny Goodman and his Orchestra had to "prove" themselves at each new location in its first year. Each success was local only—the acclaim Benny and his boys had won in the Palomar, for instance, just did not carry over to Chicago. (He was hired by the Congress's management on the advice of a few professional musicians in the Chicago local who wanted to hear the band in person!) The general public had not yet heard enough of the band's "remotes," nor listened to enough of its records, to be aware fully of what was happening.

It is while the band was at the Joseph Urban Room that Benny's use of a small group first comes to our notice. Calling the group the "Jim Dandies," Benny led a combo that included tpt, tbn, ts, and four rhythm, and alternated it occasionally with the full orchestra. He never recorded the group—but in a sense, Gene Krupa did. Substituting bassist Israel Crosby, then with Albert Ammons, Gene used Benny's "Jim Dandies" lineup to cut his very first records as a leader. Gene regarded them as some of Benny's best work on wax.

GENE KRUPA & HIS CHICAGOANS *November 18 or 19, 1935, Chicago*

Benny Goodman, clt; Nate Kazebier, tpt; Joe Harris, tbn; Dick Clark, ts; Jess Stacy, p; Allan Reuss, g; Israel Crosby, b; Gene Krupa, d.

C 90460-A PaE R2268, DE 18115, OdArg 194840, PaAu A7604, BrG A82622, OdSp 204333, PaFin DPY1052. **EP:** PaE GEP8576. **LP:** ReAu&G 1037, MFP 1069, SW 8457/8. **ET:** OWI Outpost Concert Series 13-Music of the Jazz Bands 26
  The Last Round Up

C 90461-A   same issues, except substitute OdArg 291195, and omit
             OWI ET
             Jazz Me Blues

C 90462-AA   PaE R2224, DE 18114, OdArg 194664, OdG A286082,
             Odlt A2337, OdSp 204371, DeF AM2333039. **EP:** PaE
             GEP8576. **LP:** DE DL5134, BrE LAT8561, CAP
             W2139, CID UM233039, ReAu&G 2041, EIG 054-
             06319M, TL STLJ05, SW 8457/8. **ET:** OWI Outpost
             Concert Series 4-Music of the Jazz Bands 8
             Three Little Words

C 90463-B   same issues except add **LP:** PaE PMC1222, and omit
             CAP W2139, TL STL J05 and OWI ET
             Blues Of Israel

(All matrices above are also on **LP:** EMI SHB39, PR 7644.)

BENNY GOODMAN   **November 22, 1935, Chicago**
  AND HIS ORCHESTRA

Benny Goodman, clt; Nate Kazebier, HARRY GELLER, Ralph Muzzillo, tpt;
Red Ballard, Joe Harris, tbn; Hymie Schertzer, Bill DePew, as; Art Rollini, Dick
Clark, ts; Jess Stacy, p; Allan Reuss, g; Harry Goodman, b; Gene Krupa, d.

BS 96299-1(2) VI 25215 B, HMV B8764, HMVAu EA1643, HMV Ind
               N4474, ViJap JA672. **EP:** RcaE RCX1064. **LP:** VI
               LPM2247, RcaAu L101039, Rca RDG1014, RcaFr
               741.059, ViJap RA69
               Sandman (arr FH)

BS 96500-1(2) VI 25193 B, HMVAu EA1629. **LP:** JAZ 16
               Yankee Doodle Never Went To Town - voc Helen Ward
               (arr SM)

BS 96501-1   same issues plus **LP:** ViJap RA69
               No Other One - voc Helen Ward (arr SM)

BS 96502-1   VI 25195 B. **EP:** VI EPOT 6703. **LP:** VI LPT6703, ViArg
               AYL3000-5. **ET:** AFRS "Remember," Series H-54-
               Prog. #13/14
               Eeny Meeny Miney Mo - voc Helen Ward

BS 96503-1A   VI 25258 A, HMV B8461, EIG EG3711. **EP:** VI EPOT
               6703. **LP:** VI LPT6703, ViArg AYL3000-5, RcaFr
               741.072, RcaFr FXM3-7273, HIS H623, JO 3057, VI
               VPM6063.
               Basin Street Blues - voc Joe Harris (arr FH)

BS 96504-1A   VI 25290 B, BB 10458, HMV B8480, EIG EG3777, ViJap
               JA992. **EP:** Vi EPOT 6703. **LP:** VI LPT6703, ViArg
               AYL3000-5, RcaFr 741.044, ViJap RA69, RcaFr
               PM45354, VI VPM6063
               If I Could Be With You (One Hour Tonight) (arr FH)

BS 96505-1   VI 25258 A, HMV B8461, EIG EG3711. **EP:** VI
               EPOT6703. **LP:** VI LPT6703, ViArg AYL3000-5, VI
               VPM6060, ViJap RA69 RcaBB AXM2-5515, RcaFr
               741.044, RcaFr FXM3-7273, RcaFr PM45354, TL
               STBB03
               When Buddha Smiles (arr FH)

(Matrices BS 96299 and BS 96500 are consecutive. Mxs BS 96299-1 thru BS
96504-1A are also on **LP:** RcaBB AXM2-5505, RcaG P JM2-8064.)

On Sunday, December 8 Benny and the band played for what many
consider to have been the very first jazz concert ever given in the United
States. It was sponsored by a Chicago "Rhythm Club," headed by "Squir-
rel" Ashcraft and Helen Oakley, took place in the Congress Hotel, and
originally was advertised as a "Tea Dance!" Some of the sidemen from Earl
Hines's band (Hines was in the Grand Terrace Ballroom, Chicago) joined
with Benny and his boys. The concert was a swinging success, so much so
that it led to two more in 1936. Gene Krupa remembers the concert as one of
the big thrills in his career, and thinks it was this first concert that in part was
a benefit for ailing pianist Joe Sullivan.

The band **was** beginning to catch on—readers of **Metronome Magazine** awarded "Best Swing Band" to Benny Goodman and his Orchestra,
the band's first such commendation.

Possibly influenced by the **Metronome** award, NBC began to broadcast
the band once each week from the Congress. It also transcribed the half-hour
programs onto 16" acetate discs, and eventually some of these were acquired
by a collector. In the 1970's they were sold and transferred to bootleg LP's.
The acetates were well preserved, the transfers were satisfactory, and thus
the LP's offer good audio fidelity. But beyond that these air checks from the
Urban Room provide unique Benny Goodman, such as the only known
performance by the "Jam Dandies" (an octet from within the band), and
sole extant renditions of a number of ballads, as well as premier airings of
some instrumentals.

SUSTAINING BROADCAST   *December 23, 1935, Chicago*
  NBC Radio Network

Personnel as November 22.

Let's Dance (theme)
Jingle Bells
Where Am I? - voc Helen Ward
Remember (arr FH)
The Music Goes 'Round And 'Round - voc Joe Harris
Get Happy (arr SM)
Basin Street Blues - voc Joe Harris
I've Got A Feelin' You're Foolin' - voc Helen Ward (arr SM)
That's You, Sweetheart - voc Helen Ward
Limehouse Blues
Someday, Sweetheart (arr FH)
Good-Bye (theme)

(Above on LP: SB 128.)

RCA also featured Benny on its "Magic Key of RCA" program, a weekly
commercial presentation of artists to be heard on the NBC network:

"MAGIC KEY OF RCA"   *December 29, 1935, Chicago*
  NBC Radio Network

Personnel as November 22.

Let's Dance (theme)   *(LP: GOJ 1005)*
Alexander's Ragtime Band (arr FH)   *(LP: GOJ 1005)*
The Dixieland Band - voc Helen Ward   *(LP: GOJ 1005)*

SUSTAINING BROADCAST   *January 6, 1936, Chicago*
  NBC Radio Network

Personnel as November 22, 1935.

Let's Dance (theme)
Blue Skies
With All My Heart - voc Helen Ward
Walk, Jenny, Walk (arr HH)
Rosetta (arr FH)
Bugle Call Rag (DK arr still in use)
Thanks A Million
Truckin' - voc Helen Ward
On The Alamo
Eeny Meeny Miney Mo - voc Helen Ward
Madhouse
Let's Dance/Good-Bye (themes)

(Above on LP: SB 129, CIC B7L8026)

SUSTAINING BROADCAST   *January 13, 1936, Chicago*
  NBC Radio Network

Personnel as November 22, 1935.

I Feel Like A Feather In The Breeze (arr HW)
I'm Shooting High - voc Helen Ward (arr SM)
Big John Special (arr HH)
Dear Old Southland

*(Above on LP: SB 130. Opening and closing themes, "Stompin' At The
Savoy" and "St. Louis Blues" were also performed, but only an incomplete
"Stompin'" is on the ET.)*

SUSTAINING BROADCAST   January 20, 1936, Chicago
NBC Radio Network

Personnel as November 22, 1935.

Let's Dance (theme)
Farewell Blues
I'm Shooting High - voc Helen Ward (arr SM)
Stompin' At The Savoy
Basin Street Blues - voc Joe Harris
I'm Building Up To An Awful Letdown - voc Helen Ward
Transcontinental (arr DR)
You Hit The Spot - voc Helen Ward
I Surrender, Dear
Yankee Doodle Never Went To Town - voc Helen Ward
Honeysuckle Rose - to signoff

(Above on LP: SB 131.)

BENNY GOODMAN AND HIS ORCHESTRA   **January 24, 1936, Chicago**
Personnel as November 22, 1935.

BS 96567-1(2)   VI 25245 A, ViArg 1A-0757. **EP:** VI EPOT6703. **LP:** VI
LPT6703, ViArg AYL3000-5, RD 3-76, ViJap RA69, VI
VPM6063
It's Been So Long - voc Helen Ward (arr DR)

BS 96568-1A
(2)   VI 25247 A, VI 20-1549, HMV B8480, EIG EG3777,
ViJap JA716, VI 27-0082. **EP:** VI EPA5072, VI
EPB1099, VI EPBT3029, RcaAu 20060, RcaE
RCX1033, RcaNZ RPX1358, VI 519-0010 (n/c). **LP:** VI
WPT3, VI LPT12, VI LPM1099, VI LOC1011 (n/c), VI
LSP4005(e), HMV DLP1112, HMV DLP1116, ViJap
RA69, VI VPM6040, VI CPLI-2470, VI ANLI-0973,
RcaE PL 12470, RcaE DHY0001, RcaFr 740.552,
RcaFr 741.084, RcaFr FXM3-7273, RcaFr PM45354,
RD 3-21, TL STLJ05, TL STBB03, Rca Cont 89323,
HIS M623, JO 3057. **ET:** AFRS Part 3-Station Library
"Show Biz" (n/c), AFRS Jam Session 22
Stompin' At The Savoy (arr ES)

BS 96569-2(1)   VI 25245 B, HMV B8427, ViArg 1A-0754, HMVAu
EA1721, ViJap JA836, ViJap A-1023, EIG EG3695,
HMVIt GW1386. **EP:** VI EPOT6703. **LP:** VI LPT6703,
ViArg AYL3000-5, RcaFr FXMI-7083, RcaFr
FXM3-7273, RcaG RD6, ViJap RA80, RD 3-21, TL
STLJ05, VI VPM6063
Goody-Goody - voc Helen Ward (arr HW)

BS 96570-1(2)   VI 25247 B, HMV B8427, HMVAu EA1721, ViJap JA716.
LP: VI LPM6702, RcaFr PM43173, RcaFr PM45354
Breakin' In A Pair Of Shoes (arr FH)

(Mxs BS 96567-1, BS 96568-1A, BS 96569-2 and BS 96570-1 are also on **LP:**
RcaBB AXM2-5515.)

SUSTAINING BROADCAST   February 3, 1936, Chicago
NBC Radio Network

Personnel as November 22, 1935.

Let's Dance (theme)
Dodging A Divorcee (arr SM)
The Day I Let You Get Away - voc Helen Ward
Sandman
Lights Out - voc Helen Ward
Alone - voc Helen Ward (arr SM)
Star Dust (SM arr still in use)
Eeny Meeny Miney Mo - voc Helen Ward
King Porter (Stomp)
Good-Bye (theme)

(Above on LP: SB 132)

SUSTAINING BROADCAST   February 10, 1936, Chicago
NBC Radio Network

Personnel as November 22, 1935.

"JAM DANDIES": BG, Kazebier, Harris, Clark, Stacy, Reuss, H. Goodman,
Krupa

Let's Dance (theme)
Remember
It's Great To Be In Love Again - voc Helen Ward (arr SM)
I'm Gonna Sit Right Down And Write Myself A Letter - JAM DANDIES
Troublesome Trumpet - voc Helen Ward
Alone - voc Helen Ward
Oh, Sweet Susannah - voc Helen Ward
Goody-Goody - voc Helen Ward (arr HW)
Transcontinental - to sign off

(Above on LP: SB 132.)

SUSTAINING BROADCAST   February 17, 1936, Chicago
NBC Radio Network

Personnel as November 22, 1935.

Lost - voc Helen Ward
Goody-Goody - voc Helen Ward
Star Dust (SM arr still in use)
Sandman
I Can't Give You Anything But Love, Baby - voc Helen Ward
Rosetta
You Hit The Spot - voc Helen Ward
Digga Digga Doo (arr SM)

(Above on LP: SB 130. Themes not known to exist.)

Earl Baker, whose 1926 Edison cylinders gave us our first Benny Goodman "air checks," also recorded bits and pieces of the Congress broadcasts. Ten years later he had graduated to a disc recorder, and one disc is extant. It contains fragments of: "Alexander's Ragtime Band," "I'm Shooting High," "Farewell Blues," "You Hit The Spot," "What's The Name Of That Song?", "Stompin' At The Savoy," "Sandman," "King Porter," "Rosetta" and "On the Alamo." They may well duplicate in part the same tunes on the SB LP's, but they are so brief and of such poor audio quality that it is impossible to match them.

GENE KRUPA'S SWING BAND   **February 29, 1936, Chicago**

Benny Goodman, clt; Roy Eldridge, tpt; Leon "Chu" Berry, ts; Jess Stacy, p; Allan Reuss, g; Israel Crosby, b; Gene Krupa, d; Helen Ward, voc.

BS 100012-1   VI 25276 A, ViJap JA717, ViJap A-1439, HMVAu
EA1702, HMV B8429, VSM SG555, BB 10705, BIA
231, BRS 1016. **EP:** HMV 7EG8111, RcaFr A75-492.
LP: CAM 340, RcaFr JPGH004, RD 3-25, RD 4A-005
I Hope Gabriel Likes My Music

BS 100013-1   VI 26263 B, HMVAu EA1685, HMV B8432, ViJap JA748,
ViJap A-1439. **EP:** HMV 7EG8111. **LP:** CAM 340, NM
0456
Mutiny In The Parlor - voc Helen Ward

BS 100014-1   VI 26263 A, HMVAu EA1685, HMV B8429, ViJap JA748,
ViJap A-1424. **EP:** HMV 7EG8111. **LP:** CAM 340
I'm Gonna Clap My Hands - voc Helen Ward

BS 100015-1   VI 25276 B, ViJap LM42 A, ViJap A-1424, ViCh 92-
0022, HMVAu EA1702, HMV B8432, VSM SG555, BB
10705, BIA 231, BRS 1016. **EP:** HMV 7EG8111, RcaFr
A75-492. **45:** VI 427-0137. **LP:** VI LPT26, VI WPT35,
HMV DLP1054, CAM 340, CAM 368, ViJap
RA5380-1/2, TL STLJ05
Swing Is Here

(Mxs BS 100012-1, BS 100013-1, BS 100014-1 and BS 100015-1 are also on
LP: RcaBB AXM2-5515, RcaAu VJL10382, VI LPV578, RcaFR 731.092,
RcaFR PM45354, RcaH NL42897.)

Pee Wee Erwin rejoined the band in the early months of 1936, replacing Ralph Muzzillo, but the precise date is not known. He believed he was present for the January 24 session, but the opinion here is that Muzzillo was then still in Benny's employ. In any event, let's enter him now, and at a significant time the first performance extant of ''Sing, Sing, Sing,'' with the most famous of all Goodman charts still developing, replete with Helen Ward's vocal:

SUSTAINING BROADCAST   *March 18, 1936, Chicago*
  CBS Radio Network

Personnel as November 22, 1935, except PEE WEE ERWIN, tpt, replaces Muzzillo.

Sing, Sing, Sing - voc Helen Ward (arr JM) - to station identification.

(LP: SB 105.)

BENNY GOODMAN AND HIS ORCHESTRA   March 20, 1936, Chicago

Benny Goodman, clt; Nate Kazebier, Harry Geller, Pee Wee Erwin, tpt; Red Ballard, Joe Harris, tbn; Hymie Schertzer, Bill DePew, as; Art Rollini, Dick Clark, ts; Jess Stacy, p; Allan Reuss, g; Harry Goodman, b; Gene Krupa, d.

BS 100057-1 (2,3)   VI 25279 B, BB 10461, ViArg 68-0181, HMVAu EA1725. **EP:** VI EPA5043, VI EPOT6703, RcaAu 20172, RcaE RCX1019, RcaNZ RPX1330. **LP:** VI LPT6703, ViArg AYL3000-5, ViJap RA69, RcaBB AXM2-5515, RcaBel 230.233, RcaFr 741.059, RcaFr PM45354, RcaAu VPL1-0471
Get Happy (arr SM)

BS 100058-1 (2,3)   VI 25279 A, BB 10460, HMV B8431, HMV J090, GrF K7751, ViArg 68-0181, HMVAu EA1725. **LP:** RD 25K, ViG LPM10022, ViJap RA69, RcaBB AXM2-5515, RcaFr 741.044, RcaFr PM45354, RcaAu VPL1-0471. **ET:** AFRS American Popular Music 390-Pt. 2
Christopher Columbus (HH/FH)

BS 100059-1 (2)   VI 25290 A, BB 10459, ViJap JA992. **LP:** VI LPM1239, VI VPM6040, VI DRL10062, RcaBB AXM2-5515, RcaFr 741.044, RcaFr PM45354
I Know That You Know (arr FH)

(Fletcher Henderson modified brother Horace's arrangement of ''Christopher Columbus'' for Benny's book.)

On Easter Sunday 1936 the band gave its third jazz concert in the Congress Hotel. This concert is of historic interest because it marks the first time a black musician played as a regular member of a white band before a ''live'' audience. He was, of course, Teddy Wilson, who came to Chicago from New York where he was house pianist at the ''Famous Door.'' He had been engaged to play in the concert, but he stayed on for Trio performances with Benny and Gene, and to play intermission piano between band sets in the Urban Room.

Integration of musicians today is commonplace, and has been for decades. But in 1936 it was taboo outside of recording studios and after-hours jam sessions. Not until Teddy joined the Goodman band at the Congress was a Negro a regular member of a white orchestra.

Benny's hiring Teddy was not in the interest of civil rights' ''cause,'' was not a studied attempt to break the color barrier. If any barriers were broken, they were sound barriers, the sounds produced by a clarinet, piano and drums playing in exquisite and empathetic harmony. Stated simply, Teddy's style fitted precisely with what Benny had in mind, and the pigment of his skin was of no moment. As Gene said, ''Teddy played perfectly for those Trio things. That's how we thought of him . . . as a damn' fine musician. We just never thought of him as being black.''

With Teddy in Chicago for the Easter concert, there seems no better time than now to introduce a hitherto undocumented recording session that is a major addition to the works of Benny Goodman:

John Hammond had been instrumental in bringing Teddy to Benny's attention, and in bringing about the reciprocal Goodman/Wilson—Victor/Brunswick recording sessions. But as a record contractor/producer himself, John knew that it was unlikely that accommodation would continue. Thus, fearing that Brunswick would not let its contract artist Teddy Wilson record again with Benny, John devised, contracted and produced a private studio date for the Trio. Probably in March/April 1936, he shepherded Benny, Teddy and Gene into the Grant Studio, 6006 Kenmore Avenue, Chicago, where they recorded:

BENNY GOODMAN TRIO   March/April 1936, Chicago

Benny Goodman, clt; Teddy Wilson, p; Gene Krupa, d.

''SQ-1''   UNISSUED — Test Acetate
''SQ-2''   UNISSUED — Test Acetate
     Squeeze Me

''L-1''   UNISSUED — Test Acetate
''L-2''   UNISSUED — Test Acetate
     Liza

''M-1''   UNISSUED — Test Acetate
''M-2''   UNISSUED — Test Acetate
     My Melancholy Baby

''IC-1''   UNISSUED — Test Acetate
     I'm Comin', Virginia

Faint rumors of this session had excited the author for many years; in conversations with him, Benny and Gene separately ''. . . seemed to remember something like that.'' But not until 1982 was its existence confirmed, when he was privileged to hear the discs. They are in a remarkable state of preservation (Hammond rarely played them, obviously stored them carefully), but unfortunately their labels reveal no date, order of recording, or printed or engraved matrix or take designations. Thus the assignments in the listing are arbitrary as to date and sequence of recording.

At first Hammond stipulated a date of ''. . . 1936, when the band went into the Congress for the **second** time.'' (His autobiography is unclear chronologically in this period.) Later he changed his dating to ''. . . just before the band went into the Congress,'' which would have been the first week of November, 1935. But Teddy was in New York then, and that time seems illogical. But it is admitted that the assignment here may be late by some five or six months.

In any event, unique recordings by the Benny Goodman Trio, almost half a century in concealment.

In March Benny Goodman and his Orchestra had begun its second sponsored radio series, this time for the Elgin Watch Company. The chronologically first extant air check from these programs has the band jamming ''Prairie Moon'' behind an announcer extolling the virtues of Elgin products. So—did Benny perpetrate the first ''swinging'' commercial?

''THE ELGIN REVUE''   *April 21, 1936, Chicago*
  NBC Radio Network

Personnel as March 20.

I've Found A New Baby (arr HH/FH) (LP: SB 105)
Prairie Moon (arr SM) (LP: SB 105)

(Note that like ''Christopher Columbus,'' Fletcher's arrangement is a modification of Horace's.)

There are several notes of interest applicable to the next studio session: This version of ''Remember'' was often used as the theme of the AFRS ''Jill's All Time Juke Box'' series of ET's—they are not enumerated here. ''Star Dust'' marks Victor's initial use of the ''Swing Classic'' label, although earlier recordings were repressed using this label. And ''Walk, Jennie, Walk'' may be the shortest commercially recorded BG side—1:52.

BENNY GOODMAN AND HIS ORCHESTRA   April 23, 1936, Chicago

Personnel as March 20.

BS 100379-2 (1)   VI 25320 A, HMV B8468, HMVAu EA1746, ElG EG3758, ViJap JA740, ViJap A-1442. **EP:** VI EPA5070, RcaNZ RPX1311. **LP:** VI LPM2246, Rca RDG1014, RD 3-76, RcaFr 741.059, RcaFr FXM3-7273, RcaFr PM45354, ViJap RA70
Star Dust (arr FH)

BS 100380-1 (2)   VI 25316 B, ViJap JA1100, HMV BD5090, ElG EG3689. **EP:** VI EPOT6703. **LP:** VI LPT6703, ViArg AYL3000-5
You Can't Pull The Wool Over My Eyes - voc Helen Ward (arr JM)

BS 100381-1   VI 25316 A, ViJap JA1100, HMVAu EA1730. **LP:** RD 3-76, JAZ 7
The Glory Of Love - voc Helen Ward (arr JM)
April 23, 1936, continued

April 23, 1936, continued

BS 100382-1   VI 25329 A, VI 25860, ViJap JA798, BB 10680, HMV
(2)   B8493, HMV B8810, HMVAu EA1761, GrF K8237, EIG
           EG6001, ViMex 75375. **LP:** VI LPM6702, RcaFr
           741.044, RcaFr PM45354, ViJap RA70. **ET:** many,
           AFRS Jill's Juke Box series
           Remember (arr FH)

BS 100383-1   VI 25329 B, ViJap JA798, BB 10799, HMV B8640,
(2)   HMVAu EA1761. **EP:** VI EPOT6703. **LP:** VI LPT6703,
           ViArg AYL3000-5, VI D14-B (demo), ViJap RA70,
           RcaFr 741.072, RcaAu VJL2-0425. **ET:** AFRS
           American Popular Music 390-Pt. 2
           Walk, Jennie, Walk (arr HH)

(Mxs BS 100379-2, BS 100380-1, BS 100381-1, BS 100382-1, BS 100383-1
are also on **LP:** RcaBB AXM2-5515.)

BENNY GOODMAN TRIO   **April 24, 1936, Chicago**

Benny Goodman, clt; Teddy Wilson, p; Gene Krupa, d.

BS 100395-1   VI 25333 A, HMV B8467, ViArg 68-0840, ViArg 1A-
(2)   0755, ViArg 1A-0181, ViJap JA752, ViJap A-1229,
           HMVAu EA1763, GrF K7752, EIG EG3759, HMVSw
           JK2074, HMVIt GW1321, VIMex 75375, ViJap 752 A.
           EP: VSM EMF72. **LP:** VI LPV521, VI LPV1032, RcaFr
           730.707, RcaFr FXM3-7273 RcaAu VPLI-0471.
           China Boy

BS 100396-1   VI 25345 B, ViJap JA770, BB 10723, HMV B8467,
(2)   HMVAu EA1774, ViArg 68-0841, EIG EG3759, HMVSw
           JK2074, HMVIt GW1321. **EP:** VI EPOT6703. **LP:** VI
           LPT6703, ViArg AYL3000-5, VI LPV521, VI LPV1032,
           VI VPM6063, RD 3-76, RcaFr 730.707
           More Than You Know

HELEN WARD WITH BENNY GOODMAN TRIO   **same session**

Same personnel, plus Helen Ward, voc.

BS 100397-1   VI 25324 B, ViJap JA750, ViJap A-1249. **LP:** VI LPV521,
           RcaFr 731.092
           All My Life - voc Helen Ward

(Mxs BS 100395-1, BS 100396-1 and BS 100397-1 are also on **LP:** RcaBB
AXM2-5515, ViJap 72A, RcaE RD7775, RcaFr PM43176.)

BENNY GOODMAN TRIO   **April 27, 1936, Chicago**
HELEN WARD WITH BENNY GOODMAN TRIO - BS 100502-1 only

Personnel as April 24.

BS 100500-1   VI 25333 B, VI 27-0119, VI 40-0107, VI 420-0151,
(2)   ViJap JA752, ViJap A-1229, HMV B8462, GrF K7752,
           ViArg 68-0841, ViArg 1A-0181, HMVAu EA1763, EIG
           EG3716. **45:** VI 27-0119, VI 447-0151. **EP:** VI
           EPA744, VI EPA5072, VI EPAT26, ViArg AGET5,
           RcaAu 20036, RcaE RCX1033, RcaF 85230, VSM
           EMF72, RcaNZ RPX1358. **LP:** VI LPT17, VI LPM1226,
           HMV DLPC11, RcaF LPM 1226, RcaF 430-230, VI
           LPV1009, RcaFr 730.629, RcaFr FXM3-7273, C/P
           25361, TL STLJ26. **ET:** OWI Outpost Concert Series
           No. 4 - Music Of The Jazz Bands No. 8, VOA Jam
           Session 23.
           Oh, Lady Be Good!

BS 100501-1   VI 25345 A, ViJap JA770, BB 10723, VI 27-0118, HMV
(2)   B8462, ViArg 68-0841, HMVAu EA1774, EIG EG3716,
           HMVIt GW1345. **45:** VI 27-0118. **EP:** RcaE RCX1064.
           LP: VI LPT17, VI LPM2247, HMV DLPC11, RcaAu L
           101039, VI LPV521, VI LPV1032, Rca RDG1014,
           RcaE RD7775, RcaFr 730.707
           Nobody's Sweetheart

BS 100502-1   VI 25324 A, ViJap JA750, ViJap A-1249, HMVSw
(2)   JK2301. **EP:** VI EPOT6703. **LP:** VI LPT6703, ViArg
           AYL3000-5, RcaFr 731.092
           Too Good To Be True - voc Helen Ward

(Mxs BS 100500-1, BS 100501-1 and BS 100502-1 are also on **LP:** RcaBB
AXM2 5515, RcaFr PM43176, ViJap RA72.)

"THE ELGIN REVUE"   *May 12, 1936, Chicago*
   NBC Radio Network

Personnel as March 20.

Let's Dance (theme)
House Hop
The Dixieland Band - voc Helen Ward
Farewell Blues
Let's Dance (closing theme)

(Above all on **LP:** SB 153)

The band had been booked into the Congress Hotel for one month—such
was its acceptance there that the stay had been extended to half a year. But
now the radio program, "The Elgin Revue," was shifted to New York, and
it thus became necessary for Benny to go there. Its last day at the Congress
was May 23; and curiously, that's the day Chris Griffin joined, replacing
Harry Geller.

     Glen Burrs, publisher of **Down Beat,** was high on trombonist Murray
McEachern, and recommended him to Benny. He joined the band in New
York, in time for:

"THE ELGIN REVUE"   *May 26, 1936, New York*
   NBC Radio Network

Benny Goodman, clt; Nate Kazebier, Pee Wee Erwin, CHRIS GRIFFIN, tpt; Red
Ballard, MURRAY McEACHERN, tbn; Hymie Schertzer, Bill DePew, as; Art
Rollini, Dick Clark, ts; Jess Stacy, p; Allan Reuss, g; Harry Goodman, b; Gene
Krupa, d; Helen Ward, voc.

Sing Me A Swing Song - voc Helen Ward (LP: AC 1)

BENNY GOODMAN AND HIS ORCHESTRA   **May 27, 1936, New York**

Personnel as May 26.

BS 101255-1   VI 25350 A, ASR L25531. **LP:** RcaBB AXM2-5515, RcaFr
           PM45354, JAZ 7
BS 101255-2   **LP:** VI LPT6703, ViArg AYL3000-5. **EP:** VI EPOT 6703
           House Hop (arr JM)

BS 101256-   UNISSUED
(1,2,3)   **These Foolish Things Remind Me Of You** - voc Helen
           Ward (arr JM)

BS 101257-1   VI 25340 B, BB 10462, HMV B8492. **LP:** VI LEJ5, ViG
(2)   LPM10022, RcaFr PM43173, RcaBB AXM2-5515
           Sing Me A Swing Song (And Let Me Dance) (arr JM) -
           voc Helen Ward

BS 101258-1   VI 25350 B, HMV B8764, ViJap 772 B, HMVInd N4474.
(2)   **EP:** VI EPOT6703. **LP:** VI LPT6703, ViArg AYL3000-5,
           RcaBB AXM2-5515, RcaFr 741.044, RcaFr PM45354
           (I Would Do) Anything For You (arr FH)

     The band had no permanent engagement at this time, kept busy playing
one-nighters in and around New York, and with its radio program and
recording sessions:

BENNY GOODMAN AND HIS ORCHESTRA   **June 15, 1936, New York**

Personnel as May 26.

BS 102214-2   VI 25351 A, HMV B8493. **LP:** RcaFr 741.084, JAZ 17
(1)   **In A Sentimental Mood** (arr JM)

BS 102215-1   VI 25355 A, VI 20-2407, HMV B8481, HMVAu EA1780,
(2)   ASR L25355. **EP:** VI EPB1005. **LP:** VI LPT1005, RD
           3-76, RcaFr 741.072, RcaFr FXM3-7273, RcaFr
           PM45354, JAZ 17. **ET:** AFRS American Popular Music
           390-Pt. 2, AFRS P-865, AFRS Jill's Juke Box H-46
           I've Found A New Baby (arr HH/FH)

BS 102216-1   UNISSUED
My Melancholy Baby (arr FH)

BS 102217-1   VI 25355 B, HMV B8481, HMVAu EA1780, ASR L25355.
(2)   **EP:** VI EPBT3056, HMV 7EG8142. **LP:** VI LPM1239,
VI LPT3056, ViArg AVLT3, ViJap RA70, RD 3-76, VI
DRLI-0062, RcaFr 741.084, RcaFr PM45354, HIS
H623, JO 3057, TL STBB03, C/P 25231. **ET:** VOA
Jam Session 22
Swingtime In The Rockies (arr JM)

BS 101256-4   VI 25351 B, VI 20-1557, HMV B8523, HMV J0261, EIG
EG3894. **EP:** VI EPBT3023. **LP:** VI LPT13, VI
VPM6040, RD "The Great Band Era," RcaFr 741.084,
SWE 1001, TL STBB03. **ET:** AFRS Jill's Juke Box 199
These Foolish Things Remind Me Of You - voc Helen
Ward (arr JM)

(Mxs BS 102214-2, BS 102215-1, BS 102217-1 and BS 101256-4 are also on
LP: RcaBB AXM2-5515.)

BENNY GOODMAN AND HIS ORCHESTRA   June 16, 1936, New York

Personnel as May 27.

BS 101255-3   VI 25350 A, ViJap 772 A, HMV B8569, GrF K8300. **EP:**
VSM EMF73. **LP:** RcaBB AXM2-5515, RcaFr 741.084,
JAZ 7
House Hop (arr JM)

BS 102066-X-1   VI 25363 A, HMV B8542, AFR 10-30/AFR-50. **EP:** VI
EPOT6703. **LP:** VI LPT6703, ViJap RA70, ViArg
AYL3000-5, CAM 872, C/P 7055, RD3-76, Rca E
1021, RcaFr 741.084, RcaBB AXM2-5515.
There's A Small Hotel (arr JM) - voc Helen Ward

The June 16 session obviously was a re-make date to cut those Jimmy Mundy arrangements satisfactorily. (The "X" that follows mx BS 102066 was a device Victor employed to denote re-recordings.) Unfortunately, Victor's files do not reveal an earlier BG recording of "There's A Small Hotel." This suggests that perhaps an entire Goodman session took place, but is missing from the files.

In late June the band entrained for Hollywood where it was to film its first motion picture, Paramount's "The Big Broadcast Of 1937." The band was on the West Coast on Tuesday, June 30, when it appeared on the initial broadcast of its third sponsored radio show —and the greatest of them all— CBS's "Camel Caravan." Aired by the R. J. Reynolds Tobacco Co., the "Caravan" began as an hour program, which Benny split with one of his old bosses, Nat Shilkret. Eventually the program was cut to one-half hour, and Benny had that all to himself.

This memorable series featured Benny Goodman to the end of 1939. In the jargon of the show, Professor Goodman blew through the "Swing School's" format to give everyone lessons in what jazz was all about. The curriculum consisted of a musical education taught by the Goodman faculty and guest lecturers—the BG band and invited jazzmen. Some of the best efforts of Benny Goodman and his Orchestra ever recorded come from these broadcasts, as air checks indicate. This was the Big Band Era, and great times of its enthusiasts. Tuesday nights were sacrosanct: THE band was on the air!

Collectors have audio- and video-taped almost all Benny's movies. Here is a rundown of the soundtrack of "The Big Broadcast Of 1937":

"THE BIG   *July/August, 1936, Hollywood*
 BROADCAST OF 1937"

A Paramount picture filmed in black-and-white
Release date: October 9, 1936   *Running time: 100 minutes*
Director: Mitchell Leisen   *Musical Director: Boris Morros*
Songs by Leo Robin and Ralph Rainger
Cast: Jack Benny, George Burns and Gracie Allen, Shirley Ross, Ray Milland,
Bob Burns, Martha Raye, Benny Fields, Frank Forrest, Sam Hearn, Larry
Adler, Leopold Stokowski and his Symphony Orchestra, and

BENNY GOODMAN AND HIS ORCHESTRA

Benny Goodman, clt; Nate Kazebier and/or Mannie Klein, Pee Wee Erwin,
Chris Griffin, tpt; Red Ballard, Murray McEachern, tbn; Hymie Schertzer, Bill

DePew, as; Art Rollini, Dick Clark, ts; Jess Stacy, p; Allan Reuss, g; Harry
Goodman, b; Gene Krupa, d.

Opening title music - Benny Goodman Orchestra, studio orchestra
(Hi Ho The Radio-unknown voc qtte with studio orchestra
(La Bomba-voc Frank Forrest with studio orchestra
(You Came To My Rescue - voc Shirley Ross & Frank Forrest, studio orch.
Intro to: Your Minstrel Man - voc fem trio, Benny Goodman Orchestra
(Here's Love In Your Eyes - voc Benny Fields, studio orchestra.
Here's Love In Your Eyes - Benny Goodman, clt, with studio orch. -
    harmonica solo, Larry Adler
Bugle Call Rag (arr JM) - Benny Goodman Orchestra (LP: EX 1002)
(I'm Talking Through My Heart - voc Shirley Ross, studio orchestra
(Fugue In G-Minor (Bach) - Leopold Stokowski and his Symphony Orch.
Vote For Mr. Rhythm - voc Martha Raye, poss. some members of BG
    Orch.
Cross Patch (background to dialogue) - Benny Goodman Orchestra
Here Comes The Bride - voc Martha Raye, Benny Goodman Orchestra
(Closing music - reprise of Here's Love In Your Eyes - studio orch.

One of the rarest of all Goodman recordings—only one copy is known—is a 16″ ET, one side only, 33⅓ rpm, issued by Paramount for radio promotion. It was pressed by RCA-Victor mid-October 1936, and bears a Victor matrix. On it are excerpts of dialogue by George Burns and Gracie Allen, Jack Benny, Bob Burns, et al; a song by Frank Forrest; and four partial cuts by Benny Goodman and his Orchestra.

There are differences between the ET and the film soundtrack. Martha Raye sings "You Came To My Rescue" with the BG band on the ET, but Shirley Ross does it in the film with a studio orchestra. Benny Fields does "Night In Manhattan" with the BG band, augmented by strings, on the ET; this tune is completely missing in the film.

It is not thought that the ET was recorded separately from the film. A more likely explanation is that it is a composite of "out takes," scenes cut from the film's final edition.

THE BIG BROADCAST OF 1937   July/August, 1936, Hollywood

Benny Goodman and his Orchestra - personnel as for the film, preceding

PMS 02100   You Came To My Rescue - voc Martha Raye (partial).
Here's Love In Your Eyes (partial) (arr JM)
Night In Manhattan - voc Benny Fields (partial)
Bugle Call Rag (arr JM) (partial)

Two mysterious circumstances crop up on the band's next regular studio session that are unresolved to this date:

The first is the disappearance of Jess Stacy's piano one-third through "Here's Love In Your Eyes," the second tune cut this session. Jess can be heard throughout the first tune recorded, "You Turned The Tables On Me"; but he just stops during the second, and is heard no more the balance of the date. The arrangement of "Here's Love In Your Eyes" seems to demand a vocal, but there is none. One gets the impression that Helen was late in coming in for the vocal, Jess began to ad lib thinking the recording would be aborted, and quit—but the band played on. But there is no plausible guess as to his absence on the final two tunes.

The second oddity is a two-sided, 78 rpm, 10″ shellac pressing, bearing Victor matrices PBS 97716 and PBS 97717, with a typewritten label on each side. The labels identify the tunes—PBS 97716-1, "Here's Love In Your Eye," and PBS 97717-1, "Night In Manhattan"—and the composers (Robin and Rainger), vocalist (Benny Fields), source (The Big Broadcast Of 1937), musical director (Boris Morros), and the orchestra (Benny Goodman). Benny's band is augmented by strings; and a piano is audible, but doesn't sound like Jess Stacy's.

Unquestionably, the disc stems from the movie; whether it was intended to be a complementary promotional item to the ET cited earlier is conjectural; it may have been a "vanity," or personal pressing, for Benny Fields. In any event the disc is a rarity—like the ET, only one copy is known.

Its matrices leave a gap of only two numbers from the last matrix certain to have been cut by BG on August 13, PBS 97713. That fact, and the non-appearance of Jess Stacy on this unique issue, suggest it may have been recorded August 13, also. (Neither tune is excerpted from the film soundtrack.) But this assumption is not provable, so the disc is listed separately.

BENNY GOODMAN　　　　　　　　　　**August 13, 1936, Hollywood**
AND HIS ORCHESTRA

Personnel as "The Big Broadcast Of 1937," with Mannie Klein, tpt, definite, Kazebier out.

PBS 97710-1　VI 25391 A, ViJap JA818, HMV B8516, HMVAu EA1790.
(2)　　　　　**EP:** VI EPOT6703. **LP:** VI LPT6703, ViArg AYL3000-5,
　　　　　　VI VPM6040, RD 3-76, ViJap RA80, RcaE DHY0001,
　　　　　　RcaFR 741.059, RcaBB AXM2-5532, TL STBB03
　　　　　　You Turned The Tables On Me - voc Helen Ward (arr FH)

PBS 97711-1　VI 25391 B, ViJap JA818, HMV BD5146, HMVAu
(2)　　　　　EA1815. **LP:** RcaBB AXM2-5532, RcaFr FXMI-7083,
　　　　　　JAZ 18
　　　　　　Here's Love In Your Eyes (arr JM)

PBS 97712-1　VI 25387 A, HMV B8492, HMVAu EA1815, HmVInd
(2)　　　　　NE734. **LP:** ViG LPM10025, RcaBB AXM2-5532, RcaFr
　　　　　　741.102, RcaFr PM45354, HIS H623, JO 3057
　　　　　　Pick Yourself Up (arr JM)

PBS 97713-1　VI 25387 A, ViArg 1A-0758, HMV POP166, HMVFin
　　　　　　TG265, HMVInd NE734. **45:** HMV 7M380, MPS
　　　　　　88.032-2. **EP:** VI EPB1099, RcaBel 85.508, RcaFr
　　　　　　A75307. **LP:** VI LPM1099, HMV DLP1112, HMV
　　　　　　DLP1116, VI VPM6040, RD 3-76, ViJap RA70, RcaFr
　　　　　　741.044, RcaFr PM45354, Rcalt LPM10043, RcaBB
　　　　　　AXM2-5532
　　　　　　Down South Camp Meeting (arr FH)

(Jimmy Mundy claims he arranged "You Turned The Tables On Me," but available evidence indicates it was Fletcher Henderson's chart.)

BENNY GOODMAN　　　　　　　　　　**mid-August 1936, Hollywood**
AND HIS ORCHESTRA

Personnel as August 13, plus strings, "audience," and possibly a substitute for Stacy, p.

PBS 97716-1　- no catalog number
　　　　　　Here's Love In Your Eye - voc Benny Fields

PBS 97717-1　- no catalog number
　　　　　　Night In Manhattan - voc Benny Fields

(Note that VI 25391 B is titled, "Here's Love In Your Eyes," whereas PBS 97716 is a one-eyed version.)

While filming their first motion picture, Benny and the band doubled into the Palomar, this time for triple the price they'd commanded the first time around. Were they worth it? A contemporary music/news magazine reported, "In the meantime, Benny Goodman is continuing the greatest attraction that ever played the Palomar." And it took special notice of a newcomer: "Teddy Wilson, colored pianist, has been making informal appearances as guest star with Benny's organization. This is probably the first time in Los Angeles band history that a colored musician has appeared in a white band."

Nate Kazebier was in the band when it opened at the Palomar on Wednesday, July 1, and appears on screen in "The Big Broadcast Of 1937." But while the movie was in production, he and Benny parted company abruptly; ever-reliable Mannie Klein, working regularly as a studio musician in Hollywood, took his place. It can be assumed that Klein cut some of the film's sound track, but he does not appear in the picture.

Kazebier's sudden departure has a comic aftermath. Some promotional photographs of the band, with Kazebier in them, had been taken for the movie. But more were needed; and the photographer was on hand the day Kazebier left. Where could they get a "tall, thin guy" to appear as a third trumpeter? Nothing daunted, Benny had brother Gene try on Kazebier's band uniform: "It fit perfectly," recalls Gene, "for in those days we were both thin and about the same height." The photos were taken, and forevermore Gene appears in front of brother Harry, with trumpet in hand—although he never played the instrument. The photo is in wide circulation, and is on the front cover of Volume III of Frank Driggs's reissue series, RcaBB AXM2-5532.

Sterling Bose could play trumpet, and very well indeed; and likely it is Bose who is the third trumpeter in the first example extant of Benny's new radio program, the "Camel Caravan." By this time, too, Vido Musso had replaced Dick Clark, for Vido is identifiable on the air check.

"CAMEL CARAVAN"　　　　　　　*August 18, 1936, Los Angeles*
　CBS Radio Network

Benny Goodman, clt; Pee Wee Erwin, Chris Griffin, STERLING BOSE, tpt; Red Ballard, Murray McEachern, tbn; Hymie Schertzer, Bill DePew, as; Art Rollini, VIDO MUSSO, ts; Jess Stacy, p; Allan Reuss, g; Harry Goodman, b; Gene Krupa, d; Helen Ward, voc.

Sugar Foot Stomp (arr FH) - to signoff (LP: RAD 19, SB 149)

We state positively that "Musso had replaced Dick Clark," although Victor's recording sheets for the upcoming August 21 studio session list Clark as a participant. (Trade papers of the time depicted Clark's leaving as "inexplicable," "sudden," "puzzling." Clark maintains that he wanted to stay on the West Coast and get into lucrative studio work. Gene Krupa believed that Benny and Clark were at odds, and that Benny had found a more exciting soloist in Musso.) It may be that Clark played the section work for the recording session—Musso did not read well—but without question the tenor solo on "Love Me Or Leave Me" is Vido's.

The August 21 Victor date also introduces the Benny Goodman Quartet. Lionel Hampton was then playing at the Paradise Club, John Hammond induced Benny to visit the club to hear Lionel . . . and in a tale too well known to be recounted here, Benny, Lionel and Gene played together for the first time, and Lionel was engaged for the studio session. It should be noted that, like Teddy, Lionel at this time was an "informal" member of the Goodman Gang. He will not join until November 10 as a regular member, at the Hotel Pennsylvania in New York.

BENNY GOODMAN　　　　　　　　　　**August 21, 1936, Hollywood**
AND HIS ORCHESTRA

Personnel as August 18, except possibly add Dick Clark, ts.

PBS 97748-1　VI 25411 A, HMV B8504, ViArg 68-0839, EIG EG6071,
(2)　　　　　ViJap A-1140, ViJap JA835, HMVSw JK2213. **EP:** VI
　　　　　　EPA 5092. **LP:** VI LPM1714, ViJap RA70, RcaFr
　　　　　　741.102, RcaFr FXM3-7273
　　　　　　St. Louis Blues (arr FH)

PBS 97749　never cut

PBS 97750-1　VI 25406 A, HMV B8504, EIG EG6071, HMVIt GW1519,
(2)　　　　　ViJap JA 822, **LP:** ViG LPM10022, RcaFr 741.102
　　　　　　Love Me Or Leave Me (arr FH)

PBS 97751-2　**LP:** ViG LPM10022, RcaFr 741.044
(1)　　　　　**Bugle Call Rag** (arr JM)

(Mxs PBS 97748-1, PBS 97750-1 and PBS 97751-2 are also on **LP:** RcaBB AXM2-5532, RcaFr PM45354. ViG LPM10022's liner notes erroneously list take 2 for "Love Me Or Leave Me.")

BENNY GOODMAN QUARTET　　　　　　　　　　**same session**

Benny Goodman, clt; LIONEL HAMPTON, vib; Teddy Wilson, p; Gene Krupa, d.

PBS 97752-1　VI 25398 A, ViJap JA821, ViJap A-1162, HMV B8568,
　　　　　　HMV J0229, ViArg 68-0153, ViArg 68-0915, HMVAu
　　　　　　EA1802, EIG EG3998, HMVFin TG267. **EP:** VI
　　　　　　EPAT406, VI EPB1099, HMV 7EG8003, RcaBel
　　　　　　85.507. **LP:** VI LPM1099, VI LPV1009, VI VPM6040,
　　　　　　ViJap RA72, TL STLJ05, RcaBB AXM2-5532, RcaFr
　　　　　　730.629, RcaFr FXM3-7273, JR 5036

PBS 97752-2　**LP:** FR series
　　　　　　Moon Glow

The reciprocal Victor-Goodman/Brunswick-Wilson deal was still in place, so Benny and his bandsmen once again recorded with Teddy. Note that on this August 24 session matrices LA 1160-A "You Turned The Tables On Me," and LA 1161-A, "Sing, Baby, Sing," both issued on BR 7736 et al, were also cut—but without Benny, who left the studio after satisfactory takes of matrices LA 1158 and LA 1159 had been waxed.

TEDDY WILSON AND HIS ORCHESTRA August 24, 1936, Hollywood

Benny Goodman, clt; Chris Griffin, tpt; Vido Musso, ts; Lionel Hampton, vib; Teddy Wilson, p; Allan Reuss, g; Harry Goodman, b; Gene Krupa, d; Helen Ward, voc.

LA 1158-A BR 7739, RZAu G22972, VoE S41, BrF 500679, DeSw M30389. **LP:** SONY 20AP1839, NOST 890/1
You Came To My Rescue - voc Vera Lane (Helen Ward)

LA 1159-A same 78 issues, plus Brlt 5063. **LP:** CBS 66274, SONY SONP-50332-3, SONY SOPW-9-10
Here's Love In Your Eye - voc Vera Lane (Helen Ward)

The bouncing Victor-Brunswick ball was once again in Benny's court, so back to the studios for a Trio/Quartet session. Note that "Exactly Like You" is by the Trio; Lionel sings, but does not play vibes.

BENNY GOODMAN QUARTET August 26, 1936, Hollywood

Personnel as Quartet, August 21.

PBS 97772-1 VI 25398 B, VI 40-0108, HMV B8503, HMVAu EA1802,
(2) GrFr K8085, ViJap DC13, ViJap A-1425. **EP:** VI EPB1226, VI EPBT3004, HMV 7EG8154. **LP:** VI LPM1226, VI LPT3004, VI LPV1009, HMV DLPC6, RcaFr 430.230, RcaFr LPM1226, RcaFr 730.629, RcaFr FXM3-7273, C/P 25361, RcaAu VPL1-0471 **ET:** 1955 Heart Fund (n/c).
Dinah

BENNY GOODMAN TRIO same session

As Quartet, but omit vibes. Lionel Hampton, voc.

PBS 97773-1 VI 25406 B, HMV B8503, HMVInd N4490, ViJap JA822,
(2) **LP:** VI LPV521, VI LPV1009, RcaE RD7775, RcaFr 730.629
Exactly Like You - voc Lionell (sic) Hampton

BENNY GOODMAN QUARTET same session

Personnel as Quartet, August 21. Lionel Hampton, voc.

PBS 97774-1 VI 25521 B, VI 40-0108, HMV B8563, HMV J0228,
(2) HMVAu EA1897, GrFr K8301, ViJap JA919, ViJap A-1160. **EP:** RcaE RCX1065, RcaFr A75605. **LP:** VI LPM2247, VI LPV521, VI LPV1032, TL STLJ05, RCA RDG1014, RcaAu L101039, RcaE RD7775, RcaFr 730.707
Vibraphone Blues - voc Lionel Hampton

(Mxs PBS 97772-1, PBS 97773-1 and PBS 97774-1 are also on **LP:** RcaBB AXM2-5532, RcaE RD7775, RcaFr PM43176, ViJap RA72.)

("Remember," an air check speculatively assigned earlier to "August 1936," is now correctly assigned to a broadcast of December 2, 1936, q.v.)

Pee Wee Erwin also elected to stay in California when "The Big Broadcast of 1937" was wrapped up and the band headed East. Joe Haymes's band (which a year earlier had been taken over in toto by Tommy Dorsey) supplied his replacement, Zeke Zarchey, as earlier in 1936 it had contributed Chris Griffin to Benny. Joe Haymes, provisioner to the stars. . .

Benny's portion of the "Camel Caravan" at this time was invariably broadcast from a CBS studio, not a location. Thus the air check following in all likelihood originated from New York, although the band was playing in the Steel Pier, Atlantic City, New Jersey. The Steel Pier engagement was further recognition of the rising popularity of the band—the Pier's management awarded its two choice holiday dates, the Fourth of July and Labor Day weekend, to that band then highest in the public's esteem.

"CAMEL CARAVAN" September 1, 1936, prob. New York
CBS Radio Network

Personnel as August 18, except ZEKE ZARCHEY, tpt, replaces Erwin.

Sing, Baby, Sing - voc Helen Ward (LP: SB 149, IAJRC 21.)

Sterling Bose was ailing, and during the Steel Pier stint Ziggy Elman (Harry Finkelman), a trumpeter in Alex Bartha's "house" band, filled in for him. When Benny left the Pier, he asked Ziggy to come with him as Bose's replacement. One tale of Ziggy's joining has Benny inquiring if he played

lead trumpet? "Not usually," Ziggy replied. "How well do you read?" "Not too good," Ziggy admitted. "Well, what do you do?" "I play the jazz," Ziggy answered firmly. And he did.

On September 10 the band began a two-week stand at the Ritz-Carlton Hotel, Boston. CBS broadcast it regularly from that location, and an amateur recordist in Philadelphia cut a number of incomplete acetates from the sustaining programs. A careful review of those air checks has added to, and revised, those previously noted, beginning with:

SUSTAINING BROADCAST September 16, 1936,
CBS Radio Network Ritz-Carlton, Boston

Benny Goodman, clt; Chris Griffin, ZIGGY ELMAN, Zeke Zarchey, tpt; Red Ballard, Murray McEachern, tbn; Hymie Schertzer, Bill DePew, as; Art Rollini, Vido Musso, ts; Jess Stacy, p; Allan Reuss, g; Harry Goodman, b; Gene Krupa, d; Helen Ward, voc.

Alexander's Ragtime Band (arr FH) (n/c)
You're Not The Kind - voc Helen Ward (n/c)
When Did You Leave Heaven? (n/c)
When Buddha Smiles (n/c)
Peter Piper (arr JM) (n/c)

SUSTAINING BROADCAST September 18, 1936
CBS Radio Network Ritz-Carlton, Boston

Personnel as September 16.

In A Sentimental Mood (n/c)
Riffin' At The Ritz (arr WM) (n/c)
Sometimes I'm Happy (n/c)
Sing, Sing, Sing - voc Helen Ward - to signoff

According to dialog on the September 29 "Camel Caravan" program, Bill Miller brought an untitled composition to Benny at the Ritz-Carlton. Benny had the boys run through it, liked it, and wondered what to call it. Listening to the audition, Helen Ward suggested: "Riffin' At The Ritz."

"CAMEL CARAVAN" September 22, 1936, Boston
CBS Radio Network

Personnel as September 16. TRIO: BG, Wilson, Krupa.

Walk, Jennie, Walk
Tiger Rag - TRIO (n/c)

SUSTAINING BROADCAST September 23, 1936,
CBS Radio Network Ritz-Carlton, Boston

Personnel as September 16.

Let's Dance (theme)
Sugar Foot Stomp
You Turned The Tables On Me - voc Helen Ward (n/c)

Leaving the Ritz-Carlton, the band went to New York prior to its October 1 opening in the Hotel Pennsylvania for its next weekly "Camel Caravan" broadcast:

"CAMEL CARAVAN" September 29, 1936, New York
CBS Radio Network

Personnel as September 16.

Star Dust (arr FH)
Riffin' At the Ritz (n/c)
Sing, Sing, Sing - voc Helen Ward (n/c)

BENNY GOODMAN AND HIS ORCHESTRA October 7, 1936, New York

Personnel as September 16.

BS 0798-1(2) VI 25434 B, HMV B8516, HMVAu EA1818, ViJap JA838.
LP: CAM 624, CamE 148
When A Lady Meets A Gentleman Down South - voc Helen Ward (arr JM)

BS 0799-1(2) VI 25434 A, HMV BD5152, HMVAu EA1821, ViJap JA838. **LP:** RcaFr PM43173, JAZ 19
You're Giving Me A Song And A Dance - voc Helen Ward (arr JM)

October 7, 1936, continued

October 7, 1936, continued

BS 02101-1(2) VI 25442 A, HMVAu EA1821, ViJap JA884. **EP:** VI
EPOT6703. **LP:** VI LPT6703, ViArg AYL3000-5, RcaFr
741.084, RcaFr PM45354, VI VPM6063
Organ Grinder's Swing (arr prob. JM)

BS 02102-1 same issues, except omit both RcaFr LP's
Peter Piper - voc Helen Ward (arr JM)

BS 02103-1 VI 25445 B, VI 420-0149, HMV B8640, ViArg 68-0174,
HMVAu EA1871, HMVIt AV715, ViJap JA867. **45:** 447-
0149. **EP:** VI EPA5004, VI EPB1239, VI EPBT3056,
RcaAu 20060, RcaE RCX1009, JUG 9061. **LP:** VI
LPT3056, VI LPM1239, ViArg AVLT3, VI DRLI-0062,
RcaFr 741.102, RcaFr PM45354, C/P 25231
Riffin' At The Ritz (arr WM)

BS 02104-1 VI 25445 A, HMV B8734, ViArg 25996, ViArg 68-0174,
ViJap JA867, ViJap A-1026, HMVAu EA1871, GrFr
K8179, HMVSw JK2214, HMVIt AV715, HMVFin
TG302. **45:** VI 47-2954. **EP:** VI EPOT6703. **LP:** VI
LPT6703, ViArg AYL3000-5, RcaFr 741.072, RcaFr
FXM3-7273, VI VPM6063
Alexander's Ragtime Band (arr FH)

(All issued matrices & takes above are also on **LP:** RcaBB AXM2-5532. Note
that mxs BS 0799 and BS 02101 are consecutive, and that Benny plays alto,
not clarinet, on "Riffin' At The Ritz.")

Next, the first air checks from Benny's initial stand at the Madhattan
Room of the Hotel Pennsylvania, the beginning of a series of storied engagements. Note that this listing correctly assigns "Picture Me Without You"
(mistaken for "You Forgot To Remember") to this date instead of September 23, and "Blue Skies" to this broadcast, not that of October 17.

SUSTAINING BROADCAST   *October 9, 1936, Hotel*
  CBS Radio Network   *Pennsylvania, New York*

Personnel as September 16.

Let's Dance (theme)
Alexander's Ragtime Band (n/c)
Picture Me Without You (n/c)
Blue Skies (n/c)

"CAMEL CARAVAN"   *October 13, 1936, New York*
  CBS Radio Network

Personnel as September 16.

Blue Skies
Organ Grinder's Swing
When A Lady Meets A Gentleman Down South - voc Helen Ward
Jam Session - to signoff

SUSTAINING BROADCAST   *October 21, 1936, Hotel*
  CBS Radio Network   *Pennsylvania, New York*

Personnel as September 16.

You're Giving Me A Song And A Dance - voc Helen Ward (n/c)

"CAMEL CARAVAN"   *October 27, 1936, New York*
  CBS Radio Network

Personnel as September 16.

Jam Session (LP: SB 149)

Teddy Wilson played between band sets as intermission pianist (Benny's term: "featured artist!"), as well as with the Trio, during this initial
engagement at the Hotel Pennsylvania, a subterfuge to "explain" a black
man's playing with a white band. He continued to do so into 1937, when the
author first saw the band in the Madhattan Room; and so far as he could tell,
the black/white issue meant absolutely nothing to anyone in the audience.

Helen Ward took a three-week "vacation" beginning October 24—she
was in the process of getting a divorce. Margaret McRae substituted for her.
But with a recording session scheduled during Helen's absence, Benny
seized the opportunity to bring in as vocalist Ella Fitzgerald—still today his
favorite gal singer—from Chick Webb's band, and to put his own voice on
record for the very first time for which he received label credit.

BENNY GOODMAN AND HIS ORCHESTRA   November 5, 1936, New York

Personnel as September 16. Ella Fitzgerald, Benny Goodman, voc.

BS 02458-1(2) VI 25497 A, ViJap JA1044, ViJap A-1142. **EP:** VI
EPOT6703, RcaBel 85.509. **LP:** VI LPT6703, ViArg
AYL3000-5, RcaBB AXM2-5532, ViJap RA70, RcaFr
741.059, RcaFr FXM3-7273, RcaFr PM45354
Somebody Loves Me (arr FH)

BS 02459-1(2) VI 25469 A, VI 25461 B, HMV B8535, HMVAu EA1842.
EP: VI EPOT6703. **LP:** VI LPT6703, ViArg AYL3000-5,
RcaBB AXM2-5532, RcaFr PM43173, RcaFr PM45727
'Taint No Use - voc " 'Apologetically' sung by Benny
Goodman"

BS 02460-1(2) VI 25467 A, VD 38 A, NavyVD 154, ViJap JA926, ViJap
A-1140, HMV B8569, ViArg 68-1384, ViArg 1A-0757,
ViArg 1A-0298, HMVAu EA1841, GrFr K8300, HMVSw
JK2213. **EP:** VI EPA664, VI EPA5042, RcaAu 20172,
RcaBel 85.506, RcaE RCX1026, VSM EMF73, RcaNZ
RPX1352. **LP:** VI LPM1099, ViJap RA70, RcaBB
AXM2-5532, HMV DLP1112, HMV DLP1116, RcaFr
741.102, RcaFr FXM3-7273, RcaFr PM45354, RcaFr
PM45727, RcaAu 50. **ET:** AFRS G.I. Jive 847, AFRS
Jill's All Time Juke Box H46-4, AFRS G.I. Jive
H12-449/50
Bugle Call Rag (arr JM)

BS 02461-1(2) VI 25497 B, HMV B8719, ViArg 1A-0759, HMVAu
EA1903, ViJap JA1049, ViJap A-1142, **EP:** VI
EPOT6703. **LP:** VI LPT6703, ViArg AYL3000-5, ViJap
RA70, MPS 52.026, RcaBB AXM2-5532, RcaFr
741.084, RcaFr PM45727, VI LPM6063
Jam Session (arr JM)

BS 02462 not a Goodman matrix

BS 02463-1(2) VI 25461 A, HMV B8542, ViArg 68-1539, ViArg 1A-
0544, ViJap JA1180, ViJap A-1179. **EP:** VI EPA5100,
RcaAu 20251, RcaE RCX1059, RcaNZ RPX1375. **LP:**
CAM 872, VI LPM2247, VI LSP4005(e), VI VPM6040,
VI CPLI-2470, VI ANLI-0973, ViJap RA79, RD RDA49,
RD LOP1509, Rca RDG1014, RcaE PL12470, RcaFr
731.041, RcaFr 740.552, RcaAu L101039, RcaFr
PM45727, RcaCont 89323, VI LOP1509, VI PRS356,
C/P 7055
Goodnight My Love - voc refrain (Ella Fitzgerald)

BS 02464-1(2) same 78 issues, except substitute HMV B8564 for HMV
B8542. **EP:** same issues. **LP:** VI LPM2247, VI
LSP4005(e), RcaAu L101039, ViJap RA79, RcaBB
AXM2-5532, RcaFr 731.041, RcaFR FXM3-7273,
RcaFr PM45727
Take Another Guess - voc refrain (Ella Fitzgerald) (arr
JM)

BS 02465-1 VI 25469 B, HMV B8535, HMVAu EA1842. **EP:** VI
EPA5100, RcaAu 20251, RcaE RCX1059, RcaNZ
RPX1375. **LP:** CAM 872, VI LPM2247, ViJap RA79,
RcaBB AXM2-5532, Rca RDG1014, RcaAu L101039,
RcaE 1021, RcaFr 731.041, RcaFr PM45727, TL
STBB03, RcaAu VJL2-0337, C/P 7055
Did You Mean It? - voc refrain (Ella Fitzgerald) (arr JM)

Ella was under contract to Decca, and its executives protested vehe-
mently when "Did You Mean It?" was put on the market November 25.
They demanded withdrawal of all of her vocals, and eventually Victor
recalled them. ("Did You Mean It?" was deleted from Victor's catalog on
January 20, 1937.) But then Victor engaged in some slick sleight-of-hand, to
the utter confusion of collectors ever since:

The original issue of VI 25461 A is BS 02463-1/"Goodnight My
Love," coupled with VI 25461 B BS 02464-1/"Take Another Guess." The
original issue of VI 25469 A is BS 02459-1/" 'Taint No Use," backed by VI
25469 B BS 02465-1/"Did You Mean It?"

Catalog number 25461 was then re-used. The second release couples

BS 04235-1/"Goodnight My Love," vocal by Frances Hunt (recorded January 14, 1937) with the original VI 25469's B side, "'Taint No Use."

But evidently during the re-pressing of VI 25461 "Goodnight My Love"/"'Taint No Use" someone pulled Ella's original version off the shelf, fed it to the presses, and a third copy of VI 25461 was made available.

Think this can't happen honestly? Check RcaBB AXM2-5532's track of "Goodnight My Love"—that's Frances Hunt, not Ella, as the liner notes contend, and as the producer certainly intended. (A later pressing corrected this error.)

Until the reissues of the BG-Ella sides in the 1960's, the original Victor's were collectors' prizes; and they still are, to the enthusiast who insists on first editions, not copies. But the reissues have had a curious effect: now it's the Frances Hunt vocal version of "Goodnight My Love" that's become harder to find. Which proves inherent value and rarity can be two different things.

Benny took further advantage of Helen's absence; he featured Ella on the "Camel Caravan" broadcast of November 10, singing Helen's own, "You Turned The Tables On Me." (Enough of that, said Helen; she was back with the band November 14.) And November 10 is a significant date for another reason: Lionel Hampton arrived that day to join the band. He did not, however, get to New York in time to be programmed into the "Camel Caravan"—the Trio played "Who?"

Eight days later, Lionel joined the Trio in Victor's studios. And when it came time to press the sides, these instructions were sent to the Camden, New Jersey, plant: "Individual artists' names must not be used!" So much for the Fitzgerald farce.

BENNY GOODMAN QUARTET   November 18, 1936, New York

Benny Goodman, clt; Lionel Hampton, vib; Teddy Wilson, p; Gene Krupa, d.

BS 03062-1(2)   VI 25473 A, ViJap JA885, ViJap A-1160, HMV B8531, HMVAu EA1843, HMVSw JK2072. **EP:** VI EPB1226, VI EPBT3004, HMV 7EG8154. **LP:** VI LPT3004, VI LPM1226, HMV DLPC6, RcaFr 430.230, RcaFr LPM1226, C/P 25361. **ET:** 1955 Heart Fund (n/c)
Sweet Sue-Just You

BS 03063-1(2)   VI 25473 B, ViJap JA885, HMV B8533, HMVAu EA1843. **45:** VI 47-2953. **EP:** VI EPAT406, HMV 7EG8003. **LP:** VI LPV521, JR 5036, RcaE RD7775
My Melancholy Baby

BS 03064- (1)   UNISSUED
Tiger Rag

(Mxs BS 03062-1 and BS 03063-1 are also on **LP:** VI LPV1032, ViJap RA73, RcaBB AXM2-5532, RcaFr 730.707, RcaFr FXM3-7273, RcaFr PM43176. Note that Victor's files indicate this date's "Tiger Rag"—which may be by the Trio—was released on VI 40-0106, but it is not.)

Another Wilson-BG session followed hard upon a Goodman small group date, proving Benny and Teddy still had their reciprocal agreement in force. But by now fame had caught up with Benny and he could no longer be credited by name on the label. He is pseudonymed, "John Jackson."

TEDDY WILSON   November 19, 1936, New York
AND HIS ORCHESTRA

Benny Goodman, clt; Jonah Jones, tpt; Ben Webster, ts; Teddy Wilson, p; Allan Reuss, g; John Kirby, b; Cozy Cole, d.

B 20290-1   BR 7789, VoE S49, BrF 500695, BrG A81102. **LP:** CO CL1758 (Set C3L-21), CBS BPG62037, SONY SOPH 63/64, CBS PMS93
Pennies From Heaven - voc Billie Holiday

B 20291-1   BR 7789, VoE S49, BrF 500695, BrG A81102, LuJap 60226. **LP:** CO CL1758 (Set C3L-21), CBS BPG62037, PhilCont BO7550L, FONT TFL5106, SONY SOPH63/64, CBS PMS93, SONY 20AP1839, PHIL 628084T
That's Life I Guess - voc Billie Holiday

B 20292-2   BR 7781, B1A 262, CoAu DO1662, VoE S52, BrF 500697, BrG A81103. **LP:** CBS 66274, SONY SONP 50332/3, SONY SOPW9/10
Sailin'

B 20293-1   BR 7781, B1A 262, CoAu DO1662, VoE S52, BrF 500696, BrG A81103, LuJap 60226. **LP:** CO CL1758 (Set C3L-21), CBS BPG62037, SONY SOPH 63/4, CoSP P12971, CBS PMS93, BOM P-12971
I Can't Give You Anything But Love (Baby) - voc Billie Holiday

Recently discovered acetates provide two-thirds of a half-hour Thanksgiving Eve broadcast from the Madhattan Room; but more importantly, they offer our first extant example of the Quartet at work outside the studios.

SUSTAINING BROADCAST   *November 25, 1936, Hotel*
  CBS Radio Network   *Pennsylvania, New York*

Orchestra as September 16, except possibly IRVING GOODMAN, tpt, replaces Zarchey. Quartet as November 18.

Let's Dance (theme)
Jam Session
'T'Ain't Good ('T'Ain't No Good, Like A Nickel Made Of Wood) - voc Helen Ward (arr JM)
Mean To Me (arr FH)
Goodnight My Love - voc Helen Ward
Pick Yourself Up
Sweet Sue-Just You - QUARTET

(Above on LP, JAA 49.)

BENNY GOODMAN QUARTET (sic)   December 2, 1936, New York

Benny Goodman, clt; Teddy Wilson, p; Gene Krupa, d.

BS 03064-2(3)   VI 25481 B, VI 40-0106, VI 27-0119, ViJap JA870, ViJap A-1042, HMV B8531, VIArg 1A-0753, HMVAu EA1845, HMVSw JK2072. **45:** VI 27-0119, VI 47-2954. **EP:** VI EPA744, VI EPAT26, ViArg EGET5. **LP:** VI LPT17, VI LPM1226, HMV DLPC11, RcaF 430-230, RcaF LPM1226, VI LPV1009, ViJap RA73, RcaBB AXM2-5532, RcaFr 730.629, RcaFr FXM37273, RcaFr PM43176, C/P 25361. **ET:** OWI Notes on Jazz 7
Tiger Rag

Add Lionel Hampton, vib.

BS 03514-1   VI 25521 A, ViJap JA919, ViJap A-1425. **LP:** RcaBB AXM2-5568, RcaFr FXM1-7083, RcaFr PM43176, JAZ 18.

BS 03514-2(3)   VI 25521 A, VI 40-0109, VI 420-0152, ViArg 1A-0755, ViJap 919 A, HMVAu EA1897. **45:** VI 27-0006, VI 447-0152. **EP:** VI EPAT3, VI EPAT406, VI EPA5072, HMV 7EG8003, RcaBel 85.507, RcaE RCX1033, VSM 7EGF109, RcaF 75-605, RcaNZ RPX1358. **LP:** VI LPT3, VI LPV521, VI "Life" PR125-1, VI LPV1032, RcaBB AXM2-5532, RcaE RD7775, RcaFr 730.707, RcaFr PM43176, ViJap RA73
Stompin' At The Savoy

BS 03515-1   VI 25481 A, HMV B8533, ViArg 68-0161, ViArg 68-0912, ViJap JA870, ViJap A-1042, HMVAu EA1845. **EP:** VI EPB1226, VI EPBT3004, ViArg AGET10, HMV 7EG8154. **LP:** VI LPT3004, VI LPM1226, ViJap RA73, JR 5036, HMV DLPC6, RcaF 430-230, RcaF LPM1226, VI LPV1009, RcaBB AXM2-5532, RcaFr 730.629 RcaFr PM43176, C/P 25361. **ET:** OWI Outpost Concert Series No. 23-Music Of The Jazz Bands No. 46
Whispering

(Original VI 78 release of "Tiger Rag" was labeled as by a Quartet, including vib; later VI releases of VI 25841 B corrected to Trio. Take 2 of the "Tiger" is the only take extant.)

SUSTAINING BROADCAST　　　　　　　*December 2, 1936, Hotel*
　CBS Radio Network　　　　　　　　*Pennsylvania, New York*

*Personnel as September 16, except IRVING GOODMAN, tpt, replaces
Zarchey.*

When A Lady Meets A Gentleman Down South - voc Helen Ward
Down South Camp Meeting (n/c)
Sometimes I'm Happy (n/c - intro excised)
Remember

"CAMEL CARAVAN"　　　　　　　　　*December 8, 1936, New York*
　CBS Radio Network

Personnel as December 2.

Mean To Me (arr FH) (LP: SB 149)
Darling, Not Without You - voc Helen Ward

The next record session is Helen's last with BG for some time; she left the band about December 18 to marry Albert Marx, her second husband. Apparently Benny had no vocalist for two weeks, since Margaret McCrae did not rejoin until the end of the year. Trumpeter Irving Goodman had replaced Zeke Zarchey the fourth week in November, quitting Charlie Barnet to play for his brother Benny.

Victor's recording sheets for the upcoming session indicate a recording of "Smoke Dreams," matrix T 2435-1, marked, "Hold in N.Y. for Mr. (Eli) Oberstein," a Victor executive. Dubs of this item are in the possession of collectors. It appears to have been recorded after the other titles had been completed. Its sequence of solos differs from the sequence in the released version of "Smoke Dreams"—Benny's clarinet takes the intro instead of a trumpet, and McEachern's trombone replaces Benny's lead solo.

BENNY GOODMAN　　　　　　　　**December 9, 1936, New York**
AND HIS ORCHESTRA

Personnel as December 2.

BS 03549-1	VI 25492 B, HMV B8691, HMVInd N4465. **EP:** VI EPOT6703. **LP:** VI LPT6703, ViArg AYL3000-5, RcaBB AXM2-5532, RcaFr 741.084, RcaFr PM45727 **When You And I Were Young, Maggie** (arr JM)
BS 03550-1	VI 25486 B, HMV B8547. **LP:** RcaBB AXM2-5532, JAZ 19
BS 03550-2(3)	UNISSUED (Test Pressing) **Gee! But You're Swell** - voc Helen Ward (arr JM)
BS 03551-1	UNISSUED (Test Pressing)
BS 03551-2	VI 25486 A, HMV B8547, HMVAu EA1862. **EP:** VI EPOT6703. **LP:** VI LPT6703, ViArg AYL3000-5, RcaBB AXM2-5532, VI VPM6063 **Smoke Dreams** - voc Helen Ward
BS 03552-1 (2,3,4)	VI 25492 A, HMV B8564, HMVAu EA1903. ViJap JA926. **LP:** ViG LPM10022, RcaBB AXM2-5532, RcaFr 741.084, TL STBB03, RcaFr PM45727 **Swing Low, Sweet Chariot** (arr JM)
T 2435-1	UNISSUED (test dub) **Smoke Dreams** - voc Helen Ward (incomplete)

SUSTAINING BROADCAST　　　　　　*December 9, 1936, Hotel*
　CBS Radio Network　　　　　　　　*Pennsylvania, New York*

Personnel as December 2.

Swing Low, Sweet Chariot (LP: SB 149)
When You And I Were Young, Maggie (n/c - intro excised)

"CAMEL CARAVAN"　　　　　　　　*December 15, 1936, New York*
　CBS Radio Network

Personnel as December 2.

Smoke Dreams - voc Helen Ward
An Apple A Day (LP & CAS: DRJ 40350)

Another change took place in the format of the "Camel Caravan" beginning with the broadcast of Dec. 29 (on Sept. 29, Georgie Stoll had replaced Nat Shilkret). Jack Oakie took over the master of ceremonies duties

from Rupert Hughes, and the "Caravan" was subtitled, "The Jack Oakie College Of Musical Knowledge." The show still had its one-hour length, split between Hollywood and New York.

The next session marked the appearance on record of two new vocalists. One was Margaret McCrae; the second, Jimmy Rushing, "Mr. Five By Five" from Count Basie's band, a swinging outfit Benny helped sponsor in the East. (Years later, when Benny was auditioning vocalists to take to the Brussels Fair, author Connor suggested Jimmy. From all reports, those who heard the little round man at the Fair were delighted.)

BENNY GOODMAN　　　　　　　　**December 30, 1936, New York**
AND HIS ORCHESTRA

Personnel as December 2.

BS 03872-1(2)	VI 25505 B, ViJap JA973, HMV B8595, HMVAu EA1859, GrFr K7899, EIG EG4011. **EP:** RcaE RCX1065. **LP:** VI LPM2247, CAM 872, RcaAu L101039, RcaE 1021, RcaFr 731.041, RcaFr FXM3-7273, Rca DRG1014, HIS H623, JO 3057, RcaBB AXM2-5537, RcaAu VJL2-0337, RcaFr PM45727, C/P 7055 **He Ain't Got Rhythm** - voc James Rushing (arr JM)
BS 03873-1(2)	VI 25500 A, ViJap JA911, HMV B8593, EIG EG3914. **LP:** ViG LPM10025, VI VPM6040, RcaFr FXMI-7083, RcaBB AXM2-5537 **Never Should Have Told You** - voc Margaret McCrae
BS 03874-1(2)	same 78 issues as BS 03872-1, plus ViJap A-1119. **EP:** VI EPOT6703. **LP:** VI LPT6703, ViArg AYL3000-5, RcaFr PM43173, RcaBB AXM2-5537 **This Year's Kisses** - voc Margaret McCrae
BS 03875-1(2)	same 78 issues as BS 03873-1, plus HMVAu EA2002. **LP:** ViG LPM10025, RcaFr PM43173, RcaBB AXM2-5537 **You Can Tell She Comes From Dixie** - voc Margaret McCrae

Margaret McCrae left the band as of December 31, and Frances Hunt came in from Lou Bring's Orchestra. More importantly, Harry James—like Benny, himself a Ben Pollack alumnus—joined in the first few days of 1937. Thus the new year saw Swing's greatest trumpet section intact, and James, Elman and Griffin will stay with Benny for the next two years. They are heard first in a short-wave broadcast to the BBC, via a CBS feed; but without Gene Krupa's solid backing. Gene, ill with sinusitis, was absent from January 5, to January 9. Lionel Hampton replaced him on band drums, but the small groups were drum-less:

SHORT WAVE BROADCAST　　　　　　*January 6, 1937, New York*
　BBC via CBS

Benny Goodman, clt; HARRY JAMES, Ziggy Elman, Chris Griffin, tpt; Red Ballard, Murray McEachern, tbn; Hymie Schertzer, Bill DePew, as; Art Rollini, Vido Musso, ts; Jess Stacy, p; Allan Reuss, g; Harry Goodman, b; LIONEL HAMPTON, d; FRANCES HUNT, voc.

DUET: Benny Goodman, clt; Teddy Wilson, p.
TRIO: Benny Goodman, clt; Lionel Hampton, vib; Teddy Wilson, p.

Let's Dance (theme)
Always (n/c)
When Buddha Smiles
Bugle Call Rag (n/c)
Body And Soul - DUET (LP & CAS: DRJ 40350)
Dinah - TRIO (LP & CAS: DRJ 40350)
Goodnight My Love - voc Frances Hunt (n/c - intro only)
Stompin' At The Savoy (LP & CAS: DRJ 40350)

(NOTE: Base material for the broadcast is from two sources. Complete renditions are excellent audio, the partials barely audible. Not found are, following "Stompin' At The Savoy," "Swing Low, Sweet Chariot" and the closing theme.)

The 'Thirties produced a number of trumpet triumvirates whose ensemble power and cohesion, as well as solo creativity, have not been surpassed by the four-, five-, and even six-man sections of later years. One thinks of the Ellington team, and Basie's; a few years earlier, of McKinney's and Henderson's. Of the white bands—perhaps of Crosby's trio of Spivak,

Lawson and Butterfield. All compare favorably **today**—via records and air checks—with the brass of Herman and Kenton of the '40's and '50's, and with the trumpets of an assortment of black bands over the past three decades.

Of them all, Benny Goodman's trinity of 1937–38 stands sans pareil. Listen critically and comparatively; the evidence is on record.

James led the attack. With his weird embouchure, his cheeks puffed as it stuffed with half grapefruits, Harry's contribution was the fulgurant brilliance that identified the flashing Goodman brass.

Elman commanded a bigger tone, a more powerful horn. He could, as he had said, "play the jazz": when Harry came along, Ziggy more often enhanced the section, expanding its volume to the level of a Sousa brass choir.

Griffin's role is harder to delineate. He played more melodically, at times with humor. In retrospect he seems to have been the balance wheel that regulated the section, the musicianly mucilage that kept things from coming unglued.

Each was capable of playing, and did play, lead, hot, sweet, or third trumpet, depending on the arrangement or Benny's signal. (Weary of replying to "who plays what" questions, they once formed "A Society To Prevent Anyone From Calling Any Of Us A First Trumpet Player.") But each subordinated his preference, and indeed his ego, to the section. The section was paramount; possibly that is why it is first, then and now.

BENNY GOODMAN   **January 14, 1937, New York**
AND HIS ORCHESTRA

Personnel as January 6, except Gene Krupa, d, returns.

BS 04235-1(2)   VI 25461 A. **45:** VI 447-0441. **EP:** VI EPOT6703. **LP:** VI LPT6703, ViArg AYL3000-5, VI LOP1509, RcaFr PM43173
            Goodnight My Love - voc ref (FRANCES HUNT) (arr JM)

BS 04236-1(2)   VI 25510 A, ViJap JA957, BB 10760, HMV B8753, HMVInd N4485. **EP:** VI EPOT6703. **LP:** VI LPT6703, ViArg AYL3000-5, ViJap RA70, RcaFR 741.044, RcaFr PM45727
            I Want To Be Happy (arr JM)

BS 04237-1   VI 25531 A, ViJap LM35, ViJap JA961, HMV B8719, ViArg 62-0040. **LP:** CAM 624, RcaFr 741.044, CamE CDN148, ViJap RA70 RcaFr PM45727. **ET:** VOA Jam Session 22
            Chlo-e (Song Of The Swamp) (arr FH)

BS 04238-1(2)   VI 25510 B, ViJap A-1074, ViJap JA957, BB 10760, HMV B8753, EIG EG6001. **EP:** VI EPOT6703. **LP:** VI LPT6703, ViArg AYL3000-5, RcaFr 741.059, ViJap RA70, RcaFr PM45727
            Rosetta (arr HH/FH)

(All issued mxs & takes above also on **LP:** RcaBB AXM2-5537.)

"CAMEL CARAVAN"   *January 19, 1937, New York*
   CBS Radio Network

Personnel as January 14.

I Want To Be Happy (LP & CAS: DRJ 40350)
Swing Low, Sweet Chariot (LP & CAS: DRJ 40350)

For his next studio session Teddy Wilson called on two of the distinguished voices of Count Basie's band, and the guts of its rhythm section. Benny continued to get label credit as "John Jackson" on the Brunswick releases. It fooled no one.

TEDDY WILSON   **January 25, 1937, New York**
AND HIS ORCHESTRA

Benny Goodman, clt; Buck Clayton, tpt; Lester Young, ts; Teddy Wilson, p; Freddie Green, g; Walter Page, b; Jo Jones, d.

B 20568-1   BR 7824, VoE S101, Brlt 5088. **EP:** PHIL BBE12359, PhilCont 429615BE. **LP:** SONY SONP50332, SONY SOPW9/10, CBS 66274
            He Ain't Got Rhythm - Billie Holiday

B 20569-2   BR 7824, VoE S101. **EP:** PHIL BBE12359, PhilCont 429615BE. **LP:** CO CL1758 (Set C3L21), CBS BPG62037, CBS P3M 5869, TL STLJ03
            This Year's Kisses - voc Billie Holiday

B 20570-1   BR 7859, Co 36283, CoC C6182, VoE S71, BrG A81160. **EP:** FontCont 662007TR. **LP:** CO CL1758 (Set C3L21), FONT 662007TR, CBS BPG62037, CoE 33S1034, CoFr FP1044, CoSP P12970, CBS PMS93, TL STLJ03
            Why Was I Born? - voc Billie Holiday

B 20571-1   BR 7859, CO 36207, CoC C6205, VoE S71, PhilCont B21177H, BrG A81160, CoArg 291283. **EP:** FONT TFE17010. **LP:** CO CL6040, CO CL 637, PHIL BBR8061, PHIL BBR8098, SONY SONP50332, PhilCont B07651R, PhilCont B07735R, CoJap PL2028, COR 1677, CO CB16, CO ZL1106, CBS XM10C, TL STLJ03
            I Must Have That Man! - voc Billie Holiday

(All releases above also on LP: SONY SOPH63/4, CO CG33502)

The next air check is unusual in that it offers "Good-Bye" in its entirety. This sustaining broadcast was announced by Bert Parks, later prominent as a "quizmaster" and MC of the "Miss America Pageant."

SUSTAINING BROADCAST   *January 27, 1937,*
   CBS Radio Network   *Hotel Pennsylvania, New York*

Personnel as January 14.

Sometimes I'm Happy (LP: SB 149)
Good-Bye (complete version)

"CAMEL CARAVAN"   *February 2, 1937, New York*
   CBS Radio Network

Benny Goodman, clt; Lionel Hampton, vib; Teddy Wilson, p; Gene Krupa, d.

Ida, Sweet As Apple Cider - QUARTET

"Runnin' Wild" was Gene's choice as his best studio-recorded work for Benny. From the same session, "Tea For Two" also displays an inventive Krupa adding color and an indefinable "taste" to the Quartet's efforts. All in all, probably Gene's finest Quartet session:

BENNY GOODMAN QUARTET   **February 3, 1937, New York**

Personnel as February 2.

BS 04559-2(1)   VI 25531 B, HMV B8765, HMV J0228, ViArg 62-0040, ASR L25531, GrFr K8301, ViJap JA961, ViJap A-1447. **EP:** Vi EPOT6703, RcaBel 85.509. **7" LP:** "bonus" disc, RD325 alb. **LP:** VI LPT6703, ViArg AYL3000-5, RcaFr 731.041, TL STLJ20, RD 4A-005
            Ida, Sweet As Apple Cider

BS 04560-1(2)   VI 25529 B, HMV B8563, HMV J0228, HMVInd N4485, ViJap JA941, ViJap A-1045. **EP:** VI EPOT6703, RcaBel 85.509. **LP:** VI LPT6703, VI LPV1032, JR 5036, ViArg AYL3000-5, RcaFr 730.707, RcaFr FXM3-7273
            Tea For Two

BS 04561-1   VI 25529 A, VI 40-0109, HMV B8568, HMV J0229, HMVAu EA1898, EIG EG3998, HMVFin TG267, ViJap JA941. **EP:** VI EPBT3004, VI EPB1226, HMV 7EG8180. **LP:** VI LPT3004, VI LPM1226, VI LPV1032, HMV DLP6, RcaFr LPM1226, RcaFr 430.230, RcaFr 730.707. **ET:** VOA Jam Session 23, 1955 Heart Fund (n/c)
            Runnin' Wild

(All releases above are also on **LP:** RcaBB AXM2-5537, RcaFr PM43176, ViJap RA73, VI VPM 6063.)

66

SUSTAINING BROADCAST — February 3, 1937, CBS Radio Network, Hotel Pennsylvania, New York

Personnel as January 14.

Japanese Sandman (LP & CAS: DRJ 40350)
Good-Bye (theme)

Forty-odd years later, Benny remembers the next broadcast clearly: CBS relayed it to radio station JOAK, Tokyo, for rebroadcast in Japan. Each tune was announced in English by Bert Parks, then Burton Crane translated its title into Japanese for the Empire's audience. Benny still chuckles over "Good-Bye" becoming "Sayonara":

SUSTAINING BROADCAST — February 6, 1937, CBS Radio Network, Hotel Pennsylvania, New York

Quartet as February 3. Orchestra as January 14.

Dinah - QUARTET (LP & CAS: DRJ 40350)
Good-Bye (theme) (LP & CAS: DRJ 40350)

Periodically, new gods of show business flame forth with such blazing effect that they evoke from their audiences completely uninhibited and oftimes riotous response. Thus, a Frank Sinatra has a generation swooning and screaming; an Elvis Presley is showered with autographed brassieres and teddy bears; and even the beat generation finds such an emotional kinship with a James Dean that it forgets its pose of cool insouciance, and roars its goatee off in a post-mortem paean.

We would make the point that this kind of tumultuous and demonstrative response, this hip awareness of what was new and sometimes good, this basic need to be identified personally with a brave new something, began precisely—in our time in the jazz world—on Wednesday, March 3, 1937. For it was that day that "Benny Goodman and Band" first appeared in New York's Paramount Theatre. And it was then that it all began.

When Benny "and band" were doubled from the Madhattan Room into the Paramount for a booking of two weeks, it meant little to the men but a heavier schedule and a little more loot in the pay envelope. Although the audiences at the Madhattan Room were generous with their applause, they were well-mannered and self-contained—possibly because if they were conspicuous, a waiter would appear asking about another round of drinks. Certainly there was no warning there that something big was about to happen. And the band's relatively few theatre dates to that time had been less than sensational; some had been outright disasters.

So it was that the several hundred milling teenagers crowded around the as yet unopened boxoffice that Wednesday morning took BG and Co. completely by surprise. The feature film for that week was Paramount's "Maid of Salem," co-starring Claudette Colbert and Fred MacMurray. Reportedly, it was to be a sober New England witch-hunting drama, surely nothing to attract youngsters in such pre-show proportions. "Guess every single one of our fans in New York is already here," was Benny's reaction, and the band agreed.

But as the band finished rehearsing, and gathered in the sunken pit prior to its initial appearance for the day, the current of near hysteria in the audience began to communicate itself. We can almost see Benny nervously, and characteristically, lipping his reed, Gene wiping the sweat from his hands onto his band jacket and checking his lapel watch one more time, Jess trying to get "the damn' piano stool to the right height—I'm such a little guy" . . . And as Benny snapped off the tempo for "Let's Dance," and as the band rose to stage level on the pit lift, an emotional elevator catapulted a cheering, screaming, uproarious audience right up with it.

The band responded in kind. An up-tempo "Bugle Call" followed hard upon the theme, and the crowd howled its approval. Then "Star Dust," replete with Reuss's chord—the kids were waiting for it—then Edith Mann, a long-limbed beauty who was with the Madhattan Room show, came on with her tap specialty; then the band again in "Ridin' High." By this time the "jitterbugs" were shagging in the aisles, were good-naturedly crowding to the stage imploring autographs, were chorusing in unison for "King Porter," or "Stompin'," or "House Hop." But the printed program said, "FRANCES HUNT," "(a) I've Got My Love To Keep Me Warm'" and "(b) He Ain't Got Rhythm,' " so Frances entered and did her thing to warm, but anticipatory, applause. Benny sensed things might be getting out of hand so he signalled no encore, let Fritz and Jean Hubert do their comic drunk routine and ease the tension. More warm, still anticipatorily polite, handclapping.

The Quartet was next. An extended "Tiger" followed a restrained "Body And Soul," and it became a challenge match between Quartet and audience, each trying to outperform, in its own way, the other. Then

"Stompin at the Savoy," with rivulets of sweat literally puddling onto Lionel's vibes. Then "I Got Rhythm" (grammatically. but erroneously programmed as "I've Got Rhythm") for chorus after chorus, with Gene belting a crash cymbal from its stand, Benny bending double as if to scoop another breath from the floor as he rose, and even the imperturbable Teddy smiling, actually smiling, with pride and satisfaction.

"Sing, Sing, Sing" (a 'jail and a half,' one wag called it) finished it off, finished Benny, finished Harry, finished Gene, finished the audience. Gene butt-ended his tunable toms with all his great wrist strength to start it. Benny came on, then the brass with its chilling growl, then Benny again, then Gene, then the mid-climax. Then Part Two with Vido bellowing, Gene's paradiddle break, then Harry assaulting the tune, raping it, leaving it torn and spent. Then a reflective Benny, an exuberantly experimental Benny, a crescendoing Benny, a diminuendoing Benny, and Gene to a stop. Then the cow bell alert, the band in full cry, Gene's triplets, and the thundering finale. The end, a mutual orgastic climax of band and audience, the fulfilling end to a new love affair. Then, as new lovers, rest and refreshment—for in about two hours, band and audience devour one another again.

That was Benny's opening day at the Paramount, a scene repeated each performance of every day of that engagement. While attendance at the Paramount rose to new heights, attendance at local schools fell alarmingly. Jazz musicians flocked in to see what all the excitement was about—we'll not forget Johnny Hodges and Sam Nanton (Duke was at the New Cotton Club with Ethel Waters and the Nicholas Brothers) marvelling at the power and enthusiasm of the band and the audience. And this was news, and press wires carried the story of Benny Goodman at the Paramount all over the country. This was the end of the "local success only" aspect of the band, for from this point on teenagers in every whistle stop lay in wait for the band. "Swing" truly was here.

Looking back, we can understand why there had to be an emotional explosion in the Paramount that March of 1937. First, there was the band itself, to most the greatest white jazz band ever assembled, to many the greatest of any color. It had great arrangements, great soloists, a great instrumentalist as leader; it played a new kind of exciting music with awesome authority. Second, the children of the Depression were full up with the monotony austerity had imposed upon them; they were desperate for something daring and different. (Sociologists may compare this with today's affluent children and their directionless ennui born of satiety—which was better?) And third, when the band went into the Paramount it became accessible to these youngsters for the first time; they could scrape together the 35¢ for the theatre, whereas they could not afford the tabs at the band's hotel locations.

Possibly they were not a critical mass—but explode they did.

We devote this much space to Benny's first stand at the Paramount because the film, "The Benny Goodman Story," failed completely to convey, in its Paramount scene, the almost unbearable excitement and the significance of the event. For there and then was an emotional orgy new to any band's experience; and Swing got its greatest impetus forward at that engagement. It may not be possible to tell it as it was, on film or in words, but an attempt seemed called for.

In late January Hymie Schertzer became ill, and Benny asked Toots Mondello to fill in. But Toots was busy with radio work and could not. George Koenig, who had just come to New York from Cleveland, was recommended to Benny, sat in, and got a permanent job, as Bill DePew left.

The same day the band opened at the Paramount is coincidentally the date of the first of the air checks released commercially, first by Columbia and later by MGM. Through the good offices of Bill Savory, the CBS engineer who cut most if not all of the air checks, exact dates of recording became available for almost all of them. Because there are no "alternative takes" of these air checks, because there already are duplicate releases and will be more, the catalog numbers in the text are keyed. The key to the releases follows:

COLUMBIA-SERIES AIR CHECK RELEASES

Monaural & "stereo" LP	Code
CO ML4590	1
CO ML4591	2
CO ML/OL4613	3

CO ML/OL4614	4
CO CL817	5
CO CL818	6
CO CL819	7
CO CL820	8
CBS 62853	9
CBS 63086	10
CoJap WL5089	11
CoJap WL5090	12
PHIL BBL7009	13
PHIL BBL7010	14
PHIL BBL7073	15
PHIL BBR8098	16
PHIL CONT B07006L	17
PHIL CONT B07007L	18
PHIL CONT B07116L	19
PHIL CONT B07665R	20
PHIL CONT B07735R	21
.CO CS8643	37
HA HS11271	38
CBS S63367	40
CBS S52688	41
CBSHol 88141	44
CO Alb. P4M-5678	46
CoSP P13289	47
HOM alb. HM1379	48
TL STLJ05	49
FR albums	50
SM albums	51
CBS set 66420	52

Extended Play	**Code**
CO B817	22
CO B818	23
CO A1040	24
CO A1041	25
CO A1053	26
CO B2587	27
CO BS8204	28
PHIL BBE12101	29
PHIL BBE12104	30
PHIL BBE12132	31
PHIL BBE12277	32
PHIL CONT 429008BE	33
PHIL CONT 429160BE	33AA
PHIL CONT 429161BE	33A
PHIL CONT 429175BE	34
PHIL CONT 429220BE	35
PHIL CONT 429234BE	36
CO B8203	39
PHIL CONT 429248BE	43
CoJap EM93	43A
PHIL B47012L	45

"Unique" issues, including miscellaneous 78's, disc jockey copies, EP's, LP's and ET's, are listed in full for appropriate performances.

MGM-SERIES AIR CHECK RELEASES

Monaural & "stereo" LP	**Code**
MGM E3788	101
MGM E3789	102
MGM E3790	103
MGM(E) C805	104
MGM(E) C807	105
MGM(EZ) C810	106

MGM(NZ) C6051	107
MGM(NZ) C6078	108
MGM(NZ) C6081	109
VER V8582	110
VER & VER(G) V6-8582	114
METFr&G set 262600 (2364005/6)	115
VER(E) VLP9120	116
VER(E) 2683055	117
VER 2317056	118
VER 2428502	119
HOM alb. HM1379	120
EUR1004	121

Extended Play	**Code**
MGM X3788	111
MGM X3789	112
MGM X3790	113

Additionally, **all** "MGM-SERIES" air checks are in these LP albums:

BOM 71-6502
MGM CONT 65001/2/3
SONY 36AP-1416/7

"Unique" issues, including miscellaneous 78's, disc jockey copies, EP's, LP's and ET's, are listed in full for appropriate performances.

The Columbia and Metro-Goldwyn-Mayer "live" performance releases, although air checks, are "legitimate" (authorized), issued recordings, and are so treated as to type style herein. The first tune released, in chronological order, was from a sustaining broadcast:

BENNY GOODMAN AND HIS ORCHESTRA   March 3, 1937, New York

CBS sustaining radio b' cast from the Madhattan Room. Personnel as January 14, except GEORGE KOENIG, as, replaces DePew.

XLP 11049-1A   CO Series: 1, 4, 6, 11, 14, 81, 23, 24, 26, 52
         Sometimes I'm Happy

"CAMEL CARAVAN"   *March 9, 1937, New York*
   CBS Radio Network

Orchestra as March 3. Quartet as February 3.

You Showed Me The Way - voc Frances Hunt (n/c)
Shine - QUARTET (LP & CAS: DRJ 40350)

BENNY GOODMAN QUARTET   March 11/16, 1937, New York

Spliced recording from a Mutual sustaining radio b' cast March 11 from the Madhattan Room and a "Camel Caravan" b' cast of March 16. Personnel as February 3.

59-MG-631   MGM Series: 102, 105, 108, 112, 116
         Limehouse Blues

"CAMEL CARAVAN"   *March 16, 1937, New York*
   CBS Radio Network

Orchestra as March 3. Quartet as February 3. TRIO: Goodman, Wilson, Krupa.

I Know That You Know
Body And Soul - TRIO (LP & CAS: DRJ 40350)
Limehouse Blues - QUARTET

(Note that this air check affords the full version of "Limehouse Blues," a portion of which was spliced to make up the MGM release; and that now "When Buddha Smiles" is the only Goodman rendition "missing" from this broadcast.)

On March 17 Benny was present at a "Hot Club Of New York" recording session held in the Master studios of the American Record Corporation. Contrary to rumor, Benny did not record.

"CAMEL CARAVAN"   *March 23, 1937, New York*
  CBS Radio Network

Orchestra as March 3. Quartet as February 3.

I've Got My Love To Keep Me Warm
Stompin' At The Savoy - QUARTET
Sugar Foot Stomp (n/c - intro only)

BENNY GOODMAN   **March 25, 1937, New York**
AND HIS ORCHESTRA/QUARTET

Mutual sustaining radio b' cast from the Madhattan Room. Orchestra personnel as March 3. Quartet personnel as February 3.

XLP 11049-1A   CO Series: 1, 4, 6, 8, 11, 14, 15, 18, 19, 23, 24, 27,
                37, 39, 41, 43A, 49, 52
              Down South Camp Meetin' (Orchestra)

XLP 11050-1C   CO Series: 2, 4, 6, 9, 12, 14, 18, 23, 24, 31, 36, 44,
                45, 46, 47, 52
              Runnin' Wild (Quartet)

BENNY GOODMAN AND HIS ORCHESTRA   **April 13, 1937, New York**

CBS "Camel Caravan" b' cast. Personnel as March 3.

XLP 11050-1C   CO Series: 2, 4, 6, 12, 14, 18, 23, 24, 52
              Minnie The Moocher's Wedding Day (arr HH/FH)

The next date offers both a commercially-released air check and a privately recorded air check from one broadcast. They are differentiated by means of type font:

BENNY GOODMAN AND HIS ORCHESTRA   **April 27, 1937, New York**

CBS "Camel Caravan" b' cast. Personnel as March 3.

59-MG-633B   MGM Series: 103, 106, 109, 113, 115, 118; and **LP:**
              GOJ 1028, SG 8004
              Remember

(acetate) Okey Dokey (arr FH) - voc Frances Hunt and Benny Goodman

SUSTAINING BROADCAST   *April 28, 1937,*
  CBS Radio Network   *Hotel Pennsylvania, New York*

Orchestra personnel as March 3. Quartet personnel as February 3.

Johnny One Note (n/c)
Blue Hawaii
That Foolish Feeling - voc Frances Hunt
Good-Bye (theme - to mid-broadcast break)
Trust In Me - voc Frances Hunt
Ida - QUARTET
Carelessly - voc Frances Hunt
I Want To Be Happy
More Than You Know - to signoff

(All on LP: SG 8004.)

The last day of the Madhattan Room engagement saw Benny and the band reunited with Helen Ward via a guest appearance on Martin Block's radio program. The show also featured departing vocalist Frances Hunt and her replacement, Peg LaCentra. Unfortunately, Frances's and Peg's efforts have not become available, but a song by Helen and a rendition by the Quartet were released:

BENNY GOODMAN   **April 29, 1937, New York**
AND HIS ORCHESTRA/QUARTET

WNEW "Make Believe Ballroom" radio b'cast - Orchestra personnel as March 3. Quartet, personnel as Feb. 3.

XLP 11050-1C   CO Series: 2, 4, 6, 12, 14, 18, 23, 24, 52
              You Turned The Tables On Me - voc Helen Ward
                (Orchestra)

59-MG-630B   MGM Series: 102, 105, 108, 112, 116, 117, 120, 121
              I Got Rhythm (Quartet)

SUSTAINING BROADCAST   *April 29, 1937,*
  Mutual Radio Network   *Hotel Pennsylvania, New York*

Orchestra personnel as March 3.

Let's Dance (theme)
Alexander's Ragtime Band (n/c)
Big John Special
Good-Bye (theme)

(All on LP: SG 8004.)

Leaving New York, the band went immediately to Boston's Hotel Statler, from which the next air check emanates:

SUSTAINING BROADCAST   *April 30, 1937,*
  Unknown network   *Hotel Statler, Boston*

Orchestra personnel as March 3.

Camel Hop (LP: SG 8004)

On May 11 the band returned to New York and dueled Chick Webb's band in an epic battle of swing in Harlem's Savoy Ballroom. But prior to the "cuttin' match" (Gene maintained he was never bested by a better man) it was into CBS's New York studios for the weekly "Camel Caravan," from which Benny's theme was recorded and subsequently released:

BENNY GOODMAN AND HIS ORCHESTRA   **May 11, 1937, New York**

CBS "Camel Caravan" b' cast. Personnel as March 3.

XLP 11048-1A   CO Series: 3, 11, 13, 17, 52
              Let's Dance (arr George Bassman)

The air checks in the Columbia and MGM albums are a distillate of those submitted to Benny for his approval. Some of those not chosen eventually found their way to collectors via tape, and later some of BG's "out takes," so to speak, were bootlegged on LP's. In turn, the bootleggers pirated from each other, with the result that identical air checks appear on a number of LP's: BBL/A XXII, FT 1507, JM (no #), ON 1507, BL 127.034, FEST 153, MU 153 & 30, JA 5114 and KOJ-20005. To eliminate redundancy, all of these releases are shown later as, "LP—Group A."

The first of these is also from the "Camel Caravan" broadcast of May 11. Harry James is simply magnificent on it, and the author asked Benny why he'd not selected this cut for release? "Listen to it closely, Russ—we change tempo a couple of times, and I couldn't let that get out." Maybe so; but if Harry had changed anything at all, he would have destroyed one of the best trumpet solos he ever cut.

"CAMEL CARAVAN"   *May 11, 1937, New York*
  CBS Radio Network

Personnel as March 3.

Blue Hawaii (LP: Group A)

The following week the band toured Pennsylvania, returning to New York May 18 to perform in the Roseland Ballroom and to broadcast the regular Tuesday night "Camel Caravan."

BENNY GOODMAN QUARTET   **May 18, 1937, New York**

CBS "Camel Caravan" b' cast. Personnel as Feb. 3.

59-MG-628   MGM Series: 101, 104, 107, 110, 111, 114, 116, 119
             Digga Digga Doo

BENNY GOODMAN AND HIS ORCHESTRA   **May 25, 1937, New York**

CBS "Camel Caravan" b' cast. Personnel as March 3.

59-MG-633B   MGM Series: 103, 106, 109, 113, 115, 118, 120, 121
             Chlo-e (Song Of The Swamp)

One of the Swing Era's better jazz radio programs was the Columbia Broadcasting System's weekly "Saturday Night Swing Club." Begun in 1936, it featured a house band—in its early days led by Bunny Berigan, later by Leith Stevens—and invited guests who, over time, included every star performer in Swing's galaxy.

Benny Goodman and his Orchestra were the headliners in the Stanley Theatre in Pittsburgh, Pa., when the "Club" celebrated its first anniversary with a special program beginning at midnight on June 12. Among its guests that early morning, "fed" to the network from locations throughout the Nation, were: Duke Ellington, Caspar Reardon, Adrian Rollini, Kay Thompson's Singers, Bunny Berigan, the Raymond Scott Quintet, Glen Gray, Les Lieber, the Quintette du Hot Club de France, Larry Clinton, Claude Thornhill, Ina Ray Hutton, Carl Kress and Dick McDonough, and . . . the Benny Goodman Trio and Quartet:

"SATURDAY NIGHT SWING CLUB"   *June 12, 1937, Pittsburgh*
  CBS Radio Network

Quartet personnel as February 3. TRIO: Quartet sans vibes.

There's A Lull In My Life - TRIO (LP: JAA 40, SC 1014)
Nagasaki - QUARTET (n/c) (LP: SC 1014)

The band, too, is heard from Pittsburgh, via "Camel Caravan":

BENNY GOODMAN QUARTET   June 15, 1937, Pittsburgh

CBS "Camel Caravan" b' cast. Personnel as Feb. 3

XLP 11048-1A   CO Series: 1, 3, 5, 10, 11, 13, 17, 22, 24, 30, 33A, 34,
                44, 45, 52 and **78**: PhilCont B21208H
                The Sheik Of Araby

Working its way west to its third engagement at the Palomar, the band made its last stop in Columbus, Ohio, before entraining for Los Angeles. Note that the air checks from the "Camel Caravan" originating there offer a unique performance of "I Got Rhythm" by the full orchestra.

"CAMEL CARAVAN"   *June 22, 1937, Columbus*
  CBS Radio Network

Orchestra personnel as March 3. Quartet personnel as February 3.

I Got Rhythm
A Handful Of Keys - QUARTET

Although neither has been heard on available air checks, it should be noted that Peg LaCentra left the band in late June, and Betty Van replaced her as vocalist. And before the band reaches Los Angeles, let's assess what has been happening to it:

The last two members added, James and Koenig, had entered in January and February. Thus the band had been intact for almost half a year. In those six months it had logged an impressive amount of play. Through April, six long nights each week in the Madhattan Room; as many as three sustaining broadcasts of an evening. While there, six stage shows daily in the Paramount, six days a week. Out of the Madhattan Room and on to a tour of theatres, ballrooms and hotels. Each week, every week, rehearsals and broadcasts, the "Camel Caravan." Individual, small group, and band "special performances" and personal appearances. Playing, rehearsing, experimenting and playing again.

Fifteen talented musicians and their leader had thus worked together almost without surcease, day and night, for nearly half a year. Fifteen men handpicked by Benny, the distillate of more than two years' upgrading personnel, had developed a rapport, an empathy, a mutuality of effort that blended their talents and skills into a single over-powering musical instrument. Honed by constant work, the Benny Goodman Orchestra reached its peak in mid-1937 and stayed on that glorious plateau for about the period of human gestation; then it gave birth to a new and different orchestra. This was Goodman's Golden Age; this was a great band at its very best.

At intervals over many years, the author sought additional information about Benny's "Camel Caravan" broadcasts from their sponsor, R. J. Reynolds Industries, Inc. His underlying purpose was to discover if transcriptions of the programs were lying unremarked in the company's possession. Searches by a succession of cooperative employees failed to find any.

In 1985, persistence paid off: more than 150 16-inch transcriptions (two 15-minute ETs per half-hour broadcast) were located, almost all in excellent condition. They were transferred to tape, and copies were given to Mr. Goodman, his attorney, and the author for evaluation.

In addition to providing a wealth of hitherto unheard performances by the Goodman orchestras and small groups for the period June 29, 1937 through the year 1939, the transcriptions give irrefutable evidence of the correct broadcast dates and locales of many of the air checks in the Columbia and M-G-M albums. In so doing they change some assignments in the author's "BG—On The Record," as supplied the author by the CBS engineer whose acetates were the source of those albums. In most instances the transcriptions confirm the data given to the author, but there are some

noteworthy exceptions. Notice of these reassignments will be cited as they occur.

The band opened in the Palomar on June 29, and that evening broadcast its weekly "Camel Caravan" from the CBS studios in Los Angeles. With this program, the format changed. Now it was limited to 30 minutes, solely devoted to Benny's band. MC Bill Goodwin announced the revamped program as, "The Benny Goodman Swing School."

Coincidentally, the first of the newly-discovered ETs mandates the initial reassignment: "When It's Sleepy Time Down South," previously ascribed to a "probable" date of June 3, 1937, is now proved to be from June 29:

"CAMEL CARAVAN"   *June 29, 1937, Los Angeles*
  CBS Radio Network

Benny Goodman, clt; Harry James, Ziggy Elman, Chris Griffin, tpt; Red Ballard, Murray McEachern, tbn; Hymie Schertzer, George Koenig, as; Art Rollini, Vido Musso, ts; Jess Stacy, p; Allan Reuss, g; Harry Goodman, b; Gene Krupa, d.

TRIO: Benny Goodman, clt; Teddy Wilson, p; Gene Krupa, d.
QUARTET: Benny Goodman, clt; Lionel Hampton, vib; Teddy Wilson, p; Gene Krupa, d.

Let's Dance (theme)

BENNY GOODMAN AND HIS ORCHESTRA

59-MG-632   MGM Series: 103, 106, 109, 113, 115, 117
                   Alexander's Ragtime Band

Peckin'

BENNY GOODMAN TRIO

XLP 11049-1A   CO Series: 1, 4, 5, 10, 11, 14, 18, 23, 24, 26, 44, 52,
                and **78**: PhilCont & AU B21093H

                Sweet Leilani
Stompin' At The Savoy - voc Meyer Alexander Chorus

BENNY GOODMAN QUARTET

59-MG-630B   MGM Series: 102, 105, 108, 112, 115
                   Avalon (full orchestra in coda)

(Down On The Farm - voc guest Rufe Davis, orchestra in coda - NO BG

BENNY GOODMAN AND HIS ORCHESTRA

59-MG-633B   MGM Series: 103, 106, 109, 110, 113, 114, 115, 118,
                119
                When It's Sleepy Time Down South (arr FH)

Sing, Sing, Sing
Good-Bye (theme)

As they had the year before, Benny's Good-men doubled from the Palomar to "make a movie." This one would prove to be, in the opinions of jazz critics and fans alike, the best film ever made by any of the swing bands.

"HOLLYWOOD HOTEL"   *July/August 1937, Hollywood*

A Warner Brothers-First National picture filmed in black-and-white. Release date: January 15, 1938   *Running time: 109 minutes*
Director: Busby Berkeley
Songs by Richard A. Whiting and Johnny Mercer
CAST: Dick Powell, Rosemary Lane, Lola Lane, Hugh Herbert, Edgar Kennedy, Mabel Todd, Ted Healy, Johnny "Scat" Davis, Alan Mowbray, Jerry Cooper, Frances Langford, Raymond Paige and his Orchestra, and

BENNY GOODMAN AND HIS ORCHESTRA,
  and the BENNY GOODMAN QUARTET

Personnels as June 29.

Opening title music - studio orchestra
Hooray For Hollywood - voc Johnny "Scat" Davis, Frances Langford, Harry James, Gene Krupa and chorus - BENNY GOODMAN ORCHESTRA (arr JM)

July/August 1937, continued

July/August 1937, continued

California, Here I Come - BENNY GOODMAN ORCHESTRA. Musical
  montage to:
(Hooray For Hollywood - studio orchestra
(Silhouetted In The Moonlight - studio orchestra
(I'm Like A Fish Out Of Water - studio orchestra
(Bob White - studio orchestra
(Have You Got Any Castles, Baby? - studio orchestra
(I'm Like A Fish Out Of Water - voc Dick Powell, Rosemary Lane, Ted
  Healy, Mabel Todd - studio orchestra
(Silhouetted In The Moonlight - voc Rosemary Lane - studio orchestra
I've Got A Heartful Of Music - BENNY GOODMAN ORCHESTRA
  (background)
Let That Be A Lesson To You - voc Johnny "Scat" Davis, Dick Powell,
  Rosemary Lane, Mabel Todd, Ted Healy, chorus - BENNY GOODMAN
  ORCHESTRA
Sing, Sing, Sing (arr JM) - BENNY GOODMAN ORCHESTRA
I've Got A Heartful Of Music - BENNY GOODMAN QUARTET (incorporating,
  "I Got Rhythm")
(I've Hitched My Wagon To A Star - voc Dick Powell - studio orchestra
(Silhouetted In The Moonlight - voc Frances Langford, Jerry Cooper -
  studio orchestra
(Dark Eyes - voc chorus - Raymond Paige and his Orchestra
(I've Hitched My Wagon To A Star - voc Dick Powell - studio orchestra
(Sing, You Son Of A Gun - voc Dick Powell - studio orchestra - segue to
(Hooray For Hollywood - voc Johnny "Scat" Davis and cast
(Closing title music - studio orchestra

Some notes on "Hollywood Hotel":

Portions of the sound track of "Hollywood Hotel" that include performances
by Benny Goodman are on LP: Warner Bros. 3XX2736, United Artists
LA361H, Hollywood Soundstage 5004, Extreme Rarities 1002, EOH 99601.

"Sing, Sing, Sing" is on an RCA 33⅓ rpm Test Pressing, No. VI-S-6203,
erroneously labeled as, "Christopher Columbus." The test also includes a
vocal from the Warner Bros. 1937 film "Over The Wall" ("Evidence") by Dick
Foran.

A 10" shellac pressing, labeled "Exploitation Record, Recorded and Manufactured by Decca Records, Inc., N.Y., N.Y.," was distributed to advertise the
radio program, "Hollywood Hotel." It contains four excerpts—two per side—
from the film, with voice-over announcements promoting the radio broadcasts. Side 1, matrix 75607, offers "Let That Be A Lesson To You" by Benny
Goodman, vocal by Frances Langford. It is the same version as that in the
movie, but is more complete than the soundtrack cut. The other three tracks
offer vocals by Dick Powell and Rosemary Lane, accompanied by the film's
studio orchestra.

An ALTERNATE VERSION (labeled a "rehearsal check") of "Hooray For Hollywood" is on a 10" acetate produced by Speak-O-Phone Recording Studios,
Inc., 29 W. 57 St., New York City. It is not known how this lengthier rendition
of the band's opening sequence made its way from Hollywood to New York,
and transfer there.

A promotional film soliciting contributions to the Will Rogers Memorial Hospital, titled, "Auld Lang Syne - A Tribute To Will Rogers Memorial," includes
brief excerpts of "out takes" made by Benny Goodman for "Hollywood
Hotel": "I've Got A Heartful Of Music"—orchestra; "Avalon"—Quartet, orchestra in coda; and "House Hop"—orchestra. These cuts are on LP: Extreme Rarities 1008, Hollywood Soundstage 5004.

A portion of "Sing, Sing, Sing" was dubbed into a Warner Bros. war-time
Victory Bond short, "The Shining Future." This film was re-titled, "The Road
To Victory, 1944," and was released by the U.S. Treasury Dept. as No. 98 in
its series.

"Sing, Sing, Sing" and the Quartet's "I've Got A Heartful Of Music" were
dubbed into an NBC TV special, "Music Of The 'Thirties," televised November
5, 1961. Similar dubbings may be found in other telecasts about Benny
Goodman or the Big Band era.

Davis, a trumpet player of sorts, appears to play with the Goodman band; he
does not. An attempt was made to dub his trumpet into "Sing, Sing, Sing"
late one night when Benny and the band had left the lot. When he heard of it,
Benny threatened to take the band out of the movie unless this sequence were
killed. It was, and Davis merely simulates playing with the band.

(A slightly different version of this incident is that Davis was secretly pho-
tographed "sync-ing" James's solo in "Sing, Sing, Sing," with the intention
that this film clip—not a SOUND clip—of Davis's trumpet would be dubbed

into the "Orchid Room" sequence. Whichever version is correct, Benny
considered the attempt insulting, and refused to permit such Hollywood han-
ky-panky.)

"Can't Teach My Old Heart New Tricks" was recorded by Dick Powell with
Raymond Paige and his Orchestra for the movie, but it was not used.

July 6 affords an unique opportunity to compare four versions of one
tune performed the same day. Three are the alternate takes of "Can't We Be
Friends?" from the Victor studio session, the fourth is from a "Camel
Caravan" broadcast that evening.

July 6 is also the day that the climactic "Sing, Sing, Sing" was committed to wax. With the latterday release of a Time-Life album, three takes
each of its two parts are now extant.

BENNY GOODMAN AND HIS ORCHESTRA   July 6, 1937, Hollywood

Personnel as June 29. HARRY JAMES (HJ), arr.

PBS 09569-1 (2)	VI 25621 A, ViJap JA1031, HMV B8615, HMV X4953. **EP:** VI EPOT6703. **LP:** VI LPT6703, ViArg AYL3000-5, VI LEJ6, CAM 385, CamE CDN112, RcaBB AXM2-5537, RcaFr 741.072, RcaFr PM45727
	Peckin' (arr HJ)
PBS 09570-1	VI 25621 B, ViJap JA1031, BB 10462, HMV B8615, HMVAu EA2002. **LP:** RcaBB AXM2-5537, JAZ 16
PBS 09570-2	VI 25261 B. **EP:** VI EOPT6703. **LP:** VI LPT6703, ViArg AYL3000-5, RcaBB AXM2-5568, ViJap RA71, RcaFr PM45727
PBS 09570-3	**LP:** RcaFr 741.044
	Can't We Be Friends? (arr FH)
PCS 09571-1	**LP:** RcaBB AXM2-5568, JAZ 41
PCS 09571-2	VI 36205 A, VI 25796 (abridged), VI 420-0154, VD 7A, NavyVD 177, ViJap LM9, ViJap NB6003, ViJap JB184, HMV C2936, ViArg 64-0002, ViArg 2A-0016, EIG EH1424, HMVAu EB111, HMVSw FKX23, HMVIt S10496. **45:** VI 27-0022, VI 27-0058, VI 447-0154. **EP:** VI EPAT412 (abridged), VI EPA664, VI EPA5042 (abridged), VI EPB1005, ViArg AVET3, RcaAu 20024, RcaBel 85.506, RcaE RCX1026, RcaFr 85230, RcaNZ RPX1352, VSM EMF72. **LP:** VI LPT1005, VI LPM1099, VI LSP4005(e), VI VPM6040, VI ANLI-0973, VI CPLI-2470, HMV DLP1112, HMV DLP1116, ViJap RA70, RD 3-21, RcaBB AXM2-5537, RcaAu VJL2-0337, RcaAu VPLi-0471, RcaCont 89323, RcaE PL12470, RcaFr 740.552, RcaFr 741.084, RcaFr FXM3-7273, RcaFr PM45727, RcaG VPS6043, SM 6-0610. **ET:** AFRS Jill's Juke Box 77
PCS 09571-3	**LP:** TL STBB03
	Sing, Sing, Sing - Introducing "Christopher Columbus" - Part 1 (arr JM)
PCS 09572-1	**LP:** TL STBB03, RcaBB AXM2-5568, JAZ 41
PCS 09572-2	same issues as PCS 09571-2
PCS 09572-3	**LP:** JAZ 41
	Sing, Sing, Sing - Introducing "Christopher Columbus" - Part 2 (arr JM)

(On December 27, 1937, matrices PCS 09571-2 and PCS 09572-2 were
abridged from the original recordings to produce 10" matrices BS 017695-1R
and BS 017696-1R. These "R" matrices were used to press VI 25796 A/B, a
10" disc that could be accommodated in juke boxes, then a growing market
for the recording companies. Later, some EPs were pressed from the 10"
matrices, as indicated above. Note that RcaBB AXM2-5568 and JAZ 41,
matrices PCS 09571-1 and PCS 09572-1, 3, were dubbed from copies of test
pressings, with indifferent results.)

The second "Reynolds transcription" forces our second reassignment:
"A Handful Of Keys" is from the broadcast of July 6, not July 16, as
believed earlier:

"CAMEL CARAVAN"   *same date - Los Angeles*
  CBS Radio Network

Personnels as June 29.

Let's Dance (theme)
Blue Skies
Swingtime In The Rockies
Body And Soul - TRIO
(It's A Long Way To Tipperary - voc Meyer Alexander Chorus - NO BG
(The Campbells - "Camels" - Are Coming - voc Meyer Alexander Chorus - NO BG

BENNY GOODMAN QUARTET

59-MG-632   MGM Series: 103, 106, 109, 113, 116
                 Handful Of Keys

(I Wish I Were A Tender Apple Blossom - voc guest Victor Moore, Meyer Alexander Chorus - NO BG

BENNY GOODMAN AND HIS ORCHESTRA

59-MG-629   MGM Series: 101, 104, 107, 111, 115, 118
                 Can't We Be Friends?

XLP 11050-1C   CO Series: 2, 4, 7, 8, 12, 14, 18, 20, 24, 28, 37, 38, 40, 41, 49, 52, plus **78:** CoJap L3017. **EP:** CO B819.
                 LP: PIC 240
                 Bugle Call Rag

Good-Bye (theme)

Victor's scroll label issues, prized by collectors, end with the next session, so far as BG releases are concerned. Note that Gene Krupa, stung by John Hammond's criticism that he varied the tempo on "Roll 'Em," timed the 78 with a metronome, found John's tempo was awry, not his.

BENNY GOODMAN AND HIS ORCHESTRA   July 7, 1937, Hollywood

Personnel as June 29. BETTY VAN, voc.

PBS 09576-3   VI 25627 B, VI 20-2407, HMV B8631, GrFr K8086,
(1,2)   ViJap A-1094, HMVIt GW1467. **45:** VI 27-0061. **EP:** VI
                 VI EPB1005. **LP:** VI LPT1005, ViJap RA71, RD3-45,
                 RcaBB AXM2-5537, RcaFr 741.072, HIS H623, JO
                 3057, RcaFr PM45727, RcaG "Golden Age Of Jazz."
                 ET: AFRS "Remember" H54-26, AFRS P-865
                 Roll 'Em (arr MLW)

PBS 09577-1   **LP:** RcaBB AXM2-5568 JAZ 7
PBS 09577-2   VI 25634 B. **LP:** ViG LPM10022, RD 3-76, RcaFr
(3)   741.059, RcaBB AXM2-5537, JAZ 16, RcaFr
                 PM45727
                 When It's Sleepy Time Down South (arr FH)

PBS 09578-2   VI 25627 A, VI 20-2409, HMV B8631, HMVAu EA1969,
(1,3)   HmVIt GW1467. **LP:** ViG LPM10025, RD "The Great
                 Band Era" album, VI VPM6040, RcaBB AXM2-5537,
                 RcaFr FXM1-7083. **ET:** AFRS P-863
                 Afraid To Dream - voc Betty Van

PBS 09579-2   **LP:** PHON LV50, RcaBB AXM2-5568, JAZ 16
(1)
PBS 09579-3   VI 25634 A, BB 11226, VI 20-2408, HMV B8683. **EP:** VI
                 EPBT3056, HMV 7EG8142. **LP:** VI LPT3056, VI
                 LPM1239, VI VPM6040, ViArg AVLT3, RcaBB
                 AXM2-5537, RcaFr 741.059, RcaFr PM45727, RcaAu
                 VPL1-0471, TL STBB03. **ET:** AFRS P-863
                 Changes (arr FH)

(RcaBB AXM2-5568's liner notes erroneously state "take 1" instead of take 2 for PBS 09579-2. Again, recent reissues on LP's are dubs of copies of test pressings.)

Two venerable standards receive tender loving care on the next broadcast: Harry James is excellent on "Star Dust," Teddy Wilson is outstanding on "More Than You Know." Not detailed is a comedy routine by guest Louis Alberni, after "Nagasaki."

"CAMEL CARAVAN"   *July 13, 1937, Los Angeles*
  CBS Radio Network

Personnels as June 29.

Let's Dance (theme)
Star Dust
Sugar Foot Stomp
More Than You Know - TRIO
(The Story Of The St. Louis Blues - voc Meyer Alexander Chorus - NO BG
Nagasaki - QUARTET
Truckin'

BENNY GOODMAN AND HIS ORCHESTRA

XLP 11050-1C   CO Series: 2, 4, 6, 8, 12, 14, 18, 23, 24, 28, 37, 41,
                 43A, 46, 52, and 78: CoJap L3017. **LP:** VJ "Caras."
                 ET: AFRS "American Popular Music," END-390-Part 1.
                 King Porter Stomp

Good-Bye (theme)

Vocalist Betty Van had replaced Peg LaCentra late in June; she recorded with Benny on July 7, and logs of sustaining broadcasts from the Palomar show her much in evidence through the third week of August. However, the next two "Caravans" are her only contributions to the sponsored broadcasts. She is not introduced by name, and is listed in the R. J. Reynolds' logs as, "Unannounced Female Vocalist":

"CAMEL CARAVAN"   *July 20, 1937, Los Angeles*
  CBS Radio Network

Personnels as June 29, plus Betty Van, voc.

Let's Dance (theme)
Smiles (arr JM)
Caravan (arr JM)

BENNY GOODMAN QUARTET

59-MG-628   MGM Series: 101, 104, 107, 111, 115, 117
                 Tea For Two

"The Camel Hop" - voc Meyer Alexander Chorus - BG in coda
Tiger Rag - TRIO (LP: VJ "Carras," SB 149)
After The Ball Is Over - voc guest Charlie Ruggles - BG obligato
They Can't Take That Away From Me - voc Betty Van

BENNY GOODMAN AND HIS ORCHESTRA

59-MG-628   MGM Series: 101, 104, 107, 111, 115, 118
                 Swing Low, Sweet Chariot (arr JM)

Good-Bye (theme)

Still unannounced, Betty makes her final appearance on the "Caravan." Note that "The Sheik Of Araby" is by the full orchestra:

"CAMEL CARAVAN"   *July 27, 1937, Los Angeles*
  CBS Radio Network

Personnels as June 29, plus Betty Van, voc.

Let's Dance (theme)
The Sheik Of Araby
I Can't Give You Anything But Love, Baby

BENNY GOODMAN TRIO

59-MG-630B   MGM Series: 102, 105, 108, 110, 112, 116, 119
                 Marie

They All Laughed - voc Meyer Alexander Chorus - BG obligato
I Got Rhythm - QUARTET
Afraid To Dream - voc Betty Van

                                        July 27, 1937, continued

July 27, 1937, continued
BENNY GOODMAN AND HIS ORCHESTRA

XLP 36019-1J **LP:** CO JZ1, PhilCont B07100L, PaE PMC1222,
RTB4301. **EP:** CO JZP1
Jam Session (arr JM)

Good-Bye (theme)

(Columbia releases of "Jam Session" are "bonus" records.)

BENNY GOODMAN QUARTET   **July 30, 1937, Hollywood**

Personnel as June 29.

PBS 09627-1 **LP:** RcaBB AXM2-5568, RcaFr PM43176
PBS 09627-2 VI 25644 A, HMV B8617, ViArg 60-0160, ViArg 1A-
(3)   0756, ViArg 68-0916, ViJap JA1013, ViJap A-1162,
             GrFr K7991, HMVInd N4494, HMVSw JK2297. **EP:** VI
             EPAT406, VI EPB1099, HMV 7EG8003, VSM EMF73,
             RcaBel 85.508, RcaFr 75.605. **LP:** VI LPM1099, VI
             LPV1009, VI VPM6040, ViJap RA73, VI LSP4005(e),
             HMV DLP1112, HMV DLP1116, RcaBB AXM2-5537,
             VI CLPI-2470, JR 5036, RcaFr 730.629, RcaFr
             740.552, RcaFr FXM3-7273, RcaFR PM43176, RcaE
             PL12470
             Avalon

PBS 09628-1 VI 25705 B, HMV B8689, GrFr K8068, ViJap JA1142.
             EP: RcaFr 75-605. **LP:** VI LEJ12, VI LPV1032, ViJap
             RA73, CAM 624, CamE CDN148, JR 5036, RcaBB
             AXM2-5537, RcaFr 730.707, RcaFr PM43176
PBS 09628-2 **LP:** RcaBB AXM2-5568, RcaFr PM43176
             Handful Of Keys

PBS 09632-1 same 78 issues as PBS 09627-2, except omit ViArg 1A-
             0756, and add ASR LB4958, HMVlt GW1578, ViJap
             A-1084, ViJap LM35. **EP:** VI EPB1226, VI EPBT3004,
             ViArg ACGT10, HMV7EG8154, VSM EMF73. **LP:** VI
             LPT3004, VI LPM1226, VI LPV1009, ViJap RA73,
             HMV DLPC6, JR 5036, RcaBB AXM2-5537, RcaFr
             LPM1226, RcaFr 430.230, RcaFr 730.629, RcaFr
             PM43176, JO 101.611
             The Man I Love

(Mxs PBS 09628 and PBS 09632 are consecutive. RcaBB AXM2-5568's liner
notes erroneously state "take 1" instead of take 2 for PBS 09628-2. Despite
claims of an extant take 2 of "The Man I Love," none has been located.)

Next is the last of the BG/Teddy Wilson Brunswick recording sessions.
Pseudonyms and other subterfuges are dispensed with simply: the labels
omit mention of personnel.

TEDDY WILSON AND HIS ORCHESTRA   **July 30, 1937, Hollywood**

Benny Goodman, clt; Harry James, tpt; Vido Musso, ts; Teddy Wilson, p;
Allan Reuss, g; Harry Goodman, b; Gene Krupa, d; Boots Castle, voc.

LA 1380-A **LP:** MER 3
LA 1380-B BR 7940, BrG A81338
           You're My Desire - voc Boots Castle

LA 1381-A BR 7940, BrG A81338, DeE J14
LA 1381-B **LP:** MER 3
           Remember Me - voc Boots Castle

LA 1382-A BR 7943, CoAu D01771, DeE J1, DeSw M30390
LA 1382-B **LP:** NOST 890/1, MER 3
           The Hour Of Parting (L'heure Bleu) - voc Boots Castle

LA 1383-A BR 7943, DeE J1, DeSw M30390, CoJap M415 (?). **LP:**
           SONY SONP50332/3, SONY SOPW9/10, CBS 66274,
           TL STLJ20, CO CG/KG 31617
LA 1383-B **LP:** MER 3
           Coquette

BENNY GOODMAN QUARTET   **August 2, 1937, Hollywood**

Personnel as June 29.

PBS 09633-2 VI 25660 B, HMV B8630, ViArg 63-0317, ViJap JA1266,
(1)   GrF K8085, HMVlt GW 1519. **EP:** VI EPB1226, VI
             EPBT3004, HMV 7EG8180. **LP:** VI LPT3004, VI
             LPM1226, RcaBB AXM2-5537, ViJap RA73, HMV
             DLPC6, RcaF 430-230, RcaF LPM1226, RcaFr
             731.041, RcaFr PM43684
             Smiles

PBS 09634-3 VI 25660 A, HMV B8630, ViArg 63-0317, ViJap JA1266,
(1,2)   GrF K8085. **EP:** VI EPOT6703. **LP:** VI LPT6703, ViArg
             AYL3000-5, VI LPV1032, ViJap RA73, RcaBB
             AXM2-5537, RcaBEL 230.233, RcaFr 730.707, RcaFr
             PM43684
             Liza

The August 3 "Reynolds ET" corrects another erroneous assignment:
"Twilight In Turkey" is from this broadcast, not from that of July 16. It also
adds two tunes rarely performed by the band, "The Merry-Go-Round Broke
Down" and "It Looks Like Rain In Cherry Blossom Lane":

"CAMEL CARAVAN"   *August 3, 1937, Los Angeles*
  CBS Radio Network

*Personnels as June 29, plus Betty Van, voc. QUINTET: Quartet plus Harry
James, tpt.*

Let's Dance (theme)

BENNY GOODMAN AND HIS ORCHESTRA

XLP 11049-1A CO Series: 1, 4, 5, 11, 14, 18, 22, 24, 52
              Always

The Merry-Go-Round Broke Down
Where Or When - TRIO
(Three Little Words - voc Meyer Alexander Chorus, Bill Goodwin - NO BG

BENNY GOODMAN QUINTET

59-MG-632 MGM Series: 103, 106, 109, 113, 115, 116, 117
           Twilight In Turkey

*(The Changing Of The Guard - voc guest Pat O'Malley, Meyer Alexander
  Chorus - NO BG*
It Looks Like Rain In Cherry Blossom Lane
I've Found A New Baby
Good-Bye (theme)

The next four "Camel Caravan" broadcasts are available to collectors in
their entireties; 16" monitor acetates of the August 10, 17, 24, and 31
programs were "moonlight requisitioned" and tapes made from them are in
circulation. Selections from three of these programs were issued by Columbia and MGM; these tunes are shown in the sequence in which they were
performed, and the balance of the programs are listed as air checks. Portions
of all four programs are also on bootleg LPs SB 146 & 147, and CARIB 810;
the first two, on MIR 165.

"CAMEL CARAVAN"   *August 10, 1937, Los Angeles*
  CBS Radio Network

Personnels as June 29.

Let's Dance (theme)
Remember
Me, Myself And I - voc Benny Goodman
Sailboat In The Moonlight - TRIO

BENNY GOODMAN QUARTET

XLP 11050-1C   Co Series: 2, 4, 7, 10, 12, 14, 15, 18, 19, 24, 31, 32,
36, 44, 45, 52, and **EP:** CO B819
Shine

Sing, Sing, Sing - Part 2
Good-Bye (theme)

These selections were played by his band, sans Benny:

Mother Goose Marches On - voc Meyer (later, Jeff) Alexander Chorus
Swing, Benny, Swing - voc Bloch & Sully, Meyer Alexander Chorus

BENNY GOODMAN QUARTET   **August 13, 1937, Los Angeles**

Sustaining radio b'cast from the Palomar. Personnel as June 29.

XLP 11048-1A   CO Series: 1, 3, 5, 9, 11, 13, 17, 22, 24, 29, 35, 44,
47, 52
Vibraphone Blues - voc Lionel Hampton

"CAMEL CARAVAN"   *August 17, 1937, Los Angeles*
CBS Radio Network

Personnels as June 29.

Let's Dance (theme)
That Naughty Waltz
Satan Takes A Holiday (arr JM)

BENNY GOODMAN TRIO

59-MG-632   MGM Series: 103, 106, 109, 113, 120, 121
So Rare

BENNY GOODMAN QUARTET

ZLP 12609-1A   **7" LP:** CO "Bonus Record" ZLP 12609
Liza "All The Clouds Will Roll Away"

Chlo-e (Song Of The Swamp)

BENNY GOODMAN AND HIS ORCHESTRA

XLP 11051-1B   CO Series: 2, 3, 7, 12, 13, 17, 20, 24, 33A, 52, and
78: CO DJ 48333, PHIL PB254, PhilCont & Au
B2109H: **EP:** CO B819
Caravan (arr JM)

XLP 11051-1B   CO Series: 3, 12, 13, 17, 52
Good-Bye (theme)

Once more, the band played without Benny:

Let's Have Another Cigarette - voc Meyer Alexander Chorus
Russian Swing - voc Marek Windheim & Meyer Alexander Chorus

SUSTAINING BROADCAST   *August 19, 1937, Palomar,*
CBS Radio Network   *Los Angeles*

Personnels as June 29.

Where Or When - TRIO (n/c)
Sweet Sue-Just You - QUARTET (n/c)

Betty Van's last documented appearance with the band is a sustaining broadcast of August 21; but note that for the "Camel Caravan" broadcasts of August 10 and 17, BG, guests, and the Meyer Alexander Chorus had taken the vocals. However, the voice of a petite young blonde in the chorus had caught Benny's ear (listen carefully and you may hear it too, in the chorus efforts from those two programs). Benny asked her to audition, liked what he heard, and signed her on. She made her first solo appearance on the next "Camel Caravan" broadcast: Martha Tilton, June Richmond's predecessor with Jimmy Dorsey.

"CAMEL CARAVAN"   *August 24, 1937, Los Angeles*
CBS Radio Network

Personnels as June 29.

Let's Dance (theme) (also on LP: NOST 1001, VIVA V36018)
Sometimes I'm Happy

Minnie The Moocher's Wedding Day
My Cabin Of Dreams - TRIO
Stompin' At The Savoy - QUARTET
Sailboat In The Moonlight - voc MARTHA TILTON
Roll 'Em
Good-Bye (theme)

. . . plus two selections by the band without BG:
Bye, Bye Pretty Baby - voc Meyer Alexander Chorus
Swing High, Swing Low - voc Pat O'Malley, chorus (arr JM)

Benny and the band took a quick trip to Toronto, played the Canadian Exhibition there on August 26, 27, and 28. Then back to the Palomar and the next "Camel Caravan" broadcast:

"CAMEL CARAVAN"   *August 31, 1937, Los Angeles*
CBS Radio Network

Personnels as June 29.

Let's Dance (theme)
Camel Hop (arr MLW)
La Cucaracha

BENNY GOODMAN TRIO

59-MG-628   MGM Series: 101, 104, 107, 111, 117
Whispers In The Dark

The Blue Danube - voc Meyer Alexander Chorus
Vibraphone Blues - voc Lionel Hampton - QUARTET
Swing Song - voc Pat O'Malley, Meyer Alexander Chorus
The Dixieland Band - voc Martha Tilton
House Hop
Good-Bye (theme)

(BG blows a few notes each on "Blue Danube" and "Swing Song.")

The Palomar gig ended September 4, but the band stayed on for a studio session and a final West Coast "Camel Caravan" broadcast. Guests on the "Caravan" were Red Norvo and Mildred Bailey, who had replaced Benny at the Palomar.

BENNY GOODMAN AND HIS ORCHESTRA **September 6, 1937, Hollywood**

Personnel as June 29. MARTHA TILTON, voc.

PBS 09688-2 (1)	VI 25683 A, HMV B8691, HMVInd N4465. **LP:** RD "The Great Band Era," ViG LPM10022, RcaBB AXM2-5537, RcaFr PM43173, RcaFr PM45727 **Bob White** - voc Martha Tilton (arr JM)
PBS 09689-1	VI 25678 B, VI 420-0149, ViJap 1224, A, HMV B8671, ViArg 68-0847, HMVAu EA2020, GrFr K8086, HMVInd N4464, ViJap A-1141. **45:** VI 447-0149. **EP:** VI EPA5043, VI EPB1239, VI EPBT3056, HMV 7EG8142, RcaAu 20060, RcaE RCX1019, RcaNZ RPX1330. **LP:** VI LPT3056, VI LPM1239, VI VPM6040, VI DRLI-0062, ViJap RA71, RD 3-76, RcaBB AXM2-5537, RcaFr 741.044, RcaFr FXM3-7273, RcaFr PM45727, C/P 25231
PBS 09689-2	**LP:** RcaBB AXM2-5568, JAZ 7 **Sugarfoot Stomp** (arr FH)
PBS 09690-2 (1)	VI 25678 A, ViJap 1224 B, HMV B8671, HMVInd N4464, ViJap A-1141. **EP:** VI EPOT6703. **LP:** VI LPT6703, ViArg AYL3000-5, ViJap RA71, RD 3-76, RcaBB AXM2-5537, RcaFr 741.059, RcaFr PM45727, VI VPM6063
PBS 09690-3	**LP:** VELP 1, JAZ 17 **I Can't Give You Anything But Love, Baby** - voc Martha Tilton (arr FH)
PBS 09691-1 (2)	VI 25683 B, HMV B8683. **EP:** VI EPOT6703. **LP:** VI LPT6703, ViArg AYL3000-5, RcaBB AXM2-5537, RcaFr 741.102, RcaFr PM45727, RcaAu VPLI-0471 **Minnie The Moocher's Weddin' Day** (arr HH/FH)

BENNY GOODMAN QUARTET September 7, 1937, Los Angeles

CBS "Camel Caravan" b' cast. Personnels as June 29.

59-MG-632 MGM Series: 103, 106, 109, 110, 113, 114, 119, 120, 121
Smiles

Also available from the same broadcast:

Oh, Lady Be Good! - orchestra (LP: IAJRC 21, SB 149)

Following the completion of "Hollywood Hotel" and the Palomar engagement, Benny and the band were booked into the Pan American Casino of the Dallas Exposition on September 9, where they began a ten day stand. This Texas gig is the first a mixed black-and-white orchestra played the Deep South. There was one unpleasant incident because of the racial issue, but it was quickly cleared up; and all the members of the band found they were judged as musicians, and were welcome.

SUSTAINING BROADCAST September 12, 1937, Pan-American Casino,
CBS Radio Network Dallas, Texas

Personnel as June 29.

Ida - QUARTET (LP: SB 149)

Harry James missed several days of the Dallas stand, was replaced by Freddy Baker. But he returned in time for the next "Camel Caravan" broadcast with a vengeance: He's featured on both trumpet and drums. In a remarkable demonstration of the versatility of his sidemen, Benny replicated the Raymond Scott Sextet, had each member play other than his usual instrument. Result is an unique air check, but Harry will play drums for Benny again in future.

BENNY GOODMAN AND HIS ORCHESTRA September 14, 1937, Dallas

CBS "Camel Caravan" broadcast. Personnel as June 29.

XLP 11048-1A CO Series: 1, 3, 5, 11, 13, 17, 22, 26, 26, 52
Peckin'

Also available from this broadcast:

SEXTET: Benny Goodman, ts; Murray McEachern, tpt & bells; Art Rollini, clt; Ziggy Elman, p; Allan Reuss, b; Harry James, d.

Powerhouse - SEXTET (LP: IAJRC 14, SB 149)

The band then turned east, appearing in Kansas City, Cleveland, Baltimore and Johnson City, New York. Excerpts of its "Camel Caravan" broadcasts from Kansas City and Cleveland are extant:

BENNY GOODMAN September 21, 1937, Kansas City
AND HIS ORCHESTRA

CBS "Camel Caravan" boradcast. Personnel as June 29.

59-MG-628 MGM Series: 101, 104, 107, 111, 115, 118
Madhouse

"CAMEL CARAVAN" September 28, 1937, Cleveland
CBS Radio Network

Personnels as June 29.

I'm Getting Sentimental Over You - TRIO (n/c)
I'm A Ding Dong Daddy (From Dumas) - QUARTET (n/c)

September 28 was the beginning of the fall season for radio contracts, and the "Caravan" resumed its hour-long format. For that program only, Jack Oakie and George Stoll divided honors with Benny and the band, from his remote location in Ohio. The week following, Oakie and Stoll took over the first half hour, from 9:30 to 10:00, and Benny had sole possession of the succeeding 30 minutes. This format persisted into 1938.

On October 11 Benny began another engagement in the Madhattan Room of the Hotel Pennsylvania. Murray McEachern had left October 1 to join Glen Gray, had been replaced by Vernon Brown. However, union regulations permitted Brown to play no more than three of the six evenings each week the band was in the Madhattan Room, and prevented him from recording commercially with Goodman until he had established residency. Substitutes, including McEachern, filled in for Brown at the Pennsylvania, and, on occasion, Benny used only one trombone. McEachern also came back for the Victor recording sessions of October 22 and November 12.

Through its 15-week engagement in the Madhattan Room this time around, the band was broadcast by the several networks, on a sustaining basis, at least once each evening. These "remotes" are the source of the very first bootleg LPs of Benny Goodman air checks. In the 1950s, an even dozen of Benny's half-hour broadcasts from the Pennsylvania were transferred from broadcast acetates onto 12" vinyl pressings, over time. They were sold on an "exclusive" basis—no more than 50 of each were to be produced. For those years, they were expensive, $25 each, a price that progressively eliminated "subscribers" to the series. Very few complete sets of all 12 are extant.

The original LPs have blank labels, and thus no catalog numbers; and there are no inscribed matrices. They are listed herein in order of performance (they were sold out of chronological order), and are arbitrarily numbered "LP 1," "LP 2," et cetera. In general, the original LPs offer good audio. In the 1970s, the entire set was duplicated on subsidiary bootleg LPs, SB 116-127 inclusive, with indifferent results. The SB LPs were later reprocessed and rereleased, with some improvement.

Precise personnels for all 12 of these broadcasts are uncertain, in main because of trombonist Brown's restricted participation. He is likely present for most of them; and because his replacements cannot be determined, he is credited throughout. Ziggy Elman was married on October 10, left the band then for a short honeymoon. Benny's brother Irving replaced Ziggy for those few days, and is believed present for the first broadcast, next:

BENNY GOODMAN TRIO, QUARTET October 13, 1937, New York
AND ORCHESTRA

CBS sustaining broadcast from the Madhattan Room.

Benny Goodman, clt; Harry James, IRVING GOODMAN, Chris Griffin, tpt; Red Ballard, VERNON BROWN, tbn; Hymie Schertzer, George Koenig, as; Art Rollini, Vido Musso, ts; Jess Stacy, p; Allan Reuss, g; Harry Goodman, b; Gene Krupa, d. Martha Tilton, voc.

TRIO: Benny Goodman, clt; Teddy Wilson, p; Gene Krupa, d.

QUARTET: As Trio, plus Lionel Hampton, d.

LP 1 - Side 1:
Let's Dance (theme)
In The Shade Of The Old Apple Tree (arr FH)
That Old Feeling - voc Martha Tilton
Moonlight On The Highway (arr JM)
Whispers In The Dark - TRIO
The Moon Got In My Eyes - voc Martha Tilton (arr JM)

LP 1 - Side 2:
Chlo-e
Avalon - QUARTET, plus orchestra in coda
I'd Like To See Samoa Of Samoa - voc Martha Tilton (arr JM)
Caravan
Satan Takes A Holiday (arr JM)
Good-Bye (theme)

The staff announcer on some of the broadcasts in this period identifies himself as "Melvin Allen." Later, as Mel Allen, he won considerable fame in radio and television as a sports' commentator. He is still active in the 1980s, may be heard on sports-related commercials on broadcasts and telecasts.

BENNY GOODMAN TRIO, QUARTET, October 16, 1937, New York
AND ORCHESTRA

CBS sustaining broadcast from Madhattan Room. Personnels as October 13, except possibly Elman returns.

LP 2 - Side 1
Let's Dance (theme)
House Hop
So Many Memories - voc Martha Tilton (arr JM)
My Honey's Lovin' Arms (arr FH)
Bob White - voc Martha Tilton
Roses In December - TRIO

LP 2 - Side 2
Marie (arr FH)
I'm A Ding Dong Daddy (From Dumas) - QUARTET
Loch Lomond - voc Martha Tilton, Benny Goodman (arr CT)
Roll 'Em

BENNY GOODMAN AND HIS ORCHESTRA   October 19, 1937, New York

CBS "Camel Caravan" b' cast. Personnels as October 13 except Ziggy Elman returns from his honeymoon and Irving Goodman leaves.

XLP 11048-1A   CO Series: 1, 3, 5, 11, 13, 17, 22, 24, 26, 52
Sunny Disposish (prob. arr JM)

BENNY GOODMAN TRIO   same broadcast

59-MG-631   MGM Series: 102, 105, 108, 112, 115
Remember Me

BENNY GOODMAN QUARTET   same broadcast

XLP 11051-1B   CO Series: 2, 3, 7, 10, 12, 13, 16, 17, 21, 24, 44, 52,
and **78**: PhilCont B21208H, **EP**: CO B819
Everybody Loves My Baby

Also available from this broadcast:

Rose Room (LP: SB 149)

BENNY GOODMAN TRIO, QUARTET,   *October 20, 1937, New York*
AND ORCHESTRA

CBS sustaining broadcast from the Madhattan Room. Personnels as October 19.

LP 3 - Side 1
Stardust On The Moon - voc Martha Tilton
Dear Old Southland
So Many Memories - voc Martha Tilton
One O'Clock Jump (arr CB)

LP 3 - Side 2
Body And Soul - TRIO
Me, Myself And I - voc Martha Tilton
Sweet Sue - QUARTET
When It's Sleepy Time Down South
Camel Hop (n'c)

BENNY GOODMAN TRIO, QUARTET,   *October 21, 1937, New York*
AND ORCHESTRA

Mutual sustaining broadcast from the Madhattan Room. Personnels as October 19.

LP 4 - Side 1
Let's Dance (theme)
Minnie The Moocher's Wedding Day
Afraid To Dream - voc Martha Tilton
Moonlight On The Highway
Once In A While - voc Martha Tilton (prob. arr SM)
Sugar Foot Stomp

LP 4 - Side 2
Sugar Foot Stomp (repeat from Side 1)
More Than You Know (arr FH)
The Dixieland Band - voc Martha Tilton
Jam Session (same as LP -5)
Good-Bye (theme) (same as LP -5)

(Actual broadcast of October 21 included "Pop-Corn Man" instead of the repeated "Sugar Foot Stomp," and full band versions of "The Sheik Of Araby" and "I Know That You Know," instead of "Jam Session' and "Good-Bye." It is not known why the substitutions were made.)

The band got back into Victor's studios on East 24th Street on October 22. It cut three tunes from "Hollywood Hotel," and a fourth destined to become one of the rarest and most sought after of all collectors' items, "Pop-Corn Man."

No one has yet offered a satisfactory explanation as to why "Pop-Corn Man" was killed almost immediately upon release. Known facts are that the catalog number was assigned a few days before the release date, March 14, 1938; one week later, March 21, "Pop-Corn Man" was withdrawn from the catalog, all releases were recalled (most were still in the hands of distributors, not retailers), all labels were scrapped, and masters of the take issued and masters of alternate takes were destroyed. That same day, March 21, "Always And Always" was assigned "Pop-Corn Man's" original catalog number; on March 23 "Always And Always" was listed in Victor's catalog; and on March 24, take 1 of "Always And Always" was passed as

"acceptable." Surely such haste betokens a compelling reason for "Pop-Corn Man's" summary extinction; and it might seem that some one should remember that reason. But no one has come forward with it, although there are several theories about it.

Benny says he doesn't know, that he had nothing to do with it. His position is that once he had chosen the take to be released, he had no further control over any side. Gene Krupa suggests that possibly there were copyright difficulties, but he recalls nothing in this regard about the "Man." He doesn't credit the thought that in some manner his leaving BG on March 3–18 days before the "Man" was killed—had anything to do with it.

Another theory is that the release was delayed too long, and the tune was outdated when the record was issued. Still another story is that a straight-laced RCA executive found something objectionable in the lyrics; close listening offers little substantiation to this idea. Whatever happened, and despite the reissue on CAMDEN in 1960, Benny Goodman's original recording of "Pop-Corn Man" is a celebrated rarity among collectors; not more than 10 copies are known to exist.

There is another interesting sidelight to this session. A participant claims that Harry James sat in for Gene Krupa on mx BS 015536-1 "Can't Teach My Old Heart New Tricks." He gives no reason for the substitution; but it should be acknowledged that although there is a James trumpet solo on each of the other three titles from this session, there is none on "Can't Teach. . ." Also, there is no distinctive drumming on this side that can be ascribed definitely to Krupa. And as revealed earlier, James did on occasion play drums for Benny.

BENNY GOODMAN AND HIS ORCHESTRA   October 22, 1937, New York

Personnel as October 19, except Murray McEachern, tbn, replaces Brown.

BS 015535-1   VI 25708 B, HMV B8736. **LP**: JAZ 16, RcaFr PM45727
(2)   **Let That Be A Lesson To You** - voc Martha Tilton

BS 015536-1   VI 25711 A, HMV B8735, HMVlt GW1557, ViJap
(2)   JA1280. **LP**: JAZ 16, TL STBB03
Can't Teach My Old Heart New Tricks - voc Martha Tilton

BS 015537-1   VI 25708 A, HMV B8736. **LP**: JAZ 18
(2)   **I've Hitched My Wagon To A Star** - voc Martha Tilton

BS 015538-1   VI 25808 B. **LP**: CAM 624, CamE CDN148, RcaFr
(2)   FXMI-7083, RS (no #), RcaFr PM45727
Pop-Corn Man - voc Martha Tilton

(Original issue of Vi 25808 couples "oooOO-OH BOOM!" (BS 021129) with "Pop-Corn Man." VI 25808 was later re-used to couple "oooOO-OH BOOM!" with "Always And Always" (BS 021130). Additionally, all issued takes above are on **LP**: RcaBB AXM2-5537.)

BENNY GOODMAN TRIO, QUARTET,   *October 23, 1937, New York*
AND ORCHESTRA

CBS sustaining broadcast from the Madhattan Room. Personnels as October 19. (This broadcast also on LPs MIR 154, ST 193749.)

LP 5 - Side 1
Let's Dance (theme)
In The Shade Of The Old Apple Tree
You're My Desire - voc Martha Tilton (arr JM)
Am I Blue? (arr FH)
Where Or When - TRIO
Someday Sweetheart

LP 5 - Side 2
Bob White - voc Martha Tilton
Nagasaki - QUARTET
Yours And Mine - voc Martha Tilton (arr JM)
Jam Session
Good-Bye (theme)

"CAMEL CARAVAN"   *October 26, 1937, New York*
CBS Radio Network

Personnel as October 19.

It Don't Mean A Thing (If You Ain't Got That Swing) - QUARTET

BENNY GOODMAN TRIO, QUARTET,   *October 27, 1937, New York*
AND ORCHESTRA

CBS sustaining broadcast from the Madhattan Room. Personnels as October 19.

LP 6 - Side 1
  Let's Dance (theme)
  When Buddha Smiles
  Cherry (arr JM)
  Swing Low, Sweet Chariot
  Star Dust

LP 6 - Side 2
  The Lady Is A Tramp - voc Martha Tilton
  A Handful Of Keys - QUARTET
  So Many Memories - voc Martha Tilton
  Swingtime In The Rockies

("Cherry" is from a broadcast of unknown date. In its place, actual broadcast of October 27 had "Tears In My Heart" and "Bob White.")

A delightful discovery in the hands of a collector—but not in RCA's vaults—is arbitrarily added to the next Victor recording session. (There is the chance that it is an out-take from "Hollywood Hotel," but no documentation supporting that surmise has been discovered.) Its ambience suggests nothing other than a studio recording, and its length imputes the inference that it was a rehearsal effort to establish timing and balance. Thus is appended, with reservations, a previously unsuspected version of, "Silhouetted In The Moonlight":

BENNY GOODMAN TRIO/QUARTET   October 29, 1937, New York

TRIO: Goodman, Wilson, Krupa - first two matrices.

QUARTET: Goodman, Hampton, Wilson, Krupa - third matrix.

BS 015575-1	VI 25725 A, HMV B9017, HMVFr X6461, HMVIt GW1548, HMVSw JK2301, ViJap A-1128, ViJap LM7-A, BB 11456, BRS 26. **EP:** VI EPOT6703. **LP:** VI LPT6703, ViArg AYL3000-5, VI LPV1032, RcaBB AXM2-5557, ViJap RA73, RcaFr 730.707, RcaFr PM43684, RcaBel 230.233
	Where Or When
- 0 -	Test Pressing
BS 015576-1 (2)	VI 25711 B, ViJap JA1280, HMV B8735, HMVAu EA2037, HMVIt GW 1547, GrFr K8038. **EP:** VI EPOT6703. **LP:** VI LPT6703, ViArg AYL3000-5, RcaBB AXM2-5557, RcaFr PM43684, ViJap RA73
	Silhouetted In The Moonlight - voc Martha Tilton
BS 015577-2 (1,3)	VI 25705 A, ViJap JA1142, HMV B8689, BIA 219. **LP:** VI LPV521, VI LPV1032, JR 5036, RcaBB AXM2-5557, RcaE RD7775, RcaFr 730.707, RcaFr PM43684, ViJap RA73, RcaAu VJL2-0267
	Vieni, Vieni

BENNY GOODMAN TRIO, QUARTET,   *October 30, 1937, New York*
AND ORCHESTRA

CBS sustaining broadcast from the Madhattan Room. Personnels as October 19.

LP 7 - Side 1
  Let's Dance (theme)
  Makin' Whoopee
  Farewell My Love - voc Martha Tilton (arr JM)
  The Lady Is A Tramp - voc Martha Tilton
  Oh, Lady Be Good! - TRIO

LP 7 - Side 2
  Love Me Or Leave Me
  Once In A While - voc Martha Tilton (arr SM)
  Everybody Loves My Baby - QUARTET
  You And I Know - voc Martha Tilton (arr JM)

BENNY GOODMAN AND HIS ORCHESTRA   November 2, 1937, New York

CBS "Camel Caravan" broadcast. Personnels as October 19.

59-MG-629	MGM Series: 101, 104, 107, 111, 115, 118
	Chicago (That Toddlin' Town) (arr HH)
XLP 11048-1A	CO Series: 1, 3, 5, 11, 13, 17, 22, 24, 26, 33A, 46, 49, 50 and **78:** CO DJ 48319. **ET:** VOA World of Jazz 6
	Ridin' High (arr JM)

BENNY GOODMAN TRIO   same broadcast

| XLP 11051-1B | CO Series: 2, 3, 6, 10, 12, 13, 17, 23, 24, 30, 34, 44, 45, 52, and **78:** PhilCont B21093H |
| | **Time On My Hands (You In My Arms)** |

BENNY GOODMAN AND HIS ORCHESTRA   November 3, 1937, New York

CBS sustaining broadcast from Madhattan Room. Personnel as October 19.

| XLP 11050-1C | CO Series: 2, 4, 7, 12, 14, 18, 24, 52, and **EP:** CO B819 |
| | **At The Darktown Strutters' Ball** (arr SM) |

Life Magazine ran a spread on Benny and the band at the Madhattan Room in its November 21 issue, headlined "Life Goes to A Party." In appreciation of this national recognition from a non-musical publication, Benny had Harry James set down some riffs he'd been "noodling" to return the favor, as witness this next entry:

BENNY GOODMAN TRIO, QUARTET,   *November 4, 1937, New York*
AND ORCHESTRA

Mutual sustaining broadcast from the Madhattan Room. Personnels as October 19.

LP 8 - Side 1
  Let's Dance (theme)
  Changes
  If It's The Last Thing I Do - voc Martha Tilton
  Someday Sweetheart
  So Many Memories - voc Martha Tilton
  Life Goes To A Party (arr HJ)

LP 8 - Side 2
  Life Goes To A Party (repeated from Side 1)
  Farewell My Love - voc Martha Tilton
  In The Shade Of The Old Apple Tree
  Blossoms On Broadway - voc Martha Tilton
  Walk, Jennie, Walk
  I Can't Give You Anything But Love, Baby - voc Martha Tilton

The November 6 air check-Lp listed next has added significance in that, so far as is known, it offers the only Goodman recording of "Pop-Corn Man" other than the Victor release:

BENNY GOODMAN TRIO, QUARTET,   *November 6, 1937, New York*
AND ORCHESTRA

CBS sustaining broadcast from the Madhattan Room. Personnels as October 19.

LP 9 - Side 1
  Let's Dance (theme)
  That Naughty Waltz
  Once In A While - voc Martha Tilton
  More Than You Know - TRIO
  Pop-Corn Man - voc Martha Tilton
  You Showed Me The Way - voc Martha Tilton

LP 9 - Side 2
  Blue Skies
  Vieni, Vieni - QUARTET
  If It's The Last Thing I Do - voc Martha Tilton
  Life Goes To A Party
  Good-Bye (theme)

BENNY GOODMAN AND HIS ORCHESTRA   November 9, 1937, New York

CBS "Camel Caravan" broadcast. Personnel as October 19, except WILL BRADLEY, tbn, substitutes for Vernon Brown.

XLP 11051-1B   CO Series: 2, 3, 7, 12, 13, 17, 24, 27, 52, and **EP:** CO
            B819
            Someday Sweetheart

BENNY GOODMAN AND HIS ORCHESTRA   November 12, 1937, New York

Personnel as October 22 (McEachern substituting for Brown).

BS 017039-1   VI 25720 A, ViJap 1278 B, GrFr K8126. **LP:** RcaBB
(**2**,3)   AXM2-5557, JAZ 18
            You Took The Words Right Out Of My Heart - voc
            Martha Tilton (arr FH)

BS 017040-1   same issues, except omit ViJap
(**2**,3)   **Mama, That Moon Is Here Again** - voc Martha Tilton
            (arr FH)

BS 017041-1   VI 25717 A, HMV B8745, HMVAu EA2084, ViJap
(**2**)   A-1094, **EP:** VI EPA5078, VI EPOT6703, RcaAu
            20206, RcaE RCX1036, RcaNZ RPX1360. **LP:** VI
            LPT6703, ViArg AYL3000-5, Vi SP4005(e), VI
            CPLI-2470, VI ANLI-0973, RD 3-21, RcaBB
            AXM2-5557, VI Spec Prod 20, RcaE PL12470, RcaFr
            741.072, RcaFr 740.552, RcaFr PM45727, RcaCont
            89323
            Loch Lomond - voc Martha Tilton and Benny Goodman
            (arr CT)

BS 017042-1   VI 25717 B, HMVAu EA2084, HMVSw JK2023. **EP:** VI
(**2**)   EPBT3056. **LP:** VI LPT3056, VI LPM1239, VI DRLI-
            0062, ViArg AVLT3, ViJap RA71, RD 3/4-45, RcaBB
            AXM2-5557, RcaFr 741.072, RcaG Golden Age of
            Jazz, RcaFr PM45727, C/P 25231. **ET:** AFRS American
            Popular Music 390-Pt. 2
            Camel Hop (arr MLW)

BS 017043-1   **LP:** RcaBB AXM2-5557, RcaFr FXMI-7083, RS (no #),
(**2**)   JAZ 18, RcaFr PM45727
            True Confession - voc Martha Tilton

BS 017044-2   ViC 25726 A, VI 25726 A (silver label), ViJap A-1438.
(1)   **EP:** VI EPA745, VI EPA5078, VI EPB1239, VI
            EPBT3056, RcaAu 20206, RcaE RCX1036. **LP:** VI
            LPT3056, VI LPM1239, VI "LIFE" PR125-1 (Time-
            Life), RD 3/4-45, RcaBB AXM2-5557, RcaFr 741.072,
            NM 0456, RcaG Golden Age of Jazz, C/P 25231
            Life Goes To A Party (arr HJ)

(The ViC issue antedates the U.S. VI release of take 2 of "Life Goes To A Party," and was a prized collector's item prior to microgroove issues. Perversely, the gold label VI U.S. take 3 issue is now more in demand by those who collect originals. Note that the unissued alternate take 2's in bold type above are in RCA's vaults, which offers at least the possibility of future release.)

BENNY GOODMAN AND HIS ORCHESTRA   November 13, 1937, New York

CBS sustaining broadcast from the Madhattan Room. Personnel as November 9 (Bradley substituting for Brown).

59-MG-628   MGM Series: 101, 104, 107, 111, 115, 118
            When Buddha Smiles

"CAMEL CARAVAN"   *November 16, 1937, New York*
   CBS Radio Network

Personnels as November 9 (Will Bradley - Wilbur Schwichtenburg - substituting for Brown.)

Let's Dance (theme)
Star Dust
If It's The Last Thing I Do - voc Martha Tilton
After You've Gone - TRIO

You Took The Words Right Out Of My Heart - voc Martha Tilton
Laughing At Life (arr FH)

BENNY GOODMAN QUARTET

XLP 11048-1A   CO Series: 1, 3, 5, 10, 11, 13, 17, 22, 24, 26, 29, 33A,
            35, 44, 45, 52
            Nagasaki

Mama, That Moon Is Here Again - voc Martha Tilton (arr FH)

BENNY GOODMAN AND HIS ORCHESTRA

59-MG-631   MGM Series: 102, 105, 108, 110, 112, 114, 115, 118,
            119, 120, 121
            Big John's Special (arr HH)

Good-Bye (theme)

(Complete broadcast is on LP, FAN 13-113.)

BENNY GOODMAN AND HIS ORCHESTRA   November 17, 1937, New York

CBS sustaining broadcast from the Madhattan Room. Personnel as October 19 (Brown back in).

59-MG-632   MGM Series: 103, 106, 109, 113, 115, 118
            Camel Hop

BENNY GOODMAN AND HIS ORCHESTRA   November 19, 1937, New York

Sustaining broadcast (network unknown) from the Madhattan Room. Personnel as October 19.

XLP 11051-1B   CO Series: 2, 3, 7, 12, 13, 17, 24, 33, 33A, 52, and
            78: PHIL PB254, PhilCont B21091H. **EP:** CO B819.
            ET: 1955 Heart Fund (partial)
            Star Dust

BENNY GOODMAN TRIO, QUARTET,   *November 20, 1937, New York*
   AND ORCHESTRA

CBS sustaining broadcast from the Madhattan Room. Personnels as October 19.

LP 10 - Side 1
   Let's Dance (theme)
   Laughing At Life (arr FH)
   You Took The Words Right Out Of My Heart - voc Martha Tilton (arr FH)
   Sweet Stranger - voc Martha Tilton (arr JM)
   Who? - TRIO
   Down South Camp Meeting (LP: RAD 1314)

LP 10 - Side 2
   In The Still Of The Night - voc Martha Tilton
   Limehouse Blues - QUARTET (LP: RAD 1314)
   Mama, That Moon Is Here Again - voc Martha Tilton
   Swingtime In The Rockies
   Farewell My Love - voc Martha Tilton

BENNY GOODMAN AND HIS ORCHESTRA   November 21, 1937, New York

Sustaining broadcast (network unknown) from the Madhattan Room. Personnel as October 19.

XLP 11049-1A   CO Series: 1, 4, 6, 11, 14, 18, 23, 24, 26, 52
            Sugar Foot Stomp

BENNY GOODMAN AND HIS ORCHESTRA   November 23, 1937, New York

CBS "Camel Caravan" broadcast. Personnels as November 9 (Will Bradley substituting for Brown).

XLP 11051-1B   CO Series: 2, 3, 7, 12, 13, 17 24, 46, 52, and **78:** CO
            DJ 48329. **EP:** CO B819
            Clarinet Marmalade (arr JM)

November 23, 1937, continued

November 23, 1937, continued

BENNY GOODMAN TRIO   same broadcast

XLP 11048-1A   CO Series: 1, 3, 5, 9, 11, 13, 17, 22, 24, 26, 29, 35, 44, 45, 47, 52, and LP: CO 21064
        Nice Work If You Can Get It

Also available from this broadcast:

All Of Me (prob. arr FH) (LP: "Group A")
Vieni, Vieni (LP: "Group A")

Vernon Brown left November 25 to join Mezz Mezzrow's group at the Harlem Uproar House for a brief period. His chair in the Madhattan Room was taken by Walter Mercurio of Tommy Dorsey's band . . . which did not endear Benny to Tommy. It should be borne in mind that there was sharp, often bitter, rivalry between band leaders in the late 1930's. Sidemen were becoming known by name, and to have one jump from one band to another meant losing face as well as a competent player. The situation was akin to the pirating of star athletes by professional sports teams in later years.

Trombonist Brown at times added a final "e" to his name, and it is so spelled in some publications. He was induced to do so by an astrologer who saw that "e" as essential to fame and fortune. Other jazzmen were oppositely influenced; Georg (no "e") Bruni(e)s was persuaded to drop that vowel as detrimental to his career. Sms an vn swap.

Neither Brown nor Mercurio was in the band for the next entry; Will Bradley again sat in for the "Camel Caravan" broadcast. Quite an entry it is, too, for it captures Benny's mob setting fire to that venerable old standard, "St. Louis Blues," making it a jazz holocaust, utterly cremating the tune beyond phoenix-like resurrection by those who have recorded it since.

In his liner notes for the Columbia album, George Avakian gives deserved praise to Harry, Gene, and Jess for this extended version of "St. Louis Blues." On first hearing, favorable reaction here was to Ziggy Elman's solo, so different from Sterling Bose's concept on the familiar Victor recording. It seems to us that H, G and J did set Handy's old rouser ablaze, but not until Ziggy had lighted the fuse.

Avakian also writes of "SLB," a "happy miracle which took place during a one-nighter broadcast from the Hartford (Conn.) Armory." The reader will discover other variances between this book and published material by others.

BENNY GOODMAN AND HIS ORCHESTRA   **November 30, 1937, New York**

CBS "Camel Caravan" broadcast. Personnel as November 9 (Bradley substituting for Brown-Mercurio).

XLP 11048-1A   CO Series: 1, 3, 5, 11, 13, 17, 20, 22, 24, 26, 52, and
        7" LP: CO DJ ZLP11392
        St. Louis Blues

BENNY GOODMAN QUARTET   same broadcast

XLP 11049-1A   CO Series: 1, 4, 5, 8, 10, 11, 14, 15, 18, 19, 22, 24, 26, 29, 35, 37, 38, 39, 40, 41, 43A, 44, 45, 52, and
        LP: CO Album DS144, PIC 240, and **78:** CoJap L3018
        Moonglow

Benny's next studio effort was a double date on which he cut one Quartet and three Orchestra sides. Note that take 1 of "I'm A Ding Dong Daddy (From Dumas")" was not reissued until the 1970's, and for years was much sought after by collectors. Note, too, that the liner notes in the Neiman-Marcus album err in claiming a take 3 for its track of "Life Goes To A Party"; it's take 2.

BENNY GOODMAN QUARTET   **December 2, 1937, New York**

Personnel as October 29.

BS 017451-1   VI 25725 B. **LP:** RcaBB AXM2-5568, RcaFr FXMI-7083, RcaFr PM43684, JAZ 16
BS 017451-2   VI 25725 B, HMV B8734, HMVFin TG302, HMVlt GW1548, GrFr K8068, BB 10903, ViJap A1128, ViJap LM7B, BRS 26. **EP:** VI EPOT6703, RcaFr 75651. **LP:** VI LPT6703, ViArg AYL3000-5, VI LPV521, ViJap RA74, RcaBB AXM2-5557, RcaE RD7775, RcaFr 731.041, RcaFr PM43684
        I'm A Ding Dong Daddy (From Dumas)

BENNY GOODMAN AND HIS ORCHESTRA   same session

Personnel as October 19—Brown returns on a full-time basis.

BS 017044-3   VI 25726 A (gold label), ViJap 1304 A, HMV B8727,
(4)   HMVAu EA4176. **EP:** RcaNZ RPX1360. **LP:** RcaBB AXM2-5557, RcaFr 741.072, ViJap RA71, JAZ 18, RcaFr PM45727, TL STBB03
        Life Goes To A Party

BS 017452-1   VI 25727 B, HMVAu EA2086. **LP:** RcaBB AXM2-5557,
(2)   RcaFr PM45727, JAZ 7
        It's Wonderful - voc Martha Tilton

BS 017453-1   VI 25727 A, ViJap 1278 A, GrFr K8126. **LP:** RcaBB AXM2-5557, RcaFr PM43173, RcaFr PM45727, JAZ 17
BS 017453-2   VI 25727 A. **LP:** CAM 872, RcaE 1021, C/P 7055
        Thanks For The Memory - voc Martha Tilton (arr prob JM)

BENNY GOODMAN   **December 3, 1937, New York**
   AND HIS ORCHESTRA

Personnel as October 19.

BS 017454-1   VI 25726 B, HMV B8727, HMVAu EA2086, ViJap 1304 B. **EP:** VI EPOT6703. **LP:** VI LPT6703, ViArg AYL3000-5, RcaBel 230.233, RcaBB AXM2-5557, RcaFr PM 45727, TL STBB03
BS 017454-2   **LP:** RcaFr PM43173
        If Dreams Come True (arr ES)

BS 017455-1   **LP:** RcaBB AXM2-5557, RS (no #), JAZ 7
        I'm Like A Fish Out Of Water - voc Martha Tilton (arr JM)

BS 017456-1   **LP:** RcaBB AXM2-5557, RS (no #), JAZ 7, RcaFr PM45727
        Sweet Stranger - voc Martha Tilton (arr JM)

(Lest it escape notice, remark the sole issue of take 2 of "If Dreams Come True" on an RcaFr LP. In general, it should be recognized that "legitimate" releases of alternate takes are usually-not always-from vault masters, and so offer excellent audio fidelity; the same cannot be said about bootleg issues. The serious collector, however, will consider his collection deficient without test pressings of such alternates, for they are the true "originals.")

The Quartet played a Sunday Morning Swing Concert at the Criterion Theatre, New York, December 5. It was broadcast via WNEW, Martin Block MC'ing. Unfortunately, no air checks of this program are known.

Two days later, however, Columbia and MGM offer air checks of a "Camel Caravan" broadcast. Included is an excellent version of "I've Got My Love To Keep Me Warm," which illustrates the way of the band with a ballad. Years later Harry James and Les Brown took successful aim at this tune, but both failed to match Benny's effort. One wonders why Victor didn't insist Benny record a number of these things commercially; weren't those VP's listening?

"CAMEL CARAVAN"   *December 7, 1937, New York*
   CBS Radio Network

Personnels as October 19.

Let's Dance (theme)

BENNY GOODMAN AND HIS ORCHESTRA

59-MG-630B   MGM Series: 102, 105, 108, 112, 115, 118
        Hallelujah (arr FH)

Bob White - voc Martha Tilton

BENNY GOODMAN TRIO

XLP 11050-1C   CO Series: 2, 4, 6, 9, 12, 14, 18, 23, 24, 44, 45, 47, 52, and **EP:** CO "Texaco," PHIL BBE12133, PhilCont 429248BE
        Have You Met Miss Jones

BENNY GOODMAN AND HIS ORCHESTRA

59-MG-633B   MGM Series: 103, 106, 109, 110, 113, 114, 115, 118,
119, 120, 121
I've Got My Love To Keep Me Warm (arr JM)

If Dreams Come True

BENNY GOODMAN QUARTET

XLP 11051-1B   CO Series: 2, 3, 7, 9, 12, 13, 17, 24, 44, 45, 47, 52,
and **78:** CO DJ 48331. **EP:** CO B819
Killer Diller

You're A Sweetheart - voc Martha Tilton
Sugar Foot Stomp
Good-Bye (theme)

Vido Musso left the band the day after the broadcast, and Benny
brought in his old record buddy, CBS staffer Babe Russin, to replace the
volatile Vido while the band was in and around New York.

SUSTAINING BROADCAST   *December 11, 1937, Hotel*
   CBS Radio Network   *Pennsylvania, New York*

*Benny Goodman, clt; Harry James, Ziggy Elman, Chris Griffin, tpt; Red
Ballard, Vernon Brown, tbn; Hymie Schertzer, George Koenig, as; Art Rollini,
BABE RUSSIN, ts; Jess Stacy, p; Allan Reuss, g; Harry Goodman, b; Gene
Krupa, d.*

TRIO: Benny Goodman, clt; Teddy Wilson, p; Gene Krupa, d.

*QUARTET: Benny Goodman, clt; Lionel Hampton, vib; Teddy Wilson, p; Gene
Krupa, d.*

Sweet Someone - voc Martha Tilton (LP: SB 127)

"CAMEL CARAVAN"   *December 14, 1937, New York*
   CBS Radio Network

Personnels as December 11.

Let's Dance (theme)

BENNY GOODMAN AND HIS ORCHESTRA

59-MG-629   MGM Series: 101, 104, 107, 110, 111, 114, 115, 118,
119, 120, 121
Three Little Words (arr FH)

I Wanna Be In Winchell's Column - voc Martha Tilton
Once In A While - TRIO

BENNY GOODMAN AND HIS ORCHESTRA

XLP 11051-1B   CO Series: 2, 3, 7, 12, 13, 17, 24, 52, and **EP:** CO
B819
Josephine (arr JM)

59-MG-628   MGM Series: same issues as "Three Little Words"
Dear Old Southland

BENNY GOODMAN QUARTET

XLP 11050-1C   CO Series: 2, 4, 7, 9, 12, 14, 18, 24, 31, 36, 44, 45,
47, 52, and **EP:** CO B819
My Gal Sal

You Took The Words Right Out Of My Heart - voc Martha Tilton
I've Found A New Baby (LP: SB 149)
Good-Bye (theme)

SUSTAINING BROADCAST   *December 16, 1937, Hotel*
   Mutual Radio Network   *Pennsylvania, New York*

Personnel as December 11.

One O'Clock Jump (arr CB) (LP: SB 127)

BENNY GOODMAN TRIO, QUARTET   *December 18, 1937, New York*
   AND ORCHESTRA

CBS sustaining broadcast from the Madhattan Room. Personnels as December 11.

LP 11 - Side 1:
   Let's Dance (theme)
   Big John Special
   You Took The Words Right Out Of My Heart - voc Martha Tilton
   If Dreams Come True
   Bei Mir Bist Du Schon - voc Martha Tilton (arr JM)
   Where Or When - TRIO
LP 11 - Side 2:
   At The Darktown Strutters' Ball
   I've Hitched My Wagon To A Star - voc Martha Tilton
   Dinah - QUARTET
   I Wanna Be In Winchell's Column - voc Martha Tilton (arr JM)
   All Of Me (n/c) (prob. arr FH)

Although the Quartet's version of "Bei Mir Bist Du Schon" was
recorded in two distinct halves and at separate sessions, some of the microgroove reissues listed below splice the two parts in order to present a continuous rendition. In the process. some lose a few bars from each of the original
performances.

BENNY GOODMAN QUARTET   December 21, 1937, New York

Personnel as December 11. Martha Tilton, voc.

BS 017754-1   VI 25751 A, HMV B8725, HMV A2048, HMVAu EA2048,
GrFr K8058, ViJap A1067, ViJap JA1160. **EP:** VI
EPOT6703, RcaFr 75.651. **LP:** VI LPT6703, ViArg
AYL3000-5, VI LPV521, VI CPLI-2470, RcaBB
AXM2-5557, RcaE RD7775, RcaE PL 12470, RcaFr
PM43684, RD 3-76, ViJap RA74
BS 017754-2   **LP:** RcaFr PM43684
Bei Mir Bist Du Schon (Part 1) - voc Martha Tilton

Next is the 12th and last of the original unlabeled LPs that offer half-
hour sustaining broadcasts from the Madhattan Room:

BENNY GOODMAN TRIO, QUARTET   *December 22, 1937, New York*
   AND ORCHESTRA

CBS sustaining broadcast from the Madhattan Room. Personnels as December 11.

LP 12 - Side 1:
   Let's Dance (theme)
   Life Goes To A Party
   Sweet Someone - voc Martha Tilton
   If Dreams Come True
   Can't Help Lovin' That Man - TRIO
   Good-Bye (theme) (break for station identification)
LP 12 - Side 2:
   Good-Bye (theme) (continued from Side 1)
   (Sweet) Alice Blue Gown (arr Augustus Wilson, Teddy's brother)
   Josephine
   It's Wonderful
   Avalon - QUARTET, plus band in coda
   Rockin' The Town - voc Martha Tilton (arr JM) (n/c)

Program logs for the sustaining broadcasts of December 25 (CBS), and
for January 13, 1938 (Mutual), each list Trio performances of "Once In A
While." The next entry could come from either date, because the source
acetate offers no information. But since other acetates in the group that
includes this cut are all CBS transcriptions, the choice here is for the earlier
date, Saturday evening of Chirstmas Day.

SUSTAINING BROADCAST   *December 25, 1937, Hotel*
   CBS Radio Network   *Pennsylvania, New York*

Personnel as December 11.

Once In A While - TRIO (LP: SB 149)

Should note that Jack Oakie's introductory half-hour invariably ran
overlong, with the consequence that Benny's nominal 30 minutes was short-

changed by a minute or more. Guest Bea Lillie's dialogue, monologue, and extended novelty vocal reduce the band's participation further on the next broadcast; she even joins Martha and Benny in "Bob White." Nonetheless, the program produces an unique "Sing You Sinners," hyper Hampton on "I Know That You Know," and yet another version of "Sing, Sing, Sing":

"CAMEL CARAVAN"   December 28, 1937, New York
  CBS Radio Network

Personnels as December 11.

Let's Dance (theme)
Sing You Sinners
Thanks For The Memory - voc Martha Tilton
"Rhythm" - novelty, voc guest Bea Lillie
I Know That You Know - QUARTET
Bob White - voc Martha Tilton, Bea Lillie, Benny Goodman
Sing, Sing, Sing
Good-Bye (theme)

BENNY GOODMAN QUARTET   **December 29, 1937, New York**

Personnel as December 11, plus Ziggy Elman, tpt. Martha Tilton, voc.

BS 017783-1   same issues as mx BS 017754, December 21.
(2)   **Bei Mir Bist Du Schon** (Part 2) - voc Martha Tilton

Benny's studio version of "Bei Mir Bist Du Schon" wrapped up 1937 for the Goodman Gang, and a vintage year for jazz enthusiasts: Some excellent commercial recordings, a bounteous crop of outstanding air checks, the best of the big band motion pictures—truly a year to be remembered.

The Andrews Sisters' Decca release of "Bei Mir . . ." skyrocketed the tune to the height of popularity during the winter of 1937. But the rendition the author recalls most fondly is the way the Quartet played it, sans Ziggy's trumpet, and with Benny and Lionel - not Martha - sharing the vocal. The only such reading extant is on a scratchy acetate, its sound somewhat distorted, from the next "Camel Caravan" broadcast:

BENNY GOODMAN AND HIS ORCHESTRA   **January 4, 1938, New York**

CBS "Camel Caravan" broadcast. Personnels as December 11, 1937.

59-MG-6308   MGM Series: 102, 105, 108, 110, 112, 114, 115, 118,
              119, 120, 121
              If Dreams Come True

Also available from this broadcast:

Bei Mir Bist Du Schon - voc Lionel Hampton & Benny Goodman -
  QUARTET

The same day "Hollywood Hotel" was released, January 15, was Benny's final day in the Hotel Pennsylvania; Bob Crosby's excellent group succeeded him. The next evening the roaring Goodman entourage was presented at Carnegie Hall in a performance that rocked the music world in 1938, and again 12 years later when LPs of the event were first issued.

Such is the renown and notoriety of the 1938 Carnegie Hall Concert that no extended commentary is necessary here. Irving Kolodin's notes in the original Columbia album cover the event adequately. Only a few observations seem worth adding:

The liner notes are deficient in that they omit any mention of Albert Marx's role in the preservation of the concert. Without him it would be but a nostalgic memory for the 2,500-odd who jammed Carnegie Hall that evening, for it was Marx who caused it to be recorded. Then Helen Ward's husband, Marx on his own initiative had the performance piped from a single microphone over the stage to a nearby studio. There it was transcribed onto acetates; these were then duplicated, and Marx gave Benny the set that was the source of the releases. There were no other recordings made of the concert. Newsreel motion pictures of portions of the performances were silent; when shown now on television, their accompanying sound tracks are dubbed from the Columbia album. All jazz devotees, and especially all Goodman enthusiasts, are forever indebted to Albert Marx.

Within 10 years of its initial release by Columbia on November 13, 1950, more than one million copies of recordings of the concert had been sold in the United States alone. Total sales to the present, worldwide, of all issues of the concert, in toto or in part, are incalculable. But without question, no other jazz album approaches it in terms of copies sold and in extent of distribution. Nor is any other likely to match its longevity; decades after its initial release, new reissues appear constantly.

Benny Goodman's 1938 concert album has a further distinction: It was the first "performance" (non-studio) recording ever made available to the public. Its overwhelming commercial success undoubtedly prompted release of additional "live" transcriptions by Goodman and many other artists. We are now so accustomed to the practice that we may forget their genesis, the "Benny Goodman Carnegie Hall Jazz Concert" Columbia album.

Such issues of past performances present a compensation problem: how fairly to pay the participants (and sadly now, their estates)? An ingenious solution employed here was to pay each sideman on a pro rata basis, for the number of bars he played during the entire concert. Obviously, Gene Krupa was in accord with this method.

Harry Carney's lengthy baritone solo in "Jam Session: Honeysuckle Rose" was excised from the transfer to the Columbia album. Two other tunes were deleted because of the poor condition of the acetates onto which they were transcribed. Both are available via tape or bootleg LP, however, and they are listed below, following the Columbia album's contents.

"Don't Be That Way" was first performed on the January 11 "Camel Caravan" broadcast, not (as the liner notes assert) at the concert.

BENNY GOODMAN   **January 16, 1938, New York**
The Famous 1938
CARNEGIE HALL JAZZ CONCERT

Goodman Orchestra, Trio, Quartet: Personnels as December 11, 1937.

"Sensation Rag." "When My Baby Smiles At Me": Benny Goodman, clt; Chris Griffin, tpt; Vernon Brown, tbn; Jess Stacy, p; Gene Krupa, d.

"I'm Coming Virginia": B. Goodman, clt; Bobby Hackett, tpt; Brown, tbn; Babe Russin, ts; Stacy, p; Allan Reuss, g; Harry Goodman, b; Krupa, d.

"Blue Reverie": Cootie Williams, tpt; Johnny Hodges, sop; Harry Carney, bar; Stacy, Reuss, H. Goodman, Krupa.

"Jam Session: Honeysuckle Rose": B. Goodman, clt; Harry James, Buck Clayton, tpt; Brown, tbn; Hodges, as; Lester Young, ts; Carney, bar; Count Basie, p; Freddie Greene, g; Walter Page, b; Krupa, d.

A code is employed to list the various issues of the 1938 Carnegie Hall concert: Each selection is numbered sequentially in its order of performance. (Exception: the two tunes not included in the original Columbia release; these are dealt with following the "legitimate" issues.) These numbers are then shown in parentheses following each release, to describe its contents. Matrices listed are those used by the original Columbia LP issues. Following each selection is an identification of the performing group.

FXLP 3601-1A   1. Don't Be That Way (arr ES) - Goodman orchestra
                2. One O'Clock Jump (arr CB) - Goodman orchestra
                3. Sensation Rag (erroneously titled, "Dixieland One-
                   Step" on early issues, subsequently corrected) -
                   personnel named above
                4. I'm Coming Virginia (arr Irving Riskin) - personnel
                   named above
                5. When My Baby Smiles At Me - personnel named
                   above
                6. Shine - Goodman orchestra, featuring Harry James
                7. Blue Reverie - personnel named above
                8. Life Goes To A Party - Goodman orchestra
FXLP 3602-1A   9. Jam Session: Honeysuckle Rose (arr JM) -
                   personnel named above
               10. Body And Soul - Goodman Trio
               11. Avalon - Goodman Quartet
               12. The Man I Love - Goodman Quartet
FXLP 3603-1A   13. I Got Rhythm - Goodman Quartet
               14. Blue Skies - Goodman orchestra
               15. Loch Lomond - voc Martha Tilton (& Benny
                   Goodman) - Goodman orchestra
               16. Blue Room (arr FH) - Goodman orchestra
               17. Swingtime In The Rockies - Goodman orchestra
               18. Bei Mir Bist Du Schon - voc Martha Tilton (arr JM) -
                   Goodman orchestra
               19. China Boy - Goodman Trio

FXLP 3604-1A 20. Stompin' At The Savoy - Goodman Quartet
21. Dizzy Spells - Goodman Quartet
22. Sing Sing Sing (With A Swing) (Parts I & II) - Goodman orchestra
23. Big John's Special - Goodman orchestra

LPs

CO Set SL 160, ML/OL4341 (1-8, 20-23)
CO Set SL 160, ML/OL4342 (9-19)
CO Set SL 160, ML4358 (1-8, 20-23)
CO Set SL 160, ML4359 (9-19)
CO CL814 (1-6, 9)
CO CL815 (7, 8, 10-17)
CO CL816 (18-23)
CO CL820 (1, 2, 11, 20, 22)
CO CL2483 (1)
CO CS8643 (1, 2, 11, 20, 22)
CO CS9283 (1)
CO KG31547 (1, 2, 10, 11, 13, 20, 22)
CO P4M5678 (1, 2, 10, 11, 13, 18, 20, 22)
CO PM16932 (1)
CoSP P13289 (12, 13)
CO "Dutch Boy Paints" (18)
CO 21064 (12, 13)
CBS 52368 (1)
CBS 52688 (1, 2, 11, 20, 22)
CBS 62340 (1-8 20-23)
CBS 62341 (9-19)
CBS 62708 (1)
CBS 62853 (12, 13)
CBS 63086 (10, 11, 19, 20, 21)
CBS Set 66202 (1-23)
CBS Set 66420 (1-23)
CBS 67268 (1, 2, 10, 11, 13, 20, 22)
CBSH 88141 (10, 11, 12, 13, 19, 20, 21)
CBS S63367 (9, 22)
CoCH LPC35051 (1-12)
CoJap WL5030 (1-8, 20-23)
CoJap WL5031 (9-19)
CoJap PL5039 (1, 2, 11, 20, 22)
HA HS11271 (9, 22)
HAAu HAS165 (1-8, 20-23)
HAAu HAS166 (9-19)
PHIL BBL7000 (1-8, 20-23)
PHIL BBL7001 (9-19)
PHIL BBL7073 (1, 2, 6, 11, 19, 20, 22)
PHIL BBL7441 (1-12)
PHIL BBL7442 (13-23)
PhilCont B07000L (1-8, 20-23)
PhilCont B07001L (9-19)
PhilCont B07116L (1, 2, 11, 19, 20, 22)
PhilCont B07143L (8)
PhilCont B07665R (1, 8, 14, 17)
RLM 8065 (2-n/c)
SONY 36AP-1502/3 (1-23)
SONY SOPE 55007/8 (1-23)
SONY SOPZ 801 (1-23)
SONY FCP2-1/2 (1)
SONY 30AP3090 (22)
FR Series (15, 22)
PIC 240 (9, 22)
TL STLJ05 (22)
TL STLJ19 (7)
COR KLP552 (1)
Broadcasters For Radio Free Europe (1-n/c)

45's: Singles & Extended Play

CO 45-X-39277 (1, 12)
CO 45-X-39278 (2-Pt 1, 11)
CO 45-X-39279 (2-Pt 2, 10)
CO 45-X-39280 (3, 4, 5, 9)
CO 45-X-39281 (7)

CO 45-X-39282 (8)
CO Set A1049 (1, 2, 7-12, 14-20, 22, 23)
CO Set B245 (1-12)
CO Set B246 (13-23)
CO Set B250 (1-23)
CO Set B814 (1-6, 9)
CO Set B815 (7, 8, 10-17)
CO Set B816 (18-23)
CO A1677 (22)
CO A1701 (1, 2)
CO A1788 (9)
CO A1817 (13, 21)
CO B2593 (22)
CO B2594 (1, 20)
CO B8201 (22)
CO B8202 (1, 20)
CO B8203 (2)
CO B8204 (11)
CO "Texaco" EP (14, 17)
CoJap EM92 (1, 3, 4, 5, 6, 12)
CoJap EM94 (22)
CoJap EM100 (2, 8)
CoJap LL38C (1)
CoJap LL452C (18)
CBS 5758 (1)
PHIL BBE12132 (10)
PHIL BBE12133 (13)
PHIL BBE12277 (1, 20)
PHIL BBE12400 (22)
PhilCont 429003BE (20, 21)
PhilCont 429008BE (14, 17)
PhilCont 429016BE (9)
PhilCont 429035BE (20, 21)
PhilCont 429198BE (1, 16, 18, 23)
PhilCont 429236BE (8, 22)
PhilCont 429248BE (13)
PhilCont 429433BE (1, 2, 18)
PhilCont 429434BE (3, 4, 9-Pt 1, 10, 21)
PhilCont 429435BE (6, 7, 9-Pt 2)
PhilCont 429436BE (12-15)
PhilCont 429437BE (11, 19, 22-Pt 1, 23)
PhilCont 429438BE (16, 20, 22-Pt 2)

78's

CO DJ XCO45706 (1)
CO DJ XCO45707 (10)
CO DJ XCO45708 (7)
CO DJ XCO45709 (11)
CO DJ XCO45710 (8)
CO DJ XCO45711 (8)
CoJap L3027 (3)
CoJap L3018 (12)
PhilCont B21207H (14, 17)

16" Electrical Transcriptions

AFRS "American Popular Music" Series 390, Pt. 1 (11)
AFRS Basic Music Library, Vol. No. P1763/4 (1-6, 9)
AFRS Basic Music Library, Vol. No. P1765/6 (7, 8, 11-17)
AFRS Basic Music Library, Vol. No. P1767/8 (18-23)
1955 Heart Fund (22 - n/c)

Also available from the concert:

Sometimes I'm Happy - Goodman orchestra (LP: SB 127)
If Dreams Come True - Goodman orchestra (LP: SB 127)

("Sometimes I'm Happy" was the second tune played; "If Dreams Come True" was the first encore, following "Sing, Sing, Sing." As noted, neither was of sufficient sound quality to be included in the Columbia release.)

On January 18 the "Camel Caravan" reverted once more to a full one-hour program, with Jack Oakie, MC, and George Stoll and his band sharing the broadcast with Benny. Coincidentally, the first program in the new series provides the initial example extant of a classical performance by Benny Goodman, his reading of the Mozart Quintet with his guests for the evening, the Coolidge String Quartet. And almost as if to lure Benny back into the Swing fold, the band digs in with a brilliant romp through Horace Henderson's 1935 arrangement of "Dear Old Southland."

"CAMEL CARAVAN"   *January 18, 1938, New York*
   CBS Radio Network

Personnels as December 11, 1937; and guests, the Coolidge String Quartet.

Let's Dance (theme) (LP: FAN 37-137)
Make Believe (arr FH) (LP: FAN 37-137)
Don't Be That Way
Quintet For Clarinet And Strings In A Major (Mozart) -
   Benny Goodman, clt, and the Coolidge String Quartet (LP: SB 152)
Honeysuckle Rose - QUARTET (LP: FAN 37-137)
Mama, That Moon Is Here Again - voc Martha Tilton
Dear Old Southland

Out of the Madhattan Room, Benny and the band went back into New York's Paramount Theater on January 26 for three weeks. Featured film for this engagement was Paramount's "Every Day's A Holiday," starring Mae West, who also co-authored the script.

As noted earlier, Benny made few appearances on CBS's "Saturday Night Swing Session." But he did so while at the Paramount on January 29, and one cut by the Quartet survives:

BENNY GOODMAN QUARTET   **January 29, 1938, New York**

CBS "Saturday Night Swing Club" broadcast. Regular Quartet personnel.

XLP 11049-1A   CO Series: 1, 4, 6, 9, 11, 14, 18, 23, 24, 26, 33AA,
                       43, 44, 45, 47, 52
            I'm A Ding Dong Daddy (From Dumas)

"oooOO-OH BOOM!" is featured on both of the next "Camel" broadcasts; interestingly, Benny names different band members on each. Note, too, unique performances of "Sunday In The Park," "Memphis Blues" and a full-band, non-vocal version of "Bei Mir Bist Du Schon," with extended Elman compensating for missing Martha:

"CAMEL CARAVAN"   *February 1, 1938, New York*
   CBS Radio Network

Personnels as December 11, 1937.

Let's Dance (theme)
When Buddha Smiles
Sunday In The Park - voc Martha Tilton
Don't Be That Way
oooOO-OH BOOM! - voc Martha Tilton, Benny Goodman
Dinah - QUARTET
Life Goes To A Party
Good-Bye (theme)

"CAMEL CARAVAN"   *February 8, 1938, New York*
   CBS Radio Network

Personnels as December 11, 1937.

Let's Dance (theme)
Memphis Blues
Thanks For The Memory - voc Martha Tilton
Lillie Stomp - QUARTET
Down South - novelty, voc guest Bea Lillie
If Dreams Come True
oooOO-OH BOOM! - voc Martha Tilton, Benny Goodman, Bea Lillie
Bei Mir Bist Du Schon
Good-Bye (theme)

As noted, the "Reynolds" transcriptions correct earlier assignments of a few air checks originally in the columbia and M-G-M albums. The ETs for the complete "Camel Caravan" broadcast of February 15 startled the author; its "Roll 'Em" is NOT the unmatched version in the Columbia set. As partial compensation, the program does offer as guests the Original Dixieland Jazz Band, in its only appearance in the "Caravan" series:

"CAMEL CARAVAN"   *February 15, 1938, New York*
   CBS Radio Network

Goodman personnels as December 11, 1937. "ODJB" QUINTET: Bobby Hackett, cnt; Eddie Edwards, tbn; Larry Shields, clt; Jess Stacy, p; Tony Sbarbaro, d.

Let's Dance (theme)
That Naughty Waltz
Loch Lomond - voc Martha Tilton, Benny Goodman
(Dixieland One-Step - ODJB Quintet - NO BG
I'm Comin', Virginia - Hackett w/contingent from BG band
When My Baby Smiles At Me - BG and a contingent from the band
Mood Indigo
Shine - James w/contingent from the band
Roll 'Em
Nagasaki - QUARTET
Mama, That Moon Is Here Again - voc Martha Tilton
Good-Bye (theme)

Despite intensive effort, the Columbia "Roll 'Em" cannot now be pinpointed to a specific date. The acetate from which it was transferred is inscribed only, "1938." Bill Savory believes this minimal notation reflects the likelihood that it is not from a CBS broadcast, and the certainty that it is not from any "Caravan" program. His recollection is that it is from a sustaining broadcast from the Syria Mosque in Pittsburgh, Pennsylvania, via an unknown network.

Data available to the author fail to place Benny in Pittsburgh the latter half of February 1938. The 15th was his last day in the Paramount. He recorded in New York on the 16th. He then went to Buffalo, was in Detroit on the 22nd, began a one-week stand in Philadelphia on the 26th. At a guess, he stopped off in Pittsburgh after Buffalo, on his way to Detroit.

With that understanding, the Columbia "Roll 'Em" is entered at this juncture, with the thought of assisting the collector by placing it nearest its previous assignment.

BENNY GOODMAN AND HIS ORCHESTRA   **February 1938, Pittsburgh**

Sustaining radio broadcast, unknown network. Personnel as December 11, 1937.

XLP 11049-1A   CO Series: 1, 4, 6, 11, 14, 18, 23, 26, 49, 50, 52; and
              ET: AFRS "American Popular Music" Prog. No. 419
            Roll 'Em

Here is the last studio recording date for Gene Krupa as a full-time member of the Benny Goodman orchestra. Fittingly, it waxed two of the Swing Era's most memorable compositions.

BENNY GOODMAN   **February 16, 1938, New York**
 AND HIS ORCHESTRA

Personnel as December 11, 1937.

BS 019831-1   VI 25792 A, VI 20-1549, VI 420-0152, VI D-22(demo),
                ViArg 25988, ViArg 1A-0753, ViJap LM8A, HMV
                POP166, HMVFin TG265, GrFr K8102. **45:** VI 447-
                0152, VI 27-0082, VI 47-2953, HMV 7M380. **EP:** VI
                EPA745, VI EPB1239, VI EPBT3029, RcaAu 20060,
                RcaBel 85.507, RcaFr 85.230. **LP:** VI LPT12, VI
                LPM1239, VI LPM6043, VI DRLI-0062, RcaE
                DHY0001, RcaFr 741.084, RD 3-21, TL STBB03
BS 019831-2   Test Pressing
(3)   **Don't Be That Way** (arr ES)
BS 019832-1   VI 25792 B, VD 15A, NavyVD 154B, ViJap LM8B, HMV
(2)   B8745, HMVFin TG266, GrFr K8102. **45:** VI 27—
                0061, Vi 447-0441. **EP:** VI EPB1005, VI EPAT300A,
                RcaBel 85.508, RcaFr A75.307. **LP:** VI LPT1005,
                RcaFr 741.072, HIS H623, J03057, SIG 132, RcaAu
                VPLI-0471. **ET:** AFRS GI JIVE 1200
            One O'Clock Jump (arr CB)

(Both mx BS 019831-1 and BS 019832-1 are also on **EP:** VI EPA5078, VI EPB1099, RcaAu 20206, RcaE RCX1036, RcaNZ RPX1360. **LP:** VI LPM1099, VI LSP4005(e), HMV DLP1112, HMV DLP1116, VI LPM6040, VI CPLI-2470, VI ANLI-0973, ViJap RA71, RcaBB AXM2-5557, RcaE PL 12470, RcaFr 740.552, RcaFr FXM3-7273, RcaCont 89323. Note that take 2 of "Don't Be That Way" is unissued as of this writing.)

Gene Krupa delighted in telling this story about the released version of "Don't Be That Way": After he left Benny, he formed his own band; its first engagement was the highly desirable Easter weekend booking on Atlantic City's Steel Pier. Through for the night, he and some friends heard the Victor recording of "Don't Be That Way" for the first time on his yellow Packard's radio. Gene waited for the drum break, listened to it critically, shook his head, exclaimed, "Man, that'll never make it." Not until the record ended did the announcer identify it as Benny Goodman's newest release; Gene thought it was another band's and another drummer's!

The break—an accented single stroke roll—was the first of its kind ever recorded. It caught the ear of every drummer in the land, and soon all of them added the same kind of lick to their bags of tricks. Ever since it has been a basic rhythm for all drummers.

The author sought an alternate take of "Don't Be That Way" for many years, but unfortunately was not able to get a copy until after Gene's death. Gene's drum break on it is good, certainly. . . but different. The author's wondered forever more what his good friend would have thought of it.

The band moved on to Buffalo, then to the Fox Theater in Detroit. A "Camel" broadcast from the Motor City gives us the last program extant that includes Krupa this time around, for the transcription of the March 1 "Caravan" has not yet been located. It also features outstanding Goodman clarinet, especially on "Smiles." After a relaxed start, Benny drives the Quartet through that standard.

"CAMEL CARAVAN"   *February 22, 1938, Detroit*
 CBS Radio Network

Personnels as December 11, 1937.

Let's Dance (theme)
The Blue Room
Sweet As A Song - voc Martha Tilton
China Boy - TRIO
My Melancholy Baby (arr FH)
Don't Be That Way
Smiles - QUARTET
I See Your Face Before Me - voc Martha Tilton

BENNY GOODMAN AND HIS ORCHESTRA

59-MG-629   MGM Series: 101, 104, 107, 111, 115, 116, 118
                   I Know That You Know - Orchestra w/Hampton, vib

Good-Bye (theme)

On Friday, February 26, Benny and the band began a one-week engagement at the Earle Theatre in Philadelphia. At the end of it, on March 3, Gene Krupa quit unceremoniously.

It was sad to see Benny and Gene feuding openly on stage those last few days. The audience helped widen the breach at every show; having waited impatiently through a simpering film titled "Swing It, Professor," starring Pinky Tomlin, they screamed for Gene to take off as soon as the curtain went up. Not for the band, not for the small groups, not for Benny; Gene was their idol.

Gene, perched high on his drummer's throne downstage nodded toward Benny, gestured as if to break his sticks, pantomimed "He won't let me." Groans and hoots from the crowd. For his part Benny ignored the audience, appeared totally bored whenever Gene had a drum solo, left no doubt in anyone's mind as to his reaction to the crowd's clamor for Krupa. A rupture was imminent and inevitable.

Gene's departure shook the music world, caused comment in the Nation's press. (One columnist drew a parallel between it and Edward's abdication of the throne of Great Britain.) Obviously, there was ill feeling; but less than two months later Benny dropped in unannounced on Gene and his new band in Philadelphia's Arcadia Restaurant, and each seemed genuinely pleased to see the other again.

Probably a majority of musicians who play brass, reed, or string instruments rank percussion instrumentalists somewhat lower than themselves in importance, in attainments, and in contributions to music. In part this value judgment is justifiable. It is generally conceded that more study and practice are required to play a clarinet correctly, for example, than a drum competently. Those who play non-rhythmic instruments are required to learn more of the intricacies of harmonics than the drummer, to read their scores more proficiently, to execute within stricter limitations. There is a gulf between the two.

It seems fair to say that Benny, a schooled musician who studied and practiced endlessly, subscribes to this view. (Harry James once said of Benny and his clarinet, "I think he takes the damn' thing to bed with him.")

Thus it was especially galling to him that the adulation of the audience was lavished not on his brass section, nor on his reed men, nor on himself, but on his drummer. Not, it should be understood, that his feeling arose from an attitude of personal envy, but rather from a sense of the crowd's unknowing unfairness.

It should also be understood that a criticism of non-study and non-practice cannot be applied to Krupa. Few drummers studied as hard as he, and few practiced more. And he was able to use what he learned, for he had the technique to do so. Unlike today's drummers who are mostly cymbal players, Gene played **drums.** and when he was with Goodman, no one in the world played them better. But his chosen instrument was the drum, an instrument that required less of a musical education even to play extremely well.

This is not to say that the drum and the drummer are not essential, although—as we shall see—Benny once got through a recording date successfully without a drummer. But if one listens through the years to all of Benny's bands, those that impress the most and persist through time are those that had in them a superior drummer.

The day after Krupa's leaving, the band returned to the Madhattan Room. Soon thereafter, Allan Reuss and George Koenig also left.

Lionel played band drums for the dancing crowd; but when the band was broadcast, Jo Jones, from Count Basie's group, replaced the Hamp. (Jo played very, very softly, quite unobtrusively—the word was around about Benny and loud drummers.) But Lionel got back to the drums at the shank of the evening. Between 1:00 and 1:30 the band dispersed and the Trio came on. Out came this battered set of traps that looked like Salvation Army rejects, and Benny or no, Lionel whaled hell out of them.

Although most of the band admired Jo Jones's work, Lionel got the call for the first post-Krupa recording date; this despite Jo's fellow Basie-ites, Lester Young, Freddie Green, and Walter Page sitting in. And note that one of the tunes. "oooOO-OH BOOM!" serves to introduce some of Benny's sidemen. This may have been an attempt to counter Krupa's loss by directing attention to those who remained.

BENNY GOODMAN AND HIS ORCHESTRA   March 9, 1938, New York

Benny Goodman, clt; Harry James, Ziggy Elman, Chris Griffin, tpt; Red Ballard, Vernon Brown, tbn; Hymie Schertzer, DAVE MATTHEWS, as; Babe Russin, LESTER YOUNG, ts; Jess Stacy, p; FREDDIE GREEN, g; WALTER PAGE, b; LIONEL HAMPTON, d; Martha Tilton, voc.

BS 021127-1   VI 25814 B, GrFr K8127, ViJap 10003 B. **LP:** RcaBB
                   AXM2-5557, JAZ 17
BS 021127-2   **LP:** VI LPM6703, RcaFr 741.059
                   Please Be Kind - voc Martha Tilton

BS 021128-1   VI 25814 A, HMV B8777, GrFr K8127, ViJap 10003 A.
(2)   **EP:** VI EPOT6703. **LP:** VI LPT6703, ViArg AYL3000-5,
                   RcaBB AXM2-5557, RcaFr 731.092, RcaFr
                   FXM3-7273, ViJap RA71
                   Ti-Pi-Tin

BS 021129-1   VI 25808 A, HMVAu EA2111. **LP:** ViG LPM10025, RcaBB
(2)   AXM2-5557, RcaFr PM43173, HIS H623, JO 3057
                   oooOO-OH BOOM! - voc Martha Tilton, Benny Goodman

BS 021130-1   VI 25808 B. **LP:** RcaBB AXM2-5557, RcaFr PM43173,
(2)   JAZ 18
                   Always And Always - voc Martha Tilton

BS 021131-1   VI 26088 A, HMV B8950, HMVAu EA2282. **LP:** CAM
(2)   624, CamE CDN148, RcaBB AXM2-5557, RcaFr
                   731.092
                   Make Believe (arr FH)

BS 021132-1   VI 26088 B, HMV B8852, HMVAu EA2282, HMVInd
                   N4497. **LP:** RcaBB AXM2-5557, JAZ 7
BS 021132-2   **LP:** ViG LPM10025, RcaBB AXM2-5568, RcaFr 731.092
                   The Blue Room (arr FH)

(In a conversation with the author, Hymie Schertzer denied ever having played with Dave Matthews. Victor's files say differently; and the musical press of the period took note of Hymie's leaving Benny to go with Tommy Dorsey the end of March, beginning of April.)

Curious to see how the band fared without Krupa, the author managed, despite a very limited budget, to get to the Madhattan Room in March 1938 at every opportunity. Thus he is somewhat comfortable in assigning the drums in the Quartet number to Jo Jones in this next air check, while still admitting the possibility that it could have been Harry James:

SUSTAINING BROADCAST   *March 12, 1938, Hotel*
  CBS Radio Network   *Pennsylvania, New York*

Benny Goodman, clt; Harry James, Ziggy Elman, Chris Griffin, tpt; Red Ballard, Vernon Brown, tbn; Hymie Schertzer, Dave Matthews, as; Babe Russin, ART ROLLINI, ts; Jess Stacy, p; prob. ALLAN REUSS, g; HARRY GOODMAN, b; Lionel Hampton, d.

QUARTET: Goodman, Hampton, Wilson, prob. JO JONES, d (poss. Harry James, d.)

Sweet Sue-Just You
The World Is Waiting For the Sunrise - QUARTET

Dave Tough, who was then with Bunny Berigan after long service with Tommy Dorsey, joined Benny March 19, and once again the Trio and Quartet came alive. Several critics have said that in retrospect, the addition of Tough permitted Benny to play in a more relaxed manner in Trio and Quartet performances than he had when driven by Krupa.

When Goodman approached him Tough made it very clear that "I'm no Krupa." He was not; but he was a very fine band drummer, one with that indefinable quality called "lift," a kind of buoyancy underneath the band that raised, rather than propelled it, to superior play. His style was less powerful, less technical than Gene's; his solos had a "melodic" structure, a style seldom heard today. Audiences accustomed to Gene's pyrotechnics were perplexed, sometimes puzzled, often disappointed in Dave's work. Which brings us on this story:

Dave had a puckish sense of humor. Later in the year, on Atlantic City's Steel Pier, Dave's solo on "Don't Be That Way," much different from Gene's famous break, caused an unfavorable audience reaction. This bothered Dave, so he asked Benny to play the tune again. This time, Dave came on with an open two-stroke roll, with the accents precisely where Gene had put them. To the uninitiated, it sounded the same as Gene's solo on the record, and the crowd cheered. But the band, aware that what Dave had done was much less difficult than Krupa's effort, broke up completely—Harry James literally fell off his chair. Tough merely acknowledged the plaudits with his secret little smile.

BENNY GOODMAN TRIO/QUARTET   **March 25, 1938, New York**

TRIO: Benny Goodman, clt; Teddy Wilson, p; DAVE TOUGH, d.

BS 021625-1   VI 25822 B, HMVAu EA3567, HMVSw JK2023, ViJap
                 10014 B. **EP:** VI EPOT6703, RcaBel 85.509. **LP:** VI
                 LPT6703, ViArg AYL3000-5, VI LPV1032, RcaBB
                 AXM2-5557, RcaFr 730.707, RcaFr PM43684, ViJap
                 RA74
                 Sweet Lorraine

QUARTET: Add Lionel Hampton, vib.

BS 021626-1   VI 26044 A, HMV B8872, HMVAu EA2500, HMVInd
                 N4473, HMVIt GW1700, HMVIt HN2470, ViJap 268,
                 ViJap LM29, ViJap A-1426. **LP:** VI LPV521, RcaBB
                 AXM2-5557, RcaFr 731.041, RcaFr PM43684, RcaE
                 RD7775, ViJap RA74, RcaAu YPLI-0471
BS 021626-2   **LP:** RcaFr PM43684, FR series
                 The Blues In Your Flat

BS 021627-1   same issues as BS 021626-1, except substitute **LP:**
                 RcaFr 730.629 for RcaFr 731.041
                 The Blues In My Flat - voc Lionel Hampton

BS 021628-1   **LP:** MER 3, RcaBB AXM2-5568, RcaFr PM43684
BS 021628-2   VI 26240 B, HMV B8957, HMVAu EA2551, GrFr K8374.
                 EP: VI EPOT6703. **LP:** VI LPT6703, ViArg AYL3000-5,
                 RcaBB AXM2-5557, RcaFr 731.041, RcaFr PM43684,
                 ViJap RA74
                 Sugar

BS 021629-1   VI 25822 A, BB 10903, HMV B8765, HMVAu EA3567,
(2)   ViJap 10014 A. **LP:** VI LPV521, VI LPV1032, RcaBB
                 AXM2-5557, RcaE RD7775, RcaFr 730.707, RcaFr
                 PM43684, RcaH SRS557, ViJap RA74
                 Dizzy Spells

(Some wax impressions and liner notes claim a take 2 for "Dizzy Spells"; all such claims are in error, and a take 2 is not known to have been issued.)

SUSTAINING BROADCAST   *March 26, 1938, Hotel*
  CBS Radio Network   *Pennsylvania, New York*

Personnel as March 12, except DAVE TOUGH, d, replaces Hampton, and prob. BEN HELLER, g, replaces Reuss.

Please Be Kind - voc Martha Tilton
Always And Always - voc Martha Tilton

Babe Russin left the band to return to more lucrative, less frenetic work in the studios. Bud Freeman, glad to be back with his buddy Dave Tough, quit Tommy Dorsey to join Benny, probably on March 28. At this juncture too, Ben Heller came in as Allan Reuss's permanent replacement.

The "Camel Caravan" resumed its half-hour format on March 29; Oakie and Stoll were out, and Benny's time slot was moved up from 9:30 to 10:00.

SUSTAINING BROADCAST   *March 31, 1938, Hotel*
  MUTUAL Radio Network   *Pennsylvania, New York*

Orchestra personnel as March 26, except BUD FREEMAN, ts, replaces Russin, and Ben Heller is now considered certain. Quartet personnel as March 25.

Let's Dance (theme)
Camel Hop
Something Tells Me - voc Martha Tilton (LP: SB 152)
Always And Always - voc Martha Tilton
The Man I Love - QUARTET (LP: SB 152)

Although Dave Tough had played Trio drums for the March 25 recording session, Benny usually called on Lionel Hampton to fill that role, especially for uptempo numbers and "Camel Caravan" broadcasts, per the next program. It also features Bud Freeman's first "Caravan" appearance; he, James and Tough excel in a sterling rendition of "Roll 'Em":

"CAMEL CARAVAN"   *April 5, 1938, New York*
  CBS Radio Network

Orchestra personnel as March 31. TRIO: Goodman, Wilson, Hampton, d.

Let's Dance (theme)
Makin' Whoopee (LP: SB 152)
I Fall In Love With You Every Day - voc Martha Tilton (LP: SB 152)
Tiger Rag - TRIO (LP: SB 152)
(Swing Is Here To Sway - voc, guest Eddie Cantor, The Three Marshall's,
  Camel Chorus - accomp. by studio orchestra, including strings - NO BG
How'd Ya Like To Love Me? - voc Martha Tilton
Roll 'Em
Good-Bye (theme)

SUSTAINING BROADCAST   *April 6, 1938, Hotel*
  MUTUAL Radio Network   *Pennsylvania, New York*

Orchestra personnel as March 31.

Let's Dance (theme—last few notes) (LP: SB 152)
Lullaby In Rhythm (arr ES) (LP: SB 152, SG 8004)
When Buddha Smiles (n/c) (LP: SB 152)

Benny had an idea that Dave Matthews, who'd left Jimmy Dorsey to join him, was more at home in the first alto chair, so Dave began to get more lead work. This disenchanted Hymie, so he quit. Milt Yaner, a New York studio man, took Hymie's place, in time for the band's next studio session:

BENNY GOODMAN AND HIS ORCHESTRA   **April 8, 1938, New York**

Personnel as March 31, except MILT YANER, as, replaces Schertzer.

BS 022414-1   VI 25846 B, ViJap 1258 B. **EP:** RcaE RCX1064. **LP:** VI
(2)   LPM2247, ViJap RA80, RcaAu L 101039, RcaBB
                 AXM2-5557
                 It's The Dreamer In Me - voc Martha Tilton (arr ES)

BS 022415-1   VI 25827 B, HMVAu EA2156, HMVSw JK2035. **EP:** VI
EPOT6703. **LP:** VI LPT6703, ViArg AYL3000-5, RcaFr
741.084, RcaBB AXM2-5566, ViJap RA71

BS 022415-2   **LP:** RcaBB AXM2-5568
Lullaby in Rhythm (arr ES)

BS 022416-1   VI 26089 A, HMVAu EA2307. **LP:** ViG LPM10025, RcaFr
741.102, RcaBB AXM2-5566
I Never Knew (arr FH)

BS 022417-1
(2)   VI 25827 A, HMVAu EA2156, HMVSw JK2035. **LP:**
RcaBB AXM2-5566, JAZ 19
That Feeling Is Gone - voc Martha Tilton (arr ES)

BS 022418-1
(2)   Test Pressing
Feelin' High And Happy - voc Martha Tilton

BS 022419-1
(2)   VI 26089 B, HMV B8905, ViArg 1A-0758. **LP:** ViG
LPM10025, RcaFr 741.102, RcaBB AXM2-5566 RcaFr
111
Sweet Sue-Just You

(Benny's files show two arrangements for "It's The Dreamer In Me," one by Jimmy Mundy, the other by Edgar Sampson; but there is no indication which was used for the Victor recording. (At a guess, Sampson's.) Note also that "Lullaby In Rhythm" was first titled, "Honey Chile.")

Particularly noteworthy on the next "Camel Caravan" is Vernon Brown's extended solo on "Clarinet Marmalade," possibly his best work with Goodman extant:

"CAMEL CARAVAN"   *April 12, 1938, New York*
  CBS Radio Network

Orchestra as April 8; Trio as April 5.

Let's Dance (theme)
The Blue Room
It's The Dreamer In Me - voc Martha Tilton
After You've Gone - TRIO
Feelin' High And Happy - voc Martha Tilton
Lullaby In Rhythm
My Honey's Lovin' Arms (arr FH)
Always And Always - voc Martha Tilton
Clarinet Marmalade
Good-Bye (theme)

SUSTAINING BROADCAST   *April 14, 1938, Hotel*
  MUTUAL Radio Network   *Pennsylvania, New York*

Personnel as April 8.

I Let A Song Go Out Of My Heart - voc Martha Tilton (n/c) (arr ES)

Like Babe Russin, Milt Yaner preferred the relative ease of a studio job to the frenetic life of a member of a road band, even Benny's; he left April 15. Once again Jimmy Dorsey's crew provided a needed replacement, now Noni Bernardi. He's included in the next air check; and with his entrance, the band's personnel will stay intact for a bit more than six months.

SUSTAINING BROADCAST   *April 16, 1938, Hotel*
  CBS Radio Network   *Pennsylvania, New York*

Personnel as April 8, except NONI BERNARDI, as, replaces Yaner.

I Let A Song Go Out Of My Heart - voc Martha Tilton (arr ES) (LP: SB 152)

Yaner hadn't left a moment too soon: Following the Saturday night (16th) broadcast, the band played a one-nighter in Washington on Sunday, returned to New York for its Monday "dark night," reassembled in the Madhattan Room on Tuesday, doubled into CBS's studios for its weekly "Camel Caravan." Note that Benny announces Harry James as "Ciribiribin's" arranger; the chart, which will be recorded in October, bears Fletcher Henderson's signature. Whatever, Harry's bravura execution more than compensates for a seven-second line interruption in an otherwise impeccable "Don't Be That Way" by the Quartet:

"CAMEL CARAVAN"   *April 19, 1938, New York*
  CBS Radio Network

Personnel as April 16 (Quartet as March 25).

Let's Dance (theme)
Sweet Sue-Just You (LP: SB 152)
I Let A Song Go Out Of My Heart - voc Martha Tilton
Ti-Pi-Tin (LP: SB 152)
You Couldn't Be Cuter - voc Martha Tilton (LP: SB 152)
Ciribiribin (arr FH, poss. with HJ) (LP: SB 152)
Don't Be That Way - QUARTET
Joseph, Joseph - voc Martha Tilton
Good-Bye (theme)

SUSTAINING BROADCAST   *April 21, 1938, Hotel*
  MUTUAL Radio Network   *Pennsylvania, New York*

Personnel as April 16 (Quartet as March 25).

Sometimes I'm Happy (LP: SB 152)
You Went To My Head - voc Martha Tilton (LP: SB 152)
Shine - QUARTET (n/c) (LP: SB 152)

A test pressing owned by Goodman collector Ken Crawford bears the sole enigmatic identification-2359-a meaningless number, in terms of Victor matrices. On it Martha Tilton is but dimly heard singing, "Feelin' High And Happy," but the band comes through loud and clear. On grounds that its tempo and soli are more akin to those in the released version of the tune from the next listing, it is arbitrarily assigned to April 22. It may have been an initial run through, with Martha behind a faulty microphone. . .

BENNY GOODMAN AND HIS ORCHESTRA   **April 22, 1938, New York**

Benny Goodman, clt; Harry James, Ziggy Elman, Chris Griffin, tpt; Red Ballard, Vernon Brown, tbn; Dave Matthews, Noni Bernardi, as; Art Rollini, Bud Freeman, ts; Jess Stacy, p; Ben Heller, g; Harry Goodman, b; Dave Tough, d; Martha Tilton, voc.

BS 022487-1
(2)   VI 25840 B, HMV B8853, GrFr K8177. **LP:**RD "The
Great Band Era" album, VI VPM6040, RcaBB
AXM2-5566, RcaFr FXM3-7273, ViJap RA80, JAZ 19.
ET: AFRS "Remember" series H54-Prog. 13/14
I Let A Song Go Out Of My Heart - voc Martha Tilton
(arr ES)

- "2359" -
BS 022418-3
(4)   Test Pressing
VI 25840 A. **LP:** ViG LPM10025, RcaBB AXM2-5566,
RcaFr PM43173. **ET:** AFRS "American Popular Music"
Series 390
Feelin' High And Happy - voc Martha Tilton

BS 022488-1   VI 25846 A, ViJap 1258 A. **LP:** RcaBB AXM2-5566, JAZ
19

BS 022488-2
(3)   **LP:** TL STBB03
Why'd Ya Make Me Fall In Love? - voc Martha Tilton
(arr ES)

(On what seemed substantial evidence, earlier discographies have listed as an issued record take 4 of BS 022418 "Feelin' High And Happy" from this session. For the same reason they had also listed as issued records take 4's of BS 025468 "You're Lovely Madame" and BS 025475 "I Had To Do It," both from October 3, 1938. Intensive search over four decades has failed to uncover a single copy of any of them; persons who claimed in the past to have had them now admit they do not, and never did. It must be concluded that none was issued, none exists.)

SUSTAINING BROADCAST   *April 23, 1938, Hotel*
  CBS Radio Network   *Pennsylvania, New York*

Personnel as April 22.

I'm A Ding Dong Daddy (From Dumas) - QUARTET (as March 25)
Please Be Kind - voc Martha Tilton (n/c)
Ti-Pi-Tin
Nice Work If You Can Get It - TRIO (as March 25)

Benny's next recording marked a personal triumph; in company with the Budapest String Quartet, Benny cut Mozart's Quintet for Clarinet and Strings, K. 581, and Victor released Benny's first classical album. Generally, critics judged it a competent performance, and Benny was thrilled with his acceptance into the classical field.

Benny recalls that a year earlier he had breezed into a Chicago studio, after an overnight bus trip from Wisconsin, to record this same Mozart work with the Pro Arte Quartet. With no preparation but with worlds of confidence, using the same reed he had used the night before on a dance date, Benny sat in cold. He blew a few bars—and promptly blew right out of the studio. He remembers, "I just got up and walked out. You know, they were nice guys. They just sat there and didn't do a thing to humiliate me."

For this reading Benny practiced diligently, haunted music shops for the perfect reed, sought criticism repeatedly from other clarinetists. When he entered Victor's New York Studio No. 2 this time, he was prepared.

About the issues listed: Catalog nos. 1884, 1885 and 1886 (plus the 12″ 14921) are a manual set, designated "M." Each record must be flipped separately to play in proper sequence. Catalog nos. 1887, 1888 and 1889, designated "AM," constitute a semi-automatic set for play on a record changer. Three stacked records play in sequence, but then each must be flipped individually. The "M" set is the original issue; the "AM" set was issued practically simultaneously. Later, Victor released a "DM" set, nos. 2090, 2091 and 2992, with an RCA-Victor labeling. This is a fully automatic set, in that the stacked 10″ records may be flipped as a group to continue play in proper sequence.

This work was also issued on HMVAu ED733/734/735, three 12″ 78 rpm discs, auto-coupled, but their correct matrix numbers are not known. Other releases are: HMV DB3576/3577/3578; HMV DB8548/8549/8550; HMVFr DB8548/8549/8550; and at least in part on ViJap JE167. And at long last, in 1985, RCA released this recording of the Mozart Quintet on LP, RCA AGLI-5275.

BUDAPEST STRING QUARTET   April 25, 1938, New York
AND BENNY GOODMAN

Benny Goodman, clt; and the Budapest String Quartet (Roismann, Schneider, Kroyt, Schneider).

BS 022902-2   VI 1885 A, VI 1889 A, VI 2092 A (M, AM, DM 452-3)
              Quintet For Clarinet And Strings
              2nd Movement-Larghetto

BS 022903-1   VI 1885 B, VI 1887 B, VI 2092 B (M, AM, DM 452-4)
              Quintet For Clarinet And Strings
              2nd Movement-Larghetto-concluded

BS 022904-2   VI 1884 A, VI 1887 A, VI 2090 A (M, AM, DM 452-1)
              Quintet For Clarinet And Strings
              1st Movement-Allegro

BS 022905-2   VI 1884 B, VI 1888 A, VI 2091 A (M, AM, DM 452-2)
              Quintet For Clarinet And Strings
              1st Movement-Allegro-concluded

BS 022906-1   VI 1886 A, VI 1888 B, VI 2091 B (M, AM, DM 452-5)
              Quintet For Clarinet And Strings
              3rd Movement-Menuetto

BS 022907-1   VI 1886 B, VI 1889 B, VI 2090 B (M, AM, DM 452-6)
              Quintet For Clarinet And Strings
              3rd Movement-Menuetto-concluded

CS 022908-2   VI 14921 A (M, AM, DM 452-7) 12″
              Quintet For Clarinet And Strings
              4th Movement-Allegro con variazioni-Variations 1, 2,
                and 3

CS 022909-1   VI 14921 B (M, AM, DM 452-8) 12″
              Quintet For Clarinet And Strings
              4th Movement-concluded-Variation 4-Adagio; Allegro

Also on the 25th, the jazz Quartet made a guest appearance on Eddie Cantor's popular CBS radio program, in company with Rudy Vallee, who was substituting for the vacationing Cantor. In his introduction, Vallee says to Benny, "As one clarinetist to another. . ."

"THE EDDIE CANTOR PROGRAM"   *April 25, 1938, New York*
   CBS Radio Network

Quartet personnel as March 25.

Don't Be That Way - QUARTET (LP: AC 1)

Guest Vicente Gomez plays two guitar solos following "Don't Be That Way" on the next "Camel Caravan," not detailed in our listing:

"CAMEL CARAVAN"   *April 26, 1938, New York*
   CBS Radio Network

Orchestra as April 22. TRIO: Godman, Wilson, Hampton, d.

Let's Dance (theme)
Make Believe
On The Sentimental Side - voc Martha Tilton
Don't Be That Way
Why'd Ya Make Me Fall In Love? - voc Martha Tilton

BENNY GOODMAN TRIO

59-MG-630B   MGM Series: 102, 105, 108, 112, 116
             Nobody's Sweetheart

You Had An Evening To Spare - voc Martha Tilton
House Hop
Good-Bye (theme)

The band left the Hotel Pennsylvania on April 30 and went on tour. On May 1 Benny attempted to repeat his Carnegie Hall concert in Boston's Symphony Hall. The results were disappointing; the audience got out of hand, and at one point Benny stopped the performance to insist that the rowdyism stop. And in truth, given Gene's leaving and the other personnel changes that had taken place since January 16, this band simply wasn't the magnificent orchestra that had performed in Carnegie Hall.

On May 2 the band played in the Auditorium, Worcester, Mass. On May 3 it had another one-nighter at Nuttings-On-The-Charles, Waltham, Mass. And that locale raises an issue: Benny insists that all "Camel Caravan" broadcasts were from studios, not from locations. Supporting his contention, the "Camel Caravan" program of May 3 is identified as originating in Boston. But the crowd noise suggests a location, not a studio. In deference to the announced identification, Boston is listed as the locale. Demonstrably, however, some "Camel Caravan" broadcasts in future do originate in ballrooms and other locations, and Benny's recollection does not always hold true.

"CAMEL CARAVAN"   *May 3, 1938, Boston*
   CBS Radio Network

Orchestra personnel as April 22. Quartet personnel as March 25.

I Can't Give You Anything But Love, Baby
Please Be Kind - voc Martha Tilton
Sampson Stomp (arr ES)
The Dixieland Band - voc Martha Tilton
Nagasaki - QUARTET (LP: SB 152)
Wrappin' It Up (LP: SB 152)
Good-Bye (theme)

The next "Camel Caravan" broadcast emanates from New York, where the band was playing in the Savoy Ballroom, opposite Teddy Hill and his Orchestra. Ambient sound suggests a studio origin:

"CAMEL CARAVAN"   *May 10, 1938, New York*
   CBS Radio Network

Orchestra personnel as April 22. Quartet personnel as March 25.

I've Found A New Baby
Lillie Stomp - QUARTET
One O'Clock Jump (LP: BID 5001/2)

The General Baking Company ("Bond Bread") distributed free tickets to Philadelphia's Convention Hall on May 11, where the band played for dancing; fire marshals were called in to limit attendance to the Hall's 10,000 capacity. Next day it was back to New York, and an engagement in the Roseland Ballroom, one of very few such facilities still in operation today. Once more, ambient sound indicates the next "Camel Caravan" program was broadcast from CBS's studios, not from Roseland:

"CAMEL CARAVAN"   May 17, 1938, New York
  CBS Radio Network

Orchestra personnel as April 22. Quartet personnel as March 25. Trio personnel as April 26 (Hampton on d). SEPTET: BG, James, Brown, Stacy, Heller, H.
Goodman, Tough.

I'll Always Be In Love With You (arr FH)
I Love To Whistle - voc Martha Tilton
Moon Glow - QUARTET (LP: BID 5001/2)
Star Dust (LP: BID 5001/2)
The Jazz Me Blues - SEPTET (LP: FAN 37-137)
I Let A Song Go Out Of My Heart - voc Martha Tilton
Who? - TRIO
Don't Be That Way (LP: FAN 37-137)
Good-Bye (theme)

Then to Boston and a return engagement in the Ritz-Carlton Hotel.
Benny recalls that the first time he was booked there the manager questioned, "Benny Goodman? He sounds like he oughta fight preliminaries at
the (Madison Square) Garden . . .!" Again, likely a studio origin for the
next broadcast:

"CAMEL CARAVAN"   May 24, 1938, Boston
  CBS Radio Network

Orchestra personnel as April 22. Quartet personnel as March 25.

Honeysuckle Rose (LP: FAN 37-137)
Lullaby In Rhythm (LP: BID 5001/2)
It's The Dreamer In Me - voc Martha Tilton (n/c)
Joseph, Joseph - QUARTET (LP: GOJ 1005)
King Porter Stomp

The band was in Hartford, Conn., on May 26, then went into Atlantic
City's Steel Pier on May 29 for the Memorial Day weekend. In between, it
stopped off in New York for a Victor session:

BENNY GOODMAN AND HIS ORCHESTRA   May 28, 1938, New York

Personnel as April 22.

BS 023506-1   VI 25867 A. **LP:** RcaBB AXM2-5566, JAZ 17
BS 023506-2   VI 25867 A, HMVAu EA2212. **LP:** JAZ 17
               Don't Wake Up My Heart - voc Martha Tilton (arr JM)

BS 023507-1   VI 25867 B. **LP:** RcaBB AXM2-5566, JAZ 17
(2)   **(I've Been) Saving Myself For You** - voc Martha Tilton
               (arr ES)

BS 023508-1   VI 25871 B, HMV B8798. **EP:** VI EPA745, Vi EPB1239,
               VI EPBT3056, HMV 7EG8142. **LP:** VI LPM1239, VI
               LPT3056, ViArg AVLT3, RcaBB AXM2-5566, RcaFr
               741.044, RD 3-76, ViJap RA71, TL STBB03, RcaAu
               VPLI-0471, C/P 25231
               Big John Special (arr HH)

BS 023509-1   VI 25880 A, HMV B8841, HMVAu EA2202. **LP:** ViG
               LPM10025, RcaBB AXM2-5566, RcaFr 741.084,
               RcaAu VPLI-0471
BS 023509-2   **LP:** RcaBB AXM2-5568
               My Melancholy Baby (arr FH)

BS 023510-1   VI 25880 B, HMV B8798, HMVAu EA2202. **EP:** VI
               EPA745, VI EPB1239, VI EPBT1239, VI EPBT3056.
               LP: VI LPM1239, VI LPT3056, ViArg AVLT3, RD
               3/4-45, VI DRLI-0062, RcaBB AXM2-5566, RcaFr
               741.059, ViJap RA71, RcaG Golden Age of Jazz,
               RcaAu VPLI-0471, C/P 25231. **ET:** AFRS Jill's All-
               Time Juke Box H12, Prog. 830
BS 023510-2   **LP:** RcaBB AXM2-5568
               Wrappin' It Up (arr FH)

BS 023511-1   VI 25878 B, GrFr K8177.**LP:** RcaBB AXM2-5566, JAZ 17
               What Goes On Here In My Heart? - voc Martha Tilton

Benny's files are not clear as to arranger credit for, "The Flat Foot
Floogee"; in addition to Joe Belford, there are indications that either Edgar
Sampson or Jimmy Mundy was responsible for the finished chart. In any

event, Benny recorded it May 31, then premiered it on the "Camel Caravan" broadcast the same evening.

BENNY GOODMAN AND HIS ORCHESTRA   May 31, 1938, New York

Personnel as April 22.

BS 023517-2   VI 25878 A, HMVAu EA2212. **LP:** RcaBB AXM2-5566,
(1)   JAZ 16
               A Little Kiss At Twilight - voc Martha Tilton (poss. arr
               ES)

BS 023518-2   VI 25871 A, HMV B8777, HMVIt GW 1578, GrFr K8179.
(1)   **LP:** ViG LPM10025, JA J1245, RD The Great Band
               Era, RcaBB AXM2-5566, RcaFr 741.102, RcaFr
               FXM3-7273
               The Flat Foot Floogee (voc, the band) (arr Joe Belford
               or ES/JM)

"CAMEL CARAVAN"   May 31, 1938, New York
  CBS Radio Network

Personnel as April 22.

Alexander's Ragtime Band (LP: BID 5001/2)
I Never Knew
The Flat Foot Floogee - voc, the band
Good-Bye (theme) (LP: BID 5001/2)

The band left Manhattan for a one-week stand in Cleveland's Hotel
Statler, the source of its next commercial broadcast. Rival champions of Jess
Stacy and Teddy Wilson are afforded an unique opportunity to compare the
two, for Benny features them in a duet:

"CAMEL CARAVAN"   June 7, 1938, Cleveland, Ohio
  CBS Radio Network

Orchestra as April 22. Quartet as March 25.

Let's Dance (theme)
Shine On, Harvest Moon (LP: BID 5001/2)
(I've Been) Saving Myself For You -voc Martha Tilton
The Flat Foot Floogee - voc, the band
(She's Funny That Way - piano duet, Stacy, Wilson - NO BG
It's Been So Long - voc Martha Tilton
Digga Digga Do - QUARTET (LP: BID 5001/2)
You Couldn't Be Cuter - voc Martha Tilton
I Know That You Know (LP: BID 5001/2)
Good-Bye (theme)

RCA again featured Benny on its weekly "Magic Key" broadcast,
offering two renditions by his Trio and three by his Quartet, plus a lengthy
chat with the program's host, Ben Grauer. Unfortunately, NBC's master 16"
acetates have a skip-and-repeat during Lionel's drum solo on the first tune;
judicious tape splicing, however, minimizes the damage. The Quartet's
contributions are flawless, both mechanically and musically. They highlight
Dave Tough's brilliant brush work and pounding bass drum in a driving
"Avalon" and a Mach 1-tempo "Digga Digga Do." In the author's opinion, this is Tough at his very best, with Goodman or anyone for whom he
ever played.

"MAGIC KEY OF RCA"   June 12, 1938, New York
  NBC Radio Network

Trio as April 26. Quartet as March 25.

After You've Gone - TRIO
You Leave Me Breathless - TRIO
Avalon - QUARTET
The Man I Love - QUARTET
Digga Digga Do - QUARTET

In the evening of the 12th, the Goodman Gang jousted jointly with
Count Basie's band in New York's Madison Square Garden. The proceedings were broadcast by radio station WHN, but no extant acetates have been
found. Then the band moved on to the Roof Garden of Boston's Ritz-Carlton
Hotel, opening there on the 13th. Its "Caravan" broadcast from there the
next evening highlights Teddy Wilson playing harpsichord, in a duet with
Benny:

"CAMEL CARAVAN"   June 14, 1938, Boston
  CBS Radio Network

Orchestra as April 22. Quartet as March 25.

Let's Dance (theme)
Sweet Sue-Just You
I've Got A Guy - voc Martha Tilton
Don't Be That Way
You Leave Me Breathless - DUET, Goodman, Wilson (harpsichord)
Make Believe
I've Found A New Baby - QUARTET (LP: BID 5001/2)

BENNY GOODMAN QUARTET

XLP 11049-1A   CO Series: 1, 4, 6, 11, 14, 18, 23, 24, 26, 52, and
                EP: PHIL BBE12133, PhilCont 429248BE
                I Hadn't Anyone Till You - voc Martha Tilton

Swingtime In The Rockies (LP: BID 5001/2)
Good-Bye (theme)

Discovery of complete transcriptions of the "Camel Caravan" broadcasts of June 21 and 28 belies - at least in part - contemporary music press notices that Martha Tilton took a two-week vacation at this time. She is present on both programs; Maxine Sullivan, who'd come into prominence as a result of her swinging the classics vocally, is a guest, an "extra added attraction." What may be true is that the reports are accurate, but Martha returned for the important commercial air time.

"CAMEL CARAVAN"   June 21, 1938, Boston
  CBS Radio Network

Orchestra as April 22. Trio as April 26.

Let's Dance (theme)
Smiles (arr JM)
I Hadn't Anyone Till You - voc Martha Tilton
Chinatown, My Chinatown - TRIO
This Time It's Real - voc, guest Maxine Sullivan
Paradise
Darling Nellie Gray - voc, guest Maxine Sullivan
One O'Clock Jump
Good-Bye (theme)

Another interesting "vacation" at the end of the month found Dave Tough in a brief reunion with Bunny Berigan - he is clearly identifiable on Bunny's NBC Thesaurus "Rhythm Makers" transcriptions, recorded Monday, June 27, in New York. The very next day, Dave was back in the Goodman band, in Montreal, Canada. Apparently, Dave sat in to solidify Bunny's band for its important NBC session, a favor to his immediate pre-BG boss.

Through this period, "Caravan" broadcasts emanated from whichever locations the band was playing in, not from CBS studios in those cities, Benny's recollection notwithstanding. Note that although an announcement identifies the next site as the Forum "Auditorium," a Canadian correspondent, present for the broadcast, says the correct designation is, Forum "Arena."

"CAMEL CARAVAN"   June 28, 1938, Montreal
  CBS Radio Network

Orchestra as April 22. Quartet as March 25.

Let's Dance (theme)
Changes
You Leave Me Breathless - voc Martha Tilton
Lullaby In Rhythm
Spring Is Here - voc, guest Maxine Sullivan
My Best Wishes (no vocal)
Canadian Capers - QUARTET
Fare-Thee-Well, Annie Laurie - voc, guest Maxine Sullivan
Clarinet Marmalade (LP: BID 5001/2)
Good-Bye (theme)

Despite the rising popularity of the bands of Tommy Dorsey, Artie Shaw, Glenn Miller and others, Benny's band played the prized July Fourth weekend engagement at Atlantic City's Steel Pier. Then on the next day it was in the Glen Park Casino in Williamsville, New York (near Buffalo), and the next "Caravan":

"CAMEL CARAVAN"   July 5, 1938,
  CBS Radio Network   Williamsville, New York

Orchestra as April 22. Trio as April 26. Quartet as March 25.

Let's Dance (theme)
The Blue Room (arr FH)
What Goes On Here In My Heart? - voc Martha Tilton
I Hadn't Anyone Till You - TRIO (LP: BID 5001/2)
The Flat Foot Floogee - voc, the band
Says My Heart - voc Martha Tilton
I'm A Ding Dong Daddy (From Dumas) - QUARTET
I Let A Song Go Out Of My Heart - voc Martha Tilton
Minnie The Moocher's Wedding Day (LP: BID 5001/2)
Good-Bye (theme)

On July 1 Benny had been announced as one winner of a jazz instrumentalist poll conducted by WNEW Radio's Martin Block, whose "Make Believe Ballroom" regularly featured jazz on its Wednesday evening broadcasts. That fact hints at a tenuous link to an otherwise-unassignable all-star dalliance with "I Know That You Know," for the acetate from which it comes offers no other clues:

"MAKE BELIEVE BALLROOM"   poss. July 6, 1938, New York
  WNEW Radio Broadcast

Benny Goodman, clt; Roy Eldridge, tpt; Lester Young, ts; Teddy Wilson, p;
Ben Heller, g; Sid Weiss, b; Jo Jones, d.

I Know That You Know (LP: IAJRC 14)

The band was in Quebec on July 9, at the State Park at Jones Beach, New York, on July 10. Then it returned to Manhattan for a studio session:

BENNY GOODMAN AND HIS ORCHESTRA   **July 11, 1938, New York**

Personnel as April 22.

BS 023511-2   VI 25878 B. **LP:** JAZ 17
(3)   **What Goes On Here In My Heart?** - voc Martha Tilton

BS 024020-2   VI 26000 A. **LP:** RcaBB AXM2-5566, JAZ 16
(1)   **I've Got A Date With A Dream** - voc Martha Tilton

BS 024021-2   same issues
(1)   **Could You Pass In Love?** - voc Martha Tilton

BS 023517-4   VI 25878 A. **LP:** ViG LPM10025
(3)   **A Little Kiss At Twilight** - voc Martha Tilton

(ViG LPM10025's liner notes erroneously indicate take 3 for "A Little Kiss At Twilight." Take is 4, as shown.)

For the third year in a row, Benny won Metronome's "best band" contest, announced on the next "Camel" broadcast:

"CAMEL CARAVAN"   July 12, 1938, New York
  CBS Radio Network

Orchestra as April 22, Trio as April 26. Quartet as March 25.

Let's Dance (theme)
Sugar Foot Stomp
Music, Maestro, Please - voc Martha Tilton
Dark Rapture (arr ES)
Time On My Hands - TRIO
A-Tisket, A-Tasket - voc Martha Tilton, Benny Goodman, the band (arr ES)
Margie - QUARTET
Could You Pass In Love? - voc Martha Tilton
When You And I Were Young, Maggie
Good-Bye (theme)

Following this broadcast Benny took three weeks vacation and went to Europe for the first time. The band continued its "Camel Caravan" broadcasts, with Harry James as interim leader. "Names" were needed to replace Benny, however, so Guy Lombardo was nominal leader of the July 19 broadcast, and Ben Bernie "led" the July 26 show. Jess Stacy and Dave Tough were absent the first program.

It should also be said here that, just as Gene Krupa seemed to have been the driving force behind the band during his tenure, Harry James came to the fore when Gene left. Benny's recognition of this undoubtedly led to his naming Harry as interim leader during BG's vacation. This is not to imply that Benny abdicated his position as leader; that never happened. But unquestionably it was Harry who drew the attention of the audiences when they no longer could demonstrate for Gene; and he responded by playing some of the best trumpet of his career.

"CAMEL CARAVAN"   *July 19, 1938, New York*
  CBS Radio Network

Personnel as April 22, except delete BG, and substitute Wilson, p, and Hampton, d, for Stacy and Tough. Jo Jones sits in for small group work.

I Hadn't Anyone Till You - voc Martha Tilton
Coquette - TRIO (Hampton, vib; Wilson, Jo Jones, d.)
Down South Camp Meeting
Boo Hoo
Big John Special
Wrappin' It Up

"CAMEL CARAVAN"   *July 26, 1938, New York*
  CBS Radio Network

Orchestra as April 22, except delete BG (Stacy and Tough both return). TRIO: Hampton (vib), Wilson, Tough. QUARTET: Trio plus guest Ben Bernie, v & voc.

Let's Dance (theme)
Smiles
My Best Wishes - voc Martha Tilton
The Flat Foot Floogee - voc, guest Ben Bernie, the band
Dinah - voc interjections, Ben Bernie - QUARTET
Sweet Georgia Brown - TRIO
(It's A) Lonesome Old Town
A-Tisket, A-Tasket - voc Martha Tilton, Ben Bernie, the band
Madhouse
Good-Bye (theme)

Benny returned from Europe on August 2, just in time for that evening's "Caravan" broadcast. Unaccountably, the program log written for sponsor R. J. Reynolds specifies that Jo Jones plays for the Quartet; however, on a newly-discovered transcription of the complete broadcast, announcer Dan Seymour names Dave Tough as anchorman for Benny's "Board Of Trustees." The excellent audio fidelity of these ETs permits aural identification of Tough, not possible with the privately-recorded acetates of a portion of the broadcast that heretofore were the only available source material.

"CAMEL CARAVAN"   *August 2, 1938, New York*
  CBS Radio Network

Orchestra as April 22. Trio as April 26. Quartet as March 25.

Let's Dance (theme)
Hallelujah! (arr FH)
Stop Beatin' 'Round The Mulberry Bush - voc Martha Tilton
Lambeth Walk - QUARTET
Alexander's Ragtime Band
I've Got A Date With A Dream - voc Martha Tilton
The World Is Waiting For The Sunrise - TRIO
My Walking Stick - voc Martha Tilton
Clarinet Marmalade
Good-Bye (theme)

Benny tried to repeat the Carnegie concert at Chicago's Ravinia Park on August 3, again with indifferent results. It is believed that he returned immediately to New York, and that it is the locale of an acetate dated August 5. No other written information accompanies it, but its ambient sound suggests a commercial, not a sustaining, broadcast. Since Dave Tough is not on board for the August 8 recording session, he may not be present here:

RADIO BROADCAST   *August 5, 1938, poss. New York*
  MUTUAL Radio Network

QUARTET: BG, Hampton, Wilson - unknown d, poss. Jo Jones

Dinah - QUARTET (LP: BID 5001/2)

The band had a week's engagement at Manhattan Beach in Brooklyn, August 7 through August 13, but it returned to the "Big Apple" for both a recording date on the 8th, and its "Caravan" broadcast on the 9th. Dave Tough is not on the Victor session, but is present for the broadcast.

BENNY GOODMAN AND HIS ORCHESTRA   **August 8, 1938, New York**

Personnel as April 22, except Lionel Hampton, d, replaces Tough.

BS 024472-1   Test Pressing
     You Got Me - voc Martha Tilton

BS 024473-1   Test Pressing
BS 024473-2   VI 26021 B, HMV B8841. **LP:** ViG LPM10025, RcaBB
       AXM2-5566
     Blue Interlude - voc Martha Tilton (arr Benny Carter)

"CAMEL CARAVAN"   *August 9, 1938, New York*
  CBS Radio Network

Benny Goodman, clt; Harry James, Ziggy Elman, Chris Griffin, tpt; Red Ballard, Vernon Brown, tbn; Dave Matthews, Noni Bernardi, as; Art Rollini, Bud Freeman, ts; Jess Stacy, p; Ben Heller, g; Harry Goodman, b; Dave Tough, d. Martha Tilton, voc.

TRIO: Benny Goodman, clt; Teddy Wilson, p; Lionel Hampton, d.

QUARTET: Benny Goodman, clt; Lionel Hampton, vib; Teddy Wilson, p; Dave Tough, d.

Let's Dance (theme)
Lullaby In Rhythm
You Go To My Head - voc Martha Tilton (arr ES)
Roll 'Em
Now It Can Be Told - TRIO
A-Tisket, A-Tasket - voc Martha Tilton, Benny Goodman, the band
Honeysuckle Rose - QUARTET
Blue Interlude - voc Martha Tilton
I Want To Be Happy
Good-Bye (theme)

Art Rollini is absent from the next recording session, according to Victor's files. Its recording sheets also show that only one title was recorded, an unusual circumstance. The sole tune cut is from a "Mask And Wig" production of the University of Pennsylvania; a time factor may have caused the arrangement to have been waxed separately.

BENNY GOODMAN AND HIS ORCHESTRA   **August 12, 1938, New York**

Personnel as August 9, except possibly omit Art Rollini, ts.

BS 02493-1(2)   VI 26021 A. **LP:** RcaBB AXM2-5566, JAZ 17
     When I Go A Dreamin' - voc Martha Tilton

The band then went on an extended tour, would not return to New York for more than two months. Its first stop was in the Marine Ballroom of the Steel Pier in Atlantic City. The band and the small groups are in fine fettle, and not even the pounding surf in the background detracts from their brilliance. Unfortunately, "skips-and-repeats" in a defective ET do mar portions of three tunes; cut-and-splice editing works wonders, however, and the resultant tape transfer is - almost - flawless.

"CAMEL CARAVAN"   *August 16, 1938, Atlantic City*
  CBS Radio Network

Personnels as August 9.

Let's Dance (theme)
Down South Camp Meetin'
I Let A Song Go Out Of My Heart - voc Martha Tilton
Don't Be That Way
'Swonderful - QUARTET
My Walking Stick - voc Martha Tilton
Runnin' Wild - QUARTET (LP: BID 5001/2)
I've Got a Pocketful Of Dreams - voc Martha Tilton
Three Little Words (arr FH)
Good-Bye (theme)

There is a fairly substantial report that there is extant a transcription of a sustaining broadcast from the Pier on August 20:

Let's Dance (theme); Alexander's Ragtime Band; I Hadn't Anyone Till You - voc Martha Tilton; Make Believe; Don't Be That Way; More Than You Know - TRIO; A-Tisket, A-Tasket - voc Martha Tilton, Benny Goodman, the band; Blue Interlude - voc Martha Tilton; I'm A Ding Dong Daddy (From Dumas) - QUARTET; One O'Clock Jump; Good-Bye (theme).

The author knows of no one who has this ET or a copy of it. Given such detail, however, he tends to believe it does exist.

He does know, on the other hand, that once there were TWO Coney Island's—the less famous was just outside Cincinnati, Ohio, and was the locale of the next ''Camel'' broadcast:

''CAMEL CARAVAN''   *August 23, 1938,*
  CBS Radio Network   *near Cincinnati*

Personnels as August 9.

Let's Dance (theme)
Love Me Or Leave Me (LP: FAN 37-137)
What Goes On Here In My Heart? - voc Martha Tilton
I'll Never Be The Same - TRIO
The Yam
Stop Beatin' 'Round The Mulberry Bush - voc Martha Tilton
Stompin' At The Savoy - QUARTET
So Help Me - voc Martha Tilton
Wrappin' It Up
Good-Bye (theme)

On August 26, 27 and 29 (not Sunday the 28th) the band saluted its Canadian fans at the dance pavilion of the Canadian National Exhibition in Toronto. Then it was on to The Coliseum, on the Michigan State Fairgrounds just outside Detroit, locale of its next ''Caravan'' broadcast. Note that Dan Seymour announces the Quartet's contribution as, ''Fiddle Faddle.'' When Columbia released this cut years later, it necessarily retitled it, ''Benny Sent Me,'' because Leroy Anderson had used the original title for his composition for strings in the interim.

Note also that Benny joins the sax section (on alto) for a dissertation on ''Liza,'' and that Harry blows a tasty chorus on ''I Used To Be Color-Blind'':

''CAMEL CARAVAN''   *August 30, 1938,*
  CBS Radio Network   *near Detroit*

Personnels as August 9.

Let's Dance (theme)
The March Of The Swing Parade - voc Martha Tilton (LP: Fan 37-137)
I Used To Be Color-Blind - voc Martha Tilton
At Sundown (LP: FAN 37-137)
Liza - Benny on alto, plus sax section
Russian Lullaby (LP: FAN 37-137)

BENNY GOODMAN QUARTET

XLP 11051-1B   CO Series: 2, 3, 7, 9, 12, 13, 17, 24, 33AA, 44, 45,
                 47, 52, and **EP:** CO B819
                 Benny Sent Me

When I Go A Dreamin' - voc Martha Tilton
The Yam (LP: ''Group A,'' FAN 37-137)
Good-Bye (theme)

It was home for Benny on September 2, for a week's stand at a Chicago theatre. But there is extant a portion of a sustaining broadcast of September 1, and its origin is uncertain:

SUSTAINING BROADCAST   *September 1, 1938, poss. Chicago*
  Unknown network

Personnel as August 9.

Sugar Foot Stomp (LP: BID 5001/2)
I've Found A New Baby - QUARTET (LP: SPJ 6602)
Honeysuckle Rose (n/c) (LP: BID 5001/2)

''CAMEL CARAVAN''   *September 6, 1938, Chicago*
  CBS Radio Network

Personnels as August 9.

Let's Dance (theme)
Chicago (LP & CAS: DRJ 40350)
I've Got A Date With A Dream - voc Martha Tilton
Margie (arr JM)
(In A Mist - Stacy p solo - NO BG (LP & CAS: DRJ 40350)
The Lambeth Walk - voc Martha Tilton
Shine - QUARTET (LP: BID 5001/2)

You Go To My Head - voc Martha Tilton (LP & CAS: DRJ 40350)
Madhouse
Good-Bye (theme)

(Above on LP, SC 1019)

BENNY GOODMAN AND HIS ORCHESTRA   September 12, 1938, Chicago

Personnel as August 9.

BS 025466-1 (2)	VI 26071 B, HMV HU196. **LP:** RcaBB AXM2-5566, JAZ 18
	You're A Sweet Little Headache - voc Martha Tilton
BS 025467-1 (2)	same issues
	I Have Eyes - voc Martha Tilton (arr FH)
BS 025468- (1,2)	UNISSUED
	You're Lovely Madame - voc Martha Tilton (arr ES)

Unique in the panoply of Benny Goodman's ''Camel Caravan'' broadcasts is guest Fletcher Henderson's appearance, next. ''Smack'' plays piano, both straight and swinging, to illustrate his conception of ''Blue Skies,'' then dissects the arrangement into its component brass-reed-rhythm parts. Then the full orchestra takes it out . . . an interlude that is indeed memorable. Preceding it is his new chart on ''You're Driving Me Crazy,'' which Benny will never record commercially.

''CAMEL CARAVAN''   *September 13, 1938, Chicago*
  CBS Radio Network

Personnels as August 9.

Let's Dance (theme)
Changes
A-Tisket, A-Tasket - voc Martha Tilton, the band
You're Driving Me Crazy (arr FH) (LP & CAS: DRJ 40350)

BENNY GOODMAN TRIO

59-MG-629	MGM Series: 101, 104, 107, 111, 116
	I Surrender Dear

(Fletcher Henderson, p & conversation, dissects his arrangement of, Blue Skies

BENNY GOODMAN QUARTET

59-MG-633B	MGM Series: 103, 106, 109, 113. LP & CAS: DRJ 40350.
	Some Of These Days

I Used To Be Color-Blind - voc Martha Tilton
Big John Special
Good-Bye (theme)

(Above, theme through ''I Surrender Dear'' on LP, SC 1019; balance on LP, SC 1020.)

BENNY GOODMAN AND HIS ORCHESTRA   September 14, 1938, Chicago

Personnel as August 9.

BS 025475- (1,2)	UNISSUED
	I Had To Do It - voc Martha Tilton (arr FH)
BS 025476-1 (2)	VI 26060 A, BB 10973, HMV B8827, HMVAu EA2233, HMVInd N4484, HMVSw JK2333. **EP:** VI CR-8. **LP:** ViG LPM10022, RcaBB AXM2-5566, RcaFr 741.102, RcaFr FXM3-7273. **ET:** AFRS ''Jill's All-Time Juke Box'' Series H-12 - Prog. No. 829
	Margie (arr JM)
BS 025477-1 (2)	VI 26053 B, HMVAu EA2190, GrFr K8238. **LP:** RcaBB AXM2-5566, JAZ 17
	What Have You Got That Gets Me? - voc Martha Tilton (arr ES)

BS 025478-1   VI 26060 B, BB 11226, HMV B8827, HMVAu EA2233,
(2)   HMVInd N4484, HMVSw JK2333. **LP:** ViG LPM10022,
              RcaBB AXM2-5566, RcaFr 741.102
              Russian Lullaby

Top to bottom, the next "Caravan" broadcast, from the stage of the Tower Theater in Kansas City, is noteworthy for a series of uncommon events: Announcer Dan Seymour is absent, producer Harry Holcombe substitutes. Martha is ill, misses the program; Jess fills in admirably for her one slated vocal chorus. Guitarist Benny Heller is featured in the band's "Oh, Lady Be Good!", gets all of its solo spots. Instead of the usual Quartet number, Lionel and Jess combine in a four-handed piano duet, "China Stomp"—which M-G-M will unaccountably retitle, "Space, Man." Finally, "Good-Bye" is promised in its entirety; but despite some 40 seconds over the program's permissible 30-minute limit, it's abruptly terminated two-thirds through. Add to all of that never-again performances of "Don't Let That Moon Get Away" and "Moten Swing" . . . remarkable.

"CAMEL CARAVAN"   September 20, 1938, Kansas City
  CBS Radio Network

Personnels as August 9. DUET: Hampton, Stacy, p.

Let's Dance (theme)
Russian Lullaby (LP & CAS: DRJ 40350)
I've Got A Pocketful Of Dreams (no voc) (LP & CAS: DRJ 40350)
Don't Let That Moon Get Away - TRIO
Moten Swing (LP: "Group A," FAN 37-137; LP & CAS: DRJ 40350)
Oh, Lady Be Good!
Margie (LP & CAS: DRJ 40350)
Star Dust (LP & CAS: DRJ 40350)

STACY/HAMPTON DUET

59-MG-631   MGM Series: 102, 105, 108, 112, 115, 116; SB 151
            Space, Man

Bumble Bee Stomp (arr FH or SM) (LP & CAS: DRJ 40350)
Good-Bye (n/c)

(Above on LP, SC 1021.)

As if to compensate for September 20's overrun, the next "Caravan" is foreshortened by an introductory listener alert: Hitler is threatening to invade the Sudetenland, the Munich Pact is two days ahead (dated the 29th, but signed on the 30th), Prime Minister Chamberlain's fatuous "Peace in our time" will soon be uttered . . . stay tuned. Martha's still ill, but the band, now in the Congress Hotel, is in fine form, unknowing of the holocaust in our future.

"CAMEL CARAVAN"   September 27, 1938, Chicago
  CBS Radio Network

Personnels as August 9.

Let's Dance (theme)
Rose Of The Rio Grande
Lullaby In Rhythm (LP & CAS: DRJ 40350)
The Yam
You're Blase' - TRIO (LP & CAS: DRJ 40350)
Ciribiribin (arr FH)
The Sheik Of Araby - QUARTET
Sometimes I'm Happy
One O'Clock Jump
Good-Bye (theme)

(Above on LP, SC 1021.)

Recovered from her malaise, Martha Tilton rejoins the band at the Orpheum Theater in Minneapolis; either as penance or because he's glad to have her back, Benny doubles her usual complement of vocal choruses. Dan Seymour's still missing, and Benny twits him on the air, warning him that Harry Holcombe's doing a superlative job. Dan gets back next week.

"CAMEL CARAVAN"   October 4, 1938, Minneapolis
  CBS Radio Network

Personnels as August 9.

Let's Dance (theme)
Make Believe
I Had To Do It - voc Martha Tilton (arr FH)

Take 'Em, Minnesota - voc Martha Tilton
At Long Last Love - TRIO
You're Driving Me Crazy - voc Martha Tilton (LP: BID 5001/2)
I Cried For You - feat. Dave Matthews, as
Opus 1/2 - QUARTET
Could You Pass In Love? - voc Martha Tilton
Clap Hands, Here Comes Charlie (LP: "Group A," FAN 37-137)
Good-Bye (theme)

Possibly inspired by a return to Chicago, everyone's in fine form for the next "Caravan." Both the Trio and Quartet are outstanding, and the band digs in for a one-time-only rendition of a Stephen Foster classic:

"CAMEL CARAVAN"   October 11, 1938, Chicago
  CBS Radio Network

Personnels as August 9.

Let's Dance (theme)
'Way Down Upon The Swanee River
Who Blew Out The Flame? - voc Martha Tilton (LP: SB 152)
I Know That You Know - TRIO
Someday Sweetheart (LP: SB 152)
Who'll Buy My Bublitchki? (The Pretzel Vendor Song)
The Man I Love - QUARTET
Is That The Way To Treat A Sweetheart? - voc Martha Tilton (LP: SB 152)
Bumble Bee Stomp (LP: SB 152)
Good-Bye (theme)

BENNY GOODMAN TRIO/QUARTET   **October 12, 1938, Chicago**

Personnel as August 9. TRIO: "I Must Have That Man" only.

BS 025876-1   VI 26091 B, VD 180 A, HMV B8851, HMVAu EA2283,
(2)   ViJap JA1369, ViJap A-1215. **EP:** VI EPB1226, VI
              EPBT3004, ViArg AGET10, HMV 7EG8180. **LP:** VI
              LPT3004, VI LPM1226, VI LPV1009, HMV DLPC6, RD
              3/4-45, ViJap RA74, TL STLJ05, RcaBB AXM2-5566,
              RcaFr LPM1226, RcaFr 430.230, RcaFr 730.629,
              RcaFr PM43684, RcaG Golden Age Of Jazz
              Opus 1/2

BS 025877-1   VI 26090 B, HMV B9166, HMV JO233, HMVAu EA2452,
(2)   HMVSw JK2016. **EP:** VI EPOT6703. **LP:** VI LPT6703,
              ViArg AYL3000-5, ViJap RA74, RcaBB AXM2-5566,
              RcaFr 731.041, RcaFr PM43684
              I Must Have That Man

BS 025878-2   same issues as mx BS 025876-1, except omit VD 180 A,
(1)   RD 3/4-45, TL STLJ05, RcaG Golden Age Of Jazz;
              and add **LP:** RcaFr FXM3-7273
              Sweet Georgia Brown

BS 025879-1   same issues as mx BS 025877-1, except substitute
              HMVAu EA2307 for HMVAu EA2452
BS 025879-2   **LP:** RcaBB AXM2-5568, RcaFr PM43684
              'S Wonderful

BENNY GOODMAN AND HIS ORCHESTRA   **October 13, 1938, Chicago**

Personnel as August 9.

BS 025798-1   VI 26082 A, HMV B8853. **LP:** RcaBB AXM2-5566, JAZ
(2)   17
              Is That The Way To Treat A Sweetheart? - voc Martha
              Tilton

BS 025475-3   VI 26082 B. **LP:** CAM 624, CamE CDN148, RcaBB
(4)   AXM2-5566
              I Had To Do It - voc Martha Tilton (arr FH)

BS 025468-3   VI 26053 A, HMVAu EA2190, GrFr K8238. **LP:** RcaBB
(4)   AXM2-5566, JAZ 17
              You're Lovely Madame - voc Martha Tilton (arr ES)
                                    October 13, 1938, continued

October 13, 1938, continued

BS 025799-1 VI 26087 A, VI 420-0025, HMVAu EA2281, HMVSw
(2) JK2024. **45:** VI 447-0025. **EP:** VI EPA5004, RcaE
  RCX1009, JUG EPRC9061. **LP:** VI LPM6702, RcaBB
  AXM2-5566, RcaFR 741.059
  Bumble Bee Stomp (arr FH - SM also claims)

BS 025900-1 VI 26087 B, HMV B8852, HMVAu EA2281, HMVInd
(2) N4497. **LP:** RcaBB AXM2-5567, RD 3-76, Viceroy
  Cigarette 6703, JAZ 41
  Ciribiribin (arr FH)

BS 025901-1 VI 26099 A, HMV Au, EA2635. **EP:** VI EPOT6703, HMV
(2) 7EG8029. **LP:** VI LPT6703, ViArg AYL3000-5, RcaBB
  AXM2-5567, VI VPM6063
  This Can't Be Love - voc Martha Tilton (poss. arr JL)

(Listing in order of recording; mxs BS 025799 and BS 025900 are consecutive. There seems some substance to Spud Murphy's assertion that he
"ghosted" some of the arrangements customarily credited to others.)

On its way back to New York after an absence of two months, the band
stopped off in the Boston Garden on October 24, then went into CBS's
Manhattan studios for its next "Camel Caravan" broadcast:

"CAMEL CARAVAN"   October 25, 1938, New York
  CBS Radio Network

*Personnels as August 9. Program guest Kate Smith is accompanied by her
own trio, with Benny's band in the coda.*

Margie
Small Fry - voc Kate Smith
I Got Rhythm - QUARTET
Farewell Blues (arr JM)
Good-Bye (theme)

The band opened in New York's Waldorf-Astoria Hotel Wednesday,
Octobet 26; Dave Tough failed to make the date, was summarily fired, and
once again Lionel Hampton played band drums.

"CAMEL CARAVAN"   November 1, 1938, New York
  CBS Radio Network

*Personnels as August 9, except Lionel Hampton, d, replaces Tough in the
orchestra. Guest Sister Rosetta Tharpe accompanies herself on guitar, with a
bit of a trill from Benny.*

Rock Me - voc, g, Sister Rosetta Tharpe
I Must Have That Man - TRIO
Three Little Words

On November 4 Benny appeared in New York's Town Hall with the
Budapest String Quartet, his first public recital as a classicist.
Heavyweight champion Jack Dempsey's wife Hannah Williams, who
had recorded with Benny while with Ben Pollack a dozen years' earlier,
made a guest appearance on the next "Camel Caravan" broadcast. She's
backed by the Quartet, with Harry James in his occasional role as small-
group drummer:

"CAMEL CARAVAN"   November 8, 1938, New York
  CBS Radio Network

Personnels as November 1. Harry James, d, replaces Tough in the Quartet.

Stay On The Right Side, Sister - voc Hannah Williams - QUARTET
Sing, Sing, Sing (LP: BID 5001/2)

Unique title, arrangement uncharacteristic of Benny's book—sounds
like something Jimmy Lunceford should have played—in a sustaining
broadcast from the Waldorf, next. Tune does not appear in any other program log in the author's possession.

SUSTAINING BROADCAST   November 9, 1938, Waldorf-
  Unknown radio network   Astoria, New York

Personnel as November 1.

Two Buck Stew (LP: FAN 37-137)

BENNY GOODMAN AND HIS   **November 10, 1938, New York**
  ORCHESTRA

Personnel as November 1.

BS 028942-1 VI 26099 B, HMVAu EA2546, HMVSw JK2025. **EP:** VI
(2) EPOT6703. **LP:** VI LPT6703, ViArg AYL3000-5, RcaBB
  AXM2-5567, RcaAu VPLI-0741
  Sing For Your Supper - voc Martha Tilton (arr JM)

BS 028943-1 VI 26107 A, HMV B8908, HMVAu EA2304, ViJap 1293
(2) A. **LP:** ViG LPM10022 (n/c), RcaBB AXM2-5567,
  RcaFr 741.102, RcaFr FXM3-7273, SWE 1001
  Topsy

BS 028944-1 VI 26107 B, HMV B8908, HMVAu EA2304, ViJap 1293
  B, GrFr K8373. **LP:** ViG LPM10022, RcaBB
  AXM2-5567, RcaFr 741.072, ViJap RA71
BS 028944-2 **LP:** RcaBB AXM2-5568
  Smoke House (arr FN)

(Some copies of VI 26107 B are titled, "Smoke House Rhythm," and omit BG
in the composer credits.)

"CAMEL CARAVAN"   November 15, 1938, New York
  CBS Radio Network

*Orchestra personnel as November 1. Quartet personnel as November 8. "Oh
Lady Be Good!": Buck Clayton, tpt; Herschel Evans, Lester Young, ts; Count
Basie, p; Walter Page, b; Jo Jones, d; and members of the Goodman orches-
tra sans Benny.*

Sly Mongoose (arr ES) (LP: "Group A")
Oh, Lady Be Good! - Basie, Goodman personnel, no BG
Dizzy Spells - QUARTET (LP: BID 5001/2)
Smoke House (annc'd as "Smoke House Serenade") (LP: BID 5001/2)

Benny chose Buddy Schutz, then with Gene Kardos's orchestra, to
replace Tough, and he is present on the next studio session. But in main
Lionel continued to play band drums for the "Camel Caravan" broadcasts.

BENNY GOODMAN AND HIS   **November 23, 1938, New York**
  ORCHESTRA

Benny Goodman, clt; Harry James, Ziggy Elman, Chris Griffin, tpt; Red Bal-
lard, Vernon Brown, tbn; Dave Matthews, Noni Bernardi, as; Art Rollini, Bud
Freeman, ts; Jess Stacy, p; Ben Heller, g; Harry Goodman, b; BUDDY
SCHUTZ, d; Martha Tilton, voc.

BS 028997-1 Test Pressing
BS 028997-2 VI 26110 B. **LP:** ViG LPM10022, RcaBB AXM2-5567
  I Must See Annie Tonight - voc Martha Tilton (arr FN)

BS 028998-2 VI 26110 A, HMVAu EA2309, HMVSw JK2024. **LP:**
(1) RcaBB AXM2-5567, JAZ 18
  Kind'a Lonesome - voc Martha Tilton

BS 028999-1 VI 26095 A, HMVAu EA2303. **LP:** RcaBB AXM2-5567,
  JAZ 17. **ET:** AFRS American Popular Music 390-Pt. 1
BS 028999-2 BB 11056 B. **EP:** HMV 7EG8029. **LP:** ViG LPM10022,
  RcaBB AXM2-5568, RcaFr 741.102
  My Honey's Lovin' Arms (arr FH)

BS 030308-1 VI 26095 B, BB 10973, HMV B8879, HMVAu EA2303,
  HMVFin TG264, HMVAu GA5101. **EP:** VI EPOT6703,
  RcaG 47-9293. **LP:** VI LPT6703, ViArg AYL 3000-5,
  RcaBB AXM2-5567, RcaFr 741.102
BS 030308-2 **LP:** RcaBB AXM2-5568
  Farewell Blues (arr JM)

(Last two matrices are consecutive.)

If you're a Harry Richman fan you'll love the next "Caravan"—he has
a seven-minute segment during which Benny does not play. Nor does Benny
join in with Tito and his Swingtet (3 acc, g, b), who take up another three
minutes. But The Man is sensational on "Honeysuckle Rose," and he's
followed by a spectacular Harry James. (Note that the BID release is not
quite complete.)

"CAMEL CARAVAN"   *November 29, 1938, New York*
  CBS Radio Network

Orchestra as November 23. QUARTET: Benny Goodman, clt; Lionel Hampton, vib; Teddy Wilson, p; BUDDY SCHUTZ, d.

Let's Dance (theme)
My Honey's Lovin' Arms
This Can't Be Love - voc Martha Tilton
(Medley: On The Sunny Side Of The Street - intro; The Birth Of The
(Blues/Muddy Waters/Puttin' On The Ritz/Singing A Vagabond Song/
(I Love A Parade/Lullaby Of The Leaves/Meet The Beat Of My Heart
(-voc Harry Richman, orchestral accomp. - NO BG
A Handful Of Keys - QUARTET
(Dark Eyes - Tito and his Swingtet - NO BG
Honeysuckle Rose (Hamp on d) (LP: BID 5001/2)
Good-Bye (theme)

Two undated acetates of "Camel Caravan" excerpts apparently from this time period defy specificity. One has Lionel on drums, the other has Buddy Schutz, but neither includes Bud Freeman as a soloist. On a "best guess" basis, both are assigned to November-December 1938:

"CAMEL CARAVAN"   *late 1938, New York*
  CBS Radio Network

Personnel(s) as November 1-November 23-December 12.

Farewell Blues (Hampton, d)
I Know That You Know (Schutz, d)

In an unwitting tribute to Benny's magnificent trumpet section, Bud Freeman quit the end of November, claiming "I just can't take that damn' brass blowin' my head off night after night." Unspoken was his reaction to Dave Tough's release, for balding Bud and Dave were close friends. To replace Freeman, Benny brought in Jerry Jerome from Glenn Miller's band.

BENNY GOODMAN AND HIS   **December 12, 1938, New York**
ORCHESTRA

Personnel as November 23, except JERRY JEROME, ts, replaces Freeman.

BS 030390-1   VI 26125 A, VI 420-0151, BB 11056, HMVAu EA2234.
/1A   **45:** VI 27-0059, VI 447-0151. **EP:** Vi EPBT1005, Vi
                EPB1239, HMV 7EG8029, RcaAu 20036. **LP:** VI
                LPT1005, Vi LPM1239, VI DRLI-0062, RcaBB
                AXM2-5567, RcaFr 741.059
BS 030390-2   **LP:** RcaBB AXM2-5568
                It Had To Be You (arr FH)

BS 030391-1   VI 26125 B, HMV B8878, HMVAu EA 4176. **EP:** VI
                EPOT6703. **LP:** VI LPT6703, ViArg AYL3000-5, RcaBB
                AXM2-5567, RcaFr 741.059, ViJap RA71, VI
                VPM6063
BS 030391-2   **LP:** RcaBB AXM2-5568
                Louise (arr FH)

"CAMEL CARAVAN"   *December 13, 1938, New York*
  CBS Radio Network

Personnel as December 12, except Lionel Hampton, d, on "Life Goes To A Party" only.

Let's Dance (theme)
It Had To Be You (LP: BID 5001/2)
When You And I Were Young, Maggie - clt duet, BG & Ken Murray, guest
Bach Goes To Town (arr Henry Brandt) (LP: BID 5001/2)
Life Goes To A Party

(NOTE: The author's earlier work, "BG—On The Record," assigned the MGM air check "Bach Goes To Town" to this broadcast. That version is now reassigned to the "Camel Caravan" broadcast of December 27, 1938, q.v.)

On December 14 Benny returned to New York's Town Hall, this time to illustrate a lecture by John Erskine on, "The Rise Of Jazz and Swing."

BENNY GOODMAN AND HIS   **December 15, 1938, New York**
ORCHESTRA

Personnel as December 12.

BS 030701-1   VI 26130 B, HMV B8878, HMVAu EA2305, ViJap 1354
                B. **LP:** RcaBB AXM2-5567, RcaFr FXMI-7083, JAZ 16
                Whispering (arr FH)

BS 030702-1   **LP:** CAM 624, CamE CDN148, RcaBB AXM2-5567, RcaFr
                741.072. **EP:** RcaG 47-9293
BS 030702-2   VI 26130 A, HMV B8879, HMVAu EA2305, HMVaus
(3)   GA5101, HMVFin TG264, HMVInd N4490, HMVSw
                JK2249, ViJap 1354 A. **EP:** RcaG EPA9044. **LP:** HIS
                H641, JAZ 16, TL STBB03, RcaAu VPLI-0741
                Bach Goes To Town (arr Henry Brandt)

BS 030703-1   VI 26187 B, HMV B8950. **EP:** VI EPOT6703. **LP:** VI
                LPT6703, ViArg AYL3000-5, RcaBB AXM2-5567,
                RcaFr 741.102, VI VPM6063
BS 030703-2   **LP:** BID 1004
                I'll Always Be In Love With You (arr FH)

BS 030704-1   VI 26134 B, HMV B8938, HMVAu EA2356, HMVFin
(2)   TG154, ViArg 1A-0759, GrFr K8282. **EP:** VI EJC1008.
                LP: VI LJM1008, RcaBB AXM2-5567, RcaFr
                FXMI-7083, RcaFr FXM3-7273, ViJap RA71, HIS
                H623, JO 3057
                Undecided

(RcaFr 741.072's liner notes err in listing take 2 for mx BS 030702; it is take 1.)

The author is in large measure responsible for the deliberate issue of alternate takes of Benny Goodman recordings on microgroove releases. It came about this way:

In the 1960's Victor began a program of re-releasing Goodman recordings not then on LP, as shown in his first work on Benny Goodman, "BG— Off The Record" (Gaildonna Publishers, 1958). When the first in its series, CAM 624, was distributed, the author sought from Victor the take it had used for "Bach Goes To Town." It was then discovered that issue of the alternate had been inadvertent, a mistake; the producers had had no intention of re-releasing anything other than the original issues. The author pointed out to them that the error was fortuitous, not only from a collector's standpoint, but also commercially: further releases of alternate takes would likely boost sales of such issues. They agreed, and soon alternate takes of "Please Be Kind" and "I Cried For You" appeared on RCA LP's. The practice is now widespread, and indeed is the raison d'etre of many legitimate and bootleg releases.

If you've not heard how "Undecided" was named: Benny got the tune from Charlie Shavers without a title appended; and before he could ask Shavers what it was called, Charlie had left New York. Benny wired him, asking the name of the tune, necessary because he was about to record it. Back came a telegram from Charlie, "Undecided. . ."; and that was that.

Next is Benny's first appearance extant on a "Fitch Bandwagon" broadcast, sponsored by a manufacturer of men's hair tonic. This long-running series featured all of the big bands of the Swing Era; and from time to time bandleaders acknowledged the program's efforts in their behalf by citing certain tunes, on record labels, as "Fitch Bandwagon Specials."

"FITCH BANDWAGON"   *December 18, 1938, New York*
  CBS Radio Network

Orchestra as December 12. QUARTET: BG, Hampton, Wilson, BUDDY SCHUTZ, d.

I'm A Ding Dong Daddy (From Dumas) - QUARTET (LP: BID 5001/2)
One O'Clock Jump (LP: BID 5001/2)

"CAMEL CARAVAN"   *December 20, 1938, New York*
  CBS Radio Network

Orchestra as December 12. QUARTET: BG, Hampton, Wilson, guest DON BUDGE, d.

Whispering (LP: BID 5001/2)
Dinah - QUARTET
Undecided (announced as "Undecided Now") (LP: BID 5001/2)
Hot Foot Shuffle (arr FN) (LP: "Group A," FAN 37-137)

The next studio session marks Harry James's final—and immense—contribution to the library of Benny Goodman Victor recordings as a regular member of the band. Two of the tunes are re-makes, are unissued from this date. One is extant, a test pressing given to the author by Mr. Goodman.

BENNY GOODMAN AND HIS   **December 23, 1938, New York**
ORCHESTRA

Personnel as December 12.

BS 030760-1	VI 26134 A, GrFr K8282. **EP:** HMV 7EG8029. **LP:** RcaBB AXM2-5567, JAZ 19
BS 030760-2	VI 26134 A, HMVAu EA2039. **LP:** JAZ 19
	We'll Never Know - voc Martha Tilton (arr FH)
BS 030390- (2,3)	UNISSUED **It Had To Be You** (arr FH)
BS 030391-3 (2)	Test Pressing **Louise** (arr FH)
BS 030761-1 (2)	VI 26159 B. **LP:** RcaBB AXM2-5567, JAZ 19 **Good For Nothin' But Love** - voc Martha Tilton

Here is the reassigned MGM air check, "Bach Goes To Town." A program log of the "Fitch Bandwagon" broadcast of December 18 also lists the tune's performance; but since the base material for the great bulk of the MGM air check releases was from "Camel Caravan" programs, this choice is the more logical:

BENNY GOODMAN AND HIS   **December 27, 1938, New York**
ORCHESTRA

CBS "Camel Caravan" b'cast. Personnel as December 12.

59-MG-631	MGM Series: 102, 105, 108, 110, 112, 114, 115, 116, 118
	Bach Goes To Town (arr Henry Brandt)

BENNY GOODMAN QUINTET/"TRIO"   **December 29, 1938, New York**

"TRIO" Benny Goodman, clt; Teddy Wilson, p; JOHN KIRBY, b; Lionel Hampton, d ("I Know That You Know" only).
QUINTET: Benny Goodman, clt; Lionel Hampton, vib.; Teddy Wilson, p; John Kirby, b; Buddy Schutz, d.

BS 030774-1	VI 26166 A, HMVAu EA2658, HMVSw JK2013, GrFr K8337, ViJap A1103, ViJap LM41A, BIA 224, POLY 6003. **EP:** VI EPA744, VI EPAT412, HMV 7EG8120, ViArg AVET3. **LP:** VI LPM1226, RcaBB AXM2-5567, RcaFr LPM1226, RcaFr 430.230, RcaFr 731.041, RcaFr PM43684, ViJap RA74
BS 030774-2	**LP:** TL STLJO5, RcaFr PM43684
	✓ **Pick-A-Rib, Part 1**
BS 030775-1	VI 26166 B, HMVAu EA2658, HMVSw JK2013, GrFr K8337, ViJap A1103, ViJap LM41B, BIA 224, POLY 6003. **LP:** RcaBB AXM2-5567, TL STLJO5, VIJap RA74 RcaFr PM43684, JAZ 19
BS 030775-2	**EP:** VI EPAT412, VI EPA744, HMV 7EG8120, ViArg AVET3. **LP:** VI LPM1226, RcaFr LPM1226, RcaFR 430.230, RcaFr 731.041, RcaFr PM43684
	✓ **Pick-A-Rib, Part 2**
BS 030776-1	**LP:** VI LPM6702, VI LPV521, RcaBB AXM2-5567, RcaBB AXM2-5568, RcaE RD7775, RcaFr 731.041, RcaFr PM43684
BS 030776-2	VI 26139 B, VI 40-0137, BB 11456, ViJap JA1340, ViJap A-1161, GrFr 8284, HMV B8895, HMV JO231, HMVAu EA2420, HMVInd N4491. **EP:** HMV 7EG8120. **LP:** RcaFr PM43684, ViJap RA74, JAZ 16
	⌣ **I Cried For You**

BS 030777-1	**LP:** RcaBB AXM2-5568, RcaFr PM43684
BS 030777-2	VI 26139 A, ViJap JA1340, ViJap A-1161, GrFr 8284, HMV B8895, HMV JO231, HMVAu EA2452, HMVInd N4491. **EP:** VI EPOT6703, HMV 7EG8120. **LP:** VI LPT6703, ViArg AYL3000-5, VI LPV521, RcaBB AXM2-5567, RcaBel 230.233, RcaE RD7775, RcaFr 731.041, RcaFr FXM3-7273, RcaFr PM43684, ViJap RA74, RcaG The Golden Age Of Jazz, VI VPM6063
	I Know That You Know (And You Know That I Know)

(The label on the original Victor release misidentifies "I Know That You Know" as by a Trio; in fact it is a Quartet, with bassist John Kirby added to clarinet, piano and drums. In later years Benny will frequently make this addition, to enable the drummer to keep strict tempo.

Note that some of the microgroove releases splice the assorted takes of "Pick-A-Rib" so as to give the impression of a single continuous rendition of Parts 1 and 2.)

That concluded 1938, a remarkable year, a watershed year in the career of Benny Goodman. It began auspiciously with the Swing Era's single most celebrated performance, the Carnegie Hall concert. It marked the divorcement of Goodman and Gene Krupa, perhaps that period's best-remembered association. Inexorably, it recorded a time of transition for what had been the world's greatest swing band.

Our first entry for the new year is a "Camel Caravan" broadcast. And thanks to Johnny Mercer, it is but the first of 25 consecutive, weekly broadcasts now known to be extant, and likely to become available to jazz enthusiasts in due course. For Mercer, who will share the R. J. Reynolds half-hour with Benny beginning January 3, caused each of these programs to be recorded professionally and in full, from opening to closing commercial, from "Let's Dance" to "Good-Bye." When his estate was settled (we will note his demise when it occurs, but please, not just yet), these transcriptions were purchased with the announced intention that they would be released over time on Lp.

A few random notes on the Goodman-Mercer "Camel Caravan" broadcast series:

Various half-chorus musical bridges and introductory passages are not notated; equally, singing announcements of some instrumental titles are omitted. Notices of commercial messages are excluded—and some of these may include vocal or instrumental accompaniment. Mercer's occasional topical parodies are shown throughout as, "The Blues." Lionel Hampton frequently sits in on band drums for uptempo renditions, especially when the broadcast originates in a studio (as opposed to a location); thus he is also listed in the orchestra's personnel, as well as in the small groups' complements. Finally, the personnel listings are not certain to be correct; indeed, the transcriptions themselves do not guarantee complete accuracy. But they reflect the author's best judgment, based on source material he has researched.

Here, then, the first complete 1939 Goodman-Mercer "Camel Caravan" broadcast, during which Benny is honored for having won the Paramount Theater's popularity contest for the second year running:

"CAMEL CARAVAN"   *January 3, 1939, New York*
   CBS Radio Network

Benny Goodman, clt; Harry James, Ziggy Elman, Chris Griffin, tpt; Red Ballard, Vernon Brown, tbn; Dave Matthews, Noni Bernardi, as; Art Rollini, Jerry Jerome, ts; Jess Stacy, p; Ben Heller, g; Harry Goodman, b; Buddy Schutz, Lionel Hampton, d. Martha Tilton, JOHNNY MERCER, voc. Guests: Albert Ammons, Meade Lux Lewis, p.

Let's Dance (theme)
I Can't Give You Anything But Love, Baby (Hampton on d)
Hurry Home - voc Martha Tilton
Mercer medley: Goody-Goody   )   (arr JM)
                 I'm An Old Cowhand) - voc, Johnny Mercer, Benny
                 You Must Have Been A   Goodman
                 Beautiful Baby   )
(Honky Tonk Train - Lewis p solo - NO BG
Cuckoo In The Clock - voc Johnny Mercer
Roll 'Em - orchestra plus Albert Ammons, Meade Lux Lewis, p (LP: SPJ 6602)
Good-Bye (theme)

(Above on LP, FAN 13-113, GOJ 1030.)

The reader will recall that John Kirby sat in for Harry Goodman for the studio date of December 29, 1938; brother Harry is again replaced in a small group performance on the next "Camel Caravan" broadcast. Thus we cannot be sure that he is the band's bassist at this time. Harry had a new venture, the ''Pick-A-Rib'' restaurant in Manhattan, and perhaps he was fully occupied there. But according to brother Gene Goodman, who had quit as ''band boy'' in 1936, and who was now managing the restaurant, Harry stayed with the band until late April, and did not take time off to help in the restaurant. Possibly, Benny simply wanted someone else to play bass with small groups.

January 4 was the band's last night in the Waldorf-Astoria. On January 6 Benny returned to Carnegie Hall, this time to perform a work he had commissioned from Bela Bartok, the maestro's ''Contrasts for Violin, Clarinet and Piano,'' with Bartok and Josef Szigeti.

Foretelling things to come, Benny has electric guitarist Leonard Ware as his guest on the next ''Camel'' program, along with bassist Al Hall, both of whom were playing in New York with Sidney Bechet:

''CAMEL CARAVAN''   *January 10, 1939, New York*
CBS Radio Network

Orchestra as January 3 (Harry Goodman uncertain).

TRIO: BG, Teddy Wilson, prob. Schutz

SEXTET: Benny Goodman, clt; Lionel Hampton, vib; guest Leonard Ware, elec g; Teddy Wilson, p; guest Al Hall, b; Buddy Schutz, d.

Let's Dance (theme)
Sweet Sue-Just You (Hampton on d)
Could Be - voc Martha Tilton, Johnny Mercer, Benny Goodman
Softly, As In A Morning Sunrise - TRIO (LP: GOJ 1034)
Ciribiribin
I Have Eyes - voc Martha Tilton
Umbrella Man - SEXTET (LP: GOJ 1034)
Sent For You Yesterday And Here You Come Today - voc Johnny Mercer
  (arr JM)
Good-Bye (theme)

(Above on LP, GOJ 1030.)

This broadcast also marked the final appearance of Harry James as a regular member of the Goodman orchestra. He left to form his own band, with Benny's blessing and financial assistance, two years after joining in January 1937. In retrospect, it seems incredible that his tenure with Benny was really so brief, that so much was bestowed upon posterity in so short a time.

Krupa's departure in March 1938 had changed the character of the Goodman juggernaut; never again would it be what it had been. For a brief period the band floundered; then Dave Tough came in to regroup Benny's personnel into a solid, if more loosely swinging, orchestra. The new driving force from the ranks, however, was Harry James. It was his personal brilliance, devotion to musical integrity, and appeal to the audiences that helped maintain Goodman's position atop the polls that named the Nation's foremost swing band.

This is not to deny Benny's leadership, which never waned. But in effect Benny was a playing manager; in order to have a winning team he needed accomplished performers in every position, and a star player in a key post. James was that star; his contributions made Benny's band a winner and were crucial to its acclaim by public and critics alike.

When James left, however, the band's produce began to deteriorate; the decline is noticeable through the balance of its Victor recordings, through May 1939. It still had its moments, of course, especially during performances on location and during broadcasts. But not as many of them as heretofore; no longer was there that exceptional James trumpet solo, the one that thrilled, the one that caused us to marvel, ''Oh, wow, listen to that!''

Perhaps the band's fall from the heights and James's leaving it were coincidental; it was growing old, many of its members had been with Benny for a long time. What had been its strength was becoming its weakness; playing the same arrangement for the thousandth time is not inspirational. If this is a valid supposition, then at a minimum Harry's departure merely hastened the decline. At maximum, he was responsible for it.

Change is inevitable in all of man's affairs. One must adapt to it or perish. Benny needed time to adapt; the demands made on him were as heavy as ever. But he will adapt here, as he had in the past and in future. As we shall see, he will do so before this year's end, with new stars and new arrangements, with new small groups that will again leave their mark on history. And in the process his playing will not suffer, he will still remain jazz's peerless clarinetist.

There is a last hurrah for Benny and Harry, ironically the first of Metronome Magazine's all-star recording sessions, personnel chosen by ballot by its readership. With the possible exception of Sonny Dunham and

Bob Zurke, all of the musicians on this inttial date had previously worked with Benny. Gene Krupa had won the poll as best drummer, but his band was on the West Coast, and Ray Bauduc substituted for him. The session began late at night on January 11, ran into the early morning hours of January 12.

ALL STAR BAND   **January 11 and 12, 1939, New York**

Benny Goodman, clt; Charlie Spivak, Bunny Berigan, Sonny Dunham, tpt; Tommy Dorsey, Jack Teagarden, tbn; Hymie Schertzer, as; Eddie Miller, Art Rollini, ts; Bob Zurke, p; Carmen Mastren, g; Bob Haggart, b; Ray Bauduc, d.

BS 031445-1   **LP:** JAA 40
BS 031445-2   VI 26144 A, ViArg 63-0299, ViJap LM40, GrFr K8329, HMVAu EA2306, HMV B8896. **EP:** VI EPAT30. **LP:** VI WPT30, VI LPT21, VI LPM1373, RcaBB AXM2-5568, CAM 426, CamE 122, RD 3/4-45, RcaAu L01297, RcaAu VJL2-0410, CamJap CL5039, RcaJap RA-97, RcaJap RMP5120, RcaFr 430.313, RcaFr 741.101, RcaG Golden Age Of Jazz
BS 031445-3   **LP:** VI LPV528, RcaBB AXM2-5568, RcaE RD7826, RcaFr 731.089, RcaJap RA-97
             Blue Lou (arr HH/FH)

(Fletcher Henderson modified brother Horace's original arrangement for Benny.)

Harry James replaces Charlie Spivak.

BS 031446-1   same 78, EP issues as BS 031445-2. **LP:** VI WPT30, VI LPT21, VI LPM1373, VI LPV528, Vilt LPM10041, RcaBB AXM2-5568, CAM 426, CamE 122, RD 3/4-45, RcaAu L01297, CamJap CL5039, RcaJap RA-97, RcaJap RMP5120, RcaE RD7826, RcaFr 430.313, RcaFr 731.089, RcaH SRS557
BS 031446-2   UNISSUED - Tape
             The Blues

The band next went into the Paramount Theater; music press reports have Cy Baker entering as James's replacement, and on that basis we'll include him in the personnel for the next ''Camel Caravan'' broadcast. Dave Matthews left with Harry to help him organize his new group, and Hymie Schertzer returned as lead alto.

Note that apparently the Mercer acetates for the next three ''Caravans'' either have parts that are missing or some that are faulty and cannot be mastered for LPs. This will lead to omissions, substitutions and crossdubbing of some releases. However, the acetates in possession of R. J. Reynolds Industries, Inc., are complete, and the listings following are derived from them.

''CAMEL CARAVAN''   *January 17, 1939, New York*
CBS Radio Network

Orchestra personnel as January 3 (Harry Goodman now likely), except CY BAKER, tpt, replaces James, and HYMIE SCHERTZER, as, replaces Matthews. Guests: Billie Holiday, Leo Watson, voc.

QUARTET: Goodman, Hampton, Wilson, Schutz

Let's Dance (theme)
I Can't Believe That You're In Love With Me
Deep In A Dream - voc Martha Tilton
Fralich In Swing (arr JM) (later, ''And The Angels Sing'')
I Cried For You - voc Billie Holiday (LP: IAJRC 8, MU 153, QD 16, SONY
  YBC1)
Lillie Stomp - QUARTET
Jeepers, Creepers - voc Martha Tilton, Johnny Mercer, Billie Holiday, Leo
  Watson
Hold Tight (LP: ''Group A'')
Good-Bye (theme)

Benny's brother Irving will eventually join as James's ''permanent'' replacement, but precisely when is uncertain. We continue the orchestra personnel unchanged through the Paramount engagement, with the understanding that Irving Goodman may have replaced Baker during that stand.

"CAMEL CARAVAN"　　　　　　　*January 24, 1939, New York*
　CBS Radio Network

Orchestra personnel as January 17. Guests: Joseph Szigeti, v; Andre Petri, v; The Quintones, voc.

Let's Dance (theme)
Gypsy Love Song
My Heart Belongs To Daddy - voc Martha Tilton
(Clair de Lune - duet, Szigeti, Petri - NO BG
Undecided
Shadrach - voc Johnny Mercer, The Quintones
Stompin' At The Savoy - orchestra plus Szigeti, Hampton (vib)
Wrappin' It Up
Good-Bye (theme)

As he promised on the broadcast of January 17, Mercer wrote the lyrics for "Fralich In Swing" and re-titled it, "And TheAngels Sing." Benny recalls that the arrangement was a ". . . kind of patched-together thing, but Jimmy Mundy pulled it together."

"CAMEL CARAVAN"　　　　　　　*January 31, 1939, New York*
　CBS Radio Network

Personnels as January 17. Guests: Jack Teagarden, tbn & voc; Pete Johnson, p.

Let's Dance (theme)
Hold Tight
And The Angels Sing - voc Martha Tilton (arr JM)
I Gotta Right To Sing The Blues - Jack Teagarden, tbn (intro only)
Basin Street Blues - feat. Teagarden, tbn & voc (LP: SPJ 6602, GOJ 1038)
Smoke House (announced as, "Smoke House Serenade")
Umbrella Man - QUARTET
Two Sleepy People - voc Teagarden, Mercer (special lyrics) (LP: GOJ 1038)
Roll 'Em - orchestra plus Teagarden, Johnson (LP: IAJRC 8, SPJ 6002, GOJ 1038)
Good-Bye (theme)

The band was about to embark on a lengthy theater tour; before it did so, it got in a studio session for Victor. Johnny Mercer—who'd taken over Dan Seymour's MC role when Seymour left the "Caravan" following the January 10 broadcast (Harry Holcombe joined as announcer)—now records his first vocals with Benny:

BENNY GOODMAN AND HIS ORCHESTRA　　　**February 1, 1939, New York**

Benny Goodman, clt; Ziggy Elman, Chris Griffin, IRVING GOODMAN, tpt; Red Ballard, Vernon Brown, tbn; Hymie Schertzer, Noni Bernardi, as; Art Rollini, Jerry Jerome, ts; Jess Stacy, p; Ben Heller, g; Harry Goodman, b; Buddy Schutz, d. Martha Tilton, Johnny Mercer, voc.

BS 031873-1　VI 26159 A. **LP:** RcaBB AXM2-5567, JAZ 18
(2)　　　　**(Gotta Get Some) Shut-Eye** - voc Martha Tilton (arr FH)

BS 031874-1　VI 26175 A. **LP:** CAM 624, CAM 872, CamE 148, RcaBB
(2)　　　　AXM2-5567, RcaE 1021, C/P 7055
　　　　　Cuckoo In The Clock - voc Johnny Mercer

BS 031875-1　VI 26170 A, Vi 420-0025, GrFr K8383, HMV B8926,
　　　　　HMVFin TG266, HMVNor AL2642. **45:** VI 447-0025.
　　　　　EP: VI EPA5043, VI EPB1099, RcaAu 20172, RcaBel
　　　　　85.508, RcaE RCX1019, RcaFr A75309, RcaNZ
　　　　　RPX1352. **LP:** VI LPM1099, VI LP6074, VI PRM261,
　　　　　VI LSP4005(e), VI VPM6040, VI ANLI0973, VI
　　　　　CPLI-2470, HMV DLP1112, HMV DLP1116, RcaBB
　　　　　AXM2-5567, RcaE PL12470, RcaFr FXM3-7273, RcaFr
　　　　　740.552, RD 3-21, TL STLJ05, HIST 623, JO 3057,
　　　　　VI CM0700, RcaCont 89323. **ET:** AFRS Jill's Juke Box
　　　　　H46-X8
　　　　　And The Angels Sing - voc Martha Tilton (arr JM)

BS 031876-1　VI 26170 B. **LP:** VI LPT6703, ViArg AYL3000-5, CAM
(2)　　　　872, RcaBB AXM2-5567, RcaE 1021, RcaFr 731.092,
　　　　　C/P 7055. **EP:** VI EPOT6703
　　　　　Sent For You Yesterday And Here You Come Today -
　　　　　voc Johnny Mercer (arr JM)

(Whether the unissued take 2's above any longer exist is problematical; they were not found when the Rca-Bluebird reissue series was researched.)

"CAMEL CARAVAN"　　　　　*February 7, 1939, State Theater,*
　CBS Radio Network　　　　　　　*Hartford, Connecticut*

Orchestra as February 1. Quartet as January 17. NONI BERNARDI (NB), arr.

Let's Dance (theme)
Swingin' Down The Lane
(Gotta Get Some) Shut-Eye - voc Martha Tilton
I've Found A New Baby - QUARTET (LP: GOJ 1034)
Estrellita (Little Star) (arr NB)
Cuckoo In The Clock - voc Martha Tilton
Old Folks (special lyrics) - voc Johnny Mercer, Benny Goodman
Hartford Stomp (LP: "Group A", IAJRC 8)
Good-Bye (theme)

(The chart for "Estrellita - Little Star" is no longer in Benny's book, but he believes it is one of very few written by Noni Bernardi.)

(Above on LP, GOJ 1033, SH 2102.)

On its way from Hartford to Philadelphia, where it will begin a one-week stand in the Earle Theater on Friday the 10th, the band stopped off in New York for another studio session:

BENNY GOODMAN AND HIS ORCHESTRA　　　**February 9, 1939, New York**

Personnel as February 1. NONI BERNARDI (NB), arr.

BS 033710-1　VI 26187 A, HMVSw JK2027. **LP:** JA J1245, RcaBB
　　　　　AXM2-5567, RcaFr PM43173, ViJap RA-71, JAZ 41
BS 033710-2　**LP:** BID 1004
(3)　　　　**Estrellita (Little Star)** (arr NB)

BS 033711-1　VI 26175 B. **LP:** JAZ 19
BS 033711-2　VI 26175 B, HMVAu EA2433, HMVSw JK2026. **LP:**
　　　　　RcaBB AXM2-5567, JAZ 19
　　　　　A Home In The Clouds - voc Martha Tilton (prob. arr
　　　　　BC)

"CAMEL CARAVAN"　　　　　*February 14, 1939, Earle Theater,*
　CBS Radio Network　　　　　　*Philadelphia, Pennsylvania*

Orchestra as February 1. Quartet as January 17.

Let's Dance (theme)
Undecided
A Home In The Clouds - voc Martha Tilton
Trees (arr FH) (LP: "Group A")
You're A Sweet Little Headache - voc Martha Tilton
Deep Purple - QUARTET (LP: IAJRC 8, GOJ 1034)
Hold Tight
Could Be (special lyrics) - voc Martha Tilton, Johnny Mercer, Benny Goodman
Sent For You Yesterday And Here You Come Today (no voc) (LP: IAJRC 8)
Good-Bye (theme)

(Above on LP, GOJ 1033, SH 2102.)

The careful reader may note that the listings through this period fail to cite vocal credits for the "Anything Can Swing" feature in each broadcast. Vocals by Mercer, Martha and/or the band preceding the instrumental performance, and one by Benny following it, are not part of the arrangement, and so are omitted.

"CAMEL CARAVAN"　　　　　*February 21, 1939, Shubert*
　CBS Radio Network　　　　　*Theater, Newark, New Jersey*

Orchestra as February 1. TRIO: BG, Wilson, Hampton (d).

Let's Dance (theme)
Honolulu
Hurry Home - voc Martha Tilton
Them There Eyes - voc Johnny Mercer (arr FH)
The World Is Waiting For The Sunrise - TRIO
When Buddha Smiles
Good For Nothin' But Love - voc Martha Tilton
Together
Farewell Blues
Good-Bye (theme)

"CAMEL CARAVAN"   February 28, 1939, Fox
  CBS Radio Network   Theater, Detroit

Orchestra as February 1. Quartet as January 17.

Let's Dance (theme)
Singin' In The Rain
Deep Purple - voc Martha Tilton
In The Shade Of The Old Apple Tree
I Cried For You - QUARTET
Big John Special
(What's The Reason) I'm Not Pleasin' You - voc Johnny Mercer
Bugle Call Rag
Good-Bye (theme)

The Detroit date may have been Teddy Wilson's last engagement with
Benny, for on the upcoming broadcast Benny announces that Teddy is
leaving to form his own band, and wishes him well. However, Teddy does
not appear on this program—his place in the Trio is taken by Jess Stacy—
and thus he may already have been on his way.

"CAMEL CARAVAN"   March 7, 1939, Lyric Theater,
  CBS Radio Network   Indianapolis, Indiana

Orchestra as February 1. TRIO: Goodman, Stacy, Hampton (d).

Let's Dance (theme)
Lulu's Back In Town (arr FH)
I Get Along Without You Very Well - voc Martha Tilton
Indiana - voc Johnny Mercer, Benny Goodman, chorus (special lyrics)
Exactly Like You - TRIO (LP: GOJ 1034)
Estrellita (Little Star)
(Gotta Get Some) Shut-Eye - voc Martha Tilton
One O'Clock Jump
Good-Bye (theme)

(Above on LP, GOJ 1036)

"CAMEL CARAVAN"   March 14, 1939, Stanley
  CBS Radio Network   Theater, Pittsburgh, Pa.

Orchestra as February 1. QUARTET: Goodman, Hampton (vib), Stacy, Schutz.

Let's Dance (theme)
Oh, Lady Be Good!
Cuckoo In The Clock - voc Martha Tilton
That Naughty Waltz (LP: IAJRC 8)
Pagan Love Song - QUARTET (LP: GOJ 1034)
Begin The Beguine (LP: "Group A", IAJRC 8)
You Oughta Be In Pictures ("Pittsburgh") - voc Johnny Mercer, Benny
  Goodman, chorus (special lyrics)
Sent For You Yesterday And Here You Come Today (LP: BID 5001/2)
Good-Bye (theme)

(Above on LP, GOJ 1036)

LP SB 152 includes interviews with Benny, Martha, Ziggy and a Goodman fan, reputedly conducted on March 18 during the band's next engagement at the Earle Theater in Washington, D.C. Apparently the backstage
interviews were broadcast, but if so further details are lacking.

"CAMEL CARAVAN"   March 21, 1939, Earle Theater,
  CBS Radio Network   Washington, D.C.

Orchestra as February 1. Quartet as March 14. Guests: The Joe Giordano
Swing Quartet.

Let's Dance (theme)
Gypsy Love Song
I Get Along Without You Very Well - voc Martha Tilton
Spring, Beautiful Spring
(Limehouse Blues - Giordano Swing Quartet - NO BG
Bach Goes To Town
Them There Eyes - voc Johnny Mercer (arr FH)
Deep Purple - QUARTET
The Kingdom Of Swing (LP BID 5001/2)
Good-Bye (theme)

"The Kingdom Of Swing" is Benny's musical salute to his autobiography of the same title, written in cooperation with music critic Irving
Kolodin. It was first published by Stackpole Sons, New York, printed by

The Telegraph Press, Harrisburg, Pa. According to an announcement on the
April 4 "Camel Caravan," it was on bookshelves in New York on April 5.
In 1944 it was reprinted by Editions For The Armed Services, Inc., a non-
profit agency of the Council on Books in Wartime, and was distributed to
U.S. service personnel. A second public edition was released in 1961 by the
Frederick Ungar Publishing Co., New York. All three are rather scarce, and
the first two are prized collector's items that command high prices.

"CAMEL CARAVAN"   March 28, 1939, Palace Theater,
  CBS Radio Network   Akron, Ohio

Orchestra as February 1. Trio as March 7.

Let's Dance (theme)
Clap Your Hands
And The Angels Sing - voc Martha Tilton (LP: SB 152)
Paradise (incidental singing) (LP: SB 152)
She's Funny That Way - TRIO (LP: IAJRC 8)
'T'Ain't What You Do (It's The Way How Cha Do It) - voc Johnny Mercer,
  chorus (arr JM)
Goodnight, My Love - voc Martha Tilton
Swingtime In The Rockies
Good-Bye (theme)

"CAMEL CARAVAN"   April 4, 1939, New York
  CBS Radio Network

Orchestra as February 1. Quartet as March 14. Guests: The Quintones, voc.

Let's Dance (theme)
Louise
That Sly Old Gentleman (From Featherbed Lane) - voc Martha Tilton, The
  Quintones
I'm Forever Blowing Bubbles
Opus 3/4 - QUARTET (LP: GOJ 1034)
The Kingdom Of Swing
Hold Tight
Shadrach - voc Johnny Mercer, The Quintones
I've Found A New Baby
Good-Bye (theme)

(Above on LP, GOJ 1039)

Contrary to an opinion expressed in the author's earlier work on Goodman, an air check of "Louise Tobin's Blues" is not from a "Camel Caravan" broadcast; and as a matter of fact, is not a Goodman performance at
all, but rather is by Harry James's band. But with Martha Tilton temporarily
indisposed, Harry's future wife Louise Tobin did record with Benny on his
first studio session in almost two months, next. Unfortunately, the master
was destroyed at Benny's request, no unauthorized copies of it are known to
exist, and it seems lost for all time.

BENNY GOODMAN QUARTET   **April 6, 1939, New York**

Benny Goodman, clt; Lionel Hampton, vib; Jess Stacy, p; Buddy Schutz, d.

BS 035708-1   VI 26240 A, GrFr K8374, HMVAu EA2551, HMV B8957.
                 EP: VI EPOT6703, RcaBel 230.233, RcaFr 75651. **LP:**
                 VI LPT6703, ViArg AYL3000-5, ViJap RA74, RcaBB
                 AXM2-5567, RcaFr 731.041, RcaFr PM43684
                 Opus 3/4

BS 035709   UNISSUED - master destroyed
                 I've Got An Old-Fashioned Love In My Heart - voc
                 LOUISE TOBIN

(It is assumed, but unprovable, that mx BS 035709 is by the Quartet, not the
orchestra.)

Martha Tilton returned to the band the next day to participate in a
lengthy recording session that had its unusual aspects. Benny evidently was
unhappy with two of the tunes recorded; he ordered one of them, "Them
There Eyes," destroyed, and would not authorize the issuance of another,
"The Kingdom Of Swing." The latter was first released on an AFRS ET in
the late 1940's. At about the same time, it was scheduled for commercial
issue and a catalog number—VI 20-3312—was assigned to it. At the last
minute, however, this release was cancelled. The recording then disappeared
until 1960, when RCA finally marketed it on EP and LP. But age did not
improve "The Kingdom Of Swing"; at best it is a pedestrian composition
and arrangement, unworthy of the band even at this period of its decline.

BENNY GOODMAN AND HIS ORCHESTRA   April 7, 1939, New York

Personnel as February 1.

BS 035713-1   VI 26211 B. **LP:** RcaFr FXM1-7083, JAZ 7
BS 035713-2   VI 26211 B, HMVAu EA2410. **LP:** RcaBB AXM2-5567,
              JAZ 7
              Show Your Linen, Miss Richardson - voc Johnny
              Mercer (arr FH)
BS 035714-1   VI 26211 A, HMV B8939, HMVFin TG154, poss. HMVAu
              EA2356. **LP:** RcaBB AXM2-5567, JAZ 19
BS 035714-2   VI 26211 A, HMVAu EA2356. **LP:** CAM 872, RcaE 1021,
              C/P 7055
              The Lady's In Love With You - voc Martha Tilton
BS 035715   UNISSUED - masters destroyed
(1,2)   **Them There Eyes** - voc Johnny Mercer (arr FH)
BS 035716-1   **ET:** AFRS Basic Music Library P1215. **EP:** VI EPA5100,
              RcaAu 20251, RcaE RCX1059, RcaNZ RPX 1375. **LP:**
              VI LPM2247, RcaAu L101039, RcaFr 741.072, RcaBB
              AXM2-5567
BS 035716-2   **LP:** RcaBB AXM2-5568, JAZ 19
              The Kingdom Of Swing
BS 035717-1   VI 26230 A, GrFr K8383, HMV B8926, HMVNor AL2642.
              EP: VI EPOT6703. **LP:** VI LPT6703, ViArg AYL3000-5,
              RcaBB AXM2-5567, RD 3/4-76
BS 035717-2   **LP:** RcaFr PM43173
              Rose Of Washington Square (arr FH - see note)
BS 035718-1   VI 26230 B, HMVAu EA2546. **LP:** RcaBB AXM2-5568,
(2)   JAZ 16
              The Siren's Song (arr JM)

(Jimmy Mundy claims that he, not Fletcher, arranged ''Rose Of Washington
Square,'' but Benny credits Henderson with it. Interestingly, no one claims
responsibility for the arrangement of ''The Kingdom Of Swing.'')

''CAMEL CARAVAN''   April 11, 1939, New York
  CBS Radio Network

Orchestra as February 1. Guests: Albert Ammons, Meade Lux Lewis, p.

Let's Dance (theme)

59-MG-631   MGM Series: 102, 105, 108, 110, 112, 114, 115, 116,
              118, 119
              Honeysuckle Rose (arr FH)

Tears From My Inkwell - voc Martha Tilton
Estrellita (Little Star)
Roll 'Em - voc Johnny Mercer (special lyrics) - p soli, Ammons & Lewis
Don't Worry 'Bout Me - voc Martha Tilton
Sing, Sing, Sing - feat. Hampton, d.
Good-Bye (theme)

(Above on LP, GOJ 1039.)

Evidently brother Irving elected to stay in New York when the band
went on the road, for Ed ''Corky'' Cornelius is in the trumpet section for the
next ''Camel Caravan'' broadcast. Cornelius, 24 years of age when he
joined Goodman, will die of a kidney ailment when he is only 28. Too bad;
he was a **jazz** trumpeter, and he is heard too little on record. Gene Krupa, for
one, considered Corky one of the best, and was delighted when he joined his
band and married his vocalist, Irene Daye. Listen for him:

''CAMEL CARAVAN''   April 18, 1939, Jefferson County
  CBS Radio Network   Armory, Louisville

Orchestra as February 1, except CORKY CORNELIUS, tpt, replaces I. Goodman. Quartet as March 14.

Let's Dance (theme)
Rose Of Washington Square
And The Angels Sing - voc Martha Tilton
'T'Ain't What You Do (It's The Way How Cha Do It) - voc Benny Goodman,
  chorus
The Man I Love - QUARTET

Show Your Linen, Miss Richardson - voc Johnny Mercer
Who'll Buy My Bublitchki? (The Pretzel Vendor's Song) (LP: BID 5001/2)
Pick-A-Rib
Good-Bye (theme)

''CAMEL CARAVAN''   April 25, 1939, Tobacco
  CBS Radio Network   Warehouse, Asheville, N.C.

Orchestra as April 18. Quartet as March 14.

Let's Dance (theme)
Night Must Fall
You And Your Love - voc Martha Tilton
The Beer Barrel Polka
Carolina In The Morning - voc Johnny Mercer, Benny Goodman (special
  lyrics)
Opus ¾ - QUARTET
Don't Worry 'Bout Me - voc Martha Tilton
Madhouse
Good-Bye (theme)

The poor condition of an undated acetate hinders identification of the
next air check. It is represented as having come from this period, but it may
well be from late 1946, when Stacy was again with Goodman:

SUSTAINING BROADCAST   c. April/May 1939 ???
  Unknown source

Quartet as March 14.

Sweet Lorraine - QUARTET

Probably at the end of April when the band went to Chicago, further
personnel changes occurred. Benny added a third trombone for the first time,
England's Bruce Squires, who left Gene Krupa (Gene's band was also in the
Windy City). Brother Harry quit to pay more attention to his New York
restaurant; Quinn Wilson, who'd been with Earl Hines, replaced him temporarily. And Buddy Schutz returned to Manhattan, joining Jan Savitt's
''Shuffle Rhythm'' gang then in the Blue Room of the Hotel Lincoln. Once
again, Lionel took over the big band's drum throne. But since even multi-
talented Lionel cannot play vibes and drums simultaneously, who's the
drummer on the Quartet's ''Chicago,'' in the next ''Camel Caravan'' broadcast? He plays in the style of Krupa; and with Gene in Chicago, he's a
possibility. But there is no announcement that Gene is appearing as a guest,
and surely much would have been made of such a reunion. Could it be Nick
Fatool, who will join within a few weeks, and who was capable of imitating
most drummers? Likely not, it's too early; and thus the Quartet's anchor man
is unknown.

''CAMEL CARAVAN''   May 2, 1939, Chicago
  CBS Radio Network

Orchestra as April 18, except Lionel Hampton, d, replaces Schutz; and likely
BRUCE SQUIRES, tbn, is added, and QUINN WILSON, b, replaces H. Goodman. QUARTET: Goodman, Hampton (vib), Stacy, unknown d.

Let's Dance (theme)
Jumpin' At The Woodside
The Lady's In Love With You - voc Martha Tilton
Chlo-e (Song Of The Swamp)
When Yuba Plays The Rhumba On The Tuba - voc Johnny Mercer
My Melancholy Baby
Chicago - QUARTET (LP: GOJ 1034)
And The Angels Sing - voc Martha Tilton
Clarinet Marmalade
Good-Bye (theme)

(Above on LP, GOJ 1042.)

Earlier in the day of May 2, Benny had come into Victor's Chicago
studios for a commercial recording session. New personnel made things go
less smoothly than usual, but after some hard work Benny felt reasonably
certain that they'd waxed two tunes satisfactorily, ''You And Your Love''
and ''Pick-A-Rib.'' He was about to give the downbeat for the first take of
''Who'll Buy My Bublitchki?'' when the engineers called a shamefaced
halt; their equipment had been totally inoperative, and they hadn't a thing
on wax.

So it was back into the studios May 4 for what will prove to be Benny's
last ''Benny Goodman and his Orchestra'' effort for Victor for many years;
save for an ''All Star'' date and a classical performance, he will not record
for RCA again until 1962.

A word about the original, if bootleg, release of "Pic-A-Rib," so spelled on the Jazz Unlimited label: A collectors' club, "Jazz Unlimited of Philadelphia," obtained a test pressing of matrix BS 034649-1 in June 1949. The test was dubbed onto a master, and 100 copies were pressed for distribution to the membership.

BENNY GOODMAN AND HIS ORCHESTRA   May 4, 1939, Chicago
Personnel as May 2 (Squires and Wilson certain).

BS 034649-1   JU 11A. **LP:** RcaBB AXM2-5568, RcaFr FXM1-7083,
(2,3)   RcaFr FXM3-7273
               Pic(k)-A-Rib (arr JM)

BS 034650-1   VI 26263 A. **LP:** RcaBB AXM2-5568, JAZ 19
               You And Your Love - voc Martha Tilton (arr JM)

BS 034651-2   VI 26263 B, HMVSw JK2027. **LP:** ViG LPM10022,
(1)   RcaBB AXM2-5568, RcaFr 741.102, JAZ 18
               Who'll Buy My Bublitchki? (The Pretzel Vendor Song)

(The author has a direct transfer of an RCA test inscribed mx BS 034651-1, but he finds no discernible difference between it and the issued take 2. Apparently, the inscription is in error.)

As stated earlier, Harry James's defection was in part causative of the band's descent from its lofty pinnacle as "best band in the land." Its studio recordings and air checks of the early months of 1939 evidence that noticeable decline. But now new players were helping revitalize it. It would soon have some marvelous new arrangements (by Eddie Sauter), and these will aid immeasurably. But what it needed most was someone to light the fires as James had, a superior talent other than Benny, Lionel and Jess, a commanding new voice that shouted, "Hey, let's play the jazz we're capable of." Sensitive to that need, Benny prevailed upon an old acquaintance to ignite his evolving new orchestra, bassist Artie Bernstein.

The author remembers vividly the first time he saw and heard Bernstein with the band. It was August 1939, in the Marine Ballroom of Atlantic City's Steel Pier. That room was long and wide, and its primitive public address system, speakers at the end opposite the bandstand, barely overcame the ocean's rumble as it crashed against the supporting piling below the swaying structure. Upon entering from the boardwalk end of the ballroom, he was immediately, and above all else, **physically** pressured by Bernstein's huge, pulsing sound. It was a memorable first encounter.

Bernstein left a comfortable and lucrative existence as a studio musician in Hollywood to join Benny, and he is present on the next "Camel Caravan" program. When they are both available, play the May 2 and May 9 broadcasts one after the other and note the enormous difference Bernstein makes. Of all of Goodman's—or anyone's—bassists, New York attorney Arthur Bernstein may have been the best.

Possibly within the month following the final Victor session, Jimmy Mundy left Benny's employ to arrange for Gene Krupa. When Mundy joined Goodman in 1936, he was expected to produce five charts each week for a salary of $175. When he left, he earned $700 per week for but two. His latterday claims that he occasionally sat in on alto sax for Benny's Victor sessions—"Jam Session," "Swingtime In The Rockies"—are not borne out by studio files.

Unwittingly, Benny takes another step toward an association with Charlie Christian, for electric guitarist George Rose enters the band along with Bernstein, replacing Benny Heller. He, too, debuts on the May 9 broadcast:

"CAMEL CARAVAN"   May 9, 1939, Fox Theater,
CBS Radio Network   St. Louis, Missouri

Benny Goodman, clt; Ziggy Elman, Chris Griffin, Corky Cornelius, tpt; Red Ballard, Vernon Brown, Bruce Squires, tbn; Hymie Schertzer, Noni Bernardi, as; Art Rollini, Jerry Jerome, ts; Jess Stacy, p; GEORGE ROSE, g; ART BERNSTEIN, b; Lionel Hampton, d. Martha Tilton, Johnny Mercer, voc.

QUARTET: Goodman, Rose, Bernstein, Hampton (sticks on suitcase)

QUINTET: Goodman, Hampton (vib), Stacy, Rose, Bernstein (no d)

Let's Dance (theme) (LP: SC 1021)
Trees (LP: SC 1021)
A Home In The Clouds - voc Martha Tilton (LP: SC 1021)
Mighty Lak A Rose (LP: SC 1021)
Oh, Lady Be Good! - QUARTET (LP: QD 16, GOJ 1034, SC 1021)
St. Louis Blues - voc Johnny Mercer
Old Fashioned Love - QUINTET (LP: GOJ 1034)

Pick-A-Rib
Good-Bye (theme)

(Above on LP, GOJ 1042.)

The May 9 "Camel Caravan" was Martha Tilton's finale; fittingly so, for she had first appeared with Benny on a "Camel Caravan" broadcast in August 1937. But she'll be back in the years ahead, for recording dates and concerts, but never again as a "regular." Louise Tobin replaced her, and is first heard on the next broadcast:

"CAMEL CARAVAN"   May 16, 1939, Palace
CBS Radio Network   Theater, Cleveland, Ohio

Personnels as May 9 (Hampton on d). LOUISE TOBIN, voc.

Let's Dance (theme)
Don't Be That Way
The Blues - voc Louise Tobin
Make Believe
The Sheik Of Araby - QUARTET
Alexander's Ragtime Band - voc Johnny Mercer (special lyrics)
It's Never Too Late - voc Louise Tobin (arr FH)
Sent For You Yesterday And Here You Come Today
Good-Bye (theme)

(Except for "Let's Dance," above on LP, AC 32. Some of its transfers are incomplete.)

Nick Fatool, who'd been jobbing with Bobby Hackett's big band—and who possibly is the "unknown" drummer on the May 2 Quartet performance—joined in time for the next "Caravan," now in Columbus:

"CAMEL CARAVAN"   May 23, 1939, Palace
CBS Radio Network   Theater, Columbus, Ohio

Orchestra as May 9, except NICK FATOOL, d, replaces Hampton.

QUINTET: Goodman, Hampton (vib), Stacy, Bernstein, Fatool

Let's Dance (theme)
Blue Skies
If You Ever Change Your Mind - voc Louise Tobin (arr JM)
Russian Lullaby
Boy Meets Horn
I Got Rhythm - QUINTET
Three Little Fishies - voc Johnny Mercer, chorus
Sugar Foot Stomp
Good-Bye (theme)

(Except for "Three Little Fishies" and "Good-Bye," above on LP, AC 32. Some of its transfers are incomplete.)

"CAMEL CARAVAN"   May 30, 1939, Elby Theater,
CBS Radio Network   Cincinnati, Ohio

Personnels as May 23. DUET: Goodman, Bernstein.

Let's Dance (theme)
Three Little Words
Don't Worry 'Bout Me - voc Louise Tobin
In A Little Spanish Town (arr FH)
Tea For Two - DUET
The Blues - voc Johnny Mercer
Stompin' At The Savoy - QUINTET
Louise - voc Louise Tobin (special lyrics)
Bugle Call Rag
Good-Bye (theme)

(Except for "Let's Dance" and "Good-Bye," above on LP, AC 32 & 34. Some of the transfers are incomplete.)

A chart by Eddie Sauter is in evidence on the next broadcast, apparently his first extant arrangement for Benny. Known earlier for his writing for Red Norvo, Sauter joins Goodman as staff arranger for the next several years, and will produce scores that today are deemed classics. Highly imaginative, intricate, difficult to execute, they demanded a high degree of musicianship—"We tripped over our jocks trying to play those things," Jerry Jerome once put it. Needless to say, they delighted Benny, who welcomed challenges not only for himself, but for his sidemen.

"CAMEL CARAVAN"   June 6, 1939, Paramount
  CBS Radio Network   Theater, Fort Wayne, Indiana

Personnels as May 23. EDDIE SAUTER (EdSau), arranger.

Let's Dance (theme)
Love Me Or Leave Me
The Lady's In Love With You - voc Louise Tobin
Without A Song (arr EdSau)
Memories Of You - QUINTET (LP: GOJ 1034)
The Blues - voc Johnny Mercer
And The Angels Sing - voc Louise Tobin
King Porter Stomp
Good-Bye (theme)

(Except for "Let's Dance," "The Blues" and "Good-Bye," above on LP, AC 34. Some of its transfers are incomplete.)

On its way to the Ritz-Carlton Hotel in Boston, the band stopped over in New York for its next "Caravan." There it was rejoined by Toots Mondello:

"CAMEL CARAVAN"   June 13, 1939, New York
  CBS Radio Network

Orchestra as May 23, except TOOTS MONDELLO, as, replaces Bernardi. Quintet as May 23.

Let's Dance (theme)
Sweet Sue-Just You
You And Your Love - voc Louise Tobin
Wishing - QUINTET (LP: GOJ 1034)
The Blues - voc Johnny Mercer
Mozart Matriculates (arr Henry Brandt)
One O'Clock Jump
Good-Bye (theme)

Interrupting the succession of "Camel Caravan's" is an excerpt of a midnight, sustaining broadcast from the Ritz-Carlton. Benny identifies a good version of, "Moon Glow," as by the "Quartet," but Bernstein's bass is unmistakably present:

SUSTAINING BROADCAST   June 16, 1939, Ritz-Carlton
  Unknown radio network   Hotel, Boston

Personnels as June 13.

If You Ever Change You Mind - voc Louise Tobin (n/c)
Moon Glow - QUINTET
One O'Clock Jump (n/c)

For unknown reasons, R. J. Reynolds and its advertising agency decided to switch Benny's "Camel Caravan" broadcasts from Tuesday evenings to Saturday evenings, beginning in July. Bob Crosby and his excellent orchestra were assigned the Tuesday "Camel Caravan" slot; Johnny Mercer stayed with Tuesdays, left Benny to MC Crosby's programs. Next, then, Benny's final Tuesday night "Camel Caravan":

"CAMEL CARAVAN"   June 20, 1939, Ritz-Carlton
  CBS Radio Network   Hotel, Boston

Personnels as June 13.

Let's Dance (theme)
Russian Lullaby
The Lamp Is Low - voc Louise Tobin
Down By The Old Mill Stream (arr FH)
There'll Be Some Changes Made - voc Louise Tobin (arr FH) (LP: AC 34)
China Boy - QUINTET (LP: AC 34)
The Blues ("Class Of '39") - voc Johnny Mercer (LP: AC 34)
Wrappin' It Up (LP: AC 34)
Good-Bye (theme) (LP: AC 34)

("Jumpin' At The Woodside" was not performed on this broadcast, AC 34's liner notes notwithstanding.)

Completing its engagement in the Ritz-Carlton, the band went cross country to San Francisco's "Golden Gate Exposition," opening at its Open Air Bandstand, Treasure Island, on July 2. There were major changes in its personnel before its next extant air checks:

As he had once before, Hymie Schertzer felt that two first-alto's in one band was one too many, and he stayed in New York. Buford "Buff" Estes

replaced Hymie, in from Lawrence Welk's "One and-a two" then territorial band. Art Rollini, who'd been with Benny since 1934, tired of all those one-night stands and also elected to stay in the East and free-lance; Clarence "Bus" Bassey took his tenor chair. Arnold Covarrubias, known professionally as Arnold "Covey," replaced George Rose. Fletcher Henderson had joined Benny's entourage as staff arranger June 8; ever one to experiment, Benny had begun to work Fletcher in as a pianist, first with the small groups, then with the orchestra. Jess Stacy suffered his diminished role for exactly one month, quit July 8 to return to his home in Missouri the day of Benny's first Saturday evening "Camel Caravan" broadcast. He'll join Bob Crosby in September—and get back on those Tuesday "Camel Caravan" programs.

The revised lineup is reflected in the first Saturday "Camel Caravan," broadcast in New York via NBC's radio station WEAF, from 10:00 to 10:30 p.m. Bert Parks, he of later "Miss America" fame, is the new MC:

"CAMEL CARAVAN"   July 8, 1939, Golden Gate
  NBC Radio Network   Exposition, San Francisco

Benny Goodman, clt; Ziggy Elman, Chris Griffin, Corky Cornelius, tpt; Red Ballard, Vernon Brown, Bruce Squires, tbn; Toots Mondello, BUFF ESTES, as; Jerry Jerome, BUS BASSEY, ts; FLETCHER HENDERSON, p; ARNOLD COVARRUBIAS (COVEY), g; Art Bernstein, b; Nick Fatool, d. Louise Tobin, voc.

QUINTET: Goodman, Hampton, Henderson, Bernstein, Fatool

Honeysuckle Rose
Opus 1/2 - QUINTET
Stealin' Apples (arr FH)
St. Louis Blues

(Above available only as private recordings; no "Reynolds" ET extant.)

Only the first of two "Reynolds" ETs has been located for the "Caravan" broadcast of July 15; it ends with the first portion of "Boy Meets Horn":

"CAMEL CARAVAN"   July 15, 1939, Golden Gate
  NBC Radio Network   Exposition, San Francisco

Personnels as July 8.

Let's Dance (theme)
Sugar Foot Stomp
Wishing - voc Louise Tobin
Night And Day (arr FH)
Boy Meets Horn (n/c)

As if to compensate for the missing half of the broadcast of the 15th, Reynolds's ETs include a partial transcription of a rehearsal for the succeeding program. Note that Benny elected to change the opening instrumental at air time:

"CAMEL CARAVAN" Rehearsal   July 20, 1939, NBC Studios,
                                              San Francisco

Personnels as July 8.

Let's Dance (theme)
I Can't Give You Anything But Love, Baby
Rendezvous Time In Paree - voc Louise Tobin (arr EdSau)
(When My Baby Smiles At Me - feat. Toots Mondello, voc & clt - NO BG
Undecided

The Exposition's management presented Benny with a scroll the afternoon preceding the next broadcast, honoring him as ".. . the first band leader to play before one million people in a three-week period," such was the success of his engagement on Treasure Island. And note that "Sunrise Serenade" is an extended version, caused by Benny's repeated vamping while Bert Parks goes through a lengthy introduction:

"CAMEL CARAVAN"   *July 22, 1939, Golden Gate*
NBC Radio Network   *Exposition, San Francisco*

Orchestra personnel as July 8. QUARTET: Goodman, Hampton (vib), Henderson, Fatool.

Let's Dance (theme)
Minnie The Moocher's Wedding Day
Rendezvous Time In Paree - voc Louise Tobin
(When My Baby Smiles At Me - feat. Mondello, voc & clt - NO BG
Undecided
Limehouse Blues - QUARTET
Sunrise Serenade (arr FH)
King Porter Stomp
Good-Bye (theme)

"CAMEL CARAVAN"   *July 29, 1939, Golden Gate*
NBC Radio Network   *Exposition, San Francisco*

Personnels as July 22.

Let's Dance (theme)
Indiana
The Lamp Is Low - voc Louise Tobin
(I Would Do) Anything For You
Star Dust - QUARTET
(Alexander's Ragtime Band - comedy, Mondello & Jerome - NO BG
Bach Goes To Town
After You've Gone - voc Louise Tobin (arr FH)
Jumpin' At The Woodside (arr CB/JM)
Good-Bye (theme)

An eyewitness claims Dave Tough was in the band during its month-long stand at the Exposition; it's possible (Dave had left Tommy Dorsey about mid-June, would join Jack Teagarden in August or September), but if so, it could only have been temporarily, for Benny was well satisfied with Fatool.

The band broadcast its August 5 "Camel Caravan" from the Hollywood Bowl, where it appeared with Alec Templeton. On August 10 it opened in the French Garden Room of Victor Hugo's restaurant in Beverly Hills for a week's stand. Available logs of "Camel Caravan" and sustaining broadcasts from the Exposition, the Bowl, and Victor Hugo's, however, do not include the next-listed air checks. At a guess, they are from two sustaining broadcasts from the Exposition:

SUSTAINING BROADCASTS   *mid-July - early August 1939,*
Unknown radio networks   *unknown location*

Personnel as July 8.

Trees
Sunrise Serenade
Roll 'Em (n/c)

*

The author has been unable to examine personally a number of Japanese RCA LPs that together blanket the Benny Goodman Victor recordings of 1935–1939. He is informed, however, that they all include the common issues of that period, and that none offers any matrices and takes not available on many other releases. These albums are:

RcaJap RA 5623-4, "More Original Benny Goodman" (2 LPs)
RcaJap RA 99003-4, "Benny Goodman - Best Collection" (2 LPs)
RcaJap RFC 0903-4, "The Great Collection of Benny Goodman" (2 LPs)
RcaJap RJL-2577, ". . . featuring Helen Ward"
RcaJap RMP-5111, "Benny Goodman"
RcaJap RMP-5112, "Benny Goodman's Small Groups"
RcaJap RJL-2019-20, "The Swing" (2 LP anthology, 8 BG tracks)
RcaJap RJL-2021-2, "The Swing II" (2 LP anthology, 7 BG tracks)
7" ViJap EP-1029, "Metronome All Stars, Vol. I"

THE RED-LABEL COLUMBIAS

Soon after he'd left Victor, Benny Goodman signed a recording contract with Columbia. Three months had gone by, and now he was eager to put his revitalized orchestra on wax. The glorious Victor era was over, but an exciting new one lay ahead.

The next entry is Benny's initial recording session for Columbia, the beginning of his new contract. In main, the format employed to list Columbia recordings by Benny Goodman from 1939 through 1946 is the same as that used for the Victors. The type style is retained, as are the positionings of the name of the recording group, date, location, personnel, matrix, take numbers, and catalog numbers of issued recordings. As heretofore, take numbers continue to reflect Benny's and/or (now) Columbia's, ranking of preference, as these numbers are engraved on released records or test pressings, or as they are noted in Columbia's files.

There is one major change, however. Because of additional information available from Columbia, it is possible to show the sequence of recording of the several attempts to record a given tune on a given day. The chief source of this information lies in Columbia transfers of Benny's studio sessions onto 16″ multi-track acetate discs, termed "safeties" by Columbia. (During World War II, and later, when Columbia moved its offices, many original studio transcriptions disappeared or were destroyed; the process of transferring original material to the 16″ discs was considered a "safe" means of retaining it.) All available evidence indicates that the transfers were made sequentially, and thus the "safeties" present a true order of recording.

The scheme employed to list Benny's Columbia recordings is perhaps best explained by illustration:

BENNY GOODMAN TRIO		July 32, 1939, New York

Benny Goodman, clt; unknown, p, d.

CO 10000	UNISSUED - Tape	(A)
CO 10000-bkdn	UNISSUED - Tape	(B)
CO 10000-2	UNISSUED - Test Pressing	(C)
CO 10000	UNISSUED - Co Ref	(D)
CO 10000-1	**78:** CO 54321, et al	(E)
CO 10000-3	**LP:** CO 9876, et al	(F)
CO 10000-S	**LP:** CO 12345, et al	(G)
(2,3)	**Benny's Tune**	

This hypothetical example reveals that a mythical Benny Goodman Trio attempted to record "Benny's Tune," to which Columbia had assigned matrix number CO 10000, six times on the 32nd of July, 1939. The present status of each effort is:

(A) The first run-through of "Benny's Tune" was complete, but did not please Benny. It was not good enough to make a test pressing of it for Benny's consideration, but Columbia retains a transfer of it. Copies of it are in the hands of collectors, via tape.

(B) Something went wrong with the second attempt to record "Benny's Tune," and Benny stopped the performance before the rendition was complete. Columbia retains a transfer of it, and copies of it are in the hands of collectors via tape. In studio parlance, it is known as a "breakdown," abbreviated "bkdn".

(C) The third attempt produced a version good enough to be test-pressed for Benny's consideration for release. Eventually it became his second choice, and was assigned take "2". One or more test pressings are in the hands of collectors.

(D) The fourth attempt was not wholly satisfactory, but at some point Columbia decided to transfer it to a 12″ acetate, which it called a "reference recording," rather than make a test pressing of it. A copy of such a Columbia Reference Recording ("Co Ref") is known to be in the possession of a collector.

(E) Benny selected the fifth attempt for original release on a Columbia 78 rpm shellac disc; it is inscribed take "1".

(F) Years later, Columbia chose to release the sixth attempt on 10″ LP. Since order-of-preference takes 1 & 2 already existed, Columbia assigned take "3" to this issue.

(G) Still later, Columbia re-released "Benny's Tune" on a 12″ LP. Given the facility tape affords, this time Columbia spliced what it considered to be the better parts of two recordings, a portion of the take 3 it had used for the 10″ LP, and a portion of the take 2 test pressing, which it had retained on a "safety".

The sequential listings following exhibit those details known to the author, not necessarily the full extent of Goodman's recordings for Columbia. Columbia may have in its vaults original recording acetates, or transfers of them to "safeties" or tape, that are unknown to him. Some of these may eventually surface, and then the listings will need be supplemented. But it is also unfortunately true that likely many alternate takes of issued Goodman recordings, and possibly some wholly unissued performances that Goodman made for Columbia, no longer exist in any form. What is fortunate is that so much has been preserved.

BENNY GOODMAN AND HIS ORCHESTRA	August 10, 1939, Los Angeles

Benny Goodman, clt; Ziggy Elman, Chris Griffin, Corky Cornelius, tpt; Red Ballard, Vernon Brown, Bruce Squires, tbn; Toots Mondello, Buff Estes, as; Bus Bassey, Jerry Jerome, ts; Fletcher Henderson, p; Arnold Covey, g; Art Bernstein, b; Nick Fatool, d; Louise Tobin, voc.

LA 1947-A	CO 35210, PaE R2916, CoAu DO2230, CoE DB5074, CoFr DF2731, CoNor GN5063, CoSw DZ307. **LP:** Co alb P5-15536, Fr series, SWE 1001, TAX 8021. **ET:** AFRS American Popular Music 65
LA 1947-B	**LP:** NOST 1004, PHON 7606
	There'll Be Some Changes Made - voc Louise Tobin (arr FH)
LA 1948-A	CO 35210, PaE R2916, CoE DB5074, CoFr DF2731, CoJap M383, CoNor GN5063, CoSw DZ307, VD 205 B. **EP:** CO 5-1653 (set B351). **LP:** CO CL534, FONT TFL5001, CO alb P4M-5678, HIS H623, JO 3057, SIG 132, TAX 8021. **ET:** AFRS Jill's Juke Box (G.I. Jive) 1923, AFRS American Popular Music Nos. 13, 56, 109, 535, AFRS Quarter Century of Swing 329
LA 1948-B	**LP:** PHON 7606
	Jumpin' At The Woodside (arr CB/JM)
LA 1949-A	Co 35201 B. **LP:** JAZ 50, TAX 8021, NOST 1005
	Rendezvous Time In Paree - voc Louise Tobin (arr EdSau)
LA 1950-A	CO 35201 A. **LP:** JAZ 50, TAX 8021
LA 1950-B	**LP:** PHON 7606
	Comes Love - voc Louise Tobin (arr EdSau)

(Jimmy Mundy modified Count Basie's arrangement of "Jumpin' At The Woodside.")

BENNY GOODMAN AND HIS ORCHESTRA	August 11, 1939, Los Angeles

Personnel as August 10.

LA 1951-A	CO 35362, PaE R2749, CoC 1025, CoCont DC335, CoSd DC33, CoSw MZ260, SIL 542. **EP:** CO sets B357, G4-20. **LP:** CO GL524, CO CB20, CO alb P6-14007, COR-Au KLP682, CBSSd JGL524, PhilCont B07011L, PhilCont B07670R, PhilCont B07797R, TAX 8021, BR (no #). **ET:** AFRS G.I. Jive 2258, AFRS American Popular Music Nos. 65, 536
LA 1951-B	**LP:** BID 1004
	Stealin' Apples (arr FH)

LA 1952-A	CO 35301, CoArg 291440, CoAu D02119, CoC 311. **LP:** JAZ 35, TAX 8021. **ET:** AFRS G.I. Jive Nos. 690, 1194, 1816, AFRS American Popular Music 537, OWI Outpost Concert Series 4-Music Of The Jazz Bands 8
LA 1952-B	**LP:** PHON 7606
	Boy Meets Horn
LA 1953-A	**LP:** CD D450 (The Great Bands-The Kings of Swing)
LA 1953-B	**LP:** PHON 7606, CO P3-16175
LA 1953	VD 731 B. **LP:** SB 144, SWE 1001, TAX 8021
	Bolero (arr FH)
LA 1954-A	**LP:** PHON 7606
LA 1954-B	**LP:** BID 1004
	. . . untitled blues - voc Louise Tobin

BENNY GOODMAN AND HIS ORCHESTRA   August 16, 1939, Los Angeles

Personnel as August 10.

LA 1951-C	**LP:** PHON 7606
LA 1951-D	**LP:** PHON LV50, BID 1006
	Stealin' Apples (arr FH)
LA 1962-A	CO 35319, CoArg 291229, CoAu D02371, CoCont DB5079, CoJap, Jx1128, CoNor GN5061, PaE R2921, SIL 542. **LP:** CO alb P5-15536, HIS H641, SWE 1001, TAX 8021, CO P3-16175. **ET:** AFRS The Swinging Years 204, AFRS American Popular Music 537
LA 1962-B	**LP:** PHON 7606
	Spring Song (Adapted From Mendelssohn's Spring Song) (arr FH)
LA 1963-A	CO 35211 A, CoE DB5072, CoSW MZ308, PaE R2914, PaSw PZ11271. **LP:** JAZ 50, TAX 8021
LA 1963-B	**LP:** PHON 7606
	Blue Orchids - voc Louise Tobin
LA 1964-A	CO 35410, PaE R2751, CoArg 291190, CoCont DC 336, SIL 543. **EP:** CO sets B 357 & G4-20, PHIL BBE 12048, PhilCont 429113BE. **LP:** CO GL524, CoSd JGL524, CORAu KLP682, PhilCont B07011L, PhilCont B07797R, CO alb P5-15536, CO alb P6-13975, RS (no #), TAX 8021
LA 1964-B	**LP:** NOST 1004, PHON 7606
	Night And Day (arr FH)
LA 1965-A	CO 35211 B, PaE R2914, PaSw PZ11271, CoE DB5072, CoNor GN5061, CoSW MZ308. **LP:** JAZ 50, TAX 8021
LA 1965-B	**LP:** PHON 7606
	What's New? - voc Louise Tobin (arr FH)

The band finished its one week stand in the French Garden Room of the new Victor Hugo Restaurant in Beverly Hills on August 17. During this engagement, John Hammond had Charlie Christian flown in from Kansas City to audition for Benny. On first hearing, in a studio, Benny wasn't impressed. But Hammond persisted, surreptitiously emplaced Charlie's amplifier on the bandstand, coaxed Benny into letting Charlie play with the Quintet. The very first performance of the new Sextet thrilled a cheering audience and Benny alike, and Charlie was hired on the spot.

Arnold Covey continued to play band guitar, although on occasion Charlie sat in both on location and in studios for recording sessions. Where ascertainable, these participations will be noted.

Two program logs—no air checks are extant—of radio broadcasts from Victor Hugo make no mention of Christian. Thus his first known appearance on wax is from the band's regular (now) Saturday night "Camel Caravan" program from the Hollywood Bowl:

"CAMEL CARAVAN"   *August 19, 1939, Hollywood Bowl,*
  NBC Radio Network   *Los Angeles*

Orchestra as August 10. SEXTET: Benny Goodman, clt; Lionel Hampton, vib.; Fletcher Henderson, p; CHARLIE CHRISTIAN, g.; Art Bernstein, b; Nick Fatool, d.

Flying Home - SEXTET (LP: JAA 23)
Jumpin' At The Woodside (LP: JM "Classics of Jazz Radio")

The band was really jumpin'—the next day it flew to a Sunday engagement in the Blue Moon Ballroom in Wichita, Kansas, and Charlie was back in the prairie he'd left less than two weeks earlier. On Monday another flight took it to Atlantic City's Steel Pier for a week's booking. And probably when the band left the west coast, two more more new faces appeared: Corky Cornelius took off for Mexico, and Jimmy Maxwell, a sterling first trumpeter who'll stay with Benny for years, replaced him; and Bruce Squires also departed, which brought in Ted Vesely on third trombone.

A Mutual sustaining broadcast from the Steel Pier presents the revised lineup for the first time:

SUSTAINING BROADCAST   *August 23, 1939, Steel*
  MUTUAL Radio Network   *Pier, Atlantic City*

Personnel as August 10, except JIMMY MAXWELL, tpt, and TED VESELY, tbn, replace Cornelius and Squires respectively.

Let's Dance (theme) (LP: Fan 19-119)
Down By The Old Mill Stream (arr FH) (LP: FAN 19-119)
King Porter Stomp (n/c)

The band next surfaces in Toronto, where it played the Canadian National Exhibition on August 31. It crossed the border the next day to appear at the Michigan State Fair in Detroit, from where it broadcast its weekly "Camel Caravan" program on Saturday evening:

"CAMEL CARAVAN"   *September 2, 1939, Michigan State*
  NBC Radio Network   *Fair, Detroit*

Orchestra personnel as August 23. Sextet personnel as August 19.

Let's Dance (theme)
If I Could Be With You (One Hour Tonight)
Day In, Day Out - voc Louise Tobin
Star Dust - SEXTET
The Jumpin' Jive - voc Louise Tobin (arr FH)
Sent For You Yesterday And Here You Come Today
Boy Meets Horn
I've Been There Before - voc Louise Tobin (arr EdSau)
Pick-A-Rib
Good-Bye (theme)

(Above on LP, JAZ 54.)

Benny makes special mention of "Star Dust," saying that although everyone had heard the Trio, Quartet and band play it, Charlie Christian, during a rehearsal " . . . tore out a chorus no one had ever heard before, and we thought you'd like to hear it." Thus Charlie's classic treatment of Hoagy Carmichael's standard evidently was first broadcast September 2.

Announcer Bert Parks also twits Benny about playing so many fairs, saying, ". . . and tomorrow you'll be on your way to the New York World's Fair." Possibly; but our information is that the band opened there on September 6. In any event, the next air check is from Toronto, where Benny once again was at the Canadian National Exhibition:

SUSTAINING BROADCAST   *September 4, 1939, New*
  CBC Radio Network   *Dance Pavilion, Toronto*

Personnel as August 23.

Jumpin' At The Woodside (n/c)

("What's New?" is reputedly extant from this broadcast, but the author has not located a copy.)

The band headlined the many attractions of the New York World's Fair from September 6 through September 11, and likely was broadcast from there via WNEW, New York—but no air checks of these broadcasts are known. On the 9th it went to NBC's Manhattan studios to broadcast its weekly "Camel Caravan":

"CAMEL CARAVAN"   *September 9, 1939, New York*
  NBC Radio Network

Personnels as September 2.

Let's Dance (theme)
Spring Song
Over The Rainbow - voc Louise Tobin
Jumpin' At The Woodside (LP: GOJ 1005, JAZZ MODERNE -, AC 34)
Moonlight Serenade (arr FH) (LP: AC 34)
Flying Home - SEXTET
Put That Down In Writing - voc Louise Tobin
Mozart Matriculates (LP: AC 34)
Stealin' Apples (LP: AC 34)
Good-Bye (theme) (LP: AC 34)

Opposite the bands of Teddy Wilson and Stuff Smith, Benny and his boys participated in Martin Block's "Swing Session" at the Manhattan Center on September 12. For the past week or so Chris Griffin had been ailing, and Johnny Martel substituted for him. Chris finally decided he'd had enough of all those one-nighters, and Martel replaced him in time for the band's next studio session:

BENNY GOODMAN   **September 13, 1939, New York**
AND HIS ORCHESTRA

Benny Goodman, clt; Jimmy Maxwell, Ziggy Elman, JOHNNY MARTEL. tpt; Red Ballard, Vernon Brown, Ted Vesely, tbn; Toots Mondello, Buff Estes, as; Bus Bassey, Jerry Jerome, ts; Fletcher Henderson, p; Arnold Covey, g; Art Bernstein, b; Nick Fatool, d; Louise Tobin, voc.

CO 25350-bkdn UNISSUED - Tape
CO 25350 UNISSUED - Tape
CO 25350 **LP:** PHON 7606
CO 25350 **LP:** BID 1004
CO 25350-1 CO 35241, CoE DB5077, PaE R2919. **LP:** JAZ 35, TAX 8021
    One Sweet Letter From You - voc Louise Tobin (arr FH)

CO 25351 **LP:** PHON XM79
CO 25351 **LP:** PHON 7606
CO 25351-1 CO 35445, PaE R2779, VD 205 B. **LP:** JAZ 35, TAX 8021. **ET:** AFRS American Popular Music 537, AFRS Remember 964
    Down By The Old Mill Stream (arr FH)

CO 25352-bkdn UNISSUED - Tape
CO 25352-1 CO 35230. **LP:** CO alb P5-15536, JAZ 41, TAX 8021. **ET:** AFRS Remember 69
CO 25352 **LP:** PHON 7606
    I Didn't Know What Time It Was - voc Louise Tobin (arr EdSau)

CO 25353 UNISSUED - Tape
CO 25353 **LP:** PHON 7606
CO 25353 **LP:** BID 1004
CO 25353-bkdn UNISSUED - Tape
CO 25353 UNISSUED - Tape
CO 25353-1 CO 35230. **LP:** JAZ 41, TAX 8021
    Love Never Went To College - voc Louise Tobin (arr EdSau)

CO 25354 UNSSUED - Tape
CO 25354-bkdn UNISSUED - Tape
CO 25354 **LP:** PHON 7606
CO 25354-1 CO 35241, PaE R2919, CoC 6325, CoE DB5077, CO 37246, CO DJ25354. **45:** CO 4-7-G (Set G4-3). **EP:** CO 5-1655 (Set B351). **LP:** CO GL501, CO CL534, CoE/Au 33SX1038, CO alb P6-14007, JAZ 35, TAX 8021. **ET:** AFRS American Popular Music Nos. 65 & 538, AFRS Quarter Century Of Swing 304
    Scatter-Brain - voc Louise Tobin (arr EdSau)

CO 25355-bkdn UNISSUED - Tape
CO 25355 **LP:** BID 1006
CO 25355-bkdn UNISSUED - Tape
CO 25355-1 **LP:** PHON 7610
    I've Been There Before - voc Louise Tobin

Shea's Theatre in Buffalo, New York, was Benny's next engagement, September 15 through 21. A newly-discovered transcription captures his "Camel Caravan" broadcast from that location:

"CAMEL CARAVAN"   *September 16, 1939, Buffalo*
  NBC Radio Network

Orchestra personnel as September 13. Sextet as August 19.

Let's Dance (theme)
Blue Skies
Scatter-Brain - voc Louise Tobin
The Jumpin' Jive - special lyrics, Benny Goodman, Bert Parks
The Hour Of Parting (arr EdSau)
Opus Local 802 - SEXTET
Blue Orchids - voc Louise Tobin
Bolero
Good-Bye (theme)

From Buffalo to the Orpheum Theatre in St. Paul, Minnesota, and the band's next stop on its "Caravan," featuring an amusing dissertation on the tribulations of a clarinet player, and the third in a trilogy of Alec Templeton pastiches:

"CAMEL CARAVAN"   *September 23, 1939, St. Paul*
  NBC Radio Network

Orchestra personnel as September 13. Sextet as August 19.

Let's Dance (theme)
After You've Gone (arr FH)
I Didn't Know What Time It Was - voc Louise Tobin
"Clarence Meek" - special lyrics, Benny Goodman, Bert Parks
It Had To Be You
Mendelssohn, I'll Mow You Down (arr Henry Brandt)
Opus 1/2 - SEXTET (LP: QD 16)
What's New? - voc Louise Tobin
Bugle Call Rag
Good-Bye (theme)

Alumnus Harry James, whose band was then at the College Inn of the Hotel Sherman, is Benny's guest the following week. They recreate a recording they'd made together—coincidentally, in Chicago—some 54 weeks' earlier, which Harry now used as his theme:

"CAMEL CARAVAN"   *September 30, 1939, Chicago*
  NBC Radio Network

Orchestra personnel as September 13. Sextet as August 19. Guest: Harry James, tpt.

Let's Dance (theme)
Love Never Went To College (no voc)
Melancholy Mood - voc Louise Tobin (arr EdSau)
"Steal American First" - special lyrics, Benny Goodman, Bert Parks
In An 18th Century Drawing Room (arr Henry Brandt)
Ciribiribin - feat. Harry James, tpt
Star Dust - SEXTET
The Little Man Who Wasn't There - voc Louise Tobin
Jumpin' At The Woodside
Good-Bye (theme)

A first for the band, it played a combination "Rodeo and Swing Concert" in Cleveland, Ohio's, Municipal Stadium on October 1. Then it returned to New York for two days at the World's Fair, and the first studio session for the Sextet:

BENNY GOODMAN SEXTET   October 2, 1939, New York

Benny Goodman, clt; Lionel Hampton, vib; Fletcher Henderson, p; Charlie
Christian, g; Art Bernstein, b; Nick Fatool, d.

WCO 26132-A   CO 35254, CoArg 291183, CoAu D02153, CoC 6200,
               CoE DB5075, CoInd 36721, CoJap M40, CoSw DZ207,
               CoSw MZ261, CO 36721, CO 50051, PaE R2917,
               PaFin DPY1058, Palt B71202, PaNor NPS5014, PaSw
               PZ11259. **45:** CO 4-50051, **EP:** CO B2587, CorAu
               KEP032, CorAu KEP124. **LP:** CO CL2483, CO CS9283,
               CO KG31547, Co alb P4M-5678, Co alb P6-14954,
               CBS 52368, CBS 62581, CBS 67268, Palt PMDQ8013,
               SONY SOPZ4-6, TL STLJ05, JAZ 35. **ET:** AFRS H-62,
               AFRS P-785, AFRS The Swinging Years 239, AFRS
               Downbeat 285, AFRS American Popular Music 538
WCO 26132-B   VD 731 B. **LP:** PHON 7610, SB 144
               Flying Home (as **"Homeward Bound"** on V-Disc)

WCO 26133-A   CO 35254, CoArg 291183, CoAu D02153, CoE DB5075,
               CoC 6199, CoJap M40, CoJap JX1067, CoSw DZ207,
               CoSw MZ261, CO 36720, PaE R2917, PaFin
               DPY1058, Palt B71202, PaNor NPS5014, PaSw
               PZ11259. **EP:** CorAu KEP032. **LP:** FONT TFL5067,
               FontCont 682047TL, Palt PMDQA8013, CO G30779,
               CO KG31547, CBS 62581, CBS 67233, SONY
               SOPZ4-6, STL-J12. **ET:** AFRS G.I. Jive 2248, AFRS
               American Popular Music Nos. 79, 129, 225, 548
               Rose Room (In Sunny Roseland)

WCO 26134-A   CO DJ26134, CoJap M757. **45:** CO 4-12-G (Set G4-2).
               EP: CO 5-1650 (Set B350), CoFr ESDF1025. CoJap
               EM95, PhilCont 429446BE. **LP:** CO GL500, COE
               33SX1035, CoFr FPX112, CoJap PL5004, CoJap
               PL5013, CorAu KLP675, PHIL BBL7178, PhilCont
               B07225L, ReSp LS1009, CBS 62581, SONY SOPZ4-6,
               SONY SOPM 162, RTB LPV4316
               Stardust

On October 4 the band began a lengthy engagement in the Empire Room of
the Waldorf-Astoria hotel in Manhattan; fellow-sideman from the early
'30's, rival clarinetist-leader Artie Shaw was among the celebrities in attendance. An opening night sustaining broadcast gives us these two air checks:

SUSTAINING BROADCAST   October 4, 1939, Waldorf-
  CBS Radio Network   Astoria, New York

Personnel as September 13.

Oh, You Crazy Moon - voc Louise Tobin (arr FH)
Stealin' Apples

   Next, Benny's second Carnegie Hall concert, but in company with
other orchestras, and to celebrate the 25th anniversary of ASCAP:

ASCAP's 25th   October 6, 1939, Carnegie
  ANNIVERSARY PROGRAM   Hall, New York

Orchestra personnel as September 13, except Hampton substitutes for Fatool
on d. Sextet as October 2. TRIO: BG, Henderson, Hampton, d.

Don't Be That Way
Sunrise Serenade (arr FH)
'T'Ain't What You Do (It's The Way How Cha Do It) - voc BG, chorus (arr
  JM)
Bach Goes To Town
One O'Clock Jump
The Sheik Of Araby - TRO (on 78, POLY 6007)
Flying Home - SEXTET
Star Dust - SEXTET (on 78, POLY 6007)
Sing, Sing, Sing

(In whole or in part, the performance above is on LP: Amalgamated 105, RS
(no #), CC 18 ELEC KV106, JS 67412, KOS 435, MU 30JA5181, OS 043.)

   An old friend and marvelous jazz singer, Mildred Bailey, is Benny's
guest on his first "Camel Caravan" broadcast while he is ensconced in the
Waldorf "for the winter," as he explains it. Three weeks later she will

return as featured vocalist for the balance of the Camel series, and she will
record with the band for Columbia until the advent of Helen Forrest. Not
well and under her doctor's orders to limit her activities, the "Rockin' Chair
Lady" is with Benny for only those special occasions, and does not appear at
the Waldorf. On location, Louise Tobin remained band vocalist through
October 25; ill herself, she will be replaced by June Robbins on October 26.
   Another cast change on this program has actor Ted Pierson supplanting
Bert Parks as MC, with announcer George Bryan doing the commercials.

"CAMEL CARAVAN"   October 7, 1939, New York
  NBC Radio Network

Orchestra personnel as September 13. Sextet as October 2. Guest: Mildred
Bailey, voc.

Let's Dance (theme)
Wrappin' It Up
Oh You Crazy Moon (no voc)
The Lamp Is Low - voc Mildred Bailey (LP: QD 16)
Scatter-Brain (no voc)
Memories Of You - SEXTET (LP: QD 16)
Shouting In That Amen Corner - voc Mildred Bailey
One O'Clock Jump
Good-Bye (theme)

(This broadcast and the remainder of the "Caravan" programs originated in
NBC's Studio G in Radio City.)

SUSTAINING BROADCAST   October 9, 1939, Waldorf-
  Unknown network   Astoria, New York

Personnel as October 2.

Rose Room (In Sunny Roseland) - SEXTET (LP: JAA 23, MU 30JA5181)

   Columbia Records promoted its new recording artist with a special
broadcast titled, "Columbia Records Present: Young Man With A Band."
Unfortunately, two of the only three cuts extant are very brief, one chorus of
a Septet side, and the introduction only of a band number:

"YOUNG MAN WITH A BAND"   October 13, 1939, New York
  CBS Radio Network

Orchestra as September 13. SEPTET: Benny, rhythm section, unknown tpt,
tbn.

Scatter-Brain
The Jazz Me Blues - SEPTET (n/c)
Blue Skies (n/c)

   The next "Camel Caravan" produced the first collaboration extant of
Louis Armstrong and Benny Goodman; and it offers a first rendition of the
Sextet's "AC-DC Current," so named because both Lionel's and Charlie's
instruments were electrically amplified:

"CAMEL CARAVAN"   October 14, 1939, New York
  NBC Radio Network

Orchestra as September 13. Sextet as October 2. Guests: Louis Armstrong,
tpt & voc; the Lynn Murray Choir, voc.

Let's Dance (theme)
Pick-A-Rib (LP: JM Classics of Jazz Radio)
I Didn't Know What Time It Was - voc Louise Tobin
Ain't Misbehavin' - SEXTET plus Louis Armstrong, tpt and voc - band in
  coda (LP: FDC 1017, SPJ 6602, JM as above)
Moonlight Serenade
AC-DC Current - SEXTET (LP: ELEC KV106, SPJ 6602, JM as above, WI
  196)
(Shadrach - voc Louis Armstrong, Lynn Murray Choir - w/rhythm section -
  NO BG
King Porter Stomp
Good-Bye (theme)

SUSTAINING BROADCAST   October 16, 1939, Waldorf-
  MUTUAL Radio Network   Astoria, New York

Orchestra as September 13. Sextet as October 2.

Flying Home - SEXTET (LP: ELEC KV106, SPJ 6002)
Sugar Foot Stomp
Sing, Sing, Sing - to signoff

Note the inclusion in the next studio session of recently-discovered mx WCO 26197, "Mozart Matriculates." Like "Bach Goes To Town," this pastiche was also composed by Alec Templeton, and arranged by Henry Brandt as noted earlier.

BENNY GOODMAN AND HIS ORCHESTRA   **October 20, 1939, New York**

Personnel as September 13, MILDRED BAILEY, voc.

WCO 26194-A   CO35313. **LP:** CO alb P5-15536, JAZ 35, TAX 8033. **ET:**
              AFRS American Popular Music 539
WCO 26194-B   **LP:** PHON 7610
              Make With The Kisses - voc Mildred Bailey (arr FH)
WCO 26195-A   CO 35308, CoArg 291477. **LP:** JAZ 35, TAX 8033.
              Heaven In My Arms (Music In My Heart) - voc Mildred
              Bailey
WCO 26196-A   CO 35313, CoAu D02241. **LP:** CL 1862 (Set C3L22),
              CBS PBG52100, TAX 8033. **ET:** AFRS American
              Popular Music 539
              I Thought About You - voc Mildred Bailey (arr EdSau)
WCO 26197-A   **LP:** BID 1004
              Mozart Matriculates (arr Henry Brandt)

The next "Camel Caravan" broadcast marks Louise Tobin's final appearance on the sponsored program, although she apparently continued with the band at the Waldorf until October 25. Ironically, her last contribution is "Make With The Kisses," recorded by Benny just the day before with Mildred Bailey:

"CAMEL CARAVAN"   *October 21, 1939, New York*
  NBC Radio Network

Orchestra as September 13. Sextet as October 2. Guest: Caspar Reardon, harp.

Let's Dance (theme)
Between The Devil And The Deep Blue Sea
Lilacs In The Rain - voc Louise Tobin
Opus Local 802 (arr FH)
(Effervescent Blues - Reardon, harp, w/orchestra - NO BG
Chicken Reel - orchestra plus Reardon, harp
Soft Winds - SEXTET (LP: ELEC KV106, SPJ 6602, W 196)
Make With The Kisses- voc Louise Tobin
Swingtime In The Rockies
Good-Bye (theme)

Louise Tobin is not on extant air checks from our next sustaining broadcast, nor is she listed on a program log for four other selections that were performed but have not become available:

SUSTAINING BROADCAST   *October 23, 1939, Waldorf-*
  Unknown network   *Astoria, New York*

Personnel as September 13, but omit Louise Tobin, Sextet as October 2.

Sent For You Yesterday And Here You Come Today
Memories Of You - SEXTET (LP: JAA 42, QD 16)
Make Believe (LP: BRO/RADR 100)
There'll Be Some Changes Made (LP: BRO/RADR 100)
Jumpin' At The Woodside (LP: BRO/RADR 100)
Absence Makes The Heart Grow Fonder (LP: BRO/RADR 100)

BENNY GOODMAN AND HIS ORCHESTRA   **October 24, 1939, New York**

Personnel as September 13.

WCO 26201-A   CO 35289. **LP:** JAZ 36, TAX 8033. **ET:** AFRS American
              Popular Music 539
              Faithful Forever - voc Mildred Bailey (arr EdSau)

WCO 26202-A   CO 35301, CoArg 291440, CoAu D02119, CoC 311, CoC
              6322, CoJap M260, CoJap L3016, CO 36224, Co
              37243. **7″33:** CO 1-512, CO 3-39107. **45:** CoJap
              LL20C. **EP:** CO B2594, CO B8202, CoE SEG7556,
              CoJap EM101, CBS 5758. **LP:** CO CL6100, CO CL820,
              CO CL2483, CO CS8643, CO CS9283, CO DS177, CO
              P2S-5112, CO Z173, CO D268, CO D403, CO
              KG31547, CO alb PZM5111, CO alb P2S5112, Co alb
              P755122, Co alb P2M5193, Co alb P4M5678, Co alb
              CS51506, Co alb P5-15536, CO alb PM16932, CoJap
              PL5013, CoJap ZL1027, CBS 52368, CBS 52688, CBS
              63367, CBS 67268, FONT TFL5001, HA 7336, HA
              HS11271, PIC 240, PHIL BBL7209, PhilCont
              B07228L, RLM 52310, RLM 8065, TAX 8033, T-L
              STBB03. **ET:** AIR FORCE GL 15, AFRS Jill's Juke Box
              Nos. 151 & 1816, AFRS American Popular Music Nos.
              33 & 244, AFRS The Swinging Years Nos. 45 & 218,
              AFRS Quarter Century Of Swing Nos. 7 & 96, AFRS P-
              S-39
              Let's Dance (arr George Bassman - FH)

WCO 26203-   CO 35308, CoArg 291477. **LP:** JAZ 36, TAX 8033
A/A1   **That Lucky Fellow** - voc Mildred Bailey (arr FH)

WCO 26204-A   CO 35289. **LP:** JAZ 36, TAX 8033. **EP:** AFRS American
               Popular Music Nos. 9 & 546
               Bluebirds In The Moonlight - voc Mildred Bailey (arr FH)

(George Bassman arranged the first 32 bars of "Let's Dance"; Fletcher Henderson completed it. Excerpts of Benny's theme appear on many other AFRS & related ET's, but they are not listed. Importantly, no alternate take of mx WCO 26202 has ever been found. //Takes "A" and "A1" appear indiscriminately on copies of CO 35308; they are the same recording.// Some copies of FONT and PHIL releases may substitute Gene Krupa's "After You've Gone" for "Let's Dance," in error.)

Mildred Bailey now becomes a "regular" on the "Camel Caravan" broadcasts:

"CAMEL CARAVAN"   *October 28, 1939, New York*
  NBC Radio Network

Orchestra as September 13. Sextet as October 2. Mildred Bailey, voc.

Let's Dance (theme)
Indiana
Blue Orchids (no voc)
My Last Goodbye - voc Mildred Bailey
Cherokee
Rose Room - SEXTET
Sometimes I'm Happy
Lover, Come Back To Me - voc Mildred Bailey
Jumpin' At The Woodside
Good-Bye (theme)

June Robbins replaced Louise Tobin from October 26 through the 30th, but our only air checks from this period do not include her.

SUSTAINING BROADCAST   *October 30, 1939, Waldorf-*
  Unknown network   *Astoria, New York*

Personnel as September 13, but JUNE ROBBINS, voc, replaces Louise Tobin.

Cherokee (arr EdSau)
Sugar Foot Stomp

Kay Foster replaced June Robbins on the first day of the new month; she'll appear with the band at the Waldorf until at least December 7—or possibly until the 10th, for Helen Forrest will make her debut with Benny on December 11. The sole extant air check from a broadcast of November 1 luckily offers a vocal by Miss Foster on her first night with the band.

SUSTAINING BROADCAST   *November 1, 1939, Waldorf-*
  Unknown network   *Astoria, New York*

Personnel as September 13, except KAY FOSTER, voc, replaces Tobin-Robbins.

Oh, You Crazy Moon - voc Kay Foster

"CAMEL CARAVAN" November 4, 1939, New York
NBC Radio Network

Orchestra as September 13. Sextet as October 2. Mildred Bailey, voc.

Let's Dance (theme)
Down By The Old Mill Stream
What's New? (no voc)
I Didn't Know What Time It Was - voc Mildred Bailey
Bolero
Shivers - SEXTET (LP: ELEC KV106, SPJ 6602)
Love Never Went To College (no voc)
Scatter-Brain - voc Mildred Bailey
Roll 'Em
Good-Bye (theme)

Benny performed the Mozart clarinet concerto, a standard in his classical repertoire, with the Buffalo (New York) Philharmonic Orchestra on November 5.

"CAMEL CARAVAN" November 11, 1939, New York
NBC Radio Network

Orchestra as September 13. Sextet as October 2. Mildred Bailey, voc.

Let's Dance (theme)
Don't Be That Way
A Ghost Of A Chance - voc Mildred Bailey (poss. arr EdSau)
Beyond The Moon (arr FH)
I'm A Ding Dong Daddy (From Dumas) - SEXTET
Darn That Dream - voc Mildred Bailey (arr FH)
Bach Goes to Town
Utt Da Zay - voc Mildred Bailey
Sugar Foot Stomp
Good-Bye (theme)

"CAMEL CARAVAN" November 18, 1939, New York
NBC Radio Network

Orchestra as September 13. Sextet as October 2. Mildred Bailey, voc.

Let's Dance (theme)
Scatter-Brain (no voc)
Lilacs In The Rain - voc Mildred Bailey
In The Mood (arr FH)
South Of The Border - SEXTET
Swinging A Dream - voc Mildred Bailey
Boy Meets Horn - feat. Ziggy Elman, tpt
Oh, Johnny! - voc Mildred Bailey
Sing, Sing, Sing - Lionel Hampton, d, substitutes for Fatool
Good-Bye (theme)

BENNY GOODMAN SEXTET **November 22, 1939, New York**

Personnel as October 2.

WCO 26284-A CO 35320, CoArg 291184, CoAu D02283, CoAu D03762, CoBr 30-1344, CoC 342, CoCont DC342, CoE DB3732, CoJap L3027, CoSd DS1317, PaE R2761. **45:** CoE SCM5239, CoFr SCD1011, CoJap LL20C. **EP:** CO B8204, CoE SEGC9, CoJap EM101, FontCont 462012TE, PhilCont 429157BE. **LP:** CO CL820, CO CS8643, CO KG31547, CO alb P5-15536, Co alb PM16932, CoJap ZL 1027, CBS 52688, CBS 62581, CBS 67268, SONY SOPZ4-6. **ET:** AFRS American Popular Music 541
WCO 26284-B **LP:** CO G30779, CBS 67233, SONY SOPZ4-6
Memories Of You

WCO 26285-A **LP:** BID 1002, PHON 7610
WCO 26285-B CO 35320, CoArg 291184, CoAu D02283, CoAu D03762, CoC 342, CoCont DC342, PaE R2761. **EP:** CoE SEGC9. **LP:** CO CL 1036, CBS 52538, SONY SOPZ4-6, B1D 1011. **ET:** AFRS American Popular Music 540
Soft Winds

WCO 26286-A CO 35349, CoArg 291181, CoAu D02177, CoE DB5081, CoInd DB5081, CoSw DZ319, PaE R2923, PaIt B71233. **EP:** PHIL BBE12272. **LP:** CO CL652, CO G30779, CoJap PL2037, CorAu KLP510, PHIL BBL7172, PhilCont B07247L, PhilCont B07907R, CBS 52538, CBS 62387, CBS 67233, SONY SOPZ4-6, SONY SOPM-155, SONY 20AP-1456
Seven Come Eleven

(At Lionel Hampton's suggestion, "Seven Come Eleven" was first titled, and announced as "Roast Turkey Stomp," in recognition of the Thanksgiving season. Note that CO 35349's label credits are incorrect; Henderson plays piano.)

BENNY GOODMAN AND HIS ORCHESTRA **same date**

Personnel as September 13; Mildred Bailey, voc.

WCO 26287-A CO 35331. **EP:** CoE SEG7524, CoFr ESDF1023. **LP:** CO CL 1862 (Set C3L22), CO alb P6-14954, CBS 62100, TAX 8033. **ET:** AFRS American Popular Music 541, AFRS Remember 273
WCO 26287-B **LP:** PHON 7610
Darn That Dream - voc Mildred Bailey (arr FH)

WCO 26288-A CO 35331. **LP:** CO CL 1862 (Set C3L22), CBS 62100, TAX 8033. **ET:** AFRS American Popular Music Nos. 3, 46, 192, 263, 390, 542, AFRS Remember 273
Peace, Brother! - voc Mildred Bailey (arr EdSau)

WCO 26289-A CO 35410, CoArg 291190, SIL 543. **LP:** SWE 1001, TAX 8033. **ET:** AFRS American Popular Music 542
WCO 26289-B **LP:** PHON 7610
Beyond The Moon (arr FH) (Originally titled, "Toots's Dream")

Substitute: Charlie Christian, g, for Covey

WCO 26290-A CO 35319, CoArg 291190, CoArg C10019, CoAu D02371, COE DB5079, CoJap M260, PaE R2921, SIL 542. **EP:** CO Set B357, CO Set G4-20, CO 5-2285. **LP:** CO GL524, CO CL6100, CO CL2533, CO CL777, CO alb P5-15536, Co alb P6-14007, CO G30779, CoJap PL5084, CoJap ZL1077, CorAu KLP500, CorAu KLP682, PhilCont B07011L, PhilCont B07797R, CBS 62581, CBS 67233, CBSSd JGL524, SONY SOPZ4-6, TAX 8033. **ET:** AFRS American Popular Music Nos. 56, 109, 542, AFRS Remember 962
Honeysuckle Rose (arr FH)

"CAMEL CARAVAN" November 25, 1939, New York
NBC Radio Network

Orchestra as September 13. Sextet as October 2. Mildred Bailey, voc.

Let's Dance (theme)
Sweet Sue-Just You
My Prayer - voc Mildred Bailey
Stealin' Apples
All The Things You Are - voc Mildred Bailey
Love Never Went to College (no voc)
Roast Turkey Stomp - SEXTET (LP: ELEC KV106, SPJ 6602, WI 196)
St. Louis Blues - voc Mildred Bailey - SEXTET plus orchestra
Three Little Words
Good-Bye (theme)

On the same day that the band played a benefit for the medical fund of (New York) musicians' Local 802 in Madison Square Garden, the Sextet is heard from the Waldorf:

BENNY GOODMAN SEXTET **November 27, 1939, Waldorf-**
MUTUAL Radio Network **Astoria, New York**

Personnel as October 2.

59-MG-632 MGM Series: 103, 106, 109, 110, 113, 114, 115, 116, 119, 120, 121
AC-DC Current

Benny and his Sextet doubled from the Waldorf into New York's Center Theater to open "Swingin' The Dream" on November 29. The musical by Earl Carroll and Gilbert Seldes (an adaptation of Shakespeare's "A Midsummer Night's Dream") featured some of the Nation's best jazz talent, in addition to the Sextet:

Louis Armstrong-Bottom; Bud Freeman and his Summa Cum Laude band, including: Max Kaminsky, tpt; Brad Gowans, tbn; PeeWee Russell, clt; Bud, ts; Dave Bowman, p; Eddie Condon, g; and Zutty Singleton, d; Bill Bailey - Cupid; Sonny Payne - Drummer Boy; Jackie Mabley - Quince; Maxine Sullivan - Titania; Dorothy McGuire - Helena; Dorothy, Vivian and Etta Dandridge - Pixies; Butterfly McQueen - Puck; Juan Hernandez - Oberon; and Don Voorhees and his Orchestra in the pit.

Despite that attractive cast (were it possible, what would it cost to assemble an equal one today?), "Swingin' The Dream" swung for only an unlucky 13 performances, as sparse attendance forced its cancellation.

"CAMEL CARAVAN"   December 2, 1939, New York
  NBC Radio Network

Orchestra personnel as September 13; Mildred Bailey, voc. Sextet personnel as October 2.

Zaggin' With Zig (arr EdSau)
AC-DC Current - SEXTET (LP: JAA 42)
I Know That You Know

"CAMEL CARAVAN"   December 9, 1939, New York
  NBC Radio Network

Personnel as September 13, except Lionel Hampton, p, substitutes for Henderson.

Madhouse (LP: IAJRC 21)

As the substitution of Lionel for Fletcher in the preceding air check underscores, Henderson, not in the best of health, found his multiple duties as staff arranger and pianist for both the band and the small groups much too taxing, and he asked Benny for relief. Benny's choice was a native New Yorker who'd played with the orchestras of George Hall and Mike Riley, and who was then unremarked in jazz circles: Johnny Guarnieri. Despite this pedestrian provenance, Guarnieri could play jazz, as his later work with Benny, Artie Shaw and others proved. More, he was Benny's kind of musician—thoroughly schooled, an excellent reader, able to play anything put before him the first time and without mistake. And quite frankly, he was an improvement over Fletcher, whose real forte was arranging.

Equally important, Helen Forrest joined, making her debut with Benny on December 11 at the Waldorf. She'd become at liberty when her temperamental boss, Artie Shaw, had abruptly fled the Hotel Pennsylvania to search for peace and quiet in Mexico.

A word about Helen. Or rather, a personal opinion about Helen, now a resident of California, who still today may be seen occasionally on television, in concert appearances and in some of the Nation's better supper clubs. And who sings—almost—as appealingly as ever.

The Swing Era—the mid-Thirties through the mid-Forties—was rich with exceptional female vocalists, dedicated women with inherent musical qualities in their voices, with talent enhanced by some training but ever constant work, and with style. Many come fondly to mind, the ballad singers and the jazz singers, most at least competent in either milieu: Ivy Anderson, Avis Andrews, Mildred Bailey, Irene Daye, Ella Fitzgerald, Billie Holiday, Peggy Lee, Helen O'Connell, Anita O'Day, Bea Wain, Helen Ward, and still more. To this illustrious roster we would add Helen Forrest. Her voice was full and true, her enunciation precise. She responded with full empathy to the mood of words and music, whether slow and sentimental or up-tempo and swinging. Her effort was unflagging—as successive takes of Columbia's studio sessions reveal, she was there time after time despite the physical and mental drain engendered by Benny's insistence on perfection. THIS was a band singer; Helen was a professional. Listen to her work critically; she may well have been the best of all of Goodman's vocalists.

Oddly, Benny never really thinks of Helen Forrest as having been one of "his" vocalists. Were you to ask him to name the gals who sang with his band, and not give him time to reflect, he'd mention Ella (his favorite) and Peggy and Martha and Helen Ward—but not Helen Forrest. I once pointed out to him that Helen Forrest worked for him every bit as long as did Martha Tilton; he refused to believe me until I cited the respective dates. Other than his notorious absent-mindedness (the stories are legion, and I once told him his attention span lasted as long as the interval between my saying "Peggy" and "Lee"), the only reason I can ascribe to this lack of recognition is that Helen Forrest first came to prominence as Artie Shaw's vocalist, and later

was equally well known for her work with Harry James; and that perhaps Benny considers her to have been their vocalist, and not his.

In any event, we can enjoy Helen Forrest with Benny Goodman from now until August 1941, with all those memorable performances in between.

Unlike Kay Foster's debut, the sole air check extant from a broadcast made the evening Helen Forrest joined the band does not include her. Johnny Guarnieri is recognizable however:

SUSTAINING BROADCAST   December 11, 1939, Waldorf-
  MUTUAL Radio Network   Astoria, New York

Personnel as September 13, except JOHNNY GUARNIERI, p, replaces Henderson.

Roll 'Em

"CAMEL CARAVAN"   December 16, 1939, New York
  NBC Radio Network

Orchestra personnel as December 11; Mildred Bailey, voc. Sextet personnel as October 2, except Guarnieri replaces Henderson.

Rockin' Chair - voc Mildred Bailey - orchestra plus Lionel Hampton, vib
  (n/c)
Dinah - SEXTET (LP: JAA 23, MU 30JA5181)
Big John Special

(Note that these air checks are now specified as to source and date; earlier they were assigned generally to the period of the Waldorf engagement.)

BENNY GOODMAN SEXTET   **December 20, 1939, New York**

Benny Goodman, clt; Lionel Hampton, vib; JOHNNY GUARNIERI, p; Charlie Christian, g; Art Bernstein, b; Nick Fatool, d.

WCO 26354-bkdn	**LP:** BID 1012
WCO 26354-A	CO 35349, CoArg 291181, CoAu DO2177, CoE DB5081, CoJap M757, CoSW DZ319, OdG 028429, PaE R2923, Palt B71233. **45:** CO 4-15-G (Set G4-2). **EP:** CO 5-1651 (Set B350), PhilCont 429446BE, CoFr ESDF1025. **LP:** CO GL500, CoE 33SC1035, PHIL BBL 7178, PhilCont B07225L, CoJap PL5004, CoFrFPX112, Palt PMDQ8013, ReSp 33LS1009, CorAu KLP675, CO alb P5-15536, CBS 62581, RTB 4316, SONY SOPZ4-6, SONY SOPM-162.
	Shivers
WCO 26355-A	**45:** CO 4-15-G (Set G4-2). **EP:** CO 5-1651 (Set B350), PhilCont 429446BE. **LP:** CO GL500, CoE 33SX1035, PHIL BBL7178, PhilCont B07225L, CoFr FPX112, CoJap PL5004, BID 1011, ReSp 33LS1009, CorAu KLP675, CBS 52538, RTB 4316, SONY SOPZ4-6, SONY SOPM-162
	AC-DC Current
WCO 26356-A	**LP:** PHON LV50, TL STLJ05, PHON 7610
	I'm Confessin'

SUSTAINING BROADCAST   December 21, 1939, Waldorf-
  CBS Radio Network   Astoria, New York

Personnel as December 11; HELEN FORREST, voc.

Does Your Heart Beat For Me? - voc Helen Forrest. (LP: IAJRC 21)

December 24 found Benny once more at Carnegie Hall, this time with the Sextet including Fletcher Henderson on piano. The Christmas Eve performance was the second of John Hammond's annual "Spirituals To Swing" concerts. In addition to the selections listed, Benny's men jammed with some of the other performers on "Oh, Lady Be Good!"—sans BG.

BENNY GOODMAN SEXTET   **December 24, 1939, New York**

Personnel as October 2 (Henderson, p).

K80P-8898-1	**LP:** VANG VRS8523 A, TR 35/064, FONT TFL5187, VANG VSD47/48, CBS 51WQ16007
	I Got Rhythm; Flying Home; Memories of You

K80P-8900-1   **LP:** VANG VRS8524 A, TR 35/065, FONT TFL5188,
VANG VSD47/48, CBS 51WQ16007
Stompin' At The Savoy; Honeysuckle Rose

("Memories Of You" is also on SR InternationalG 70674.)

Charlie Christian is given label credit as guitarist for the next studio session by the orchestra; he is not, however, aurally identifiable on any side, and the belief expressed earlier that Covey continued to play with the band seems confirmed. This date does mark the recording debut of Helen Forrest with Benny Goodman, and the initial waxing of a manuscript by a new arranger, Les Hite (LH).

BENNY GOODMAN AND HIS ORCHESTRA   December 27, 1939, New York

Personnel as December 11; HELEN FORREST, voc; LES HITE (LH), arr.

WCO 26365-A   CO 35362, PaE R2749, CoAu D02136, CoCont DC335,
CoFr DF3088, CoSw MZ260. **LP:** SWE 1001, TAX
8033.
Opus Local 802 (FH)

WCO 26366-A   CO 35356, CoAu D02230. **LP:** CO KG32822, JOY 6012,
TAX 8033
Busy As A Bee (I'm Buzz, Buzz, Buzzin') - voc Helen
Forrest (arr FH)

WCO 26367-A   CO 35396, PaE R2769, CoArg 291461, CoAu D02466.
LP: CO alb P5-15536, JAZ 36, TAX 8033
Board Meeting (arr LH)

WCO 26368-A   CO 35356, PaE R2769, CoJap M161. **LP:** SWE 1001,
TAX 8033
Zaggin' With Zig (arr EdSau)

Benny's association with the R.J. Reynolds Tobacco Company expired with the broadcast of December 30's "Camel Caravan," after 182 programs spread over three and a half years. It was the longest-running commercially-sponsored series featuring one orchestra continuously, and it captured the greatest of the swing bands in some of its finest moments. All jazz fans will ever be indebted to those professional and amateur recordists who preserved portions of those performances for posterity. Unfortunately, our only mementos of the final broadcast are of poor audio quality:

"CAMEL CARAVAN"   *December 30, 1939, New York*
   NBC Radio Network

Orchestra as December 11. Sextet as December 20.

Pick-A-Rib - SEXTET (LP: AC 34)
One O'Clock Jump (n/c) (LP: AC 34)

"FITCH BANDWAGON"   *December 31, 1939, Waldorf-*
   CBS Radio Network   *Astoria, New York*

Sextet as December 20.

Till Tom Special - SEXTET

The band left the Waldorf January 1, played a theater date, then gave a swing concert in New York's Town Hall on January 10. On the 15th it went into NBC's studios in Rockefeller Center for a special short-wave broadcast to Sweden, Norway and Denmark, from which countries it was rebroadcast regionally over their facilities. Swedish engineers preserved about 10 minutes' of the half-hour program:

SHORT-WAVE BROADCAST   *January 15, 1940, Rockefeller*
   via NBC   *Center, New York*

Personnel as December 27, 1939.

Let's Dance (theme)
Scatter-Brain
Indian Summer - voc Helen Forrest (n/c)
One O'Clock Jump (n/c - "Two O'Clock" coda only)
Good-Bye (theme)

BENNY GOODMAN AND HIS ORCHESTRA   January 16, 1940, New York

Personnel as December 27, 1939.

WCO 26416-A   CO 35374, PaE R2969. **LP:** CO KG32822, JOY 6012
What's The Matter With Me? -voc Helen Forrest (arr FH)

WCO 26417-A   CO 35374. **LP:** JAZ 50, JOY 6012
What'll They Think Of Next - voc Helen Forrest (arr FH)

WCO 26418-A   CO 35543, PaE R2760, CoCont DC341, **EP:** CO B357,
CO G4-20, PhilCont 429008BE. **LP:** CO GL524, CorAu
KLP682, CBSSd JGL524, PhilCont B07011L, PhilCont
B07797R
Can't You Tell? (arr FH)

WCO 26419-A   **LP:** PHON 7610
Squeeze Me (arr FH)

("Can't You Tell?" derives from Fletcher Henderson's, "I'm Rhythm Crazy Now.")

Troubled by sciatica, a recurring ailment that will plague him for years, Benny gave the band a few days off and went to Florida for sun, salt water swimming and rest. But it was quickly back to work: a week in the Strand Theater, Portland, Maine, beginning January 21; one-nighters, February 2, 3, 4, and 5, at the Georgetown University Prom in Washington, D.C., the Winter Carnival Ball in Schenectady, New York, the County Center in White Plains, New York, and the Willard Hotel, again in Washington.

Then it was a three-part recording session for Benny in Columbia's New York studios. First, two sides with the second annual Metronome magazine all star jazz poll winners; next, three sides with his orchestra; and finally, ending a long day before the microphones, two cuts with the Sextet, these with Count Basie sitting in for Guarnieri:

METRONOME ALL STAR BAND   February 7, 1940, New York

Benny Goodman, clt; Charlie Spivak, Ziggy Elman, Harry James, tpt; Jack Teagarden, Jack Jenney, tbn; Toots Mondello, Benny Carter, as; Eddie Miller, Charlie Barnet, ts; Jess Stacy, p; Charlie Christian, g; Bob Haggart, b; Gene Krupa, d.

WCO 26489-
bkdn   **LP:** BID 1012
WCO 26489-A   CO 35389, CoArg 291180, CoAu D02107, CoJap M233,
PaE R2746, Palt B71082, PaSW PZ11172, VD 894 B.
LP: CO CL2528, HA HL7044, SONY SONP-50419, JO
101.611, QD 009, TAX 8039
WCO 26489-B   **LP:** PHON 7610
King Porter Stomp (arr FH)

METRONOME ALL STAR NINE   same date

Goodman, James, Teagarden, Carter, Miller, Stacy, Christian, Haggart, Krupa.

WCO 26490-
bkdn   **LP:** BID 1012
WCO 26490-A   same issues as WCO 26489-A, except VD 879 B instead
of VD 894 B, plus **78**, CoJap S10009
WCO 26490-B   **LP:** CO G30779, SONY SONP-50419, CBS 67233, TAX
8039
All Star Strut

BENNY GOODMAN AND HIS ORCHESTRA   same date

Benny Goodman, clt; Jimmy Maxwell, Ziggy Elman, IRVING GOODMAN, tpt; Red Ballard, Vernon Brown, Ted Vesely, tbn; Toots Mondello, Buff Estes, as; Bus Bassey, Jerry Jerome, ts; Johnny Guarnieri, p; Arnold Covey, g; Art Bernstein, b; Nick Fatool, d; Helen Forrest, voc.

WCO 26491-A   CO 35391, CoJap M259, **EP:** CO 5-1654 (Set B351). **LP:**
CO CL534, CO CL607, Co alb P5-15536, JOY 6012
How High The Moon - voc Helen Forrest (arr EdSau)

WCO 26492-A   Co 35396, CoArg 291461. **LP:** JAZ 36, JOY 6012
Let's All Sing Together - voc Helen Forrest (arr FH)

WCO 26493-A   CO 35391. **LP:** NOST 890/1, CO KG32822, JOY 6012
The Fable Of The Rose - voc Helen Forrest (arr EdSau)

February 7, 1940, continued

February 7, 1940, continued
BENNY GOODMAN SEXTET   same date

Benny Goodman, clt; Lionel Hampton, vib; COUNT BASIE, p; Charlie Christian, g; Art Bernstein, b; Nick Fatool, d.

WCO 26494-A   CO 35404, PaE R2752, PaSw PZ11133, CoArg 291316,
               CoC 912, CoCont DC337, CoCont DC603, CoFr BF581,
               Colt DQ2529, CoJap M325, CO 37512. **EP:** CO Set
               B504, ReSp SEML34017. **LP:** CO CL652, CorAu
               KLP510, PHIL BBL7172, PhilCont B07247L, PhilCont
               B07907R, CO G30779, CBS 52538, CBS 62387, CBS
               67233, SONY SOPZ4-6, SONY SOPM-155, SONY
               20AP-1456
               Till Tom Special

(Basie's intro is excised on CO CL652 - same take, A.)

WCO 26495-A   **LP:** BID 1009
WCO 26495-B   CO 35404, PaE R2752, PaSw PZ11133, CoArG 291261,
               CoAu D02136, CoCont DC337, CoCont DC603, CoFin
               DYC167, CoFr BF581, Colt D02529, CoJap M452, BIA
               260A. **EP:** CO B2011, ReSp SEML34017. **LP:** CO
               CL652, CorAu KLP510, PHIL BBL7172, PhilCont
               B07247L, PhilCont B07907R, CO G30779, CBS
               52538, CBS 62387, CBS 67233, SONY SOPZ4-6,
               SONY SOPM-155, SONY 20AP-1456 TL STLJ22. **ET:**
               Air Force GL-15, AFRS/T P-GL-16
               Gone With "What" Wind

The band left New York the next day to begin a one-week engagement at the Stanley Theater, Pittsburgh, on February 9. Succeeding week-long stands were at the Lyric Theater, Indianapolis, opening on February 16, and at the Chicago Theater in Benny's hometown, starting February 23. Through this period Jimmy Maxwell and Irving Goodman were absent because of illness; Chris Griffin and Corky Cornelius substituted for them. But both regular trumpeters recovered in time to make the March 1 studio recording session.

Before we get to March, however, let's dispose of an air check erroneously ascribed in a bootleg LP's liner notes to, "Benny Goodman and his Orchestra, February 1940." The cut is "Melancholy Baby," vocal by Mildred Bailey, first released on JP 11, later on STO 3112. It's not by Goodman at all, but rather by Bob Crosby, who featured Mildred Bailey on his "Dixieland Music Shop" broadcasts for R. J. Reynolds in 1940.

BENNY GOODMAN AND HIS ORCHESTRA   March 1, 1940, Chicago

Personnel as February 7 Goodman orchestra.

WC 2971 A   CO 35426, CoC 8, PaE R2751, CoCont DC336. **LP:** CO
             KG32822, JOY 6012
             Shake Down The Stars - voc Helen Forrest (arr EdSau)

WC 2972 A   CO 35426, CoC 8, CoAu D02466. **LP:** JAZ 36, JOY 6012
             Be Sure - voc Helen Forrest (arr FH)

WC 2973 A   CO 35445, PaE R2779, SIL 544, **LP:** CO KG32822, JOY
             6012
             Yours Is My Heart Alone - voc Helen Forrest (arr FH)

WC 2974 A   CO 35420. **EP:** CoE SEG7536. **LP:** JAZ 36, JOY 6012
             The Sky Fell Down - voc Helen Forrest (arr FH)

WC 2975 A   CO 35420, CO 39478, **45:** CO 4-39478. **EP:** CoE
             SEG7536. **LP:** JAZ 41, JOY 6014
             It Never Entered My Mind - voc Helen Forrest

WC 2976 A   Co 35543, PaE R2760, CoCont DC341. **LP:** JAZ 42, JOY
             6014
             Once More - voc Helen Forrest (arr Budd Johnson)

The next day, March 2, the band got another two-weeks' vacation. Benny's sciatica (or so it was then diagnosed) had become so painful that he had to go to the mineral springs spa in Hot Springs, Arkansas, for additional treatment.

The band reassembled March 19 to open in the Cocoanut Grove of the Hotel Ambassador in Los Angeles. Les Robinson, as, replaced Estes; and Christian replaced Covey on guitar in the band, on some broadcasts.

SUSTAINING BROADCAST   *March 19, 1940, Cocoanut*
  NBC Radio Network   *Grove, Los Angeles*

Orchestra as March 1, except LES ROBINSON, as, replaces Estes, and Charlie Christian likely shares guitar work with Covey. SEXTET: BG, Hampton, Guarnieri, Christian, Bernstein, Fatool.

Gone With "What" Wind - SEXTET (LP: SPJ 6602, WI 196)
Blue Skies

SUSTAINING BROADCAST   *March 20, 1940, Cocoanut*
  Unknown network   *Grove, Los Angeles*

Personnel as March 19.

Memories Of You - SEXTET

SUSTAINING BROADCAST   *March 23, 1940, Cocoanut*
  NBC Radio Network   *Grove, Los Angeles*

Personnel as March 19.

Smiles (n/c - intro excised)
Good-Bye (theme)

SUSTAINING BROADCAST   *March 30, 1940, Cocoanut*
  NBC Radio Network   *Grove, Los Angeles*

Personnel as March 19.

Big John Special (n/c - intro excised)

SUSTAINING BROADCAST   *March/April 1940, Cocoanut*
  Unknown network   *Grove, Los Angeles*

Personnel as March 19.

I've Found A New Baby
Make With The Kisses (n/c - intro only)

SUSTAINING BROADCAST   *April 6, 1940, Cocoanut*
  ABC Radio Network   *Grove, Los Angeles*

Personnels as March 19.

Shake Down The Stars - voc Helen Forrest
Gone With "What" Wind - SEXTET (LP: JAA 23, MU 30JA5181)

BENNY GOODMAN AND HIS ORCHESTRA   April 10, 1940, Los Angeles

Personnel as March 19.

WCO 26714-A   CO 35472. **LP:** JAZ 41, JOY 6014
               Buds Won't Bud - voc Helen Forrest (arr FH)

WCO 26715-A   CO 35461. **LP:** JAZ 41, JOY 6014
               Devil May Care - voc Helen Forrest (arr Ralph
               Hallenbeck)

WCO 26716-A   CO 35472. **LP:** CO KG32822, CO alb P5-15536, JOY
               6014
               I'm Nobody's Baby - voc Helen Forrest (arr FH)

WCO 26717-A   CO 35527, PaE R2767, CoC 24, CoCont DC343, CO
               37513. **EP:** CO 5-1653 (Set B351). **LP:** CO CL534
               Cocoanut Grove (arr EdSau)

BENNY GOODMAN SEXTET   same date

Personnel as March 19.

WCO 26718-A   CO 35466, PaE R2733, CoArg 291222, CoAu D02400,
               CoCont DC338, SIL 545. **EP:** CoE SEGC11. **LP:**
               PhilCont B07907R, Co alb P5-15536, CBS 62581,
               SONY SOPZ4-6, JAZ 41
               The Sheik

WCO 26719-A   CO 35466, CO 36722, PaE R2733, CoArg 291222, CoAu
               D02400, CoBr 30-1344, CoC 6201, CoCont DC338,
               CoJap M204, SIL 545. **EP:** CoE SEGC11, FONT
               TFE17079, FONT 462065TE. **LP:** CO CL541, CBS
               52538, SONY SOPZ4-6, BID 1011
               Poor Butterfly

SUSTAINING BROADCAST　　　　　　　*April 12, 1940, Cocoanut*
　NBC Radio Network　　　　　　　　　*Grove, Los Angeles*

Personnels as March 19.

Minnie The Moocher's Wedding Day
Too Romantic - voc Helen Forrest (arr EdSau)
Cocoanut Grove
Sometimes I'm Happy
The Sheik (Of Araby) - SEXTET (LP: JAA 23, MU 30JA5181, JM (no #),
　GOJ 1005)
Roll 'Em (LP: JM (no #)
Good-Bye (theme)

SUSTAINING BROADCAST　　　　　　　*April 13, 1940, Cocoanut*
　NBC Radio Network　　　　　　　　　*Grove, Los Angeles*

Personnel as March 19.

In The Mood (arr FH) (LP: FT 1513, BIL 127.034, ON 1513)
Good-Bye (theme)

Probably in mid-April, Arnold Covey left; George Rose, whose place Covey had taken a year earlier, returned. But Charlie Christian now records with the band as well as with the Sextet, and likely plays for all the broadcasts.

BENNY GOODMAN AND HIS ORCHESTRA　　April 16, 1940, Los Angeles

Personnel as March 19; Christian on g.

WCO 26739-A	**LP:** PHON 7610
	I Can't Love You Any More - voc Helen Forrest (arr FH)
WCO 26740-A	CO 35527, PaE R2767, CoC 24, CoCont DC343. **EP:** CO 5-1655 (Set B351). **45:** CO 4-8-G (set G4-3). **LP:** CO GL501, CO CL534, Co alb P6-14954, CoE 33SX1038
	The Hour Of Parting (arr EdSau)
WCO 26741-A	CO 35461. **LP:** JAZ 41, JOY 6014
	Ev'ry Sunday Afternoon - voc Helen Forrest (arr FH)
WCO 26742-B	CO 35497, CoE DB2463, CoG DW5225, Colt CQ1875, CoJap M159, CoNor GNS5099. **45:** CO Set G4-20. **EP:** CO Set B357, PHIL BBE12104, PhilCont 429175BE. **LP:** CO GL524, CorAu KLP682, PHIL BBR8071, PhilCont B07011L, PhilCont B07664R, PhilCont B07797R, CBSSd JGL524
	Crazy Rhythm (arr FH)

(A vinyl test pressing of WCO 26742 is falsely inscribed, take "A". It was pressed when CO GL524 was being assembled and was then misidentified. No true take A has been found.)

BENNY GOODMAN SEXTET　　　　　　　　　same date

Personnel as March 19.

WCO 26743-B	CO 35482, PaE R2757, CoArg 291224, CoCont DC340, Colt 2971, CoJap M160. **EP:** CoE SEGC10. **LP:** CBS 62581, SONY SOPZ4-6, JAZ 41
	I Surrender, Dear

(Some copies of CO 35482 were issued with an indicated take "A." There is no musical difference between their cuts of "I Surrender, Dear" and the true take "B.")

WCO 26744-B	CO 35482, CO 36722, PaE R2757, CoArg 291224, CoAu D03134, CoC 6201, CoCont DC340, CoJap M137, CoJap JX1128, CoSd DS1317. **EP:** CoE SEGC10, CorAu KEP032. **LP:** FONT TFL5067, FontCont 682047TL, CO G30779, CBS 62581, CBS 67233, SONY SOPZ4-6. **ET:** AFRS P-785
	Boy Meets Goy (Grand Slam) (Boy Meets Girl)

("Boy Meets Goy" is the title used for the original issue of mx WCO 26744; later releases are titled, "Grand Slam" and "Boy Meets Girl." //A vinyl test pressing of WCO 26744 is falsely inscribed, take "A". No true take A has been found.)

The next air check has been reassigned from an earlier-posited date of "October-December 1939"; it is from the current period, possibly from a broadcast of April 26. A reputed air check of "Busy As A Bee" from the Cocoanut Grove has not been confirmed, and is omitted.

SUSTAINING BROADCAST　　　　*poss. April 26, 1940, Cocoanut*
　Unknown network　　　　　　　　　*Grove, Los Angeles*

Personnel as March 19.

The Sheik (Of Araby) - SEXTET (n/c)

SUSTAINING BROADCAST　　　　　　*April 27, 1940, Cocoanut*
　NBC Radio Network　　　　　　　　　*Grove, Los Angeles*

Personnels as March 19; Christian on band g.

Poor Butterfly - SEXTET
It Never Entered My Mind - voc Helen Forrest
Big John Special - segue to,
Good-Bye (theme)

On May 1 Benny performed the Mozart concerto in the Hollywood Bowl, Leopold Stokowski conducting. Using a format he will repeat many times in future, Benny featured the band and Sextet in the second half of a classical/jazz concert. The West Coast press acclaimed the evening a "phenomenal success."

The next studio session is highly unusual from several standpoints: It marks Benny's only extant collaboration with debonair Fred Astaire, who not only sings but also tap dances on a Goodman recording. The 78 release of Astaire's sides places his name above Benny's on its labels, an extraordinary concession. Lionel plays vibes with the orchestra on one cut, an addition Benny frequently made during performances and broadcasts, but rarely on record. The matrix for a (contemporaneously) unissued side recorded but a few weeks earlier is not carried forward; a new matrix is used. And a new arranger, Dudley Brooks (DB), contributes a chart; he'll soon join as pianist.

Twenty-odd years later when the original Quartet gathered in RCA's studios for their "Together Again!" reunion, there was general agreement that they should record some "new" tunes. Early on, Benny suggested, "Who Cares?". Turning to the author, Benny said, "I never recorded that, did I, Russ?" I reminded him of the Astaire side. He was silent for a moment, then growled, "That one don't count." So they cut it.

FRED ASTAIRE WITH　　　　　　　　May 9, 1940, Los Angeles
　BENNY GOODMAN AND ORCHESTRA (1)
BENNY GOODMAN AND HIS ORCHESTRA (2)
FRED ASTAIRE WITH BENNY GOODMAN AND HIS SEXTET (3)

Personnel as March 19; Christian on g. Add Lionel Hampton, vib, mx WCO 26809. FRED ASTAIRE, voc; DUDLEY BROOKS (DB), arr.

WCO 26807-A (1)	CO 35517, CoE DB1943, **LP:** NOST 890/1, CO 20164, CBS 66316
	Who Cares (So Long As You Care For Me) - voc Fred Astaire (arr EdSau)
WCO 26808-A (2)	CO 35487, CoC 7. **LP:** CO KG32822, JOY 6014
	The Moon Won't Talk - voc Helen Forrest (arr EdSau)
WCO 26809-A (3)	CO 35517, CoE DB1943, CoJap M556. **LP:** NOST 890/1, CBS 66316
	Just Like Taking Candy From A Baby - voc & tap dancing, Fred Astaire (arr FH)
WCO 26810-A (2)	CO 35497, CoBr 50482. **LP:** CO KG32822, JOY 6014
	Mister Meadowlark - voc Helen Forrest (arr DB)
WCO 26811-A (2)	CO 35487, CoC 7. **LP:** JAZ 42, JOY 6014
	I Can't Love You Any More (Any More Than I Do) - voc Helen Forrest (arr FH)

Benny and Joseph Szigeti had commissioned Bela Bartok to compose a work for violin, clarinet and piano. In a sense it was an act of charity, for Bartok had fallen on hard times, and both Goodman and Szigeti wanted to encourage and sustain him. They were nonplussed when they saw the intricate and difficult work for the first time—"Looked like fly specks all over the sheets," Benny recalls. But they persevered and gave it its premier performance in Columbia's studios:

BELA BARTOK,   May 13, 1940, Los Angeles
JOSEPH SZIGETI, BENNY GOODMAN

Benny Goodman, clt; Joseph Szigeti, v; Bela Bartok, p.

WXCO 26819-A   CO 70362-D (Set X-178), CO 70666-D (Set MX-178),
                CoAu LOX485, CoFr 264681, ReSp M10015. **LP:** CO
                ML2213, ODY 32160220
                Contrasts For Violin, Clarinet and Piano
                I - Verbunkos (Recruiting Dance) (Beginning)

WXCO 26820-A   same issues, except substitute CO 70667-D for CO
                70666-D
                Contrasts for Violin, Clarinet and Piano
                I - Verbunkos (Recruiting Dance) (Conclusion)
                II - Piheno (Relaxation) (Beginning)

WXCO 26821-A   CO 70363-D (Set X-178), CO 70667-D (Set MX-178),
                CoAu LOX 486, CoFr 264682, ReSp M10016. **LP:** CO
                ML2213, ODY 32160220
                Contrasts for Violin, Clarinet and Piano
                II - Piheno (Relaxation) (Conclusion)
                III - Sebes (Fast Dance) (Beginning)

WXCO 26822-C   same issues except CO 70666-D for CO 70667-D
                Contrasts For Violin, Clarinet and Piano
                III - Sebes (Fast Dance) (Conclusion)

(Separation of the movements applies only to the 78 rpm issues, not the LP's. Despite claims to the contrary, no alternate takes of these matrices have been discovered.)

The next engagement was in the Peacock Court of the Mark Hopkins Hotel in San Francisco, from which we have two broadcasts via the Don Lee-Mutual network:

SUSTAINING BROADCAST   *May 28, 1940, Mark*
  Don Lee-MUTUAL Radio Network   *Hopkins, San Francisco*

Personnels as March 19 (Christian, band g.)

Let's Dance (theme)
Big John Special
The Hour of Parting
Seven Come Eleven - SEXTET
Where Do I Go From You? - voc Helen Forrest
Good-Bye (theme)

(Broadcast on LP: AC 16; GOL 15077 (sans "Good-Bye"))

SUSTAINING BROADCAST   *June 4, 1940, Mark*
  Don Lee-MUTUAL Radio Network   *Hopkins, San Francisco*

Personnels as March 19 (Christian, band g.)

Let's Dance (theme)
Board Meeting
Where Do I Go From You? - voc Helen Forrest
Six Appeal - SEXTET
Star Dust
Good-Bye (theme)

(Broadcast on LP: AC 16; GOL 15077 (sans "Let's Dance," "Where Do I Go From You?"))

St. Catherine's Hotel on Catalina Island was the band's next stop, beginning June 5. Sam Donahue sat in on tenor sax for a few days, but he does not record with the band, nor is he aurally identifiable on the few extant air checks from that location. Apparently Johnny Guarnieri remained with the band (he will shortly join Artie Shaw), but for an unknown reason Dudley Brooks replaced him for the next Sextet session:

BENNY GOODMAN SEXTET   June 20, 1940, Los Angeles

Personnel as March 19, except DUDLEY BROOKS, p, replaces Guarnieri.

WCO 26940-A   Co 35553, CoArg 291293, CoArg 291750, PaAu A7433,
               PaE R2770, Palt B71235, OdG 026922, BIA 260B. **LP:**
               CO CL652, CorAu KLP510, Palt PMDQ8013, PHIL
               BBL7172, PhilCont B07247L, PhilCont B07907R, CO
               G30779, CBS 52538, CBS 62387, CBS 67233, SONY
               SOPZ4-6, SONY SOPM155, SONY 20AP-1456
               Six Appeal (originally titled, "My Daddy Rocks Me")

WCO 26941-A   CO 35553, CoArg 291293, CoArg 291763, CoC 912,
               CoJap M205, PaE R2770, Palt B71235, OdG 026922,
               CO 37512. **EP:** FontCont 462012TE. **LP:** CO alb
               P5-15536, CBS 52538, SONY SOPZ4-6, JAZ 42
               These Foolish Things

WCO 26942   **LP:** CO G30779, CBS 67233, SONY SOPZ4-6
               Good Enough To Keep

SUSTAINING BROADCAST   *June 22, 1940, St. Catharine's*
  Unknown network   *Hotel, Catalina, California*

Personnel as March 19, except probably Brooks on p.

Honeysuckle Rose - SEXTET (n/c)
Six Appeal - SEXTET (n/c) (LP: JAA 23, MU 30JA5181)

The next two orchestra sides are reassigned from a date previously believed to have been "October-December 1939":

SUSTAINING BROADCAST   *June 30, 1940, St. Catharine's*
  NBC Radio Network   *Hotel, Catalina, California*

Personnel as March 19/June 22 (pianist uncertain).
Wrappin' It Up
Devil May Care - voc Helen Forrest (n/c)

In all probability, the next cut is also from the June 30 broadcast, preceding. The program log for that broadcast lists, "Dear Old Southland" as by the Sextet. Clearly, the air check is, "AC-DC Current." But immediately following the performance, an announcer mistakenly identifies the tune as having been . . . "Dear Old Southland."

SUSTAINING BROADCAST   *June 30, 1940, St. Catharine's*
  NBC Radio Network   *Hotel, Catalina, California*

Personnel as March 19/June 22 (pianist uncertain).

AC-DC Current - SEXTET (LP: JAA 23, MU 30JA5181)

It is not known whether Guarnieri returned especially for the next studio session, or whether he and Brooks had been swapping performances during the gig at St. Catharine's. In either event he does leave Goodman's employ at this time to go with Artie Shaw for some six or seven months, but he will be back.

BENNY GOODMAN AND HIS ORCHESTRA   July 3, 1940, Los Angeles

Personnel as March 19 (Guarnieri returned for this studio session).

WCO 26980-A   CO 35574, CoC 38. **LP:** JAZ 50, JOY 6014
               I Can't Resist You - voc Helen Forrest (arr EdSau)

WCO 26981-A   same issues, plus **LP:** CO P14302
               Dreaming Out Loud - voc Helen Forrest (arr EdSau)

WCO 26982-A   CO 35594, CoC 50. **LP:** JAZ 50, JOY 6014
               Li'l Boy Love - voc Helen Forrest (arr LH)

WCO 26983-A   **LP:** CO alb P5-15536, PHON 7610
WCO 26983-B   CO 35594, CoC 50. **LP:** JAZ 50
               Nostalgia (Waltz) (arr EdSau)

On July 10 Benny's sciatica became so painful that an immediate operation was deemed necessary; he flew to the Mayo Clinic, Rochester, Minnesota, where surgery was performed July 12. His orchestra finished out the week at the Casino—Kay Kyser conducted—then disbanded. Guarnieri, Vernon Brown, Bus Bassey, Les Robinson, Jerry Jerome and Nick Fatool went over to Artie Shaw who, since his return to the band business, had been using studio men primarily to make records. Ziggy Elman, Jimmy Maxwell, Charlie Christian, Art Bernstein and Lionel Hampton—all of whom Benny considered key performers—stayed on salary, went back to New York where they jobbed around until the "Old Man" could return to action.

The operation was successful, and August and September found Benny recuperating. But Ziggy tired of the relative inactivity, and late in August succumbed to Tommy Dorsey's blandishments and joined TD's crew. In October Lionel got the urge to form his own band; as in Harry James's case, the Hamp got Benny's OK, financial help, and advice.

Benny got back into harness in October: on October 18, the big band played a prom date for Washington & Lee University; on the 25th, a prom for Lehigh University; and on the 27th, it was in the Arena in New Haven, Conn. He gigged in and around New York, with both a small group and a big band. Instrumentalists were shuffled in and out, as Benny sought the best men available. Some of the more noteworthy of his sidemen in October were: Jimmy Maxwell, Irving Goodman, tpt; Lou McGarity, tbn, who joined for the first time October 25; Skippy Martin, Gus Bivona, as; Sam Donahue, ts; Teddy Wilson, Bernie Leighton, p; Charlie Christian, g; Art Bernstein, b; Dave Tough, Harry Jaeger, d.

For some time Benny had admired the "growl" trumpet work of one of Duke Ellington's men, "Cootie" Williams. With the Duke's assent, Benny talked to Cootie, offered him a one-year contract. Williams agreed to it, and left the Duke to join Benny "officially" on November 6.

On October 28 Benny went to Columbia's New York studios to rehearse a new seven-man "sextet," and acetates of at least a portion of this rehearsal were cut. Years later they were discovered by a collector—along with other Columbia-recorded Goodman material—in the discard pile of a used-goods store in lower Manhattan. He was secretive about their contents, and this led to an inaccurate detailing of their particulars in an earlier work by the author. Eventually the owner sold the rights to tape them to an independent record producer, who then released them on LP.

The acetates are marked "10-28-40," followed by an inscription that appears to be, "NG (possibly, "BG") date." No other information is on them—no notice of matrices, takes, tune titles, personnel. The first cut does not include Benny, and so is not listed below; it is titled by the producer, "Ad Lib Blues," and evidently was a warm-up for the sidemen and the engineers. Two cuts are derivatives of "Dickie's Dream," and these are retitled by the producer, "Charlie's Dream" and "Lester's Dream," for obvious reasons. The other two tunes bear their normal titles.

Benny has little recollection of this studio session. A few days earlier (October 24) he and Charlie had sat in with Count Basie's orchestra, then the headline attraction at the Apollo Theater. Likely that had influenced him to record with some of the Count's men. But for what purpose, he now has no idea.

In any event, a star-studded new beginning in the studios for Benny, after an absence of almost four months:

BENNY GOODMAN SEPTET
October 28, 1940, New York

Benny Goodman, clt; Buck Clayton, tpt; Lester Young, ts; Count Basie, p; Charlie Christian, g; Walter Page, b; Jo Jones, d.

-0-   **LP:** JAA 6
"Charlie's Dream"

-0-   **LP:** JAA 6, **EP:** PHON XM-EPH81
I Never Knew

-0-   **LP:** JAA 6
"Lester's Dream"

-0-   **LP:** JAA 6
Wholly Cats

(Second-generation - unauthorized transfers from the JAA LP - cuts are on **LP:** JD 7997.)

Continuing his association with the Count, Benny appeared at a Democratic presidential campaign rally in Madison Square Garden, in support of the reelection of President Roosevelt:

"DEMOCRATIC RALLY"   *November 4, 1940, New York*
ABC-NBC-MUTUAL, independent radio networks

Benny Goodman, clt; Count Basie, p; Charlie Christian, g; Walter Page, b; Jo Jones, c.

Gone With "What" Wind (LP: BEP 14800, FAN 19-119, QD 16)

Cootie Williams's contract with Benny began November 6, and the next day the new "Sextet" recorded for the first time. Discovery of the "junk pile" acetates mentioned above adds to what was previously known about this session, but it is a mixed blessing: their releases on a JAA LP are splices of various performances, and they require a cumbersome and lengthy explanation.

BENNY GOODMAN AND HIS SEXTET FEATURING COUNT BASIE
November 7, 1940, New York

Benny Goodman, clt; Cootie Williams, tpt; George Auld, ts; Count Basie, p; Charlie Christian, g; Art Bernstein, b; Harry Jaeger, d.

CO 29027	**LP:** JAA 6
CO 29027	**LP:** CO G30779, CBS 67233, SONY SOPZ4-6
CO 29027	**LP:** CO G30779, CBS 67233, SONY SOPZ4-6, Co alb CG33566, CBS 88225
CO 29027-bkdn	UNISSUED - Tape
CO 29027-1	CO 35810, VD 880 A, CoArg 291182, CoAu D02650, CoJap M452, CoSd 1539, PaE R2787, Palt B71190, PaSw PZ11250. **EP:** PHIL BBE 12272. **LP:** CO CL652, CorAu KLP510, Palt PMDQ8013, PHIL BBL7172, PhilCont B07247L, PhilCont B07907R, CBS 52538, CBS 62387, SONY SOPZ4-6, SONY SOPM155, SONY 20AP-1456
CO 29027-2	CO 35810. **LP:** TL STLJ05

Wholly Cats

CO 29028	**LP:** JAA 6
CO 29028	**LP:** CO G30779, CBS 67233, SONY SOPZ4-6
CO 29028-1	CO 35810, CoArg 291182, CoJap M453, CoSd 1539, PaE R2787, Palt B71190, PaSw PZ11250. **LP:** CO CB-20, CO KL5142, Palt PMDQ8013, CBS 62581, SONY SOPZ4-6

Royal Garden Blues

CO 29029-1	CO 35901, CO 36723, VD 714 B, CoArg 291282, CoC 190, CoC 6202, CoH DCH301, CoJap M204, PaAu A7433, PaE R2961, PaSw PZ11249. **45:** CO 4-13-G Set G4-2). **EP:** CO 5-1652 (Set B350), CoFr ESDF1025. **LP:** CO CB-20, CO GL500, CO G30779, Co alb P4M-5678, CoE 33SX1035, CoFr FPX112, CoJap PL5004, PHIL BBL7178, PhilCont B07225L, ReSp 33LS1009, CorAu KLP675, CBS 62581, CBS 67233, SONY SOPZ4-6, SONY SOPM-162, TL STLJ05, SB 144, RTB LPV4316. **ET:** VOA World Of Jazz 1

As Long As I Live

CO 29030-S(a)	**LP:** JAA 6 (splice - a, b - see notes)
CO 29030-S(b)	**LP:** JAA 6 (splice - b, a - see notes)
CO 29030-S(c)	**LP:** JAA 6 (splice - c, d - see notes)
CO 29030	UNISSUED - Tape
CO 29030-S(d)	**LP:** JAA 6 (splice - d, c - see notes)
CO 29030	UNISSUED - Tape
CO 29030-1	Co 35901, VD 714 B, CoArg 291282, CoAu D02650, CoC 190, CoC 6202, CoJap M191, BIA 240A. **45, EP, LP:** same issues as CO 29029-1, except **omit** CO alb P4M-5678, TL STLJ05; and **add EP,** CoJap EM45. **ET:** Air Force GL-15

Benny's Bugle

(NOTES: Track "(a)" is a lengthy rehearsal, consisting of individual practice, some 10 group rehearsals of the introduction to "Benny's Bugle," and miscellaneous rehearsal of the middle portion of the tune. The **2nd** intro becomes the first half of JAA 6 - Side 2, Track 1; it is spliced to the latter portion of "(b)," which is the first complete rendition of the tune.

Track "(c)" is the second complete rendition. Its first portion, through Christian's first chorus, is the first half of JAA 6 - Side 2, Track 4; it is spliced to the second portion "(d)," which is the third complete rendition. Unlettered listings above are miscellaneous rehearsals between full renditions. //Portions of the material on JAA 6 were dubbed onto **LP:** JD 7997.)

Within a week Benny assembled his new big band in the same Columbia studios to record its first sides. Note that Fletcher Henderson, who continued as staff arranger for the band but who would not play piano for it regularly, nevertheless sits in to record his own composition. "Notes To You," now retitled, "Henderson Stomp." Also, Cootie Williams for some reason does not take part in Benny's first 12″ jazz side for Columbia, "The Man I Love." Even without Cootie, the trumpet section is potent, with Alec Fila (in from Bob Chester's band - remember "Octave Jump"?) joining Jimmy Maxwell and brother Irving.

The session also introduces Lou McGarity, possibly Benny's best trombonist ever, Jack Teagarden excepted; and Georgie Auld, one of the better tenor men to play for Goodman over the years. Auld, who had been with both the Berigan and Shaw bands, and who just before joining Benny had been jobbing with Teddy Wilson, took great pride in his work. He **swung,** he was a schooled musician (on occasions when Shaw was ill, Auld led that band), and unfortunately his work is today largely overlooked.

BENNY GOODMAN AND HIS ORCHESTRA　　　　November 13, 1940, New York

Benny Goodman, clt; Alec Fila, Jimmy Maxwell, Cootie Williams, Irving Goodman, tpt; Lou McGarity, Red Gingler, tbn; Skip Martin, Gus Bivona, Bob Snyder, as; George Auld, Jack Henderson, ts; Bernie Leighton (sometimes, Layton), p; Mike Bryan, g; Art Bernstein, b; Harry Jaeger (sometimes, Yaeger- and married to Helen Forrest), d; Helen Forrest, voc.

CO 29062-1	CO 35820, CoArg 291289, CoAu D02241, CoC 157, SIL 544, PaE R2794, PaInd DPE17. **LP:** CO KG32822, JOY 6014
CO 29062	**LP:** PHON 7610
CO 29062	**LP:** BID 1009
CO 29062-bkdn	UNISSUED - Tape
CO 29062	UNISSUED - Tape
	Nobody - voc Helen Forrest (arr EdSau)

Williams, tpt, out

XCO 29063-2	CO 55001, CO 55038, CoC 25011. **45:** CO 4-9-G (Set G4-3). **EP:** CO 5-1654 (Set B351). **LP:** CO GL501, CO CL534, CoE 33SX1038, FR series, CO PM16932, JOY 6014
XCO 29063-bkdn	UNISSUED - Tape
XCO 29063-1	CO 55001, CoArg 264015, CoAu DOX681, CoJap SW282, PaE E11450. **LP:** JAZ 50
XCO 29063	**LP:** PHON 7610
	The Man I Love - voc Helen Forrest (arr EdSau)

Williams returns; Henderson, p, replaces Leighton

CO 29064	**LP:** PHON 7610
CO 29064	UNISSUED - Tape
CO 29064	UNISSUED - Tape
CO 29064-1	CO 35820, CoArg 291290, CoC 157, PaE R2794, PaInd DPE17. **LP:** CO CB-4, CO CB-20, PhilCont B07670R, JAZ 42, FR series. **ET:** AFRS American Popular Music Nos. 39, 60, 93, AFRS Downbeat 348
CO 29064	**LP:** BID 1009
CO 29064-S	**45:** CO Set G4-20. **EP:** CO Set B357. **LP:** CO GL524, CBSSd JGL524, CorAu KLP682, PhilCont B07011L, PhilCont B07797R (spliced in part from cut on BID 1009, immediately preceding)
	Henderson Stomp (arr FH)

Leighton returns, replacing Henderson

XCO 29065	**LP:** BID 1009
XCO 29065-bkdn	UNISSUED - Tape
XCO 29065-1	CO 55001, CoArg 264009, CoAu DOX681, PaE E11450. **45:** CO 4-10-G (Set G4-3). **LP:** CO GL501, CO CL2126, CO CL2483, CO CS8926, CO CS9283, CoE 33SX1038, CO KG31547, CO alb P4M-5678, FR series, CBS 52368, CBS 67268, SONY SOPL-193. **ET:** Air Force GL-15
XCO 29065-2	**LP:** PHON 7610, TL STLJ05
	Benny Rides Again (arr EdSau)

On November 17 Benny performed another combined classical/jazz concert, this time with the Rochester (New York) Philharmonic Orchestra and his band. The next day he repeated a benefit performance for Local 802's medical fund that he'd done a year earlier:

"LOCAL 802 MEDICAL FUND BENEFIT"　　　November 18, 1940, Manhattan Center, New York
Unknown network

Personnel as November 13.

Don't Be That Way (n/c - excerpt only)
The Man I Love - voc Helen Forrest

The new "Sextet," Count Basie included, is heard for the first time on radio via Martin Block's program:

"THE MAKE BELIEVE BALLROOM" WNEW Radio　　November 19, 1940, New York

Personnel as November 7.

Benny's Bugle (LP: JAA 23, SPJ 6602)
Wholly Cats (LP: JAA 23, MU 30JA5181)
Honeysuckle Rose (LP: JAA 23, MU 30JA5181)

Robert Dewees "Cutty" Cutshall, who'd been with Jan Savitt's band, replaced Red Gingler before the next studio session, and for the next year and a half (until Cutty's induction into the U.S. Army) Benny will have his finest two-man, jazz-oriented trombone team ever. Lou McGarity's excellence is generally acknowledged, and deservedly so, but Cutty's work is relatively overlooked. Both played similar gutty, tailgate trombone, so much alike that it is often difficult to distinguish one from the other. A good man for Goodman, Cutty Cutshall.

BENNY GOODMAN AND HIS ORCHESTRA　　　　November 29, 1940, New York

Personnel as November 13, except CUTTY CUTSHALL, tbn, replaces Gingler.

CO 29177-1	CO 35869, PaAu A7502, CoC 703. **LP:** CO alb P5-15536, JOY 6016, RLM 8065
CO 29177-2	**LP:** CO KG32822, Coalb P6-14954, CO 6P6465
	Taking A Chance On Love - voc Helen Forrest (arr FH)
CO 29178-1	**LP:** PHON 7610
CO 29178-2	CO 35869, PaAu A7502, CoC 703. **LP:** CO KG32822, JOY 6016
	Cabin In The Sky - voc Helen Forrest (arr FH)
CO 29179-bkdn	UNISSUED - Tape
CO 29179-	**LP:** PHON 7612
CO 29179-1	**LP:** CO GL 524, CorAu KLP682, PhilCont B07011L, PhilCont B07797R, CBSSd JGL524. **45:** CO Set G4-20. **EP:** CO Set B357, PHIL BBE12048, PhilCont 429113BE
CO 29179-2	CO 35863, CoArg 291234, CoArg 291759, CoC 178. **LP:** JAZ 50
	Frenesi (arr FH)
CO 29180-1	CO 35863, CoArg 291289, CoC 178. **LP:** CO KG32822, JOY 6016
CO 29180-2	**LP:** PHON 7612
	Hard To Get - voc Helen Forrest (arr EdSau)

The author has been unable to verify the continued existence of an acetate containing a portion of a CBS "We The People" broadcast of December 10, including a partial rendition of "Flying Home" by the Septet, and conversation between Benny and the program's commentator, Deems Taylor. It was reliably reported as extant at one time, but its present status is unknown.

Benny returned to Carnegie Hall December 12 and 13 to perform Debussy's "First Rhapsody For Clarinet" and Mozart's "Concerto In D Major" with the Philharmonic-Symphony Orchestra of New York, John Barbirolli conducting.

An acetate bearing a date of December 12 has Benny on an NBC "Symphony Hour" broadcast, performing the third movement of Mozart's "Concerto For Clarinet And Orchestra In A." Efforts to verify the accuracy of the notations on the disc have been unavailing; but there is no evidence to the contrary, so:

"NBC SYMPHONY ORCHESTRA"   *December 12, 1940, New York*
  NBC Radio Network

Benny Goodman clt, and the Philharmonic Symphony Orchestra of New York, John Barbirolli conducting.

Third Movement, Concerto For Clarinet And Orchestra, In A, K.632 (Mozart)

On the 16th, Benny recorded the Debussy opus for Columbia, and it was released on a 12" 78. Portions of a rehearsal in the studio prior to the recording have been obtained by collectors, and are in circulation via tape. So far, so good.

Columbia's master list of matrices to which the author had access, however, fails to include matrices applicable to his very first recording of the Mozart Concerto In A. Benny has a tape of the recording, but it does not reveal which matrices were used for the three movements of the work. Thus they are bracketed here to show the recording in its entirety.

BENNY GOODMAN (CLARINET) and the   **December 16, 1940, New York**
PHILHARMONIC-SYMPHONY
ORCHESTRA OF NEW YORK, John Barbirolli, Conductor

Benny Goodman, clt, and the Philharmonic-Symphony Orchestra of New York, John Barbirolli, conducting.

XCO 29448- through XCO 29455	UNISSUED **Concerto For Clarinet And Orchestra, In A, K.622 (Mozart)** **First Movement: Allegro** **Second Movement: Adagio** **Third Movement: Rondo: Allegro**
-0- XCO 29461-1	UNISSUED (Rehearsal) - Tape CO 11517-D, CoAu LOX521. **ET:** 1955 Heart Fund (n/c) **First Rhapsody For Clarinet (Beginning)**
-0- XCO 29462-1	UNISSUED (Rehearsal) - Tape CO 11517-D, CoAu LOX521 **First Rhapsody For Clarinet (Conclusion)**

(Matrices XCO 29456 through XCO 29460 are likely non-Goodman recordings, but their details are not known.)

The author feels strongly that the historical importance of Benny's initial recording of the Mozart Concerto In A warrants its release by Columbia. Efforts to this end are being made by Mr. Goodman; but given the state of the record industry in 1986, early success seems unlikely.

The band had no lengthy engagements at this time; the contemporary music-press reported college proms and other one-nighters, mainly in the eastern U.S.

Cootie Williams is not audibly identifiable on the majority of the orchestra's studio recordings in this period, but in the absence of specific information to the contrary, he is continued in the personnel listings.

BENNY GOODMAN AND HIS   **December 18, 1940, New York**
ORCHESTRA

Personnel as November 29.

CO 29255-1	CO 35910. **LP:** NOST 1004, JOY 6016 **These Things You Left Me** - voc Helen Forrest (prob arr EdSau)
XCO 29256- bkdn	UNISSUED - Tape
XCO 29256(a)	UNISSUED - Tape
XCO 29256-1	CO 55002, VD 299 B, NavyVD 79 B, CoArg 264009. **LP:** SONY SOPL193
XCO 29256-S (a,1)	**LP:** CO GL523, PHIL BBL7043, PhilCont B07010L. **45:** CO 7-1500
XCO 29256	**LP:** CO PG33405 **Superman** (arr EdSau)

(CO GL523 et al's version is a splice of "(a)" - beginning, through passage preceding Auld's solo - and take 1 from that point to conclusion.)

XCO 29257-1	CO 55002, CoArg 264015. **45:** CO 7-1500. **LP:** CO GL523, PHIL BBL7043, PhilCont B07010L, JOY 6016 **More Than You Know** - voc Helen Forrest (arr EdSau)
CO 29258(a)	**LP:** BID 1004
CO 29258-1	**LP:** PHON 7612
CO 29258-2	TEST PRESSING
CO 29258-S (a,1)	**LP:** CO GL523, PHIL BBL7043, PhilCont B07010L, PhilCont B07145L, SONY SOPL193, CO PG33405, FR series **Moonlight On The Ganges** (arr EdSau)

(CO GL523 et al's version is a splice of "(a)" - beginning, through half of Benny's solo - and take 1 from that point to conclusion.)

Ken Kersey replaced Count Basie for the Septet's next studio session; and a plethora of recent discoveries and multiple splicings entail lengthy explanation as accompaniment to his debut with the group. Much simpler is the tale of "Gilly"; recorded here under title of "Gone With What Draft," Benny renamed it in honor of one of his stepdaughters when it was first released on LP on September 7, 1951. His other children, daughters Rachel and Benjie, and stepdaughters Shirley and Sophia, are similarly commemorated on record. In 1975, Benny had all five recordings—"Gilly," "Rachel's Dream," "Benjie's Bubble," "Shirley Steps Out" and "Hi 'Ya, Sophia"—repressed on one LP as a birthday present for his wife and their mother, Alice.

BENNY GOODMAN AND HIS SEXTET   **December 19, 1940, New York**

Personnel as November 7, except KEN KERSEY, p, replaces Basie.

CO 29259	**LP:** JAA 6 (Side 1, Track 7)
CO 29259(a)	**LP:** JAA 6 (Side 2, Track 7)
CO 29259(b)	**LP:** JAA 6 (Side 2, Track 5)
CO 29259-bkdn	**LP:** CBS 62581
CO 29259-bkdn	**LP:** CBS 62581
CO 29259(c)	**LP:** JAA 6 (see explanation)
CO 29259-1	**LP:** CO G30779, SONY SOPZ4-6, CBS 62581, CBS 67233, BID 1004 **Breakfast Feud**

(JAA 6, Side 2, Track 7 uses "(a)" as its base, then splices onto it a chorus by Charlie Christian from "(c)". Similarly, JAA 6, Side 2, Track 5 uses "(b)" as its base, then splices onto it a chorus by Charlie Christian from "(c)". //Takes used for JAA 6, Side 1, Track 7; and for CO G30779 et al are each single, unspliced performances. //Liner notes for BID 1004 are in error; take cited above is on that LP.)

CO 29260	**LP:** JAA 6 (Side 1, Track 6)
CO 29260-bkdn	UNISSUED - Tape
CO 29260	**LP:** JAA 6 (Side 2, Track 2)
CO 29260-1	CO 36755, CoArg 291600, CoE DB3350. **LP:** FONT TFL5067, FontCont 682047TL, CO G30779, SONY SOPZ4-6, CBS 62581, CBS 67233. **ET:** OWI Notes On Jazz 7 **I Can't Give You Anything But Love, Baby**
CO 29261-bkdn	UNISSUED - Tape
CO 29261	**EP:** CoE SEG C11. **LP:** BID 1011
CO 29261-2	CO DJ 29261-2. **LP:** JAA 6 (Side 2, Track 8)
CO 29261-1	CO DJ 29261-1. **45:** CO 4-11-G (Set G4-2). **EP:** CO 5-1562 (Set B350), PhilCont 429446BE. **LP:** CO GL500, CoE 33SX1035, CoFr FPX112, CoJap PL5004, PHIL BBL7178, PhilCont B07225L, CO G30779, CorAu KLP675, CBS 52538, CBS 67233, SONY SOPZ4-6, SONY SOPM-162, RTB LPV4316 **Gilly**

(Note discovery of CO DJ 29261-2 - most unusual, an alternate take on a second copy of a disc jockey release - which causes removal of a "take 2" designation for the CoE EP, as listed in an earlier work.)

BENNY GOODMAN AND HIS   **December 20, 1940, New York**
ORCHESTRA

Personnel as November 29.

CO 29262-bkdn UNISSUED - Tape
CO 29262   **LP:** PHON 7612 (voc. Helen Forrest, chorus)
CO 29262-2   CO 35910. **LP:** JAZ 50, JOY 6016
CO 29262-1   **LP:** CO alb P5-15536
               Yes, My Darling Daughter - voc Helen Forrest (and BG,
                  Williams, chorus)

CO 29274   UNISSUED - Tape
CO 29274   **LP:** BID 1009
CO 29274-1   CO 35916, CoArg 291234, CoArg 291666, CoAu
               D02345, CoC 203. **LP:** JAZ 42, JOY 6016
CO 29274-2   **LP:** PHON 7612
               I'm Always Chasing Rainbows - voc Helen Forrest (arr
                  EdSau)

CO 29275   **LP:** BID 1009
CO 29275   UNISSUED - Tape
CO 29275-1   CO 35916, CoArg 291262, CoAu D02345, CoC 203.
               12"78: AFRS G.I. Jive 141. **45:** CO Set G4-20. **EP:** CO
               Set B357, PHIL BBE12048, PhilCont 429113BE. **LP:**
               CO GL524, CBSSd JGL524, CorAu KLP682, PhilCont
               B07011L, PhilCont B07797R
CO 29275-2   **LP:** PHON 7612
               Somebody Stole My Gal (arr FH)

CO 29276-1   CO 35937, CoC 219, CoSw DZ313. **LP:** JAZ 42, JOY
               6016
               I Left My Heart In Your Hand - voc Helen Forrest

(Matrices CO 29263 through CO 29273 are not Goodman items.)

Origin of the next air check is not known, and the pianist and drummer are uncertain, but believed to be Leighton and Jaeger, respectively:

RADIO BROADCAST   *December 25, 1940 - location unknown*
  Unknown network

Benny Goodman, clt; Cootie Williams, tpt; George Auld, ts; Charlie Christian, g; Art Bernstein, b; poss. Bernie Leighton, p and Harry Jaeger, d.

Wholly Cats - to signoff

The band played a one-nighter at the Sunnybrook Ballroom in Pottstown, Pa., on New Year's Eve, a modest gig for that one evening in all the year when every band in the land is working. Benny's operation in July and the uncertainty of his return to full activity had caused reluctant cancellation of his future bookings. But he's back in business now, and the desirable dates will come.

Likely soon after the first of the new year, two luminaries of earlier Goodman bands returned to the fold - Teddy Wilson and Dave Tough. Both were present for Benny's initial studio session of 1941, along with arranger Margie Gibson (MG), who contributes a chart for the first time, "Let The Door Knob Hitcha," which was first titled, "That's The Girl":

BENNY GOODMAN AND HIS ORCHESTRA   **January 14, 1941, New York**

Personnel as November 29, 1940, except TEDDY WILSON, p, replaces Leighton, and DAVE TOUGH, d, replaces Jaeger. MARGIE GIBSON (MG), arr. Cootie Williams, voc.

CO 29502   **LP:** PHON 7612
CO 29502   **LP:** BID 1009
CO 29502-1   CO 35962, CoArg 291276, CoC 243, CoSd DS1454,
               CoSw DZ 313. **LP:** CO alb P5-15536, JAZ 50
               Let The Door Knob Hitcha - voc Cootie Williams (arr
                  MG)

CO 29503   **LP:** PHON 7612
CO 29503   **LP:** BID 1009
CO 29503-1   CO 35937, CoC 291, CoSw DZ313, SIL 572, PaE R2802,
               Palnd DPE18. **LP:** JAZ 42, JOY 6016
               I Hear A Rhapsody - voc Helen Forrest (arr EdSau)

CO 29504   **LP:** CO KG32822
CO 29504-1   CO 36002, CoArg 291276, CoC 265, CO 36680, CoC
               715. **LP:** JOY 6016
               It's Always You - voc Helen Forrest (arr EdSau)

CO 29505   **LP:** PHON 7612
CO 29505   **LP:** BID 1009
CO 29505-1   CO 35992, CoC 257. **LP:** JAZ 50, JOY 6016
               Corn Silk - voc Helen Forrest (arr EdSau)

CO 29507   **LP:** BID 1009
CO 29507   **LP:** PHON 7612
CO 29507-1   CO 35977, CoC 250. **LP:** JAZ 51, JOY 6016
               Birds Of A Feather - voc Helen Forrest (arr FH)

(Matrices CO 29505 and CO 29507 are consecutive.)

Despite the fact that Wilson and Tough are now back with Benny, Basie and his drummer, Jo Jones, are on the next Septet sides. The author has no explanation for this substitution, for certainly both Teddy and Dave were more than competent in small group work.

Even more difficult to explain is the multiple splicing that occurs in a reprise of "Breakfast Feud." The several interpolations of soli by Charlie Christian suggest the possibility that as many as six takes may have been the sources from which the two sets of LP releases have been comprised. The base material has not been available to the author as of this writing (1986), and further effort to sort out this matrix will be made.

BENNY GOODMAN AND HIS   **January 15, 1941, New York**
SEXTET FEATURING COUNT BASIE

Personnel as November 7, 1940. except JO JONES, d, replaces Jaeger.

CO 29512-1   **LP:** PHON 7612, BID 1006
CO 29512-2   CO 36039, CoArg 291223, BIA 240. **45:** CO 4-12-G (Set
               G4-2). **EP:** CO 5-1652 (Set B350), PHIL BBE12189,
               PhilCont 429410BE. **LP:** CO GL500, CoE 33SX1035,
               CoFr FPX112, CoJap PL5004, PHIL BBL7178, PhilCont
               B07225L, CorAu KLP675, SONY SOPZ4-6, SONY
               SOPM-155, SONY 20AP-1456, RTB LPV4316, TL
               STLJ22. **ET:** Air Force GL-15
CO 29512-S(a) **LP:** CO CL652, CorAu KLP510, PHIL BBL7172, PhilCont
               B07247L, CBS 62387, SONY SOPZ4-6, SONY
               SOPM-162. **EP:** CO Set B504
CO 29512-S(b) **LP:** CO G30779, CBS 67233
               Breakfast Feud

(CO CL652 et al - "(a)" above: Intro through Christian's **1st** solo is excerpted from a take different from takes 1 & 2. Christian's **2nd** solo is excerpted from a take different from takes 1 & 2. Auld's solo and the rideout are from a take different from takes 1 & 2. This combination opens up a possibility of four unnumbered takes from this session. CO G30779 et al - "(b)" above: Intro through Christian's **1st** solo is different from takes 1 & 2, and the take or takes used for CO CL652 et al, "(a)". Christian's **2nd** and **3rd** soli are the **same** as his 1st and 2nd soli on CO CL652 et al. Christian's **4th** solo and Auld's solo and the rideout are excerpted from CO 29512-1.)

CO 29513-1   CO 35938, CoArg 291261, CoJap M454, PaAu A7423,
               PaE R2798, Palnd DPE12, VD 55 B, CO 37513. **45:**
               CO 4-14-G (Set G4-2). **EP:** CO 5-1650 (Set B350). **LP:**
               CO GL500, CoE 33SX1035, CoFr FPX112, CoJap
               PL5004, ReSp 33LS1009, PHIL BBL7178, PhilCont
               B07183L, PhilCont B07225L, CO G30779, CO alb
               P4M-5678, CorAu KLP675, CBS 62581, CBS 67233,
               SONY SOPZ4-6, SONY SOPM-162
               On The Alamo

CO 29514-1   CO 36029, CoArg 291223, CoArg 291763, CoC 6200,
               CoH DCH301, CoJap M161, PaE R2961, PaSw
               PZ11249, CO 36721. **EP:** FONT TFE17079, FONT
               462065TE. **LP:** CBS 62581, SONY SOPZ4-6
CO 29514-2   **LP:** CO G30779, CBS 67233, SONY SOPZ4-6, SM
               P6-11891
               I Found A New Baby

CO 29519-bkdn UNISSUED - Tape
CO 29519 **LP:** JAA 6 (Side 2, Track 3), PHON 7612
CO 29519-1 CO 35938, CoArg 291316, PaAu A7423, PaE R2798, Palnd DPE12. **LP:** PhilCont B07907R, BID 1011, JAZ 42
CO29519-3 **LP:** CO CL652, CorAu KLP510, PHIL BBL7172, PhilCont B07247L, CBS 52538, CBS 62387, SONY SOPZ4-6, SONY SOPM-155, SONY 20AP-1456. **EP:** CO Set B504
    Gone With What Draft

(Matrices CO 29515 through CO 29518 are non-Goodman items.)

Despite his illness-induced absence from the big band scene in 1940, Benny again led Metronome magazine's all-star poll as top jazz clarinetist, and the next day he waxed two of his arrangements with the other winners. It marked his first performance with Buddy Rich, whose supremacy on his instrument is destined to endure almost as long as Benny's. They will record and perform together but a few times in future; unfortunate, when one considers that these two giants could have, and should have, produced memorable music together.

In 1977, when arrangements for the 40th anniversary concert in Carnegie Hall were begun, the author suggested that Benny hire Buddy for the job, if he were available. At first Benny accepted the thought favorably; the inquiry reached Buddy in Canada, where he was then appearing with his own big band. Yes, he could make the date, came the response; and Buddy added, "And tell Benny I'll play 'Sing, Sing, Sing' like it's never been played before!" Well, that did it; Benny recoiled at the thought of still another crowd pleasing tub-thumper overwhelming his music, and Buddy was not hired. Too bad; would have made that concert.

METRONOME ALL STAR BAND   January 16, 1941, New York

Benny Goodman, clt; Harry James, Ziggy Elman, Cootie Williams, tpt; Tommy Dorsey, J.C. Higginbotham, tbn; Toots Mondello, Benny Carter, as; Coleman Hawkins, Tex Beneke, ts; Count Basie, p; Charlie Christian, g; Art Bernstein, b; Buddy Rich, c.

OA 060331-1 VI 27314 A, VI 42-0036, HMV B9195, HMVAu EA3004, ViArg 1AC-0069. **45:** VI 27-0036, VI 447-0199. **EP:** VI EPAT30. **LP:** VI LPT21, CAM 426, CamE CDN122, CamJap CL5039, RcaJap RA-97, RcaJap RMP5120, RD 3/4-45, RcaFR 430.313, RcaFR 731.089, ViJap RA5380-1/2, RcaG Golden Age of Jazz. **ET:** (12") U.S. War Dept. Sound Off 8
    Bugle Call Rag

OA 060332-1 same issues, except add (78) ViJap A-1337, and omit **45:** VI 447-0199, **LP,** RcaFR 430.313, ViJap, and **ET.**
    One O'Clock Jump

The band had an unusual three-day stand at the Providence Theater, Providence, Rhode Island, beginning January 17 (still struggling to pick up bookings), and then it returned to New York for its next studio session. Columbia's files show that Hymie Schertzer replaced Skippy Martin for the first tune only, but Hymie maintained that he played for all of them. We'll go with the written record.

BENNY GOODMAN AND HIS ORCHESTRA   January 21, 1941, New York

Personnel as January 14, except HYMIE SCHERTZER, as, and COUNT BASIE, p, replace Martin and Wilson on the first title only.

CO 29529-1 CO 36022, CoArg 291275. **LP:** JAZ 42
CO 29259 UNISSUED - Tape
CO 29259 UNISSUED - Tape
CO 29259-2 **LP:** PHON 7612
    I'm Not Complainin' (arr ES)

Martin and Wilson return, replacing Schertzer and Basie

CO 29530 **LP:** PHON 7612
CO 29530 UNISSUED - Tape
CO 29530 UNISSUED - Tape
CO 29530-1 CO 36180, CoArg 291191, CoSd DS1369, PaE R2835, Palnd DPE33. **LP:** JAZ 42
CO 29530 **LP:** CO PG33405
    Time On My Hands (arr EdSau)

CO 29531 **LP:** PHON 7612
CO 29531-1 CO 35977, CoC 250. **LP:** JAZ 51, JOY 6016
    You're Dangerous - voc Helen Forrest

CO 29532 **LP:** PHON 7612
CO 29532-1 CO 35992, CoC 257. **LP:** JAZ 51, JOY 6016
    The Mem'ry Of A Rose - voc Helen Forrest (arr EdSau)

Latter-day discovery of a Goodman Columbia recording that was not assigned a matrix more than compensates for the reassignment of a cut thought earlier to have come from the studio session of January 28, next. The tunes in question are, 1, "Jenny," which can be placed correctly because of recorded dialog between the musical performances, despite its having no matrix; and 2, "Afraid To Say Hello," which now is moved to the studio session of February 19.

BENNY GOODMAN AND HIS ORCHESTRA   January 28, 1941, New York

Benny Goodman, clt; Alec Fila, Jimmy Maxwell, Cootie Williams, Irving Goodman, tpt; Lou McGarity, Cutty Cutshall, tbn; Gus Bivona, LES ROBINSON, as; George Auld, Jack Henderson, ts; Skippy Martin, bar; Teddy Wilson, p; Mike Bryan, g; Art Bernstein, b; Dave Tough, d; Helen Forrest, voc.

CO 29577-bkdn **LP:** PHON 7615
CO 29577 **LP:** PHON 7615
CO 29577-bkdn UNISSUED - Tape
CO 29577-1 CO 35944, CoC 235. **LP:** JAZ 42, JOY 6019
    This Is New - voc Helen Forrest (arr EdSau)

-0- **LP:** BID 1006
-0-bkdn **LP:** BID 1006 (actually a rehearsal, not a breakdown)
-0- **LP:** BID 1006, PHON 7615
    Jenny - voc Helen Forrest, Benny Goodman, chorus

CO 29578 **LP:** MER 11
CO 29578 **LP:** PHON 7615
CO 29578-bkdn UNISSUED - Tape
CO 29578-bkdn UNISSUED - Tape
CO 29578-1 CO 35962, SIL 572, VD 233 A, NavyVD 13 A, CoArg 20363, CoBr 30-1440, CoC 243, CoJap M270, CoSd DS1454, CoSW DZ314. **EP:** CoE SEG7556. **LP:** CL6100, CO CL2533, CO "Texaco" LP, 1960 Heart Fund LP, JOY 6019
    Perfidia (Tonight) - voc Helen Forrest (arr EdSau)

CO 29579-bkdn UNISSUED - Tape
CO 29579 **LP:** PHON 7615
CO 29579-1 CO 35944, CoBr 30-1412, CoC 235, HA 1012, CO 38821, CoC 1546. **EP:** CO 1-642. **7"33:** CO 3-38821. **LP:** CO KG32822, CO alb P5-15536, JOY 6019
    Bewitched - voc Helen Forrest (arr EdSau)

Benny did land a prestigious job the end of the month: the "President's Birthday Ball" in Washington on January 30, a charity event begun by Franklin Roosevelt to raise funds to combat infantile paralysis, with which he was afflicted. And on February 2 the band was playing in the Golden Gate Ballroom in New York City, which may be the point of origin of the next air check, but that is uncertain.

Even less certain is Benny's exact lineup for the next several weeks; Bob Snyder will return as Martin leaves, and Toots's brother Pete will replace Jack Henderson. The piano stool will revolve wildly, with Bill Rowland, Milt Raskin and Johnny Guarnieri occupying it at different times. But precisely when these changes took place is not known.

SUSTAINING BROADCAST   *February 4, 1941, poss. Golden*
   Unknown network   *Gate Ballroom, New York*

Personnel as January 28, except JOHNNY GUARNIERI, p, replaces Wilson.

Stealin' Apples (n/c)

On February 10 Benny began another commercial radio series, "What's New?", and for yet another cigarette—Old Gold. The program lasted for 13 weeks, and was broadcast via New York radio station WJZ only. Its format had Benny discoursing on new bands, new records and new kinds of dancing between selections. He seemingly had little input to the script, for on the first show he breaks up when he recites that one of the best new bands is . . . Tony Pastor's!

Those familiar with the author's earlier work on Goodman will note many new inclusions in the "What's New?" listings, and some performance reassignments. Both are caused by better information received post-publication of "BG—On The Record." LP issues of some of the cuts will help collectors identify some of the reassignments.

"WHAT'S NEW?"   *February 10, 1941, New York*
  WJZ Radio (NBC)

Orchestra as January 28, except JOHNNY GUARNIERI, p, replaces Wilson. SEPTET: BG, Williams, Auld, Guarnieri (NOT Basie, as earlier believed), Christian, Bernstein, Tough.

Let's Dance (theme)
Benny Rides Again
Sunrise Serenade
There'll Be Some Changes Made - voc Helen Forrest
Wholly Cats - SEPTET (LP: TRIB - no #)
Perfidia - voc Helen Forrest
Flying Home - SEPTET plus Red Norvo, xylo - orch. in coda (LP: TRIB - no #)
Let's Dance (theme)

Note that Bill Rowland replaces Guarnieri on this "Fitch Bandwagon" broadcast:

"FITCH BANDWAGON"   *February 16, 1941, New York*
  NBC Radio Network

Orchestra as January 28, except BILL ROWLAND, p, replaces Wilson. SEPTET: BG, Williams, Auld, Rowland, Christian, Bernstein, Tough.

Let's Dance (theme)
Perfidia - voc Helen Forrest
Let The Door Knob Hitcha - voc Cootie Williams
Gone With What Draft - SEPTET
These Things You Left Me - voc Helen Forrest
. . . intro, "Scarecrow," a bridge to:
Benny Rides Again

And now Milt Raskin replaces Rowland; but Guarnieri will be back, two days later.

"WHAT'S NEW?"   *February 17, 1941, New York*
  WJZ Radio (NBC)

Orchestra as January 28, except MILT RASKIN, p, replaces Wilson. SEPTET: BG, Williams, Auld, Raskin, Christian, Bernstein, Tough. TRIO: BG, guest Teddy Wilson, Tough.

Let The Door Knob Hitcha (no voc) (announced as, "That's The Girl")
Ida - TRIO
Breakfast Feud - SEPTET (LP: TRIB - no #)
Scarecrow (arr BH)
Let's Dance (theme)

(That may be Wilson instead of Raskin in the Septet's "Breakfast Feud.")

BENNY GOODMAN AND HIS ORCHESTRA   February 19, 1941, New York

Benny Goodman, clt; Alec Fila, Jimmy Maxwell, Cootie Williams, Irving Goodman, tpt; Lou McGarity, Cutty Cutshall, tbn; Les Robinson, Gus Bivona, as; George Auld, Pete Mondello, ts; Bob Snyder, bar; Johnny Guarnieri, p; Mike Bryan, g; Art Bernstein, b; Dave Tough, d; Helen Forrest, voc. BUSTER HARDING (BH) is a new arranger.

CO 29774	**LP:** PHON 7615
CO 29774-1	CO 36012, CoArg 291290, CoC 273, CoSw MZ251. **LP:** CO KG32822
CO 29774	**LP:** BID 1009
CO 29774	UNISSUED - Tape
CO 29774-bkdn	UNISSUED - Tape
CO 29774-bkdn	UNISSUED - Tape
CO 29774-2	CO 36012. **LP:** JAZ 51, JOY 6019

    Lazy River - voc Helen Forrest (arr EdSau)

CO 29775	**LP:** PHON 7615
CO 29775	**LP:** TL STLJ05
CO 29775-bkdn	UNISSUED - Tape
CO 29775	**LP:** BID 1009
CO 29775-1	CO 36180, CoArg 291191, CoSd DS1369, PaE R2835, Palnd DPE33, VD 849 B. **LP:** CO PG33405, FR series, SB 144

    Scarecrow (arr BH)

CO 29776	**LP:** PHON 7615
CO 29776	UNISSUED - Tape
CO 29776	UNISSUED - Tape
CO 29776-bkdn	UNISSUED - Tape
CO 29776-1	CO 36067, CoArg 291208, CoBr 30-1440, CoFr DF336, CoSw DZ336, PaE R2805, Palnd DPE22. **LP:** CO KG32822, CO alb P5-15536, JOY 6019

    Yours - voc Helen Forrest (arr MG)

CO 29777	**LP:** PHON 7615
CO 29777-1	CO 36002, CoArg 291210, CoC 265. **LP:** JAZ 51, JOY 6019

    You Lucky People You - voc Helen Forrest (arr EdSau)

-0-	**LP:** PHON 7615

    Afraid To Say Hello - voc Helen Forrest (prob arr EdSau)

("Afraid To Say Hello" is now assigned to this date because its source is a Columbia Reference Recording whose reverse is the alternate take of CO 29776 from which PHON 7615 was transferred, and because its overall "sound" seems more in keeping with the other cuts from this date. //Note that Dave Tough named "Scarecrow" as his best-ever side with Goodman; the several takes extant substantiate his opinion.)

Identity of the band pianist on the next "What's New?" broadcast is uncertain; it may well have been Milt Raskin, with Guarnieri having returned only for the February 19 studio session. Note that the mid-broadcast "Let's Dance" is not an introductory theme, but rather a musical explanation of the tune's historical development. Also, the title, "What's New—It's You," is taken from a program log; its acetate is of such poor audio quality that it prevents confirmation of that title.

"WHAT'S NEW?"   *February 24, 1941, New York*
  WJZ Radio (NBC)

Orchestra personnel as February 19, with poss. Milt Raskin on p. SEPTET: BG, Williams, Auld, guest Count Basie, Christian, Bernstein, Tough.

Frenesi
The Moon Won't Talk - voc Helen Forrest (n/c)
Let's Dance
(The Fives - Basie w/rhythm - NO BG)
Gone With What Draft - SEPTET (LP: TRIB - no #)
What's New—It's You (?)
Let's Dance (closing theme)

"WHAT'S NEW?"   *March 3, 1941, New York*
  WJZ Radio (NBC)

Personnel as February 19, except SKIP MARTIN, as, replaces Robinson, and MILT RASKIN, p, replaces Guarnieri. SEPTET: BG, Williams, Auld, Raskin, Christian, Bernstein, Tough. Guest, Jack Teagarden, tbn & voc.

Swing Low, Sweet Chariot
My Sister And I - voc Helen Forrest (n/c) (arr EdSau)
Chonk, Charlie, Chonk (later, "Solo Flight") (LP: BEP 14800, QD 16) (arr JM)
Oh! Look At Me Now - voc Helen Forrest (arr EdSau)
Jack Hits The Road - voc, tbn, Jack Teagarden (LP: QD 16)
Six Appeal - SEPTET (LP: TRIB—no # - as "My Daddy Rocks Me")
Take It - voc, the band (arr MG)

BENNY GOODMAN AND HIS ORCHESTRA   March 4, 1941, New York

Personnel as February 19, except SKIP MARTIN, as replaces Robinson (Guarnieri on p).

CO 29862   **LP:** PHON 7615
CO 29862-1   CO 36012, CoArg 291275, CoC 273, CoSw MZ251. **LP:** CO KG32822, Joy 6019
     Oh! Look At Me Now - voc Helen Forrest (arr EdSau)

CO 29863   **LP:** BID 1009
CO 29863   **LP:** PHON 7615
CO 29863-1   CO 36067, CoArg 291208, CoAu DO 2992, CoBr 50482, CoC 304, CoFr DF336, CoSw DZ336, PaE R2805, PaInd DPE22. **LP:** CO "Texaco," SWE 1001
     Take It - voc ensemble (arr MG)

CO 29864-1   CO 36022, CoArg 291209. **LP:** JAZ 42, JOY 6019
     My Sister And I -voc Helen Forrest (arr EdSau)

Charlie Christian, g, replaces Bryan

CO 29865-1   CO 36684, CoC 719, OdNor D50253, PaE R2978, PaSw PZ11077. **LP:** CO G30779, CBS 62581, CBS 67233, SONY SOPZ4-6, TL STLJ12
CO 29865-2   **LP:** CO CL652, CorAu KLP510, PHIL BBL7172, PhilCont B07247L, CBS 52538, CBS 62387, SONY SOPZ4-6, SONY SOPM-155, SONY 20AP-1456, PHON 7615
     Solo Flight (arr JM) (originally titled, "Chonk, Charlie, Chonk")

"WHAT'S NEW?"   March 10, 1941, New York
WJZ Radio (NBC)

Personnel as March 4. SEPTET: BG, Williams, Auld, Guarnieri, Christian, Bernstein, guest Gene Krupa, d.

Mellow Gold
It All Comes Back To Me Now - voc Helen Forrest
Drumboogie - voc Helen Forrest, band. Gene Krupa on d.
Flying Home - SEPTET (LP: JAA 23, MU 30JA5181)
Perfidia - voc Helen Forrest
Let's Dance (theme)

Interest in Charlie Christian was such that in 1955, when Columbia assembled its memorial LP CL652 in his honor (released April 11), it included in it portions of the rehearsal that preceded the March 13, 1941 studio session. Almost 25 years later, additional segments of the rehearsal were discovered and released on LP, BID 1006. Since Benny had not yet arrived and did not participate in the rehearsal, the various releases are not detailed herein. The issues are, however, recommended to collectors generally, and are a "must" for the Christian fan.

Note that discovery of a test pressing of take 1 of the hyphenated "A Smo-o-o-oth One," released on LP BID 1004, relegates the release on LP CO CL652 et al to an unnumbered take, or possibly a splice from an unnumbered take.

BENNY GOODMAN AND HIS SEXTET   March 13, 1941, New York

Benny Goodman, clt; Cootie Williams, tpt; George Auld, ts; Johnny Guarnieri, p; Charlie Christian, g; Art Bernstein, b; Dave Tough, d.

CO 29942-1   **LP:** BID 1004
CO 29942-2   CO 36099, CoArg 291473, CoJap M325, CoSw DZ334, PaE R2816, Palt B71083, VD 187 A. **45:** CO 4-16-G (Set G4-2). **EP:** CO 5-1651 (Set B350), CO B2011, PHIL BBE 12277. **LP:** CO GL500, CoE 33SX1035, CoFr FPX112, CoJap PL5004, PHIL BBL7178, PhilCont B07109L, PhilCont B07225L, Palt PMDQ8013, CorAu KLP675, CBS 67268, SONY SOPZ4-6, SONY SOPM-162, RTB LPV4316, JO 101.611. **ET:** Air Force GL-18.
CO 29942   **LP:** CO CL652, CorAu KLP510, PHIL BBL7172, PhilCont B07247L, CO KG31547, CO alb P4M-5678, CBS 62387, SONY SOPZ4-6, SONY SOPM-155
     A Smo-o-o-oth One (originally titled, "Moppin' It Up")

CO 29943-1   CO 36099, CoArg 291473, CoC 6199, CoJap M160, CoSw DZ334, PaE R2816, PaFin DPY1060, Palt B71083, CO 36720, VD 253 A, NavyVD 33 A. **LP:** PHIL BBL7356, PhilCont B07907R, Palt PMDQ8013, TL STLJ05, RTB LPV4316, JO 101.611, SB 142. **ET:** AFRS H-62
CO 29943-2   **LP:** PHON 7615
CO 29943-S(a)   **LP:** CO CL652, CorAu KLP510, PHIL BBL7172, PhilCont B07247L, CBS 52688, CBS 62387, SONY SOPZ4-6, SONY SOPM-155. **EP:** PHIL BBE12272
CO 29943-S(b)   **LP:** CO G30779, CBS 67233, SONY SOPZ4-6
     Good Enough To Keep (later issues, **Airmail Special**)

(CO CL652 et al, "(a)" above, consists of CO 29943-2 in its entirety, plus Christian's solo, Benny's solo, and the rideout from CO 29943-1. CO G30779 et al, "(b)" above, begins with the intro through Christian's first solo from CO 29943-2. Then, with the first four bars of Christian's beginning solo excised, this splice continues with CO 29943-1 from that point to completion.)

Sometime in March Billy Butterfield, available when Artie Shaw again disbanded, joined as Alec Fila left to go with Will Bradley. Bob Snyder departed, Skip Martin moved over to baritone, and Les Robinson returned once again on alto. It is not known when these changes became effective—they are present for the next studio session—so the personnel for March 17's "What's New?" broadcast is uncertain.

Two days before it, however, Benny reciprocated for Gene Krupa's guest appearance on the March 10 "What's New?" program:

"MATINEE AT   March 15, 1941, Cedar Grove, N.J.
THE MEADOWBROOK"
CBS Radio Network

Benny Goodman, ts, with Gene Krupa and his Orchestra. TRIO: Benny Goodman, clt; Bob Kitsis, p; Gene Krupa, d.

Georgia On My Mind (LP: IAJRC 17)
Ida, Sweet As Apple Cider - TRIO

"WHAT'S NEW?"   March 17, 1941, New York
WJZ Radio (NBC)

Orchestra personnel as March 4/March 27. Septet as March 13. Guest, Coleman Hawkins, ts.

Let's Dance (theme)
Deep River (alternate title, "Dear Old Southland")
Walkin' By The River - voc Helen Forrest (arr EdSau)
Benny Rides Again
The Wise Old Owl- voc Helen Forrest (arr EdSau)
(Georgia On My Mind - guest Coleman Hawkins, ts, w/orch.—NO BG)
Good Enough To Keep—SEPTET (LP: JAA 23, MU 30JA5181)
Take It - voc, the band - to signoff

It is reasonable to assume that some of the personnel changes to be noted in the studio session of March 27 had taken place in time for the next "What's New?" broadcast, but there is no certain evidence to verify that assumption.

"WHAT'S NEW?"   March 24, 1941, Manhattan Center, New York
WJZ Radio (NBC)

Personnel as March 4/March 27.

Oh! Look At Me Now - voc Helen Forrest (n/c)
Superman

BENNY GOODMAN AND HIS ORCHESTRA   March 27, 1941, New York

Benny Goodman, clt; BILLY BUTTERFIELD, Jimmy Maxwell, Irving Goodman, tpt; Lou McGarity, Cutty Cutshall, tbn; LES ROBINSON, Gus Bivona, as; George Auld, Pete Mondello, ts; SKIP MARTIN, bar; Johnny Guarnieri, p; Mike Bryan, g; Art Bernstein, b; Dave Tough, d; Helen Forrest, voc.

CO 30069	**LP:** PHON 7615
CO 30069	**LP:** BID 1009
CO 30069-1	CO 36050, CoC 297, CoJap M213, CoSd DS1299, PaE R2802, Palnd DPE18. **LP:** CO KG32822, CO alb P5-15536, JOY 6019, RLM 8065
	Amapola (Pretty Little Poppy) - voc Helen Forrest (arr MG)
CO 30070-2	**LP:** PHON 7615
CO 30070	**LP:** BID 1009
CO 30070-1	CO 36050, CoArg 291209, CoC 297, CoSd DS1299. **45:** CO 7-1502. **LP:** CO GL523, PHIL BBL7043, PhilCont B07010L
	Intermezzo (A Love Story) (arr EdSau)

Add Cootie Williams, tpt.

CO 30071	**LP:** PHON 7615
CO 30071-1	CO 36755, CoArg 291600. **LP:** CO PG33405, SWE 1001
	Fiesta In Blue (originally titled, "Cootie Growls") (arr JM)
CO 30072	**LP:** PHON 7616
CO 30072	**LP:** BID 1009
CO 30072-bkdn	UNISSUED - Tape
CO 30072-1	HA 1061. **LP:** EPIC EE22025, EpicAu ELP3648, EpicFr/H EPC80056
	Cherry (arr JM)

Jimmy Mundy's arrangement of "Cherry" had been in Benny's book as long ago as the Victor days; he played it occasionally, but did not record it because he did not particularly like it. He was prevailed upon to record it for Columbia on the March 27 session, but then refused to authorize its release. Even when Columbia first issued it post-World War II, he still thought it pedestrian, and told Columbia Harry James's version was better.

Speaking of Harry, he was Benny's guest on the next "What's New?" broadcast, which now originated in New York's Manhattan Center. A program log shows Harry performing his "Jeffrey's Blues" with Benny's band, and replacing Cootie Williams in the Septet for a romp through, "Moppin' It Up." Unfortunately, neither of these cuts has been found; the one selection extant from this program, however, has a brief trumpet "alert" that may well be Harry's:

"WHAT'S NEW?"   March 31, 1941, Manhattan Center, New York
  WJZ Radio (NBC)

Personnel as March 27. Guest, Harry James, tpt.

The Jazz Me Blues

"WHAT'S NEW?"   April 7, 1941, Manhattan Center, New York
  WJZ Radio (NBC)

Orchestra as March 27. Septet as March 13. SEXTET: BG, Guarnieri, Christian, Bernstein, plus guests Will Bradley, tbn, and Ray McKinley, voc & d.

Swing Low, Sweet Chariot
My Sister And I - voc Helen Forrest (n/c)
Cootie Growls (Fiesta In Blue) (LP: QD 16)
Wholly Cats - SEPTET (LP: JAA 23, MU 3OJA5181)
Negra Soy (later, "Something New") (arr EdSau) (n/c)
Southpaw Serenade - voc Ray McKinley - SEXTET (QD 16, BAND 7128)
Air Mail Special (arr JM)

"WHAT'S NEW?"   April 14, 1941, Manhattan Center, New York
  WJZ Radio (NBC)

Orchestra as March 27. Septet as March 13. Guest, Mildred Bailey, voc.

Blues My Naughty Sweetie Gives To Me
When You And I Were Young, Maggie
Lazy River - voc Helen Forrest
Breakfast Feud - SEPTET (LP: SPJ 6602, WI 196)

There'll Be Some Changes Made - voc Mildred Bailey (LP: QD 16)
Intermezzo
Benny's Bugle
Let's Dance (theme)

"WHAT'S NEW?"   April 21, 1941, Manhattan Center, New York
  WJZ Radio (NBC)

Personnel as March 27.

Board Meeting
Yours - voc Helen Forrest
Take It - voc, the band

"WHAT'S NEW?"   April 28, 1941, Manhattan Center, New York
  WJZ Radio (NBC)

Orchestra as March 27. Septet as March 13. Guests, Delta Rhythm Boys, voc.

Good Evenin', Good Lookin'! - voc Helen Forrest (arr JM)
La Golondrina
(Give Me Some Skin - voc, Delta Rhythm Boys - NO BG)
Everything Happens To Me - voc Helen Forrest
Song Of The Islands - SEPTET (LP: TRIB - no #)
Air Mail Special
Let's Dance (theme)

   To this point listings for "What's New?" broadcasts have been in main substantiated by program logs, in part by dated acetates. The cuts following are not so confirmed, but are believed to have been from "What's New?" broadcasts to date:

"WHAT'S NEW?"   February-April 1941, New York
  WJZ Radio (NBC)

Septet as March 13. Orchestra personnel appropriate to the period.

Ida - SEPTET (LP: JAA 23, MU 3OJA5181)
(Georgia On My Mind - p solo, guest Art Tatum - NO BG)
Board Meeting (poss. from February 17)
The Glory Of Your Love (?-title-?) (n/c)

   On April 29 Benny returned to Carnegie Hall as a soloist, this time to perform Prokofieff's "Variations On Yiddish Themes." Then on May Day the band helped celebrate the 18th Annual Shenandoah Apple Blossom Festival in Alexandria, Virginia, and was broadcast from the Armory there:

SUSTAINING BROADCAST   May 1, 1941, Alexandria, Va.
  MUTUAL Radio Network

Orchestra as March 27. Septet as March 13.

Benny Rides Again
Cootie Growls
Moppin' It Up - SEPTET (Later, "A Smo-o-o-oth One")
Air Mail Special - to signoff

   Dave Tough is present on the May 1 broadcast, but during much of April he was in and out of the band—for example, Benny's stand at the Paramount beginning April 11 found both Nick Fatool and Don Carter substituting for him on different shows. But apparently he was in shape (sober) to have played for all the "What's New?" broadcasts in April.

   He is, however, absent from the last "What's New?" program, and from here forward there is no evidence that he's with the band. In May or June he rejoined Joe Marsala, then in August went with Artie Shaw.

   Jo Jones sat in for the May 5 studio session and final "What's New?" broadcast; and somewhat mysteriously. Teddy Wilson filled in on both for Guarnieri—but John will be back. Temporarily too, Jimmy Horvath replaced Gus Bivona on alto.

BENNY GOODMAN AND HIS ORCHESTRA   May 5, 1941, New York

Personnel as March 27, except JIMMY HORVATH, as, TEDDY WILSON, p, and JO JONES, d, replace Bivona, Guarnieri and Tough respectively.

CO 30419-bkdn	UNISSUED - Tape
CO 30419-1	CO 36136, CoC 341. **LP:** JAZ 42, JOY 6019
CO 30419-2	**LP:** PHON 7616
	Good Evenin', Good Lookin'! - voc Helen Forrest (arr JM)

CO 30420-bkdn   UNISSUED - Tape
CO 30420-bkdn   UNISSUED - Tape
CO 30420   **LP:** PHON 7616
CO 30420-1   CO 36209, CoC 370. **LP:** NOST 890/1, CO PG33405
                 Something New (Negra Soy) (arr EdSau)

CO 30421-1   CO 36254, CoC 399, PaAu A7507, PaE R2827, PaSw
                     PZ11124. **LP:** CO PG33405
                 Air Mail Special (arr JM)

CO 30422-   UNISSUED - Tape (4 aborted attempts, each
bkdns   progressively longer)
CO 30422   UNISSUED - Tape
CO 30422-bkdn   UNISSUED - Tape
CO 30422-1   **LP:** PHON 7616
CO 30422   UNISSUED - Tape
CO 30422-2   CO 36136, CoC 341. **LP:** JAZ 42, JOY 6019
                 **I Found A Million Dollar Baby (In The Five And Ten
                 Cent Store)** - voc Helen Forrest (arr EdSau)

-0-   **LP:** PHON 7616
                 Don't Be That Way

("Don't Be That Way" is noted on Columbia's recording sheets as, "For Mr. Wallerstein - Test 104." It likely was not intended as a recording for release, and may have been a gift for Edward "Ted" Wallerstein, once Victor's, and now Columbia's president.)

Gene Krupa, whose band was at the Hotel Pennsylvania, was Benny's guest on the final "What's New?" broadcast. His presence reunited the original Trio, and he, Benny and Teddy do an amusing little skit about their credentials when seeking a job. The juxtaposition of Gene's appearance following the studio recording of "Don't Be That Way," drums by Jo Jones, and their work on the broadcast permits immediate comparison of two of Swing's finest drummers.

"WHAT'S NEW?"   *May 5, 1941, New York*
  WJZ Radio (NBC)

Orchestra as studio session this date. TRIO: BG, Wilson, guest Gene Krupa. SEPTET: BG, Williams, Auld, Wilson, Christian, Bernstein, Jones. Lloyd "Skippy" Martin (SkM) contributes his first known arrangement.

Walkin' By The River - TRIO (EP: PHON BG01)
Hot-Cha-Chornya - TRIO
Fancy Meeting You - voc Helen Forrest
Superman (LP: FAN 19-119, QD 16)
G'Bye Now - voc Helen Forrest
Flying Home - SEPTET, orch. in coda (LP: QD 16)
Let's Dance (theme)

The next fix on the band's shifting personnel is provided by Columbia's files, detailing the studio session of June 4. But contemporary press reports, and identifying announcements on several extant air checks, indicate earlier occurrence, and these are shown in the next listing. A notable loss was the departure of Art Bernstein in May, off to Hollywood, there to do studio work with other fine musicians who'd quit the band business for more money and less hassle. He'll be missed.

Entrepreneur Monte Proser had a grand idea: book not one, but three, big bands into spacious Madison Square Garden, provide continuous music for dancing, and reap the profits. Thus Benny, Charlie Barnet and Larry Clinton all were engaged for his "Dance Carnival," and the experiment began. Unfortunately, not even those "names" filled the cavernous Garden, and the venture quickly folded. Fortunately, however, portions of a number of Benny's broadcasts from the Garden were captured, beginning with:

SUSTAINING BROADCAST   *May 28, 1941, Madison*
  MUTUAL Radio Network   *Square Garden, New York*

Benny Goodman, clt; Billy Butterfield, Cootie Williams, CHRIS GRIFFIN, tpt; Lou McGarity, Cutty Cutshall, tbn; Les Robinson, GENE KINSEY, as; George Auld, Pete Mondello, ts; Skip Martin, bar; JOHNNY GUARNIERI, p; Charlie Christian, g; WALTER IOOSS, b; NICK FATOOL, d; Helen Forrest, voc.

SEPTET: BG, Williams, Auld, Guarnieri, Christian, IOOSS, FATOOL.

Benny's Bugle - SEPTET (LP: JAA 23, MU 30JA5181)
Concerto For Cootie
One O'Clock Jump

SUSTAINING BROADCAST   *May 30, 1941, Madison*
  Unknown radio network   *Square Garden, New York*

Personnel as May 28.

Tuesday At Ten (arr SkM)
Bewitched - voc Helen Forrest (n/c)

SUSTAINING BROADCAST   *May 31, 1941, Madison*
  Unknown radio network   *Square Garden, New York*

Personnel as May 28.

Good Evenin', Good Lookin'! - voc Helen Forrest (n/c)

SUSTAINING BROADCAST   *June 1, 1941, Madison*
  MUTUAL Radio Network   *Square Garden, New York*

Personnel as May 28.

When The Sun Comes Out (arr EdSau) - intro only, segue to,
Good-Bye (theme)

SUSTAINING BROADCAST   *June 2, 1941, Madison*
  MUTUAL Radio Network   *Square Garden, New York*

Personnel as May 28.

Negra Soy ("Something New") (n/c -intro excised)
Superman
Soft As Spring - voc Helen Forrest (arr EdSau)
Sing, Sing, Sing
Sugar Foot Stomp - to signoff

It almost seems a contractual reason prevented Nick Fatool from recording with Benny at this time; although he is with the band before and after the next studio session, J.C. Heard, who'd been with Teddy Wilson's group, makes the date.

Recent discovery of an almost-complete version of "Tuesday At Ten" on a Columbia Reference Recording lends substance to an earlier unconfirmed report that one take of that tune was recorded June 4. Its overall sound is different from the two existing cuts made June 11, and it offers soli by George Auld rather than by Lou McGarity. For those reasons it is assigned here:

BENNY GOODMAN AND HIS ORCHESTRA   **June 4, 1941, New York**

Personnel As May 28, except J.C. HEARD, d, replaces Fatool.

CO 30598   UNISSUED - Tape
CO 30598   **LP:** PHON 7616
CO 30598-1   CO 36209, CoC 370. **LP:** CO KG32822, JOY 6109
                 When The Sun Comes Out - voc Helen Forrest (arr
                     EdSau)

CO 30599   UNISSUED - Tape
CO 30599   UNISSUED - Tape
CO 30599   **LP:** PHON 7616
CO 30599   UNISSUED - Tape
CO 30599   UNISSUED - Tpae
CO 30599-1   CO 36284, CoArg 291299, CoBr 30-1412, CoC 411, **LP:**
                     CO alb P5-15536, CO alb P6-14538, JAZ 51, JOY
                     6019
                 (When Your Heart's On Fire) Smoke Gets In Your Eyes
                 - voc Helen Forrest (arr EdSau)

-0-   UNISSUED - Co Ref
                 Tuesday At Ten (arr SkM)

SUSTAINING BROADCAST   *June 6, 1941, Madison*
  MUTUAL Radio Network   *Square Garden, New York*

Personnel as May 28 (Fatool returns).

Negra Soy ("Something New")
When The Sun Comes Out - voc Helen Forrest (n/c)
Stealin' Apples (LP: JOY 1097)
(When Your Heart's On Fire) Smoke Gets In Your Eyes - voc Helen Forrest
Rose Room - SEPTET

(JOY 1097's liner notes ascribe "Stealin' Apples" to July 5 in error.)

Next are some undated air checks considered certain to have come from Monte Proser's "Dance Carnival" in Madison Square Garden:

SUSTAINING BROADCASTS　　　　　*May/June 1941, Madison*
　MUTUAL Radio Network　　　　　*Square Garden, New York*

Personnel as May 28.

Solo Flight (LP: JAA 23, MU 30JA5181, BEP 14800)
Sing, Sing, Sing - to signoff
Sugar Foot Stomp
One O'Clock Jump - to signoff

Now some undated airchecks considered likely to have come from the "Dance Carnival," although some of them have been assigned differently by others:

SUSTAINING BROADCASTS　　　　　*May/June 1941, Madison*
　MUTUAL Radio Network　　　　　*Square Garden, New York*

Personnel as May 28.

Don't Be That Way (LP: JAZ 35)
Intermezzo (LP: JAZ 35)

Intermezzo

SUSTAINING BROADCASTS　　　　　*May/June 1941, Madison*
　Unknown networks　　　　　*Square Garden, New York*

Personnel as May 28.

Flying Home (orchestra)
Negra Soy ("Something New")
Superman
Caprice XXIV Paganini (arr SkM) (n/c)
The Hour Of Parting (n/c)
La Rosita (arr EdSau) (n/c)
Stompin' At The Savoy - SEPTET (n/c)

Finally for this period, an undated air check that has puzzled the author for some 20 years or more. He long believed that it was from late 1937 or early 1938, and that the drummer on this good version of "Sing, Sing, Sing" was Gene Krupa. Good friends with Gene, a kind of Salvation Army-type drummer himself, he'd long prided himself on his ability to distinguish one drummer from another. He now has a hunch that the drummer was . . . Nick Fatool, and that the cut is from a broadcast from the Garden in 1941. One minor reason for so believing is that Fatool could imitate any drummer's style, as witness his work on the Glen Gray re-creations of Big Band Era hits, note for note transcriptions of the originals. Here, then, the enigmatic "SSS":

SUSTAINING BROADCAST　　　　　*May/June 1941, Madison*
　Unknown network　　　　　*Square Garden, New York*

Personnel as May 28.

Sing, Sing, Sing

Knocked out of the Garden by insufficient attendance and about to go on the road, Chris Griffin, Johnny Guarnieri and likely Nick Fatool preferred to stay in New York; Jimmy Maxwell, Mel Powell and Big Sid Catlett replaced them, in time for the next studio session. As they say, that was a trade that hurt no one.

Goodman fans are divided in their opinions as to which pianist was Benny's best: was it Jess Stacy (the author's favorite), Teddy Wilson (universally acclaimed) or Mel Powell (whose reputation is still growing, 40 years later)? Each had his—many—moments of transcendence, and each has left a legacy of genius. Few would quarrel that these three, who all came to prominence with Benny, would make anyone's list of the 10 best big band and small group pianists in all Jazz history. Benny knew how to pick 'em.

But he had help in choosing Mel. Because Guarnieri was on notice, someone recommended to Benny that he audition a youngster whose name meant nothing to him. Where could he hear him? Don't know, the kid isn't playing anywhere at the moment. Well, how about in my booker's office building, there's a small studio on one of the floors? OK—and an audition was arranged in Music Corporation of America's suite, with their personnel nearby and passing through as, ". . . this big, blonde kid, couldn't have been more than 17, and was really nervous," solo'd for the Man. "Well, I couldn't decide," recalls Benny, "I didn't know what the hell to think of him, although I did think he had some talent. So I turned to one of the

stenographers who was sitting there, and I asked her, 'Do you like him?' And she said, 'Yes!' And that was it, and I took him on."

All hail The Unknown Stenographer, Mel's sponsor so long ago.

BENNY GOODMAN AND HIS ORCHESTRA　　　June 11, 1941, New York

Benny Goodman, clt; JIMMY MAXWELL, Billy Butterfield, Cootie Williams, tpt; Lou McGarity, Cutty Cutshall, tbn; Les Robinson, Gene Kinsey, as; George Auld, Pete Mondello, ts; Skip Martin, bar; MEL POWELL, p & arr (MP); Charlie Christian, g; Walter Iooss, b; SID CATLETT, d; Helen Forrest, voc.

CO 30648　　　**LP:** PHON 7616
CO 30648-2　　CO 36254, PaAu A7507, PaE R2827, PaSw PZ11124,
　　　　　　　CoC 399. **LP:** JAZ 51
　　　　　　　Tuesday At Ten (arr SkM)

CO 30649　　　**LP:** PHON 7616
CO 30649　　　UNISSUED - Tape
CO 30649-1　　CO 36219, CoC 377. **45:** CO 7-1501. **EP:** PhilCont
　　　　　　　429129BE. **LP:** CO GL523, PHIL BBL7043, PhilCont
　　　　　　　B07010L, JOY 6019
　　　　　　　Soft As Spring - voc Helen Forrest (arr EdSau)

CO 30650　　　**LP:** PHON 7616
CO 30650　　　UNISSUED - Tape
CO 30650　　　UNSSUED - Tape
CO 30650-1　　**LP:** CO KG32822
CO 30650-bkdn　UNISSUED - Tape
CO 30650-2　　CO 36219, CoC 377. **LP:** CO alb P5-15536, JOY 6021
CO 30650　　　UNISSUED - Tape
　　　　　　　Down, Down, Down (What A Song!) - voc Helen Forrest
　　　　　　　& ensemble (arr EdSau)

CO 30651-bkdn　UNISSUED - Tape
CO 30651-1　　CO 36284, CoArg 291262, CoC 411, CoE DB2797, CoFr
　　　　　　　BF407, CoNor GNS5103. **LP:** JAZ 51
CO 30651-2　　**LP:** CO GL523, PHIL BBL7043, PhilCont B07010L, CO
　　　　　　　"Texaco". **45:** CO 7-1502. **EP:** CO B356
　　　　　　　La Rosita (arr EdSau)

The band put in a week at the Cedar Point Ballroom, Sandusky, Ohio, beginning June 14; it may be from there that this undated air check emanated:

SUSTAINING BROADCAST　　　　　*poss. mid-June 1941,*
　Unknown radio network　　　　　*Sandusky, Ohio*

Personnel as June 11/July 6.

La Rosita
Caprice XXIV Paganini

During this brief midwestern tour, Charlie Christian became ill and left the band, never to return. His malady was diagnosed as tuberculosis in Bellevue Hospital in New York, and from there he was transferred to Seaview Sanitarium in Staten Island. He will never recover. Tommy Morgan (elli) joined in his stead—so phrased, because no one could really replace him. Charlie died of tuberculosis March 2, 1942.

Other changes occurred; logically, and expediently, likely by the end of June. Les Robinson decided to stay in New York, and Clint Neagley, who'd been working with Gene Krupa, returned to the fold. So did Vido Musso who, after a long stint with Harry James, had failed in a brief attempt to lead his own big band. His return was necessitated by the defection of Georgie Auld, who'd elected to go back to his old boss, Artie Shaw. Music-press reports had Don Carter coming in on band drums, leaving Sid Catlett free for small group work—but Sid played with the orchestra during broadcasts. (The author saw the band several times in July and on each occasion, broadcasts or no, Catlett was the only drummer in evidence.) And vocalist Tommy Taylor began his four and a half months with the band on the July 4 weekend.

A dated acetate that is not confirmed by a broadcast log finds the new bandsmen at work on Atlantic City's Steel Pier:

SUSTAINING BROADCAST   *July 6, 1941, Atlantic City, N.J.*
  MUTUAL Radio Network

*Benny Goodman, clt; Billy Butterfield, Cootie Williams, Jimmy Maxwell, tpt;
Lou McGarity, Cutty Cutshall, tbn; Gene Kinsey, CLINT NEAGLEY, as; Pete
Mondello, VIDO MUSSO, ts; Skip Martin, bar; Mel Powell, p; TOMMY MOR-
GAN (ELLI), g; Walter Iooss, b; Sid Catlett, d; Helen Forrest, TOMMY TAY-
LOR, voc.*

Let's Dance (theme)
Don't Be That Way (LP: HR 5004)
Smoke Gets In Your Eyes - voc Helen Forrest
Tuesday At Ten (n/c)

On Thursday, July 10, Benny gave a combined classical/jazz concert in
the Robin Hood Dell (an outdoor auditorium) in Philadelphia. He played the
Mozart Concerto with the Philadelphia Orchestra, Edwin McArthur conducting. Benny then conducted the orchestra in Stravinsky's "Tango," with
Vido Musso featured on tenor. Finally the band took over. All of this was
broadcast, but unfortunately no transcriptions of it are extant. But another
broadcast from the Steel Pier was captured in part on acetate:

SUSTAINING BROADCAST   *July 12, 1941, Atlantic City, N.J.*
  Unknown network

Personnel as July 6.

Tuesday At Ten (n/c)
*When The Sun Comes Out - voc Helen Forrest; voc interjections, Sid
  Catlett*
Negra Soy ("Something New")
Roll 'Em (LP: HR 5004)
Embraceable You - feat. Jimmy Maxwell, tpt

Another classical/jazz concert was given in New York's Lewishon
Stadium on July 14, this time with the New York Philharmonic Orchestra,
Reginald Stewart conducting. Then the band headed west to an eventual
engagement in the Panther Room of Chicago's Hotel Sherman. Likely as it
did so, some of the men chose to stay on the East Coast, and more personnel
changes took place. These are reflected in the next air check listing, the first
in a series of seven commercial programs for the Holland Furnace Company,
titled, "House Warming":

"HOUSE WARMING"   *July 17, 1941, prob. Chicago*
  Unknown network

*Benny Goodman, clt; Billy Butterfield, Cootie Williams, Jimmy Maxwell, AL
DAVIS, tpt; Lou McGarity, Cutty Cutshall, tbn; Skip Martin, Clint Neagley, as;
Vido Musso, GEORGE BERG, ts; CHARLES "CHUCK" GENTRY, bar; Mel
Powell, p; Tommy Morgan, g; JOHN SIMMONS, b; Sid Catlett, d; Helen
Forrest, Tommy Taylor, voc.*

Tuesday At Ten

"HOUSE WARMING"   *July 24, 1941, Chicago*
  Unknown network

Personnel as July 17.

Daddy - voc Helen Forrest

"HOUSE WARMING"   *July 31, 1941, Chicago,*
  Unknown network

Personnel as July 17.

A Smo-o-o-oth One (orchestra - arr EdSau)
Anything - voc Tommy Taylor (arr EdSau)

And from the same date, our first sustaining broadcast from the
Sherman:

SUSTAINING BROADCAST   *July 31, 1941, Hotel*
  NBC Radio Network   *Sherman, Chicago*

Personnel as July 17.

Flying Home (orchestra - arr SkM) (LP: HR 5004)
Soft As Spring - voc Helen Forrest (n/c)
Something New (n/c)
A Smo-o-o-oth One - to signoff (orchestra)

On August 1 Helen Forrest gave four weeks' notice. Although she'd
been troubled (and briefly hospitalized) with an ulcer, that was not her

reason for leaving: she had an opportunity to join her one true love, Harry
James, and she seized it. Thus she does not appear on the new band's first
studio session in Chicago, and her recording days with Benny are over.

BENNY GOODMAN AND HIS ORCHESTRA   August 1, 1941, Chicago

Personnel as July 17.

CCO 3925-1	CO 36305, CoC 426. **EP:** CoE SEG7536. **LP:** JAZ 51
	From One Love To Another (Danza Lucumi) - voc Tommy Taylor
CCO 3926-1	same issues
	Anything - voc Tommy Taylor (arr EdSau)
CCO 3927-1	CO 36379, CoArg 291336, CoC 458, PaAu A7477. **LP:** CO PG33405
	The Count (arr MP? - poss. MLW)
CCO 3928-1	**LP:** PHON 7616
CCO 3928-2	CO 36421, CoArg 291336, CoC 494, PaAu A7434. **LP:** CO CL6100, CO CL2533, CO PG33405, CO alb P5-15536, SWE 1001
	Pound Ridge (originally titled, "Same Time Tomorrow")

There is some dispute over arranger credit for, "The Count." Collectors point out striking similarities between Benny's version and Andy Kirk's
(DE 18123), recorded in November 1940, long before Mel Powell joined the
band. Benny insists that his was written by Mel, and not by Mary Lou
Williams, believed to have written Kirk's. Other like instances occur: for
example, Skippy Martin's chart on "Tuesday At Ten" for Benny was
recorded by Count Basie on January 28, 1941 (OK 6071), and they are one
and the same.

Although Helen does not again record with Benny, she continues to
appear with him, both in the Sherman and on the "House Warming" programs and sustaining broadcasts. According to a program log, she did so as
late as August 17, two days after Peggy Lee had made her first record with
the band. That is her last logged performance, but she claims Benny had her
sit on the bandstand until the end of the Sherman engagement, but did not
permit her to sing. Benny says he does not remember it that way.

SUSTAINING BROADCAST   *August 8, 1941, Hotel*
  Unknown network   *Sherman, Chicago*

Personnel as July 17.

Superman
It's So Peaceful In The Country - voc Helen Forrest (arr EdSau)
Flying Home (orchestra)
Let's Dance (theme)

SUSTAINING BROADCAST   *August 10, 1941, Hotel*
  NBC Radio Network   *Sherman, Chicago*

Personnel as July 17.

Let's Dance (theme) (LP: FT 2501)
The Count
Time Was - voc Tommy Taylor
Clarinet A La King (arr EdSau)
Soft As Spring - voc Helen Forrest
Perfidia - voc Helen Forrest
Caprice XXIV Paganini (arr SkM)
Anything - voc Tommy Taylor
A Smo-o-o-oth One (orchestra)

(This broadcast is on LP, FAN 19-119.)

Broadcast logs, as well as extant air checks, show not a single instance
of a small group performance throughout the Sherman engagement. For
whatever reason, Benny offered the orchestra exclusively during July, August and September, according to all available evidence.

Although working in the Sherman, Benny stayed in the Ambassador
Hotel in Chicago. When Helen gave notice he listened the more carefully to
a youngster singing in a trio in the Ambassador, one Norma Egstrom. Benny
liked what he heard, saw in the petite blonde an exciting, if as yet un-
polished, talent. He offered her a contract, she accepted, and went along
with the suggestion that she adopt a new name as she began her new job:
Peggy Lee.

Peggy's first recording session with the band was August 15. Two tunes
are certain to have been recorded, and it was speculated that a third, a V-

Disc version of, "Buckle Down, Winsocki," might also have been cut at the same time. Further research, however, now more positively points to a date in October for that recording, and it no longer is assigned to August 15.

BENNY GOODMAN AND HIS ORCHESTRA　　　**August 15, 1941, Chicago**

Personnel as July 17, except PEGGY LEE, voc, replaces Forrest.

CCO 3950-1	**LP:** PHON 7616
CCO 3950-2	CO 36359, CoC 439. **EP:** CO B1636, CorAu KEP057. **LP:** HA HL7005, HA HL7255, HA HA30024, CorAu KLP799, CBSH S52866, SONY SOPJ22-23, SONY 20AP-1486, HALLMARK 503
	Elmer's Tune - voc PEGGY LEE
CCO 3951-1	**LP:** CO PG33405
	The Birth Of The Blues (arr EdSau)

SUSTAINING BROADCAST　　　　　　*August 17, 1941, Hotel*
　NBC Radio Network　　　　　　　　　*Sherman, Chicago*

Personnel as July 17 (Forrest still performing with the band).

Tuesday At Ten

　　The next set of undated air checks, many of them of poor audio quality and incomplete, is believed to have come from the Sherman while Helen was still with the band:

SUSTAINING BROADCASTS　　　　*July 25-August 17, 1941, Hotel*
　NBC Radio Network　　　　　　　　*Sherman, Chicago*

Personnel as July 17.

Let's Dance (theme)
Flying Home (orchestra)
From One Love To Another (n/c - intro only)
Take It - voc, the band
Intermezzo (n/c - intro only)
Benny Rides Again
Soft As Spring (n/c - intro only)
Daddy (n/c - ending only)
A Smo-o-o-oth One (orchestra)
It's So Peaceful In The Country - voc Helen Forrest (n/c)

BENNY GOODMAN AND HIS ORCHESTRA　　　**August 20, 1941, Chicago**

Personnel as August 15 (Lee in, Forrest out).

CCO 3951-2	CO 36359, CoC 439, PaE R2830, PaInd DPE31, PaSw PZ11260. **LP:** JAZ 51
	The Birth Of The Blues (arr EdSau)
CCO 3980-1	**LP:** CO PG33405, Co alb P6-14954, reputedly FR series
CCO 3980-2	**LP:** PHON 7616
	Clarinet A La King (arr EdSau)
CCO 3981-1	**LP:** PHON 7616
	My Old Flame - voc Peggy Lee (arr EdSau)
CCO 3982-1	CO 36379, CoC 458, CO 39034. **LP:** SONY SOPJ22-23, NOST 890/1. **ET:** Air Force GL 18
	I See A Million People (But All I Can See Is You) - voc Peggy Lee (arr EdSau)

　　Music press reports at this time claimed Benny recorded some sides with vocals by Peggy for World Transcriptions. Benny has no recollection of such a session, cannot imagine under what circumstances it would have occurred.

SUSTAINING BROADCAST　　　　　　*August 24, 1941, Hotel*
　NBC Radio Network　　　　　　　　　*Sherman, Chicago*

Personnel as August 15.
Flying Home (orchestra)
From One Love To Another (Danza Lucumi) - voc Tommy Taylor (n/c)
A Smo-o-o-oth One (orchestra)
Daddy - voc Peggy Lee (n/c)

　　No clues tell us whether the next clutch of undated air checks from the Sherman are pre- or post-Peggy. First three cuts are via NBC, the rest via unknown networks.

SUSTAINING BROADCASTS　　　　*July 25 - August 28, 1941, Hotel*
　　　　　　　　　　　　　　　　　　　　Sherman, Chicago

Personnel as July 17/August 15.

Via NBC Radio Network:
Anything - voc Tommy Taylor (n/c)
Don't Be That Way
A Smo-o-o-oth One (orchestra) - to signoff (n/c - intro clipped)

Via unknown radio networks:
The Count (poss. "House Warming" source)
Flying Home (orchestra)
Lazy River (no voc)] (from one program, poss. August 28)
Pound Ridge (n/c)]
Something New

　　John Simmons remained in Chicago when the band left the Sherman; Marty Blitz replaced him. It went first to Toronto, appeared at the Dance Pavilion of the Canadian National Exhibition on August 30. Early in September Benny was guest soloist with the Dayton Symphony Orchestra, Dayton, Ohio. Then it was on to a four-week stand at Frank Dailey's Meadowbrook, in Cedar Grove, N.J. An earlier assumption that opening night was the 16th is now disproved, for there is a broadcast from the 11th:

SUSTAINING BROADCAST　　　*September 11, 1941, Cedar Grove, N. J.*
　MUTUAL Radio Network

Personnel as August 15, except MARTY BLITZ, b, replaces Simmons.

Tuesday At Ten (n/c) (LP: HR 5004)
When The Sun Comes Out - voc Peggy Lee (LP: HR 5004)
A Smo-o-o-oth One (orchestra) (LP: HR 5004)
. . . intro only, unidentified tune
From One Love To Another (Danza Lucumi) - voc Tommy Taylor (n/c)
Roll 'Em (LP: HR 5005 - splice)
Good-Bye (theme)

　　Every Saturday afternoon CBS aired a special "Matinee at the Meadowbrook" broadcast, featuring comedy (Eddie Mayhoff, others) sports' scores (Mel Allen, others) and the band in residence. On his first "Matinee," Benny does something special, too—a "History Of Swing," in which segments of the band play "Rockin' Chair" in the styles of the ODJB, Paul Whiteman, Red Nichols, Kay Kyser and Guy Lombardo, and finally, Benny Goodman:

"MATINEE AT THE　　　　　*September 13, 1941, Cedar Grove, N. J.*
　MEADOWBROOK"　　*CBS Radio Network*

Personnel as September 11.

The Count
"A History Of Swing"
It's So Peaceful In The Country - voc Peggy Lee
Superman
Caprice XXIV Paganini
Clarinet A La King (n/c - intro clipped)

　　Source acetates for the next grouping of "Matinee at the Meadowbrook" air checks are unclear as to date, whether the broadcast of the 13th or the 20th. On the slim basis that Benny is unlikely to have repeated a "History Of Swing" interlude, and that the (upcoming) program of the 20th seems "full," a lucky 13 is the choice here. It may well be, of course, that some of the cuts are from the 13th, and some from the 20th; or that some may be from an intervening sustaining broadcast. In any event, all are from this period.

"MATINEE AT THE　　　　*September 13/20, 1941, Cedar Grove, N.J.*
　MEADOWBROOK"　　*CBS Radio Network*
or
SUSTAINING BROADCAST(S)　　　　　*mid-September 1941, Cedar*
　CBS, other network(s)　　　　　　　　　　*Grove, N.J.*

Personnel as September 11.

Rockin' Chair
. . . unknown tune (n/c)
Caprice XXIV Paganini (n/c)
A Smo-o-o-oth One (orchestra)
I Don't Want To Set The World On Fire - voc Peggy Lee
Flying Home (orchestra)

SUSTAINING BROADCAST   September 14, 1941, Cedar Grove, N.J.
    MUTUAL Radio Network

Personnel as September 11.

Benny Rides Again (LP: HR 5004)
A Smo-o-o-oth One (orchestra)
Take It - voc, the band
Concerto For Cootie (LP: HR 5004)
Roll 'Em - to signoff (LP: HR 5005 - splice)

SUSTAINING BROADCAST   September 16, 1941, Cedar Grove, N.J.
    MUTUAL Radio Network

Personnel as September 11.

The Count (LP: HR 5004)
Smoke Gets In Your Eyes - voc Peggy Lee (LP: HR 5004)
The Earl (arr MP) (LP: HR 5004)
Let's Do It - voc Peggy Lee (arr MP) (n/c)
Roll 'Em (LP: HR 5005)
The Birth Of The Blues (LP: HR 5004)
Same Time Tomorrow (later, "Pound Ridge") (LP: HR 5004)
Good-Bye (theme)

SUSTAINING BROADCAST   September 17, 1941, Cedar Grove, N.J.
    CBS Radio Network

Personnel as September 11.

Let The Door Knob Hitcha - voc Cootie Williams
Caprice XXIV Paganini
I See A Million People - voc Peggy Lee
Clarinet A La King
Something New - to signoff

SUSTAINING BROADCAST   September 19, 1941, Cedar Grove, N.J.
    CBS Radio Network

Personnel as September 11.

Let's Dance (theme)
Flying Home (orchestra)
A Smo-o-o-oth One (orchestra)
The Earl
Let The Door Knob Hitcha - voc Cootie Williams - to signoff

"MATINEE AT THE   September 20, 1941, Cedar Grove, N.J.
    MEADOWBROOK"   CBS Radio Network

Personnel as September 11.

The Earl
It's So Peaceful In The Country - voc Peggy Lee
Delilah (arr EdSau)
Time Was - voc Tommy Taylor
Tuesday At Ten
Intermezzo
Benny Rides Again (LP: HR 5005)

(Above all on LP, JOY 1056, 1097. The latter LP also has "Let's Dance (theme)", taken from the broadcast of September 27, and "Caprice XXIV Paganini" and a closing theme, "Let's Dance (theme)", taken from the broadcast of October 4, q.v.)

SUSTAINING BROADCAST   September 21, 1941, Cedar Grove, N.J.
    MUTUAL Radio Network

Personnel as September 11.

One O'Clock Jump
I'm Here (arr MP)
Concerto For Cootie - to signoff

SUSTAINING BROADCAST   September 23, 1941, Cedar Grove, N.J.
    MUTUAL Radio Network

Personnel as September 11.

The Earl
If It's True - voc Tommy Taylor
Roll 'Em
One O'Clock Jump - to signoff

(Above on LP, HR 5005. "Roll 'Em" is spliced.)

Benny's next recording session is celebrated among collectors as unique, "The Drum-less Date." And with good cause: the only contemporary release from the session, OK 6474, presented the Goodman orchestra sans batterie, a startling event. Microgroove issues into the late 1970's of various takes of the five tunes recorded on September 25 confirmed the absence of drums. "Safeties" in Columbia's possession, containing further unreleased material, offer not a single side with drums.

But all of that would change in 1984 with access to Columbia safeties no longer in the studio's vaults. Five takes and two aborted efforts of the first two tunes recorded at the session negate the "drum-less" tag, for Jo Jones's tubs are unmistakably present on them.

When first it appeared that Benny had recorded without Sid Catlett, the music press speculated that Benny was disenchanted with Big Sid, had hired Jo Jones to replace him for the recording session. To explain Jones's apparent non-participation, the press reported that Jones did not then carry a Local 802 (New York) musicians' union card, and that at the last minute union officials forbade him to record.

Years ago, when the author first broached the matter to Mr. Goodman, Benny wasn't explicit about Catlett's missing the date: "Maybe he was sick; I don't remember." As to Jones's seeming nonemployment, Benny said no, he didn't think the union had anything to do with it. It was his custom, as I should know, to rehearse the several sections of his orchestra separately. He said he did so on this session; and when he added the rhythm section, ". . . the drums just didn't sound right. Somehow, they didn't fit in with Mel's new arrangements. So I tried a couple of takes without them, and it came out all right."

Stimulated in 1985 by revelation that newly-discovered takes from this session include Jones, Benny dug a bit deeper into his memory: "Y'know, we were recording in Leiderkranz Hall, and the acoustics there were very 'hard.' Sound just bounced off those walls, the whole place reverberated. Jo's drums just went 'boom,' 'boom,' 'boom,' no matter what the engineers did. So I simply decided we'd go ahead without them, and it sounded better."

So much for Jones; Benny's recollections in his regard, almost a quarter-century apart, are consistent. But what about Catlett? Was he irked with Big Sid's propensity to throw in "fills" and accents whenever he felt like it, no matter what the score called for? (The author recalls witnessing a club date of Louis Armstrong's, Catlett on drums, and ever-tolerant Louis telling him right on the stand, "For Christ's sake, Sidney, keep it down!") Was Benny fed up with Sid's overdrumming? "No, not at all, I thought he was an excellent drummer. I heard him for the first time in some little club in Harlem, and I thought he was marvelous." (When speaking about musicians, and especially when his remarks may be published, Benny can be very, very diplomatic.).

Catlett was indeed an "excellent drummer." A large man, addicted to green chalk-stripe suits and wide flowered ties, he enjoyed life and he played drums enthusiastically, at times loud and long. He had a bubbly sense of humor and he played with what Chicago musicians call "a lot of side," a kind of stagey exhibitionism. His droll, "Watch the drummer, boy!", his use of an oversized powder puff with which he patted his armpits, his trick of tossing a drumstick high overhead and catching it seemingly without looking—marking the catch with a heavy foot on the bass drum—were mannerisms knowing audiences came to look for. Then when the tune Benny programmed challenged his ability, he played (as musicians say) "his ass off." (One of the author's fond memories of Big Sid is his imaginative workout on "Sing, Sing, Sing," in a manner totally different from Krupa's conception. Another is an instance when Catlett substituted for an ailing Chick Webb—a hard act to follow—and Chick's band applauding him onstage after the first set.) Big Sid Catlett, a big man with a big talent.

(Discographical note: Throughout this work, the several takes of any given tune recorded by Goodman for Columbia at any one session are grouped together, almost invariably. This mode is employed for simplicity's sake, so that the reader may see all of the known efforts to obtain a satisfactory recording of one composition, in a single, unbroken listing. It also demonstrates, so far as can be ascertained, the sequence in which the several takes were performed, for any given tune. This arrangement, however, may not reflect the true order-of-performance for the entire session: On occasion, Benny would first record one of more takes of tune ''A,'' switch to one or more takes of tune ''B,'' then eventually return to an additional take or takes of tune ''A.'' Because of the drums/no drums character of the September 25 studio date, the listing reflects the order-of-performance for the entire session.)

BENNY GOODMAN   **September 25, 1941, New York**
  AND HIS ORCHESTRA

Benny Goodman, clt; Billy Butterfield, Cootie Williams, Jimmy Maxwell, Al Davis, tpt; Lou McGarity, Cutty Cutshall, tbn; Skip Martin, Clint Neagley, as; Vido Musso, George Berg, ts; Chuck Gentry, bar; Mel Powell, p; Tommy Morgan, g; Marty Blitz, b; Jo Jones, d. Tommy Taylor, Peggy Lee, voc.

CO 31363	UNISSUED - Tape
CO 31363	UNISSUED - Tape
	How Deep Is The Ocean - voc Peggy Lee (arr EdSau)
CO 31364-bkdn	UNISSUED - Tape
CO 31364	UNISSUED - Tape
CO 31364	**LP:** BID 1014
CO 31364-bkdn	UNISSUED - Tape
CO 31364	UNISSUED - Tape
	The Earl (arr MP)

Jones out; no drums for balance of session

CO 31364-1	VD 425 A, NavyVD 205 A. **45:** CO 409-G (Set G4-3). **LP:** EPIC EE22025, EPICAu ELP3648, EPICFr/H 80056, TL STLJ05, PHON 7616
	The Earl (arr MP)
CO 31363-bkdn	UNISSUED - Tape
CO 31363	**LP:** PHON 7616
CO 31363-bkdn	UNISSUED - Tape
CO 31363-1	**LP:** NOST 1004, BID 1014
	How Deep Is The Ocean - voc Peggy Lee (arr EdSau)
CO 31364-bkdns	UNISSUED - Tape (3 consecutive aborted attempts)
CO 31364-2	OK 6474, CoC 587, CoSd DS1372, PaE R2843, PaInd DPE44, PaIt B71222. **EP:** CO 5-1654 (Set B351). **LP:** CO GL501, CO CL534, CO ''Texaco,'' CO PG33405, FONT TFL 5067, FontCont 682047TL, FR series
	The Earl (arr MP)
CO 31365	**LP:** PHON 7617
CO 31365	**LP:** BID 1014
CO 31365-bkdn	UNISSUED - Tape
CO 31365-1	**LP:** CO GL523, PHIL BBL7043, PhilCont B07010L. **45:** Co 7-1501
	'Tis Autumn - voc Tommy Taylor (arr EdSau)
CO 31366-1	**LP:** PHON 7617
CO 31366-2	**LP:** CO GL523, HA HL7005, CorAu KLP799, PHIL BBL7043, PhilCont B07010L, SONY SOPJ 22/23, SONY 20AP-1486, HALLMARK 503. **45:** CO 7-1502
	That's The Way It Goes - voc Peggy Lee (arr EdSau)
CO 31367-1	**LP:** CO alb P6-14538
CO 31367-bkdns	UNISSUED - Tape (3 consecutive aborted attempts)
CO 31367-2	OK 6474. **LP:** EPIC EE22025, EPICAu ELP3648, EpicFr/H 80056, CO KG31547, CO alb P5-15536, CO alb P4M-5678, CBS 67268, SONY SOPJ 22/23, SONY 20AP-1486
	Let's Do It (Let's Fall In Love) - voc Peggy Lee (arr MP)

(The original issue from this session is Benny's first on the 35-cent Okeh label, not the more expensive Columbia, a strategical move to counter RCA's low-priced Bluebird releases. // ''Let's Do It'' began as a head arrangement, with the band vamping behind Peggy's bluesy vocal. When it was decided to record the tune, Mel Powell committed it to manuscript.)

Whatever the reason for Sid Catlett's absence on the September 25 recording session, he's back on drums the very next night:

SUSTAINING BROADCAST   *September 26, 1941, Cedar Grove, N.J.*
  Unknown network

Personnel as September 25, except Sid Catlett, d.

Delilah

The announcer's introduction of ''The Count'' on the next ''Matinee at the Meadowbrook'' specifies that the arrangement is by Mary Lou Williams. So despite Benny's contention, she should be credited for the chart, and not Mel Powell.

''MATINEE AT THE   *September 27, 1941, Cedar Grove, N.J.*
  MEADOWBROOK''   *CBS Radio Network*

Personnel as September 26.

Let's Dance (theme) (LP: JOY 1056, 1097)
The Count
From One Love To Another (Danza Lucumi) - voc Tommy Taylor
Let The Door Knob Hitcha - voc Cootie Williams (LP: SB 158)
That's The Way It Goes - voc Peggy Lee (n/c)
Caprice XXIV Paganini
A Smo-o-o-oth One (orchestra)
Let's Dance (theme) - to signoff

SUSTAINING BROADCAST   *September 27, 1941, Cedar Grove, N.J.*
  Unknown network

Personnel as September 26.

I Got It Bad (And That Ain't Good) - voc Peggy Lee (arr EdSau)
Roll 'Em (n/c)

SUSTAINING BROADCAST   *September 28, 1941, Cedar Grove, N.J.*
  CBS Radio Network

Personnel as September 26.

Delilah (n/c - intro excised)
Benny Rides Again
The Count
The Earl
A Smo-o-o-oth One (orchestra) - to signoff

SUSTAINING BROADCAST   *September 28, 1941, Cedar Grove, N.J.*
  MUTUAL Radio Network

Personnel as September 26.

(few bars each, I Got It Bad (And That Ain't Good), I'm Here, La Rosita)
Roll 'Em
Good-Bye (theme)

Access to Columbia safeties in private hands for the September 25 session led to further revelations: from the same source, safeties from the Goodman sessions of October 2, 8, 21 and 28, 1941, and for three dates in 1942 became available. Importantly, the safeties for October 2 add still more takes of ''Clarinet A La King'' to those previously known, emphasizing Benny's determination to record Sauter's composition to his complete satisfaction.

(Collectors should note that various claims of a 78 rpm release of take 1 of ''Clarinet A La King'' from this session appear unfounded, for none has been located on any label. Similarly, reports of a take 2 release of ''Clarinet A La King'' on CoC 566 are unconfirmed. The original release on OK 6544, take 2, is rare; it and the take 4 issue of ''Let's Do It'' on OK 6474 are the scarcest of all of Goodman's Okeh's from the 1940's.)

BENNY GOODMAN AND HIS ORCHESTRA   **October 2, 1941, New York**

Personnel as September 26.

CO 31390-1	CO 36411, CoArg 291359, CoAu DO2992, CoC 487, CoJap M258, PaE R2830, PaInd DPE31, PaSw PZ11260. **LP:** EPIC EE22025, EPICAu ELP3648, EPICFr/H 80056, CO P3-16175
	Caprice XXIV Paganini (arr SkM)

CO 31391-1   CO 36421, CoArg 291322, CoC 494. **LP:** Co alb
P6-14954, EPIC EE22025, EPICAu ELP3648, EPICFr/H
80056, HA HL7148, HA 30024, CBSH 52866, SONY
SOPJ 22/23, SONY 20AP-1486
I Got It Bad (And That Ain't Good) - voc Peggy Lee (arr
EdSau)

CO 31392-   UNISSUED - Tape (2 consecutive aborted attempts)
bkdns
CO 31392   **LP:** BID 1014
CO 31392-1   CO 36754. **EP:** CO B1636. **LP:** HA HL7005, CorAU
KLP799, Co ''Bernz-O-Matic,'' CO D499, CO alb
P2M-5267, CO IP6466, HA 30024, CBSH 52866,
SONY SOPJ 22/23, SONY 20AP-1486, NOST ''Those
Wonderful Stars of Yesteryear'' alb, HALLMARK 503
My Old Flame - (voc Peggy Lee - not credited on
original issue) (arr EdSau)

CO 31393-   UNISSUED - Tape (2 consecutive aborted attempts)
bkdns
CO 31393-1   **LP:** PHON 7617
CO 31393   **LP:** BID 1014
CO 31393-2   OK 6544. **LP:** EPIC EE22025, EPICAu ELP3648,
EPICFr/H 80056, CO KG31547, CO alb P5-15536, CO
alb PM-16932, SONY SOPL-193
CO 31393   **LP:** BID 1014
Clarinet A La King (arr EdSau)

CO 31402-2   **LP:** PHON 7617
CO 31402-1   CO 36411, CoArg 291322, CoC 487. **LP:** EPIC EE22025,
EPICAu ELP3648, EPICFr/H 80056
I'm Here (arr MP)

(Matrices CO 31394 through CO 31401 are not Goodman recordings.)

SUSTAINING BROADCAST   *October 3, 1941,*
  Unknown network   *Cedar Grove, N.J.*

Personnel as October 2.

Tuesday At Ten

''MATINEE AT THE MEADOWBROOK''   *October 4, 1941,*
  CBS Radio Network   *Cedar Grove, N.J.*

Orchestra as October 2. TRIO: Goodman, Powell, Catlett

Ida - TRIO (LP: SB 158, HR 5005)
Delilah (LP: SB 158)
Clarinet A La King (LP: SB 158)
Soft As Spring - voc Peggy Lee (LP: SB 158)
Let's Dance (intermission theme - rhythm section only)
I'm Here (LP: SB 158, HR 5005)
Caprice XXIV Paganini (LP: JOY 1097)
Let's Dance (theme) (LP: JOY 1056, 1097)

SUSTAINING BROADCAST   *October 7, 1941,*
  Unknown network   *Cedar Grove, N.J.*

Personnel as October 2.

Rose Room (LP: QD 16)

Source material in Columbia's possession available to the author presents conflicting evidence in regard certain Goodman matrices recorded in October 1941. A voluminous listing of all Columbia-related matrices, published in-house and used internally, is at odds with markings on 16" safeties for this period in Columbia's vaults. Especially mystifying are inconsistencies between the two sources for matrices CO 31426, ''Shady Lady Bird,'' and CO 31427, ''Buckle Down Winsocki.''

Aural identifications, principally those of drummers Sid Catlett or Ralph Collier and vocalists Tommy Taylor or Tommy Dix, indicated that the published listing was at best incomplete. This determination caused a re-alignment of affected matrices, as they appeared in the author's earlier, ''BG - On The Record.'' These logical inferences were valid up to a point, but were not fully explanatory; there still seemed to be something missing.

Discovery of Columbia 16" safeties in private hands in 1984 supplied that missing link. Together with the safeties still at Columbia, they stipulate

when, and in what order, the several takes of ''Shady Lady Bird'' and ''Buckle Down Winsocki'' were recorded. And they resolve a question that has troubled Goodman collectors for over 40 years: Benny did indeed record a two-part ''Roll 'Em'' for Columbia.

Without specifying the date of the recording, magazines published in the fall of 1941 reported that Benny had waxed the Mary Lou Williams classic in Liederkranz Hall. Thorough search of Columbia's vaults in the '50s and '60s failed to produce the recording; obvious, now, it had been removed. Columbia's matrix listing omitted any notice of it; that, too, is now explained, for the cuts were not assigned matrices.

Even today, Benny has no recollection of having recorded ''Roll 'Em'' for Columbia, can't think why he would have attempted to do so, given his definitive and successful Victor release. (The May 5, 1941 Columbia recording of ''Don't Be That Way'' was not assigned a matrix, either. Could ''Roll 'Em'' have also been cut at the request of a Columbia executive, for his personal use?) Withal, a significant addition to Mr. Goodman's works, and an enigma finally resolved.

BENNY GOODMAN AND HIS ORCHESTRA   **October 8, 1941, New York**
Personnel as October 2. CLIFF JENKINS (CJ), arr. And to his other talents, add Benny Goodman, whistle-blower.

CO 31363-bkdn   UNISSUED - Tape
CO 31363-3   CO 36754. **LP:** EPIC EE22025, EPICAu ELP3648,
EPICFr/H 80056, CO alb P6-14007, CO alb P4M-5678,
SONY SOPJ 22/23
How Deep Is The Ocean - voc Peggy Lee (arr EdSau)

CO 31426-bkdn   UNISSUED - Tape
CO 31426   UNISSUED - Tape
CO 31426-bkdn   UNISSUED - Tape
CO 31426   UNISSUED - Tape
CO 31426   UNISSUED - Tape
CO 31426-bkdn   UNISSUED - Tape
CO 31426-1   CO 36429 (''small-type'' label)
Shady Lady Bird - voc Peggy Lee

CO 31427   UNISSUED - Tape
CO 31427   UNISSUED - Tape
CO 31427-   UNISSUED - Tape (2 consecutive aborted attempts)
bkdns
CO 31427-1   VD 55A. **ET:** AFRS Jill's Juke Box H46-98, AFRS G.I.
(XP 33332-1)   Jive 742
Buckle Down, Winsocki - voc Tommy Taylor & chorus
(arr CJ)

-0- bkdn   **LP:** BID 1014
-0-   **LP:** BID 1014
Roll 'Em - Part 1

-0-   **LP:** BID 1014
Roll 'Em - Part 2

(The V-Disc release of ''Buckle Down, Winsocki'' inserts the comma as shown, the original Columbia release does not.)

SUSTAINING BROADCAST   *October 8, 1941, Cedar Grove, New Jersey*
  CBS Radio Network

Personnel as October 2.

Clarinet A La King (LP: HR 5005)
I'm Here (LP: HR 5005)
Let The Door Knob Hitcha - voc Cootie Williams (LP: QD 16, HR 5005)
Let's Dance (theme)

October 8 was the last day of Benny's engagement in the Meadowbrook; Tommy Dorsey, with Frank Sinatra, Connie Haines, Ziggy Elman and Buddy Rich, replaced him. Crossing the river back into Manhattan, Benny began a lengthy stand in the Terrace Room of the Hotel New Yorker the very next day. But before we pick him up there it is necessary to catalog some air checks from undated acetates, all believed to have originated in the Meadowbrook during Big Sid's tenure with the band. They are listed alphabetically:

SUSTAINING BROADCASTS *September 11 - October 8, 1941,*
Various radio networks *Cedar Grove, New Jersey*

Personnel as September 26.

The Count (n/c)
Don't Be That Way
The Earl
I'm Here (via CBS)
I'm Not Complainin'
A Smo-o-o-oth One (orchestra)
Sing, Sing, Sing (LP: HR 5005-splice)
Sing, Sing, Sing

Precisely when Catlett—and Taylor, Blitz and Skip Martin—left the band is not known, but all had been replaced by our next evidence of the band's activity, its re-make studio session of October 21. Note that Columbia's files do not include Cootie Williams in the personnel for this session (or the studio date of October 23); the listing here conforms to Columbia's information. But in fact Cootie did stay on until October 31, the full extent of his year's contract, and personnels for broadcasts until the end of the month reflect his presence.

BENNY GOODMAN AND HIS ORCHESTRA **October 21, 1941, New York**

Benny Goodman, clt; Billy Butterfield, Jimmy Maxwell, Al Davis, tpt; Lou McGarity, Cutty Cutshall, tbn; Clint Neagley, JULIE SCHWARTZ, as; Vido Musso, George Berg, ts; Chuck Gentry, bar; Mel Powell, p. Tom Morgan, g; SID WEISS, b; RALPH COLLIER, d; Peggy Lee, voc.

CO 31426 UNISSUED - Tape
CO 31426 UNISSUED - Tape
CO 31426-3 CO 36429, CoC 502. **LP:** EPIC EE22025, EPICAu ELP3648, EPICFr/H 80056, SONY SOPJ22/23
CO 31426-2 **LP:** PHON 7617
Shady Lady Bird - voc Peggy Lee

CO 31427 UNISSUED - Tape (voc, Tommy Dix & chorus)
CO 31427 UNISSUED - Tape (voc, Tommy Dix & chorus)
CO 31427-3 **LP:** PHON 7617 (voc, Tommy Dix & chorus)
CO 31427-2 CO 36429, CoC 502. **LP:** JAZ 51 (voc, Tommy Dix & chorus)
CO 31427-5 **LP:** EPIC series only, as mx CO 31426-3 (voc, Benny Goodman & chorus)
CO 31427 UNISSUED - Tape (voc, Benny Goodman & chorus)
Buckle Down Winsocki (voc credits as above) (arr CJ)

CO 31367-3 **LP:** VELP 1, PHON 7617
CO 31367-4 OK 6474, CoArg 291353, CoC 587, CO 38281, CoC 6400. **LP:** CO CL6033, Phil Cont B07626R, CoJap PL5046, SONY SOPJ22/23. **EP:** CO B406
Let's Do It (Let's Fall In Love) - voc Peggy Lee (arr MP)

(Re-make mxs CO 31426 and CO 31427 are listed first in order to emphasize their reassignment to this date; re-make mx CO 31367 may have been re-corded before them during this session. Tommy Dix is not included in the orchestral personnel listing because he apparently was engaged for the studio date only, and was not a member of the entourage.)

The first in an impressive array of extant air checks from this stand in the Terrace Room of the Hotel New Yorker was broadcast by CBS the evening of the studio session:

SUSTAINING BROADCAST *October 21, 1941, Hotel*
CBS Radio Network *New Yorker, New York*

Orchestra personnel as studio session this date, plus Cootie Williams, tpt.
TRIO: BG, Powell, Collier

Clarinet A La King
The Earl
From One Love To Another (Danza Lucumi) (n/c - intro only)
Ida - TRIO
Moon And Sand (arr EdSau) (n/c - intro only)

SUSTAINING BROADCAST *October 22, 1941, Hotel*
Unknown network *New Yorker, New York*

Personnel as October 21.

Moon And Sand (LP: FAN 19-119)
Superman (n/c)

Another re-make session took place the next day, October 23. Columbia's file material advises that only one tune was recorded, which seems unlikely; would Benny go through the hassle of assembling the band in the studio to cut one tune? To "balance" the date, an otherwise-unassignable recording of "I'll Get By," about which the files offer no information at all, is appended here.

A second unusual circumstance arises from the session: A 12″ test pressing, clearly inscribed CO 31393-1, recently available, was found upon examination to have been cut this date. There is no explanation for the assignment of a take 1, other than that it was a mistake; it is identical to one cut on a safety recording. Its discovery reduces the number of extant recordings of "Clarinet A La King" made at this session to three, not four, as was earlier believed.

BENNY GOODMAN AND HIS ORCHESTRA **October 23, 1941, New York**

Personnel as studio session of October 21.

CO 31393 UNISSUED - Tape
CO 31393-"1" **LP:** PHON 7617
CO 31393-3 OK 6544, CoArg 291368, CoArg 292105, Co Arg C10019B, CoC 566, CoJap S10010, CoSd DS1372, OdG 028129, PaAu A7490, PaE R2843, PaInd DPE44, PaIt B71222. **45:** CO 4-G-6 (Set G4-3). **LP:** CO GL501, CoE 33SX1038, CBS 66267, SONY SOPL-193
Clarinet A La King (arr EdSau)

. . . and from an unknown date,

-0-bkdn UNISSUED - Co Ref
-0- **LP:** PHON 7617
-0-bkdn UNISSUED - Co Ref
-0-bkdn UNISSUED - Co Ref
I'll Get By

"FITCH BANDWAGON" *October 26, 1941, New York*
NBC Radio Network

Personnel as CBS broadcast of October 21.
QUARTET: BG, McGarity, Powell, Collier.

Let's Dance (theme)
Delilah
The Shrine Of St. Cecilia - voc Peggy Lee (arr EdSau) (LP: SB 158)
Clarinet A La King
I'm Here
You and I - QUARTET
A Smo-o-o-oth One (orchestra) (n/c - intro clipped)
Let's Dance (theme)
"Fitch Bandwagon" theme

SUSTAINING BROADCAST *October 27, 1941, Hotel*
Unknown Network *New Yorker, New York*

Personnel as CBS broadcast of October 21.

The Man I Love - voc Peggy Lee
I Got It Bad (And That Ain't Good) - voc Peggy Lee
Sometimes I'm Happy
One O'Clock Jump
Good-Bye (theme)

For several months our only evidences of small group performances have been a few air checks of performances by Trios and a Quartet. Now Benny records his new Sextet for the first time:

BENNY GOODMAN SEXTET　　　　　　**October 28, 1941, New York**

Benny Goodman, clt; Lou McGarity, tbn; Mel Powell, p; Tom Morgan, g; Sid Weiss, b; Ralph Collier, d.

CO 31609-1　**LP:** FONT TFL5067, FontCont 682047TL, EPIC EE22025, EPICAu ELP3648, EPICFr/H 80056, NOST 1004
CO 31609-bkdn　UNISSUED - Tape
CO 31609-bkdn　UNISSUED - Tape
CO 31609-2　OK 6486, CoArg 291330, CoC 532, CoSd DS1366, CoJap M454, PaE R2838, PaInd DPE35, HA 1011. **LP:** CO D449, CO alb P2M-5267, SONY 20AP-1810, JAZ 51
CO 31609　**LP:** BID 1002
CO 31609　**LP:** PHON LV-50, PHON 7617, BID 1004
　　　　If I Had You

CO 31610-1　OK 6486, CoArg 291330, CoArg 291750, CoC532, CoJap M324, CoSd DS1366, PaE R2838, PaFin DPY1009, PaInd DPE35, HA 1011. **EP:** FontCont 462012TE. **LP:** EPIC EE22025, EPICAu ELP3648, EPICFr/H 80056, SONY 20AP-1810
CO 31610　7" **LP:** EPH82. **LP:** BID 1002
CO 31610　**LP:** PHON LV-50, PHON 7617, BID 1002
CO 31610-2　**LP:** BID 1004
CO 31610-bkdns　UNISSUED - Tape (3 consecutive aborted attempts)
　　　　Limehouse Blues

SUSTAINING BROADCAST　　*October 30, 1941, Hotel*
　MUTUAL Radio Network　　*New Yorker, New York*

Personnel as CBS broadcast of October 21.

Let's Dance (theme)
Caprice XXIV Paganini

　　As noted, Cootie's last day with the band was October 31. Two undated air checks from the Hotel New Yorker complete his year's contribution:

SUSTAINING BROADCASTS　　*October 9–31, 1941, Hotel*
　Unknown network　　*New Yorker, New York*

Personnel as CBS broadcast of October 21.

Benny Rides Again
Concerto For Cootie

SUSTAINING BROADCAST　　*November 1, 1941, Hotel*
　MUTUAL Radio Network　　*New Yorker New York*

Personnel as studio session, October 21.

Caprice XXIV Paganini (LP: SB 158)
That Did It, Marie - voc Peggy Lee (arr MP) (LP: SB 158)
Good-Bye (theme)

SUSTAINING BROADCAST　　*November 7, 1941, Hotel*
　MUTUAL Radio Network　　*New Yorker, New York*

Orchestra as studio session, October 21. Sextet as October 28.

More Than You Know - voc Peggy Lee
If I Had You - SEXTET
Sing, Sing, Sing
Why Don't We Do This More Often? - voc Peggy Lee (n/c)

BENNY GOODMAN AND HIS ORCHESTRA　November 13, 1941, New York

Personnel as studio session, October 21.

CO 31741-2　**LP:** CO CL6048, PHON 7617
CO 31741-1　OK 6497, CoC 539, CO 37244, CO 38198, CoC 6323. **LP:** SONY SOPJ22/23, SONY 20AP-1486, JAZ 67
　　　　Somebody Else Is Taking My Place - voc Peggy Lee

CO 31742　7" **LP:** PHON MLP80
CO 31742-1　OK 6562, CoArg 291375, CoC 579, CO 38283, CoArg 291666, CoC 6402. **LP:** CO CL6033, PhilCont B07626R, CoJap PL5046, SONY SOPJ22/23, JAZ 67
CO 31742-bkdn　UNISSUED - Tape
CO 31742-bkdn　UNISSUED - Tape
CO 31742-2　**LP:** PHON 7617
　　　　Somebody Nobody Loves - voc Peggy Lee (arr EdSau)

CO 31743　**LP:** PHON 7617
CO 31743-2　OK 6544, CoArg 291405, CoC 566. **LP:** JAZ 51
CO 31743-bkdn　UNISSUED - Tape
CO 31743-1　**LP:** CO CL6100, CorkAu KLP799, HA HL7005, SONY SOPJ22/23, SONY 20AP-1486, HALLMARK 503. **EP:** CoE SEG7556
　　　　How Long Has This Been Going On? - voc Peggy Lee (arr MP)

CO 31744-bkdn　**LP:** PHON 7617
CO 31744　**LP:** PHON 7617
CO 31744-1　OK 6497, CoArg 291375, CoC 539, CO 37244, CoC 6323. **LP:** CorAu KLP799, HA HL7005, SONY SOPJ22/23, SONY 20AP-1486, HALLMARK 503
　　　　That Did It, Marie - voc Peggy Lee (arr MP)

(Note that new information now credits Mel Powell, not Eddie Sauter, for the arrangement of "That Did It, Marie"; and that Peggy reverses the fifth and sixth lines of "Somebody Else Is Taking My Place," take 1 vs take 2. A test pressing confirms that this transposition is "genuine," not a matter of an inadvertent tape splice to prepare CO CL6048. HA HL7005 deletes the intro and first chorus of "That Did It, Marie.")

SUSTAINING BROADCAST　　*November 13, 1941, Hotel*
　MUTUAL Radio Network　　*New Yorker, New York*

Personnel as November 13 studio session.

The Count
Somebody Else Is Taking My Place - voc Peggy Lee
Good-Bye (theme)

　　The Coca Cola Company began its five-year series of "Spotlight Band" broadcasts on November 3, featuring Kay Kyser; Benny's first appearance was November 14. Over the years he will broadcast for Coca Cola an even two dozen times. Fortunately, acetates of some selections from most of the programs are extant, and during World War II AFRS transcribed some of the broadcasts. Unfortunately, advice from Coca Cola in 1986 is that it does not have transcriptions of any of the hundreds of programs that it sponsored.

　　Monday through Friday, "Spotlight Band" broadcasts were 15 minutes in length; on Saturday, the "band of the week" got a full half hour. The broadcasts originated from locations, not studios; and here's Benny's first, from the Terrace Room of the Hotel New Yorker:

"SPOTLIGHT BANDS"　　*November 14, 1941, Hotel*
　MUTUAL Radio Network　　*New Yorker, New York*

Personnel as November 13.

Let's Dance (theme)
Let's Do It (Let's Fall In Love) - voc Peggy Lee
One O'Clock Jump
Good-Bye (theme)
"Spotlight Bands" theme

SUSTAINING BROADCAST　　*November 16, 1941, Hotel*
　MUTUAL Radio Network　　*New Yorker, New York*

Personnel as November 13, plus ART LONDON (later, Lund), voc. Sextet as October 28.

Henderson Stomp
I'm Here
A Sinner Kissed An Angel - voc ART LONDON
Limehouse Blues - SEXTET

Precisely when Art London joined the band is not known, but program logs prior to the 16th do not include him, and the broadcast just listed may mark his very first day.

SUSTAINING BROADCAST   *November 22, 1941, Hotel*
 CBS Radio Network   *New Yorker, New York*

Personnel as November 16.

Henderson Stomp
Buckle Down Winsocki - voc Art London (to station break)
Winter Weather - voc Peggy Lee, Art London (from station break)

Nor is it known when the personnel changes reflected in the next studio session occurred. We are approaching the United States' entry into World War II, ''draft'' calls were impinging on staffing of all enterprises more frequently, and new faces will appear in the band more often than heretofore.

As evidence of Art London's recent arrival, note the multiple takes needed to produce a version of ''Winter Weather'' that Benny found acceptable:

BENNY GOODMAN AND HIS ORCHESTRA **November 27, 1941, New York**

Benny Goodman, clt; Jimmy Maxwell, Al Davis, JOE FERRANTE, tpt; Lou McGarity, Cutty Cutshall, tbn; Clint Neagley, SOL KANE, as; Vido Musso, George Berg, ts; Chuck Gentry, bar; Mel Powell, p; Tom Morgan, g; Sid Weiss, b; Ralph Collier, d; Peggy Lee, Art London, voc.

CO 31811-bkdn	UNISSUED - Tape
CO 31811	**LP:** PHON 7617
CO 31811	UNISSUED - Tape
CO 31811-bkdn	UNISSUED - Tape
CO 31811-bkdn	UNISSUED - Tape
CO 31811	UNISSUED - Tape
CO 31811-bkdn	UNISSUED - Tape
CO 31811-1	OK 6516, CoC 552, CO 38283, CoC 6402. **LP:** CO CL6033, PhilCont B07626R, CO alb P5-15536, CoJap PL5046, SONY SOPJ22/23, JAZ 67, JOY 6015, SONY 20AP-1486. **EP:** CO B406
	Winter Weather - voc Peggy Lee and Art London (arr MP)
CO 31812	**LP:** PHON 7620
CO 31812	UNISSUED - Tape
CO 31812-2	OK 6516, CoC 552. **LP:** EPIC EE22025, EPICAu ELP3648, EPICFr/H 80056, SONY SOPJ22/23
	Ev'rything I Love - voc Peggy Lee (arr EdSau)

(Some issues of OK 6516 erroneously back ''Winter Weather'' with Tommy Tucker's ''I Don't Want To Walk Without You,'' mx CO 31843-1.)

SUSTAINING BROADCAST   *November 29, 1941, Hotel*
 MUTUAL Radio Network   *New Yorker, New York*

Personnel as November 27.

Buckle Down Winsocki - voc Art London
Don't Take Your Love From Me - voc Art London
I'm Here
Ev'rything I Love - voc Peggy Lee
Henderson Stomp - to signoff

Benny appeared as guest soloist with the Rochester, New York, Symphony Orchestra on Sunday, November 30, and then it was back to the New Yorker:

SUSTAINING BROADCAST   *December 1, 1941, Hotel*
 CBS Radio Network   *New Yorker, New York*

Orchestra as November 27. Sextet as October 28.

. . . few bars only, The Man I Love
Who Can I Turn To? - voc Art London
Limehouse Blues - SEXTET
One O'Clock Jump
Sing, Sing, Sing (n/c)

SUSTAINING BROADCAST   *December 2, 1941, Hotel*
 CBS Radio Network   *New Yorker, New York*

Orchestra as November 27. Sextet as October 28.

. . . few bars only, I See A Million People (But All I Can See Is You)
Where Or When - SEXTET
How Long Has This Been Going On? - voc Peggy Lee
Stealin' Apples (n/c)
Good-Bye (theme)

SUSTAINING BROADCAST   *December 4, 1941, Hotel*
 Unknown network   *New Yorker, New York*

Personnel as November 27.

Benny Rides Again (n/c)

''SPOTLIGHT BANDS''   *December 5, 1941, Hotel*
 MUTUAL Radio Network   *New Yorker, New York*

Orchestra as November 27. Sextet as October 28.

After You've Gone
Ev'rything I Love - voc Peggy Lee (n/c)
Limehouse Blues - SEXTET (LP: FAN 19-119)
The Earl (LP: FAN 19-119)
Good-Bye (theme) (LP: FAN 19-119)
''Spotlight Bands'' theme

SUSTAINING BROADCAST   *December 6, 1941, Hotel*
 MUTUAL Radio Network   *New Yorker, New York*

Personnel as November 27.

I'm Here
Ev'rything I Love - voc Peggy Lee (n/c)
The Earl - to signoff

SUSTAINING BROADCAST   *December 6, 1941, Hotel*
 Unknown network   *New Yorker, New York*

Personnel as November 27.

After You've Gone

(This cut may be from the MUTUAL broadcast, preceding.)

SUSTAINING BROADCAST   *December 9, 1941, Hotel*
 CBS Radio Network   *New Yorker, New York*

Personnel as November 27.

. . . final chorus only, Stealin' Apples
Somebody Else Is Taking My Place - voc Peggy Lee
. . . few bars only, Tuesday At Ten
Someone's Rocking My Dreamboat - voc Art London (arr MP)
Good-Bye (theme)

Bernie Privin may have replaced Joe Ferrante in the trumpet section prior to the next studio session; indeed, Ferrante may have been present only for the studio date of November 27. However, there is no concrete evidence of either supposition, and Privin's entrance is held until now.

BENNY GOODMAN AND HIS **December 10, 1941, New York**
ORCHESTRA

Personnel as November 27, except BERNIE PRIVIN, tpt, replaces Ferrante.

CO 31942-1	OK 6534, CoC 558. **LP:** JAZ 67, JOY 6015
CO 31942-bkdns	UNISSUED - Tape (3 consecutive aborted attempts)
CO 31942	**LP:** PHON 7620
	Someone's Rocking My Dreamboat - voc Art London (arr MP)
CO 31943	**LP:** PHON 7620
CO 31943	UNISSUED - Tape
CO 31943	UNISSUED - Tape
CO 31943-bkdn	UNISSUED - Tape
CO 31943-1	OK 6562, CoC 579. **LP:** JAZ 67, JOY 6015
	Let's Give Love A Chance - voc Art London (arr EdSau)

CO 31944	**LP:** PHON 7620
CO 31944	UNISSUED - Tape
CO 31944-1	CO 36580, CoC 654, CO 38280, CoC 6399. **LP:** CO CL6033, PhilCont B07626R, CO alb P-14007, CoJap PL5046, SONY SOPJ22/23, JAZ 67

Not Mine - voc Peggy Lee (arr EdSau)

CO 31945-bkdn	UNISSUED - Tape
CO 31945-1	**LP:** PHON 7620
CO 31945-2	**LP:** CO GL523, CorAu KLP799, PHIL BBL7043, PhilCont B07010L, HA HL7005, HA 30024, CBSH 52866, SONY SOPJ22/23, HALLMARK 503. **45:** CO 7-1502

Not A Care In The World - voc Peggy Lee (arr EdSau)

CO 31946-bkdn	UNISSUED - Tape
CO 31946-bkdn	**LP:** PHON 7620
CO 31946	UNISSUED - Tape
CO 31946	**LP:** PHON 7620
CO 31946	UNISSUED - Tape
CO 31946-1	OK 6534, CoC 558. **LP:** JAZ 67, JOY 6015

You Don't Know What Love Is - voc Art London (arr EdSau)

(Acquisition and comparison of a test pressing of mx CO 31945-1 with an unnumbered cut on a Columbia safety recording proved that they were one and the same, and thus an alternate take believed earlier to exist is eliminated.)

Dates of the next two listings, 13 and 14 (Sunday) December, are taken from the source acetates. It is possible that only one broadcast is involved, that of the 13th. Such discrepancies are not unusual, especially when a broadcast began at 12:00 midnight—recordists seemed wont to note the date of the prior day, not the new morning.

SUSTAINING BROADCAST	December 13, 1941, Hotel
Unknown network	New Yorker, New York

Personnel as December 10.

Buckle Down Winsocki - voc Art London

SUSTAINING BROADCAST	December 14, 1941, Hotel
CBS Radio Network	New Yorker, New York

Personnel as December 10.

The Earl
Sing, Sing, Sing
Good-Bye (theme)

SUSTAINING BROADCAST	December 19, 1941, Hotel
Unknown network	New Yorker, New York

Personnel as December 10.

Benny Rides Again (n/c)
Clarinet A La King

SUSTAINING BROADCAST	December 20, 1941, Hotel
CBS Radio Network	New Yorker, New York

Personnel as December 10.

Let's Dance (theme)
Caprice XXIV Paganini
At The Darktown Strutters' Ball - voc Art London (arr MP)

BENNY GOODMAN (& HIS) SEXTET December 24, 1941, New York

Personnel as October 28, plus Cutty Cutshall, tbn. Peggy Lee, Lou McGarity, voc.

CO 32051-1	OK 6533, CoC 572, CoJap M324, PaE R2845, PaInd DPE46, PaIt B71223, PaSw PZ11010, CO 38821, CoC 1546, HA 1012. **7″ 33:** CO 3-38821, Co 1-642. **EP:** CO B2556, PHIL BBE12172. **LP:** SONY SOPJ22/33, SONY 20AP-1486, JAZ 67

Blues In The Night - voc Peggy Lee, Lou McGar(r)ity

CO 32052-1	OK 6553, CoC 572, CoJap M203, PaE R2845, PaInd DPE46, PaIt B71223, PaSw PZ11010, CO 38821, CoC 6400. **7″ 33:** CO 3-38821. **45:** CoJap LL39-C. **EP:** CO B2556, CO B406, PHIL BBE12172, CoJap EM95. **LP:** CO CL6033, PhilCont B07626R, CoJap PL5046, SONY SOPJ22/23, SONY 20AP-1486, ''GE special,'' JAZ 67
CO 32052	**LP:** PHON 7620, BID 1002

Where Or When - voc Peggy Lee

Omit Cutty Cutshall, tbn.

CO 32053	**LP:** PHON 7620, BID 1002
CO 32053-1	CO 36617, CoArg 291553, CoC 665, PaE R2858 (some copies, false take 2), CoJap M203, CoSd DS1497, PaFin DPY1009, PaInd DPE58, OdG 208209, CO 37246, CO 37514, CO 38210, CO 38282, CoC 975, CoC 6325, CoC 6401. **45:** CoJap LL39-C. **EP:** CO B2556, PHIL BBE12172, CoJap EM95. **LP:** CO CL6033, CoJap PL5046, TL STLJ05, SONY SOPJ22/23, SONY 20AP-1486, JA 67. **ET:** War Dept. G. I. Jive H-12-406
CO 32053	**LP:** BID 1004

On The Sunny Side Of The Street - voc Peggy Lee

SUSTAINING BROADCAST prob.	December 27, 1941, Hotel
CBS Radio Network	New Yorker, New York

Personnel as December 10.

Ramona (arr EdSau)

A number of undated acetates are believed to have been recorded from the Hotel New Yorker in the period November/December 1941. Note that at this time the location is sometimes identified as the ''Ice'' Terrace Room of the Hotel New Yorker (a small rink had been constructed, and ice-skating chorus girls performed as part of the floor show), but the radio announcers are inconsistent in this regard.

SUSTAINING BROADCAST	November/December 1941, Hotel
MUTUAL Radio Network	New Yorker, New York

Personnel appropriate to this period.

I'm Here
Limehouse Blues - SEXTET
Clarinet A La King
Where Or When - SEXTET

SUSTAINING BROADCAST	November/December 1941, Hotel
NBC Radio Network	New Yorker, New York

Personnel appropriate to this period.

Clarinet A La King
Ida - TRIO (BG, Powell, Collier)
Caprice XXIV Paganini - to close

SUSTAINING BROADCAST	November/December 1941, Hotel
CBS Radio Network	New Yorker, New York

Personnel appropriate to this period.

Where Or When - SEXTET - to signoff

Male vocalist on ''My Blue Heaven,'' following, is not Art London, is not identified by announcement or notation on the source acetate; sounds like Danny Kaye. . .? Performance of this arrangement at this time seems wholly out of chronological order, but it is listed here on the basis of supplied information.

SUSTAINING BROADCAST   *November/December 1941, Hotel*
  CBS Radio Network   *New Yorker, New York*

Personnel appropriate to this period.

My Blue Heaven - voc ?
At The Darktown Strutters' Ball - voc Art London
Buckle Down Winsocki - voc Art London
After You've Gone - voc Art London
Winter Weather - voc Peggy Lee, Art London
Good-Bye (theme)

Cuts following are all via Mutual, but from more than one broadcast:

SUSTAINING BROADCASTS   *November/December 1941, Hotel*
  MUTUAL Radio Network   *New Yorker, New York*

Personnel appropriate to this period.

After You've Gone (LP: JAZ 35)
Good-Bye (theme) (LP: JAZ 35)
On The Sunny Side Of The Street - voc Peggy Lee - SEXTET (n/c)
Take It - voc, the band
Let's Give Love A Chance (arr EdSau) (n/c)
Roll 'Em
Good-Bye (theme)

Finally, two cuts via unknown networks:

SUSTAINING BROADCASTS   *November/December 1941, Hotel*
  Unknown networks   *New Yorker, New York*

Personnel appropriate to this period.

That Did It, Marie - to şignoff
Sing, Sing, Sing

On the last day of the year, Benny participates in his final Metronome All-Star session . . . at least, the beginning of it:

METRONOME ALL STAR BAND   **December 31, 1941, New York**

Benny Goodman, clt; Harry James, Cootie Williams, Roy Eldridge, tpt; J. C. Higginbotham, Lou McGarity, tbn; Toots Mondello, Benny Carter, as; Vido Musso, Tex Beneke, ts; Count Basie, p; Freddie Green, g; Doc Goldberg, b; Gene Krupa, d.

CO 32079   **LP:** PHON 7620
CO 32079-1   CO 36499, CoAu D02481, CoC 601, CoJap M234, PaE R2967, Palt B71103, PaSw PZ11210, PaE DP253. **LP:** SONY SONP-50419, JO 101.611, QD 008, JAZ 67, TAX 8039
CO 32079-2   **LP:** CO CL2528, HA HL7044, SONY SONP-50419, QD 009, TAX 8039
           Royal Flush

CO 32080   **LP:** PHON 7620
CO 32080   **LP:** PHON 7620
CO 32080-1   **LP:** HA HL7044, SONY SONP-50419, QD 009, TAX 8039
           Dear Old Southland

"SPOTLIGHT BANDS"   *January 1, 1942, New York*
  MUTUAL Radio Network

Personnel as December 10, 1941.

"Spotlight Bands" theme
Don't Be That Way (LP: SB 158)
The Count (LP: SB 158)
Blues In The Night - voc Peggy Lee, Lou McGarity (LP: SB 158)
Clarinet A La King
Good-Bye (theme) (LP: SB 158)

Benny went on a solo tour the first two weeks of the new year, appearing as guest clarinetist with municipal symphony orchestras in cities in the eastern United States. He began in Cleveland, Ohio, on the 4th, with the Cleveland Symphony Orchestra, Arthur Rodzinski conducting. Following were Pittsburgh, Pa. (6th), Youngstown, Ohio (7th), Toledo, Ohio (8th), Cincinnati, Ohio (9th), Washington (10th), and Dayton, Ohio (12th). He then returned to New York to resume his interrupted engagement in the Hotel New Yorker.

An acetate clearly, but mistakenly, dated "January 10, 1942" led to an earlier belief that Benny and the band appeared on Jack Benny's radio program at this time. Not so—the acetate's date is in error by a full year, and his guest shot is deferred until January 10, 1943, q.v.

The first order of business in Manhattan was a studio date with his own band, and then a wrapup of the Metronome All Star session:

BENNY GOODMAN AND HIS ORCHESTRA   **January 15, 1942, New York**

Personnel as December 10, 1941 (but see paragraph following session).

CO 32238-1   VD 409 A, NavyVD 189 A. **7"33:** CO 1-514. **EP:** CO B301, CorAu KEP057, FONT TFE17022. **LP:** CO CL6048, CO alb P5-15536, CO alb PM-16932
           Jersey Bounce (arr MP)

CO 32239-1   OK 6580, CoC 604. **LP:** SONY SOPJ22/23, JAZ 67
           The Lamp Of Memory (Incertidumbre) - voc Peggy Lee (arr EdSau)

CO 32240-2   **LP:** SONY SOPJ22/23
CO 32240-1   CO 36580, CoArg 291385, CoC 654. **LP:** JAZ 67, JOY 6015
           If You Build A Better Mousetrap - voc Peggy Lee and Art London (arr EdSau)

CO 32241-1   CO 36699, CoArg 291575, CoC 726, CoInd DB30220, OdNor D50253, PaE R2978, PaSw PZ11077, CO DJ32241. **45:** CO 4-G-6 (Set G4-3). **EP:** CO 5-1654 (Set B351). **LP:** CO GL501, CO CL534, CoE 33SX1084, CO "bonus" GB-4, CBSSw 52964
CO 32241-2   VD 425 A, NavyVD 205 A. **LP:** PHON 7620
           At The Darktown Strutters' Ball (arr MP)

CO 32242-1   **LP:** SONY SOPJ22/23
           When The Roses Bloom Again - voc Peggy Lee

(Acquisition of a test pressing of mx CO 32242-1 proved it to be the same as an unnumbered take on a CO safety recording, and a supposed alternate is eliminated.)

Clarinetist, baritone-saxophonist Artie Baker is firm in his contention that he recorded with the band this session, an assertion not confirmed by Columbia's files. Further, he claims that he played with the band for a short time in the New Yorker, and relates this anecdote: Benny occasionally did not play the first set of a location gig, and Lou McGarity led the band in his stead. One night, Lou asked Art to lead, and he did so—on clarinet. He recalls he was solo'ing on "Someone's Rocking My Dreamboat" when Benny walked in, and that was the end of that. As he says, he was with the band but briefly. Apocryphal? Would seem so, according to Columbia. Possible? Yes. And with this caveat: the circumstances may apply to the remake date for "Jersey Bounce," January 23.

Note that takes 1 and 3 of "I Got Rhythm," following, are interchanged from previous listings, to bring them into accord with an order-of-recording:

METRONOME ALL STAR LEADERS   **January 16, 1942, New York**

Benny Goodman, clt; Cootie Williams, tpt; J. C. Higginbotham, tbn; Benny Carter, as; Charlie Barnet, ts; Count Basie, p; Alvino Rey, g; John Kirby, b; Gene Krupa, d.

CO 32261-1   **LP:** SONY SONP-50419, TAX 8039
CO 32261-2   CO 36499, CoC 601, CoJap M234, PaE R2967, Palt B71103, PaSw PZ11210, PaE DP253. **LP:** SONY SONP-50419, QD 008, TAX 8039
CO 32261-3   **LP:** CO CL2528, HA HL7044, SONY SONP-50419, QD009, TAX 8039. **78** (reputedly), CoAu D02481
           I Got Rhythm

SUSTAINING BROADCAST   *January 17, 1942, Hotel*
  prob. CBS Radio Network   *New Yorker, New York*

Personnel as December 10, 1941.

Jersey Bounce
Sing, Sing, Sing

SUSTAINING BROADCAST   *January 20, 1942, Hotel*
  CBS Radio Network   *New Yorker, New York*

Personnel as December 10, 1941.

Blues In The Night - voc Peggy Lee, Lou McGarity
Tuesday At Ten
How Do You Do Without Me? - voc Peggy Lee
Stealin' Apples - to signoff

    Should point out that, in retrospect, Ralph Collier was playing very well for Benny at this time. At this writing (1986) a realtor in California, Collier has never been accorded the credit due him. And note that although the issue CO 36588 is listed by Columbia as a release for "Jersey Bounce" from the upcoming studio date, it does not exist; it was scheduled to be released, but was cancelled.

BENNY GOODMAN AND HIS ORCHESTRA   January 23, 1942, New York

Personnel as December 10, 1941 (with possibly ART BAKER, bar, replacing Gentry).

CO 32238-2   OK 6590, CoArg 291359, CoC 609, CoMex 2071, PaAu
             A7434, CO 37245, CO 38062, CoC 728, CoC 6324,
             CO 50023. **45:** CO 4-38062, CO 4-39741, CO
             4-50023. **EP:** CO B2523. **LP:** CO CL6212, CO CL605,
             CO CL611, CO CL1687 (Set C2X), COJap PL2006, CO
             CL2483, CO CS9283, CO DS289 (Set P7S 5122), CO
             alb PZM-5111, CO alb P2S-5112, CO D269, CO KG
             31547, CO PG33405, CO alb P4M-5678, CBS 52368,
             CBS 67268, CO alb P6-14954, RLM 8065. **ET:** AFRS
             Jill's All Time Juke Box H46-No. 9, OWI Outpost
             Concert Series 4-Music of the Jazz Bands 8, AFRS
             G.I. Jive 1207
             Jersey Bounce (arr MP)

CO 32242-2   OK 6580, CoC 604. **LP:** JAZ 67, JOY 6015
             When The Roses Bloom Again - voc Art London (prob.
             arr EdSau)

CO 32318-2   OK 6606, CoArg 291368, CoC 619. **LP:** JAZ 68, JOY
             6015

CO 32318   **LP:** PHON 7620
             A Zoot Suit (For My Sunday Gal) - voc Art London (arr
             MP)

CO 32319-1   CoArg 20.323. **EP:** CO 7-1500, PhilCont 429129BE. **LP:**
             CO GL523, PHIL BBL7043, PhilCont B07010L, CO alb
             P6-14538, JOY 6015
             Tangerine - Art Lund (arr EdSau)

(Note tht the first release of "Tangerine" was May 1, 1953, on LP, CO CL523; and that by then Art had forsaken "London" for "Lund.")

    Lending some credence to Baker's claim is Chuck Gentry's leaving the band to join Jimmy Dorsey, sometime in late January or early February. The precise date is not known, and so Gentry is continued in Benny's employ until the studio session of February 5.

SUSTAINING BROADCAST   *January 24, 1942, Hotel*
  CBS Radio Network   *New Yorker, New York*

Personnel as December 10, 1941.

Star Dust (n/c)
Ramona
Blues In The Night - voc Peggy Lee, Lou McGarity
Stealin' Apples - to signoff

SUSTAINING BROADCAST   *January 31, 1942, Hotel*
  Unknown network   *New Yorker, New York*

Personnel as December 10, 1941.

Jersey Bounce
Sing, Sing, Sing

    It is uncertain whether "Body and Soul," next listed, is from this February 2 Coca Cola broadcast, or from its broadcast of March 2.

"SPOTLIGHT BANDS"   *February 2, 1942, Hotel*
  MUTUAL Radio Network   *New Yorker, New York*

Personnel as December 10, 1941.

"Spotlight Bands" theme
Henderson Stomp
Jersey Bounce (n/c - intro excised)
Body And Soul - TRIO (BG, Powell, Collier)

SUSTAINING BROADCAST   *February 3, 1942, Hotel*
  CBS Radio Network   *New Yorker, New York*

Personnel as December 10, 1941.

Somebody Nobody Loves - voc Peggy Lee
I'm Here

    In little more than half a year Mel Powell's work with Benny had so promulgated his reputation that a record date of his own was inevitable. Benny agreed to participate—under the pseudonym of "Shoeless John Jackson"—and Mel's septet convened in Studio B, Decca's complex, 50 W. 57th Street in Manhattan, under the aegis of Milt Gabler:

MEL POWELL AND HIS ORCHESTRA   February 4, 1942, New York

Benny Goodman, clt; Billy Butterfield, tpt; Lou McGarity, tbn; George Berg, ts; Mel Powell, p; Al Morgan, b; Carl Donnell "Kansas" Fields, d.

76986-A   CMS 543A, CMS 7531A. **LP:** MS S/6011, CMS 14943,
           LON 5005, DeG 6.24063
           When Did You Leave Heaven

76987-A   CMS 544A, CMS 7532A. **LP:** MS S/6009, CMS 14943,
           LON 5005, JA 1216, DeG 6.24063
           The World Is Waiting For The Sunrise

76988-A   CMS 543A, CMS 7531B. **LP:** CMS 14943, LON 5005,
           DeG 6.24063

76988-B   **LP:** PHON LV-50, BID 1011
           Blue Skies

76989-A   CMS 544B, CMS 7532B. **LP:** MS S/6011, CMS 14943,
           LON 5005, JA 1216, DeG 6.24063
           Mood At Twilight

SUSTAINING BROADCAST   *February 4, 1942, Hotel*
  CBS Radio Network   *New Yorker, New York*

Personnel as December 10, 1941.

The Earl
A Zoot Suit (For My Sunday Gal) - voc Art London
Stealin' Apples - to signoff

    Th next day's studio date produced an hilarious breakup during the many attempts to get Eddie Sauter's difficult chart of "Ramona" on wax, and Columbia saw fit to issue it as a bonus record some dozen years after its recording. And note that the cancelled 78, CO 36588, applies equally here to "A String Of Pearls," for it was the scheduled flip side of "Jersey Bounce."

BENNY GOODMAN AND HIS ORCHESTRA   February 5, 1942, New York

Benny Goodman, clt; Jimmy Maxwell, Al Davis, Bernie Privin, tpt; Lou McGarity, Cutty Cutshall, tbn; Clint Neagley, Sol Kane, as; Vido Musso, George Berg, ts; ART RALSTON, bar; Mel Powell, p; Tom Morgan, g; Sid Weiss, b; Ralph Collier, d; Peggy Lee, Art London, voc.

CO 32383	**LP:** PHON 7620
CO 32383	UNISSUED - Tape
CO 32383-1	OK 6590, PaAu A7490, CoC 609, CoJap M191, VD 409 A, NavyVD 189 A, CO 37245, CO 38062, CoC 728, CoC 6324, CO 50023. **45:** CO 4-38062, CO 4-50023. **7"33:** CO 1-514. **EP:** CO B2523, CorAu KEP057, FONT TFE17022. **LP:** CO CL 6048, CO CL611, FONT TFL5067, FontCont 682047TL, CO KG31547, CO PG33405, CO alb P5-15536, CO alb P4M-5678, CBS 67268, RD 166, "GE special"

A String Of Pearls (arr MP)

CO 32384-bkdns	UNISSUED - Tape (2 consecutive aborted attempts)
CO 32384	**LP:** CO PG33405
CO 32384-bkdn	UNISSUED - Tape
CO 32384	**LP:** PHON 7620
CO 32384-bkdn	UNISSUED - Tape
CO 32384-1	OK 6606, CoC 619, CO 38280, CoC 6399. **LP:** CO CL6033, PhilCont B07626R, CoJap PL5046, SONY SOPJ22/23, JAZ 68. **ET:** Air Force GL 18. **EP:** CO B406

My Little Cousin - voc Peggy Lee (arr MP)

CO 32385	**LP:** PHON 7620
CO 32385-bkdns	UNISSUED - Tape (2 consecutive aborted attempts)
CO 32385	UNISSUED - Tape
CO 32385-bkdn	UNISSUED - Tape
CO 32385-bkdn	**LP:** BID 1006
CO 32385-2(a)	**7"33:** CO ZLP13905. **LP:** BID 1006
CO 32385-1(b)	CoArg 20.323 B, CoJap L3006
CO 32385-S(a,b)	**LP:** CO GL523, PHIL BBL7043, PhilCont B07010L. **EP:** CO 7-1500, PhilCont 429129BE

Ramona (arr EdSau)

(CO LP GL523 et al splices the first half of mx CO 32385-2, "(a)" above (through Benny's solo) to the last half of mx CO 32385-1, "(b)" above.)

SUSTAINING BROADCAST   *February 6, 1942, Hotel*
MUTUAL Radio Network   *New Yorker, New York*

Personnel as February 5.

My Little Cousin - voc Peggy Lee
Jersey Bounce (n/c - intro only)

SUSTAINING BROADCAST   *February 7, 1942, Hotel*
Unknown network   *New Yorker, New York*

Personnel as February 5.

Take It - voc, the band

SUSTAINING BROADCAST   *February 14, 1942, Hotel*
CBS Radio Network   *New Yorker, New York*

Personnel as February 5.

Blues In The Night - voc Peggy Lee, Lou McGarity
Sing, Sing, Sing - to signoff

SUSTAINING BROADCAST   *February 14, 1942, Hotel*
MUTUAL Radio Network   *New Yorker, New York*

Personnel as February 5.

How Long Has This Been Going On? - voc Peggy Lee
Jersey Bounce
The Count
Good-Bye (theme)

Benny broadcast for Coca Cola on February 17, the date of our next air checks. But the overall ambience of these cuts suggests a sustaining broadcast from the Terrace Room, not a "Spotlight Bands" program.

SUSTAINING BROADCAST   *February 17, 1942, Hotel*
Unknown network   *New Yorker, New York*

Personnel as February 5. SEXTET: BG, McGarity, Powell, Morgan, Weiss, Collier.

After You've Gone
Skylark - voc Peggy Lee
If I Had You - SEXTET
Ev'rything I Love - voc Peggy Lee

(If a "SPOTLIGHT BANDS" broadcast, the network is MUTUAL, the location the same.)

SUSTAINING BROADCAST   *February 20, 1942, Hotel*
Unknown network   *New Yorker, New York*

Personnel as February 5.

Down South Camp Meeting

SUSTAINING BROADCAST   *February 21, 1942, Hotel*
Unknown network   *New Yorker, New York*

Sextet as February 17.

Limehouse Blues - SEXTET

Before we post our final February air check, we must note that during the month (date unknown) Benny appeared in—more properly, played in—another movie, "Syncopation." His participation was prompted by his selection as best clarinetist in the **Saturday Evening Post's** "All-American Jazz Band" poll.

The sequence featuring the contest's winners, which serves as an epilogue for the film, was recorded at the Fox-Movietown studios in Manhattan. But Benny had recorded his solo with his own rhythm section separately, and it was dubbed into the movie's soundtrack. Benny missed filming the sequence, and an actor named Paul Rickey, with back to the camera, masquerades as Benny on screen.

Eddy Duchin was the Post's readership's choice as pianist(!), but ex-Tommy Dorsey pianist Howard Smith substituted for him when the jazz winners' sequence was recorded. Further, although the Duke's Rex Stewart has a speaking and playing role in the film Bunny Berigan actually cut all of the soli that Rex appears to perform.

"SYNCOPATION"   *February 1942, New York*

An RKO-Radio motion picture filmed in black-and-white
Released May 22, 1942
Producer-Director: William Dieterle
CAST: Adolphe Menjou, Jackie Cooper, Bonita Granville, George Bancroft, Todd Duncan, Connee Boswell, Rex Stewart, the Hall-Johnson Choir, and

THE SATURDAY EVENING POST ALL-AMERICAN JAZZ BAND:

Benny Goodman, clt; Harry James, tpt; Jack Jenney, tbn; Charlie Barnet, ts; Joe Venuti, v; Howard Smith, p; Alvino Rey, g; Bob Haggart, b; Gene Krupa, d.

Blues - untitled

SUSTAINING BROADCAST   *February 28, 1942, Hotel*
CBS Radio Network   *New Yorker, New York*

Personnel as February 5.

Let's Give Love A Chance - voc Art London
Henderson Stomp - to signoff

"SPOTLIGHT BANDS"
MUTUAL Radio Network

March 2, 1942, Hotel
New Yorker, New York

Personnel as February 5. TRIO: BG, Powell, Collier.

Body And Soul - TRIO   (see February 2)
A String Of Pearls
We'll Meet Again - voc Peggy Lee (n/c)
Benny Rides Again (n/c)

SUSTAINING BROADCAST
CBS Radio Network

March 4, 1942, Hotel
New Yorker, New York

Personnel as February 5.

Moonlight On The Ganges - to signoff

SUSTAINING BROADCAST
Unknown network

March 5, 1942, Hotel
New Yorker, New York

Personnel as February 5.

My Little Cousin - voc Peggy Lee (n/c)
The Lamp Of Memory (Incertidumbre) - voc Peggy Lee (n/c)
Mandy Is Two - voc Peggy Lee (n/c)

SUSTAINING BROADCAST
Unknown network

March 6, 1942, Hotel
New Yorker, New York

Personnel as February 5.

Clarinet A La King (n/c)
Jersey Bounce (r/c)

SUSTAINING BROADCAST
Unknown network

March 7, 1942, Hotel
New Yorker, New York

Personnel as February 5.

Before (Rachmaninoff Special) (arr Toots Camarata)

BENNY GOODMAN SEXTET   March 10, 1942, New York

Benny Goodman, clt; Lou McGarity, tbn; Mel Powell, p & cel; Tom Morgan, g; Sid Weiss, b; Ralph Collier, d; Peggy Lee, voc.

CO 32593   **LP:** BID 1002, PHON 7644
CO 32593-1   CO 36594, CoArg 291445, CoAu D03134, CoJap M159, CoSd DS1497, PaE R2858 (shows false take 2), PaInd DPE58, OdG 028209, CO 36723, CO 39478, CoC 6202. **45:** CO 4-39478. **EP:** FontCont 462012TE. **LP:** CO alb P5-15536, SONY 20AP-1810, JAZ 68. **ET:** AFRS Downbeat 206/207
              The Wang Wang Blues

(A report that EP CorAu KEP032 uses the first take of "The Wang Wang Blues," as issued on BID 1002 et al above, is unverified. If untrue, EP CorAu KEP032 should be added to the releases for mx CO 32593-1.)

CO 32594   **LP:** BID 1002, PHON 7644
              The World Is Waiting For The Sunrise

BENNY GOODMAN QUARTET   same session

As Sextet, less McGarity, Morgan.

CO 32594   **LP:** BID 1002, PHON 7644
CO 32594-1   CO 36684, CoArg 291553, CoC 719, CoJap M323, PaE R3002, PaNor NPS5015, PaSw PZ11099, CO 50051, CoJap L3012. **45:** CO 4-50051. **EP:** CO B2523, CorAu KEP057, FONT TFE17022, FONT TFE17079, FontCont 462065TE. **LP:** CO alb P5-15536, SONY 20AP-1810, JAZ 68. **ET:** AFRS Downbeat 206/207
              The World Is Waiting For The Sunrise

BENNY GOODMAN SEXTET   same session

McGarity, Morgan return. Powell plays celeste on "The Way You Look Tonight."

CO 32595-1   CO 36594, CoArg 291455, CO 38282, CoC 6401. **EP:** CO B2556, CO B406, PHIL BBE12172. **LP:** CO CL6033, PhilCont B07626R, CBSH 52866, CoJap PL5046, HA HL7148, HA 30024, SONY SOPJ22/33, SONY 20AP-1486
              The Way You Look Tonight - voc Peggy Lee

-0-   **LP:** EPIC EE22025, EPICAu ELP3648, EPICFr/H 80056, SONY 20AP-1810, PHON 7644
              St. Louis Blues

("St. Louis Blues" was not assigned a matrix, per Columbia's files.)

    The band's personnel had been remarkably stable throughout its split five-month engagement at the New Yorker, especially so in view of voluntary enlistments in, and Selective Service calls to, the Nation's armed services. Changes are reflected, however, in the next studio session; but even these might have been caused by Benny's leaving the Ice Terrace Room, and the desire of some of the men to remain in New York rather than go on the road.

    Note that OK 6652, below, was the last in the series of Goodman Okeh's issued, and that it is scarce.

BENNY GOODMAN AND HIS ORCHESTRA   March 12, 1942, New York

Benny Goodman, clt; Jimmy Maxwell, Bernie Privin, JOHN NAPTON, tpt; Lou McGarity, Cutty Cutshall, tbn; Sol Kane, BUD SHIFFMAN, as; Vido Musso, George Berg, ts; Art Ralston, bar; Mel Powell, p; Tom Morgan, g; Sid Weiss, b; Ralph Collier, d; Peggy Lee, Art London, voc; TUTTI (TOOTS) CAMARATA (TC), arr.

CO 32600-1   OK 6644, CoC 639. **LP:** EPIC EE22025, EPICAu ELP3648, EPICFr/H 80056
CO 32600-bkdn UNISSUED - Tape
CO 32600   **LP:** PHON 7644
              Before (Rachmaninoff Special) (arr TC)

CO 32601   **LP:** PHON 7644
CO 32601   UNISSUED - Tape
CO 32601-bkdn UNISSUED - Tape
CO 32601   UNISSUED - Tape
CO 32601-1   OK 6652, CoArg 291385, CoC 648, CO 36590. **LP:** HA HL7005, CorAu KLP799, SONY SOPJ22/23, HALLMARK 503
              I Threw A Kiss In The Ocean- voc Peggy Lee

CO 32602   **LP:** PHON 7644
CO 32602-bkdn UNISSUED - Tape
CO 32602-1   OK 6644, CoC 639. **EP:** CO B1636. **LP:** HA HL7005, CorAu KLP799, HA 30024, CBSH 52866, SONY SOP322/23, SONY 20AP-1486, HALLMARK 503
              We'll Meet Again - voc Peggy Lee

CO 32603   **LP:** PHON 7644
CO 32603-bkdns UNISSUED - Tape (2 consecutive aborted attempts)
CO 32603-1   OK 6652, CoC 648, CO 36590. **LP:** HA HL7005, CorAu KLP799, HA 30024, CBSH 52866, SONY SOPJ22/23, SONY 20AP-1486, HALLMARK 503
              Full Moon (Noche de Luna) - voc Peggy Lee

(HA releases of "Full Moon" excise intro and first chorus.)

CO 32604-2   **LP:** NOST 1004, PHON 7644
CO 32604-1   **LP:** CO alb P5-15536, SONY SOPJ22/23
              There Won't Be A Shortage On Love - voc Peggy Lee

-0-   **LP:** EPIC EE22025, EPICAu ELP3648, EPICFr/H 80056, PHON 7644
              Peter And The Wolf (prob. arr MP)

("Peter And The Wolf" was not assigned a matrix, per Columbia's files. Note that a mechanical flaw in the source safety recording—a repeat—was edited out of the tape transfer from which the LP's were made.)

This same day, March 12, was the band's last day in the Hotel New Yorker. Before we continue its odyssey, however, it is necessary to list some undated acetates of air checks believed to have originated in the Ice Terrace Room the first two-and-a-half months of 1942. They are listed in alphabetical order; and unfortunately, most are of poor audio quality.

SUSTAINING BROADCASTS   January-March 1942, Hotel
  CBS, unknown networks   New Yorker, New York

Personnels appropriate to the period.

After You've Gone - voc Art London (n/c)
Blues In The Night - voc Peggy Lee, Lou McGarity (n/c)
The Count (n/c)   (CBS)
The Earl   (CBS)
Henderson Stomp
I'm Here
Jersey Bounce   (CBS)
Limehouse Blues - SEXTET (n/c)   (CBS)
Not Mine - voc Peggy Lee (n/c)   (CBS)
One O'Clock Jump
Somebody Nobody Loves - voc Peggy Lee (n/c)   (CBS)
That Did It, Marie - voc Peggy Lee (n/c)   (CBS)
When The Roses Bloom Again - voc Art London (n/c)
When The Roses Bloom Again - voc Art London (n/c)   (CBS)
You And I - voc Art London - SEXTET (n/c)
Good-Bye (theme)   (CBS)

Out of the New Yorker, Benny gave the boys a two-week vacation, for the engagement had been a long one. Besides—never one to waste a minute—he had a personal engagement in view: On March 21 he married a very gracious lady, Alice Hammond Duckworth, in Reno, Nevada. Sister to John Hammond, descendant of Cornelius Vanderbilt, the very social Alice Hammond will be a good wife to Benny, and a good influence upon him, for the next several decades.

But, back to work in April. A report that the band's first post-hiatus booking was in Atlantic City at the Steel Pier seems on reflection dubious, for normally the Pier began its "season"—save for the Easter weekend— the end of May, the Memorial Day holiday. In any event, the band did a week in the Center Theater in Passaic, New Jersey, beginning April 2. On the 9th it opened a week's stand in the Earle Theater, Philadelphia, from whence it broadcast for Coca Cola:

"SPOTLIGHT BANDS"   April 10, 1942, Earle Theater,
  MUTUAL Radio Network   Philadelphia, Pa.

Personnel similar to that of March 12.

Jersey Bounce
Good-Bye (theme)
"Spotlight Bands" theme

Benny crossed the Delaware River to Camden, New Jersey, where the band played in the Stanley Theater for one week, beginning April 15. From its closing there until its next studio date in New York its locations are unknown, but in that interim it broadcast twice for Coke:

"SPOTLIGHT BANDS"   April 24, 1942, unknown location
  MUTUAL Radio Network

Personnel similar to that of March 12.

A String of Pearls
If You Build A Better Mousetrap - voc Peggy Lee & Art London

"SPOTLIGHT BANDS"   April 30, 1942, unknown location
  MUTUAL Radio Network

Personnel similar to that of March 12.

A Smo-o-o-oth One (orchestra)
Moonlight On The Ganges

SUSTAINING BROADCAST   May 11, 1942, unknown location
  Unknown radio network

Personnel similar to that of March 12.

We'll Meet Again - voc Peggy Lee (n/c)

The point should be made that, especially in this wartime period, personnel listings for air checks can only be approximations; no records exist

(Benny's files regarding payrolls, contracts and the like were destroyed long ago) to tell us precisely who was in the band on a given location date. Fortunately, studio recording sheets do give us specifics, and personnel listings may be derived from them for air checks with some assurance of accuracy. But evidently not even the studio data are infallible, and from time to time deviations from them are suggested.

Cutty Cutshall joined the U.S. Army in May, thus breaking up the peerless trombone twosome. And Ralph Collier left before the next Columbia date, but the cause of his departure is not known.

BENNY GOODMAN AND HIS ORCHESTRA   **May 14, 1942, New York**

Personnel as March 12, except CHARLIE CASTALDO, tbn, replaces Cutshall, and ALVIN STOLLER, d, replaces Collier.

CO 32793   LP: BID 1014
CO 32793-1   **LP:** SONY SOPJ22/23, CO alb P5-15536, PHON 7644
       You're Easy To Dance With - voc Peggy Lee

CO 32794-bkdn   UNISSUED - Tape
CO 32794   **LP:** PHON 7644
CO 32794-1   CO 36617, CoArg 291405, CoC 665. **EP:** CO B1636. **LP:**
       HA HL7005, CorAu KLP799, CO alb P2S-5112, CO alb
       P7S-5122, CO alb PZM-5111, CO alb P2M-5193, CO
       alb DS295, CO D404, CO Z173, CBSH 52866, SONY
       SOPJ22/23, TULIP 106, HALLMARK 503
       All I Need Is You - voc Peggy Lee (poss. arr Dave
       Matthews)

(One take of "All I Need Is You" earlier listed for this date is now reassigned to the session of June 17.)

CO 32795-bkdns   UNISSUED - Tape (3 consecutive aborted attempts)
CO 32795   UNISSUED - CO REF
CO 32795-bkdns   UNISSUED - Tape (2 consecutive aborted attempts)
CO 32795   UNISSUED - Tape
CO 32795   UNISSUED - Tape
CO 32795-bkdn   UNISSUED - Tape
CO 32795-1   **LP:** VELP 1, PHON 7644
       I've Got A Gal In Kalamazoo - voc Art London (arr MP)
CO 32796   UNISSUED - Tape
CO 32796-bkdn   UNISSUED - Tape (2 consecutive aborted attempts)
CO 32796   UNISSUED - Tape
CO 32796-bkdn   UNISSUED - Tape
CO 32796-1   **LP:** PHON 7644
       Take Me - voc Art London (arr MP)

(All cuts of "I've Got A Gal In Kalamazoo" from this session are sans the "Remember" intro appended to the arrangement as cut on June 17.)

The very next day Benny took his Selective Service physical examination. He was excused from military service because of his history of chronic sciatica. But Art London passed his physical with flying colors, and Dick Haymes replaced him May 27 as the band went into the Paramount in New York. Haymes was also reported as having appeared with the band at the Steel Pier in Atlantic City on an unspecified date, but this has failed verification.

On June 3 another of the immortals of jazz passed away—Bunny Berigan. Thus, only three months after Charlie Christian's death (March 2), a Goodman alumnus leaves us and is heard no more, save on all those wonderful records and air checks he left us as a legacy.

Bunny's demise had an immediate effect on Benny's band; Vido Musso left to take over the Berigan band intact, on June 6, and complete its contracted engagements.

The next Columbia session reflects further personnel changes, and it is stressed that some of the musicians only recorded with the band, were not included in the orchestra as it appeared in the Paramount and on the road. The author recalls a one-nighter in the Sunnybrook Ballroom, Pottstown, Pa., probably in May before the Paramount gig, when a local drummer, Bob Sheble, had trouble with the triplets Gene played in the coda of "Sing, Sing, Sing." He also remembers Lou McGarity introducing him to Peggy Lee during an intermission with a tentative date in the offing; and that Vido Musso, who acted as Peggy's unofficial bodyguard, talked her out of it.

Wouldn't have had Bunny die any earlier than he did, but certainly wish Vido had left a few weeks sooner. . .

Note that one take of "All I Need Is You," earlier believed to have been recorded May 14, is now assigned to June 17:

BENNY GOODMAN AND HIS ORCHESTRA   June 17, 1942, New York

Benny Goodman, clt; Bernie Privin, COOTIE WILLIAMS, TONY FASO, tpt; Lou McGarity, Charlie Castaldo, tbn; Bud Shiffman, HYMIE SCHERTZER, as; George Berg, JERRY JEROME, ts; JOHNNY McAFEE, bar; Mel Powell, p; DAVE BARBOUR, g; Sid Weiss, b; Alvin Stoller, d; Peggy Lee, DICK HAYMES, voc; DON KIRKPATRICK (DoKi), JOHNNY THOMPSON (JT), arr.

CO 32794   **LP:** PHON 7644
      All I Need Is You - voc Peggy Lee (poss. arr Dave Matthews)

CO 32795-2   CO 36622, CoC 668. **LP:** JOY 6009
      I've Got A Gal In Kalamazoo - voc Dick Haymes (arr MP)

CO 32796-bkdn UNISSUED - CO REF
CO 32796   **LP:** PHON 7644
CO 32796   UNISSUED - Tape
CO 32796-2   CO 36613, CoArg 291391, PaAu A7461. **LP:** JAZ 68, JOY 6009
      Take Me - voc Dick Haymes (arr MP)

CO 32923   UNISSUED - CO REF
CO 32923   **LP:** PHON 7648
CO 32923-1   CO 36622, CoC 668, CoMex 1901, CO 37514, CoC 975. **LP:** NOST 890/1, JOY 6009
      Serenade In Blue - voc Dick Haymes (arr JT)

CO 32924-1   CO 36613, CoArg 291391. **EP:** CO 5-1653 (Set B351). **LP:** CO CL534, PhilCont B07648R, CO PG33405
      Idaho - voc Dick Haymes (arr DoKi)

(Note that Johnny Thompson, not Eddie Sauter as earlier believed, is credited with the arrangement of "Serenade In Blue.")

Dick Haymes had a great voice; would it be considered heresy to say it was better than Sinatra's? Not that he had Frank's style, phrasing; but voice, oh, yes!

June 25 was the last day in the Paramount, and the band went on another theater tour. One engagement was a week's stand in the Metropolitan Theater, Boston, beginning July 16. The day after the Boston gig ended, BG did a one-nighter (July 23) at Canobie Lake Park, Canobie Lake, New Hampshire. A letter of agreement for that Thursday night appearance specifies that Mr. Goodman will receive ". . . 60% of the gross gate receipts, with a minimum guarantee of $1,250," and that he is to provide ". . . 15 musicians plus vocalist." In the 1980s, a Goodman small group would command 10 times that minimum for a single concert; who says the big bands will come back?

Back to New York, and a newly-revised studio date, made possible by access to Columbia safety recordings in private hands. Half the band was now "new" faces, and there may be one more than Columbia's files name: Jimmy Maxwell is adamant that his teacher, trumpeter Benny Baker who regularly played with the New York Philharmonic, recorded with the band on this session. He remembers clearly sitting next to Baker as the band cut, "After You've Gone." So certain is he of Baker's presence that Baker is here added to the personnel, and Lawrence Stearns's participation is considered questionable:

BENNY GOODMAN AND HIS ORCHESTRA   July 27, 1942, New York

Benny Goodman, clt; Tony Faso, JIMMY MAXWELL, prob. BENNY BAKER, LAWRENCE STEARNS (?), tpt; Lou McGarity, Charlie Castaldo, tbn; Hymie Schertzer, CLINT NEAGLEY, as; JON WALTON, LEONARD SIMS, ts; BOB POLAND, bar; Mel Powell, p; Dave Barbour, g; CLIFF HILL, b; HOWARD "HUD" DAVIES, d. Peggy Lee, voc. RICHARD MALTBY (RiM), arr.

CO 33047   **LP:** BID 1014
CO 33047-1   CO 36652, CoC 694, PaE R2864, PaSw PZ11055. **45:** CO 4-10-G (Set G4-3). **EP:** CO 5-1653 (Set B351), CO B2523, FONT TFE17022. **LP:** CO GL501, CO CL534, CO CL2483, CO CS9283, CoE 33SX1038, CBS 52368, CO KG31547, CO PG33405, CO alb P5-15536, CBS 67268, CO alb P4M-5678
      Six Flats Unfurnished (arr RiM)

CO 33048   **LP:** BID 1014
CO 33048-bkdn UNISSUED - Tape
CO 33048   UNISSUED - Tape
CO 33048-1   CO 36652, CoC 694, PaAu A7477, PaE R2864, PaSw PZ11055, CO 37243, CoC 6322, CO 38198. **LP:** CO CL 6048. War Dept. Sound Off 17, CBS 67268, TL STLJ05, CO DS860, CO alb PM-16932, RD 166. **ET:** AFRS Jill's All Time Juke Box H46-9, AFRS Hi Neighbor Series 17-3
CO 33048-2   VD 233 B, Navy VD 13 B. **EP:** CO B2587. **LP:** CO KG31547, HA 30024, CO alb P6-14538, CBSH 52866, SONY SOPJ22/23, SONY 20AP-1486, CO alb P4M-5678. **ET:** AFRS Yank Swing Sessions 41, 51
      Why Don't You Do Right (?) - voc Peggy Lee (arr MP)

(CO 36652 title omits the question mark, V-Disc 233 B includes it.)

CO 33049   UNISSUED - Tape
CO 33049-bkdn UNISSUED - Tape
CO 33049   **LP:** BID 1014
CO 33049-bkdn UNISSUED - Tape
CO 33049   **LP:** BID 1014
CO 33049-1   CO 36699, CoArg 291575, CoC 726, CoInd DB30220. **EP:** CO B2533. **LP:** CO CL6100, CO CL2533, FONT TFL5001 (some copies only; most erroneously include Sextet version from February 4, 1945), CBSSw 52964, CO alb P5-15536, JAZ 68
      After You've Gone (arr FH)

(Take of "Why Don't You Do Right?" included in FR series is not known. This expensive set of reissues has not been available for examination.)

A recording ban—a dispute between the musicians' union and the record companies caused the union to forbid its members to record until certain financial agreements were concluded - began August 1. Before it could take effect, Benny hastened to get in one final studio session:

BENNY GOODMAN AND HIS ORCHESTRA   **July 30, 1942, New York**

Personnel as July 27, but with Stearn's presence likely. Baker out. BUZZ ALSTON, voc.

CO 33067	**LP:** PHON 7648
CO 33067	LP: BID 1014
CO 33067-bkdn	UNISSUED - Tape
CO 33067	UNISSUED - Tape
CO 33067	UNISSUED - Tape
CO 33067-1	CO 36641, CoArg 291430, CoC 675. **LP:** CO alb P5-15536, JAZ 68

              Dearly Beloved - voc Buzz Alston (arr EdSau)

CO 33068	**LP:** PHON 7648
CO 33068-bkdn	UNISSUED - Tape
CO 33068	LP: BID 1014
CO 33068-1	CO 36641, CoArg 291430, CoC 675. **LP:** JAZ 68

              I'm Old Fashioned - voc Buzz Alston

CO 33069	UNISSUED - Tape
CO 33069-bkdn	UNISSUED - Tape
CO 33069-1	**LP:** PHON 7648

              Let's Say A Prayer - voc Peggy Lee

CO 33070	LP: BID 1014
CO 33070-bkdn	UNISSUED - Tape
CO 33070	**LP:** PHON 7648
CO 33070-bkdns	UNISSUED - Tape (2 consecutive aborted attempts)
CO 33070-1	CO 36680, CoC 715. **45:** CO 4-8-G (Set G4-3). **EP:** CO 5-1655 (Set B351). **LP:** CO GL501, CO CL534, CoE 33SX1084, CO PG33405, TL STLJ05, FR series, SM 6-0610, CO alb PM-16932. **ET:** AFRS G.I. Jive H12-447

              Mission To Moscow (arr MP)

(Note that the new vocalist's name really was Philip "Buzz" **Aston** - no "l". Columbia's labels err.)

The proscription imposed by James C. Petrillo, president of the American Federation of Musicians to which the great majority of professionals belonged, forbade recording for commercial purposes by the membership. But it did permit union members to record for agencies of the United States Government, provided certain conditions were observed: The participants could not be compensated; royalty payments to the copyright owners of the compositions recorded must be waived; and the recordings could not be sold to civilians, but could only be distributed to members of the armed forces.

These restrictions did not deter civilian bandsmen, for they were eager to contribute to the war effort as best they might. Besides, cynically, they had an interest in keeping their names before that segment of their public now in military service, and records for the troops would help accomplish that purpose.

Thus, Benny will make no sanctioned recordings for commercial release until November 1944. Fortunately for the Goodman enthusiast, the next 27-odd months are not barren. He will record directly for Departments and other established agencies of the government, and for the Armed Forces Radio Service, a new agency commissioned to facilitate recording and distribution of authorized records to the various services. Further, the governmental agencies, principally AFRS, will transcribe some of his radio broadcasts onto 16″ electrical transcriptions; and these, and V-Discs, will eventually become prized possessions of collectors, even if illegally held. He will make motion pictures; and in time copies of the films, and transcriptions of their sound tracks, will circulate among collectors. And, adding considerable bulk and hours of excellent music to the aforementioned media, will be acetates taken from radio broadcasts by amateurs; bless them.

It may be, too, that Mr. Petrillo's dictate was not observed without exception. There is some evidence that the bands on occasion made some studio recordings not intended for the armed services. This possibility will be explored.

In all, the recording ban will not silence Benny Goodman. And that's as well, for he rarely played better than he will play during the War Years, next in our chronology.

THE WAR YEARS—V-DISCS AND AFRS TRANSCRIPTIONS

Mel Powell left the band in August to enlist in the U.S. Army, but really to join Glenn Miller's all-star AAF orchestra. Bill Clifton replaced him, and it may be he who is present on the first air check extant for the Petrillo-ban period. The band was playing in the Chicago Theater, but this War Bonds program was broadcast from outdoors:

"BOND WAGON DRIVE"　　　　　　August 10, 1942, Chicago
　Radio Station WGN

Personnel as July 30, except poss. BILL CLIFTON, p, replaces Powell.

Let's Dance (theme)
Idaho
These Foolish Things - voc Peggy Lee
After You've Gone

(Above on LP, AC 16.)

Then it was on to Hollywood for a musical about a modeling agency, "The Powers Girl." Here pianist Jimmy Rowles, who was playing with Lester and Lee Young's group in Los Angeles, joined the band. But to get the job, he first had to audition. Jimmy tells this story about his first encounter with Benny:

The audition was set for MCA's offices in Beverly Hills, in a studio local musicians had cynically named "The Blood Room," because so many of them had sweated blood in it while demonstrating their talents for potential employers. Benny met Jimmy there, asked him what he'd like to play, just the two of them. Jimmy appeared to mull this over, but in reality he knew what he would choose, if Benny asked. It was a piece with which he was completely familiar, a routine he'd developed with Lester: "Body And Soul" in the key of E, or four sharps. Customarily, the tune is played in either C-natural or D-flat. To play it in Jimmy's key, E, forced Benny to transpose to six sharps, and he was somewhat at a loss trying to keep up with Jimmy. Rowles recalls, "I played the hell out of it while Benny struggled. I had him at a helluva disadvantage, which I had planned." Impressed with Jimmy's apparent skill, Benny hired him then and there.

Just out of Woody Herman's band, and in demand as a studio stalwart, lefthander Frankie Carlson was hired to play drums for the film . . . or at least for its sound track. To the best of the author's recollection (eventually a video cassette may settle the question), Carlson does not appear on screen. Hud Davies does; and a correspondent insists that Louis Bellson is seen in a Quintet performance. Thus, a trio of tympanists in our personnel for . . .

"THE POWERS GIRL"　　　　　　September 1942, Hollywood

An United Artists motion picture filmed in black-and-white.
Release date: January 15, 1943　　　*Running time: 93 minutes*
Director: Norman Z. McLeod　　　*Producer: Charles R. Rogers*
Songs by Kim Gannan and Jules Styne
CAST: George Murphy, Anne Shirley, Carole Landis, Dennis Day, Alan Mowbray, and

BENNY GOODMAN AND HIS ORCHESTRA:

Personnel as July 30, except JIMMY ROWLES, p, replaces Powell; and FRANKIE CARLSON and/or LOUIS BELLSON, added on d.

QUINTET: BG, Rowles, Barbour, Hill, and Davies, Carlson or Bellson

(Opening title music: studio orchestra
Let's Dance: Benny Goodman Orchestra
Roll 'Em: Benny Goodman Orchestra
. . . unidentified title: Benny Goodman Orchestra (as choir sings, "Flow Gently, Sweet Afton")
I Know That You Know - QUINTET (LP: EX 1004)
(Three Dreams: studio orchestra
(You're Out Of This World-voc Dennis Day: studio orchestra
(Three Dreams-voc Dennis Day: studio orchestra

One O'Clock Jump: Benny Goodman Orchestra
The Lady Who Didn't Believe In Love-voc Peggy Lee: Benny Goodman Orchestra
(Closing title music: studio orchestra

An acetate of poor quality, represented as from an unidentified studio source in 1941, is believed by the author to be an out-take from "The Powers Girl":

poss. out-take, "THE POWERS GIRL"　　September 1942, Hollywood

Personnel as preceding

You're Out Of This World-voc Peggy Lee

The band returned to Manhattan, opened in the Hotel New Yorker on October 9. Personnel changes were in progress: it is assumed that Louis Bellson is now permanent, and that Al Klink is in the lineup on an undated air check broadcast from the Ice Terrace Room prior to October 16, when Lou McGarity will leave:

SUSTAINING BROADCAST　　　　　early October 1942, Hotel
　Unknown radio network　　　　　　New Yorker, New York

Personnel as "The Powers Girl," except AL KLINK, ts, replaces Sims, and Louis Bellson, d, is certain.

Blues In the Night-voc Peggy Lee, Lou McGarity

Lou McGarity quit on the 16th to go with Raymond Scott's CBS house band before a tour of duty with the U.S. Navy. He'll be back. And Lawrence Stearns also left, and was replaced by a powerful young trumpeter who'll become prominent in the post-war period, Conrad Gozzo.

Coca Cola had switched from the Mutual Network to ABC's Blue Network for its "Spotlight Bands" programs, and Benny appeared on the new network for Coke on October 17. It was the 24th program in its new series, now titled, "The Victory Parade Of Spotlight Bands." One or both of the following two cuts, from undated acetates, may be from that broadcast; but since this is uncertain, they are shown as emanating from the New Yorker:

SUSTAINING BROADCASTS　　　　　mid-October 1942, Hotel
　Unknown radio networks　　　　　New Yorker, New York

Personnel as "early October," with possibly CONRAD GOZZO, tpt, replacing Stearns, and EARL LeFAVE, tbn, replacing McGarity.

Dearly Beloved (arr EdSau)
Cow Cow Boogie - voc Peggy Lee

SUSTAINING BROADCAST　　　　　　October 19, 1942, Hotel
　CBS Radio Network　　　　　　　New Yorker, New York

Benny Goodman, clt; Jimmy Maxwell, Tony Faso, Conrad Gozzo, tpt; Charlie Castaldo, Earl LeFave, tbn; Hymie Schertzer, Clint Neagley, as; Jon Walton, Al Klink, ts; Bob Poland, bar; Jimmy Rowles, p; Dave Barbour, g; Cliff Hill, b; Louis Bellson, d; Peggy Lee, voc.

QUINTET: BG, Rowles, Barbour, Hill, Bellson

Cow Cow Boogie - voc Peggy Lee (LP: JSSd AA510)
I Know That You Know - QUINTET (n/c - middle break)
Praise The Lord And Pass The Ammunition - voc Peggy Lee, band (LP: JSSD AA510)
Let's Dance (mid-broadcast theme)
I Came Here To Talk For Joe (n/c - intro only)

Benny performed Gershwin's "Rhapsody In Blue" for the first time on radio with Toscanini, no less—and to his huge embarrassment blew a clinker in the opening clarinet passage. In part, Benny feels the maestro was

139

responsible; he assumed there would be a rehearsal, but Toscanini said no, just come in and play. In any event, he will redeem himself some ten weeks later.

"NBC SYMPHONY HOUR" November 1, 1942, New York
  NBC Radio Network

Benny Goodman, clt, and the NBC Symphony Orchestra, Arturo Toscanini, conducting. Earl Wild, p.

Rhapsody In Blue

SUSTAINING BROADCAST November 11, 1942, Hotel
  CBS Radio Network New Yorker, New York

Personnel as October 19.

Can't We Be Friends?
Clarinet A La King (n/c)
I Had The Craziest Dream - to signoff

SUSTAINING BROADCAST November 12, 1942, Hotel
  CBS Radio Network New Yorker, New York

Personnel as October 19.

Let's Dance (theme)
Down South Camp Meeting
Velvet Moon
Mr. Five By Five - voc Peggy Lee (LP: JSSd AA510)
Liza (arr HH) (n/c)
Take Me
Mission To Moscow
Let's Dance (mid-broadcast theme)
Six Flats Unfurnished
I Had The Craziest Dream - voc Peggy Lee

SUSTAINING BROADCAST November 20, 1942, Hotel
  Unknown radio network New Yorker, New York

Personnel as October 19.

9:20 Special (arr SkM or BH)

(There are two arrangements in Mr. Goodman's library for "9:20 Special," one by Skippy Martin, the other by Buster Harding. It is not known which was used for this performance.)

Wholesale personnel changes occurred at about this time, probably near or at the end of the month. Bob Crosby had disbanded, Jess was available, and he replaced Rowles in time to appear on Mutual's "Stage Door Canteen," mc'd by Rudy Vallee:

"STAGE DOOR CANTEEN" December 2, 1942, New York
  MUTUAL Radio Network

QUINTET: BG, JESS STACY, Barbour, Hill, Bellson.

I Know That You Know - QUINTET

The other replacements included Jack Jenney, a marvelous trombonist, who joined when Earl LeFave left. As had Lou McGarity, Jimmy Maxwell moved over to the house band at CBS; and both Tony Faso (Joseph Fasulo) and Bob Poland departed, but with unknown destinations. We assume that all substitutions had taken place by the time of our next air checks, although Jimmy Maxwell believes he stayed with the band until New Year's Eve.

SUSTAINING BROADCAST December 3, 1942, Hotel
  Unknown network New Yorker, New York

Benny Goodman, clt; Conrad Gozzo, CARL POOLE, STEVE STECK, tpt; Charlie Castaldo, JACK JENNEY, tbn; Hymie Schertzer, Clint Neagley, as; Jon Walton, Al Klink, ts; TED GODDARD, bar; Jess Stacy, p; Dave Barbour, g; Cliff Hill, b; Louis Bellson, d; Peggy Lee, voc.

QUINTET: BG, Stacy, Barbour, Hill, Bellson

Oh, Lady Be Good! - QUINTET
Why Don't You Do Right? - voc Peggy Lee (n/c)

"SPOTLIGHT BANDS" December 11, 1942, New York
  Blue Network

Personnel as December 3.

Sugar Foot Stomp (LP: JOY 1073)
Goodbye (theme)

Here's our first "AFRS" original ET; in fact, it was issued by the Special Service Division of the War Department. It is the first of three guest appearances Benny will make on NBC's hugely popular Sunday evening program featuring Jack Benny, Mary Livingston, Dennis Day, Rochester, announcer Don Wilson, and this evening's guest, Gary Cooper. Phil Harris and his Orchestra were regularly on these programs, but for the next several they are missing.

JACK BENNY No. 7 **December 13, 1942, New York**
Orchestra personnel as December 3, augmented by unknown strings.

SS-12-13-42-1 **ET:** War Department Special Service Division Jack Benny No. 7 - Part 1
  Hallelujah!
  I Had The Craziest Dream - voc Dennis Day (augmented orchestra)

SS-12-13-42-2 **ET:** As preceding, except: Part 2
  After You've Gone
  One O'Clock Jump (to close)

(A clarinet obligato at the end of "I Had The Craziest Dream" would seem to qualify this tune as a Goodman item. Full program is on LP, JOY 1073.)

United Artists built a musical around Hollywood's mecca for servicemen, its Stage Door Canteen, where the stars and starlets entertained troops fortunate enough to go on leave in Tinsel City. One of a huge number of entertainers to appear briefly in the film, Benny had his contribution filmed in New York sometime in December, because wartime travel restrictions and his commitment to the New Yorker prevented him from going to California.

"STAGE DOOR CANTEEN" December 1942, New York

An United Artists motion picture filmed in black-and-white.
Release date: July 1943 Running time: 132 minutes
Director: Frank Borzage Producer: Sol Lesser
CAST: Lon McAllister, William Terry, Cheryl Walker, principal roles. Cameo appearances by Harpo Marx, Ray Bolger, Gracie Fields, Edgar Bergen (and Charlie McCarthy and Mortimer Snerd), Katharine Cornell, Ethel Waters, Yehudi Menuhin, Gypsy Rose Lee, Ed Wynn, Tallulah Bankhead, Ralph Bellamy, Georgie Jessel, Gertrude Lawrence, Ethel Merman, Alfred Lunt and Lynn Fontanne, Judith Anderson, Katherine Hepburn, Martha Scott, Lanny Ross, Ina Claire, Jane Cowl and Kenny Baker; and the orchestras of Count Basie, Xavier Cugat, Kay Kyser, Guy Lombardo, Freddy Martin, and

BENNY GOODMAN AND HIS ORCHESTRA:

Personnel as December 3.

Why Don't You Do Right? - voc Peggy Lee
Bugle Call Rag

(Above on LP, CURTAIN CALLS 100-11/12.)

Benny broadcast for Coca Cola on Christmas Day and again on December 29, but no air checks from either are known to exist.
The two Benny's, Goodman and Jack, got together again on the 27th, but it is uncertain whether BG brought his band along: the two orchestral numbers are used almost as themes, and are partial renditions. Both may be by a studio orchestra, with Benny simply fronting it. The Quintet, however, is all his:

"THE GRAPE NUTS PROGRAM, December 27, 1942, Vanderbilt
  STARRING JACK BENNY" Theater, New York
  NBC Radio Network

Benny Goodman, clt, and possibly a studio orchestra.
QUINTET: As December 3, with possibly KENNY UNWIN, d, replacing Bellson

For Me And My Gal (n/c)
Oh, Lady Be Good! - QUINTET (n/c - voice over)
Alabamy Bound (n/c)

The Paramount Theater offered what has become an historic stage show beginning December 30; Benny Goodman and his Orchestra were the headliners, but a featured performer stole the show: Frank Sinatra. Frank had left Tommy Dorsey's band the end of September (replaced by Dick Haymes, who had also followed Sinatra into Harry James's orchestra), had had a few minor engagements, but this was his first major booking as a "single." So popular was he that when Benny's four-week stand ended, Frank stayed on for another month, appearing then with Johnny Long and his Orchestra.

There are no known recordings of any kind of Benny and Frank together at the Parmount. There are, however, a number of undated acetate air checks believed to have originated in the New Yorker in late 1942 and early 1943. They are listed next, and show a collective personnel for the band, reflecting the numerous changes reported by the music press in this period. The press also indicated that Benny employed as many as seven brass, five reeds and five rhythm (if both baritone and bass saxes were present simultaneously) while in the Paramount.

SUSTAINING BROADCASTS   late November 1942-early 1943,
  CBS Radio Network   Hotel New Yorker, N.Y.

Benny Goodman, clt; Gozzo, Poole, Steck, SOL LaPERCHE, LEE CASTLE (Castaldo), YANK LAWSON, tpt; Charlie Castaldo, Jenney, MIFF MOLE, tbn; Schertzer, Neagley, HANK D'AMICO, HEINIE BEAU, as; Walton, Klink, ZOOT SIMS, BOB TAYLOR, ts; Goddard, JOE RUSHTON, bar or b-sax; Stacy, p; Barbour, g; Hill, SID WEISS, b; Bellson, KENNY UNWIN, d; Peggy Lee, voc.

QUINTET: BG, Stacy, Barbour, Hill or Weiss, Bellson or Unwin

Alabamy Bound
Why Don't You Do Right? - voc Peggy Lee - to signoff
Don't Get Around Much Any More - voc Peggy Lee - to signoff

SUSTAINING BROADCASTS   late November 1942-early 1943, Hotel
  Unknown radio networks   New Yorker, New York

Personnel as for CBS broadcasts, preceding.

Six Flats Unfurnished
Why Don't You Do Right? - voc Peggy Lee
Why Don't You Do Right? - voc Peggy Lee (n/c)
I Lost My Sugar 'n Salt Lake City - voc Peggy Lee
I Lost My Sugar 'n Salt Lake City - voc Peggy Lee (n/c)
The Count (n/c)
Rose Room - QUINTET (n/c)
That Soldier Of Mine - voc Peggy Lee (n/c)
After You've Gone (n/c)

Next is the re-dated Jack Benny program, once thought to have been broadcast a year earlier. Possibly with a studio orchestra rather than this own band, BG plays a new version of "Bugle Call Rag," arranger unknown. An introductory "Hallelujah!" and a closing "Rosie The Riveter," both with announcements over them, have no Goodman soli, and it is questionable if Benny participated in either. Dennis Day sings "Moonlight Becomes You," accompanied by an orchestra with strings, and this is not considered a Goodman item.

"THE GRAPE NUTS PROGRAM,   January 10, 1943, Vanderbilt
  STARRING JACK BENNY"   Theater, New York
  NBC Radio Network

Benny Goodman, clt, and possibly a studio orchestra.

Hallelujah! (? BG ?) (n/c - voice over)
Bugle Call Rag
Rosie The Riveter (? BG ?) (n/c - voice over)

We may not yet be finished with January 10; there is reason to believe two Goodman renditions, formerly assigned to a date of "Spring 1943," may have taken place this date. And there is some evidence that a newly-discovered duet by Benny and an unidentified pianist, playing an unannounced composition, may also be from January 10.

Two cuts are from a sponsored series, "The Cresta Blanca Carnival," broadcast weekly via Mutual. It regularly featured Morton Gould and his Orchestra, Oscar Levant, Clifton Fadiman, George S. Kaufman, Walter O'Keefe, and guests. Maestro Gould, a longstanding friend of Benny's, still active and now living in New York, assures the author that all of the "Cresta Blanca" programs originated in Manhattan. This eliminates a putative date of "Spring 1943," because Benny leaves New York the end of January, does not return until midyear. And it supports a written inscription on an acetate of one of the tunes.

One cut is on an "AFRS" 16" transcription, generically titled, "Your Broadway And Mine," and it finds Benny performing "Rhapsody In Blue" flawlessly, the second time around. It is the only rendition by Benny on the ET. The other is the Quintet's "Rose Room," via the acetate cited above. However, there is a report that two-12" Army Service Forces discs offer both performances. Because the author has been unable to confirm this claim, these discs are shown as possible subsidiary issues.

YOUR BROADWAY AND MINE,   ? January 10, 1943, New York
  Program No. 16

Benny Goodman, clt; Oscar Levant, p; and a studio orchestra conducted by Morton Gould.

YTNY 1734-1A   ET: War Department Special Service Division present
                    Your Broadway And Mine Program No. 16, Part 2
                    Rhapsody In Blue

(Reputedly on 12"-78, Army Service Forces Special Services Program, mx D5-TC 428/429.)

"THE CRESTA BLANCA   ? January 10, 1943, New York
  CARNIVAL" MUTUAL Radio Network

Benny Goodman, clt; Jess Stacy, p; Dave Barbour, g; prob. Sid Weiss, b; prob. Louis Bellson or Kenny Unwin, d.

Rose Room - QUINTET

(Reputedly on 12"-78, Army Special Services Program, mx D5-TC 426/427.)

The flip side of the acetate bearing "Rose Room" has on it a tune unfamiliar to the author, played by Benny and a pianist. Both the composition and the piano style appeal to the author as something Alec Templeton might have written and played. But there's that "January 10" date . . . If the pianist is Levant, then the "Cresta Blanca" broadcast is likely the source. Therefore,

? "THE CRESTA BLANCA   ? January 10, 1943, New York
  CARNIVAL" MUTUAL Radio Network

Benny Goodman, clt; possibly Oscar Levant, p.

. . . unidentified tune - DUET

Out of the New Yorker, finished at the Paramount, Benny went first to Chicago for an engagement at the Chicago Theater. While there he broadcast at least twice for Coca Cola, from a facility reserved for military personnel, the Servicemen's Center No. 2. The Coca Cola Company is to be commended not only for its sponsorship of these programs, but also because it stood the expenses involved in transporting the bands to the locations, and paid the leaders for an evening's performance.

"SPOTLIGHT BANDS"   February 6, 1943, Chicago
  Blue Network

Personnel drawn from that for "CBS - late November 1942-early 1943." Bellson on d.

Bugle Call Rag (LP: JOY 1073)
Good-Bye (theme)

"SPOTLIGHT BANDS"   February 13, 1943, Chicago
  Blue Network

Personnel as February 6.

Don't Be That Way
I Had The Craziest Dream (n/c)
Clarinet A La King
As Time Goes By - voc Peggy Lee (n/c)

A week later Benny again was featured by Coca Cola, but from a location unknown to the author; it may well have been Chicago, although he'll be on the West Coast on the 23rd.

"SPOTLIGHT BANDS"   February 20, 1943, unknown location
  Blue Network

Personnel as February 6.

Stealin' Apples
Down South Camp Meeting
I've Found A New Baby

Benny and key members of the band flew to California to begin an engagement at the Hollywood Palladium on February 23, and to make another movie. A broadcast from the Palladium displays his revamped lineup:

SUSTAINING BROADCAST   February 28, 1943, Hollywood
  Unknown radio network   Palladium, Hollywood

Benny Goodman, clt; Lee Castle, RAY LINN, BOBBY GUYER, tpt; Charlie Castaldo, Miff Mole, tbn; Hymie Schertzer, LEONARD KAYE, as; Jon Walton, Bob Taylor, ts; Joe Rushton, b-sax; Jess Stacy, p; BART ROTH, g; GUS VAN CAMP, b; Louis Bellson, d; Peggy Lee, voc.

TRIO: BG, Stacy, Bellson

SEXTET: BG, Rushton, Stacy, Roth, Van Camp, Bellson

I Love A Piano - voc Peggy Lee and Benny Goodman

The only known copy of the Armed Forces Radio Service's chronologically first "live" recording of Benny Goodman is, unfortunately, so badly mutilated that its identifying inscriptions have been obliterated, and it took endless hours of repeated playing to produce a tape of it. More time was then required to pitch-correct and equalize segments of that tape, then multiple splicing was needed to produce a coherent transfer. What emerges from all of this is, apart from the music, conversation that reveals Peggy was recently married to David Barbour — which helps date the ET:

AFRS DOWNBEAT No. 25   **c. February/March 1943, Los Angeles**
Personnel as February 28.

(-?-)   ET: AFRS Downbeat No. 25 - Part 1
             Let's Dance (theme)
             Air Mail Special (LP: SWH 46)
             You'd Be So Nice To Come Home To
             9:20 Special
             I Don't Believe In Rumors-voc Peggy Lee

(-?-)   ET: as above, except Part 2
             I Love A Piano-voc Peggy Lee, Benny Goodman (LP:
               SWH 46)
             I'm Just Wild About Harry (arr EdSau) (LP: SWH 46)
             Why Don't You Do Right?-voc Peggy Lee (LP: SWH 46)
             Stealin' Apples - to signoff (LP: SWH 46)

("Air Mail Special" is also on ET, AFRS Basic Music Library No. P-6.)

Trumpeter Jimmy Pupa is known to have played with the band while it was at the Palladium; but now Benny is carrying only five brass, and Pupa is believed to have been a substitute.

SUSTAINING BROADCAST   March 10, 1943, Hollywood
  Unknown radio network   Palladium, Hollywood

Personnel as February 28.

Henderson Stomp
. . . unidentified title (possibly, "If I Knew Then") (n/c)
Rosie The Riveter - voc Benny Goodman
A Smo-o-o-oth One
Sugar (arr FH)
At The Darktown Strutters' Ball (n/c)

SUSTAINING BROADCAST   March 13, 1943, Hollywood
  CBS Radio Network   Palladium, Hollywood

Personnel as February 28.

Bugle Call Rag
Don't Get Around Much Any More - voc Peggy Lee (n/c)
Good-Bye (theme)

SUSTAINING BROADCAST   March 14, 1943, Hollywood
  Unknown radio network   Palladium, Hollywood

Personnel as February 28.

Great Guy (n/c)

SUSTAINING BROADCAST   March 20, 1943, Hollywood
  CBS Radio Network   Palladium, Hollywood

Personnel as February 28.

Drip-Drop - voc Benny Goodman (n/c - middle break)
Slender, Tender and Tall - voc Peggy Lee
Air Mail Special
Good-Bye (theme)

"Slender, Tender And Tall" (and she was, then) is Peggy's final known rendition as a regular member of Benny's entourage. With her (first) husband, Dave Barbour, out of the band, she'd given Benny three weeks' notice on March 1. For some 20 months Peggy had been a stalwart performer and the band's foremost popular attraction; now it was time for her to capitalize personally on the public's acceptance. An alumna of the 1937 Goodman Gang, Frances Hunt, replaced her and is heard on the next air check:

SUSTAINING BROADCAST   March 24, 1943, Hollywood
  CBS Radio Network   Palladium, Hollywood

Personnel as February 28, except FRANCES HUNT, voc, replaces Peggy Lee.

Miss Daffodil (arr Johnny Thompson)
You Turned The Tables On Me - voc Frances Hunt
After You've Gone
Good-Bye (theme)

SUSTAINING BROADCAST   March 28, 1943, Hollywood
  Unknown radio network   Palladium, Hollywood

Orchestra as March 24. Sextet as February 28.

Oh, Lady Be Good! - SEXTET
As Time Goes By - voc Frances Hunt
But Not For Me - voc Frances Hunt (arr EdSau)
Miss Daffodil
Sugar Foot Stomp

SUSTAINING BROADCAST   March 31, 1943, Hollywood
  CBS Radio Network   Palladium, Hollywood

Personnel as March 24.

A Smo-o-o-oth One
I'm Just Wild About Harry
After You've Gone
I've Been Saving Myself For Bill - voc Frances Hunt
Clarinet A La King
Good-Bye (theme)

A few air checks believed to be from the Palladium engagement are undated:

SUSTAINING BROADCAST(S)   March 1943, Hollywood
  Unknown radio network(s)   Palladium, Hollywood

Instrumental personnel as February 28.

Stealin' Apples (n/c)
Sugar Foot Stomp
Can't We Be Friends?
Air Mail Special (n/c)
Honeysuckle Rose - TRIO

Benny's precise itinerary at this juncture is unknown to the author (he was in the U.S. Army himself, had been since late 1942). Benny did open in the Casino Gardens on April 23, but just when he had left the Palladium is unascertained. The next broadcast from the Palladium marks a full six weeks for this engagement, and it may have been the final one:

SUSTAINING BROADCAST   April 5, 1943, Hollywood
  CBS Radio Network   Palladium, Hollywood

Personnel as March 24.

Air Mail Special
You'll Never Know - voc Frances Hunt (n/c - line interruption)
At The Darktown Strutters' Ball
Why Don't You Do Right? - voc Frances Hunt
Miss Daffodil
I've Found A New Baby (n/c)

Jack Teagarden reputedly sat in with the band for one set during its Palladium engagement. Unfortunately, none of the extant air checks reveals his presence. Too bad; what a prize that would be, two of the titans of the trombone together with Benny, Big Tea and Miff, an opportunity muffed.

Through the latter part of March and into April, while the band was at the Palladium, it doubled into 20th Century-Fox's studios for another musical extravaganza, this one in color. Benny sings, and his band is heard throughout the film, even if some of its performances are partials, and background for dialogue. Originally titled, "The Girl He Left Behind (Him)," here is:

"THE GANG'S ALL HERE"   *March/April 1943, Hollywood*

A 20th Century-Fox motion picture filmed in color.
Release date: December 24, 1943   *Running time: 103 minutes*
Director: Busby Berkely   *Producer: William Le Baron*
Songs by Leo Robin and Harry Warren
CAST: Alice Faye Carmen Miranda, James Ellison, Eugene Pallette, Edward Everett Horton, Charlotte Greenwood, Tony DeMarco, Sheila Ryan, Phil Baker, and

BENNY GOODMAN AND HIS ORCHESTRA: Personnel as March/April Palladium engagement, except HAROLD PEPPIE, tpt, replaces Linn, and EDDIE MILLER, ts, records the tenor sax solos (although Bob Taylor appears on screen).

(Let's Dance and opening title music: studio orchestra
(You Discover You're In New York - voc Carmen Miranda & Phil Baker: studio orchestra
Let's Dance: Benny Goodman Orchestra
Minnie's In the Money - voc Benny Goodman (arr EdSau): Benny Goodman Orchestra
A Journey To A Star: Benny Goodman Orchestra (background to dialogue)
Soft Winds (arr FH): Benny Goodman Orchestra (background to dialogue)
(The Lady In The Tutti-Frutti Hat - voc Carmen Miranda: studio orchestra
(A Journey To A Star - voc Alice Faye: studio orchestra
. . . unidentified rhythm tune: Benny Goodman Orchestra (background to dance by Charlotte Greenwood and Charles Saggau)
No Love, No Nothin' - voc Alice Faye: Benny Goodman Orchestra (augmented by strings) (LP: CITADEL 6004)
. . . unidentified rhythm tune: Benny Goodman Orchestra
No Love, No Nothin': Benny Goodman Orchestra (background to dialogue)
No Love, No Nothin': Benny Goodman Orchestra (background to dance by Sheila Ryan and Tony DeMarco)
Minnie's In The Money: Benny Goodman Orchestra (background for Miriam Lavelle dance)
Paducah - voc Carmen Miranda & Benny Goodman (arr EdSau): Benny Goodman Orchestra (augmented by Latin-type group)
(A Journey To A Star - voc Alice Faye & choir: studio orchestra
(The Polka Dot Polka - voc Alice Faye: studio orchestra
A Journey To A Star - voc the cast, including Benny Goodman, each of whom sings one line of the chorus: studio orchestra

(Portions of the sound track are on LP, SH 2009, CIF 3003.)

To help promote the film, 20th Century-Fox produced four—possibly, five—two-sided 78 rpm shellac 10″ discs for distribution to radio stations. Two of them feature Benny Goodman. Their labels are white, and they are printed in black: "Beverly Hills, California" "TITLE" "ARTIST" "PICTURE," plus a 20th Century-Fox insignia. Imprints (in appearance, as if applied by mimeograph) fill in the Title, Artist and Picture blanks. Collectors are advised that these are rare recordings.

THE GANG'S ALL HERE   **March/April 1943, Hollywood**

Personnel as for the motion picture, "The Gang's All Here." Carmen Miranda, Benny Goodman, voc.

TCF 233   TCF 233
        Let's Dance/Minnie's In The Money - voc Benny Goodman (arr EdSau)

(TCF 234, reverse of TCF 233, has a vocal by Alice Faye, accompanied by a studio orchestra)

TCF 237   TCF 237
        Paducah - voc Benny Goodman (arr EdSau)

TCF 238   TCF 238
        Paducah - voc Carmen Miranda

(Note that each side's "matrix" is the same as its catalog number.)

The other known 20th Century-Fox discs publicizing this film are TCF 235/236, Parts 1 and 2 of "The Lady In The Tutti-Frutti Hat," vocal by Carmen Miranda, accompanied by a studio orchestra - no BG; and TCF 241, "You Discover You're In New York," instrumental by a studio orchestra - no BG. If TCF 241 has a reverse, its contents are not known. And there is no information on what would appear to be a missing disc in the series, TCF 239/240.

Benny remained in California after the movie was completed for an excellent reason: Alice gave birth to their first daughter, Rachel, on May 2 in Los Angeles. Alice and Benny had rented an apartment in the Los Angeles district, and stayed there for some time after the baby's birth.

Little is known of Benny's activities for the next month and a half. He recalls that the band played for service personnel at various military installations, but the specifics have faded with the passing years. Nor have any air checks surfaced that would throw some light on this period. But in main Benny stayed at home with Alice and Rachel.

He next is heard on a "Spotlight Bands" program from Princeton University, Princeton, New Jersey, on June 26 (previously thought to have been broadcast June 21). Princeton, as did many colleges and universities throughout the war, had opened its ivied halls to military trainees studying under the aegis of the government, and Benny entertained a Naval Training unit there. AFRS transcribed the broadcast in part. Note the revamped lineup, which included vocalist E'Lane McAfree, reputedly a wealthy debutante who sang with the band just for kicks; and a privately-recorded air check that adds to the ET's contents:

AFRS SPOTLIGHT BANDS No. 84   **June 26, 1943, Princeton, N.J.**

Benny Goodman, clt; Lee Castle, Bobby Guyer, RALPH MUZZILLO, tpt; Charlie Castaldo, Miff Mole, tbn; Hymie Schertzer, EDDIE ROSA, as; Bob Taylor, HERBIE HAYMER, ts; Joe Rushton, b-sax; Jess Stacy, p; ALLAN REUSS, g; SID WEISS, b; ERNIE AUSTIN or LES BRAUN, d; E'LANE McAFREE, voc.

SS-6-21-9   **ET:** AFRS Spotlight Bands No. 84
        After You've Gone
        Honky Tonk Train Blues (featuring Jess Stacy) (**LP:** JOY 1073)
        But Not For Me - voc E'Lane McAfree (arr EdSau)
        Henderson Stomp

Also available from this broadcast:

Bugle Call Rag

On June 28 Benny and the band began a lengthy engagement at the Astor Roof, Hotel Astor, Manhattan. George Wettling joined, and together with Stacy, Reuss and Weiss, gave Benny the best rhythm section he'd had for more than a year. Supported by this solid foundation, Benny blew on an undated air check some of the finest clarinet of his career, chorus after chorus of "Stealin' Apples." This extended performance is recommended to jazz enthusiasts of all persuasions as a supreme example of Benny's invention and virtuosity, a true classic:

SUSTAINING BROADCAST   *early July 1943, Hotel Astor*
CBS Radio Network   *New York*

Instrumental personnel as June 26, except GEORGE WETTLING, d, replaces either Austin or Braun.

Stealin' Apples (LP: JSFr/Sd AA510, GOJ 1005, JM "Classics of Jazz Radio," JAZ 27)
Good-Bye (theme) (LP: JSFr/Sd AA510, GOJ 1005, JM "Classics of Jazz Radio," JAZ 27)

We specify "instrumental personnel" above because Benny changed vocalists almost weekly at this time—Susie Allen replaced E'Lane McAfree, she in turn was supplanted by Monica Lewis. Neither appears on verified air checks; the few vocals on acetate the first month of the Astor stand are by Benny himself.

Nor is it known how long Wettling remained with the band. In reviewing this period with Benny, the author suggested that the drummer on some of the air checks sounded like Ray McKinley. And Benny agreed—he did recall that McKinley, under whatever circumstances, had played for him at the Astor. But save for the few air checks that seem to include McKinley—and lacking specific advice to the contrary—Wettling is continued in the listings for most of the Astor engagement.

SUSTAINING BROADCAST   early July 1943, Hotel Astor
   Unknown radio network   New York

Personnel as CBS ''early July'' broadcast.

After You've Gone

SUSTAINING BROADCAST   July 14, 1943, Hotel Astor
   Unknown radio network   New York

Personnel as CBS ''early July'' broadcast.

Honky Tonk Train (n/c)
Stealin' Apples (n/c)

Frank Sinatra, who had replaced Barry Wood as one of the vocalists on the ''Your Hit Parade'' broadcasts in March, landed his own radio program in May, ''Broadway Bandbox.'' The Benny Goodman Trio made a guest appearance with him; and the drummer here may well be McKinley:

"BROADWAY BANDBOX"   July 16, 1943, New York
   CBS Radio Network

Benny Goodman, clt; Jess Stacy, p; possibly Ray McKinley, d.

Rose Room - TRIO (LP: GOJ 1002)
Oh, Lady Be Good! - TRIO (LP: GOJ 1002)

The author is unable to verify a claim that there are extant air checks from the Astor on the 16th, also. Tune titles reported are: And Russia Is Her Name; Bugle Call Rag; In My Arms; It Can't Be Wrong; Mexico Joe; Stealin' Apples; and Sugar Foot Stomp. Monica Lewis is cited as vocalist for the ballads.

SUSTAINING BROADCAST   July 23, 1943, Hotel Astor
   CBS Radio Network   New York

Personnel as CBS ''early July'' broadcast.

At The Darktown Strutters' Ball (n/c)
Henderson Stomp (n/c)
Minnie's In The Money - voc Benny Goodman (n/c)
I've Found A New Baby - to signoff

SUSTAINING BROADCAST   July 24, 1943, Hotel Astor
   Unknown radio network   New York

Personnel as CBS ''early July'' broadcast.

Air Mail Special (n/c)

SUSTAINING BROADCAST   July 26, 1943, Hotel Astor
   Unknown radio network   New York

QUINTET: Benny Goodman, clt; Jess Stacy, p; Allan Reuss, g; Sid Weiss, b; probably George Wettling, d.

Oh, Lady Be Good! - QUINTET

SUSTAINING BROADCAST   July 27, 1943, Hotel Astor
   CBS Radio Network   New York

Personnel as CBS ''early July'' broadcast, except possibly Ray McKinley on d.

Roll 'Em
Do Nothing Till You Hear From Me - voc Benny Goodman
At The Darktown Strutters' Ball
Minnie's In The Money - voc Benny Goodman
Good-Bye (theme)

Carol Kay(e)—a gal afflicted with the Vernon Brown(e)-George Bruni(e)s ''to 'e' or not to 'e' '' syndrome—debuts on our next air check. Evidently she and male vocalist Ray Dorey joined the band at about the same time, for his first extant vocal comes two days later. They'll stay for awhile.

SUSTAINING BROADCAST   July 28, 1943, Hotel Astor
   MUTUAL Radio Network   New York

Personnel as July 27 (Wettling or McKinley), plus CAROL KAY(E), voc.

Don't Be That Way (n/c-coda only)
Clarinet A La King (n/c)
Thank Your Lucky Stars - voc Carol Kay(e)
Some Sunny Day (arr EdSau) (n/c)

SUSTAINING BROADCAST   July 29, 1943, Hotel Astor,
   Unknown radio network   New York

Personnel as July 28.

Sugar Foot Stomp

SUSTAINING BROADCAST   July 30, 1943, Hotel Astor,
   CBS Radio Network   New York

Personnel as July 28, plus RAY DOREY, voc. Quintet as July 26, except prob. McKinley, d.

After You've Gone (n/c - intro excised)
But Not For Me - voc Carol Kay(e)
Oh, Lady Be Good! - QUINTET
Time Stands Still - voc Ray Dorey (arr EdSau) (n/c)
Do Nothing Till You Hear From Me - voc Carol Kay(e)
Roll 'Em (n/c)

SUSTAINING BROADCAST   August 2, 1943, Hotel Astor
   MUTUAL Radio Network   New York

Personnel as July 30.

Down South Camp Meeting
Good-Bye (theme)

The band doubled from the Roof Garden into the Paramount beginning August 4. According to contemporary press reports, the band ended its engagement at the Astor on the 7th. If those accounts are accurate, the next air check is from the band's last day in the hotel.

SUSTAINING BROADCAST   August 7, 1943, Hotel Astor
   Unknown radio network   New York

Orchestra as July 30. QUINTET: BG, Stacy, Reuss, Weiss, unknown d.

Blue Lou (n/c - intro excised)
Oh, Lady Be Good! - QUINTET

The news stories also announced an altered lineup in the Paramount, two new trombonists and the return of drummer Ernie Austin. The notable addition is Bill Harris, who had been with bands led by fellow-Philadelphian Buddy Williams, and with Bob Chester. Because of the recording ban, Harris's work with Goodman will go largely unremarked; he will attain lasting fame with Woody Herman. But he'll be back with Benny in the late 1950's, for a series of stellar performances.

Harris is unmistakably present on the next four sets of air checks. One set is undated, but its source acetates list the Astor as the point of origination. The other three are dated: August 17, 18, and 20. Their recordist states positively that they, too, are from the Astor. If he is correct, the closing date of August 7 is wrong.

Other material supplied by that recordist has been found as he had specified it, in accord with other references. Therefore his designation is accepted. But we will compromise with the press, and adopt its personnel listings.

SUSTAINING BROADCAST   August 17, 1943, Hotel Astor
   Unknown radio network   New York

Benny Goodman, clt; Lee Castle, Bobby Guyer, Ralph Muzzillo, tpt; BILL HARRIS, AL MASTREN, tbn; Hymie Schertzer, Eddie Rosa, as; Bob Taylor, Herbie Haymer, ts; Joe Rushton, b-sax; Jess Stacy, p; Allan Reuss, g; Sid Weiss, b; ERNIE AUSTIN, d; Carol (Kay(e), Ray Dorey, voc.

I'm Just Wild About Harry
Pur Your Arms Around Me - voc Carol Kay(e) (n/c)
One O'Clock Jump (n/c)

SUSTAINING BROADCAST   August 18, 1943, Hotel Astor
   Unknown radio network   New York

Personnel as August 17.

At The Darktown Strutters' Ball (n/c)
Stealin' Apples (n/c)

SUSTAINING BROADCAST   August 20, 1943, Hotel Astor,
   MUTUAL Radio Network   New York

Personnel as August 17.

Down South Camp Meeting (n/c)

SUSTAINING BROADCAST　　　　　　*August 1943, Hotel Astor*
　Unknown radio network　　　　　　　　　　　*New York*

Personnel as August 17.

Bugle Call Rag
Roll 'Em
Honky Tonk Train

Introduction of a studio recording of "Henderson Stomp" by Benny Goodman, its provenance not established, is advisable at this juncture. It is on a 10″ acetate, recorded on one side only at 78 rpm, bearing the label of Associated Recording, New York. Typewritten on the label is, "Lee Castaldo, trumpet." A handwritten inscription adds, "Jess Stacy." The three soli in the performance are clearly ascribable to Stacy, Goodman and Castaldo (better known as Castle). No other instrumentalist is identifiable. Drumming throughout has no especial characteristics that would permit its attribution to a recognizable tympanist. Whether or not Gene Krupa is the drummer is the key to dating this recording.

Castle and Stacy were together in the band only for the year 1943. Krupa will join September 21. If he is not present, this version of "Henderson Stomp" was waxed in the period January-early September, 1943. If Gene does participate, then likely the recording was made on December 9, 1943, and is an alternate take of the "Henderson Stomp" released on V-Disc 159 A. (There are three known alternates to the V-Disc, none of which has been accessible to the author.) Because the acetate's "Henderson Stomp" has much the sound and "feel" of the V-Disc, the author inclines to this latter view.

Withal, a hitherto-undisclosed "Henderson Stomp," unquestionably a studio recording made during the Petrillo recording ban, 1942–1944:

BENNY GOODMAN ORCH.　　? January - December 9, 1943, New York

Personnel appropriate to the period cited, including Lee Castle, tpt, and Jess Stacy, p.

- 0 -　　　　UNISSUED - Acetate
Henderson Stomp

Gene Krupa returned to the band as a full-time, salaried sideman on September 21. There is a tale behind his return.

Gene had been in prison. He had been convicted in San Francisco on a charge of contributing to the delinquency of a minor, was fined $500, and was incarcerated for 84 days. His initial arrest came about when police officers raided a ballroom in which his band was playing and found marijuana. The drug was not in Gene's possession, but rather was discovered on the person of his "band boy." Later, the authorities learned that the band boy was both a minor and a draft dodger; although an alien, he was subject to military conscription, which he had evaded. These factors led to Gene's re-arrest, for he was held legally responsible for the boy's conduct. He was tried, convicted and imprisoned. He appealed; after a term of confinement he was freed on the basis that he had been placed in double jeopardy. His orchestra disbanded, his savings spent on lawyers' fees, Gene packed his drums and looked for work. Benny, who had visited him in prison and who had helped him through his difficulties, hired him immediately.

Those are the facts of Gene's imprisonment. Note that he was not brought to trial on a charge of either possession or use of drugs. He was never charged with that offense. The charge was as stated above, and nothing more. And the appeal process established that the charge on which he was convicted was legally defective, and he was fully exonerated.

There is more to the story, and even a background to it:

Today, nonprescriptive use of narcotics of all kinds is commonplace, world-widespread. There are those who now openly advocate decriminalization of the use of one drug especially, marijuana. That attitude did not obtain 40-odd years ago. The Nation was at war, marijuana was universally recognized as a harmful substance, its use was condemned as unpatriotic, sabotage of the war effort.

Jazz musicians as a class were then believed by the public likely to be addicted to the weed. Gene Krupa was particularly suspect: his antics at the drums, the facial contortions, the nervous energy, the sweat . . . surely he smoked marijuana. And why wasn't he in military service? There had to be a reason, and it must be drugs.

Did Gene ever smoke "tea"? Yes, he admitted that he had, but he added that it was never a habit. (Many musicians would say the same. Even Benny confesses that he tried marijuana . . . once. He said ". . . it put me right out of my mind, and I never smoked another one. How can you play and smoke those things? Impossible.") Gene's "addiction" was to Dewars Scotch, a taste he kept all his life. In some 37 years' time, the author never saw Gene use Cannabis; not in Gene's home nor in the author's, not a

hundred times over backstage in clubs, ballrooms and theaters, not in hotel and motel rooms (listening to, or watching, Chicago Cub baseball games, if they were on), not ever, anywhere, anytime. But he dearly loved Dewars, and many's the bottle he and the author killed between them.

(Once, the author feared a fifth of Dewars was about to finish them off, not the reverse. Gene's wife Ethel had just died, and the author went to Yonkers to try to console him. They commiserated, they drank, they reminisced, they drank, and they skipped both lunch and dinner. Finally the booze was gone, and the author dimly remembered he had to get back to Manhattan. Gene immediately insisted that he would drive him into town, it's the only way to go. Now, Gene was short, possibly five feet five or so; and when he wheeled his seven-passenger Caddy limousine out of the garage, it filtered through to the author that Gene could barely see over its dashboard, if indeed he could see at all. Given Gene's stature, the scotch, and twilight traffic on the Hudson River Parkway, that was a trip to induce two to take the pledge. But we never did.)

But the public believed—and much of it today casually assumes—that Gene was hung up on hemp. In part, the press fostered this opinion; and Gene always felt that it was the press, by magnifying and potboiling the incident in California, that was ultimately responsible for his imprisonment.

He said that a friend privy to police activity warned him that a raid by narcotics officers was imminent. He thereupon ordered his band boy to search everywhere for the weed, and to flush whatever he found down a toilet. The boy did as he was told, up to a point: he kept the marijuana he found rather than destroy it. Still, he, Gene, had none in his possession, and he was let go.

A national chain of newspapers would not let go, however; it kept the incident alive. When the band boy failed to appear for sentencing, and his minority and evasion of the draft came to light, it trumpeted these facts and brought pressure upon the authorities to prosecute Gene. Some six months after the event, Gene was hauled back to California, and this time he went to jail.

This episode had a lasting effect on Gene; he never really forgot it. One example: he was one of nine or ten (forget which) brothers and sisters. Between them, all who married produced only one grandchild; evidently, something inherent prevented them from having children. Ethel and Gene loved children, and they often thought about adoption. But each time they did, Gene wondered if he'd be judged "unfit" because of his arrest, and reluctantly they would decide not to expose themselves to possible rejection. (Gene and his second wife did adopt two children, Mary Grace and an infant boy, Bee Gee - how about that? By then Gene said he didn't give a damn.) Another: Ed Murrow had a TV show in the middle-50's, "Person To Person"; its format had Ed "visit" the homes of the famous, let the public see where and how they lived. Murrow asked Gene several times if he would agree to the cameras looking in on Ethel and Gene at 10 Ritchie Drive, Yonkers. The answer was always no. Gene respected Ed, but the specter of San Francisco was ever present.

If fickle, the public is also ambivalent. While persisting in its mistaken perception that Gene smoked marijuana, it nonetheless welcomed him warmly as a performer. And no one deserved their patronage more. A man of character and integrity, Gene Krupa, as all who knew him well will testify. And in our recitation, now he's back with Benny.

First evidence extant of Gene's reunion with Benny is a "Spotlight Bands" 25-minute broadcast from Cornell University, Ithaca, New York. Under the aegis of the United Service Organizations Inc., the band was on a two-week tour of military installations (Army and Navy units were in training at Cornell). Gene was so grateful to be free and behind his Slingerlands once more that he donated his salary for the tour to the U.S.O.

There is reason to believe that the first portion of this broadcast was transcribed by AFRS onto one of its 15-minute ETs, "Spotlight Bands No. 162." However, the author has searched in vain for this putative ET, knows no one who has a copy, and perforce must list the broadcast as an air check:

"SPOTLIGHT BANDS"　　　　　*September 25, 1943, Ithaca, N.Y.*
  Blue Network

Personnel as August 17, except GENE KRUPA, d, replaces Austin.

QUINTET: BG, Stacy, Reuss, Weiss, Krupa

"Spotlight Bands" theme
After You've Gone
A Journey To A Star-voc Ray Dorey (n/c - line interruption)
Three Little Words - QUINTET
Minnie's In The Money-voc Benny Goodman
I've Found A New Baby
"Spotlight Bands" theme

(Above on LP, FAN 27-127. "After You've Gone," "Three Little Words" and "I've Found A New Baby" on LP, JS AA510, GOL 15078. "Minnie's In The Money" on LP, JS AA510. "I've Found A New Baby" on LP, SWT 103.)

Benny's next broadcast for Coca Cola is from the Armory in Springfield, Massachusetts. AFRS transcribed the program's first 15 minutes onto an ET; the balance is shown as air checks, in their order of performance.

AFRS SPOTLIGHT BANDS No. 165　　　**September 29, 1943,**
　　　　　　　　　　　　　　　　　　　Springfield, Ma.

Personnel as September 25.

SS-9-29-11　　**ET:** AFRS Spotlight Bands No. 165
　　　　　　"Spotlight Bands" theme
　　　　　　Sugar Foot Stomp
　　　　　　No Love, No Nothin'-voc Ray Dorey
　　　　　　Sweet Georgia Brown - QUINTET
　　　　　　Sunday, Monday And Always-voc Ray Dorey (arr FH)
　　　　　　Paducah-voc Benny Goodman

Available as air checks:
Clarinet A La King
Good-Bye (theme)
"Spotlight Bands" theme

(Complete broadcast on LP, FAN 27-127. "Sugar Foot Stomp," "Sweet Georgia Brown" and "Clarinet A La King" on LP, SWT 103. "Sugar Foot Stomp" on LP, DAN 5002.)

At the end of the U.S.O. tour, Benny returned to the Ice Terrace Room of the Hotel New Yorker. Hired initially only for the tour, Gene tentatively agreed to join Tommy Dorsey, whose band was in Benny's old stamping grounds, the Hotel Pennsylvania. Benny, delighted to have Gene back, asked him to stay. However, the managements of both hotels resisted Gene's presence, fearful that it would elicit adverse publicity because of Gene's troubles on the West Coast. Benny and Tommy each espoused Gene's cause, but their respective employers would not be persuaded, and Gene was in limbo.

But Benny was determined to have Gene or no one; and so he opened in the New Yorker on Thursday, October 7, without a drummer. Thus the first known air check from this engagement features a small Goodman group and full orchestra, both sans batterie:

SUSTAINING BROADCAST　　　　*October 9, 1943, Hotel*
  Unknown radio network　　　　*New Yorker, New York*

QUARTET: BG, Stacy, Reuss, Weiss. ORCHESTRA: See listing for October 13, but omit Krupa.

Honeysuckle Rose - QUARTET (n/c)
Let's Dance (mid-broadcast theme) (LP: JOY 1073)

On Sunday night Benny appeared on Jimmy Melton's "Texaco Star Theater" program as guest soloist with Al ("no relation") Goodman's Orchestra. An extant acetate offers only a portion of the Mozart Concerto, but it seems highly unlikely that Benny would have performed the opus in its entirety.

"TEXACO STAR THEATER"　　　*October 10, 1943, New York*
  NBC Radio Network

Benny Goodman, clt, and Al Goodman's Orchestra.

Concerto for Clarinet and Orchestra in A Major, K.622 (Mozart) (n/c)

The New Yorker's management capitulated—does anyone think Benny would have lost this argument?—and Gene rejoined the band on Columbus Day, October 12. But there is still a reluctance to advertise his presence; to the best of the author's recollection, Krupa's name is never mentioned on any of the extant broadcasts. That omission is unusual, and is not thought to be mere happenstance.

AFRS transcribed a Wednesday evening broadcast, and the personnel listing reflects the several changes that likely occurred when the band began its engagement at the New Yorker:

AFRS ONE NIGHT STAND No. 36　　　**October 13, 1943, New York**

Benny Goodman, clt; Lee Castle, Ralph Muzzillo, CHARLIE FRANKHOUSER, tpt; Bill Harris, MARK BENNETT, tbn; Hymie Schertzer, Eddie Rosa, as; Bob Taylor, AL KLINK, ts; ERNIE CACERES, bar; Jess Stacy, p; Allan Reuss, g; Sid Weiss, b; Gene Krupa, d; Carol Kay(e), Ray Dorey, voc.

TRIO: BG, Stacy, Krupa

QUARTET: BG, Stacy, Weiss, Krupa

QUINTET: BG, Stacy, Reuss, Weiss, Krupa

SSR-10-13-10　　**ET:** AFRS One Night Stand No. 36 - Part 1
　　　　　　Mission To Moscow
　　　　　　No Love, No Nothin' - voc Ray Dorey
　　　　　　You're Driving Me Crazy (arr FH)
　　　　　　Henderson Stomp

SSR-10-13-11　　**ET:** as above, except Part 2
　　　　　　Do Nothing Till You Hear From Me - voc Benny
　　　　　　　Goodman
　　　　　　Oh, Lady Be Good! - TRIO
　　　　　　Speak Low - voc Ray Dorey
　　　　　　Stealin' Apples

("Mission To Moscow" is also on **ET**, AFRS Yank Swing Session H/2-No. 79; and **LP**, JS AA510, QD 042. "You're Driving Me Crazy" is also on **ET**, AFRS One Night Stand No. 45, Navy Dept. 15, AFRS Basic Music Library P83/84, AFRS G.I. Jive 15; and **LP**, QD 042. "Henderson Stomp" and "Do Nothing Till You Hear From Me" are also on **LP**, QD 042. "Oh, Lady Be Good!" is also on **ET**, AFRS Basic Music Library P83/84; and **LP**, QD 042.)

The broadcast listed next was once extant via a Columbia Reference Recording, as the latter portion of a 15-minute segment of a half-hour broadcast, the full final 15 minutes. However, only three of the nine cuts listed are in general circulation among collectors, and these come from a different source. These three are denoted by asterisk; the author cannot verify the present existence of the cuts not so indicated.

SUSTAINING BROADCAST　　　　*October 16, 1943, Hotel*
  CBS Radio Network　　　　　*New Yorker, New York*

Personnel as October 13.

Minnie's In The Money - voc Benny Goodman
No Love, No Nothin' - voc Ray Dorey
Good-Bye (mid-broadcast theme)
Let's Dance (mid-broadcast theme)
* Three Little Words - QUARTET
A Journey To A Star - voc Ray Dorey
* After You've Gone
*Good-Bye (theme)

AFRS ONE NIGHT STAND No. 26　　　**October 21, 1943, New York**

Personnel as October 13.

SSR-10-21-3　　**ET:** AFRS One Night Stand No. 26 - Part 1
　　　　　　Let's Dance (theme)
　　　　　　I'm Just Wild About Harry (arr EdSau) (Also on ET,
　　　　　　　AFRS BML P6)
　　　　　　No Love, No Nothin' - voc Ray Dorey
　　　　　　Minnie's In The Money - voc Benny Goodman
　　　　　　Speak Low - voc Ray Dorey

SSR-10-21-4   **ET:** as above, except Part 2
Don't Be That Way
I'll Be Around - voc Carol Kay(e)
Stealin' Apples
(I'm Just Wild About Harry - partial repeat from Part 1)
Good-Bye (theme)

(With the exception of the themes, ET is also on **LP,** DON 1100, KOS 1100, MIR 135; and on tape, Radio Yesteryear 1054. "I'm Just Wild About Harry," "Minnie's In The Money," "Don't Be That Way" and "Stealin' Apples" are on **LP,** QD 042. Additionally, "Minnie's In The Money" is on **LP,** JAZ 3; and "Stealin' Apples" is on **LP,** SWT 103.)

Although unannounced, Gene revitalizes a masterpiece in inimitable fashion:

SUSTAINING BROADCAST   *October 22, 1943, Hotel*
   CBS Radio Network   *New Yorker, New York*

Personnel as October 13.

Sing, Sing, Sing

Benny made additional personnel changes the last week in October, and these are reflected in the next listing. This lineup will remain intact for the balance of the New Yorker engagement.

SUSTAINING BROADCAST   *October 30, 1943, Hotel*
   CBS Radio Network   *New Yorker, New York*

Benny Goodman, clt; Lee Castle, Ralph Muzzillo, Charlie Frankhauser, tpt; Bill Harris, H. COLLINS, tbn; Hymie Schertzer, LEONARD KAYE, as; Al Klink, ZOOT SIMS, ts; Ernie Caceres, bar; Jess Stacy, p; Allan Reuss, g; Sid Weiss, b; Gene Krupa, d; Carol Kay(e), Ray Dorey, voc.

Small groups as October 13.

Limehouse Blues - TRIO
I'll Be Around (r/c)
One O'Clock Jump - to signoff

Yes, that's a very young Zoot Sims playing for Benny in 1943; unfortunately, what will become his highly individual style is not often identifiable on air checks from this period. But he'll work with Benny in later years, and make his presence felt. Too, the next-to-last tune in the next listing is the same "Katusha" (but not the same arrangement) that will delight the Soviets during Benny's tour of the USSR in 1962.

SUSTAINING BROADCAST   *October 31, 1943, Hotel*
   CBS Radio Network   *New Yorker, New York*

Personnel as October 30.

After You've Gone
Rosie The Riveter - voc Benny Goodman
Sugar Foot Stomp
I Lost My Sugar In Salt Lake City - voc Benny Goodman
Katusha
At The Darktown Strutters' Ball

AFRS transcribed a loosely-swinging rendition of "Three Little Words" from a broadcast from the New Yorker, and released it as a V-Disc. Unfortunately, the date of the broadcast from which it was taken is not known, and it can only now be assigned to the period October 7-December 11. Note that AFRS mistakenly lists the group as a "Sextette"; it is in fact the Quintet:

BENNY GOODMAN SEXTETTE (sic)   **October 7–December 11, 1943, New York**

Quintet as October 13.

VP 211   VD 88 A. **LP:** SPJ 6605, JS AA509, JSJap 15PJ16,
         Three Little Words

SUSTAINING BROADCAST   *November 1, 1943, Hotel*
   Unknown radio network   *New Yorker, New York*

Personnel as October 30.

Complainin' (n/c)
Down South Camp Meeting (n/c)

On November 4 the "March Of Time" assembled an illustrious group at 1697 Broadway for the purpose of filming, "Orchestra Leaders Discussing The Next Army Hit Kit." Leading the discussion was Capt. Harry Salter of the Special Service Division of the War Department. His panel members were Tommy Dorsey, Fred Waring, Paul Whiteman, and . . . Benny Goodman. Sorry to say, the author recalls nothing of this film, although he spent some ten months with Special Service in France in 1944 and 1945. Nor has he found anyone with a copy of it. No original music by the artists present is in the film, so its absence is no great loss.

The same day, however, there is one tune extant from a broadcast from the Ice Terrace Room:

SUSTAINING BROADCAST   *November 4, 1943, Hotel*
   Unknown radio network   *New Yorker, New York*

Personnel as October 30.

Seven Come Eleven (arr EdSau) (LP: FAN 27-127)

SUSTAINING BROADCAST   *November 5, 1943, Hotel*
   Unknown radio network   *New Yorker, New York*

Personnel as October 30.

Bidin' My Time (prob. arr Alec Wilder, transcribed by Luther Henderson, Jr.)
Dinah - voc Ray Dorey
Oh, Lady Be Good! - TRIO
Down South Camp Meeting
Bugle Call Rag
Mission To Moscow (LP: SWT 103)
Seven Come Eleven - to theme
Good-Bye (theme)

SUSTAINING BROADCAST   *November 7, 1943, Hotel*
   CBS Radio Network   *New Yorker, New York*

Personnel as October 30.

Bugle Call Rag
Dinah (n/c)
Mission To Moscow
Bidin' My Time (n/c)

From the purist's point of view, AFRS began a vexing practice that ever since has impeded positive detailing of its ET releases; it intercut broadcasts, cross-splicing performances from one broadcast to another. Thus on this next ET, the bulk of which is from a broadcast of November 9, "You're Driving Me Crazy" is from the earlier broadcast of October 13, and "Henderson Stomp" is duplicated on its ET for the broadcast of November 17. In a few instances, such as this case, privately-recorded acetates serve to determine the correct dates of AFRS ET cuts. But there are regrettably few such "companion" acetates, and in main AFRS ET's can only be displayed on the basis of their contents.

AFRS ONE NIGHT STAND No. 45   **November 9, 1943, New York**

Personnel as October 30.

SSR-11-9-5   **ET:** AFRS One Night Stand No. 45 - Part 1
Let's Dance (theme)
I'm Here
Dinah - voc Ray Dorey
Do Nothing Till You Hear From Me - voc Benny Goodman
Henderson Stomp

SSR-11-9-6   **ET:** as above, except Part 2
Sing, Sing, Sing
My Heart Tells Me - voc Carol Kay(e)
(You're Driving Me Crazy)

("I'm Here" is also on **ET,** War Dept. Yank Swing Session 83. "Do Nothing Till You Hear From Me" is also on **ET,** AFRS G.I. Jive 647. "Henderson Stomp" is also on **ET,** AFRS One Night Stand No. 53, AFRS Basic Music Library P83/84; and **LP,** SWT 103. "Sing, Sing, Sing" is also on **LP,** SWT 103. "You're Driving Me Crazy" is also on **ET,** AFRS One Night Stand No. 36, Navy Dept. 15, AFRS Basic Music Library P83/84, AFRS G.I. Jive 15; and **LP,** QD 042.)

SUSTAINING BROADCAST　　　　　*November 10, 1943, Hotel*
　CBS Radio Network　　　　　　*New Yorker, New York*

Personnel as October 30.

Let's Dance (theme)
Bugle Call Rag
Sunday, Monday And Always - voc Ray Dorey (n/c)

SUSTAINING BROADCAST　　　　　*November 13, 1943, Hotel*
　CBS Radio Network　　　　　　*New Yorker, New York*

Personnels as October 30.

Let's Dance (theme)
Love Me Or Leave Me
Oh, Lady Be Good! - TRIO
Speak Low - voc Ray Dorey (to mid-broadcast break)
Let's Dance (mid-broadcast theme)
Seven Come Eleven
Shoo Shoo baby - voc Benny Goodman
One O'Clock Jump - to signoff

The MARCH OF TIME surveyed music in wartime America, and on November 16 (confirmed by a recently-discovered "cameraman's dope sheet") filmed Benny at work in the Ice Terrace Room. The short subject also depicts Professor Goodman lecturing at Juilliard; he was appointed to the faculty there November 3. Original title of the movie was "Upbeat in Music"; its better-known title, "Music in America," was not copyrighted until September 3, 1946, and is applied to the MARCH OF TIME's "Home Forum Edition" re-release.

"UPBEAT IN MUSIC"　　　　　*November 16, 1943, Hotel*
　("MUSIC IN AMERICA")　　　　*New Yorker, New York*

A MARCH OF TIME short subject, Volume 10, No. 5, filmed in black-and-white
Release date: December 31, 1943
CAST: Original Dixieland Jazz Band, Serge Koussevitsky, an Eddie Condon group, Marian Anderson, Bea Wain, The Juilliard Quartette, the Metropolitan Opera Company, Art Tatum, George Gershwin (film clip), Perry Como, James C. Petrillo, and

BENNY GOODMAN AND HIS ORCHESTRA

Personnel as October 30.

Henderson Stomp (n/c)

(Also available are poor-quality audio out-takes of additional portions of "Henderson Stomp" and brief excerpts of "Mission To Moscow.")

AFRS ONE NIGHT STAND No. 53　　　**November 17, 1943, New York**

Personnels as October 30.

SSR-11-17-1　　**ET: AFRS One Night Stand No. 53 - Part 1**
　　　　　　　At The Darktown Strutters' Ball
　　　　　　　Honeysuckle Rose - TRIO
　　　　　　　Tomorrow - voc Carol Kay(e) (arr EdSau)
　　　　　　　Do Nothing Till You Hear From Me - voc Benny
　　　　　　　　Goodman

SRR-11-17-2　　**ET: as above, except Part 2**
　　　　　　　Mission To Moscow
　　　　　　　My Heart Tells Me - voc Carol Kay(e)
　　　　　　　I've Found A New Baby
　　　　　　　Minnie's In The Money - voc Benny Goodman
　　　　　　　(Henderson Stomp)

("Honeysuckle Rose" is also on **LP,** QD 042, SWT 103. "Do Nothing Till You Hear From Me" is also on **LP,** SWT 103. "My Heart Tells Me" is also on **ET,** AFRS G.I. Jive 654. "I've Found A New Baby" is also on **LP,** SWT 103. "Minnie's In The Money" is also on **ET,** AFRS G.I. Jive 659. "Henderson Stomp" is also on **ET,** AFRS One Night Stand No. 45, AFRS Basic Music Library P83/84; and **LP,** SWT 103.)

The next listing may be an amalgam of two broadcasts. The first three tunes are via CBS, the rest may be from another network. In the absence of evidence to the contrary, however, the listing is shown as one program.

SUSTAINING BROADCAST　　　　　*November 20, 1943, Hotel*
　CBS Radio Network　　　　　　*New Yorker, New York*

Personnel as October 30.

Put Your Arms Around Me - voc Carol Kay(e)
Stealin' Apples
The Very Thought Of You - voc Ray Dorey (n/c)
Sweet Georgia Brown (n/c)
How Sweet You Are - voc Ray Dorey
Air Mail Special
No Love, No Nothin' - voc Ray Dorey
With My Head In The Clouds
I've Found A New Baby - to signoff

SUSTAINING BROADCAST　　　　　*November 27, 1943, Hotel*
　CBS Radio Network　　　　　　*New Yorker, New York*

Personnels as October 30.

Sweet Georgia Brown (n/c)
Speak Low - voc Ray Dorey (n/c)
Sometimes I'm Happy (n/c)
Honeysuckle Rose - QUARTET
Mission To Moscow
No Love, No Nothin' - voc Ray Dorey
Air Mail Special
Good-Bye (theme)

Each Sunday NBC broadcast a pop music and jazz-oriented program titled, "The Chamber Music Society Of Lower Basin Street." Benny appeared with the series' mainstays, "Professor" Paul Lavalle and his "Woodwindy Ten" on November 28:

"CHAMBER MUSIC SOCIETY OF　　*November 28, 1943, New York*
　LOWER BASIN STREET"
　NBC Radio Network

Benny Goodman, clt, and Paul Lavalle and his orchestra.

Dinah - voc Benny Goodman
Concerto in D Minor (Bach)

SUSTAINING BROADCAST　　　　　*November 30, 1943, Hotel*
　CBS Radio Network　　　　　　*New Yorker, New York*

Personnels as October 30.

Love Me Or Leave Me
Do Nothing Till You Hear From Me - voc Benny Goodman
Seven Come Eleven
Limehouse Blues - TRIO (n/c)
Stealin' Apples

A number of U.S. Government-produced transcriptions of performances by Benny Goodman cannot be precisely dated, and are herewith generally assigned to the period November–December 1943, prior to December 12. The first of these is AFRS ET Basic Music Library P83/84, which has one rendition by Goodman on its Side 1, and four on Side 2. Three of the four cuts on Side 2 have already been assigned to their correct broadcast dates; the other two are:

AFRS BASIC MUSIC　　　**November–December 1943, New York**
LIBRARY P83/84

Personnel as October 30.

SSL-109　　**ET: AFRS Basic Music Library P83/84 - Side 1**
　　　　　After You've Gone

SSL-110　　**ET: as above, except Side 2**
　　　　　Dinah - voc Ray Dorey

(Ambient sound suggests both cuts are location, not studio, recordings; both may be from the Hotel New Yorker, but that is uncertain. Note that AFRS uses the titles, "Basic Music Library" and "Basic Musical Library" indiscriminately; in this work, the first is employed throughout.)

There are two original-issue ET's for the next listing; their only difference is the issuing agency. One is the Office Of War Information (OWI), the other the Voice Of America (VOA). Both employ the legend, "Outpost

Concert Series No. 11, Music Of The Jazz Bands No. 22.'' The ''matrix number'' for the OWI ET is listed here.

All three cuts are from a broadcast, or broadcasts, from the Hotel New Yorker.

OWI No. 17-L-88 /   **November–December 1943, Hotel**
VOA Outpost Concert   **New Yorker, New York**
SERIES No. 11, MUSIC OF THE JAZZ BANDS No. 22

Personnel as October 30.

WL-88   **ET:** OWI No. 17-WL-88 / VOA
         Down South Camp Meetin'
         I'll Be Around - voc Carol Kay
         Seven Come Eleven (arr EdSau)

(Note that Benny's first - NBC Thesaurus - recording used the title, ''Down South Camp Meetin','' but that his Victor recording is spelled, ''Down South Camp Meeting.'' The latter title appears more frequently. Above on LP, SWT 103.)

Two acetates, both in poor condition, offer undated air checks from the New Yorker, likely from broadcasts during November or December:

SUSTAINING BROADCAST(S)   *November–December 1943, Hotel*
  Unknown radio network(s)   *New Yorker, New York*

Personnels as October 30.

Limehouse Blues - QUARTET
Stealin' Apples (n/c)

In the first week in December Benny took part in a ''Command Performance'' presentation, transcribed by NBC especially for U.S. military personnel. Whether the program was broadcast in the United States is not known, but there are some indications that it was. Benny has one tune on each of the two sides of the 30-minute ET. Joining him in this special program for the troops are announcer Paul Douglas, Fred Allen, Gypsy Rose Lee, Ginny Simms, Lauritz Melchior and the Golden Gate Quartet.

NAVY DEPARTMENT   **December 1943, New York**
  AFRS COMMAND PERFORMANCE, UNIT 4

Personnel as October 30.

H-18-98 - Pt. 1   **ET:** Navy Department - AFRS Command Performance
                      Unit 4 - A
                      Limehouse Blues - TRIO

H-18-98 - Pt. 2   **ET:** as above, except Unit 4 - B
                      Air Mail Special

(This ET is reliably reported to be duplicated on **ET**, AFRS Command Performance No. 98. A copy has not been available to the author, and he can give no further details.)

Benny next went into Columbia's Liederkranz Hall for a V-Disc session. Note that there are extant (on 16″ studio acetates) alternate takes of each of the issued V-Discs, plus a wholly-unreleased performance of a big band chart believed to have been written by Eddie Sauter:

BENNY GOODMAN AND HIS ORCHESTRA   **December 9, 1943, New York**

Personnel as October 30.

-0-   UNISSUED - acetate
XP 33399-1   VD 159 B
(VP 409)   **Dinah** - voc Benny Goodman

-0-   UNISSUED - acetates - 3 alternates, 2 bkdns
XP 33400-1   VD 159 A
(VP 408)   **Henderson Stomp**

-0-   UNISSUED - acetates - 2 takes
         'Way Down Yonder In New Orleans (arr prob. EdSau)

BENNY GOODMAN, GENE KRUPA AND   **same session**
  JESS STACEY (sic)

Goodman, Stacy, Krupa.

-0-   UNISSUED - acetate
XP 33400-1   VD 159 A
(VP 408)   **Limehouse Blues**

(V-Disc 159 A/B is also on **LP:** ELEC KV119, JS AA509, JSJap 15PJ16, SPJ6605, SB 142.)

The highly successful New Yorker engagement ended December 11; closing night produced this air check:

SUSTAINING BROADCAST   *December 11, 1943, Hotel*
  CBS Radio Network   *New Yorker, New York*

Personnels as October 30.

Mission To Moscow
No Love, No Nothin' - voc Ray Dorey
Bidin' My Time
Stealin' Apples
Limehouse Blues - TRIO
My Heart Tells Me - voc Carol Kay(e)
Don't Be That Way
Seven Come Eleven - to signoff

The sound quality of some of the air checks from this New Yorker engagement is so poor that, had they been from another period, they might have been omitted. They are included because this Goodman orchestra, of the fall and winter of 1943, unrecorded commercially, merits the fullest representation. Although it was together but a few months, it was one of Benny's best bands.

The rhythm section, three-quarters of it the same as that of Benny's standard, the Victor-era section, was outstanding. Krupa, who felt the need to reestablish his reputation and renew his self-esteem, never worked harder. Stacy rarely played more melodiously. Reuss never more rhythmically. Joined with Sid Weiss, a bassist superior to Harry Goodman of 1935–1939, they were a formidable foursome.

The trumpets, admittedly no match for the team of James, Elman and Griffin, were firm and swung as a section. The trombones offered Willard ''Bill'' Harris, who would become **the** trombonist of the 'Forties and 'Fifties. Hymie Schertzer again led a superior reed section, with Sims and Klink estimable substitutes for Rollini-Musso-Russin-Freeman. Given a bit more time to mesh these talents, a few new manuscripts the caliber of earlier Henderson/Mundy/Sauter arrangements, professional studio sound reproduction, and commercial distribution of their produce, this band would have been one of the memorable ones.

It was a band infused with the spirit of the times. The Nation's military fortunes were rising. Employment was full and money was plentiful. Because of the war, personal relationships were transitory; this impermanence led to a don't-give-a-damn attitude, a joie de vivre that caused the musicians to go all out today and save nothing for tomorrow. It was a time when civilian performers felt a compulsion to justify their exemption from military service; Benny's bandsmen worked hard at their trade, but withal enjoyed it. From audacity to zest, this orchestra pulled out all the stops.

But perhaps its greatest claim to fame is Benny himself. Backed by a Gibraltar-solid rhythm section and seemingly infected by an attitude of tempori parendum, Benny, supported yet degage, played every conceivable note the clarinet is capable of, stripped his instrument and his invention until there was simply nothing left. No more the 16- or 32-bar solos of a few years before; ''Stealin' Apples'' or ''After You've Gone'' now brought forth chorus upon chorus, one building on another to the apogee of virtuosity. Gene never worked harder? **Benny** never worked harder. Or played better.

On furlough, the author was privileged to watch, and to listen to this marvelous orchestra, and to renew his war-and-jail interrupted friendship with Gene. And, to suffer his first Goodman ''ray'': There was a small space behind Gene's kit on the elevated bandstand, and the author sat there to talk with Gene between numbers, and to watch his every display of technique. (''Don't you know how to play that, Russ? It's easy—look.'' And he'd play the lick s-l-o-w-l-y, and as often as necessary, until Russ could understand how to stroke it.) Well, Benny kicked off ''Mission To Moscow''—never forget it—and we were still talking, and there were no drums. Came the ''ray,'' equally distributed between us, and ''Oh, Christ!'' from Gene, and he beat that snare as if it were at fault. Used a ''Roll 'Em'' accented two-stroke roll he sometimes used on the ''Mission,'' sorry there are no good recordings of it. Whaled the hell out of it, and take that, Benny.

One night, when the band had finished a set and dispersed on Benny's "Take five," Gene remained on his drummer's throne, regarding his tubs almost meditatively. All alone, he began a brush beat, for he wanted to play. Jess, ever Gene's good friend, slid back onto the piano bench and joined in.

Benny, seated ringside with some friends and watching this duet somewhat quizzically, returned to the bandstand, picked up his stick, and now it was a trio. Bill Harris, a kind of "grey" guy really, until that horn was in his hands, slipped in inconspicuously. Weiss and Reuss were next, then—think it was Frankhauser, but may have been Castaldo—a trumpet came on and it was a ball, with about eight of them in a kind of cutting contest, the rest of the band beaming and egging them on, the delighted audience applauding and jostling its way to the fore, the author enraptured, but still on the floor behind Gene.

That went on for what seemed about 20 minutes. Then Benny waved a halt, motioned the full band to return, and faced Gene: "Hey, Gene, I think they'd like to hear 'Sing, Sing, Sing'—how's about it?"

Oh, they blew, man, they blew!

Out of the New Yorker on the 11th, the band took Sunday off, then appeared in the Arena in Washington, D.C., on the 13th, and at another Palomar—this one in Norfolk, Va.—on the 14th. From there it was a short hop to Annapolis, Md., and a date with the midshipmen of the U.S. Naval Academy.

Whether Gene Krupa was with the band after it left the New Yorker is open to question. There is some indication that he joined Tommy Dorsey's band at the Paramount in New York on December 12. (Benny's band did not have an engagement on the 12th; it is possible that Gene worked with Tommy on that day, went back to Benny for the balance of the week. If so, he would return to the Dorsey band quickly, remain with it until June 1944.) AFRS transcribed a "Spotlight Bands" broadcast from the Academy; unfortunately, its contents do not include drumwork so distinctive that it can positively be ascribed to Krupa, or to anyone else. Thus his presence on it is uncertain.

In addition to the ET, privately-recorded acetates of portions of the broadcast not transcribed by AFRS are listed in performance order:

AFRS SPOTLIGHT BANDS No. 232   December 15, 1943, Annapolis, Md.

Personnels as October 30, but uncertain drums.

SS-12-16-13   **ET:** AFRS Spotlight Bands No. 232
"Spotlight Bands" theme
Mission To Moscow
Seven Come Eleven
Do Nothing Till You Hear From Me - voc Benny Goodman
No Love, No Nothin' - voc Ray Dorey
Honeysuckle Rose - TRIO (n/c)
Stealin' Apples
"Spotlight Bands" theme

("Seven Come Eleven" is also on ET, War Dep't. Yank Swing Session 88; and on LP, QD 042.)

Also on December 15, a recording cohort of Benny's an unlucky 13 years' earlier, Thomas Wright "Fats" Waller, died of pneumonia at age 39 on the Santa Fe Flier at the train station in Kansas City.

If Gene was with Benny in Annapolis, then likely it was his final association with him for 1943. He is not believed to have been with Goodman for theater dates of one week each, beginning December 17 at the Hippodrome in Baltimore; December 24 at the Earle in Philadelphia; and at the Stanley in Pittsburgh, December 31. (No known recordings from any of these engagements are extant to confirm or deny Krupa's presence.) Benny and key members of the band then headed for Hollywood.

Gene had a persuasive reason for not going to California: to appear there so soon after the damaging press his arrest had caused was unthinkable. Accepting Tommy Dorsey's standing offer to join his band also gave him pause. As noted, Gene's presence with Benny at the New Yorker was unadvertised, unannounced; the audiences were relatively small. To appear at the Paramount with Tommy meant exposure on a much larger scale, even if once again his presence would not be publicized. But he had to work, and whatever the reaction might be, he would somehow cope with it. So once more the pit lift in the Paramount rose to stage level . . . and as the audience recognized Gene it rose en masse to give him a standing ovation. Gene wept with relief and joy.

In his earlier work on Goodman, the author ascribed "I've Found A New Baby," transcribed onto AFRS ET Command Performance No. 208 et al, to the period November–December 1943, New York. It is now reas-

signed to mid-January 1944, Hollywood. Further, he now believes that "Rachel's Dream," also per Command Performance No. 208 et al, is NOT the version piped in via radio to the Esquire Jazz Concert of January 18, 1944, at the Metropolitan Opera House in New York. The ET cut is reassigned also to mid-January 1944, Hollywood. The rendition broadcast to the Esquire Concert is listed as a privately-recorded acetate, January 18, 1944, from Los Angeles.

The several ETs that offer both "Rachel's Dream" and "I've Found A New Baby," in toto seem to present far too many performers for but a single program. (AFRS may have cross-dubbed them from more than one source.) Arbitrarily, AFRS ET Command Performance No. 155, headlined by Bob Hope and Bing Crosby, and featuring Ann Sheridan, the Andrews Sisters and GI-cartoonist Bill Mauldin, is shown as the original release for "Rachel's Dream." AFRS ET Command Performance No. 208, whose cast includes Judy Garland, Danny Kaye, Lauritz Melchior, Maxine Sullivan, Hoagy Carmichael and Lina Romay, is accredited for "I've Found A New Baby," to differentiate:

AFRS COMMAND PERFORMANCE No. 155   mid-January 1944, Hollywood

Benny Goodman, clt; Jess Stacy, p; Sid Weiss, b; MOREY FELD, d.

H-18-155-1   **ET:** AFRS Command Performance No. 155 - Part 1
Rachel's Dream - QUARTET

(Also on ET, AFRS Command Performance No. 208, (Navy)AFRS Command Performance 12 (matrix H-18-102), War Dep't. Yank Swing Session 123; and on LP, AC 27, FDC 1007, JO 3132, MU 30JA5146, PAL 30, RAD 5051, SA 6923, SB 155, SWH 46, WI 248.)

AFRS COMMAND PERFORMANCE No. 208   mid-January 1944, Hollywood

Benny Goodman, clt; JOHNNY DEE, FRANK BERARDI, MICKEY MANGANO, tpt; Bill Harris, AL MASTREN, tbn; HEINIE BEAU, EDDIE ROSA, as; Al Klink, Zoot Sims, ts; EDDIE BEAU, bar; Jess Stacy, p; Allan Reuss, g; Sid Weiss, b; MOREY FELD, d.

H-18-208-1   **ET:** AFRS Command Performance No. 208 - Part 1
I've Found A New Baby

(Also on ET, AFRS Command Performance No. 155, (Navy)AFRS Command Performance 12, AFRS G.I. Jive 660; and on LP, DAN 5002.)

The two contemporaneous versions of "Rachel's Dream" are quite similar, but they are different. To the best of the author's knowledge, the cut listed next is extant only via acetate; he cannot confirm a vague report that it may be on AFRS ET One Night Stand No. 188, which he has not heard:

STUDIO BROADCAST   *January 18, 1944, Los Angeles*
   Unknown radio network

Personnel as "mid-January 1944."

Rachel's Dream - QUARTET

(Transmitted to the Esquire All-American Jazz Concert, Metropolitan Opera House, New York.)

Benny's remote participation in Esquire's concert was triggered by his selection as the Nation's top jazz clarinetist by the magazine's "board of experts." (He'll win the gold award the next two years, too.) The award was determined by ballot in December, a month when he was also named as **Down Beat's** "King Of Swing"—for the fifth time.

Benny began another film for 20th Century-Fox in February. Originally titled, "Moment For Music," the script was based on a story by Richard English. Benny collaborated on the scenario, and in part it was autobiographical. But that was largely changed, and the film when released was called:

"SWEET AND LOWDOWN"   *February 1944, Hollywood*

A 20th Century-Fox picture filmed in black-and-white
Release date: September 1944   Running time: 75 minutes
Director: Archie Mayo
Songs by Mack Gordon and Jimmy Monaco
CAST: Linda Darnell, Jack Oakie (as Benny's real-life band boy-photographer, "Popsie" Randolph), Lynn Bari, James Caldwell, Allyn Joslyn, the Pied Pipers, and

BENNY GOODMAN AND HIS ORCHESTRA

Personnel as "mid-January 1944")
(Bill Harris recorded all of the trombone soli supposedly played on screen by actor Caldwell; and Lorraine Elliott dubbed in for Lynn Bari's "vocals.")

Opening title music - I've Found A New Baby: Benny Goodman Orchestra (n/c)
I'm Making Believe: Benny Goodman, clt; Bill Harris, tbn; Jess Stacy, p.
Jersey Bounce: Benny Goodman Orchestra
Hey, Bub, Let's Have A Ball - voc Lorraine Elliott, Pied Pipers, BG: Benny Goodman Orchestra
No Love, No Nothin': Benny Goodman Orchestra (background to dialogue)
(I'm Making Believe: p solo
Ten Days With Baby - voc Lorraine Elliott (arr JT): Benny Goodman Orchestra
Let's Dance: Benny Goodman Orchestra
I'm Making Believe - voc Lorraine Elliott (arr EdSau): Benny Goodman Orchestra
Ten Days With Baby: intro, BG (musical montage, to Latin-American type band)
The World Is Waiting For The Sunrise: Benny Goodman Quartet
Rachel's Dream (n/c): Benny Goodman Quartet
Minuet movement, Quintet For Clarinet And Strings In A (Mozart): Benny Goodman, clt; Louis Kaufman, 1st v; John Pennington, 2nd v; Paul Robyn, viola, Lauri Kennedy, cel;
(Chug, Chug, Choo-Choo, Chug - voc Lorraine Elliott, Pied Pipers: studio orchestra
(Hey, Bub, Let's Have A Ball - voc Lorraine Elliott: studio orchestra
Ten Days With Baby: Benny Goodman Orchestra (montage)
I've Found A New Baby: Benny Goodman Orchestra (as opening number - n/c)
I'm Making Believe: Benny Goodman Orchestra

Two of the tunes featured in "Sweet And Lowdown" are on a V-Disc. "Ten Days With Baby" was recorded by the orchestra for the film, but is an alternate take to the version in the sound track. The Quartet's "Rachel's Dream" is the same version as that in the movie, but is complete; the sound track's cut is edited. Note that the artist credit on the V-Disc label does not cite the Quartet.

BENNY GOODMAN AND HIS BAND   February 1944, Hollywood

Personnel as "Sweet And Lowdown."

D7-TC-7338-1C	VD 779 A	
(JB-378)	**Ten Days With Baby** - (voc Lorraine Elliott) (arr JT) (orchestra)	
- same	VD 779 A	
	Rachel's Dream (Quartet)	

(Both cuts are on **LP**, DeG 12005, JS AA509, JSJap 15PJ16, SPJ 6605, SB 144. Additionally, "Ten Days With Baby" is on **LP**, WI 196, SWH 46. A claim that this version of "Rachel's Dream" is on **ET**, War Dep't. Yank Swing Session 123—and not that on the Command Performance ETs—cannot be confirmed.)

While Benny is in Hollywood, it seems appropriate to bring this notice to the attention of film buffs:

Sometime in 1944 Warner Bros. produced a two-reeler titled, "The Shining Future," for Canada's Sixth Victory Loan Drive. Its large cast included Olive Blakeney, Jack Carson, Bing Crosby, Deanna Durbin, Cary Grant, Harry James, James Lydon, Irene Manning, Herbert Marshall, Dennis Morgan, Harold Peary, Frank Sinatra, and . . . Benny Goodman. The film was then edited down to one reel, was retitled, "The Road To Victory," and was released under the aegis of the U.S. Treasury Department in support of its Fifth War Loan Drive. Benny's footage in "The Shining Future" was omitted from "The Road To Victory."

The author does not know what Benny's contribution to the film might have been; he has never seen the original, uncut version. He assumes that it may have been other than original music—possibly news clips, or excerpts from Benny's feature films. Continuing research is warranted.

For some months prior to "Sweet And Lowdown," Benny had been at odds with his booking agency, MCA—the Music Corporation of America. He had sought several times to terminate his long-term contract with MCA, but to no avail. Upon finishing the movie, he doubled his efforts to do so, but failed once more. Thereupon, on March 9, Benny disbanded unceremoniously and flew to New York.

Jess Stacy tried to keep the band together, but soon gave up and joined Horace Heidt, whose personnel also included Shorty Sherock, Joe Rushton and Frankie Carlson. (In June, Jess married vocalist Lee Wiley in Los Angeles.) Bill Harris stayed on the West Coast, worked with Charlie Barnet and Freddie Slack, jobbed around, joined Woody Herman in August. Allan Reuss went with Harry James. Some of the men went back to studio work in Hollywood, and some others eventually returned to New York on their own.

Nothing is heard of Benny until May, when he appeared on two "Philco Hall Of Fame" radio programs, broadcast on Sunday evenings via the Blue Network. The first of these (advanced from an earlier assumed date of July 15, 1944), featuring Deems Taylor, comedian "Doc" Rockwell, Connie Boswell and Paul Whiteman and his Orchestra, is on an AFRS ET:

(Replaces Burns & Allen No. 61)
AFRS RADIO HALL OF FAME   May 7, 1944, New York

Benny Goodman, clt; Teddy Wilson, p; Sid Weiss, b; Cozy Cole, d.

SS-12-20-7	**ET:** AFRS Radio Hall Of Fame - Part 1 **Body And Soul**
SS-12-20-8	**ET:** as above, except Part 2 **Who?**

Not on the ET, but available as an air check:

After You've Gone

(All above on LP, SB 145.)

Speculation that Benny might have been the clarinetist on Mildred Bailey's V-Disc 524 A, "Downhearted Blues," has been scotched—no BG.

The author has been unable to locate a copy of an AFRS ET for the next "Philco Hall Of Fame" broadcast, although he suspects one may exist, possibly under the title, "AL JOLSON." Privately-recorded acetates provide two Goodman efforts:

"PHILCO HALL OF FAME"   May 28, 1944, Convention
Blue Network   Hall, Philadelphia, Pa.

Quartet as May 7.

I Surrender, Dear (LP: SB 145)
Hallelujah!

Benny went to work in earnest in June, rehearsing a big band recruited from New York radio studios, many of the men former regulars in his several orchestras. Occasion was participation in Walt Disney's imaginative cartoon, "Make Mine Music," which originally was titled, "Swing Street."

"MAKE MINE MUSIC"   June 12, 1944, New York

An RKO-Radio animated color cartoon
Release date: May/June 1946   Running time: 74 minutes
Producer: Walt Disney
CAST: The Andrews Sisters, Jerry Colonna, Nelson Eddy, Sterling Holloway, The King's Men, Andy Russell, Dinah Shore (with David Lichine and Tania Riabouchinska), and

BENNY GOODMAN AND HIS ORCHESTRA

Benny Goodman, clt; Billy Butterfield, Charlie Shavers, Mickey McMickle, tpt; Vernon Brown, Jack Satterfield, tbn; Hymie Schertzer, Jules Rubin, as; Art Rollini, Don Byas, ts; Ernie Caceres, bar; Teddy Wilson, p; Allan Reuss, g; Sid Weiss, b; Cozy Cole, d.

BENNY GOODMAN QUARTET: BG, Wilson, Weiss, Cole

All The Cats Join In (arr JT)
After You've Gone - QUARTET

Several aspects of "Make Mine Music" are worth noting:

Benny's segment (which was later re-released as a short subject titled, "Two For The Record") was recorded at the Fox-Movietone studios in New York. Reputedly, Evelyn Knight provided a vocal for "All The Cats Join In" at this session; but if it were made, it was not used. In Hollywood, June Hutton and the Ken Darby Singers recorded the tune a capella, and their vocal was superimposed on Benny's instrumental version for the sound track.

Two tunes from the movie were released on a 10" 78 whose label bears no manufacturer's identification, only the legend, "From Walt Disney's

'Make Mine Music'.'' ''All The Cats Join In'' offers a good clarinet solo, and ''Two Silhouettes'' has a vocal by Peggy Lee. Charles Wolcott and his Orchestra is credited with both performances. The several coincidences— the clarinet, Peggy Lee, the selections from a film in which Benny participated—have caused collectors to wonder if this record is actually by Benny Goodman. It is not, nothing more than a curious coincidence.

Years later, Capitol issued Benny's original cuts on an EP titled ''Two For The Record,'' in conjunction with release of a cartoon short with the same title. However, there are differences between the sound track and EP versions: ''All The Cats Join In'' has no vocal on the EP; the EP omits Benny's introductory ''One, two, three'' count to ''After You've Gone''; and the tempi for the EP tracks are noticeably faster. These variants should not mislead the listener; the underlying Goodman cuts are identical, EP vis a vis sound track.

BENNY GOODMAN AND HIS ORCHESTRA　　　**June 12, 1944, New York**

Personnel as ''Make Mine Music.''

| 12368 | **EP:** CAP EAP1-519, CAP EAP1-409, CapAu CEP030. **LP:** CAP T409, CapE LC6831, CAP M11061, CAP 5CO5280854, CapCont 80854, CapJap 50059, EMI 85165M, BomG 665992. **ET:** Here's To Veterans 107 (excerpt) |
| | **All The Cats Join In** (arr JT) |

BENNY GOODMAN QUARTET　　　　　　　**same date**

Personnel as ''Make Mine Music.''

| 12451 | **EP:** CAP EAP1-519, CAP EAP1-441, CapAu CEP030. **LP:** CAP T409, CapFr 81713, EMI 52715, EMI 81713, SW 1380. **ET:** AFRS P4223 |
| | **After You've Gone** |

(BomG and EMI issues are also on cassette, similarly numbered.)

Turnabout is excellent play, and Benny next appeared on Mildred Bailey's new radio program, as she had on his ''Camel Caravan'' broadcasts in late 1939:

''THE MILDRED BAILEY SHOW''　　　　　*June 21, 1944, New York*
CBS Radio Network

Benny Goodman, clt; Teddy Wilson, p; GORDON ''SPECS'' POWELL, d.

Poor Butterfly - TRIO
The World Is Waiting For The Sunrise - TRIO

(A report that Benny also played ''Henderson Stomp,'' backed by Paul Baron and his Orchestra on this date is not borne out by a full half-hour transcription of the program.)

Benny duplicated the two tunes performed on the June 21 broadcast for V-Disc, but the exact date of these studio recordings is not known:

BENNY GOODMAN TRIO　　　　**prob. late June 1944, New York**

Personnel as June 21.

| XP 33649-1 (VP 777) | VD 274 A, NavyVD 54 A **Poor Butterfly** |
| same | same issues **The World Is Waiting For The Sunrise** |

(Both cuts also on **LP:** JS AA509, JSJap 15PJ16, SPJ 6605, SB 142, WI 196)

The same Trio then played the same two tunes a third time, and again the date of this performance is unknown. This program links Benny for the first time with Ed Sullivan, then a gossip columnist and later the impressario of a long-running TV variety show. In behalf of U.S. Navy recruiting, the ET also offers contributions by Raymond Scott and his Orchestra, and some unintentional dialogue bloopers by Messrs. Goodman and Sullivan:

U.S. NAVY WAVES PRESENT　　　**prob. early July 1944, New York**
SOMETHING FOR THE GIRLS PROGRAM No. 13 - PART 1

Personnel as June 21.

| YTNY 3113-1A | **ET:** U.S. Navy Waves Present Something For The Girls Program 13 - Part 1 **Poor Butterfly** **The World Is Waiting For The Sunrise** |

In his earlier works on Benny Goodman the author expressed a belief that certain V-Discs were not from a radio broadcast of July 31, 1944. Reassessment—and indeed, more careful cross-referencing—following publication of those books confirms that the broadcast is certainly the source of the V-Discs in question.

The program is the first in a series promulgated by AFRS, ''For The Record,'' broadcast via WEAF in New York and the NBC Radio Network nationally. The series featured various artists over time, originated mainly in New York, and was broadcast on Monday evenings. The initial program offered an orchestra comprised of studio musicians, assembled by Hymie Schertzer and George Simon, and led by Benny, plus vocalists Mildred Bailey, Perry Como and Carmen Miranda.

Transcriptions of the broadcast itself put Benny's performances in this order: ''After You've Gone,'' ''There'll Be A Jubilee,'' ''Goodbye Sue,'' ''Hallelujah,'' ''These Foolish Things,'' ''At The Darktown Strutters' Ball'' and the closing theme. In listing the V-Disc and AFRS ET releases, the author changes the order to show the issues according to inscribed matrix numbers. And he does not include ''Tico, Tico,'' vocal by Carmen Miranda, probably backed by Benny's band—no Goodman clarinet is in evidence throughout that rendition.

To compensate for his arbitrary rearrangement, the author can offer a previously undocumented rehearsal of the program, refuting assertions that none exists. The source is one side of a 16″ acetate recorded by NBC. (Its reverse has the final 15 minutes of ''The Mildred Bailey Show'' of October 20, 1944. This odd mix of NBC/CBS broadcast material likely came about because of AFRS's participation in both programs.) The ''For The Record'' side is a rehearsal of the first part of that program. Here, too, Benny announces the band's personnel, and includes Charlie Shavers, who is not named on the V-Disc labels. And evidently because Perry Como had not yet arrived, Benny himself does a ''mock'' vocal on, ''Goodbye Sue.'' The disc is not dated, but likely the rehearsal was the same day as the broadcast.

All in all, a noteworthy addition to Goodmania:

REHEARSAL, ''FOR THE RECORD''　　　*July 31, 1944, New York*

Benny Goodman, clt; Charlie Shavers, Yank Lawson, Roy Eldridge, Mickey McMickle, tpt; Vernon Brown, Ward Silloway, tbn; Hymie Schertzer, Reggie Merrill, as; Art Rollini, Wolfe Tayne, ts; Ernie Caceres, bar; Teddy Wilson, p; Tommy Kay(e), g; Gene Traxler, b; Specs Powell, d; Mildred Bailey, Benny Goodman, voc.

QUARTET: BG, Wilson, Traxler, Powell

After You've Gone
There'll Be A Jubilee - voc Mildred Bailey
Goodbye, Sue - voc Benny Goodman
Hallelujah! - QUARTET

BENNY GOODMAN AND HIS　　　　　**July 31, 1944, New York**
**　V-DISC ALL STAR BAND**

Personnel as rehearsal this date, plus Perry Como, voc (Shavers omitted from VD labels).

| D4-TC-283-1 (VP 848) | VD 322 B, NavyVD 117 A. **ET:** AFRS Jubilee H-11/Prog. 168, War Dep't. Yank Swing Session 115. **LP:** DAN 5002, ELEC KV119, GOJ 1017, JS AA509, JSJap 15PJ16, SPJ 6605, WI 196 **After You've Gone** |
| D4-TC-284-1A (VP 849) | VD 312 A, NavyVD 92 A. **LP:** ELEC KV 119, SB 142 **Goodbye Sue** - voc Perry Como |

BENNY GOODMAN AND HIS V-DISC ALL STARS　　　**same date**

Same personnel. Mildred Bailey, voc.

| D4-TC-285-1 (VP 850) | VD 494 B. **LP:** same issues as ''After You've Gone,'' except omit GOJ **There'll Be A Jubilee** - voc Mildred Bailey |

BENNY GOODMAN AND HIS V-DISC ALL STAR BAND same date

Same personnel. Mildred Bailey, voc.

D4-TC-290-1C (VP 859)	VD 302 A, NavyVD 82 A. **ET:** OWI Outpost Concert Series No. 24-Record No. No. 17-2473-Music of the Jazz Bands No. 47; AFRS Basic Music Library P239. **LP:** ELEC KV119, JS AA509, JSJap 15PJ16, SPJ 6605 **These Foolish Things Remind Me Of You** - voc Mildred Bailey (arr JM)

BENNY GOODMAN AND HIS V-DISC QUARTETTE same date

Quartet as rehearsal.

D4-TC-290-1C (VP 859)	VD 302 A, NavyVD 82 A. **ET:** AFRS Basic Music Library P307, War Dep't. Yank Swing Session 120. **LP:** JS AA509, SPJ 6605, SWH 46, JSJap 15PJ16 **Hallelujah**

BENNY GOODMAN AND HIS ORCHESTRA same date

Same personnel.

SSL-631-RE	**ET:** AFRS Basic Music Library P307, AFRS Jubilee H-11/Prog. 168. **LP:** GOJ 1017, Quicksilver 5046 **At The Darktown Strutters' Ball**

The author cannot support a claim that the Goodman Quartet recorded "Lover" and "Someday Sweetheart" for AFRS at "about this period." He has an acetate that offers those two tunes, both recorded by a group consisting of clarinet, piano, bass and drums; and tapes of this acetate have circulated among collectors as authentic Goodman items. But the clarinetist is Peanuts Hucko, not Benny. Thus, reports of unissued Goodman V-Discs of "Lover" and "Someday Sweetheart" may be false.

Chronologically, a compound error needs be disposed of at this juncture. Earlier the author had speculated that three cuts on an AFRS ET—"Exactly Like You," "Sweet Georgia Brown," and "Rose Room"—were "probably" recorded in May 1945. A more recent publication places them in "August 1944." Neither is correct; those cuts, and others, were recorded January 11, 1946, q.v.

It now appears likely that two other V-Discs, once assigned to an "October 1944" date, are in fact from a "For The Record" broadcast of September 25, 1944. Press reports listing that program failed to give its contents, and privately-recorded air checks of the broadcast itself have eluded the author's search.

(THE) BENNY GOODMAN QUINTET September 25, 1944, New York

Benny Goodman, clt; RED NORVO, vib; Teddy Wilson, p; SID WEISS, b; MOREY FELD, d.

D4-TC-444-1 (VP 942)	VD 366 A, NavyVD 148 A. **LP:** ARISTON 12015, JS AA509, SPJ 6608, JSJap 15PJ16 **Sweet Georgia Brown**
same	same issues as "Sweet Georgia Brown," plus **ET:** AFRS Basic Music Library P307 **(The) Sheik Of Araby**

Benny's new group, sans Red Norvo, went to New Orleans as the star attraction of the first in what was hoped would be a series of concerts sponsored by the National Jazz Foundation. The concerts were presented in the cradle of jazz's Municipal Auditorium on October 4 and 5, and were broadcast "live" by local radio station WWL. (While in the Bayou State, Benny made a side trip to the U.S. Naval Station at Algiers, and performed for the personnel there. So far as is known, this presentation was not recorded or broadcast.) The broadcasts were then transcribed, at least in part, onto 13 twelve-inch two-sided acetates. One set is privately held, and another is believed to be in the Library of Congress. Benny's selections are on sides 13 through 20 inclusive, and sides 22 through 26; the others feature a "New Orleans Jazz Band," comprised of local musicians. The acetates are not dated, and thus may be from either or both October 4, 5; the listing following conforms to the order of the acetates:

"NATIONAL JAZZ FOUNDATION" October 4/5, 1944, Municipal
Radio Station WWL Auditorium, New Orleans

Benny Goodman, clt; Teddy Wilson, p; Sid Weiss, b; Morey Feld, d.

(Sides 13–20)
Limehouse Blues
Embraceable You
After You've Gone
Body And Soul
'Way Down Yonder In New Orleans
Rose Room
The World Is Waiting For The Sunrise

(Sides 22–26)
Hallelujah!
The Man I Love
Boogie Woogie
Honeysuckle Rose
On The Sunny Side Of The Street

Back to New York and another V-Disc session, again with the addition of Red Norvo who was still a regular on the "Mildred Bailey Show." Recent research has pinpointed the recording dates of this and the following set of V-Discs (heretofore ascribed to "October 1944" and "January 1945"—the latter because of the applied "D5" control numbers); and adds the certain existence of alternate takes, on studio acetates:

(THE) BENNY GOODMAN QUINTET October 11, 1944, New York

Personnel as September 25.

-0-	UNISSUED - acetate
D4-TC-446-1A (VP 944)	VD 344 A, NavyVD 124 A. **LP:** ARISTON 12015, DAN 5002, JS AA509, JSJap 15PJ16, SPJ 6608, SB 142 **Untitled** (later, "Slipped Disc")
D4-TC-447-1 (VP 945)	VD 394 A, NavyVD 174 A. **LP:** same issues as VD 344 A, et al, "Untitled" **Rose Room**
-0-	UNISSUED - acetate
D5-TC-199-1C (VP 1245)	VD 446 A, NavyVD 226 A. **LP:** same issues as VD 344 A, et al, "Untitled," except substitute ELEC KV119 for JS AA509, omit JSJap **Just One Of Those Things**

A 16" acetate, inscribed "D5-TC-426," includes a portion of "Rose Room," above. Dialogue indicates that the disc is part of an AFRS production titled, "So This Is Music," featuring Benny Goodman, Oscar Levant and Clifton Fadiman. No counterpart issued AFRS ET has been located, but research is continuing. And note also that the author cannot verify that a number of other Goodman V-Discs, reputedly including "Undecided," "Oomph Fah Fah," "Under A Blanket Of Blue," "Four Or Five Times," "How Am I To Know?," "I'll Never Be The Same" and "Between The Devil And The Deep Blue Sea," were also cut October 11. Effort to locate acetates of these titles has so far proved unavailing.

(THE) BENNY GOODMAN QUINTET October 17, 1944, New York

Personnel as September 25.

-0-	UNISSUED - breakdown and alternate - acetate
D5-TC-199-1C (VP 1245)	VD 446 A, NavyVD 226 A. **ET:** War Dep't. Yank Swing Session 123. **LP:** DAN 5002, ELEC KV119, SB 142 **Rachel's Dream**
D5-TC-232-1B (VP 1271)	VD 475 A, NavyVD 255 A. **LP:** same issues as VD 446 A, "Rachel's Dream" **Let's Fall In Love**

The author has no knowledge of other cuts reputedly made October 17, but it does seem likely that Benny would record more than two selections only—simply wouldn't have been worth the effort to quit at that point.

Earlier in October Liggett & Meyers, who had sponsored Glenn Miller's civilian band on radio, approached Benny about a new Chesterfield program. It would feature Benny and Oscar Levant, and the title penciled in was, "The Benny Goodman - Oscar Levant Show." Was Benny interested? He was, and immediately assembled a full orchestra, replete with strings, from New York studio musicians. Ed Herlihy was signed as announcer, and a boy-girl vocal group, christened the "Chesterfieldians," completed the package.

The entire cast went into the studios on October 23 for an audition . . . and the whole project ended there. For reasons unknown, L&M cancelled the program, and Benny of course disbanded. Fortunately, acetate transcriptions of the rehearsal survive:

"THE BENNY GOODMAN-   *October 23, 1944, New York*
* OSCAR LEVANT SHOW"*

Benny Goodman, clt, and a full orchestra, personnel unknown.

QUINTET: As September 25.

Let's Dance (theme) - full orchestra, plus Oscar Levant, p (LP: GOJ 1017)
Dance With A Dolly - voc, The Chesterfieldians - full orchestra
My Ideal - full orchestra
Limehouse Blues - QUINTET
(Prelude No. 3 (Gershwin) - Oscar Levant, p solo
Big John Special - orchestra sans strings (LP: SB 145)
Good-Bye (theme) - full orchestra (LP: SB 145)

Belated discovery of an AFRS ET makes it the base issue for the next Goodman recordings, and subordinates a 12″ 78 release bearing an OWI label, "General Stockpile Series Dance Music #15 - Dance Music Part 1 of 3," and its reverse, ". . . -Part 2 of 3." ("Part 3 of 3" in this series offers Paul Baron and his Orchestra's, "Four In A Bar," composed and arranged by Eddie Sauter — but without Benny's participation.)

The complete ET is a transcription of CBS's October 27 broadcast of, "The Mildred Bailey Show." Only Side 2 - final 15 minutes of the half-hour broadcast - is detailed, because Benny does not appear on Side 1. An introductory "Let's Dance" by Paul Baron's band is the final cut on Side 1; but it is sans BG.

AFRS MILDRED BAILEY SHOW No. 4   October 27, 1944, New York

Benny Goodman, clt; with Paul Baron and his Orchestra, including Charlie Shavers, Chris Griffin, tpt; Red Norvo, vib; Teddy Wilson, p; Remo Palmieri, g; Al Hall, b; Specs Powell, d; and unknown 2 tpt, 3 tbn, 5 reeds, strings.

QUINTET: Personnel as September 25.

SSR-11-12-9   **ET:** AFRS Mildred Bailey Show No. 4 - Part 2
               Henderson Stomp (orchestra) (Also on **78**, OWI release
                  as above, "1 of 3")
               Rachel's Dream - Opus 2 - QUINTET (Also on **78**, OWI,
                  "2 of 3")

("Rachel's Dream - Opus 2" is actually, "Slipped Disc.")

Note that some copies of the OWI release bear a pasted-over label reading, "American Information Center MUSIC LIBRARY No. GSS 23a, General Stockpile Series, Dance Music No. 15." Reason for this alteration is unknown. Also, press listings for Mildred's radio program bill it as, "Music Till Midnight."

WNEW's Martin Block hosted NBC's "For The Record" broadcast of November 6, and once again Benny was a featured performer, along with Alec Templeton, George Paxton and his Orchestra-Liza Morrow, vocals, and announcer Jack Costello.

A 16″ acetate confirms that one cut, the Quintet's "Avalon," which is on an AFRS ET, is from the broadcast. Curiously, a companion track on the AFRS ET is not on the acetate; the acetate includes Alec Templeton's "Impression Of A Tenor Sax Player" and "Impression Of Crooners," but not "Improvisation"—which features Benny, along with Templeton and Morey Feld. The author has no explanation for this discrepancy.

AFRS BASIC MUSIC LIBRARY P244   November 6, 1944, New York

Personnel as September 25.

SSL-472   **ET:** AFRS Basic Music Library P244 (cut 4)
            Avalon - QUINTET

Possibly from this broadcast:

AFRS BASIC MUSIC LIBRARY P244   same date

Benny Goodman, clt; Alec Templeton, p; Morey Feld, d.

SSL-472   **ET:** as above (cut 1)
            Improvisation (LP: SWH 46)

Despite cancellation of the Chesterfield radio series, things started swinging for Benny in November. His Quintet, now with Red Norvo a full-time member, went into rehearsal for Billy Rose's new revue, "The Seven Lively Arts." And best news of all, the record ban had ended, and Benny resumed his interrupted contract with Columbia. Two of the three tunes recorded this initial post-ban session were featured in, "The Seven Lively Arts." The third, "After You've Gone," produced two rare original releases, one on ET, and the other on a little-known 45 rpm commercial issue.

BENNY GOODMAN QUINTET   November 16, 1944, New York

Personnel as September 25. Peggy Mann, voc.

CO 33816	**LP:** PHON 7648
CO 33816-1	CO 36767, CoArg 291625, CoC 742. **LP:** FontCont 68204TL, FONT TFL5067, SONY 20AP-1810, JAZ 68, JOY 6044. **ET:** AFRS Basic Music Library P287
	Ev'ry Time We Say Goodbye - voc Peggy Mann (arr EdSau)
CO 33817	**LP:** BID 1002
CO 33817	UNISSUED - Tape
CO 33817	UNISSUED - Tape
CO 33817	**LP:** MER 11
CO 33817	UNISSUED - Tape
CO 33817	UNISSUED - Tape
CO 33817-1	**ET:** AFRS Basic Music Library P307. **LP:** VELP 1, PHON 7648
CO 33817-2	**45:** CO 4-11-G (Set G4-2). **LP:** BID 1011
	After You've Gone
CO 33818	**LP:** PHON 7648, BID 1002
CO 33818	UNISSUED - Tape
	Only Another Boy And Girl - voc Peggy Mann (arr EdSau)

"The Seven Lively Arts" opened in Philadelphia November 24, with a cast that included Bea Lillie, Bert Lahr, "Doc" Rockwell, Alicia Markova, Anton Dolin, Nan Wynn, Dolores Gray, and Benny Goodman and his Quintet. Additionally, Benny performed movements from von Weber's concerto with the pit orchestra, as part of this talent-laden extravaganza. In passing, we note that Benny had first been employed by Napoleon-sized, ex-speed typist Rose just about a decade earlier, the "Music Hall" engagement.

Before his next studio session, Benny changed vocalists: Jane Harvey replaced Peggy Mann. And if Benny can change his mind, so can the author: some cuts of "Rachel's Dream" are now removed from this date to the studio session of May 7, 1945, q.v. And one cut of "Only Another Boy and Girl," on an AFRS ET, seems open to question here—more following.

BENNY GOODMAN QUINTET   December 21, 1944, New York

Personnel as September 25. JANE HARVEY, voc.

CO 34030-bkdn	UNISSUED - Tape
CO 34030	UNISSUED - Tape
CO 34030	UNISSUED - Tape
CO 34030	UNISSUED - Tape
CO 34030-bkdn	UNISSUED - Tape
CO 34030-2	**LP:** BID 1002
CO 34030-bkdn	UNISSUED - Tape
CO 34030-1A	**LP:** PHON 7648
	Rachel's Dream
CO 34031	UNISSUED - Tape
CO 34031	UNISSUED - Tape
CO 34031	**LP:** BID 1011
CO 34031-bkdn	UNISSUED - Tape
CO 34031-2	Co 36767, CoArg 291625, CoC 742. **LP:** SONY 20AP-1810, JAZ 68
CO 34031-5	**LP:** FONT TFL5067, FontCont 662003TR, PHON 7648
	Only Another Boy And Girl - voc Jane Harvey (arr EdSau)

It may be a quibble, but an AFRS ET cut of "Only Another Boy And Girl" is different in tempo from all other cuts shown above, has no vocal reprise, and Red's vibes are recorded more prominently. Further - although it is not an absolute criterion - the ET cut is not included in tape transfers of the sequential Columbia "safeties." Thus it seems prudent to list it separately, origin uncertain, rather than as a Columbia commercial recording:

(THE) BENNY GOODMAN QUINTET   prob. December 1944, New York

Personnel as September 25. Jane Harvey, voc.

-0-   **ET:** AFRS Basic Music Library P287
          Only Another Boy And Girl - voc Jane Harvey

Likely before the end of the year, Benny's new Quintet appeared on an AFRS-transcribed program mc'd by Gertrude Niessen—who fumbled the introduction. Its date is unknown—it may have originated on an NBC broadcast of December 23 that included Benny, but that is only speculation.

AFRS MAIL CALL   prob. December 1944, New York
SERIES H-1, PROGRAM No. 117

Quintet as September 25.

ND4-   **ET:** AFRS Mail Call Series H-1, Program No. 117 - Part 1
NM-9469-1   **After You've Gone**

Benny made a solo appearance—no Quintet—on Mildred Bailey's "Music Till Midnight" program of January 5. Also, there seems a good possibility that the one cut available from this broadcast may be on an AFRS ET, but the author is unable to confirm such a release.

"MUSIC TILL MIDNIGHT"   *January 5, 1945, New York*
CBS Radio Network

Benny Goodman, clt, and Paul Baron and his Orchestra.

Moonlight On The Ganges

Uniquely, and curiously, Benny Goodman, Louis Armstrong and Duke Ellington recorded together on January 17, 1945. It came about this way:

The occasion was the Second Annual Esquire All-American Jazz Concert. With contest winner Armstrong in New Orleans, winner Ellington in Los Angeles, and winner Goodman in the Metropolitan Opera House in New York, it was decided to pipe each of three separate concerts to the other locations via radio. AFRS transcribed the entire broadcast.

Louis had the first half-hour, Duke the second, and Benny a final 15 minutes. In order to lend continuity to the whole, Louis's solo trumpet and Benny's solo clarinet were transmitted to Los Angeles as the Ellington orchestra played his then theme, "Things Ain't What They Used To Be." But as Benny listened via earphones to Louis blending with Duke, he heard his clarinet intro bounce back from the public address system in the hall in Los Angeles. Thinking that this was Louis's contribution, he repeated his phrase, thus "answering" himself.

The ET listed first is the Duke's segment; Benny's only performance on it is in "Things Ain't What They Used To Be." Others on this ET are MC, Danny Kaye; commentary, Leonard Feather; award presentations by Judy Garland, Lena Horne and Billy Strayhorn; and performances by contest winners Ellington, Willie Smith, Anita O'Day and Art Tatum.

AFRS ONE NIGHT STAND No. 485   January 17, 1945,
New Orleans, Los Angeles, New York

Benny Goodman, clt; Louis Armstrong, tpt; and Duke Ellington and his Orchestra.

SSC-1-22-2   **ET:** AFRS One Night Stand No. 485—Part 2
            Things Ain't What They Used To Be

(Also on **LP:** DLT 50104, FDC 1009, PAL 30, SA 6924, SB 219.)

Others on Benny's ET, next, are: awards, Jack Benny and Bea Lillie; and performances by contest winners Edmond Hall, Oscar Pettiford, Coleman Hawkins and (Sgt.) Buck Clayton. Benny, Teddy Wilson and Red Norvo were "Gold" (first place) award winners on their respective instruments in Esquire's poll.

AFRS ONE NIGHT STAND No. 490   January 17, 1945, New York

Benny Goodman, clt; Red Norvo, vib; Teddy Wilson, p; Sid Weiss, b; Morey Feld, d. Mildred Bailey, voc.

SSC-1-27-1   **ET:** AFRS One Night Stand No. 490 — Part 1
            Air Mail Special
            Downhearted Blues-voc Mildred Bailey (& ensemble)

SSC-1-27-2   **ET:** as above, except Part 2
            The World Is Waiting For The Sunrise

(Duplicated on **ET,** AFRS One Night Stand No. 916. Parts 1 & 2, with over-pressed matrices SSC-3-29-1/2; and **LP,** DLT 50104, FDC 1008, JS AA510, PAL 30, SA 6924, SB 219. "Air Mail Special" (as "Esquire Jump") and "The World Is Waiting For The Sunrise" are also on **ET,** AFRS Basic Music Library P224; and **LP,** WI 248. "Downhearted Blues" is also on **LP,** KOJ 20035.)

Mildred is marvelous on "Downhearted Blues"—one of the author's favorites. Sadly it is her last collaboration with Benny; ill with diabetes and a cardiac condition, she will die on December 12, 1951. Farewell, Mrs. Swing . . . you were one of the great ones. And on record, you *are*, and forever will be, one of the great ones.

Late in January Mike Bryan was added to the Quintet, and Slam Stewart replaced Sid Weiss. Both debut on the next Columbia session, beginning with a re-make of the Quintet's "After You've Gone".

BENNY GOODMAN SEXTET   February 4, 1945, New York

Benny Goodman, clt; Red Norvo, vib; Teddy Wilson, p; MIKE BRYAN, g; SLAM STEWART, b; Morey Feld, d. Jane Harvey, voc.

CO 33817-
Bkdn   UNISSUED — Tape

CO 33817   **LP:** BID 1002, PHON 7648

CO-33817-
Bkdns   UNISSUED — Tape (2 consecutive aborted attempts)

CO 33817-3   CO 36781, VD 519 A, CoC 747, OdG 0-28429, PaE R2983, PaNor NPS5017 PaSw PZ11086. **EP:** CO 5-1650 (Set B350). PHIL BBE12189, PhilCont 429410BE. **LP:** CO GL500, CoE 33SX1035, CoFr FPX112, CoJap PL5004, FONT TFL5001 (see note), PHIL BBL7178, PhilCont BO7225L. PhilCont B 13201R, ReSp 33LS1006, CBS 52965, CBS 67268, COR KLP675, CO KG31547, CO alb P4M-5678, CoH 33QX12016, SONY SOPM-162, TL J14, RTB LPV4316
            After You've Gone

(Some copies of FONT TFL5001 substitute the full band version, mx CO 33049-1)

CO 34263   **LP:** BID 1002

CO 34263-2   **ET:** AFRS Basic Music Library P384. **LP:** PHON 7648, BID 1011

CO 34263   **LP:** BID 1011

CO 34263-
Bkdn   **LP:** BID 1011

CO 34263-1   CO 36817, CO DJ "Special," CoArg 291646, OdG 0-28398, OdSp 184889, PaE R3007, PaFin DPY 1070, Palt B71230, PaSw PZ11106, PHIL JAZ107. **45:** CO 4-16-G (Set G4-2), Phil Cont 322212BE. **EP:** CO 5-1651 (Set B-350), CoJap EM101, PHIL BBE12189, PhilCont 429410BE. **LP:** CO GL500, CO "Texaco," CoE 33SX1035, CoFr FPX112, CoJap PL 5004, PHIL BBL7178, PhilCont BO7225L, ReSp 33LS1009, CBS 52965, COR KLP675, SONY SOPM-162, RTB LPV4316, TL J14
            Slipped Disc

CO 34264-1   Co 36817, VD 519 A, CoArg 291646, CoJap M453, OdSp 184741, PaE R3010, Palt B71230, PaNor NPS5015, PaSw PZ11109. **LP:** FONT TFL5067, FontCont 682047TL, CBS 52965, CO alb P5-15536, SONY 20AP-1810, JAZ 68. **ET:** AFRS Basic Music Library P384
            Oomph Fah Fah

February 4, 1945, continued

February 4, 1945, continued

CO 34265	UNISSUED — Tape
CO 34265-Bkdn	UNISSUED — Tape
CO 34265-1	CO 36923, CoAu DO3115, CoC 6226, OdF 281786, PaE R3008, PaSw PZ11107. **45:** CO 4-36923. **LP:** CO CL 6052, CO CL2564, CoE 33S1048, CoFr FP 1031, FONT TFR6006, FontCont 662003TR, Colt QS6033, CBS 52965, SONY 20AP-1810, JAZ 68. **ET:** AFRS G.I. Jive 2273
CO 34265-Bkdn	UNISSUED — Tape
CO 34265-2	CoBr 30-1276. **LP:** PHON 7648, BID 1002
	She's Funny That Way-voc Jane Harvey
CO 34266	**LP:** PHON 7648, BID 1004
	Body And Soul

BENNY GOODMAN TRIO   **same session**

Benny Goodman, clt; Teddy Wilson, p; Morey Feld, d.

CO 34266	**LP:**PHON 7648
CO 34266	UNISSUED — Tape
CO 34266-1	CO 36781, CoC 747, CoJap M323, OdG 0-28343, PaE R2983, PaFin DPY 1060, PaSw PZ11086. **LP:** FONT TFL5067, FontCont 682047TL, CBS 52965, SONY 20AP-1810, JAZ 68
CO 34266	UNISSUED — Tape
	Body And Soul

Although he stayed with "The Seven Lively Arts" into March, Benny began to assemble a big band in February. He believed that when the war was over, the big bands would regain their pre-war preeminence. For a few years at least, his judgment was sound.

Thus with the record ban over, a new orchestra in prospect, and V-E Day but a few months off, it is time to end the WAR YEARS' stage of Benny Goodman's career and begin the POSTWAR COLUMBIA phase. Collectors and Goodman fans alike owe their gratitude to AFRS for providing so much of Benny's work on record over the past two and one-half years, filling the void created by the Petrillo prohibition. And supplementing the commercial recording that now resumes, AFRS continues to add Goodman material that otherwise would be non-existent.

One postscript to the WAR YEARS' era: Benny's new Sextet gave a jazz concert in Rochester, New York, on February 18. It was not broadcast; and sadly, this is decades before the advent of hand-held cassette recorders . . .

POSTWAR COLUMBIAS AND THE "BENNY GOODMAN SHOW"

Although many of the Nation's better jazz instrumentalists were still in its Armed Services, Benny was able to assemble at least a "representative" Goodman orchestra for his first big band commercial recording of the post-ban period. Note that Saul "Sonny" Berman, who will have a brief but meteoric career with Woody Herman, is in the personnel. But despite an exchange of letters between Berman and Goodman that indicate tenure, Sonny may not have remained with the band much beyond this studio session. Note too that Teddy Wilson, who along with Red Norvo was with Benny on a full-time basis (Mildred's radio program having folded February 9), does not play band piano, nor does Slam Stewart play bass. At this time, both performed with the small groups only.

BENNY GOODMAN AND HIS ORCHESTRA   February 25, 1945, New York

Benny Goodman, clt; Vincent Badale, Sonny Berman, Tony Faso (Joseph Fasulo), Alex Clozzo, tpt; James "Trummy" Young, Bill Pritchard, Don Matthew, tbn; Bill Shine, Aaron Sachs, as; Stan Kosow, Al Epstein, ts; Danny Bank, bar; Charlie Queener, p; Mike Bryan, g; Clyde Lombardi, b; Morey Feld, d. Jane Harvey, BOB HAYDEN, voc.

CO 34292-1	VD 485 B. **EP**: CoE SEG7556, **LP**: CO CL6100, CO CL2533, CO CL967, FONT TFL5001, PHON 7648. **ET**: AFRS Basic Music Library P288
CO 34292	UNISSUED—Tape
CO 34292	UNISSUED—Tape
CO 34292-2	CO 36787, CoE DB2333, CoSw DZ504, ReSp C8830. **LP**: JAZ 68
	You Brought A New Kind Of Love To Me-voc Jane Harvey (arr FH)
CO 34293	UNISSUED—Tape
CO 34293-Bkdn	UNISSUED—Tape
CO 34293-2	CO 36787. **ET**: AFRS Basic Music Library P288. **LP**: NOST 1004
CO 34293	UNISSUED—Tape
CO 34293-Bkdns	UNISSUED—Tape (2 consecutive aborted attempts)
CO 34293-1	**LP**: PHON 7650
CO 34293	UNISSUED—Tape
CO 34293	UNISSUED—Tape
	Close As Pages In A Book-voc Jane Harvey (arr EdSau)
CO 34294-1	**ET**: AFRS Basic Music Library P287. **LP**: PHON 7650
CO 34294-2	CO 36790
	(I Love You-I Love You-I Love You) Sweetheart Of All My Dreams-voc Bob Hayden
CO 34295-1	CO 36790, VD 485 B, PaAu A7563. **ET**: AFRS Basic Music Library P288
CO 34295-2	**LP**: PHON 7650
	Ev'ry Time (Ev'ry Time I Fall In Love)-voc Jane Harvey (arr ES)

We would point out that it is highly unlikely that, after a lengthy struggle with "Close As Pages . . .", the band suddenly became so proficient that it quickly knocked off two acceptable takes of each of the next two selections. Rather, these are the only takes that exist, to the best of the author's knowledge.

Once again, the author speculates that AFRS may also have transcribed onto an ET the next listing, which is based on a privately-recorded acetate.

Note too that dialogue on the acetate suggests that Benny performed another selection prior to the one listed following; the author has no other information about it.

"THE JERRY WAYNE SHOW"   March 5, 1945, New York
    Unknown radio network

Benny Goodman, clt, and a studio orchestra, possibly Al Goodman's.

Dizzy Fingers

Victory-in-Europe Day was still two months away, the troops were still in the camps, and Benny launched another big band tour to provide them entertainment. The Fitch Shampoo people caught up with one engagement, and Coca Cola "Spotlighted" Benny on two; and AFRS transcribed all three. The AFRS ET's are edited, and some of the performances are not on them; however, copies of the full broadcasts are available. Those tunes not on the ET's are listed in their order of performance, in a distinguishing type face.

AFRS BANDWAGON No. 144   March 11, 1945, Camp Shanks, New York

Personnel as February 25, except Berman is uncertain; AL MASTREN, tbn. replaces both Pritchard and Matthew; and OTIS KIBBER, ts, replaces Al Epstein. Dick Powell (Fitch's MC), voc.

SS-3-11-21 (C1393)	**ET**: AFRS Bandwagon No. 144 ("Fitch Bandwagon" theme - dubbed) **Let's Dance** (theme) **Somebody Stole My Gal** *I'm Making Believe-voc Jane Harvey* **Clarinade** (arr MP) **King Porter Stomp** (update FH arr) **Ev'ry Time We Say Goodbye**-voc Dick Powell, chorus (arr ES) *Good-Bye (theme)* ("Fitch Bandwagon" theme-dubbed

(Above on **LP**, SB 145.)

Note that the Sextet's "Slipped Disc," broadcast from Camp Kilmer, New Jersey, has Clyde Lombardi on bass, not Slam Stewart:

AFRS SPOTLIGHT BANDS No. 623   March 15, 1945, Camp Kilmer, New Jersey

Personnel as March 11.

SEXTET: BG, Norvo, Wilson, Bryan, LOMBARDI, Feld.

SS-3-16-8	**ET**: AFRS Spotlight Bands No. 623 *"Spotlight Bands" theme* **Let's Dance** (theme) **Frenesi** **Ev'ry Time (Ev'ry Time I Fall In Love)**-voc Jane Harvey (**LP**: JS AA510) *Sweetheart Of All My Dreams-voc Bob Hayden* **Slipped Disc**—SEXTET (**LP**: JS AA510) *Close As Pages In A Book-voc Jane Harvey* **King Porter Stomp** *Good-Bye (theme)* *"Spotlight Bands" theme*

(Above on **LP**, GOJ 1024. Note that "Sweetheart Of All My Dreams" is so announced, omitting its introductory, "(I Love You-I Love You-I Love You)".)

A studio date interrupted Benny's tour of military bases. Berman is certainly out of the band by now, for Stan Fishelson replaces him as a fourth trumpet. Several of the men who made the February 25 Columbia session now return, which suggests Benny's touring band was different from his recording orchestra, probably because studio commitments prevented some of the sidemen from traveling.

BENNY GOODMAN AND HIS ORCHESTRA   March 17, 1945, New York

Benny Goodman, clt; Vince Badale, Al Cuozzo, Tony Faso, STAN FISHELSON, tpt; Trummy Young, SY SHAEFFER, BILL PRITCHARD, tbn; Bill Shine, Aaron Sachs, as; Stan Kosow, AL EPSTEIN, ts; Danny Bank, bar; Charlie Queener, p; Mike Bryan, g; Clyde Lombardi, b; Morey Feld, d. Jane Harvey, Bob Hayden, voc. SONNY SKYLAR (SS), arr.

CO 34474-1	**LP**: PHON 7650
CO 34474-2	TEST PRESSING
	Two Little Fishes And Five Loaves Of Bread-voc Jane Harvey
CO 34475-1	VD 535 B. **45**: CO 4-7-G (Set G4-3). **EP**: CO 5-1655 (Set B351). **LP**: CO GL501, CO CL534, CoE 33SX1034, CBSSw 52964, CO PG33405, SB 143. **ET**: AFRS Basic Music Library P384
	Clarinade (arr MP)
CO 34476-Bkdn	UNISSUED—Tape (voc, Jane Harvey, Benny Goodman)
CO 34476	**LP**: PHON 7650 (voc, Jane Harvey, Benny Goodman)
CO 34476-1	**LP**: CO alb P6-14538 (voc, Jane Harvey, Benny Goodman)
CO 34476	UNISSUED—Tape (voc, Jane Harvey, Bob Hayden)
CO 34476	UNISSUED—Tape (voc, Jane Harvey, Benny Goodman)
CO 34476	**LP**: FR "Hidden Treasure Of The Big Band Era" (voc Jane Harvey, BG)
	Gotta Be This Or That (vocals as above) (arr SS)
CO 34477-Bkdn	UNISSUED—Tape
CO 34477-	**LP**: CO "Star Time" XLP 32642, Vol. 1; PHON 7650
CO 34477-Bkdns	UNISSUED—Tape (2 consecutive aborted attempts)
CO 34477-2	**LP**: CO GL523, CO CB14, PHIL BBL7043, Phil Cont B07010L, CO PG33405. **EP**: CO 5-1652 (Set B351), PhilCont 429129BE, CO 21064. **ET**: VOA World Of Jazz 9
	Love Walked In (arr EdSau)

(The 3-minute arrangement of "Gotta Be This Or That" is Sonny Skylar's; Edgar Sampson added to it to produce the extended version. CO Lp alb P6-14014, not obtained by the author reputedly includes a take of "Love Walked In." FONT TFL5067's liner notes err; its "Clarinade" is from the session of May 16, q.v.)

A compound error in the author's earlier work shows Coca Cola broadcasts from March 20 and 21; there is only one, March 20, from the Naval Air Station at Lakehurst, New Jersey, now the Nation's only facility for lighter-than-air craft. Too, the false, "March 20" entry erroneously mixed performances from the March 15 broadcast and the true March 20 program.

Those sponsors' themes—"Fitch Bandwagon" and "Spotlight Bands" identifying signatures—are troublesome to detail. When they are extant from acetates of the actual broadcasts, they are played by the orchestra then appearing. But when they are from AFRS ET's, they seem to have been dubbed from a standard track, and are not performed by the orchestra on that date's program. Also, collectors should distinguish between catalog numbers on AFRS ET's, and performance numbers announced on Coca Cola broadcasts. As an example, the March 20 broadcast next was the 782nd broadcast in the "Spotlight Band" series; but it was the 627th ET in AFRS's ET set. AFRS began its releases with the March 22, 1943 broadcast by Hal McIntyre for the Atlanta-based soft-drink company.

AFRS SPOTLIGHT BANDS No. 627   March 20, 1945, Lakehurst, New Jersey

Personnel As March 15/17.

QUINTET: BG, Norvo, Wilson, Stewart, Feld (no g).

SS-3-21-5	**ET**: AFRS Spotlight Bands No. 627
	"Spotlight Bands" theme
	Let's Dance (theme)
	Spring Song (LP: GOL 55001)
	You Brought A New Kind Of Love To Me-voc Jane Harvey
	Seven Come Eleven (**LP**: GOL 55001, JS AA510)
	Love Walked In
	After You've Gone - QUINTET
	Gotta Be This Or That-voc Jane Harvey, Benny Goodman (**LP**: JS AA510)
	Good-Bye (theme)
	"Spotlight Bands" Theme

(Above on **LP**, GOJ 1024.)

Benny closed out "The Seven Lively Arts" March 24 and on March 28 opened in the Paramount Theater in New York with his orchestra and Sextet. Fishelson is not reported in press accounts of the personnel for this engagement, and likely Benny played the date with only three trumpets. Al Mastren is noted as one trombonist, and the tenors were Otis Kibber and Al Young, at least for some of the performances. Once again, it is stressed that Benny's road band was different from his studio orchestra.

We next pick up Benny a month later at a marathon session for Columbia, with what must have been an excruciating effort to record a satisfactory take of "June Is Bustin' Out All Over," with new vocalist Kay Penton. Its ten complete performances and four aborted takes are likely the most attempts Benny ever made to record one tune at one session. And it was all in vain: none merited his approval, there would be no contemporary commercial release. AFRS did issue one track on an ET, and in later years Columbia reissued it, and Phontastic released an alternate. But at the time - nothing.

BENNY GOODMAN AND HIS ORCHESTRA   April 27, 1945, New York

Benny Goodman, clt; Vince Badale, Al Cuozzo, Tony Faso, Stan Fishelson, tpt; Trummy Young, EDDIE AULINO, CHAUNCEY WELSCH, tbn; Aaron Sachs, RAY BELLER, as; Stan Kosow, Al Epstein, ts; Danny Bank, bar; Charlie Queener, p; Mike Bryan, g; Clyde Lombardi, b; Morey Feld, d. Bob Hayden, KAY PENTON, voc.

CO 34477	**LP**: PHON 7650
CO 34477-Bkdn	UNISSUED - Tape
CO 34477	UNISSUED - Tape
CO 34477	UNISSUED - Tape
	Love Walked In-voc Bob Hayden
CO 34645	**LP**: PHON 7650
CO 34645	UNISSUED—Tape
CO 34645	UNISSUED—Tape
CO 34645-Bkdns	UNISSUED—Tape (4 consecutive aborted attempts)
CO 34645	UNISSUED—Tape
CO 34645	UNISSUED—Tape
CO 34645-1	**ET** AFRS Basic Music Library P385. **LP**: CO alb. P5-15536
CO 34645	UNISSUED—Tape
CO 34645	UNISSUED—Tape
CO 34645	UNISSUED—Tape
CO 34645	UNISSUED—Tape
	June Is Bustin' Out All Over-voc Kay Penton (arr ES)

(When CO released CO alb P5-15536, this 6th full cut became take-of-preference "I".)

Add Red Norvo, vib; and substitute Slam Stewart, b, for Lombardi.

CO 34646- Bkdn	UNISSUED—Tape
CO 34646	**LP**: PHON 7650
CO 34646- Bkdns	UNISSUED - Tape (2 consecutive aborted attempts)
CO 34646-1	CO 36813, VD 513 A, Navy VD 273 A, CoAu D02821, CoC 753, CoFr DF 3088.**LP**: CO CL6048, SB 142. **ET**: AFRS Basic Music Library P385, AFRS Jill's Juke Box 150, AFRS G.I. Jive 2227 **Gotta Be This Or That (Part 1)**-voc Benny Goodman (arr SS/ES)
CO 34647	**LP**: PHON 7650
CO 34647- Bkdn	UNISSUED - Tape
CO 34647	UNISSUED - Tape
CO 34647-1	same 78 rpm issues as CO 34646-1, **LP**: CO CL6048, SB 142, RAD 31. **ET**: AFRS Basic Music Library P385, AFRS "New Year's Eve Dancing Party" H-9-124, AFRS G.I. Jive 2228 **Gotta Be This Or That (Part 2)** (arr SS/ES)
CO 34646/7	**LP**: PHON 7650 **Gotta Be This Or That**-voc Benny Goodman, Trummy Young (n/c) (arr SS/ES)

Columbia's acetates simply could not accommodate the continuous, Part 1/2, take of "Gotta Be This Or That," listed last above; it is incomplete. Too bad, the band was swinging. Note that simulated crowd noise was dubbed into the AFRS ET's track of Part 2, fooling some collectors into believing that it was a live performance; and that Part 2 of CO 36813, the original issue, bears the legend, 'Featuring the Goodman Trio'.

The reader may recall that material once believed to have been recorded December 21, 1944, has been reassigned to the next studio session. The initial take and ts following breakdown of "Rachel's Dream," next, are the cuts involved.

BENNY GOODMAN SEXTET   **May 7, 1945, New York**

Benny Goodman, clt; Red Norvo, vib; Teddy Wilson, p; Mike Bryan, g; Slam Stewart, b; Morey Feld, D.

CO 34030	**LP**: TL STL J05
CO 34030- Bkdn	UNISSUED—Tape
CO 34030-3A	**LP**: PHON 7650
CO 34030-4	CO 36925, CoAu D03115, CoC 6228, PaE R3008, PaSw PZ11107. **45**: CO 4-36925. **EP**: FONT TFE17184. **LP**: CO CL6052, CO CL2564, CO "Texaco," CoE 33S 1048, CoFr FP 1031, FONT TFR 6006, FontCont 662003TR, SONY 20AP-1810. **ET**: AFRS G.I. Jive 2252 **Rachel's Dream**
CO 34673-1	CO 36924, CoAu D03155, CoC 6227, CoJap M556, PaE R3022, PaSw PZ11155. **45**: CO 4-36924. **EP**: FONT TFE17184. **LP**: CO CL6052, CoE 33S1048, CoFr FP 1031, FONT TRF6006, Font Cont 662003TR, CO alb P5-15536, SONY 20AP-1810. **ET**: Dept. Of State "Notes On Jazz", No. 11, AFRS G.I. Jive 2252
CO 34673-2	**LP**: BID 1002 **Just One Of Those Things**

It was at this juncture that the author's earlier work listed AFRS-released Sextet performances of "Exactly Like You," "Sweet Georgia Brown" and "Rose Room." He reminds the reader that this entry is reassigned correctly to January 11, 1946, q.v.

BENNY GOODMAN AND HIS ORCHESTRA   **May 16, 1945, New York**

Benny Goodman, clt; Vince Badale, Al Cuozzo, Tony Faso, FRANK LePINTO, tpt; Trummy Young, Eddie Aulino, Chauncey Welsch, tbn; Aaron Sachs, BILL SHINE, as; Stan Kosow, Ray Beller, ts; Danny Bank, bar; Charlie Queener, p; Mike Bryan, g; Clyde Lombardi, b; Morey Feld, d. Kay Penton, voc.

CO 34475-3	**LP**: PHON 7650
CO 34475-4	CO 36823, CoArg 291653, OdSp 184741, PaE R3010, PaSw PZ11109. **EP**: CO 5-1655 (Set B351). **LP**: FONT TFL5067, FontCont 682047TL **Clarinade** (arr MP)
CO 34645-4	CO 36823, CoArg 291649 **June Is Bustin' Out All Over**-voc Kay Penton (arr ES)
CO 34713-1	**LP**: PHON 7650
CO 34713-2	TEST PRESSING **Ain't Misbehavin'**-voc Kay Penton

Benny's next major engagement was in Manhattan's 400 Restaurant (some announcements have it, "400 Club"), and his stay provides us with an array of air checks, many of them recently discovered. Unfortunately, few of the source acetates are dated, and the majority of broadcasts can only be ascribed to the period May-June 1945. Also, we cannot be fully assured that the orchestra personnel listed (as for the May 16 Columbia session) is correct—again, the road band/studio orchestra condition. Note that whenever Part 2 of "Gotta Be This Or That" is performed, it should be understood that Norvo and Stewart join the band for that rendition; the listings omit this reiteration.

SUSTAINING BROADCAST   *May 24, 1945*
  Blue Radio Network   *400 Restaurant, New York*

Orchestra as May 16, plus Bob Hayden, voc.
Sextet as May 7.
TRIO: BG, Wilson, Feld

Let's Dance (theme)
Somebody Stole My Gal
June Is Bustin' Out All Over-voc Kay Penton
After You've Gone - SEXTET
Gotta Be This Or That, Parts 1 & 2 - voc Benny Goodman
Close As Pages In A Book-voc Kay Penton
Ev'ry Time (Ev'ry Time I Fall In Love)-voc Kay Penton
Body And Soul - TRIO
Frenesi - to signoff

SUSTAINING BROADCAST   *May 29, 1945*
  MUTUAL Radio Network   *400 Restaurant, New York*

Personnels as May 24.

Let's Dance (theme) (**EP**: PHON BG01)
Slipped Disc - SEXTET (**EP**: PHON BG01)
Gotta Be This Or That, Part 1 - Part 2 (n/c) - voc Benny Goodman
Just One Of Those Things - SEXTET (**EP**:PHON BG01)
Clarinet A La King (**EP**: PHON BG01; **LP**:PHON 7605)
Good-Bye (theme) (**EP**: PHON BG01)

SUSTAINING BROADCAST   *prob. June 2, 1945*
  CBS Radio Network   *400 Restaurant, New York*

Personnels as May 24.

Let's Dance (theme)
Don't Be That Way
June Is Bustin' Out All Over-voc Kay Penton
After You've Gone - SEXTET

SUSTAINING BROADCAST   June 2, 1945
  MUTUAL Radio Network   400 Restaurant, New York

Personnels as May 24.

Clarinade
Slipped Disc - SEXTET
Air Mail Special (**LP**: PHON 7605)
Play, Fiddle, Play - feat. Slam Stewart, b
Frenesi
King Porter Stomp
Good-Bye (theme)

SUSTAINING BROADCAST   May/June 1945
  CBS Radio Network   400 Restaurant, New York

Personnels as May 24.

Let's Dance (theme)
Just One Of Those Things - SEXTET
Clarinade (**LP**: PHON 7605)
Good-Bye (theme)

SUSTAINING BROADCAST   May/June 1945
  MUTUAL Radio Network   400 Restaurant, New York

Personnels as May 24.

Let's Dance (theme)
Somebody Stole My Gal
Limehouse Blues - SEXTET
Star Dust

SUSTAINING BROADCAST   May/June 1945
  MUTUAL Radio Network   400 Restaurant, New York

Personnels as May 24.

Air Mail Special
Oomph Fah Fah - SEXTET
Limehouse Blues - SEXTET
Good-Bye (theme)

SUSTAINING BROADCAST   May/June 1945
  MUTUAL Radio Network   400 Restaurant, New York

Personnels as May 24.

Let's Dance (theme)
Stompin' At The Savoy
The Man I Love - feat. Red Norvo, vib
Somebody Stole My Gal
Good-Bye (theme)

SUSTAINING BROADCAST   May/June 1945
  MUTUAL Radio Network   400 Restaurant, New York

Personnels as May 24.

Let's Dance (theme)
Don't Be That Way
Clarinade
Rachel's Dream - SEXTET (**LP**: PHON 7605)
Oomph Fah Fah - SEXTET (**LP**: PHON 7605)
Gotta Be This Or That, Parts 1 & 2 - voc Benny Goodman
Good-Bye (theme)

SUSTAINING BROADCAST   May/June 1945
  MUTUAL Radio Network   400 Restaurant, New York

Personnels as May 24.

Slipped Disc - SEXTET
Gotta Be This Or That, Parts 1 & 2 - voc Benny Goodman
Oomph Fah Fah - SEXTET
Good-Bye (theme)

SUSTAINING BROADCAST   May/June 1945
  MUTUAL Radio Network   400 Restaurant, New York

Personnels as May 24.

Let's Dance (theme)
It's Only A Paper Moon (arr FH) (**LP**: PHON 7605)
Gotta Be This Or That, Part 1 (n/c), Part 2 - voc Benny Goodman
Slipped Disc - SEXTET
Don't Blame Me-voc Bob Hayden (arr FH)
June Is Bustin' Out All Over - segue to
Good-Bye (theme)

SUSTAINING BROADCAST   May/June 1945
  Unknown radio network   400 Restaurant, New York

Personnels as May 24.

Let's Dance (theme)
Air Mail Special
Slipped Disc - SEXTET
The World Is Waiting For The Sunrise - SEXTET

SUSTAINING BROADCAST   May/June 1945
  Unknown radio network   400 Restaurant, New York

Gotta Be This Or That, Part 2
Stompin' At The Savoy (n/c - intro clipped)
After You've Gone - SEXTET
King Porter Stomp

SUSTAINING BROADCAST   May/June 1945
  Unknown radio network   400 Restaurant, New York

Personnels as May 24.

Don't Be That Way

SUSTAINING BROADCAST   May/June 1945
  Unknown network (MUTUAL?)   400 Restaurant, New York

Flying Home
Slipped Disc - SEXTET (n/c - intro only)

SUSTAINING BROADCAST   May/June 1945
  Unknown radio networks   400 Restaurant, New York

Personnel as May 24.

Slipped Disc - SEXTET (ABC network?)
The World Is Waiting For The Sunrise - SEXTET (Mutual network?)
Just One Of Those Things - SEXTET

Milton Berle—in a few years, "Mr. Television," and that medium's first great star—was host of the 7th War Loan Bond Drive in the Paramount Theater on June 5. Named "Glenn Miller Day" in honor of the celebrated bandleader who disappeared over the English Channel on December 15, 1944, the lengthy program featured ex-Millerites Marion Hutton and Chief Petty Officer Tex Beneke, comedian Joe Besser, vocalist Johnny Johnston, and Benny Goodman and his Orchestra and Sextet. Radio station WNEW and NBC broadcast the event.

The listing below includes only those performances in which Benny and/or his sidemen play. And a sidelight: Benny claims that "Moonlight Serenade" is Fletcher Henderson's arrangement (and such a chart was in Benny's book), but the version here is Miller's:

"GLENN MILLER DAY" WNEW and   June 5, 1945
  NBC Radio Network   Paramount Theater, New York

Personnels as May 24.

Moonlight Serenade (theme)
Don't Be That Way (**LP**: RAD, METRONOME, SG 8009)
Don't Sit Under The Apple Tree-voc Marion Hutton, Tex Beneke (no BG clt)
  (**LP**: SG 8009)
The World Is Waiting For The Sunrise - SEXTET (**LP**: RAD, METRONOME,
  SG 8009)
Love-voc Johnny Johnston (no BG clt)
Gotta Be This Or That (shortened version, Parts 1 & 2)-voc Benny
  Goodman (**LP**: RAD, METRONOME, SG 8009)
Good-Bye (theme)

The next studio date finds the reeds playing musical chairs, with this result:

BENNY GOODMAN AND HIS ORCHESTRA   June 18, 1945, New York

Benny Goodman, clt; Vince Badale, Al Cuozzo, Tony Faso, Frank LePinto, tpt; Trummy Young, Eddie Aulino, Chauncey Welsch, tbn; HYMIE SCHERTZER, RAY ECKSTROM (sometimes, "Eckstrand"), as; Bill Shine, AL EPSTEIN, ts; Danny Bank, bar; Charlie Queener, p; Mike Bryan, g; Clyde Lombardi, b; Morey Feld, d. DOTTIE REID, voc.

CO 35010-1	**ET**: AFRS Basic Music Library P384. **LP**: CO alb P5-15536, RLM 8065
CO 35010-2	CO 36843, CoJap M177. **ET**: AFRS G.I. Jive 1070
	It's Only A Paper Moon-voc Dottie Reid (arr FH)
CO 35011-1	**LP**: PHON 7650
	My Head Says Yes (But My Heart Says No)-voc Dottie Reid (arr EdSau)
CO 35012-1	UNISSUED - Test Pressing
CO 35012-2	**LP**: PHON 7650
	How Little We Know-voc Dottie Reid
CO 35013-1	**ET**: AFRS Basic Music Library P385. **LP**: NOST 1004
CO 35013-2	CO 36843, VD 535 B. **LP**: FEST alb 214, SB 143
	I'm Gonna Love That Guy-voc Dottie Reid

(Note that the French Festival release erroneously credits Lena Horne with Dottie Reid's vocal on, "I'm Gonna Love That Guy.")

The band began a two-month theater tour in the Earle Theater, Philadelphia, on July 5, did another week in the Michigan Theater in Detroit on July 13, then went to Chicago for two weeks in the Chicago Theater, beginning July 20. Benny's birthplace was also headquarters for the AFM's Caesar Petrillo, and while there Benny appealed to the music czar to settle his dispute with his booking agency, MCA. Petrillo arranged a settlement between the disputants on July 31, and the contract was dissolved. Reputedly, it cost Benny a bundle to get free.

The King was in residence in three "Palaces" in two weeks in August: the Palace Theater in Cleveland, Ohio, beginning August 3, then a split week in Palace theaters in Toledo, Ohio and Columbus, Ohio, beginning August 10 and 14, respectively.

A baffling air check, via acetate, circulates among collectors; good balance, good audio quality, sounding much like a cut from a sponsored broadcast rather than from a sustaining radio program. Various ascriptions have been made for the vocalist, but the author leans toward Dottie Reid. The chart is Jimmy Mundy's original arrangement, and Liza Morrow will perform it later this year, but this doesn't sound like Liza. Thus,

RADIO BROADCAST   *poss. June-August 1945,*
Unknown radio network   *unknown location*

Personnel for this period.

These Foolish Things-voc Dottie Reid (?)

The Glenn Miller Orchestra returned from Europe August 12, and most of the men went on 30-day furloughs prior to discharge. Benny immediately persuaded Mel Powell to rejoin as staff arranger, and for the time being, as pianist with the small groups. (The author was privileged to spend some time with Mel, Ray McKinley, Peanuts Hucko and others in the band in Paris over the V-E Day period in May, and can attest that without Glenn, the group swung much more loosely, in more ways than one. Benny's tough? Miller was THE disciplinarian, more Army officer than bandleader; freed from his restraint, the men really enjoyed all Paris had to offer . . .) Mel's back on piano for the next Sextet session in the studios, following two cuts by the full orchestra:

BENNY GOODMAN AND HIS ORCHESTRA   August 29, 1945, New York

Benny Goodman, clt; Vince Badale, Tony Faso, Frank LePinto, CHRIS GRIFFIN, tpt; Trummy Young, Eddie Aulino, Chauncey Welsch, tbn; Hymie Schertzer, GERALD SANFINO, as; Bill Shine, Al Epstein, ts; Danny Bank, bar; Charlie Queener, p; Mike Bryan, g; Clyde Lombardi, b; Morey Feld, d.

CO 35141	UNISSUED -Tape
CO 35141	**LP**: PHON 7652
CO 35141-Bkdn	UNISSUED -Tape
CO 35141-1A	PaE R3000, OdSp 204359, PaSw PZ11097. **45**: CO Set G4-20. **EP**: CO Set B357, PHIL BBE12048, PhilCont 429113BE. **LP**: CO GL524, CO "Texaco," CorAu KLP682, PhilCont B07011L, PhilCont B07797R, CBSSd 524
	Just You, Just Me (arr FH)

Substitute Slam Stewart, b, for Lombardi

CO 35142-2B	**LP**: PHON 7652
CO 35142-1	**7″ 33⅓**: CO Bonus Record ZLP 13906. **LP**: CO alb P5-15536, CBS 52964
	Baby, Won't You Please Come Home (arr FH)

(Note that recent release CO alb P5-15536 now designates its issue as take-of-choice "1"; and that some test pressings marked CO 35142-**1C** are identical to those marked CO 35142-2B)

BENNY GOODMAN SEXTET   same session

Benny Goodman, clt; Red Norvo, vib; MEL POWELL, p; Mike Bryan, g; Slam Stewart, b; Morey Feld, d.

CO 35143	**7″ 33⅓**: PHON MX EPA4
CO 35143-1	CO 36922, VD 556 A, CoBr 301302, CoC 6225, CoJap M555, CoJap L3020, OdFr 281786, OdG 0-28343, PaE R3022, PaSw PZ11155. **45**: CO 4-36922. **LP**: CO CL6052, CO CL2564, CoE 33S1048, CoFr FP1031, FONT TFR6006, FontCont 662003TR, CBS 52965, SB 143. **ET**: AFRS G.I. Jive 2252, AFRS G.I. Jive 2273, Dept. Of State Notes On Jazz 11
CO 35143-2	**LP**: PHON LV-50, PHON 7652, BID 1004, SONY 20AP-1810
	Tiger Rag
CO 35144-1	CO 36925, VD 556 A, CoArg 291726, CoAu D03142, CoC 6228, PaE R3002, PaFin DPY1019, PaSw PZ11099. **45**: CO 4-36925, **EP**: FONT TFE17184. **LP**: CO CL6052, CO CL2564, CoE 33S1048, CoFr FP1031, FONT TFR6006, FontCont 662003TR, CBS 52965, CO alb P4M-5678, SONY 20AP-1810, SB 143. **ET**: Dept. Of State Notes On Jazz 11, AFRS G.I. Jive 2252
CO 35144-2A	**LP**: BID 1004, PHON 7652
	Shine

The author recalls Mel playing an Olde English folk ditty, "Oranges and Lemons," with small groups from the Miller band, and now he adapts it to his first chart for Benny after his return from Europe, "My Guy's Come Back." It's sung by Benny's new vocalist, Liza Morrow, who had been singing on the "Gloom Chasers" radio program, and who was pressed into service when Dottie Reid missed the studio date. Trummy Young left to form his own band, and Sy Shaeffer rejoined as his replacement. Note that Powell substitutes on band piano here—probably because of his arrangement—although Charlie Queener is still the regular pianist for the orchestra.

BENNY GOODMAN　　　　　　　**September 12, 1945, New York**
　AND HIS ORCHESTRA

Personnel as August 29, except SY SHAEFFER, tbn, replaces Young; and Mel Powell, p, substitutes for Queener. LIZA MORROW, Voc.

CO 35190-1	VD 585 A. **ET**: AFRS Basic Music Library P493. **LP**: CO alb P5-15536, SB 143
CO 35190-2	CO 36874, CoBR 301184, CoC 766, OdSp 204359, PaE R3000, PaSw PZ11097, History In Sound 1941
	My Guy's Come Back-voc Liza Morrow (arr MP)
CO 35191-1A	**LP**: NOST 1004
CO 35191-2	**LP**: PHON 7652
	That's All That Matters To Me-voc Liza Morrow (poss. arr MP)

Interesting occurrence on the next Sextet session: Using a different matrix, Benny records a 10″ and a 12″ version of, "I Got Rhythm," and both were released. And note a previously-undisclosed take of the shorter cut.

BENNY GOODMAN SEXTET　　　　　**September 18, 1945, New York**

Personnel as August 29 Sextet.

CO 35206	**7″ 33⅓**: PHON MX EPH85
CO 35206-1	CO 36922, CoArg 291726, CoAu D03142, CoBr 30-1276, CoC 6225, OdFr 281785, OdSp 204344, PaE R3014, PaSw PZ11111. **45**: CO 4-36922. **LP**: CO CL6052, CO CL2564, CoE 33S1048, CoFr FP1031, Colt QS6033, FONT TFR6006, FontCont 662003TR, CBS 52965, CO alb P4M-5678, SONY 20AP-1810. **ET**: AFRS G.I. Jive 2273, Dept. Of State Notes On Jazz 11
	Ain't Misbehavin'
CO 35207-1	**LP**: PHON 7652
CO 35207-2	CO 36923, CoArg 291697, CoAu D03155, CoC 6226, OdG 0-28398. OdSp 184889, PaE R3007, PaFin DPY 1070, PaSw PZ11106. **45**: CO 4-36923. **LP**: CO CL6052, CoE 33S1048, CoFr FP1031, FONT TFR6006, FontCont 662003TR, Colt QS6033, CO 21064. **ET**: AFRS G.I. Jive 2273
	I Got Rhythm
XCO 35208-1	CO 55038, VD 601 B. CoC 25011, CoJap SW282. **LP**: CBS 52965, CO alb P5-15536, SONY 20AP-1810, SB 143
	I Got Rhythm

Hymie Schertzer returned to studio work, and Bill Shine gave up his tenor chair to replace him; Bud Freeman, a Goodman associate from the Pollack days and Benny's 1938 orchestra, filled in on tenor. Note that the only original releases from this abbreviated session were on V-Disc.

BENNY GOODMAN　　　　　　　**September 19, 1945, New York**
　AND HIS ORCHESTRA

Personnel as September 12, except Bill Shine moves to as, replacing Schertzer; BUD FREEMAN, ts, joins; and Charlie Queener resumes band piano.

CO 35209-1B	VD 574 A. **LP**: SB 143-
CO 35209-2A	**LP**: NOST 1004, PHON 7652
	Fishin' For The Moon-voc Liza Morrow
CO 35210-?	VD 585 A. **LP**: SB 143
	Give Me The Simple Life-voc Liza Morrow

(To the best of the author's knowledge, Columbia never assigned a "take-of-preference" number to this cut of mx CO 35210.)

Five days later, Benny returned to the studios for a triple-header, recording with his Quintet, Sextet and orchestra. Off to this unusual start, things got more complex, compounded by a recent discovery:

A previously-unknown Columbia "safety" provides five full, and two aborted, additional takes of "Liza." Presumably they are transferred in order-of-performance. The safety does not, however, include released takes 1 and 2 of "Liza"; and the new cuts find a bass, probably Slam Stewart, in

and out of these performances. Thus it is not known at which point takes 1 and 2 were recorded. They are listed below following the "new" material.

The safety also includes two previously-undocumented cuts of "King Porter Stomp" by the orchestra. So far as it is known, no matrix number was assigned by Columbia to this recording. It may be that Benny did not intend this version for release, but simply ran through the old standard for some unknown reason. The cuts are listed in order-of-performance, since they were recorded just prior to, "Lucky."

Takes 1 and 2 of "Liza" have an interesting lineage: Take 1 was first issued commercially in England, then on V-Disc, eventually on a Columbia LP. To introduce the LP, Columbia pressed several tunes from it onto 78 rpm singles, sent them to disc jockeys. The DJ release of "Liza" was an alternate take of the version on the LP; a test proved it to be, take 2.

Take 1 of the Sextet's "China Boy" was released on CO 36924 et al, including a **vinyl** edition of V-Disc 627 B. In some manner, a **shellac** pressing of V-Disc 627 B was also distributed; mysteriously, its take was an alternate, take 2. This is the only instance known to the author wherein a single V-Disc catalog number applies to alternate versions of the given performance.

Finally, despite some assertions to the contrary, there were no contemporary releases of the orchestra's "Lucky" (later titled, "You're Right - I'm Wrong") from this session. Initial commercial release waited until Benny was satisfied with a take re-made almost three months later, December 19.

BENNY GOODMAN (AND HIS) QUINTET　　**September 24, 1945, New York**

Benny Goodman, clt; Red Norvo, vib; Mel Powell, p; Mike Bryan, g; Morey Feld, d.

CO 35234	**LP**: BID 1012
CO 35234	**LP**: BID 1012
	Liza (All the Clouds'll Roll Away)

Add b; probably Slam Stewart.

CO 35234-bkdn	**LP**: BID 1012
CO 35234	**LP**: BID 1012
CO 35234	**LP**: BID 1012
CO 35234-bkdn	**LP**: BID 1012
CO 35234	**LP**: BID 1012
	Liza (All the Clouds'll Roll Away)

Omit b.

CO 35234-1	CoE DB 2287, VD 627 B, Co Jap M205, CoNor GNS5082, CoSw DZ461, FONT JAZ107, ReSp C8787, **45**: CO 4-14-G (set G4-2), PhilCont 322212BF. **EP**: CO 5-1652 (set B350), PHIL BBE12189, PhilCont 429410BE. **LP**: CO GL500, CoE 33SX1035, CoFr FPX112, CoJap PL5004, PHIL BBL7178, PhilCont B07225L, ReSp 33LS1009, CO KG31547, CO alb P4M-5678, COR KLP 675, CBS 52965, CBS67268, RTB LPV4316, SONY SOPM-162, CO 21064
CO 35234-2	CO DJ 78 rpm (advertising CO LP GL500). **LP**: PHON 7652, SB 143
	Liza (All The Clouds'll Roll Away)

BENNY GOODMAN (AND HIS) SEXTET　　　　　**same session**

Personnel as Quintet, plus Slam Stewart, b.

CO 35235-1	CO 36924, VD 627 B (vinyl), CoArg 291697, CoBr 301302, CoC 6227, CoJap M555, OdFr 281785, OdSp 204344, PaE R3014, PaFin DPY1019, PaSw PZ11111. **45**: CO 4-36924. **EP**: FONT TFE17184. **LP**: CO CL6052, CO CL2654, CoE 33SX1048, CoFr FP1031, FONT TFR 6006, FontCont 662003TR, CBS 52965, Co alb P4M-5678, SONY 20AP-1810, SB 143. **ET**: AFRS G.I. Jive 2252
CO 35235-2	VD 627 B (shellac only). **LP**: PHON 7652
	China Boy

BENNY GOODMAN AND HIS ORCHESTRA same session

Personnel as September 19, except BERNIE PRIVIN, tpt, replaces Griffin, and TOMMY REO, tbn, replaces Welsch.

CO 35236-1	CO 36874, VD 574 A, CoBr 301184, CoC 766, CoMex 2071. **LP**: Co alb P6-14954, CO PM16932, CO 2P6264, CO 6P6465, RLM 8065, FEST alb 214, SB 143
CO 35236-2	UNISSUED - Test Pressing
	Symphony-voc Liza Morrow
-0-	UNISSUED—Tape
-0-	UNISSUED—Tape
	King Porter Stomp
CO 35237-1	**LP**: NOST 1004
CO 35237-2	**LP**: PHON 7652
	Lucky (later, "You're Right - I'm Wrong") (arr ES)

(FEST alb 214 lists Lena Horne as vocalist on "Symphony," in error.)

Little is known of Benny's activities for the next two months. On October 23 the band opened the renovated Arena in Niagara Falls, Ontario; and on the 27th he appeared as soloist with the Kansas City Philharmonic, in Kansas City, performing the Mozart Concerto, von Weber's Concertina, and his concert arrangement of "Dizzy Fingers." We next pick him up in Columbia's studios, with (almost) a brand new band:

BENNY GOODMAN AND HIS ORCHESTRA November 20, 1945, New York

Benny Goodman, clt; Tony Faso, JOHN BEST, CONRAD GOZZO, LOUIS MUCCI, tpt; KAI WINDING, CHAUNCEY WELSCH, EARL (DICK) LeFAVE, tbn; Bill Shine, Gerry Sanfino, as; STAN GETZ, EMMET CARL, ts; Danny Bank, bar; Charlie Queener p; Mike Bryan, g; BARNEY SPIELER, b; Morey Feld, d. Liza Morrow, voc.

CO 35210-3	CO 36908, CoArg 291675, CoC 779. **LP**: NOST 890/1
CO 35210-4	**LP**: CO alb P6-14538, CO alb P5-15536, PHON 7652
	Give Me The Simple Life-voc Liza Morrow

(CO alb P5-15536's liner notes misidentify its track of CO 35210-4 as the, "V-Disc take.")

CO 35443-1	CoE DB2416, CoAu SV55, CoSd 1750. **LP**: FONT TFL5067, FontCont 68204TL, Co alb P5-15536, CO 21064, SWE 1001, SB 144
CO 35443-2	**LP**: VELP 1, PHON 7652
	Fascinating Rhythm (arr FH)
CO 35444-1	CO 36908, CoArg 291675, CoC 779. **LP**: NOST 1004, SB 144
CO 35444-2	PaAu A7583. **LP**: PHON 7652
	I Wish I Could Tell You-voc Liza Morrow

The band made a hurried trip to Chicago to play its "Harvest Moon Festival" on the 24th, returned to New York in time to appear on NBC's & Philip Morris's 'Johnny Presents' radio program on the 27th. No air checks identified to this broadcast are known, and it may be that only the Sextet, not the full orchestra, performed. The next night the entire Goodman troupe opened in the Terrace Room of the Mosque Theater building, in Newark, New Jersey.

Through the course of the three weeks-plus engagement, various comings-and-goings were reported in the press. Given Goodman's penchant for using some specialists when recording (other than sidemen regularly employed), and the failure of extant air checks to make every member of the orchestra audibly identifiable, the full band personnel for the Mosque Theater stand is collective. But some changes can be noted with assurance:

Charlie Queener, Slam Stewart and Morey Feld apparently left Benny's employ before the engagement began, because none is heard on any broadcast. And contrary to the author's earlier opinion, Red Norvo stayed with Benny until Benny left the New York area and went to the West Coast. Powell and Barney Spieler played in both the band and the Sextet, and Benny's new drummer was Bob Sheble, although it is reliably reported (and he seems identifiable on some air checks) that Dave Tough sat in on occasion.

Dave never beat his battle with the bottle, and his addiction caused physical problems, forcing him to leave Woody Herman's First Herd in September. He was working with Joey Marsala's small group in and around

New York, and he helped Eddie Condon open his new club there in December. Thus he was close to Newark (if memory serves, believe he was living in Newark at the time) and filling in with Benny seems a likely possibility. Ironically, Dave's destiny was linked with Newark; injuries sustained in a fall there three years from now will cause his death, December 6, 1948.

SUSTAINING BROADCAST November 28, 1945
  MUTUAL Radio Network Terrace Room, Newark, N.J.

Benny Goodman, clt; John Best, Conrad Gozzo, BERNIE PRIVIN, and BILLY BUTTERFIELD or Tony Faso, tpt; Kai Winding, Chauncey Welsch, Dick LeFave, tbn; Bill Shine, Gerry Sanfino, as; Stan Getz and PEANUTS HUCKO or Emmet Carl, ts; Danny Bank, bar; Mel Powell, p; Mike Bryan, g; Barney Spieler, b; BOB SHEBLE, poss. DAVE TOUGH, d. Liza Morrow, voc.

SEXTET: BG, Red Norvo, Powell, Bryan, Spieler, Sheble. (Tough not identifiable)

Fascinating Rhythm
*After You've Gone - SEXTET (**LP**: PHON 7605)*
Flying Home
Clarinade - to fade

SUSTAINING BROADCAST November 29, 1945
  CBS Radio Network Terrace Room, Newark, N.J.

Personnels as November 28.

Let's Dance (theme)
Frenesi (n/c - intro clipped)
*Slipped Disc - SEXTET (**LP**: PHON 7605)*
King Porter Stomp

SUSTAINING BROADCAST December 1, 1945
  NBC Radio Network Terrace Room, Newark, N.J.

Personnel as November 28.

Let's Dance (theme)
Somebody Stole My Gal
Aren't You Glad You're You?-voc Liza Morrow
Fascinating Rhythm
Seven Come Eleven
It's Only A Paper Moon-voc Liza Morrow
King Porter Stomp
Good-Bye (theme)

SUSTAINING BROADCAST December 6, 1945,
  CBS Radio Network Terrace Room, Newark, N.J.

Personnel as November 28 (Sheble now certain).

You Brought A New Kind Of Love To Me-voc Liza Morrow
Symphony-voc Liza Morrow
Clarinet A La King (incorporating, "Oh, Baby!")
Tuesday At Ten
How Deep Is The Ocean? (no voc)
Flying Home - to signoff

SUSTAINING BROADCAST prob. December 7, 1945
  CBS Radio Network Terrace Room, Newark, N.J.

Personnels as November 28.

Seven Come Eleven
The World Is Waiting For The Sunrise - SEXTET
Clarinade (n/c - intro only)
Air Mail Special
("Rose Room" is announced, but program immediately segue's to
Good-Bye (theme)

England's Alistair Cooke was the erudite and witty host of a prerecorded radio series titled, "(The) Kings Of Jazz." The programs offered the best of American jazz, and were rebroadcast in suave Mr. Cooke's native Great Britain. The Christmas Day broadcast, rebroadcast via BBC on February 8, 1946, was transcribed in G. Schirmer's New York studios on December 8. It found Benny's Trio and Sextet in top form; and a recent LP release, transferred directly from the original Schirmer transcriptions, matches the performance with excellent audio fidelity:

"(THE) KINGS OF JAZZ"   *December 8, 1945, New York*

Sextet as November 28.

TRIO: Goodman, Powell, Sheble

After You've Gone - SEXTET
Body and Soul - TRIO
Slipped Disc - SEXTET
Liza - TRIO
Confessin' - SEXTET
The World Is Waiting For The Sunrise - SEXTET
Stompin' At The Savoy - SEXTET
Somebody Loves Me - SEXTET
Good-Bye (theme) - SEXTET

*(Above on **LP**: BID 1012.)*

SUSTAINING BROADCAST   *December 15, 1945,*
  NBC Radio Network   *Terrace Room, Newark, N.J.*

Personnel as November 28.

Lucky (later, "You're Right-I'm Wrong")
Tuesday At Ten
My Guy's Come Back-voc Liza Morrow (n/c)

Two years earlier, Benny had appeared on James Melton's radio program; the author suspects that AFRS transcribed it, but has no physical evidence to support his belief. His next known guest slot is on ET, however, from a broadcast of December 16. Benny and mellifluous Irish tenor and antique car collector Jimmy Melton went back a long way together; he'd accompanied Melton on two record dates for Columbia in 1929.

JAMES MELTON No. 77   **December 16, 1945, New York**

Benny Goodman, clt, and a studio orchestra conducted by David Brookman.

SS-12-16-11A   **ET**: AFRS James Melton No. 77 - Part 1
                 Let's Dance

SS-12-16-12A   **ET**: as above, except Part 2
                 The Man I Love

Benny interrupted the Mosque engagement for a recording session, felt he needed a better drummer for the date, got the very best: Buddy Rich. Buddy, who'd recently left Tommy Dorsey and was in the process of assembling his own - first - big band, remembers the gig very well, and is fond of telling this tale.

He had long admired Goodman, and still holds him in high regard . . . as a musician, as a jazz clarinetist without equal. He was pleased that Benny had called upon him, and there was no discussion of salary for the gig. A few weeks later, he received Benny's check—and it was for scale, not a penny more than union rules required. Buddy exploded, "Hell, I pay more for my shirts than this," and returned the check uncashed. The kicker? Benny kept it.

In any event, the one side from this session that was released contemporaneously in the United States was the only one on which Rich soloed, "Rattle And Roll." Coincidentally, its arranger and composer (although both Benny and Count Basie are additionally credited) was Buck Clayton, a sergeant in the U.S. Army, then stationed just before his discharge at nearby Camp Kilmer, New Jersey.

BENNY GOODMAN AND HIS ORCHESTRA   December 19, 1945, New York

Personnel as orchestra, November 28, except Butterfield and Hucko definite (Faso and Carl out), and BUDDY RICH, d, replaces Sheble for the recording session only. BUCK CLAYTON (BuC), arr.

CO 35237-3   **LP**: VELP 1, PHON 7652
CO 35237-4   CoE DB2443, CoAu SV55. **7" 33 and 45:** CO "Priceless
                 Editions" PE 10. **LP**: SWE 1001
               Lucky (as "You're Right-I'm Wrong" on PE 10) (arr ES)
CO 35523-1   CO 36988, VD 683 B, CoC 815, CoE DB2333, CoFr
                 BF135, CoSw DZ504, ReSp C8830. **LP**: FONT
                 TFL5067, NOST 1004, DAN VC5003, SWE 1001
               Rattle And Roll (arr BuC)
CO 35524-1   **LP**: PHON 7652
CO 35524-2A   UNISSUED - Test Pressing
               Sweet I've Gotten On You-voc Liza Morrow

The next evening's broadcast brought Art Lund back to the fold, if only temporarily: program logs and extant air checks for the balance of the Terrace Room engagement fail to show his presence. According to the announcer, Lund had just returned from military service (he was a Naval lieutenant), and apparently is here as a guest. He will rejoin Benny formally the end of the month.

SUSTAINING BROADCAST   *December 20, 1945,*
  MUTUAL Radio Network   *Terrace Room, Newark, N.J.*

Personnels as November 28.

I'm Always Chasing Rainbows-voc Art Lund
Lucky
*Rattle And Roll (**LP**: PHON 7605)*
*Rose Room - SEXTET (**LP**: PHON 7605)*
*Flying Home (**LP**: PHON 7605)*
*King Porter Stomp (**LP**: PHON 7605, SWT 103)*
Good-Bye (theme)

SUSTAINING BROADCAST   *December 21, 1945,*
  CBS Radio Network   *Terrace Room, Newark, N.J.*

Personnel as November 28.

Give Me The Simple Life-voc Liza Morrow
Lucky
Star Dust
King Porter Stomp
Clarinade
Baby, Won't You Please Come Home (arr FH)
It's Been A Long, Long Time-voc Liza Morrow
Good-Bye (theme)

A number of extant air checks certain to have originated in the Terrace Room are undated, and must be ascribed to the period, November 28 - December 23, the final day of the engagement. They begin with a broadcast transcribed by AFRS:

AFRS MAGIC CARPET 199A   **November 28/December 23, 1945**
                                    Terrace Room, Newark, N.J.

Personnel as November 28.

U 6567-1   **ET**: AFRS Magic Carpet 199A
             Let's Dance (theme)
             Don't Be That Way (LP: PHON 7603)
             You Was Right, Baby-voc Liza Morrow (LP: PHON 7603)
             Seven Come Eleven (LP: PHON 7603)
             I'm In The Mood For Love-voc Liza Morrow (n/c)

SUSTAINING BROADCAST   *Nov. 28/Dec. 23, 1945,*
  ABC Radio Network   *Terrace Room, Newark, N.J.*

Personnel as November 28.

Lucky
Clarinet A La King
My Guy's Come Back-voc Liza Morrow (n/c - Intro only)

SUSTAINING BROADCAST   *Nov. 28/Dec. 23, 1945,*
  ABC Radio Network   *Terrace Room, Newark, N.J.*

Personnel as November 28.

Let's Dance (theme)
Stompin' At The Savoy (misintroduced as, "King Porter Stomp")
My Guy's Come Back-voc Liza Morrow (n/c - ending only)
Air Mail Special
Gotta Be This Or That, Part 2 - to signoff

SUSTAINING BROADCAST   *Nov. 28/Dec. 23, 1945,*
  ABC Radio Network   *Terrace Room, Newark, N.J.*

Personnel as November 28.

Flying Home
Clarinet A La King (incorporating, "Oh, Baby!")
Tuesday At Ten
Good-Bye (theme)

SUSTAINING BROADCAST | Nov. 28/Dec. 23, 1945,
ABC Radio Network | Terrace Room, Newark, N.J.

Personnel as November 28.

Lucky
Clarinade (n/c - intro only)
King Porter Stomp
Good-Bye (theme)

SUSTAINING BROADCAST | Nov. 28/Dec. 23, 1945,
MUTUAL Radio Network | Terrace Room, Newark, N.J.

Personnel as November 28.

Seven Come Eleven
The Man I Love - feat. Red Norvo (no vocal)
Somebody Stole My Gal

SUSTAINING BROADCAST | Nov. 28/Dec. 23, 1945,
MUTUAL Radio Network | Terrace Room, Newark, N.J.

Personnel as November 28.

You Brought A New Kind Of Love To Me-voc Liza Morrow (n/c)
I'm Here
King Porter Stomp - to signoff

SUSTAINING BROADCAST | Nov. 28/Dec. 23, 1945,
Unknown radio network | Terrace Room, Newark, N.J.

Personnel as November 28.

I'm Always Chasing Rainbows (no vocal)
Clarinade (n/c - intro only)
Rattle And Roll (n/c - ending only)

SUSTAINING BROADCAST | Nov. 28/Dec. 23, 1945,
Unknown radio network | Terrace Room, Newark, N.J.

Personnel as November 28.

Let's Dance (theme)
These Foolish Things-voc Liza Morrow (n/c - intro clipped)
One O'Clock Jump (n/c - intro clipped)

An unlabeled acetate affords an air check dated December 25; it offers no other information save a handwritten opinion that the pianist is Johnny Guarnieri. The announcer's introduction indicates that the program is sponsored . . . On that basis, the air check is ascribed to the Philip Morris broadcast on which Benny is known to have appeared; and we leave the judgment as to whether the pianist is Guarnieri, or Mel Powell, to the listener:

"JOHNNY PRESENTS" | December 25, 1945, New York
NBC Radio Network

Benny Goodman, clt; Mel Powell or JOHNNY GUARNIERI, p; Bob Sheble, d.

Home

Back on solid ground, we find Benny in Columbia's studios the next day for a classical performance of the Brahms' Sonata with Nadia Reisenberg:

BENNY GOODMAN, NADIA REISENBERG   **December 26, 1945, New York**

Benny Goodman, clt; Nadia Reisenberg, p.

XCO 35536-1B | CO 71816-D (Set MM 629-1), CoC 15983 (Set D 170-1)
**Brahms - Sonata No. 2 In E-Flat Major
For Clarinet and Piano, Opus 120, No. 2
First Movement: Allegro amabile (Beginning)**

XCO 35537-1A | CO 71817-D (Set MM 629-2). CoC 15984 (Set D 170-2)
**Brahms - Sonata No. 2 In E-Flat Major
For Clarinet and Piano, Opus 120, No. 2
First Movement: Allegro amabile (Conclusion)**

XCO 35538-2D | CO 71818-D (Set MM 629-3), CoC 15985 (Set D 170-3)
**Brahms - Sonata No. 2 in E-Flat Major
For Clarinet and Piano, Opus 120, No. 2
Second Movement: Allegro appassionato (Beginning)**

XCO 35539-2A | CO 71818-D (Set MM 629-4), CoC 15985 (Set D 170-4)
**Brahms - Sonata No. 2 In E-Flat Major
For Clarinet and Piano, Opus 120, No. 2
Second Movement: Allegro appassionato (Conclusion)
Third Movement: Andante con moto (Theme and
Variations) (Beginning)**

XCO 35540-1B | CO 71817-D (Set MM 629-5), CoC 15984 (Set D 170-5)
**Brahms - Sonata No. 2 In E-Flat Major
For Clarinet and Piano, Opus 120, No. 2
Third Movement: Andante con moto (Theme and
Variations) (Continued)**

XCO 35541-1B | CO 71816-D (Set MM 629-6), CoC 15983 (Set D 170-6)
**Brahms - Sonata No. 2 In E-Flat Major
For Clarinet and Piano, Opus 120, No. 2
Third Movement: Andante con moto (Theme and
Variations) (Conclusion)**

(Above is also on **LP**, CO CL629.)

Probably in December, Benny was interviewed by Russ Hughes for a broadcast series titled, "Song And Dance Parade." The sponsor of the transcribed program was the magazine, The Saturday Evening Post. Between talk, Hughes spun records. In part, the transcription was broadcast January 16, 1946, via radio station WJR, Detroit, Michigan.

A report that BG is on AFRS ET Basic Music Library P566 is in error. The ET is represented as a transcription of Esquire's Third Annual All-American Jazz Festival, held in New York in December. Its label lists Benny Goodman as clarinetist; but the recordings on it are the Metronome All-Star Victor studio recordings of "Look Out" and "Metronome All Out," which of course feature clarinetist Buddy DeFranco.

Before we leave 1945, and as a bridge to 1946, we list two air checks whose acetates offer no information at all. They may have originated in the Terrace Room engagement just ended, or the Meadowbrook stand upcoming—or from a source whose identity is beyond conjecture . . . ?

RADIO BROADCASTS | poss. 1945/1946,
Unknown radio networks | locations unknown

Benny Goodman and his Orchestra: personnel unknown.

I Can't Believe That You're In Love With Me
Clarinet A La King

Benny went directly from New York to the West Coast where he began an engagement in the Meadowbrook Gardens, Culver City, Calif., on January 3. A broadcast via the Mutual-Don Lee network finds a few new faces in the band:

SUSTAINING BROADCAST | January 3, 1946
MUTUAL-Don Lee Radio Network | Meadowbrook Gardens,
| Culver City, Calif.

Benny Goodman, clt; Bernie Privin, John Best, DALE "BRODIE" SCHROFF, tpt; Chauncey Welsch, Kai Winding, tbn; Bill Shine, Gerry Sanfino, as; Stan Getz, HOWARD "GISH" GILBERTSON, ts; Danny Bank, bar; Mel Powell, p; Mike Bryan, g; Barney Spieler, b; CHARLIE GREEN d. Liza Morrow, ART LUND, voc.

QUINTET: BG, Powell, Bryan, Spieler, Green.

Let's Dance (theme)
Who's Sorry Now?-voc Liza Morrow (arr MP)
Clarinade
I'm Always Chasing Rainbows-voc Art Lund
Runnin' Wild - QUINTET
Good-Bye (theme)

(Above on **LP**, MARK 736)

An undated 16" acetate offers another 15-minute broadcast via Mutual-Don Lee. It may also have come from opening night, but that is uncertain. If not, it most likely was from early in January:

SUSTAINING BROADCAST
MUTUAL-Don Lee Radio Network

*early January 1946,
Meadowbrook Gardens,
Culver City, Calif.*

Personnels as January 3.

*Let's Dance (theme)
Somebody Stole My Gal
Symphony-voc Liza Morrow
Runnin' Wild - QUINTET
King Porter Stomp - to signoff*

(Above on LP, MARK 736. Note that the Lp appends "Good-Bye" from the January 3 broadcast to this "early January" transcription.)

Discovery of two 16″ acetates, respectively inscribed, "Master Acetate No. 4" and "Master Acetate No. 5," resolves earlier erroneous attributions of V-Discs and AFRS ET's to "prob. May 1945." They pinpoint a recording date of January 11, and further provide continuity between the cuts in which the musicians practice, and Benny and the producer get testy with each other over what tunes might be played.

The material is listed in order-of-recording, via the 16″ discs. "Matrix" numbers are taken from released V-Discs and AFRS ET's.

BENNY GOODMAN QUINTET   January 11, 1946, Hollywood

Benny Goodman, clt; Mel Powell, p; Mike Bryan, g; Barney Spieler, b; JOHNNY DeSOTO, d.

"matrices" per releases	ET: AFRS Basic Music Library P570 (mx SSL-1138). 78: VD 644 B (mx D6-TC-5062-1G/JDB29). LP: PHON 7654, DAN 5002, ELEC KV119, SB 143 **Exactly Like You**
"	ET: AFRS Basic Music Library P570 (mx SSL-1138). LP: PHON 7654 **Sweet Georgia Brown**
"	ET: AFRS Basic Music Library P597 (mx SSL-1179). 78: VD 694 B (mx D6-TC-5296-1A/JDB117). LP: PHON 7654, DAN 5002, ELEC KV119, SB 143 **Oh Lady Be Good** (sic)

BENNY GOODMAN TRIO   same session

Benny Goodman, clt; Mel Powell, p; Johnny De Soto, d.

| XP 35739-1C (JDB23) | VD 615 A. LP: PHON 7654, DAN 5002, ELEC KV119, SB 143 **I Want To Be Loved** |

BENNY GOODMAN QUINTET   same session

As "Exactly Like You."

| - 0 - | LP: PHON 7654 **"The Blues In B Flat"** |
| SSL-1138 | ET: AFRS Basic Music Library P570. LP: PHON 7654 **Rose Room** |

(Note that PHON 7654 transcribes the material between the selections listed above.)

The next date of which we are certain is January 14, but the identity of the drummer is unknown—when announcing the members of the Quintet, Benny fails to name him. It may be Charlie Green, Johnny DeSoto, or even a "Charlie Perry," cited by some press reports as in the band during the Meadowbrook engagement.

SUSTAINING BROADCAST
MUTUAL-Don Lee Radio Network

*January 14, 1946
Meadowbrook Gardens,
Culver City, Calif.*

Personnels as January 3, except unknown d.

*Somebody Stole My Gal (n/c - intro excised)
My Guy's Come Back-voc Liza Morrow (LP: RED 1001)
Body And Soul - QUINTET (LP: RED 1001, Quicksilver 5046)
I'm Always Chasing Rainbows-voc Art Lund (LP: RED 1001)
Oh, Lady Be Good! - QUINTET (LP: Quicksilver 5046)
Waitin' For The Train To Come In-voc Art Lund*

*Rattle And Roll
I Wish I Could Tell You-voc Liza Morrow - segue to,
Good-Bye (theme)*

(Except "Somebody Stole My Gal", "Body And Soul" and "I'm Always Chasing Rainbows," above on LP, GOJ 1017.)

Next is a spate of AFRS-transcribed material, and only the date of the first ET is known. It comes from Nelson Eddy's Sunday evening series, and offers an amusing build-up and intro to, "Shortnin' Bread":

AFRS NELSON EDDY PROGRAM No. 48   January 20, 1946, Hollywood

Benny Goodman, clt, and a studio orchestra conducted by Robert Armbruster. Nelson Eddy, voc.

| SS-1-20-7 | ET: AFRS Nelson Eddy Program No. 48 - Part 1 **More Than You Know** **Shortnin' Bread**-voc Nelson Eddy |

(Benny does not appear on Part 2 of the ET.)

Probably in the latter half of January, Benny participated in another of NBC's broadcasts to the Armed Forces, along with Gene Krupa and his Trio (Gene's new band was in the Hollywood Palladium), Lena Horne, Joe Liggins and his Honeydrippers, Slam and Bam, Art Tatum, and MC Ernie "Bubbles" Whitman. A transcription of the actual short-wave broadcast has been unavailable to the author, and thus his listing, via AFRS material, may not be in order-of-performance, given AFRS's penchant for intercutting. Also, a reputed ET, AFRS Jubilee Program No. 167, has not been located, and its contents are unknown.

Only those selections in which Benny or his orchestra participate are listed. In the absence of certainty, performances are omitted; e.g., Lena Horne's "My Silent Love," whose orchestral accompaniment cannot be positively identified, and some opening and closing program themes that may have been dubbed into the ET's from another source.

AFRS JUBILEE SERIES H-11 PROGRAM No. 166   January 1946, Hollywood

Personnels as January 14.

| HD-6- MM-4605-1 | ET: AFRS Jubilee Series H-11 Program No. 166 - Part 1 **One O'Clock Jump** (theme - prob. BG orchestra) **Lucky (You're Right-I'm Wrong)** **More And More**-voc Lena Horne |
| HD-6- MM-4606-1 | ET: as above, except Part 2 **Runnin' Wild** - QUINTET **Come To Baby Do**-voc Lena Horne (78: VD 614 B (mx D6-TC-5064-1B/JDB31)) **King Porter Stomp** - coda only - BG orchestra plus Gene Krupa, Joey Preston, d **Rattle And Roll** **Good-Bye** (theme - 1st note only - segue to "Jubilee" theme) |

(Excerpts from the above are also on LP, PHON 7603, RS unnumbered 12″, DAN 5002, GOJ 1017, SB 143, Quicksilver 5046. Note that Lena Horne's VD 631 (also on AFRS Basic Music Library P116) "Mad About The Boy"/"Why Shouldn't I" is not from this program, and her accompaniment is not by Benny Goodman. Preston is a nine-year-old who swaps single-strokes with Gene.)

AFRS JUBILEE SERIES H-11 PROGRAM No. 168   January 1946, Hollywood

Personnel as January 14.

| HD-6- MM-4690-1 | ET: AFRS Jubilee Series H-11 Program No. 168 - Part 1 **One O'Clock Jump** (theme - see Program No. 166) **Let's Dance** (theme) **Who's Sorry Now?**-voc Liza Morrow (arr MP) |
| HD-6- MM-4691-1 | ET: as above, except Part 2 **I'm Always Chasing Rainbows**-voc Art Lund **Good-Bye** (theme) |

(The reader will recall that some tracks on this ET are from an NBC "For The Record" broadcast of July 31, 1944, q.v. Orchestral accompaniment for Lena Horne's "My Silent Love" on this ET does not seem to be Goodman's. Excerpts from this ET are on LP, GOJ 1017.)

The next AFRS "Goodman" ET is a hodge-podge of dubbed Columbia records ("Let's Dance," "Wang Wang Blues" and "The World Is Waiting For The Sunrise") and original performances. Their ambience suggests that the originals are AFRS-produced studio recordings, certainly not excerpts from sustaining broadcasts. They may come from the "Jubilee" program preceding, but the guess here is that they are from a different session, date unknown. Benny's chit chat with announcer Al Buffington may have been recorded January 23, when Benny's spoken intros to various V-Discs from this period were cut.

AFRS DOWNBEAT SERIES H-7 PROGRAM No. 206/207 January 1946, Hollywood

Personnel as January 14.

H-7 206 **ET**: AFRS Downbeat Series H-7 Program No. 206
Somebody Stole My Gal (**ET**: AFRS Basic Music Library P597)
Moonlight On The Ganges (**ET**: AFRS Basic Music Library P533)
It's The Talk Of The Town-voc Art Lund (arr MP) (**ET**: AFRS Basic Music Library P533)

H-7 207 **ET**: AFRS Downbeat Series H-7 Program No. 207
Who's Sorry Now?-voc Liza Morrow (**78**: VD 760 B (mx D7-TC-7131-1C/JDB348)) (**ET**: AFRS Basic Music Library P533.)

(Intro to "Who's Sorry Now?" on AFRS Downbeat 207 is clipped, but otherwise it is the same version as the V-Disc and AFRS BML P533. "Somebody Stole My Gal" is erroneously ascribed to a "Quintet" on AFRS BML P597. Excerpts from the two-sided ET above are also on **LP**, PHON 7603, DAN 5002, JAZ 27, SB 144)

Those who have been waiting with forbearance for the entrance of Lou McGarity and vibraphonist Johnny White into the Goodman roster must still wait the arrival of McGarity, for he is unidentifiable until the Columbia session the end of this month. But their patience is in part rewarded: Johnny White joins on the 26th, and a transcribed broadcast features him on his first night with the band.

SUSTAINING BROADCAST *January 26, 1946,*
MUTUAL-Don Lee Radio Network *Meadowbrook Gardens, Culver City, Calif.*

Personnel as January 14, with DeSoto, d.

SEXTET: BG; JOHNNY WHITE, vib; Powell, Bryan, Spieler, DeSoto.
TRIO: BG, Powell, DeSoto.

Swing Angel
Oh, Baby! - SEXTET
Limehouse Blues - SEXTET
Clarinade
Sweet Lorraine - TRIO - segue to,
Good-Bye (theme)

(Above on LP, JOY 1056, JOY 1097.)

Two hitherto-undocumented AFRS ET's are undated, but come from the period January 26 through January 29, because they include White but fail to give evidence of McGarity. Again, AFRS's disturbing practice of intercutting selections from one program to another prevents our saying, "This ET is from one broadcast." Quite obviously, the reprise in each ET following "Seven Come Eleven" is not, sequentially, in accord with the selections preceding it on either ET, and it may come from still another broadcast from Culver City. Too, the selections on these ET's should be cross-checked carefully with other ET's from this period, to determine if there are duplications; the author may have missed some.

AFRS MAGIC CARPET No. 220 January 26–29, 1946, Culver City, California

Personnels as January 26.

U 7346 **ET**: AFRS Magic Carpet No. 220
(SUR 2-5-6) **Let's Dance** (theme)
Sweetheart-voc Art Lund (arr MP)
Oh, Baby! - SEXTET
I Wish I Could Tell You-voc Liza Morrow
Swing Angel - to signoff
reprise: **Seven Come Eleven** (same as on **ET**, AFRS Magic Carpet No. 225)

AFRS MAGIC CARPET No. 225 January 26–29, 1946, Culver City, California

Personnels as January 26

U 7490 **ET**: AFRS Magic Carpet No. 225
(SUR 2-10-1) **Let's Dance** (theme)
Give Me The Simple Life-voc Liza Morrow
After You've Gone - SEXTET
It's The Talk Of The Town-voc Art Lund (arr MP)
Incognito-to signoff (prob. arr BuC)
reprise: **Seven Come Eleven** (same as on **ET**, AFRS Magic Carpet No. 220)

The bulk of the material on the next ET is from a broadcast of January 27 from the Meadowbrook Gardens. But its penultimate "Don't Be That Way" is brought forward from December 1945's AFRS Magic Carpet 199A ET, and its reprise, "Moonlight On The Ganges," is a partial repeat from Side 1. Further, Mel Powell's solo on "I'll Remember April," may also be heard on ET's under dates of February 2, 1946 and June 5, 1946, q.v.

AFRS ONE NIGHT STAND No. 856 January 27, 1946, Culver City, California

Personnels as January 26.

SSC-1-28-1 **ET**: AFRS One Night Stand No. 856 - Part 1
Let's Dance (theme)
Who's Sorry Now?-voc Liza Morrow (**LP**: PHON 7603)
Moonlight On The Ganges
I Wish I Could Tell You-voc Liza Morrow
Stompin' At The Savoy - SEXTET

SSC-1-28-2 **ET**: as above, except Part 2
Sweetheart-voc Art Lund (**LP**: JS 508)
I'll Remember April - Powell solo
Incognito
(**Don't Be That Way** - ET, AFRS Magic Carpet No. 199A)
reprise: **Moonlight On The Ganges** - Part 1

After so much "free" recording for AFRS, Benny decided it was about time he made some commercial sides for Columbia. To do so he revamped his orchestra for the studio date by adding Hollywood sideman Mannie Klein to his trumpet section, revising his trombone section—McGarity now enters—and bringing back drummer Ralph Collier. And the session would feature a chart by an arranger new to the band, Sonny Burke, that would become very popular with his post-war audiences, "On The Alamo."

"On The Alamo" also presents a discographical problem: How to list a recently-discovered, 12" shellac test pressing, clearly inscribed with a take "1," when the released 78 Columbia is also inscribed take 1—and the two are different? There seems no rational explanation for this oddity, and no infallible method of listing it that will obviate misinterpretation—other than to make this prior explanation.

BENNY GOODMAN AND HIS ORCHESTRA January 30, 1946, Los Angeles

Benny Goodman, clt; Bernie Privin, John Best, Brodie Schroff, MANNIE KLEIN, tpt; LOU McGARITY, HOYT BOHANNON, tbn; Bill Shine, Gerry Sanfino, as; Stan Getz, Gish Gilbertson, ts; Danny Bank, bar; Mel Powell, p; Mike Bryan, g; Barney Spieler, b; RALPH COLLIER, d. Liza Morrow, Art Lund, voc SONNY BURKE (SB), arr.

HCO 1670-1	**LP**: PHON 7652
	Sweetheart-voc Art Lund (arr MP)
HCO 1671-1	CO 36955, CoC 795, CoE DB2416, **LP**: CBS 52964, JOY 6015. **ET**: AFRS Basic Music Library P582
HCO 1671-2	VD 805 B (mx D7-TC-7353-1/JB387). **LP**: NOST 1004, SB 144
	It's The Talk Of The Town-voc Art Lund (arr MP)

Add: (Earl) DICK LeFAVE, tbn.

HCO 1672-1	CO 36955, CoArg 291653, CoC 795, CoE DB2443. **LP**: FONT TFL5067, FontCont 682047TL, SWE 1001. **ET**: AFRS Basic Music Library P582
	Swing Angel (arr BuC)
HCO 1673-1 (12″)	**LP**: PHON 7654
HCO 1673-1 (10″)	CO 36988, CoC 815, PaE R3018. **LP**: CO CL6100, CO CL2533, CBS 52964, JOY 6015
	On The Alamo-voc Art Lund (arr SB)

In passing, it should be noted that, contrary to published reports, Benny does not perform "Sweetheart" in Metro-Goldwyn-Mayer's motion picture, "The Hoodlum Saint." Benny had no association with that 1946 movie.

AFRS took one final swipe at Benny for the month of January; He appeared on Frank's "Songs By Sinatra" ABC radio program that Wednesday evening, and the program is on ET:

AFRS FRANK SINATRA SHOW No. 20   January 30, 1946, Los Angeles

Benny Goodman, clt; Johnny White, vib; Mel Powell, p; Mike Bryan, g; Barney Spieler, b; Ralph Collier, d. Frank Sinatra, voc.

HD-6- MM-4790-1 (SSV 2-2-1)	**ET**: AFRS Frank Sinatra Show No. 20 - Part 1 **Stompin' At The Savoy** (n/c) **After You've Gone** (n/c) **I Only Have Eyes For You**-voc Frank Sinatra (**LP**: ARTISTRY 106)
HD-6- MM-4791-1 (SSV 2-2-2)	**ET**: as above, except Part 2 **Runnin' Wild**

January 30 was the final day of the Meadowbrook Gardens engagement; Benny next began a brief stand at the Mission Beach Ballroom, in Mission Beach, San Diego, on Saturday, February 2. It seems likely that Benny carried three trumpets and two trombones for this engagement, and that he added two brass for studio sessions only. AFRS transcribed an opening night broadcast onto ET:

AFRS ONE NIGHT STAND No. 872   February 2, 1946, San Diego

Personnel probably as January 30 Columbia session, except trumpets are Privin, Best and Schroff only; and trombones are McGarity and LeFave only.

SEXTET: Personnel as January 30 Sinatra broadcast.

SSC-2-13-1	**ET**: AFRS One Night Stand No. 872 - Part 1 **Let's Dance** (theme) **Lucky (You're Right-I'm Wrong)** (**I'll Remember April** - Powell solo (dubbed from January 27, 1946, q.v.) **Oh, Lady Be Good!** - SEXTET **Rattle And Roll** (**LP**: PHON 7603)

SSC-2-13-2	**ET**: as above, except Part 2 **After You've Gone** - SEXTET (dubbed to June 5, 1946, q.v.) **I Wish I Could Tell You**-voc Liza Morrow **On The Alamo**-voc Art Lund **Who's Sorry Now?**-voc Liza Morrow (**Hallelujah!** - Powell, Collier **Good-Bye** (theme)

BENNY GOODMAN AND HIS ORCHESTRA February 6, 1946, Los Angeles

Personnel as January 30 Columbia session, except NATE KAZEBIER, tpt, replaces Klein, and EDDIE BENSON, tbn, replaces Bohannon, joining McGarity and LeFave. JOHNNY THOMPSON (JT), arr.

HCO 1684-1	CO 37053, CoC 828, PaAu A7583. **LP**: JOY 6015
	I Don't Know Enough About You-voc Art Lund

Add: Johnny White, vib.

HCO 1685-1	CO 36967, CoArg 291649, CoC 805, CoE DB2463, CoG DW 5225, Colt CQ1875, CoNor GNS5099, PaAu A7563. **LP**: FONT TFL5067, FontCont 682047TL, CBS 52964, CO alb P5-15536. **ET**: AFRS Basic Music Library P597
	All The Cats Join In-voc Liza Morrow and Benny Goodman (and ensemble)

February 10 was the last day of the Mission Beach Ballroom contract, and shortly thereafter, with most of the band intact, Benny flew to New York where he would begin a lengthy engagement in the Paramount Theater on February 27. The evening before the Paramount inaugural he appeared as guest on Chesterfield's CBS radio program, "Supper Club," and AFRS transcribed it:

AFRS SUPPER CLUB No. 262   February 26, 1946, New York

Benny Goodman, clt; Mel Powell, p; COZY COLE, d.

(mx unknown)	**ET**: AFRS Supper Club No. 262 **I Can't Give You Anything But Love, Baby** **Sweet Georgia Brown**

The author has been unable to obtain from Columbia any further information on the recording session of March 8, following; it seems unlikely that Benny would wax but one tune that day. He is, however, able to add one previously-undocumented alternate take to the Sextet's lone, "Don't Be A Baby, Baby";

BENNY GOODMAN SEXTET   March 8, 1946, New York

Benny Goodman, clt; Johnny White, vib; Mel Powell, p; Mike Bryan, g; Barney Spieler, b; Cozy Cole, d. Art Lund, voc.

CO 35952	UNISSUED - Co Ref
CO 35952-3	CO 36967, CoArg 291662, CoC 805. **ET**: CoE SEG7524, CoFr ESDF1023. **LP**: SONY 20AP-1810, JOY 6015
	Don't Be A Baby, Baby-voc Art Lund

The same personnel (sans Lund) recorded one cut that to date has only surfaced on an AFRS ET. Whether it stems from the abbreviated Columbia session of March 8, or whether it comes from an AFRS studio session is unknown. If either or neither, this time period is likely correct.

AFRS BASIC MUSIC LIBRARY P597   prob. March 1946, New York

Instrumental personnel as March 8.

SS1-1179	**ET**: AFRS Basic Music Library P597 **Running Wild**

(The ET's label adds a final "g" to "Runnin'.")

The author's earlier work on Goodman speculated that a Department of State ET that includes one track by, "Benny Goodman, Clarinetist; Ted Dale Orchestra," might also have been recorded in March 1946. Wrong—by some two years. Its "Rose Room" is from an April 19, 1948 broadcast of the "Buddy Clarke - (Carnation Milk) Contented Hour," q.v.

The condensed milk company adds to our discontent: A report that the Library of Congress has, or at one time had, a Voice Of America transcription of a "Contented Hour" broadcast of April 15, 1946, still eludes confirmation. Reputedly, it offers Benny with the program's studio orchestra performing, "More Than You Know" and "Dizzy Fingers." Efforts to determine the validity of this report are continuing.

April 16 marked the end of the Paramount engagement. From there the band went first to the Earle Theater in Philadelphia; the author, just out of military service, renewed acquaintances with Lou McGarity, and was pleasantly surprised by Louis Bellson's improvement on the tubs, evidenced in an extended, "Oh, Baby!". Bellson (Balassoni), who'd been with Goodman in 1942–1943, first attracted notice when he'd won a drum contest sponsored by Slingerland. The contest's requirements were two: play the drums, and look like Gene Krupa! Louis did resemble, Gene, sort of . . .

Following the week at the Earle, the band went to Boston. Then it returned to New York, in anticipation of its engagement at the 400 Restaurant. The band's complement had changed over time—an important defection was Stan Getz's leaving to join Gene Krupa; ironically, Gene's band preceded Benny's in the 400—and its revised personnel is reflected in the next studio session, two days before it settled down in the 400. Note that in compensation for Getz's absence, Cutty Cutshall returns.

BENNY GOODMAN AND HIS ORCHESTRA — May 14, 1946, New York

Benny Goodman clt; Bernie Privin, John Best, Nate Kazebier, JIMMY BLAKE, tpt; Lou McGarity, CUTTY CUTSHALL, tbn; ADDISON COLLINS, Fr-h; Bill Shine, JOHN PRAGER, as; Gish Gilbertson, CLIFF STRICKLAND, ts; Danny Bank, bar; Mel Powell, p; Mike Bryan, g; Barney Spieler, b; LOUIS BELLSON, d; Johnny White vib. Art Lund, Johnny White, voc. Johnny White (JW) arr

XCO 36286	**LP**: PHON 7654
XCO 36286-Bkdn	UNISSUED - Tape
XCO 36286-1	CO 55039, PaE E11453. **LP**: CO CL6048, CBS 52964, FR series
XCO 36286-2	CO 55039, PaE E11453, CoC 25020, PaE DPX40. **LP**: TL STLJ05

Oh, Baby! (Part 1)-voc Benny Goodman (arr MP)

XCO 36287	**LP**: PHON 7654
XCO 36287-2	CO 55039, CoC 25020, PaE DPX40, poss. PaE 11453. **LP**: TL STLJ05
XCO 36287	UNISSUED - Tape
XCO 36287-1	CO 55039, PaE E11453, **LP**: CO CL 6048, CBS 52964, FR series
XCO 36287	UNISSUED - Tape

Oh, Baby! (Part 2) (arr MP)

CO 36288-1	CO 37053, CoArg 291676, CoC 828, PaE R3018, Palt B71199. **EP**: CO B461. **LP**: CO CL599, CBS 52964, JOY 6015

Blue Skies-voc Art Lund

CO 36289-1	**EP**: CoE SEG7524, CoFr ESDF1023. **LP**: PHON 7654

I Ain't Mad At Nobody-voc Johnny White (arr JW)

A plethora of reasonably good-audio-quality acetates provides a panorama of Benny's four-week gig at the 400, beginning with a broadcast from opening night. Note that over time some changes take place, and these are suggested in the collective personnel for the first listing. Note too that some of the orchestral performances (e.g., "Oh, Baby!") include Johnny White, and that his participation is not separately shown, but is understood.

SUSTAINING BROADCAST poss.
MUTUAL Radio Network
May 16, 1946,
400 Restaurant, New York

Orchestra: As May 14, except DICK MAINS, tpt; LARRY MOLINELLI, as; RALPH LaPOLLA as/bar, may substitute in the respective sections.

SEXTET; BG, White, Powell, Bryan, Spieler, Bellson

All The Cats Join In (n/c - intro only)
Don't Be A Baby, Baby-voc Art Lund
Tiger Rag - SEXTET
Come Rain Or Come Shine-voc Art Lund
Oh, Baby!, Parts 1 & 2 (n/c)

SUSTAINING BROADCAST
Unknown radio network
May 19, 1946,
400 Restaurant, New York

Personnels as May 16.

Mission To Moscow
Rattle And Roll
I Got Rhythm - SEXTET
Love Doesn't Grow On Trees (n/c - intro only)
Ain't Misbehavin' - SEXTET
It's The Talk Of The Town-voc Art Lund (n/c)
On The Alamo-voc Art Lund
Who's Sorry Now? (complete - to signoff)

SUSTAINING BROADCAST
Unknown radio network
May 19, 1946,
400 Restaurant, New York

Personnels as May 16.

All The Cats Join In-voc ensemble
After You've Gone - SEXTET
Blue Skies-voc Art Lund
Just One Of Those Things - SEXTET
Lucky (You're Right-I'm Wrong)

SUSTAINING BROADCAST
NBC Radio Network
May 22, 1946,
400 Restaurant, New York

Personnels as May 16.

Let's Dance (theme)
Just You, Just Me
Fly By Night
They Say It's Wonderful - TRIO
Swing Angel
Sentimental Baby-voc Art Lund
The World Is Waiting For The Sunrise - SEXTET
Fascinating Rhythm
Good-Bye (in its entirety)

SUSTAINING BROADCAST
ABC Radio Network
May 22, 1946,
400 Restaurant, New York

Personnels as May 16.

Let's Dance (theme)
*Something New (**LP**: PHON 7605)*
More Than You Know
*Tiger Rag - SEXTET (**LP**: PHON 7605)*
Don't Be A Baby, Baby-voc Art Lund (n/c)
Oh, Baby!, Parts 1 & 2-voc Benny Goodman

Next, a previously-undocumented ET, transcribed from NBC's "Teen Timers Club," a program featuring vocalist John Conte at this time, and invited guests. Note that Benny's clarinet is not heard during Conte's vocals with the full band.

AFRS TEEN TIMERS CLUB No. 10 — May 25, 1946, New York

Personnels as May 16, John Conte, voc.

U 59859 (SUR 8-1-7)	**ET**: AFRS Teen Timers Club No. 10

Somebody Loves Me-voc John Conte
All The Cats Join In
Full Moon And Empty Arms-voc John Conte
Tiger Rag - SEXTET
. . . reprise, **All The Cats Join In**

SUSTAINING BROADCAST
Unknown radio network
May 28, 1946,
400 Restaurant, New York

Personnels as May 16.

I'm Here
I've Got The Sun In The Morning-voc Art Lund (n/c)
Oh, Lady Be Good! - SEXTET
Don't Be A Baby, Baby-voc Art Lund
Laughin' On The Outside (Cryin' On The Inside)-voc Art Lund
I Don't Know Enough About You-voc Art Lund
Oh, Baby! - Part 2

SUSTAINING BROADCAST   *May 30, 1946,*
  CBS Radio Network   *400 Restaurant, New York*

Personnels as May 16.

Let's Dance (theme - final note only)
Gotta Be This Or That, Part 1-voc Benny Goodman (n/c)
Sweet Georgia Brown - SEXTET (n/c - intro clipped)
More Than You Know
All The Cats Join In-voc ensemble
Fly By Night - to signoff

SUSTAINING BROADCAST   *May 31, 1946,*
  ABC Radio Network   *400 Restaurant, New York*

Personnels as May 16.

Oh, Baby!, Part 1-voc Benny Goodman
Can't Help Lovin' Dat Man (n/c - ending excised)
Just One Of Those Things - SEXTET - to signoff

SUSTAINING BROADCAST   *May/June 1946,*
  Unknown radio network   *400 Restaurant, New York*

Personnel as May 16.

On The Alamo-voc Art Lund (n/c - middle excised)

SUSTAINING BROADCAST   *June 2, 1946,*
  CBS Radio Network   *400 Restaurant, New York*

Personnels as May 16.

Clarinade
After You've Gone - SEXTET
Blue Skies-voc Art Lund
Daily Blues
In Love In Vain-voc Art Lund
Fly By Night

Discovery of a half-hour 16″ transcription of NBC's "Bell Telephone Hour" broadcast of June 3, 1946, eliminates speculation that some of the performances on that program might have come from a broadcast of July 29, and relegates previously-known releases to the status of subsidiary issues:

AFRS MUSIC FROM AMERICA No. 188   **June 3, 1946, New York**

Orchestra: Benny Goodman, clt, with Donald Voorhees and his Bell Telephone Orchestra.

SEXTET: As May 16.

SS-6-3-7   **ET**: AFRS Music From America No. 188 - Part 1
(D 4131)   **Concertino for Clarinet and Orchestra, von Weber**

SS-6-3-8   **ET**: as above, except Part 2
(D 3560)   **Hymn To The Sun, Rimsky-Korsakoff** (arr Simeon
                  Bellison)
                I Only Have Eyes For You
                After You've Gone - SEXTET
                . . . reprise, **I Only Have Eyes For You**

("After You've Gone" and the Concertino are also on **ET**, Dept. of State Great Artists Concert No. 28 (mx QND6-MM-10285-1/17-3920). The Concertino and "Hymn To The Sun" are also on **ET**, AFRS Basic Music Library SPX11 (mx SSLX-31). "After You've Gone" is also on **LP**, JS AA508, and reputedly, CBS 67268.)

SUSTAINING BROADCAST   *June 4, 1946,*
  NBC Radio Network   *400 Restaurant, New York*

Personnels as May 16.

Frenesi
On The Sunny Side Of The Street - SEXTET
Sentimental Baby-voc Art Lund - to signoff

SUSTAINING BROADCAST   *June 5, 1946,*
  Unknown radio network   *400 Restaurant, New York*

Personnels as May 16.

Lulu's Back In Town (arr FH)
I Ain't Mad At Nobody-voc Johnny White
It Couldn't Be True-voc Art Lund
Shine - SEXTET
It's The Talk Of The Town-voc Art Lund (n/c)
Body And Soul - TRIO
Swing Angel - to signoff

AFRS transcribed a different broadcast of June 5 from the 400, following. Recall that some of its cuts have been dubbed in from earlier ET's, and note that some are dubbed from this ET to a later one:

AFRS ONE NIGHT STAND No. 1024   **June 5, 1946, New York**

Personnels as May 16.

SSC-SP-7-2-1   **ET**: AFRS One Night Stand No. 1024 - Part 1
                Let's Dance (theme)
                Who's Sorry Now?
                Don't Be A Baby, Baby-voc Art Lund
                All The Cats Join In-voc ensemble (**LP**: PHON 7603, JS
                  AA508)
                (**After You've Gone** - SEXTET - from ET, AFRS One
                  Night Stand No. 872)
                (**I'll Remember April** - Powell solo - from ET, AFRS One
                  Night Stand No. 856)

SSC-SP-7-2-2   **ET**: as above, except Part 2
                I've Got The Sun In The Morning-voc Art Lund (**LP**:
                  PHON 7603)
                I Got Rhythm - SEXTET
                I'm Always Chasing Rainbows-voc Art Lund (**LP**: JS
                  AA508)
                Fly By Night - to AFRS signoff (**LP**: JS AA508)

("I'm Always Chasing Rainbows" and "Fly By Night" are dubbed to AFRS One Night Stand No. 1046, June 12, 1946, q.v.)

SUSTAINING BROADCAST   *June 7, 1946,*
  ABC Radio Network   *400 Restaurant, New York*

Personnels as May 16.

They Say It's Wonderful - TRIO
Oh, Baby!, Parts 1 & 2-voc Benny Goodman
Good-Bye (theme)

SUSTAINING BROADCAST   *June 11, 1946,*
  NBC Radio Network   *400 Restaurant, New York*

Personnels as May 16.

Let's Dance (theme)
Stompin' At The Savoy
On The Alamo-voc Art Lund
Rattle And Roll
The World Is Waiting For The Sunrise - SEXTET

Certainly worth mentioning is Lou McGarity's trombone through this period—tremendous, and possibly the best of his career. A persuasive example is to be heard in "Who's Sorry Now?" on the foregoing air checks and ET, and on the upcoming ET, which incidentally ends the listings for this Goodman gig at the 400. Evidently an AFRS engineer shared this view, for he dubbed this particular cut into an AFRS ET whose other selections are from November 1, four and one-half month's worth of memory later.

The whole band is more difficult to evaluate. With the possible exception of the reeds, its personnel was very strong—Best, Privin, Kazebier, McGarity, Cutshall, Powell, Bellson, these are names to conjure musical magic with. But somehow this band never produced really great music, on record or in person. Perhaps it was the lack of outstanding new arrangements—or tunes, for that matter. Perhaps it was that when this band played the old charts, comparisons inevitably were made with the original performances; the new were not the equal of the old. Perhaps it was a matter of aging, tiring . . . Perhaps it was that bands with younger personnel, Kenton, Herman, were playing a more daring kind of jazz, and that Benny's band

P2166-5

On the set of ''The Big Broadcast of 1937,'' July 1936. Privately, Benny was of two minds about his first feature film: He was delighted with the recognition his music was achieving, dismayed that its presentation here was so severely limited. (Photo, Paramount)

Two of the great ones: George Gershwin congratulates Benny Goodman on his orchestra's
huge success at the Madhattan Room, Winter 1936. In 1930, Benny had been in the pit for
the Gershwins' "Strike Up The Band," for which the composer occasionally played piano.
(Photo, courtesy Benny Goodman)

Opening sequence of ''Hollywood Hotel,'' widely acclaimed as the quintessential big band film. One reason may be its spontaneity: Benny insisted that the cameras capture his superbly talented musicians ''live,'' no matter the technical difficulties.   (Photo, Vitaphone, Inc.)

The Quartet as they appear in ''Hollywood Hotel.'' Half a century later, their studio and performance recordings remain exemplars for the small groups that succeeded them. (Photo, Vitaphone, Inc.)

Benny never thought of Helen Forrest as "his" vocalist, although her tenure with Goodman was as long as Martha Tilton's. Her rapture here, and the many great performances they made together, belie their fragile relationship.   (Photo, Metronome)

Just four months after his Mayo Clinic operation caused him to disband, Benny returns with a
new complement to record for Columbia. Cootie Williams (not shown) also joined, leaving
Duke Ellington for a year's stay with Goodman.   (Photo, courtesy Frank Driggs)

The years of World War II proved to be Benny's most prolific Hollywood period; he was featured in six movies between 1942 and 1944. The band on the set of ''The Powers Girl,'' September 1942.

(Photo, United Artists)

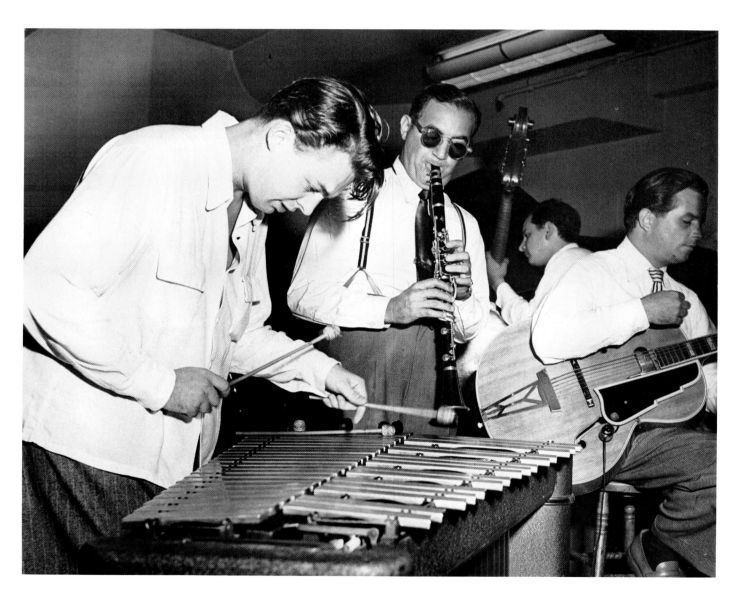

From left, Johnny White, Benny, Trigger Alpert, and Mike Bryan broadcast ''live'' during
radio station WNEW's 24-hour tribute, ''Benny Goodman Day,'' July 24, 1946. An excellent
tape of the broadcast is extant.   (Photo, Conrad Eiger)

Charlie Barnet, Tommy Dorsey, Louis Armstrong, and Lionel Hampton surround Benny Goodman, in his role as the long-haired Professor Magenbruch, on the set of ''A Song Is Born,'' July 1947. With a rhythm section added, they constituted the film's ''Leaders' Orchestra.''   (Photo, RKO-Goldwyn)

Ala Dizzy Gillespie: Francis Beecher, Clyde Lombardi, Wardell Grey, Sonny Igoe, and
Benny sport berets to prove that they, too, play Bop. Crosley Radio broadcast their December
1948 efforts from New York's famed "Stork Club."   (Photo, Popsie)

Benny's bop band at the Hollywood Palladium, March 1949. Benny much preferred his customary swing mode, but ironically, the Armed Forces Radio Service chose to record this band extensively during the engagement.   (Photo, courtesy Benny Goodman)

Benny, Clyde Lombardi, Sonny Igoe, Nancy Reed, Dick Hyman (hidden), Zoot Sims, and Roy Eldridge rehearse in New York prior to a Spring 1950 tour of England, Scandinavia, and the Continent. Lombardi and Igoe would be replaced before the Sextet left for England, April 15. (Photo, courtesy Benny Goodman)

For many years, following the early death of his father, Benny was the principal support of his mother, brothers, and sisters. Here Mrs. Goodman, Benny, and sister Ethel celebrate the release of ''The Benny Goodman Story,'' 1956. (Photo, courtesy Benny Goodman)

Goodwill ambassador Goodman delights his hosts by joining a Burmese dancing troupe,
Rangoon, New Year's Day, 1957. An adept dancer himself, Benny insisted his music was
intended more for the ballroom than the concert stage.
(Photo, courtesy Benny Goodman)

Benny's favorite jazz vocalist was Ella Fitzgerald, who ''. . . uses her voice like I play my clarinet.'' Here they rehearse for the 1958 ''Swing Into Spring'' television special, accompanied by Teddy Wilson and Arvell Shaw.   (Photo, Popsie)

At the New York supper club ''21,'' Donna Musgrove, Peggy Lee, and Helen Ward help Benny cut the cake marking his ''25'' years in show business, 1959. The inscription was understated by more than a decade, for Benny played professionally in the early '20s. (Photo, Popsie)

As a gag, Benny dressed in a Disneyland Band parade uniform to welcome wife Alice and daughters Rachel and Benjie to the amusement center, June 1961. The gag worked: they swept past without recognizing him . . . (Photo, courtesy Benny Goodman)

Prime Minister Harold MacMillan of Great Britain, President John F. Kennedy, Benny, Teddy
Wilson, Ed Shaughnessy, George Duvivier, and publicist Larry Meeks at Washington's
Overseas Press Club, April 27, 1962. The Quartet entertained the two heads of state at the
Club's annual luncheon. (Photo, Vincent A. Finnigan)

A joyous Joya Sherrill swings offstage to the appreciative applause of the audience, and Benny's acknowledging, ''Good, good!,'' Moscow, July 1962. A last-minute Goodman choice to make the Russian tour, Joya delighted the Soviet citizenry and the sidemen alike. (Photo, courtesy Benny Goodman)

Ziggy Elman, Chris Griffin, George Koenig, Martha Tilton, Gene Krupa, and Vernon Brown
surround Lionel Hampton, WNEW's William B. Williams, Benny, and Jess Stacy at Benny's
30th anniversary party for his first Carnegie Hall concert, January 16, 1968.   (Photo, Popsie)

Teddy Wilson, Benny, Gene Krupa, and Lionel Hampton at Madison Square Garden, September 21, 1972. In poor health, Gene had put his own kit in storage, borrowed Buddy Rich's drums for this cameo appearance. (Photo, courtesy Benny Goodman)

Count Basie, Benny, Ella Fitzgerald, Doc Severinson, Joe Williams, and Duke Ellington in the finale of the ''Timex All Star Special,'' October 23, 1972. Most of the performances were videotaped the day before, but Benny insisted his Quartet be recorded ''live.''
(Photo, NBC)

From left, John Bunch, Benny, Bucky Pizzarelli; second row, Peter Appleyard, Muriel Zuckerman, Mrs. Pizzarelli, Ethel Goodman, Slam Stewart; top row, John McLevy (with hat). At first Benny didn't want to go, but he had a great time in a Hamburg night club, December 1973.   (Photo, courtesy Benny Goodman)

Rehearsal at Carnegie Hall, September 13, 1974: Benny, Bucky Pizzarelli, Slam Stewart, Zoot
Sims, Grady Tate, Urbie Green, and Peter Appleyard. Goodman's Carnegie Hall concerts
invariably sold out within days of their announcement, and this one was no exception.
(Photo, Jack Bradley)

George Benson, Red Norvo, Jo Jones, Milt Hinton, Teddy Wilson, and Benny rehearse for the
  Public Broadcasting System's tribute to John Hammond, September 10, 1975. The three-hour
television program celebrated Hammond's 40-plus years as a record producer.
(Photo, WTTV, Chicago)

Veterans Day, 1976: Lionel and Teddy join the author as the century-old Lotus Club names
Benny its ''Man Of The Year.'' In keeping with the spirit of the day, the author's gentle roast
of Benny's foibles did not lead to hostilities between them.   (Photo, courtesy Lotus Club)

Wayne Andre, Benny, and Jack Sheldon try to ''get something going'' during the 40th Anniversary Concert, Carnegie Hall, January 1978. Internationally anticipated, it proved an uneven reprise of the 1938 classic it commemorated.   (Photo, Donna Connor)

John Bunch, Benny, Michael Moore, Bucky Pizzarelli, and Ron Davis entertain guests at the
Rainbow Grill, October 1979, at a press party announcing publication of *Benny: King of Swing*,
a pictorial biography (Thames & Hudson, Ltd./William Morrow & Co., Inc.).
(Photo, Donna Connor)

Vocalist Carrie Smith elicits a hearty chuckle from Benny during a rehearsal at Yale University, December 8, 1985. Bassist Murray Wall and tenor saxophonist Ken Peplowski are behind Benny, guitarist Lou Chirillo is obscured by Carrie.   (Photo, Brian Berry)

The band in concert at Yale University, December 8, 1985. Top row: Bellson, Sandke, Eckert, Mosello, Cohen. Second row: Wall, Bert, Barrett (hidden), Pring. Front: Chirillo, Peplowski, Stuckey, Wilson (behind Benny), Nash, Bank. Aronov off camera.   (Photo, Brian Berry)

This charming photograph of Benny's last studio recording session captures the sheer joy he felt whenever he was playing. Interestingly, the photographer is the grandson of classical pianist Nadia Reisenberg, with whom Benny performed in the late 1940s. (Photo, Steve J. Sherman)

The Final Concert: Benny addresses his last audience, June 7, 1986, Wolf Trap, Vienna, Virginia. Photo from the collection of tenor saxophonist Ted Nash, taken by Goodman aide Lloyd Rauch.

was no longer No. 1 without dispute, and did not have to play its guts out night after night to maintain that exalted standing. The American way of life is predicated on competition. In earlier days, competition helped make its music great.

The Sextet played creditably. More than that—it played with precision and polish; the Sextet's rendition of "After You've Gone" on the Bell Telephone ET is faultless. And possibly that capsulates the Sextet's produce and its problem—it played faultlessly, but not excitingly. It's as if it were composed of six Teddy Wilsons, all performing without mistake; sometimes, perfection can be boring. Not that this Sextet was boring, for it was not perfect. But it seemed always to produce the expected, and seldom a surprise. Maybe that's it—this Sextet rarely surprised. Lou McGarity did.

Benny, as ever, played excellently. His solos were well-conceived, well-rounded, sleek. When necessary (or so it seems in retrospect) they were dazzling displays of virtuosity, testifying to Benny's complete control of his instrument. To some this is the acme of perfection—flawless technique, a capability beyond that of other clarinetists. Were there no other Goodman solos than those of 1946, then they would be the standard to which all other jazz clarinet work would be compared.

But that's just the trouble; Goodman is his own standard. Begin with Dodds and Tesch think through Shaw, Bigard and DeFranco to Bilk, Collette, Giuffre and Scott . . . Goodman is his own standard. He played over many years, and his work in any one period must be compared with his work in another, for that is the only meaningful comparison. And his work in 1946 suffers by self-comparison. For whatever reason—a personal thing, the environment, his band—Benny was not stimulated. And his work does not inspire. But remember, the caveat—self-comparison.

AFRS ONE NIGHT STAND No. 1046   June 12, 1946, New York

Personnels as May 16.

SSC-7-24-1   **ET**: AFRS One Night Stand No. 1046 - Part 1
Let's Dance (theme)
Who's Sorry Now?
On The Alamo-voc Art Lund
Tiger Rag - SEXTET
(**I'm Always Chasing Rainbows**-voc Art Lund - from ET, AFRS One Night Stand No. 1024)

SSC-7-24-2   **ET**: as above, except Part 2
(**Fly By Night** - from ET, AFRS One Night Stand No. 1024)
Love Doesn't Grow On Trees-voc Art Lund
Sing, Sing, Sing - Part 1, and Part 2 to fade

("Who's Sorry Now?" is dubbed to AFRS One Night Stand No. 1197, November 1, 1946. q.v. Five cuts, "Who's Sorry Now?" through "Fly By Night," are also on **LP**, JS AA508.)

The next day Benny was back in the studios for another abbreviated recording session; Columbia's files indicate that only one tune was cut. Again, this seems highly unlikely, but further research has discovered nothing more. One remotely possible explanation is that Columbia's brass speculated that a "hot" new tune seemed headed to the top of the pop charts, and there was a rush to record it. But, "Pity The Poor Lobster". . . . ? To the best of the author's knowledge, this opus has never been reissued in any form, anywhere. Not even the pirates have seen fit to bootleg, "Pity The Poor Turkey."

BENNY GOODMAN AND HIS ORCHESTRA   June 13, 1946, New York

Personnel as May 14, except DICK MAINS, tpt, replaces Blake; and RALPH LaPOLLA, as/bar replaces Bank. No vibes. Art Lund, voc.

CO 36519-1   CO 37077, PaAu A7587
Pity The Poor Lobster-voc Art Lund

Out of the 400, and for the balance of the month, Benny is known to have appeared with the NBC Symphony Orchestra, Howard Barlow conducting. No air checks of this performance are known. He also was featured with the Memphis Symphony Orchestra in Dunbar Bowl, Memphis, Tennessee; that recital is not believed to have been broadcast.

On July 1 Benny and the band began a series of weekly broadcasts that started out as a summer replacement for the popular quiz program, "Information Please." Normally, this would have meant only a 13-week engagement. But Goodman was retained when the format of the program was changed with the advent of the fall radio season, and he continued to broad-

cast to the end of June 1947. Thus, what began as three month's air time stretched into a full year.

The series is not well known, even to ardent Goodman enthusiasts. Thus it is not remarkable that only a handful of collectors are aware that this series produced the greatest number of electrical transcriptions Goodman ever recorded—42 certain, and 44 possible, AFRS 16" ET's.

All of the ET's are labelled "BENNY GOODMAN SHOW," and are numbered 1 through 50. Six, however, are falsely labelled; they offer no BG at all, but rather the orchestras of Al Sack and Ray Bloch. Two ET's have never been located, Numbers 14 and 42. What should be "Number 14" is available via NBC acetates: the ET itself may exist. "Number 42," however, probably was never cut; if there is a "Number 42," it does not include material by BG.

So far as it is known, all of the ET's bear matrix numbers that seem to relate to AFRS rebroadcast dates. (The author has access to some of the ET's, and tapes of the Goodman material on all 42 certain ET's.) Valid "BENNY GOODMAN SHOW" ET's Numbers 1 through 24 have actual broadcast dates inscribed on them, with one transposition. Those beyond Number 24 are thought not to have actual broadcast dates inscribed.

NBC carried the program nationally on Monday evenings from 9:30 to 10:00, Daylight Saving Time. (This was changed to Eastern Standard Time when appropriate.) The first 10 programs, July 1 through September 2, originated in New York and were announced as, "The Benny Goodman Music Festival." The first four apparently were unsponsored; commencing with the fifth, the Mobil Oil Company picked up the tab for the entire series.

On September 9, in Hollywood, Benny joined with Danish humorist-pianist Victor Borge in a new format announced as, "The Victor Borge Show Starring Benny Goodman." The probable reason for the merger was that NBC had a contract with Borge for 44 shows, and this program constituted a device to satisfy that contract.

AFRS did not transcribe the first two Hollywood broadcasts, those of September 9 and 16. Instead, the AFRS series of ET's labelled, "BENNY GOODMAN SHOW" for Programs No. 11 and 12 employ replacement music by Al Sack and Ray Bloch.

Beginning with Program No. 13, September 23, the series of ET's includes Borge-Goodman material through Program No. 20, November 11 (assuming the existence of ET No. 14). Then, evidently, AFRS did not transcribe the Borge-Goodman broadcasts of November 18 and 25; but this time AFRS substituted *three* replacement ET's, Numbers 21, 22, and 23, again by Sack and Bloch. The broadcast of December 2 became "BENNY GOODMAN SHOW - Prog. #24." Then, although no broadcast date intervened between this program and the next in the series, Program No. 25 once more contains replacement music by Bloch.

"BENNY GOODMAN SHOW - Prog. #26" was transcribed for the broadcast of December 9; but the broadcasts of December 16, 23, and 30 were omitted entirely by AFRS. Beginning with Program No. 27, January 6, 1947, the series continues in sequence and without interruption, through Program No. 41, April 21, 1947.

The Borge-Goodman broadcast of April 28, 1947 (which would have been ET "Number 42") was preempted for a report on the Moscow Conference by Secretary Of State Gen. George C. Marshall. No replacement ET by AFRS has been located.

The series resumes with Program No. 43, May 5, 1947, and once more continues sequentially through Program No. 50, June 23, 1947. Number 50 is the last known ET, although there was one more Borge-Goodman broadcast, June 30, 1947, which terminated the program. It is unlikely that AFRS transcribed this broadcast; private air checks of it are available.

Only material that includes Benny Goodman is listed. AFRS engineers cross-dubbed BG's efforts throughout the series, perhaps to "fill" air time taken up by commercials. These repeats are indicated following the ET's contents. All selections are by Benny's full band, unless otherwise indicated. Personnels are approximations based on aural evidence, known personnel for commercial recording sessions, and reports in trade papers. "The Mobilgas Orchestra" includes strings, was Benny's regular lineup plus a string section.

Here, then, the initial "BENNY GOODMAN SHOW," with alumna Martha Tilton as Benny's first guest; and including Peter Donald as MC and Bud Collyer as announcer for the New York-based broadcasts.

AFRS BENNY GOODMAN SHOW - PROGRAM #1 July 1, 1946, New York

Benny Goodman, clt; Bernie Privin, John Best, Nate Kazebier, Dick Mains, tpt; Lou McGarity, Cutty Cutshall, tbn; Addison Collins, Fr-h; Larry Molinelli, and John Prager or HYMIE SCHERTZER, as; Gish Gilbertson, Cliff Strickland, ts; Ralph LaPolla, as/bar, or JOHN PEPPER, bar; JOE BUSHKIN, p; Mike Bryan, g; Barney Spieler or JACK LESBERG, b; Louis Bellson, d; Johnny White, vib. Art Lund, voc. Guest: Martha Tilton, voc.

QUINTET: BG, Bushkin, Bryan, Spieler or Lesberg, Bellson

SEXTET: Quintet plus White

"MOBILGAS ORCHESTRA": Benny Goodman Orchestra augmented by strings.

SSC-SP-7-18-3　**ET**: AFRS Benny Goodman Show, Program #1 - Part 1
Let's Dance (theme)
Somebody Stole My Gal
On The Sunny Side Of The Street - QUINTET plus orchestra
And The Angels Sing-voc, guest Martha Tilton
More Than You Know - Mobilgas Orchestra - BG, clt (arr DR)

SSC-SP-7-18-4　**ET**: as above, except Part 2
I Got Rhythm - SEXTET
I Don't Know Enough About You-voc Art Lund
Sing, Sing, Sing,
. . . reprise, **On The Sunny Side Of The Street**

(Although the Mobil Oil Company likely did not begin to sponsor these broadcasts until the July 29 program, the term "Mobilgas Orchestra" is used for sake of convenience. "Somebody Stole My Gal" is dubbed to Program #s 2, 43. "On The Sunny Side Of The Street" is dubbed to Program #43. "More Than You Know" is dubbed to Program #5. "I Got Rhythm" is dubbed to Program #4. Various excerpts from this ET are on **LP**, FH 23, FH 37, JOY 1082, PHON 7603, SB 151, SWH 17.)

Privately-recorded acetates of the broadcast of July 1 confirm that the AFRS ET conforms to the actual program. Unfortunately, the great bulk of the "Benny Goodman Show" AFRS ET's are not subject to similar confirmation; the author has found relatively few applicable acetates. Thus the reader—and the collector—is reminded that the listings herein for the "Benny Goodman Show" are based on the contents of the ET's; he is cautioned that the listings may not reflect accurately the contents of the respective broadcasts.

The observant collector will also note that Joey Bushkin is now a Goodmanite, that Mel Powell left the band sometime in June. And it is reiterated that Johnny White occasionally plays vibes with the orchestra—as in "My Sugar Is So Refined" and "Oh, Baby!," next—but that his participation is not separately displayed.

AFRS BENNY GOODMAN SHOW—Program #2 July 8, 1946, New York

Personnels as July 1. EVE YOUNG, voc. Guest: Johnny Mercer, voc.

SSC-7-25-3　**ET**: AFRS Benny Goodman Show, Program #2 - Part 1
Let's Dance (theme)
I Know That You Know
Ain't Misbehavin'
My Sugar Is So Refined-voc, guest Johnny Mercer

SSC-7-25-4　**ET**: as above, except Part 2
Dizzy Fingers - Mobilgas Orchestra - BG, clt
I Don't Know Why-voc Eve Young
Oh, Baby!-voc Benny Goodman
(Somebody Stole My Gal - from ET, Program #1)
. . . reprise, **I Know That You Know**

("I Know That You Know" is dubbed to Program #s 6, 16, 44. Various excerpts from this ET are on **LP,** DAN 5002, FH 37, JS AA508, PHON 7603.)

Discovery of an AFRS ET supplants as original issue what previously was an acetate "collectible." Note that now there is substantial evidence that this NBC broadcast originated in Boston, not New York, and that change is also made:

AFRS VAUGHN MONROE No. 1　　July 11, 1946, Boston

Benny Goodman, clt; Joe Bushkin, p; Louis Bellson, d.

SS-7-25-15　**ET**: AFRS Vaughn Monroe 1 - Part 1
Sweet Georgia Brown

SS-7-25-16　**ET**: as above, except Part 2
St. Louis Blues

Sorry, no Goodman accompaniment to any of Vaughn's vocals on the half-hour program. Too bad—he sang "Star Dust," and THAT would have been a collectors' item.

AFRS BENNY GOODMAN SHOW - Program #3 July 15, 1946, New York

Personnels as July 1. Guest: Nadia Reisenberg, p.

SSC-8-1-3　**ET**: AFRS Benny Goodman Program #3 - Part 1
Let's Dance (theme)
After You've Gone
Just One Of Those Things - SEXTET
The Man I Love - Mobilgas Orchestra
Blue Skies-voc Art Lund

SSC-8-1-4　**ET**: as above, except Part 2
Rondo: Third Movement, von Weber's Duo Concertante for Piano and Clarinet, Opus 48, in E-Flat Major - Benny Goodman, clt, and guest Nadia Reisenberg, p.
Rattle And Roll
. . . reprise, **After You've Gone**

(The Rondo is dubbed to Program #7.)

BENNY GOODMAN AND HIS ORCHESTRA　　July 18, 1946, New York

Orchestra personnel as July 1, with Schertzer, Pepper and Lesberg certain, replacing Prager, La Polla and Spieler, respectively.

CO 36658-2　CO 37077, CoArg 291676, PaAu A7587
Love Doesn't Grow On Trees-voc Art Lund

CO 36659-1　LP: PHON 7654
CO 36659-2　UNISSUED - Test Pressing
Fly By Night

AFRS BENNY GOODMAN SHOW - Program #4 July 22, 1946, New York

Orchestra as July 18. Guest: Helen Ward, voc.

SEXTET: BG, White, Bushkin, Bryan, Lesberg, Bellson

SSC-8-8-3　**ET**: AFRS Benny Goodman Show, Program #4 - Part 1
Let's Dance (theme)
Hallelujah! (arr BuC) (**ET**: Dept. Of State Dance Program No. 24)
Love Me Or Leave Me
Linger In My Arms A Little Longer-voc, guest Helen Ward
Tiger Rag - SEXTET (ET: Voice Of America American Jazz Program No. 25)

SSC-8-8-4　**ET**: as above, except Part 2
I've Got The Sun In The Morning-voc Art Lund
(I Got Rhythm - SEXTET - from ET, Program #1)
Seven Come Eleven
Good-Bye (theme)
. . . reprise, **Hallelujah!**

("Love Me Or Leave Me" is dubbed to Program #18. "Seven Come Eleven" is dubbed to Program #9. Various excerpts from this ET are on LP, FH 23, SB 154, SWH 17.)

New York radio station WNEW, long a Goodman champion (its studios are practically around the corner from Benny's offices and apartment), paid him an around-the-clock tribute on July 24. Benny took the Sextet along when he visited Martin Block's "Make Believe Ballroom," with resultant good humor and good music:

"MAKE BELIEVE BALLROOM"   *July 24, 1946*
WNEW Radio   *WNEW Studios, New York*

Sextet as July 22, except TRIGGER ALPERT, b, replaces Lesberg.

Let's Dance (theme)
After You've Gone
St. Louis Blues (LP: VELP 1)
On The Sunny Side Of The Street
I Got Rhythm
Rose Room
Limehouse Blues

As he had often done before, Benny invited Gene Krupa to be his guest on the—now—Mobil Oil program. But whether he realized it or not, this appearance was going to cost Gene: Lou McGarity was about decided to forsake the band for another more lucrative stint in the Hollywood studios, and Leon Cox, from Gene's band, will replace him in August.

AFRS BENNY GOODMAN SHOW - Program #5   July 29, 1946, New York

Orchestra as July 18. Eve Young, voc. Sextet as July 22. Guest: Gene Krupa, d.

TRIO: BG, Bushkin, guest Gene Krupa

SSC-8-15-3   **ET**: AFRS Benny Goodman Show, Program #5 - Part 1
     Let's Dance (theme)
     All The Cats Join In-voc ensemble
     If I Had You
     Who Do You Love, I Hope-voc Eve Young
     I Want To Go Where You Go-Then I'll Be Happy - TRIO
      (ET: Voice of America Jazz Program No. 25)

SSC-8-15-4   **ET**: as above, except Part 2
     (**More Than You Know**—from ET, Program #1)
     Sometimes I'm Happy—voc Eve Young—SEXTET
     Don't Be That Way—feat. Krupa, Bellson
     Good-Bye (theme)
     . . . reprise, **(I Want To Go Where You Go) Then I'll Be Happy**

("All The Cats Join In" is dubbed to Program #10. Various excerpts from this ET are on **LP**, Quicksilver 5040, SB 151, FH 17, SWH 37.)

Before McGarity leaves the band, we must list an ET cut whose provenance is unknown. The Voice Of America American Jazz Program No. 25 ET includes five Goodman tracks. Four are transfers from "Benny Goodman Show" programs 4, 5 and 7. The fifth, "Rattle And Roll, has not been matched to performances of that tune on other ET's, Goodman-Borge broadcasts, or private air checks. Its ambience suggests it was performed before a large audience, not in a studio—sounds similar to cuts from Benny's military camp broadcasts, for example. Lou solo's, so does Joey Bushkin, and Bellson is unmistakable—which pretty much delimits this version to the month of July, or early August:

VOICE OF AMERICA   July/early August 1946,
JAZZ PROGRAM No. 25   unknown location

Personnel as July 1–July 18.

DS-D26214   **ET**: Voice of America American Jazz Program No. 25—
     Track 1
     Rattle And Roll

Note that arranger credit for "Sweet Lorraine," next, now goes to Hugo Winterhalter. Further examination of Eddie Sauter's chart showed his omitted a French horn, whereas Winterhalter's includes that part.

AFRS BENNY GOODMAN SHOW - Program #6   August 5, 1946, New York

Orchestra as July 18/August 7. Sextet as July 22. HUGO WINTERHALTER (HW). arr.

SSC-8-22-3   **ET**:AFRS Benny Goodman Show, Program #6 - Part I
     Let's Dance (theme)
     I'm Just Wild About Harry
     Sweet Lorraine (arr HW) (**ET**: Dept. Of State Dance Program No. 34)
     (**I Know That You Know** - from ET, Program #2)
     My Blue Heaven-voc Art Lund

SSC-8-22-4   **ET**: as above, except Part 2
     South America, Take It Away-voc Eve Young
     Flying Home - SEXTET plus orchestra
     Good-Bye (theme)
     . . . reprise, **I'm Just Wild About Harry**

("Flying Home" is dubbed to Program #8.)

BENNY GOODMAN AND HIS ORCHESTRA   August 7, 1946, New York

Benny Goodman, clt; John Best, Nate Kazebier, Dick Mains, MICKEY McMICKLE, tpt; Cutty Cutshall, LEON COX, tbn; Addison Collins, Fr-h; Hymie Schertzer, Larry Mollinelli; as; Cliff Strickland, LESTER CLARK, ts; AL KLINK, bar; Joe Bushkin, p; Mike Bryan, g; BARNEY SPIELER, b; Louis Bellson, d. Art Lund, Eve Young, voc.

CO 36736-1   CO 37149, CoC 842
     A Kiss In The Night-voc Art Lund

CO 36737-1   CO 37149, CoAu DO3018, CoC 842
     For You, For Me, For Evermore-voc Eve Young (arr EdSau)

CO 36738-1   VD 719 A. **LP**: CBS 52964, SB 144
CO 36738-2   **LP**: PHON 7654
     Put That Kiss Back Where You Found It-voc Benny Goodman

CO 36739-1A   **LP**: PHON 7654
CO 36739-2   CO 37091, CoC 834
     My Blue Heaven-voc Art Lund

(Johnny White, vib, remains with the orchestra, but does not participate here.)

NBC's "Teen Timers Club" radio program had Benny as its guest on August 10, but efforts to locate a possible AFRS ET, or privately-recorded air checks, of the broadcast have been unsuccessful.

AFRS BENNY GOODMAN SHOW - Program #7   August 12, 1946, New York

Orchestra personnel as August 7. Guest: Count Basie, p.

SEXTET: BG, White, Bushkin, Bryan, BARNEY SPIELER, Bellson

SSC-8-29-3   **ET**: AFRS Benny Goodman Show, Program #7 - Part I
     Let's Dance (theme)
     Great Day (arr JT)
     To Each His Own-voc Art Lund
     (**Rondo** - from ET, Program #3)
     Rachel's Dream - SEXTET (**ET**: Voice of America American Jazz Program No. 25, Dept. of State Dance Program No. 34)

SSC-8-29-4   **ET**: as above, except Part 2
     Mad Boogie - feat. Count Basie, p (**ET**: Voice of America American Jazz Program No. 25)
     Doin' What Comes Nat'rally-voc Eve Young
     One O'Clock Jump - feat. Count Basie, p. (**ET**: Dept. of State Dance Program No. 34)
     Good-Bye (theme)

("Great Day" is dubbed to Program #18. Various excerpts from this ET are on **LP**, GOJ 1004, JS AA508, FH 37, SWH 17, Quicksilver 5046.)

There had been another addition to the Goodman menage, but she'll not play cello professionally for many years—Benjie Goodman, Alice and Benny's second child. We mention it because the next ''Benny Goodman Show'' premiere's ''Under The Double Eagle,'' which Benny will re-title, ''Benjie's Bubble,'' when he records Joey Bushkin's chart for Columbia some 10 days later.

AFRS BENNY GOODMAN SHOW - Program #8   August 19, 1946, New York

Personnels as August 12. Joe Bushkin (JB), arr. Guests: The Stuyvesant String Quartet.

SSC-9-5-3   **ET**: AFRS Benny Goodman Show, Program #8-Part 1
Let's Dance (theme)
Under The Double Eagle (arr JB)
Indian Summer (arr EdSau)
(**Flying Home** - SEXTET plus orchestra - from ET, Program #6)

SSC-9-5-4   **ET**: as above, except Part 2
Ain't Misbehavin'-voc Art Lund - SEXTET plus orchestra
Rendezvous With Benny -Benny Goodman, clt, and the Stuyvesant String Quartet (arr Alan Shulman)
Oh, Baby! (no vocal)
Good-Bye (theme)

(''Oh, Baby!'' is dubbed to Program #9, and is also on **LP**, FH 23.)

AFRS BENNY GOODMAN SHOW - Program #9   August 26, 1946, New York

Orchestra as August 7. Guest: Peggy Lee, voc.

QUINTET: BG, Bushkin, Bryan, Spieler, Bellson

SSC-9-12-3   **ET**: AFRS Benny Goodman Show, Program #9 - Part 1
Let's Dance (theme)
A String Of Pearls
Mean To Me
Why Don't You Do Right?-voc, guest Peggy Lee
(**Seven Come Eleven** - from ET, Program #4)

SSC-9-12-4   **ET**: as above, except Part 2
I Don't Know Enough About You-voc, guest Peggy Lee, Art Lund - QUINTET
(**Oh, Baby!** - from ET, Program #8)
Benny Rides Again
Good-Bye (theme)
. . . reprise, **Benny Rides Again**

BENNY GOODMAN AND HIS ORCHESTRA   August 29, 1946, New York

Personnel as August 7.

CO 36738-3   CO 37091, CoAu D03018, CoC 834
Put That Kiss Back Where You Found It - voc Art Lund

CO 36767-1   CO 37187, CoC 846, CoJap M383. **LP**: FR series
Benjie's Bubble (arr JB)

AFRS BENNY GOODMAN SHOW - Program #10   September 2, 1946, New York

Personnels as August 12. Guest: Nadia Reisenberg, p.

SSC-9-19-3   **ET**: AFRS Benny Goodman Show, Program #10 - Part 1
Let's Dance (theme)
Lulu's Back In Town (arr FH)
If You Were the Only Girl In The World-voc Art Lund
Shine - SEXTET

SSC-9-19-4   **ET**: as above, except Part 2
Beethoven's Variations On A Theme From Don Giovanni by Mozart, transcribed by Simeon Bellison - Benny Goodman, clt, Nadia Reisenberg, p
(**All The Cats Join In** - from ET, Program #5
Stealin' Apples
. . . reprise, **Lulu's Back In Town**

(''If You Were The Only Girl In The World'' is dubbed to Program #16. ''Shine'' is dubbed to Program #13, and is also on **LP**, SWH 17.)

The 10th program ended Benny's sole proprietorship of the Mobilgas broadcasts. Now it was necessary that he go to Hollywood for the fall radio season, there to inaugurate an altered format, jointly with Victor Borge and announcer Don Wilson. Succeeding broadcasts would be retitled, ''The Mobilgas Program, Presenting The Victor Borge Show, Starring Benny Goodman.'' En route, Benny performed two concerts in Detroit's Music Hall.

Benny recalls that the band was pretty much intact as it moved from coast to coast. It seems likely, however, that both Hymie Schertzer and Al Klink, in demand for radio work in New York, remained in Manhattan; that may also be true of Lester Clark and Mickey McMickle. There is no substantive ''fix'' on the personnel until a Columbia session in the middle of October. Logically (principally because of contractual terms), the certain personnel of the studio date are advanced herein to ''early October 1946,'' the putative date of an AFRS ET, Magic Carpet 514. Until then, personnel listings are approximations, combinations of the listings for August 12 and ''early October.''

The first two broadcasts from Hollywood were apparently not transcribed by AFRS. (Curiously, there are two AFRS ''Benny Goodman Show'' ET's for what should have been the broadcasts of September 9 and September 16—but the AFRS labels are in error, for the ET's feature the orchestras of Al Sack and Ray Bloch, respectively.) But NBC did transcribe the broadcasts onto 16'' acetates:

''THE VICTOR BORGE SHOW,   *September 9, 1946, Hollywood*
STARRING BENNY GOODMAN''
NBC Radio Network

Personnels as August 12/''early October.'' Guest: Lana Turner.

Under The Double Eagle
St. Louis Blues - SEXTET
I Know That You Know
Good-Bye (theme)

NBC's promotional series, ''Parade of Stars,'' solicited Benny's help in advertising its new Goodman-Borge programs. Likely in mid-September it recorded his comments about the Monday night broadcasts, and his introductions to his recordings of, ''Rattle And Roll,'' ''It's The Talk Of the Town,'' ''Don't Be A Baby, Baby'' and ''Swing Angel.'' The 15-minute program was transcribed onto an Orthacoustic ET, mx ND-6-MM-9876. It should be noted that this ET contains no original music; a more interesting one will turn up later.

Benny had begun 1946 with an engagement at the Meadowbrook Gardens in Culver City; now he returns, opening there on September 12. Our first evidence of his work this time is a privately-recorded acetate:

SUSTAINING BROADCAST   *September 14, 1946,*
MUTUAL-Don Lee Radio Network   *Meadowbrook Gardens,*
Culver City, Calif.

Personnel as September 9.

Rose Room - SEXTET

NBC used two 16'' acetates to transcribe its half hour broadcasts; recorded standard groove at 33⅓ rpm, each one-sided disc runs for approximately 15 minutes. Missing as of this writing is the acetate for the second half of the September 16 broadcast; the first disc ends with applause following ''Embraceable You.'' But all is not lost: NBC ''borrowed'' Benny's performances from the September 16 program for its ''Parade Of Stars'' promo, which it broadcast on September 17. Together, the NBC acetate and privately-recorded acetates of the ''Parade Of Stars'' presentation yield all of Benny's performances, save for the closing theme:

"THE VICTOR BORGE SHOW,   September 16, 1946, Hollywood
  STARRING BENNY GOODMAN"
NBC Radio Network

*Personnels as September 9. Don Wilson announces "Embraceable You" as
". . . Benny Goodman and his band join forces with the Mobilgas orchestra . . ."—the band, then, augmented by strings. Guest: Hal Perry.*

Carioca
Embraceable You - "Mobilgas Orchestra" - BG, clt
Why Does It Get So Late So Early?-voc Art Lund, Eve Young - SEXTET

AFRS recorded some of Benny's broadcasts from the Meadowbrook,
transcribed them onto its "Magic Carpet" 15-minute ET's. The engineers
persisted in cross-dubbing—what would those characters have created if
tape had been then available?—and thus "Stealin' Apples" is from an
unknown date, whereas the bulk of the ET is from September 20:

AFRS MAGIC CARPET 482   **September 20, 1946, Culver City**

Personnels as September 9.

SUR 10-11-6   **ET**: AFRS Magic Carpet 482
(U-66978)   **Let's Dance** (theme)
                 Under The Double Eagle
                 This Is Always-voc Eve Young
                 I Want To Go Where You Go-Then I'll Be Happy -
                   SEXTET
                 My Blue Heaven-voc Art Lund (announced as, "Blue
                   Skies")
                 Good-Bye (theme)
                 Stealin Apples - to fade

("Under The Double Eagle" is dubbed to AFRS Magic Carpet 508. "Stealin'
Apples" is also on ET, AFRS Magic Carpet 514. "Under The Double Eagle"
and "(I Want To Go Where You Go) Then I'll Be Happy" are also on **LP**, JS
AA508. "Under The Double Eagle" is also on **LP**, DAN 5002.)

SUSTAINING BROADCAST   *September 21, 1946,*
  Unknown radio network   *Meadowbrook Gardens,*
                                       Culver City, Calif.

Personnel as September 9.

A'Huggin' And A 'Chalkin'-voc Art Lund (n/c - intro clipped) **(LP**: SB 156)
Good-Bye (theme) **(LP**: SB 156)

SUSTAINING BROADCAST   *September 22, 1946,*
  MUTUAL-Don Lee Radio Network   *Meadowbrook Gardens,*
                                       Culver City, Calif.

Personnel as September 9.

I Never Knew (arr SkM)

AFRS resumed transcribing the Mobilgas broadcast series with Program No. 13. "Thirteen" proved unlucky for Marlene Dietrich, for she was
unable to appear as scheduled; Lucille Ball substituted for her.

Note that although the actual broadcasts are announced as, "The Victor
Borge Show Starring Benny Goodman," the ET's continue to be titled, the
"Benny Goodman Show." Those engineers got something right . . .

AFRS BENNY GOODMAN SHOW - Program #13   **September 23, 1946,**
                                              Hollywood

Personnels as September 9. Guest: Lucille Ball.

SSC-10-10-3   **ET**: AFRS Benny Goodman Show, Program #13 - Part 1
                 Let's Dance (theme)
                 Zing Went The Strings Of My Heart
                 (Shine - SEXTET - from ET, Program #10)
                 Blue Skies-voc Art Lund

SSC-10-10-4   **ET**: as above, except Part 2
                 I Want To Go Where You Go-Then I'll Be Happy -
                   SEXTET
                 Good-Bye (theme)

(Various excerpts from this ET are on **LP,** SB 154, SWH 3.)

Dates on the next two sets of air checks come from the bootleg Lp that
includes them; the author cannot attest to their accuracy. In some instances,
dates listed on other releases of this label have been incorrect, as demonstrated by program logs. Further, the author suggests using both a good
equalizer and a variable-pitch turntable when playing these cuts.

SUSTAINING BROADCAST   *September 27, 1946,*
  Unknown network   *Meadowbrook Gardens,*
                                       Culver City, Calif.

Personnel as September 9.

Love Doesn't Grow On Trees-voc Art Lund (n/c - intro clipped)
Don't Be That Way
Clarinade
Old Buttermilk Sky-voc Art Lund
Good-Bye (theme)

(Above and following air checks on LP, SB 154.)

SUSTAINING BROADCAST   *September 28, 1946,*
  Unknown network   *Meadowbrook Gardens,*
                                       Culver City, Calif.

Personnels as September 9.

For You, For Me, For Evermore-voc Eve Young
Shine - SEXTET
Sing, Sing, Sing (n/c)

Tommy Dorsey had also latched onto a summer replacement radio
program (for Fred Allen), but his was about to end. Sponsored by the makers
of "Tender Leaf Tea" (where are you now, when the big bands need you?),
and broadcast via NBC on Sunday evenings. Tommy's contract expired with
the program of September 29. Benny is his guest that final night; and note
that Benny brought along his own charts of "Clarinade" and "Hora Staccato," the latter replete with strings, by Jeff Alexander.

"THE TOMMY DORSEY SHOW"   *September 29, 1946,*
  NBC Radio Network   *Hollywood*

*Benny Goodman, clt, with Tommy Dorsey and his Orchestra, probably includ-
ing: Charlie Shavers, Ziggy Elman, Mickey Mangano, John Dougherty, tpt;
Tommy Dorsey, John Youngman, Charles LaRue, Eddie Benson, tbn; Abe
Most, clt & as; Louis Prisby, Martin Berman, as; Boomie Richman, Livio
Fresk, ts; John Potoker, p; Sam Herman, g; Sid Block, b; Alvin Stoller, d.*

Clarinade
Hora Staccato (arr JEFF ALEXANDER)

Here's the second "Magic Carpet" ET. The date of its broadcast is not
known; but it is introduced before the end of September because it still offers
the Sextet that includes both Mike Bryan and Barney Spieler.

AFRS MAGIC CARPET 508   **late September 1946, Culver City**

Personnels as September 9.

SUR-11-6-6   **ET**: AFRS Magic Carpet 508
(U-70992)   **Let's Dance** (theme)
(D-8749)   **I Know That You Know**
                 Love Doesn't Grow On Trees-voc Art Lund
                 I Want To Go Where You Go-Then I'll Be Happy -
                   SEXTET
                 Why Does It Get So Late So Early?-voc Eve Young, Art
                   Lund - SEXTET
                 (Under The Double Eagle - from ET, AFRS Magic Carpet
                   482)

Recently-discovered NBC acetates of the September 30 Goodman-
Borge broadcast confirm a previously-held but unproven supposition: this
program is the original source of the "Poor Butterfly" rendition that is
included in the AFRS ET's for its "Benny Goodman Show" Nos. "20" and
29. Thus it must now be assumed that either AFRS did transcribe this
broadcast, or failing that, had access to these NBC acetates. (The former
seems the more likely.) However, all efforts to locate a counterpart AFRS
ET for the September 30 airing—what would be AFRS "Benny Goodman
Show No. 14"—have been in vain. Apparently, AFRS did not press a "No.
14" ET.

"THE VICTOR BORGE SHOW,   *September 30, 1946,*
   STARRING BENNY GOODMAN"   *Hollywood*
 NBC Radio Network

Personnels as September 9. The "Mobilgas Orchestra" is introduced as, ". . . the augmented Goodman band." Guest: Slim Gaillard.

Rosalie
Poor Butterfly - "Mobilgas Orchestra" - BG, clt
Rachel's Dream - SEXTET
Good-Bye (theme)

("Poor Butterfly" is dubbed to Program Nos. "20" and 29.)

A hitherto-undocumented AFRS transcription of a sustaining broadcast from the Meadowbrook Gardens is undated; our best judgment places it in the first few days of October. This arbitrary assignment conveniently permits updating Benny's personnel, essentially bringing it forward from the certain complement of the October 15 Columbia studio session:

AFRS MAGIC CARPET 514   **early October 1946, Culver City**

Benny Goodman, clt; John Best, Nate Kazebier, Dick Mains, DALE PIERCE, tpt; Cutty Cutshall, Leon Cox, tbn; Addison Collins, Fr-h; Larry Molinelli, BILL SHINE, as; Cliff Strickland, ZOOT SIMS, ts; JOHN ROTELLA, bar; Joe Bushkin, p. BARNEY KESSEL, g; HARRY BABASIN, b; Louis Bellson, d. Art Lund, Eve Young, voc. Johnny White, vib. where applicable.

SEXTET: BG, White, Bushkin, Kessel, Babasin, Bellson

SUR 11-12-6	**ET:** AFRS Magic Carpet 514
(U-71102)	**Let's Dance** (theme)
(D-8750)	**Under The Double Eagle**
	This Is Always-voc Eve Young
	Rattle And Roll (LP: SB 156)
	Just One Of Those Things - SEXTET (LP: SB 156)
	Pity The Poor Lobster-voc Art Lund - to signoff
	Stealin' Apples - to fade

("Stealin' Apples" is also on ET, AFRS Magic Carpet 482, September 20.)

AFRS BENNY GOODMAN SHOW - Program #15   **October 7, 1946,**
                                                           Hollywood

Personnels as "early October." Guest: Edward G. Robinson.

SSC-10-24-3	**ET:** AFRS Benny Goodman Show, Program #15 - Part 1
	After You've Gone
	Pity The Poor Lobster-voc Art Lund
	St. Louis Blues - SEXTET
SSC-10-24-4	**ET:** as above, except Part 2
	The Sheik Of Araby - SEXTET
	Good-Bye (theme)

(Various excerpts from this ET are on **LP**, GOJ 1005, SWH 3, SWH 17.)

The next NBC "Parade Of Stars" presentation is a curious admixture of the new and the old, insofar as Benny is involved. Dialogue between him and Borge duplicates script material from two prior Goodman-Borge shows; and his Sextet's "The Sheik Of Araby" mirrors its rendition in the immediately preceding Goodman-Borge broadcast of October 7. But this is all "live" stuff—the words are the same, the tune is the same, but the executions of both are different from their predecessors.

This is a radical departure from the two "Parade Of Stars" promo's cited earlier. The first, the Orthacoustic ET, offered only dubs of his commercial recordings, along with Benny's voice tracks. The second, counterpart to the Goodman-Borge broadcast of September 16, dubbed in performances from that broadcast. Now we have Goodman and Borge "live," but duplicating pieces of dialogue and a Sextet performance previously broadcast . . . Odd, too, is NBC's dating of this third "Parade Of Stars" broadcast: October 13, a Sunday. Its September 16 counterpart "rebroadcast" (so announced) is dated September 17, a Tuesday. "Pity The Poor Lobster," indeed; pity the poor discographer.

"PARADE OF STARS"   *October 13, 1946, Hollywood*
 NBC Radio Network

Personnel as "early October."

The Sheik Of Araby - SEXTET

AFRS BENNY GOODMAN SHOW - Program #16   **October 14, 1946,**
                                                     Hollywood

Personnels as "early October." Guest: Charlie "Finnegan" Cantor

SSC-10-31-3	**ET:** AFRS Benny Goodman Show, Program #16 - Part 1
	King Porter Stomp (LP: FH 37)
	(If You Were The Only Girl In The World-voc Art Lund - from ET, Program #10)
	Hora Staccato - Mobilgas Orchestra - BG, clt (arr Jeff Alexander)
SSC-10-31-4	**ET:** as above, except Part 2
	Honeysuckle Rose - SEXTET (LP: SWH 3)
	(I Know That You Know - from ET, Program #2)
	Good-Bye (theme)

From the first Victor date forward, Benny had limited his studio recordings to performances with his regular personnel: various small group combinations, and an orchestra composed of 13–17 brass, reed and rhythm instruments. But other of the swing bands had added strings for both recording sessions and location engagements, and their ventures had gotten Benny's attention. He enjoyed leading the "Mobilgas" orchestra, and had had some arrangements written especially for it. With Columbia's eager assent, he felt that these charts should be recorded.

The men who comprised the string session were recruited from the Hollywood studios. Some of them likely appeared on the "Benny Goodman Show" broadcasts as members of the large orchestra, but it is emphasized that Benny did not employ them for his night club and other appearances. They were present for recording purposes only.

Collectors are advised that the original issues of "That's The Beginning Of The End," Australian Columbia D03129 and French Columbia B597, are quite rare and difficult to find in any condition.

BENNY GOODMAN AND HIS ORCHESTRA   **October 15, 1946,**
                                                      Los Angeles

Personnel as Orchestra, "early October," augmented by: Victor Arno, Harry Bluestone, Howard Halber, Dan Lube, Mischa Russell, Marshall Sosson, v; Allen Herschmann, Paul Robyn, viola; Cy Bernard, Arthur Kafton, cel. JEFF ALEXANDER, (JA), arr.

HCO 2083-1	CO 37207, CoArg 291706, CoC 848, CoSd DS1709, CoE DB2326, CoMex 1901, CoSw DZ495, ReSp C8768. **7"-33:** CO 1-512, CO 3-37207. **ET:** AFRS P722.
	Hora Staccato (arr JA)
HCO 2084-1	HA 1061, CoSd DS1709, CoE DB2326, CoSw DZ495, ReSp C8768
HCO 2084-2	**LP:** CO CL541, CO alb P4M-5678, **EP:** CO 5-1798 (Set B363)
	Poor Butterfly
Omit strings.	
HCO 2085-1	UNISSUED - Test Pressing
HCO 2085-2	CoAu DO3129, CoFr BF97
	That's The Beginning Of The End-voc Eve Young

AFRS BENNY GOODMAN SHOW - Program #17   **October 21, 1946,**
                                                     Hollywood

Personnels as "early October," except possibly CLINT BELLEW, as, replaces Shine. Guests: Marlene Dietrich, Eileen Wilson, voc.

SSC-11-7-3	**ET:** AFRS Benny Goodman Show, Program #17 - Part I
	Hallelujah!
	Put That Kiss Back Where You Found It-voc, guest Eileen Wilson
SSC-11-7-4	**ET:** as above, except part 2
	I'll Always Be In Love With You - SEXTET
	Good-Bye (theme)

("Hallalujah!" is dubbed to Program #s 18, 24, "I'll Always Be In Love With You" is also on **LP**, SB 156, SWH 3.)

The next day's studio session is Benny's final date for Columbia for almost four years. Perhaps the end of his contract is the reason Columbia did not release either of two excellent sides by the Sextet in the United States. One, ''Honeysuckle Rose,'' was scheduled for release, and catalog number CO 37974 was assigned to it; but it was cancelled.

BENNY GOODMAN AND HIS ORCHESTRA October 22, 1946, Los Angeles

Orchestra personnel as ''early October,'' except CLINT BELLEW, as, replaces Shine.

HCO 2110-2   CO 37207, CoArg 291706, CoC 848. **EP**: CoE SEG7524, CoFr ESDF1023. **LP**: FONT TFL5067, FontCont 682047TL
    Man Here Plays Fine Piano-voc Eve Young (arr JB)

HCO 2111-1   CO 37187, CoC 846, CoFr BF135, CoJap M259
    A Gal In Calico-voc Eve Young

BENNY GOODMAN SEXTET same session

Sextet personnel as ''early October.''

HCO 2112-1   CoC 1025. **LP**: BID 1011
    I'll Always Be In Love With You

HCO 2113-1   CoE DB2287, CoArg 292105, CoArg 20.363B, CoNor GNS5082, CoSw DZ461, ReSp C8787. **LP**: BID 1011
    Honeysuckle Rose

Because both Borge and Goodman had engagements in the East, their radio program was relocated to New York. On the way cross-country, Benny played concerts in the Denver Auditorium, Denver, Colorado, on October 23; in the Turnpike Ballroom (early Howard Johnson?) Lincoln, Nebraska, October 25; and in the Temple of the Knights of Ak-Sar-Ben, Omaha, Nebraska, on October 26.

Big, blond, engaging Art Lund remained in Hollywood to try his luck in the movies. But according to Benny, the band's personnel remained ''about the same,'' as it moved east. Absence of a recording contract and its attendant personnel listing precludes confirmation of his recollection, and press reports of exits and entrances through the next month are of little help. Not until the beginning of December can we list the band's composition with some assurance.

Here is the first of seven Goodman-Borge broadcasts to originate in New York:

AFRS BENNY GOODMAN SHOW - Program #18 October 28, 1946, New York

Personnels as October 22. Guest: Basil Rathbone. DICK KOHLER, voc.

SSC-11-14-3   **ET**: AFRS Benny Goodman Show, Program #18 - Part 1
    (**Great Day** - from ET, Program #7)
    Carioca

SSC-11-14-4   **ET**: as above, except Part 2
    Flying Home - SEXTET
    Buckle Down Winsocki-voc Dick Kohler & ensemble
    (**Hallelujah!** - from ET, Program #17
    (. . . reprise, **Love Me Or Leave Me** - from ET, Program #4)

(''Flying Home'' is dubbed to Program #s ''19,'' 24; and is also on **LP**, FH 1974, SWH 3.)

Although the AFRS ''Benny Goodman Show'' ET's do not present the Goodman-Borge programs as broadcast, they do reflect a condition that made Benny unhappy: his performances were being limited to no more than three renditions per half hour. Borge and his guests were taking up more and more of each broadcast; and although Benny was included in many of the skits, he resented not being able to play. Benny recalls a constant tug of war between the producers, and a shifting emphasis as to who was the ''star of the program.'' AFRS's practice of cross-dubbing in fact, then, gives us more Goodman than actually occurred, and thanks to them. Perhaps announcements are indicative of AFRS's opinion. When Bud Collyer is heard to announce the broadcasts ''live,'' it's ''The Victor Borge Show Starring Benny Goodman.'' But when an AFRS announcer's introduction is dubbed in, it's ''The Benny Goodman-Victor Borge Show.''

Benny and the band began a six-week engagement in the 400 Restaurant on October 31. Frequent broadcasts from there make up for his dimin-

ished participation on the Mobil program. Chronologically, our first air check from the 400 is on an AFRS ET.

AFRS ONE NIGHT STAND No. 1197 November 1, 1946, New York

Personnels as October 28.

SSC-12-22-1   **ET**: AFRS One Night Stand No. 1197 - Part 1
    Let's Dance (theme)
    A String Of Pearls
    For You, For Me, For Evermore-voc Eve Young
    Flying Home - SEXTET
    Tiger Rag - SEXTET

SSC-12-22-2   **ET**: as above, except Part 2
    Put That Kiss Back Where You Found It-voc Eve Young
    Hora Staccato
    (**Who's Sorry Now?** - ET, AFRS One Night Stand No. 1046)
    Love Doesn't Grow On Trees-voc Dick Kohler
    St. Louis Blues - SEXTET (n/c)

(''Flying Home'' and ''Hora Staccato'' are dubbed to ET, AFRS One Night Stand No. 1229.)

AFRS transposed the dates, catalog and matrix numbers, on its next two ''Benny Goodman Show'' transcriptions. Its ''Program #20'' is actually the 19th broadcast in the series, and its ''Program #19'' is the 20th. The ET's are listed herein in proper sequence, but the erroneous catalog and matrix numbers are shown as they appear on the discs.

AFRS BENNY GOODMAN SHOW - Program #20 November 4, 1946, New York

Personnels as October 28. Guest: Elsa Maxwell.

SSC-11-28-3   **ET**: AFRS Benny Goodman Show, Program ''#20'' - Part 1
    Old Buttermilk Sky
    Stealin' Apples

SSC-11-28-4   **ET**: as above, except Part 2
    (**Poor Butterfly** - from September 30 broadcast)
    Good-Bye (theme)

(''Old Buttermilk Sky'' is dubbed to Program #41, ''Poor Butterfly'' is dubbed to Program #29, ''Old Buttermilk Sky'' is also on **LP**, YB 467.)

SUSTAINING BROADCAST   *November 7, 1946,*
  CBS Radio Network   *400 Restaurant, New York*

Personnels as October 28.

The More I Go Out With Somebody Else-voc Eve Young
Rose Room - SEXTET
Benjie's Bubble
The Things We Did Last Summer-voc Eve Young
I Never Knew (I Could Love Anybody)-voc Eve Young (arr EdSau)
This Is Always-voc Eve Young
The Sheik Of Araby - SEXTET
Everybody Loves My Baby-voc Eve Young - to signoff

SUSTAINING BROADCAST   *November 9, 1946,*
  MUTUAL Radio Network   *400 Restaurant, New York*

Personnels as October 28.

Don't Be That Way
Oh, Baby!-voc Benny Goodman - Parts 1 & 2
Poor Butterfly - SEXTET
The More I Go Out With Somebody Else-voc Eve Young
Good-Bye (theme)

Next is the second of the ''Benny Goodman Show'' ET's whose program numbers are transposed by AFRS. Its final tune, ''Red Horse Boogie,'' is a salute to the sponsor's trademark (remember ''Camel Hop,'' ''Mellow Gold''?). It swings, and in general, the band seems a lot more loose during this engagement at the 400, if less technically brilliant than in the spring.

AFRS BENNY GOODMAN SHOW - Program #19   **November 11, 1946, New York**

Personnels as October 28. Guest: Shirley Booth.

SSC-11-21-3   **ET**: AFRS Benny Goodman Show, Program "#19" - Part 1
    I May Be Wrong (arr FH)
    For You, For Me, For Evermore-voc Eve Young

SSC-11-21-4   **ET**: as above, except Part 2
    (**Flying Home** - SEXTET - from ET, Program #18)
    Red Horse Boogie - SEXTET
    Good-Bye (theme)

("Red Horse Boogie" is dubbed to Program #26; and is also on **LP**, FH 1974, SWH 3.)

AFRS's next "One Night Stand" ET, most of which seems to be from a single broadcast from the 400, is undated, but still includes Joey Bushkin. Therefore it is assigned to the period prior to November 14, when Jess Stacy replaced Bushkin.

AFRS ONE NIGHT STAND No. 1229   **early November, 1946, New York**

Personnels as October 28.

SSC-1-23-1   **ET**: AFRS One Night Stand No. 1229 - Part 1
    Let's Dance (theme)
    Rattle And Roll
    Just Squeeze Me-voc Eve Young
    Honeysuckle Rose - SEXTET
    Put That Kiss Back Where You Found It-voc Eve Young

SSC-1-23-2   **ET**: as above, except Part 2
    (**Hora Staccato** - ET, AFRS One Night Stand No. 1197)
    Exactly Like You - SEXTET
    A Gal In Calico-voc Eve Young
    (**Flying Home** - SEXTET - ET, AFRS One Night Stand No. 1197)
    One O'Clock Jump (n/c)

("Rattle And Roll," "Honeysuckle Rose" and "Exactly Like You" are dubbed to ET, AFRS One Night Stand No. 1260. Additionally, "Rattle And Roll" is dubbed to ET, AFRS One Night Stand No. 1300.)

Should note in passing that Bushkin acquitted himself well while with Goodman—good work throughout, and on occasion exceptional soli, such as in the November 7 air check of, "The Sheik Of Araby." Almost as if challenged by his predecessor, Jess will play some of the finest piano of his career during this four-month reunion with Benny.

SUSTAINING BROADCAST   *November 14, 1946,*
   CBS Radio Network   *400 Restaurant, New York*

Personnels as October 28, except JESS STACY, p, replaces Bushkin in the orchestra and small groups.

Benny Rides Again
Rose Room - SEXTET

AFRS ONE NIGHT STAND No. 1260   **November 15, 1946, New York**

Personnels as November 14.

SSC-2-23-1   **ET**: AFRS One Night Stand No. 1260 - Part 1
    Let's Dance (theme)
    Rosalie
    Somewhere In The Night
    Hora Staccato
    (**Rattle And Roll** - ET, AFRS One Night Stand No. 1229)

SSC-2-23-2   **ET**: as above, except Part 2
    St. Louis Blues - SEXTET
    A Gal In Calico-voc Eve Young
    Sweet Georgia Brown - SEXTET
    (**Exactly Like You** - SEXTET - ET, AFRS One Night Stand No. 1229)
    (**Honeysuckle Rose** - SEXTET - ET, AFRS One Night Stand No. 1229)

AFRS "Benny Goodman Show" ETs numbered "Programs 21, 22 and 23" feature the orchestras of Al Sack and Ray Bloch, not Benny Goodman. (As noted in the preamble to this Goodman-Borge series, at this juncture AFRS produced three ETs as substitutes for two Goodman-Borge broadcasts. Further along, the reader will note that the AFRS ETs for the consecutive Goodman-Borge broadcasts of December 2 and December 9 are numbered "Program No. 24" and "Program No. 26," respectively. AFRS's intervening "Benny Goodman Show - Program No. 25" ET again offers the orchestra of Ray Bloch, not Benny Goodman.)

Although AFRS evidently did not transcribe the Goodman-Borge broadcasts of November 18 and 25, NBC did. Here's the first, via NBC's 16" acetates:

"THE VICTOR BORGE SHOW,   *November 18, 1946,*
   STARRING BENNY GOODMAN"   *New York*
   NBC Radio Network

Personnels as November 14. Guest: Monty Wooley.

You Brought A New Kind Of Love To Me (no vocal) (LP: SB 155)
The World Is Waiting For The Sunrise - SEXTET
Good-Bye (theme)

On November 18 and 19 Benny was guest soloist with the NBC Symphony, Leonard Bernstein conducting. He performed a work he had commissioned from Alex North, "Revue For Clarinet And Orchestra." Whether this first public presentation of the North opus was broadcast is not known; no transcriptions of any kind have come to light.

SUSTAINING BROADCAST   *November 20, 1946,*
   MUTUAL Radio Network   *400 Restaurant, New York*

Personnels as November 14.

Sweet Lorraine - SEXTET
The Count
Stealin' Apples
China Boy - SEXTET
Tuesday At Ten - to signoff

SUSTAINING BROADCAST   *November 21, 1946,*
   CBS Radio Network   *400 Restaurant, New York*

Personnels as November 14.

Rosalie
I'll Always Be In Love With You - SEXTET
Somebody Loves Me - SEXTET
Embraceable You

A dated acetate confirms that the bulk of the next undated AFRS ET comes from a broadcast of November 22. An announcer informs us that this is the premiere performance of "Lonely Moments," a signal that Benny is building a new book for the band, that it will be oriented toward "bop." Note, too, that the announcer says Eve Young will sing, "(I Sent You) A Kiss In The Night," but she does not—this version is an instrumental.

AFRS ONE NIGHT STAND No. 1300   **November 22, 1946, New York**

Personnels as November 14.

SSC-4-4-1   **ET**: AFRS One Night Stand No. 1300 - Part 1
    Let's Dance (theme)
    Somebody Stole My Gal
    For You, For Me, For Evermore-voc Eve Young
    On The Sunny Side Of The Street - SEXTET
    (**Rattle And Roll** - from ET, AFRS One Night No. 1229)

SSC-4-4-2   **ET**: as above, except Part 2
    Lonely Moments (arr MLW)
    I Sent You-A Kiss In The Night-voc Eve Young
    Honeysuckle Rose - SEXTET
    (**Sing, Sing Sing** - from ET, AFRS One Night Stand No. 1046)

Next, NBC's transcription of the Goodman-Borge broadcast of November 25. Note that through this period Bud Collyer announces the programs as, "The Mobilgas Program, presenting the Victor Borge Show, starring Benny Goodman."

''THE VICTOR BORGE SHOW,   *November 25, 1946,*
  STARRING BENNY GOODMAN''   *New York*
  NBC Radio Network

Orchestra as November 14. QUINTET: Goodman, Stacy, Kessel, Babasin, Bellson. Guest: Keenan Wynn.

The Count
The Whistling Blues (later, ''Whistle Blues'') (arr MLW)
September Song - QUINTET (LP: SB 155)
Good-Bye (theme)

Recent discovery of an AFRS ET upgrades what previously was believed to exist only as a privately-recorded air check. But the acetates are still important: AFRS omits an intermediate performance (''Rainy Night In Rio''), signs off on a partial, ''Stompin' At The Savoy,'' thus omitting the actual conclusion, ''Flying Home'':

AFRS MAGIC CARPET No. 812   November 29, 1946, New York

Personnels as November 14.

U99779	**ET**: AFRS Magic Carpet No. 812
(SUR 9-15-4)	**Let's Dance** (theme)
(D-18749)	**Clarinade**
	Love Doesn't Grow On Trees-voc Eve Young
	On The Sunny Side Of The Street - SEXTET
	Whistle Blues
	A Rainy Night In Rio-voc Eve Young
	Stompin' At The Savoy (n/c - to AFRS signoff)
	Stompin' At The Savoy (complete)
	Flying Home - SEXTET - to ABC signoff

SUSTAINING BROADCAST   *November 30 1946,*
  MUTUAL Radio Network   *400 Restaurant, New York*

Personnels as November 14.

Benjie's Bubble
Put That Kiss Back Where You Found It-voc Eve Young
Jersey Bounce
Love Doesn't Grow On Trees-voc Eve Young
Sweet Lorraine - SEXTET
The World Is Waiting For The Sunrise - SEXTET
Whistle Blues - to signoff

Benny treated himself to a pre-Christmas present on the first of December: retaining only Nate Kazebier and the rhythm section, and Johnny White and Eve Young, Benny put together a whole new band:

AFRS BENNY GOODMAN SHOW - Program #24   December 2, 1946, New York

Benny Goodman, clt; Nate Kazebier, VAN RASEY, RAY LINN, tpt; LOU McGARITY, RED BALLARD, TOMMY PEDERSON, tbn; SKEETS HERFURT, HEINIE BEAU, as; BABE RUSSIN, JACK CHANEY, ts; CHUCK GENTRY, bar; Jess Stacy, p; Barney Kessel, g; Harry Babasin, b; Louis Bellson, d; Johnny White, vib. Eve Young, voc. Guest: Basil Rathbone.

SEXTET: BG, White, Stacy, Kessel, Babasin, Bellson
QUINTET: as Sextet, sans vibes

SSC-12-26-3	**ET**: AFRS Benny Goodman Show, Program #24—Part 1
	(**Hallelujah!**—from ET, Program #17)
	Swanee River (arr FH)
SSC-12-26-4	**ET**: as above, except Part 2
	I've Found A New Baby—QUINTET
	(**Flying Home**—from ET, Program #18)
	. . . reprise, **I've Found A New Baby**—QUINTET

(Benny blows a few bars of the, ''Hungarian Dance'' preceding ''I've Found A New Baby.'' ''I've Found A New Baby'' is also on **LP**, SB 155.)

SUSTAINING BROADCAST   *December 4, 1946,*
  MUTUAL Radio Network   *400 Restaurant, New York*

Personnels as December 2.

If I'm Lucky-voc Eve Young (arr EdSau)
Where Or When—SEXTET
Whistle Blues
Benjie's Bubble
Stealin' Apples—to signoff

Don Wilson, the Goodman-Borge program West Coast announcer, appears on the next broadcast, possibly in preparation for the show's removal once again to Hollywood:

AFRS BENNY GOODMAN SHOW - Program #26   December 9, 1946, New York

Personnels as December 2. Guest: Rise Stevens.

SSC-1-9-3	**ET**: AFRS Benny Goodman Show, Program #26—Part 1
	Somebody Stole My Gal
SSC-1-9-4	**ET**: as above, except Part 2
	Hora Staccato
	(. . . reprise, **Red Horse Boogie**—from ET, Program ''#19'')

(''Somebody Stole My Gal'' is dubbed to Program #27; and is also on **LP**, FH 37, Quicksilver 5046.)

The date of the next, and our final, broadcast from the 400 is unknown:

SUSTAINING BROADCAST   *December 1946,*
  CBS Radio Network   *400 Restaurant, New York*

Personnel as December 2.

Fly By Night (n/c)
Can't Help Lovin' That Man
Oh, Baby!-voc Benny Goodman—Part 1—to signoff

With the next broadcast, the Goodman-Borge series relocates permanently to Hollywood. AFRS did not transcribe the broadcasts of December 16, 23 and 30, but NBC did. However, even these full half-hour transcriptions offer few clues to the band's personnel. Contemporary press reports cite several replacements, but they are not specific as to dates. It is assumed that likely changes occurred when the band went west—some of the sidemen elected to stay in New York. On that premise, our listing shows a revamped lineup, with the understanding that some of the new faces might not have appeared until later in the month.

''THE VICTOR BORGE SHOW,   *December 16, 1946,*
  STARRING BENNY GOODMAN''   *Hollywood*
  NBC Radio Network

Benny Goodman, clt; Nate Kazebier, GEORGE WENDT, ZEKE ZARCHEY, JOE TRISCARI, tpt; Lou McGarity, Red Ballard, BILL SCHAEFER, tbn; Skeets Herfurt, Heinie Beau, as; Babe Russin, Jack Chaney, ts; Chuck Gentry, bar; Jess Stacy, p; Barney Kessel, g; Harry Babasin, b; SAMMY WEISS, d; Johnny White, vib. Guest: Vera Vague.

QUINTET: BG, White, Stacy, Kessel, Babasin, Weiss
SEXTET: As Quintet, sans vibes

I Never Knew (I Could Love Anybody) (LP: SB 156)
Where Or When - SEXTET (LP: SB 156)
Benjie's Bubble (LP: SB 156)

''THE VICTOR BORGE SHOW,   *December 23, 1946,*
  STARRING BENNY GOODMAN''   *Hollywood*
  NBC Radio Network

Personnels as December 16. Guests: Anita O'Day, voc; the Mitchell Boys' Choir.

Winter Wonderland
The Christmas Song-voc Anita O'Day (LP: SB 156)
The World Is Waiting For The Sunrise - SEXTET (LP: SB 155)

That was Johnny White's final appearance with Benny. Now, ''the new Benny Goodman Quintet'' is featured on a special CBS Christmas Day broadcast:

"CHRISTMAS PROGRAM"
  CBS Radio Network
December 25, 1946,
Hollywood

Quintet as December 16.

Honeysuckle Rose - QUINTET

"THE VICTOR BORGE SHOW,
  STARRING BENNY GOODMAN"
  NBC Radio Network
December 30, 1946,
Hollywood

Personnels as December 16. JEANNIE McKEON, voc. Guest: Lauritz Melchior.

A Gal In Calico-voc Jeannie McKeon (LP: SB 156)
September Song - QUINTET
burlesque, "South America, Take It Away" - voc Benny Goodman, Lauritz
  Melchior, Victor Borge
Good-Bye (theme)

Walter Huston's Brunswick recording of "September Song" is justly famed as a sensitive reading of Kurt Weill's and Maxwell Anderson's classic; and a year from now, Harry James's swinging version will top the charts of Columbia's hits. But for sheer poetry of expression, an emotional, exultant paean, Jess's solo in the Quintet's rendition deserves equal recognition.

AFRS BENNY GOODMAN SHOW - Program #27   **January 6, 1947,**
Hollywood

Personnels as December 16, 1946. Guest: Judy Canova.

SSC-1-16-3   **ET**: AFRS Benny Goodman Show, Program #27—Part 1
       Great Day
       Guilty-voc Jeannie McKeon (arr JT)

SSC-1-16-4   **ET**: as above, except Part 2
       Slipped Disc—QUINTET
       (**Somebody Stole My Gal**—from ET, Program #26)

("Great Day" is also on **LP**, FH 23, FH 1974, SB 156, YB 467. "Guilty" is also on **LP**, YB 467. "Slipped Disc" is also on **LP**, SB 155, SWH 17.)

From this juncture forward the author has not had visual access to the AFRS "Benny Goodman Show" ET's. Therefore, their matrix numbers have in main been determined by extrapolation, and may not be accurate.

AFRS BENNY GOODMAN SHOW - Program #28   **January 13, 1947,**
Hollywood

Personnels as December 16, 1946. Guest: Kay Kyser.

SSC-1-23-3   **ET**: AFRS Benny Goodman Show, Program #28—Part 1
       Lonely Moments (arr MLW)

SSC-1-23-4   **ET**: as above, except Part 2
       For Sentimental Reasons-voc Jeannie McKeon
       I'll Always Be In Love With You—QUINTET

("Lonely Moments" is also on **LP**, FH 23, FH 1974. "I'll Always Be In Love With You" is also on **LP**, SB 155, SWH 17.)

AFRS BENNY GOODMAN SHOW - Program #29   **January 20, 1947,**
Hollywood

Orchestra personnel as December 16, 1946, except ALLAN REUSS, g, replaces Kessel. TOMMY TODD (TT), arr. Guests: Hedda Hopper, Art Lund, voc.

SEXTET: BG; ERNIE FELICE, acc; Stacy, Reuss, Babasin, Weiss

SSC-1-30-3   **ET**: AFRS Benny Goodman Show, Program #29—Part 1
       The One I Love Belongs To Somebody Else-voc, guest
          Art Lund (arr TT)
       Dizzy Fingers (arr TT)

SSC-1-30-4   **ET**: as above, except Part 2
       At Sundown—SEXTET
       (**Poor Butterfly**-from September 30, 1946, broadcast)

("The One I Love . . ." and "At Sundown" are also on **LP**, YB 467. Additionally, "At Sundown" is also on **LP**, SB 155.)

In newspaper parlance, "30" signifies "the end." Coincidentally, the "Benny Goodman Show—Program #30," ends the "POSTWAR CO-LUMBIAS" section of this work, and serves as a springboard to, "THE CAPITOL SERIES":

AFRS BENNY GOODMAN SHOW - Program #30   **January 27, 1947,**
Hollywood

Personnels as January 20, MATT DENNIS, voc. Guest: William Bendix.

SSC-2-6-3   **ET**: AFRS Benny Goodman Show, Program #30—Part 1
       Clarinade
       You Broke The Only Heart That Ever Loved You-voc
          Matt Dennis

SSC-2-6-4   **ET**: as above, except Part 2
       Memories Of You—SEXTET

("Memories Of You" is dubbed to Program #36; and is also on **LP**, SB 155. "Clarinade" is also on **LP**, FH 37. "You Broke The Only Heart . . ." is also on **LP**, SB 156.)

THE CAPITOL SERIES

Were one to suggest that Benny Goodman's Capitol-era band of four decades ago was his last traditional big band, casual fans as well as collectors—and perhaps Benny himself—would demur. Their justifiable objection on all counts to that thrice-qualified judgment might well be expressed in a single expletive, "Absurd!"

In one sense the suggestion is demonstrably inapt, and readily so. "Last" and "big" may be dismissed summarily: Everyone knows that in 1962 Benny toured the Soviet Union as leader of an orchestra that included seven brass, five reeds, four rhythm, two vocalists, a second pianist, and one vibraphonist. That's fifteen years later than his band that produced the Capitol series, and big by any standard.

As for "traditional . . ." The Benny Goodman Orchestra of 1947–1949 was the least characteristic of all of Benny's bands. Although its instrumentation was BG-conventional, the music it played was far removed from Benny's established swing style. This band was imitative, it did not trade on the heritage of Goodman's past glory. This band played BOP, deliberately, unmistakably, almost exclusively. It forsook its standard and accepted arrangements of "King Porter" and "Jersey Bounce" and the others, and read them as they had been rewritten by new people named Johnny Thompson, Tommy Todd and Chico O'Farrell. And this was no experimental dalliance—it lasted two full years.

But in another sense the suggestion has merit. The Capitol-series band was a traditional Goodman band in that it was a regularly constituted orchestra whose members were relatively permanent, under contract for a period of time, and on salary. It was a road band that worked a routine schedule of supper clubs and night clubs, dance halls and college proms, theatres and, only incidentally occasional sessions in recording studios. It was not a special-purpose orchestra organized specifically to satisfy a limited recording contract, a concert tour, or a television series. This was a band in the tradition of bands as they were for Benny in the 'Thirties and 'Forties—a band that went where the work was no matter what it was, a band that played month-long stands and one-nighters indiscriminately and as they were booked. It was a band of troubadors who slept in buses, played pinochle in hotel rooms, and drank bourbon in both.

In this sense Benny's Capitol-recording band was his last big band. Certainly he had full orchestras in the 'Fifties, 'Sixties, and 'Seventies, and even one in the 'Eighties. But these latter were organized for specific and limited purposes, although on occasion they persisted beyond those purposes. For there were at work socio-economic forces that mandated the majority of the big bands out of existence.

One of the most puissant of these forces was the coming of age of network television. This had multiple consequences. It provided the American public with twenty-four hour home entertainment, varied, convenient, and free. This sounded the death knell of "live" stage shows on other than a star-system, limited appearance basis only. The vaudeville circuit blew its fuse, and the lights went out on the dance bands. Variety theatres became variety stores, Palladiums parking lots, dance halls discount marts. There were fewer and ever fewer places in which the big bands could perform.

Radio's product was sound, and the big bands prospered. TV's stock is sight, and the no-funny hats, music-only swing bands weren't especially photogenic. Sponsors read the ratings and learned that television was not the medium for a big band; "acts" were needed to sustain the interest of general audiences. Acts grew in importance, bands dwindled. Which acts became paramount, whose orchestra immaterial. No longer was a girl named Peggy Lee a vocalist with the Benny Goodman Orchestra. Benny Goodman was a guest on the "Peggy Lee TV Special."

Not that television could do without musicians; on the contrary it required the best. It could afford to pay top dollar for unfailing competency, and it recruited those most competent from the ranks of the big bands. No matter to name musicians that they became anonymous and disappeared from the Metronome and Down Beat polls. As Hollywood studio musicians had discovered earlier, their compensation was more money, a sane physical existence, a permanent home and a conventional family life. Musicians' wives cheered while road band leaders cut their own income to compete for able sidemen willing to endure the rigors of one-nighters.

Television was not the only culprit in the demise of the big bands. Nor was it the first. One might pinpoint Frank Sinatra's leaving Tommy Dorsey as the epoch of the individual performer. Certainly the diffusion of sideman talent had begun earlier—Krupa, James, Hampton, Wilson, to name only a few and only from Benny's band. If nothing else, money prevented the assemblage of such talent again. And tastes in music had been evolving; the public once again was seeking something new, something different. Perhaps its postwar affluence made it want to forget its prewar preferences and performers along with its prewar poverty.

Nor did network television spring full-blown from experimental laboratories overnight, so to speak, in 1947–1949. Its maximum impact was later. But television's minds were ahead of its onstream technology. The producers had also read the ratings, and they were planning for the future. Their plans did not include programming the big bands as they had been programmed in radio.

It is doubtful if the band leaders were fully cognizant of the underlying causes of what was happening. Possibly no one at that time understood them. But the results were readily apparent—fewer opportunities for the big bands, fewer locations, fewer radio broadcasts, fewer record sales. And something had to be done.

Goodman was a bit more insulated from the economic consequences of the advent of television and the other factors that were changing the big bands' milieu. His past success assured some momentum generally, and at the beginning of 1947 he had a commercial radio program that had a half year yet to run. But Benny is an astute businessman, and it is likely he had some appreciation of the evolving environment for the big bands.

He was also fully aware that musical modes were changing, and he had never been one to shrink from new challenges. If a new style was what was wanted, that new style he would play. Not that he would compromise his integrity to pander to the crowd; Benny is an obsessively proud man who felt he could damn' well play bop as well as anyone. And besides, it might be fun.

Thus Benny's bop band. A controversial chapter in his long career, certainly. Few Goodman enthusiasts champion this band, but those few are ardent. They do not include the majority of collectors, the author, or Benny Goodman.

BENNY GOODMAN AND HIS ORCHESTRA   January 28, 1947, Hollywood

Benny Goodman, clt; Nate Kazebier, George Wendt, Zeke Zarchey, Joe Triscari, tpt; Red Ballard, Lou McGarity, Bill Schaefer, tbn; Skeets Herfurt, Heinie Beau, as; Babe Russin, Jack Chaney, ts; Chuck Gentry, bar; Jess Stacy, p; Allan Reuss, g; LARRY BREEN, b; Sammy Weiss, d. JOHNNY MERCER, Matt Dennis, voc.

1609-4L-1	CAP 374. EP: CAP EAP 1-409. LP: CAP T409, CapE LC6831, CapJap ECJ50059, CapJap ECJ50074. ET: AFRS P-771
1609-alt.	LP: EMI-F 1551563
	Lonely Moments (arr MLW)
1610-4R-2	CAP 376. LP: CapE LC6601. ET: Air Force G1-15. AFRS P-771
	It Takes Time-voc Johnny Mercer (arr TT)
1611	UNISSUED-Tape
	Moon-Faced, Starry-Eyed-voc Matt Dennis (arr JT)
1612-2R-2	CAP 374. EP: CAP EAP 2-409. LP: CAP H409, CAP T409, CapE LC6601, CapE LC6831, CapG LCA409, CapJap ECJ50059, AMI 850019. ET: AFRS P-771
	Whistle Blues (arr MLW)
1619-4R	CAP 376
	Moon-Faced, Starry-Eyed-voc Matt Dennis (arr JT)

(Matrix 1619 may have been recorded January 29, after it was decided that mx 1611 was unsatisfactory. Intervening matrices are not Goodman's.)

Precise personnel for Goodman's band over the next six weeks is not known. The listing following is a collective one; sidemen in bold type are likely present.

AFRS BENNY GOODMAN SHOW - Program #31　　**February 3, 1947,**
Hollywood

Benny Goodman, clt; **Nate Kazebier,** George Wendt, Zeke Zarchey, Joe Triscari, JOHN BEST, GEORGE SEABURG, FRANK BEACH, tpt; **Lou McGarity, TOMMY PEDERSON,** Red Ballard, Bill Schaefer, RAY SIMS, tbn; **Heinie Beau,** Skeets Herfurt, GUS BIVONA, as; **Babe Russin,** Jack Chaney, ZOOT SIMS, ts; **Chuck Gentry,** bar; **Jess Stacy,** p; **Allan Reuss,** g; **HARRY BABASIN,** b; **TOMMY ROMERSA,** d. Jeannie McKeon, voc. Guests: Jimmy Durante, Phil Silvers.

SEXTET: BG, Felice, Stacy, Reuss, Babasin, Romersa

SSC-2-13-3	**ET:** AFRS Benny Goodman Show, Program #31 - Part 1 **'Swonderful** (arr TT) **Oh, But I Do**-voc Jeannie McKeon (arr TT)
SSC-2-13-4	**ET:** as above, except Part 2 **Toscanini, Iturbi And Me**-voc Jimmy Durante, Phil Silvers—Mobilgas Orchestra - BG, clt **The Anniversary Song** - SEXTET

("'Swonderful" is dubbed to Program #47; and is also on **LP**, FH 23. "The Anniversary Song" is also on **LP**, YB 467.)

On an unknown date, probably early in February, Benny and his Sextet appeared at a military installation near Los Angeles on a program that also included Frank Sinatra, Johnny Mercer, Marilyn Maxwell, Dave Barry and announcer-MC Gene Norman. AFRS transcribed that portion of the program that was broadcast:

AFRS COMMAND PERFORMANCE No. 272　　**prob. early February 1947**
near Los Angeles

Sextet personnel as February 3.

H-11, 1	**ET:** AFRS Command Performance No. 272 - Part 1 **Sweet Georgia Brown** - SEXTET
H-11, 2	**ET:** as above, except Part 2 **I Know That You Know** - SEXTET

AFRS BENNY GOODMAN SHOW - Program #32　　**February 10, 1947**
Hollywood

Personnels as February 3. Guest: Billie Burke.

SSC-2-20-3	**ET:** AFRS Benny Goodman Show, Program #32 - Part 1 **Jalousie** (arr TT) **Moon-Faced, Starry-Eyed**-voc Jeannie McKeon
SSC-2-20-4	**ET:** as above, except Part 2 **Sweet Georgia Brown** - SEXTET (**Red Horse Boogie** - SEXTET - From ET, Program "#19")

("Jalousie" is dubbed to Programs #39, #45, #50; and is also on **LP**, SB 156, YB 467. "Moon-Faced, Starry-Eyed" is also on **LP**, FH 23. "Sweet Georgia Brown" is also on **LP**, SB 155.)

Should note that through here Jess Stacy is uninfluenced by the trend to bop, and played as he always had—beautifully.

In this period the band appeared at the Meadowbrook Gardens, and also played a number of one-nighters in and around Los Angeles. To date no air checks from any of these engagements have come to the author's attention. Our only "live" Goodman material comes from the Goodman-Borge broadcasts, via AFRS's ET's. It may be that as early as the beginning of 1947 fewer remote "wires" were available to the big bands.

Having recorded his big band for Capitol, Benny next took his small group into its studios. For some inexplicable reason, guitarist Allan Reuss was not included, and Benny's first small group sides for Capitol are by a Quintet:

BENNY GOODMAN QUINTET　　**February 12, 1947, Hollywood**

Goodman, Felice, Stacy, Babasin, Romersa.

1631	CAP 15768. **EP:** CAP EBF 295. **LP:** CAP H295, CAP P395, CAP T395, CAP T669, CapAu CLP501, CapAu ENC508, CapE LC6810, CapG H295, AMI 850019, SW 1364, EMI-F 1551563 **Sweet Georgia Brown**

1632	**LP:** CAP H479, CAP T669, CapE LC6680, CapE LC6810, CapE VMPM1002, CapNZ CLP037, SW 1381, EMI-F 1551563. **EP:** CAP EAP 1-479, CapG EBF 1-479. **I'll Always Be In Love With You**
1633	**LP:** CAP H441, CAP T441, CapE LC6620, SW 1381, EMI-F 1551563. **EP:** CAP EAP 2-441, CapFr&G EBF 1-441. **ET:** AFRS P-4224
1633-2R	UNISSUED - Test Pressing **Sweet Lorraine**
1634	**LP:** CAP H479, CAP T449, CAP T669, CapE LC6680, CapE LC6810, CapNZ CLP037, BomG 665950, EMI 1C054-85161, SW 1381, EMI-F 1551563. **EP:** CAP EAP 1-479, CapG EBF 1-479 **St. Louis Blues**

(NOTE: "St. Louis Blues" is also on BomG and EMI cassettes, complementary to their LP's. Because the author has never found any alternate takes or otherwise-unissued material on cassettes, they are not listed further in this work.)

AFRS BENNY GOODMAN SHOW - Program #33　　**February 17, 1947,**
Hollywood

Personnels as February 3. Guests: Quentin Reynolds, Benay Venuta.

SSC-2-27-3	**ET:** AFRS Benny Goodman Show, Program #33 - Part 1 **'Way Down Yonder In New Orleans** (arr FH) **It Takes Time**-voc Benny Goodman (arr TT)
SSC-2-27-4	**ET:** as above, except Part 2 **St. Louis Blues** - SEXTET

("'Way Down Yonder . . ." is also on **LP**, YB 467. "St. Louis Blues" is also on **LP**, SB 155.)

Benny's next efforts for Capitol mixed classical music and jazz in one session; an unusual event in the studio, but a combination that mirrored some of his "live" performances. He first recorded the Rondo movement of von Weber's "Grand Duo Concertante for Piano and Clarinet" with Nadia Reisenberg, repeating their duet on the third "Benny Goodman Show" broadcast some eight months earlier. This two-part recording has not been released by Capitol at this writing, but a very few collectors have tape transfers of it. He ended the day's date with one side each by his Quintet and his Trio:

BENNY GOODMAN, and NADIA REISENBERG　　**February 19, 1947,**
Hollywood

Benny Goodman, clt; Nadia Reisenberg, p.

1656	UNISSUED - Tape **Grand Duo Concertante for Piano and Clarinet, Opus 48, In E-Flat Major** (von Weber) **Third Movement: Rondo - Beginning**
1657	UNISSUED - Tape **Grand Duo Concertante for Piano and Clarinet, Opus 48, In E-Flat Major** (von Weber) **Third Movement: Rondo - Conclusion**

BENNY GOODMAN QUINTET　　**same session**

Personnel as February 12.

1658-3R-1	CAP B20130. **LP:** CAP H479, CapE LC6680, CapNZ CLP037, SW 1381, EMI-F 1551563. **EP:** CAP EAP 1-479, CapG EBF 1-479 **I Know That You Know**

BENNY GOODMAN TRIO　　**same session**

Goodman, Stacy, Romersa.

1659	**LP:** CAP H295, CAP P395, CapAu CLP501, CapAu ENC508, CapE LC6557, CapG H295, SW 1364, EMI-F 1551563, PAU 9031 **I Can't Get Started**

AFRS BENNY GOODMAN SHOW - Program #34 February 24, 1947, Hollywood

Personnels as February 3. Guest: Ralph Edwards.

SSC-3-5-3   **ET:** AFRS Benny Goodman Show, Program #34 - Part 1
             Canadian Capers (arr TT)
             Maybe You'll Be There-voc Jeannie McKeon

SSC-3-5-4   **ET:** as above, except Part 2
             I Know That You Know - SEXTET

("Canadian Capers" is dubbed to Program #49; and is also on **LP,** SB 156 and YB 467 (as 'Moonlight Saving Time"!). "Maybe You'll Be There" is also on **LP,** FH 23 and SB 156. "I Know That You Know" is also on **LP,** SB 155.)

There was no Goodman-Borge broadcast March 3. Its time slot was preempted by the Bell Telephone Company for a special program celebrating the centennial anniversary of Alexander Graham Bell. There is no known AFRS replacement ET for this date.

Another Alexander—Alexandria, really, Jess Alexandria Stacy, his full name—was about to celebrate, too: in May he'll form his own regrettably short-lived and illrecorded big band. Possibly in anticipation thereof, pianist-arranger Tommy Todd replaces Jess on the next Capitol session:

BENNY GOODMAN QUARTET   March 7, 1947, Hollywood

Goodman; TOMMY TODD, p; Babasin, Romersa.

1698-4L-2   CAP 394, CapE CL13073, CapG CL 15286. **LP:** CAP
             H441, CAP T441, CapE LC6620, SW 1380. **EP:** CAP
             EAP 1-441, CapFr&G EBF 2-441. **ET:** AFRS P-785,
             AFRS P-4223
             The Lonesome Road

BENNY GOODMAN QUINTET   same session

Goodman, Felice, Todd, Babasin, Romersa.

1699-5R-2   same issues, except omit CapE & CapG 78's; and **LP,**
             substitute SW 1381 for SW 1380 and add EMI-F
             1551563
             Fine And Dandy

Jess is back three days later for the Goodman-Borge broadcast; his conception and "sound" are unmistakable in both the big band and sextet renditions. As much as any pianist's, Jess's timbre, his Klangfarbe, is unique. The author once persuaded a very accomplished pianist, both an accompanist and teacher of some repute, to try to duplicate a Stacy solo. Although he could "play like" Hines and Wilson and Waller, and gave a fairly good representation of Tatum and Peterson, he simply could not simulate that solo. He played all the notes easily enough—it simply sounded different. He said he thought there must be something in the bone-and-muscle structure of Jess's hands that enabled him to play as he did, and that anyone with a different manual formation would produce a different timbre. Interestingly, the author once asked Jess if he could account for his unexampled sound; Jess, a modest man, said he thought it had something to do with his hands. . .

AFRS BENNY GOODMAN SHOW - Program #35 March 10, 1947, Hollywood

Personnels as February 3. Guests: Beryl Davis, Dennis Day.

SSC-3-12-3   **ET:** AFRS Benny Goodman Show, Program #35-Part I
             You Turned The Tables On Me-voc Beryl Davis -
                SEXTET
             Jack, Jack, Jack (announced as, "Tuo Tuo Guerro")
                (arr TT)

(No Goodman renditions on Part 2 of this ET)

("You Turned The Tables On Me" is also on **LP,** SB 155, SWH 17. "Jack, Jack, Jack" is also on **LP,** FH 23, FH 1974, YB 467.)

Jess Stacy is not audibly identifiable on the next Goodman-Borge broadcast. Perhaps the omission of piano soli in both the big band and Quintet performance is indicative of his absence, and he is no longer considered among Goodman's personnel.

AFRS BENNY GOODMAN SHOW - Program #36 March 17, 1947, Hollywood

Orchestra personnel as February 3, except AL HENDRICKSON, g, likely replaces Reuss, and Tommy Todd or JIMMY ROWLES, p, replaces Stacy. Guest: Jan Clayton.

Quintet: Goodman, Felice, Todd or Rowles, Babasin, Romersa.

SSC-3-19-3   **ET:** AFRS Benny Goodman Show, Program #36 - Part 1
             In A Shanty In Old Shanty Town (arr FH)
             Fine And Dandy - QUINTET

SSC-3-19-4   **ET:** as above, except Part 2
             (**Memories Of You -** SEXTET - from ET, Program #30)

("In A Shanty . . ." is also on **LP,** SB 156, YB 467. "Fine And Dandy" is also on **LP,** SWH 17.)

On March 20 Benny and Peggy Lee were guests on "Sound Off With Mark Warnow," a radio interview show. No acetates of this broadcast are known to exist.

AFRS BENNY GOODMAN SHOW - Program #37 March 24, 1947, Hollywood

Orchestra personnel as March 17, including Hendrickson and Rowles. Guest: Arthur Treacher.

Sextet: BG, Felice, Rowles, Hendrickson, Babasin, Romersa.

SSC-3-26-3   **ET:** AFRS Benny Goodman Show, Program #37 - Part 1
             Tattletale (arr TT and Charlie Shavers)

SSC-3-26-4   **ET:** as above, except Part 2
             The Lonesome Road - SEXTET

("The Lonesome Road" is dubbed to Program #40.)

AFRS BENNY GOODMAN SHOW - Program #38 March 31, 1947 Hollywood

Personnels as March 24. Guest: Shirley Ross.

SSC-4-2-3   **ET:** AFRS Benny Goodman Show, Program #38 - Part 1
             Whistle Blues (announced as, "Whistling Blues")

SSC-4-2-4   **ET:** as above, except Part 2
             The Bannister Slide - SEXTET

(Shirley Ross reputedly sang, "Somebody Loves Me," with unknown accompaniment on this broadcast, but the rendition is not on the ET. "The Bannister Slide" is dubbed to Program #48; and is also on **LP,** SWH 17.)

BENNY GOODMAN DUO   April 6, 1947, Hollywood

Benny Goodman, clt; Jimmy Rowles, p.

1842   **LP:** CAP H441, CAP T441, CapE LC6620, SW 1380,
             EMI-F 1551563. **EP:** CAP EAP 2-441, CapFr&G EBF
             2-441. **ET:** AFRS P-4224.
             Mean To Me

BENNY GOODMAN TRIO   same session

Benny Goodman, clt; Jimmy Rowles, p; Tommy Romersa, d.

1843-4D-3   CAP B20125, CAP 15767, CapG C20125. **LP:** CAP H295,
             CAP H441, CAP T441, CAP P 395, CAP T395, CAP
             T669, CapAu CLP501, CapAu ENC508, CapE LC6620,
             CapG H295, SW 1364, EMI-F 1551563. **EP:** CAP EAP
             1-441, CAP EBF295, CapFR&G 1-441. **ET:** AFRS
             P-4223.
             Puttin' On The Ritz

1844   **LP:** CAP H295, CAP P395, CAP T395, CAP T669, CapAu
             CLP501, CapAu ENC508, CapE LC6557, CapE LC6810,
             CapG H295, SW 1346, EMI-F 1551563
             I Never Knew

April 6, 1947, continued

April 6, 1947, continued

BENNY GOODMAN DUO   **same session**

Goodman, Rowles.

1845-6D-2   CAP B20124, CapG 20124. **LP:** CAP H441, CAP T441,
                   CapE LC 6620, SW 1380. **EP:** CAP EAP 1-441. Cap Fr
                   & G EBF 1-441. **ET:** AFRS G.I. Jive 2058, AFRS G.I.
                   Jive 2111
                   Lazy River

AFRS BENNY GOODMAN SHOW - Program #39   April 7, 1947 Hollywood

Personnels as March 24. Guest: Lionel Barrymore.

SSC-4-9-3   **ET:** AFRS Benny Goodman Show, Program #39 - Part 1
                   Linda

SSC-4-9-4   **ET:** as above, except Part 2
                   How High The Moon - SEXTET
                   (**Jalousie** - from ET, Program #32)

("Linda" is also on **LP,** FH 23, YB 467. "How High The Moon" is also on **LP,**
SWH 17.)

Note that apparently (we do not have copies of the programs as broadcast) Benny's tune allotment was dwindling down to a precious few, two
original performances per show. AFRS's engineers enhanced his role by 50
per cent by cross-dubbing; despite the disputes between the pro- and anti-
Goodman factions among the producers, AFRS believed it knew what the
GI's wanted. Also, if the arrangement of "Remember" in Program #40
sounds different, it is—this is a new chart of the old standard by Tommy
Todd:

AFRS BENNY GOODMAN SHOW - Program #40   **April 14, 1947,**
                                                   Hollywood

Personnels as March 24. Guest: Irving Berlin.

SSC-4-16-3   **ET:** AFRS Benny Goodman Show, Program #40 - Part 1
                   Remember (arr TT)

SSC-4-16-4   **ET:** as above, except Part 2
                   Puttin' On The Ritz - SEXTET
                   (**The Lonesome Road** - SEXTET - from ET, Program
                   #37)

("Remember" is also on **LP,** FH 37, Quicksilver 5046. "Puttin' On The Ritz"
is also on **LP,** SWH 17.)

BENNY GOODMAN SEXTET   **April 17, 1947, Hollywood**

Personnel as March 24.

1834-5D-10   CAP B20127, **LP:** CAP H479, CAP T668, CapE LC6680,
                   CapNZ CLP037, SW 1381, EMI-F 1551563. **ET:** CAP
                   EAP 1-479, CapG 1-479
                   The Bannister Slide

BENNY GOODMAN QUARTET   **same session**

Goodman, Rowles, Babasin, Romersa.

1848-3D-1   CAP B20126, CapE CL13141. **LP:** CAP H441, CAP T441,
                   CapE LC6620, SW 1380, BomG 665984, EMI
                   IC054-85164. **EP:** CAP EAP 2-441, CapFr&G EBF
                   1-441. **ET:** AFRS G.I. Jive 2058, AFRS P-4224.
                   Benny's Boogie

BENNY GOODMAN SEPTET   **same session**

As Sextet, plus RAY SIMS, tbn.

1849-3D-1   CAP B20126, CapE CL13206, CapE F15478. **LP:** CAP
                   H202, CAP P395, CapAu CLP501, CapAu ENC508,
                   CapE LC6526, SW 1364. **EP:** CAP EBF 202. **45:** CAP
                   SET CCF 202. **ET:** AFRS G.I. Jive 2058, AFRS G.I.
                   Jive 2111
                   How High The Moon

(Intervening matrices above are not Goodman's. The seemingly out-of-order
mx 1834 may well represent a re-make from an earlier, but unknown, session.
Detail here may differ from that shown in liner notes of various releases, but is
believed correct.)

AFRS BENNY GOODMAN SHOW - Program #41   **April 21, 1947,**
                                                   Hollywood

Orchestra as March 24. Guest: Craig Rice.
Trio: Goodman, Rowles, Romersa.

SSC-4-23-3   **ET:** AFRS Benny Goodman Show, Program #41 - Part 1
                   Clarinet A La King
                   (**Old Buttermilk Sky** - from ET, Program "#20")

SSC-4-23-4   **ET:** as above, except Part 2
                   Lazy River - TRIO

("Clarinet A La King" is dubbed to Program #46; and is also on **LP,** FH 23,
FH 1974. "Lazy River is also on **LP,** FH 1974, SWH 3.)

Benny broadcast several times for the U.S. Department of State in
April, commentary interspersed with recordings. So far as it is known, there
was no original music on any of these programs, and no transcriptions of the
broadcasts have been located.

BENNY GOODMAN QUINTET   **April 23, 1947, Hollywood**

Goodman, Felice, Rowles, Babasin, Romersa.

1858-4D-5   CAP B20127. **LP:** CAP H479, CAP T668, CapE LC6680,
                   CapNZ CLP037, SW 1381, EMI-F 1551563. **EP:** CAP
                   EAP 2-479, CapG EBF 2-479. **ET:** AFRS G.I. Jive
                   2058, AFRS G.I. Jive 2111 (n/c)
                   Music Maestro Please

Hendrickson replaces Felice.

1859   CAP 15767. **LP:** CAP H295, CAP P395, CAP T395, CAP
                   T668, CapAu CLP501, CapAu ENC508, CapE LC6557,
                   CapG H295, SW 1364. **EP:** CAP EBF 295.
                   Makin' Whoopee

BENNY GOODMAN AND HIS ORCHESTRA   **April 24, 1947, Hollywood**

Benny Goodman, clt; Nate Kazebier, John Best, George Seaburg, Frank
Beach, tpt; Lou McGarity, Tommy Pederson, Ray Sims, tbn; Heinie Beau, Gus
Bivona, as; Babe Russin, Zoot Sims, ts; Chuck Gentry, bar; Tommy Todd, p;
Al Hendrickson, g; Harry Babasin, b; Tommy Romersa, d. LILLIAN LANE,
voc.

1867-6L   CAP 416. **ET:** AFRS P-845
                   I Want To Be Loved-voc Lillian Lane (arr TT)

1868-3R   CAP 416. **LP:** CAP H409, CAP T409, CapE LC6601,
                   CapFr C05481713, CapG LCA409, CapJap ECJ50059,
                   EMI 1C054-81713, EMI-F 1551563. **EP:** CAP - EAP
                   1-409. **ET:** AFRS P-845
                   Mahzel (Means Good Luck) (arr TT)

1869-1L2   CAP 15111
                   Have You Ever Been Told-voc Lillian Lane

(Matrices 1870, 1871 and 1872 are not by Goodman.)

1873-9R   CAP B439, CapNZ CP127. **LP:** CAP H409, CAP T409,
                   CapE LC6601, CapE VMPM1002, CapG LCA409,
                   CapJap ECJ50059, EMI-F 1551563. **EP:** CAP EAP
                   2-409. **ET:** AFRS P-845
                   Tattletale (arr TT & Charlie Shavers)

(Matrices 1874 and 1875 are used for a 78 rpm CAP promo, titled "Greetings
from Capitol Artists to all Music Dealers," distributed to the NAMM convention in Chicago, June 1947. Excerpts from Capitol recordings, including a
portion of Benny's "Makin' Whoopee," intersperse commentary on its two
sides.)

There is a report that Benny appeared at a "Just Jazz" concert in
Pasadena's Civic Auditorium on April 29, and some support for a belief that
"The Lonesome Road," which is on an AFRS ET, is from that concert.
Given AFRS's penchant for cross-dubbing, the supposition is a possibility.
But in view of the personnel on that cut, it is assigned herein to the concert of
June 23, q.v.

Trade papers of the period listed various personnel changes in Benny's
band, but none specified dates of the entrances and exits. Thus once again
the next roster is collective. Musicians whose names are in bold type are

believed certain in a complement that included Goodman and four trumpets, three trombones, five reeds and four rhythm.

"Stealin' Apples" on the next AFRS ET sounds oddly out of keeping with the band's style at this time, as if it had been dubbed from another and earlier source. If so, that source has not been ascertained. Note that there was no Goodman-Borge broadcast on April 28; the time slot was preempted for an address by Secretary of State George C. Marshall. No AFRS ET has been discovered for what would have been Program No. 42.

AFRS BENNY GOODMAN SHOW - Program #43   May 5, 1947, Hollywood

Benny Goodman, clt; **John Best, George Seaburg, Frank Beach**, Nate Kazebier, IRVING GOODMAN, tpt; **Lou McGarity, Tommy Pederson,** Ray Sims, HOYT BOHANNON, tbn; **Heinie Beau, Gus Bivona**, as; Babe Russin, Zoot Sims, HERBIE HAYMER, STAN GETZ, ts; **Chuck Gentry**, bar; **Jimmy Rowles**, p; **Al Hendrickson**, g; **Harry Babasin**, b; **Tommy Romersa**, d. Guests: none listed.

QUINTET: Goodman, Rowles, Hendrickson, Babasin, Romersa.

SSC-5-7-3   **ET**: AFRS Benny Goodman Show, Program #43 - Part 1
    Mahzel (Means Good Luck)
    (**Somebody Stole My Gal** - from ET, Program #1)
    (**On The Sunny Side Of The Street** - from ET, Program #1)

SSC-5-7-4   **ET**: as above, except Part 2
    Stealin' Apples
    After You've Gone - QUINTET

("Mahzel" is also on **LP**, FH 23, FH 1974.)

AFRS BENNY GOODMAN SHOW - Program #44   May 12, 1947, Hollywood

Personnels as May 5. Guest: Jimmy Dykes.

SSC-5-14-3   **ET**: AFRS Benny Goodman Show, Program #44 - Part 1
    Chicago (arr - see note)

SSC-5-14-4   **ET**: as above, except Part 2
    Air Mail Special - QUINTET
    (**I Know That You Know** - from ET, Program #2)

(Fletcher Henderson is usually given credit for this version of "Chicago," but there is some evidence that Tommy Todd was its arranger.)

AFRS BENNY GOODMAN SHOW - Program #45   May 19, 1947, Hollywood

Personnels as May 5. Guest: Frances Langford, voc.

SSC-5-21-3   **ET**: AFRS Benny Goodman Show, Program #45 - Part 1
    Jack, Jack, Jack
    (**Jalousie** - from ET, Program #32)

SSC-5-21-4   **ET**: as above, except Part 2
    Between The Devil And The Deep Blue Sea-voc Frances Langford - Mobilgas Orchestra - BG, clt
    Flying Home - QUINTET

AFRS BENNY GOODMAN SHOW - Program #46   May 26, 1947, Hollywood

Personnels as May 5. Guest: Louella Parsons.

SSC-5-28-3   **ET**: AFRS Benny Goodman Show, Program #46 - Part 1
    I Want To Be Loved-voc Lillian Lane

SSC-5-28-4   **ET**: as above, except Part 2
    Love Is Just Around The Corner - QUINTET
    (**Clarinet A La King** - from ET, Program #41)

("I Want To Be Loved" is also on **LP**, FH 37.)

Capitol was making progress in its efforts to compete with RCA, Columbia and Decca in the jazz field, and had signed some outstanding artists. It displayed their talents in its own all-star date, which incidentally reunited Benny and Red Norvo, whose association stretched over many decades.

Note that an introductory phrase, "Happy am I, happy am I," to "Happy Blues" appears on some microgroove releases, but is excised from the original 78 rpm Capitol issue. These are not alternate takes; save for that elision, all known issued versions are identical.

THE HOLLYWOOD HUCKSTERS   May 29, 1947, Hollywood

Benny Goodman, clt; Charlie Shavers, tpt; Benny Carter, as; Dave Cavanaugh (DC), ts & arr; Joe Koch, bar; Red Norvo, xylo & vib; Jimmy Rowles, p; Irving Ashby, g; Red Callender, b; Lee Young, d. Benny Goodman, Stan Kenton, voc.

2006-2D-4   CAP 48013, CapG C80156. **45:** CAP 7-1230, CapC 7C-593. **EP:** CAP EAP 2-441. **LP:** CAP T441, CapJap ECJ50077, SW 1381, TOSH CR 8811, INT 25039. **ET:** AFRS P-4225
    I Apologize (arr DC)

2007-4D-5   CAP A40022, CapE 13067, CapG C40022. **45:** CapAu,Sd,Sw 7-C40022. **EP:** CAP EBF 322. **LP:** CAP H322, CapE LC6563, CapE VMPM1002, CapJap ECJ50077, TOSH CR8811, INT 25039. **ET:** AFRS P-847
    Them There Eyes (arr DC)

2008-1D-11   CAP A40022, CapE 13067, CapG C40022. **45:** CAP 7-1230, CapAu,Sd,Sw 7C-40022, CapC 7C-593. **LP:** CapE VMPM1002, CapJap ECJ50077, TOSH CR8811, BAND 7106, INT 25039. **ET:** AFRS P-847
    Happy Blues-voc Benny Goodman, Stan Kenton (arr DC)

Capitol's files for Benny's June 5 recording session likely represents the band's personnel for the next Goodman-Borge broadcast, and it is listed for that program. Note that many of the men also recorded with Woody Herman for his Columbia studio session of May 7. This suggests that Benny really had no fixed lineup for his orchestra at this time, save for a few men he had under contract. In large measure they were studio musicians, hired for the broadcasts and recording sessions.

AFRS BENNY GOODMAN SHOW - Program #47   June 2, 1947, Hollywood

Benny Goodman, clt; John Best, George Seaburg, Frank Beach, Irving Goodman, tpt; Lou McGarity, Tommy Pederson, Hoyt Bohannon, tbn; Heinie Beau, Gus Bivona, as; Herbie Haymer, Stan Getz, ts; Chuck Gentry, bar; Jimmy Rowles, p; Al Hendrickson, g; Harry Babasin, b; DON LAMOND, d. Matt Dennis, voc. RALPH BURNS (RB), arr. Guest: Peter Lorre.

QUINTET: Goodman, Rowles, Hendrickson, Babasin, Lamond.

SSC-6-4-3   **ET**: AFRS Benny Goodman Show, Program # 47 - Part 1
    Skeleton In The Closet-voc Matt Dennis (arr RB)
    ('**Swonderful** - from ET, Program #31)

SSC-6-4-4   **ET**: as above, except Part 2
    Cherokee - QUINTET

Throughout this work song titles are shown as they appear on the labels of releases; thus, "King Porter" may be listed for one issue, "King Porter Stomp" for another—but both are Jelly Roll Morton's classic. In this next studio date, a fairly recent English LP titles the tune, "8, 9 And Ten," just reversing the new York Times's style manual for numbers. Capitol's files show the title as, "Eight, Nine And Ten." Further, it was originally a two-part composition: "No, Baby, No" was recorded as Part 1 of "Eight, Nine And Ten," but was retitled before it was released.

BENNY GOODMAN AND HIS ORCHESTRA   **June 5, 1947, Hollywood**

Personnel as June 2. Benny Goodman, Lillian Lane, voc.

2022-7D-10   CAP B20124, CapG C20124. **ET:** AFRS G.I. Jive 2111
           No, Baby, No-voc Benny Goodman (arr - see note)

2023   **LP:** CapE VMPM1002
           8, 9 And Ten (arr RB)

2024   **LP:** CapE VMPM1002
           The Best Things In Life Are Free-voc Lillian Lane (arr
           TT)

2025-1D-1   CAP B439, CapNZ CP127. **EP:** CAP EAP 1-409. **LP:** CAP
           H409, CAP T409, CapE LC6601, CapE LC6831, CapG
           LCA409, CapJap ECJ50059, EMI-F 1551563. **ET:** AFRS
           P-845
           Dizzy Fingers (arr TT)

2026-2D-9   CAP B20125, CAP 57-733, CapAu&NZ CP142, CapC
           C151, CapE CL13142, CapG C20125. **EP:** CAP EAP
           2-409. **LP:** CAP H409, CAP T409, CapE LC6601, CapE
           LC6831, CapJap ECJ50059, AMI 850019, CONTOUR
           (PIC), 2870443, EMI 64035. **ET:** AFRS G.I. Jive 2111,
           Voice of the Army 499 (''Melody Moderne'')
           Chicago (arr - see note)

(Both Ralph Burns and Tommy Todd supplied arrangements for Part 1 (''No, Baby, No'') of ''Eight, Nine and Ten,'' but only Burns is known to have provided a chart for Part 2. It is not known whose arrangement was used for the issued ''No, Baby, No.'' And note too that Tommy Todd, not Fletcher Henderson, may be responsible for this arrangement of ''Chicago.'')

BENNY GOODMAN SEXTET   **June 6, 1947, Hollywood**

Benny Goodman, clt; Red Norvo, vib; Jimmy Rowles, p; Al Hendrickson, g; Harry Babasin, b; Don Lamond, d.

2030-5D-6   CAP 15166. **EP:** CAP EAP 2-479, CapG EBF 2-479. **LP:**
           CAP H479, CAP T668, CapE LC6680, CapNZ CLP037,
           SW 1381, EMI-F 1551563, INT 25039
           Cherokee (Indian Love Song)

(Matrices 2031 through 2033 are not by Goodman, were used for a children's album.)

2034-4D-1   CAP 15286, CapE F15477, CapG C80015. **EP:** CAP
           EBF202. **LP:** CAP H202, CAP P395, CAP T395, CAP
           T668, CapAu CLP501, CapAu ENC508, CapE LC6526,
           SW 1364, INT 25039
           The Maids Of Cadiz

2035-2D-1   same issues as ''Cherokee''
           Love Is Just Around The Corner

2036   **LP:** CAP T669, CapE LC6810, SW 1381, INT 25039
           I Know That You Know

AFRS BENNY GOODMAN SHOW - Program #48 June 9, 1947, Hollywood

Orchestra as June 2. Sextet as June 6. No guests listed.

SSC-6-11-3   **ET:** AFRS Benny Goodman Show, Program #48 - Part 1
           Dizzy Fingers

SSC-6-11-4   **ET:** as above, except Part 2
           (**The Bannister Slide** - from ET, Program #38)
           Just One Of Those Things - SEXTET

AFRS BENNY GOODMAN SHOW - Program #49   **June 16, 1947,**
                                               Hollywood

Personnels as June 9. Guest: Clifton Webb.

SSC-6-18-3   **ET:** AFRS Benny Goodman Show, Program #49 - Part 1
           Mahzel (Means Good Luck)

SSC-6-18-4   **ET:** as above, except Part 2
           I Know That You Know - SEXTET
           (**Canadian Capers** - from ET, Program #34)

Together with an all-star octet led by Benny Carter, and performances by Peggy Lee and Erroll Garner, Benny's Trio and Sextet were transcribed by AFRS as they appeared at a ''Just Jazz'' concert on the day of the next Goodman-Borge broadcast. The concert was in part, at least, broadcast via an unknown network, and acetates of the broadcast provide one Goodman rendition that AFRS failed to include in its ET's:

AFRS JUBILEE SERIES H-18, Program No. 261   **June 23, 1947**
                                       Civic Auditorium, Pasadena

Sextet as June 9.

D-19968   **ET:** AFRS Jubilee Series H-18, Program No. 261 - Part 1
           After You've Gone - SEXTET

AFRS JUBILEE SERIES H-18, Program No. 262   **same date**

Sextet as June 9. TRIO: Goodman, Rowles, Lamond.

D-19971   **ET:** AFRS Jubilee Series H-18, Program No. 262 - Part 2
           Puttin' On The Ritz - TRIO
           The Lonesome Road - SEXTET

Also extant as an air check from this concert:
Air Mail Special - SEXTET

(''Puttin' On The Ritz'' is also on **LP**, SWH 17.)

Here is the last Goodman-Borge broadcast transcribed by AFRS, and the penultimate broadcast in the series:

AFRS BENNY GOODMAN SHOW - Program #50   **June 23, 1947,**
                                               Hollywood

Personnels as June 9. Guest: Marjorie Main.

SSC-6-25-3   **ET:** AFRS Benny Goodman Show, Program #50 - Part 1
           (**Jalousie** - from ET, Program #32)
           Tattletale

SSC-6-25-4   **ET:** as above, except Part 2
           Sweet Georgia Brown - SEXTET
           Red Horse Boogie - SEXTET (voice over)

On occasion AFRS transcribed the Borden Company's ''Carnation Contented Hour,'' but no ET has ever been discovered for Benny's appearance on the next broadcast. An amateur recordist captured it in part:

''CARNATION CONTENTED HOUR''   *June 27, 1947,*
  CBS Radio Network   *Hollywood*

Benny Goodman, clt, and a studio orchestra.

Sweet Sue-Just You (n/c - few notes only)
Canadian Capers

The final Goodman-Borge broadcast was June 30; ''Dr. I.Q.'' took over its time slot the following week. So far as it is known AFRS did not transcribe this program, but two cuts are extant via acetates:

''THE VICTOR BORGE SHOW   *June 30, 1947,*
  STARRING BENNY GOODMAN''   *Hollywood*
  NBC Radio Network

Personnels as June 9. Guests unknown.

Ev'rything I've Got (Belongs To You) (arr RB)
Dardanella - SEXTET

The date of the next air check is known, but its source is not. It may have come from a location in Crescent City, California, for Benny had an engagement there beginning in late June:

SUSTAINING BROADCAST   *July 2, 1947,*
  Unknown radio network   *location unknown*

Personnel as June 9.

Just One Of Those Things - SEXTET

Benny spent most of July satisfying some classical commitments as a soloist. He performed for three days with the New Orleans Symphony, then on July 17 appeared with the Buffalo Symphony. He returned to the West Coast the end of the month to reassemble his bop band. The reconstituted orchestra was in the Meadowbrook Gardens, Culver City, on August 3.

But his chief reason for a return to California was to make what will be his last appearance as an actor in a motion picture . . . "A Song Is Born." And with that statement the author admits to having perpetrated an inexcusable gaffe in his earlier work on Goodman, for in "BG - On The Record" he mistakenly dated the film as July/August 1948, instead of 1947. That false premise triggered other errors, as we shall see; and hopefully this treatise will set them all to rights.

Initially titled "That's Life," "A Song Is Born" is a re-make of the 1941 RKO-Radio production "Ball Of Fire" that starred Gary Cooper and Barbara Stanwyck, with BG alumnus Gene Krupa and his Orchestra. Both films are based on a story by Billy Wilder and Thomas Monroe, "From A To Z." Here is a sequential resume of Goodman's musical portion of the movie, followed by a summation of the contributions of the other instrumental and vocal performers:

"A SONG IS BORN"   *July/August 1947, Hollywood*

An RKO—Samuel Goldwyn motion picture filmed in Technicolor.
Release date: October 1948
Director: Howard Hawks   *Producer: Samuel Goldwyn*
Musical direction: Emil Newman, Hugo Friedhofer
                          Orchestrations: Sonny Burke
Songs by Don Raye and Gene DePaul
CAST: Danny Kaye, Virginia Mayo, Hugh Herbert, Steve Cochrane, J. Edward Bromberg, Felix Bressart, O.Z. Whitehead and Ludwig Stossel, plus Louis Armstrong, Buck and Bubbles, Jeri Sullivan (voice dub for Virginia Mayo), The Golden Gate Quartet, the Page Cavanaugh Trio, and the orchestras of Charlie Barnet, Tommy Dorsey, Lionel Hampton, Mel Powell, and Russo and the Samba Kings; and in the role of "Professor Magenbruch," Benny Goodman.

BENNY GOODMAN SEXTET: Benny Goodman, clt; Lionel Hampton, vib; Mel Powell, p; Al Hendrickson, g; Harry Babasin, b, Louis Bellson, d.

"LEADERS' ORCHESTRA": Benny Goodman, clt; Louis Armstrong, tpt; Tommy Dorsey, tbn; Charlie Barnet, ts; Lionel Hampton, vib; Mel Powell, p; Al Hendrickson, g; Harry Babasin, b, Louis Bellson, d.

portion, Mozart Clarinet Concerto - Benny Goodman, clt, and a string quartet
portion, "Anitra's Dance" - Benny Goodman, clt, and Buck Washington, p
. . . few bars, unidentified classical composition - Benny Goodman, clt, and a string quartet
Stealin' Apples - BENNY GOODMAN SEXTET
*A Song Was Born-voc Louis Armstrong, Jeri Sullivan, the Golden Gate Quartet - LEADERS' ORCHESTRA, plus other musicians to fill (**LP:** RARE RECORDS 6, PUMPKIN 109)*
*Flying Home (n/c - interrupted by dialog) - LEADERS' ORCHESTRA, plus members of Lionel Hampton's orchestra (**LP:** RARE RECORDS 6)*

Non-Goodman performances, in main brief excerpts, with dialog over, include:

Louis Armstrong Nonet: Louis Armstrong, tpt; Vic Dickenson, tbn, Barney Bigard, clt; Benny Carter, as; Lionel Hampton, vib; Phil Moore, p; Irving Ashby, g; Charlie Drayton, b; Zutty Singleton, d:
*Goldwyn Stomp (**LP:** PUMPKIN 109, RARE RECORDS 6)*
Charlie Barnet and his Orchestra:
Redskin Rhumba
Tommy Dorsey and his Orchestra:
I'm Getting Sentimental Over You (theme); segue to, Marie
Golden Gate Quartet:
unidentified spiritual; Jericho
Mel Powell and his Orchestra:
Muskrat Ramble
Jeri Sullivan and the Page Cavanaugh Trio, plus studio orchestra.
Daddy-O
. . . and tout les ensemble, sans Benny Goodman:
incidental music throughout; Anvil Chorus

The author is willing to share the blame for his misdating of "A Song Is Born" with Capitol Records, for he now believes information it supplied was faulty. He was advised that Capitol matrices 3426 and 3427, applied to the two-sided 78 rpm release of the title song, "A Song Was Born," were recorded August 9, 1948, along with matrix 3421, assigned to a then-unissued performance, that presumably included Goodman, "Goldwyn Stomp." These matrices are out of sequence with Capitol's numbering in 1947 (the next Goodman studio recording for Capitol, August 11, 1947, bears matrix 2149); but they are in accord with Capitol matrices for August 1948. Given that it would have been wholly unlikely that the cast of the

movie could have been reassembled a year later merely to make a record, the date of the movie thus became July/August 1948.

But the author is now convinced that matrices 3421, 3426 and 3427 are pressing matrices, assigned at the time existing material was processed for issuance. Thus August 9, 1948 is the date CAP 10172, "A Song Was Born," was put into manufacture, not when it was recorded. This assumption obviates the matrix discrepancy and reassembly of the cast.

Further, matrix "3421," at least, was not recorded in Capitol's studios. Discovery of two, two-sided Samuel Goldwyn Studios Reference Recordings provided the author with his first audition of that matrix. Later, it was released on **LP**, TOSHIBA CR8811. Given the two, several things came to light: One, the cuts on the Goldwyn 12" acetate and the Toshiba LP are identical. Two, the title supplied by Capitol is wrong; the tune is "Muskrat Ramble," not "Goldwyn Stomp." Three, although the Mel Powell movie sequence of "Muskrat Ramble" is abridged, it is the same take as that on the Goldwyn/Toshiba discs. And four, Goodman is not in that group. Nor are Armstrong, Dorsey or Barnet. Its personnel, for those interested, should be reconstituted based on visual identification afforded by the film itself.

More of the Goldwyn Reference Recordings later. But first, let's enter "Capitol's" recording of "A Song Was Born." It is different from the take used in the film. And note that although the film is titled "A Song Is Born," its title song uses the past tense:

A SONG WAS BORN   **July/August 1947, Hollywood**

Personnel as "Leaders' Orchestra" in the film "A Song Is Born," plus unknown musicians to fill it. Note that "The Brazilians" are given label credit for participation, but that they are not identifiable on the recording.

"3426"   CAP 10172. **LP:** CapJap EDJ50077
           A Song Was Born, Part I-voc Golden Gate Quartet, Jeri
              Sullivan, Louis Armstrong

"3427"   same issues
           A Song Was Born, Part II

(Although "A Song Was Born" is not included in the two Goldwyn Reference Recordings, the author believes it likely that it was recorded in the Goldwyn studios, not in Capitol's.)

Benny blows an especially imaginative chorus on Part II of "A Song Was Born," above. Not even the Goodman traditionalist should dismiss his work while he was in his bop period.

As indicated in the listing for the film, the musical performances in main are fragmentary; and further research has revealed that some of those that sound complete are indeed edited, abridged, when compared with other source material. These elisions, coupled with the film's voice-overdubbing and interruptions, make it difficult to compare one "version" of a tune with another. Thus the author cannot say for certain that the next entry of the title tune is dubbed directly from the sound track, but he believes that it is. The original issue on a 12" Japanese Victor is rare, but it does provide good sound:

A SONG WAS BORN   **July/August 1947, Hollywood**

Personnel as "Leaders' Orchestra" in the film "A Song Is Born," plus unknown musicians to fill.

M-233   ViJap NB-6013. **LP:** RcaFr FXMI-7083
           A Song Was Born-voc Golden Gate Quartet, Jeri
              Sullivan, Louis Armstrong

To promote the film via radio, RKO-Goldwyn distributed three 16" electrical transcriptions bearing WOR label credits. (WOR is the call letters of a then-independent radio broadcasting station located in Newark, New Jersey, affiliated with the Mutual Broadcasting System.) One, No. 1168, contains only voice tracks by Goodman, Armstrong, Hampton, Tommy Dorsey and Barnet, no music. The other two are two-sided, and are numbered 3177 A/B, and 3207 A/B. They each offer partial and complete renditions of selections from, "A Song Was Born," but both are necessary to obtain full versions of all the selections. Benny has voice tracks on 3177 A and 3207 B. Dorsey has voice tracks on 3177 B; and both Dorsey and Barnet have voice tracks on 3207 A.

Painstaking reassessment of selections common to the WOR transcriptions, Goldwyn acetates and a rather poor-quality print of the film persuades the author that the Sextet's "Stealin' Apples," and Armstrong-Hampton's "Goldwyn Stomp," are identical takes, ET's vis a vis the film. He is less certain of "Flying Home" and "A Song Was Born," ET's vis a vis film; some passages in each sound the same, some dissimilar—perhaps cross-dubbing was employed. But in any event, the dedicated Goodman collector should have copies of the ET's because they provide complete versions of the tunes, whereas the film offers edited cuts.

A SONG IS BORN - WOR

Appropriate personnels as per the film, "A Song Is Born."

3177-A   **ET:** A Song Is Born, WOR 3177 - Part A
(Intro; announcement; Goodman voice track)
Flying Home (n/c)
Stealin' Apples
(Daddy-O)
(Goldwyn Stomp)
A Song Was Born (n/c)
Flying Home (n/c)

3177-B   **ET:** as above, except Part B
(Intro; announcement; Dorsey voice track)
Flying Home (n/c)
(I'm Getting Sentimental Over You; Marie)
(Redskin Rhumba (n/c))
Stealin' Apples
A Song Was Born
(I'm Getting Sentimental Over You)

(Note that all three tracks of "Flying Home," above, are incomplete. A full version is on WOR 3207-A, next. Also, edited cuts of "A Song Was Born" are on LP, RcaFr NL 89279-2 and PUMPKIN 109.)

A SONG IS BORN - WOR   July/August 1947, Hollywood

Appropriate personnels as per the film, "A Song Is Born."

3207-A   **ET:** A Song Is Born, WOR 3207 - Part A
(Announcement; Barnet, Dorsey themes, voice tracks)
Flying Home
Stealin' Apples
(I'm Getting Sentimental Over You; Marie)
(Redskin Rhumba)
(Goldwyn Stomp (n/c))

3207-B   **ET:** as above, except Part B
(Goldwyn Stomp (n/c))
(Goodman voice track)
(Daddy-O (n/c))
Stealin' Apples
(Goldwyn Stomp (n/c))

(Note that Louis's and Lionel's "Goldwyn Stomp" is incomplete on all three tracks above; a complete version is on WOR 3177-A, preceding. Interestingly, the Sextet's "Stealin' Apples" is the only selection recorded in its entirety each time it appears on the WOR transcriptions.)

A SONG IS BORN - WOR   July/August 1947, Hollywood

Voice tracks only - no music.

13-1168-A   **ET:** A Song Is Born, WOR 1168 - Part A
(Voice tracks by Goodman, Armstrong, Hampton, T. Dorsey, Barnet)

We are not yet finished with "A Song Is Born." Having just reduced the various "different" performances by Benny by virtue of cross-referencing, it is now the author's pleasant obligation to add a brand new one: an alternate take of the Sextet's "Stealin' Apples."

One of the Goldwyn Reference Recordings mentioned above contains four cuts, two on each side. They are "Redskin Rhumba"-"Goldwyn Stomp/Stealin' Apples" -"Muskrat Ramble." All of these are the same as the respective performances in the film, on the WOR ET's, and the Toshiba LP. The second has but two cuts. Its Side A has a repeat of, "Redskin Rhumba." But—at last—its second side has a noticeably different version of the Waller masterpiece, and one of Benny's favorite tunes, "Stealin' Apples."

The discs are not inscribed with matrix or take numbers. But before each selection is played, a voice announcement specifies the number of the recording. This number is used below as both a "matrix" and a "catalog"

number, for purposes of certain identification, although they may not be necessary; the disc may be unique.

A SONG IS BORN - GOLDWYN   July/August 1947, Hollywood

Benny Goodman, clt; Lionel Hampton, vib; Mel Powell, p; Al Hendrickson, g; Harry Babasin, b; Louis Bellson, d.

3200 DS-24   Samuel Goldwyn Studios Reference Recording 3200 DS-24
Stealin' Apples - SEXTET

"Hi 'Ya Sophia" next, pays tribute to one of Alice's daughters from her first marriage; as noted earlier, Benny has memorialized each of his children by naming recordings for them. Note that Red Norvo replaces Lionel Hampton in Benny's "A Song Is Born" Sextet; Lionel's contract with Decca prevented him from recording with Benny for Capitol.

THE BENNY GOODMAN SEXTET   August 11, 1947, Hollywood

Benny Goodman, clt; Red Norvo, vib; Mel Powell, p; Al Hendrickson, g; Harry Babasin, b; Louis Bellson, d. Al Hendrickson, voc.

2149   CAP B462, CapE CL13136, CapNZ CP131, CapE F15477.
45: CAP set CCF202. **EP:** CAP EBF202. **LP:** CAP H202, CAP P395, CAP T395, CAP T668, Cap AuCLP50I,CapAu ENC508, CapE LC6526, SW 1364, EMI-F 1551563, INT 25039
Hi 'Ya Sophia

2150   CAP B462
Baby, Have You Got A Little Love To Spare-voc Al Hendrickson

BENNY GOODMAN SEXTET   August 25, 1947, Hollywood

Personnel as August 11, except ARTIE SHAPIRO, b, replaces Babasin.

2198   CAP 15008, CapE F15476. **45:** CAP set CCF202. **EP:** CAP EBF202. **LP:** CAP H202, CAP P395, CAP T395, CAP T668, CapE LC6526, CapE VMPM1002, SW 1364, EMI-F 1551563, INT 25039
Nagasaki

Capitol assembled some of its recording stars for a patriotic tribute, and Benny joined the group:

PAUL WESTON AND HIS ORCHESTRA   September 12, 1947, Hollywood

Benny Goodman, clt, and Paul Weston and his Orchestra.

2247   CAP 15003
The Freedom Train-voc Johnny Mercer, Peggy Lee, Margaret Whiting and the Pied Pipers

BENNY GOODMAN SEXTET   September 22, 1947, Hollywood

Personnel as August 25, except JOE MONDRAGON, b, and TOMMY ROMER-SA, d, replace Shapiro and Bellson respectively. Al Hendrickson, voc.

2261-4D-5   CAP 15286, CapE CL13073, CapE F15476, CapG CL15286, CapG C80-15208. **45:** CAP set CCF202. **EP:** CAP EBF202. **LP:** CAP H202, CAP P395, CAP T395, CAP T668, CapAu CLP50I, CapAu ENC508, CapE LC6526, CapE VMPM1002, SW 1364, INT 25039
The Varsity Drag

2262   CAP 15008, CapE CL13022
Gonna Get A Girl-voc Al Hendrickson

Benny evidently sensed that his big band bop recordings weren't all that popular with the public, so for his next Capitol date he had Fletcher Henderson write five new arrangements for the orchestra. They are more conventional than the scores Benny had been playing, but they are something short of classic Hendersonia:

BENNY GOODMAN AND HIS ORCHESTRA   October 23, 1947, Hollywood

Benny Goodman, clt; George Seaburg, Frank Beach, Irving Goodman, VERNON "JAKE" PORTER, tpt; Lou McGarity, Tommy Pederson, HERBIE HARPER, tbn; Gus Bivona, JACK DUMONT, as; BABE RUSSIN, BUMPS MEYERS, ts; Chuck Gentry, bar; Mel Powell, p; Al Hendrickson, g; ARTIE SHAPIRO, b; Tommy Romersa, d. Al Hendrickson, EMMA LOU WELCH, voc.

2370	CAP 15208, CapE CL13003, CapFr 15208319, CapG C80-15208. **LP:** CapE LC6520. **ET:** 1949 American Cancer Society (n/c) **On A Slow Boat To China**-voc Al Hendrickson (arr FH)
2371	CAP 15020, CapG C15020. **EP:**CAP EAP 2-409, CAP EBF241. **LP:**CAP H241, CAP T409, CAP T795, CapE LC6520, CapE LC6831, CapFr C054-81713, CapJap ECJ50059, AMI 850019, EMI 64-704, EMI IC054-52715, EMI IC054-81713 **Sweet And Lovely** (arr FH)
2372	CAP 15020, CapE CL13022, CapG C15020 **Oooh! Look-a There, Ain't She Pretty?**-voc Emma Lou Welch (arr FH)

Add Red Norvo, vib.

2373	CAP 57-733, CapC C151, CapE CL13264, CapNZ CP 131. **EP:** CAP&FR EAP 1-409. **LP:** CAP H409, CAP T409, CapE LC6601, Cap E LC6831, CapFr C054-81713, CapG LCA409, CapJap ECJ50059, EMI IC054-52715, EMI IC054-81713, EMI-F 1551563 **Back In Your Own Back Yard** (arr FH)

Norvo out.

2374	**LP:** CAP H409, CAP T409, CapE LC6601 CapE LC6831, CapG LCA409, CapJap ECJ50059, AMI 850019. **EP:** CAP&Fr EAP 409, CAP EBF 241 **Wrap Your Troubles In Dreams (And Dream Your Troubles Away)** (arr FH)

Immediately following this session Benny flew to Virginia Beach, Virginia, where he had a one-week engagement at the Surf Beach Club for the orchestra. How many of those who made the record date accompanied him is not known, but it seems likely that some of them stayed behind because of movie studio commitments. Benny disbanded at the end of the Surf Beach Club stand, and for the next year he will work primarily with small groups, although he will record with big bands assembled for those studio dates. This might seem the end of Benny's big bands, but it is not; a new one will emerge in December 1948, playing on the road, recording for Capitol, and boppin' more than ever.

Out of the big band business temporarily, Benny's first move was to get together with Teddy Wilson, and with Jimmy Crawford, a "fly" drummer who had propelled the great Jimmy Lunceford orchestra (Lunceford had collapsed while signing autographs in a record store in Oregon, and had died on July 12, 1947). Before the new Trio recorded for Capitol, it appeared on Buddy Clark's "Carnation Contented Hour" broadcast weekly via NBC on Monday evenings. AFRS transcribed the program, but its ET reverses the Part 1 and Part 2 inscriptions. This listing corrects the reversal:

AFRS MELODY HOUR No. 216   November 3, 1947, New York

Benny Goodman, clt; Teddy Wilson, p; Jimmy Crawford, d.

D-20093 (SSR-11-10-3)	**ET:** AFRS Melody Hour No. 216-Part 1 **Poor Butterfly** - TRIO
D-20094 (SSR-11-10-4)	**ET:** as above, except Part 2 **After You've Gone** - TRIO

("Poor Butterfly" is also on LP: MARK 678.)

For the first time, Benny recorded in Capitol's New York studios. Note that matrices 1999 and 2500 are consecutive.

BENNY GOODMAN TRIO   November 7, 1947, New York

Personnel as November 3.

1996	CAP 15888. **45:** CAP set CCF343. **EP:** CAP EBF 2-343. **LP:** CAP H343, CapE LC 6565, CapE VMPM1002, SW 1380 **Blue (And Broken Hearted)**
1997	CAP 15888. **45:** CAP set CCF343. **EP:** CAP EBF 1-343. **LP:** CAP H343, CAP T669, CapE LC6565, CapE LC6810, SW 1380, EMI-F 1551563 **After Hours**
1998	**LP:** CAP T795 ("History Of Jazz No. 3"), SW 1380 **All I Do Is Dream Of You**
1999	**LP:** CAP H343, CAP H479, CAP T669, CapE LC6565, CapE LC6680, CapE LC6810, CapeE VMPM1002, SW 1380. **EP:** CAP EAP 2-479, CAP EBF 1-343 **I'll Never Be The Same**
2500	CAP 15887. **45:** CAP set CCF343. **EP:** CAP EBF 2-343. **LP:** CAP H343, CapE LC6565, SW 1380 **Bye Bye Pretty Baby**
2501	**LP:** CAP H441, CAP T441, CapE LC6620, CapE VMPM1002, SW 1380, EMI-F 1551563. **EP:** CAP EAP 2-441, CapFr&G EBF 2-441. **ET:** AFRS P-4224 **Shoe Shine Boy**

(Above all on LP, PAU 9031.)

When introduced on Fred Allen's popular Sunday evening radio program, Benny blows a few comic notes with the studio orchestra. Then the Trio performs:

"THE FRED ALLEN SHOW"   *November 16, 1947,*
NBC Radio Network   *New York*

Intro, Benny Goodman, clt, and a studio orchestra. Trio personnel as November 3.

. . . intro—Benny Goodman, clt, and a studio orchestra
All I Do Is Dream Of You—TRIO

BENNY GOODMAN TRIO   November 17, 1947, New York

Personnel as November 3.

2517	CAP 15888. **45:** CAP set CCF343. **EP:** CAP EBF 2-343. **LP:** CAP H343, CapE LC6565, SW 1380, PAU 9031 **At Sundown**
2518	same issues as preceding, except substitute CAP 15887 for CAP 15888 **When You're Smiling (The Whole World Smiles With You)**
2519	CAP 15886. **EP:** CAP EBF241, CAP EBF 1-343. **LP:** CAP H241, CAP H343, CAP T669, CapE LC6520, CapE LC6565, CapE LC6810, SW 1380, PAU 9031 **All I Do Is Dream Of You**
2520	**LP:** CAP H343, CAP T669, CapE LC6565, CapE LC6810, CapeE VMPM1002, EMI-F 1551563, PAU 9031. **EP:** CAP EBF 2-343 **Stompin' At The Savoy**

(CapE LP VMPM1002's liner notes erroneously show a date of November 7 for "Stompin' At The Savoy.")

Benny had a contractual obligation to Capitol for additional big band recordings. To satisfy it he returned to Hollywood, there to reunite with some of the studio musicians who'd worked with him earlier in the year. The first side offers unusual instrumentation along with a new Mel Powell arrangement of a Goodman classic:

BENNY GOODMAN AND HIS ORCHESTRA November 25, 1947, Hollywood

Benny Goodman, clt; John Best, tpt; Ed Kuszborski (Kusby), tbn; Jack Cave, Fr-h; Louella Howard, fl; Virginia Majewski, viola; George Smith, Nick Mumulo, as; Bumps Meyers, ts; Chuck Gentry, bar; Red Norvo, vib; Mel Powell, p; Al Hendrickson, g; Artie Shapiro, b; Dick Cornell, d. Emma Lou Welch, voc.

2599   CAP 15044. **LP:** EMI-F 1551563. **ET:** AFRS P966
            You Turned The Tables On Me-voc Emma Lou Welch
             (arr MP)

Next was a combined Sextet/orchestra session, including a bow to step-daughter Shirley. Note that a tape transfer of the studio master, in the hands of a few collectors, proves that ''Keep Me In Mind'' is by the Sextet—with a vocal by ''guest'' Peggy Lee—and not by the big band, as earlier believed:

BENNY GOODMAN SEXTET December 2, 1947, Hollywood

Benny Goodman, clt; Red Norvo, vib; Mel Powell, p; Al Hendrickson, g; Artie Shapiro, b; Tommy Romersa, d. Peggy Lee, voc.

2721   UNISSUED—Tape
            Keep Me In Mind-voc Peggy Lee

2722   CAP 15069. **LP:** EMI-F 1551563, INT 25039
            Shirley Steps Out

BENNY GOODMAN AND HIS ORCHESTRA same session

Personnel as November 25, except SINCLAIR LOTT, Fr-h, LOUIS KIEVMAN, viola, PAUL McLARAND, as, and JACK DUMONT, as, replace Cave, Howard, Majewski, Smith and Mumulo, respectively. Peggy Lee, The Sportsmen, voc. ''The Sportsmen'' are not given label credit, but are listed only as a, ''Quartette.''

2723   CAP 15030, CapE CL13003, CapFr 15030318. **ET:** AFRS
            P951
            For Every Man There's A Woman-voc Peggy Lee (arr
             MP)

Best, Lott, Kievman, McLarand, Dumont, Meyers out.

2724   CAP 15044. **ET:** AFRS P966
            Give Me Those Good Old Days-voc, quartette (arr MP)

Fletcher Henderson is reputed to have arranged ''I'm In A Crying Mood,'' and he may have done so. But is seems highly unlikely his chart was employed for Benny's unreleased performance of the tune, for it is by a Septet (miscounted by Capitol as a ''Sextet,'' a frequent occurence by all of the record companies). A tape transfer of the studio master reveals that it is an excellent rendition, with a soulful vocal by Emma Lou Welch, and one wonders why it has never been issued:

BENNY GOODMAN (& HIS) SEXTET December 9, 1947, Hollywood

Benny Goodman, clt; Jake Porter, tpt; Red Norvo, vib; Mel Powell, p; Allan Reuss, g; Artie Shapiro, b; Bill Douglass, d. Emma Lou Welch, voc.

2794   UNISSUED—Tape
            I'm In A Crying Mood-voc Emma Lou Welch

2795   **LP:** CAP H322, CAP T441, CapE LC6563, SW 1381,
            EMI-F 1551563. **EP:** CAP EBF 322, CAP EAP 2-441.
            ET: AFRS P4224
            High Falutin'

Porter out.

2796   CAP 15766. **EP:** EBF 295. **LP:** CAP H295, CAP P395,
            CAP T395, Cap T668, CapAu CLP501, CapAu ENC508,
            CapE LC6557, SW 1364
            That's A Plenty

Allan Reuss's presence two days later is inconsistent. Capitol LP H295's liner notes omit him from the first tune, add him for the third—but he is not clearly identifiable on either. He is heard, however, on the unreleased ''You Took Advantage Of Me.'' Note that Ralph Burns is now believed to have provided a small-group arrangement for ''Behave Yourself,'' which Benny sings rather appealingly.

BENNY GOODMAN SEXTET/SEPTET December 11, 1947, Hollywood

Personnel as ''I'm In A Crying Mood,'' December 9, except omit Reuss.

2830   CAP 15766. **EP:** CAP EBF 295. **LP:** CAP H295, CAP
            P395, CAP T395, CAP T668, CapAu CLP501, CapAu
            ENC508, CapE LC6557, SW 1364, EMI-F 1551563
            Henderson Stomp

Add Allan Reuss, g.

2831   UNISSUED—Tape
            You Took Advantage Of Me

Reuss questionable.

2832   CAP 15768. **EP, LP:** same as ''Henderson Stomp,''
            except omit CAP T668, EMI-F 1551563
            Behave Yourself-voc Benny Goodman (prob. arr RB)

Benny returned to New York's Town Hall for a classical recital on December 15, came back to the West Coast for another big band session for Capitol two days before Christmas:

BENNY GOODMAN AND HIS ORCHESTRA December 23, 1947, Hollywood

Benny Goodman, clt; John Best, Jake Porter, Irving Goodman, Ray Linn, tpt; Herbie Harper, Tommy Pederson, Hoyt Bohannon, tbn; Jack Kelson, Nick Mumulo, as; Pete Pumiglio, Bumps Meyers, ts; Chuck Gentry, bar; Mel Powell, p; Al Hendrickson, g; Red Callender, b; Bill Douglass, d. Emma Lou Welch, voc.

3054   CAP 15208, CapG C80-15208
            I Hate To Lose You (I'm So Used To You Now)-voc
            Emma Lou Welch

3055   **LP:** CAP H409, CAP T409, CapE LC6601, CapE LC6831,
            CapE VMPM1002, CapG LCA409, CapJap ECJ50059,
            AMI 850019. **EP:** CAP EAP 2-409
            Muskrat Ramble (arr FH)

3056   **LP:** CapE VMPM1002
            Am I Blue?-voc Emma Lou Welch (arr FH)

3057   CAP 15111. **LP:** EMI-F 1551563
            The Blues Jumped Up And Got Me- voc Emma Lou
            Welch (arr FH)

The author's prior work on Goodman listed a Gene Norman ''Just Jazz'' concert as of ''January 1948.'' Later information specifies the correct date as, December 27, 1947. Others on that program with Benny, and appearing on AFRS's several transcriptions of the event, included vocalist Kay Starr, pianist Pete Johnson, and ''The All-Stars,'' featuring Ernie Royal, tpt; Wardell Gray, Vido Musso, ts; Arnold Ross, p; Barney Kessel, g; Harry Babasin, b; Don Lamond, d. Johnny Mercer has a high old time singing with Benny's Quintet.

Three AFRS ET's are needed to afford all known Goodman performances that were transcribed. A fourth—AFRS Just Jazz Series H-83, Program NO. 3, Parts 1 & 2, bearing matrices D-23609, D-23610—duplicates the material on the three that are detailed herein:

AFRS JUBILEE SERIES H-11, Program No. 271 December 27, 1947,
                                     Shrine Auditorium, Los Angeles

Benny Goodman, clt; Red Norvo, vib; Mel Powell, p; Red Callender, b; Lee Young, d. Johnny Mercer, voc.

D-20842   **ET:** AFRS Jubilee Series H-11, Program No. 271—Part 2
            After You've Gone
            Sent For You Yesterday And Here You Come Today-voc
            Johnny Mercer

(Part 1 of this ET, mx D-20841, contains no Goodman performances. ''After You've Gone'' is also on **ET,** AFRS Just Jazz, Series H-83, Program No. 3; and on **LP,** JAZ 58, JOY 5014. ''Sent For You Yesterday . . .'' is also on **ET,** AFRS Just Jazz, Series H-83, Program No. 16; and on **LP,** JAZ 58, JOY 5014, SWH 3.)

AFRS JUBILEE SERIES H-11, Program No. 299 same concert

Personnel as preceding.

D-29257 **ET:** AFRS Jubilee Series H-11, Program No. 299—Part 1
Air Mail Special
Rose Room

D-29258 **ET:** as above, except Part 2
The World Is Waiting For The Sunrise
Flying Home

(All of the above are also on **ET,** AFRS Just Jazz, Series H-83, Program No. 3 ("Flying Home" is incomplete); and on **LP,** JOY 5014, SWH 3. "Air Mail Special" and "Flying Home" are also on **LP,** FH 1974.)

AFRS JUST JAZZ SERIES H-83, Program No. 16 same concert

Personnel as preceding.

D-30903 **ET:** AFRS Just Jazz Series H-83, Program No. 16—Part 1
Jingle Bells-voc Johnny Mercer

D-30904 **ET:** as above, except Part 2
Sugar Blues-voc Johnny Mercer
Sent For You Yesterday And Here You Come Today-voc Johnny Mercer

Add: Ernie Royal, tpt; Wardell Gray, Vido Musso, ts.

I Never Knew (to fade)

("Sent For You Yesterday . . ." is also on **ET,** AFRS Jubilee Series H-11, Program No. 271.)

Caesar Perillo did it again—the czar of the American Federation of Musicians decreed another recording ban, this one to begin the first day of the new year. Capitol had Benny beat the deadline with a mixed recording session, the big band and the Quintet. We say "Quintet" despite Capitol's insistence that guitarist Al Hendrickson is present. He is not audible; and otherwise the group is the same as that that played the "Just Jazz" concert on December 27. Note that the personnel for the two orchestral recordings are not known; Capitol was not able to supply that information. Both cuts are heavily scored, largely for strings, and there are no identifiable soli other than Goodman's. It is likely that the personnel included those musicians with whom he had recorded earlier in the month.

BENNY GOODMAN AND HIS ORCHESTRA December 30, 1947, Hollywood

Benny Goodman, clt, and an orchestra including strings, personnel unknown. Emma Lou Welch, voc. PAUL NEW (PW), arr.

3147 CAP 15030, CapFr 15030318. **ET:** AFRS P951
Beyond The Sea (La Mer) (arr PN)

3148 UNISSUED—Tape
Darn That Dream-voc Emma Lou Welch (arr PN)

BENNY GOODMAN SEXTET (sic) same session

Personnel as December 27 Quintet.

3149 CAP 15069, CapE F15478. **45:** CAP set SSF202. TOSH CR1035. **EP:** CAP EBF 202. **LP:** CAP H202, CAP P395, CAP T395, CAP T668, CapE LC6526, SW 1364, TOSH CR8810, EMI-F 1551563, INT 25039
The World Is Waiting For The Sunrise

Little is known of Benny's activities for the first several months of 1948. He is reputed to have appeared with the New Orleans Symphony, and with the Buffalo Symphony, as he had in July 1947; but that is suspect, because their "seasons" usually were in the same months, year after year. He is said to have first encountered Swedish clarinetist Stan Hasselgard at Club 47 in Los Angeles in February, where the tow-headed youngster was then playing, and to have offered him a job on the spot. That tale likely has merit, for Benny had Hasselgard in his small group (along with vibraphonist Johnny White and Mel Powell, and unknown musicians) on March 26, when he participated in a "Just Jazz" concert in San Diego's Russ Auditorium; and again on March 27, when the group appeared in the Civic Auditorium in Pasadena. The author believes that either or both of these concerts may have

been recorded—and may even have been broadcast—but no transcriptions or air checks that would substantiate his opinion have surfaced.

But AFRS comes through, as it had during the 1942–1943 recording ban, and locates Benny for us in April. It transcribed another Goodman appearance on Buddy Clark's "Carnation Contented Hour," but released only one cut on a Department of State ET. A Trio performance from the same program is extant via a privately-recorded air check:

DEPARTMENT OF STATE, OFFICE OF INTERNATIONAL INFORMATION AMERICAN PERSONALITIES PARADE—Program No. 1 April 19, 1948
New York

"Benny Goodman, clarinetist; Ted Dale Orchestra."

DS-594, **ET:** Department of State, Office of International
DS-35906 Information American Personalities Parade, Program No. 1—Cut No. 1
Rose Room

Also extant from the same "Carnation Contented Hour" broadcast, via NBC:

Benny Goodman, clt; Mel Powell, p; Irv Cottler, d.

The World Is Waiting For The Sunrise—TRIO (n/c)

Also in April Benny appeared with the American Art Quintet and pianist Ingolf Dahl in a benefit performance for the Idyllwild Music and Arts School, but the date and the location of the concert are not known. Early in May he began to rehearse a new Septet, and on May 10 he took it, and vocalist Muriel Jayne, into Carnegie Hall for its first engagement. Then on May 24 the Septet opened a two-week stand in the Click, a restaurant-supper club in Philadelphia.

The Septet featured Benny's protege, Stan Hasselgard. They played so much alike at the Click that it takes an experienced ear to distinguish one from the other. Benny took an interest in the young Swedish star and gave him numerous solo opportunities, especially during performances that were not broadcast—The Man took over when they were on the air, and Hasselgard is heard less frequently. But Benny held him in high regard, and was visibly shaken when Stan was killed in an automobile accident, November 23, 1948.

Benny broadcast frequently from the Click and home recordists were kept busy. One Philadelphian had a tape recorder, a new device not in general use among amateurs until some five years later. His paper-backed tapes held up fairly well—to the author's knowledge, they are the first tapes of Goodman broadcasts ever made by a non-professional—but provided indifferent sound quality. Another had professional-type disc recording gear, and his acetates afford excellent audio fidelity. Unfortunately, mis-dating on the tapes led to erroneous assignment of this material in the author's earlier work on Goodman. The broadcasts are now correct as listed below.

Louis Armstrong's All-Stars, including Jack Teagarden, Barney Bigard, Earl Hines, Arvell Shaw, Sid Catlett and vocalist Velma Middleton, were at Ciro's, a Philadelphia bistro, the second week of Goodman's engagement at the Click. The two groups visited back and forth—Benny's Teddy Wilson especially welcomed getting together with Louis's "Fatha" Hines, whose style influenced Teddy—but these "Meetings At The Summit" never occurred when either group was broadcast. Too bad . . . ; but acetates of Benny's and Louis's separate broadcasts stir memories of a stellar couple of weeks in the City of Brotherly Love.

Note that now Benny uses "Stompin' At The Savoy" as his opening theme, forsaking "Let's Dance." Wardell Gray's tenor is not audible on all of the full group renditions, but he is listed as present. Teddy Wilson is mistakenly introduced as "Teddy Williams" on occasion, but this Teddy has never been known to spit at an audience.

Note, too, that excerpts from the Click broadcasts are on Dragon (Sweden) and Swedisc (Japan) LP's—there's a switch. An attempt is made to match the LP tracks with appropriate performances, but there is no guarantee that these assignments are correct. Swedisc is dubbed from Dragon, which in turn was dubbed from tapes, possibly generations removed, supplied by the author to a collector before the broadcasts were realigned. Realignment changed the dates of some performances, and this information was not available to the bootleggers. Thus data herein may differ from LP liner notes.

Here, then, an extensive array of Benny Goodman and Ake "Stan" Hasselgard, thanks to the efforts of enthusiasts Harry Foster (tape) and Virgil Thomas (disc). They knew what to record, even if they sometimes forgot when they recorded it:

SUSTAINING BROADCAST   May 24, 1948, Click, Phila.
  NBC Radio Network

Benny Goodman, clt; Stan Hasselgard, clt; Wardell Gray, ts; Teddy Wilson, p;
Billy Bauer, g; Arnold Fishkind, b; Mel Zelnick, d. Patti Page, voc.

TRIO: Goodman, Wilson, Zelnick
QUARTET: Goodman, Wilson, Fishkind, Zelnick
QUINTET: Goodman, Wilson, Bauer, Fishkind, Zelnick

Stompin At The Savoy (theme)
Limehouse Blues
Body And Soul - TRIO
On The Sunny Side Of The Street-voc Patti Page
Cookin' One Up (**LP:**DR 16, SWD 25-9008)
Poor Butterfly - QUINTET
After You've Gone
Good-Bye (theme)

SUSTAINING BROADCAST   May 27, 1948, Click, Phila.
  CBS Radio Network

Personnels as May 24.

Swedish Pastry (**LP:**DR 16, SWD 25-9008)
All The Things You Are (**LP:**DR 16, SWD 25-9008)
You Turned The Tables On Me-voc Patti Page
Where Or When - TRIO
The World Is Waiting For The Sunrise - QUARTET
The Man I Love-voc Patti Page
Mary's Idea (**LP:**DR16, SWD 25-9008)
Don't Blame Me-voc Patti Page
Good-Bye (theme)

SUSTAINING BROADCAST   May 28, 1948, Click, Phila.
  CBS Radio Network

Personnels as May 24.

Swedish Pastry (**LP:**DR 16, SWD 25-9008)
There's A Small Hotel - TRIO
On The Sunny Side Of The Street-voc Patti Page
Body And Soul - TRIO
The World Is Waiting For The Sunrise - QUARTET
It Had To Be You-voc Patti Page
After You've Gone (**LP:**SWD 25-9016)
Good-Bye (theme)

SUSTAINING BROADCAST   May 29, 1948, Click, Phila.
  CBS Radio Network

Personnels as May 24.

Bye, Bye Pretty Baby (**LP:**DR 16, SWD 25-9008)
I'm In The Mood For Love-voc Patti Page
Mary's Idea (**LP:**DR 16, SWD 25-9008)
Just One Of Those Things - QUINTET
Mel's Idea (**LP:** DR 16, SWD 25-9008)

SUSTAINING BROADCAST   May 29, 1948, Click, Phila.
  NBC Radio Network

Personnels as May 24.

Bye, Bye Pretty Baby
He's Funny That Way-voc Patti Page
Mary's Idea
I'm In The Mood For Love-voc Patti Page
Just One Of Those Things - QUINTET
Mel's Idea (**LP:** DR 16, SWD 25-9008)

SUSTAINING BROADCAST   June 1, 1948, Click, Phila.
  NBC Radio Network

Personnels as May 24.

Mary's Idea (**LP:**SWD 25-9016)
If I Had You-voc Patti Page - TRIO
Indiana
Poor Butterfly - QUARTET
Don't Blame Me-voc Patti Page
Bye Bye Blues (**LP:**DR 16, SWD 25-9008)

AFRS transcribed a CBS broadcast from the Click, as it was aired, no cross-dubbing, except for a reprise of "Limehouse Blues" to end Part 2. It thus missed the final tune, "There's A Small Hotel," which, however, is extant via acetate. Also, AFRS excised the intro of the opener, "Limehouse Blues," but it too is available on acetate. Thus a combination of the ET and acetates provides the complete half-hour program.

AFRS ONE NIGHT STAND No. 1722   **June 3, 1948, Philadelphia**

Personnels as May 24.

D-28487   **ET:** AFRS One Night Stand No. 1722 - Part 1
           Limehouse Blues (n/c - intro excised - complete on
             acetate)
           The Man I Love-voc Patti Page
           Indiana
           Confess-voc Patti Page - QUINTET

D-28488   **ET:** as above, except Part 2
           Bye Bye Blues
           Little White Lies-voc Patti Page
           Mel's Idea
           Body And Soul - TRIO
           . . . reprise, **Limehouse Blues**
Also extant from the same sustaining broadcast, via CBS:

There's A Small Hotel - QUARTET (to signoff)

(The **ET** is also on **LP**, DAN 5023, DON 1100, JOY 1082, MIR 135, "Mel's Idea" is also on **LP**, DR 29.)

Each Saturday afternoon at 1:00 o'clock the Click offered a special matinee presentation, to which its management invited other artists then appearing elsewhere in Philadelphia. Its special guest June 5 was Pearl Bailey—if memory serves, not yet Mrs. Louis Bellson—and Pearl does her popular plaint, "Tired," with Benny:

SUSTAINING BROADCAST   June 5, 1948, Click, Phila.
  CBS Radio Network

Personnels as May 24. Guest: Pearl Bailey, voc.

Indiana (**LP:** DR 16, SWD 25-9008)
Confess-voc Patti Page and Benny Goodman
Tired-voc Pearl Bailey
There's A Small Hotel—TRIO
You Turned The Tables On Me-voc Patti Page
Good-Bye (theme)

Then a Saturday evening broadcast, Benny's last from the Click:

SUSTAINING BROADCAST   June 5, 1948, Click, Phila.
  NBC Radio Network

Personnels as May 24.

Swedish Pastry (n/c - ending excised) (**LP:** DR 16, SWD 25-9008)
You Go To My Head-voc Patti Page
Lullaby In Rhythm (**LP:** DR 16, SWD 25-9008)
If I Had You-voc Patti Page - TRIO
Confess-voc Patti Page and Benny Goodman—QUINTET

To wrap up the festivities at the Click, two partial acetates of "Limehouse Blues," both final tunes from broadcasts whose dates are unknown. The first is from a CBS broadcast, the second from NBC:

SUSTAINING BROADCASTS   May/June 1948, Click, Phila.
  CBS/NBC Radio Networks

Septet as May 24.

Limehouse Blues (n/c - ending only) (to signoff)
Limehouse Blues (n/c - ending only) (to first note of, "Good-Bye")

On June 26 Benny and a revamped Septet inaugurated a summer series programmed by radio station WNEW, New York. Its half-hour broadcasts on Saturday evenings originated in the Westchester County Center, White Plains, New York. Benny's two broadcasts were announced as, "The Benny Goodman Show."

For the first time, Benny has a female instrumentalist as a regular member of his orchestra, pianist/composer/arranger Mary Lou Williams. Mary Lou is no problem—but trumpeter Red Rodney is. Contemporary press reports had Red (Robert Chudnick) playing with Benny in White Plains, but his horn is certainly not prominent in the first broadcast, and there's not a hint of it in the second. Repeated listening to "Indiana" from the June 26 air check, using an equalizer with various settings, suggests there's a trumpet in that rendition. On that basis—and because of the press reports—he is included in the June 26 personnel.

Bootleg LP's also add to the confusion. One, especially, confounds collectors. Its format suggests that its origin is Sweden; it is not, it was manufactured in the United States. Further, this LP—TRIBUTE FROM SWEDEN (TRIB) UNNNUMBERED—re-titles "Mary's Idea" to "Stompin' Slow," "Swedish Pastry" to "Swedish Sweets," and "Blue Views" to "Blues For Sweden." Apparently, all of this subterfuge was an attempt to avoid penalty for the unauthorized use of this material. And note also that DR 29 lists "Indiana" as "Donna Lee."

With those caveats in mind, here's Benny from the Westchester County Center:

"THE BENNY GOODMAN SHOW"   *June 26, 1948,*
WNEW Radio   *White Plains, N.Y.*

Benny Goodman, clt; Stan Hasselgard, clt; RED RODNEY, tpt(?); Wardell Gray, ts; MARY LOU WILLIAMS, p; Billy Bauer, g; CLYDE LOMBARDI, b; Mel Zelnick, d. JACKIE SEARLE, DOLLY HUSTON, voc.

QUARTET: Goodman, Williams, Lombardi, Zelnick.

Stompin' At The Savoy (theme)
Mary's Idea (LP: DAN 5003, DR—, SWD 25-9016, TRIB—)
S'pos'n-voc Jackie Searle
There's A Small Hotel - QUARTET
Mel's Idea (LP: DAN 5003)
You Turned The Tables On Me-voc Dolly Huston
Swedish Pastry (LP: DAN 5003, DR 29, SWD 25-9016, TRIB—)
Indiana (LP: same issues)
Good-Bye (theme)

"THE BENNY GOODMAN SHOW"   *July 3, 1948,*
WNEW Radio   *White Plains, N.Y.*

Personnels as June 26, except omit Red Rodney.

Stompin' At The Savoy (theme)
Bye Bye Blues (LP: DAN 5003, DR—, SWD 25-9016, TRIB—)
Wrap Your Troubles In Dreams-voc Jackie Searle
Blues Views (LP: TRIB—)
It's The Talk Of The Town-voc Dolly Huston
Mel's Idea (LP: DR 29)
Don't Blame Me-voc Jackie Searle
After You've Gone
Good-Bye (theme)

At the end of the July 3 broadcast, Benny invites the audience to return to the Westchester County Center next Friday evening, and then says ". . . see you . . . on WNEW at 8:00 p.m. next Saturday." The author has not located a transcription of that broadcast (July 10), nor any for possible broadcasts from White Plains on July 17 and July 24, "Benny Goodman Day" at the Center, and likely his final appearance there. It is suggested, however, that two tracks on a SUNBEAM LP are from one of those dates, although this is by no means certain; these cuts may have been recorded as V-Discs.

POSSIBLY: "THE BENNY GOODMAN SHOW"   *July 1948,*
WNEW Radio   *White Plains, N.Y.*

Personnel as July 3, but with Hasselgard's presence questionable.

I Can't Give You Anything But Love, Baby-voc Jackie Searle (LP: SB 144)
Bye-Bye Blues (LP: SB 144)

Nor is the author able to pinpoint the recording date or dates of the next two V-Discs. One source has it that "Benny's Bop" (in reality, "Limehouse Blues") was cut on August 20. The author believes, however, that both were cut earlier, likely in July while Benny was in and around New York, and after Hasselgard had departed.

The author is also unable to confirm other titles recorded for AFRS by Benny's bop Sextet at this time, as suggested in a V-Disc/AFRS discography. He is, however, able to offer two alternate takes of "Benny's Bop," newly-found and important additions to Goodmania during this period when commercial recordings were banned by the AFM:

BENNY GOODMAN SEXTET   **prob. July 1948, New York**

Benny Goodman, clt; Wardell Gray, ts; Mary Lou Williams, p; Billy Bauer, g; Clyde Lombardi, b; Mel Zelnick, d.

- 0 -	UNISSUED - Studio acetate	
- 0 -	UNISSUED - Studio acetate	
J-640-	VD 880 A	
USS-1070	**Benny's Bop**	

(The **V-Disc** is also on **LP:** DAN 5003 (as, "Wardell's Riff"), ELEC KV119.)

V-Disc 880 is very scarce; the author found it to be the most difficult of all Goodman V-Discs to acquire. Almost, but not quite, equally rare is Goodman V-Disc 88, "Three Little Words."

In all likelihood, the next V-Disc was cut at the same session as "Benny's Bop," although Benny uses an "arrangement" he will wax for Capitol in April 1949. Note that the label credits a Sextet, but that the group actually is a Quartet:

BENNY GOODMAN AND SEXTET (sic)   **prob. July 1948, New York**

Benny Goodman, clt; Mary Lou Williams, p; Clyde Lombardi, b; Mel Zelnick, d.

J661-1091	VD 890 B	
	There's A Small Hotel	

("There's A Small Hotel" is also on **LP:** SB 144.)

Nothing is known of Benny's activities in August 1948; the recording ban keeps him out of Capitol's studios, and eliminates that "fix" on his whereabouts and associations. He may well have hied himself off to Newfoundland for some fishing, still one of his favorite pastimes. Or maybe he just spent some pleasant hours with Alice, Rachel and Benjie.

Although the recording ban is still in effect, Benny does make a recording in Capitol's studios September 9—Mr. Petrillo granted special dispensation, because all proceeds from the sale of the record, included in Capitol album CC 106, went to a charity, the Damon Runyon Cancer Fund. The problem is, where was the recording made, in Hollywood or in New York?

Some collectors believe it was made in New York, given the side's matrix and a belief that Benny would not have travelled to California simply to cut one tune. Capitol, however, says Hollywood, and on a broadcast of September 17, Benny says when introducing Wardell Gray, ". . . a boy I brought back with me from California." The weight of evidence seems to be with the West Coast:

BENNY GOODMAN SEPTET   **September 9, 1948, Hollywood**

Benny Goodman, clt; Fats Navarro, tpt; Wardell Gray, ts; Gene DiNovi, p; Mundell Lowe, g; Clyde Lombardi, b; Mel Zelnick, d.

2974	CAP 10173. **LP:** CapE T20578, CapEur 80.854, TOSH CR8024, OD SCO 52-80854, Cap Jap ECJ50074, INT 25039
	Stealin' Apples

Here's the broadcast referred to in the paragraph above. MC Ted Husing had won fame as a sportscaster; Count Basie, who sits in for the second tune, then had his band in New York's Royal Roost:

"THE TED HUSING SHOW"   *September 17, 1948,*
WMGM Radio   *New York*

Benny Goodman, clt; Wardell Gray, ts; Gene DiNovi, p; BILLY BAUER, g; Clyde Lombardi, b; Mel Zelnick, d.

Stealin' Apples

Count Basie, p, substitutes for DiNovi:

WMGM Jump (LP: DAN 5003)

When Husing asks Goodman what he thinks of "bebop," the retort implies . . . not much. Nevertheless, Benny's new big band, which he began to assemble in October, was the boppin'est of them all. None of Benny's sidemen from the '30's and the early '40's were called back; and to provide suitable vehicles for his modernists, Goodman commissioned Arturo "Chico" O'Farrell (C O'F) to put together a new book, all bop. Even longtime Goodman favorites such as "Don't Be That Way," "Air Mail Special" and others were not exempt, were re-scored a la BOP.

The band broke in with a series of engagements in the Middle Atlantic states and New England in November, even got to Canada—the Arena, Niagara Falls, Ontario, on November 26. Then it had a full week in the

Persian Terrace Room of the Hotel Syracuse, Syracuse, New York, from whence come our next air checks:

SUSTAINING BROADCAST   *December 1, 1948,*
  NBC Radio Network   *Hotel Syracuse, Syracuse, N.Y.*

Benny Goodman, clt; Howard Reich, Doug Mettome, Al Stewart, Nick Travis, tpt; Milt Bernhart, Eddie Bert, George Monte, tbn; Mitch Goldberg, Angelo Cicalese, as; Wardell Gray, Eddie Wasserman, ts; Larry Molinelli, bar; Buddy Greco, p; Francis Beecher, g; Clyde Lombardi, b; Sonny Igoe, d. Buddy Greco, Terry Swope, The Clarinaders, voc.

SEXTET: Goodman, Gray, Greco, Beecher, Lombardi, Igoe.

Clarinet A La King
You Turned The Tables On Me-voc, The Clarinaders

SUSTAINING BROADCAST   *December 2, 1948,*
  NBC Radio Network   *Hotel Syracuse, Syracuse, N.Y.*

Personnels as December 1.

Clarinet A La King
Don't Worry 'Bout Me-voc Buddy Greco
Indiana - SEXTET (**LP:** SWT 111)
You Turned The Tables On Me-voc Terry Swope and The Clarinaders
Chico's Bop (arr C O'F) (announced as, "The Chico Bop") (**LP:** SWT 111)
They Didn't Believe Me-voc Terry Swope
Undercurrent Blues - to signoff (arr C O'F)

SUSTAINING BROADCAST   *December 5, 1948,*
  NBC Radio Network   *Hotel Syracuse, Syracuse, N.Y.*

Personnels as December 1.

Wrap Your Troubles In Dreams-voc Terry Swope (**LP:** SWT 111)
Don't Be That Way
Guilty-voc Buddy Greco and The Clarinaders
Bedlam - SEXTET (**LP:** SWT 111)
Rebecca-voc Buddy Greco (**LP:** SWT 111)
I'll See You In My Dreams-voc Terry Swope and The Clarinaders
Air Mail Special (**LP:** SWT 111)
Good-Bye (theme)

The band's next major engagement was in Manhattan's Paramount Theater, where it opened December 15. While there Benny recorded a 15-minute program in Columbia's studios for the National Foundation for Infantile Paralysis, which each year conducted a "March Of Dimes" fund raising campaign. The program was distributed to radio stations via a 16″ transcription, asking that they give it air time as an aid in soliciting donations. Note that AFRS excerpted one of the tunes, pressed it as a V-Disc. The V-Disc listing is repeated, but it should be understood that it, and its counterpart on the ET, are identical.

New York pianist Dick Katz adds a grace note to the "March Of Dimes" session. Brought in to fill the piano bench while Buddy Greco sang, Dick has an acetate of "I'll See You In My Dreams" that is an alternate take of the version on the ET. It is shown below in italics.

1949 MARCH OF DIMES   **December 1948, New York**
BENNY GOODMAN AND HIS ORCHESTRA

Personnel as December 1, plus Dick Katz, p, on "I'll See You In My Dreams" and "Don't Worry 'Bout Me."

YTNY 10328-1   **ET: 1949 March Of Dimes**
                Let's Dance (theme)
                A String Of Pearls
                I'll See You In My Dreams-voc, The Clarinaders
                Undercurrent Blues (arr C O'F) (see also VD 903 A,
                    following)
                Don't Worry 'Bout Me-voc Buddy Greco
                Good-Bye (theme)

("A String Of Pearls" and "I'll See You In My Dreams" are also on LP: GOL 55001. For LP releases of "Undercurrent Blues," see V-Disc listing, below.)

alternate take   *I'll See You In My Dreams*-voc, The Clarinaders

BENNY GOODMAN AND HIS ORCHESTRA   **December 1948, New York**

Personnel as December 1.

J-686 1116   VD 903 A (also on 1949 March Of Dimes ET, above)
                 Undercurrent Blues

(The V-Disc is also on LP: DAN 5003, ELEC 119, SB 144.)

Likely at about this time, Benny and announcer Ed Herlihy recorded voice tracks for the American Cancer Society's 1949 fund drive. They are on the Society's 16″ ET, matrix 8760-A, interspersing dubs of CO 35301, "Let's Dance," and CAP 15208, "On A Slow Boat To China."

To the best of the author's knowledge, the first extant example of a Goodman appearance on commercial television is his visit to Ed Sullivan's long-running "Toast Of The Town" program. Unfortunately, the exact date of this telecast is not known. It likely occurred while Benny was at the Paramount, for it has been and remains Benny's practice to guest on radio or television concurrently with an engagement he then has, to advertise it to potential audiences.

"TOAST OF THE TOWN"   *December 1948, New York*
  CBS Television Network

Benny Goodman, clt; Buddy Greco, p; Francis Beecher, g; Clyde Lombardi, b; Sonny Igoe, d.

Indiana
On A Slow Boat To China-voc Buddy Greco

While at the Paramount, Benny and his Sextet "doubled" into the Stork Club, the first—and only—time he is known to have performed in that renowned Manhattan night club. At least one partial rendition is extant from his appearance there:

SUSTAINING BROADCAST   *December 1948,*
  CROSLEY Radio Network   *Stork Club, N.Y.*

Sextet as December 1.

How High The Moon (n/c)

Two other cuts by the Sextet, likely from this time period, may also have originated in the Stork Club. But they are on acetates that bear no information, and so are listed generally:

SUSTAINING BROADCAST(S)   *December 1948/January 1949*
  Unknown radio network   *location?*

Sextet as December 1.

Indiana
Limehouse Blues

A severe case of bronchitis caused Benny to miss the last few days of the Paramount engagement in early 1949, and Gene Krupa fronted the band in his absence (if memory serves, Gene had just finished a lengthy stand at Frank Dailey's Meadowbrook). Not fully recovered, and against medical advice, Benny insisted on leading the band when it was chosen—along with the orchestras of Guy Lombardo, Xavier Cugat, and some Washington-local groups—to play the Inaugural Ball in Washington's National Guard Armory on January 20.

NBC broadcast the proceedings, but unfortunately Benny's portion of the program is buried beneath chit-chat between President Truman's sister Mary, and television personality Mary Margaret McBride. Only Benny's final selection, "Rose Room," is completely free of their overriding chatter:

"INAUGURAL BALL"   *January 20, 1949,*
  NBC Radio Network   *National Guard Armory, Washington*

Personnels as December 1, 1948.

Let's Dance (theme)
Jersey Bounce
Don't Worry 'Bout Me-voc Buddy Greco
Buckle Down, Winsocki-voc Buddy Greco
Rose Room - SEXTET

Benny's health worsened, he was forced home to recuperate, and Buddy Greco led the band as it worked its way through a series of one-nighters to the West Coast. Benny rejoined it there; and with the recording ban ended, resumed recording for Capitol. Capitol now employed tape facilities, and for the first time Benny was recorded commercially on the new medium.

If there is any doubt about Goodman's intention to play bop, note the legend on the label of CAPITOL 15409 from this session: "Undercurrent Blues - Bop Instrumental."

BENNY GOODMAN AND HIS ORCHESTRA   February 10, 1949, Hollywood

Personnel as December 1, 1948, except ARNOLD ROSS, p, substitutes for Greco on mx 3959, on which Greco sings. Note that trumpeter Al Stewart is also known as Al Goldberg, a name sometimes listed for this session. Buddy Greco, "THE SINGERS," voc.

3958	CAP 15409, CapAu&NZ 142, CapE CL 13136, CapFr 15611, CapFr 15409317, CapG C80016. **45:** CapDen F4100. **EP:** CAP EBF 235. **LP:** CAP H235, CAP T667, CapE LC6510, CapE T20578, CapEur 80.854, CapG LCA235, CapJap ECJ40001, TOSH CR8024, OD SC052-80854 Here's To Vets 107-1389, EMI-F 1551563, INT 25039, CapJap ECJ50074
	Undercurrent Blues (arr C O'F)
3959	CAP 15409, CapFr 15409317, CapG C80016. **LP:** CapJap ECJ40001. **ET:** AFRS Basic Music Library 1293
	Ma Belle Marguerite-voc Buddy Greco and The Singers

(Note that although Capitol label-credits the vocal group as, "The Singers," they are announced on broadcasts as, "The Clarinaders.")

Following a tour of California and the Pacific Northwest in February, Benny's boppers went into the Hollywood Palladium March 1 for the ensuing month, from where they were on radio extensively. Save for the addition of bongo player Louis Martinez (it's hard to imagine Benny with TWO drummers), the band's personnel was remarkably static. That may reflect the dwindling number of big bands still working, and fewer and fewer opportunities for brass and reed sidemen to find gainful employment.

Benny's library no longer has in it many of the arrangements that will be listed in the broadcasts following. It is believed that the bulk of them were written by Chico O'Farrell, for he did not commission any other arranger at this time.

SUSTAINING BROADCAST   March 4, 1949,
  CBS Radio Network   Hollywood Palladium, Hollywood

Personnels as December 1, 1948, plus LOUIS MARTINEZ, bo, on some selections

SEPTET: Goodman, Mettome, Gray, Greco, Beecher, Lombardi, Igoe.

Let's Dance (theme)
A String of Pearls
My Darling, My Darling-voc Buddy Greco
Trees
Am I Blue?-voc The Clarinaders
Flying Home - SEPTET
Buckle Down, Winsocki-voc Buddy Greco
Ma Belle Marguerite-voc Buddy Greco and The Clarinaders
Undercurrent Blues
Good-Bye (theme)

SUSTAINING BROADCAST   March 6, 1949,
  CBS Radio Network   Hollywood Palladium, Hollywood

Personnels as March 4.

*Bugle Call Rag (**LP:** SWT 111)*
Don't Worry 'Bout Me-voc Buddy Greco
*Star Dust (**LP:** SWT 111)*
Once In Love With Amy-voc Buddy Greco
Trees
Indiana - SEPTET
Undercurrent Blues

Should make it clear that many of the standards played at this time are not the familiar, classic arrangements. These are new charts.

And now AFRS swings into action, transcribing a number of the sustaining broadcasts from the Palladium onto 16" ET's. And once again it does some cross-dubbing that makes it impossible, when no confirming acetates are at hand, to be completely certain that the performances are from the dates given.

AFRS ONE NIGHT STAND No. 1901   March 8, 1949, Hollywood

Personnels as March 4.

D-40375	**ET:** AFRS One Night Stand No. 1901 - Part 1
	Let's Dance (theme)
	Chico's Bop
	It Takes A Woman To Take A Man-voc Terry Swope
	It Isn't Fair-voc Buddy Greco
	Trees
D-40376	**ET:** as above, except Part 2
	After You've Gone - SEPTET
	Am I Blue?-voc. The Clarinaders
	Undercurrent Blues
	Good-Bye (theme)
	. . . reprise, **Chico's Bop**

("Let's Dance," "Trees" and "Undercurrent Blues" are dubbed to Program No. 1911. "Chico's Bop," "It Takes A Woman . . . ," "Trees," "After You've Gone" and "Undercurrent Blues" are also on **LP:** SWT 100. "Undercurrent Blues" is also on **LP:** DAN 5003)

AFRS ONE NIGHT STAND No. 1911   March 11, 1949, Hollywood

Personnels as March 4.

D-41115	**ET:** AFRS One Night Stand No. 1911 - Part 1
	(Let's Dance (theme) - from ET, Program No. 1901)
	I've Got My Love To Keep Me Warm (prob arr TT)
	Someone Like You-voc Buddy Greco
	I'll See You In My Dreams-voc. The Clarinaders
	Intermezzo
D-41116	**ET:** as above, except Part 2
	Sweet Georgia Brown - SEPTET
	It Takes A Woman To Take A Man-voc Terry Swope
	(Undercurrent Blues - from ET, Program No. 1901)
	Good-Bye (theme)
	(Trees - from ET, Program No. 1901)

("Intermezzo" is dubbed to Programs No. 1931, 1957. "Sweet Georgia Brown" is also on **LP:** DAN 5003, SWT 100.)

AFRS ONE NIGHT STAND No. 1931   March 15, 1949, Hollywood

Personnels as March 4.

RL-12295	**ET:** AFRS One Night Stand No. 1931 - Part 1
	Don't Be That Way
	Do, Do, Do-voc Buddy Greco
	Shishkabop (arr C O'F)
	Am I Blue?-voc, The Clarinaders
RL-12296	**ET:** as above, except Part 2
	Bedlam - SEPTET
	Lover Man-voc Terry Swope
	Undercurrent Blues
	(Intermezzo - n/c - from ET, Program No. 1911)

("Don't Be That Way," "Shishkabop" and "Undercurrent Blues" are also on **LP:** SWT 111.)

SUSTAINING BROADCAST   March 19, 1949
  Unknown radio network   Hollywood Palladium, Hollywood

Personnel as March 4.

After You've Gone - SEPTET (n/c)

Once again Benny was a guest on Buddy Clark's radio program, this time appearing with his Quartet. Note that both selections are reputedly on a MARK '56 LP, catalog number unknown—the author has been unable to obtain a copy of this release.

"CARNATION CONTENTED HOUR" — March 21, 1949,
 NBC Radio Network — Hollywood

QUARTET: Goodman, Greco, Lombardi, Igoe.

There's A Small Hotel - QUARTET
Sweet Georgia Brown - QUARTET

AFRS ONE NIGHT STAND No. 1946 — March 22, 1949, Hollywood

Personnels as March 4.

D-43747   **ET:** AFRS One Night Stand No. 1946 - Part 1
    (Let's Dance - original CO 78 rpm recording, complete)
    I've Got My Love To Keep Me Warm
    It Isn't Fair-voc Buddy Greco and The Clarinaders
    Undercurrent Blues

D-43748   **ET:** as above, except Part 2
    So In Love-voc Terry Swope
    Blue Lou - SEPTET
    Don't Worry 'Bout Me-voc Buddy Greco
    El Greco (arr C O'F)
    (. . . reprise, **Let's Dance,** CO recording - n/c)

("Blue Lou" is also on **LP:** SWT 100. "I've Got My Love . . ." and "Don't Worry 'Bout Me" are also on **LP:** SWT 111.)

Should note that all of the AFRS ET's from the Palladium this time around are taken from CBS broadcasts.

After a lapse of a month and a half, Benny returned to Capitol's studios:

BENNY GOODMAN AND HIS ORCHESTRA — March 24, 1949, Hollywood

Personnel as March 4, except BUD HERMANN, p, substitutes for Greco on matrices 4115, 4116 and 4117, on which Buddy sings.

4114   CAP 57-568, CapE CL13141, CapG C80086. **LP:** CapJap
    ECJ40001, CapJap ECJ50074, INT 25039, EMI-F
    1551563. **ET:** AFRS Basic Music Library 1293
    —**Shishkabop** (arr C O'F)

4115   same issues as mx 4114, except substitute CapE
    CL13125 for CapE CL13141, omit EMI-F, INT
    —**Having A Wonderful Wish (Time You Were Here)**-voc
    Buddy Greco

4116   CAP 57-576. **LP:** CapJap ECJ40001
    —**That Wonderful Girl Of Mine**-voc Buddy Greco

4117   CAP 860, CapE CL13325. **LP:** CapJap ECJ40001
    —**It Isn't Fair**-voc Buddy Greco and The Singers

For several reasons, the date indicated by AFRS for the next-listed ET seems wrong. Its release number, "No. 1974," is out of sequence, for the succeeding ET is, "No. 1957." Similarly, its matrices are higher than those of the following transcription. Finally, if its date is correct, then its contents involve reverse dubbing; that is, performances on later ET's are brought forward, a process that seems highly unlikely. Unfortunately, the author has no companion acetates that might date the bulk of this broadcast correctly. Therefore, AFRS's dating is listed, but is questionned.

AFRS ONE NIGHT STAND No. 1974 — ? March 25, 1949, Hollywood

Orchestra as March 4. Quartet as March 21.

D-45160   **ET:** AFRS One Night Stand No. 1974 - Part 1
    Let's Dance (theme)
    Undercurrent Blues
    Do, Do, Do-voc Buddy Greco
    Trees
    There's A Small Hotel - QUARTET

D-45161   **ET:** as above, except Part 2
    Jersey Bounce
    El Greco
    Lover Man-voc Terry Swope
    King Porter Stomp
    Clarinade (n/c)

("Let's Dance" and "El Greco" are also on **ET,** AFRS One Night Stand No. 1994, q.v. "Clarinade" is also on **ET,** AFRS One Night Stand No. 1957, q.v.

"Undercurrent Blues" and "El Greco" are also on **LP:** FH 1974. "Jersey Bounce" and "King Porter Stomp" are also on **LP:** DAN 5003, SWT 100. "Trees" and "El Greco" are also on **LP:** SWT 100. The **ET** is on **LP:** JAZ 57.)

SUSTAINING BROADCAST — March 26, 1949,
 Unknown radio network — Hollywood Palladium, Hollywood

Personnel as March 4.

Bedlam - SEPTET (n/c - portion of p solo excised)

AFRS ONE NIGHT STAND No. 1957 — March 29, 1949, Hollywood

Personnels as "? March 25."

D-44443   **ET:** AFRS One Night Stand No. 1957 - Part 1
    Undercurrent Blues
    So In Love-voc Terry Swope
    Shishkabop
    Fresh Fish-voc, The Clarinaders (arr C O'F)

D-44444   **ET:** as above, except Part 2
    There's A Small Hotel - QUARTET
    Someone Like You-voc Buddy Greco
    Clarinade
    If I Could Be With You (One Hour Tonight)-voc Buddy
    Greco
    (Intermezzo - n/c - from ET, Program No. 1911)

("Clarinade" is also on **ET,** AFRS One Night Stand No. 1974, q.v. The **ET** is on **LP:** DAN 5023.)

Neither Benny nor Capitol saw fit to release contemporaneously three of four sides recorded the next studio session. But the thorough Japanese did, on an LP released in the late 1970's:

BENNY GOODMAN AND HIS ORCHESTRA — March 31, 1949, Hollywood

Personnel as March 4, except BILL BYERS, tbn, replaces Bernhart, and Martinez, bo, is not present.

4126   **LP:** CapJap ECJ40001, CapJap ECJ50074
    Fresh Fish-voc, The Singers (arr C O'F)

4127   CAP 57-576, CapE CL13125. **LP:** CapEur 80.854. OD
    SC05280854, CapJap ECJ50074. **ET:** AFRS G.I. Jive
    2297
    —**The Huckle-Buck**-voc, The Singers

4128   **LP:** CapJap ECJ40001, CapJap ECJ50074
    Trees

4129   **LP:** CapJap ECJ4001
    Don't Worry 'Bout Me-voc Buddy Greco

AFRS ONE NIGHT STAND No. 1994 — April 1, 1949, Hollywood

Orchestra as March 31. Septet as March 4.

D-46630   **ET:** AFRS One Night Stand No. 1994 - Part 1
    Let's Dance (theme)
    Chico's Bop
    That Wonderful Girl Of Mine-voc Buddy Greco
    Sweet Georgia Brown - SEPTET
    If I Could Be With You (One Hour Tonight)-voc Buddy
    Greco
    El Greco

D-46631   **ET:** as above, except Part 2
    Undercurrent Blues
    It Takes A Woman To Take A Man-voc Terry Swope
    Trees
    Clarinade
    Good-Bye (theme)

("Let's Dance" and "El Greco" are also on **ET,** AFRS One Night Stand No. 1974, q.v. "Chico's Bop" is also on **LP:** BBL/A 2204.)

Before we take leave of Benny at the Palladium, we must dispose of a few air checks extant via acetate, none of them dated, all reputedly from this engagement. That is a bit suspect, because the small group renditions seem to be by a Sextet, whereas Benny more frequently played with a Septet. Nonetheless . . .

SUSTAINING BROADCAST(S)   *March/April 1949,*
  Unknown radio networks   *Hollywood Palladium, Hollywood*

Personnel appropriate to the period.

Let's Dance (theme)
Swedish Pastry - SEXTET (n/c)
Just An Idea - SEXTET (n/c)
Six Flats Unfurnished

(Surely those Sextet performances are from an earlier period- . . . ?)

Finally—Benny will leave April 4—our last dated air check from the Palladium:

SUSTAINING BROADCAST   *April 2, 1949,*
  Unknown radio network   *Hollywood Palladium, Hollywood*

Personnel as March 4.

Blue Lou - SEPTET (n/c—middle break)

Thanks to trombonist Eddie Bert, a previously-undisclosed studio session can now be added to Goodman's Capitol recordings. The information had not been forthcoming from Capitol when the author wrote his earlier work on Goodman. Nor had the Japanese discovered the session when they prepared their survey releases. But Bert's personal files insisted that he had recorded with Benny on April 12, 1949, and they even named the tunes— "Bop Hop," "Trees," "Star Dust," "Lover Man" and "Dreazag."

Eventually, the author was able to obtain tape transfers of four of the selections named by Bert. According to Capitol, they are in consecutive matrix order—but they omit "Star Dust," the middle recording cited by Bert. If "Star Dust" was not assigned a matrix, assuming that it was performed, it may mean that Benny simply ran through it, decided then and there that he did not wish to record it for release.

In any event, four out of five isn't too shabby:

BENNY GOODMAN AND HIS ORCHESTRA   **April 12, 1949, Hollywood**

Personnel as March 31.

4195-take 2	UNISSUED - Tape	
	Bop Hop	
4196	UNISSUED - Tape	
	Trees	
4197	UNISSUED - Tape	
	Lover Man-voc Terry Swope	
4198	UNISSUED - Tape	
	Dreazag	

Semantically, Capitol could be correct when it labeled the Septet's next issues, "Benny Goodman and his Sextet." But if one accepts that designation, then Capitol should have given label credit to "Benny Goodman and his Trio" for the Quartet side, to be consistent:

BENNY GOODMAN AND HIS SEXTET (sic)   **April 14, 1949, Hollywood**

Septet as March 4.

4203   CAP 57-621, CapE CL 13206, CapG C80021. **LP:** CapEur
             80.854, OD SC052-80854, EMI-F 1551563, CapJap
             ECJ50074, Here's To Vets-107-1389
         Bedlam

BENNY GOODMAN (AND HIS) QUARTET   **same session**

Quartet as March 21.

4204   CAP 57-60009, CapC C143. **LP:** CAP H202, CAP P395,
             CAP T395, CAP T669, CapE LC6526, CapE LC6810,
             SW 1364, EMI-F 1551563. **ET:** Voice Of The Army No.
             499 ("Melody Moderne")
         There's A Small Hotel

BENNY GOODMAN AND HIS SEXTET   **same session**

4205   CAP 57-621, CapE CL13142, CapG C80021. **LP:** CapJap
             ECJ50074
         Oo-Bla-Dee-voc Buddy Greco

4206   CAP 567-60009, CapC C143. **45:** CapDen F4100. **LP:**
             CAP H202, CAP P395, CAP T395, CapE LC6526,
             CapEur 80.854, SW 1364, Here's To Vets 107-1389,
             OD SC052-80854 (n/c), EMI-F 1551563, CapJap
             ECJ50074
         Blue Lou

Out of the Palladium, the band is known to have performed in San Diego's Pacific Square Ballroom, then to have turned east. It played a private dance in Russell, Kansas on April 25, at the Rainbow Ballroom in Denver on April 26, the Pla-Mor Ballroom in Kansas City on April 27, and for the University of Minnesota in Minneapolis on April 30. On May 1 it was in Devine's Ballroom in Milwaukee. Its one-nighter hegira also included unknown locations in Reno, Nevada; Boulder City, Nevada; Salt Lake City, Utah; and Rochester, Minnesota.

It had three theater dates in May: St. Louis Theater, St. Louis, 5-11; Circle Theater, Indianapolis, 19-25; and the Riverside Theater, Milwaukee, May 26-June 2. We lose sight of it until June 18, when it broadcast from the Hershey Park Ballroom, Hershey, Pa.:

SUSTAINING BROADCAST   *June 18, 1949,*
  CBS Radio Network   *Hershey Park Ballroom, Hershey, Pa.*

Orchestra as March 31. Septet as April 14.

Undercurrent Blues
Bedlam - SEPTET (n/c)
Chico's Bop - to signoff

One week later the band was in The Armouries, in Hamilton, Ontario. According to an eyewitness, the instrumental personnel was unchanged from that of seven months earlier. The only difference noted: The Modernaires had replaced The Clarinaders/"Singers."

At the end of June Benny gave the orchestra a six-week vacation, for he had booked the Septet for a tour of England and the Continent. When they learned of his plans, officials of Great Britain's musicians' union John Bullishly said no. British musicians needed the work, and Mr. Goodman would be permitted to bring only his pianist. On July 7 Benny and Buddy flew to London, where Benny hired The Skyrockets to tour with him. On July 18 Benny, Buddy, and The Skyrockets began a two-week engagement in London's Palladium.

On July 21 Benny's English-flavored group appeared on a BBC radio program hosted by Ben Lyons, husband of film star Bebe Daniels, and an actor of sorts himself:

"HI GANG - THE BEN LYONS PROGRAM"   *July 21, 1949, London*
  BBC Radio Network

Benny Goodman, clt & voc, accompanied by a studio orchestra (presumably all-British)

Put Your Shoes On, Lucy-voc Benny Goodman

Benny Goodman, clt; Buddy Greco, p; Pete Chilver, g; Charlie Short, b; "Flash" Winston, d.

The World Is Waiting For The Sunrise - QUINTET

At the end of the Palladium engagement, Benny cancelled the balance of the tour, finding currency conversion difficulties and European travel restrictions unpalatable—or in his words, "Who needs it?" He vacationed briefly on the Riviera, returned to the United States August 12, summoned his orchestra to return to work. One of its first jobs was a two-week engagement at the Surf Beach Club, Virginia Beach, Virginia. We are not certain of the exact lineup of the band at this time, so the personnel listed is collective:

SUSTAINING BROADCAST   *August 27, 1949,*
  NBC Radio Network   *Virginia Beach, Virginia*

Benny Goodman, clt; Howard Reich, Doug Mettome, Al Stewart, Nick Travis, JOHN WILSON, ZIGGY SCHATZ, tpt; Eddie Bert, George Monte, Bill Byers, MARIO DAONE, tbn; Mitch Goldberg, Angelo Cicalese, as; Wardell Gray, Eddie Wasserman, ts; Larry Molinelli, JOE CASALARO, bar; Buddy Greco, p; Francis Beecher, g; BOB CARTER, b; Sonny Igoe, d. Buddy Greco, EMILY LONG, The Clarinaders, voc.

QUARTET: Goodman, Greco, Carter, Igoe

SEPTET: Goodman, Mettome, Gray, Greco, Beecher, Carter, Igoe

Let's Dance (theme)
*The Huckle-Buck-voc, The Clarinaders (**LP:** DAN 5003)*
Don't Worry 'Bout Me-voc Buddy Greco
Clarinet A La King
Some Enchanted Evening-voc Emily Long
*A String Of Pearls (**LP:** DAN 5003)*
There's A Small Hotel - QUARTET
*Blue Lou - SEPTET (**LP:** DAN 5003)*
Fiesta Time (arr C O'F)
Good-Bye (theme)

*(Above on **LP**, MIR 154, ST 193749.)*

Save for Miss Long, whose one vocal is a disaster and who does not appear again, the band was in fine form after its long layoff. The rhythm section, especially Carter and Igoe, provide a strong if modern foundation for the four trumpets, three trombones and five reeds that Benny carried at this time.

SUSTAINING BROADCAST   *September 3, 1949,*
  NBC Radio Network   *Virginia Beach, Virginia*

Personnels as August 27.

Let's Dance (theme)
Six Flats Unfurnished
I Didn't Know What Time It Was-voc Buddy Greco
Blue Lou - SEPTET
There's A Small Hotel - QUARTET
Lover, Come Back To Me-voc Buddy Greco
*Clarinet A La King (**LP:** RAR 22)*
*Good-Bye (in its entirety) (**LP:** RAR 22)*
Undercurrent Blues - to signoff

The band put in a week at the Town Casino, Buffalo, New York, beginning September 19, returned to Manhattan for a week at the Roxy Theater. Personnel for the Roxy engagement was the same as that for the upcoming Capitol session save that Bob Davies was on baritone (vocalist Dolly Huston had replaced Emily Long as early as the Town Casino stint).

Note that an additional matrix, 4291, is appended to what was previously known of this Capitol date. This version of "Spin A Record" is different from the performance that was released, and is extant via tape transfer from the studio master. Its vocal group is not named, but we use the designation applied by Capitol on issues from the October 27 session.

BENNY GOODMAN AND HIS ORCHESTRA   October 15, 1949, N.Y.

Benny Goodman, clt; Doug Mettome, Al Stewart, John Wilson, Sigmund (Ziggy) Schatz, tpt; George Monte, Bill Byers, Mario Daone, tbn; Mitch Goldberg, Angelo Cicalese, as; Wardell Gray, Eddie Wasserman, ts; Joe Casalaro, bar; Buddy Greco, p; Francis Beecher, g; Bob Carter, b; Sonny Igoe, d. Buddy Greco, DOLLY HUSTON, THE HEATHERTONES, voc.

4288   CAP 57-758, CapC 78-163. **LP:** CapEur 80.854, CapJap
                   ECJ40001, OD SC052-80854, EMI-F 1551563, CapJap
                   ECJ50074, INT 25039. **ET:** AFRS 2318
                   Egg Head

4289   CAP 828. **45:** CAP F828. **LP:** CapJap ECJ40001
                   Little Girl, Don't Cry-voc Buddy Greco

4290   CAP 57-758, CapC 78-163. **LP:** CapJap ECJ40001,
                   CapJap ECJ50074. **ET:** AFRS 2316
                   Why Don't We Do This More Often-voc Dolly Huston

4291   UNISSUED - Tape
                   Spin A Record-voc Buddy Greco and The Heathertones

Benny's final session in THE CAPITOL SERIES presents a vexing problem that is as yet unresolved. Years ago, when the facts should have been fresh, Capitol informed the author that the title of unissued matrix 4306 was "Get Yourself Another Fool," vocals by Buddy Greco and The Heathertones. In the late 1970's, a Japanese LP included what ostensibly was mx 4306; but the tune is "I Had Someone Else Before I Had You"—and its lyrics do not offer the line, "Get Yourself Another Fool," or anything like it. Thereupon the author applied to Capitol for a tape transfer of studio master 4306; when received, it proved to be identical to the Japanese issue of "I Had Someone Else Before I Had You."

Therefore, the listing below is revised from earlier accounts of this session to substitute one title for another for matrix 4306, and "Get Yourself Another Fool" continues to perplex the author.

BENNY GOODMAN AND HIS ORCHESTRA   October 27, 1949, N.Y.

Personnel as October 15, except ZOOT SIMS, ts, replaces Gray, and BOB DAVIES, bar, replaces Casalaro.

4304   CAP 57-788, CapE CL 13325. **LP:** CapJap ECJ40001. **ET:**
                   Voice Of The Army No. 499 ("Melody Moderne")
                   Brother Bill-voc Buddy Greco and The Heathertones

4305   CAP 828. **45:** CAP F828. **LP:** CapJap ECJ4001
                   Spin A Record-voc Buddy Greco and The Heathertones

4306   **LP:** CapJap ECJ40001
                   I Had Someone Else Before I Had You-voc Dolly Huston

4307   CAP 860, CAP 57-788, CapE CL13264. **45:** CAP F860.
                   LP: CapJap ECJ40001. **ET:** Voice Of The Army No.
                   499 ("Melody Moderne")
                   You're Always There-voc Buddy Greco and The
                   Heathertones

????   UNISSUED, possibly not recorded
                   Get Yourself Another Fool-voc Buddy Greco and The
                   Heathertones (arr C O'F)

The October 27 Capitol date writes finis to Benny's two-year dalliance with bop; when the session was completed, he promptly disbanded. Retaining only Buddy Greco, Bob Carter and Sonny Igoe, Benny flew to the Philippines in November for a brief concert tour (no recordings of these appearances are known to exist). When he resumes playing in 1950, he will return to his standard swing style.

At the outset of THE CAPITOL SERIES, the point was made that this era also marked Benny's last attempt to lead a traditional big band, "traditional" in the sense that it was not organized with a specific engagement in mind, but rather played wherever it was booked, in theaters, night clubs, a diminishing number of ballrooms, whatever. From this point forward, Benny will assemble an orchestra for a special purpose only, and with its termination clearly in view from the start. The reader may differ with this assessment, but it seems valid to the author.

THE 1950'S—CONCERTS, TELEVISION AND "THE BENNY GOODMAN STORY"

Home from the Philippines, Benny studied with peerless classical clarinetist Reginald Kell; Benny denies his liaison with the English master altered his technique in any appreciable way, as some have claimed. Otherwise, Benny was largely inactive in the early months of 1950. On January 18 he recorded some voice tracks for a recruiting transcription, Voice Of The Army No. 499 ("Melody Moderne"); dialog between him and announcer Joe Ripley intersperse four of his Capitol records. On one occasion whose date is not known, he, Lionel Hampton and drummer Charlie Perry joined Mel Powell at Yale University for a concert in New Haven. No recordings of that concert are known to exist.

Inactivity is anathema to Benny Goodman, even today; he may grumble—and the growls are more frequent as he grows older—but he is happiest when he is working. He needed a new challenge, and the aborted European tour of the previous fall still rankled. He began to plan another, this time with the problems of union acceptance, currency conversion and travel restrictions resolved in advance. Promoters responded enthusiastically to his solicitations, and a tour covering Great Britain, Scandinavia, Italy, Switzerland, Belgium, and a final concert in Paris, was rapidly developed.

Taking with him Roy Eldridge, Zoot Sims, Dick Hyman and Eddie Shaughnessy, Benny flew to London on April 15. Bassist Charlie Short, whom Benny had hired the previous July for the Palladium engagement in London, joined him there. The group is first heard on but one track of an esoteric Department of State transcription, whose precise date is not known. Other than this, the ET's claim to fame is an impossibly long title:

DEPARTMENT OF STATE   **mid-April 1950, London**
THE VOICE OF AMERICA
"FUN WITH MUSIC" - WHAT IS JAZZ? Program No. 43
BENNY GOODMAN SEXTET

Benny Goodman clt; Roy Eldridge, tpt; Zoot Sims, ts; Dick Hyman, p; Charlie Short, b; Eddie Shaughnessy, d.

DS-2072   ET: Department of State, etc. Program No. 43 - Cut 1
            The Blues

Precise dates and locations of many of the engagements are not known. The group did perform in Copenhagen on April 21; and it is believed that the versatile Belgian, Jean "Toots" Thielmanns, joined it there. Toots, who arranges and composes in addition to playing guitar and harmonica, now lives in the United States, in the New York area. From Denmark the - now - Septet flew to Stockholm, for a concert in Stockholm's Konserthuset on April 24. Upon his arrival at the Bromma airfield, Benny was interviewed briefly, and a minute's worth of the interview appeared on Swedish TV.

Radio Sweden recorded the Konserthuset concert in its entirety on acetate, and still has the discs in its library, in excellent condition. Some notes about these 12" recordings are in order: They reveal that the first portion of the concert was presented to the Konserthuset audience only; the middle portion was broadcast by Radio Sweden; and the final segment of the concert was again limited to the immediate audience. In the first portion, Roy's "Rockin' Chair" is terminated after the first few bars; either the recording process was stopped at this point so that the engineers could prepare for the broadcast, or perhaps a disc is missing. The last tune broadcast, "Boogie Woogie," has a closing announcement over it, and the performance is not quite complete; but an audience recording of the concert offers the select on in full. In the third segment, Benny announces he will play "Poor Butterfly" in response to a request; the requestor was Olof Palme, who in future will become Sweden's Prime Minister, and who will be assassinated in 1986. Finally, cheers for Benny's Septet are led by Swedish vocalist Alice Babs, who one day will record with Duke Ellington.

Here, then, the Konserthuset concert of April 24, separated into its three parts, with those performances that do not include Benny shown in parentheses:

STOCKHOLM CONCERT   April 24, 1950,
                           Konserthuset, Stockholm

Benny Goodman, clt; Roy Eldridge, tpt; Zoot Sims, ts; Dick Hyman, p; Toots Theilmanns, g & hca; Charlie Short, b; Eddie Shaughnessy, d. Nancy Reed, Roy Eldridge, voc.

QUARTET: Goodman, Hyman, Short, Shaughnessy

Konserthuset audience only:

Stompin' At The Savoy (theme)
After You've Gone—QUARTET
Body And Soul—QUARTET
On The Sunny Side Of The Street—QUARTET
(Rockin' Chair—Eldridge w/rhythm—n/c, intro only

Radio Sweden broadcast:

Stompin' At The Savoy (theme)
Air Mail Special
Let Me Off Uptown-voc Nancy Reed, Roy Eldridge
The World Is Waiting For The Sunrise—QUARTET
(Star Dust—Theilmanns, hca, w/rhythm—NO BG
(Honeysuckle Rose—Hyman w/d—NO BG
(Lover—Hyman p solo—NO BG
Boogie Woogie

Konserthuset audience only:

Poor Butterfly—QUARTET
I've Found A New Baby
Where Or When-voc Nancy Reed—QUARTET
I Can't Give You Anything But Love, Baby-voc Nancy Reed
(All The Things You Are—Sims w/rhythm—NO BG
Indiana
(Hi Ho Trailus) Boot Whip-voc Roy Eldridge
Flying Home
. . . cheers for Benny, Alice Babs; Benny says "Thanks" in Swedish
Stompin' At The Savoy (theme)

About the only thing that detracts from the Konserthuset concert is Eddie Shaughnessy's attempt to play two bass drums, which he fails to do successfully. As a matter of fact, not even Buddy Rich was proficient with the double basses, about the only drum technique he never quite mastered. Louis Bellson was better; but best of all was relatively less known Dave Black, as exampled by his work with the "Duke."

It was once believed that a portion of a concert broadcast by Swiss Radio was an extract of the Konserthuset concert. Not so; the broadcast is from a concert given in Zurich, whose date unfortunately is not known:

ZURICH CONCERT   May 1950, Zurich
  Swiss Radio

Personnels as April 24.

Stompin' At The Savoy (theme)
After You've Gone—QUARTET
(All The Things You Are—Sims w/rhythm—NO BG
(How High The Moon—Theilmanns, hca, w/rhythm—NO BG
(Rockin' Chair—Eldridge w/rhythm—NO BG
Just One Of Those Things—QUARTET

The Septet is reported to have been in Belgium from May 28 through June 5, but no recordings of its work while there are known to the author. Apparently, Thielmanns left the tour there, for his guitar and harmonica are not evident on air checks from the final concert in Paris. Neither is Charlie Short's bass audible; and thus he, too, is omitted from the personnel.

At least in part, the Paris concert, at the Palais de Chaillot, was broadcast by a French radio network. Extant recordings were taken off the air onto acetates. Because of disc limitations, intro's of some of the selections are clipped, and some have their middle portions excised. But overall, their quality is good, and they are a worthwhile souvenir of Benny's farewell to Europe in 1950:

PARIS CONCERT-Palais de Chaillot   June 8, 1950, Paris
  French Radio

Benny Goodman, clt; Roy Eldridge, tpt; Zoot Sims, ts; Dick Hyman, p; Eddie Shaughnessy, d. Nancy Reed, Roy Eldridge, voc.

TRIO: Goodman, Hyman, Shaughnessy

After You've Gone—TRIO
Body and Soul—TRIO
The World Is Waiting For The Sunrise—TRIO
Air Mail Special (n/c—middle break)
I've Found A New Baby (n/c—middle break)
Flying Home (n/c—middle break)
. . . unannounced tune, possibly "Boogie Woogie" (n/c—middle break)
(Rockin' Chair—Eldridge w/rhythm—NO BG
(Knock Me A Kiss-voc Roy Eldridge—Eldridge w/rhythm—NO BG
(Honeysuckle Rose—Hyman w/d—NO BG
(I Would Do) Anything For You-voc Nancy Reed
Let Me Off Uptown-voc Nancy Reed, Roy Eldridge (n/c)
I Can't Give You Anything But Love, Baby-voc Nancy Reed (n/c—intro only)

Benny returned to the United States June 20, took the group into New York's mammoth Radio City Music Hall on July 9. That same day he was guest soloist with the NBC Symphony, and its Sunday broadcast was recorded privately:

"THE NBC SYMPHONY HOUR"   July 9, 1950, New York
  NBC Radio Network

Benny Goodman, clt; and the NBC Symphony Orchestra, Arthur Fiedler conducting.

Beyond The Sea (arr Paul New)
Tzena, Tzena, Tzena (arr . . . Ross)
Finale, Concerto No. 1 For Clarinet And Orchestra (von Weber)

Classical recitals shared Benny's attention in August while he rehearsed a new Sextet for what would become his first sponsored series on television. The hour-long programs were titled "Star Time," and featured comedian Lew Parker and comedienne-vocalist Frances Langford as the quarreling "Bickersons," along with invited guests. Benny's participation began September 5 and lasted for 13 weeks. All of his performances were recorded privately, and appear below. These listings are revised from those shown in the author's previous work, and include some additional selections.

"STAR TIME"   September 5, 1950, New York
  DUMONT Television Network

Benny Goodman, clt; Terry Gibbs, vib; Teddy Wilson, p; Johnny Smith, g; Bob Carter, b; Terry Snyder, d. Frances Langford, voc. Guests: Ben Blue, Kathryn Lee.

Slipped Disc
Come Rain Or Come Shine-voc Frances Langford

Those interested in sound-on-film should note that kinescopes of the "Star Time" telecasts are extant, and some have been acquired by collectors. Their quality is not equal to later videotapes, but is acceptable, and they are desirable collectors' items.

"STAR TIME"   September 12, 1950, New York
  DUMONT Television Network

Sextet personnel as September 5. Benny Goodman, clt, and a studio orchestra. Guests: David Burns, Dick Haymes, dancer Kathryn Lee.

Preludes II, III (Gershwin) - Benny Goodman, clt, and a studio orchestra
Three Little Words - SEXTET

"STAR TIME"   September 19, 1950, New York
  DUMONT Television Network

Personnels as Sept. 12. Guests: David Burns, Dick Haymes.

Get Happy - SEXTET
Body And Soul - SEXTET
Somebody Loves Me-voc Dick Haymes - SEXTET
I've Got Music In My Heart-voc Dick Haymes, Frances Langford, Lew Parker - Benny Goodman, clt, and a studio orchestra

"STAR TIME"   September 26, 1950, New York
  DUMONT Television Network

Sextet as September 5. Guest: Harry Brooks.

Just One Of Those Things
(Honeysuckle Rose - Wilson p solo - NO BG
Maybe My Baby Loves Me-voc Frances Langford
Temptation Rag

Reevaluation of base material removed "After You've Gone" from the telecast of September 26, reassigned it to a non-"Star Time" telecast of October 8, q.v.

"STAR TIME"   October 3, 1950, New York
  DUMONT Television Network

Sextet as September 5. Guest: James Jewell.

Lullaby Of The Leaves
Blues In The Night
After You've Gone

The name of the program and the place of origin of the next listing are unknown. It was transcribed from a telecast via WFIL-TV, at the time the affiliate of the Dumont Television Network in Philadelphia.

TELECAST-WFIL-TV, Phila.   October 8, 1950,
Sextet as September 5.   unknown location

After You've Gone

For his first commercial recordings in almost a year, Benny added Nancy Reed and Jimmy "Rickey" Ricks to his "Star Time" Sextet:

BENNY GOODMAN & his SEXTET   **October 10, 1950, New York**

Personnel as September 5. Nancy Reed, "Rickey," voc.

CO 44431-1   CO 39045, CO DJ 39045, CoC 1650, CoE DB2797, CoFr
              BF407, CoH DCH70, CoJap M462. **EP:** CO 1-889, CoE
              SEGC11. **LP:** HA HL7278, CBS 52405
              Oh Babe-voc Rickey, Nancy Reed

CO 44432-1   **LP:** HA HL7278, CO alb P5-15536, CBS 52405
              You're Gonna Lose Your Gal-voc Rickey

CO 44433-1   CO 39045, CO DJ 39045, CoC 1650, CoH DCH70, CoJap
              M462. **45:** CO 3-39045. **EP:** CO 1-889. **LP:** HA
              HL7278, CBS 52405
              Walkin' With The Blues-voc Rickey

Designation, "The Opener," is arbitrarily applied to the first selection played on the "Star Time" telecast the evening of the Columbia session. Note that the unknown trombonist on "Jazz Me Blues" may be Lou McGarity—sounds a lot like him:

"STAR TIME"   October 10, 1950, New York
  DUMONT Television Network

Sextet, orchestra personnels as September 12. SEPTET: Unknown tpt, tbn replace vib in Sextet. Guests: Peter Hamilton, Arnold Stang.

"The Opener"-voc Frances Langford, Lew Parker - Benny Goodman, clt, and a studio orchestra
Memories Of You - SEXTET
Blue Skies-voc Frances Langford - SEXTET
The Jazz Me Blues - SEPTET
The World Is Waiting For The Sunrise - SEXTET

"STAR TIME"   October 17, 1950, New York
DUMONT Television Network

Personnels as September 12. Guest: Sam Levenson.

It's Only A Paper Moon
Limehouse Blues
Jamboree Jones-voc Lew Parker & chorus - SEXTET plus studio orchestra

"STAR TIME"   October 24, 1950, New York
DUMONT Television Network

Personnel as September 5, plus Jimmy Ricks ("Rickey"), voc. Guests: Sam Levenson, Danny Scholl.

Oh Babe-voc Jimmy Ricks
Air Mail Special

"STAR TIME"   October 31, 1950, New York
DUMONT Television Network

Personnel as September 5.

Rose Room
Temptation Rag

On November 5 Benny once again was guest soloist on NBC's "Symphony Hour" broadcast. The U.S. Department of State transcribed the program onto two 16" "Voice Of America" transcriptions. Chronologically, these are the last "live" Benny Goodman 16" ET's known to the author; in 1951, U.S. Government agencies began to employ tape to record broadcasts and telecasts, and in main distributed them via 12" LP's.

The broadcast marks Benny's initial "recording" of Aaron Copland's "Concerto For Clarinet And String Orchestra," which he had commissioned in 1947. (ET labels identify the composition as "Concerto For Clarinet And Orchestra"—no strings attached.) This performance came just one week before the composer's 50th birthday.

The program also included Bartok's "Two Rumanian Dances"; these are on the second ET, along with the conclusion of the Copland concerto. Benny is heard but briefly in the Bartok works, for their solo clarinet passages are limited. Their inclusion, however, presents Benny in vehicles he rarely performs.

DEPARTMENT OF STATE   November 5, 1950, New York
THE VOICE OF AMERICA
CONCERTO SERIES, Program No. 44

Benny Goodman, clt, and the NBC Symphony Orchestra. Fritz Reiner conducts the Copland concerto; harpist is Edward Vito, pianist is Joseph Kahn. Milton Katims conducts the Bartok "Dances."

DS-2366   **ET:** Department of State, Voice Of America, Concerto Series, Program No. 44 - Part I of II
Copland: Concerto for Clarinet and Orchestra (Beginning)

DS-2367   **ET:** Department of State, Voice Of America, Concerto Series, Program No. 44 - Part II of II - cut 1
Copland: Concerto for Clarinet and Orchestra (Conclusion)

      ET: as above, except Cut 2
Bartok: Two Rumanian Dances

"STAR TIME"   November 7, 1950, New York
DUMONT Television Network

Benny Goodman, clt; Terry Gibbs, vib; Teddy Wilson, p; Johnny Smith, g; Bob Carter, b; CHARLIE SMITH, d, replaces Snyder. Guests: Danny Scholl, Jack Gilford.

On The Sunny Side Of The Street
Rachel's Dream

"STAR TIME"   November 14, 1950, New York
DUMONT Television Network

Sextet as November 7. Orchestra: Benny Goodman, clt, and a studio orchestra. Guests: Jack Gilford, Alan Ross.

Sing, Sing, Sing - Benny Goodman, clt, and a studio orchestra
Avalon
Just One Of Those Things-voc Frances Langford
China Boy

Next, Benny's commercial recording of the Copland concerto, with the maestro conducting; and now the harp and piano get label credit:

✓ **AARON COPLAND - CONCERTO FOR**   November 15, 1950, New York
CLARINET AND STRING ORCHESTRA
(WITH HARP AND PIANO)

Benny Goodman, clt, with Aaron Copland conducting The Columbia String Orchestra (With Harp and Piano).

FXLP 4408-1   **LP:** CO ML4421, CoJap WL5102, CBS BLG72218
Concerto For Clarinet And String Orchestra (With Harp and Piano)

(Retaining its catalog number, CBS later released the concerto in a "stereo" mode, **LP:** CBS S72218.)

"STAR TIME"   November 21, 1950, New York
DUMONT Television Network

Personnel as November 7. Guests: Jon Hall, Ronnie Cunningham, Jack Cassidy.

These Foolish Things
Honeysuckle Rose

Seemingly impossibly, a few copies of CO 39121 were released that backed "Lullaby Of The Leaves" with, "The Boy Next Door," by Eddie Duchin - "impossibly," because the label lists "Temptation Rag," and the matrix and take inscribed at its periphery are correct for the Goodman recording. Columbia has no explanation as to how this might have occurred.

Note that further comparison persuades that a test pressing of matrix CO 44675, showing take 1A, is identical to the LP release, which Columbia designates take 3. This is not an uncommon occurrence; it happens when an unissued recording is made into a test pressing for evaluation prior to release. The LP take was the third take recorded; it is the first in order-of-preference.

BENNY GOODMAN SEXTET   November 24, 1950, New York

Personnel as November 7. Nancy Reed, The Pastels, voc.

CO 44674-1   CO 39121, CoC 1693, CoCont DC647, CoE DB3350, CoFr DF3483, CoNor GNS5104. **EP:** CoE SEGC10. **LP:** HA HL7225, CO alb P5-15536
Lullaby Of The Leaves

CO 44675-3   **LP:** HA HL7278, CO alb P5-15536, CBS 52405
Then You've Never Been Blue-voc Nancy Reed

CO 44676-1A   **LP:** HA HL7278, CBS 52405
Walkin'-voc, The Pastels

CO 44677-1   CO 39121, CoC 1693, CoCont DC647, CoE DB3315, CoFin DYC146, CoFin DYC167, CoFr DF3483, Colt 2641, CoNor GNS5104. **45:** CoCont SCM5053, CoG SCMW104. **EP:** CoE SEGC10, ReSp SEML34017. **LP:** HA HL7225
Temptation Rag

Next is Benny's final appearance on "Star Time"—the program was renewed, but the Sextet, having completed its 13-week contract, was not. Fittingly, the last selection he plays on the series (recently uncovered when all of the "Star Time" material was reviewed) has a brilliant burst of clarinet, something to remember him by:

"STAR TIME"   *November 28, 1950, New York*
  DUMONT Television Network

Personnels as November 14. Guest: Charlie Cantor.

Stompin' At The Savoy
I Want To Be Happy
I've Got Music In My Heart-voc tout les ensemble - Benny Goodman, clt,
  and a studio orchestra - to signoff

The Sextet dispersed, and Benny did little for the balance of the year. He appeared as soloist with the Philadelphia Orchestra, in Billy Penn's Town's Academy of Music, on December 11, but no recordings of the event are known to exist. That's unfortunate, because he performed another work he had commissioned, the Hindemith Clarinet Concerto.

He began 1951 with a classical recording session in Columbia's studios; two sessions, in fact, for two were required to complete this version of the Mozart opus:

BENNY GOODMAN, Clarinet, and the   **January 4, 1951, New York**
AMERICAN ART QUARTET

Benny Goodman, clt; Eudice Shapiro, Robert Sushel, v; Virginia Majewski, viola; Victor Gottlieb, cello.

XLP 7249-1   **LP:** CO ML4483, Side 1. **ET:** 1955 Heart Fund (n/c)
                Quintet For Clarinet And Strings In A Major (K.581)
                First Movement: Allegro - Band 1
                Second Movement: Larghetto - Band 2

BENNY GOODMAN, Clarinet, and the   **January 15, 1951, New York**
AMERICAN ART QUARTET

Personnel as January 4.

XLP 7250-1   **LP:** CO ML4483, Side 2
                Quintet For Clarinet And Strings In A Major (K.581)
                Third Movement: Minuetto)
                   Trio 1) - Band 1
                   Trio 2)
                Fourth Movement: Allegretto con variazioni - Band 2

On February 14 Benny began a two-week engagement at the El Rancho Vegas, in the then gambling capitol of the U.S., Las Vegas, Nevada. His new Sextet included Johnny White, vib; Paul Smith, p; Milt Norman, g; Morty Corb, b; Bill Douglass, d; and vocalist Nancy Reed. Prices were going up—reportedly, Benny received $7,000 per week. Twenty years later, Goodman small groups will command that much and more for a one-nighter.

Benny's next known appearance on television was March 21, when he was chosen to inaugurate a new series sponsored by a manufacturer of watchbands. Watch this band that Hymie Schertzer assembled from the cream of New York studio musicians for Benny:

"KREISLER BANDSTAND"   *March 21, 1951, New York*
  ABC Television Network

Benny Goodman, clt; Bernie Privin, Doc Severinson, Jimmy Maxwell, tpt; Will Bradley, Lou McGarity, Cutty Cutshall, tbn; Hymie Schertzer, Bill Stegmeyer, as; Al Klink, Boomie Richman (sometimes, Richmond), ts; Teddy Wilson, p; Johnny Smith, g; Eddie Safranski, b; Jo Jones, d. Peggy Lee, Mel Torme, voc.

TRIO: Goodman, Wilson, Torme (d)

SEXTET: Goodman; Terry Gibbs, vib; Wilson, Smith, Safranski, Jones

Let's Dance (theme)
Why Don't You Do Right?-voc Peggy Lee
(Isn't This A Lovely Day? (poss arr SM) - accomp. to tap-dancing - NO BG
After You've Gone - SEXTET
(Where Or When-voc Peggy Lee, accomp. Wilson, Jones - NO BG
China Boy - TRIO
You're Getting To Be A Habit With Me-voc Mel Torme
Gotta Be This Or That-voc Benny Goodman - to close

The overwhelming majority of Benny Goodman collectors are jazz enthusiasts. To possess complete collections of his works they buy his classical recordings, even if they never play them. Their guide to acquisition is his name on the record label or its LP sleeve, not the sound of his clarinet. Who of us can distinguish among classical clarinetists?

Thus it is understandable that Goodman collectors in toto missed the

original release of Benny's next classical recording; his name is not on its label and is not prominent on its jacket. It is mentioned but once, buried in the final paragraph of the liner notes: ". . . and performed by a virtuoso orchestra that includes as clarinetist Benny Goodman."

The original 10″ LP is exceptionally rare and a copy in excellent condition commands a premium price. The recording (Benny's first with Leonard Bernstein and the only Goodman performance of this work extant) has been re-released on 12″ LPs. Not even these are widely known as Goodman recordings, for on them Benny gets no mention at all.

LEONARD BERNSTEIN conducting   **March 22, 1951, New York**
THE COLUMBIA CHAMBER ORCHESTRA

Benny Goodman, clt; and the Columbia Chamber Orchestra, Leonard Bernstein conducting.

XCO 45465-1)
XCO 45466-1)   **LP:** CO ML2203 (10″); CO CL920, PhilCont NO2600R
               (12″)
XCO 45467-1)   **Milhaud - La Creation Du Monde (1923)**
XCO 45468-1)

(Pressing matrix of the 10″ LP is: LP 6635; pressing matrix of the CO 12″ LP is: SLP 38384.)

Fletcher Henderson, Benny's longtime arranging genius, had suffered a cerebral hemorrhage in December 1950, then a second seizure six weeks later. His funds were exhausted. Radio station WNEW disc jockey Martin Block solicited Benny's aid in playing a benefit for "Smack," and Benny agreed immediately. Together they rounded up the original Goodman Trio, added other well-known musicians, and on April 1 broadcast on Henderson's behalf via WNEW.

The program was transcribed onto a limited-edition premium-priced LP by Columbia. All proceeds of its sale went to Henderson; the musicians got nothing. A little over a year later Columbia reissued the record on its regular label at retail, a practice viewed dimly by those who, in good faith, had paid a high price for the first issue. Given the date of the broadcast, it was April Fool! for collectors.

THE BENNY GOODMAN TRIO   **April 1, 1951, New York**
plays for FLETCHER HENDERSON

Benny Goodman, clt; Teddy Wilson, p; Gene Krupa, d.

XTV 14888-2   **LP:** MB 1000-Side 1, CO CL516, CoAu&E 33(0)SX1020,
               CoFr FPX114, CoJap PL5001, SONY SONP-50203,
               SONY SOPM-181, SONY 20AP-1438, TAX 8041. **EP:**
               CO set G4-14, CoJap EM85. **78:** CoJap L3019
               China Boy

               same issues, plus **LP:** FONT TFR6022, FontCont
               662019TR, CO alb P6-14954
               Body And Soul

               same issues as "China Boy," except delete CoJap 78 &
               EP; and add **ET:** AFRS Jazz Club USA 29
               Runnin' Wild

Add Eddie Safranski, b.

               same issues as "China Boy," except delete **78**, Co Jap
               L3019
               On The Sunny Side Of The Street

Add Johnny Smith, g.

               same issues as "Body And Soul," except delete **78**,
               CoJap L3019; and add **ET:** AFRS Jazz Club USA 29
               After You've Gone

Add Lou McGarity, tbn.

               same issues as "After You've Gone," except delete **EP**,
               CoJap EM85
               Basin Street Blues

Trio only - Goodman, Wilson, Krupa

XTV 14889-2   **LP:** MB 1000-Side 2, CO CL516, CoAu&E 33(0)SX1020, FONT TFR6022, FontCont 662019TR, SONY SONP-50203, SONY SOPM-181, SONY 20AP-1438, TAX 8041. **EP:** CO set G4-14, ReSp 34065. **ET:** AFRS Jazz Club USA 29
Rose Room

Add Buck Clayton, tpt; Johnny Smith, g; Eddie Safranski, b.

same issues as ''Rose Room,'' except delete **EP**, ReSp 34065; and add **LP:** CO alb P4M-5678
Honeysuckle Rose

Trio only - Goodman, Wilson, Krupa

same issues as ''Rose Room,'' except delete FONT and FontCont LP's, and AFRS ET, and add **LP:** CO alb P4M-5678
I Found A New Baby (sic)

Add Clayton, McGarity, Smith, Safranski.

same issues as ''Rose Room''
One O'Clock Jump

The spring months of 1951 saw Benny conduct a classical music recording program for WNEW-BMI titled ''The Benny Goodman Music Festival.'' Benny's role was to introduce and discuss various performances; between his commentary, stations that subscribed to the WNEW-BMI service played the recordings in question. Benny's announcements and commentary were transcribed onto two LP's for distribution to subscribers, both labeled ''The Benny Goodman Music Festival - A BMI service in cooperation with WNEW, New York.'' Seven tracks of announcements are on a two-sided 10″ LP, bearing matrices ''BG 101, BG 102.'' A 12″ two-sided LP, with matrices ''BG 103, BG 104,'' contains one track for each of the seven programs in the series. The final track on this LP is titled ''Interview With BG''; on it Benny answers questions put to him by local announcers, as supplied by a text that accompanied the LP. The commentary is interesting, and tapes of the LP's are worthwhile.

To further revival of interest in a failing Fletcher Henderson, Benny next assembled an orchestra to record some old and new arrangements ''Smack'' had written for Goodman:

BENNY GOODMAN AND HIS ORCHESTRA   April 26, 1951, New York

Benny Goodman, clt; Billy Butterfield, Chris Griffin, Jimmy Maxwell, tpt; Lou McGarity, Cutty Cutshall, Will Bradley, tbn; Hymie Schertzer, Al Klink, as; Peanuts Hucko, Boomie Richman (Richmond), ts; Art Drellinger, bar; Stan Freeman, p; Johnny Smith, g; Bob Haggart, b; Terry Snyder, d.

CO 45670-1   CO 39416, CoC 1781, CoCont DC575, CoH DCH131, CoJap L3012. **45:** CO 4-39416. **EP:** CO B2587, CoE SEG 7549, CoJap EM56. **LP:** HA HL7190, HA HS11090, CO alb P13371, CBS 52340, CBS 21124
Down South Camp Meetin' (arr FH)

CO 45671-1   CoH DCH229, CoSw DS2058. **EP:** CoE SEG7574, Font Cont 462034TE. **LP:** HA HL7225
Mean To Me (arr FH)

CO 45672-1   CO 39416, AFR 10-41/AFR 81 (B8193), CoArg 291851, CoAu DO3562, CoC 1781, CoCont DC592, CoFin DYC137, CoG DW5166, CoH DCH131, CoJap M648, CoMex 2120. **45:** CO 4-39416. **EP:** CoE SEG7549, CoJap EM56. **LP:** HA HL7190, HA HS11090, Co alb P13371, CoJap PL2029, CBS 52340, CBS 21124
South Of The Border (Down Mexico Way) (arr FH)

CO 45673-1   CoArg 291851, CoAu DO3562, CoCont DC592, CoFin DYC137, CoG DW5166, CoH DCH229, CoJap ME83, CoSw DZ863. **EP:** CoE SEG7549, CoJap EM56. **LP:** HA HL7225
Muskat (Muskrat) Ramble (arr FH)

BENNY GOODMAN AND HIS ORCHESTRA   April 29, 1951, New York

Personnel as April 26.

CO 45674-1   **LP:** HA HL7225
Lulu's Back In Town (arr FH)

CO 45675-Bkdn   UNISSUED - Co Ref

CO 45675-1   CoG DW5105, CoJap ME83, CoSw DZ863. **EP:** CoE SEG7574, FontCont 462034TE. **LP:** HA HL7225
Stardust (arr FH)

CO 45676-1   CO 39513, AFR 10-55/AFR 105, CoC 1822, CoFr BF454, CoMex 2120. **45:** CO 4-39513. **EP:** CoE SEG7574, FontCont 462034TE. **LP:** HA HL7190, HA HS11090, CO alb P13371, CBS 52340, CBS 21124
Wrappin' It Up (The Lindy Glide) (arr FH)

CO 45677-1   CO 39564, CoC 1850, CoCont DC575, CoE DB3732, CoFr BF454, CoG DW5105, CoNor GNS5103. **45:** CO 4039564, CoE SCM5259, CoFr SCDF1011. **EP:** CoE SEG7574, FontCont 462034TE. **LP:** HA HL7190, HA HL7255, HA HS11090, Co alb P13371, CBS 52340, CBS 21124
King Porter Stomp (arr FH)

(A CO Reference Recording is extant that offers a false start of ''Stardust,'' mx CO 45675.)

May and early June saw Benny working with a Sextet whose complement was the same as that for the Columbia session next, save that Eddie Safranski replaced Sid Weiss in the studios. Note that matrices for the two unissued sides are unknown, and that Sid Bulkin is sometimes spelled ''Balkin'':

BENNY GOODMAN SEXTET   June 13, 1951, New York

Benny Goodman, clt; Terry Gibbs, vib; Paul Smith, p; Johnny Smith, g; Eddie Safranski, b; Sid Bulkin, d. Nancy Reed, voc.

CO 45842-1   CO 39564, CoC 1850, CoFr BF498, CoH DCH157, CoJap M648. **45:** CO 4-39564. **EP:** CoE SEG7549, CoE SEGC9, FONT TFE17079, FontCont 462065TE, CoJap EM56. **LP:** HA HL7225
Farewell Blues

CO 45843-1   CO 39513, CoC 1822, CoFr BF498, CoH DCH157. **45:** CO 4-39513. **EP:** CoE SEGC9. **LP:** HA HL7278, CBS 52405. **ET:** Air Force GL-18
Toodle-Lee-Yoo-Doo-voc Nancy Reed

- ? -   UNISSUED
By The Fireside-voc Nancy Reed

- ? -   UNISSUED
Who?

Two days later Benny was in Philadelphia with Gibbs, Paul Smith, Weiss and an unidentified drummer, appearing in a benefit performance for an ethnic newspaper, the Phila. Enquirer. Later in the month he was guest soloist with the Philadelphia Symphony Orchestra, and in July he was featured artist with the Denver Symphony Orchestra. On July 15 he made a guest appearance on Peggy Lee's radio program:

''THE PEGGY LEE (REXALL) SHOW''   *July 15, 1951, New York*
   CBS Radio Network

Benny Goodman, clt, and Russ Case and his Orchestra.

*Clarinade (**LP:** GOJ 1005)*
*Toodle-Lee-Yoo-Doo-voc Peggy Lee (**LP:** GOJ 1005)*
Good-Bye (in its entirety)

August was a vacation month; Benny went back to work in September. There is some evidence that NBC recorded a Hollywood Bowl concert (for AFRS) that saw Benny sit in with Johnny Green and his Orchestra, and that also featured Bob Hope and Les Brown and his ''Band Of Renown,'' and Lionel Barrymore reciting ''Peter And The Wolf.'' Efforts to learn more about this engagement, and to verify the recording, have failed.

The date of this next entry has been revised from September 28, as once believed, to September 22:

"THE KEN MURRAY SHOW"   *September 22, 1951, New York*
  CBS Television Network

Benny Goodman, clt, and a studio orchestra.

SEXTET: *Benny Goodman, clt; Terry Gibbs, vib; Bernie Leighton, p; Johnny Smith, g; Eddie Safranski, b; Terry Snyder, d.*

The Man I Love
The World Is Waiting For The Sunrise - SEXTET
Three O'Clock In The Morning - Goodman, Ken Murray clt duet
Stompin' At The Savoy - SEXTET plus orchestra

Benny next cut three more big band sides for Columbia, the first of which was initially released by Playboy Magazine on its label. Benny's inclusion in this album was the result of his having been chosen "best clarinetist" in Playboy's first annual jazz poll. He will win that honor many times, and along with Armstrong, Basie, Brubeck, Ray Charles, John Coltrane, Ellington, Ella Fitzgerald, Frank Sinatra and others, he is enshrined in Playboy's "Jazz Hall Of Fame."

BENNY GOODMAN AND HIS ORCHESTRA September 26, 1951, New York

Personnel as April 26, except substitute BERNIE PRIVIN and CARL POOLE, tpt, for Maxwell. Nancy Reed, voc.

CO 47080-1   **LP:** PB 31957, HA HL7190, HA HS11090, CoE
              33CX1529, CO alb P13371, CO alb P5-15536, CBS
              52340, CBS 21124
              When Buddha Smiles (arr FH)

Delete Billy Butterfield.

CO 47081   **LP:** HA HL7225
              Sunrise Serenade (arr FH)

CO 47082   UNISSUED - CO Ref
              You Can't Pull The Wool Over My Eyes-voc Nancy Reed
              (arr JM)

An unsubstantiated report indicates that sometime in October Benny waxed some ". . . titles never previously recorded for recruiting shows called 'Star On Parade.'" The author can offer no further information on this assertion, save to refer the reader to additional discussion as of June/July 1952 in this work. His only certain entry for October 1951 is NBC's "The Big Show":

"THE BIG SHOW"   *October 21, 1951, New York*
  NBC Radio Network

Benny Goodman, clt, with Meredith Willson's Orchestra.

The Man I Love
Dizzy Fingers

Two days later, Benny was guest soloist with the Philadelphia Orchestra in Worcester, Massachusetts. We then lose sight of him until December, when he appeared on a television series that had famous people present relatives. Benny introduced his stepdaughter Gilly on the program hosted by Peter Lind Hayes and Mary Healy, then performed with a Trio:

"STAR OF THE FAMILY"   *December 2, 1951, New York*
  CBS Television Network

Benny Goodman, clt; Bernie Leighton, p; Terry Snyder, d.

The Sheik Of Araby

Benny's next studio session was in Hollywood, where he recorded four tunes of a projected eight-track 10″ LP to be titled "Let's Hear The Melody." The remaining tunes were not recorded until almost three months later.

BENNY GOODMAN WITH STRINGS   December 19, 1951, Los Angeles

Benny Goodman, clt; Hal Diner, Bill Schaefer, Al Thompson, tbn; George Kast, Samuel Cytron, Mischa Russell, Felix Slatkin, Paul Nero, Sam Middleman, Dave Frisina, Marshall Sosson, Ted Rosen, v; David Sterkin, Maurice Perlmutter, viola; Cy Bernard, Armand Kaproff, cello; Paul Smith, p; George Van Eps, g; John Ryan, b; Nick Fatool, d.

RHCO   CO DJ 2185, CoJap M750. **45:** CO set G4-13. **EP:** CO
10063-1B   set B352. **LP:** CO GL102, CO CL6302, CO
                demonstration LP D2, Co alb P4M-5678, CoJap
                PL5046, PHIL BBR8064, PhilCont B07649R, PhilCont
                B07728R
              Moonglow

RHCO   same issues as "Moonglow," except omit 78's, and
10064-1B   substitute LP PhilCont B07078L for PhilCont B07728R
              Georgia On My Mind

RHCO   same issues as "Georgia On My Mind," except omit LP,
10065-1B   PhilCont B07078L
              I Gotta Right To Sing The Blues

RHCO   same issues as "I Gotta Right to Sing The Blues"
10066-1B   **I Didn't Know What Time It Was**

The new year began with Benny performing with the Philadelphia Orchestra January 2. He stayed over to record with a segment of the Orchestra the next day, then returned on February 17 to complete the session. It is not known how many tunes were recorded, nor on which day; none was ever issued, and Columbia's files are vague about these sessions. Three selections are extant on a test pressing LP.

The recording "studio" was Philadelphia's Academy Of Music, an auditorium widely acclaimed for its near-perfect acoustical qualities. (Thirteen years later, when setting up for a classical/jazz concert, Benny had the author sit in various locations in the Academy to test the sound. They agreed mutually that no public address system was needed, and none was used for the performance.) All of the tunes recorded were to have constituted a Columbia album tentatively titled "Goodman At The Pops." The extant cuts sound fine, and it is a mystery why this project never reached fruition.

"Henderson Stomp" (not "Stealin' Apples," as misidentified in an earlier biodiscography) uses Fletcher Henderson's 1940 arrangement, rescored to include the Orchestra's instrumentation. Arranger credits for the other two tunes follow their titles.

GOODMAN AT THE POPS   January 3-February 17, 1952, Phila.

Benny Goodman, clt; and the Philadelphia "Pops" Orchestra, Alexander Hillsberg conducting.

LP 9097-2C   UNISSUED - Test Pressing
              Henderson Stomp
              I Only Have Eyes For You (arr Ralph Wilkinson)
              Dizzy Fingers (arr Will Beittel)

On January 26 Benny was interviewed on radio by jazz critic George Simon. And on an unknown date in March, Benny appeared on television in Chicago on a program titled "Pace Of Chicago": he performed with a group including Doc Evans, cnt; Max Miller, vib; Ralph Blank, p; Ed Stapleton, b; and Red Saunders, d. Unfortunately, no air checks of either program have been located, and the author can offer no additional information.

Also in March, completion of the "Let's Hear The Melody" album:

BENNY GOODMAN WITH STRINGS   March 5, 1952, Los Angeles

Personnel as December 19, 1951, except: Eudice Shapiro, Harry Blueston and Robert Sushel, v, replace Kast, Frisina and Sosson; Virginia Majewski, viola, replaces Perlmutter; Victor Gottlieb, cello, replaces Kaproff; and Morty Corb b, replaces Ryan.

RHCO   CoJap L3016. **45:** CO set G4-13, CoJap LL38C. **EP:** CO
10139-1B   set B352, CoJap EM101. **LP:** CO GL102, CO CL2483,
                CO CL6302, CO CS9283, CoJap PL5046, PHIL
                BBR8064, PhilCont B07649R, CBS 52368. **ET:** 1955
                Heart Fund (n/c)
              Goodbye (arr Thomas Goodman)

RHCO 10140-1A	**45:** CO set G4-13. **EP:** CO set B352. **LP:** CO GL102, CO CL6302, CoJap PL5046, PHIL BBR8064, PhilCont B07649R, CO 21064 **Embraceable You**
RHCO 10141-1A	same issues as "Embraceable You," plus **78,** CO DJ 241; **LP,** CO alb P4M-5678 **Lover, Come Back To Me**
RHCO 10142-1A	same issues as "Embraceable You," plus **78,** CO DJ 241; **LP,** CO alb P4M-5678 **If I Had You**

On April 12, in Columbia's New York studios, Benny recorded the voice track that introduces Columbia's "1937-1938 Jazz Concert No. 2" album. His voice is dubbed into the introductory "Let's Dance" track.

"THE KATE SMITH SHOW"   *May 7, 1952, New York*
  NBC Television Network

Benny Goodman, clt, and a studio orchestra.

SEXTET: Benny Goodman, clt; Terry Gibbs, vib; Bernie Leighton, p; Mundell Lowe, g; Sid Weiss, b; Don Lamond, d.

Lover Come Back To Me
The World Is Waiting For The Sunrise - SEXTET

Benny next flew to Florida for a solo appearance with the Miami Symphony and a brief vacation. He then returned to New York for a big band studio session. Before detailing it however, we must deal with a recording session about which little is known:

Benny has a photo whose caption reads, "PROGRAM 591 - STARS ON PARADE - The U.S. Army and U.S. Air Force Recruiting Service presents 'The KING SWINGS AGAIN' starring BENNY GOODMAN, with MEL POWELL, SYD WEISS, MUNDELL LOWE, and TERRY SNYDER." The notice's type style and stock are identical to those that frequently accompanied electrical transcriptions distributed by U.S. Government agencies.

The author has not located a copy of "Stars On Parade No. 591," if indeed an ET or LP so designated was released. Benny was working with the personnel cited in mid-1952, as evidenced by recording sessions and extant air checks. Thus the photograph—and the recording session—is listed at this juncture. (The reader will recall a similar entry as of October 1951—if there was but one session, that date may be nearer the mark.) Further information is being sought.

BENNY GOODMAN AND HIS ORCHESTRA   **May 28, 1952, New York**

Benny Goodman, clt; Bernie Privin, Chris Griffin, Mickey McMickle, Ricky Trent, tpt; Lou McGarity, Cutty Cutshall, Will Bradley, tbn; Hymie Schertzer, Al Klink, as; Peanuts Hucko, Boomie Richman (Richmond), ts; Art Drellinger, bar; Mel Powell, p; Mundell Lowe, g; Jack Lesberg, b; Terry Snyder, d.

CO 47458-S	**LP:** HA HL7190, HA HS11090, HA HS11271, CO P13371, CBS 52340, CBS 63367, PIC 240, CBS 21124 **I'm Gonna Sit Right Down And Write Myself A Letter** (arr FH)
CO 47459	UNISSUED **My Honey's Lovin' Arms** (arr MP)

(The author has not been able to obtain a copy of matrix CO 47459, but understands the version remaining in Columbia's possession is a splice of two or more takes, as is the release of "I'm Gonna Sit . . .".)

On June 7 Benny appeared at the Brooklyn Dodgers' baseball stadium, Ebbets Field, with Morton Gould and the New York Philharmonic. A month later he is seen on television with both a Jazz Trio and a Classical Trio:

"CELEBRITY TIME SUMMER CONCERT"   *July 6, 1952, New York*
  CBS Television Network

Benny Goodman, clt; Mel Powell, p; Terry Snyder, d.

Avalon - JAZZ TRIO

Benny Goodman, clt; Yehudi Menuhin, v; Leon Pommers, p.

Trio-Finale, Suite For Clarinet, Violin And Piano (Milhaud) - CLASSICAL TRIO

(THE NEW) BENNY GOODMAN SEXTET   **July 29, 1952, New York**

Benny Goodman, clt; Terry Gibbs, vib; Teddy Wilson, p; Mundell Lowe, g; Sid Weiss, b; Terry Snyder, d.

CO 48131	**EP:** CO B1633. **LP:** CO CL552, CO D404, CO alb P2M-5193, CoJap PL5010, HA HL7278, PHIL BBL7021, PHIL BBR8085, PhilCont B07024L, PhilCont B07050L, PhilCont B07706R, CBS 52405 **I've Got A Feeling I'm Falling**
CO 48132	**EP:** CO B1633. **LP:** CO CL552, CoJap PL5010, HA HL7278, CBS 52405, PHIL BBL7021, PhilCont B07024L, PhilCont B07519L. **ET:** Treasury Department Guest Star 555 **Bye Bye Blues**
CO 48133	**EP:** CO B1633, PHIL BBE12104, PhilCont 429175BE. **LP:** CO CL552, CO CB4, CoJap PL5010, HA HL7225, PHIL BBL7021, PhilCont B07024L **I'll Never Be The Same**
CO 48134	**EP:** CO B1561, DoJap EM1, PHIL BBE12001, PhilCont 429016BE. **LP:** CO CL552, CoJap PL5010, HA HL7278, PHIL BBL7021, PhilCont B07024L, CBS 52405. **ET:** Treasury Department Guest Star 555 **Between The Devil And The Deep Blue Sea**

(THE NEW) BENNY GOODMAN SEXTET   **July 30, 1952, New York**

Personnel as July 29, except DON LAMOND, d, replaces Snyder.

CO 48135	CoJap M807. **EP:** CO B1845. **LP:** CO CL552, CoJap PL5010, PHIL BBL7021, PhilCont B07024L, PhilCont B07519L. **ET:** Treasury Department Guest Star 555 **Under A Blanket Of Blue**
CO 48136	UNISSUED **East Of The Sun (And West Of The Moon)** (see comment below)
CO 48137	UNISSUED **Four Or Five Times** (see comment below)
CO 48138	**EP:** CO B1845. **LP:** CO CL552, CoJap PL5010, PHIL BBL7021, PhilCont B07024L, PhilCont B07519L **How Am I To Know?**
CO 48139	**EP:** CO B1561, CoJap EM1, PHIL BBE12001, PhilCont 429016BE. **LP:** CO CL552, CO Texaco LP, Co alb P4M-5678, CoJap PL5010, PHIL BBL7021, PhilCont B07024L **Undecided**
CO 48140	UNISSUED -unknown title

("East Of The Sun" and "Four Or Five Times" were re-recorded October 22. Columbia's files indicate the issued versions are from that date, including both takes of "Four Or Five Times.")

Benny assembled a new Sextet for a two-week engagement in The Forum, St. John, New Brunswick, beginning August 1. As vocalist, he hired attractive Jan Crockett, who'd been named "Miss Florida" for 1951. On an unknown date during the fortnight, radio station CHSJ featured the group in a 30-minute broadcast "live" from The Forum. Despite an occasional drop-out (the broadcast was transcribed onto acetates), a tape of the program affords excellent audio:

SUSTAINING BROADCAST   *first half August 1952, The Forum,*
  Radio Station CHSJ   *St. John, New Brunswick, Canada*

Benny Goodman, clt; Don Elliott, tpt & mellophone; Terry Gibbs, vib; Jimmy Lyons, p; Sid Weiss, b; Sid Bulkin, d. Jan Crockett, voc.

Stompin' At The Savoy (theme)
After You've Gone
Rose Room
'Deed I Do-voc Jan Crockett
Poor Butterfly
Just One Of Those Things
If I Had You
Bye Bye Blues
That Old Feeling-voc Jan Crockett
The World Is Waiting For The Sunrise
Good-Bye (theme)

The Sextet then moved to the Blue Note in Chicago for two weeks, opening there on August 15. Sid Bulkin was replaced by Morey Feld, and the addition of guitarist Don Roberts increased the group to a Septet. Two NBC broadcasts from the Blue Note are extant; the first has excellent sound, the author's copy of the second is poor.

SUSTAINING BROADCAST   *August 20, 1952,*
  NBC Radio Network   *Blue Note, Chicago*

Personnel as "first half August 1952," except add DON ROBERTS, g, and substitute MOREY FELD, d, for Bulkin.

Stompin' At The Savoy (theme)
After You've Gone
If I Had You
Bye Bye Blues
Poor Butterfly (mistakenly announced as, "Rose Room")
Avalon
Good-Bye (theme)

(Above on **LP:** *MARK 736, JAZ 36)*

SUSTAINING BROADCAST   *August 27, 1952,*
  NBC Radio Network   *Blue Note, Chicago*

Personnel as August 20.

Sweet Georgia Brown
Memories Of You
Just One Of Those Things
If I Had You
Flying Home

Magnecord, then a manufacturer of quality audio equipment, is known to have taped the Septet in stereo during performances at the Blue Note. For years collectors sought Magnecord's reels numbered 43 through 46 - even that much was known - to no avail. However, in 1983, and again in 1986, copies of some of those tapes became available to the author. Well recorded, the group is in good form: as ever, Benny plays superlatively, Don Elliott supplies arresting interpolations, and seldom-heard Jimmy Lyons is a revelation. Somewhat mysteriously, midway through copy reel No. 1 the club's manager is heard to say during "Good-Bye" that the past two weeks have been the happiest in the Blue Note's history. Then somewhat extravagantly, Benny replies that they've been the happiest of his life, too.

BENNY AT THE BLUE NOTE: *August 28, 1952,*
  MAGNECORD TAPES   *Blue Note, Chicago*

Septet as August 20. SEXTET: Septet sans Elliott. Jan Crockett, voc.

Tea For Two (n/c - intro excised)
Rose Room
Bye Bye Blues
Flying Home
Good-Bye (theme)
Them There Eyes-voc Jan Crockett
That Old Feeling-voc Jan Crockett
After You've Gone
(Tenderly - Elliott (mel) w/rhythm, vib in coda - NO BG
Just One Of Those Things
Body And Soul
Sweet Georgia Brown

After You've Gone
If I Had You
Air Mail Special
Avalon
Moon Glow
Don't Be That Way
(This Can't Be Love - Lyons w/rhythm - NO BG
These Foolish Things
'Deed I Do-voc Jan Crockett
Sugar-voc Jan Crockett
The World Is Waiting For The Sunrise - SEXTET

A week at the Colonial Tavern in Toronto, Canada, followed the Blue Note engagement. Benny is reported to have appeared in Fort Wayne, Indiana, and Hartford, Connecticut, at this time, but precisely where, when and with whom is not known. On September 19 he was the guest on a CBS Radio panel show, "Right You Are," which was broadcast from New York; panelists were James A. Michener, Betty Furness and Lyman Bryson. Unbelievably, Benny portrayed Franklin Roosevelt's famous pooch, "Fala."

Possibly in the fall of 1952—and possibly as late as spring/summer 1953—Benny and Teddy Wilson appeared on Faye Emerson's CBS Television series, "Wonderful Town." These programs highlighted major American cities; the subject of the telecast that included Benny was, naturally, Chicago. All efforts to pin down the date have been unavailing. Since this period is believed to be the earliest that Benny's participation could have occurred, the performance is inserted here:

"WONDERFUL TOWN"   *Fall 1952 - Summer 1953, New York*
  CBS Television Network

Benny Goodman, clt; Teddy Wilson, p; unknown b, d.

Rose Room
. . . few bars, unidentified tune

Next is the remake session necessary to record satisfactory takes of "East Of The Sun" and "Four Or Five Times." Two takes of the latter were released, both on a Columbia EP. Since EP's do not bear markings that make it possible to distinguish one from another, collectors could not visually select the two different versions issued under the same catalog number. They had to buy multiple copies, listen to them, and hope eventually to find alternate versions.

They are arbitrarily identified here as takes, "1," "2." Take "1" is the shorter rendition, by about 50 seconds. On it Benny can be heard to say, "Take it, Jack." On take "2," he exclaims, "Take it, boy." Take "1" has only been found on the EP, not on other releases, and is a rare collectors' item.

(THE NEW) BENNY GOODMAN SEXTET   **October 22, 1952, New York**

Benny Goodman, clt; Terry Gibbs, vib; Lou Stein, p; Allen Hanlon, g; Eddie Safranski, b; Don Lamond, d.

CO 48136-R   CoJap M807. **EP:** CO B1845. **LP:** CO CL552, CO alb P4M-5678, CoJap PL5010, HA HL7225, PHIL BBL7021, PhilCont BO-P07024L-R, PhilCont B07519L
    East Of The Sun (And West Of The Moon)

CO 48137-R(1)   **EP:** CO B1845
CO 48137-R(2)   **EP:** CO B1845. **LP:** CO CL552, CoJap PL5010, HA HL7278, PHIL BBL7021, PhilCont B07024L, CBS 52405. **ET:** Treasury Department Guest Star 555
    Four Or Five Times-voc Benny Goodman

Immediately following the Sextet session, a party celebrating release of the Goodman Columbia air checks album attracted alumni and friends to the studio. For the last time an ailing Fletcher Henderson was reunited with Benny and others of his orchestra who had become famous partially as a result of his arrangements. Fletcher died some nine-plus weeks later, on December 29. Benny was an honorary pallbearer at his funeral on January 2 in New York, and then Swing's greatest arranger, Fletcher Hamilton Henderson, Jr., was interred in a cemetery at his birthplace, Cuthbert, Georgia.

Metronome's January 1953 edition featured Benny on its cover, and in its lead story. On the 25th, jazz buff Alistair Cooke played host to the original Trio on television:

"OMNIBUS"   *January 25, 1953, New York*
   NBC Television Network

Benny Goodman, clt; Teddy Wilson, p; Gene Krupa, d.

. . . few bars, introduction
China Boy
Nice Work If You Can Get It
Memories Of You
The World Is Waiting For The Sunrise

It was back to the studios in February for a date with a charming alumna, Helen Ward, and a memorial session for Fletcher. Note that the original release of "Wolverine Blues" was a promo, "Priceless Editions," issued both as a 7" LP and a 45.

BENNY GOODMAN AND HIS ORCHESTRA   February 23, 1953, New York

Benny Goodman, clt; Billy Butterfield, Chris Griffin, Jimmy Maxwell, tpt; Lou McGarity, Cutty Cutshall, Bobby Byrne, tbn; Hymie Schertzer, Milt Yaner, as; Boomie Richman (Richmond), Al Klink, ts; Bernie Leighton, p; Barry Galbraith, g; Eddie Safranski, b; Don Lamond, d. Helen Ward, voc.

CO 48873-1A   **7"33:** CO PE 10. **45:** CO 4-PE 10. **LP:** HA HL7190, HA HS11090, CO P13371, CBS 52340
         Wolverine Blues (arr FH)

CO 48874-1A   **45:** CO set G4-20. **EP:** CO B1743, CO set B357. **LP:** CO GL524, CO P13371, HA HL7190, HA HS11090, CorAu KLP682, PhilCont B07011L, CBS 52340, CBSSd JGL524
         You're A Heavenly Thing-voc Helen Ward (arr FH)

CO 48875-1A   PhilAu B21051H. **45:** CO set G4-20. **EP:** CO set B357, PhilCont set KD147. **LP:** CO GL524, CO Texaco LP, CO P13371, CoJap L3006, HA HL7190, HA HS11090, CorAu KLP682, PhilCont B07011L, PhilCont B07797R, CBS 52340, CBSSd JGL524, CBS 21124

CO 48875-1B   CO 39976, CO DJ39976, CoCh 291866, PhilCont B21051H. **45:** CO 4039976. **EP:** CO B1743
         What A Little Moonlight Can Do-voc Helen Ward (arr FH)

(Note that a take 1A issue on PhilAu B21051H is reported, has not been verified, and is therefore suspect. Also, CO DJ39976 copies may bear "1A" or "1D" inscriptions, but are in fact true 1B releases.)

CO 48876-1A   CO 39976, CO DJ 39976, CoCh 291866, PhilCont B21051H. **45:** CO 4-39976, CO set G4-20. **EP:** CO B1743, CO set B357. **LP:** CO GL524, CO Texaco LP, CO P13371, CO alb P6-14538, HA HL7190, HA HS11090, CorAu KLP682, PhilCont B07011L, CBS 52340, CBSSd JGL524, CBS 21124
         I'll Never Say "Never Again" Again-voc Helen Ward (arr FH)

(Note that the inscription "1D" appears on some copies of CO DJ39976, but that they are true 1A releases.)

BENNY GOODMAN AND HIS ORCHESTRA   March 4, 1953, New York

Personnel as February 23, except WILL BRADLEY, tbn, replaces Cutshall and Byrne; Klink plays as, Yaner leaves, and SAM MAROWITZ, ts, enters.

CO 48913   UNISSUED
         Keep Smiling At Trouble-voc Helen Ward (arr FH)

CO 48914   **EP:** CO B1743. **LP:** CO Z-173
         I've Got A Feeling I'm Falling-voc Helen Ward (arr FH)

CO 48915   UNISSUED
         It's Been So Long-voc Helen Ward (arr ?)

(As noted for the original Victor release of "It's Been So Long," its arrangement was once believed to have been written by David Rose, but there was some evidence that the score was Fletcher's. Benny's election to record the tune again at this time—if the unheard arrangement is the same as the original—tilts credit for it more toward Henderson. Note that the matrices assigned to the unissued sides may be reversed.)

"NEW YORK HERALD TRIBUNE FORUM"   *March 21, 1953, New York*
   WNYC Radio

Benny Goodman, clt; Teddy Wilson, p; Morey Feld, d.

After You've Gone
Memories Of You
On The Sunny Side Of The Street
The World Is Waiting For The Sunrise

The enormous success of his Carnegie Hall Concert and "Jazz Concert No. 2" albums made new fans for Benny throughout the world and rekindled the interest of those nearing middle age who had caught him the first time around. Buoyed by the popular and critical acclaim accorded his Victor-era orchestra all over again, Benny decided in February to get the old gang on the road once more, for a six-week tour of the United States.

His first task was to assemble those of his original personnel who were still playing well and who could get free of their various commitments. Two key sidemen, Harry James and Lionel Hampton, were unavailable for different reasons. Chris Griffin, Hymie Schertzer and Babe Russin were unable to leave their staff positions with the networks for so long a period. Jess Stacy had a number of contractual obligations as a solo performer on the West Coast. Benny's brother Harry, head of a New York music publishing firm, could not neglect his responsibilities.

Thus faced with finding suitable replacements, Benny sought out musicians with whom he was familiar, men he knew were capable of recreating the sound of his original orchestra. Teddy Wilson and Gene Krupa had responded enthusiastically, and their enlistment influenced others to join. At length, this personnel was set:

Benny Goodman, clt; Charlie Shavers, Ziggy Elman, Al Stewart, tpt; Vernon Brown, Rex Peer, tbn; Clint Neagley, Willie Smith, as; George Auld, Sol Schlinger (an outstanding New York classicist) ts; Teddy Wilson, p; Steve Jordan, g; Israel Crosby, b; Gene Krupa, d. And as vocalist, lovely Helen Ward.

With the band in rehearsal and engagements becoming firm, Benny yet had qualms about the magic of the Goodman name: would it still attract paying customers? As he had been for the 1938 Carnegie concert, Benny was persuaded to augment and diversify the appeal of the tour "package." To guarantee its success—or so it was believed—Louis Armstrong and his All Stars were added to the program.

Benny insisted that the band play three break-in engagements before the formal tour began. It did so on April 10, 11 and 12, in Manchester, New Hampshire, Portland, Maine and New London, Connecticut respectively—and without Louis; his All Stars joined for the first concert on April 15, at the Arena in New Haven. On the 16th, 17th and 18th, the tour moved on to the Mosque in Newark, New Jersey; Carnegie Hall; and the Met Theater in Providence, Rhode Island. The next scheduled engagement was in Boston's Symphony Hall, April 19. Benny never made it. Upon reaching the Ritz-Carlton Hotel in Boston that Saturday morning he collapsed, unable to breathe normally, was put in an oxygen tent. Rumors that he had suffered a heart attack proved unfounded. He recovered, of course—but he never rejoined the tour.

Those interested in a detailed account of the aborted tour—from his point of view—are recommended to John Hammond's autobiography, "John Hammond On Record," The Ridge Press, 1977.

In any event, the tour continued with Gene taking charge. It was a financial success, but less than that as an artistic triumph, a faithful re-creation of the Benny Goodman Orchestra that had owned the Swing Era. For without Benny's watchful eye (for which read, "The Ray"), some sloppy performances resulted. The author heard Gene explode one night, "For Christ's sake, this is supposed to be the Benny Goodman Orchestra—let's try to sound like it!", as one of the "big names" failed to execute properly. "Integrity" was ever more than just a word to Gene Krupa.

There are no commercial recordings of the 1953 concert tour. One of the sidemen taped some of the performances, but these have not become available to the author. It is not known if the tapes embrace any of the engagements in which Benny participated. If they do, they would be worthwhile; if not, their unavailability is no great loss.

Benny did little else the balance of 1954. His one significant effort was in behalf of mental health. Employing his first and middle names as a pseudonym—"Ben David"—Benny contributed to the sound track of a documentary film sponsored by mental health authorities of the states of California, Connecticut, Delaware, Maryland, Michigan, Nevada and Rhode Island. Just over an hour in length, the film deals sympathetically with disturbed personalities and their treatment. The sound track includes almost 50 minutes' background music, untitled, written expressly for the film by Mel Powell. It was recorded in Manhattan during the winter of 1953-1954:

"THE LONELY NIGHT"   *Winter, 1953-1954, New York*
An Associated Producers motion picture filmed in black-and-white.
Producers: Irving Jacoby and Willard Van Dyke
Running time: 62 minutes   *Release date: March 27, 1954*
Music composed by Mel Powell   *Cameraman: Richard Leacock*

ORCHESTRA PERSONNEL: Benny Goodman, clt; Mel Powell, p; Bob Haggart, b; Terry Snyder, d; and The New Music Quartet-Broadus Earle, 1st v; Matthew Raimondi, 2nd v; Walter Trampler, viola; Claus Adam, cello.

Untitled compositions as background

Benny made a fresh start on New Year's Day:

"THE MARTIN BLOCK SHOW"   *January 1, 1954, New York*
  ABC Television Network

Benny Goodman, clt; Teddy Wilson, p; Gene Krupa, d.
Avalon
Memories Of You
The World Is Waiting For The Sunrise

Benny next recorded four Trio sides for Capitol, only one of which has been issued at this writing. Tape transfers from studio masters of the other three suggest they deserve release:

BENNY GOODMAN TRIO   **January 28, 1954, New York**

Benny Goodman, clt; Mel Powell, p; Eddie Grady, d.

20333	**LP:** CAP T441, CAP T669, SW 1380, EMI-F 1551563. **EP:** CAP EAP 1-441, CAP EAP 1-519, CapAu CEP030. **ET:** Air Force GL-15, AFRS P4223, AFR&TS P-GL-16 **There'll Be Some Changes Made**
20334	UNISSUED - Tape **Everything I Have Is Yours**
20335	UNISSUED - Tape **But Not For Me**
20336	UNISSUED - Tape **Margie**

Precise information about Benny's activities in much of 1954 is sketchy. He, together with Charlie Shavers, Mel Powell, guitarist Ron Roberts, Israel Crosby and Morey Feld, played a 10-day engagement at Chicago's Blue Note, beginning April 16. Once more, as in 1952, some of the performances were taped on location, are reputedly on Magnecord reels numbered 120, 121, 122 and 123. But again, their contents and present repository (if they still exist) are unknown.

On May 5 Benny flew to Canada to appear as soloist the next day with the Toronto Symphony, Sir Ernest MacMillan conducting. Later in the month he was featured with the Birmingham, Alabama, symphony orchestra. No recordings of these recitals are known. Unknown, too, is the exact date (believed to be either June 7 or 14) of a reunion of the original Quartet: Benny, Lionel, Teddy and Gene played a benefit for the N.A.A.C.P. in Manhattan's Basin Street, a night club that championed jazz. The author has not been able to confirm rumors that the benefit was recorded—but he suspects it was.

Substituting Steve Jordan for Ron Roberts, Benny and his "Blue Note" Sextet began a play-for-pay engagement at Basin Street on July 13. To promote this presentation, he appeared on Steve Allen's "Tonight Show" the evening preceding:

"THE TONIGHT SHOW"   *July 12, 1954, New York*
  NBC Television Network

Benny Goodman, clt; Mel Powell, p; Morey Feld, d.
Liza
Nice Work If You Can Get It
I've Found a New Baby

On August 7 a concert in the Hollywood Bowl featured Benny as soloist with a symphony orchestra conducted by Leroy Anderson, and in a jazz segment with Teddy Wilson and Louis Bellson. He appears then to have been dormant until October, when his "Basin Street" Sextet was booked into the Last Frontier Hotel, in Las Vegas, Nevada. On the first of November he, Mel and Gene played some jazz and had some fun on TV:

"THE SID CAESAR SHOW"   *November 1, 1954, New York*
  NBC Television Network

TRIO: Benny Goodman, clt; Mel Powell, p; Gene Krupa, d.

ORCHESTRA: TRIO plus a studio orchestra, including Charlie Shavers, tpt; Sid Caesar, ts.

After You've Gone - TRIO
Sing, Sing, Sing - ORCHESTRA

Edward R. Murrow's "Person To Person" TV cameras visited the Goodman home in Stamford, permitting Benny to show viewers his trout pond, and presenting an opportunity to play a few bars of Mozart with daughter Rachel:

"PERSON TO PERSON"   *November 5, 1954, Stamford, Conn.*
  CBS Television Network

Benny Goodman, clt; Rachel Goodman, p.

. . . portion, final movement, Concerto For Clarinet And Orchestra In A, K. 622

Almost 10 months had elapsed since Benny's initial 1954 date for Capitol. Now, in 10 days' time, Benny would cut 19 small group and big band sides in four recording sessions. The results were packaged in an album titled "B.G. in HI-FI," subtitled "BENNY GOODMAN, HIS ORCHESTRA, AND HIS COMBOS." Considering the haste with which they were made, they're not all that bad, and the sound quality is excellent. Note that some of the unissued cuts are, via tape transfer from the studio masters, in the hands of a few collectors:

B.G. in HI-FI   **November 8, 1954, New York**

Benny Goodman, clt; Charlie Shavers, tpt; Mel Powell, p; George Duvivier, b; Jo Jones, d.

20527	**EP:** CAP & CAPEur sets EAP/EBF565. **LP:** CAP W565, CAP T&D1514, CAP TCO&DTCO1983, CAP set STFL293, CapE LCT6012, EMI C-048/C-148, EMI-F 1551563. **ET:** Air Force GL-15, AFR&TS P-GL-16 **Airmail Special**
20528	UNISSUED - Tape **Ain't Misbehavin'**

Add Steve Jordan, g.

20529	same issues as mx 20527, except omit **LP**, CAP set STFL293, and both ET's; and add **ET**, Civil Defense Stars For Defense 91, AFRS P4226 **Get Happy**
20530	UNISSUED - Tape **Slipped Disc**

If you thought you recognized "Jersey Bounce" in Jake Lamotta's filmed biography, "The Raging Bull," it's a dub from this next session:

B.G. in HI-FI   **November 9, 1954, New York**

Benny Goodman, clt; Chris Griffin, Ruby Braff, Bernie Privin, Carl Poole, tpt; Will Bradley, Cutty Cutshall, Vernon Brown, tbn; Hymie Schertzer, Paul Ricci, as; Boomie Richman, Al Klink, ts; Sol Schlinger, bar; Mel Powell, p; Steve Jordan, g; George Duvivier, b; Bobby Donaldson, d.

20531	same issues as mx 20527, except omit both ET's; and add **12"** ET, National Guard Session 209 **Jersey Bounce**
20532	**EP:** CAP & CAPEur sets EAP/EBF565. **LP:** CAP W565, CapE LCT6012. **ET:** AFRS P4226 **When I Grow Too Old To Dream** (arr FH)
20533	same issues as mx 20531, plus **LP**, PIC SPC3270; **12"** ET, 1957 Christmas Seal; and **ET**, AFRS P4226 **You Brought a New Kind Of Love To Me** (arr FH)
20534	same issues as mx 20527, except omit both ET's; and add **45**, CapE 45CL14258; **EP**, CapE EAP4-1514; **LP**, CAP T&ST1386 **Blue Lou** (arr Neal Hefti)

20535	CAP 3043, CapFr&H 3043. **45:** CAP F3043, CAP DJ20535, CapE 45CL14258, TOSH CR1036. **EP:** CAP & CAPEur sets EAP/EBF565. **LP:** CAP W565, CAP T&ST 1386, CAP T&D1514, CAP TCO&DTCO1983, CAP set STFL293, CapE LCT6012, EMI C-048/C-148. **12″ET:** National Guard Session 212. **ET:** Treasury Department Guest Star 432, AFRS P4225

Jumpin' At The Woodside

20536	**EP:** CAP & CAPEur sets EAP/EBF565, CAP set FDM706, CapE EAP4-1514. **LP:** CAP W565, CAP S706, CAP T&ST1386, CAP T&D1514, CAP TCO&DTCO1983, CAP set STFL293, CAP SL6716, CapE LCT6012, CapE LCT6104, CapFr W706, CapFr CO54.81713, EMI 62524, EMI 1C054.52715, EMI 1C054.81713, PIC SPC3270. **12″ET:** National Guard Session 211. **ET:** Treasury Department Guest Star 432, AFRS P4225, AFR&TS 4621/4622

Stompin' At The Savoy

20537	**EP:** CAP & CAPEur sets EAP/EBF565, CapE EAP EAP4-1514. **LP:** CAP W565, CAP T&D1514, CAP TCO&DTCO1983, CAP set STFL293, CapE LCT 6012, EMI C-048–C-148, PIC SPC3270, EMI-F 1551563. **12″ET:** 1957 Christmas Seal

Sent For You Yesterday And Here You Come Today

(It is stressed that all of these Capitol recordings were taped monaurally; "stereo" LP releases are processed to simulate true channel separation. Thus no distinction is made in these listings between monaural and "duophonic" (i.e., fake stereo) LP's. And to repeat: latterday cassette releases, such as PIC CS1154, contain no additional releases or alternate takes of previously issued material, and are omitted.)

B.G. in HI-FI   **November 16, 1954, New York**

Benny Goodman, clt; Mel Powell, p; Bobby Donaldson, d.

20547	**LP:** PAU 9031

Rose Room

20548	same EP and LP issues as mx 20537, except omit PIC SPC3270, EMI-F 1551563. Add **ET,** AFRS P4225

What Can I Say After I Say I'm Sorry?

Add Ruby Braff, :pt; George Duvivier, b.

20549	**EP:** CAP & CAPEur sets EAP/EBF565. **LP:** CAP W565, CAP T&D1514, CAP TCO&DTCO1983, CapE LCT6012, EMI C-048/C-148, EMI-F 1551563. **12″ET:** 1957 Christmas Seal. **ET:** Civil Defense Stars For Defense 91, AFRS P4226

Rock Rimmon (arr MP)

20550	**EP:** CAP & CAPEur sets EAP/EBF565. **LP:** CAP W565, CapE LCT6012. **ET:** Civil Defense Stars For Defense 91, Treasury Dept. Guest Star 432

You're A Sweetheart

("You're a Sweetheart" is also on a souvenir recording presented to the King of Thailand by Benny Goodman.)

B.G. in HI-FI   **November 17, 1954, New York**

Personnel as November 9.

20551	same issues as mx 20537, except omit **EP,** CapE EAP4-1514, EMI-F 1551563

Somebody Stole My Gal

20552-Bkdn	UNISSUED - Tape
20552	UNISSUED - Tape

(I Would Do) Anything For You

20553	**EP:** CAP & CAPEur sets EAP/EBF565. **LP:** CAP W565, CapE LCT6012, EMI-F 1551563

Big John's Special

20554	CAP 3043, CapFr&H 3043. **45:** CAP F3043, CAP DJ20554, CapE 45CL14258. **EP:** CAP & CAPEur sets EAP/EBF565. **LP:** CAP W565, CAP T&D1514, CAP TCO&DTCO1983, CAP set STFL293, CapE LCT6012, EMI C-048/C-148, PIC SPC3270, EMI-F 1551563. **12″ET:** 1957 Christmas Seal (n/c), National Guard Sessions 209/210/211/212. **ET:** AFRS P4225, AFRS&TS P-GL-13, Treasury Dept. Guest Star 432

Let's Dance

(Generally, "Let's Dance" was edited in time to provide the opening tracks for the LP issues shown above. The shortened version was assigned an arbitrary matrix, 13220. The 78 rpm releases are complete versions, but are inscribed erroneously with the edited matrix number. "Let's Dance" is also on the souvenir record given to the King of Thailand.)

Charities next occupied Benny, and two of his endeavors suggest a third was performed at this time. On November 22 he, Teddy Wilson and Gene Krupa participated in a benefit for Oran "Hot Lips" Page—the trumpeter had succumbed to a coronary November 5. And likely in late November or early December, he recorded a half-minute spot announcement for the National Foundation for Infantile Paralysis's annual campaign. (It appears as Track 15 on side 2 of the 1955 "March Of Dimes" LP, titled, "Discs For Dimes.")

Given that the original Trio was working together, and that Benny cut a voice track for the "March Of Dimes," late November/early December 1954 is the author's choice as the time the Trio filmed a promotional "short" in behalf of the N. F. I. P. He has an audio tape of the film's sound track, but has little other information about it. Here, then, a previously-undocumented film of the Trio in action in 1954:

"MARCH OF DIMES"   *November/December 1954, New York*

Benny Goodman, clt; Teddy Wilson, p; Gene Krupa, d.

Stompin' At The Savoy (theme)
Nice Work If You Can Get It
Avalon

Benny also did some promotional work for the American Heart Association: On November 24, he and announcer-commentator Milton Cross recorded a conversation about Benny's works in New York. It was released on the 1955 Heart Fund 16″ ET, "Heart To Heart," Program Three, ET II, interspersed with commercial Goodman recordings. These cuts are listed in the text where appropriate. And a sad note to end 1954: Lee Morse died on December 16.

Beginning the new year, Benny performed in Carnegie Hall on January 19 with a "Symphony Of The Air" concert orchestra. He returned to Carnegie just three days later, as guest soloist with the New York Philharmonic. And possibly at this time, he is reported to have appeared on a television program titled, "What Is Jazz?", performing "Prelude, Fugue and Riffs" with its composer, Leonard Bernstein. The author has been unable to obtain further information about this reputed telecast.

February's Good Housekeeping Magazine profiled Benny in an article titled, "The Benny Who Never Changed His Tune," by its music editor, George Marek. And in proof thereof, Benny assembled and rehearsed a new Octet for a series of 10 weekend-only engagements in New York City's Basin Street West, beginning February 25/26. New Yorker Magazine reviewed "Benny At Basin Street" in its March 19 issue, and enthused about the group's fresh sound. On the evenings of March 25 and 26, Benny employed some engineers from Columbia to tape all of the performances for his future use; he has in his possession 28 - 10″ reels and 16 - 7″ reels recorded that March weekend. In early 1967 he released the tapes to Book-of-the-Month Club, Inc. Selected cuts were issued originally by the Club in December 1967, on three 12″ "Classics Record Library" LP's in one album.

The original-issue monaural and stereo LP's share common catalog numbers, and these catalog numbers are also employed as "matrix numbers." (Unless specifically shown otherwise, all performances are considered to have been by the Octet; at times it is difficult to hear all of the instruments, particularly the tenor saxophone and the guitar.) The Club release is the base issue, and its "matrix numbers" are displayed, along with its LP side designations. Three subsidiary albums are known to have duplicated the Club release in toto, and these are listed following the Club album.

Additional secondary releases excerpt selected tracks from the Club album. To facilitate their identification, the performances are numbered consecutively, as they appear on the Club album. Tracks appearing on the secondary releases are:

EUROPE (It.) 1045: 4, 8, 16, 20, 23
FONTANA (Eur.) 9290-401-5215: 5, 6, 7, 13, 14, 17, 20, 24
HALL OF MUSIC 1379: 4, 8, 16, 20, 23
JAZZ MASTERS (H) 6433-551: 1, 2, 6, 10, 13, 14, 26
PHILIPS H72-CU235: 4, 5, 6, 7, 8, 9, 10, 13, 14, 15, 17, 19, 20, 21, 24
PHILIPS (Fr.) 6610017: 1, 2, 4, 5, 6, 9, 10, 13, 14, 15, 16, 17, 19, 20, 26, 29
MERCURY 6433551: 1, 2, 6, 10, 13, 14, 17, 26

Further, five Japanese releases offer random excerpts from the Club original. Their tracks are:

FONTANA (Jap.) StLP PAT-16: 1, 2, 5, 10, 11, 15, 16, 22, 26, 29
FONTANA (Jap.) StLP PAT-1020: same as StLP PAT-16, above
PHILIPS (Jap.) LP 28PP-29: 4, 5, 8, 10, 13, 16, 19, 28, 29
PHILIPS (Jap.) alb. FDX-9039-40: 2, 4, 5, 8, 10, 11, 13, 15, 16, 17, 19, 22, 26, 27, 28, 29
PHILIPS (Jap.) 7" LP: 1, 10, 16, 29

(Various cassette releases, such as FON 7263-425-5215, offer no additional or alternate material, and are not detailed.)

BENNY GOODMAN   March 25/26, 1955, New York
Plays An Album Of Swing Classics

Benny Goodman, clt; Ruby Braff, tpt; Urbie Green, tbn; Paul Quinichette, ts; Teddy Wilson, p; Perry Lopez, g; Milt Hinton, b; Bobby Donaldson, d.

QUINTET: Goodman, Wilson, Lopez, Hinton, Donaldson

RL 7673-1   **LP & StLp:** CRL album RL7673, Side 1: PHIL 870000/1/2, PHILFr 6379.001/2/3, PHONOGRAM (Jap) SFL9087/8/9
1 **Don't Be That Way**
2 **Rose Room**
3 **Between The Devil And The Deep Blue Sea**
4 **Body And Soul** - QUINTET
5 **After You've Gone** - QUINTET

RL 7673-2   **LP & StLp:** same issues as above (CRL - Side 2)
6 **Slipped Disc**
7 **On The Alamo**
8 **Just One Of Those Things** - QUINTET
9 **Blue And Sentimental** - feat. Quinichette
10 **Airmail Special**

RL 7673-3   **LP & StLp:** same issues as above (CRL - Side 3)
11 **I Found A New Baby** - QUINTET
12 **As Long As I Live**
13 **Flying Home**
14 **'Deed I Do**

RL 7673-4   **LP & StLp:** same issues as above (CRL - Side 4)
15 **Avalon**
16 **Memories Of You**
17 **Stompin' At The Savoy**
18 **If I Had You**
19 **Sing, Sing, Sing**

RL 7673-5   **LP & StLp:** same issues as above (CRL - Side 5)
20 **Oh, Lady Be Good!** - QUINTET
21 **Stairway To The Stars** - Green w/rhythm section - NO BG
22 **Honeysuckle Rose**
23 **Nice Work If You Can Get It** - QUINTET
24 **Rosetta**

RL 7673-6   **LP & StLp:** same issues as above (CRL - Side 6)
25 **Mean To Me**
26 **Shine**
27 **Night And Day**
28 **One O'Clock Jump**
29 **Good-Bye**

(Note that the Club's stereo LP's have an "S" preceding the catalog and "matrix" numbers; and that the LP couplings are, 1-6, 2-5, 3-4.)

In 1979 Benny was persuaded to release an album that was to be advertised extensively on television; its sales met with indifferent results. The three-record set offered one LP containing duplicates from the MGM "air checks" album, a second containing material previously released from the 1958 Brussels engagement—and a third derived from this 1955 Basin Street West stand. This LP includes cuts from the Club album (as shown above), but also offers five cuts not in that release. Because four of its titles—bear in mind that these are different performances—are the same as those in the Club album, the track positions are identified:

BENNY GOODMAN   March 25/26, 1955, New York
- GOLDEN ANNIVERSARY COLLECTION

Personnels as Club album.

V-10366   **LP:** HOM HMI 1379 - record 2, side C
As Long As I Live (track 2)
After You've Gone - QUINTET (track 5)

V-10367   **LP:** as above, except side D
If I Had You (track 3)
On The Sunny Side Of The Street (track 4)
Avalon (track 5)

(The Hall Of Music LP is duplicated on EUROPA (It) 1045.)

Six years after release of the "Golden Anniversary Collection" album, Benny was approached by the Musical Heritage Society with a proposal he found even more appealing: The Society had learned that Benny had recorded various classical compositions privately over the years, and that they had never been issued. If Benny had tapes of them, would he care to have them digitally remastered and made available to the public?

Benny located several tapes, found them quite good in terms of performance and audio quality. In 1985, four of the compositions were presented in the Society's two-LP album, "Benny Goodman - Private Collection," under its "Musicmasters" label.

Unfortunately, precise details about the recordings are lacking. In the early 1980s, Benny had disposed of the great bulk of his files for the years prior to 1977, so that invaluable source of discographical information could no longer be consulted. However, Bill Savory (the engineer responsible for the Columbia and M-G-M air checks albums and other Goodman recordings) recalls that at least Side 4 of the album was recorded in Carl Fischer Recital Hall, New York, in March 1955. Savory, then chief engineer for Angel Records, mastered the session.

(Savory also believes that the cellist was Peter Maag, younger brother of Fritz Maag, who is credited in the album's liner notes.)

BENNY GOODMAN - PRIVATE COLLECTION   March 1955, New York

Benny Goodman, clt, with the Berkshire String Quartet: Urico Rossi, Albert Lazan, v; David Dawson, viola; either Fritz or Peter Maag, cel.

MM 20104 B   **LP:** MM 20104 B - Side 4. **CD:** MM 60103Y
Clarinet Quintet in B-Flat Major, Op. 34 (von Weber)
1. **Allegro**
2. **Fantasia** (Adagio ma non troppo)
3. **Menuetto** (Capriccio presto)
4. **Rondo** (Allegro giocoso)

(Note that the reproduction is in "stereo," but that the original recording is in the monaural mode.)

At the same session, Benny also recorded the Beethoven Trio. But it is Savory's judgment that the Musicmasters' release is not from the March date, but rather from a re-recording made in Benny's studio in Stamford, later in the year. (It may well have been post-September, when Benny had returned from Hollywood, and had formally established his own Park Recording Company.) Once again, Savory engineered the taping, this time with Benny's newly-purchased recording gear. Because its date is not ascertainable, the release is introduced at this juncture:

BENNY GOODMAN - PRIVATE COLLECTION post-March 1955, Stamford

Benny Goodman clt; Fritz or Peter Maag, cel; Leon Pommers, p.

MM 20104 A **LP:** MM 20104 A - Side 3
  Trio in B-Flat Major for Piano, Clarinet and Cello, Op. 11 (Beethoven)
  1. **Allegro con brio**
  2. **Adagio**
  3. **Allegretto** (Theme and Variations)

(For the other contents of this album, see under May 1957.)

While at Basin Street West, Benny appeared on television with Martha Raye, the comedienne who had been in the cast of Benny's first feature film, "The Big Broadcast Of 1937." Leather-lunged Martha seemed to appreciate jazz; and when she wasn't clowning, she sang fairly well.

"THE MARTHA RAYE SHOW" April 12, 1955, New York
  NBC Television Network

Benny Goodman, clt; Teddy Wilson, p; Milt Hinton, b; Bobby Donaldson, d.

Don't Be That Way (**LP:** GOJ 1010)
Runnin' Wild (**LP:** GOJ 1010)

Add Urbie Green, tbn.

As Long As I Live-voc Martha Raye

Probably in May or June Benny and actor John Conte recorded a conversation that was used to promote the sale of U.S. Savings Bonds via Treasury Department ET, "Guest Star" No. 432. Their dialogue is interspersed with Benny's commercial recordings, taken from CAP LP 565. Credits are listed in the text where appropriate.

Universal-International's "The Benny Goodman Story" next commanded Benny's attention, and June found him in Hollywood as production on the film began. To promote the movie and Steve Allen's selection to play the lead, Gene Krupa appeared on Allen's "Tonight Show" on June 27, played two tunes with a quintet from the studio orchestra. Then Benny, the original Trio, and other musicians he'd chosen for the sound track were guests on a TV special starring Benny's biographical alter ego:

"(STEVE) ALLEN IN MOVIELAND" July 2, 1955, Hollywood
  NBC Television Network

TRIO: Benny Goodman, clt; Teddy Wilson, p; Gene Krupa, d.

China Boy

OCTET: Benny Goodman, clt; Buck Clayton, tpt; Urbie Green, tbn; Stan Getz, ts; Steve Allen, Teddy Wilson, p; George Duvivier, b; Gene Krupa, d.

Slipped Disc

DUET: Goodman, Allen, clt.

Moon Glow

To our mind, "The Benny Goodman Story" suffered from two basic faults. First, it was a sugared-over, inaccurate recital of fiction rather than fact. Some of the incidents it depicts never happened; some that did were distorted. Surely there was enough drama in Benny's early life and struggle to the top to provide sufficient material for an honest biographical portrayal. (Twenty-odd years later the author, together with Morton Gould and Teddy Wilson, paid tribute to Benny at an annual meeting of the Lotus Club, a century-old New York patron of the arts, that honored Benny as its "Man Of The Year." The author chose to "roast" Benny—but gently!; and in speaking of "The Benny Goodman Story," characterized it as, ". . . the 'Jimmy Dorsey Story,' or perhaps the 'Artie Shaw Story'- for whatever it was, it certainly wasn't a story about Benny Goodman." All assembled, including Benny and Alice Goodman, heartily agreed.)

Second, the film simply missed recapturing the spirit, excitement and great music produced by Benny Goodman's 1935-1938 Orchestra and small groups. This failure to re-create the original Goodman produce reinforces our opinion that it is not possible, no matter how great the effort, to assemble even the finest of musicians for a period of a few weeks, and expect that they will duplicate the sound of an orchestra that was together for as many years. Not even Hollywood can create that illusion.

Whatever its historical inaccuracies and musical shortcomings, "The Benny Goodman Story" does provide an abundance of Benny's clarinet for his fans; and as it appears on television the world over, it continues to provide royalties to Benny. For those reasons, all of us are grateful to Universal-International.

The author's gratitude to U-I is tempered, however, by the omission of Jess Stacy from the sound track. In his view, Jess was as much responsible for the original orchestra's success as any of the key sidemen. Benny hired Jess to play for the orchestra; Jess also asked for a speaking role in the film, which would have raised his salary considerably. The producers evidently would not agree, so Jess quit. U and I will never agree on that decision.

"THE BENNY GOODMAN STORY" June/July/August 1955, Hollywood

A Universal-International motion picture filmed in color

Director, Screenwriter: Valentine Davies
Producer: Aaron Rosenberg
Music Supervisor: Joseph Gershenson
Additional music: Henry Mancini
Release date: February 1956
CAST: Steve Allen (as Benny Goodman); Donna Reed (Alice Hammond); Berta Gersten (Mom Goodman); Robert F. Simon (Pop Goodman); Herbert Anderson (John Hammond); Hy Averback (Willard Alexander); Wilton Graff (John & Alice's father); David Kasday (Benny at age 10); Barry Truex (Benny at age 16); Dick Winslow (Gil Rodin); Sammy Davis, Sr. (Fletcher Henderson); and as themselves, Kid Ory, Ben Pollack, Harry James, Ziggy Elman, Lionel Hampton, Teddy Wilson, Gene Krupa and Martha Tilton.

Full Orchestra selections were recorded by this collective personnel:

BENNY GOODMAN ORCHESTRA: Benny Goodman, clt; Chris Griffin, Buck Clayton, John Best, Conrad Gozzo, Irving Goodman, and possibly Ray Linn, tpt; Murray McEachern, Urbie Green, Jimmy Priddy, tbn; Hymie Schertzer, Blake Reynolds, as; Babe Russin, Stan Getz, ts; Teddy Wilson, p; Allan Reuss, g; George Duvivier, b; Gene Krupa, d.

BENNY GOODMAN TRIO: Goodman, Wilson, Krupa
BENNY GOODMAN QUARTET: Goodman; Lionel Hampton, vib; Wilson, Krupa
BENNY GOODMAN OCTET: Goodman, Clayton, Green, Getz, Wilson, Reuss, Duvivier, Krupa

Let's Dance and opening title music: Benny Goodman Orchestra and studio orchestra
. . . clarinet exercise: first Steve Allen; then Goodman
(By The Sea: studio group (lake steamer sequence)
Original Dixieland One-Step: Goodman, Ory, studio group (lake steamer sequence)
Good-Bye: Goodman clt solo (rooftop sequence)
Montage-Waitin' For Katie/If You Knew Susie/'Way Down Yonder In New Orleans: Goodman and studio group (Ben Pollack sequence)
(On The Sunny Side Of The Street: Wilson, p (background)
. . . portion, Mozart Clarinet Concerto: Goodman and strings (John Hammond sequence)
(Let's Dance: studio orchestra (Kel Murray sequence)
Slipped Disc: Goodman OCTET
Let's Dance: Benny Goodman Orchestra (radio broadcast sequence)
Goody-Goody: Benny Goodman Orchestra
Stompin' At The Savoy: Benny Goodman Orchestra
Memories Of You: Goodman TRIO (party sequence)
One O'Clock Jump: Benny Goodman Orchestra (Palomar Ballroom sequence)
Memories Of You: Benny Goodman Orchestra
Avalon: Goodman QUARTET (Catalina Island sequence)
It's Been So Long: Benny Goodman Orchestra (background)
Let's Dance: Benny Goodman Orchestra (Paramount Theater sequence)
Bugle Call Rag: Benny Goodman Orchestra (Paramount Theater sequence)
Don't Be That Way: Benny Goodman Orchestra (Carnegie Hall rehearsal)
Good-Bye: Goodman and studio orchestra (Mom Goodman sequence)
Shine: Harry James, tpt, and the Benny Goodman Orchestra (Carnegie Hall sequence)
Sensation Rag: Goodman OCTET (Carnegie Hall sequence)
And The Angels Sing-voc Martha Tilton: feat. Mannie Klein, tpt, with the Benny Goodman Orchestra (Ziggy Elman seen on screen) (Carnegie Hall sequence)
Moon Glow: Goodman QUARTET (Carnegie Hall sequence)
Sing, Sing, Sing: Harry James, tpt, and the Benny Goodman Orchestra (Carnegie Hall sequence)

June/July/August 1955, continued

June/July/August 1955, continued
Memories Of You: Goodman TRIO and studio orchestra (Carnegie Hall sequence and closing music)
Don't Be That Way: Benny Goodman Orchestra (reprise)

(Most of the Benny Goodman performances in the film are condensed versions or partial renditions. Other bits and pieces of music are scattered throughout.)

The film's sound track had obvious appeal to jazz fans, and Decca Records, Inc., by then a division of MCA, was chosen to release it on record. Because many of the musicians had exclusive recording agreements with companies other than Decca, clearances had to be obtained from those companies. Eventually Decca was able to do so, and it issued the tunes from the film's sound track on LP and tape. Subsidiary issues followed.

Decca's choice as the releasing agency posed a problem for discographers, for over the years Decca has been unresponsive to inquiries about personnel, dates, locations, and the like. Thus precise facts about the recordings are lacking; why, for example, Buck Clayton (who is obviously present) is not given credit in Decca's liner notes, or why there are minor discrepancies in the performances, sound track vis a vis LP, are unexplained. From other sources, it was determined that the sound track was recorded in Universal-International's studios, in about two weeks' time in August.

Still, the Decca releases are the "originals," and they are the base upon which the listing herein is constructed. Contemporary releases that duplicate the Decca issues in toto are listed following the Decca issues. To facilitate identification of additional releases, the tunes are numbered consecutively as they appear on the Decca LP's. These releases, and the tracks appearing on them, are:

45: Universal-International 78191 (promo for DJs): 12
Universal-International 78192 (promo for DJs): 2
Universal-International 78193 (promo for DJs): 6
DeJap DS-606: 1, 13

EP: BrE OE9220: 1, 2, 3, 4
BrE OE9221: 5, 6, 7, 8
BrE OE9222: 9, 10, 11, 12
BrE OE9223: 13, 14, 15
BrE OE9224: 16, 17, 18
BrE OE9225: 19, 20, 21
BrFr 10043: 6, 18, 20, 21
BrFr 10044: 1, 11, 17
BrFr 10045: 3, 7, 12
BrFr 10046: 9, 10, 13, 14
DE ED797: 1 thru 8, inclusive
DE ED798: 9 thru 15, inclusive
DE ED799: 16 thru 21, inclusive
DeJap DEP-87: 1, 2, 11, 12
DeJap DEP-88: 13, 14, 15
DeJap DEP-89: 16, 21

ET: AFR&TS P4621/4622: 1, 2, 6, 7, 11, 12, 13, 16, 17

LP: BrFr 86043: 1, 3, 6, 7, 11, 12, 17, 20, 21
BrFr 87006: 2, 4, 5, 8, 9, 10, 13, 14, 15, 16, 18, 19
CRL set 0042.029 COPS8940: 1, 2, 3, 4, 5, 6, 17, 18, 19, 20, 21
CrlE set CP11/CP17: all except 6 ("Bugle Call Rag")
DE set DXB188: all except 6 ("Bugle Call Rag")
DeJap JDL-2046: 1, 2, 11, 12, 13, 15, 17
DeJap JDL-7001: 1 thru 12, inclusive
DeJap JDL-7002: 13 thru 21, inclusive
DeJap SDL-16: 1 thru 12, inclusive
DeJap SDL-20: 13 thru 21, inclusive
DeJap DSL-11: 1 thru 12, inclusive
DeJap DSL-12: 13 thru 21, inclusive
DeJap SDW-10003: 13, 14, 21
DeJap DW-11: 13, 14, 21
DeJap SDW-10007: 1, 2, 6, 11
DeJap SDW-10075: 9, 12, 15, 16
DeJap SDL-10175: 1, 3, 6, 7, 9, 11, 12, 13, 14, 15, 16, 21
EMI 1C054-81713: 1, 2, 4, 7, 12, 13, 16, 17, 21
McaG & Jap MAPS1009: 1 thru 12, inclusive
McaJap 9034-5 and McaJap 8305-6: both, 1 thru 21, inclusive
McaJap 7013 and McaJap 7216: both, 1, 3, 6, 7, 9, 11, 12, 13, 14, 15, 16, 20, 21
McaJap MCF-8004: 13

McaJap 10020: 1, 13
McaJap 9131: 1, 7, 11, 12, 13, 15
McaJap 9018: 15
McaJap 3003: 2
McaJap 10012: 1, 2, 3, 6, 7, 9, 11, 12, 13, 14, 17, 18, 20, 21
Universal-International DCLA1119 (promo for DJs): various n/c cuts

(As heretofore, cassettes containing no additional or alternative issues, such as McaJap VCM3605, CRL 0642.029 COPS 8940, EMI 1C228-81713, are not detailed.)

THE BENNY GOODMAN STORY   **August 1955, Hollywood**

Personnels as "The Benny Goodman Story" sound track, preceding.

MG 4514T1   **LP:** DE DL8252, BrE LAT8102, CID UMT263602. **StLp:** DE DL78252, CRL set COPS5162D, TOSH set CR8042. **StT:** DE ST74-8252.
1 **Let's Dance**
2 **Down South Camp Meetin'**
3 **King Porter Stomp**
4 **It's Been So Long**
5 **Roll 'Em**
6 **Bugle Call Rag**

MG 4515T8   same issues
7 **Don't Be That Way**
8 **You Turned The Tables On Me**-voc Martha Tilton
9 **Goody Goody**
10 **Slipped Disc** - OCTET
11 **Stompin' At The Savoy**
12 **One O'Clock Jump**

MG 4616T3   **LP:** DE DL8253, BrE LAT8103, CID UMT263603. **StLp:** DE DL78253, CRL set COPS5162D, TOSH set CR8024, **StT:** ST74-8253.
13 **Memories Of You** - TRIO
14 **China Boy** - TRIO
15 **Moonglow** - QUARTET
16 **Avalon** - QUARTET

MG 4617T1   same issues
17 **And The Angels Sing**-voc Martha Tilton - feat. Mannie Klein, tpt solo
18 **Jersey Bounce**
19 **Sometimes I'm Happy**
20 **Shine** - feat. Harry James, tpt solo
21 **Sing, Sing, Sing (With A Swing)** - feat. Harry James, tpt solo

We are finished with Decca, but not yet with "The Benny Goodman Story," for there is additional material extant from it.

Universal-International's promotional kit for disc jockeys included three 7" 45's, six sides in all. Three of the sides are shown preceding the Decca listings. Two others, on U-I 78196/78197, offer a "Personal Interview with Benny Goodman, Parts One, Two and Three." These are voice tracks by Benny, answers to questions put to him by DJ's, suggested in an included folder. Interesting to some collectors, but not to all. But the final side, on U-I 78189, provides a portion of a tenor solo by Stan Getz that is different from his work in the film or on the DE-based release. Speculatively, it may be that this bit was excised from the film/LP version, but it is different:

THE BENNY GOODMAN STORY   **August 1955, Hollywood**

Personnel as "The Benny Goodman Story" sound track, preceding.

- 0 -   **45:** U-I 78189
Sing, Sing, Sing (With A Swing)

Of even greater interest is the fairly recent discovery of performances for "The Benny Goodman Story" that are neither in the film nor on the commercial releases. These out-takes are on Universal-International studio reference 12" acetates. One, recorded at 78 rpm, has back-to-back cuts by the Trio. A second, recorded at 33⅓ rpm, offers two sides featuring the Octet. The third, at 78 rpm, provides a complete take, by the orchestra, of a tune not on the LP's, and only partially in the movie. (Its reverse, "One O'Clock Jump," is the same as that released commercially.)

Thus, major additions to the known works of Benny Goodman, especially of his small groups. And a hint that there may be more, yet undiscovered, somewhere in Hollywood.

THE BENNY GOODMAN STORY   August 1955, Hollywood

Personnels as "The Benny Goodman Story" sound track, preceding.

- 0 -   Universal-International Studio Reference Recording
Oh, Lady Be Good! - TRIO
Body And Soul - TRIO

- 0 -   Universal-International Studio Reference Recording
Honeysuckle Rose - OCTET
On The Sunny Side Of The Street - OCTET

- 0 -   Universal-International Studio Reference Recording
Memories Of You

Upon his return to New York from Hollywood, Benny received approval of his application to the American Federation of Musicians for a license to establish his own recording company, Park Recording, Inc. Under its aegis he recorded four tunes with a new Septet and two ex-Goodman vocalists. None has ever been released, the master tapes are ". . . somewhere in the studio," a combined recording facility/storage structure adjacent to his home in Stamford:

THE BENNY GOODMAN SEPTET   September 8, 1955, New York

Benny Goodman, clt; Ruby Braff, tpt; Urbie Green, tbn; Dave McKenna, p; Steve Jordan, g; Tommy Potter, b; Bobby Donaldson, d. Nancy Reed, Art Lund, voc.

- 0 -   UNISSUED
Soft Lights-voc Nancy Reed
Easy To Love-voc Art Lund
Oh, By Jingo!-voc Art Lund
It's Bad For Me-voc Nancy Reed, Benny Goodman - Tape

Benny liked "It's Bad For Me," determined to get it on wax, sold Columbia on the idea. But Rosemary Clooney had a bigger "name" than Nancy Reed, and she was chosen to record its vocal. Note that the 78 rpm issues from this session, and one coupling from the next, are the last Goodman original-issue 78's released by Columbia. In the mid-Fifties turntables accommodating 45's and LP's were commonplace, and from this point forward, in the U.S. at least, microgroove was the way to go.

THE BENNY GOODMAN SEXTET   November 14, 1955, New York
with ROSEMARY CLOONEY

Benny Goodman, clt; Buck Clayton, tpt; Urbie Green, tbn; Dick Hyman, p; Aaron Bell, b; Bobby Donaldson, d. Rosemary Clooney, voc. Dick Hyman (DH), arr.

CO 54293-1   CO 40616, PHIL 21798H, PHIL PB547. **45:** CO 4-40616, PhilCont B21798F. **EP:** CO B2107, PHIL BBE12038, PhilCont 429167BE. **LP:** CO CL2572
It's Bad For Me-voc Rosemary Clooney (and Benny Goodman) (arr DH)

CO 54294-1   CO 40625, CoJap L3029. **45:** CO 4-40625. **EP:** CO B2107, CoJap EM108, PHIL BBE12038, PhilCont 429167BE. **LP:** CO CL2572, COR KP030, CO alb P4M-5678
Goodbye-voc Rosemary Clooney (arr DH)

CO 54295-1   **LP:** CO CL2572, CO alb P4M-5678. **EP:** CO B2107, CoJap EM108, PHIL BBE12038
That's A' Plenty

THE BENNY GOODMAN TRIO   same session
with ROSEMARY CLOONEY

Goodman, Hyman, Donaldson. Rosemary Clooney, voc.

CO 54296-1   same issues as "It's Bad For Me," plus **78**, CoJap L3029; **EP**, CoJap EM108; **LP**, CO alb P4M-5678, PHIL BBR 8084, PhilCont BO7151L
Memories Of You-voc Rosemary Clooney

Two more tunes were needed to fill a 10" LP, so Benny returned to the studios December 6. Titled "Date With The King," it is the last original-issue 10" LP of Goodman recordings released in the United States. Later LP's are all 12".

Note the seeming out-of-numerical-sequence matrix numbers; Columbia assures that they are correct.

BENNY GOODMAN SEXTET   December 6, 1955, New York

Benny Goodman, clt; Buck Clayton, tpt; Urbie Green, tbn; CLAUDE THORN-HILL, p; Aaron Bell, b; Bobby Donaldson, d.

CO 54220   **LP:** CO CL2572
Can't We Talk It Over

CO 54221-1   CO 40625. **45:** CO 4-40625. **EP:** CoJap EM108, PhilCont 429167BE. **LP:** CO CL2572, COR KP030
A Fine Romance

The next day Benny began a four-part session for Capitol that supports an idea that he was disappointed with "The Benny Goodman Story" sound track—many of its tunes were duplicated. He prefers these versions, and remarked that he was especially pleased with Harry James's work, thought he played as well as ever.

Once again, the titles recorded are numbered consecutively, and secondary releases that excerpt tracks from the base Capitol issues are shown next:

78: CapE CI 14570 - 3, 11   **45:** CapE 45CL 14570 - 3, 11
EP: CapH HF36 - 32
  TOSH 1032 - 5, 6
  TOSH 1035 - 7, 9
  TOSH 1036 - 15
  TOSH 1037 - 4, 21
LP: CapFr CO54-81713)
  EMI 1C054-52715   ) 1, 3, 5, 6, 9, 11, 14, 15, 18, 21
  EMI 1C054-81713   )
  EMI 64704 - 1, 9, 11
  SW 1381 - 18, 19, 21

Note that some of the commercially unreleased cuts, particularly those by the small groups, have become available to a few collectors via tape transfer from the studio masters.

MR. BENNY GOODMAN December 7, 1955, New York

Benny Goodman, clt; Chris Griffin, Billy Butterfield, Bernie Privin, tpt; Urbie Green, Will Bradley, tbn; Hymie Schertzer, Phil Bodner, as; Al Klink, Peanuts Hucko, ts; Dick Hyman, p; Tony Mottola, g; Milt Hinton, b; Bobby Donaldson, d. Martha Tilton, voc.

20931 LP: CAP S706, CapAu VMP1072, CapE LCT6104, CapFr W706. EP: CAP set FDM706, CAP set FBF1-706
1 **Down South Camp Meetin'**

20932 UNISSUED
2 **Don't Be That Way**

Add Harry James, tpt.

20933 same issues
3 **And The Angels Sing**-voc Martha Tilton

James out.

20934 same issues
4 **Good-Bye**

James returns.

20935 same issues
5 **Sing, Sing, Sing** (Part 1)

20936 same issues
6 **Sing, Sing, Sing.** (Part 2)

MR. BENNY GOODMAN December 8, 1955, New York

Personnel as December 7, except trumpets are Griffin, Butterfield, CARL POOLE, JIMMY MAXWELL and RUBY BRAFF.

20937 same issues as mx 20931, "Down South Camp Meetin'"
7 **Bugle Call Rag**

Add Harry James, tpt; Braff out.

20938 same issues
8 **Shine**

20945 same issues
9 **One O'Clock Jump**

Braff returns; James out.

20946 UNISSUED - Tape
10 **King Porter Stomp**

(Intervening matrices 20939 through 20944 are not by Benny Goodman.)

MR. BENNY GOODMAN December 12, 1955, New York

Benny Goodman, clt; Doc Severinson, Bernie Glow, John Durante, tpt; Urbie Green, Lou McGarity, tbn; Hymie Schertzer, Milt Yaner, as; Peanuts Hucko, Boomie Richman, ts; Sol Schlinger, bar; Morrie Wechsler, p; Al Caiola, g; George Duvivier, b; Don Lamond, d.

20932 same issues as mx 20931, "Down South Camp Meetin'," plus LP, EMI-F 1551563
11 **Don't Be That Way**

20946 UNISSUED
12 **King Porter Stomp**

The last Capitol session in this series also provides the last original-issue 78 rpm record by Benny Goodman released in the United States, CAP 3331, "Sometimes I'm Happy"/"Goody Goody." Many collectors regret their passing, believing that the good ones offered superior reproduction.

MR. BENNY GOODMAN December 14, 1955, New York

Orchestra personnel as December 12.

20946 UNISSUED (takes 3 through 8)
13 **King Porter Stomp**

20947 same issues as mx 20931, "Down South Camp Meetin'":
14 **It's Been So Long**

20948 same issues
15 **Let's Dance**

(Matrices 20949 and 20950 apparently were not used.)

20951 CAP 3331, CapE CL14531. 45: CAP F3331, CAP DJ20951, CapE 45CL14531. LP: CAP W2140, EMI 62524, CAP SL6716
16 **Sometimes I'm Happy**

20952 CAP 3331, CapE CL14531. 45: CAP F3331, CAP DJ20952
17 **Goody-Goody**-voc Benny Goodman

BENNY GOODMAN QUINTET same session

Benny Goodman, clt; Lionel Hampton, vib; Mel Powell, p; George Duvivier, b; Bobby Donaldson, d.

20953 same issues as mx 20931, "Down South Camp Meetin'," plus LP, EMI-F 1551563
18 **Avalon**

20954 same issues, except omit EMI-F
19 **Moonglow**

20955 UNISSUED - Tape
20 **Alicia's Blues**

20956 same issues
21 **Memories Of You**

20957 same issues
22 **China Boy**

20958 UNISSUED - Tape
23 **Seven Come Eleven**

20959 UNISSUED - Tape
24 **I Got Rhythm**

That evening, Benny appeared on Steve Allen's telecast with a re-vamped Quintet. The Carnegie Hall sequence from "The Benny Goodman Story" was shown and Benny, Allen, John Hammond and Skitch Henderson discussed the movie and old times. The Quintet played two tunes, was joined for two more by Sol Yaged (Allen's clarinet instructor for the film), Doc Severinson, Lou McGarity, and comedian Sid Caesar, an ex-tenor saxophonist:

"THE STEVE ALLEN SHOW" *December 14, 1955, New York*
NBC Television Network

Benny Goodman, clt; Buck Clayton, tpt; Urbie Green, tbn; Teddy Wilson, p; unknown, b; Don Lamond, d.

*Honeysuckle Rose (**LP:** GOJ 1010)*
Memories Of You (Clayton, Green in coda only)

SEXTET plus Doc Severinson, tpt; Lou McGarity, tbn; Sol Yaged, clt; Sid Caesar, ts; unknown b.

One O'Clock Jump - segue to, Stompin' At The Savoy (to close)

Critic-commentator-disc jockey Willis Conover regularly broadcast music-and-talk programs over the Voice Of America radio network, good jazz and intelligent comment. Some of his early shows were transcribed onto 16" ET's; later, 12" ET's and LP's came into vogue, and finally tape was employed to distribute the programs.

Conover interviewed Benny during the winter of 1955-1956. A resultant hour-long broadcast was heard January 27, 1956, covering Benny's career from the Pollack days to "The Benny Goodman Story." A tape of the show is extant, but it is not known if a recording was made and distributed. From the same interview a follow-up program was broadcast February 3, 1956. This talk-only show was transcribed onto a 12" disc labeled, "Music USA - Program 401-B." All of this material is interesting, and is recommended to collectors.

For its 1956 dealer promotion, Columbia released a 12" LP titled "Columbia Retailer," that celebrated Benny's 25th year of recording for its labels. Fragments of "Let's Dance" (CO air checks album), "Basin Street Blues" (Charleston Chasers), "Don't Be That Way" and "Sing, Sing, Sing" (both Carnegie Hall), and "Memories Of You" (Goodman-Clooney) are included.

Steve Allen taped interviews with Gene Krupa, John Hammond, Helen

Ward, Teddy Wilson, Hymie Schertzer and Lionel Hampton in the winter of 1955-1956; they reminisce about their days with Benny. These conversations were broadcast February 1, 1956, as a promotional effort for the Heart Fund. Collectors will find this non-music broadcast worthwhile.

Coincidentally, Benny was in Chicago February 1, and while there appeared on NBC's "Adults Only" telecast together with Steve Allen, to promote the just-released "The Benny Goodman Story." Benny arrived late in the hour-long program, but did get in one tune with the Art Van Damme Quintet, and acknowledges that early in his career he played in a pit orchestra in a Chicago theater with Joseph Galicio, now music director for "Adults Only":

"ADULTS ONLY"   *February 1, 1956, Chicago*
  NBC Television Network

Benny Goodman, clt, and the Art Van Damme Quintet

Memories Of You

Making it a triple-header for February 1, Benny chatted with Len O'Connor on his "News On The Spot" radio program, WMAQ, Chicago, for five minutes about the old days in the Windy City.

Drumbeating for "The Benny Goodman Story" included "The Kings of Swing," an article in the January 20 edition of Collier's Magazine, in which Benny and Steve Allen talk about "That Old Gang Of Mine"; the February 8 and 22 issues of Down Beat, largely given over to Benny's career, and John Hammond's two columns on "New Facts About Swing's King"; the February 21 edition of Look Magazine, with its feature story on, "Life With A King"; and the March issue of Metronome, dedicated to Benny and "The Benny Goodman Story."

While all of this was going on, Benny had a new big band in rehearsal. The author attended some of the tryouts in the Waldorf-Astoria in New York, and recalls Benny had trouble getting a drummer he liked. It got to the point that Benny had Peanuts Hucko rehearse the band while he auditioned drummers. His test was the paradiddle that Krupa employed to introduce the trumpet solo in "Sing, Sing, Sing." If the drummer didn't know that lick, his career with Goodman ended right there. The author also remembers that Benny was so impressed with then-unknown trumpeter Mel Davis—who had hitchhiked to Manhattan for an audition—that he offered him a year's contract on the spot. Davis later would go with the NBC staff in New York and play for the network's major telecasts.

The new band woodshedded in New England, playing in the Bradford Hotel, Boston, on February 3; for the Roseland Ball in Taunton, Mass., on February 4; and in Waterbury, Conn., Worcester, Mass., and Manchester, New Hampshire, on February 5, 6 and 7, respectively. It then opened on February 9 in the Waldorf-Astoria with this personnel; Benny Goodman, clt; Jimmy Maxwell, Mel Davis, Fern Caron, tpt; Urbie Green, Rex Peer, tbn; Walt Levinsky, Al Block, as; Budd Johnson, Sol Schlinger, ts; Hank Jones, p; Steve Jordan, g; Irv Manning, b; Mousey Alexander, d; and Mitzi Cottle, voc. So far as it is known, the band never was on the air during this engagement, and there are no extant air checks.

The third week of April saw the band on tour. Maxwell, Green, Schlinger and Manning, in demand as staff musicians, remained in New York; Al Maiorca, Harry DiVito, Bill Slapin and Whitey Mitchell, respectively, replaced them. They played for the University of Minnesota on April 21, were in Milwaukee the 22nd, did proms for Purdue University (April 27), University of Detroit (May 4 and 5), and V.P.I. (May 11). Their May 12 Saturday night gig at the Sunnybrook Ballroom in Pottstown, Pa., was the scene of a monumental traffic jam, so great was the demand to see Benny Goodman. The band got there early, but Benny was an hour late, victim of the traffic tieup he had created. It was an unseasonably warm evening, Sunnybrook was not then airconditioned, and after the first set Benny and the sidemen all removed their jackets. The overflow audience got a big kick out of Benny's wide red suspenders. . .

Back in New York, Benny recorded the band for his Park Recording Company. Five tapes' worth were cut, but all that is known to exist now are one issued and three unreleased sides, plus one alternate take.

BENNY GOODMAN AND HIS ORCHESTRA   May 17, 1956, New York

Benny Goodman, clt; Jimmy Maxwell, Mel Davis, Fern Caron, Al Maiorca, tpt; Rex Peer, Harry DiVito, tbn; Walt Levinsky, Al Block, as; Budd Johnson, Bill Slapin, ts; Hank Jones, p; Steve Jordan, g; Irv Manning, b; Mousey Alexander, d. Marilyn "Mitzi" Cottle, voc.

U-9666   **LP:** CHESS LP1440, BARCLAY (Fr) 84.103,
              BELLAPHON(G) BJS4025. **StLp:** CHESS S1440,
              ChessH 9283047. **StT:** CADET-Bel Canto ST-112.
              12"ET: AFR&TS P7705
-0-   UNISSUED - Tape
              Fascinating Rhythm

              UNISSUED
              Delia's Gone-voc Mitzi Cottle
              The Earl - Tape
              More Than You Know-voc Mitzi Cottle

(The tapes have no matrices; "U-9666," above, is Chess's pressing matrix.)

The band had a few dates in June; it played for The Citadel June 1, was in Dayton, Cleveland and Canton, Ohio, on the 22nd, 23rd and 24th, respectively. But Benny is next in evidence as a soloist, at the Berkshire Festival, at Tanglewood in Lenox, Massachusetts. Two of these performances were recorded and released by RCA-Victor:

MOZART CONCERTO FOR CLARINET   July 9, 1956, Lenox, Mass.
AND ORCHESTRA, IN A, K.622

Benny Goodman, clt, and the Boston Symphony Orchestra, Charles Munch, conducting.

G2RP-7023-1   **LP:** VI LM2073, RcaAu L16060, RcaE RB16013, RcaFr
                  630.398. **StLp:** VI VICS1402, ETR 826765, RCA
                  AGL1-5275. **StT:** VI DCS39
                  First Movement: Allegro
                  Second Movement: Adagio
                  Third Movement: Rondo: Allegro

MOZART CLARINET QUINTET   July 12, 1956, Lenox, Mass.
IN A, K.581

Benny Goodman, clt, and the Boston String Quartet: Richard Burgin, 1st v; Alfred Krips, 2nd v; Joseph dePasquale, viola; Samuel Mayes, cel.

G2RP-7024-1   **LP:** VI LM2073, RcaAu L16060. **StLp:** VI VICS1402, ETR
                  826765
                  First Movement: Allegro
                  Second Movement: Larghetto
                  Third Movement: Menuetto
                  Fourth Movement: Allegretto con Variazioni

Benny next appeared in Washington's Carter Barron Ampitheater July 14–17; and after that, so far as it is known, took the balance of the summer off. He seems to have been idle until—possibly—the last week in September. "Possibly," because there is some evidence, which the author has been unable to confirm, that on two dates late that month Benny recorded Morton Gould's "Derivations For Clarinet And Band" for Capitol and for the first time. Reputedly, sketchily, the available information is:

BENNY GOODMAN   September 24, 1956, New York

Benny Goodman, clt, and unknown orchestral accompaniment.

              UNISSUED
              Derivations For Clarinet And Band
21341   **I - Warm-up**
21342   **III - Rag**

BENNY GOODMAN   September 29, 1956, New York

Benny Goodman, clt, and unknown orchestral accompaniment.

              UNISSUED
              Derivations For Clarinet And Band
21343   **IV - Ride-Out**
21344   **II - Contrapuntal Blues**

The band regrouped in November; ahead was a tour of the Far East, under the joint auspices of the Department of State of the United States, and the American National Theater and Academy (ANTA). Its initial engagement would be at the U.S. exhibit at Thailand's Constitution Fair in Lumpini Park, Bangkok, for two weeks. Following that it would go to Phnom Penh, Singapore (Christmas Eve), Kuala Lumpor, Rangoon (New Year's Day), Hong Kong, Seoul and Tokyo. It would be Benny's first venture into the Orient, and he looked forward to it eagerly.

The hegira was East-to-East in a sense, for it began in New Jersey, a jazz concert at Princeton University on November 9. On the 15th, it was another jazz concert in Buffalo, New York's Kleinhans Music Hall; on the 17th, there was a repeat in Brooklyn's Academy of Music. Then it was "Westward, Ho!," for concerts in Seattle (21st), Portland (22nd), Vancouver, B.C. (23rd), Spokane (24th), San Diego (29th), Los Angeles (30th), and finally, San Francisco on December 1. On the 2nd of December, the band left the West Coast and flew to Thailand. While in Vancouver, Benny granted an interview to William Bellman of the Canadian Broadcasting Corporation. A five-minute tape of the broadcast is extant, but the date of its airing is not known. And in November and December, Willis Conover broadcast an interview with Benny about plans for the Far East trip via the Voice Of America radio network.

Since publication of "BG - On The Record," the author has become privy to taped performances of the Goodman entourage during its last several days in Thailand. They were made, with Benny's permission, by a Swiss national with business interests in Bangkok, Kurt A. Mueller. First cut monaurally on an Ampex reel recorder and stereophonically on a Magnecord staggered-head machine, transfers of the tapes were later presented to Mr. Goodman and the author. At times both recorders were in operation simultaneously, while at others only one machine was in use; the listings below are composite, combining the produce of both recorders. In general, the sound quality of the tapes is excellent, although on occasion vocals are dimly heard because of fixed microphone placement.

Mr. Mueller has supplied the English translations of some of the Thai titles, at least two of which were composed by Phumiphol Aduljej, the King of Thailand. A good friend of Benny and the author, Mr. Mueller has also provided some of the concert tapes that will be listed in the 'Seventies and 'Eighties. For his past and continuing efforts, collectors owe him their thanks.

For the first time in print, then, Benny Goodman at the Constitution Fair, Lumpini Park, Bangkok, 1956:

CONSTITUTION FAIR CONCERT   Lumpini Park, Bangkok
                                             1st Show, December 14, 1956

Benny Goodman, clt; Mel Davis, John Frosk, Billy Hodges, tpt; Rex Peer, Jack Rains, tbn; Peanuts Hucko, Al Block, as; Budd Johnson, Bill Slapin, ts; Hank Jones, p; Steve Jordan, g; Israel Crosby, b; Mousey Alexander, d. Dottie Reid, voc. BUDD JOHNSON (BJ), arr.

TRIO: Goodman, Jones, Alexander
QUARTET: Goodman, Jones, Crosby, Alexander
OCTET: Goodman, Davis, Peer, Johnson, Jones, Jordan, Crosby, Alexander

Let's Dance (theme)
Lao Duang Duen ("Laotian Moonlight"; alternately, "The Beautiful Moon
   Of Lao")
Yarm Yen ("In The Evening" - composed by the King of Thailand)
Medley: 'Swonderful-voc Dottie Reid
        Please Be Kind-voc Dottie Reid
        Loch Lomond -voc Dottie Reid
        I Let A Song Go Out Of My Heart-voc Dottie Reid
        Bei Mir Bist Du Schon-voc Dottie Reid
Kanueng Kruang ("Humming The Thoughts")-voc Dottie Reid
Sugar Foot Stomp (n/c - intro clipped)
Somebody Else Is Taking My Place-voc Dottie Reid
A String Of Pearls
Mack The Knife (Moritat) (arr BJ)
One O'Clock Jump
After You've Gone (n/c - intro clipped)
Can't We Be Friends?
Sweet Georgia Brown - TRIO
Medley: Rose Room - TRIO
        If I Had You - TRIO
        Just One Of Those Things - TRIO
On The Sunny Side Of The Street - TRIO
King Porter Stomp

Benny isn't about to try to pronounce the titles of the Thai tunes; in the next performance, he announces them as, "Number 1, Number 2, Number 3."

CONSTITUTION FAIR CONCERT   Lumpini Park, Bangkok
                                             2nd Show, December 14, 1956

Personnels as preceding.

Let's Dance (theme)
Bugle Call Rag (n/c - intro clipped)
Down South Camp Meetin'
Roll 'Em
Medley: 'Swonderful-voc Dottie Reid
        Please Be Kind-voc Dottie Reid
        Loch Lomond-voc Dottie Reid
        I Let A Song Go Out Of My Heart-voc Dottie Reid
        Bei Mir Bist Du Schon-voc Dottie Reid
        And The Angels Sing-voc Dottie Reid
Lao Duang Duen
Sai Fon ("Rainfall" - composed by the King of Thailand)
Yarm Yen
The World Is Waiting For The Sunrise - TRIO
Memories Of You - TRIO
Oh, Lady Be Good! - TRIO
The Blues - OCTET
Flying Home - OCTET
Sing, Sing, Sing - Part 1 (n/c - intro clipped)
Sing, Sing, Sing - Part 2
Thai National Anthem

CONSTITUTION FAIR CONCERT   Lumpini Park Bangkok
                                             1st Show, December 15, 1956

Personnels as December 14.

Let's Dance (theme)
Don't Be That Way
King Porter Stomp
Lao Duang Duen
Trigger Fantasy - feat. Israel Crosby
Roll 'Em
'Swonderful-voc Dottie Reid
And The Angels Sing-voc Dottie Reid
One O'Clock Jump

Benny wasn't feeling well, and so he cut short the first performance of December 15. He began the second program that day, but following "Sugar Foot Stomp" he left the bandstand, and Peanuts Hucko assumed leadership. Hucko continued to play section alto, but also took up his clarinet when the occasion arose.

CONSTITUTION FAIR CONCERT   Lumpini Park, Bangkok
                                             2nd Show, December 15, 1956

Personnels as December 14.

Let's Dance (theme)
Bugle Call Rag
Down South Camp Meetin'
Yarm Yen
Sugar Foot Stomp

Goodman leaves.

(Medley: This Is My Lucky Day - voc Dottie Reid
         Please Be Kind - voc Dottie Reid
         Loch Lomond - voc Dottie Reid
         I Let A Song Go Out of My Heart-voc Dottie Reid
         Bei Mir Bist Du Schon - voc Dottie Reid
         And The Angels Sing - voc Dottie Reid
(Big John Special
(Mack The Knife (Moritat)
(Perdido - OCTET - Hucko plays clt
(. . . announcement that Mr. Goodman is ill)

Benny did not appear for the last concert that was recorded, the 1st show of December 16. But before we get to it we must list some undated material that includes Goodman. The first is part of a concert performance in Lumpini Park:

CONSTITUTION FAIR CONCERT   Lumpini Park, Bangkok
                                             2nd Show, December 1956

Personnels as December 14.

Anything Goes - voc Dottie Reid
King Porter Stomp
Kanueng Kruang (no vocal)
Kanueng Kruang-voc Dottie Reid
Stompin' At The Savoy
Flying Home - OCTET
One O'Clock Jump
Thai National Anthem

NBC recorded Benny in Bangkok for a shortwave broadcast that was on the air in the United States on New Year's Day 1957. It featured an unique Sextet: Benny, his rhythm section, and His Majesty Phumiphol Aduljej on soprano sax. The King, a devoted jazz fan who presented Benny with a medal for coming to Thailand, plays, as one of the sidemen remarked, ". . . okay, for a King." And he was delighted with a special pressing of two Capitol sides that Benny gave him, "Let's Dance" and "You're A Sweetheart."

"PARADE OF BANDS"   December 1956, Bangkok
    NBC Radio Network   Broadcast January 1, 1957

Orchestra personnel as December 14. SEXTET: Goodman, Phumiphol Aduljej, ss; Jones, Jordan, Crosby, Alexander.

Down South Camp Meetin'
On The Sunny Side Of The Street - SEXTET
Roll 'Em
Lao Duang Duen (Benny announces as, "The Beautiful Moon Of Lao")
    (n/c)
One O'Clock Jump
Good-Bye (theme)

The United States Information Service, in cooperation with the Voice Of America, produced a three-reel, black-and-white film of Benny's Thai odyssey, "Benny Goodman in Bangkok." The narrative portion of the film is in the Thai language, but the locations of Benny's several performances are clearly identified. The first segment is from a concert in Lumpini Park; the second is filmed in the Paholyothin Studios; and the third is from a concert in a Bangkok ballroom. Here are the musical segments of the film:

"BENNY GOODMAN IN BANGKOK"   December 1956, Bangkok
    A USIS-VOA three-reel film, black-and-white

Lumpini Park episode: Personnel as December 14.

Let's Dance (theme)
Bugle Call Rag
Down South Camp Meetin'
Easy To Love-voc Dottie Reid
Sing, Sing, Sing - Part 2

Paholyothin Studios episode (identified as the, "Thai Army Television Show"): Benny Goodman, clt, and Thai musicians, singers, dancers, featuring Thai vocalist Surophol.

Traditional Thai song
Popular Thai song
Ramwong song

Bangkok Ballroom episode: Benny Goodman Orchestra and the (Thai) Prasarn Mitr Orchestra. Lao Duang Duen

And finally from Bangkok, the first performance on December 16; Benny, still under the weather, does not participate; Peanuts Hucko leads the band, plays both alto sax and clarinet:

CONSTITUTION FAIR CONCERT   Lumpini Park, Bangkok
                                             1st Show, December 16, 1956

Personnels as December 14, except omit Benny Goodman.

(Let's Dance (theme)
(Stealin' Apples
(Roll 'Em
(Flying Home - OCTET - Hucko, clt
(One O'Clock Jump
(Thai National Anthem

Some years ago, a search of Benny's files uncovered evidence that he had in storage tapes of the band's performances on January 1, 1957, in Rangoon, Burma. Alphabetically, the included tunes were listed as:

Air Mail Special; And The Angels Sing-voc Dottie Reid; Bei Mir Bist Du Schon-voc Dottie Reid; Bugle Call Rag; Cherry Pink And Apple Blossom White; Don't Be That Way; Down South Camp Meetin'; Flying Home; I Let A Song Go Out Of My Heart-voc Dottie Reid; Just One Of Those Things-BG, rhythm; King Porter Stomp; Let's Dance; Loch Lomond-voc Dottie Reid and Benny Goodman; Memories Of You - BG, rhythm; One O'Clock Jump; Please Be Kind-voc Dottie Reid; Que Sera Sera; Roll 'Em; Rose Room (indicated as by the orchestra); Sing, Sing, Sing; Sugar Foot Stomp; Sweet Georgia Brown - BG, rhythm; 'Swonderful-voc Dottie Reid; Take The A Train - Octet; Tea For Two - Quartet; That's A Plenty - Octet; untitled blues - "Rangoon Blues."

The tapes, if indeed they once were in Benny's possession, cannot now be located. Benny says that he did not commission any recordings during the entire Far East tour. He was aware, of course, of recordings being made by others, but has no recollection of any in Rangoon.

Since some of the tunes listed are unique, do not appear in any other extant transcriptions from this tour; and because the listings, now not to be found, were in some detail, the judgment here is that the tapes were cut. A search for them will continue.

Dogged research by Japanese enthusiast Yasuo Segami discovered specific information about Benny's itinerary following the Rangoon engagement: The band arrived in Hong Kong on January 4, gave one concert there on each of the following four days, then left for Seoul (via Taipei) on January 9. (No recordings of the Hong Kong appearances are known to the author.) A scheduled concert in Seoul was cancelled, and the band flew on to Haneda airport in Japan, arriving a day early on January 10. Sponsored by Sankei-Jiji, a Tokyo newspaper, the band would perform six concerts in four days, beginning January 12, in Sankei Hall. On January 16, a final hour-long concert would be both broadcast and televised from NHK Hall.

Still unknown, however, is the date of a broadcast transcribed by the Armed Forces (radio) Network. It could have been excerpted from any of the concerts preceding that of the 16th, and possibly from either the afternoon or evening concert of January 12. Since members of the Japanese royal family and the American ambassador to Japan attended the evening performance, it seems a likely candidate for the AFN broadcast.

TOKYO CONCERT   mid-January 1957, Tokyo
    AFN radio broadcast   Sankei Hall

Broadcast date unknown. Personnels as December 14, 1956.

Let's Dance (theme)
Bugle Call Rag
Roll 'Em
'Swonderful-voc Dottie Reid
Medley: Please Be Kind-voc Dottie Reid
        Bei Mir Bist Du Schon-voc Dottie Reid
        And The Angels Sing-voc Dottie Reid
The World Is Waiting For The Sunrise - QUARTET
Just One Of Those Things - QUARTET
One O'Clock Jump
Sing, Sing, Sing
(. . . presentation, interview - Goodman, AFN staff announcer
Sent For You Yesterday And Here You Come Today
King Porter Stomp (n/c)

On the afternoon of January 16, Benny, Mel Davis, Budd Johnson and Mousey Alexander and some Japanese musicians gathered in Esuya, the Ginza, Tokyo, for what is described as a "memorial party." The U.S. Information Service was on hand, filmed portions of the event to produce a 16mm short titled, "Benny In Tokyo." Although the author has not viewed the film, his audio tape of its sound track is believed to be complete:

"BENNY IN TOKYO"   January 16, 1957, Esuya, Tokyo
   A USIS film in black-and-white.

Benny Goodman, Shoji Suzuki, clt; Mel Davis, Fumio Nanri, tpt; Budd Johnson, Akira Miyazawa, ts; prob. Hank Jones, p; Takeshi Ueda, b; Mousey Alexander, George Kawaguchi, d.

  . . . drum soli, Alexander & Kawaguchi
Air Mail Special
Honeysuckle Rose
. . . drum soli, Alexander & Kawaguchi

Benny Goodman, clt, and a Japanese string quartet

Quintet For Clarinet And Strings In A Major (Mozart)

Reminiscing later about his performance with the string quartet, Benny remarked that he had been quite hesitant about appearing with them. He takes classical music very seriously, questioned the competence of a group he had never heard. He was delighted to find them excellent musicians, their reading of the Mozart opus flawless.

That evening, Benny gave his final concert of the Far East tour:

TOKYO CONCERT   January 16, 1957, Sankei Hall, Tokyo
  NHK Radio & Television

Personnels as December 14, 1956.

Let's Dance (theme)
(. . . introduction - Benny speaks in English, Japanese
Bugle Call Rag
One O'Clock Jump
Trigger Fantasy - feat. Israel Crosby
'Swonderful-voc Dottie Reid
Please Be Kind-voc Dottie Reid
Loch Lomond-voc Dottie Reid
Bei Mir Bist Du Schon-voc Dottie Reid
And The Angels Sing-voc Dottie Reid
Sweet Georgia Brown - QUARTET
Memories Of You - TRIO
Medley: Rose Room - QUARTET
      If I Had You - QUARTET
      Just One Of Those Things - QUARTET
Air Mail Special - OCTET
"N H K Blues" (traditional blues) - OCTET
That's A Plenty - OCTET
Sing, Sing, Sing - Parts 1 and 2
Good-Bye (theme)

Benny and Alice returned to the United States separately from the band, finally reached New York on January 23. There he was promptly interviewed by Willis Conover for a 15-minute conversation that was broadcast over the Voice Of America radio network. The program was transcribed onto a 12" ET labeled, "Music USA, Program No. 707-B."

The band went back to work in February. Some personnel changes were made, and these are reflected in Benny's first television appearance in the U.S. for 1957:

"THE ED SULLIVAN SHOW"   February 10, 1957, New York
  CBS Television Network

Benny Goodman, clt; JIMMY MAXWELL, BUCK CLAYTON, NICK TRAVIS, tpt; Rex Peer, FRANK REHAK, tbn; Al Block, RED PRESS, as; Budd Johnson, SOL SCHLINGER, ts; Hank Jones, p; Steve Jordan, g; IRV MANNING, b; Mousey Alexander, d.

TRIO: Goodman, Jones, Alexander

Let's Dance (theme)
Memories Of You - TRIO
Just One Of Those Things - TRIO
Sing, Sing, Sing

(Except for "Let's Dance," above on LP, GOJ 1010.)

Prior to a four-week engagement at the Waldorf-Astoria that began March 11, the band played some concert/dance dates in the East. One was at Rhodes-On-The-Pawtuxet, Cranston, Rhode Island. Here a collector smuggled in a hand-held tape recorder and taped several sets surreptitiously. This early instance of an unauthorized audience-recording of a Goodman performance is the precursor of many that lie ahead, especially in the 1970's, when the availability of cassette recorders facilitated the practice. The author has not heard this transcription, and so cannot comment on its audio quality.

DANCE — RHODES-ON-THE-PAWTUXET   February 23, 1957
                                                     Cranston, R.I.

Personnel as February 10, except MEL POWELL, p, replaces Jones; and possibly EDDIE BERT, tbn, replaces Rehak. Lynn Taylor, voc. GEORGE WILLIAMS (GW), CHARLES H. COOPER (CHC), arr.

Riding High
Delia-voc Lynn Taylor and Benny Goodman
Down South Camp Meetin'
I'll Never Say "Never Again" Again-voc Lynn Taylor
King Porter Stomp
You Hit The Spot-voc Lynn Taylor (arr GW)
If I Could Be With You (One Hour Tonight)
Goody-Goody-voc Benny Goodman
The Earl
Always
Oh, Baby!
How Long Has This Been Going On?-voc Lynn Taylor
And The Angels Sing-voc Lynn Taylor
Mission To Moscow
Was That The Human Thing To Do?-voc Lynn Taylor (arr CHC)
Jersey Bounce
Big John Special

Collectors disagree, sometimes to the point of fisticuffs, about which Goodman performance of a given tune is "best"—a futile exercise, but seemingly an unending one. However, the choice of the worst-ever extant version of "Sing, Sing, Sing" is surely limited to two performances of that warhorse on Perry Como's television programs in 1957. Here is the first travesty:

"THE PERRY COMO SHOW"   March 23, 1957, New York
  NBC Television Network

Benny Goodman, clt; Mel Powell, p; Roy Burnes, d.

Medley: The Man I Love
       Embraceable You
       Oh, Lady Be Good!
       Somebody Loves Me
       Liza

(Above on LP, GOJ 1010.)

TRIO plus Mitchell Ayres's studio orchestra

Sing, Sing, Sing-voc Benny Goodman, Perry Como, Ed Wynn, Anna Maria Alberghetti, Andy Williams and chorus

The Waldorf-Astoria engagement ended April 6, no recordings from that stand are known to the author. The band then went on the road, but under the leadership of trombonist Urbie Green, and most likely with different personnel. Benny elected to stay in the New York area, content to do some television shows and some private recording. It was intimated that the band that accompanied him on Kate Smith's program, next, was the one that had toured southeast Asia. It was not; its only recognizable members, Mel Powell and Roy Burnes, were not on the Far East tour:

"THE KATE SMITH SHOW"   April 28, 1957, New York
  ABC Television Network

Benny Goodman, clt; Mel Powell, p; Roy Burnes, d; plus full orchestra, personnel unknown.

Let's Dance (theme)
Bugle Call Rag
Medley: Memories Of You - TRIO
      Stompin' At The Savoy - TRIO
      The World Is Waiting For The Sunrise - TRIO
One O'Clock Jump

A playback of "The Kate Smith Show" convinced Benny that he should record the Trio for his own Park Recording Company. He did, in his studio at his home in Stamford, where the tape is now stored. Recent access to the tape alters the contents previously reported, show that the Trio cut two medleys, one of Gershwin tunes, the other of Rodgers-Hart compositions:

THE BENNY GOODMAN TRIO   May 16, 1957, Stamford

Benny Goodman, clt; Mel Powell, p; Roy Burnes, d.

- 0 -   UNISSUED-Tape
Medley: **The Man I Love**
      (Embraceable You (Powell solo)
      Oh, Lady Be Good!
      Somebody Loves Me
      Liza

- 0 -   UNISSUED-Tape
Medley: **Where Or When**
      I Didn't Know What Time It Was
      There's A Small Hotel
      (This Can't Be Love (Powell, Burnes)
      Sing For Your Supper
      Blue Room

Benny also put his converted-garage studio in Stamford to another use on an uncertain date in May: He recorded two works by Johannes Brahms. As noted previously (March 1955), these tapes were remastered and released in 1985 by the Musical Heritage Society. And as before, the LP is identified as "stereo," but the original recording was monaural.

BENNY GOODMAN - PRIVATE COLLECTION   May 1957, Stamford

Benny Goodman, clt, with the Berkshire String Quartet: Urico Rossi, Albert Lazan, v; David Dawson, viola; Fritz Maag, cel; Leon Pommers, p. TRIO: Goodman, Maag, Pommers.

MM 20103 A   **LP:** MM 20103 A - Side 1. **CD:** MM 60103Y
      Trio in A Minor for Clarinet, Cello and Piano, Op. 114
      (Brahms)
      1. **First movement**
      2. **Adagio**
      3. **Andantino grazioso**
      4. **Allegro**

MM 20103 B   **LP:** MM 20103 B - Side 2
      Quintet in B Minor for Clarinet and String Quartet, Op. 115 (Brahms)
      1. **Allegro**
      2. **Adagio**
      3. **Andantino**
      4. **Con moto**

There is little recorded evidence of Benny's activities for the next 12 months; not until he accepts another commission from the U.S. State Department will we find him at work in earnest. In main, the gap is bridged by television appearances, beginning with:

"THE RAY BOLGER SHOW"   June 13, 1957, New York
  NBC Television Network

Benny Goodman, clt; Mel Powell, p; Roy Burnes, d.

I Know That You Know
Where Or When
Swanee
Memories - accomp. Ray Bolger, tap dancing

"THE STEVE ALLEN SHOW"   July 7, 1957, New York
  NBC Television Network

Benny Goodman, clt, plus rhythm section from studio orchestra, including Jack Cummings, d.

Medley: Fascinating Rhythm
    Bidin' My Time
    I've Got A Crush On You

. . . unknown title - Quintet plus Steve Allen, clt

Benny Goodman, clt, and the studio orchestra

St. Louis Blues
Let's Dance (theme)

The band on Benny's next television appearance was billed as his; if so, it was assembled from Local 802 musicians especially for the show:

"CRESCENDO"   September 29, 1957, New York

Benny Goodman, clt, and a full orchestra, including Urbie Green, tbn, and Roy Burnes, d.

Let's Dance (theme) (**LP:** GOJ 1010)
Don't Be That Way (**LP:** GOJ 1010)

"The Benny Goodman Orchestra," without Benny and led by Urbie Green, broadcast via the Canadian Broadcasting Corporation on October 18 from the Lido Deck, Brant Inn, Burlington, Ontario. An air check of a portion of the last tune, "King Porter Stomp," and the closing theme, "Good-Bye," is extant.

Here's the other Como TV massacre of "Sing, Sing, Sing":

"THE PERRY COMO SHOW"   October 19, 1957, New York
  NBC Television Network

Benny Goodman, clt; Mel Powell, p; unknown, b; Roy Burnes, d.

Medley: After I Say I'm Sorry
    If I Had You
    How High The Moon
    I Know That You Know

(Above on LP, GOJ 1011.)

Sing, Sing, Sing-voc Perry Como, Tony Bennett, Diana Dors, Jackie Miles & chorus - QUARTET plus Mitchell Ayres's studio orchestra, including Don Lamond, d.

(A few bars of an introductory "Let's Dance" probably includes Benny.)

On October 21 Benny MC'd the New York Herald Tribune's Second Annual Fresh Air Fund. The charity affair presented musical performances by groups of amateurs who regularly worked for advertising agencies. Benny joined in for three selections.

The event was taped and pressed in part onto a 12" LP, which was then sold by mail in an effort to raise additional contributions. It failed to sell well, and is now a desirable collectors' item.

Accompanying Benny on his first two tunes are Irving Townsend, then Columbia's A&R chief; writer-critic George Simon; Walter Newton, Wee Television, and then Helen Ward's husband; Layton Guptil, American Artists' Magazine; and Helen Ward. On the final tune, almost everyone present joined in, on a day when spirits were not only high, but flowed freely:

2nd. ANNUAL HERALD TRIBUNE   October 21, 1957, New York
FRESH AIR FUND JAZZ CONCERT

Benny Goodman, clt, and "aghast commentary," accompanied by Irving Townsend, clt; Layton Guptil, p; Walter Newton, b; George Simon, d. Helen Ward, voc.

T-959   **LP:** GOTH GRC-4775-B
      Batten, Barton, Durstine and Osborne Blues-voc Helen Ward (**LP:** JAZ 27)
      Embraceable You-voc Helen Ward (**LP:** JAZ 27)
      Blues

In the latter part of the year Benny did some more work for charity, this time in aid of fund solicitation to combat tuberculosis. His remarks, interspersed with recordings from his Capitol LP, W565, are on a 12" LP, "Christmas Seal Sale 1957," mx H8-MR-7877-1D.

"THE BIG RECORD (THE PATTI PAGE SHOW)"   December 4, 1957,
  CBS Television Network   New York

Benny Goodman, clt; Hank Jones, p; Bobby Donaldson, d.

Medley: Somebody Loves Me - TRIO
    Body And Soul - TRIO
    Stompin' At The Savoy - TRIO
    Sweet Georgia Brown - TRIO

Jones, Donaldson join Vic Schoen and his studio orchestra:

Gotta Be This Or That-voc Patti Page, Benny Goodman

St. Louis Blues - TRIO
Basin Street Blues-voc Patti Page - TRIO
China Boy - tap dancing, Will Mastin, Sr. - TRIO (one chorus)

The Birth Of The Blues-voc & tap dancing, Sammy Davis, Jr. - TRIO plus Vic Schoen Orchestra

"LOOK HERE"   December 15, 1957, New York
NBC Television Network

Benny Goodman, clt; Hank Jones, p; Arvell Shaw, b; Roy Burnes, d.

Rose Room
(Inside And Outside The Waldorf - Jones, Shaw, Burnes - NO BG
Oh, Lady Be Good!

(Benny is also interviewed at length by the program's host, Martin Agronsky.)

On December 27 the results of Down Beat magazine's 21st annual poll were announced; over the years, Benny had won more individual and group popularity contests than any other musician. Thereupon he was elected to Down Beat's "Hall Of Fame" at a ceremony at the Berklee School Of Music in Boston, joining previous enrollees Louis Armstrong, Duke Ellington, Stan Kenton, Glenn Miller and Charlie Parker.

"The Benny Goodman Orchestra," still led by Urbie Green and sans Benny, broadcast from Chicago's Aragon Ballroom on New Year's Eve. An extant air check includes "Auld Lang Syne," "Don't Be That Way," "You Turned The Tables On Me" and "One O'Clock Jump."

Jimmy Dorsey, Benny's ex-roommate and competitor for studio dates in the late '20's and '30's had died of cancer June 12, 1957. The American Cancer Society's 1958 Cancer Crusade marked his passing with an ET labelled, "A Tribute To Jimmy Dorsey." It offered reminiscences by Benny, Jackie Gleason, Gene Krupa, Connie Boswell and Helen O'Connell.

January 1958 was the 20th anniversary of Benny's first Carnegie Hall concert. To commemorate it, WNEW disc jockey William B. Williams broadcast a five-minute interview with Benny. There would be a more elaborate commemoration 10 years later.

In February Benny contracted for an hour-long television special for the Texaco Company. Part of his agreement called for some spot commercials for Texaco, including one tune for an advertising EP. For this purpose, Benny assembled an all-star band in Columbia's transcription studios. Two tunes were cut; both were released originally on a Columbia 45, which has become a fairly scarce item:

BENNY GOODMAN AND HIS ORCHESTRA   **February 25, 1958, New York**

Benny Goodman, clt; Doc Severinson, Bernie Glow, Buck Clayton, tpt; Chauncey Welsch, Eddie Bert, Bill Byers, tbn; Hymie Schertzer, Walt Levinsky, as; Al Klink, Boomie Richman, ts; Sol Schlinger, bar; Hank Jones, p; Tony Mottola, g; George Duvivier, b; Roy Burnes, d.

CO 60487	**45:** CO 4-41148. **LP:** SWE 1001
	Back In Your Own Backyard (arr FH)
CO 60488	**45:** CO 4-41148. **EP:** CO "Texaco" ZTEP 27372. **LP:** CO "Texaco" LP
	Swing Into Spring (arr Ralph Burns)

To promote his Texaco special, Benny appeared on two television "talk" shows. A 15-minute interview on the "Hy Gardner Calling" program was televised April 2 via the Dumont Television Network. A brief chat with Jack Paar on NBC's "Tonight Show" was on the air April 7. The day before, the Philadelphia Inquirer featured an article titled, "Dr. Goodman Prescribes More Jazz." On April 9, Benny swung into Spring:

"SWING INTO SPRING"   April 9, 1958, New York
NBC Television Network

Benny Goodman, clt; Harry James, Billy Butterfield, Buck Clayton, tpt; Lou McGarity, Urbie Green, Eddie Bert, tbn; Hymie Schertzer, Walt Levinsky, as; Zoot Sims, Al Klink, ts; Sol Schlinger, bar; Hank Jones, p; Kenny Burrell, g; George Duvivier, b; Roy Burnes, d. Ella Fitzgerald, Jo Stafford, chorus, Ray Eberle, the McGuire Sisters, voc. Ralph Burns (RB), arr. Dave Garroway, commentator. Orchestra is augmented with strings for some selections.

QUINTET: Goodman, Red Norvo, vib; Teddy Wilson, p; Arvell Shaw, b; Burnes.
SEXTET: Quintet plus Harry James.

Let's Dance (theme)
("Swing Into Spring" medley - augmented Goodman orchestra, but NO BG:
  (It's Delovely-voc Ella Fitzgerald
  (Ciri Biri Bin - feat. Harry James
  (?? Sugar In The Morning ??-voc, the McGuire Sisters
  (It's Almost Like Being In Love-voc Jo Stafford

Ridin' High-voc Ella Fitzgerald (arr (George Williams) (LP: GOJ 1005)
Sometimes I'm Happy
Don't Be That Way
Rachel's Dream - QUINTET (LP: GOJ 1005)

("Big Band" medley - Goodman orchestra, but NO BG (LP: GOJ 1010)
  (Careless - segue to Moonlight Serenade - segue to Blue Champagne-voc Ray Eberle
  (I'm Getting Sentimental Over You - segue to Let's Get Away From It All-voc Jo Stafford, chorus

King Porter Stomp (LP: GOJ 1010)

Medley: I Gotta Right To Sing The Blues-voc Ella Fitzgerald
    Limehouse Blues
    How Come You Do Me Like You Do?-voc Jo Stafford
    Poor Butterfly - SEXTET
    Hard-Hearted Hannah-voc Ella Fitzgerald
    I Got It Bad (And That Ain't Good)-voc Jo Stafford
    St. Louis Blues-voc Ella Fitzgerald & Jo Stafford

(Medley on LP, GOJ 1010.)

Spring Rhapsody - augmented Goodman orchestra, conducted by Ralph Burns (arr RB)
(Blue Skies-voc, the McGuire Sisters - Goodman orchestra, but NO BG
(I'd Rather Lead A Band-voc, the McGuire Sisters - Goodman orchestra, but NO BG
Gotta Be This Or That-voc Benny Goodman, Jo Stafford, Ella Fitzgerald, the McGuire Sisters, chorus - QUINTET plus orchestra (LP: GOJ 1010)
Good-Bye (theme) (LP: GOJ 1010)
"Swing Into Spring" - to close

(The television program is also on LP, SH 2057.)

Cunningham and Walsh, then Texaco's advertising agency, transcribed the telecast onto a two-sided 12" LP, distributed very few copies of it to top Texaco, NBC and agency executives, a few of the performers and Benny's staff. Needless to say, it is rare and a desirable collectors' item. Its contents are listed below sans the detail shown for the telecast; but it should be understood that the included selections are identical.

SWING INTO SPRING   **April 9, 1958, New York**

Personnel as for "Swing Into Spring" telecast.

C&W 1683A	**LP:** C&W 1683A (monaural)
	Let's Dance (theme)
	Medley: It's Delovely-voc Ella Fitzgerald
	Ciri Biri Bin
	?Sugar In The Morning?-voc the McGuire Sisters
	It's Almost Like Being In Love-voc Jo Stafford
	Ridin' High-voc Ella Fitzgerald
	Sometimes I'm Happy
	Don't Be That Way
	Rachel's Dream - QUINTET
	Medley: Careless
	Moonlight Serenade
	Blue Champagne-voc Ray Eberle
	I'm Getting Sentimental Over You
	Let's Get Away From It All-voc Jo Stafford, chorus
	King Porter Stomp

C&W 1683B   **LP:** C&W 1683B

    Medley: I Gotta Right To Sing The Blues-voc Ella
        Fitzgerald
        Limehouse Blues
        How Come You Do Me Like You Do?-voc Jo
        Stafford
        Poor Butterfly
        Hard-Hearted Hannah-voc Ella Fitzgerald
        I Got It Bad-voc Jo Stafford
        St. Louis Blues-voc Ella Fitzgerald & Jo Stafford
    Spring Rhapsody
    Blue Skies-voc, the McGuire Sisters
    Gotta Be This Or That-voc Benny Goodman, Jo Stafford,
      Ella Fitzgerald, the McGuire Sisters, chorus
    Good-Bye (theme)
    Swing Into Spring

Benny taped some voice tracks for the Federal Civil Defense Administration in April, spun some of his commercial recordings, chatted with announcer Jay Jackson. The whole is on a "Stars For Defense" ET, Program No. 91.

The author was present April 15 when Benny rehearsed a new big band. (He was impressed with the band, and equally with the suitcase-sized tape recorders Westinghouse engineers had on hand. Benny marveled at the quality of the playback, as did the author; try as he might, he could not get copies.) Another venture for the U.S. State Department was in prospect: an extensive tour of Europe, finishing in the U.S. exhibit at the Brussels World's Fair. The itinerary included performances in Stockholm, Copenhagen, Oslo, Hamburg, Berlin, Frankfurt, Zurich, Amsterdam, Blokker, Cologne, Munich, Vienna, Karlsruhe, Essen, Dusseldorf, Hanover . . . and finally, Brussels.

On its way overseas, the Goodman Trio was taped by an unknown television network at Idlewild (later, JFK International) Airport:

TV NEWS - Unknown network   *early May 1958, New York*

Benny Goodman, clt; Roland Hanna, p; Roy Burnes, d.

. . . riffs

A May 9, 1958 air check by the "BG All Stars," circulating among collectors via generations-removed tape, is erroneously credited by a few to Benny Goodman. Not so; clarinetist is Heinie Beau.

There are a number of Goodman concert performances extant from the European tour, most of them from Brussels, but the first is from Berlin. Portions of the concert were broadcast at least twice by the Armed Forces Network (AFN), and latterly additional selections have been released on bootleg LP's. More may be in the offing; and thus it seems prudent to list the concert in full, indicating by means of symbols the two certain AFN broadcasts, current releases, and unissued selections as of this writing:

DEUTSCHLAND HALLE CONCERT   *May 10, 1958, Berlin*

Benny Goodman, clt; Taft Jordan, John Frosk, Emmet (E.V.) Perry, Billy Hodges, tpt; Rex Peer, Vernon Brown, Willie Dennis, tbn; Ernie Mauro, Al Block, as; Zoot Sims, Seldon Powell, ts; Gene Allen, bar; Roland Hanna, p; Billy Bauer, g; Arvell Shaw, b; Roy Burnes, d. Ethel Ennis, Jimmy Rushing, voc.

Arrangers: Gil Evans (GE), Sid Feller (SF), Thomas Goodman (TG), Bobby Gutesha (BoG), Fred Norman (FN), George Williams (GW), possibly Johnny Thompson (JT).

TRIO: Benny Goodman, clt; Roland Hanna, p; Roy Burnes, d.
QUARTET: TRIO plus Arvell Shaw, b.
QUINTET: QUARTET plus Billy Bauer, g.
OCTET: QUINTET plus John Frosk (alternately, Taft Jordan), tpt; Zoot Sims, ts; Gene Allen, bar.
NONET: OCTET plus Willie Dennis (alternately, Rex Peer), tbn.

* = broadcast by AFN on November 11, 1958
 # = broadcast by AFN on an unknown date
+ = not broadcast, but later issued on LP
0 = not broadcast, not on LP

* Let's Dance (theme)
* Bugle Call Rag (arr GW)
** Don't Be That Way (**LP:** SWH 7)*
* St. Louis Blues

* One O'Clock Jump (arr GW)
0 This is My Lucky Day-voc Ethel Ennis (arr GE)
0 Medley: I Gotta Right To Sing The Blues-voc Ethel Ennis
*   I Hadn't Anyone Till You-voc Ethel Ennis*
*   I've Got You Under My Skin (arr BoG)-voc Ethel Ennis*
0 The Song Is Ended-voc Ethel Ennis (arr TG-FN)
0 King Porter Stomp
* Memories Of You—TRIO
* If I Had You—TRIO
* The World Is Waiting For The Sunrise—QUARTET
(Intermission)

** Roll 'Em (**LP:** SWH 7)*
 # Baby (Bye, Bye Baby)-voc Jimmy Rushing (poss arr JT)
*# Mr. Five By Five-voc Jimmy Rushing (poss arr JT) (**LP:** SWH 7)*
0 I'm Coming, Virginia-voc Jimmy Rushing (poss arr FH)
0 Jimmy's Blues-voc Jimmy Rushing
0 A Fine Romance-voc Ethel Ennis & Jimmy Rushing (arr SF)
0 Harvard Blues-voc Jimmy Rushing
0 . . . unindentified title—OCTET
*+ Flying Home—NONET (arr GW) (**LP:** SWH 7)*
* Sing, Sing, Sing
* . . . reprise, Roll 'Em (AFN November 11 broadcast)

Almost a year and a half after the event, the American Broadcasting Company televised brief portions of two concerts given in Holland. One was May 14 in the Concertgebow, Amsterdam; the second the day following in Blokker. The program was televised in the United States October 3, 1959.

"JOHN GUNTHER'S HIGH ROAD"   *dates, locales below*
  ABC Television Network

Televised October 3, 1959. Personnels as May 10.

One O'Clock Jump (n/c)   *May 14, 1958, Amsterdam*
Let's Dance (theme)
A Fine Romance-voc Ethel Ennis & Jimmy Rushing (n/c)

One O'Clock Jump   *May 15, 1958, Blokker*
Memories Of You
Sing, Sing, Sing (n/c)

On a date unknown to the author, Bremen Radio broadcast an interview given by Benny to Dr. Ingolf Wachler; a tape of it is extant.

The engagement at the American Pavilion of the Brussels World's Fair began Sunday, May 25, ended Saturday, May 31. (Benny celebrated his 49th birthday May 30.) It was underwritten by the Westinghouse Broadcasting Company, then operators of a network of radio and television stations in the United States, as a public service for the U.S. State Department. Westinghouse engineers recorded the Brussels concerts extensively, as we shall see.

A new European television network, Eurovision, was the first on the air with a telecast of the Brussels concerts. On August 5 it inaugurated simultaneous service to Belgium, England, France and Italy with a program likely, but not certainly, composed of performances from more than one concert. Note that the reed section is augmented by the addition of Hans Koller, a European tenor saxophonist, who joined the band May 27, remained to the end of the engagement:

BRUSSELS EUROVISION TELECAST   *May 25–31, 1958*
  Eurovision Television Network   *Brussels*

Televised August 5. Personnels as May 10, plus probably HANS KOLLER, ts, in the orchestra.

Let's Dance (theme)
Bugle Call Rag
St. Louis Blues
This Is My Lucky Day-voc Ethel Ennis
The Song Is Ended-voc Ethel Ennis
One O'Clock Jump
Mr. Five By Five-voc Jimmy Rushing
I'm Coming, Virginia-voc Jimmy Rushing
A Fine Romance-voc Ethel Ennis & Jimmy Rushing
Harvard Blues-voc Jimmy Rushing

(Jimmy Rushing can be heard to announce, "Chicago," after "Harvard Blues," but that performance is not on the author's audio tape of the telecast.)

According to its announcer, NBC's telecast of concert performances from Brussels begins with selections from the first appearance on opening day, ends with two tunes from Benny's final appearance, this time at the Grand Place, not the American Pavilion. (There is some confusion here—the announcer also claims that the final day was Benny's birthday. Not so; his birthday is May 30, the engagement ended May 31.) Note that the last tune, ''Brussels Blues,'' is the track that appears on Time-Life's album, ''The Swing Era—Benny Goodman Into The '70s, The King In Person''; its source has eluded identification by collectors:

BRUSSELS NBC TELECAST   May 25–31, 1958
   NBC Television Network   Brussels

Televised December 7, 1958. Personnels as May 25-31 Eurovision telecast.

Let's Dance (theme)
One O'Clock Jump
Goin' To Chicago-voc Jimmy Rushing
Poor Butterfly—QUARTET
Stealin' Apples
The World Is Waiting For The Sunrise—QUARTET (n/c)

Benny Goodman, clt, and the Belgian National Symphony Orchestra
Concerto For Clarinet And Orchestra In A, K.622 (Mozart) (n/c)

Sing, Sing, Sing
I Gotta Right To Sing The Blues-voc Ethel Ennis
Roll 'Em
Bugle Call Rag
Let's Dance (theme)

STL-2-354-B2   **LP:** TL STA354 (Side 2, Track 5)
           Brussels Blues-voc Jimmy Rushing

Two European radio broadcasts, previously undocumented, are next. The first, transcribed by Radio France (Radio-diffusion Francaise), was broadcast on a date unknown to the author:

BRUSSELS FRENCH RADIO BROADCAST   May 25–31, 1958
   Radio France Network   Brussels

Broadcast date unknown. Personnels as May 25-31 Eurovision telecast.

Who Cares?—NONET (w/Frosk, Dennis) (arr BoG)
When You're Smiling (arr GW)
Sent For You Yesterday And Here You Come Today-voc Jimmy Rushing
Balkan Mixed Grill (arr BoG)
'Deed I Do-voc Ethel Ennis (arr BoG)
There's No Fool Like An Old Fool-voc Ethel Ennis
One O'Clock Jump
Soon—NONET (w/Frosk, Dennis) (arr BoG)
Goin' To Chicago-voc Jimmy Rushing
I'm Coming, Virginia-voc Jimmy Rushing
A Fine Romance-voc Ethel Ennis & Jimmy Rushing
Sing, Sing, Sing—to fade

BRUSSELS AFN RADIO BROADCAST   May 25–31, 1958
   AFN, Germany   Brussels

Broadcast January 1, 1959. Personnels as May 25-31 Eurovision telecast.

Let's Dance (theme)
Bugle Call Rag
St. Louis Blues
One O'Clock Jump
When You're Smiling
This Is My Lucky Day-voc Ethel Ennis
Medley: I Hadn't Anyone Till You-voc Ethel Ennis
        I've Got You Under My Skin-voc Ethel Ennis
There's No Fool Like An Old Fool-voc Ethel Ennis
'Deed I Do-voc Ethel Ennis
Balkan Mixed Grill
Mr. Five By Five-voc Jimmy Rushing
I'm Coming, Virginia-voc Jimmy Rushing
Harvard Blues-voc Jimmy Rushing
On The Sunny Side Of The Street-voc Jimmy Rushing—QUARTET plus
   orchestra in code

(This broadcast concluded with the recording, ''Back In Your Own Backyard.'' CO 4-41148.)

Westinghouse's technicians kept their tape recorders seemingly in continual use during the Brussels engagement. The resultant tapes served a

number of purposes: They were used for a series of radio broadcasts via Westinghouse stations in the United States. They were the basis of a two-12″ LP Columbia album, ''Benny In Brussels.'' They constituted a 12″ promotional LP, advertising Westinghouse products, an album titled, ''Benny Goodman Plays World Favorites In High-Fidelity.'' And Westinghouse also used its tapes to produce a souvenir album for distribution to executives of its radio and television network; a five-12″ LP set titled the same as the Columbia release, ''Benny In Brussels.''

The souvenir LP's are red vinyl, bear labels printed in purple type on a white background that list tunes and vocalists where appropriate. They are packaged in a stock album onto which has been pasted a printed cover, in pink with red printing. The cover shows a well-known caricature of Benny and has the legend, ''W B C'' and ''BENNY IN BRUSSELS.''

To distinguish among the several LP sets, the Westinghouse five-LP souvenir album is identified as, ''WBIB''; the Westinghouse promotional single-LP is shown as, ''WWF.'' The commercially-released Columbia album bears its title, ''Benny In Brussels,'' as on CO LPs CL 1247, CL 1248 et al. (In that regard, it should be noted that there may be duplications of performances among the telecasts, broadcasts and LP releases that are not shown herein. Effort has been made to so cross-reference the material, but the poor audio quality of some of the broadcasts, particularly the domestic Westinghouse air checks, makes it difficult to do so.)

Here, then the Westinghouse souvenir album, among the rarest of Goodman collectors' items; the author knows of only three sets in the hands of collectors. When the author apprised Benny of its existence, he was startled; he had never before been informed that such an album had been pressed and distributed.

WESTINGHOUSE—BENNY IN BRUSSELS (WBIB)   **May 25-31, 1958**
                                                            Brussels

Personnels as May 25-31 Eurovision telecast. Add P. LEEMANS (PL), arr.

PO 1-5217-1   **LP:** WBIB 1—Side I
             Let's Dance (theme)
             Bugle Corps. Rag (arr GW) (also **LP**, WWF et al)
             Don't Be That Way (also on **LP**, CO CL1247 et al)
             Stompin' At The Savoy
             Honeysuckle Rose—QUARTET
             Mean To Me—OCTET (also on **LP**, WWF)
             There Will Never Be Another You—QUARTET plus
               sax

(The title, ''Don't Be That Way,'' is not listed on the label. The transfer here is the most complete—see discussion preceding CO listings. And note that Jimmy Mundy's arrangement is altered, possibly by George Williams. ''Bugle Corps. Rag'' is really ''Bugle Call Rag.'')

PO 1-5217-2   **LP:** WBIB 1—Side II
             Roll 'Em
             Baby (Bye, Bye, Baby)-voc Jimmy Rushing
             I'm Comin', Virginia-voc Jimmy Rushing (poss. arr FH)
             Harvard Blues-voc Jimmy Rushing
             Goin To Chicago-voc Jimmy Rushing

PO 1-5217-3   **LP:** WBIB 2—Side III
             One O'Clock Jump (arr GW)
             Poor Butterfly—QUARTET (also on **LP**, WWF)
             Stealing Apples (also on **LP**, CO CL1248 et al)
             If I Had You—QUARTET

PO 1-5217-4   **LP:** WBIB 2—Side IV
             Soon—NONET (w/Frosk, Peer) (arr BoG)
             Who Cares?—NONET (w/Frosk, Peer) (arr BoG)
             St. Louis Blues
             When You're Smiling (arr GW)
             Sent For You Yesterday-voc Jimmy Rushing
             Pennies From Heaven-voc Jimmy Rushing—OCTET (arr
               BoG)

PO 1-5217-5   **LP:** WBIB 3—Side V

Mr. 5 x 5 (sic)-voc Jimmy Rushing (poss. arr JT)

Let's Just Be Friends (actually, "Can't We Be Friends?")—QUARTET

Hallelujah—QUINTET (also on **LP**, CO CL1247 et al)

Avalon—QUARTET (also on **LP**, WWF)

(All The Things You Are—Sims w/rhythm—No BG

PO 1-5217-6   **LP:** WBIB 3 - Side VI

What A Diff'rence A Day Made - QUARTET plus alto sax (arr BoG)

(The) Lady Is A Tramp - QUARTET

Memories Of You - QUARTET)

Medley: The Man I Love   )

       (Oh,) Lady Be Good!) - QUARTET

       Somebody Loves Me)

       I Got Rhythm   )

There's No Fool Like An Old Fool - voc Ethel Ennis

PO 1-5217-7   **LP:** WBIB 4—Side VII

This Is My Lucky Day-voc Ethel Ennis (arr GE)

Medley: I've Got A Right To Sing The Blues-voc Ethel Ennis

       I Hadn't Anyone Till You-voc Ethel Ennis

       I've Got You Under My Skin (arr (BoG)-voc Ethel Ennis

How Long Has This Been Going On?-voc Ethel Ennis

Paratrooper's March (as "March of The Belgian Paratroops" on CO CL1248 et al) (arr PL)

Flying Home—NONET (alto sax replaces trumpet) (arr GW)

PO 1-5217-8   **LP:** WBIB 4—Side VIII

(A) String Of Pearls

More Than You Know—QUINTET (also on **LP**, CO CL 1247 et al)

Jubilee (arr GW) (also on **LP**, CO CL1247 et al)

Balkan Mixed Grill (arr BoG)

The World Is Waiting For The Sunrise—QUARTET

A Fine Romance-voc Jimmy Rushing & Ethel Ennis (arr SF)

PO 1-5217-9   **LP:** WBIB 5—Side IX

(On The) Sunny Side Of The Street-voc Jimmy Rushing—QUARTET

I'm Confessin'-voc Jimmy Rushing—QUARTET

Brussels Blues-voc Jimmy Rushing—QUINTET (also on **LP**, CO CL1247 et al)

The Song Is Ended-voc Ethel Ennis (arr TG-FN)

Sometimes I'm Happy

Sing, Sing, Sing

Good-Bye (theme)

A few notes on the Westinghouse-Benny In Brussels album, preceding: The second side of WBIB 5—what would be Side X—is blank. For obvious reasons, minor changes have been made in the titles that appear on the WBIB labels. Composition of the small groups was fluid—the listener may hear different personnel or instrumentation than are shown herein. Cross-references are limited to WWF and CO releases; duplications occurring in the Westinghouse radio broadcasts are shown there. Finally, "Brussels Blues" is in main a rendition by Jimmy Rushing and the Quintet, but other members of the band join in for the last few choruses.

Columbia's releases are next, and they, too, require some explanations: Columbia's files insist that all of the tunes it issued were recorded May 25, Benny's first day at the Fair. (If so, then delete Hans Koller, ts. from the personnel.) On the other hand, fragmentary documentation in Mr. Goodman's office indicates the Columbia releases are from various dates. Because so many of the tunes were played more than once, it has not been possible to pin down individual cuts to specific dates.

For the first time we encounter "alternate takes" in monaural LP's versus stereo LP's. One is truly different: the monaural "Let's Dance" is from a different concert than is the stereo "Let's Dance." There is even a "third take" of "Let's Dance," in a sense—the Philips stereo LP excises the spoken introduction that is on its Columbia counterpart.

The other "alternates" are matters of editing. One has to do with "Don't Be That Way." The WBIB track has five drum breaks in its coda; the Columbia monaural LP has three; and the Columbia stereo LP has but two—but they are all one and the same performance. Similarly, the Columbia stereo LP track of "Brussels Blues" is complete, whereas the Columbia monaural LP omits a portion of Jimmy Rushing's vocal, and a few bars of Goodman's final clarinet passage.

To eliminate needless redundancy and to simplify listing the 22 possible cuts stemming from the original Columbia releases and subsidiary issues, the tunes are numbered consecutively, as they appear on the Columbia LP's. Numbered tracks are then credited to the releases, following:

MONAURAL LP's:

CO CL1247, CO CL1265 (set C2L16), PHIL BBL7299, Phil Cont BO 7391L: 1, 4, 6, 7, 9-13, incl.

CO CL1248, CO CL1266 (set C2L16), PHIL BBL7300, PhilCont BO7392L: 14-22, incl.

PhilCont B07397L: 1, 4, 11, 12, 15, 17, 20. PhilCont B07519L: 6, 10, 11, 15

WBIB: 4 (5 drum breaks), 6, 8 (complete), 10, 12, 14, 20. WWF: 21.

HOM 1379, EUR 1031: 2, 4, 14, 18, 21, 22. NARAS Chevrolet: 4

STEREO LP's:

CO CS8075: 2, 5, 6, 7, 8, 10-22, incl. PHIL SBBL536: 3, 5, 8, 11, 12, 15, 17, 20, 22, TL STA354: 2, 14. CO P6-14954: 14. CO 21064: 17.

45: CoJap LL452C—16

EP's: PHIL BBE12358, PhilCont 429600BE—4, 10, 11, 15

ET's: 1959 Easter Seal—6, 7, 16   1959 March Of Dimes—7

1961 Christmas Seal—4, 22

Air Force "Manhattan Melodies" 189, "Army Bandstand" 23—21 (both ET's, n/c)

Note that the Columbia monaural LP matrices are shown as primaries, the stereo LP matrices in parentheses.

COLUMBIA—BENNY IN BRUSSELS   May 25-31, 1958, Brussels

Personnels as May 25-31 Eurovision telecast (with and without Hans Koller, ts). Add DAVID BEE (DB), arr.

XLP 44070	**LP:** CO and related monaural LP releases
	1 **Let's Dance**—with spoken intro (theme)
(XSM 44509)	**StLp:** CO CS8075 and related LP's
	2 **Let's Dance**—with spoken intro (theme)
- 0 -	**StLp:** PHIL SBBL536 (spoken intro excised)
	3 **Let's Dance** (theme)
XLP 44070	**LP:** CO and related "three drum break" releases (WBIB has 5)
	4 **Don't Be That Way**
(XSM 44509)	**StLP:** CO and related "two drum break" releases
	5 **Don't Be That Way**
XLP 44070	**LP, StLP:** CO and related LP's, EP's, ET's
(XSM 44509)	6 **Hallelujah**—QUINTET
	7 **Obsession** (arr DB)
(XSM 44509)	**StLP:** CO CS8075, PHIL SBBL536 (complete version, as on WBIB LP)
	8 **Brussels Blues**-voc Jimmy Rushing—QUINTET (orchestra in coda)
XLP 44070	**LP:** CO and related monaural LP's (excised version)
	9 **Brussels Blues**-voc Jimmy Rushing—QUINTET (orchestra in coda)
XLP 44071	**All** relevant issues
(XSM 44510)	10 **More Than You Know**—QUINTET
	11 **The World Is Waiting For The Sunrise**—QUINTET
	12 **Jubilee**
	13 **Roll 'Em**

May 25–31, 1958, continued

May 25–31, 1958, continued

XLP 44194	**All** relevant issues	
(XSM 44511)	14	**Stealin' Apples**
	15	**Memories Of You**—QUINTET
	16	**Balkan Mixed Grill**
	17	**Gershwin Medley:**
		The Man I Love-QUINTET
		Oh, Lady Be Good(!)-QUINTET
		Somebody Loves Me-QUINTET
		I Got Rhythm-QUINTET
XLP 44195	**All** relevant issues	
(XSM 44512)	18	**St Louis Blues**
	19	**Mr. Five By Five**-voc Jimmy Rushing
	20	**March Of The Belgian Paratroops**
	21	**One O'Clock Jump**
	22	**Good-Bye** (theme)

One of the better promotional releases ever to come to the author's attention is Westinghouse's, ''Benny Goodman Plays World Favorites In High-Fidelity.'' Its initial recording, its transfer and pressing are all excellent, and its included tracks display the musicians in good form. Another plus is that all but two of the performances can be pinpointed to exact dates; these follow the titles:

BENNY GOODMAN PLAYS WORLD   **May 25-31, 1958**
FAVORITES IN HIGH-FIDELTY   **Brussels**

Personnels as May 25-31 Eurovision telecasts.

XTV 27713   **LP:** WWF—Side 1
        One O'Clock Jump (also on **LP**, CO CL1248 et al)
        Balkan Mixed Grill (May 27) (also on **ET**, ''Army
          Bandstand'' 23 (n/c), Air Force ''Manhattan Melodies''
          189 (n/c)
        Avalon—QUARTET (May 28) (also on **LP**, WBIB)
        Poor Butterfly - QUARTET (May 28) also on **LP**, WBIB)
        You're Driving Me Crazy—QUARTET (May 26) (also on
          ET, ''Army Bandstand'' 23 (n/c), Air Force
          ''Manhattan Melodies'' 189 (n/c)

XTV 27714   **LP:** WWF—Side 2
        Bugle Call Rag (May 25) (also on **LP**, WBIB et al)
        Mean To Me—OCTET (May 26) (also on **LP**, WBIB)
        King Porter Stomp (May 28) (also on **LP**, HOM 1379,
          EUR 1031)
        Sing, Sing, Sing (also on **LP**, HOM 1379, EUR 1031;
          ET, Air Force ''Manhattan Melodies'' 189 (n/c)

(The WWF LP is also bootlegged on **LP:** MU 30JA5194, EXPLOSIVE(Fr) 528.008. It seems ironic that the original Westinghouse LP sold for $1.00, and the inferior copies for so much more.)

While Benny is still physically at the American Pavilion, let's pick up a brief bit of film that Ed Sullivan ''shewed'' on his telecast of June 15, 1958:

''THE ED SULLIVAN SHOW''   *May 30, 1958, Brussels*
  CBS Television Network

Televised June 15. Benny Goodman and actor William Holden, clts, and the orchestra.

Colonel Bogey March

Now Benny is on his way home, and when he gets there he'll be able to hear tapes of his concerts broadcast on Westinghouse radio stations throughout the United States. The author can list several; unfortunately, his copies are of such poor audio quality that they prevent accurate comparison with all of the Brussels material that has gone before. Not only would cross-referencing have been possible were the tapes in better condition, but precise identifications might be made—dimly, Benny is heard to announce the personnels of some of the small group performances.

Before leaving this band, it is appropriate to say in retrospect, ''It was pretty good.'' It had been together less than two months, but in that time it had worked intensively. Many of the sidemen were Goodman alumni, thoroughly familiar with the old arrangements; and they executed the new ones creditably. A plus factor was Roy—sometimes, Leroy—Burnes. It has been

stressed earlier that a Goodman orchestra always performed better when a superior drummer was behind it, and that holds true for this band. And finally, Benny seemed in good spirits throughout the tour, played well himself, seemed to enjoy Jimmy Rushing's vocals hugely and responded to them. In part, the author takes credit for that: When the personnel for the tour were being assembled, Benny remarked that he had in mind asking Joe Williams along, and what did I think? Yes, Joe Williams is great, I admire his work; but how about Jimmy Rushing, European audiences might be more familiar with him? Benny mulled that over, decided it had merit, and Jimmy Rushing it was. Sorry, Joe.

And so, the Westinghouse radio broadcasts, in the order in which they were aired. And if good tapes are still in existence, effort should be made to acquire them:

BRUSSELS REBROADCAST   *May 25-31, 1958*
  WESTINGHOUSE Radio Network   *Brussels*

Broadcast June 2. Personnels as Eurovision telecast, May 25-31.

Let's Dance (theme)
Bugle Call Rag
There's No Fool Like An Old Fool-voc Ethel Ennis
Stealin' Apples
*You're Driving Me Crazy—QUARTET (also on **LP**, WWF)*
Sing, Sing, Sing—Part 2

BRUSSELS REBROADCAST   *May 25-31, 1958*
  WESTINGHOUSE Radio Network   *Brussels*

Broadcast June 3. Personnels as Eurovision telecast, May 25-31.

Let's Dance (theme)
When You're Smiling
Sent For You Yesterday And Here You Come Today-voc Jimmy Rushing
Pennies From Heaven-voc Jimmy Rushing
Goin' To Chicago-voc Jimmy Rushing
*Soon—OCTET (also on **LP**, WBIB)*
Who Cares?—OCTET (poss. same as WBIB)
St. Louis Blues (poss. same as WBIB)
This Is My Lucky Day-voc Ethel Ennis
'Deed I Do-voc Ethel Ennis
I Hadn't Anyone Till You-voc Ethel Ennis
I've Got You Under My Skin-voc Ethel Ennis
Mr. Five By Five-voc Jimmy Rushing
I'm Coming, Virginia-voc Jimmy Rushing
One O'Clock Jump (n/c)
*Let's Dance (theme) (also on **LP**, CO CL 1247 et al)*

BRUSSELS REBROADCAST   *May 25-31, 1958*
  WESTINGHOUSE Radio Network   *Brussels*

Broadcast June 4. Personnels as Eurovision telecast, May 25-31.

Let's Dance (theme)
*Bugle Call Rag (also on **LP**, WBIB, WWF)*
There's No Fool Like An Old Fool-voc Ethel Ennis
*Stealin' Apples (also on **LP**, WBIB, CO CL1248 et al)*
Roll 'Em
Baby (Bye, Bye Baby)-voc Jimmy Rushing
Harvard Blues-voc Jimmy Rushing
A Fine Romance-voc Ethel Ennis & Jimmy Rushing
Don't Blame Me—QUARTET
*Hallelujah—QUINTET (also on **LP**, WBIB, CO CL1247 et al)*
*Poor Butterfly—QUARTET (also on **LP**, WBIB, WWF)*
*Avalon—QUARTET (also on **LP**, WBIB, WWF)*
Let's Dance (closing theme)

BRUSSELS REBROADCAST   *May 25-31, 1958*
  WESTINGHOUSE Radio Network   *Brussels*

Broadcast date unknown. Personnels as Eurovision telecast, May 25-31.

*One O'Clock Jump (n/c) (also on **LP**, WWF, CO CL1248 et al)*
Mr. Five By Five-voc Jimmy Rushing (n/c)
I'm Coming, Virginia-voc Jimmy Rushing
Harvard Blues-voc Jimmy Rushing

Copies of many of Westinghouse's tapes of the May 1958 tour that culminated in Brussels are in Benny's possession. At this writing (1986) he is evaluating them for the purpose of possible release. One of the tapes, from a performance in the American Pavilion on May 28, has been audited. To write finis to the Brussels engagement, here are the details:

BRUSSELS CONCERT   *May 28, 1958, Brussels*

Personnels as Eurovision telecast, May 25-31.

Roll 'Em
Baby-voc Jimmy Rushing
Pennies From Heaven-voc Jimmy Rushing
I'm Coming, Virginia-voc Jimmy Rushing
Goin' To Chicago-voc Jimmy Rushing
Don't Blame Me-QUARTET (n/c)

Benny relaxed at home in June; rest was in order following his strenuous European tour. But its huge success prompted organizers of "The Newport (Rhode Island) Jazz Festival" to invite him to participate in the star-studded July 4 weekend bash. He agreed, hastily assembled a big band comprised of available members of his Brussels entourage and New York staff musicians, plus Martha Tilton. His contract specified that he appear Friday, July 4 at 8:30 p.m., in Freebody Park. (His performance is elsewhere dated July 5. However, an eyewitness who meticulously "logged" the complete Goodman concert confirms the July 4 date, which is shown herein.)

Benny rehearsed his reorganized orchestra July 1; just where the rehearsal took place is not known, but a tape of a portion of it is extant. It is noteworthy for Roland Hanna's work in "Oh, Lady Be Good!," where he plays an unusual chorus in the "locked hands" style popularized by Lionel Hampton's Milt Buckner:

NEWPORT JAZZ FESTIVAL REHEARSAL   *July 1, 1958*
                                    unknown location

Personnels probably as July 4, 1958, q.v.

Let's Dance (theme)
St. Louis Blues
One O'Clock Jump
Mr. Five By Five - voc Jimmy Rushing
Medley: The Man I Love   )
        Oh, Lady Be Good!   ) - QUARTET
        Somebody Loves Me)
        I Got Rhythm   )
And The Angels Sing - voc Martha Tilton - breakdown
And The Angels Sing - voc Martha Tilton (n/c)

CBS broadcast the opening half-hour of the July 4 Goodman concert. More correctly, it taped the first 30 minutes for broadcast, but its delayed presentation ended with Martha Tilton's "And The Angels Sing." Eliminated from the broadcast were the final tune, "Bugle Call Rag," and the theme, "Good-Bye." The date of the CBS broadcast is uncertain. It may well have been July 5, thus giving rise to confusion over the true date of the performance.

"THE NEWPORT JAZZ FESTIVAL"   *July 4, 1958*
   CBS Radio Network   *Newport, Rhode Island*

Possibly broadcast July 5. Benny Goodman, clt; Billy Butterfield, Bernie Glow, Doc Severinson, Taft Jordan, tpt; Eddie Bert, Vernon Brown, Frank Rehak, tbn; Skippy Colluccio, Ernie Mauro, as; Rudy Rutherford, Buddy Tate, ts; Gene Allen, bar; Roland Hanna, p; Kenny Burrell, g; Henry Grimes, b; Roy Burnes, d. Jimmy Rushing, Martha Tilton, voc.

QUARTET: Goodman, Hanna, Grimes, Burnes

Let's Dance (theme)
St. Louis Blues
One O'Clock Jump
Mr. Five By Five-voc Jimmy Rushing
Medley: The Man I Love   )
        Oh, Lady Be Good!   ) - QUARTET
        Somebody Loves Me)
        I Got Rhythm   )
And The Angels Sing - voc Martha Tilton (to signoff)

(Portions of the broadcast are also on LP, GOJ 1011.)

Columbia Records recorded the Goodman concert in its entirety, along with the performances of the other participants. Its intention was to release an LP titled, "Benny In Newport." But the playbacks pleased neither Benny

nor Columbia, and the release was cancelled—wisely so, for the band did not perform well, as contemporary reviews in the press, and the CBS broadcast, clearly attest. Columbia did, however, include two Goodman tracks in an two-LP Newport album marketed in 1983:

BENNY GOODMAN AND HIS ORCHESTRA   **July 4, 1958**
                                           Newport, Rhode Island

Personnel as preceding.

BL-38263-1C   **St LP:** CO C2-38262
                  Boogie Woogie-voc Jimmy Rushing
                  Cherokee (arr George Williams)

In addition to the selections shown for the broadcast and the CO issue, Benny also played: "Don't Be That Way," "Brussels Briefing," "Bach Goes To Town," "I'm Coming, Virginia," "Harvard Blues," "Swonderful," "Loch Lomond," "Please Be Kind," "I Let A Song Go Out Of My Heart," "Bei Mir Bist Du Schon," "A Fine Romance," "More Than You Know," "You're Driving Me Crazy," "Body And Soul," "Sing, Sing, Sing," "Macedonian Lullaby," "One O'Clock Jump" and "Good-Bye," in that order. They are listed on the assumption that Columbia has these cuts on tape, and that some of them may eventually be released.

On July 6 Benny appeared as a "mystery guest" on the "What's My Line?" television program, but no tape of his non-playing appearance is in the hands of collectors.

Benny found it increasingly advantageous to record for his own Park Recording Company. He hired engineers, leased recording facilities, and paid his sidemen directly. In this manner he had full control over the material, and he could release it to the record company of his choice for distribution.

From this point forward all of the mastering is done on tape, and the "matrix numbers" that appear on issued recordings are pressing numbers.

Note the unusual instrumentation on this session, recorded in the Metropolitan Studios, 255 E. 67th Street, New York:

BENNY GOODMAN AND HIS ORCHESTRA   **July 7, 1958, New York**

Benny Goodman, clt; Emmet (E.V.) Perry, Taft Jordan, Buck Clayton, Billy Butterfield, tpt; Vernon Brown, Eddie Bert, Harry DeVito (sometimes DiVito), tbn; Gene Allen, bar; Roland Hanna, p; Kenny Burrell, g; Henry Grimes, b; Roy Burnes, d. Martha Tilton, voc.

—0—   UNISSUED
                  Nobody's Heart-voc Martha Tilton (arr SF)
                  You Couldn't Be Cuter-voc Martha Tilton (arr SF)

Perry, Jordan, Clayton out; Butterfield sole remaining tpt.

—0—   UNISSUED
                  Oh! Gee, Oh! Joy-voc Martha Tilton (arr GW)
                  My Lover-voc Martha Tilton (arr GW) - Tape

Benny reverted to conventional instrumentation for the next studio date, this time in Capitol's New York facilities—but still under the banner of Park Recording Co., Inc.

BENNY GOODMAN AND HIS ORCHESTRA   **July 14, 1958, New York**

Benny Goodman, clt; Emmet (E.V.) Perry, Taft Jordan, Buzz King, John Frosk, tpt; Vernon Brown, Eddie Bert, Harry DeVito, tbn; Ernie Mauro, Skippy Colluccio (sometimes, Galluccio), as; Buddy Tate, Dick Hafer, ts; Gene Allen, bar; Roland Hanna, p; Chuck Wayne, g; Henry Grimes, b; Roy Burnes, d. ANDRE PREVIN (AP), arr.

PB-1958-201   **LP:** PB 1958
                  The King And Me (Brussels Briefing) (arr AP)

—0—   UNISSUED
                  Cherokee (arr GW)
                  Macedonia Lullaby (arr BoG)

The next three sessions for Park Recording Company were cut in Capitol's Hollywood studios, for Benny had gone to the West Coast for some personal appearances. He assembled a big band of Hollywood staff musicians, half of them former members from years gone by. The new arrangements of the Victor-era tunes may also have been performed at the July 4 Newport Jazz Festival, but this is not certain.

BENNY GOODMAN AND HIS ORCHESTRA September 2, 1958
Hollywood

Benny Goodman, clt; Mannie Klein, Conrad Gozzo, Irving Goodman, Don Fagerquist, tpt; Joe Howard, Murray McEachern, Milt Bernhart, tbn; Herb Geller, Bud Shank, as; Buddy Collette, Dave Pell, ts; Chuck Gentry, bar; Russ Freeman, p; Al Hendrickson, g; Leroy Vinnegar, b; Frank Capp, d. Martha Tilton, voc.

—0— UNISSUED
Bei Mir Bist Du Schon-voc Martha Tilton (arr GW)
I Let A Song Go Out Of My Heart-voc Martha Tilton (arr GW)
Loch Lomond-voc Martha Tilton (arr SF)-Tape

BENNY GOODMAN QUINTET September 3, 1958
Hollywood

Benny Goodman, clt; Andre Previn, p; Barney Kessel, g; Leroy Vinnegar, b; Frank Capp, d.

—0— UNISSUED
It's All Right With Me
Easy To Love
Who?

Note that more than one record company is involved in the authorized distribution of the sides from the next session and those that follow; and that as heretofore, "matrices" listed are those of the monaural LP for each tune.

BENNY GOODMAN QUINTET September 4, 1958, Hollywood

Personnel as September 3.

XLP 45585 **LP:** CO CL1324, PHIL BBL7318, PhilCont B07511L, NARC KM89-1006, SONY SOPZ31. **StLp:** CO CS8129, HA HS11271, PHIL SBBL539, SONY SOPZ31, CBS 63367, PIC 240. **StT:** CO L2C44
You'd Be So Nice To Come Home To

XLP 45586 Same issues, except omit NARC LP, PIC **StLp's**
Having A Ball

U 9667 **LP:** CHESS 1440, GALA SPK708, BARCLAY(Fr) 84.103, BELLAPHON(G) 4025. **StLp:** CHESS S1440, ChessH 9283047. **StT:** CADET—Bel Canto ST112. **ET:** AFR&TS P7705/7706
Everything I've Got

U 9667 Same issues, except omit BELLAPHON(G) **LP;** and add: **LP:** PB 1959, GALA SPK1003; **7"LP:** GALA FPK703, POP PARADE(E) BPC711, POP RECORD CIRCLE(H) HPK716. **EP:** JA(G) SJS743
Stereo Stomp

("GALA" and both "POP" releases are issues by English and Continental jazz clubs.)

Benny had worked for composer-orchestra leader Johnny Green back in the '30's, probably had recorded with him in 1934. Now he appears on Green's television program:

"MUSIC USA—THE JOHNNY GREEN SHOW" September 8, 1958
CBS Television Hollywood

Benny Goodman, clt; Russ Freeman, p; Barney Kessel, g; Leroy Vinnegar, b; Frank Capp, d.

Poor Butterfly
Avalon

Andre Previn, p, replaces Freeman.

It's All Right With Me (announced as "It's The Right Time")
Coquette

(All tunes except "Coquette" are on **LP**, FEST 246, RAR 30, KOS_____)

There was hopeful speculation in the music press that Benny might resume full time with a big band while on the West Coast, but nothing came of this wishful thinking, and he returned to the East and some more studio sessions for Park Recording.

The first session resulted in a very rare release, Benny's first and only attempt to distribute records on his own. As a favor to the producer of the Broadway show, "The World Of Susie Wong," he cut both a vocal and an instrumental version of "How Can You Forget," to be used as background music on stage. Benny liked the sides enough to have them pressed back-to-back on a new label, "BG." He then tried to market the 45 rpm disc through selected distributors. But sales were disappointing, and Benny quickly abandoned the record wholesaling business. Most of the pressings of his BG-label "How Can You Forget" were then destroyed, but a few were given to friends as souvenirs. A very few eventually got into the hands of collectors.

(Equally rare is the only other release on the "BG" label, another 45 featuring the Vinny Parle Orchestra. Fortunately for the collector, this release does not include Benny Goodman as a performer, but only as a producer.)

For his first Eastern recording date, Benny elected to use his own facilities in Stamford; five weeks later, he would continue in a commercial studio in Manhattan. Those present in Stamford included guitarist Carl Bogart, but he cannot be heard in the five issued sides and one alternate take available to the author. Thus the group is listed below as a Quartet, not as a Quintet, so billed on some releases.

The last tune cut this session, "I'm Beginning To See The Light," was never authorized for release. A low-fi cut of the Ellington opus first appeared on a GALA bootleg LP, later on other labels. Benny has no idea how the jazz club responsible for the GALA release obtained the material. . .

THE BENNY GOODMAN QUARTET October 7, 1958, Stamford

Benny Goodman, clt; Andre Previn, p; Red Mitchell, b; Frank Capp, d. Helen Ward, voc. (Guitarist Carl Bogart inaudible.)

- 0 - UNISSUED - Tape
45-1A-N2 **45:** BG 45-1B
How Can You Forget-voc Helen Ward

45-1-Side B **45:** BG 45-1A
How Can You Forget

U 9667 **LP:** CHESS 1440, GALA SPK1003, GALA SPK708, BELLAPHON(G) 4025, BARCLAY(Fr) 84.103. **StLp:** CHESS S1440, ChessH 9283047. **7"LP:** POP PARADE(E) BPS711, POP RECORD CIRCLE(H) HPK716, GALA FPK703. **StT:** CADET-Bel Canto ST112. **EP:** JA(G) SJS743. **ET:** AFR&TS P7705/7706
All The Things You Are

U 9667 same issues, except omit **7"LP**, GALA FPK703
It Could Happen To you

SPK1003-121 **LP:** GALA SPK1003, GALA SPK708, B1D 1011. **7"LP:** POP PARADE(E) BPS711, POP RECORD CIRCLE(H) HPK716. **EP:** JA(G) SJS743
I'm Beginning To See The Light

Probably in October, Benny taped some voice tracks for the U.S. Treasury Department's Savings Bond Division. His conversation with announcer Del Sharbutt is interspersed with some of his 1952 Columbia Sextet sides. Resultant ET is, "Guest Star," No. 555.

Benny recorded the next four sessions in Engineers' Hall, New York; the first of them produced another unique release on the GALA label:

THE BENNY GOODMAN ORCHESTRA November 15, 1958, New York

Benny Goodman, clt; John Frosk, Allen Smith, Emmet (E.V.) Perry, Benny Ventura, tpt; Rex Peer, Hale Rood, Buster Cooper, tbn; Herb Geller, Jimmy Sands (Santucci), as; Bob Wilber, Arthur Clark(e), ts; Pepper Adams, bar; Russ Freeman, p; Turk Van Lake, g; Milt Hinton, b; Shelly Manne, d. Donna Musgrove, voc.

U 9666 **LP:** CHESS 1440, BARCLAY(Fr) 84.103, BELLAPHON(G) 4025. **7"LP:** GALA FPK703. **StLp:** CHESS S1440, ChessH 9283047. **StT:** CADET-Bel Canto ST112. **ET:** AFR&TS P7705/7706
Oh Baby

U 9666 same issues, except omit **7"LP, ET**
Mission To Moscow

—0— UNISSUED
How Long Has This Been Going On?-voc Donna
  Musgrove
How Deep Is The Ocean?-voc Donna Musgrove

FPK703-11 **7"LP:** GALA FPK703
Autumn Nocturne (arr BoG)

XLP 45585 **LP:** CO CL1324, CO JJ1, PHIL BBL7318, PhilCont
  B07511L. **StLp:** CO CS8129, CO JS1, PHIL SBBL539,
  SONY SOPZ31. **StT:** CO L2C44
Happy Session Blues (arr BoG)

(Releases other than CHESS variously credit, "Benny Goodman & His
Orch./Orchestra.")

THE BENNY GOODMAN ORCHESTRA   **November 17, 1958, New York**

Personnel as November 15, except GEORGE DUVIVIER, b, replaces Hinton.

U 9666 same issues as "Mission To Moscow," November 15
Benny Rides Again

U 9666 same issues
The Earl

—0— UNISSUED
The King And Me (Brussels Briefing)

BENNY GOODMAN AND HIS ORCHESTRA   **November 18, 1958, New York**

Personnel as November 17.

XLP 45585 **LP:** CO CL1324, PHIL BBL7318, PhilCont B07511L.
  StLp: CO CS8129, PHIL SBBL539, TL STA354. **StT:**
  CO L2C44
King And Me (Brussels Briefing)

XLP 45585 same issues, except omit **StLp**, TL STA354
What A Diff'rence A Day Made (arr BoG)

XLP 45586 same issues as "What A Diff'rence A Day Made"
Batunga Train (arr BoG)

XLP 45586 **LP:** CO CL1324, CO CL2483, PHIL BBL7318, PhilCont
  B0711L, NARC KM8P-1006, CBS 52368. **StLp:** CO
  CS8129, CO CS9283, PHIL SBBL539, CO KG31547,
  Co a1b P4M5678. **StT:** CO L2C44
Clarinet A La King

XLP 45586 same issues as "King And Me," CO CL1324 et al
Macedonia Lullaby

(THE) BENNY GOODMAN (SWING) QUINTET   **November 19, 1958
New York**

Benny Goodman, clt; Russ Freeman, p; Turk Van Lake, g; George Duvivier, b;
Shelly Manne, c.

XLP 45585 **LP:** CO CL1324, PHIL BBL7318, PhilCont B07511L,
  PhilCont B07519L. **StLp:** CO CS8129, PHIL SBBL539,
  SONY SOPZ31. **StT:** CO L2C44
Indian Summer

XLP 45586 same issues, plus **LP**, NARC KM8P1006
Diga Diga Do

U 9667 **LP:** CHESS 1440, GALA SPK1003, GALA SPK708,
  BARCLAY(Fr) 84.103, BELLAPHON(G) 4025. **7"LP:**
  GALA FPK703, POP PARADE(E) BPS711, POP
  RECORD CIRCLE(H) HPK716. **StLp:**CH S1440, ChessH
  9283047. **EP:** JA(G) SJS743. **StT:** CADET-Bel Canto
  ST112. **ET:** AFR&TS P7705/7706

—0— **LP:** BID 1011
Whispering

U 9667 **LP:** CHESS 1440, GALA SPK1003, GALA SPK708,
  BARCLAY(Fr) 84.103, BELLAPHON(G) 4025. **7"LP:**
  GALA FPK703, **StLp:** CHESS S1440, ChessH 9283097.
  45: CHESS 1742. **StT:** CADET-Bel Canto St112. **ET:**
  AFRS&TS p7705/7706
You Do Something To Me

Benny taped two sets of voice tracks in New York in the winter of
1958-1959. One set—Benny's responses to questions put by local announcers, in a memo accompanying the release—is on a 1959 "March Of
Dimes" ET. It also includes his recording of "Obsession" from the Columbia Brussels album.

The second is on a 12" LP, issued to radio stations in conjunction with
his M-G-M "Treasure Chest" album. Its title may be the longest ever:
"B/G Himself Answers Your Questions About His Original Performance
Recordings, 1937-1938."

On the second and third days of the new year Benny took first an Octet,
then a Septet, into Engineers' Hall for morning and afternoon recording
sessions. At this writing, only one side has been released, this on an unauthorized LP. Mr. Goodman's files indicate that two tunes had arrangements
by different writers, but do not specify which—or if both—were used.

THE BENNY GOODMAN OCTET   **January 2, 1959, New York**

Benny Goodman, clt; Urbie Green, tbn; Zoot Sims, ts; Russ Freeman, p; Turk
Van Lake, g; Chuck Wayne, elec g; George Duvivier, b; Don Lamond, d. AL
COHN (AC), TURK VAN LAKE (TVL), arr. Donna Musgrove, voc.

- 0 - UNISSUED
The Nearness Of You-voc Donna Musgrove
Taking A Chance On Love-voc Donna Musgrove (poss.
  arr FN)
It Never Entered My Mind-voc Donna Musgrove (poss.
  arr AC or TVL)
Just One Of Those Things-voc Donna Musgrove
I Gotta Right To Sing The Blues-voc Donna Musgrove
  (poss. arr AC or TVL)
What Is This Thing Called Love?-voc Donna Musgrove

- 0 - **LP:** BID 1011
I Never Knew [Jam Session]

THE BENNY GOODMAN SEPTET   **January 3, 1959, New York**

Benny Goodman, clt; Urbie Green, tbn; Zoot Sims, ts; Russ Freeman, p;
Chuck Wayne, g; Milt Hinton, b; Don Lamond, d. Donna Musgrove, voc.

- 0 - UNISSUED
Spring Is Here-voc Donna Musgrove
Diga Diga Do (arr AC)

Comedian Garry Moore's television variety program featured a weekly
salute to a selected year in the past. Benny got in the act for 1929—30 years
late. Note his strange musical bedfellows on the first tune:

"THE GARRY MOORE SHOW"   *January 6, 1959, New York*
  NBC Television Network

Benny Goodman, clt; Rudy Vallee, as; Milt Kamen, Fr-h; Garry Moore, d.

Sweet Sue-Just You

Benny Goodman, clt, w/rhythm section from studio orchestra

*Whispering (also on **LP:** FEST 246, RAR 30, KOS — —)*

*Benny Goodman, clt; Urbie Green, tbn; Zoot Sims, ts; Russ Freeman, p; Don
Lamond, d; plus unidentified tpt, g, b, presumably from the studio orchestra*

*Diga Diga Do (also on **LP:** FEST 246, RAR 30, KOS — —)*

Benny Goodman, clt, and the studio orchestra

*Medley: (You Were Meant For Me-voc Dorothy Collins - NO BG
    Ain't Misbehavin'
    (Louise-voc Rudy Vallee - NO BG
    More Than You Know-voc Dorothy Collins
    Star Dust
    (Keep Your Sunny Side Up-voc Garry Moore - NO BG
    (Why Was I Born?-voc Dorothy Collins - NO BG
    (Happy Days Are Here Again-voc Milt Kamen - NO BG
    (My Time Is Your Time-voc Rudy Vallee - NO BG*

Possibly on the same day Benny joined Garry Moore in taping an ET for the 1959 Easter Seal Campaign. It is labeled ''Garry Moore's Easter Seal Bandstand-Transcription #3,'' offers joint introductions of selections from the Columbia Brussels album.

Benny journeyed to Springfield, Illinois on February 8 to appear as guest soloist with the Springfield Symphony. Two selections, Haydn's Symphony No. 31, and Brahms's Symphony No. 1, were recorded, under unknown auspices. A tape is in Benny's library.

Next for Benny was the second—and unfortunately, last—television special for Texaco. This program was also transcribed and pressed onto a 12" LP by Texaco's advertising agency, and similarly given to a few executives and cast members. First, the television program:

''SWING INTO SPRING''   *April 10, 1959, New York*
  CBS Television Network

Benny Goodman, clt; Buck Clayton, John Frosk, Irwin Berger, Allen Smith, tpt; Urbie Green, Hale Rood, Buster Cooper, tbn; Hymie Schertzer, Gerald Sanfino, as; Babe Clarke, Herb Geller, ts; Pepper Adams, bar; Hank Jones, p; Kenny Burrell, g; Jack Lesberg, b; Roy Burnes, d; Phil Kraus, percussion. Ella Fitzgerald, Peggy Lee, Donna Musgrove, the Hi-Lo's, chorus, voc. Ralph Burns, arr & music director. Producer, Lawrence White.

QUARTET: Benny Goodman, clt; Andre Previn, p; Jack Lesberg, b; Shelly Manne, d.
QUINTET: Quartet plus Lionel Hampton, vib.

Let's Dance (theme)
Swing Into Spring - voc chorus
Medley: 'Swonderful - voc Ella Fitzgerald)
        Things Are Swingin' - voc Peggy Lee) - QUINTET plus orchestra
        'Swonderful - voc Ella & Peggy)
Theme from von Weber Concertino, Op. 26 (Adagio, Andante)
  - BG clt & accomp
Bach Goes To Town
Swing Low, Sweet Clarinet - voc chorus
Air Mail Special - QUINTET
Why Don't You Do Right? - voc Peggy Lee
Like Young-voc chorus - incl. Previn, p (poss arr AP)
Mountain Greenery - voc Ella Fitzgerald
Ah! Men, Ah! Women - voc Benny, Ella, Peggy - Previn p accomp
I Must Have That Man - voc Ella Fitzgerald - QUARTET
Medley: Sweet Georgia Brown - voc Benny   )
        I'm Just Wild About Harry - voc Peggy   )
        Sweet Lorraine - voc Benny   ) - QUINTET
        The Gentleman Is A Dope - voc Ella   )
        When A Woman Loves A Man - voc Peggy)
        The Glory Of Love - voc Benny, Ella, Peggy)
Medley: Let's Dance (theme)
        A String of Pearls
        Goody-Goody - voc, the Hi-Lo's
        You Turned The Tables On Me - voc Donna Musgrove, The Hi-Lo's
        One O'Clock Jump
Swing Into Spring - voc Peggy, Ella, the Hi-Lo's, chorus
'Swonderful (special lyrics) - voc Peggy, Ella, the Hi-Lo's, chorus
Good-Bye (theme)
Swing Into Spring

Here is the souvenir LP. Note that the selections are numbered, but that they are in a somewhat different order than they were performed on television. (The show was ''live,'' not on tape, there are no different ''takes.'') Some of the selections are not credited on the label, and these are preceded by a bracket. Instrumental and vocal credits are not listed; they are identical to those in the air check listing.

SWING INTO SPRING   **April 10, 1959, New York**
Personnels as for the television program, preceding.

A&R 2000   **LP:** Swing Into Spring - Side 1
             (Let's Dance - theme
             1. **Good Evening** and **'S Wonderful**
             (Things Are Swingin'
             2. **Three Faces Of Spring**
                A. **Concertina For Clarinet**
                B. **Bach Goes To Town**
                C. **Swing Low Sweet Clarinet**
             3. **Ah Men, Ah Women Medley**
                A. **Ah Men, Ah Women**
                (I Must Have That Man
                B. **Sweet Georgia Brown**
                C. **Wild About Harry**
                D. **Sweet Lorraine**
                E. **The Gentleman Is A Dope**
                F. **Woman Loves A Man**
                G. **Glory Of Love**

A&R 2001   **LP:** as above, except Side 2
             1. **Air Mail Special**
             2. **Why Don't You Do Right**
             3. **Mountain Greenery**
             4. **Junior Prom Medley**
                A. **String Of Pearls**
                B. **Goody-Goody**
                C. **You Turned The Tables On Me**
                D. **One O'Clock Jump**
             5. **Swing Into Spring: ['Swonderful] Goodbye**

General Artists Corp. ''packaged'' Dakota Staton, the Ahmad Jamal Trio and Benny Goodman and his Orchestra for a three-week tour of the U.S. and Canada that began April 24 in Hershey, Pa. Some of Benny's sidemen were Taft Jordan, tpt; Rex Peer, tbn; Herb Geller, Bob Wilber and Pepper Adams, saxes; Hank Jones, p; Turk Van Lake, g; Scotty Lofaro, b; Roy Burnes, d; and Donna Musgrove, voc. Tenor saxophonist Buddy Tate played some of the dates.

A week before the tour began, Benny rehearsed his band in New York; a tape of a portion of the rehearsal is extant:

GENERAL ARTISTS' TOUR REHEARSAL   *April 17, 1959, New York*

Benny Goodman, clt, and his Orchestra, probably including Taft Jordan, tpt; Rex Peer, tbn; Herb Geller, Bob Wilber, Pepper Adams and possibly Buddy Tate, reeds; Hank Jones, p; Turk Van Lake, g; Scotty Lofaro, b; Roy Burnes, d; and others unknown.

Mission To Moscow
Bach Goes To Town (arr Ralph Burns)
Clarinet A La King - false start
Clarinet A La King - breakdown
Clarinet A La King (arr Walter Fuller)

The jazz tour was in the Montreal Forum on April 26. The next day Henry Whiston of the Canadian Broadcasting Corp. interviewed Benny in the Queen Elizabeth Hotel in Montreal; various excerpts of the interview were broadcast via CBC over time. On the 28th the ''Benny Goodman Presents America's Top Jazz Concert'' was in the Maple Leaf Gardens in Toronto, and on the 29th it performed in the Kleinhans Music Hall in Buffalo, New York. No recordings of any of these concerts are known to the author.

Upon his return to New York City Benny cut some voice tracks for the National Association For Retarded Children's 1959 campaign. They are on a 12" LP, NARC KM8P-1006, in between some of Benny's commercial recordings.

Benny visited London in late June, returned to the United States to go into Basin Street East July 13 for two weeks with Charlie Shavers, Mel Powell, Steve Jordan, Israel Crosby and Morey Feld. There are no known recordings from this engagement. On August 8 he appeared with the Berkshire String Quartet in the Guild Hall, New Caanan, Conn. There daughter Rachel made her debut, playing Debussy's ''Premiere Rhapsodie'' with Dad and David Dawson of the Berkshire group.

We find Benny next in Miami, Florida, recording on three consecutive days with Bill Harris, Flip Phillips and a rhythm section comprised of local musicians. None of these sides has been released, the tapes are in Benny's vault in Stamford. Possibly as many as half of the arrangements may have been either Harris's or Phillip's, for they do not appear anywhere in Goodman's files.

THE BENNY GOODMAN SEPTET   August 15, 1959, Miami

Benny Goodman, clt; Bill Harris, tbn; Flip Phillips, ts; Martin Harris, p; Al Simi, b; Robert S. Binnix, Leo Robinson, unknown instruments, presumably g, d.

- 0 -   UNISSUED
             I Want To Be Happy (arr AC)
             Sometimes I'm Happy (arr AC)
             Time On My Hands (arr AC)
             Tenbone - Tape

THE BENNY GOODMAN SEPTET   August 16, 1959, Miami

Personnel as August 15.

- 0 -   UNISSUED
             Sleep
             Tea For Two (arr AC)
             Yardbird Suite [Rosetta]
             Splanky
             Sweet Miss
             The Best Things In Life Are Free

THE BENNY GOODMAN SEPTET   August 17, 1959, Miami

Personnel as August 15.

- 0 -   UNISSUED
             Someone To Watch Over Me
             Broadway - Tape
             Dark Shadows - Tape
             The Deacon And The Elder

Benny spent the latter part of September rehearsing a group headed by Red Norvo, in preparation for a month's tour of Europe. It began October 3 in Munich, and covered 20 cities in 21 playing days (two dates in Paris) in Germany, Sweden, France, Switzerland and Austria.

Several of the concerts were recorded and (at least in part) were rebroadcast via radio. (None is known to have been broadcast "live.") They reveal Benny playing exceptionally well, inventive, exciting, technically flawless clarinet. The extant tapes, taken as a whole, may well represent his personal post-World War II best. They are recommended without reservation to collectors. They begin with a concert in the State Hall of Freiburg, Germany, as rebroadcast on a German radio network:

FREIBURG REBROADCAST   *October 15, 1959,*
German Radio Network   *Stadthalle, Freiburg*

Broadcast date not known. Benny Goodman, clt; Jack Sheldon, tpt; Bill Harris, tbn; Jerry Dodgion, as & fl; Flip Phillips, ts; Red Norvo, vib; Russ Freeman, p; Jimmy Wyble, g; Red Wootten, b; John Markham, d. Anita O'Day, voc. FRED KARLIN (FK), BILL STEGMEYER (BS), BOB WILBER (occasionally, "Wilbur") (BW), arr.

SEXTET: Goodman, Norvo, Freeman, Wyble, Wooten, Markham.
SEPTET: Sextet plus Sheldon

(NORVO SEXTET: Norvo, Dodgion, Freeman, Wyble, Wootten, Markham - NO BG

(NOTE that John Poole, d, replaces Markham on all Anita O'Day vocals.

B-Flat Blues-voc Anita O'Day
Breakfast Feud (arr BW)
After You've Gone - SEXTET
Honeysuckle Rose-voc Anita O'Day (arr FK)
Gotta Be This Or That-voc Anita O'Day, Benny Goodman
Air Mail Special (head arrangement)
Rachel's Dream - SEXTET
Get Happy - SEPTET (prob. arr MP)
(Everything I've Got Belongs To You - NORVO SEXTET
Raising (alternately, "Raze") The Riff (arr FK)
(Come Rain Or Come Shine-voc Anita O'Day - NO BG, Norvo

The next rebroadcast is from Stockholm's Concert Hall, was presented on Anita's birthday, which the band celebrated in song. Anita spotted Zoot Sims, then living in Sweden, in the audience, and he joined her for a rousing rendition of "Four Brothers." Unfortunately, Swedish Radio did not include it in its broadcast.

Unfortunate, too, was the deteriorating relationship between Benny and Anita halfway through the tour; her autobiography describes it in bitter terms, claiming in essence that Benny resented the applause her work elicited, taking the spotlight from him. But Muriel Zuckerman, for 30-odd years Benny's secretary, accountant, financial advisor and booking agent, remembers it differently. Anita was an admitted heroin addict, and drugs were something Benny simply would not tolerate. Too bad—in the author's opinion, Anita was a great jazz vocalist, with Krupa, with Kenton, any time, anywhere. But her relationship was doomed from the start, and the fault was certainly not all Benny's.

STOCKHOLM REBROADCAST   *October 18, 1959, Konserthuset,*
Swedish Radio Network   *Stockholm*

Broadcast date not known. Personnels as October 15.

Sing, Sing, Sing, Part 2 (n/c - announcer's voice over)
Air Mail Special
Rachel's Dream - SEXTET
Memories Of You - SEXTET
(Everything I've Got Belongs To You - NORVO SEXTET
(Tenbone - feat. Harris, Phillips - NO BG
Honeysuckle Rose-voc Anita O'Day (arr FK)
. . . few bars, Happy Birthday
Come Rain Or Come Shine-voc Anita O'Day (arr FK)
Let Me Off Uptown-voc Anita O'Day, Jack Sheldon
You Turned the Tables On Me-voc Anita O'Day
Tea For Two-voc Anita O'Day
Slipped Disc - SEXTET
A Smo-o-o-oth One (arr FK)

There appear to have been (at least) three rebroadcasts of selections from the concert in Bremen's Die Glocke Concert Hall the next day; some of the tunes are duplicated in the several airings. They are combined below in what would be a reasonable concert order-of-performance:

BREMEN REBROADCASTS   *October 19, 1959, Die Glocke,*
German Radio Network   *Bremen*

Broadcast dates unknown. Personnels as October 15.

Let's Dance (theme) (arr BS)
Air Mail Special
Rachel's Dream - SEXTET
Memories Of You - SEXTET
Slipped Disc - SEXTET
Get Happy - SEXTET
(Everything I've Got Belongs To You - NORVO SEXTET
(Don't Get Around Much Anymore - NORVO SEXTET
(Tenbone - feat. Harris, Phillips - NO BG
Raising The Riff
Gotta Be This Or That-voc Anita O'Day, Benny Goodman
Between The Devil And The Deep Blue Sea
Marching And Swinging (arr FK)
Jammin' (alternately, "Jam") On The Breaks (arr FK)
Breakfast Feud
Medley: Don't Be That Way   )
*   Stompin' At The Savoy   )*
*   On The Sunny Side Of The Street)   ) (arr BS)*
*   Rose Room - contra melody, In A Mellotone)*
*   Moon Glow   )*
*   Sing, Sing, Sing   )*
I Want To Be Happy (arr AC or BS)
When You're Smiling
Good-Bye (arr BS)

The concert in Berlin's Sportpalast was taped in its entirety by either or both Armed Forces (Radio) Network (AFN)/German radio personnel. AFN rebroadcast excerpts from the latter portion of the concert, but Benny and one of the sidemen each has excellent stereo tapes of the complete performance, as does the author. In recent years cuts not broadcast by AFN have appeared on bootleg LP's (liner notes claim that the original material exists only on acetates, and this is not true). Because the concert is extant in its entirety, it is so listed below; selections broadcast by AFN—and they are in order-of-performance—are preceded by an asterisk:

BERLIN CONCERT   October 22, 1959, Sportpalast,
  AFN partial rebroadcast   Berlin

AFN broadcast date unknown. Personnels as October 15. TRIO: Goodman, Freeman, Markham.

  . . . introductions
Let's Dance (theme)
*Air Mail Special (**LP:** SWH 7)*
*Rachel's Dream - SEXTET (**LP:** SWH 37)*
Memories Of You - TRIO
*Slipped Disc - SEXTET (**LP:** SWH 24)*
*(Billie's Bounce - feat. Freeman w/rhythm - NO BG (**LP:** SWH 24)*
*Get Happy - SEPTET (**LP:** SWH 24)*
*(. . . unidentified tune - NORVO SEXTET (**LP:** SWH 37)*
(Don't Get Around Much Anymore - NORVO SEXTET
*(Tenbone - feat. Harris, Phillips - NO BG (**LP:** SWH 24)*
*Raisin' The Riff (**LP:** SWH 24)*
*(Honeysuckle Rose-voc Anita O'Day - NO BG (**LP:** SWH 24)*
(Come Rain Or Come Shine-voc Anita O'Day - NO BG
*Medley: *Ooh, Hot Dog-voc Anita O'Day) (**LP:** SWH 37)*
         *Let Me Off Uptown-voc Anita O'Day, Jack Sheldon (**LP:** SWH 37)*
*Gotta Be This Or That-voc Anita O'Day, Benny Goodman (**LP:** SWH 7)*

Intermission

Between The Devil And The Deep Blue Sea (LP:** SWH 7)*
*Go, Margot, Go (**LP:** SWH 24)*
*Marching And Swinging
*Jammin' On The Breaks (**LP:** SWH 37)*
*Body And Soul - SEXTET
After You've Gone - SEXTET
*When You're Smiling - SEXTET (**LP:** SWH 37)*
*(But Not For Me - voc Anita O'Day - NO BG, Norvo (arr FK)
*(Four Brothers - voc Anita O'Day - NO BG (**LP:** SWH 37)*
*You Turned The Tables On Me - voc Anita O'Day - accomp. Goodman,
     Sheldon, Phillips, rhythm
*Medley: *Don't Be That Way*   )*
        Stompin' At The Savoy   )
        *On The Sunny Side Of The Street   ) *(**LP:** SWH 37)*
          *Rose Room - contra melody, In A Mellotone)
          Moon Glow   )
          Sing, Sing, Sing   )*
*I Want To Be Happy (**LP:** SWH 37)*
*Breakfast Feud (**LP:** SWH 24)*
Good-Bye (theme)

The AFN rebroadcast's "Moon Glow" is incomplete, clipped by closing announcements.)

The penultimate stop on the tour was Basel, Switzerland; so far as extant performances are concerned, the Swiss engagement was the ultimate concert. Almost an hour and a half in length, a tape of the concert provides moments in jazz that, were they more widely known, would be cherished as bench marks against which to measure clarinetists for all time.

Benny is . . . Benny. Superb. From the opening "Air Mail Special" he serves notice that this is his concert. Highlights are a matter of personal choice, for every selection has something to recommend it. We choose "Go, Margot, Go," which Benny dedicates ". . . uh, to the great German movie actress, Margot Hielscher." Again, his devastating chorus that slices laser-like through Fred (Benny sometimes announces him as, "Phil") Karlin's "Marching And Swinging." Then, a numbing, absolutely anesthetizing brace of choruses on, "Breakfast Feud," that has the audience overroaring Flip's following solo. And what might be described as a blues of maturity and consummate accomplishment, "Body And Soul."

Benny's support is inspired; as so often happens in jazz and in man's other pursuits, one stellar performance begets another. It's as if everyone agreed, "This night is for our epitaphs, so let's do it all." Norvo, Harris and Phillips are excellent throughout. Russ Freeman picks his spots, Sheldon and Dodgion surpass themselves, the rhythm section both undergirds and accents. As for Anita . . . just great. Despite her addiction, her fuliginous voice is another jazz instrument in the uptempo, "Four Brothers." And despite her rancor, she admits today that ". . . Benny had the potential for a memorable group among the people he'd hired." That potential was realized in Basel.

Looking back to what he has chronicled, and thinking ahead to the

performances to come, the author would name this concert as Benny's best, from the end of World War II to the end of his career.

BASEL REBROADCAST   October 28, 1959, Basel
  Swiss Radio Network

Broadcast date unknown. Personnels as October 15.

Let's Dance (theme)
Air Mail Special
Rachel's Dream - SEXTET
Memories Of You - SEXTET
Slipped Disc - SEXTET
Get Happy - SEPTET
(Everything I've Got Belongs To You - NORVO SEXTET
(Don't Get Around Much Anymore - NORVO SEXTET
(Tenbone - feat. Harris, Phillips - NO BG
Go, Margot, Go
Marching And Swinging
Breakfast Feud
(But Not For Me-voc Anita O'Day - NO BG
(Four Brothers-voc Anita O'Day - NO BG
You Turned The Tables On Me-voc Anita O'Day (BG in coda)
Body And Soul - SEXTET
I Want To Be Happy

The last engagement on the tour was in Vienna. No recordings of that concert are known, but on the morning of the performance Benny appeared "live" on Austrian television, chatting with announcer Gunther Schifter, and offering a free sample:

VIENNA TELECAST   October 30, 1959, Vienna
  Austrian Television Network

SEXTET plus Flip Phillips, ts.

Rachel's Dream

Immediately upon his return from Europe, Benny was booked into Ralph Watkins's Manhattan bistro, Basin Street East, for three weeks beginning November 5. The group remained intact except for Russ Freeman—Gene DiNovi replaced him—and, of course, Anita. Benny quickly resumed a practice he'd begun in the '20's, recording tunes from Broadway shows, this time in the Olmsted Studios, 80 W. 40th Street. The subject now was Rodgers and Hammerstein's, "The Sound Of Music":

BENNY GODMAN AND HIS ORCHESTRA   November 11, 1959, New York

Benny Goodman, clt; Jack Sheldon, tpt; Bill Harris, tbn; Jerry Dodgion, as; Flip Phillips, ts; Red Norvo, vib; Gene DiNovi, p; Jimmy Wyble, g; Red Wootten, b; John Markham, d.

- 0 -   UNISSUED
              No Way To Stop It (arr FK)
              So Long, Farewell (arr FK)
              My Favorite Things (arr FK)
              The Sound Of Music (arr FK)
              Sixteen Going On Seventeen (arr FK)

BENNY GOODMAN AND HIS ORCHESTRA   November 12, 1959, New York

Personnel as November 11.

- 0 -   UNISSUED
              Raze The Riff (arr FK)
              So Long, Farewell

For some reason, the band sounded better "live" in Basin Street East than it sounded on the playback tapes of the two sessions in Olmsted's. (Frankly, it sounded much better playing jazz than it did the tunes from "The Sound Of Music.") So the very next day Benny had two shows in Basin Street East taped "live" for Park Recording, playing the tunes he'd featured in Europe. None of these cuts has been released officially, but tapes of some of the material are in the possession of a few collectors. The privately-circulated recordings are listed first, following, and are notated, "Tape." Those performances that have not escaped from Benny's library are then listed alphabetically, for it is not known in which order they were recorded.

BENNY GOODMAN AND HIS ORCHESTRA   November 13, 1959, New York

Orchestra as November 11. SEXTET: Goodman, Norvo, rhythm section. SEPTET: Sextet plus Sheldon.

- 0 -   UNISSUED - Tape
               Let's Dance (theme)
               Raze The Riff
               Avalon - SEXTET
               Poor Butterfly - SEXTET
               When You're Smiling - SEXTET
               (**My Funny Valentine** - Dodgion (flt), Norvo, rhythm
                    section - NO BG
               Marchin' And Swingin'
               (**Sleep** - Phillips, Harris, rhythm section - NO BG
               Get Happy - SEPTET
               Medley: **Don't Be That Way**
                       Stompin' At The Savoy
                       On The Sunny Side Of The Street
                       Rose Room / In A Mellotone
                       Moon Glow
                       One O'Clock Jump
                       Sing, Sing, Sing

(NOTE: Bill Stegmeyer arranged the "Don't Be That Way" - "Sing, Sing, Sing" medley.)

- 0 -   UNISSUED
               Benny's Bugle
               Blue And Sentimental
               Body And Soul
               Don't Get Around Much Any More (arr BS)
               Everything I've Got Belongs To You - SEXTET
               Gotta Be This Or That
               Memories Of You - SEXTET
               No Way To Stop It (arr FK)
               Rachel's Dream
               Sweet And Lovely
               Tenbone
               Trigger Fantasy - feat. Wootten (arr Irv Manning)

(Benny's files specify instrumentation for only a few of the unheard recordings; it seems likely that not all are by the full group, and it is possible that he is not on some of the tunes on the three tapes in his possession.)

Believe it or not, there's still a third Perry Como version of, "Sing, Sing, Sing." This last is not quite as bad as the other two, but it's still a travesty. Redeeming a portion of the telecast is Benny's Basin Street East troupe:

"THE PERRY COMO SHOW"   *November 18, 1959, New York*
  NBC Television Network

Benny Goodman, clt, and Mitchell Ayres and his Orchestra.

Sing, Sing, Sing-voc Perry Como, Celeste Holm, Connie Francis, chorus

Goodman Orchestra as November 11

Medley: Memories Of You
        Don't Be That Way
        Stompin' At The Savoy
        On The Sunny Side Of The Street
        Moon Glow
        One O'Clock Jump
        After You've Gone

Combined Goodman, Ayres orchestras

Now You Has Jazz (w/interpolations of sundry other tunes)-voc Como, Holm, chorus

Even if a modicum of the magic that had struck at Basel was missing at Basin Street, still the tapes recorded there November 13 were superior to those recorded in the studios November 11 and 12. That being the case, perhaps the score of "The Sound of Music" should be cut "live" . . . Benny tried it, liked it, with this result:

BENNY GOODMAN AND HIS ORCHESTRA   November 20, 1959, New York

Personnel as November 11, except Sheldon, Harris and Phillips do not play on, "An Ordinary Couple," "Climb Every Mountain" and "Do-Re-Mi."

59-MG-650   **LP:** MGM E3810, MGM (E) C858. **StLp:** MGM S3810,
                 MGM (E) CS6033, MGM (E) 2353123. **StT:** MGM
                 STC3810. **StCas:** MGM (E) 3110233
              No Way To Stop It
              Sixteen Going On Seventeen
              So Long, Farewell
              Climb Every Mountain (arr FK)

59-MG-651   same issues
              The Sound Of Music
              My Favorite Things (arr FK)
              An Ordinary Couple (arr FK)
              Maria (arr FK)
              Do-Re-Mi (arr FK)

("The Sound Of Music" and "Do-Re-Mi" are also on **StLp**, TL STA354. "So Long, Farewell" and "Do-Re-Mi" are also on an MGM DJ release, 59-XY-1150/1151.)

"The World's Largest Department Store," Macy's, annually sponsors a Thanksgiving Day parade in New York, and portions of the extravaganza are usually televised. Benny appeared on a float in the 1959 parade, and is heard as he passes the cameras. The announcer heralds the group as the Benny Goodman Sextet, but only four instruments are audible:

"MACY'S THANKSGIVING DAY PARADE"   *November 27, 1959, New York*
  NBC Television Network

Benny Goodman, clt; unknown p, b, d.

The World Is Waiting For The Sunrise (n/c)

At the conclusion of the Basin Street East engagement, Red Norvo took the group to Las Vegas, there to work with Frank Sinatra at the Sands Hotel. Benny remained in New York and began a further series of appearances on television.

The first in the series reunited Benny, Lionel, Jess and Gene. The author was a guest at several of the rehearsals and was impressed, first with how well this Quartet meshed after so long an interval, and second, with the respect accorded Benny. Up the ranks from stagehands to producers, the technicians thought nothing of calling personalities like Sir John Gielgud, Peggy Lee and Eva Gabor, who were also in the cast, by their first names: "Hey, John, over here." Benny, however, was invariably addressed as, "Mr. Goodman." The only other jazz musician the author ever saw treated with equal deference was Louis "Mr. Armstrong."

(The author also remembers that there was a stunning redhead at the first rehearsal, trying out for the chorus. Her abundant charms caught everyone's eyes, including long looks from Peggy Lee and Eva Gabor. She was nowhere in sight at the second rehearsal, and Peggy and Eva seemed smug.)

One reason the Quartet played so well was the Goodman penchant for perfection. All present thought the first rehearsal was fine; but Benny wasn't satisfied, "suggested" they get together for some private practice in a salon off Park Recording's offices across from Carnegie Hall. Gene and the author arrived first, then Jess, then Lionel; promptly at 2:00 p.m., Benny and his personal manager strode in. By 2:45 they'd accomplished what Benny wanted, and he was ready to pack it in. But Gene said, "Hey, Ben (Gene always called him 'Ben,' was the only one who got away with it), it's been a long time—let's play." And play they did, past four o'clock when members of a large orchestra started filtering into the hall for their scheduled rehearsal. What had been an audience of two quickly grew to a cheering section of 30-odd, some of the best staff musicians in New York, all urging the Quartet on, and the hell with time, rehearsals, further commitments and dinner. For this is when Benny is at his best—playing for kicks with musicians his equal, playing for an audience that can appreciate what's happening, forgetting about camera angles and audio levels, not worrying about mistakes . . . It was something to witness, and something ever to regret: it was not recorded.

"THE BIG PARTY"   *December 17, 1959, New York*
   CBS Television Network

Benny Goodman, clt; Lionel Hampton, vib; Jess Stacy, p; Gene Krupa, d.

Avalon   )
*Where Or When) (**LP:** FEST 246, RAR 30, KOS —)*
I Got Rhythm   )

(Benny also appears with an unidentified pianist accompanying Sir John Gielgud's recitation of Lorenzo's speech from Act V, Scene 1 of, "The Merchant Of Venice." The selection is a portion of a work by Brahms.)

The day of the rehearsals for "The Big Party" had an evening to remember, too. Columbia Pictures had scheduled a private screening of its soon-to-be-released, "The Gene Krupa Story," and Gene invited Jess and the author to come along. We did, assembled in a small studio near 50th and Seventh Avenue, with Sal Mineo (who shook hands limply), the female lead (who kissed wetly), some Columbia brass and Gene. The projector rolled; and soon Jess and the author were rolling in the aisles. "Hell, that can't be Bix—he's dead." "Is that supposed to be Frank Sinatra?" "Christ, that's all wrong." These and similar remarks from us drew censorious warnings from the Columbia people. Finally the film bumbled its way to "The End," and Jess and the author headed for the elevators (Lionel was playing in town, and we'd promised we'd come see him). But newsmen crowded in to interview Gene and the actors, and our exit was temporarily blocked. Surrounded by the press, Gene saw us, said, "Hey, how'd you like it?" The author was speechless, but Jess came up with, "Well, the music was pretty good." And we left.

There is one more bit of recorded Goodmania to be logged before the 1950's are closed out, although when it was taped is unknown: A Portuguese "Office Of War Information" 12″ ET has commercially-released Goodman records interspersed with an interview between Benny and an announcer named "George." Benny replies in English to questions put to him in Portuguese.

And that's the 1950's. An uneven, albeit momentous, decade in Benny Goodman's career. Europe, "Star Time," the Henderson commemoration, "The Benny Goodman Story," Bangkok and Tokyo, "Swing Into Spring," Brussels, Basin Street East and West, lots of television, that marvelous concert in Switzerland. Not too much hard work, really, considering Benny's regimen in the '30's and '40's. All in all it had been a ball, and perhaps Revlon's, "The Big Party," sums it up best.

THE 1960's—ANOTHER "MISSION TO MOSCOW" AND A GRAND REUNION

The new decade found Benny without a group of his own for the first four months of 1960, but he is in evidence on television and radio. His initial guest appearance reunited him with an orchestra leader for whom he had worked on radio, thirty years' earlier:

"THE BELL TELEPHONE HOUR"   January 29, 1960, New York
   NBC Television Network

Benny Goodman, clt, and the Bell Telephone Orchestra, Donald Voorhees, conductor.

Concertino For Clarinet And Orchestra In C-Major (von Weber)
Don't Be That Way - segue to One O'Clock Jump coda

"THE DINAH SHORE CHEVY SHOW"   February 28, 1960, New York
   NBC Television Network

Benny Goodman, clt; Jess Stacy, p; Rowland "Rolly" Bundock, b; Jack Sperling, d.

("Let's Dance" - CO record
These Foolish Things   *(LP: FEST 246, RAR 30, KOS —)*
That's A-Plenty   "   "   "   "
Slipped Disc - "scat" voc Dinah Shore   "   "   "   "
After You've Gone - voc Dinah Shore   "   "   "   "
. . . various short Goodman clt passages

Probably in March, Benny and Gene Krupa taped some voice tracks for Radio Free Europe, "answering" questions put to them via local announcers from a prepared list. The 12″ ET contains a portion of "Don't Be That Way," from the 1938 Carnegie Hall concert.

Arthur Godfrey, who had first come into prominence when he broadcast an emotional description of President Roosevelt's funeral cortege, was one of television's biggest stars in the 1950's. When his program's popularity waned in that medium, he reversed the usual procedure and took it to radio. It was the housewives' delight, and "The Old Redhead" had a new career.

A jazz fan, the quondam ukelele plucker staffed his studio orchestra with excellent musicians, some of them Goodman alumni. Thus it was somewhat in the nature of a reunion when Benny jammed at length with Godfrey's group. Too much material for one program, the tape was split into two and broadcast on successive days. The music is excellent, the reminiscences are fun to listen to, and a complete tape of Benny's appearance on Godfrey's CBS show is recommended:

"THE ARTHUR GODFREY SHOW"   April 27, 1960, New York
   CBS Radio Network

Benny Goodman, clt, and Arthur Godfrey's studio orchestra: Johnny Parker (Plonsky), tpt; Lou McGarity, tbn; Johnny Mince, clt & as; Lee Irwin, ts; Lud Flato, glockenspiel; Dick Hyman, p; Remo Palmieri, g; Arthur Godfrey, uke; Gene Traxler, b; Joe Marshall, d. Melissa "Frankie" Crockett, Johnny Nash, Arthur Godfrey, voc.

QUARTET: Goodman, Hyman, Traxler, Marshall
QUINTET: Quartet plus Parker
SEXTET: Quartet plus Mince, Godfrey
SEPTET: Quintet plus Palmieri, Godfrey

Broadcast April 28:

Let's Dance (theme)
Lulu's Back In Town (arr Dick Hyman)   *(LP: OM 2903)*
(Things Are Swingin' - voc Frankie Crockett - NO BG
Let's Dance (theme - 2nd half of broadcast)
The Lady Is A Tramp (arr Dick Hyman)

(Good-Bye - voc Johnny Nash - NO BG
Jungle Cock Blues - SEXTET   *(LP: OM 2903)*
It's All Right With Me - QUARTET   "   "   "   "
My Gal Sal - voc Arthur Godfrey

Broadcast April 29:

Let's Dance (theme)
As Long As I Live - voc Arthur Godfrey
Climb Every Mountain-QUARTET   *(LP: OM 2903)*
I'm Nobody's Baby   "   "   "   "
Somebody's Wrong - voc Arthur Godfrey
I Let A Song Go Out Of My Heart - QUINTET
At Sundown - voc Arthur Godfrey - SEPTET   *(LP: OM 2903)*

(April 29 broadcast is also on LP, JAZ 27.)

Red Norvo returned to the East with his small group; Benny added Urbie Green and Flip Phillips, took them all to Atlantic City's Warner Theater in May, then into Basin Street East in June for a three-week engagement. There are no known recordings from Basin Street, but the group does appear on television:

"THE ED SULLIVAN SHOW"   June 19, 1960, New York
   CBS Television Network

Benny Goodman, clt; Jack Sheldon, tpt; Urbie Green, tbn; Jerry Dodgion, as & fl; Flip Phillips, ts; Red Norvo, vib; John Bunch, p; Jimmy Wyble, g; John Mosher, b; John Markham, d. Maria Marshall, voc.

SEXTET: Goodman, Norvo, rhythm section

Don't Be That Way (theme)
The World Is Waiting For The Sunrise - SEXTET
Poor Butterfly - SEXTET
Bill Bailey, Won't You Please Come Home?-voc Maria Marshall (arr FK)
I Want To Be Happy (arr AC or BS)

Finished at Basin Street, the band played at the Westbury Music Fair, Westbury, Long Island, on June 23; at the Oakdale Musical Theater in Wallingford, Conn., on June 26; and at the Carousel Music Theater in Framingham, Mass., on July 3.

Next it recorded in Columbia's studios at 207 E. 30th Street for Park Recording. The date produced a minor controversy.

Ahead (September 2) is a Columbia release of this basic group taped "live" at Ciro's in Hollywood—for the most part. One of its tracks is "I Want To Be Happy." At one time there was speculation that it was from a session at Harrah's Club, Lake Tahoe, Nevada, but this now seems unlikely. "I Want To Be Happy" was also recorded in the studio on July 6; and a recently-discovered "Artist's Card" (a file record of releases and attendant information) insists that the July 6 studio cut is the one on the Columbia issues.

The studio cut has not been available to the author. He believes, as does Benny, that "I Want To Be Happy" on Columbia LP CL 1579 et al is from Ciro's, September 2; thus it is listed as "unissued" from July 6. Note, however, that two takes of "My Baby Done Tol' Me" and one of "I Can't Believe That You're In Love With Me" are in the hands of a few collectors.

BENNY GOODMAN AND HIS ORCHESTRA   July 6, 1960, New York

Benny Goodman, clt: Jack Sheldon, tpt; Urbie Green, tbn; Jerry Dodgion, as & flt; Flip Phillips, ts; Red Norvo, vib: John Bunch, p; Jimmy Wyble, g; John Mosher, b; John Markham, d. Maria Marshall, Jack Sheldon, voc. PETER MATZ (PM), RED WOOTTEN (RW), arr.

- 0 -   UNISSUED
          I Want To Be Happy (arr AC or BS)

- 0 -   UNISSUED - Tape
          I Can't Believe That You're In Love With Me-voc Maria
          Marshall (arr PM)

- 0 -   UNISSUED
          St. James Infirmary (arr BS)
          Too Many Tears (arr BS)
          Air Mail Special (arr BS)

- 0   UNISSUED - Tape (2 takes)
          My Baby Done Tol' Me-voc Jack Sheldon

- 0   UNISSUED
          Between The Devil And The Deep Blue Sea (arr RW)

July 6 was a busy day for Benny. In addition to a split session at the studio (the first ended with "Too Many Tears"), Benny attended a reception for King Phumiphol Aduljej of Thailand given by the governor of New York State, then entertained his royal friend from Bangkok at a party in the penthouse auditorium of the Goodman apartment in the Manhattan House. His Majesty caused some diplomatic and Secret Service consternation by interrupting a tight schedule to arrive early and stay late.

On hand to greet the King were the Goodman group and Jonah Jones, Teddy Wilson and Gene Krupa. Naturally, they played; and naturally, too, the King joined in, as he had in Bangkok in 1956. Too bad someone didn't record it . . .

But someone did.

Despite his assertion in "BG—On The Record" to the contrary, the author learned subsequently that portions of the royal jam session were recorded, and that a tape of the proceedings is extant. Although the performances on the tape are incomplete, the audio quality is excellent, suggesting that the recording gear was something more than a small portable machine with a built-in microphone. Benny is heard to announce that the King will be given a recording of the event, adding to the belief that the taping was done professionally. (It is also believed that the King was given a tape copy, not a pressed recording. Whether the souvenir given the King is more complete than the tape the author was privileged to hear is not known.)

Thus, Benny and the King of Siam, one more time.

PRIVATE PARTY, KING OF THAILAND   *July 6, 1960, New York*

Benny Goodman, clt; Phumiphol Aduljej, as; Red Norvo, vib; Teddy Wilson, p; Gene Krupa, d.

Sweet Georgia Brown (n/c)

Goodman; Jack Sheldon, tpt; Urbie Green, tbn; the King, Jerry Dodgion, as; Flip Phillips, ts; Norvo, Wilson; Jimmy Wyble, g; Krupa.

Oh, Lady Be Good! (n/c)

Sheldon, Green, Dodgion, Phillips, Wyble; uncertain p, d (possibly John Bunch and John Markham, respectively, not Wilson and Krupa).

(Once In A While (n/c)—NO BG
(Memories Of You (n/c)—NO BG

The following week the band moved into the Palmer House in Chicago. While in his home town Benny introduced the new Selmer Series IX clarinet at the National Association of Music Merchants' Trade Show.

New York's Lewisohn Stadium was the next stop, July 19; the bill was split between jazz and classical music, and Benny was solo clarinetist with Alfredo Antonini's Stadium Symphony Orchestra. Then it was on to Boston for an engagement at George Wein's Storyville. Ending the month, the band travelled to Roberts Stadium, Evansville, for the Indiana Jazz Festival. CBS broadcast part of the concert.

"INDIANA JAZZ FESTIVAL"   *July 30, 1960,*
CBS Radio Network   *Evansville, Indiana*

Orchestra as July 6 (studio), except RUSS FREEMAN, p, and RED WOOTTEN, b, replace Bunch and Mosher, respectively.

SEXTET: Goodman, Norvo, rhythm section

I Want To Be Happy
Poor Butterfly—SEXTET
After You've Gone—SEXTET
I Can't Believe That You're In Love With Me-voc Maria Marshall
Bill Bailey, Won't You Please Come Home?-voc Maria Marshall
(Tenbone—feat. Green, Phillips—NO BG
Medley: Don't Be That Way
    Stompin' At The Savoy
    On The Sunny Side Of The Street
    Rose Room—contra melody, In A Mellotone
    Moon Glow
    One O'Clock Jump
Sing, Sing, Sing—to closing announcement

Two days later the group played at the Brandywine Music Circus in Concordville, Pa., where it was recorded from the audience with a spring-powered, battery-activated reel recorder. Because of varying pitch, poor balance and extraneous noise, such recordings are rarely satisfying. Given suitable acoustic ambience, cassette recorders in general use in the 1970's and beyond will produce better results.

But such early audience tapes are worthwhile for their informational purposes; note that this one reveals that in the two days that had elapsed since the CBS broadcast from Evansville, John Bunch had replaced Freeman:

BRANDYWINE CONCERT   *August 1, 1960,*
Concordville, Pa

Personnels as July 30, except JOHN BUNCH, p, replaces Freeman in the orchestra and Sextet.

Rachel's Dream—SEXTET
Memories Of You—SEXTET
After You've Gone—SEXTET
(Tenbone—feat. Green, Philips—NO BG
I Can't Believe That You're In Love With Me-voc. Maria Marshall
But Not For Me-voc Maria Marshall
Poor Butterfly—SEXTET
Breakfast Feud
Willow Weep For Me (arr BS)
Avalon—SEXTET

Next, Benny returned to Columbia's 30th Street studios to try to capture there what was happening on the road. There is no claim that any of these cuts were used in the coming Columbia release, and all of them are considered unissued (one take of "St. Louis Blues" is held by a few collectors):

BENNY GOODMAN AND HIS ORCHESTRA   **August 3, 1960, New York**

Personnel as July 6 studio.

—0—   UNISSUED
          Willow Weep For Me (arr BS)
          Breakfast Feud (head arr)
          St. Louis Blues-voc Maria Marshall (head arr)—TAPE
          As Long As I Live (arr BS)
          Raze The Riff (arr FK)
          Sing, Sing, Sing

BENNY GOODMAN SEXTET   **August 4, 1960, New York**

Personnel as August 1 Sextet, except JOHN MOSHER, b, replaces Wootten.

—0—   UNISSUED
          Sweet Georgia Brown
          My Funny Valentine
          After You've Gone

With a few changes in personnel, the band embarked on a tour of the United States and Canada. Its precise itinerary is unknown, but one certain engagement was in Ciro's, in Hollywood, over the long Labor Day weekend. According to LP liner notes (disputed by an "Artist's Card" in regard to one tune, as we have seen), the band recorded the full contents of a Columbia album there. Columbia's files specify the date to have been Friday, September 2. So we'll begin our tour with ''Benny Goodman Swings Again—recorded live on the West Coast'':

BENNY GOODMAN AND HIS ORCHESTRA   September 2, 1960, Hollywood

Benny Goodman, clt; Jack Sheldon, tpt; MURRAY McEACHERN, tbn; Jerry Dodgion, as & fl; Flip Phillips, ts; Red Norvo, vib; RUSS FREEMAN, p; Jimmy Wyble, g; RED WOOTTEN, b; John Markham, d. Maria Marshall, voc.

QUINTET: Goodman, rhythm section
SEXTET: Quintet plus Norvo

XLP 51692   **LP**: CL CL1579, CO CL2483, PHIL BBL7449, CBS 62708. **StLp**: CO CS8379, CO CS9283, PHIL SBBL605, CBS 52368, CO alb P4M-5678, CL C10259 (and cassette, 8-track, same catalog number). **StT**: CO CQ359, CBS 67209
Air Mail Special (arr BS)

same issues, except omit **StT**: CBS 67209
Slipped Disc—SEXTET

LP: CO CL1579, PHIL BBL7449. **StLp**: CO CS8379, PHIL SBBL605, CO C10259 (et al). **StT**: CO CQ359
Gotta Be This Or That-voc Benny Goodman

same issues as ''Gotta Be This Or That,'' plus **ET**: 1961 Christmas Seal Campaign
Where Or When—QUINTET

same issues as ''Gotta Be This Or That''
I Want To Be Happy (arr AC or BS)

XLP 51693   same issues as ''Gotta Be This Or That,'' plus **StLp**: HA HS11271, CBS 63367, PIC 240
After You've Gone—QUINTET

same issues as ''Gotta Be This Or That''
Waiting For The Robert E. Lee-voc Maria Marshall (arr BS)

same issues as ''After You've Gone''
Bill Bailey Won't You Please Come Home-voc Maria Marshall (arr FK)

same issues as ''Air Mail Special,'' except omit **StLp**: CO alb P4M-5678; **StT**: CBS 67209. And add **StLp**: CO P7S-5122, CO DS292
Sing, Sing, Sing (With A Swing) (Interpolation: ''Christopher Columbus'')

(See following paragraphs for comment on ''Gotta Be This Or That,'' ''Waiting For The Robert E. Lee,'' and ''Bill Bailey Won't You Please Come Home.'')

In addition to appearing in Ciro's during this tour of the west, the group also had engagements in the Hollywood Bowl, and in Harrah's Club in Lake Tahoe; indeed, the Columbia release's cover includes a photo of Harrah's marquee. And Benny has a tape whose container is labeled, ''Harrah's, Lake Tahoe, September 1960.'' No other information is on or in the box.

The tape gives every indication of being continuous; its 11 tunes seem to comprise one set. Six of the titles on the tape are not included in the Columbia release. Two that are, ''Air Mail Special'' and ''Where Or When,'' are distinctly different performances from their counterparts on the Columbia LP. The remaining three are interesting:

''Gotta Be This Or That'' is the same ''take,'' Columbia LP/BG tape—save that the CO track edits out a chorus by Jimmy Wyble that follows Benny's vocal, and also excises about half of McEachern's solo.

''Waiting For The Robert E. Lee'' seems identical.

Save for a different reprise, ''Bill Bailey . . .'' also seems the same, LP vis a vis the tape. Given the facility for splicing tape affords, an altered ending would have been a simple matter to achieve.

It is possible that the container is mislabeled, that Benny's tape is a test of an LP assembled for his OK, that it has nothing to do with Harrah's. Much more likely is that Columbia's ''Gotta Be . . .'' and ''Waiting . . .'' were not performed in Ciro's, but rather in Harrah's; and that may also be true of at least portions of ''Bill Bailey . . .''. In any event, it's all good music, and here's Benny's tape as it winds through:

BENNY GOODMAN   September 1960, Harrah's, Lake Tahoe
Personnels as September 2.

- 0 -   **UNISSUED** - Tape
Air Mail Special
Avalon - SEXTET
Where Or When - QUINTET
The World Is Waiting For The Sunrise - SEXTET
(**I'll Remember April** - Norvo, Dodgion, rhythm section - NO BG
(**Tenbone** - feat. Sheldon, Phillips - NO BG, Norvo
(**You Took Advantage Of Me**-voc Maria Marshall - full group sans BG
(**But Not For Me**-voc Maria Marshall - full group sans BG

CO Series releases - ?
Waiting For The Robert E. Lee-voc Maria Marshall
Bill Bailey Won't You Please Come Home-voc Maria Marshall
Gotta Be This Or That-voc Benny Goodman

A concert in the Queen Elizabeth Theatre in Vancouver, British Columbia, was taped in its entirety from the audience, with mixed results: portions are fair audio, parts are poor. Amusing special lyrics on ''Nice Work If You Can Get It'' make the tape worthwhile:

QUEEN ELIZABETH CONCERT   *September 19, 1960, Vancouver*

Personnels as September 2. NORVO SEXTET: Norvo, Dodgion, rhythm section.

Let's Dance (theme) (arr BS)
Air Mail Special
Poor Butterfly - SEXTET
The World Is Waiting For The Sunrise - SEXTET
Memories Of You - SEXTET
After You've Gone - SEXTET
(Red Eye - NORVO SEXTET
(Tenbone - feat. Sheldon, Phillips - NO BG
I Can't Believe That You're In Love With Me-voc Maria Marshall
St. Louis Blues-voc Maria Marshall
Bill Bailey, Won't You Please Come Home?-voc Maria Marshall

Medley: Don't Be That Way   )
*   Stompin' At The Savoy   )*
*   On The Sunny Side Of The Street   )*
*   Rose Room - contra melody, In A Mellotone) (arr BS)*
*   Moon Glow   )*
*   One O'Clock Jump   )*
*   Sing, Sing, Sing   )*

Intermission

Strike Up The Band
St. James Infirmary (arr BS)
Rachel's Dream - SEXTET
These Foolish Things - SEXTET
Slipped Disc - SEXTET
(Tenderly - McEachern w/rhythm - NO BG
(Danny Boy - McEachern w/rhythm - NO BG
You Took Advantage Of Me-voc Maria Marshall (arr FK)
But Not For Me-voc Maria Marshall
Stormy Weather-voc Maria Marshall (arr BS)
Nice Work If You Can Get It-voc Benny Goodman (special lyrics)
Gotta Be This Or That-voc Benny Goodman
I Want To Be Happy (arr BS)
Good-Bye (theme) (arr BS)

The group had one last fling this time around; following the Bell Telephone telecast, next, Norvo took it to Las Vegas:

"THE BELL TELEPHONE HOUR"   *September 30, 1960, New York*
  CBS Television Network

Orchestra, Sextet as September 2. QUINTET: Goodman, Norvo, Freeman, Wootten, Markham.

September Song - QUINTET
The World Is Waiting For The Sunrise - SEXTET
Bill Bailey, Won't You Please Come Home?-voc Maria Marshall
I Want To Be Happy

*(All On **LP**: FEST 246, RAR 21, KOS—)*

Benny did not work regularly the balance of 1960, occupied himself with miscellaneous activities. At this time he may have recorded the voice tracks for a Federal Civil Defense ET, "Stars For Defense - Program No. 91." In addition to his promo's, the ET has two tracks from his Capitol LP, W565.

In October he flew to the West Coast to perform both the Copland Concerto and the von Weber Concertino with Milton Katims and the Seattle Symphony Orchestra. Later in the month he went to Chicago to tape jazz and classical segments for Ed Sullivan's TV show:

"THE ED SULLIVAN SHOW"   *mid-October 1960, Chicago*
  CBS Television Network

Televised November 6, 1960. Benny Goodman, clt; Dave Grusin, p; Karl Kiffe, d; unknown vib, b.

*Runnin' Wild (**LP**: FEST 246, MU 30JA5195, RAR 21, KOS—)*

Benny Goodman, clt, and the Chicago Fine Arts Quartet: Leonard Sorkin, 1st v; Abraham Loft, 2nd v; Irving Ilmer, viola; George Sopkin, cel.

Quintet In B For Clarinet And Strings, Opus 115 (Brahms) (excerpt)

On October 22 Benny taped Dave Grusin, p; George Catlett, b; and Stu Martin, d, in his Stamford studio, playing "Stella By Starlight," "Till My Lover Is Gone" and an untitled blues. Benny acted as recording engineer only, did not play himself.

He returned to Carnegie Hall November 16 to perform the Copland Concerto with The Orchestra Of America. The concert was broadcast only in the New York area:

SUSTAINING BROADCAST   *November 16, 1960, New York*
  WNYC Radio Station

Benny Goodman, clt, and The Orchestra Of America, Richard Korn, conductor.

Concerto For Clarinet And String Orchestra With Harp And Piano (Copland)

The Territory of Hawaii had been admitted to the Union as its 50th state in 1959; possibly with this in mind, Columbia induced Benny to record what it hoped would be an LP of Polynesian-type tunes in January 1961. Bill Stegmeyer was commissioned to write (at least) 10 new arrangements, and some of the better musicians in the New York area were recruited to execute them. The project seemed full of promise; but to date, none of the sides has been authorized for release.

Benny says that he never really thought much of the idea. However, at the author's urging that he consider OK'ing them for release, he has listened to some of the material several times in recent years. His opinion remains unchanged; they're not good enough to issue. The author begs to differ; he has heard a few of the cuts, and thinks they're interesting. Besides, they would afford another chance to listen to Lou McGarity, Zoot Sims, Toots Mondello and the others, playing some different compositions. Perhaps in the future Benny can be persuaded . . .

Some of the material is available to collectors; but none is from the first or second sessions.

BENNY GOODMAN   **January 12, 1961, New York**

Benny Goodman, clt; Bernie Privin, tpt; Lou McGarity, tbn; Toots Mondello, as; Zoot Sims, ts; Henry Rowland, p; Tony Mottola, g; Arnold Fishkind, b; Morey Feld, d; Eddie Costa, vib. All arrangements are by Bill Stegmeyer.

CO 65875   UNISSUED
           Hawaiian War Chant

CO 65876   UNISSUED
           South Sea Island Magic

CO 65877   UNISSUED
           The Moon Of Manakoora

CO 65878   UNISSUED
           On The Beach At Waikiki

BENNY GOODMAN   **January 16, 1961, New York**

Benny Goodman, clt; Bernie Privin, tpt; Lou McGarity, tbn; Toots Mondello, as; JEROME RICHARDSON, ts; ROCKY COLUCCIO, p; AL CASAMENTI, g; BOB HAGGART, b; Morey Feld, d; Eddie Costa, vib. All arrangements by Stegmeyer.

CO 65891   UNISSUED
           My Little Grass Shack

CO 65892   UNISSUED
           Song Of The Islands

CO 65893   UNISSUED
           Sweet Leilani

In some fashion, three cuts from the January 24 "Hawaiian" session were smuggled out of Columbia, bootlegged onto a promotional LP for an installer of home swimming pools. Zoot Sims, for one, was incensed at this unauthorized release, made threats about prosecution. But as is so often the case in such matters, there seems little chance to recover the costs of litigation against such perpetrators, let alone compensation for damages, and so nothing gets done. In any event, a desirable extract of Benny's "Hawaiian period" for collectors:

BENNY GOODMAN   **January 24, 1961, New York**

Personnel as January 12, except GEORGE DUVIVIER, b, replaces Fishkind. All arrangements by Stegmeyer.

CO 65929   UNISSUED
           Too Many Tears

CO 65930   UNISSUED
           Willow Weep For Me

CO 65931   UNISSUED
           Blue Hawaii

CO 65892-1   **LP**: GRIV - Side 2
           Song Of The Islands

CO 65891   UNISSUED
           My Little Grass Shack

CO 65877-3   **LP**: GRIV - Side 2
           The Moon Of Manakoora

CO 65893   UNISSUED
           Sweet Leilani

CO 65878-3   **LP**: GRIV - Side 2
           On The Beach At Waikiki

One of the tapes from this time period in Benny's library is absent any information whatsoever; its container offers no clues as to date, locale, personnel or matrices. It includes but one performance subject to direct comparison with a known quantity: "On The Beach At Waikiki," as released from the session of January 24. Concept and execution of these two performances are quite different, and the author is unable to say with certainty that the tenor saxophone solo in it is by Richardson or Sims. Overall, the tape gives the "feel" of a rehearsal preceding a recording session. If the tenor Richardson, the date of this tape is c. January 16; if Sims, c. January 24.

BENNY GOODMAN - Rehearsal ?   **January 16–24, 1961, New York**

Personnel as January 16/January 24. All arrangements by Stegmeyer.

- 0 -   UNISSUED - Tape
      Little Hula Hands
      On The Beach At Waikiki (breakdown, complete version,
        repeat ending)
      Sweet Leilani (breakdown, 3 complete versions)
      Blue Hawaii
      My Little Grass Shack

As they had a dozen years earlier, union rules governing exchanges of musicians prevented Benny from undertaking a planned tour of Great Britain in January 1961. His immediate itinerary in disarray, Benny played a benefit for the New York Philharmonic at the Waldorf-Astoria, jamming with Lionel Hampton, Teddy Wilson and Morey Feld; no tapes of this performance are known. On February 8 the toy department of Macy's huge New York department store saw the original Quartet, plus Jimmy Rushing, re-united. A report that AFR&TS recorded Benny, Lionel, Teddy, Gene and Jimmy "in concert" at Macy's has not been confirmed; nor has a recent search located a tape of the event once listed in an inventory of Benny's library. He does, however, have a tape of a radio interview he gave Jack Sperling on February 16.

In late February, he and Jimmy Rushing flew to Las Vegas. There he assumed leadership once again of Red Norvo's group, now joined by Charlie Shavers and Zoot Sims. The aforementioned inventory also included notice of two tapes recorded at the Desert Inn, March 3 and March 5. These tapes, too, have not been located.

On March 9 Benny began a three-week stand in Basin Street East with Red Norvo's Nonet. Its personnel included Buddy Childers, tpt; Carl Fontana, tbn; Jerry Dodgion, as & fl; Zoot Sims, ts; John Bunch, p; Jimmy Wyble, g; Chuck Israel, b; and Dottie Dodgion (Jerry's wife), d. (Mickey Sheen replaced Dottie on March 15.) Vocalists were Jimmy Rushing and Maria Marshall. No recordings of this engagement at Basin Street East have been discovered.

On April 2 Benny played a benefit for the New York YMHA in the Kaufman Concert Hall, performing Morton Gould's "Derivations." This concert was taped, and at one time Benny's library included a copy; it, too, seems now to have disappeared. The next day the Goodman Sextet joined other celebrities to pay tribute to Jack Benny in Carnegie Hall. Part of the program was televised:

"CARNEGIE HALL SALUTES JACK BENNY"   *April 3, 1961, New York*
   CBS Television Network

First televised September 27, 1961. Second telecast, July 31, 1962.

Benny Goodman, clt; Red Norvo, vib; John Bunch, p; Jimmy Wyble, g; Red Wootten, b; Mickey Sheen, d.

The World Is Waiting For The Sunrise

(The Sextet also played "The Man I Love," but this was not televised.)

Taking only guitarist Jimmy Wyble and drummer Mickey Sheen with him, Benny went West in May for his first engagement at Walt Disney's imaginative amusement park, "Disneyland." There he recruited sidemen from the Hollywood studios. Personnel fluctuated wildly, and over the course of the stand included: John Audino, Frank Beach, Mannie Klein, Cappy Lewis, Ray Triscari, George Werth, tpt; Ed Anderson, Pete Carpenter, Dick Nash, Bob Pring, tbn; Morey Crawford, Skeets Herfurt, Bill Hood, Plas Johnson, Les Robinson, Bill Usselton, reeds; Jimmy Rowles, Ray Sherman, p; Johnny Gray, Tommy Tedesco, Jimmy Wyble, g; Morty Corb, b; Stan Levey, Mickey Sheen, d.

NBC-Westinghouse filmed a performance at the Orange County, California entertainment center either in late May or early June; at least one print, titled "NBC-Westinghouse Preview Theater (Benny Goodman), No. 1715," is in the hands of a collector. On September 15 NBC televised the half-hour program. As it had for the Brussels engagement, Westinghouse once again produced a 12" LP, taken from the film, that was given to various executives and performers associated with the event. But this LP was to serve as more than a mere souvenir; it was a "promo" to interest potential sponsors in a television series featuring Benny Goodman. Unfortunately, nothing came of it.

Here is the LP. It should be understood that the selections on it are also in circulation among collectors via tapes of the telecast:

THE BENNY GOODMAN SHOW   **late May/early June 1961,**
                                               Disneyland

Benny Goodman, clt; Cappy Lewis, Mannie Klein, John Audino, George Werth (sometimes, "Worth"), tpt; Bob Pring, Pete Carpenter, tbn; Les Robinson, Skeets Herfurt, as; Morey Crawford, Bill Usselton, ts; Bill Hood, bar; Ray Sherman, p; Tommy Tedesco, g; Morty Corb, b; Stan Levey, d.

"Benny Goodman and his Dixieland Group": Goodman, Lewis, Pring, rhythm section

QUINTET: Goodman, Sherman, Tedesco, Corb, Levey

BGTV1A   **LP:** Westinghouse BGTV1A - Side 1
            Let's Dance (theme)
            Ridin' High
            Stealin' Apples
            (Wake Up, Wake Up, Darlin' Cora-voc The Yachtsmen -
              no BG
            You Turned The Tables On Me
            That's A Plenty-Benny Goodman and his Dixieland
              Group

BGTV1B   **LP:** Westinghouse BGTV1B - Side 2
            Medley: **September Song**   )
                       All The Things You Are) - QUINTET
                       Avalon   )
            Roll 'Em
            Good-Bye (in its entirety)

(Small group performances above are also on **LP:** OM 2903.)

There was another delayed telecast of the band from this engagement at Disneyland. "Delayed," indeed—it was not televised until June 12, 1964, which preceded by one day another Goodman gig at Disneyland, one week beginning June 13. This coincidence caused collectors to believe the telecast was somehow from the 1964 stand. Not so; it was filmed over three days in 1961, June 12, 13 and 14. Sponsored by Colgate-Palmolive-Peet, offering in addition to Goodman's the orchestras of Count Basie, Duke Ellington and Wayne King, mc'd by Paul Whiteman, the 1961 material was televised by Hollywood station KTTV, Channel 11, now a Metromedia affiliate. This telecast was to promote Benny's 1964 Disneyland gig:

"COLGATE-PALMOLIVE-PEET SHOW"   *June 12–14, 1961, Disneyland*
   KTTV-TV

Benny Goodman, clt; Cappy Lewis, George Werth, FRANK BEACH, RAY TRISCARI, tpt; Pete Carpenter, ED ANDERSON, DICK NASH, tbn; Les Robinson, Skeets Herfurt, as; Morey Crawford, PLAS JOHNSON, ts; Bill Hood, bar; JIMMY ROWLES, p; JOHNNY GRAY, g; Morty Corb, b; MICKEY SHEEN, d.

QUINTET: Goodman, Rowles, Gray, Corb, Sheen

Let's Dance (theme)
I've Found A New Baby - QUINTET
I Surrender, Dear - QUINTET
Sing, Sing, Sing (n/c)

(Mickey Sheen recalls that this taping was done by a recording company then owned by comedian Red Skelton, from a huge trailer parked near the bandstand.)

As early as the late 1930's, Benny had delighted in performing in amusement parks—was thrilled by the roller-coasters. In July he took a big band into Disneyland's then East Coast counterpart, Freedomland. On the 25th he taped the band "live"; eventually excerpts from his tapes were released in an omnibus album assembled by Reader's Digest; they are on Side 1 of Record 5 which bears the title, "Let's Take A Sentimental Journey - Benny Goodman Swings Again":

BENNY GOODMAN AND HIS ORCHESTRA
July 25, 1961,
Freedomland, New York

Benny Goodman, clt; Jimmy Nottingham, Doc Severinson, Carl Poole, George Triffon, tpt; Jack Satterfield, Jack Rains, Jack Schnupp, tbn; Ray Beckenstein, Anthony Saffer, as; Wolfe Tannenbaum, Sheldon Russell, ts; Billy Rowland, p; Carl Kress, g; Jack Highborn, b; Joe Marshall, d. Lynn Roberts, voc.

XIRS-9679-4S   **StLp:** RD alb 4-84-5 (Record, 5, Side 1)
Sugar Foot Stomp
The Blue Room
I'll Never Say "Never Again" Again-voc Lynn Roberts
East Of The Sun (And West Of The Moon)
Always
Roll 'Em

Sometime in the summer Benny performed at a New York children's hospital for the benefit of the New York Federation of Jewish Philanthropies. He was accompanied by an unknown pianist and a "rhythm section" comprised of young patients with triangles, rattles and assorted other noisemakers. The recital was televised locally in New York as a "Twelve Star Salute," with off-camera narration by Danny Kaye. Televising stations include WABC-TV, December 9; WCBS-TV, December 17; WPIX, December 30; WNEW-TV, January 6, 1962; and WNBC-TV and WOR-TV, January 21, 1962:

"TWELVE STAR SALUTE"   *Summer 1961, New York*
 Various television stations

Televised various dates. Benny Goodman, clt; unknown p, "rhythm section."

The Sidewalks Of New York
Moritat (Mack The Knife)
I Can't Give You Anything But Love, Baby

Benny returned to Freedomland's "Moon Bowl" in September with an orchestra completely different from the one he'd had there in July. He recorded this band also, and has in his library four 10″ and three 7″ reels of those performances, all unreleased as of this writing.

CBS taped the band September 7 for its series of U.S. Savings Bonds broadcasts in behalf of the U.S. Treasury Department. It also aired the first three selections from its tape on another of its sustaining programs, "Kaleidoscope," a weekly program that promoted coming CBS radio shows. (This "Kaleidoscope" broadcast was September 10.) Then the Office of Armed Forces Information & Education - Department of Defense got in the act, put the entire program on a 12″ LP that was distributed by the U.S. Government's Armed Forces Radio & Television Service:

BENNY GOODMAN   September 7, 1961,
Freedomland, New York

Benny Goodman, clt; Ernie Royal, Bernie Privin, Nick Travis, tpt; Frank Rehak, Wayne Andre, tbn; Hymie Schertzer, Red Press, as; Al Klink, John Murtaugh, ts; Hank Jones, p; Billy Bauer, g; Jack Lesberg, b; Sol Gubin, d. Lynn Roberts, voc.

GXTV866E   **LP:** AFR&TS One Night Stand No. 5480
RR-HW-A-6   ("One Night Stand" recorded theme - no BG
END-25-5480   **Let's Dance** (theme)
(11-17-61)   **Big John Special**
      You Brought A New Kind Of Love To Me-voc Lynn
        Roberts
      Stealin' Apples
      I'll Never Say "Never Again" Again-voc Lynn Roberts
      I Can't Get Started (arr JL)
      Sugar Foot Stomp
      King Porter Stomp - to signoff
      ("One Night Stand" recorded theme - no BG)

Not to be outdone by CBS, NBC also broadcast Benny from the Bronx. It, too, had a promotional series, titled "Monitor":

"MONITOR"   *September 9, 1961, Freedomland, New York*
 NBC Radio Network

Personnel as September 7.

Let's Dance (theme)
At The Darktown Strutters' Ball
Somebody Else Is Taking My Place-voc Lynn Roberts
Roll 'Em
My Reverie (arr JL) **(LP:** OM 2903)
Down South Camp Meetin'
(I Would Do) Anything For You - to signoff

Probably in the early fall, Benny recorded a voice track for the upcoming Christmas Seal campaign. It appears as track 9 of a 12″ LP issued by that charity for the year 1961.

Benny next reassembled the original Trio for an appearance on the "Bell Telephone Hour" telecast of October 27:

"THE BELL TELEPHONE HOUR"   *October 27, 1961, New York*
 NBC Television Network

Benny Goodman, clt; Teddy Wilson, p; Gene Krupa, d.

Avalon
Body And Soul
China Boy
Poor Butterfly
I Can't Give You Anything But Love, Baby
The Sheik Of Araby

*(Above selections are on **LP:** FEST 246, RAR 30, KOS_____)*

Possibly because of New Haven's proximity to his home in Stamford, Benny seems long to have had an intermittent association with Yale University, occasionally as guest lecturer. (Twenty-one years from now, Yale will confer an honorary doctorate upon him.) But his relationship with the Ivy League university in 1961 was that of jazz & classical clarinetist performing in ivied Woolsey Hall for faculty and students. In return, Yale presented Benny with a stereo tape of an excellent concert:

BENNY GOODMAN   *November 3, 1961, New Haven*
 AT YALE UNIVERSITY

Benny Goodman, clt, and the Yale University "Pops" Band, under the direction of Keith Wilson, conductor.

Concertino For Clarinet And Orchestra in C-Major (von Weber)

Benny Goodman, clt; Buck Clayton, tpt; Harry Sheppard, vib; Derek Smith, p; Howie Collins, g; Arvell Shaw, b; Mousey Alexander, d.

QUINTET: Goodman, Smith, Collins, Shaw, Alexander
SEXTET: Goodman, Sheppard, rhythm section

Sweet Georgia Brown
Memories Of You
Medley: Oh, Lady Be Good!   )
        Moritat (Mack The Knife)   ) - QUINTET
        I Can't Give You Anything But Love, Baby)
Avalon - SEXTET
Rose Room - SEXTET
I Can't Believe That You're In Love With Me
That's A-Plenty

Benny Goodman Septet and the Yale University "Pops" Band

Medley - A Tribute To Benny Goodman (arr Dick Hyman)
      Pushin' Sand
      Air Mail Special
      A Smo-o-o-oth One
      Flying Home
      Slipped Disc

With his "Yale Septet" as a nucleus, Benny had assembled a big band for a three-week tour of South America. The tour began November 7, included engagements in Buenos Aires, Montevideo, Santiago, Rio de Janeiro and Sao Paulo. No concert recordings have surfaced from South America, but Benny did tape a rehearsal in Carrol's, a studio in Manhattan, the day following the performance in New Haven. The tape was not intended for future release, and so is not considered a studio session, is categorized as an "air check":

BENNY GOODMAN   *November 4, 1961, New York*

Benny Goodman, clt; Buck Clayton, Nick Travis, Al DeRisi, tpt; Sonny Russo, Rex Peer, tbn; Jerry Dodgion, Herb Geller, as; Tommy Newsom(e), John Murtaugh, ts; Derek Smith, p; Howie Collins, g; Arvell Shaw, b; Mousey Alexander, d. Maria Marshall, voc.

SEXTET: Goodman; Harry Sheppard, vib; Smith, Collins, Shaw, Alexander
DUET: Goodman, Collins

Let's Dance (theme)
Bugle Call Rag - false start
Bugle Call Rag
Down South Camp Meetin'
After You've Gone
I Can't Believe That You're In Love With Me-voc Maria Marshall
Bill Bailey, Won't You Please Come Home?-voc Maria Marshall
Shine
Memories Of You—SEXTET
Avalon—SEXTET
The Man I Love—DUET—vib in coda
Sweet Georgia Brown—SEXTET (n/c)

("Shine" is the 1938 Carnegie Hall version, presumably with Buck Clayton playing the Armstrong-James trumpet intro.)

While Benny was away, This Week Magazine's November 12 issue highlighted an article by Benny and Les Lieber, "BG Picks 60 'Greatest Jazz Of All Time' Records." Obviously Benny sanctioned the article, but one suspects Benny in main merely assented to Les's choices. Benny has rarely voiced his personal preferences in public; he has on occasion done so in private conversations, but even then one senses his reluctance. The author has found that, over time, Benny has but three jazz favorites he will cite consistently: his 1937 band, trumpeter Bunny Berigan, and vocalist Ella Fitzgerald. Less often, he will name Bix Beiderbecke, Jack Teagarden, Johnny Hodges, Teddy Wilson and Gene Krupa. From time to time he will mention others, such as Lionel Hampton, Harry James, Jess Stacy, Charlie Christian and Lester Young; and that's about it. But above all, that '37 band, Bunny and Ella.

On December 2 Benny played a classical/jazz concert in Stratford, Conn., for the Vassar Club of Fairfield County. He performed von Weber's Grand Duo Concertante and Beethoven's Trio in B-flat Major, Opus 11, with pianist Bernard Greenhouse and cellist Paul Olanofsky. The jazz portion featured Benny, Derek Smith, Howie Collins, Whitney Mitchell (b), Mousey and Jimmy Rushing. No recordings of the concert are known.

On December 14 the author, with a new edition of his 1958 "BG-Off The Record" ever then in mind, taped a lengthy interview with Benny in his New York apartment. Winding up the year on December 31, Benny granted a telephone interview from his Stamford home to Ted Husing. The subject matter was, "A Tribute To Glenn Miller." It is available on tape, but when and from where it was broadcast is not identified.

The new year began auspiciously—but unfortunately, unrecorded—as Benny performed with the celebrated Pablo Casals in Puerto Rico on January 20. Senor Casals had been invited to appear in the United States, but declined to do so because of his political convictions.

Returning to New York, Benny videotaped a panel discussion for NBC's "Open Mind" series on January 31. The program was telecast at 3:00 p.m. on February 4, but collectors missed this one, and no air checks of it are known to exist.

On March 9 Benny realized an ambition he had nurtured for many years. The Nation's press announced that he had been chosen to tour the Soviet Union, his ancestral homeland, as a cultural ambassador of the United States Department of State. His selection as the first government-sponsored jazz emissary to penetrate the Iron Curtain was generally applauded, but did cause a brief controversy. Some felt that Benny's brand of music was not representative of the then current mainstream of jazz, and that a more "modern" group should have been named. Others believed that a Negro orchestra, such as Duke Ellington's or Count Basie's, might better have been chosen, as evidence of the Nation's growing recognition of racial relationships.

Those who so cavilled were quickly reminded that Goodman's style was ambient, that for more than three decades it had encompassed the several periods of popular American music; and that Benny more than any other leader had pioneered racial integration by example, not merely by advocacy. These factors, plus his time-tested ability to discipline disparate personalities, and the sheer magic of the Goodman name, effectively silenced the opposition. Benny began laying plans for the tour.

Once again, Benny was front page news. The several media sought him out for interviews and personal appearances. They provide us with a number

of air checks prior to the tour. The first was a 20-minute interview with Willis Conover, host of the CBS Radio Network's "House Of Sounds." The program was taped in New York March 20, broadcast over the full network March 24. He did not play on that program, but did on the next:

"CALENDAR"   *March 26, 1962, New York*
  CBS Television Network

Benny Goodman, clt; Hank Jones, p; Trigger Alpert, b; Sonny Igoe, d.

. . . unannounced title, intro only
Mission To Moscow

(There is some evidence that this performance was pre-taped March 16, but that has not been confirmed.)

On April 17 Benny rehearsed his new band in Carroll's Studio, Manhattan. He has a 7″ tape of the rehearsal; the author has not heard it, and cannot detail its contents. He next appeared on the "Bell Telephone Hour" with most of the musicians who will accompany him to the USSR. The program was taped during the two days immediately preceding the telecast. One of the rehearsal sessions has become available to collectors. It offers performances by a small group, and is of especial interest because these cuts were not televised:

"THE BELL TELEPHONE HOUR"—REHEARSAL   *April 26, 1962,*
  NBC Studios   *New York*

Benny Goodman, clt; John Bunch, p; Bill Crow, b; Mel Lewis, d.

Avalon—breakdown
Avalon
Medley: Body And Soul
        Rose Room
        Don't Be That Way
        China Boy

Late in 1968 the Longines Symphonette Society released a six-LP set titled, "The Best of The Telephone Hour." It is made up of 50-odd excerpts of "The Bell Telephone Hour" broadcasts and telecasts over the years. One track only, the next to the last cut on Side 2 of Record 5, is by Benny Goodman. Curiously, this transfer excises a trombone solo and one of two tenor saxophone solos from the rendition as it was recorded and televised. The release is shown in the order in which it was performed:

"THE BELL TELEPHONE HOUR"   *April 25–26, 1962,*
  NBC Television Network   *New York*

Telecast April 27.

Benny Goodman, clt; Jimmy Maxwell, Clark Terry, John Frosk, Doc Severinson, tpt; Willie Dennis, Jimmy Knepper, Bob Alexander, tbn; Jerry Dodgion, Phil Woods, as; Zoot Sims, Tommy Newsom, ts; Gene Allen, bar; John Bunch, p; Turk Van Lake, g; Bill Crow, b; Mel Lewis, d. Anna Moffo, voc.

Let's Dance (theme)
Mission To Moscow (**LP**: FEST 246, RAR 21, KOS_____, MU 30JA5195)
Clarinet A La King (**LP**: FEST 246, RAR 21, KOS_____)
Medley: Embraceable You-voc Anna Moffo
        'Swonderful-voc Anna Moffo

LWS 386B-2   **LP & "StLp"**: LSS SYS5116 - Side 2, Record 5
                King Porter Stomp

("King Porter Stomp" is also on **LP**: FEST 246, RAR 21, KOS_____, MU 30JA5195.)

The day of the delayed telecast, April 27, Benny was the honored guest at the White House correspondents' annual dinner, invited at the express invitation of President John F. Kennedy. Reciprocally, Benny, Teddy Wilson, George Duvivier and Ed Shaughnessy entertained the President, Prime Minister Harold MacMillan of Great Britain, and other guests of the newsmen.

Late in April WNBC Radio taped a Goodman monologue in New York, broadcast it in eleven 10-minute segments, May 14 through May 18, May 21 through May 25, and May 28. A tape of the full series, more than 90 minutes in length, is both interesting and entertaining, and is recommended to collectors. Benny divests himself of some reminiscences, anecdotes, and (for him) some surprisingly candid opinions.

On May 4 Benny taped another interview with Willis Conover, this time for radio broadcast via the Voice Of America. No dates of broadcasts nor private air checks of this conversation are known to the author.

Benny appeared on "PM," a presentation of the Westinghouse Television Network, on May 7. MC Mike Wallace, later notorious for his interviews on CBS's "60 Minutes," posed questions to Benny, Morton Gould, Gene Krupa, Tyree Glenn and Hal Davis (a public relations man long associated with Goodman, and a fellow traveler on the Russian tour). Included on the telecasts is a taped segment of Benny's return to his alma mater, Chicago's Harrison High, on the occasion of its 50th anniversary the previous month. Benny does not play on this telecast, but Gene Krupa does, joining the Tyree Glenn Quartet for a romp through "Avalon."

Following rehearsals in the Essex House, Benny left New York May 15 for a week's engagement at the Seattle World's Fair, with the personnel for his Russian trip just about set; Joe Newman, Jimmy Maxwell, John Frosk, Joe Wilder, tpt; Willie Dennis, Wayne Andre, Jim Winters, tbn; Jerry Dodgion, Phil Woods, as; Zoot Sims, Tommy Newsom, ts; Gene Allen, bar; Teddy Wilson, p; Turk Van Lake (Vanig Hovsepian), g; Bill Crow, b; Mel Lewis, d; Vic Feldman, vib; and Joya Sherrill, voc.

En route the band played at the University of Illinois On May 18; Keel Auditorium, St. Louis, May 19; and in the Opera House, San Francisco, May 20. From May 21 through May 26 the band appeared at the Seattle World's Fair. (No recordings from any of these performances are known.) Immediately after the final performance in Seattle the band flew to New York where Jimmy Knepper replaced Jim Winters, and John Bunch was added as band pianist, freeing Teddy Wilson to work only with the small groups.

Benny, the band and a small entourage enplaned for the Soviet Union May 27. The first engagement was May 30, Benny's 53rd birthday, in Moscow's Sports Palace. Premier Nikita Khrushchev, top Communist party members and other Soviet officials preempted most of the seats, and the Russian proletariat waited impatiently for their turn to listen to American jazz.

Concerts at Sochi, Tblisi (Tiflis), Tashkent, Leningrad and Kiev followed. Then the band returned to Moscow for five performances in the Sports Palace, July 3 through July 8, omitting July 4. On July 4 Benny was a guest of the United States Embassy at its annual Independence Day reception. It was then that the "confrontation" between Benny and Nikita Khruschev took place. They discussed jazz and modern art. The Russian premier said he did not like either; Benny defended both.

The National Broadcasting Company videotaped an assortment of the performances throughout the tour. It blended these tapes with excerpts from many other sources, and televised the resultant "The World Of Benny Goodman" on January 24, 1963. Because that program has so many diverse dates of origin, it is listed herein as of the date of the telecast.

Benny audiotaped a number of the concerts for his own Park Recording Company—in Tblisi June 12 and 13, in Tashkent June 16, in Kiev June 30, and in Moscow in July. Unreliable Soviet electric service and other difficulties aborted some of his taping, but those that were successful are in his library. The several tapes from the July performances in Moscow were released to RCA-Victor and from these the original issues were excerpted and transferred. Specific dates of the individual cuts are not known, but all were recorded during the final week in Moscow.

Most of the releases known to the author contain all of the material included in the initial Rca-Victor LP album issues; a few subsidiary LP's excerpt tracks from the "originals." As heretofore, each tune is numbered sequentially as it is transferred onto the Rca-Victor monaural LP set, and these numbers are plotted against the various releases. "Matrix" numbers—actually, pressing numbers—listed are those for the Rca-Victor monaural LP's. Known issues are:

LP, all cuts: VI alb LOC 6008-1/2, RcaE alb RD7536/7, RcaFr alb 430.358/9, RcaG alb RD2005, ViJap RA5169/70.
StLp, all cuts: VI alb LSO 6008-1/2, VI alb APL2-0824, ViJap alb RJL 2001/2, RcaE alb SF7536/7, RcaFr alb ABL2-0824, ViJap SHP5138/9.
StT, all cuts: VI FTO 6003.

7″ **LP:** VI 1-6008 - 5, 18, 19, 20

LP: SR International G77643 - 1, 3, 7, 8, 9, 10, 11, 13, 16, 17, 20, 21
RcaFr 730.629 - 8
RcaFr FXM3-7273 - 12, 14

StLp: RD RDA3-76 - 1
TL STA354 - 16, 20, 21

BENNY GOODMAN IN MOSCOW — July 3, 5–8, 1962, Moscow

Benny Goodman, clt; Joe Newman, Jimmy Maxwell, John Frosk, Joe Wilder, tpt; Willie Dennis, Wayne Andre, Jimmy Knepper, tbn; Jerry Dodgion (fl), Phil Woods, as; Zoot Sims, Tommy Newsom(e), ts; Gene Allen, bar; John Bunch, p; Turk Van Lake, g; Bill Crow, b; Mel Lewis, d. Teddy Wilson, p, and Vic Feldman, vib, some orchestral renditions.

QUINTET: Goodman, Wilson, Van Lake, Crow, Lewis
SEPTET: Goodman, Newman, Feldman, Bunch, Van Lake, Crow, Lewis
OCTET: Septet plus Sims

Arrangers: John Bunch (JB), Tadd Dameron (TD), Joe Lip(p)man (JL), Joe Newman (JN), Tommy Newsom(e) (TN), Bob Prince (BP).

NO7P-31-2S   **LP:** VI LOC 6008-1, et al
1 **Let's Dance** (theme)
2 **Mission To Moscow**
3 **Meet The Band**-narration, Benny Goodman (arr BP)
4 **(I Got It Bad And That Ain't Good** - Newman w/rhythm - NO BG
5 **Why You?** (arr JB)
6 **Titter Pipes** (arr TN)

NO7P-32-2S   **LP:** VI LOC 6008-2, et al
Medley - QUINTET
7   **Avalon**
8   **Body And Soul**
9   **Rose Room**
10   **The World Is Waiting For The Sunrise**
11 **Bei Mir Bist Du Schon** - SEPTET
12 **Stealin' Apples**

NO7P-33-2S   **LP:** VI LOC 6008-2, et al
13 **Feathers** (arr JB)
14 **On The Alamo** - OCTET
15 **Midgets** - OCTET (arr JN)
16 **One O'Clock Jump**

NO7P-34-4S   **LP:** VI LOC 6008-1, et al
17 **Bye Bye Blackbird** (arr JB)
18 **Swift As The Wind** (arr TD)
19 **Fontainebleau** (arr TD)
20 **Meadowland** (arr JL)
21 **Good-Bye** (in its entirety)

("Body And Soul," and excised versions of "Mission To Moscow" and "The World Is Waiting For The Sunrise" are also on a 12″ **ET**, National Guard "Guard Session" 210.)

Despite Khruschev's expressed dislike for Benny's brand of music, which then became the party line, those Russians fortunate enough to obtain seats to the concerts welcomed the band enthusiastically. Their enthusiasm is not shared by the majority of Goodman fans; their lack of interest in it is evidenced by the relative paucity of reissues of the original Rca-Victor tracks. That's too bad, for it was a good band that featured several exciting soloists, and offered some scintillating Goodman—his work on "Midgets," for example. More of the band's efforts during the tour of the USSR deserve to be heard.

Benny recalls that tape recorders were in plain sight in the audiences at almost every concert, so obviously there is a great deal of material extant in the Soviet Union. But despite inquiries and promises, the author has not yet received any of these concert recordings from behind the Iron Curtain. Those sources cannot be counted upon, so we must look to material brought back to the United States that so far is unissued.

On speculation, a major American record company in the late '70's blended unissued performances from the Russian tour with released material from the Brussels engagement, sufficient for a single 12″ LP. At this writing, the gamble has not paid off, and it appears that the project is dead. To the best of the author's knowledge, not even a "demonstration" LP was pressed; the assembled material is only on a master tape. A very few collectors have copies of the tape, and it is listed next. (The Brussels tracks—"King Porter Stomp," "Balkan Mixed Grill," "Bugle Call Rag" and "One O'Clock Jump," all on the Westinghouse-WWF ". . . Plays World Favorites . . ." LP—are not included.) It seems likely that the renditions are from the July concert series in Moscow, but that cannot be proved.

BENNY GOODMAN - RUSSIAN TOUR   **May 30–July 8, 1962, USSR**

Orchestra and Octet personnels as Rca-Victor releases, preceding. Add Joya Sherrill, voc.

SEXTET: Goodman, Feldman, Bunch, Van Lake, Crow, Lewis

- 0 -   UNISSUED - Tape
             Don't Be That Way
             Lullaby Of Birdland
             St. Louis Blues-voc Joya Sherrill
             The Man I Love - SEXTET
             Honeysuckle Rose - OCTET
             Caravan - OCTET
             How High The Moon

Before leaving the Moscow scene, there is a serio-comic incident to report. The Department of State had purchased copies of the author's "BG - Off The Record" to be distributed as gifts to Soviet citizens. Prior to the first concert at Sochi, trumpeter Joe Newman gave one to a Russian named Valentin, in front of the hotel in which the band was quartered. No sooner had he done so than two husky plainclothesmen appeared from out of the shadows, heaved Valentin into a motorcycle with sidecar attached, whisked him off into the black Soviet night. Alarmed, Newman asked a bystander, "What are they going to do with him?" The reply was an ominous, "We'll be lucky if we ever see him again." American press services carried the story as evidence of official Soviet efforts to keep the citizenry at arms' length from band members. Later in the tour this attitude was relaxed, and the sidemen had some jam sessions with local talent in Russian equivalents of U.S. night clubs.

Benny vacationed briefly in England, returned to the U.S. July 18. The July 6 issue of Life Magazine offered photo coverage of the tour, "Benny Goodman Swings Through Russia." The fall edition of Selmer's house organ, Encore, headlined its account, "Benny Goodman Swings The Iron Curtain Open." WNEW Radio, New York, interviewed Benny at the airport when he returned. Next, he made an unannounced appearance on CBS-TV's panel quiz show, "What's My Line?" Collectors missed taping that program. A rumored guest appearance on the same network's "Calendar" has not been confirmed. On July 24 Benny met with President Kennedy to report on the Russian tour. Near the end of July he taped an eighteen-second voice track for the 1962 Christmas Seal campaign.

On July 28, proclaimed "Benny Goodman Day" in Connecticut by Governor Dempsey, Benny began a two-month tour with a concert in the Yale Bowl, New Haven. Personnel included: Cootie Williams, Jimmy Nottingham, George Triffon, "Flea" Campbell, Harold Lieberman, tpt; Rex Peer, Jim Winters, Dick Brady, tbn; Carl Parks, Buddy Saffer, as; Tommy Newsom(e), Dick Hafer, ts; Gene Allen, bar; Teddy Wilson, p; Turk Van Lake, g; Tommy Bryant, b; Phil Faila, d; and Sandy Stewart, voc. Dates in Colorado Springs, Colorado; the Ravinia Festival, Highland Park, Illinois; and the Stony Brook Festival, Stony Brook, Long Island, New York, followed. The only extant audience recording from this tour is a tape of the August 3rd Ravinia concert, but its audio quality is so poor that it is not detailed herein.

Benny returned to Freedomland August 11 for five days with the band pretty much intact. Two radio broadcasts from this engagement are extant. Curiously, their programs are identical, the only instance known to the author that this occurred:

SUSTAINING BROADCAST   *August 11, 1962,*
  ABC Radio Network   *Freedomland, New York*

Personnel as Yale Bowl concert, July 28, except GENE QUILL, as, replaces Parks, and OLIVER JACKSON, d, replaces Faila.

Let's Dance (theme)
Love For Sale
I've Got A Lot Of Livin' To Do-voc Sandy Stewart
Clarinade
Early Autumn (arr Joe Lippman)
Chicago-voc Sandy Stewart
Dancing In The Dark (poss. arr Deane Kincaide)
One O'Clock Jump
Good-Bye (theme)

SUSTAINING BROADCAST   *August 12, 1962,*
  WNEW Radio   *Freedomland, New York*

Personnel as August 11.

Let's Dance (theme)
Love For Sale (LP: OM 2903)
I've Got A Lot Of Livin' To Do-voc Sandy Stewart
Clarinade (Benny announces as, "Clarinet A La King")
Early Autumn (LP: OM 2903)
Chicago-voc Sandy Stewart
Dancing In The Dark (LP: OM 2903)
One O'Clock Jump
Good-Bye (theme)

The band then flew to the West Coast for five days in Disneyland, beginning August 29. It returned east for dates in Knoxville, Tenn.; Greensboro, N.C.; the University of Maryland, College Park, Md.; Newport, R.I.; and the Carousel Music Theater, Framingham, Mass., from September 5 through September 9. Benny taped the September 6 concert in Greensboro's Memorial Coliseum for Park Recording Company, but the tape's contents are not known.

Benny's back ailment flared up again and he disbanded. Although he would spend some time in hospital in October, he was out of action but briefly. He assembled a new small group around Bobby Hackett, and booked it and the Berkshire String Quartet for a combined jazz and classical tour. Bobby's year-long contract guaranteed him $1,000 per week.

The jazz group's first date was a benefit for the Wyltwyk School for Boys at Lincoln Center, New York, on October 3. This engagement is believed to be the source of a 12" LP promoting U.S. Air Force Reserve recruitment. Announced by TV's "Sergeant Friday," Jack Webb, the LP offers several five-minute spots for radio broadcasts, one of which is Benny's:

WEEKEND SOUND FLIGHT '63   **poss. October 3, 1962, New York**

Benny Goodman, clt; Bobby Hackett, tpt; Modesto Bresano, ts; John Bunch, p; Steve Swallow, b; Ray Mosca, d.

XPB 498-P1   LP: Weekend Sound Flight '63—Part 3
               I've Found A New Baby

Benny chatted with Johnny Carson on NBC-TV's "The Tonight Show" on October 10, but did not perform. He underwent treatment for his slipped disc, then recuperated the balance of the month. The jazz and classical tour resumed in November with a date at the Mosque Theater in Newark. Benny then made solo appearances with the Baltimore Symphony, both in Baltimore and in Annapolis, Maryland, site of the U.S. Naval Academy. We next hear him via "The Today Show," enjoying playing with Lionel and Gene, and discussing the author's "BG-Off The Record" with Hugh Downs:

"THE TODAY SHOW"   *November 9, 1962, New York*
  NBC Television Network

Benny Goodman, clt; Lionel Hampton, vib; Hank Jones, p; Slam Stewart, b; Gene Krupa, d.

Avalon
Seven Come Eleven

The tour continued, included appearances with the Oklahoma Symphony, Oklahoma City; the San Antonio Symphony, San Antonio, Texas; the Philharmonic Symphony of Westchester, New York; the Academy of Music, Philadelphia; Yale University, New Haven (with guests Mel Powell and Jimmy Rushing); and in Symphony Hall, Boston. The Philadelphia concert, January 22, was recorded from the audience, but the tape is not of sufficient quality to warrant inclusion herein. Through January, the various television networks plugged racial integration with a photograph of the original Quartet, and a portion of the Victor recording of "Runnin' Wild."

On January 24 NBC televised "The World Of Benny Goodman," a documentary centered around the Russian tour. It was written by Joseph Liss, directed and produced by Eugene S. Jones, narrated by Alexander Scourby, and has additional background music by Robert Emmet Dolen. The hour-long telecast offered film clips, kinescopes and videotapes from many sources; brief identifications follow the tune titles:

"THE WORLD OF BENNY GOODMAN"   *various dates,*
NBC Television Network   *locations*

Televised January 24, 1963.

Sing, Sing, Sing-clt solo excerpt—background to introduction
Pop Goes The Weasel/traditional Russian song—clt solo, Moscow street
  scene
Opening night in Moscow, May 30, 1962:
  Meet the Band—Goodman narration
  Let There Be Love-voc Joya Sherrill (arr Joe Lippman)
  Original Dixieland One-Step
(Film clip, "New Orleans," feat. Louis Armstrong
Film clip, "Hollywood Hotel":
  I've Got A Heartful Of Music
  Sing, Sing, Sing
1945 CO recording,
  The World Is Waiting For The Sunrise—SEXTET
Stamford sequence, Benny Goodman, clt;
  Rachel Goodman, p; Aldo Parisot, cel.:
  Trio For Clarinet, Piano And Cello—Beethoven
1958 CO Brussels recording,
  Brussels Blues-voc Jimmy Rushing
Jam session with the King of Thailand, December 1956
1956 VI recording, Concerto For Clarinet And Orchestra - Mozart
Harrison High School reunion sequence, April 1962
Goodman's New York office sequence
Essex House rehearsal sequence, May 1962:
  Meadowland
  Dark Eyes
Willis Conover interview, May 1962
Derivations (Gould) rehearsal - Goodman, clt; Morton Gould, p.
Essex house rehearsal sequence, May 1962:
  . . . unknown title
"Character study"-reminiscences about Benny by Popsie Randolph, Peggy
  Lee, Aaron Copland, Dave Brubeck, Teddy Wilson, Gilbert Seldes, Willis
  Conover, John Hammond, Gene Krupa and Sol Hurok
Seattle World's Fair sequence, May 1962:
  Swift As The Wind
  Titter Pipes
Moscow concert sequence, May 30, 1962:
  One O'Clock Jump
Sochi concert sequence, June 1962
  Who Cares?-voc Joya Sherrill (arr BoG)
  Sing, Sing, Sing
Tblisi concert sequence, June 1962:
  . . . untitled blues-Turk Van Lake, g solo
  As Long As I Live - SEXTET
  King Porter Stomp
  . . . unidentified title
  Autumn Leaves-sidemen jam with Russian group-NO BG
Tashkent concert sequence, June 1962:
  Rose Room-QUARTET
  Bugle Call Rag
  Let's Dance (theme)
. . . plus assorted snippets of Goodman renditions even more brief than
  those listed above. Save for the penultimate "Bugle Call Rag," which is
  reasonably complete, all performances are seconds-long excerpts.

On February 1 the Sextet-Benny, Hackett, Bresano, Bunch, Mosca, and Jimmy Rowser, b, and the Berkshire String Quartet performed in Chicago's Opera House. The program was taped from the audience; but a review of the tapes now eliminates them from inclusion herein because of their poor audio quality. Next stop was Cleveland's Music Hall; and—at least—a portion of the jazz half of the program was broadcast:

CLEVELAND BROADCAST   *February 3, 1963, Cleveland, Ohio*
WJW Radio

Benny Goodman, clt; Bobby Hackett, tpt; Modesto Bresano, ts & fl; John Bunch, p; Steve Swallow, b; Ray Mosca, d. Charles DeForrest, voc.

QUARTET: Goodman, Bunch, Swallow, Mosca

Liza
Medley: Poor Butterfly   )
       Avalon   ) *- QUARTET*
       Sweet Lorraine   )
       The World Is Waiting For The Sunrise   -   )
(Lazy Afternoon - Hackett w/rhythm - NO BG, Bresano
(St. Louis Blues - Hackett w/rhythm - NO BG, Bresano
This Could Be The Start Of Something - voc Charles DeForrest
I Left My Heart In San Francisco - voc Charles DeForrest
Bye, Bye Blackbird - voc Charles DeForrest
Rachel's Dream
(Father Time - Bunch w/rhythm - NO BG, Hackett, Bresano
I've Found A New Baby
. . . interview, BG, local announcer

A tape of the classical portion of February 3 engagement in Cleveland, also recorded by radio station WJW and once in Benny's library, has eluded recent search. It is not known if this performance with the Berkshire String Quartet was broadcast.

The next stop on the classical-jazz tour was a benefit for Rotary in Benny's home town, Stamford. Benny had the entire concert recorded professionally in stereo, and has the resultant tapes in his collection. Additionally, Bobby Hackett taped the jazz segment. Tapes of Benny and the Berkshire String Quartet are unavailable, but a combination of the Goodman-Hackett recordings offers the bulk of the Sextet's performance:

ROTARY CONCERT   *February 7, 1963, Stamford*

Personnels as February 3.

Liza
Medley: Poor Butterfly   )
       Avalon   )
       Sweet Lorraine   ) *- QUARTET*
       The World Is Waiting For The Sunrise)
(Lazy Afternoon - Hackett w/rhythm - NO BG, Bresano
St. Louis Blues
(Father Time - Bunch w/rhythm - NO BG, Hackett, Bresano
Rachel's Dream
(Easy Living - Bresano (fl) w/rhythm - NO BG, Hackett
I've Found A New Baby (n/c)
Medley: Don't Be That Way
       Stompin' At The Savoy
       Jersey Bounce
       Moon Glow
       One O'Clock Jump
       Air Mail Special
Oh, Lady Be Good!

Some twenty-seven and a half years after its initial recordings for Victor, the original Quartet reassembled for another RCA session. The author attended the first of four dates needed to satisfy Benny that sufficient material was on tape to produce an LP. The first session went something like this:

Assembled at 2:00 p.m. First tune was "Together," a theme for the reunion. The Quartet played it for balance, changed the "arrangement" slightly, was ready for the first take at 2:30. By three o'clock it had cut three full takes and three that were aborted. The next 40 minutes were spent listening to playbacks and rehearsing the next tune, "Who Cares?" Lionel claimed never to have heard the tune before, but the author reminded him that he had cut it years before with Benny and the orchestra and Fred Astaire, for Columbia. (Benny said testily that one didn't count.) Between 3:42 and 4:18, four takes were on tape.

Benny next called for "September Song"—it was rehearsed, but not recorded, until 4:40. Between then and 5:15 four takes were cut. Every one save Teddy Wilson then left the studio for dinner. Teddy stayed behind to swap ideas at the piano with Thelonius Monk, who had gotten through the strict security set up to guarantee the Quartet some privacy.

The Big Four reassembled at 6:15, began rehearsing "Just One Of Those Things." Take 1 was taped at 6:38. Another rehearsal followed, then recording resumed at 7:09. This take was aborted. Between 7:11 and 7:30

two good takes were taped. The last—take 4—was almost 10 minutes in length. Lionel had suggested that the normal-length version be supplemented with a kind of "Sing, Sing, Sing" reprise, introduced by Gene's tom toms. Benny said "Let's try it," and seemed to like the results. So did all present—Gene thought this version could serve as the projected album's initial track. However, it was not released; more about that later.

It was getting on to 8:00 p.m., Benny wanted to continue, but Gene had to get to the Metropole where he had begun a lengthy stand with his own group. (A temporary band boy he had hired, when asked to take Gene's clothes to a tailor for cleaning and pressing, had stolen them and had disappeared. Gene needed to scare up some new threads quickly.) So Benny said "OK, let's cut one more tune and then call it quits." Beginning at 7:55, the Quartet ran through an initial version of "Love Sends A Little Gift of Roses," then quickly dispersed.

Despite the interest of collectors and jazz fans alike, there have been no further releases, legitimate or bootleg, of material from the Quartet's "Together Again!" sessions beyond the contemporary RCA and subsidiary issues. Benny is not averse to a supplemental release, but there is a problem: the master tapes, recorded at 30 IPS in stereo, seem to have gotten lost somewhere in RCA's vaults. Until they are located, it seems unlikely that additional releases will be forthcoming.

Simultaneously with the recording of the master tapes, a duplicate set—for at least the first two sessions—was prepared for Benny. Years later, these duplicates were discovered to be blank; evidently the subsidiary recorder hadn't been working. Benny does have, however, backup tapes of "acceptable" cuts from February 13 and 14. He also has a 7″ reel containing two takes from February 13, one from February 14, three from August 26 and one from August 27. This small reel was a "demo" from RCA, suggesting versions that might be released in a second album; some of the cuts are spliced.

The author has heard both the backup and demo tapes. The listings that follow incorporate this unissued material. Cuts on either the backup or demo tapes are identified as "UNISSUED-takes 1, 2, etc.-Tape." Unreleased titles are identified simply as, "UNISSUED." "Matrices" for released material are pressing numbers; where known, takes for the issued recordings are added to "matrix" numbers.

TOGETHER AGAIN!   February 13, 1963, New York
THE BENNY GOODMAN QUARTET

Benny Goodman, clt; Lionel Hampton, vib; Teddy Wilson, p; Gene Krupa, d.

- 0 -	UNISSUED - takes 1, 3, 6 - Tape **Together**
- 0 -	UNISSUED - takes 1, 2 - Tape **Who Cares?**
P4RM-6-74-2S	**LP:** VI LPM2698, RcaE RD7618, RcaE RD7630. **StLp:** VI LSP2698, RcaE SF7618, RcaE SFSJ7630, RcaE/F 89304, RcaJap RJL2510, RcaJap RCA6217, RcaJap PG30. **StT:** VI FTP1200. **StCas:** RcaG VCS67045. **CD:** RcaJap R32J1015 **Who Cares?**
- 0 -	UNISSUED - takes 1, 2, 3, 4 - Tape **September Song**
- 0 -	UNISSUED - takes 1, 3, 4 - Tape **Just One Of Those Things**
- 0 -	UNISSUED - take 1 - Tape **Love Sends A Little Gift Of Roses**

(Take 4 of "Just One Of Those Things" on the backup tape is the unedited, 10-minute complete version. On the demo tape, the final three minutes are deleted.)

TOGETHER AGAIN!   February 14, 1963, New York
THE BENNY GOODMAN QUARTET

Personnel as February 13.

- 0 -	UNISSUED - takes 2, 3, 4, 5 - Tape **Love Sends A Little Gift Of Roses**
-0-	UNISSUED-takes 5, 6, 8, 9-Tape **Dearest**
P4RM-6-74-2S-10	same issues as releases for "Who Cares?" **Dearest**
-0-	UNISSUED-takes 1, 3, 4-Tape **Oh, Gee, Oh, Joy!**
-0-	UNISSUED-takes 1, 2, 3-Tape **Bernie's Tune**
-0-	UNISSUED-takes 1, 2-Tape **East Of The Sun**

(Producer George Avakian is heard to designate the first take of "Love Sends A Little Gift Of Roses" on this session as "Take 1," thus ignoring the take recorded February 13. However, written material accompanying the backup takes begins with the proper number in sequence, 2. The RCA demo tape identifies the tune as, "Love BRINGS A Little Gift Of Roses.")

Within a week Benny switched from jazz to classical and from RCA to Columbia, and a new recording of the Copland Concerto:

BENNY GOODMAN, Clarinetist   February 20, 1963, New York
AARON COPLAND conducting the COLUMBIA SYMPHONY STRINGS

Benny Goodman, clt, and the Columbia Symphony Strings, Aaron Copland conducting.

XLP 75063	**LP:** CO ML5897, CO ML6205. **StLp:** CO MS6497, CO MS6805, CBS S72469 **Concerto For Clarinet And String Orchestra** (with Harp and Piano)

Little is known of Benny's activities until April 10, when he appeared in Carnegie Hall on a program in honor of French composer Francis Poulenc, who had died earlier in the year. He and Leonard Bernstein performed an unpublished work of Poulenc's, and a stereo tape of the recital is in Benny's library:

POULENC MEMORIAL CONCERT   *April 10, 1963, New York*

Benny Goodman, clt; Leonard Bernstein, p.

Sonata For Clarinet And Piano (Poulenc)

In September 1956 Benny had recorded Morton Gould's "Derivations For Clarinet And Band" for Capitol, but had refused to permit its release; he says that a strong bass is essential to a successful performance of the composition he had commissioned, and the Capitol recording is deficient in that regard. Now, needing a companion piece for an LP that would include the Copland opus, Benny once more recorded his friend's "Derivations," nine years after it had been written:

BENNY GOODMAN, Clarinet Soloist   April 25, 1963, New York
MORTON GOULD conducting COLUMBIA JAZZ COMBO

Studio personnel, possibly similar to that of May 6, 1963.

XLP 111223	**LP:** CO ML6205. **StLp:** CO MS6805, CBS S72469 **Derivations For Clarinet And Band** **I - Warm-up** **II - Contrapuntal Blues** **III - Rag** **IV - Ride-Out**

(An excerpt is also on a Columbia "sampler" LP, SOG-1.)

Some 14 years earlier, Woody Herman had commissioned Leonard Bernstein to write a composition for his Herd, "Prelude, Fugue And Riffs," but—to the best of the author's knowledge—Woody never put it on wax. Now Benny would record the Bernstein work, and not once, but twice.

Benny recalls that prior to the upcoming Columbia session he had recorded Bernstein's "Prelude" for his Park Recording Company. Specifics, such as date, studio and personnel, are unknown, for tapes of this initial effort are not now at hand. Benny does say that his version is superior to Columbia's which he faults because of inadequate execution by the lead trumpeter.

The search for Benny's tapes goes on. Until they are found, we must be content with the Columbia release:

BENNY GOODMAN, Clarinet Soloist   **May 6, 1963, New York**
LEONARD BERNSTEIN conducting COLUMBIA JAZZ COMBO

Benny Goodman, clt; Carl Poole, Joe Ferrante, John Frosk, Clyde Reisinger, Irving Markowitz, tpt; Will Bradley, Buddy Morrow, Frank Saracco, Dick Hickson, tbn; Toots Mondello, Paul Ricci, as; Bill Slapin, Romeo Penque, ts; Sol Schlinger, bar; Bernie Leighton, p; Homer Mensch, b; Sol Gubin, d; Joe Venuto, percussion.

XLP 78342-1A   **LP:** CO ML6077, CO ML6205. **StLp:** CO MS6677, CO
                 MS6805, CBS S72406, CBS S72469. **StT:** CO MQ698.
                 StCAS: CO RMQ698.
                 Prelude, Fugue And Riffs

A week later Benny returned to Basin Street East with an excellent group that included Bobby Hackett, Modesto Bresano and Tyree Glenn. Also on the bill for the three-week engagement was a vocalist destined for greatness, in one of her earliest professional appearances, Barbra Streisand.

Benny did not record any of the performances from this stand at Basin Street, but Bobby Hackett did, at least once. His tape, in true stereo, exhibits Benny and his sidemen in top form; noteworthy among a succession of polished performances is Glenn's wah-wah trombone burlesque of "Volare." But first among equals is Miss Streisand, whose range, control, dynamics, power and sensitivity are thrilling to hear:

BASIN STREET EAST PROGRAM   *mid-May 1963, New York*

Benny Goodman, clt; Bobby Hackett, tpt; Tyree Glenn, tbn & vib; Modesto Bresano, ts & fl; John Bunch, p; Jimmy Rowser, b; Ray Mosca, d. Barbra Streisand, voc.

QUARTET: Goodman, Bunch, Rowser, Mosca.
QUINTET: Quartet plus Glenn, vib.

I've Found A New Baby
Oh, Lady Be Good! - QUARTET
The World Is Waiting For The Sunrise - QUINTET
(Lazy Afternoon - Hackett w/Glenn (vib), rhythm - NO BG, Bresano
St. Louis Blues
Rachel's Dream
(Volare - Glenn w/rhythm - NO BG, Hackett, Bresano
(Kiss Me Tonight - Glenn w/rhythm - NO BG, Hackett, Bresano
Liza
Bei Mir Bist Du Schon
(When The Sun Comes Out-voc Barbra Streisand - NO BG
(My Honey's Lovin' Arms-voc Barbra Streisand - NO BG
(Cry Me A River-voc Barbra Streisand - NO BG

On May 27 Benny taped an interview for WCBS Radio's "The Bob Maxwell Show." His remarks about the Russian tour, a few reminiscences, and a plug for his upcoming summer concerts in Stamford were broken up into three segments, broadcast in New York only on May 27, 28 and 29. On June 6 he appeared on WOR-TV's "Hy Gardiner Show," discussed the bands of the '30's with MC Gardiner, bandleaders Xavier Cugat and Peter Duchin, and disc jockey Martin Block. He next took a small group, in main the same as the Basin Street East Septet, to Mexico. He has a tape of a rehearsal recorded June 14 in the Terrazza Casino, Mexico City, but its particulars are not known.

Benny next took his small group into the Shoreham Terrace Hotel in Washington, D.C., for one week. While in the Nation's capital they were videotaped doing two tunes for "The Lively Ones," a summer replacement series on the NBC television network. The performances were televised a month apart:

"THE LIVELY ONES"   *July 9, 1963, Washington*
  NBC Television Network

Benny Goodman, clt; Bobby Hackett, tpt; Rex Peer, tbn; Modesto Bresano, ts & fl; John Bunch, p; Jimmy Rowser, b; Ray Mosca, d.

Televised July 25, 1963:

There'll Be Some Changes Made

Televised August 22, 1963:

I've Found A New Baby

*(Both above on **LP**, FEST 246, RAR 30, KOS_____.)*

Benny had inaugurated what would be an annual series of "Benny Goodman Presents" concerts in late June in Stamford. He appeared with guest artists Isaac Stern, Rudolf Serkin, Morton Gould, and the Berkshire String Quartet; it is assumed that some of these performances were recorded, but recent search has not located any tapes. There is evidence that four reels' worth of concerts given by his Septet, and one reel containing a performance by the Dave Brubeck Quartet, were at one time in his library, but these too have not been found. Only one tape is now known to exist; an excerpt from Brubeck's engagement, it offers Bobby Hackett sitting in with Brubeck for one selection, and Hackett and Benny joining forces with the Brubeck Quartet for two extended renditions:

"BENNY GOODMAN PRESENTS"   *July 12, 1963,*
                                         Stamford

Benny Goodman, clt; Bobby Hackett, tpt; and the Dave Brubeck Quartet: Dave Brubeck, p; Paul Desmond, as; unknown b; unknown d (sounds like Joe Morello).

(Poor Butterfly - Hackett w/Brubeck, unknown b, d - NO BG
Sweet Georgia Brown
On The Sunny Side Of The Street (n/c)

Because their various commitments had prevented reassembling earlier, more than six months had elapsed since the Quartet had been in Rca-Victor's 24th Street studios. They met again in late August to provide more material for the "Together Again!" album.

The author has been unable to find any "backup" tapes for these sessions. But four tunes are on the "demo" tape, and these are included in the listings:

TOGETHER AGAIN!   **August 26, 1963, New York**
THE BENNY GOODMAN QUARTET

Benny Goodman, clt; Lionel Hampton, vib; Teddy Wilson, p; Gene Krupa, d.

P4RM-6074-2S   **LP:** VI LPM2698, RcaE RD7618, RcaE RD7630. **StLp:** VI
               LSP2698, RcaE SF7618, RcaE SFSJ7630, RcaE/F
               89304, RcaJap RJL2510, RcaJap RCA6217, RcaJap
               PG30. **StT:** VI FTP1200. **StCas:** RcaG VCS67045. **CD:**
               RcaJap R32J1015
               Seven Come Eleven

P4RM-6074-2S   same issues as "Seven Come Eleven"
               I've Found A New Baby

P4RM-6074-2S   same issues as "Seven Come Eleven"
               Somebody Loves Me

- 0 -   UNISSUED - take 3 - Tape
               Somebody Loves Me

P4RM-6074-2S   same issues as "Seven Come Eleven"
               Say It Isn't So

P4RM-6074-2S   same issues as "Seven Come Eleven" plus **StLp:** TL STA
               354, RcaFr FXM3-7273
               Runnin' Wild

P4RM-6075-2S   same issues as "Seven Come Eleven"
               I'll Get By

P4RM-6075-2S   same issues as "Seven Come Eleven"
               Four Once More

- 0 -   UNISSUED - splice, take 3, plus last 3/4 bars of first
               chorus from take 2 - Tape
               But Not For Me

- 0 -   UNISSUED - take 5 - Tape
               It's All Right With Me

               UNISSUED
               It Had To Be You

(Notes accompanying the demo tape identify the released take of "Somebody Loves Me" to be take 1½. The author has no explanation for the fraction.)

TOGETHER AGAIN!   August 27, 1963, New York
THE BENNY GOODMAN QUARTET

Personnel as August 26.

P4RM-6075-2S   same issues as "Seven Come Eleven," August 26
                I Got It Bad And That Ain't Good

- C -   UNISSUED
                Soft Lights And Sweet Music

- C -   UNISSUED - Take 3½ - Tape
                Liza

- C -   UNISSUED
                Nice Work If You Can Get It

- C -   UNISSUED
                From This Moment On

- 0 -   UNISSUED
                If Dreams Come True

WNEW Radio's William B. Williams taped an interview with the members of the Quartet during this studio session. It was broadcast January 5, 1964, following release of the "Together Again!" album, and excerpts from it are used as background to the dialogue.

Continuing his association with H. & A. Selmer, Inc., Benny went into the Edison Studios in the Bronx, New York, on September 26 to participate in an advertising film for the band instrument manufacturer. He improvises a few clarinet passages and speaks of the benefits deriving from a musical education:

"ADVENTURES IN SHARPS AND FLATS"   September 26, 1963,
                                             Bronx, New York

A Reid H. Ray Film Industries, Inc. motion picture filmed in color
Director: Joseph C. Spery   Musical Director: Jack Shaindlin
Music composed by: Robert Ward   Running time: 22:30 minutes

CAST: Benny Goodman, clt; Richard Franko Goldman, three unidentified actors

Clarinet solo - Benny Goodman

Benny and daughter-pianist Rachel performed together at the American Shakespeare Festival Theater in Stratford, Conn., on October 5. He then rehearsed a new jazz group for a two-month tour beginning in November. He took one of its members, pianist Marian McPartland, with him for an appearance on the "Tonight Show"—and some publicity for his upcoming concerts:

"THE TONIGHT SHOW"   October 24, 1963, New York
NBC Television Network

Benny Goodman, clt; Marian McPartland, p; and regular members of Skitch Henderson's studio orchestra, including in part Doc Severinson, Clark Terry, tpt; Buddy Morrow, tbn; Hymie Schertzer, as; Al Klink, ts; Bob Haggart, b; Bobby Rosengarden, d.

Don't Be That Way
King Porter Stomp

On October 30 Benny broadcast a roundtable discussion with MC Bob Maxwell, Jack Cassidy and ex-Goodmanite Buddy Greco on New York radio station WABC's "Sounding Board." Possibly late in October or early in November, Benny also taped a half-hour interview with disc jockey Fred Robbins; it was broadcast on WNEW's "The Fred Robbins Show" in November.

Benny kicked off another jazz-and-classics tour (billed as "The Worlds Of Benny Goodman") November 1 in Philadelphia's Academy of Music. Bobby Hackett's one-year contract had expired and was not renewed; in his stead, Red Norvo returned. The new group included Red, Modesto Bresano, Marian McPartland, Jimmy Wyble, Gene Cherico on bass, and Bobby Donaldson. The Berkshire String Quartet continued to provide the classical part of the program.

(As observed earlier, the Academy of Music is noted for its marvelous acoustics; sound from its stage can be heard clearly anywhere in the auditorium without amplification. That fact is central to this story: Benny and Red long used a routine on "Gotta Be This Or That" that ends in a challenge match between them. The climax comes when Red rips the strung-together metal bars off the resonator of his vibes and in mock anger slings them at

Benny. During the rehearsal at the Academy Benny wasn't sure he wanted to do that bit—they'd done it so many times before. But Red thought it was good stage "business," wanted to keep the routine in. The issue still wasn't settled at show time, 8:00 p.m., but Benny confidently expected Red to omit the theatrics. Thus it came as a complete surprise when Red went right ahead, slid the bars at Benny's legs, causing him to jump aside to avoid being hit. Leaving stage left, Red said to the rest of the group, "I told that ****** ****** I'd do it!", using an unprintable compound noun common among musicians. Given the Academy's unforgiving acoustical properties, mothers in the fifth balcony heard every word.)

To the best of the author's knowledge, there are no tapes of the Academy of Music concert, nor of concerts in Philharmonic Hall, Lincoln Center, New York, and the Donnelly Theater, Pittsburgh, also performed in November. But the jazz portion of the program in Houston's Music Hall was recorded, and the tape's audio quality is quite good:

HOUSTON CONCERT   November 28, 1963, Houston

Benny Goodman, clt; Modesto Bresano, ts & fl; Red Norvo, vib; John Bunch, p; Jimmy Wyble, g; Gene Cherico, b; Bobby Donaldson, d.

QUINTET: Goodman, Bunch, Wyble, Cherico, Donaldson
SEXTET: Quintet plus Norvo
BG/McP QUINTET: Goodman, Marian McPartland, p; Wyble, Cherico, Donaldson
TRIO: McPartland, Cherico, Donaldson - NO BG

I've Found A New Baby
Medley: Oh, Lady be Good!)
        But Not For Me   ) - QUINTET
        I Got Rhythm   )
(Shepherd's Blues - Bresano (fl) w/rhythm - NO BG, Norvo
Rachel's Dream
(I Surrender, Dear - Norvo w/rhythm - NO BG, Bresano
(Red Eye - Norvo w/rhythm - NO BG, Bresano
Medley: Avalon   )
        Poor Butterfly   ) - SEXTET
        The World Is Waiting For The Sunrise)
(Tonight - TRIO - NO BG
(Love For Sale - TRIO - NO BG
On The Sunny Side Of The Street - BG/McP QUINTET

John Bunch reenters; McPartland remains:
"Houston Blues"
Honeysuckle Rose (aborted)
Medley: Don't Be That Way
        Stompin' At The Savoy
        One O'Clock Jump
        Honeysuckle Rose
Good-Bye (theme)
How High The Moon (encore)

In December Benny was guest soloist with the New Orleans Symphony, and with the Cincinnati (Ohio) Symphony; he also was a judge of the annual Intercollegiate Jazz Competition held that year in Grossinger's famed resort in New York's Catskills. In mid-month (December 16) he taped the jazz and classical concert his twin groups performed in Tulsa, Oklahoma; contents of the tape are not known.

The untimely deaths of two major jazz musicians, both intimately associated with the career of Benny Goodman, got 1964 off to a shocking start. On January 4 Arthur Bernstein died in California a month before his 55th birthday. A Hollywood studio staff musician since just before World War II, the Brooklyn-born attorney was, in the author's opinion, certainly Benny's best-ever bassist. His contributions to Benny's records and air checks give lasting testimony to his power and skill.

Eleven days later Benny was further stunned by news of the demise of Jack Teagarden; he would be an honorary pallbearer when Jack was laid to rest in Forest Lawn Cemetery in Los Angeles. Jack and Benny went back a long way together, and it was fitting that they be together at the end. A huge talent, possibly the best jazz trombonist of all time, and a very likable man: Weldon Leo "Jack" Teagarden, dead of bronchial pneumonia January 15, 1964, in the cradle of jazz, New Orleans.

In between these two sad events, Benny and Gene Krupa appeared once again on the "John Lissner and Jazz" radio program. A tape of their conversations is extant, broadcast in January 12.

Benny seems to have been idle for the next several weeks; we next find him in Japan in late February with a Quartet. The group was well received and was recorded on three occasions by Toshiba, then Capitol's Japanese affiliate. Selections from a concert at the Kosei Nenkin Auditorium in Tokyo were released by the parent company:

MADE IN JAPAN   **February 25, 1964, Tokyo**
THE BENNY GOODMAN QUARTET

Benny Goodman, clt; Dick Shreve, p; Monty Budwig, b; Colin Bailey, d.

T1-2282-G2   **LP:** CAP T2282. **StLp:** CAP ST2282
                  Cheek To Cheek (also on **StLp:** TL STA354)
                  Like Someone In Love (also on **StLp:** TL STA354, PIC SPC3270)
                  Close Your Eyes (also on **StLp:** PIC SPC3270)
                  As Long As I Live
                  Stompin' At The Savoy (also on **StLp:** TL STA354)

T2-2282-G2   **LP:** CAP T2282. **StLp:** CAP ST2282
                  My Melancholy Baby (also on **12"ET:** National Guard "Guard Session" 211)
                  Memories Of You
                  I've Got The World On A String
                  You're Blase (also on **StLp:** PIC SPC3270)
                  Dinah
                  Good-Bye (also on **12"ET:** Nat'l Guard "Guard Session" 212; on **StLp:** PIC SPC3270)

Toshiba also taped the two-hour concert given the next day in the same auditorium, and another lengthy concert in Tokyo's Sankei Hall on March 9. The tapes were recorded for Capitol, not Park Recording, but Benny has copies of them, a dozen reels in all. Tunes are identified for each of the reels, but their dates and locations are not. A very few collectors have dubs of one of them, numbered "Reel #4920" by Capitol:

BENNY GOODMAN QUARTET   *February 25 or 26, 1964,*
                                       Kosei Nenkin Auditorium; or,
                        March 9, 1964, Sankei Hall, both Tokyo

Personnel as February 25.

Linger Awhile
Memories Of You
There's A Small Hotel
I'm Through With Love
Tangerine
You're Blase
I've Got The World On A String
Stompin' At The Savoy
The World Is Waiting For The Sunrise

Benny also has two reels of tape of a rehearsal of the Japanese quartet; these, too, are undated, bear only the notation, "Studio 3." (Benny now has no idea as to when or where these tapes were recorded.) For the most part, the Toshiba-Capitol tapes and Benny's rehearsal tapes contain Goodman-familiar material; and understandably, the titles repeat from concert to concert and tape to tape. However, there is a "Tempura Blues" on several of the tapes; and one tape features Benny and the Tokyo Royal Philharmonic Orchestra, Hidemaro Konoe conducting, performing the Mozart clarinet concerto.

Stateside once more, Benny soloed April 29 at New York's Lincoln Center in the premiere performance of George Balanchine's "Clarinade." Then on May 2 Benny and daughter Rachel gave a recital at the Sanders Theater, Cambridge, Mass. The concert was a benefit for the Lili Boulanger Memorial Fund.

In appreciation of his and Rachel's appearance, the Harvard Radio Broadcasting Company, Inc. (a student/faculty organization) recorded the concert monaurally and gave Benny a tape of it. (Engineers were Wolcott B. Dunham, Jr. and Thomas P. Owen; T'ing C. Pei was the producer.) Benny liked the tape, had Capitol transfer it onto a 12" LP for his private use. He then gave copies of the LP to a few friends:

LILI BOULANGER   **May 2, 1964, Cambridge, Mass.**
MEMORIAL FUND RECITAL

Benny Goodman, clt; Rachel Goodman, p.

RB-3258   **LP:** CAP Private Release - Side 1
                 Sonata For Clarinet And Piano, Opus 120, No. 1 (Brahms)
                 Allegro Appassianato
                 Andante Un Poco Adagio
                 Allegretto Grazioso
                 Vivace

RB-3259   same issue, except Side 2
                 Sonata For Clarinet And Piano, (Bohuslav Martinu)
                 Moderato
                 Allegro
                 Andante
                 Poco Allegro

                 Grand Duo Concertante For Clarinet And Piano, Opus 48 (von Weber)
                 Andante con Moto
                 Rondo Allegro

On May 6 the "Japanese Quartet" (Shreve, Budwig and Bailey) played a benefit for the Wyltwyck School in Carnegie Hall. The New York press mistakenly advertised the group as the original Quartet.

Five weeks later Benny is back in Disneyland for a week's engagement beginning June 13 with a big band recruited from the Hollywood studios. On three consecutive days he recorded some new arrangements for Park Recording Company in Capitol's studios; eventually, he sold the tapes to Capitol, which then released an LP. Still later, the tapes were reviewed by Time-Life in preparation for its "The King In Person - Benny Goodman Into the '70s" album, and some alternate takes and previously unissued selections from the June 1964 sessions found favor.

HELLO BENNY! BENNY GOODMAN   **June 16, 1964, Hollywood**

Benny Goodman, clt; Tony Terran, Ray Triscari, Jimmy Zito, tpt; Bob Edmondson, Vern Friley, tbn; Skeets Herfurt, Herb Steward, as; Teddy Edwards, Bob Hardaway, ts; Pete Jolly, p; Benny Garcia, g; Monty Budwig, b; Colin Bailey, d. Tommy Newsom(e), GERALD WILSON (GW), BILL HOLMAN (BH), arr.

T1-2157-G2   **LP:** CAP T2157. **StLp:** CAP St2157. **StT:** CAP ZT2157.
            12" ET: National Guard "Guard Session" 212
            Hello, Dolly! (arr TN)

STL-6-354   **StLp:** TL STA354 - Side 6
            Hello, Dolly!

T2-2157-F1   **LP:** CAP T2157. **StLp:** CAP St2157. **StT:** CAP ZT2157
            Hallelujah, I Love Her So (arr GW)

STL-5-354   **StLp:** TL STA354 - Side 5
            Fascinating Rhythm (arr TN)

- 0 -   UNISSUED
            People

STL-1-354   **StLp:** TL STA354 - Side 1
            Charade (arr TN)

(Pianist Paul Smith was also hired for the date, but did not perform.)

HELLO BENNY! BENNY GOODMAN   **June 17, 1964, Hollywood**

Personnel as June 16.

T1-2157-G2   same issues as "Hallelujah, I Love Her So"
            La Boehm (arr TN)
            People (arr TN)
            Call Me Irresponsible (arr BH)

STL-2-354   **StLp:** TL STA354 - Side 2
            Call Me Irresponsible

T1-2157-F1	same issues as "Hallelujah, I Love Her So"
	The Girl From Ipanema (also on StLp: TL STA354— Side 6)
	Them There Eyes (arr FH)
- 0 -	UNISSUED
	A Room Without Windows (arr TN)
	Charade
	Wives and Lovers (arr TN)
	Sukiyaki (arr TN)

HELLO BENNY! BENNY GOODMAN   June 18, 1964, Hollywood

Personnel as June 16.

T1-2157-G2	**LP:** CAP T2157. **StLp:** ST2157. **StT:** CAP ZT2157. **12"**
	ET: National Guard "Guard Session" 211
	Great Day (arr FH)
T2-2157-F1	same issues, except omit 12" ET
	The Pink Panther Theme (arr JL)
	The Lamp Is Low (arr FH)

There are also "live" recordings from this engagement at Disneyland; save that they were taped June 16 and 17, nothing else is known about them. It may be that Benny wanted the band recorded on location as well as in the studio, a practice he'd begun at Basin Street. Their fair audio quality, however, suggests that this isn't the case. In any event, air checks from Anaheim:

DISNEYLAND PERFORMANCES   *June 16 & 17, 1964, Anaheim, California*

Personnel as June 16 Capitol recordings. TRIO: Goodman, Jolly, Bailey.

Hello, Dolly!
Memories Of You - TRIO
People
Blue Skies
Stealin' Apples
Can't We Be Friends?
The Girl From Ipanema
Fascinating Rhythm
A String Of Pearls
St. Louis Blues
Roll 'Em
Wrappin' It Up
Them There Eyes
Stolen Love
Pink Panther Theme
Pink Panther Theme
Can't We Be Friends?
Good-Bye (in its entirety)
Good-Bye (in its entirety)

(The renditions of "Pink Panther Theme" are consecutive; the band botches the ending of the first cut, and Benny repeats the entire arrangement. The two versions of "Good-Bye" seem to come from different sets.)

Benny returned to his home in Stamford and the second in the annual "Benny Goodman Presents" series immediately after the Disneyland engagement. He has the tapes from a performance labeled simply, "Decormier," dated June 19; their contents are not known. Similarly, two tapes dated June 26, bearing the legend, "Stravinsky Violin Concerto," are also unaudited. Two tapes dated July 3 feature vocalist Tony Bennett, backed by a small group (probably a Quartet) led by Benny; these too have not been heard. But one reel by the Goodman Quartet, in stereo, opens with a blazing "Avalon," ends with a stunning version of "I've Found A New Baby." In between, Benny calls on Bobby Hackett, who does three tunes with the rhythm section sans Benny. The tape carries a date of "June 1964," and there is no file material that specifies it further.

"BENNY GOODMAN PRESENTS"   *late June 1964, Stamford*

Benny Goodman, clt; Frank Pizzeri (sp?), p; Monty Budwig, b; Colin Bailey, d.

Avalon
You're Blase
Night And Day (n/c)
(My Funny Valentine - Hackett w/rhythm - NO BG
(Just You, Just Me - Hackett w/rhythm - NO BG
(Perdido - Hackett w/rhythm - NO BG
Melancholy Baby
I've Found A New Baby

The audience-recorded tape listed next has not been available to the author, but he has been assured that its audio quality is satisfactory:

MYSTIC SEAPORT CONCERT   *July 10, 1964, Mystic Seaport, Conn.*

Benny Goodman, clt; Bobby Hackett, tpt; Teddy Edwards, ts; Vince Guaraldi, p; Monty Budwig, b; Colin Bailey, d. Marilyn Moore, voc.

QUARTET: Goodman, Guaraldi, Budwig, Bailey.

Great Day
Memories Of You - QUARTET
Night And Day - QUARTET
I Can't Get Started - feat. Hackett
I'm A Woman-voc Marilyn Moore
Sunset Eyes - feat. Edwards
Stompin' At The Savoy
Them There Eyes-voc Marilyn Moore
Honeysuckle Rose
Good-Bye (theme)

(Benny also performed with pianist Constance Keene—Grand Duo Concertante, and a work by Stravinsky—but these selections were not recorded.)

The next day, July 11, Benny returned to the Rockrimmon Festival for a performance with pianist Peter Serkin and the Toho-Gakuen Symphony Orchestra of Japan. At one time his library included three tapes of this concert, but they have eluded recent search.

A sad note in August: on the fifth, the fabled Paramount Theater in New York closed its doors forever.

August 22 was "Benny Goodman Day" at the New York World's Fair, and Benny helped commemorate the event by presenting a concert with a big band and a Quartet. He was interviewed on New York radio station WCBS's "Jack Sterling Show." The press noted that he had performed at every world's fair since the 1939 New York World's Fair. News telecasts showed Benny in action on the bandstand, and there is extant a seconds-brief air check from one of them:

NEWS TELECAST   *August 22, 1964, New York*
  Unknown TV network

Personnel unknown.

Big John Special (n/c)

As he had in other years, Benny appeared at a Democratic Party rally this national election year in New Rochelle, New York. The proceedings were taped from the audience:

DEMOCRATIC PARTY RALLY   *September 10, 1964, New Rochelle, New York*

Benny Goodman, clt; Lionel Hampton, vib; unknown p, b, d.

Avalon
Don't Be That Way
Medley: One O'Clock Jump
  Hello, Dolly!

Benny flew to London to appear on BBC Television's "Gala Performance," a variety program that also included as guests a Russian ballet company, a Milanese soprano, and a harpist. Introduced by actor Andrew Cruickshank, Benny performed with various complements of British musicians:

"GALA PERFORMANCE" September 25, 1964,
BBC-TV2 BBC-TV Centre, London

Televised October 23, 1964. Benny Goodman, clt, and the Pro Arte Orchestra, Stanford Robinson, conducting.

Concertino For Clarinet And Orchestra, Opus 26 (von Weber)

Benny Goodman, clt; Ronnie Scott, ts; Bill LeSage, vib; Colin Purbrook, p; Dave Green, b; Jackie Dougan, d.

Avalon - SEXTET
Poor Butterfly - SEXTET

Benny Goodman, clt, and a studio orchestra (including strings)

I Gotta Right To Sing The Blues (arr TN)
Indiana - SEXTET (as for "Avalon")

Benny vacationed for several weeks in Great Britain. Home, he obliged the New York Advertising Club by performing once again for the Herald Tribune Fresh Air Fund luncheon on October 26, joined by Bobby Hackett, Cutty Cutshall, Marian McPartland and drummer Cliff Leeman. Unlike the same charity affair seven years' earlier, this one did not produce an LP. No private recordings are known.

While in London, Benny had taped two "talk shows" for BBC Radio. One, titled "Hear Me Talking," was first broadcast November 9. It offered a monologue, discussion of several artists and their recordings, and Benny's reminiscences about his relationships with some of the performers. The second, titled "Frankly Speaking," was initially broadcast January 8, 1965. A trio of British interviewers put sharp questions to Benny, some of them bordering on the insulting. To his credit, Benny held his temper, fielded the questions adroitly, acquitted himself well. Copies of both programs are recommended listening.

Also interesting is an article in the February 1965 issue of the magazine "House Beautiful," titled "The American Talent For Jazz." Interviewed by Carroll Calkins, Benny speculates on why jazz began in the United States rather than elsewhere.

Benny was relatively idle for the first half of 1965. We first hear him on the "Tonight Show," chatting with host Johnny Carson and announcer Jack Haskell, then leading the studio orchestra in an extended performance:

"THE TONIGHT SHOW" March 22, 1965, New York
NBC Television Network

Benny Goodman, clt, and the "Tonight Show" studio orchestra, including: Doc Severinson, Bernie Privin, 2 unknown tpt; 3 unknown tbn; Hymie Schertzer, Stan Webb, as; Al Klink, Tommy Newsom(e), ts; unknown bar; unknown p, g; Julio Ruggerio, b; Ed Shaughnessy, d.

SEXTET: Goodman; Joe Newman, tpt; unknown, p, g; Ruggerio, Shaughnessy.
QUARTET: as Sextet, sans Newman, g

"Tonight Show" theme
Let's Dance (theme)
Don't Be That Way
It's Been So Long - SEXTET
Stealin' Apples
The Preacher
Where Or When - QUARTET
Stompin' At The Savoy (to signoff)

Columbia conceived a "Meeting At The Summit" LP, showcasing Benny with various conductors; several tracks were in the vaults, one more was needed. Benny again elected to record a composition that had been commissioned (and this time, recorded) by Woody Herman. Two unusual incidents occurred: One, Columbia Television filmed portions of the recording session for a documentary on Igor Stravinsky. And two, the "Andante" movement of the Stravinsky opus was recorded last, after Benny had left the studio; Charles Russo played its clarinet parts.

BENNY GOODMAN, Clarinet Soloist April 25, 1965, New York
IGOR STRAVINSKY conducting COLUMBIA JAZZ COMBO

Benny Goodman, Charles Russo, clt; Doc Severinson, Bernie Glow, tpt; Buddy Morrow, tbn; Charles Russo, Bill Slapin, ts; Sol Schlinger, bar; contractor Loren Glickman, bassoon; Dick Hyman, p; Barry Galbraith, g; Bobby Rosengarden, percussion; others unknown.

XLP 111223 **LP:** CO ML6205. **StLp:** CO MS6805, CO M30579, CBS S72469
Ebony Concerto
I- Allegro Moderato
II - Andante
III - Moderato; Con moto

Early in May, Benny returned to "Melodyland" in Disneyland with an 18-piece orchestra, again recruited from the film studios. Co-starring with him for the week's stand was alumna Peggy Lee. Speculation that Capitol would record the combination both "live" and in its studios never materialized. No private air checks of the engagement are known.

The third annual "Benny Goodman Presents" - "Rockrimmon Festival" concerts in Stamford occupied Benny in June and early July. In addition to classical artists, Benny offered the Stan Getz Quartet and Duke Ellington and his Orchestra, each for one evening's recital. A high point of the Ellington concert for Goodman fans came when Benny went onstage following intermission, picked up Jimmy Hamilton's clarinet, wailed through an impromptu blues with the Duke's men. Benny has three tapes of the 1965 Festival, including one of that lucky - 7/11 - performance with Ellington.

On July 12 Rachel Goodman was interviewed by Les Crane on ABC-TV's "Night Life," and had some nice things to say about her Dad.

Benny next appeared at the Stratford Festival Concert in Ontario, Canada. The classical portions of the concert were recorded and delayed-broadcast by the Canadian Broadcasting Corp. Included is a conversation between Benny and Lou Appelbaum, a Canadian composer and conductor; Benny has some interesting remarks about Bela Bartok. Benny's jazz Trio—pianist Derek Smith, drummer Mousey Alexander—also performed; but their efforts, if taped by CBC, were not broadcast.

STRATFORD FESTIVAL July 25, 1965, Stratford, Ontario
CBC Radio Network

Broadcast August 1. Benny Goodman, clt; Oscar Shumsky, 1st v; Lee Foley, 2nd v; Les Maliwheny (sp?), viola; Lynn Harold, cel.

Quintet For Clarinet And Strings In A Major (Mozart)

Benny Goodman, clt; Oscar Shumsky, v; Mario Bernardi, p.

Contrasts For Violin, Clarinet And Piano (Bartok)

Benny's next broadcast was "live" from Sheep Meadow in New York's Central Park.

CENTRAL PARK CONCERT August 17, 1965, New York
WNYC Radio

Benny Goodman, clt, and the New York Philharmonic Orchestra, Seiji Ozawa, conducting.

Concerto For Clarinet And Orchestra In A Major (Mozart)

On August 31 New York radio station WCBS's "The Talk Of New York" featured a 25-minute interview between Benny and Bill Randle. A week later Benny went to the West Coast and taped a program with Danny Kaye for his television series. Benny's sidemen were once more from the Hollywood studios; he had no regularly constituted group at this juncture.

"THE DANNY KAYE SHOW" September 17, 1965, Hollywood
CBS Television Network

Televised October 13. Benny Goodman, clt, and a studio orchestra.

*Let's Dance (theme) (**LP:** MU 30JA5195)*

Benny Goodman, clt; Lou Levy, p; Al Hendrickson, g; Max Bennett, b; Colin Bailey, d.

Poor Butterfly
The World Is Waiting For The Sunrise (omit g)

*(Both above on **LP:** FEST 246, RAR 21, KOS_____, MU 30JA5195.)*
(Benny also blows a few notes as intro to "Hi Ya, Sophia," in main a vocal by Danny Kaye and Katerina Valenti.)

Likely in late September or in October, in New York, Benny recorded some voice tracks with Martin Block for the National Guard; Bob Considine does additional narration. Intermixed with Goodman commercial recordings, the dialogue is on a 12″ LP/ET, matrix GXCSV 108153-1A. The disc has four 15-minute programs, numbered GS 209 through GS 212, two per side; its overall title is "Guard Session."

"The Bell Telephone Hour" next claimed Benny's attention; he assembled a big band for his segment. He has a same-day rehearsal tape, but its contents are not known.

"THE BELL TELEPHONE HOUR"   *October 24, 1965, New York*
  NBC Television Network

Benny Goodman, clt; Snooky Young, Yank Lawson, Joe Newman, Dick Perry, tpt; Chauncey Welsch, Wayne Andre, Sonny Russo, tbn; Hymie Schertzer, Romeo Penque, as; Al Klink, Tommy Newsom(e), ts; Don Ashworth, bar; Hank Jones, p; Gene Bertoncini, g; Bob Haggart, b; Bobby Rosengarden, d.

STRING GROUP: Goodman, Jones, Bertoncini, Haggart, Rosengarden, strings from Don Voorhees' Bell Telephone orchestra

Let's Dance (theme) (LP: MU 30JA5195, FEST 246, RAR 21, KOS_____)
I Walk With You (A Walk In The Black Forest) (arr TN): (LP: as "Let's Dance")
Yesterday - STRING GROUP (arr TN) (LP: RAR 21, KOS _____)
King Porter Stomp (LP: MU 30JA5195, FEST 246, KOS _____)

Another big band, this one comprised of musicians whose home base was Las Vegas, for an engagement in the Blue Room of the Hotel Tropicana over the Christmas-New Year's holiday season was picked up by NBC for its New Year's Eve broadcast. Alumnus George Auld, then a resident of the casino center, may have helped put together an orchestra that included some name musicians, but its one extant air check is undistinguished:

"NBC PARADE OF BANDS"   *December 31, 1965, Las Vegas*
  NBC Radio Network

Benny Goodman, clt; Jack Sheldon, Bobby Shew, Wes Hensel, Carl Saunders, tpt; Carl Fontana, Jim McQuary, Jim Guinn, tbn; John Bambridge, Raoul Romero, as; George Auld, Jay Corey, ts; Steve Perlow, bar; Lou Levy, p; Don Overberg, g; Monty Budwig, b; Colin Bailey, d. Mavis Rivers, voc.

Let's Dance (theme) (LP: BT 6)
King Porter Stomp (LP: BT 6)
Medley: Fiddler On The Roof (LP: BT 6)   )
    Matchmaker, Matchmaker (LP: BT 6)) (arr TN)
    Bei Mir Bist Du Schon (LP: BT 6))
(Blame It On My Youth - voc Mavis Rivers, accomp. rhythm section - NO BG
(Love You Madly - voc Mavis Rivers - NO BG
One O'Clock Jump (n/c - interrupted by news bulletin)
Good-Bye (theme)

Columbia Television's Stravinsky special, including the "Ebony Concerto" excerpt noted earlier, was televised March 3, 1966. Less than three weeks later, Benny rehearsed a small group in a studio in Brooklyn for another "Bell Telephone Hour" telecast:

BELL TELEPHONE REHEARSAL   *March 22, 1966, Brooklyn*

Benny Goodman, clt; Dick Hyman, p; Charlie Byrd, g; Bob Haggart, b; Ed Shaughnessy, d.

Bye Bye Blues
The Shadow Of Your Smile
Great Day
Bye Bye Blues
The Shadow Of Your Smile
Great Day

Three days later, in the same studio, the Quintet was taped for the telecast:

"THE BELL TELEPHONE HOUR"   *March 25, 1966, Brooklyn*
  NBC Television Network

Televised March 27. Personnel as March 22.

Great Day
The Shadow Of Your Smile
Air Mail Special

(Above on LP: FEST 246, RAR 21, KOS_____, MU 30JA5195.)

Benny was on radio the same day as the telecast: WOR's Martin Block interviewed him briefly for his "Martin Block Show." On March 29 Benny attended the opening of a new Manhattan bistro, Church's Composite. While there he and some amateur musicians improvised. New York radio station WCBS broadcast comment by Les Lieber, Mike Wallace and Gene Shepherd; underneath the chatter Benny's non-pro's can be heard dimly in a few bars of "Honeysuckle Rose."

Early in May Benny made a non-playing appearance on a television panel program, "To Tell The Truth." ("Will the real Benny Goodman please stand up?") No extant air checks of this tasty tidbit are known. On May 11 New York radio station WOR's Jack O'Brien interviewed Benny for his "Critics Circle" broadcast. William B. Williams had Benny and Harry James on his May 16 "And All That Jazz-Sunday News Close-up" WNEW Radio feature; Benny's segment was taped the day before. A report that Benny also appeared on the then Philadelphia-based "Mike Douglas Show" on May 16 is false; neither Benny's nor Douglas's files show any evidence of his participation in the Westinghouse Television series on that day. Besides, it was a Sunday, and Douglas usually did not do any taping on the Sabbath.

All of this activity heralded Benny's initial engagement in Rockefeller Center's Rainbow Grill, with a new group that will stay intact for some time. The ubiquitous William B. Williams was on hand to broadcast one set opening night:

SUSTAINING BROADCAST   *May 19, 1966,*
  WNEW Radio   *Rainbow Grill, New York*

Benny Goodman, clt; Adolphus "Doc" Cheatham, tpt; Hank Jones, p; Al Hall, b; Morey Feld, d. Annette Saunders, voc.

Indiana (LP: OM 2903)
Cheerful Little Earful-voc Annette Saunders (LP: OM 2903)
You Turned The Tables On Me-voc Annette Saunders
It's A Most Unusual Day-voc Annette Saunders (LP: OM 2903)
(When Sunny Is Blue - feat. Cheatham - NO BG
A Handful Of Keys (LP: OM 2903)
Body And Soul
Medley: Don't Be That Way
    Stompin' At The Savoy (to signoff)

On May 28 Benny was interviewed by New York radio station WQXR's Lloyd Moss; a tape of the broadcast circulates among collectors. At about this time Hank Jones left, was replaced by Herbie Hancock; and guitarist Les Spann joined. Both were in the group June 3 and 4 when Benny recorded the three shows each evening for Park Recording. The resultant six hours' worth of material is in his library in Stamford, and none of it has been released at this writing. Contents of three of the tapes are known:

BENNY GOODMAN SEXTET   *June 3, 1966, New York*

Benny Goodman, clt; Doc Cheatham, tpt; Herbie Hancock, p; Les Spann, g; Al Hall, b; Morey Feld, d. Annette Saunders, voc.

Keepin' Out Of Mischief Now
Broadway-voc Annette Saunders
Look For The Silver Lining-voc Annette Saunders
Oh, Lady Be Good!
Good-Bye (theme)

BENNY GOODMAN SEXTET   *June 4, 1966, New York*

Personnel as June 3.

I Can't Get Started - feat. Cheatham - BG in coda
As Long As I Live
Sunny Disposish
Satin Doll
"That's All!"
Medley: Don't Be That Way
    Stompin' At The Savoy
    Lullaby in Rhythm

("That's All!" is a two-note signoff characteristic of Benny's, heard at the end of many of his concert appearances.)

Cheatham's varied trumpet—open, muted, high- and low-register—added a surprising amount of coloration to this small group. The author was present as Benny's guest for several sets, liked what he heard, found the audiences particularly enthusiastic about the one-time leader of Cab Calloway's brass section. In his judgment, selected excerpts from Benny's tapes deserve commercial release.

Wrapping up this engagement, the June 11 edition of Saturday Review profiled, ''Goodman At The Rainbow Grill.'' Then it was ''Goin' To Chicago'' for Benny's Quintet—for whatever reason, he chose to go without a pianist—where he appeared in the Windy City's Orchestra Hall on consecutive days for combined classical-jazz concerts. Chicago radio station WFMT-FM taped the first concert in its entirety, but broadcast only the classical segment, and that about 10 months' later:

SUSTAINING BROADCAST　　　　　　　　　　June 15, 1966,
　WFMT-FM　　　　　　　　　　　　Orchestra Hall, Chicago

Broadcast April 9, 1967. Benny Goodman, clt, with the Chicago Symphony Orchestra, Morton Gould conducting.

Chicago (mock version) (arr Morton Gould)
Concerto For Clarinet And Orchestra, Opus 57 (Nielsen)

The second concert was taped from the audience; its audio quality is fair:

ORCHESTRA HALL CONCERT　　　　　　　　June 16, 1966, Chicago

Benny Goodman, clt; Doc Cheatham, tpt; Les Spann, g; Al Hall, b; Morey Feld, d.

Avalon
(When Sunny Is Blue - feat. Cheatham - NO BG)
These Foolish Things Remind Me Of You - feat. Cheatham - BG in coda
Satin Doll
Sweet Georgia Brown
Medley: Don't Be That Way
　　　　Stompin' At The Savoy
　　　　Lullaby in Rhythm

Benny Goodman, clt, with the Chicago Symphony Orchestra, Morton Gould conducting.

Chicago (mock version)
Concerto For Clarinet And Orchestra, Opus 57 (Nielsen)

The performances of the Nielsen opus pleased Benny and RCA Victor, and it was decided to record the difficult work while Benny and the orchestra were in good form. The careful splicing produced a product that critics complimented:

BENNY GOODMAN, Clarinetist　　　　　　**June 18, 1966, Chicago**
CHICAGO SYMPHONY ORCHESTRA, Morton Gould, Conducting

Benny Goodman, clt, and the Chicago Symphony Orchestra, Morton Gould conducting.

TRRM-5830-1S　　**LP:** VI LM2920, RcaE RB6701. **StLp:** VI LSC2920, RcaE SB6701
　　　　　　　　Concerto for Clarinet And Orchestra, Op. 57

Possibly to provide relief from the demanding Nielsen concerto. Morton Gould's humorous arrangement of ''Chicago'' was also taped. Years later this version was relased on an RCA Special Products LP, whose sales' profits were donated to the Chicago Symphony. This premium-priced LP was sold privately, advertised little, and is rare:

BENNY GOODMAN, Clarinetist　　　　　　**June 18, 1966, Chicago**
CHICAGO SYMPHONY ORCHESTRA, Morton Gould, Conducting

Benny Goodman, clt, and the Chicago Symphony Orchestra, Morton Gould conducting.

DPL1-0245B-1　　**StLp:** RCA Special Products DPL1-0245 - Side 2, Track 1
　　　　　　　　Chicago (arr Morton Gould)

Returning to Stamford and the Rockrimmon Festival, Benny recorded daughter Rachel performing the von Weber Trio with Fritz Maag and Paul Dunkel. On July 1 the Quintet appeared in the Ezio Pinza Theater of the Stamford Nature Museum, and Benny taped that concert, too. A friend suggested that one of the improvisations might be used as a jingle to advertise a well-known brand of Scotch. The intent was to give a one-sided disc to liquor distributors and retailers. But the project came to naught because liquor control laws in the several states generally forbid the use of premiums to promote the sale of alcoholic beverages.

Benny did appear in magazine advertisements for Haig & Haig's pinch bottle; but it would have been nice to have had a record:

BENNY GOODMAN QUINTET　　　　　　　July 1, 1966, Stamford
Personnel as June 16.

Inch Of Pinch
Medley: Don't Be That Way
　　　　Stompin' At The Savoy
　　　　Lullaby In Rhythm

Add Charlie Byrd, g.

. . . untitled blues

On July 26 an unknown station's news telecast offered a brief videotape of Benny performing with a symphony orchestra; nothing else is known of this concert. Next, with Bernie Leighton added on piano, his now-Sextet flew to Belgium for afternoon and evening performances at the International Jazz Festival at Comblain-La-Tour. Belgian Radio and Television (R-T-B) taped the festival in its entirety. Excerpts of Benny's concerts are in the hands of collectors, although it is uncertain when—or even if—the material was broadcast or televised by R-T-B.

The National Broadcasting Company was also on hand with videotape equipment. It recorded Benny's activities from the time he got off the jet in Belgium, capturing him sight-seeing, in rehearsal the day before the concert, and at both the afternoon and evening performances. Selected clips eventually became a ''Bell Telephone Hour'' telecast:

''THE BELL TELEPHONE HOUR''　　　　　　August 6–7, 1966,
　NBC Television Network　　　　　　　　Comblain-La-Tour

Televised February 26, 1967. Benny Goodman, clt; Doc Cheatham, tpt; Bernie Leighton, p; Les Spann, g; Al Hall, b; Morey Feld, d.

Rehearsal sequence, August 6:

Air Mail Special (n/c)
The World Is Waiting For The Sunrise (n/c)
The Monk Swings (alternately, ''The Swinging Monk'')

Afternoon concert, August 7:

The World Is Waiting For The Sunrise
The Swinging Monk

Evening concert, August 7:

Bill Bailey, Won't You Please Come Home

(As background to narration, brief bits of other Sextet renditions, including ''I'm Confessin','' are also audible.)

INTERNATIONAL JAZZ FESTIVAL　　　　　　August 7, 1966,
　R-T-B Network　　　　　　　　　　　Comblain-La-Tour

Broadcast, telecast date(s) unknown. Personnel as ''The Bell Telephone Hour,'' preceding:

Afternoon concert:

Avalon
I Can't Get Started - feat. Cheatham - BG in coda
These Foolish Things Remind Me Of You
Air Mail Special
Memories Of You
Medley: Don't Be That Way
　　　　Stompin' At The Savoy
　　　　Lullaby In Rhythm
The Swinging Monk
The World Is Waiting For The Sunrise
Sweet Georgia Brown

Evening concert:

Just One Of Those Things
Bye, Bye Blackbird - feat. Spann
I'm Confessin' - feat. Cheatham - BG in coda
Bill Bailey, Won't You Please Come Home
Medley: Don't Be That Way
　　　　Stompin' At The Savoy
Liza

(Matching tunes on ''The Bell Telephone Hour'' telecast and the R-T-B tapes are identical performances.)

John "Bucky" Pizzarelli, g, and Joe Dumont, b, replaced Spann and Hall respectively, and Hank Jones returned when Benny began a four-week engagement in the Empire Room of the Waldorf-Astoria Hotel, New York, October 31 through November 26. While there, Benny appeared on television, but without his Sextet:

"THE TONIGHT SHOW"   November 16, 1966, New York
   NBC Television Network

Benny Goodman, clt, and the "Tonight Show" studio orchestra, including: Clark Terry, tpt, Hymie Schertzer, as; Al Klink, ts; Bucky Pizzarelli, g; Ed Shaughnessy, d; and Milton Delugg, conductor.

Let's Dance (theme)
Down South Camp Meetin'
Sing, Sing, Sing (LP: GOJ 1005)

Benny taped his Sextet "live" at the Empire Room on November 22, but says the recording's audio quality is poor. On November 30 two "BG's" got together: he played for an anniversary celebration of a fashionable New York women's department store, Bergdorf-Goodman. A tape of the event is labeled, "Noisy," a reference to the guests' background chatter. But it is noteworthy for two unusual medleys, unique combinations of selections, and for Doc Cheatham's recreation of Harry James's 1938 Carnegie concert interpretation of "Shine":

BERGDORF-GOODMAN PARTY   November 30, 1966, New York

Benny Goodman clt; Doc Cheatham, tpt; Hank Jones, p; Bucky Pizzarelli, g; Al Hall, b; Morey Feld, d.

TRIO: Goodman, Jones, Feld
QUARTET: Trio plus Pizzarelli

Medley: Exactly Like You
        On The Sunny Side Of The Street
        You Turned The Tables On Me
        Love Me Or Leave Me
Shine
Body And Soul - TRIO
Air Mail Special
Sing, Sing, Sing
Yesterday - QUARTET
Medley: Bye, Bye Blackbird
        It Had To Be You
        Sunday
        Jersey Bounce
        Don't Be That Way
        Stompin' At The Savoy

Retaining only Cheatham from his Waldorf group, Benny opened a two-week stand in the Blue Room of the Hotel Tropicana in Las Vegas on December 23. All three major U.S. radio networks broadcast his new Sextet on New Year's Eve. Because of time constraints, CBS pre-recorded its broadcast:

SUSTAINING BROADCAST   December 27, 1966, Las Vegas
   CBS Radio Network

Broadcast December 31–January 1, 1967. Benny Goodman, clt; Doc Cheatham, tpt; Ross Tompkins, p; Bob Morgan, g; Bill Tackus, b; Mousey Alexander, d. Jan Tober, voc.

QUINTET: Goodman, Tompkins, Morgan, Tackus, Alexander.

Let's Dance (theme)
Avalon
I Got Rhythm - QUINTET
Why Don't You Do Right?-voc Jan Tober
The Swinging Monk
Air Mail Special
Sing, Sing, Sing
The World Is Waiting For The Sunrise
One O'Clock Jump (to signoff)

("Avalon" through "Sing, Sing, Sing," above, on LP: BT 6.)

SUSTAINING BROADCAST   December 31, 1966, Las Vegas
   NBC Radio Network

Personnel as December 27.

Let's Dance (theme)
Avalon
Medley: Exactly Like You
        On The Sunny Side Of The Street
        You Took Advantage Of Me
        Love Me Or Leave Me
Why Don't You Do Right?-voc Jan Tober
The Swinging Monk
Good-Bye (theme)

SUSTAINING BROADCAST   December 31, 1966, Las Vegas
   ABC Radio Network

Personnels as December 27.

Let's Dance (theme)
Sweet Georgia Brown
Shine - feat. Cheatham
Body And Soul - QUINTET
Air Mail Special
On A Wonderful Day Like Today-voc Jan Tober
Memories Of You - QUINTET
Just In Time-voc Jan Tober
I Can't Get Started - feat. Cheatham - BG in coda
One O'Clock Jump
Rose Room - QUINTET
Auld Lang Syne
. . . untitled blues; segue to,
Don't Be That Way (to signoff)

(Above on LP: SG 8010.)
(Depending on the time zone of the reception area, all three Las Vegas broadcasts could have been heard on either December 31, 1966, or January 1, 1967.)

Benny has a tape of the Sextet's first show at the Tropicana on January 7, but its contents are unknown. Leaving Las Vegas, he played a benefit for the National Jewish Hospital in Denver, with the Sextet intact. Next stop was the Chateau Madrid in Fort Lauderdale, Florida, for one week ending January 25. Pizzarelli and Dumont replaced Vegas-oriented Morgan and Tackus for this engagement.

Benny's first recorded effort for 1967 was another advertising jingle for an alcoholic beverage—beer. Two cuts, one with an announcement superimposed, were pressed onto a 12" LP that was distributed to radio stations for broadcast (laws governing beer are less stringent than those regulating hard liquor). The label's "BBDO" designation refers to the F & M Schaefer Brewing Company's advertising agency, Batten, Barton, Durstine and Osborn:

BENNY GOODMAN -   February 10, 1967, New York
F & M SCHAEFER BREWING CO.

Benny Goodman, clt; Phil Kraus, vib; Derek Smith, p; Bucky Pizzarelli, g; Milt Hinton, b; Don Lamond, d.

A&R 3035A   LP: BBDO A&R 3005A
             Schaefer Jingle - Cut 3 #S-105

A&R 3035B   LP: BBDO A&R 3005B
             Schaefer Jingle - Cut 3 #S-106

On February 15 Benny appeared in Atlantic City's cavernous Convention Hall for the American Association of School Administrators, with a Sextet comprised of Cheatham, Tompkins, Pizzarelli, Hinton and Lamond. Then, to celebrate the 25th anniversary of their marriage, Benny and Alice flew to London, then to Marrakech, Morocco in late March. While in London they visited daughter Rachel, who was studying there.

Benny was asked to address an assembly of underprivileged children at the George Gershwin Junior High School in New York on April 21. He'd much prefer to play than speak, so he took along a Quartet (Pat Rebillot, p; Charlie Haden, b; Lenny Seed, d) and vocalist Carole Ventura. A 30-minute jam session resulted, but no one taped it. He did tape a practice session of the von Weber concerto in his New York apartment on April 27, however.

His next endeavor took Benny to a regional UHF television station. There he made a pilot tape, the first in a series of programs to be titled, "The

Art Of Performing.'' Intent of the series was to present artists from various fields to audiences of participating stations that formed an "educational network." Format of Benny's program centered on improvisation: He explained how jazz musicians extemporize, then he and his group played to illustrate his comments. He also solicited observations from them about "their feelings toward jazz," and what motivated them to improvise. Having in mind Benny's general attitude toward drummers caused the author to chuckle: Eddie Shaughnessy remarks that his association with Benny taught him ". . . what not to play."

The project never came to fruition, and the pilot tape has never been televised. For years the only knowledge of "The Art Of Performing" came from a note in Benny's files. Eventually a persistent collector obtained a copy of the videotape; its video portion contains a few "blips," but its excellent audio track reveals that the Septet performed beautifully. Just over 30 minutes in length, the tape ends rather awkwardly, apparently unedited; and it does not include a final "Stompin' At The Savoy," which according to Benny's files, had been pre-programmed.

"THE ART OF PERFORMING"   *May 4, 1967, Newark, N.J.*
  WNJU-TV - Channel 47

Benny Goodman, clt; Clark Terry, tpt & Flugelhorn; Zoot Sims, ts; Hank Jones, p; Gene Bertoncini, g; Milt Hinton, b; Eddie Shaughnessy, d.

Let's Dance (theme)
Always (begun by Jones's solo piano in waltz tempo, picked up by the full Septet in fox-trot tempo)
Rose Room - incorporating, In A Mellotone
How High The Moon - segue to,
Ornithology ("ala Charlie Parker")
Air Mail Special

Benny flew to Chicago to appear in concert with the Chicago Symphony Orchestra May 13. Both the noon rehearsal and evening performance were taped from the audience with good results:

ORCHESTRA HALL REHEARSAL   *May 13, 1967, Chicago*

Benny Goodman, clt, and the Chicago Symphony Orchestra, Jean Martinon conducting.

Clarinet Concerto No. 1 in F Minor, Op. 73 (von Weber)

ORCHESTRA HALL CONCERT   *May 13, 1967, Chicago*

Benny Goodman, clt, and the Chicago Symphony Orchestra, Jean Martinon conducting.

Clarinet Concerto No. 1 in F Minor, Op. 73 (von Weber)

Benny then recorded the concerto for RCA-Victor:

BENNY GOODMAN, Clarinet   **May 16, 1967, Chicago**
CHICAGO SYMPHONY ORCHESTRA, Jean Martinon, Conductor

Benny Goodman, clt, and the Chicago Symphony Orchestra, Jean Martinon conducting.

URRS-1692-2S   **StLp:** VI LSC3052, RcaJap RVC2105, RCA AGL1-3788
                Clarinet Concerto No. 1 in F Minor, Op. 73
                I - Allegro
                II - Adagio ma non troppo
                III - Rondo:Allegretto

Benny was one of the judges of the "Miss U.S.A." beauty contest in Miami, Florida. CBS-TV televised the May 20 finals; and alert Goodman fans taped Benny's question to the eventual winner. How alert can one get?

Bobby Byrne, ex-Jimmy Dorsey trombonist responsible for that marvelous solo on "Long John Silver" from long ago, was now Artists & Repertoire chief of Command Records. Would Benny be interested in recording with a group assembled by Command? He would, and cut three tunes on the initial studio date. But he didn't like the results, asked Command not to release any of the sides. Thereupon Command put them aside; but one cut was "accidently" issued on a sampler LP of artists under contract. This LP is scarce:

BENNY GOODMAN AND HIS ORCHESTRA   **May 31, 1967, New York**

Benny Goodman, clt; Billy Butterfield, tpt; Jean "Toots" Theilmanns, g & hca; Hank Jones, p; Milt Hinton, b; Ed Shaughnessy, d.

RS 921   **StLp:** CMND COM-18 SD (Command Popular Preview
                 '67, Vol. 2)
                Beyond The Sea (La Mer)

- 0 -   UNISSUED
                Ridin' High
                Stars Fell On Alabama

Benny was interviewed for 25 minutes about his upcoming Rainbow Grill engagement on a WOR Radio morning program, "The Martha Deane Program," on June 9. That evening, he, Hank Jones, Gene Bertoncini, George Duvivier and Joe Marshall helped entertain the King and Queen of Thailand, in the United States on an official visit, at New York's Metropolitan Museum of Art. No tapes of the event are known.

In support of Israel's war against the Arab Nations, Benny, Joe Newman, Zoot Sims, Bernie Leighton, Bertoncini, Duvivier, Marshall and vocalist Lynn Roberts performed in Madison Square Garden on June 11. They played one number only, "And The Angels Sing." No private recording has come to light.

On June 12 Benny was again interviewed about his Rainbow Grill engagement, this time on New York radio station WQXR's "The Duncan MacDonald Program."

With trumpeter Jimmy Nottingham, Sims, Leighton, Bertoncini, Duvivier, Marshall and vocalist Lynn Roberts, Benny began a three-week engagement in the Rainbow Grill on June 13. Nottingham was in the group for the first four nights only, through June 16. Joe Newman then replaced him.

A report that NBC Radio's "Monitor" broadcast Benny "live" from the Grill on June 17 is unconfirmed. Muriel Zuckerman, then Benny's secretary, says she had no record of it, that it didn't happen. Still the rumor persists; inquiries to NBC have elicited polite acknowledgement, but no information.

The Rainbow Grill is atop Rockefeller Center, on the 65th floor. For his next television appearance, Benny moved vertically—down 50-odd floors to the studio then the source of the "Tonight Show." But Benny went alone, without his Septet, possibly because each guest on the program is paid . . .

"THE TONIGHT SHOW"   *June 20, 1967, New York*
  NBC Television Network

Benny Goodman, clt, and the "Tonight Show" studio orchestra, Milton DeLugg, conductor.

*A String Of Pearls (**LP:** FEST 246, MU 30JA5195, RAR 21, KOS—)*

Goodman; Johnny Carson, wire brushes on galvanized bucket; four rhythm, orchestra in coda:

Sweet Georgia Brown

Bertoncini left to honor a prior commitment, was replaced by Attila (sometimes, "Attile") Zoller. With Newman, Sims, Leighton, Zoller, Duvivier, Marshall and vocalist Lynn Roberts, Benny taped three shows each evening, June 28 and 29, for Park Recording. Stimulated by a group he enjoyed, comfortable in a setting he likes, "The Man" was at the top of his form. Highlights of the first two shows on the 28th, in the author's view, were a memorable "St. Louis Blues," an exciting first-set reading of "Between The Devil And The Deep Blue Sea," and "Sweet Georgia Brown," Charleston-styled, that brought the second set audience roaring to its feet. (Benny invites everyone to dance, but most just listen.) Standing ovations at that time were passe in New York, but this audience blew its cool, the author included.

At this writing only three cuts from Benny's tapes have been released, in a Time-Life album issued in 1972. All three are from June 28; "Undecided" and "Seven Come Eleven" from the second set, "A Smo-o-o-oth One" from the third:

BENNY GOODMAN Into The '70s   **June 28, 1967, New York**
THE KING IN PERSON

Benny Goodman, clt; Joe Newman, tpt; Zoot Sims, ts; Bernie Leighton, p; Attila Zoller, g; George Duvivier, b; Joe Marshall, d.

STL-4-354-B2   **StLp:** TL STA354 (Side 4, Track 5)
                Undecided

STL-5-354-A1   **StLp:** TL STA354 (Side 5, Track 4)
Seven Come Eleven

STL-1-354-A1   **StLp:** TL STA354 (Side 1, Track 5)
A Smo-o-o-oth One

Contents of several of the tapes are known. These are listed below in hopes that excerpts from them may be released in future. None, however, may ever come from Bell Sound's initial recordings, those from the first show on June 23; those that the author has heard are distorted.

June 28 - First Show, First Reel:

Let's Dance (theme)
Between The Devil And The Deep Blue Sea
Oh, Lady Be Good!
This Is The Life-voc Lynn Roberts
The Lady Is A Tramp-voc Lynn Roberts
I Will Wait For You
Polka Dots And Moonbeams - feat. Zoller - group in coda
Sweet Georgia Brown
I've Found A New Baby
A Man And A Woman - QUINTET - Goodman, rhythm section
Somebody Loves Me

(Documentation accompanying the tapes is not clear; the final four tunes, above, may be from the second show on June 28.)

June 28 - Third Show, First Reel:

But Not For Me
A Smo-o-o-oth One (**StLp:** TL STA354)
Mr. And Mrs. Fitch
I've Found A New Baby
Willow Weep For Me
Embraceable You

June 29 - Second Show, First Reel:

The Girl From Ipanema
I've Got The World On A String
I Will Wait For You
The Man I Love
Exactly Like You
I Love Paris
Darn That Dream

Had they been oriented toward the audience, Bell's microphones might have picked up a decades-old tradition among Goodman sidemen that is little known to his fans. Possibly Harry James began it, or perhaps it even preceded him. It occurs during Benny's closing signature, "Good-Bye," whose opening phrase, vocally, is "I'll never forget you." Immediately following is a bridge, three notes, 'da da daaah," which is repeated. Some sideman long ago found that interval the perfect time to serenade the audience, "Go to hell, go to hell." In the Grill on the 28th as Benny's guest, Helen Ward carried on the custom . . .

(Speaking of Harry James, did you ever listen *carefully* to his Columbia 36466 recording of "The Devil Sat Down And Cried"? Rig your equalizer to emphasize mid and upper octaves and go through the first full set of vocals—Forrest, Haymes, James, ensemble. There follows a bridge led by a strong trombone, then a kind of Texas-style cowboy "Eeyow." In the slight interval before the next phrase, a sideman makes a singular sexual suggestion . . .)

Trombonist Urbie Green had replaced tenor saxophonist Sims for the last two evenings of the Rainbow Grill engagement. Now Benny had his own group with which to fulfill his obligation to Command, and he returned to the studios on June 30, building an album around the theme, Paris.

The several subsidiary releases of the Command recordings are more easily detailed by numbering the selections consecutively, and posting the issues to these numbers:

StLp: CMND RS 921 SD - 1-12, inclusive
    ABC30014   )
    ABC-Dunhill ABCX773) - 1, 2, 3, 4, 6, 7, 8, 10, 11, 12
    Pathe (Fr) ABCX773)
    PIC 3529 - 2, 3, 4, 5, 7, 8, 9, 10, 12 (also on PIC StCas CS-3611)
    SR International (G) - 1-12, inclusive

StT: CMND CMC921 - 1-12, inclusive

45: CMND 45-4108 - 1, 7 (little known, and a desirable collectors' item)

BENNY GOODMAN AND HIS ORCHESTRA   **June 30, 1967, New York**

Benny Goodman, clt; Joe Newman, tpt; Urbie Green, tbn; Bernie Leighton, p; Attila Zoller, g; George Duvivier, b; Joe Marshall, d.

RS 921   **StLp:** CMND RS 921 SD and related issues
    1 **Mimi**
    2 **A Man And A Woman**
    3 **I Will Wait For You**

BENNY GOODMAN AND HIS ORCHESTRA   **July 6, 1967, New York**

Personnel as June 30.

RS 921   **StLp:** CMND RS 921 SD and related issues
    4 **I Love Paris**
    5 **I Wish You Love**
    6 **Under Paris Skies**
    7 **Petite Fleur (Little Flower)**

BENNY GOODMAN AND HIS ORCHESTRA   **July 7, 1967, New York**

Personnel as June 30.

RS 921   **StLp:** CMND RS 921 SD and related issues
    8 **Autumn leaves**
    9 **How 'Ya Gonna Keep 'Em Down On The Farm (After They've Seen Paree)**
    10 **C'est Si Bon**
    11 **C'est Magnifique**
    12 **April In Paris**

Like the Moscow tour recordings, the Command sides enjoy little popularity among collectors. The author recommends another hearing; some are quite good, and that old chestnut, "How 'Ya Gonna Keep 'Em Down On The Farm," is a real rowser.

But that recommendation applies only to the Septet sides; Benny's two big band recordings for Command are pretty bad. The intent was good—Israeli tunes, given that the Sinai Peninsula was still in the headlines. And the personnel was exemplary. But the results—unworthy of the intent and the participants:

BENNY GOODMAN AND HIS ORCHESTRA   **August 2, 1967, New York**

Benny Goodman, clt; Mel Davis, Flea Campbell, Joe Newman, Jimmy Nottingham, tpt; Urbie Green, Lou McGarity, Jack Schnupp, tbn; Toots Mondello, Jerry Sanfino, as; Tommy Newsom(e), Buzz Brauner, ts; Billy Roland, p; Gene Bertoncini, g; Jack Lesberg, b; Joe Marshall, d; Bobby Donaldson, bongos. Sid Feller (SF), arr.

RS 4104   **45:** CMND 45-4104
    Hava Nagila (arr SF)

RS 4104   same issue
    Peace (Hevenu Shalom A'Leychem) (arr SF)

"ET No. 4" issued by the American Bankers' Association is not a Goodman item, despite the legend covering one track that reads, "Lynn Roberts seen with Benny Goodman at Rockefeller's Rainbow Grill." Lynn cut the track in August with non-Goodman personnel, for the ABA's promotional advertising.

Benny's next public appearance was August 5, with daughter Rachel and the Berkshire String Quartet at Music Mountain, Falls Village, Conn. No tapes of the concert are known. Tapes abound, however, of his next appearance on television, in celebration of Illinois's sesquicentennial:

"I REMEMBER ILLINOIS"   *August 21, 1967, New York*
  NBC Television Network

Televised February 18, 1968. Benny Goodman, clt; Teddy Wilson, p; George Duvivier, b; Gene Krupa, d.

A Handful Of Keys
Chicago (**LP:** GOJ 1005)

Benny began a three-week vacation August 28, flying first to Europe and then to Israel for his initial visit there. Returning home, he appeared on the campus of the University of California at Los Angeles (UCLA) with a chamber group, Henri Temianka conducting, for the premiere American performance of a new work by Malcolm Arnold, "Three Pieces For Clarinet And String Orchestra." The author is unaware of any tapes of the recital.

His recurrent problem with a slipped disc caused Benny to cancel a jazz concert tour that was to have begun October 27 in Pittsburgh, Pa. Rest, sunshine and swimming in salt water usually bring relief, so he went to his and Alice's island retreat in the Caribbean, St. Martin's (St. Maarten's), Dutch West Indies.

New York radio station WNEW, long a champion of Benny Goodman—its offices and studios are around the corner, practically, from Benny's Manhattan House apartment—gave a "New Year's Eve Party" on the afternoon of December 20. Locale was the Riverboat, then a new cafe-restaurant at the base of the Empire State Building. Benny played for an hour; an edited tape was broadcast early in the morning of New Year's Day:

"NEW YEAR'S EVE PARTY"　　　　　　*December 20, 1967, New York*
　WNEW Radio

Broadcast January 1, 1968. Benny Goodman, clt; Joe Newman, tpt; Urbie Green, tbn; Bernie Leighton, p; Gene Bertoncini, g; George Duvivier, b; Sol Gubin, d. Lynn Roberts, voc.

QUINTET: Goodman, Leighton, Bertoncini, Duvivier, Gubin.

Don't Be That Way
Yesterday - QUINTET
Ode To Billy Joe - feat. Newman - BG, Green in coda
The Lady Is A Tramp-voc Lynn Roberts
Basin Street Blues
Air Mail Special
Auld Lang Syne
Stompin' At The Savoy
Good-Bye (theme)

Tuesday, January 16, 1968, was the 30th anniversary of world-renowned Benny Goodman swing concert in Carnegie Hall. He celebrated the event with a dinner party in the roof garden atop his apartment in Manhattan's East Sixties. Sidemen in his Carnegie Hall orchestra, others who participated in the concert, and Helen Ward and Martha Tilton were invited, together with members of his family, personal staff, personal friends, and other musicians of later Goodman vintage. Periodical, press, radio and television personnel were on hand in impressive number, and the gathering was publicized throughout the Nation.

Not all of Benny's bandsmen could attend. Harry James, just out of hospital following minor surgery, was recuperating at his home in Las Vegas. Red Ballard's interior decorating service kept him in California. Babe Russin and Allan Reuss could not break playing engagements on the West Coast, and Teddy Wilson had similar obligations in the East. Harry Goodman, head of Regent Music, was in Europe on a business trip.

Those of his band who were present, with their then current vocations, were:

Ziggy Elman - proproprietor of a Santa Monica, Calif., music store.
Chris Griffin - CBS staff musician, New York, and a partner with Pee-
　Wee Erwin in a music school in Teaneck, N.J.
Vernon Brown - ABC staff musician, New York.
Hymie Schertzer - NBC staff musician, New York.
George Koenig - proprietor of a Hillside, N.J., music store.
Art Rollini - wholesale florist, Long Island, N.Y.
Jess Stacy - cosmetics, West Coast - "I sell wigs for Max Factor!"
Gene Krupa - inactive following hospitalization for emphysema.
Lionel Hampton - touring with his Octet.
Helen Ward (then Mrs. Walter Newton) - housewife, Chappaqua, N.Y.
Martha Tilton - California resident, inactive musically.

Disc jockey William B. Williams taped interviews during the party with Benny, the sidemen, John Hammond and Sol Hurok for New York radio station WNEW. Consensus comment was that it was gratifying that all the members of Benny's band were alive and well 30 years later; that everyone but Benny was "scared to death" when it came time to go onstage at Carnegie; and that of all the stars in that band, a little guy from Missouri had stolen the concert—Jess Stacy.

Excerpts of the interviews were blended with tracks from Columbia's Carnegie Hall album, and a composite tape was broadcast via WNEW on January 27. The tape was then transferred to three sides (fourth side blank) of a two-12" LP set titled, "One More Time! - Benny Goodman." Benny autographed this souvenir album and gave copies to those who were guests at the celebration.

Following a buffet dinner, Benny, Lionel, Jess, Gene and Ruby Braff jammed for more than an hour. (Photographer, ex-Goodman band boy "Popsie" Randolph hadn't gotten Gene's drums set up when they began to play. Critic George Simon accompanied the group on cymbal before Gene

could participate.) Jess, especially, played beautifully, all the more remarkable because he had not performed professionally in a half dozen years.

The author taped the jam session in its entirety on a portable Uher reel-to-reel recorder; a CBS news telecast at 11:00 p.m. offered snippets of "Avalon," "Body And Soul" and "(I Would Do) Anything For You." Here's the author's tape:

30TH ANNIVERSARY PARTY　　　　　*January 16, 1968, New York*

Benny Goodman, clt; Ruby Braff, tpt; Lionel Hampton, vib; Jess Stacy, p.

. . . untitled blues (warmup)
Sweet Lorraine

Add Gene Krupa, d, midway through next selection.

I Want To Be Happy
If I Had You
Avalon
Someday Sweetheart
Rosetta
Body And Soul - TRIO - Goodman, Stacy, Krupa
(I Would Do) Anything For You
Don't Be That Way
Stompin' At The Savoy

On newsstands in May, the June issue of Esquire Magazine offered a two-page color photograph of the Carnegie concert personnel, and a brief article by George Frazier.

Benny taped an interview March 11 about an upcoming benefit in Lincoln Center for the Medical Center of New York University. The tape was broadcast March 15 on "The Martha Dean Program," WOR Radio, New York. Before that concert, he appeared on television with Merv Griffin:

"THE MERV GRIFFIN SHOW"　　　　　*March 14, 1968, New York*
　METROMEDIA Television Network

First televised March 15 via WNEW-TV, New York. Additional telecasts later via various Metromedia and independent stations.

Benny Goodman, clt, and Mort Lindsey's studio orchestra: Bill Berry, Danny Stiles, tpt; Bill Watrous, tbn; Shelly Gold, Roger Pemberton, as; Dick Hafer, ts; Richie Kamuca, ts & bar; Mort Lindsey, p; Jim Hall, g; Art Davis, b; Jake Hanna, d.

Medley: They All Laughed
　　　Love Walked In
　　　Fascinating Rhythm

Benny underwrote "An Evening With Benny Goodman" to raise funds for NYU's Medical Center on March 17 in Philharmonic Hall, Lincoln Center, New York. He performed von Weber's Clarinet Concerto in E-Flat with the Chamber Symphony of Philadelphia, Anshel Brusilow conducting. Licia Albanese sang several arias by Puccini and Villa-Lobos with the Chamber Symphony in Part II of the concert. Part III offered Benny, Joe Newman, Zoot Sims, Lionel Hampton, Teddy Wilson, Gene Bertoncini, George Duvivier and Bobby Donaldson in a jazz recital. To lock it up, the entire company then joined in a salute to George Gershwin.

Benny had made arrangements to record the event; at the last minute a craft union—not the musicians' union—forbade it. Since taping from the audience is prohibited in Lincoln Center, there is no recorded evidence of an exceptional "evening with Benny Goodman."

His health improved, Benny rescheduled the jazz tour his slipped disc had caused him to cancel the previous winter. His personnel for the initial two dates in April did not satisfy him, so he replaced them with Joe Newman, Zoot Sims, Roland Hanna, Toots Theilmanns, bassist Ben Tucker and Bobby Donaldson. Toots tells this story about an incident in Indianapolis, where the group was playing during the Democratic presidential primary contest between Robert Kennedy and Eugene McCarthy:

Benny's group jumped on the Kennedy bandwagon—literally, a flatbed truck—and toured the city, their music and messages amplified by an on-board public address system. The McCarthy advocates had a similar setup; and inevitably the two trucks passed each other. When they did, a McCarthy man shouted a suggestion that Benny perform a solo sexual act. Engrossed in playing, Benny did not hear the remark clearly, asked the sidemen what was said; but no one was willing to tell him. Later, the trucks passed again, the suggestion was repeated, and this time Benny heard it. Benny roared with laughter.

In his role of college professor on the "Camel Caravan" broadcasts, Benny frequently was addressed as, "Doctor." That title became his officially in May, when the honorary degree of LL.D. was conferred upon him by the Illinois Institute of Technology. The good Doctor then appeared with the Chicago Symphony in Orchestra Hall on May 11. The concert was taped from the audience, again with good results:

ORCHESTRA HALL CONCERT   May 11, 1968, Chicago

Benny Goodman, clt, and the Chicago Symphony Orchestra, Jean Martinon conducting.

Clarinet Concerto No. 2 in E-Flat, Op. 74 (von Weber)

Benny stayed the weekend in Chicago, then recorded the Concerto on Monday, thus providing a second side for an RCA-Victor LP he'd begun a year earlier:

BENNY GOODMAN, Clarinet   **May 13, 1968, Chicago**
CHICAGO SYMPHONY ORCHESTRA
Jean Martinon, Conductor

Benny Goodman, clt, and the Chicago Symphony Orchestra, Jean Martinon, conductor.

WRRS-4136-1S   **StLp:** VI LSC3052, RcaJap RVC2105, RCA AGL1-3788
Clarinet Concerto No. 2 in E-Flat, Op. 74
I - Allegro
II - Andante con moto
III - Alla Polacca

On June 18 Benny flew to Europe to appear in concerts in Vienna (June 27) and in Rotterdam (June 29). The Austrian concert was videotaped and first televised May 30, 1969, Benny's 60th birthday and publication date of "BG—On The Record." As an encore to the Mozart concerto, Benny obliged the audience in the Grosser Musikvereinssaal with two jazz soli:

VIENNA CONCERT   June 27, 1968, Vienna
    Austrian Television Network

Benny Goodman, clt, and the Wiener Barockensemble, Theodor Guschlbauer conducting.

Concerto For Clarinet And Orchestra In A Major (Mozart)

Benny Goodman, solo clarinet:

Sweet Georgia Brown
Don't Be That Way

While Benny was in Europe, Ziggy Elman died of a liver ailment June 26 in the Sepulveda Veterans Hospital in California at age 54. Thus within six months of the Carnegie anniversary party at which everyone was grateful that all had survived, Ziggy passed away. He had been ill for some time—indeed, he had left the party early—and his death was not unexpected. But it shocked nevertheless, for he was a relatively young man.

In July, Benny resumed his jazz tour in the United States, playing engagements in Columbia, Md. and Flint, Mich. He was guest soloist at a classical concert in the Nation's capital on July 7. A scheduled appearance at Temple University's Ambler, Pa., campus on July 14 was cancelled when driving rain threatened to collapse the canvas over the outdoor theater.

On August 16 another of Benny's illustrious alumni passed away—Robert Dewees "Cutty" Cutshall, dead of a heart attack at age 56 in Toronto, Canada, where he had been performing with Eddie Condon.

The next day Benny appeared with the Cleveland Symphony, Aaron Copland conducting, in the Blossom Music Center in Cleveland, Ohio. The concert was taped and broadcast by a Cleveland radio station in 1973, but it was first broadcast in New York on an unspecified date in October:

SUSTAINING BROADCAST   August 17, 1968, Cleveland
    WNCN Radio, New York

Broadcast in New York in October. Benny Goodman, clt, and the Cleveland Symphony Orchestra, Aaron Copland conducting.

Concerto for Clarinet and (String) Orchestra (with Harp and Piano) (Copland)

On August 24 Benny was guest soloist with a contingent from the Philadelphia Orchestra, Stanislaw Skrowaczewski conducting, in Saratoga Springs, New York. (The famed New York spa has for years been the summer vacation and workshop locale of members of the Philadelphia Orchestra.) Benny and Alice then jetted to St. Martin's for the months of September and October.

Benny's new RCA classical album was released in November. New York radio station WQXR interviewed him November 7 about the LP, broadcast the tape December 17. Bob Adams of New York radio station WNYC interviewed Benny on the same subject on November 20; the author has not located a recording of the interview, if the tape was broadcast.

For many years Benny had contributed his time, talent and money to a host of charitable causes. In recognition thereof, the New York Philanthropic League honored him December 8 with its 57th Annual Achievement Award for his preeminence in ". . . personal attainment and active concern for the public welfare." Following the presentation, Benny went again to St. Martin's.

Benny was inactive for much of 1969; indeed there is little worth noting until June. On January 29 he played a jazz/classical benefit for the Institute of International Education's 10th Annual Diamond Ball at the Plaza Hotel, New York. There are no known recordings of the Sextet's performance that evening that featured Joe Newman, Derek Smith, Gene Bertoncini, George Duvivier and Bobby Donaldson; nor is there any of Benny's work with the Felix Galimar String Quartet. Three months later to the day he was a guest of President Nixon at the White House for a celebration of Duke Ellington's 70th birthday; some of the guests performed, but Benny did not.

WOR Radio's Bill Mazur interviewed Benny June 17 for a same-day broadcast from a new New York restaurant, the Steer Palace. On June 19 and 21 Benny performed classical works with Aaron Copland at the Garden State Arts Center in Holmdale, N.J.; no recordings are known. Likely toward the end of the month, Al McDowell of WFIL-TV, Philadelphia, pretaped an interview with Benny that was televised on the station's "Summer '69" program on July 4.

Groups led by Benny and by Lionel Hampton performed separately at the Schaefer (beer) Music Festival, Wollman Memorial Rink, Central Park, New York on June 26. The quality of an audience-recording of Benny's portion is poor, and because of that normally would be excluded from this work. However, one cut does appear on a bootleg LP; and Lionel joins Benny's group for its concluding number. For those reasons, here are the details:

SCHAEFER MUSIC FESTIVAL   June 26, 1969,
                                        Central Park, New York

Benny Goodman, clt; Joe Newman, tpt; Kai Winding, tbn; Zoot Sims, ts; Hank Jones, p; Toots Theilmanns, g & hca; Jack Lesberg, b; Bobby Donaldson, d. Lynn Roberts, voc.

QUINTET: Goodman, Jones, Theilmanns, Lesberg, Donaldson.
SEXTET: Quintet plus Newman

Sweet Georgia Brown
Avalon - QUINTET
Yesterday - QUINTET
The World Is Waiting For The Sunrise - QUINTET
The Girl From Ipanema-voc Lynn Roberts
(The Shadow Of Your Smile-voc Lynn Roberts, w/rhythm - NO BG)
It's A Most Unusual Day-voc Lynn Roberts
Medley: Don't Be That Way
        Stompin' At The Savoy
(Bluesette - Theilmanns w/rhythm - NO BG)
(Summertime - Theilmanns w/rhythm - NO BG)
Ode To Billy Joe - SEXTET
St. Louis Blues (**LP:** OM 2903)

Add Lionel Hampton, vib.

Air Mail Special

On June 30 Benny taped an interview for the "Peter Lind Hayes-Mary Healy Show" for WOR Radio; the principals discussed the new bio-discography, "BG—On The Record." On July 5 Benny was featured soloist with the Zagreb Symphony Orchestra, Jimmy DePriest conducting, at Temple University's Ambler, Pa., facility. Again, no known recordings. His next performance did produce a tape—two, in fact; both rehearsal and concert—recorded from the audience. In part a benefit performance celebrating the 80th anniversary of Chicago's Hull House (BG, alumnus), the concert at Ravinia Park, in Highland Park, Ill., featured a good Goodman group: Jimmy Nottingham, Urbie Green, Jerome Richardson (ts), Derek Smith, Bucky Pizzarelli, Jack Lesberg, Mousey Alexander and vocalist Lynn Roberts. But the quality of the tapes is poor, and they are not detailed herein. Date was July 23.

Salmon fishing in New Brunswick, British Columbia, next occupied Benny. Then on August 14 he taped a 5-minute interview for Mike Wallace's radio program; the author does not have a copy of it. On the 28th he appeared "live" on WOR's "The Martha Deane Program," giving radio listeners another rundown on "BG—On The Record." We next locate him in Louisville, Kentucky's, Art Center with Aaron Copland on September 20; nothing on tape from that concert. On the 30th he attended a testimonial for brother-in-law John Hammond at the Essex House in New York, but did not play.

Benny went back to work in October with a vengeance. For the first time in over five years—if one discounts those two Israeli tunes for Command—he recorded a big band in a studio. Befitting his reentry into the jazz orchestra orbit, everything about the project was new. Well, almost everything; most of the sidemen, assembled with Hymie Schertzer's help, were tried and true Goodman alumni. But all the tunes were contemporary compositions, never before in the Goodman library. They were charted by arrangers who had not worked for Benny previously. They were recorded in RCA's just-opened studios at 1133 Avenue of the Americas (6th Avenue). And they would be released by Reader's Digest, a new sponsor for Benny Goodman.

The author attended two of the recording sessions. Enthusiasm was high, everyone was pleased with the results, so much so that the sidemen stayed on to listen to the playbacks, despite commitments elsewhere. And on the third date, the author witnessed a remarkable example of the competency of professional musicianship:

The last tune recorded that day was "Spinning Wheel," arranged by Frank Foster, who was in the control room watching and listening. The band ran through it once; and then there was silence. Finally Benny said, nodding toward Foster, "I'm sorry, but that's not for us," meaning, that's not the Goodman style. More silence. Then Hymie said, "Look, Benny, if we do this, here . . . ," taking a pencil and making some changes on the arrangement before him, and fingering them on his horn. Then someone else, believe it was Buddy Morrow, said, "That's right; then if we do this . . ." And so it went, for no more than 10 minutes certainly, and possibly not longer than five, with others contributing suggestions. In that brief time the arrangement was rewritten, Benny said OK, and the band put it on 16-track tape. Remarkable.

Given Reader's Digest's mammoth marketing facilities, its several albums that issued these Goodman sides were commercial successes. However, like the material from the Moscow tour, these recordings have not been especially popular with Goodman collectors. Perhaps Benny's gut feeling about "Spinning Wheel" applied generally: not the Goodman style, not what we expect of him. But there may be another factor: The playbacks on the Studio C monitors sounded great; as noted, the performers delayed moving on to listen to them, they were so good. Somehow, that sound just doesn't come through on the LP's.

Two albums embrace all of the tunes cut: RD4-106, "Happiness Is . . . Up, Up And Away With The Happy Hits Of Today," and RD4-112, "The Big Bands Are Back - Swinging Today's Hits." RD4-169, "Great Songs! Great Bands!", RD "Dance Party" and RD "All-Star Jazz Festival" are secondary releases. A recent bootleg LP, English Bulldog BDL 1038, contains all of the cuts.

Each tune was recorded more than once; counting aborted takes—"breakdowns"—the number of takes for a given tune is shown in parentheses following its title. In most cases, the last take recorded of each tune was the one that was issued.

BENNY GOODMAN AND HIS ORCHESTRA   October 7, 1969, New York

Benny Goodman, clt; Bernie Glow, Joe Newman, Snooky Young, John Frosk, tpt; Buddy Morrow, Lou McGarity, Chauncey Welsch, Paul Faulise, tbn; Hymie Schertzer, Walt Levinsky, as; Frank Wess, Al Klink, ts; Sol Schlinger, bar; Derek Smith, p; Bucky Pizzarelli, g; Milt Hinton, b; Grady Tate, d. Frank Foster (FF), Walt Levinsky (WL), Sammy Lowe (SL), Claus Ogerman (CO), arr.

XR1S-9511   **StLp:** RD4-112 (Record 6, Side 1, Track 3), RD4-169, RD "Dance Party"
Windy (6 takes) (arr WL)

XR2S-9684   **StLp:** RD4-106 (Record 7, Side 2, Track 3), RD4-169
Good Morning Starshine (8 takes) (arr CO)

XR1S-9507   **StLp:** RD4-112 (Record 4, Side 1, Track 5), RD4-169
Aquarius (4 takes) (arr WL)

BENNY GOODMAN AND HIS ORCHESTRA   October 8, 1969, New York

Personnel as October 7.

XR2S-9683   **StLp:** RD4-106 (Record 7, Side 1, Track 2)
Love Theme From "Romeo And Juliet" (6 takes) (arr CO)

XR2S-9686   **StLp:** RD4-106 (Record 8, Side 2, Track 3), RD4-169
I'll Never Fall In Love Again (# takes unknown) (arr CO)

- 0 -   UNISSUED
Up, Up And Away (1 take) (arr SL)

BENNY GOODMAN AND HIS ORCHESTRA   October 9, 1969, New York

Personnel as October 7.

XR1S-9501   **StLp:** RD4-112 (Record 1, Side 1, Track 4), RD4-169, RD "Dance Party"
Watch What Happens (6 takes) (arr WL)

XR2S-9686   **StLp:** RD4-106 (Record 8, Side 2, Track 6), RD4-169
Both Sides Now (6 takes) (arr CO)

XR2S-9678   **StLp:** RD4-106 (Record 4, Side 2, Track 6)
You've Made Me So Very Happy (7 takes) (arr FF)

XR2S-9673   **StLp:** RD4-106 (Record 2, Side 1, Track 6), RD4-034
Up, Up And Away (1 take) (arr SL)

XR2S-9677   **StLp:** RD4-106 (Record 4, Side 1, Track 6), RD4-169
Spinning Wheel (3 takes) (arr FF)

(The seventh take of "You've Made Me So Very Happy" was a recording of the last few choruses of the arrangements; likely the issued version is a splice of the sixth take and this ending.)

Thinking ahead, believe the October 9 session was Benny's last with Lou McGarity. A good ol' boy from Georgia, he of those curly, golden locks, Lou was now white-haired and bearded, and not in the best of health. But he still played well, for Benny and for "The World's Greatest Jazz Band," with which he worked regularly. A heart attack will lay him low in Blues Alley, Washington, and he will pass on on August 28, 1971. Robert Louis McGarity, one of the great ones.

Ten tunes were on tape for Reader's Digest; Benny made it an even dozen with two more by his Sextet:

(THE) BENNY GOODMAN SEXTET   October 10, 1969, New York

Benny Goodman, clt; Urbie Green, tbn; Derek Smith, p; Toots Theilmanns, hca & g; Milt Hinton, b; Grady Tate, d.

XR1S-9510   **StLp:** RD4-112 (Record 5, Side 2, Track 5), RD4-169, RD "Dance Party"
Bluesette

XR1S-9503   **StLp:** RD4-112 (Record 2, Side 1, Track 5), RD4-169, RD "All-Star Jazz Festival"
Monday, Monday

("Monday, Monday" is also on **LP**, RcaG "The Golden Age Of Jazz," (GJAZ 039). Both tunes are also on the English Bulldog issue, BDL 1038.)

On October 14 Benny appeared in a recital of classical music in the Portland City Hall Auditorium, Portland, Maine. Two days later he flew to London, for what was intended to be a two-week visit to a city he enjoys. While there he was approached by Philips: Would he be available to listen to a big band comprised of British musicians, assembled by Frank Leidy, playing some arrangements written by local talent? He would. Would he consider recording with them? He did; for upon hearing them for the first time, his immediate reaction was, "Hey, these guys are good!" And they were; and Philips's superior recording and transfer of the material provide good listening.

LONDON DATE   **October 28, 1969, London**
BENNY GOODMAN & HIS ORCHESTRA

Benny Goodman, clt; Kenny Baker, Bert Ezard, Tommy McQuator, Derek Healey, tpt; Lad Eusby, Johnny Marshall, Jackie Armstrong, Chris Smith, tbn; Bob Burns, Don Honeywill, as; Tommy Whittle, Frank Reidy, ts; Roy Willox, bar: Bill McGuffie, p; Judd Proctor, g; Lennie Bush, b; Ronnie Stephenson, d. Peter Knight (PK), Harry South (HS), Wally Stott (WS), arr.

- 0 -   **StLp:** PHIL 6308023, PhilG 6308023D MEGA M51-5002, PHIL 9282003, TL STA354. **StCas:** PHIL 7108019
I Talk To The Trees (arr WS)

same issues as "I Talk To The Trees," except omit TL STA354
I Will Wait For You (arr WS)

same issues as "I Talk To The Trees"
This Guy's In Love With You (arr PK)

same issues as "I Will Wait For You"
Yesterday (arr WS)

("Matrix" numbers are the same as the catalog number of the initial Philips release.)

A month would go by before Benny returned to Philips' studios in Stanhope House, Stanhope Place, London W.2, to provide sufficient additional material for an album. And he would take with him some of Fletcher Henderson's charts, to supplement those by the British arrangers. Meanwhile, he inaugurated the new Performing Arts Center in Milwaukee, Wisc., aided by Joe Newman, Chauncey Welsch, Frank Foster (ts), Roland Hanna, Toots Theilmanns, Bucky Pizzarelli, Bob Cranshaw (b) and Bobby Rosengarden. The author has an audience-recorded tape of the concert, but its quality is not up to the standard set for inclusion herein. Opening day was November 7. On the 16th he fronted a big band at Philharmonic Hall, Lincoln Center, as part of a revue titled, "The Heyday Of Rodgers And Hart." There was critical praise for his performance, but no recordings. Then it was back to London:

LONDON DATE   **November 27, 1969, London**
BENNY GOODMAN & HIS ORCHESTRA

Personnel as October 28.

- 0 -   **StLp:** PHIL 6308023, PhilC 6308023D, MEGA M51-5002, PHIL 9282003, TL STA354. **StCas:** PHIL 7108019
On A Clear Day (arr HS)

same issues as "On A Clear Day," except omit TL STA354
That My Love (Los Reyes Magos) (arr PK)

same issues as "That My Love"
Liza (All The Clouds'll Roll Away) (arr FH)

same issues as "That My Love"
(What Can I Say) After I Say I'm Sorry (arr FH)

Eight tunes were successfully on tape; a few more were needed for an LP's worth. Benny elected to do these with a small group, possibly because no more attractive new arrangements were on hand. Note that these cuts are by an Octet, although liner notes still credit an "orchestra":

LONDON DATE   **November 28, 1969, London**
BENNY GOODMAN & HIS ORCHESTRA

Benny Goodman, clt; Kenny Baker, tpt; George Chisholm, tbn; Tommy Whittle, ts; Bill McGuffie, p; Judd Proctor, g; Lennie Bush, b; Ronnie Stephenson, d.

- 0 -   UNISSUED
Mr. & Mrs. Fitch

StLp: PHIL 6308023, PhilG 6308023D MEGA M51-5002, PHIL 9282003. **StCas:** PHIL 7108019
You Took Advantage Of Me

same issues
Octopus's Garden (arr PK)

same issues
It's Easy To Remember (arr PK)

Thus the British band, 1969. But it is a precursor of things to come, for Benny had an idea he'd like to lead such a band on a tour of the Continent. He'll be back early next year.

Before closing out the decade of the '60's, a few random notes:

Sometime in the Fall-Winter of 1969, WCBS Radio (New York) announcer Jeff Scott interviewed Benny, and over time excerpts of his tape were broadcast on that station. And likely in the same period, Benny cut some voice tracks for the National Guard. They appear on two 12" LP/ET's: Cut No. 9 on "Spots For The Guards" GVL NG 500A/B; and Cuts 5, 10 and 15 on "Spots For The Guards" GXTV 220203-1A. And despite his English connection, Benny endorsed the liquor "Irish Mist" in space advertising in some national periodicals.

A quick review finds high spots, low spots and some sad notes in Benny's personal history of the turbulent 1960's. The Arthur Godfrey program comes to mind, some good dates with Red Norvo, the concert at Yale, the Russian tour, the Quartet Together Again!, Basin Street and Barbra, recording with the Chicago Symphony, some exciting things from the Rainbow Grill, and of course the old gang reunited if only for gin and gab . . . On the other hand, those two big band cuts for Command; bad. And what a trombone section we lost: Jack and Cutty. And one of the most powerful trumpets ever, stilled for all time, Ziggy.

But musicians look ahead, never back (the only musician ever to ask the author about old recordings was the Duke's Harry Carney, who collected Ellington's sides). So we'll join Benny in anticipating more good times in the 'Seventies.

THE 1970'S—CONCERTS, CASSETTES AND CARNEGIE, FORTY YEARS LATER

AUTHOR'S NOTE:

As the 1970's moved forward, cassette and micro-cassette recorders got progressively better, smaller and cheaper. As they did so, their unauthorized use to tape Goodman's concert appearances from the audience grew commensurately. Despite proscriptions posted and enforced against these devices, it is likely that from early in the decade on, every one of Benny Goodman's concerts was recorded clandestinely.

The author has a representative sample of such tapes in his library. For many reasons—auditoria acoustics, type of equipment, location of the recordist, etc.—the audio fidelity of these tapes varies greatly. In this work, those tapes that afford reasonably satisfactory listening are described in detail; those whose sound quality is poor are not, but notice is given that they are extant. If the author does not have a tape of a given concert, only the date and location of the performance, and personnel who appeared in it, are noted.

The reader, and especially the collector, should bear these things in mind: One, the author's judgment is subjective; his "poor" may be someone else's "acceptable." Two, although tapes in circulation among collectors generally are from a common source, certainly alternative cassette recordings of any given concert are likely extant; their sound quality may be better or worse than the author's copy. And three—in all likelihood, someone out there has a cassette recording of a concert that the author lacks. Goodman's itineraries should be used to search them out.

* * *

Pleased by the technical expertise of the English musicians, impressed by their discipline, and delighted that they swung, Benny had Frank Reidy assemble a big band of Britain's best for a tour of the Continent that would present 15 concerts in eight countries in less than a month's time. On February 4 Benny revealed some of the particulars on BBC Radio, in an interview with Gordon Kitchen.

First stop was Zurich, February 5, in Kongresshaus; the next day the band appeared in Geneva's Victoria Hall. Our first audience-recorded tape is from the Teatro Lirico in Milan, February 8:

MILAN CONCERT   February 8, 1970, Milan

Benny Goodman, clt; Gregg Bowen, Derek Watkins, John McLevy, tpt (McLevy doubles on Flugelhorn; his name sometimes is spelled, McLeavy); Keith Christie, Nat Peck, Jimmy Wilson, tbn; Bob Burns, Don Honeywill, as; Frank Reidy, Bob Efford, ts; Dave Willis, bar; Bill McGuffie, p; Bucky Pizzarelli, acou g; Louis Stewart, elec g; Lennie Bush, b; Bobby Orr, d. Barbara Jay (Mrs. Tommy Whittle), voc. E. T. Harney (ETH), Kenny Knepper (KK), Peter Knight (PK), Bill McGuffie (BM), Harry South (HS), Wally Stott (WS), arr.

QUINTET: Goodman, McGuffie, Pizzarelli, Bush, Orr.

SEXTET: Quintet plus Stewart.

OCTET: Sextet plus either McLevy or unspecified tbn, and either Burns or Reidy.

Let's Dance (theme)
Bugle Call Rag
This Guy's In Love With You (arr PK)
Stealin' Apples
(On A Clear Day - voc Barbara Jay (arr HS) - no audible BG
(The Look Of Love - voc Barbara Jay - no audible BG
(The Moment of Truth - voc Barbara Jay (arr HS) - no audible BG
(Satin Doll - Pizzarelli, Stewart, rhythm - NO BG
That My Love (Los Reyes Magos) (Missa Creole) (arr WS)
(Willow Weep For Me - feat. Watkins - NO BG

King Porter Stomp
. . . reprise, King Porter Stomp

Intermission

Don't Be That Way
("Turkish March" - Orr, ballpoint pen on dentures - NO BG
Yesterday (arr WS)
(Dear Dave - feat. McGuffie - NO BG
Sometimes I'm Happy
Roll 'Em
Soon It's Gonna Rain - voc Barbara Jay (arr KK)
? "I Don't Know" - voc Barbara Jay
? "I'm All Smiles" - voc Barbara Jay (arr KK)
Rose Room - SEXTET
The World Is Waiting For The Sunrise - SEXTET
It's Easy To Remember - SEXTET
Air Mail Special - OCTET
Sing, Sing, Sing - Part 1
Sing, Sing, Sing - Part 2 (n/c)
(I Would Do) Anything For You
Good-Bye (theme)
One O'Clock Jump (encore)

From Milan the band went to the Palace Hotel in Gstaad on the 13th, then performed the next day in London's Royal Festival Hall; a tape of the complete concert from London does not meet the author's standard for detailing herein. It was on to Bucharest on the 16th, back to the Tivoli in Copenhagen on the 18th, and then to Stockholm on the 20th.

Benny recorded the performance in Stockholm's Concert Hall in its entirety. Later, he authorized a LONDON release of selections from the concert; subsidiary issues followed. Still later, two selections not on the London release were included in a TIME-LIFE album. Adding to dissemination of the Stockholm concert, the Armed Forces Network rebroadcast selections from it soon after the performance itself; the exact date (or dates) of the AFN radio broadcast is not known.

The listing below is derived from the Bell Sound Studio master tapes, and is in program order. Neither the London-and-related LP's, nor the AFN broadcast, follows that order. LP side-and-track identifications, as they appear on the primary London release, are listed for each tune. The AFN broadcast is dealt with separately, following the Bell Sound Studio master listing. Unissued selections as of this writing are shown in italics. LP pressing matrices are meaningless, and are omitted.

The primary release is an album containing two-12" stereo LP's, LONDON SPB 21, titled, "Benny Goodman Today." Subsidiary releases that duplicate the London album are: DeE DDS-3, DeEur DS3129-1/2, DeG 6.28121DP. Two selections in a Time-Life album, and duplicates on other London releases, are separately noted.

BENNY GOODMAN AND HIS ORCHESTRA   February 20, 1970, Stockholm

Personnels as February 8.

-0-   **StLp:** LON SPB 21, etc. Also on **StLp:** LON MIP-1-9311
       Let's Dance (theme) - Side 1, Track 1

       StLp: TL STA 354
       Bugle Call Rag - Side 2, Track 5

       This Guy's In Love With You (arr PK)

       StLp: LON STA354
       Stealin' Apples - Side 1, Track 5

       (Theme from Villa Lobos - Pizzarelli solo - NO BG
       (Satin Doll - Pizzarelli, Stewart w/rhythm - NO BG

StLp: LON SPB 21, etc.
(Willow Weep For Me - feat. Watkins (arr ETH) - NO BG - Side 2, Track 2 - also on **CD,** LON 820 044-2
Roll 'Em - Side 3, Track 3 - also on **StLp,** LON MIP-1-9311; **CD,** LON 820 044-2
Poor Butterfly - QUINTET - Side 3, Track 1 - also on **StLp,** LON MIP-1-9311
Body And Soul - Burns w/rhythm, BG in coda - Side 2, Track 4

Air Mail Special - QUINTET

StLp: LON SPB 21, etc. Also on **StLp:** LON MIP-1-9311
Blue Skies - Side 3, Track 4

StLp: TL STA 354
King Porter Stomp - Side 1, Track 4

StLp: LON SPB 21, etc.
Don't Be That Way - Side 2, Track 1

Yesterday (orch. - arr Tommy Newsome)

StLp: LON SPB 21, etc.
(Dear Dave - feat. McGuffie (arr BM) - NO BG - Side 3, Track 2

Sometimes I'm Happy
That My Love (Los Reyes Magos) (Missa Creole) (arr WS)

StLp: LON SPB 21, etc.
(Baubles, Bangles And Beads - feat. McLevy - NO BG - Side 1, Track 4
If I Had You - QUINTET - Side 1, Track 3
Sweet Georgia Brown - QUINTET - Side 1, Track 2

It's Easy to Remember - SEXTET

StLp: LON SPB 21, etc.
("Turkish March" - feat Orr - NO BG - Side 4, Track 2
Sing, Sing, Sing - Side 4, Track 3 & 4
One O'Clock Jump - Side 3, Track 5 - also on **CD,** LON 820 044-2
A String Of Pearls - Side 2, Track 5 - also on **CD,** LON 820 044-2
Big John Special - Side 2, Track 3
Good-Bye - Side 4, Track 5
(I Would Do) Anything For You (encore) - Side 4, Track 1

The AFN broadcast of the Stockholm concert presented the selections in this order: Let's Dance, Sweet Georgia Brown, If I Had You, Baubles, Bangles And Beads, Stealin' Apples, Don't Be That Way, Willow Weep For Me, Big John Special, and (I Would Do) Anything For You. Collectors are cautioned that this broadcast is sometimes misrepresented as having originated at a concert in Berlin on March 20, 1971.

Benny was quite pleased with the Stockholm London album, considered it his best original release in years. Once, when he and the author were arguing the merits of English vis a vis American jazz musicians, Benny turned on his stereo, made the author listen closely to the Swedish album. Halfway through he queried, "There; they don't sound like foreigners, do they!"

The author's tape of the next concert, February 22 in Gotenbourg's Concert Hall, just misses the quality level set for detailing herein. A tentative booking in Paris's Salle Pleyel on February 24 was cancelled, so the band moved instead to the Bayerischer Hof in Munich:

MUNICH CONCERT February 26, 1970, Munich

Personnels as February 8.

Let's Dance (theme)
Bugle Call Rag
Stealin' Apples
(Willow Weep For Me - feat. Watkins - NO BG
Poor Butterfly - QUINTET
Stompin' At The Savoy - QUINTET
The World Is Waiting for the Sunrise - QUINTET
Sometimes I'm Happy
Roll 'Em
(Baubles, Bangles And Beads - feat. McLevy - NO BG
King Porter Stomp

Body And Soul - Burns w/rhythm - BG in coda
That My Love (Los Reyes Magos) (Missa Creole)
("Turkish March" - feat. Orr - NO BG
Sing, Sing, Sing

At this point the concert ended, and Benny invited the audience to dance:

Don't Be That Way
Rose Room - QUINTET plus Burns
A String Of Pearls
(Quiet Nights Of Quiet Stars - Stewart w/rhythm - NO BG
One O'Clock Jump
This Guy's In Love With You (n/c - intro only)

Benny granted a brief interview while at the Bayerischer Hof; it was televised February 27 on a program titled, "Die Drehscheibe" via ZDF-TV (Zweites Deutsches Fernsehen). In addition to questions-and-answers, it includes "Stealin' Apples" from the Munich concert. Then it was on to the Musikhalle in Hamburg:

HAMBURG CONCERT February 28, 1970, Hamburg

Personnels as February 8.

Let's Dance (theme)
Bugle Call Rag
This Guy's In Love With You
Stealin' Apples
(Theme from Villa Lobos - Pizzarelli solo - NO BG
(Satin Doll - Pizzarelli, Stewart rhythm - NO BG
(Willow Weep For Me - feat. Watkins - NO BG
Roll 'Em
Poor Butterfly - QUINTET
Avalon - SEXTET
(Body And Soul - Burns w/rhythm - NO BG
Blue Skies
King Porter Stomp

Intermission.

Don't Be That Way
Yesterday
(Dear Dave - feat. McGuffie - NO BG
Sometimes I'm Happy
(Baubles, Bangles And Beads - feat. McLevy - NO BG
(I Can't Give You Anything But Love, Baby - feat. McLevy - NO BG
And The Angels Sing
That My Love (Los Reyes Magos) (Missa Creole)
Stompin' At The Savoy - SEXTET
Air Mail Special - SEXTET
One O'Clock Jump
("Turkish March" - feat. Orr - NO BG
Sing, Sing, Sing
A String Of Pearls
Good-Bye (theme)

Last stop on the tour was Berlin's Sportpalast, March 3. Counting the two themes, Armed Forces Network broadcast a dozen selections from the concert; these are shown in order-of-broadcast by numbers preceding the tunes in the listing.

BERLIN CONCERT March 3, 1970, Berlin

Personnels as February 8. AFN broadcast was March 9, 1970.

1. *Let's Dance (theme)*
   Bugle Call Rag
   Stealin' Apples
   (Theme from Villa Lobos - Pizzarelli solo - NO BG
   (Satin Doll - Pizzarelli, Stewart w/rhythm - NO BG
3. *(Willow Weep For Me - feat. Watkins - NO BG*
   Avalon - QUINTET
4. *Poor Butterfly - QUINTET*
   Stompin' At The Savoy - QUINTET
5. *The World Is Waiting For The Sunrise - QUINTET*
   Roll 'Em
6. *(Body And Soul - Burns w/rhythm - NO BG*
7. *This Guy's In Love With You*
2. *King Porter Stomp*

Intermission.

March 3, 1970, continued

March 3, 1970, continued
8. Don't Be That Way
   Yesterday
9. (Baubles, Bangles And Beads - feat. McLevy - NO BG
   (I Can't Give You Anything But Love, Baby - feat. McLevy - NO 3G
10. That My Love (Los Reyes Magos) (Missa Creole)
    (Dear Dave - feat. McGuffie - NO BG
    Sometimes I'm Happy
    Oh, Lady Be Good! - QUINTET
    Memories Of You - QUINTET
    Air Mail Special - SEXTET
    ("Turkish March" - feat. Orr - NO BG
11. Sing, Sing, Sing
    One O'Clock Jump
12. Good-Bye (theme)

(The AFN's "Sing, Sing, Sing" has minor elisions; some portions of the soli
are edited out. Note, too, that AFN may also have broadcast additional selections from the Berlin concert at a different time, for it taped the concert in its
entirety. Benny's library includes a copy of the AFN master tape, from which
this listing is taken.)

Benny spent much of the late spring and early summer of 1970 fishing,
playing golf, enjoying the good life with Alice in Stamford and Manhattan.
On May 4 he was interviewed on WOR's "The Martha Deane Show." Two
days later, May 6, he and Peter Serkin played a benefit for the scholarship
fund of the Manhattan School of Music in Lincoln Center's Alice Tully Hall;
no tapes of the performance are known. On May 22 the Canadian Broadcasting Corporation's FM network presented a "sampler" program, "Bright
Lights - Hail To The King," as introduction to a 13-week review of Goodman's life that was broadcast beginning October 3, 1970, ended December
26, 1970. Benny, John Hammond, George Avakian, Marian McPartland
and others are interviewed between illustrative Goodman recordings. On
June 8 Benny was interviewed via telephone by radio station WTIC's Arnold
Dean. Together with comments from Harry James and Gene Krupa, Benny's
remarks were broadcast on an unknown date by the Hartford, Conn., station.

By July Benny had had enough of inactivity, and he began to schedule
another European tour, this time limited to Italy, Switzerland and Spain. It
would be the English big band again, with but few changes in personnel:
Derek Watkins was on tour with Johnny Cash, and Kenny Baker replaced
him. Wives were not permitted to accompany the musicians, and Bob Efford
refused to go without his. Nat Peck wasn't invited. Replacements for Efford
and Peck were Peter Hughes and John Marshall, respectively. At the last
minute, Keith Bird took Don Honeywill's chair.

Plans to visit Spain were abandoned, and the itinerary developed thus:
In Italy, August 9 & 10, the Lido Theatre in Venice; 11th and 12th, Livor-
nia; 14th, Lignano Sabbiadora; 15th, Riccone; 16th, Monticatine; 17th,
Viareggio; 19th, San Remo. A detour to Ascona in Switzerland on August
21 preceded the final date, August 23, in Varese, Italy.

The author has only one tape from the August 1970 tour, but circumstances surrounding it are interesting. Benny agreed to do a telecast from
"La Bussola," a nightclub in Focette, Viareggio. Set to begin, he was
informed by local union officials that the sidemen would have to be paid
twice—once for the performance itself, then a second time because of the
telecast. "No way," Benny decided, and the telecast was in jeopardy. Then
he had an idea: the big band would play the first tune, but without the
cameras rolling. Then he'd bring on a small group, and Italy's Secondo
Canale (Second Channel) could tape its performances for the better part of an
hour. Off with the cameras, and the orchestra would return to complete the
concert. OK? "Si"—and that's the way it was, and he'd reduced the extra
fees by two-thirds:

"LA BUSSOLA" TELECAST   August 17, 1970, Viareggio
   Secondo Canale TV

Televised April 13, 1971.

Benny Goodman, clt; John McLevy, tpt; Bill McGuffie, p; Louis Stewart, g;
Lennie Bush, b; Bobby Orr, d.

QUINTET: Goodman, McGuffie, Stewart, Bush, Orr.

Avalon - QUINTET
Poor Butterfly - QUINTET
(Theme from "Black Orpheus" - Stewart w/rhythm - NO BG
Sweet Georgia Brown - QUINTET
(Baubles, Bangles And Beads - feat. McLevy - NO BG
The World Is Waiting For The Sunrise - QUINTET
Stompin' At The Savoy - QUINTET

(My) Secret Love
Memories Of You - QUINTET
Rose Room - QUINTET
Honeysuckle Rose
Good-Bye (theme) - QUINTET

("My Secret Love" is so announced, but the title is more often listed as,
"Secret Love.")

Back to the U.S. in September, Benny would not perform again for five
months; again, rest, physical recreation, and visiting art museums, one of his
favorite pastimes. The October 29 edition of Down Beat includes an interview by John McDonough in which Benny speaks of the February-March
tour. The Sunday New York Times, November 29, has a lengthy article by
John Lissner that reviews two albums, Reader's Digest RDA 76A, "Swing
Hits," and Time-Life STA 345, "The Swing Era, Volume I." The first
reissues (along with tracks by T. Dorsey, Miller and Shaw) Goodman studio
recordings, and Benny had no problem with that. The second, however,
"recreates" Benny's recordings, has—excellent—studio musicians playing
the Goodman arrangements note for note, including the soli. That didn't sit
too well. Why not, instead, market an album with original Goodman material in it? Time-Life agreed, and negotiations were begun that resulted in the
eventual release of TL STA 354, "Benny Goodman Into the '70s, The King
In Person."

Benny took Derek Smith, Bucky Pizzarelli, Georgie Duvivier and
Grady Tate into New York's Waldorf-Astoria for a single performance on
January 29, 1971, but its purpose has been forgotten. Then it was off to
London February 6 to set in motion a new tour of the Continent with the
English band. On the 10th, in London's Grosvenor House where he custom-
arily stayed, Benny gave an interview to the BBC's Bruce Wyndham. It was
broadcast via BBC Radio 1's "Night Ride" on February 16.

To kick off the 1971 European tour, Benny flew to Munich to appear as
guest soloist with Max Greger's studio orchestra on a ZDF television
program:

"DREI MAL NEUN" ZDF-TV   March 4, 1971, Munich

Benny Goodman, clt, and a studio orchestra led by Max Greger. Wim Thoelke
conducts an interview with Goodman.

Let's Dance (theme)
Memories Of You
Don't Be That Way

The band joined Benny in Oberschwabenhalle in Ravensburg, Germany, the next day for the initial concert. On March 6 it performed in the
Kongresshalle-Deutsche Museum in Munich. Together with an interview
granted by Benny to a staff member, the Armed Forces Network broadcast a
portion of the concert in Frankfurt's Jahrhunderthalle on the 7th:

FRANKFURT CONCERT   March 7, 1971, Frankfurt
   AFN Radio Network

Broadcast March 14. Benny Goodman, clt; Gregg Bowen, Derek Watkins,
John McLevy, tpt (McLevy doubles on Flugelhorn); Keith Christie, Jock Bain,
Jimmy Wilson, tbn; Bob Burns, Dennis Walton, as; Bob Efford, Duncan
Lamont, ts; Dave Willis, bar; Bill McGuffie, p; Louis Stewart, g; Lennie Bush,
b; Bobby Orr, d.

QUINTET: Goodman, McGuffie, Stewart, Bush, Orr.

SEPTET: Quintet plus McLevy, Burns.

Don't Be That Way
Yesterday
(Dear Dave—feat. McGuffie—NO BG
I Will Wait For You
A String Of Pearls
Stompin' At The Savoy—QUINTET
The Man I Love—QUINTET
King Porter Stomp

Following Frankfurt were concerts in the Rosengarten-Musenal in
Mannheim March 9, in the Liederhalle in Stuttgart March 10, and in the
Mercatorhalle in Duisburg March 11. A performance in the Meister-
singerhalle in Nurnberg on March 12 was recorded satisfactorily from the
audience.

NURNBERG CONCERT   March 12, 1971, Nurnberg

Personnels as March 7.

Let's Dance (theme)
Bugle Call Rag
This Guy's In Love With You
Stealin' Apples
(A Man And A Woman—Stewart w/rhythm—NO BG
(Willow Weep For Me—feat. Watkins—NO BG
Roll Em'
Oh, Lady Be Good!—QUINTET
Poor Butterfly—QUINTET
Honeysuckle Rose—QUINTET
Avalon—QUINTET
King Porter Stomp

Intermission.

Don't Be That Way
Yesterday
(Dear Dave—feat. McGuffie—NO BG
(I Would Do) Anything For You
(Baubles, Bangles And Beads—feat. McLevy—NO BG
I Can't Give You Anything But Love, Baby—feat. McLevy—BG in coda
Sweet Georgia Brown—QUINTET
Memories Of You—QUINTET
Stompin' At The Savoy—QUINTET
(Body And Soul—Burns w/rhythm—NO BG
("Turkish March"—feat. Orr—NO BG
Sing, Sing, Sing
A String Of Pearls
One O'Clock Jump
Good-Bye (theme)
Big John Special (encore)

Next stop was Dusseldorf's Rheinhalle, March 15; there an unfortunate accident boded ill for the balance of the tour. Just prior to the concert, Benny was in his dressing room, practicing, seated on a three-legged stool. The stool slipped out from under him on the terrazzo floor, and he fell heavily onto his back. Given his long history of a back ailment, little else could have happened that would have been so incapacitating. But true to the traditions of show business, he went ahead with the performance, although eyewitnesses plainly saw that he was in agony.

Despite the injury, he persisted with concerts in the Stadthalle in Braunschweig on the 17th, and in Hanover's Stadthalle-Kuppelsaal on the 18th. The quality of the author's tape of the Hanover engagement does not warrant its inclusion herein. A better tape is available from the next concert, in the Musikhalle in Hamburg:

HAMBURG CONCERT   March 19, 1971, Hamburg

Personnels as March 7.

Let's Dance (theme)
Bugle Call Rag
This Guy's In Love With You
Stealin' Apples
(Quiet Nights Of Quiet Stars—Stewart w/rhythm—NO BG
(Willow Weep For Me—feat. Watkins—NO BG
Roll 'Em
Poor Butterfly—QUINTET
Oh, Lady Be Good!—QUINTET
Avalon—QUINTET
(Body And Soul—Burns w/rhythm—NO BG
Blue Skies
King Porter Stomp

Intermission.

Don't Be That Way
Yesterday
(Dear Dave—feat. McGuffie—NO BG
(I Would Do) Anything For You
(Baubles, Bangles And Beads - feat. McLevy - NO BG
(I Can't Give You Anything But Love, Baby - feat. McLevy - NO BG
Sweet Georgia Brown - QUINTET
Memories Of You - QUINTET
("Turkish March" - feat. Orr - NO BG
Sing, Sing, Sing

A String Of Pearls
One O'Clock Jump
Big John Special
Good-Bye (theme)

What would prove to be the final concert was given the next day in Berlin's Sportpalast. The author's tape's quality is marginal—dropouts, incomplete renditions—but since it is in the last of this series, it is detailed:

BERLIN CONCERT   March 20, 1971, Berlin

Personnels as March 7.

Let's Dance (theme)
Bugle Call Rag
This Guy's In Love With You
Stealin' Apples
(Quiet Nights Of Quiet Stars—Stewart w/rhythm—NO BG
(Willow Weep For Me—feat. Watkins—NO BG
Roll 'Em
Poor Butterfly—QUINTET
Avalon—QUINTET
Stompin' At The Savoy—QUINTET
(Body And Soul—Burns w/rhythm—NO BG
Blue Skies (n/c—ending clipped)
King Porter Stomp

Intermission.

Don't Be That Way
Yesterday
(Dear Dave—feat. McGuffie—NO BG
(I Would Do) Anything For You
(Baubles, Bangles And Beads—feat. McLevy—NO BG
(I Can't Give You Anything But Love, Baby—feat. McLevy—NO BG
Sweet Georgia Brown—QUINTET
Memories of You—QUINTET
(announced, but not taped—"Turkish March"
Sing, Sing, Sing (n/c)

Treatment for his injury had proved ineffective, and now the pain was excruciating; Benny had little choice but to cancel the balance of the tour, dates in Stockholm, Gotenbourg, Copenhagen, Forest National-Brussels, Paris and London. On March 21 he flew to Frankfurt, from there immediately jetted back to the United States. He simply stopped over in New York, caught another plane to his "R&R facility" in St. Martin's. He would not return to Manhattan until Easter Sunday, April 11.

Benny's next engagement was as guest soloist with the Winnipeg Symphony Orchestra in Manitoba on May 4; the files fail to disclose whether he kept the date. Our next evidence of Benny back at work finds him on television:

"THE DAVID FROST SHOW"   June 4, 1971, New York
   METROMEDIA Television Network

Televised July 7, 1971, via WNEW-TV, New York; and at various times by other independent television stations.

Benny Goodman, clt; Derek Smith, p; Bucky Pizzarelli, g; Milt Hinton, b; Grady Tate, d.

I Want To Be Happy
Medley: Don't Be That Way
        Stompin' At The Savoy
The Man I Love
The World Is Waiting For The Sunrise—to close

A sad note, June 7—Ben Pollack committed suicide by hanging in Palm Springs, California, where for some years he had managed a restaurant.

On June 10 Benny was interviewed in his New York apartment by Garry Moore and Ludmilla Obolensky for the Voice of America. It is not known when or if portions of the tape were broadcast by VOA. But all collectors seem to have a tape of Benny's first television appearance with Dick Cavett:

"THE DICK CAVETT SHOW"　　　　　*July 21, 1971, New York*
　ABC Television Network

Televised July 22, 1971, via WABC-TV, New York; and at various times by other ABC-TV network stations.

Benny Goodman, clt; Bucky Pizzarelli, g; Milt Hinton, b; Bobby Rosengarden, d.

Here, There And Everywhere
Oh, Lady Be Good!
Something

Benny Goodman, clt, and Bobby Rosengarden's studio orchestra.

Let's Dance (theme)
Don't Be That Way
Stealin' Apples

On July 28 Westdeutscher Rundfunk, Second Program (WDR II) broadcast an interview of Benny by Dieter Broer titled, "Swinging Reminiscences." The program was rebroadcast August 3 by Radio Bremen. It is not known when the interview was recorded. A month later, August 28, Lou McGarity passed away, as noted earlier.

The author's tape of (a portion of ?) the September 11 Richmond Jazz Festival, Richmond Coliseum, Richmond, Virginia, is excluded because of its poor quality.

Taking only Derek Smith along, Benny appeared on a Canadian television program with Guido Basso's studio orchestra.

"IN THE MOOD"　　　　　*September 28, 1971, Toronto*
　CBC Television Network

Televised September 30. Benny Goodman, clt; Derek Smith, p; and Guido Basso's Orchestra.

QUARTET: Goodman, Smith, unknown b, d.

Let's Dance (theme)
King Porter Stomp
Avalon—QUARTET
Don't Be That Way
On A Clear Day
Stealin' Apples
Good-Bye (theme)

Possibly because the April 1 engagement in Royal Albert Hall had been cancelled as a result of his back injury in Dusseldorf, Benny flew to Great Britain for a mini-tour. He was whisked from the airport to the BBC studios, was interviewed there by Kenneth Allsop; the interview was televised on BBC-TV's "24 Hours" the same day, September 29. Then it was off to The Dome in Brighton, for a reunion with the British band.

BRIGHTON CONCERT　　　　　*September 30, 1971, Brighton*

Benny Goodman, clt; Derek Watkins, John McLevy, Tommy McQuator, tpt; Nat Peck, Keith Christie, Jimmy Wilson, tbn; Bob Burns, Don Honeywill, as; Bob Efford, Frank Reidy, ts; Dave Willis, bar; Bill McGuffie, p; Judd Proctor, g; Lennie Bush, b; Bobby Orr, d.

QUINTET: Goodman, McGuffie, Proctor, Bush, Orr.

Let's Dance (theme)
Sweet Georgia Brown—QUINTET
Poor Butterfly—QUINTET
Don't Be That Way
On A Clear Day (arr Wally Stott)
(Willow Weep For Me—feat. Watkins—NO BG
Roll 'Em
(Body And Soul—Burns w/rhythm—NO BG
Rose Room—QUINTET
Avalon—QUINTET
Blue Skies
Stealin' Apples

Intermission.

King Porter Stomp
That My Love (Los Reyes Magos) (Missa Creole)
(Dear Dave—feat. McGuffie—NO BG
I Will Wait For You (arr Peter Knight)
(Bangles, Baubles And Beads—feat. McLevy—NO BG
(I Can't Give You Anything But Love, Baby—feat. McLevy—NO BG

(I Would Do) Anything For You
The Man I Love—QUINTET
The World Is Waiting For The Sunrise—QUINTET
("Turkish March"—feat. Orr—NO BG
Sing, Sing, Sing
A String Of Pearls
One O'Clock Jump
Good-Bye (theme)

With but slight alteration, the Brighton concert was repeated in London's Royal Albert Hall:

LONDON CONCERT　　　　　*October 2, 1971, London*

Personnels as September 30.

Let's Dance (theme)
Sweet Georgia Brown—QUINTET
Poor Butterfly—QUINTET
Don't Be That Way
On A Clear Day
(Willow Weep For Me—feat. Watkins—NO BG
Roll 'Em
(Body And Soul—Burns w/rhythm—NO BG
Blue Skies
Memories Of You—QUINTET
Avalon—QUINTET
Stealin' Apples

Intermission.

King Porter Stomp
That My Love (Los Reyes Magos) (Missa Creole)
(Dear Dave—feat. McGuffie—NO BG
I Will Wait For You
(Baubles, Bangles And Beads—feat. McLevy—NO BG
(I Can't Give You Anything But Love, Baby—feat. McLevy—NO BG
The Man I Love—QUINTET
Oh, Lady Be Good!—QUINTET
Stompin' At The Savoy—QUINTET
("Turkish March"—feat. Orr—NO BG
Sing, Sing, Sing
A String Of Pearls
One O'Clock Jump
Good-Bye (theme)

Pianist Bill McGuffie discussed his association with Benny October 3 via BBC Radio. He'll be back, but the rest of the British band will not; the October 2 concert was its finale.

Benny's English experiment, begun modestly as nothing more than a recording session, had extended for two full years, had blanketed Britain and Western Europe in the course of four concert tours. It was a controlled experiment in a sense, patterned after prototype Goodman successes: A stable complement of technically competent musicians, some capable of jazz, playing exciting new charts and the tested standards. It had something more: For the sidemen, the thrill, the learning experience, the lasting endorsement of working with the master. For Benny, the challenge, the incentive of collaborating with fresh new instrumentalists.

Decades earlier, a similar blend would have percolated, fermented, matured with age into vintage Goodman. But here the distillation process was immediate; the fizz, the sparkle, was all there at the beginning, time merely diminished it. The range of improvisation was limited, repetition bred boredom; familiarity led to a lack of discipline, drinking became excessive. It was time to end the experiment, and Benny realized it.

One relationship that Benny will retain for as long as either can perform is with Hans Moennig, a pipe-smoking ancient who repairs reed instruments; "the best in the world," according to Benny. His second-floor walkup in Philadelphia is something out of Dickens, cluttered beyond belief with cigar boxes overflowing with keys and felts and washers and barrels and the myriad parts incidental to his trade. Lath and plaster suspend dangerously from the ceiling, loose floorboards will trip you, the toilet's a disaster, the 'phone rings but can't be found. There's no priority here; if a high school student is first in line, Hans will discuss his needs for hours while Benny browses among instruments a century old, and memorabilia almost equally elderly. But when Benny's time comes, it's a joy to watch two craftsmen at work, each fingering and blowing clarinets alternately, coming to agreement on minutely precise adjustments.

On one pilgrimage to Moennig's, Benny detoured to Westinghouse's Philadelphia affiliate, KYW-TV, conversed with Mr. & Mrs. (Pearl Bailey) Louis Bellson, played with Louis and studio personnel.

"THE MIKE DOUGLAS SHOW"   *October 11, 1971, Philadelphia*
  WESTINGHOUSE Television Network

Televised October 18 via KYW-TV; and on various stations on that date and others.

Benny Goodman, clt; Joe Harnell, p; Bobby DiNardo, g; Jimmy DiJulio, b; (guest) Louis Belson, d.

The Man I Love
Oh, Lady Be Good!

Benny appeared in Hackensack, New Jersey on October 14 with Urbie Green, vibraphonist Peter Appleyard, Derek Smith, Gene Bertoncini, George Duvivier, and Gene Traxler's son Ronnie, drums; we've no tape of the performance. He taped an interview for WOR Radio October 20; it was broadcast on "The Martha Deane Show" October 22. On the 25th he granted an interview to syndicated columnist Dan Lewis, which appeared in various newspapers soon thereafter. And sometime in this period Benny videotaped a question-and-answer program for Public Service Television, "Vibrations." Its telecast was delayed until May 5, 1972.

An American Broadcasting Company news telecast, whose date is unknown, captured Benny in rehearsal for his next engagement in the Rainbow Grill:

NEWS TELECAST   *October 1971, New York*
  ABC Television Network

Benny Goodman, clt; Urbie Green, tbn; Peter Appleyard, vib; Al Caiola, g.

Oh, Lady Be Good! (n/c)
Stompin' At The Savoy (n/c)

Then CBS Radio featured the Septet in promotional broadcasts for U.S. Savings Bonds from the Grill:

"U.S. SAVINGS BONDS"   *October 27, 1971, New York*
  CBS Radio Network

Broadcast October 31. Benny Goodman, clt; Urbie Green, tbn; Peter Appleyard, vib; Derek Smith, p; Al Caiola, g; George Duvivier, b; Ronnie Zito, d.

QUINTET: Goodman, Smith, Caiola, Duvivier, Zito.

I Want To Be Happy
If I Had You - QUINTET
(The Song Is You - Green w/rhythm - NO BG
A Smo-o-o-oth One
(Fascinating Rhythm - Appleyard w/rhythm - NO BG
(Tin Roof Blues - Appleyard w/rhythm - NO BG - to signoff

"U.S. SAVINGS BONDS"   *November 3, 1971, New York*
  CBS Radio Network

Broadcast November 6. Personnels as October 27.

I Want To Be Happy
(Star Dust - Green w/rhythm - NO BG
A Smo-o-o-oth One
The Man I Love - QUINTET
(Fascinating Rhythm - Appleyard w/rhythm - NO BG, - to signoff

Two tunes recorded from the audience during the first set on November 5 are extant, but their poor audio quality precludes their listing herein. Slightly better are audience recordings of a portion of the first set, and the full second set, made the next night. They are minimally satisfactory, but are detailed to illustrate a typical program:

RAINBOW GRILL   *November 6, 1971, New York*

Personnels as October 27.

1st Set:

I Want To Be Happy
A Smo-o-o-oth One
Fascinating Rhythm - feat. Appleyard - BG in coda
(Autumn Leaves - Smith w/d - NO BG
Rose Room - QUINTET
(Tin Roof Blues - feat. Appleyard - NO BG (n/c, intro only)
Slipped Disc

(In all likelihood, NBC Radio, via its "Monitor" program, broadcast the first 15 minutes of the first set—an announcer can be heard during "Autumn Leaves." A tape of this broadcast has eluded the author.)

2nd Set:

I Want To Be Happy
Star Dust - feat. Green - BG in coda
The Girl From Ipanema
A Smo-o-o-oth One
Fascinating Rhythm, feat. Appleyard - BG in coda
Tin Roof Blues - feat. Appleyard - BG, Green in coda
The Man I Love - QUINTET
Love For Sale - feat. Appleyard - BG, Green in coda
Slipped Disc
I'm A Ding Dong Daddy (From Dumas)

(At this point the "concert" portion of the performance ended, and Benny invited the audience to dance. The author, his wife and daughter were among those who did.)

Medley: Don't Be That Way
      Stompin' At The Savoy
(Out Of Nowhere - feat. Appleyard - NO BG, segue to,
How High the Moon
(I Fall In Love Too Easily - Green w/rhythm - NO BG
(Watch What Happens - Caiola w/rhythm - NO BG
Memories Of You - QUINTET
Sweet Georgia Brown
Good-Bye (theme)
Avalon (encore)
Good-Bye (theme)

The next listing is a composite of a broadcast and an audience recording of the first set, November 10. Through the closing announcement during "Satin Doll," the source is a CBS radio broadcast. Then the cassette tape carries the performance through to its end:

"U.S. SAVINGS BONDS"   *November 10, 1971, New York*
  CBS Radio Network

Broadcast November 13. Personnels as October 27.

I Want To Be Happy
(The Shadow Of Your Smile - Green w/rhythm - NO BG
I'm A Ding Dong Daddy (From Dumas)
(Satin Doll - feat. Appleyard - NO BG - to signoff

Audience Recording:

(Satin Doll - conclusion - feat. Appleyard - NO BG
Tin Roof Blues - feat. Appleyard - BG in coda
(Love For Sale - Smith w/d - NO BG
Medley: Soon
      Somebody Loves Me
      Fascinating Rhythm
      Oh, Lady Be Good!
Medley: Don't Be That Way
      Stompin' At The Savoy
Raindrops Keep Fallin' On My Head
A Smo-o-o-oth One
Good-Bye (theme)
Sweet Georgia Brown (encore)
Good-Bye (theme)

Not feeling well, Benny went to his home in Stamford after the final set at the Grill on the 10th. His malaise worsened, and the next morning Alice drove him to the New York University Hospital, where he was treated for an acute intestinal virus. He thus missed the 11th, but did return to the Grill—for one set only, each night—on the 12th and 13th, the end of the engagement. On both the the 12th and 13th, Buddy Morrow and Gene Bertoncini remained, and Benny's slightly revised Septet played four tunes at the Gershwin Memorial Concert in New York's Philharmonic Hall. No tapes of this event are known to exist.

The Time-Life album, "Benny Goodman Into the '70s - The King In Person," was in prospect, and Benny decided to record some small group material for it. For that purpose, he assembled Green, Appleyard, Smith, Caiola and two of Appleyard's Canadian compadres in the former Columbia facility, now the A&R Studios, 799 Seventh Avenue, on December 1. They warmed up with "A Smo-o-o-oth One" and "Oh, Lady Be Good!" beginning at 2:20 p.m., then began to tape "I'm A Ding Dong Daddy (From Dumas)." The first four takes were by the full group, the next six without Green. (Green and the author watched the proceedings from the control booth. The author observed that things were going badly; Green would not voice an opinion, certainly would not criticize.) Six more takes followed, these with the original Quartet format, clarinet, vibes, piano, drums. It was now 4:15, and Benny had had enough. He didn't like the studio itself, was dissatisfied with the grouping of the instruments, found the piano out-of-tune, wanted the drums muffled. They'd take a break, come back at 5:30 (in a different studio, same address) and try again. And to finish it off, they'd return the next day at 9:00 a.m. The author went home.

Eventually, Benny salvaged five 10″ reels of material from these sessions. From them 10 cuts were programmed onto a demonstration tape. From these, two were selected for release in the Time-Life album. (It cannot now be determined when either was recorded, the evening of December 1 or the morning of December 2.) The contents of the demonstration tape follow, with take numbers and Benny's reel numbers in the positions usually occupied by matrix numbers:

BENNY GOODMAN SEXTET   **December 1 or 2, 1971, New York**

Benny Goodman, clt; Peter Appleyard, vib; Derek Smith, p; Al Caiola, g; Don Thompson, b; Howie Reay, d.

Reel 2, take 2	UNISSUED - Tape	**Soon**
Reel 2, take 2	StLp: TL STA354 - Side 3, Track 5	**I'm A Ding Dong Daddy (From Dumas)**
Reel 1, take 3	UNISSUED - Tape	**Opus 1/2**
Reel 2, take 2	StLp: TL STA354 - Side 3, Track 2	**The Shadow Of Your Smile**
Reel 2, take 1	UNISSUED - Tape	**Close To You**
Reel 1, take 5	UNISSUED - Tape	**Slipped Disc**
Reel 1, take 5	UNISSUED - Tape	**Fascinating Rhythm**
Reel 2, take 1	UNISSUED - Tape	**What Is This Thing Called Love?**
Reel 2, take 1	UNISSUED - Tape	**It's Impossible**
Reel 2, take 2	UNISSUED - Tape	**A Smo-o-o-oth One**

Additionally, alternate takes of two of the cuts on the demo tape are in the hands of a few collectors. Their takes are specified, but not the master reels from which they come:

Reel ?, take 1	UNISSUED - Tape	**Soon**
Reel ?, take 1	UNISSUED - Tape	**Opus 1/2** (breakdown in coda)

Did Benny ever make a "square" record? Musically, it's arguable; physically, it's not: Either late in 1971, or more likely, early in 1972, he cut a voice track in support of education for the Music Educators 1972 national conference, "Music Power." His remarks, over "Let's Dance" from the February 20, 1970 Stockholm concert, are on an EVA-TONE "Sound Sheet," Side 1, Track 1—and the flimsy LP is a perfect square in shape.

Europe beckoned; despite problems with money conversion and the rigors of one-nighters, the audiences were eager and enthusiastic, and they stimulated Benny. But this time it would be a small group comprised principally of musicians from the 'States, with only the pianist and bassist from Great Britain. The native contingent left late on February 24 for Amsterdam, rehearsed there on the 25th, joined with the Englishmen for the initial concert in Amsterdam's Concertgebow on the 26th. We hear them first in a lengthy, if delayed, telecast from the Theater National Populaire in Paris:

PARIS CONCERT   *February 28, 1972, Paris*
  ORTF II Television

Televised May 27, 1972. Benny Goodman, clt; Zoot Sims, ts; Peter Appleyard, vib; Bill McGuffie, p; Bucky Pizzarelli, g; Hal Gaylor, b; Mousey Alexander, d. Lynn Roberts, voc.

TRIO: Goodman, McGuffie, Alexander
QUARTET: Trio plus Pizzarelli
QUINTET: Quartet plus Gaylor
SEXTET: Quintet plus Appleyard

I Want To Be Happy
Memories Of You - QUARTET
Slipped Disc
(The Girl From Ipanema - Pizzarelli w/rhythm - NO BG
Medley: Don't Be That Way
        Stompin' At The Savoy
(Jitterbug Waltz - Sims w/rhythm - NO BG
Emily - feat. Sims - BG "tag" in coda
I'll Remember April - QUINTET plus Sims
Honeysuckle Rose
(All The Things You Are - McGuffie w/rhythm - NO BG
I'm A Ding Dong Daddy (From Dumas) - SEXTET
Rose Room - SEXTET
After You've Gone
I've Found A New Baby
If I Had You - SEXTET
Air Mail Special
Avalon - SEXTET
Poor Butterfly - SEXTET
The Man I Love - QUINTET
Medley: Somebody Loves Me - full group
        Fascinating Rhythm - SEXTET
        Oh, Lady Be Good! - full group
You Turned The Tables On Me - voc Lynn Roberts
The Lady Is A Tramp - voc Lynn Roberts
After I Say I'm Sorry - voc Lynn Roberts
A Smo-o-o-oth One
The World Is Waiting For The Sunrise - SEXTET
Sweet Georgia Brown
Tin Roof Blues - segue to, Hamp's Boogie - to close

The group flew to Manchester, England, for its next engagement in the King's Hall, Belle Vue. On arrival at Ringway Airport, Benny was interviewed by Alan Sykes, Radio Manchester; their conversation was broadcast that day, March 1. An audience-recorded tape of that evening's concert is extant, but its poor quality precludes detailing herein. A minimally-satisfactory tape is available from the next day in Royal Albert Hall:

LONDON CONCERT   *March 3, 1972, London*

Personnels as February 28. DUET: Goodman, McGuffie.

I Want To Be Happy
Poor Butterfly - SEXTET
(Jitterbug Waltz - Sims w/rhythm - NO BG
A Smo-o-o-oth One
Sweet Georgia Brown
Tin Roof Blues - Appleyard w/rhythm - BG in coda
Avalon - SEXTET
You Turned The Tables On Me - voc Lynn Roberts
(Here's That Rainy Day - voc Lynn Roberts, rhythm accomp.
The Lady Is A Tramp - voc Lynn Roberts
Memories of You - QUARTET
I've Found A New Baby
Honeysuckle Rose

Intermission.

Medley: Don't Be That Way
        Stompin' At The Savoy
The Man I Love - SEXTET
Somebody Loves Me - QUINTET plus Sims
(Fascinating Rhythm - Appleyard w/rhythm - NO BG
(Summertime - McGuffie w/rhythm - NO BG
Oh, Lady Be Good!
(I'm Not In Love Any More - Pizzarelli w/d - NO BG
Rose Room - SEXTET

The World Is Waiting For The Sunrise - SEXTET
(Emily - Sims w/rhythm - NO BG)
(I'll Remember April - Sims w/rhythm - NO BG)
If I Had You
I'm A Ding Dong Daddy (From Dumas)
After You've Gone
Good-Bye (theme)
Air Mail Special (encore)

The September 28, 1972 edition of Britain's "Rolling Stone" offers James Horwitz's hour-by-hour tour with the group from Manchester to London. Interesting, insightful account.

Germany and Switzerland were next, concerts in the Rosengarten Musensaal, Frankfurt, on March 5; the Lichtsburgsaal, Essen, March 6; the Beethovensaal, Bonn, March 7; the Congresshalle, Zurich, March 9; and the Deutsche Museum, Munich, March 10. Our next tape is from Hamburg's Musikhalle:

HAMBURG CONCERT   *March 11, 1972, Hamburg*

Personnels as February 28; Duet as March 3.

Flying Home
The Man I Love - QUARTET
A Smo-o-o-oth One
(Jitterbug Waltz - Sims w/rhythm - NO BG)
Runnin' Wild
Tin Roof Blues - Appleyard w/rhythm - BG in coda
You Turned The Tables On Me - voc Lynn Roberts
Here's That Rainy Day - voc Lynn Roberts - QUINTET
The Lady Is A Tramp - voc Lynn Roberts
After I Say I'm Sorry - voc Lynn Roberts
(All The Things You Are - McGuffie w/rhythm - NO BG)
Memories Of You - QUARTET
Sweet Georgia Brown

Intermission.

Medley: Don't Be That Way
*   Stompin' At The Savoy*
Avalon - SEXTET
(People Will Say We're In Love - Pizzarelli w/d - NO BG)
(Lush Life - Pizzarelli solo - NO BG)
(Out of Nowhere - Appleyard w/rhythm - NO BG)
If I Had You
(Emily - Sims w/rhythm - NO BG)
After You've Gone
Where Or When - DUET
Shine
Body And Soul - DUET
The Sheik Of Araby
(On The Trail - Sims w/rhythm - NO BG)
The World Is Waiting For The Sunrise - SEXTET
As Long As I Live - QUARTET
(Fascinating Rhythm - Appleyard w/rhythm - NO BG)
Oh, Lady Be Good!
Good-Bye (theme)

Benny was in good humor, the Septet in good form—auspices for a concert recording. The next engagement was in Copenhagen's Tivoli Theatre, and Decca put the proceedings on tape. On June 22 Benny and an executive from Decca-London Records auditioned the masters, decided which tracks to release. Result was the two-LP LONDON album, BP 44182/83, "On Stage with Benny Goodman and his Sextet - Recorded 'Live' in Copenhagen." The album was duplicated in toto on subsidiary releases DeE DKL 4/1–4/2, and World Record Club (Au) RO3177/78. One track, "Where Or When," is also on a London StLp, MIP-1-9311.

Swedish Television videotaped the concert; excerpts were televised twice, on an unknown date and on September 25, 1972. Together, the two telecasts offer three tunes not included in the London album: "The Man I Love," "Summertime" and "Someday Sweetheart." And of course, the concert was taped from the audience; a poor-quality cassette offers additional tunes, in neither the London album nor in the Swedish telecasts.

The listing following is in order-of-performance. Side and track identifications are shown for the London album; pressing matrices are ignored as meaningless. Tunes not in the London album are shown in italics, and are identified as to source. The two Swedish telecasts are detailed separately, after the composite listing.

BENNY GOODMAN: **March 13, 1972, Copenhagen**
TIVOLI THEATRE CONCERT

Personnels as February 28.

-0-   **StLp:** LON SP 44182, etc.
       I Want To Be Happy - Side 1, Track 1

       The Man I Love - TRIO (TV)

       StLp: LON SP 44182, etc.
       A Smo-o-o-oth One - SEXTET - Side 1, Track 2
       (Jitterbug Waltz - Sims w/rhythm - NO BG - Side 1, Track 3

       (Tin Roof Blues - Appleyard w/rhythm - NO BG (Aud.)

       StLp: LON SP 44182, etc.
       Shine - QUINTET - Side 2, Track 1
       My Funny Valentine - TRIO - Side 2, Track 2

       You Turned The Tables On Me - voc Lynn Roberts (Aud.)
       Here's That Rainy Day - voc Lynn Roberts (Aud.)
       The Lady Is A Tramp - voc Lynn Roberts (Aud.)

       StLp: LON SP 44182, etc.
       Rose Room -QUINTET - Side 2, Track 4

       StLp: LON SP 44183, etc.
       The Sheik Of Araby - Side 1, Track 5

       StLp: LON SP 44182, etc.
       Where Or When - TRIO - Side 1, Track 4
       Honeysuckle Rose - Side 2, Track 5

       StLp: LON SP 44183, etc.
       I've Found A New Baby - Side 1, Track 1
       Memories Of You - QUINTET - Side 1, Track 2
       Flying Home - Side 1, Track 3

       (Emily - Sims w/rhythm - NO BG (Aud.)

       StLp: LON SP 44183, etc.
       It Had To Be You - QUINTET plus Sims - Side 2, Track 1
       *(Too Close For Comfort** - Sims w/rhythm - NO BG - Side 2, Track 2

       Gershwin medley:
       StLp: LON SP 44182, etc.
       *(Soon** - TRIO - Side 2, Track 5
       *(Somebody Loves Me** - QUINTET plus Sims - Side 2, Track 5
       *(Fascinating Rhythm** - SEXTET - Side 2, Track 5

       ((Summertime - McGuffie w/rhythm - NO BG (TV)

       StLp: LON SP 44182, etc.
       *(Oh, Lady Be Good!** - Side 2, Track 3

       (unannounced Pizzarelli solo - NO BG (Aud.)

       StLp: LON SP 44183, etc.
       Medley: **Don't Be That Way**   ) - Side 1, Track 4
              Stompin' At The Savoy)

       Someday Sweetheart - QUINTET (TV)

       StLp: LON SP 44183, etc.
       After You've Gone - Side 2, Track 3
       Moon Glow - Side 2, Track 4
       Runnin' Wild - Side 2, Track 5
       Good-Bye (theme) - Side 2, Track 6

(NOTE: The London album jacket prefixes its catalog number with "SB"; the LP's use the prefix, "SP,").

The first Swedish telecast, date unknown, offered: I Want To Be Happy, The Man I Love, A Smo-o-o-oth One, Jitterbug Waltz, Soon, Somebody Loves Me, Fascinating Rhythm, Summertime and Oh, Lady Be Good! The second, televised September 25, 1972, included: I've Found A New Baby, Memories Of You, Flying Home, Don't Be That Way/Stompin' At The Savoy, Someday Sweetheart and After You've Gone. Tape copies of both offer excellent audio fidelity. As noted, the audience-recorded cassette is poor. The latter's cuts are detailed because Decca, and likely Swedish TV, recorded them, and there is the possibility that good sound copies may one day be available.

From Copenhagen the Septet went to Cologne on March 15, appeared in the Stadthalle Kuppelsaal in Hanover on the 16th, then performed in Vienna's Concert House on the 18th. A concert in the Rheinhalle, Dusseldorf, scheduled for March 19 was cancelled. The final performance was in Berlin's Philharmonia Hall, from which a ''fair'' audience tape is extant:

BERLIN CONCERT   March 21, 1972, Berlin

Personnels as February 28.

I Want To Be Happy
Poor Butterfly - SEXTET
(Jitterbug Waltz - Sims w/rhythm - NO BG
A Smo-o-o-oth One
Tin Roof Blues - SEXTET
The Sheik Of Araby
You Turned The Tables On Me - voc Lynn Roberts
(Here's That Rainy Day - voc Lynn Roberts, w/rhythm - NO BG
The Lady Is A Tramp - voc Lynn Roberts
I've Got The World On A String - voc Lynn Roberts
(All The Things You Are—McGuffie w/rhythm - NO BG
I've Found A New Baby
Avalon - SEXTET
(Out Of Nowhere - Appleyard w/rhythm - NO BG
(Emily - Sims w/rhythm - NO BG
The Man I Love - QUARTET
Somebody Loves Me - QUINTET plus Sims
Fascinating Rhythm - SEXTET
Oh, Lady Be Good!
After I Say I'm Sorry - voc Lynn Roberts
'Deed I Do - voc Lynn Roberts
Memories Of You - QUARTET
Sweet Georgia Brown
Medley: Don't Be That Way
        Stompin' At The Savoy
Runnin' Wild
Good-Bye (theme)

Benny returned to the U.S. March 25, tended to business in New York for a week, then vacationed in St. Martin's April 2 to April 16. A month later he was in Chicago to testify at hearings convened by the Windy City's Board of Education, examining its plans to eliminate all music programs from the schools after June 30. ''Tragic,'' said Benny. Back to Manhattan, and a call from his French connection: Would he, his friend Ambassador Tom Watson inquired, be gracious enough to play a benefit for the American Hospital in Paris? But of course; and it was off to the City of Light and a date in the Theatre de la Musique May 27, Bob Hope emcee'ing.

The author has no recordings of the charity affair itself, but: because Benny's sidemen were native sons, Swedish Television videotaped them from Stockholm to their introduction to Benny in Paris, kept the cameras rolling through rehearsals in Selmer's Paris studios on May 25 and 26. Almost five months' later, it televised some 40 minutes' worth of its footage:

"BENNY GOODMAN IN PARIS"   May 25–26, 1972, Paris
   Swedish TV

Televised October 10, 1972. Benny Goodman, clt; Lars Erstrand, vib; Rolf Larsson, p; Nicke Wohrmann, g; Arne Wilhelmsson, b; Pelle Hulten, d.

TRIO: Goodman, Larsson, Hulten.

(. . . "the swingin' Swedes," enroute: fragments of "Topsy"
(. . . Muriel Zuckerman introduces the group to Benny; brief bits of "Three
   Little Words" and an untitled blues
Sweet Georgia Brown
April In Paris - TRIO
Poor Butterfly
After You've Gone
Fascinating Rhythm
'Swonderful
The Man I Love

How come the Swedes, whom Benny'd never seen? A ''sound'' reason: he'd admired their work on an LP on which they'd backed Swedish clarinetist Ove Lind. ''Like to play with those guys sometime''—and he did.

Benny flew to New York May 28; a brief respite, then a guest ap-

pearance on Dick Cavett's program, delay-telecast the same day because of a Presidential address. During general discussion, Sex reared its lovely head; Benny's erudite contribution was, ''Well, I've got a sextet . . .'' Note that Benny is not the clarinetist in the introductory, ''Let's Dance,'' and that it is omitted for that reason:

"THE DICK CAVETT SHOW"   June 1, 1972, New York
   ABC Television Network

Benny Goodman, clt; Derek Smith, p; George Duvivier, b; Bobby Rosengarden, d.

I've Got The World On A String
Shine

Another benefit, this time for Phoenix House (drug rehabilitation), took Benny, Derek Smith, Bucky Pizzarelli, Milt Hinton and Grady Tate to Roseland Ballroom on June 5. There are no known tapes of this performance. Some ten weeks shy of his 70th birthday, James Andrew ''Jimmy'' Rushing, who'd made a big hit with Benny at the Brussels Fair in 1958, passed away. An engagement at Waterloo Village, Stanhope, New Jersey, on June 24 had to be cancelled because of flood conditions resulting from Hurricane Agnes. It was rescheduled for July 8. (A remarkable coincidence will find Hurricane Gloria causing another cancellation at Waterloo Village 13 years from now.) Before the ''rain date,'' however, Benny appeared as guest clarinetist and conductor in Central Park on Independence Day, where he featured a new medley written for him by Peter Knight:

"NAUMBURG MEMORIAL CONCERT"   July 4, 1972, New York
   WNYC-FM Radio

Benny Goodman, clt, and the Naumburg Symphony Orchestra, Jonathan Sternberg conducting.

Clarinet Concerto No. 1 In F Minor, Op. 73 (von Weber)
Medley: Poor Butterfly   )
        The Man I Love   )
        If I Had You   ) (arr PK)
        My Funny Valentine)
        Don't Be That Way)

(Benny conducted the orchestra's rendition of Malcolm Arnold's "Four Scottish Dances, Op. 84," but did not play.)

The July 8 performance at Waterloo Village featured Benny, Buddy Morrow, Peter Appleyard, Roland Hanna, Bucky Pizzarelli, George Duvivier and Bobby Rosengarden. An audience recording is extant, but its quality is poor. Too bad—Hanna played a startling chorus on ''Stompin' At The Savoy,'' causing Benny to stare in frank admiration.

Substituting Urbie Green for Morrow and Derek Smith for Hanna in the group he'd had at Waterloo Village, Benny played a private party in Cleveland, Tennessee on July 29; no recordings are known. A cassette tape is extant from the August 12 Jazz Festival in Concord, California, where Benny used Green, Appleyard, Smith, Rosengarden, guitarist Joe Pas (alternatively spelled both ''Pass'' and ''Paz'') and bassist Monty Budwig. Its poor quality prevents its inclusion in this work.

Taking only Appleyard and Smith along, Benny next appeared with Guido Basso's orchestra at the Canadian National Exhibition's band shell in Toronto, Canada, on August 18, 19 and 20. Audience recordings of all three concerts are extant, but are excluded because of their poor quality. However, the Canadian Broadcasting Corp. taped the concerts, and eventually aired excerpts from them:

"SHOWCASE '73 - BENNY GOODMAN AT THE 'EX'"
   CBC-FM Radio   August 18–20, 1972, Toronto

Broadcast January 12, 1973. Benny Goodman, clt; Peter Appleyard, vib; Derek Smith, p; and the Guido Basso Orchestra, including in part: Guido Basso, tpt; Bob McConnell tbn; Moe Koffman, as & fl; Jerry Todd, ts; Ed Bickert, g; Don Thompson, b; Ron Rooley, d.

QUINTET: Goodman, Smith, Bickert, Thompson, Rooley
SEXTET: Quintet plus Appleyard

(. . . introduction and Basso theme - NO BG
Let's Dance (theme)
Don't Be That Way
I Want To Be Happy - SEXTET
Rose Room - SEXTET
Love For Sale - QUINTET feat. Smith - BG in coda
(Swingin' Shepherd Blues - Koffman, fl, w/rhythm - NO BG

Roll 'Em
Stealin' Apples
A String Of Pearls
King Porter Stomp
Fascinating Rhythm - SEXTET
Oh, Lady Be Good! - SEXTET
Stompin' At The Savoy - SEXTET
Good-Bye (theme)
. . . Don't Be That Way (reprise)

(The introduction is from the concert on the 19th, and portions of the dialogue in the second half hour of the broadcast are from the 18th. Poor quality of the audience recordings prevents further certain cross-referencing.)

Benny was guest soloist with the Milwaukee Philharmonic, Andre Kostelanetz conducting, at the Dade County Coliseum in Madison, Wisconsin on August 30. On September 1 his Sextet—Appleyard, Smith, Pizzarelli, Duvivier and Rosengarden—appeared in Ames, Iowa. Tapes of neither performance are known. There is an audience recording of the original Quartet's reunion (Benny, Lionel, Teddy and Gene) at the finals of the 38th annual Harvest Moon Ball, Madison Square Garden, September 21; but its quality is such that their "Avalon," "Stompin' At The Savoy" and an untitled improvisation can barely be heard.

Benny's intense concentration gives rise to occasional memory lapses that are legendary among musicians who have worked for him, and family and friends. For example, at the Madhattan Room in 1937, the author vividly recalls Benny pointing to the next soloist, gesturing, stammering, "Hey, uh, trumpet player . . ."—he was signalling Harry James. Less privileged to witness these temporary mental blocks ordinarily is the casual fan; but on his next television appearance with Dick Cavett, Benny's quirk was exposed, so to speak, to millions: Providently visiting the men's room before making his entrance, Benny came on camera to a nationwide audience . . . with his fly open. To his credit, Cavett dealt with the situation with wit and tact, minimizing Benny's embarrassment.

"THE DICK CAVETT SHOW"   October 16, 1972, New York
ABC Television Network

Televised October 20. Benny Goodman, clt; Derek Smith, p; Bucky Pizzarelli, g; George Duvivier, b; Bobby Rosengarden, d.

Medley: As Long As I Live
        I Guess I'll Have To Change My Plans
        Manhattan

Add Billy Watrous, tbn (from the studio orchestra):

Sweet Georgia Brown

A week later, the Timex Corporation "gave a party" for its sales personnel, key distributors and guests. Supplying the entertainment were the orchestras of Count Basie and Duke Ellington, vocalists Ella Fitzgerald and Joe Williams, Dave Brubeck's and Tommy Flanagan's small groups, Willie "The Lion" Smith, an all-star group that included MC Doc Severinsen, Dizzy Gillespie, Max Kaminsky, Bobby Hackett, Tyree Glenn, Barney Bigard, Earl Hines, Arvell Shaw and Barrett Deems—and the Original Benny Goodman Quartet. Philharmonic Hall at Lincoln Center would accomodate the gala, and executive producers Burt Rosen and Dave Winters would tape the performances for a television "special." So far, so good.

Benny, however, was not enthusiastic about reuniting the Quartet. Save for their cameo appearance at the Harvest Moon Ball, they'd not played together for 10 years, had rarely seen each other in that time. He felt that he and the sidemen he'd employed recently would provide better music; they were mutually responsive, knew what each other could and would do. He believed nostalgia was the reason for insistence upon the Quartet, a poor motive in his view. There were bound to be contractual difficulties; it was all-or-none, giving one member an opportunity to demand—and get—several times the stipend for one night that he then was receiving for a full week's work.

His demurrers notwithstanding, the producers insisted. "Okay," said Benny, "but we'll have to rehearse." On Sunday afternoon before the Monday evening performance, Benny and the author taxied to the Wellington Hotel, there to meet with Lionel, Teddy and Gene—and a surprise! bassist George Duvivier. On this point Benny was adamant; he was accustomed to a bass behind him, he thought Gene, obviously not in the best of health, could use some support, and it would be an augmented Quartet. The doors to the Wellington's ground floor studio were locked and the now-five man Quartet began to rehearse before an audience of one, the author.

There was the usual tuning up and moving about, then Benny set the tempo, as he usually does, by tapping his foot, and they were off on "Ava-

lon." If nothing else, this very first runthrough proved to the author that there was more than mere mystique to the Quartet; despite their different personalities, despite a decade's hiatus, they meshed and swung.

But Benny wasn't satisfied, the old bugaboo cropped up: "Gene, why don't you play that like you played it on the record? You used brushes, didn't you?" "No, Ben, I used sticks." Appeal to the author; he used sticks. "Well, okay, let's try it again." "Avalon," take 2. "Gene, could you play that a little softer?" That did it: "Ben, you've been telling me that for 25 years. If you don't like the way I play, get yourself another drummer." Gene stands up; author grabs him. Benny apologizes: "Gene, I'm sorry, I'm sorry; I just thought it would sound better if you played a little softer." And truthfully, he probably did. Benny gets so immersed in his music that sensitivities, intrapersonal relationships, simply do not exist.

The storm broken, the air cleared, the rehearsal went ahead without further incident. On appeal from Teddy, his son was admitted, and secretary Muriel Zuckerman appeared with some papers for Benny to sign. An hour and a half break for dinner. Reassemble at seven, and a surprise for Benny: Technicians swarming, . . . a request . . . to tape the Quartet now, not tomorrow night, we'll blend it into the tape for television. "Either you tape us live, or we don't play—and I mean it." Something in Benny's tone and demeanor convinced the producers that he was in earnest. But note that some of the other sequences seen on television were videotaped on Sunday, are not from the Monday evening performance in Philharmonic Hall.

At last, "live" Benny Goodman from Lincoln Center.

"TIMEX ALL-STAR SWING FESTIVAL"   October 23, 1972, New York
NBC Television Network

First televised November 29, 1972, via NBC-TV. Rerun on Public Broadcasting Service network television stations in March 1977, and in some foreign countries still later.

Benny Goodman, clt; Lionel Hampton, vib; Teddy Wilson, p; George Duvivier, b; Gene Krupa, d.

Avalon
Moon Glow
I'm A Ding Dong Daddy (From Dumas)

Combined Basie & Ellington orchestras, others, BG in coda:

One O'Clock Jump - to close

(As an encore to "I'm A Ding Dong Daddy (From Dumas)," the Quartet-plus-one performed an untitled improvisation that is not included in the videotape.)

Watch it—we've still not finished with Timex. Producers Rosen and Winters caused a 12" souvenir LP to be pressed, presented copies to some of the performers. It contains excerpts from the videotape, offers two of Benny's numbers on its Side 2:

TIMEX ALL STAR SWING FESTIVAL   October 23, 1972, New York
Personnel as for the television program, preceding.

TX 1129B-1   **StLp:** Limited Edition A Winters-Rosen Production Side 2
                 Avalon - BENNY GOODMAN QUARTET
                 I'm A Ding Dong Daddy (From Dumas)
                 -BENNY GOODMAN QUARTET

October 28 found Benny in Denver as guest soloist with the Denver Symphony, Bryan Pressman conducting; the next day his Sextet performed for Colorado State University. No tapes of either concert are known. On November 8 Jack Ellsworth interviewed Benny in New York; results were broadcast on Patchogue, New York's radio station WALK-FM on March 13 and 15, 1973. At the end of the month, the Lotus Club feted Benny; he took along Derek Smith, Bucky Pizzarelli, Milt Hinton and Bobby Rosengarden and returned the compliment. Again, no known tapes. He finished out the year on Pearl Harbor Day, December 7, with an engagement whose details are missing.

The new year began tragically with the death of one of Swing's, and Benny's, better arrangers: Edgar Sampson died after a lengthy illness on January 16. An amputee since the '60s, Sampson has been musically inactive for much of the last decade of his life.

On January 27 Benny, Stan Getz, Appleyard, Smith, Pizzarelli, Duvivier and Rosengarden played the first Goodman engagement of 1973 at Hartford, Connecticut. No tapes of the concert, which also featured Benny as soloist with the Hartford "Pops" Symphony, are known.

The original Quartet reunited February 16, this time to pay homage to Lionel Hampton, honored at the National Urban League Guild's 33rd annual Beaux Arts Ball for his work in behalf of low-income housing in Harlem.

The grand ballroom of New York's Waldorf-Astoria Hotel overflowed with more than 2,000 celebrants as the Quartet performed for almost an hour and a half. They began with "Avalon" (Teddy was late in arriving; Lionel's pianist, Zeke Mullins, filled in), ended with a lengthy "Flying Home," in which they were joined by Illinois Jacquet, who recreated his famous chorus. Eyewitnesses noted tape recorders sprinkled throughout the audience, but to date no recordings have become available to the author.

There is, however, an "acceptable" tape extant from an engagement two days' later in Atlantic City's Chalfont-Haddon Hall Hotel, now a gambling casino:

CHALFONT-HADDON HALL CONCERT   February 18, 1973, Atlantic City

Benny Goodman, clt; Billy Watrous, tbn; Peter Appleyard, vib; Derek Smith, p; Bucky Pizzarelli, g; George Duvivier, b; Bobby Rosengarden, d.

TRIO: Goodman, Smith, Rosengarden
QUINTET: Trio plus Pizzarelli, Duvivier
SEXTET: Quintet plus Appleyard

Avalon - SEXTET
Memories Of You - TRIO
The World Is Waiting For The Sunrise - SEXTET
(Warm Valley - Watrous w/rhythm - NO BG
Rose Room
Tin Roof Blues - SEXTET (BG in coda)
Medley: Don't Be That Way
      Stompin' At The Savoy
(Love For Sale - Smith w/rhythm - NO BG
Yesterday - QUINTET
Sweet Georgia Brown
Poor Butterfly - SEXTET
Honeysuckle Rose
I Will Wait For You
Oh, Lady Be Good!
Moon Glow - SEXTET
Just One Of Those Things - SEXTET
Body And Soul - QUINTET
You Took Advantage Of Me - SEXTET
I've Found A New Baby

"Australia? Never been there, but why not?," was Benny's reaction to an offer to tour "down under," and a revamped Septet was on its way March 2. The first stop was in Sydney's Hordern Pavilion, from where the concert was both televised and broadcast later:

SYDNEY CONCERT   March 6, 1973, Sydney
  AUSTRALIAN TV & Radio

Benny Goodman, clt; Zoot Sims, ts; Peter Appleyard, vib; Derek Smith, p; Joe Pas, g; Monty Budwig, b; Ron Stevenson, d.

QUINTET: Goodman, Smith, Pas, Budwig, Stevenson
SEXTET: Quintet plus Appleyard

Televised April 18:

I Want To Be Happy
A Smo-o-o-oth One
(Jitterbug Waltz - Sims w/rhythm - NO BG
Poor Butterfly - QUINTET
Avalon - SEXTET
(Tangerine - Pas w/rhythm - NO BG
Medley: The Man I Love - QUINTET
      (Somebody Loves Me - Sims w/rhythm - NO BG
      (Fascinating Rhythm - Appleyard w/rhythm - NO BG
      (Summertime - Smith w/rhythm - NO BG
      Oh, Lady Be Good!
Sweet Georgia Brown

Intermission; end of first telecast.

Televised April 25:

Medley: Don't Be That Way
      Stompin' At The Savoy
(Emily - Sims w/rhythm - NO BG
Shine - SEXTET
Tin Roof Blues - SEXTET (BG in coda)
It Had To Be You - SEXTET
Seven Come Eleven

(Autumn Leaves - Smith w/rhythm - NO BG
Memories Of You - QUINTET
I'm A Ding Dong Daddy (From Dumas)
Honeysuckle Rose
Sing, Sing, Sing
One O'Clock Jump
Good-Bye (theme)

Next engagement in the Apollo Stadium in Adelaide offers a cassette taped from the audience that is minimally satisfactory. Only those performances that included Benny were recorded, those that featured the sidemen without him were not, save for Appleyard's "Tin Roof Blues":

ADELAIDE CONCERT   March 10, 1973, Adelaide

Personnels as March 6.

I Want To Be Happy
A Smo-o-o-oth One
Poor Butterfly - QUINTET
Avalon - SEXTET
Medley: The Man I Love - QUINTET
      (Somebody Loves Me - Sims w/rhythm - NO BG
      (Fascinating Rhythm - Appleyard w/rhythm - NO BG
      (Summertime - Smith w/rhythm - NO BG
      Oh, Lady Be Good!
It Had To Be You - QUINTET
Sweet Georgia Brown
Medley: Don't Be That Way
      Stompin' At The Savoy
Memories Of You - QUINTET
I've Found A New Baby
(Tin Roof Blues - Appleyard w/rhythm - NO BG
Yesterday - QUINTET
Seven Come Eleven
If I Had You
Indiana
I'm A Ding Dong Daddy (From Dumas)
Good-Bye (theme)

The author has no recording of the ensuing concert in Melbourne's Festival Hall, but while there Benny granted an interview to Jeff Manion. The tape was broadcast via Radio 3AW on March 31. The final concert, in Brisbane's Festival Hall, provided a bonus. Skitch Henderson was in Australia to conduct the Queensland Symphony Orchestra, and Benny invited him to join for one number:

BRISBANE CONCERT   March 13, 1973, Brisbane

Personnels as March 6.

I Want To Be Happy (n/c - intro clipped)
A Smo-o-o-oth One (n/c - ending clipped)
(Jitterbug Waltz - Sims w/rhythm - NO BG
Poor Butterfly - QUINTET
Avalon
(Tangerine - Pas w/rhythm - NO BG
Medley: The Man I Love - QUINTET
      Somebody Loves Me - QUINTET plus Sims
      (Fascinating Rhythm - Appleyard w/rhythm - NO BG
      (Summertime - Smith w/rhythm - NO BG
      Oh, Lady Be Good!

Skitch Henderson, p, replaces Smith in the Quintet:
Memories Of You - QUINTET

Smith replaces Henderson:
Sweet Georgia Brown

Intermission.

Medley: Don't Be That Way
      Stompin' At The Savoy
Body And Soul - QUINTET
It Had To Be You - QUINTET plus Sims
(Emily - Sims w/rhythm - NO BG
Tin Roof Blues - SEXTET (BG in coda)
(Out of Nowhere - Appleyard w/rhythm - NO BG
Yesterday - QUINTET
I'm A Ding Dong Daddy (From Dumas)
(You And Me - Pas w/rhythm - NO BG

(Love For Sale - Smith w/rhythm - NO BG
More Than You Know - QUINTET
I've Found A New Baby (n/c)

A month elapses, and now it's "Down South" instead of "down under," and an hour's concert in New Orleans's Municipal Auditorium:

JAZZ HERITAGE FESTIVAL — April 11, 1973, New Orleans

Benny Goodman, clt; Urbie Green, tbn; Zoot Sims, ts; John Bunch, p; Bucky Pizzarelli, g; Milt Hinton, b; Bobby Rosengarden, d.

QUINTET: Goodman, Bunch, Pizzarelli, Hinton, Rosengarden

Indiana - QUINTET
(Things Ain't What They Used To Be - Bunch w/rhythm - NO BG
Here's That Rainy Day - QUINTET
Avalon - QUINTET
(Jitterbug Waltz - Sims w/rhythm - NO BG
(Star Dust - Green w/rhythm - NO BG
Sweet Georgia Brown
Medley: Don't Be That Way
      Stompin' At The Savoy
Undecided
Memories Of You - QUINTET
The World Is Waiting For The Sunrise - QUINTET
I've Found A New Baby
Good-Bye (theme)

Friday the 13th of April proved somewhat unlucky; the author has no recording of a benefit performance Benny and his New Orleans personnel played for Skills Unlimited in the Knights of Columbus Hall, Patchogue, Long Island. He does have, however, a souvenir program compiled by Jack Ellsworth (Shiebler) that offers some seldom-seen photographs of Goodman.

On April 26 Benny was guest soloist with the Des Moines (Iowa) Symphony, Arthur Fiedler conducting. On the 29th he did another benefit for a synagogue in Short Hills, New Jersey, with Bunch, Pizzarelli, Hinton and Rosengarden. He took the same rhythm section to New York's Plaza Hotel May 10, where he was honored for his charitable works by the Dutch Treat club. The author has no recordings from any of those events; the next, chronologically, is from television:

"THE TODAY SHOW" — May 30, 1973, New York
  NBC Television Network

Benny Goodman, clt; Peter Appleyard, vib; John Bunch, p; Bucky Pizzarelli, g; Milt Hinton, b; Bobby Rosengarden, d.

Sweet Georgia Brown
Lazy River
Medley: Don't Be That Way
      Stompin' at The Savoy
Undecided
Sweet Lorraine

The "Today Show" appearance served to announce Benny's return to the Rainbow Grill, May 31 through June 16, with Bobby Hackett added to the personnel on the telecast. Urbie Green also joined for the final week; at the same time, Slam Stewart replaced Hinton, who had a prior commitment to go to Europe with Pearl Bailey. To the best of the author's knowledge, there were no broadcasts from the Grill this time around, and no audience recordings have come to his attention. His only evidence of this engagement is a CBS-TV news clip of Goodman, Hackett and the rhythm section rehearsing "Sweet Lorraine."

Earlier in June, Mundelein College of Chicago had conferred an honorary doctorate upon Benny. On June 22, the governor of Connecticut cited Benny for his cultural contributions. A week later, the original Quartet made the first of its final three appearances. But before it appeared in Carnegie Hall as part of George Wein's Newport Jazz Festival (long since removed to Manhattan), it rehearsed in CBS's studios. CBS-TV network news programs televised half-minute excerpts of its videotape, but a half hour's worth of the rehearsal is extant via audio tape:

CARNEGIE HALL REHEARSAL — June 27, 1973, New York

Benny Goodman, clt; Lionel Hampton, vib; Teddy Wilson, p; Gene Krupa, d.
Various segments of:

Sing, Sing, Sing
Avalon
Dizzy Spells (several cuts)

China Boy (intro only)
Flying Home (intro only)
Bei Mir Bist Du Schon
Melancholy Baby
Sing, Sing, Sing (two cuts)
Good-Bye (several cuts - Lionel and Teddy both play piano)

The concert itself was taped in its entirety by NBC, which then broadcast excerpts from it via its "Monitor" radio program. The listing following is that of the NBC master tape; the "Monitor" excerpts are shown in their order-of-broadcast by numbers preceding the appropriate tunes:

CARNEGIE HALL CONCERT — June 29, 1973, New York

Benny Goodman, clt; Lionel Hampton, vib; Teddy Wilson, p; Slam Stewart, b; Gene Krupa, d.

QUARTET: Goodman, Wilson, Stewart, Krupa

    I'm A Ding Dong Daddy (From Dumas)
3,8 Moon Glow
  1 ("C" Jam Blues - segue to,)
    (One O'Clock Jump   ) -Wilson, Stewart, Krupa - NO BG
  7 Memories Of You
  5 Bei Mir Bist Du Schon
  2 Oh, Lady be Good! - QUARTET
  4 Medley: Don't Be That Way
        Stompin' At The Savoy
  6 (How High The Moon - Hampton, Wilson, Stewart, Krupa
    - NO BG
    Body And Soul - QUARTET
  9 After You've Gone
    Sing, Sing, Sing
 10 Avalon (encore)

(For the most part, the "Monitor" excerpts are partial renditions.)

Gene was visibly failing on this, the first night of the 10-day Newport Jazz Festival. Just prior to the Wednesday afternoon rehearsal, he'd been in hospital for the better part of a month, where his condition had been diagnosed as "benign leukemia." In truth, the rehearsal took place, in his words, ". . . to see if I could hack it. You don't often get to play with guys of this caliber, and I didn't want to hang them up." He didn't; he played well. And that's not a judgment tempered by his illness, or by his enforced absence from the drums. He played well. There are times when the spirit overcomes all else.

Longtime Goodman observers were startled by Benny's uncharacteristic behavior on stage that Friday evening. He seemed to meditate for endless minutes between renditions, stared into space while the audience tittered restlessly. He fiddled with his reed, adjusted it, blew into it, readjusted it; he moved his stool about, seemingly dissatisfied with this location or that. He mugged, imitated Groucho Marx, complete with bobbing eyebrows and lascivious leer, something he may never have done before or since. And when he walked off stage after "Sing, Sing, Sing," which he fully intended would end the concert, he returned at once when he realized Gene was exhausted, could not rise from his drummer's throne. Unannounced, there was an encore; and then he and Lionel got on either side of Gene and supported him into the wings. He had succeeded in what he had set out to do: at the sacrifice of his dignity—which is very important to Benny Goodman—his comportment had given Gene time to gather himself together between selections.

Backstage after the concert the author's wife embraced Gene: "Be careful, Georgia, you'll get what I've got." And then, "Well, Russ, what did you think?" "Great, Gene, great!" (Benny had the better adjective; he called Gene's performance "heroic.") Looking back: "Y'know, that fire I had; I lost your book. Can you get me another copy?" (Some three months earlier, fire had gutted his home in Yonkers. He'd lost the mementoes of a lifetime.) "Sure, hell, no problem." And looking ahead: 'Did you see these new sticks I'm using? They're ironwood (actually, the trade mark is "durawood"), Slingerland had 'em made especially for me. I've only got one pair. But if you get me a copy of your book, I'll get a pair for you." "Gene, thanks; but if you get another pair, you keep them. You're gonna need more than one pair."

Heroic indeed. But oh, so sad.

On July 1 Benny appeared at the South Shore Music Circus, Cohasset, Massachusetts, with Ed Polcer, tpt; George Masso, tbn; Al Klink, ts; Peter Appleyard, vib; John Bunch, p; Bucky Pizzarelli, g; Arvell Shaw, b; and Ron Traxler, d. The next day the same group—save that Zoot Sims replaced Klink—performed at the Garden State Arts Center in Holmdel, New Jersey. The author does not have an audience recording of either concert.

Oakland University in Rochester, Michigan, next presented the Goodman Septet (no guitar) at its "Meadow Brook Festival" in the Baldwin Pavilion. An audience recording captured most of the concert:

MEADOW BROOK FESTIVAL   *July 13, 1973, Rochester, Michigan*

Benny Goodman, clt; Ed Polcer, tpt; George Masso, tbn; Peter Appleyard, vib; John Bunch, p; Slam Stewart, b; Ron Traxler, d.

QUARTET: Goodman, Bunch, Stewart, Traxler
QUINTET: Quartet plus Appleyard

Let's Dance (theme)
Undecided
Lazy River
(Tin Roof Blues—Appleyard w/rhythm—NO BG (n/c)
(unidentified Bunch solo—NO BG
Sweet Lorraine—QUARTET
(The One I Love—Masso w/rhythm—NO BG
A Handful Of Keys—QUINTET
Oh, Lady Be Good!—feat. Stewart; full group in coda
Medley: Don't Be That Way
*   Stompin' At The Savoy*
After You've Gone
Avalon
(That Old Feeling—Polcer w/rhythm—NO BG
(Fascinating Rhythm - Appleyard w/rhythm - NO BG
Memories Of You—QUARTET
Bei Mir Bist Du Schon
That's A Plenty
Good-Bye (theme)
Sweet Georgia Brown (encore)

Two days later the original Quartet-plus Slam Stewart ("our designated hitter," Benny announced, borrowing a term from baseball) made the second of its three farewell appearances at Ravinia, Highland Park, Illinois. Benny did everything he could to make Gene comfortable: had a cabulance meet his plane at O'Hare, provided a couch backstage, saw that his every need was accommodated.

With an ear to history, a selfish interest and a presentiment of the inevitable, the author had suggested to Benny that the Ravinia concert should be recorded professionally; if given permission, a sound engineer from Chicago was set to tape the performance. Benny investigated, found contractual and other reasons made the project infeasible. Disappointed but not daunted, the engineer bribed a Ravinia employee, smuggled his equipment into the park and tapped into the public address system. The concert began, the tape rolled, a monitor assured that the sound was excellent—through the first three tunes. But then the jerry-built, jury-rigged tap went awry, the tape aborted—and the public address system quit completely, bringing anguished cries from the audience. The engineer and his gear beat a hasty retreat, chased by the now-fearful park employee.

But not to worry: A composite tape, blended from three separate cassette recordings (one from a recorder secreted under Teddy's piano, the other two in the audience) and the engineer's reel, when equalized and corrected for pitch, preserve the concert for posterity:

RAVINIA CONCERT   *July 15, 1973, Highland Park, Illinois*

Benny Goodman, clt; Lionel Hampton, vib; Teddy Wilson, p; Slam Stewart, b; Gene Krupa, d.

QUARTET: Goodman, Wilson, Stewart, Krupa

Avalon
Moon Glow
I'm A Ding Dong Daddy (From Dumas)
(Medley: Sophisticated Lady)—Wilson, Stewart, Krupa—NO BG
*   Take The "A" Train)*
How High The Moon-feat. Hampton—Goodman in coda
Memories Of You—QUARTET
Oh, Lady Be Good!—feat. Stewart—ensemble in coda
Don't Be That Way
Hamp's Boogie-segue to, The Blues
After You've Gone
I Got Rhythm
Good-Bye (theme)

Down Beat presented its 1972 "Hall Of Fame" award to Gene Krupa during the concert. Gene acknowledged his gratitude, said it was ". . . appropriate to get it while playing for the people of Chicago . . . and with the Benny Goodman Quartet." Appropriately, Benny played "Memories Of

You" after the presentation. All very appropriate, but in the author's view, why wasn't the award given Gene years earlier? Why wait until he was dying?

Benny, Hackett, trombonist Dick Rath, Appleyard, Bunch, Al Caiola, Arvell Shaw and drummer Joe Corsello were in the Eastman Theater in Rochester, New York on July 28; the author knows of no tape of that concert. But thanks to Bobby Hackett and his trusty Tandberg, there is an excellent recording of Benny's next engagement, in the Cape Cod Coliseum. As we've seen (Basin Street East, mid-May 1963), on occasion Bobby would set up his stereo recorder and tape some of his appearances with Benny. This date posed him no problems in logistics, for at the time Bobby was a Cape Cod resident.

CAPE COD COLISEUM CONCERT   *August 12, 1973,*
South Yarmouth, Mass.

Benny Goodman, clt; Bobby Hackett, tpt; George Masso, tbn; Peter Appleyard, vib; John Bunch, p; Bucky Pizzarelli, g; Slam Stewart, b; Ronnie Bedford, d.

DUET: Goodman, Pizzarelli
QUINTET: Duet plus Bunch, Stewart, Corsello

Let's Dance (theme)
Undecided
The Good Life - Hackett w/rhythm - BG obligato in coda
A Smo-o-o-oth One
The One I Love Belongs To Somebody Else - Masso w/rhythm - BG,
*   Hackett in coda*
Tin Roof Blues - Appleyard w/rhythm - BG obligati (n/c)
(Fascinating Rhythm - Appleyard w/rhythm - NO BG
(. . . unannounced Pizzarelli solo - NO BG
Here, There And Everywhere - DUET
(Oh, Lady Be Good! - Stewart w/rhythm - NO BG
All The Things You Are - QUINTET plus Hackett
Avalon
Rose Room
Medley: Don't Be That Way
*   Stompin' At The Savoy*
(The Duke - Bunch solo - NO BG
Memories Of You - QUINTET
Poor Butterfly - Hackett, Pizzarelli duet - full group in coda
Misty - Pizzarelli, Hackett duet - BG, rhythm in coda
If I Had You
(Play, Fiddle, Play - Stewart w/rhythm - NO BG (n/c)
Bei Mir Bist Du Schon
Indiana - Appleyard w/rhythm - BG in coda
Sweet Lorraine - QUINTET
I'm Coming, Virginia
Good-Bye (theme)
That's A Plenty (encore)

Evidence of Benny's notorious memory lapses is clearly audible on the tape: Following "Memories Of You," Benny announces that Bucky and Bobby will perform. "What'll we play, Professori?" Bobby asks Benny. Pizzarelli murmurs, "Somebody requested 'Poor Butterfly.'" Benny responds, "I just played that." "No, you didn't," Hackett demurs. "What did I play?" Benny questions. Hackett settles it: "Memories Of You."

It's time now, sadly, to say "Good-Bye" to Gene Krupa, for next is the final assembly of the original Quartet. Once again, there is intrigue behind the recording:

The concert was given in the Performing Arts Center, Saratoga Springs, New York, long the summer residence of members of the Philadelphia Orchestra. The Center's management on occasion records classical performances there, and offers them for broadcasting to FM stations throughout the United States. Possibly for this reason it resolutely opposes audience recordings, has its ushers confiscate any tape device discovered on the persons of patrons entering the open-air facility. Further, cameras are similarly banned.

A journalist, however, given some freedom of movement because of his profession managed to place a cassette recorder on stage just prior to the concert. He then attempted to take some photographs; apprehended, he was evicted, his film exposed; and the recorder ran on unattended. It was discovered and impounded; eventually it was returned to Goodman's office. Miraculously, the cassette was intact; unfortunately, it had run out, did not capture the encore, "Stompin' At The Savoy," in its entirety.

Here, then, the clandestine cassette from Saratoga, the last recording of the original Benny Goodman Quartet; and so far as the author knows, the last recording of Gene Krupa:

SARATOGA CONCERT August 18, 1973, Saratoga Springs, New York

Personnels as July 15.

Avalon
Moon Glow
(Oh, Lady Be Good!—Stewart solo—NO BG
(St. Louis Blues—Wilson, Stewart, Krupa—NO BG
(How High The Moon—Hampton, Wilson, Stewart, Krupa—NO BG
Sweet Lorraine—QUARTET
Dinah
Rose Room
I'm A Ding Dong Daddy (From Dumas)
Memories Of You
I Got Rhythm
Stompin' At The Savoy (encore—n/c)

(It is believed that Performing Arts Center personnel recorded Benny's guest appearance with resident Philadelphia Orchestra members prior to the jazz concert. But if so, no tape of the von Weber concerto is in Benny's library, and no broadcast is known.)

Perhaps the Fates intervened: the on-stage recorder was so positioned that it picked up Gene's drums more clearly than the other instruments. And it is obvious listening to that tape and reliving those moments, that Gene was laboring. After the concert, backstage, with Gene struggling to sit up on the couch provided for him, it was manifest that the blood transfusions, drugs and other treatment being given him were not effective. Little was said, just some pleasantries; what was there to say? We embraced, mumbled our good-byes, both of us choked up. And then that final poignant moment: "Here, Russ, here's those sticks I promised you. I won't be needing them any-more."

A satisfactory cassette is extant from Benny's next engagement, in Philadelphia's outdoor Robin Hood Dell:

PHILADELPHIA CONCERT August 21, 1973, Phila.

Benny Goodman, clt; Bobby Hackett, Ed Polcer, tpt; George Masso, tbn; Al Klink, ts; Peter Appleyard, vib; John Bunch, p; Wayne Wright, g; Slam Stewart, b; Joe Corsello, d.

QUINTET: Goodman, Bunch, Wright, Stewart, Corsello

Let's Dance (theme)
Undecided
(The Good Life—Hackett w/rhythm—NO BG
The One I Love Belongs To Somebody Else—Masso w/rhythm - BG in coda
Memories of You—QUINTET
Honeysuckle Rose
(Oh, Lady Be Good!—Stewart w/rhythm - NO BG
I'm Getting Sentimental Over You—Wright w/rhythm—BG obligato
(Tin Roof Blues—Appleyard w/rhythm—NO BG (n/c)
(Fascinating Rhythm—Appleyard w/rhythm—NO BG
Don't Be That Way
Avalon
That's A Plenty
Good-Bye (theme)
Sweet Georgia Brown (encore)
Good-Bye (theme)

The same group sans Polcer and Appleyard played two days later in Chautauqua, New York. Note that purists may cavil that Hackett more frequently is known as a cornetist. Benny invariably introduced him as a "trumpeter," and that instrument is listed for Hackett throughout this work.

CHAUTAUGUA CONCERT August 23, 1973, Chautauga, New York

Personnel as August 21, except omit Polcer.

TRIO: Goodman, Bunch, Corsello
QUARTET: Trio plus Stewart
QUINTET: Quartet plus Wright

Let's Dance (theme)
Undecided
(The Good Life—Hackett w/rhythm—NO BG
The One I Love Belongs To Somebody Else—feat. Masso—full group in coda
Memories Of You—TRIO
'Swonderful
(Oh, Lady Be Good!—Stewart w/rhythm—NO BG
The Flat Foot Floogie—Stewart w/rhythm—BG in release

The Girl From Ipanema—feat. Klink—full group in coda
(I'm Getting Sentimental Over You—Wright w/rhythm—NO BG
Body And Soul—QUARTET—full group in coda
Sweet Georgia Brown

Intermission.

Avalon
(All The Things You Are—Hackett w/rhythm—NO BG
The Man I Love
I Got It Bad (And That Ain't Good)—feat. Klink—full group in coda
Medley: Don't Be That Way
        Stompin' At The Savoy
That's A Plenty
Good-Bye (theme)
Oh, Lady Be Good! (encore)

Rather a rollicking concert, that; although the audience recording certainly isn't of studio quality, it clearly evidences that everyone is having a good time, playing well. Hackett seemed to inspire Goodman whenever they were together, and Leroy "Slam" Stewart pleased crowds wherever he appeared. When Benny had needed to replace Hinton at the Rainbow Grill in June, the author enthusiastically endorsed the Rochester, New York resident as his substitute.

With only Ed Polcer, George Masso, Peter Appleyard and Joe Corsello along, Benny returned to the band shell of the Canadian National Exhibition in Toronto for two dates with Guido Basso's orchestra. (An announcer identifies Basso's personnel; their names are spelled phonetically, and some of them likely are incorrect.) Both concerts were taped successfully from the audience:

"BENNY AT THE 'EX' - I August 31, 1973, Toronto

Benny Goodman, clt; Ed Polcer, tpt; George Masso, tbn; Peter Appleyard, vib; Joe Corsello, d; and members of Guido Basso's Orchestra, including: Guido Basso, Arnie Chaikovski, Eric Travert, tpt; Bob McConnell, Teddy Rudderman, tbn; Moe Koffman, Greg Wilkins; Jerry Williams, Eugene Amaro, Jerry Potts (Todd?), reeds; Jimmy Dale, p; Ed Bickert, g; Don Thompson, b.

DUET: Goodman, Bickert
SEXTET: Goodman, Appleyard, Dale, Bickert, Thompson, Corsello
OCTET: Sextet plus Polcer, Masso

Let's Dance (theme)
After You've Gone - OCTET
Mission To Moscow
(The One I Love Belongs To Somebody Else - Masso w/rhythm - NO BG
A String Of Pearls
(Indiana - Appleyard w/rhythm - NO BG
Stompin' At The Savoy - SEXTET - Polcer, Masso in coda
(That Old Feeling - Polcer w/rhythm - NO BG
Don't Be That Way
Memories Of You - DUET
King Porter Stomp
(I Can't Believe That You're In Love With Me - Bickert w/rhythm - NO BG
Sometimes I'm Happy
Sing, Sing, Sing
Good-Bye (in its entirety)
Big John Special (encore)

"BENNY AT THE 'EX' - II September 1, 1973, Toronto

Personnels as August 31.

Let's Dance (theme)
A String Of Pearls
Mission To Moscow
Undecided - OCTET
The One I Love Belongs To Somebody Else - Masso w/SEXTET
(Fascinating Rhythm - Appleyard w/rhythm - NO BG
Rose Room - OCTET
King Porter Stomp
(That Old Feeling - Polcer w/rhythm - NO BG
Wolverine Blues (arr George Masso) - OCTET
Sweet Georgia Brown - OCTET
Sing, Sing, Sing
Good-Bye (theme)
Don't Be That Way (encore)

The Canadian Broadcasting Corporation recorded both concerts in stereo, broadcast a composite tape as part of its "Showcase" series later in the year.

"SHOWCASE '73 - BENNY AT THE 'EX'"
CBC-FM Radio   *August 31–September 1, 1973, Toronto*

Broadcast October 27. Personnels as August 31 audience recording.

Let's Dance (theme)
Mission To Moscow
A String Of Pearls
(Indiana - Appleyard w/rhythm - NO BG
Stompin' At The Savoy - SEXTET - Polcer, Masso in coda
(That Old Feeling - Polcer w/rhythm - NO BG
Don't Be That Way
Memories Of You - DUET
King Porter Stomp
(I Can't Believe That You're In Love With Me - Bickert w/rhythm - NO BG
Sometimes I'm Happy
Sing, Sing, Sing
Undecided - OCTET
Wolverine Blues - OCTET - to signoff

*(All selections above are from the concert of August 31 except "Undecided"
and "Wolverine Blues," which are from the concert of September 1.)*

Benny's files reveal little activity for the next two months. On September 29 he played a benefit for the American Shakespeare Theatre's Student Audience Program—"An Evening With Benny Goodman At Stratford"—in Stratford, Connecticut. A cassette recording of the concert is extant, but has not been heard by the author, and its quality is not known. The program included ten of the selections repeated at Benny's next engagement, played by the same personnel:

IOWA STATE CONCERT   *October 6, 1973, Ames, Iowa*

*Benny Goodman, clt; Ed Polcer, tpt; George Masso, tbn; Al Klink, ts; John
Bunch, p; Wayne Wright, g; Slam Stewart, b; Joe Corsello, d.*

TRIO: Goodman, Bunch, Corsello

Let's Dance (theme)
Undecided
(The One I Love Belongs To Somebody Else - Masso w/rhythm - NO BG
(Dream A Little Dream Of Me - Wright w/rhythm - NO BG
Sing
(That Old Feeling - Polcer w/rhythm - NO BG
—performed, but not taped: Oh, Lady Be Good! - Stewart w/rhythm - NO
   BG
Here's That Rainy Day - Goodman, Bunch
Medley: Don't Be that Way
        Stompin' At The Savoy
Avalon
Wolverine Blues
A Smo-o-o-oth One
—performed, but not taped: The Girl From Ipanema - Klink w/rhythm - NO
   BG
Memories Of You - TRIO
Honeysuckle Rose
That's A Plenty
Bei Mir Bist Du Schon
Good-Bye (theme)

Gene Krupa died Tuesday, October 16, at his home in Yonkers, of leukemia and coronary disfunctions acerbated by the disease. A requiem Mass was said on Thursday at St. Denis Roman Catholic Church in Yonkers. His body was flown to Chicago on Saturday; following a mass at the Immaculate Conception Church there, it was interred in the Krupa family plot in Calumet City, Illinois. He was survived by his brother Jules and his two adopted children Mary Grace and Beegee. A memorial service was held October 29 at St. Peter's Lutheran Church in Manhattan; Jo Jones paid a musical tribute to Gene.

The last half-dozen were not the happiest of Gene's 64 years. Unwell (a heart attack in 1960; emphysema; a disc operation that had "frozen" his spinal column), playing poorly by his standards, he'd given up his recurring engagements at the Metropole on Seventh Avenue in 1967. He stayed away from music for three full years, then eased back on a limited basis. His second marriage, to Patricia (Patti) Bowler, ended in divorce. His son Beegee, adopted as an infant, was discovered to be mentally impaired before the age of two.

But through all this his innate good humor, his interest in current events, his warm and genuine welcome to old friends never flagged. He rarely spoke of his personal problems, instead talked about the jazz he had served all of his adult life. In the end, it sustained him.

Gene Krupa, January 15 1909–October 16, 1973. He will not be forgotten.

Benny's Septet was in the Westchester County Center in White Plains, New York, on November 3; no tapes from the concert are extant. New York's Jazz Museum, then on West 55th Street, opened November 27 with a prominent display of Goodman memorabilia; Benny was interviewed there by Milton Lewis, and the videotape appeared on ABC-TV's "Eyewitness News" that evening. At about this time he videotaped a segment for Peggy Lee's recognition on the television program, "This is Your Life." He flew to London at the end of the month for a brief concert tour; while there he was interviewed by Peter Clayton of BBC Radio 3. The interview was broadcast on Boxing Day, December 26.

There are extant two audience recordings of this limited European tour. The first concert was also videotaped by the German television network. Zweites Deutsches Fernsehen (ZDF). The concert is listed in its entirety; the portions televised by ZDF are indicated by numbers showing the order in which they were televised, preceding appropriate selections.

HAMBURG CONCERT   *December 8, 1973, Musikhalle, Hamburg*

Numbered selections televised by ZDF-TV on February 24, 1974.

*Benny Goodman, clt; John McLevy, tpt; George Masso, tbn; Al Klink, ts & fl;
Peter Appleyard, vib; John Bunch, p; Bucky Pizzarelli, g; Slam Stewart, b; Joe
Corsello, d.*

QUINTET: Goodman, Bunch, Pizzarelli, Stewart, Corsello
SEXTET: Quintet plus Appleyard

 1 Let's Dance (theme)
 2 Avalon - SEXTET
 3 (Baubles, Bangles And Beads - McLevy w/rhythm - NO BG
    Moon Glow - SEXTET
    Sing
 4 (Oh, Lady Be Good! - Stewart w/rhythm - NO BG
    (The Girl From Ipanema - Klink w/rhythm - NO BG
 5 A Handful Of Keys - SEXTET
    (Love Song - Pizzarelli solo - NO BG
 8 That's A Plenty

Intermission.

 9 Medley: Don't Be That Way
           Stompin' At The Savoy
 6 You Must Meet My Wife - QUINTET
    Tin Roof Blues - Appleyard w/rhythm - BG, others in coda
    Poor Butterfly - SEXTET
10 After You've Gone
    (The Duke - Bunch solo - NO BG
 7 Fascinating Rhythm - Appleyard w/rhythm - BG in coda
    . . . reprise, Fascinating Rhythm - SEXTET
    A Weekend In The Country
    Memories Of You - QUINTET
    Seven Come Eleven
11 Bei Mir Bist Du Schon
    Good-Bye (theme)

*(Televised cuts on **LP,** SG 8006.)*

Alto saxophonist Bob Burns and drummer Bobby Orr, members of Benny's erstwhile English big band, made guest appearances with the Nonet at the Royal Albert Hall, following intermission:

LONDON CONCERT   *December 10, 1973, London*

Personnels as December 8.

Let's Dance (theme)
Avalon - SEXTET
(Baubles, Bangles And Beads - McLevy w/rhythm - NO BG
Moon Glow - SEXTET
A Handful Of Keys - SEXTET
(Oh, Lady Be Good! - Stewart w/rhythm - NO BG
Sing
(The Girl From Ipanema - Klink w/rhythm - NO BG
(Love Song - Pizzarelli solo - NO BG
Poor Butterfly - SEXTET
That's A Plenty

Intermission.

Medley: Don't Be That Way
       Stompin' At The Savoy
Tin Roof Blues - Appleyard w/rhythm - BG in coda
Spain - SEXTET plus McLevy, Klink (fl)
Memories Of You - QUINTET
(The Duke - Bunch solo - NO BG
A Weekend In The Country
(Body And Soul - guest Bob Burns, as w/rhythm - NO BG
Fascinating Rhythm - Appleyard w/ rhythm - BG in coda
Sing, Sing, Sing
("Turkish March" / Nola - guest Bobby Orr, d solo - NO BG
After You've Gone
Good-Bye (theme)

Benny's initial engagement for 1974 was both ambitious and complex. He signed with York Enterprises, Inc., to produce an hour-long television special for Monsanto Corporation. The program would consist of excerpts from three separate performances, each with different personnel, each from a different locale. The first, featuring an Octet and guest vocalist Mel Torme, would be played before an audience of invited guests in the Rainbow Room (not the Rainbow Grill) at Rockefeller Center on the afternoon of January 19. Through the week beginning Sunday, January 20, his Quartet would be videotaped at his home in Stamford, and he would also record a duet with his daughter, Rachel Goodman Weismann. A concert in Carnegie Hall on Sunday evening, January 27, with a big band and guests Cleo Laine and her husband Johnny Dankworth, would complete the project.

(Interrupting this schedule, Benny's Monsanto-Rainbow Room Octet—except Wayne Wright substituting for Pizzarelli—appeared January 21 in Ottawa's National Arts Centre. The author has no tape of this concert.)

The program is listed as televised. Personnels for each of the three source performances are identified by date and location. Dates in parentheses following each of the first nine selections permit cross-referencing. From "Let's Dance" on, all selections are from Carnegie Hall, January 27. Some of the performances are edited, may be splices of more than one "take," may have portions deleted.

The "Monsanto Special" was first televised March 31, 1974, via NBC-TV. It was shown on other television networks on later dates.

"MONSANTO SPECIAL - BENNY GOODMAN"
  NBC Television Network   January 1974 - see specifics

January 19, 1974, Rainbow Room, Rockefeller Center, New York

Benny Goodman, clt; Bobby Hackett, tpt; Zoot Sims, ts; Red Norvo, vib; Hank Jones, p; Bucky Pizzarelli, g; Slam Stewart, b; Grady Tate, d. Mel Torme, voc.

  QUARTET: Goodman, Jones, Stewart, Tate
  SEXTET: Quartet plus Hackett, Pizzarelli
  SEPTET: Sextet plus Sims

Week of January 20, 1974, Stamford, Conn.

Goodman, Jones, Pizzarelli, Tate. Guests: Cleo Laine, voc; John Dankworth, as.
DUET: Goodman, Rachel Goodman Edelson, p.

January 27, 1974, Carnegie Hall, New York

Benny Goodman, clt; Marvin Stam, Johnny Frosk, Chris Griffin, Bernie Privin, tpt; Paul Faulise, Buddy Morrow, Eddie Bert, tbn; Toots Mondello, Walt Levinsky, as; Zoot Sims, Al Klink, ts; Sol Schlinger, bar; Hank Jones, p; Bucky Pizzarelli, g; Slam Stewart, b; Grady Tate, d. Guests: Cleo Laine, voc; John Dankworth, as.

Bugle Call Rag (voice over) (January 27)
I Know That You Know (week of January 20)
(Feeling Good - voc Cleo Laine; Dankworth w/rhythm - NO BG (week of January 20)
Bei Mir Bist Du Schon - SEPTET (Norvo solo deleted) (January 19)
Slipped Disc (January 19)
You Must Meet My Wife - QUARTET (January 19)
Nice Work If You Can Get It - voc Mel Torme - SEXTET (January 19) (splice, two cuts)
Oh, Lady Be Good! - voc Mel Torme - SEPTET (January 19)
Rondo, Duo Concertante for Piano and Clarinet - DUET (week of January 20) (edited)
Let's Dance (theme)
King Porter Stomp
Send In The Clowns (arr Jonathan Tunic)

(Ridin' High - voc Cleo Laine - Dankworth w/orch. - NO BG
(I'm Gonna Sit Right Down And Write Myself A Letter - voc Cleo Laine - Dankworth w/orch. - NO BG
Stealin' Apples (edited)
Gotta Be This Or That - voc Benny Goodman - orch. plus Norvo (edited)
Sing, Sing, Sing (edited - Part I plus coda, Part II)
Good-Bye (theme)

On February 9 a revamped Goodman Octet appeared in Sarasota, Florida: no tape is available from that concert. A minimally-satisfactory cassette is extant from its next engagement:

CHALFONT-HADDON HALL CONCERT   February 17, 1974, Atlantic City

Benny Goodman, clt; Bernie Privin, tpt; Al Klink, ts; Peter Appleyard, vib; John Bunch, p; Bucky Pizzarelli, g; Slam Stewart, b; Joe Corsello, d.

TRIO: Goodman, Bunch, Corsello
QUINTET: Trio plus Pizzarelli, Stewart

Let's Dance (theme)
I Know That You Know - QUINTET
Am I Blue? - QUINTET
(Play, Fiddle, Play - Stewart w/rhythm - NO BG
(Fascinating Rhythm - Appleyard w/rhythm - NO BG
I Can't Believe That You're In Love With Me - feat. Privin - BG in coda
(The Girl From Ipanema - Klink w/rhythm - NO BG
Here's That Rainy Day - QUINTET
Medley: Don't Be That Way
       Stompin' At The Savoy
(unannounced Pizzarelli solo - NO BG
After You've Gone
Bei Mir Bist Du Schon
Tin Roof Blues - Appleyard w/rhythm - BG in coda
Memories Of You - TRIO
Honeysuckle Rose
Sing, Sing, Sing
Poor Butterfly
Sweet Georgia Brown
Good-Bye (theme)

A tape of Benny's next engagement, March 1 in Toronto's Massey Hall, fails the standards for inclusion herein. Too bad; it was a good group, with Hackett and Paul Quinichette added to Appleyard and the rhythm section. Somewhat better is a cassette from Benny's succeeding appearance in Philadelphia's Academy of Music:

PHILADELPHIA CONCERT   March 24, 1974, Phila.

Benny Goodman; clt; Frank Williams, tpt; Zoot Sims, Paul Quinichette, ts; Hank Jones, p; Bucky Pizzarelli, Remo Palmieri, g; Slam Stewart, b; Grady Tate, d.

TRIO: Goodman, Jones, Tate
QUINTET: Trio plus Palmieri, Stewart
SEXTET: Quintet plus Pizzarelli
SEPTET: Quintet plus Williams, Sims

I Know That You Know - QUINTET
Am I Blue? - QUINTET
Avalon - SEPTET
(Blue And Sentimental - Quinichette w/rhythm - NO BG
(Oh, Lady Be Good! - Stewart w/rhythm - NO BG
(Satin Doll - Pizzarelli, Palmieri w/rhythm - NO BG
Here's That Rainy Day - SEXTET
Honeysuckle Rose
(I Can't Give You Anything But Love, Baby - Williams w/rhythm - NO BG
Memories Of You - TRIO
I've Found A New Baby
Medley: Don't Be That Way
       Stompin' At The Savoy
(Emily - Sims w/rhythm - NO BG
If I Had You - SEXTET
You Must Meet My Wife - TRIO
(The Very Thought Of You - Jones solo - NO BG
(Sunday - Quinichette w/rhythm - NO BG
(Meditation - Williams w/rhythm - NO BG
Bei Mir Bist Du Schon
Sweet Georgia Brown
One O'Clock Jump
Good-Bye (theme)

We've no tapes of the next five Goodman concerts: March 31, the Waldorf-Astoria; a benefit in Carnegie Hall April 3 for the New York University Medical Center; another benefit, Chicago's Lincoln Academy, April 20; Glen Cove, New York, April 27; and one more benefit, Temple Sinai, in Stamford on May 5. (There is extant a cassette of part of the April 3 program. The author hasn't heard it, but is advised that its quality is poor.) But almost every Goodman aficionado has a tape of Benny's guest appearance with the renowned Boston Pops Orchestra, for it has been shown many times on the Nation's "educational" Public Television network:

"EVENING AT THE 'POPS'" — *May 9, 1974,*
National Public Television — *Symphony Hall, Boston*

First televised July 14, 1974; repeated in succeeding years.

Benny Goodman, clt, and the Boston Pops Orchestra, Arthur Fiedler conducting.

Concertino For Clarinet And Orchestra In C Major, Op. 26 (von Weber)

Medley: Poor Butterfly
The Man I Love
If I Had You
My Funny Valentine
Don't Be That Way

Recordings of Benny's appearances in Atlantic City, May 13; a private party for the Deere Co. in Moline, Illinois, May 22; a benefit in Stratford, Connecticut, June 2; as host of a municipal party in New York on June 11; and the Schaefer Festival in Central Park, June 12, have eluded the author. On June 17, Gil Rodin, responsible for Benny's hiring by Ben Pollack almost 50 years earlier, died in California at age 64.

Benny's next concert was as a guest with the Cleveland Summer Orchestra, and with his own Quintet, in the Blossom Music Center in Cayuga Falls, Ohio. A barely acceptable cassette is extant:

BLOSSOM MUSIC CENTER CONCERT — *June 25, 1974, Cayuga Falls, Ohio*

Benny Goodman, clt, and the Cleveland Summer Orchestra.

Medley: Poor Butterfly
The Man I Love
If I Had You
My Funny Valentine
Don't Be That Way

Benny Goodman, clt; Hank Jones, p; Bucky Pizzarelli, g; Slam Stewart, b; Ronnie Bedford, d.

I Know That You Know
(Play, Fiddle, Play - Stewart w/rhythm - NO BG
Satin Doll
You Must Meet My Wife
(Maple Leaf Rag - Jones solo - NO BG
Sweet Georgia Brown
Good-Bye (theme)

A tape at the lower level of our standard is available from Benny's next concert, at suburban Washington's arts complex in Vienna, Virginia, Wolf Trap Farm Park:

WOLF TRAP CONCERT — *June 29, 1974, Vienna, Virginia*

Benny Goodman, clt; Chris Griffin, tpt; Urbie Green, tbn; Zoot Sims, ts; Peter Appleyard, vib; Hank Jones, p; Bucky Pizzarelli, g; Slam Stewart, b; Grady Tate, d.

QUINTET: Goodman, Jones, Pizzarelli, Stewart, Tate

I Know That You Know—QUINTET
You Must Meet My Wife—QUINTET
That's A Plenty
(Star Dust—Green w/rhythm—NO BG
(Fascinating Rhythm—Appleyard w/rhythm—NO BG
You Turned The Tables On Me—QUINTET
Entertainer Rag
I Can't Get Started—feat. Griffin—full group in coda
Honeysuckle Rose (n/c)
Memories Of You—QUINTET
Medley: Don't Be That Way
Stompin' At The Savoy
Good-Bye (theme)

The reader may be puzzled by the constantly changing personnel, and their varying number, that Benny employed through these later years. The reasons were in main economic. He worked intermittently, only as often as he chose; it made no sense to have sidemen under contract who would be idle most of the time. Since they were employed elsewhere, their availability for a given Goodman date was a matter of chance. Their number was in part dependent upon the fee offered for the engagement, which in turn was a factor of seating capacity and the prices of tickets—the greater the combination, the larger the fee. In general, his contracts called for a minimum guarantee or a percentage of the gross, whichever was greater, a common practice in the entertainment business.

The author has no recording of Benny's next engagement in East Meadow, Long Island on July 5, but does have a listenable tape from the one following, the Meadow Brook Festival in Rochester, Michigan. This cassette gives evidence of a practice Benny would employ in the 'Seventies and beyond: He would greet the audience at the start of a concert, on occasion play one selection with his rhythm section. Then he would leave while the section entertained for half an hour or so, up to a brief intermission. More often, he would introduce the group, leave, return following the intermission.

This work omits such preliminaries. It does, however, include performances by featured sidemen without Goodman's participation, when these occur while Benny is on stage.

MEADOW BROOK CONCERT — *July 12, 1974, Rochester, Michigan*

Benny Goodman, clt; Chris Griffin, tpt; Urbie Green, tbn; Zoot Sims, ts; Peter Appleyard, vib; Hank Jones, p; Bucky Pizzarelli, g; Slam Stewart, b; Ronnie Bedford, d.

QUINTET: Goodman, Jones, Pizzarelli, Stewart, Bedford
SEXTET: Quintet plus Appleyard

I Want To Be Happy—SEXTET
Here's That Rainy Day—QUINTET
I Know That You Know—QUINTET
(Star Dust—Green w/rhythm—NO BG
That's A Plenty
I Can't Get Started—feat. Griffin—BG in coda
Fascinating Rhythm—Appleyard w/rhythm—BG in coda
You Must Meet My Wife—QUINTET
(Satin Doll—Pizzarelli w/rhythm—NO BG
Medley: Don't Be That Way
Stompin' At The Savoy
(Play, Fiddle, Play—Stewart w/rhythm—NO BG (n/c)
Slipped Disc
Memories Of You—QUINTET
Sweet Georgia Brown
Entertainer Rag
I've Found A New Baby
Good-Bye (theme)
Honeysuckle Rose (encore)

Engagements in Ambler, Pennsylvania (Temple Music Festival), July 15; Rockland County, New York, July 24; Rochester, New York, July 27; the White Mountain Festival in New Hampshire, August 9; Saratoga, New York, August 13; with the Denver Symphony in Denver, August 17; and rehearsals and performances with the San Francisco Symphony, August 23–35, produced no tapes that have come to the author. As stated before, it is more than likely that almost all of Benny's performances were recorded from the audience, and for that reason his known itineraries are noted.

Audience recordings made in Carnegie Hall are rarely satisfactory; the auditorium's acoustical properties almost make its management's enforced ban unnecessary. Benny's next appearance there produced some clandestine cassettes, but their quality is poor. Fortunately, there is a professional tape of the concert:

CARNEGIE HALL CONCERT — *September 13, 1974, New York*

Benny Goodman, clt; Chris Griffin, tpt; Urbie Green, tbn; Zoot Sims, ts; Peter Appleyard, vib; Hank Jones, p; Bucky Pizzarelli, g; Slam Stewart, b; Grady Tate, d.

TRIO: Goodman, Jones, Tate
QUINTET: Trio plus Pizzarelli, Stewart
SEXTET: Quintet Plus Appleyard

I Want To Be Happy - QUINTET
Body And Soul—TRIO
Avalon—SEXTET

(unannounced selection feat. Sims w/rhythm—NO BG
That's A Plenty
(Star Dust—Green w/rhythm—NO BG
(Big Noise From Winnetka—Stewart w/rhythm—NO BG
Send In The Clowns—TRIO

Bobby Hackett, tpt, joins, participates in all full-group performances.

(The Good Life—Hackett w/rhythm—NO BG
All The Things You Are—Hackett w/rhythm—BG obligato
Slipped Disc
(Satin Doll—Pizzarelli w/rhythm—NO BG
Entertainer Rag
Sweet Georgia Brown
Medley: Don't Be That Way
        Stompin' At The Savoy
After You've Gone
Good-Bye (theme)

Two nights later Benny again performed for the Schaefer Music Festival in Manhattan's Central Park, but the author has no recording of the open air concert.

Next were two consecutive evenings at the Valley Forge Music Circus, and there is a satisfactory audience recording extant for each:

VALLEY FORGE MUSIC CIRCUS   September 27, 1974, Devon, Pa.

Benny Goodman, clt; Chris Griffin, tpt; Mickey Gravine, tbn; Al Klink, ts; Peter Appleyard, vib; Hank Jones, p; Bucky Pizzarelli, g; Slam Stewart, b; Ronnie Bedford, d.

QUINTET: Goodman, Jones, Pizzarelli, Stewart, Bedford
SEXTET: Quintet plus Appleyard

I Want To Be Happy - QUINTET
Body And Soul - QUINTET
Bei Mir Bist Du Schon - QUINTET
That's A Plenty
Poor Butterfly - SEXTET
(Big Noise From Winnetka - Stewart w/rhythm - NO BG
Medley: Don't Be That Way
        Stompin' At The Savoy
Avalon - SEXTET
(Nuages - Pizzarelli w/rhythm - NO BG
Send In The Clowns - QUINTET
(Maple Leaf Rag - Jones solo - NO BG
Entertainer Rag
(The Girl From Ipanema - Klink w/rhythm - NO BG
Memories Of You - QUINTET
Sweet Georgia Brown
Slipped Disc
Good-Bye (theme)

VALLEY FORGE MUSIC CIRCUS   September 28, 1974, Devon, Pa.

Personnels as September 27.

After You've Gone - QUINTET
Lazy River - QUINTET
Avalon - SEXTET
(I Can't Get Started - Griffin w/rhythm - NO BG
That's A Plenty
(Oh, Lady Be Good! - Stewart w/rhythm - NO BG
(Tangerine - Pizzarelli w/rhythm - NO BG
Slipped Disc (n/c)
Medley: Don't Be That Way
        Stompin' At The Savoy
(The Girl From Ipanema - Klink w/rhythm - NO BG
Send In The Clowns - QUINTET
(That's All - Gravine w/rhythm - NO BG
Bei Mir Bist Du Schon (n/c)
Sweet Georgia Brown
Memories Of You - QUINTET
Honeysuckle Rose
I've Found A New Baby
Good-Bye (theme)

Nine days later Benny's Septet was in Finland where it was joined by Britain's John McLevy. Swedish Television videotaped the concert, televised it in two segments the following year:

HELSINKI CONCERT   October 7, 1974, Helsinki
   Swedish TV

Televised in two segments, January 28 and February 11, 1975.

Benny Goodman, clt; John McLevy, tpt; Al Klink, ts; Peter Appleyard, vib; Hank Jones, p; Bucky Pizzarelli, g; Slam Stewart, b; Ronnie Bedford, d.

QUARTET: Goodman, Jones, Stewart, Bedford
QUINTET: Quartet plus Pizzarelli
SEXTET: Quintet plus Appleyard

I Want To Be Happy - QUINTET
Body And Soul - QUARTET
Avalon - SEXTET
(Oh, Lady Be Good! - Stewart w/rhythm - NO BG
Send In The Clowns - QUARTET
(The Very Thought Of You - Jones solo - NO BG
Medley: Don't Be That Way
        Stompin' At The Savoy
That's A Plenty
Slipped Disc
I've Found A New Baby
Memories Of You - QUARTET
Honeysuckle Rose
Good-Bye (theme)

And a satisfactory cassette from Royal Albert Hall:

LONDON CONCERT   October 12, 1974, London

Personnels as October 7.

I Want To Be Happy - QUINTET
Here's That Rainy Day - QUINTET
Avalon - SEXTET
(Baubles, Bangles And Beads - McLevy w/rhythm - NO BG
(The Girl From Ipanema - Klink w/rhythm - NO BG
That's A Plenty
(Play, Fiddle, Play - Stewart w/rhythm - NO BG
Send In The Clowns - QUINTET
Medley: Don't Be That Way
        Stompin' At The Savoy
(Satin Doll - Pizzarelli w/rhythm - NO BG
Slipped Disc
(The Very Thought Of You - Jones solo - NO BG
Honeysuckle Rose
Sing, Sing, Sing
Sweet Georgia Brown
Good-Bye (theme)

No recording of the Newtown Arts Festival October 19, but an acceptable tape from Benny's next engagement in Maryland a week later:

SHADY GROVE CONCERT   October 26, 1974, Gaithersburg, Md.

Benny Goodman, clt; Marvin Stam, tpt; Mickey Gravine, tbn; Al Klink, ts, fl; Hank Jones, p; Bucky Pizzarelli, g; Slam Stewart, b; Ronnie Bedford, d.

QUINTET: Goodman, Jones, Pizzarelli, Stewart, Bedford

I Want To Be Happy - QUINTET (n/c - intro clipped)
You Must Meet My Wife - QUINTET
I Know That You Know - QUINTET
That's A Plenty
Poor Butterfly - QUINTET
Seven Come Eleven
Entertainer Rag
Medley: Don't Be That Way
        Stompin' At The Savoy
The World Is Waiting For The Sunrise - QUINTET
Avalon - QUINTET - full group in coda
Slipped Disc
Sing, Sing, Sing
And The Angels Sing - QUINTET
Sweet Georgia Brown

Benny played a benefit to solicit funds for Cystic Fibrosis research in New York on November 1. He next appeared November 9 at West Point, and November 11 in Montreal. From there he went to El Paso, Texas, and a date with the El Paso Symphony, November 16. Two consecutive evenings on Long Island followed; the second provides a good audience recording:

WESTBURY MUSIC FAIR   November 30, 1974, Long Island, N.Y.

Benny Goodman, clt; Bobby Hackett, tpt; Mickey Gravine, tbn; Al Klink, ts;
Hank Jones, p; Bucky Pizzarelli, g; Slam Stewart, b; Ronnie Bedford, d.

QUINTET: Goodman, Jones, Pizzarelli, Stewart, Bedford

I Want To Be Happy - QUINTET
Like Someone In Love - QUINTET
I Know That You Know - QUINTET
(The Good Life - Hackett w/rhythm - NO BG
All The Things You Are - Hackett w/rhythm - BG in coda
That's A Plenty
(That's All - Gravine w/rhythm - NO BG
Medley: Don't Be That Way
        Stompin' At The Savoy
(The Girl From Ipanema - Klink w/rhythm - NO BG
Slipped Disc
(Oh, Lady Be Good! - Stewart w/rhythm - NO BG
Send In The Clowns - QUINTET
Avalon
(A Day In The Life Of A Fool - Pizzarelli w/rhythm - NO BG
Bei Mir Bist Du Schon
Entertainer Rag
Sweet Georgia Brown
Sing, Sing, Sing
Honeysuckle Rose
Good-Bye (theme)

Benny finished out the year in Sioux City, Iowa, on December 5. First
engagement in 1975 was a private party in Charlottesville, Virginia, on
January 18. No known recordings from those concerts, but a satisfactory
tape from his next appearance, in the Miami Beach Auditorium on January
31, has been located:

MIAMI BEACH CONCERT   January 31, 1975, Miami Beach, Fla.

Benny Goodman, clt; Marvin Stam, tpt; Urbie Green, tbn; Frank Wess, ts;
Hank Jones, p; Bucky Pizzarelli, g; Slam Stewart, b; Ray Mosca, d.

DUET: Goodman, Jones
QUINTET: Goodman, Jones, Pizzarelli, Stewart, Mosca

I Want To Be Happy - QUINTET
Here's That Rainy Day - QUINTET
The World Is Waiting For The Sunrise - QUINTET
(Star Dust - Green w/rhythm - NO BG
(What A Diff'rence A Day Made - Wess w/rhythm - NO BG
That's A Plenty
(Oh, Lady Be Good! - Stewart w/rhythm - NO BG
(Polka Dots And Moonbeams - Stam w/rhythm - NO BG
Medley: Don't Be That Way
        Stompin' At The Savoy
(Satin Doll - Pizzarelli w/rhythm - NO BG
Send In The Clowns - DUET
(Maple Leaf Rag - Jones solo - NO BG
Honeysuckle Rose
Poor Butterfly - QUINTET
Bei Mir Bist Du Schon
After You've Gone
Sing, Sing, Sing
Good-Bye (theme)

Three and a half months will pass before we next hear Benny Good-
man, for there are no known recordings of his engagements until May 12.
His itinerary from February through April included appearances in San
Salvador with Aaron Copland and the Brazil Symphony on February 22 and
23; in Palm Beach, Florida, March 16; The Air Force Ball in the Americana,
Manhattan, March 21; in Montreal, March 29; in Meridian, Mississippi,
April 5; in Lincoln Center, April 9; and a benefit for Temple Sinai, in Lynn,
Massachusetts, April 19.

Almost 40 years earlier "Professor" Goodman had lectured "Camel
Caravan" audiences on the intricacies of Swing. Now in earnest, he addressed an assembly convened by the Department of Music of the University
of Chicago, tootling away to illustrate clarinet technique, and answering
questions. The lengthy May 12 program was recorded, and portions of it
were broadcast later on the University's own radio station, as part of a series
titled, "From The Midway." Interesting listening, recommended to collectors.

Benny next appeared on two consecutive evenings at Nanuet's Star
Theater, and an excellent-quality tape of each is available. Note that trumpeter Mel Davis is in the group the first night, but absent the second:

NANUET CONCERT   May 16, 1975, Nanuet, New York

Benny Goodman, clt; Mel Davis, tpt; Urbie Green, tbn; Zoot Sims, ts; Hank
Jones, p; Bucky Pizzarelli, g; Slam Stewart, b; Ronnie Bedford, d.

QUINTET: Goodman, Jones, Pizzarelli, Stewart, Bedford

I Want To Be Happy—QUINTET
Here's That Rainy Day—QUINTET
Avalon—QUINTET
The World Is Waiting For The Sunrise—QUINTET
(Stairway To The Stars—Green w/rhythm—NO BG
Slipped Disc
(Emily—Sims w/rhythm—NO BG
That's A Plenty
(Oh, Lady Be Good!—Stewart w/rhythm—NO BG
Send In The Clowns—QUINTET
Medley: Don't Be That Way
        Stompin' At The Savoy
(The Very Thought Of You - Jones solo—NO BG
Bei Mir Bist Du Schon
Memories Of You—QUINTET
Honeysuckle Rose
Nuages—QUINTET, feat. Pizzarelli
I've Found A New Baby
Sing, Sing, Sing
Good-Bye (theme)

NANUET CONCERT   May 17, 1975, Nanuet, New York

Personnels as May 16, except omit Davis.

After You've Gone—QUINTET
Lazy River—QUINTET
The World Is Waiting For The Sunrise—QUINTET
Undecided
A Smo-o-o-oth One
(Stairway To The Stars—Green w/rhythm—NO BG
(Emily—Sims w/rhythm—NO BG
Indiana
(Big Noise From Winnetka - Stewart w/rhythm—NO BG
Send In The Clowns—QUINTET
Medley: Don't Be That Way
        Stompin' At The Savoy
One O'Clock Jump
(The Very Thought Of You—Jones solo—NO BG
Avalon
Sing, Sing, Sing
Medley: And The Angels Sing
        Bei Mir Bist Du Schon
Air Mail Special
Good-Bye (theme)

Another two-nighter followed, this in the Front Row Theater in
Cleveland, Ohio. These concerts were also recorded from the audience, but
with minimally-satisfactory results:

CLEVELAND CONCERT   May 23, 1975, Cleveland

Benny Goodman, clt; Urbie Green, tbn; Zoot Sims, ts; Hank Jones, p; Remo
Palmieri, g; Slam Stewart, b; Ronnie Bedford, d.

QUINTET: Goodman, Jones, Palmieri, Stewart, Bedford

After You've Gone—QUINTET
Lazy River—QUINTET
The World Is Waiting For The Sunrise—QUINTET
Undecided
(Stairway To The Stars—Green w/rhythm—NO BG
A Smo-o-o-oth One
Indiana
(Emily—Sims w/rhythm—NO BG
Medley: Don't Be That Way
        Stompin' At The Savoy
(Big Noise From Winnetka - Stewart w/rhythm - NO BG
Send In The Clowns - QUINTET
Medley: Don't Be That Way
        Bei Mir Bist Du Schon
(Maple Leaf Rag - Jones solo - NO BG
One O'Clock Jump
Poor Butterfly - QUINTET

Sweet Georgia Brown
Sing, Sing, Sing
Good-Bye (theme)

CLEVELAND CONCERT   *May 24, 1975, Cleveland*

Personnels as May 23.

I Want To Be Happy - QUINTET
Body And Soul - QUINTET
After You've Gone - QUINTET
Undecided
(Stairway To The Stars - Green w/rhythm - NO BG
Air Mail Special
(Big Noise From Winnetka - Stewart w/rhythm - NO BG
(Maple Leaf Rag - Jones solo - NO BG
Send In The Clowns - QUINTET
(The Man I Love - Sims w/rhythm - NO BG
Indiana
One O'Clock Jump
Avalon
Medley: Don't Be That Way
*   Stompin' At The Savoy*
Moon Glow - QUINTET
I've Found A New Baby
Sing, Sing, Sing (n/c - ending excised)
Good-Bye (theme)

The four consecutive concerts preceding clearly illustrate Benny's programming concept: There would be variety, but many of the same selections would be performed at every concert. And most would be Goodman standards, few would be current compositions. The author repeatedly argued that Benny should play new tunes, but each time Benny demurred. Audiences expected to hear certain tunes; if they did not, they shouted their requests. The fact that the author, a collector, had had enough of the "Don't Be That Way/Stompin' At The Savoy" medley wasn't persuasive; an audience in Cleveland might be hearing it for the very first time. Besides, Benny just didn't like what was being written. Oh, a Beatles' tune, a melody by Sondheim, yes; but the bulk of current work, no. The format would persist.

Listening to those concerts educes another conclusion. Now in his middle sixties, Benny still played very well, IF—if he was physically comfortable, and if his sidemen were enthusiastic. Yes, a "Send In The Clowns" was highly structured, and he would play it note for note night after night. But he played the jazz tunes differently, as his imagination was stimulated by what he heard from his group, or if he felt the need to improvise something startling in order to inspire them. Good jazz is a mutual endeavor, but it needs a leader. Benny was ever that.

The nation's bicentennial celebration offered brief radio testimonies by a host of celebrities. On May 31 Benny's transcribed comments about a Revolutionary event were broadcast on the series, "A Bicentennial Minute."

The first two weeks of June found Benny in the American West: the Circle Star Theater, San Carlos, California, the 7th and 8th; in Anchorage, Alaska, the 10th and 11th; and in Fairbanks, Alaska, on the 13th. The only recording the author has from this tour is a barely-acceptable cassette from the first engagement. It is listed primarily because Urbie Green—what can be heard of him—is in good form.

SAN CARLOS CONCERT   *June 7, 1975, San Carlos, Calif.*

Benny Goodman, clt; Urbie Green, tbn; Zoot Sims, ts; Hank Jones, p; Joe Pas, g; Slam Stewart, b; Ronnie Bedford, d.

DUET: Goodman, Jones
QUINTET: Goodman, Jones, Pas, Stewart, Bedford

I Want To Be Happy—QUINTET (n/c—intro clipped)
Lazy River—QUINTET
After You've Gone—QUINTET
Undecided
(Stairway To The Stars—Green w/rhythm—NO BG
(The Man I Love—Sims w/rhythm—NO BG
Send In The Clowns—DUET
Indiana
(Big Noise From Winnetka—Stewart w/rhythm—NO BG
Medley: Don't Be That Way
*   Stompin' At The Savoy*
Air Mail Special
(The Very Thought Of You - Jones solo—NO BG

One O'Clock Jump (n/c)
Avalon (n/c—intro clipped)
Sing, Sing, Sing
Good-Bye (theme)

Recordings of Benny's appearances in Saratoga, New York, June 22, and in Manhattan, June 28, have not surfaced. The next in the author's possession is a fair quality cassette from the Temple University Music Festival:

TEMPLE MUSIC FESTIVAL   *July 2, 1975, Ambler, Pa.*

Benny Goodman, clt; Urbie Green, tbn; Zoot Sims, ts; Hank Jones, p; Bucky Pizzarelli, g; Slam Stewart, b; Ronnie Bedford, d.

DUET: Goodman, Pizzarelli (1), Jones (2)
QUINTET: Goodman, Jones, Pizzarelli, Stewart, Bedford

I Want To Be Happy—QUINTET
Nuages—DUET (1)
After You've Gone—QUINTET
Undecided
(How Long Has This Been Going On?—Green w/rhythm—NO BG
Indiana
(Big Noise From Winnetka—Stewart w/rhythm—NO BG
Somebody Loves Me—Sims w/QUINTET
I've Found A New Baby
(Medley: unidentified tune/Lazy River—Pizzarelli w/rhythm—NO BG
Medley: Don't Be That Way
*   Stompin' At The Savoy*
Send In The Clowns—DUET (2)
Love Me Or Leave Me
Seven Come Eleven
Avalon
Sing, Sing, Sing
Good-Bye (theme)
Oh, Lady Be Good! (encore)

A tape from Benny's next engagement, July 5 at Wolf Trap Farm, Vienna, Virginia, is omitted because of its poor sound. Concerts July 13 in Cohasset, New York, and July 18, in Franconia, New Hampshire, offer no tapes known to the author. His next is from the Ravinia Festival; its recordist deliberately omitted performances by Urbie, Slam, Bucky and Peter that did not include Benny. But he did capture a presentation of the first American Music Congress award to Mr. Goodman.

RAVINIA CONCERT   *July 27, 1975, Highland Park, Illinois*

Benny Goodman, clt; Warren Vache, tpt; Urbie Green, tbn; Carmen Leggio, ts; Peter Appleyard, vib; Hank Jones, p; Bucky Pizzarelli, g; Slam Stewart, b; Ronnie Bedford, d.

DUET: Goodman, Jones
QUINTET: Goodman, Jones, Pizzarelli, Stewart, Bedford
SEXTET: Quintet plus Appleyard

I Want To Be Happy - QUINTET
Body And Soul - QUINTET
The World Is Waiting For The Sunrise - QUINTET
Moon Glow - SEXTET
Avalon - SEXTET
Undecided
(Struttin' With Some Barbecue - Vache w/rhythm - NO BG
Nuages - QUINTET
That's A Plenty
Medley: Don't Be That Way
*   Stompin' At The Savoy*
Send In The Clowns - DUET
Seven Come Eleven
Sing, Sing, Sing
Sweet Georgia Brown
Good-Bye (theme)

No recording of the Interlochen Music Camp (near Detroit) concert of July 30 is known, and a cassette of Benny's August 1 participation in the Central Park Schaefer Music Festival is omitted because of its poor quality. His succeeding engagement produced a satisfactory tape, albeit with some excisions and dropouts:

MEADOW BROOK FESTIVAL   *August 8, 1975, Rochester, Michigan*

Benny Goodman, clt; Urbie Green, tbn; Zoot Sims, ts; Peter Appleyard, vib; Hank Jones, p; Bucky Pizzarelli, g; Slam Stewart, b; Ronnie Bedford, d.

QUINTET: Goodman, Jones, Pizzarelli, Stewart, Bedford

I Know That You Know - QUINTET
Ain't Misbehavin' - QUINTET
The World Is Waiting For The Sunrise - QUINTET
Undecided
(How Long Has This Been Going On? - Green w/rhythm - NO BG
Indiana (bad intro)
(Big Noise From Winnetka - Stewart w/rhythm - NO BG—dropouts)
(Emily - Sims w/rhythm - NO BG
Avalon
(unidentified Pizzarelli solo - NO BG
Medley: Don't Be That Way
        Stompin' At The Savoy
(Fascinating Rhythm - Appleyard w/rhythm - NO BG
Honeysuckle Rose
Send In The Clowns - QUINTET
That's A Plenty
One O'Clock Jump (dropouts)
Sing, Sing, Sing
Good-Bye (theme)
Sweet Georgia Brown (encore)

Benny took a week off, went fishin' in Goose Bay, Labrador. His first date upon his return marked the initial appearance of Connie Kay, noted for his work with the Modern Jazz Quartet. Site was a tent in under-reconstruction Waterloo Village.

WATERLOO VILLAGE CONCERT   *August 23, 1975, Stanhope, New Jersey*

Benny Goodman, clt; Urbie Green, tbn; Frank Wess, ts; Peter Appleyard, vib; John Bunch, p; Bucky Pizzarelli, g; Slam Stewart, b; Connie Kay, d.

QUINTET: Goodman, Bunch, Pizzarelli, Stewart, Kay

I Want To Be Happy - QUINTET
Here's That Rainy Day - QUINTET
Avalon - QUINTET
It's Easy To Remember - QUINTET
After You've Gone - QUINTET
Undecided
(Star Dust - Green w/rhythm - NO BG
Indiana
(What A Diff'rence A Day Made - Wess w/rhythm - NO BG
Send In The Clowns - QUINTET
Medley: Don't Be That Way
        Stompin' At The Savoy
(Nuages - Pizzarelli w/rhythm - NO BG
(Oh, Lady Be Good! - Stewart w/rhythm - NO BG
Poor Butterfly - QUINTET
Seven Come Eleven
Sing, Sing, Sing
Good-Bye (theme)
Sweet Georgia Brown (encore)

Then to Philadelphia's outdoor Robin Hood Dell, and a cassette that lacks "Sing, Sing, Sing," performed just before the closing theme:

ROBIN HOOD DELL CONCERT   *August 25, 1975, Phila.*

Benny Goodman, clt; Warren Vache, tpt; Urbie Green, tbn; Zoot Sims, ts; Hank Jones, p; Bucky Pizzarelli, g; Slam Stewart, b; Ronnie Bedford, d.

DUET: Goodman, Jones
QUINTET: Goodman, Jones, Pizzarelli, Stewart, Bedford

I Want To Be Happy - QUINTET
Here's That Rainy Day - QUINTET
Avalon - QUINTET
Undecided
(Star Dust - Green w/rhythm - NO BG
That's A Plenty (n/c - middle break)
(Emily - Sims w/rhythm - NO BG
The Man I Love - Sims w/QUINTET
Satin Doll - Pizzarelli w/rhythm - BG in coda
Seven Come Eleven

(Big Noise From Winnetka - Stewart w/rhythm - NO BG
Struttin' With Some Barbecue - Vache w/rhythm - BG in coda
Send In The Clowns - DUET
(Oh, Look At Me Now! - Jones solo - NO BG
Indiana
Medley: Don't Be That Way
        Stompin' At The Savoy
Good-Bye (theme)

A date in Scranton, Pennsylvania August 31 provides no audience cassette; then Benny will leave the concert trail for a full month. But in between there's a television show, and—for the first time in almost five years—a studio recording session.

John Hammond, then a vice president of Columbia Records, was nearing retirement. To mark his noteworthy contributions to music, especially jazz, over 40-odd years, the Public Broadcasting System memorialized him in a three-hour television special. The program offers conversations with various of John's friends and associates; film clips of Bessie Smith, Billie Holiday and Lester Young; and "live" performances by Helen Humes, Marion Williams, his son Johnny Hammond, Bob Dylan and Sonny Terry; and by Benny Morton, Benny Carter, Red Norvo, Teddy Wilson, Jesse Dixon, George Benson, Milt Hinton, Jo Jones—and Benny Goodman.

The program was videotaped in the studios of WTTV, Chicago. Prior to its performances that appear on the telecast, the Goodman group rehearsed for about half an hour. An excellent-quality audio tape of the rehearsal is in possession of a few collectors:

REHEARSAL, "THE WORLD OF JOHN HAMMOND"   *September 10, 1975,*
                                                  Chicago

Benny Goodman, clt; Teddy Wilson, p; George Benson, g; Milt Hinton, b; Jo Jones, d.

Body And Soul

Add Red Norvo, vib.

After I Say I'm Sorry
Avalon
Seven Come Eleven

Immediately following the rehearsal—which includes individual instrumental practice and various partial versions of the tunes listed—the Sextet performed for the cameras:

"SOUNDSTAGE - THE WORLD OF JOHN HAMMOND"
   PBS Television Network   *September 10, 1975, Chicago*

Televised in two one-and-one-half hour segments in December 1975 and January 1976 over PBS network stations. Some of the telecasts were also simulcast via PBS FM radio stations.

Benny Goodman, clt; Red Norvo, vib; Teddy Wilson, p; George Benson, g; Milt Hinton, b; Jo Jones, d.

After I Say I'm Sorry
Sweet Lorraine
Avalon
Seven Come Eleven

("Seven Come Eleven" is a splice; the master tape reveals a false start—someone was in the wrong key.)

As if to compensate for his long absence from the studios, Benny's 1975 recordings for Columbia are listed in full detail; the complete sessions are on tape, and these have been audited. Since the tapes included producer Teo Macero's spoken designations of the successive takes, they are listed below. Doing so causes a departure from previous practice in this work; Teo "counts" breakdowns, whereas prior to this listing the author did not accord them that status.

In 1976, Columbia prepared an LP test pressing for Benny's approval. He decided that the material wasn't worthy of release, refused to approve it, and the projected issue was cancelled. Some collectors obtained tape copies of the demo LP. Eventually Benny succumbed to Columbia's blandishments, and an LP was issued in 1982. It was then discovered that four of the tracks on the demo LP were not included in the Columbia release. Those four tracks are designated, "Demo LP." The eight tracks on the demo LP that are duplicated on the release are shown in parentheses.

Additionally, one otherwise-unissued track was released on a limited-edition, 50-copy, private LP. Too, some of the tracks on the Columbia release are edited versions. These and other particulars are noted as they occur:

BENNY GOODMAN QUINTET   September 15, 1975, New York

Benny Goodman clt; Hank Jones, p; Bucky Pizzarelli, g; Milt Hinton, b; Grady Tate, d.

CO 117173-1-bkdn	UNISSUED—Tape
CO 117173-2	UNISSUED—Tape
CO 117173-3	UNISSUED—Tape
CO 117173-4	UNISSUED—Tape
CO 117173-5	UNISSUED—Tape
	Alone Together
CO 117174-1	UNISSUED—Tape
CO 117174-2	**StLp:** PHON LV-50
CO 117174-3	**StLp:** CO FC38265 (also on demo LP)
	Send In The Clowns
CO 117175-1	UNISSUED—Tape
CO 117175-2-bkdn	UNISSUED—Tape
CO 117175-3	UNISSUED—Tape
CO 117175-4	UNISSUED—Tape
CO 117175-5-bkdn	UNISSUED—Tape
CO 117175-6	UNISSUED—Tape
CO 117175-7	UNISSUED—Tape
CO 117175-8	UNISSUED—Tape
	Slow Drag
CO 117173-6-bkdn	UNISSUED—Tape
CO 117173-7	UNISSUED—Tape
CO 117173-8	**StLP:** CO FC38265 (also on demo LP)
	Alone Together

(Macero identifies takes 6, 7 and 8 of "Alone Together" as "Remakes 1,2,3." To avoid confusion, the original sequence is continued.)

CO 117176-1	UNISSUED—Tape
	Here's That Rainy Day
CO 117177-1	UNISSUED—Tape
	(What Can I Say) After I Say I'm Sorry

(Benny experiments with two alternate endings following the full performance of, "After I Say I'm Sorry.")

CO 117178-1	UNISSUED—Tape
CO 117178-2	UNISSUED—Tape
	My One And Only Love
CO 117179-1-bkdn	UNISSUED—Tape
CO 117179-2	UNISSUED—Tape
CO 117179-3	**StLP:** CO FC38265
	And The Angels Sing

(The CO release of "And The Angels Sing" is edited by elimination of a solo by Pizzarelli, and abbreviation of the coda by about 40 seconds.)

CO 117180-1	**StLP:** CO FC38265 (also on demo LP)
	I Only Have Eyes For You

Columbia's liner notes for "Seven Come Eleven," first track up at the next session and title song for the album, include Basie trombonist Al Grey in error. He is not present for any of the six takes recorded. But George Benson is, and produces a swinging solo. Prior to the session, Benny had Gene Bertoncini work with George in Benny's New York apartment, to help him with his reading.

BENNY GOODMAN SEXTET   September 23, 1975, New York

Benny Goodman, clt; John Bunch, p; Bucky Pizzarelli, George Benson, g; Ron Carter, b; Grady Tate, d.

CO 122743-1-bkdn	UNISSUED—Tape
CO 122743-2	UNISSUED—Tape
CO 122743-3	UNISSUED—Tape
CO 122743-4-bkdn	UNISSUED—Tape
CO 122743-5	UNISSUED—Tape
CO 122743-6	**StLP:** CO FC38265 (also on demo LP)
	Seven Come Eleven

BENNY GOODMAN SEPTET   same session

Sextet plus Al Grey, tbn.

CO 122744-1	**StLp:** CO FC38265 (also on demo LP)
	A Smo-o-o-oth One
CO 122745-1-bkdn	UNISSUED—Tape
CO 122745-2	UNISSUED—Tape
CO 122745-3	**StLP:** CO FC38265 (also on demo LP)
	Sweet Lorraine

(Note that Benson may not be present for all takes of "Sweet Lorraine." His guitar is not audibly identifiable on any of them.)

CO 122746-1	**StLP:** CO FC38265
CO 122746-2	**LP:** Demo LP
	You Are The Sunshine Of My Life

(The CO release of "You Are The Sunshine Of My Life" is edited by elimination of an eight bar intro, and halving of soli by both Grey and Pizzarelli.)

CO 122747-1	UNISSUED—Tape
CO 122747-2-bkdn	UNISSUED—Tape
CO 122747-3-bkdn	UNISSUED—Tape
CO 122747-4	**StLP:** CO FC38265 (also on demo LP)
	I Cover The Waterfront

Benny's appearances with symphony orchestras in Peoria (September 30) and Rockford, Illinois (October 2) preceded a two-day stint for the Selmer Company on October 3 and 4. Following were dates with the Cincinnati (Ohio) Symphony on October 5, a concert at Centre College in Lexington, Kentucky on October 10, and an engagement in Lawrence, Kansas on October 25. He returned to New York for a private party in New York's Century Club, of which he is a member, on October 29. No tapes from any of those performances are in the author's possession. But he has satisfactory cassettes from Benny's two appearances at the Valley Forge Music Circus:

VALLEY FORGE MUSIC CIRCUS   *October 31, 1975, Devon, Pa.*

Benny Goodman, clt; Warren Vache, tpt; Urbie Green, tbn; Peter Appleyard, vib; Hank Jones, p; Bucky Pizzarelli, Gene Bertoncini, g; Slam Stewart, b; Connie Kay, d.

QUINTET: Goodman, Jones, Pizzarelli, Stewart, Kay
SEXTET: Quintet plus Appleyard

After You've Gone - QUINTET
Body And Soul - QUINTET (n/c - middle elision)
Poor Butterfly - QUINTET
Avalon - SEXTET
(I Can't Get Started - Green w/rhythm - NO BG
That's A Plenty (n/c)
(Play, Fiddle, Play - Stewart w/rhythm - NO BG
Seven Come Eleven
(Emily - duet, Pizzarelli, Bertoncini - NO BG
Medley: Don't Be That Way
     Stompin' At The Savoy
(Someday You'll Be Sorry - Vache w/rhythm - NO BG
(Fascinating Rhythm - Appleyard w/rhythm - NO BG
     October 31, 1975, continued

October 31, 1975, continued
Send In The Clowns - QUINTET
Indiana
Stealin' Apples
Sing, Sing, Sing
Good-Bye (theme)

VALLEY FORGE MUSIC CIRCUS   *November 1, 1975, Devon, Pa.*

Personnels as October 31, except omit Pizzarelli, and substitute Bertoncini as appropriate.

I Want To Be Happy - QUINTET
Here's That Rainy Day - QUINTET
The World Is Waiting For The Sunrise - QUINTET
(I Can't Get Started - Green w/rhythm - NO BG
That's A Plenty
(Big Noise From Winnetka - Stewart w/rhythm - NO BG
Avalon
(Struttin' With Some Barbecue - Vache w/rhythm - NO BG
Medley: Don't Be That Way
       Stompin' At The Savoy
(Fascinating Rhythm - Appleyard w/rhythm - NO BG
Send In The Clowns - QUINTET
Indiana
Poor Butterfly - QUINTET
Honeysuckle Rose
Sing, Sing, Sing
Sweet Georgia Brown
Good-Bye (theme)

On November 6 Benny performed with the Nashville, Tennessee symphony orchestra, and on the 8th he was in Plainfield, New Jersey, playing jazz. November 14 was his friend Aaron Copland's 75th birthday; BBC-TV 2 televised "Happy Birthday, Aaron Copland" on the 16th, a salute to the famed composer that included a videotaped testimonial by Benny. And on the 14th, he was back in Columbia's studios. His group now was an Octet with Joe Venuti; and so far as the author knows, it was Venuti's last recording session.

BENNY GOODMAN OCTET   **November 14, 1975, New York**

Benny Goodman, clt; Urbie Green tbn; Joe Venuti, v; Peter Appleyard, vib; Hank Jones, p; Bucky Pizzarelli, g; Slam Stewart, b; Grady Tate, d.

CO 122665-1	UNISSUED—Tape
CO 122665-2	UNISSUED—Tape
CO 122665-3 bkdn	UNISSUED—Tape
CO 122665-4	**LP:** Demo LP
	Soft Winds
CO 122666-1- bkdn	UNISSUED—Tape
CO 122666-2	UNISSUED—Tape
CO 122666-3	**StLp:** CO FC38265
	Slipped Disc

(The CO release of "Slipped Disc" abridges Venuti's solo.)

(A single take of "Big Noise From Winnetka" followed "Slipped Disc," and was included in the demo LP. It was assigned matrix number CO 122667-1, and was recorded by Stewart, Jones and Tate only—no BG.)

CO 122668-1	**LP:** Demo LP
	Nuages
CO 122669-1	UNISSUED—Tape
CO 122669-2- bkdn	UNISSUED—Tape
CO 122669-3	**StLp:** CO FC38265 (also on demo LP)
	Limehouse Blues

(At this point all of the tracks on both the Columbia release and the demonstration LP have been accounted for. There remain, however, additional cuts on the master tapes. For various reasons, some of them contradictory of one another, the author cannot certify that his listing is in true order-of-performance. Nor is he certain that all of the matrix numbers are correct. The producer announces the same number for two different tunes, and omits

mention of the matrix assigned a third; this latter is extrapolated, and shown in quotations for that reason.)

CO 122666-4- bkdn	UNISSUED—Tape
CO 122666-5- bkdn	UNISSUED—Tape
CO 122666-6	UNISSUED—Tape
	Slipped Disc

(Only the Quintet - Benny and the rhythm section - perform the aborted "What I Did For Love," next. It may have been intended as a selection for the full Octet, but midway through Benny stops, says to the producer, "Teo, I don't think . . .", and the rendition ends.)

"CO 122670"- bkdn	UNISSUED—Tape
	What I Did For Love

(Clearly, producer Macero states that the matrix for "Shivers," next, is CO 122671. At its conclusion, he then repeats that matrix for the final cuts on the master tapes, two brief versions of "I Never Knew." Arbitrarily but logically, the next consecutive matrix number is listed here for the last efforts of a rather lengthy recording session.)

CO 122671-1- bkdn	UNISSUED—Tape
CO 122671-2	UNISSUED—Tape
CO 122671-3	UNISSUED—Tape
CO 122671-4	UNISSUED—Tape
	Shivers
CO 122672-1- bkdn	UNISSUED—Tape
CO 122672-2- bkdn	UNISSUED—Tape
	I Never Knew

(Stomping his foot to set the tempo for "I Never Knew," Benny says, "Here we go—let's get out of here." Again, only the Quintet is heard in the first breakdown, quickly aborted. Venuti and Green, but not Appleyard, are audible in the second breakdown; this, too, is wrapped up quickly. Benny and Teo thank the participants, the session ends, and someone says, "Don't forget the (tax) withholding slips." And that's it, Benny's last recording date for Columbia in 1975.)

Jazz concerts on November 15 in Rockaway Park, New York, and on November 19 in San Antonio, Texas, took Benny on the road again. He then appeared with the Danville (Illinois) Symphony, on November 30. No tapes of these three engagements have been made available to the author. To complete this schedule for 1975, Benny performed at the Westbury Music Fair on successive evenings. Both concerts afford cassette recordings of good quality:

WESTBURY MUSIC FAIR   *December 5, 1975, Long Island, N.Y.*

Benny Goodman, clt; Warren Vache, tpt; Mickey Gravine, tbn; Al Klink, ts; Peter Appleyard, vib; Hank Jones, p; Gene Bertoncini, g; Slam Stewart, b; Connie Kay, d.

QUINTET: Goodman, Jones, Bertoncini, Stewart, Kay
SEXTET: Quintet plus Appleyard

After You've Gone - QUINTET
Here's That Rainy Day - QUINTET
Lazy River - QUINTET
Avalon - SEXTET
(The Girl From Ipanema - Klink w/rhythm - NO BG
That's A Plenty
(That's All - Gravine w/rhythm - NO BG
Medley: Don't Be That Way
       Stompin' At The Savoy
(Struttin' With Some Barbecue - Vache w/rhythm - NO BG
Send In The Clowns - QUINTET
Big Noise From Winnetka - Stewart w/rhythm - BG in coda
Indiana
Sweet Lorraine - QUINTET
(Fascinating Rhythm - Appleyard w/rhythm - NO BG
Sweet Georgia Brown
Sing, Sing, Sing
Honeysuckle Rose
Good-Bye (theme)

WESTBURY MUSIC FAIR   December 6, 1975, Long Island, N.Y.

Personnels as December 5:

After You've Gone - SEXTET
Moon Glow - SEXTET
Avalon - SEXTET
Body And Soul - QUINTET
Honeysuckle Rose - SEXTET
(The Lady's In Love With You - Klink w/rhythm - NO BG
That's A Plenty
(That's All - Gravine w/rhythm - NO BG
(Oh, Lady Be Good! - Stewart w/rhythm - NO BG
Medley: Don't Be That Way
        Stompin' At The Savoy
Send In The Clowns - QUINTET
(Struttin' With Some Barbecue - Vache w/rhythm - NO BG
Indiana
(Fascinating Rhythm - Appleyard w/rhythm - NO BG
Sing, Sing, Sing
Good-Bye (theme)
Sweet Georgia Brown - segue to, One O'Clock Jump (encore)

Benny's first date in 1976 was a concert for Butler University, in Clowes Memorial Hall in Indianapolis; a reasonably good cassette is extant:

BUTLER UNIVERSITY CONCERT   January 15, 1976, Indianapolis

Benny Goodman, clt; Warren Vache, tpt; George Masso, tbn; Al Klink, ts; Peter Appleyard, vib; John Bunch, p; Bucky Pizzarelli, g; Slam Stewart, b; Connie Kay, d.

DUET: Goodman, Pizzarelli
QUINTET: Goodman, Bunch, Pizzarelli, Stewart, Kay
SEXTET: Quintet plus Appleyard

After You've Gone - SEXTET
Body And Soul - SEXTET
Avalon - SEXTET
(The Girl From Ipanema - Klink w/rhythm - NO BG
That's A Plenty
(Just You, Just Me - Vache w/rhythm - NO BG
Medley: Don't Be That Way
        Stompin At The Savoy
Here, There And Everywhere - DUET
(The One I Love Belongs To Somebody Else - Masso w/rhythm - NO BG
Indiana
(Play, Fiddle, Play - Stewart w/rhythm - NO BG
Rose Room - QUINTET
The World Is Waiting For The Sunrise - SEXTET
(Nuages - Pizzarelli solo - NO BG
(Fascinating Rhythm - Appleyard w/rhythm - NO BG
Moon Glow - SEXTET
Sing, Sing, Sing
Honeysuckle Rose
Seven Come Eleven
Good-Bye (theme)

After a date in Buffalo on the 16th, for which there is no known recording, Benny went to California on the 25th for an appearance with the Los Angeles Symphony, Aaron Copland conducting. The performance was videotaped, and was televised and simulcast in March on various television and radio stations. Credits shown are those for the author's tape:

COPLAND CONCERT   January 27–28, 1975, Los Angeles

Televised via WNET-TV, New York and simulcast via WQXR-FM, New York, on March 17.

Benny Goodman, clt, and the Los Angeles Symphony Orchestra, Aaron Copland conducting.

Concerto For Clarinet And (String) Orchestra (With Harp And Piano)
  (Copland)

A satisfactory cassette is available from Benny's next engagement, at Kennedy Center in Washington:

KENNEDY CENTER CONCERT   February 6, 1976, Washington, D.C.

Benny Goodman, clt; Bobby Hackett, tpt; George Masso, tbn; Al Klink, ts; Peter Appleyard, vib; Hank Jones, p; Bucky Pizzarelli, g; Slam Stewart, b; Grady Tate, d.

TRIO: Goodman, Jones, Tate
QUARTET: Trio plus Stewart
SEXTET: Quartet plus Appleyard, Pizzarelli

I Want To Be Happy - SEXTET
Body And Soul - TRIO
Taking A Chance On Love - SEXTET
Don't Blame Me - TRIO
Avalon - SEXTET
(The Good Life - Hackett w/rhythm - NO BG
Indiana
(The One I Love Belongs To Somebody Else - Masso w/rhythm - NO BG
That's A Plenty
(Play, Fiddle, Play - Stewart w/rhythm - NO BG
Send In The Clowns - QUARTET
Medley: Don't Be That Way
        Stompin' At The Savoy
(The Very Thought Of You - Jones solo - NO BG
Air Mail Special
(Fascinating Rhythm - Appleyard w/rhythm - NO BG
Honeysuckle Rose
Sing, Sing, Sing
Good-Bye (theme)

The author has no tape of a concert in Lakeland, Florida on February 10. Unluckily, his cassette of the Carnegie Hall concert on Friday the 13th is too poor for inclusion herein, a date that saw Roy Eldridge join the group that had appeared in Kennedy Center (with Urbie Green replacing Masso). Engagements in Symphony Hall, Boston, February 14; the Place des Artes, Montreal, February 15; in Springfield, New Jersey, February 29; in Calgary, Canada, March 6; and in Spokane, Washington's Opera House on March 7 produced no recordings known to the author. His next is from the Orpheum Theater in Omaha, Nebraska:

OMAHA CONCERT   March 12, 1976, Omaha

Benny Goodman, clt; Warren Vache, tpt; Urbie Green, tbn; Peter Appleyard, vib; Hank Jones, p; Gene Bertoncini, g; Slam Stewart, b; Grady Tate, d.

TRIO: Goodman, Jones, Tate

Lover, Come Back To Me (n/c)
(Just You, Just Me - Vache w/rhythm - NO BG
(unidentified tune - Green w/rhythm - NO BG
Medley: Don't Be That Way
        Stompin' At The Savoy
Indiana
(Oh, Lady Be Good! - Stewart w/rhythm - NO BG
Tin Roof Blues - Appleyard w/rhythm - BG accomp. - segue to, Flying
  Home
(The Very Thought Of You - Jones solo - NO BG
Poor Butterfly - TRIO
That's A Plenty
One O'Clock Jump
Sing, Sing, Sing
Good-Bye (theme)

(At least one selection preceded the incomplete "Lover, Come Back To Me," was missed by the recordist)

A week later, March 19, Benny appeared in Ottawa, Canada, but there's no cassette from that concert. His next performance, however, not only produced some audience recordings, but also a souvenir LP. The occasion was a surprise birthday party for jazz critic Herb Caen of the San Francisco "Examiner," an old friend and longtime booster of Benny Goodman. The celebration was taped professionally in true stereo, was eventually transferred to a 12" LP as an added present for Caen, and a memento of the event for the participants. Recorded in San Francisco's Great American Music Hall, the disc is rare, obviously, and its acquisition will challenge Goodman collectors:

CAEN BIRTHDAY PARTY   March 31, 1976, San Francisco

Benny Goodman, clt; Jack Sheldon, tpt; Dick Nash, tbn; Lou Levy, p; Eddie Duran, g; Bob Dougherty, b; Louis Bellson, d. Merv Griffin, voc.

QUARTET: Goodman, Levy, Dougherty; guest Herb Caen, d.
QUINTET: Goodman, Levy, Duran, Dougherty, Bellson

-0-   **StLP:** HERB CAEN RECORDS, BG 33176 - Side 1
         Avalon - QUINTET
         Poor Butterfly
         Just One Of Those Things
         Medley: Don't Be That Way
                 Stompin' At The Savoy

-0-   **StLP:** as above, except Side 2
         On The Alamo
         Seven Come Eleven
         The Shadow Of Your Smile - voc Merv Griffin
         As Long As I Live - QUARTET
         Sweet Georgia Brown

Taped the week before, interviews with Benny and producer Hal Davis were broadcast on John Lissner's ''The Swing Era'' on April 15, via New York radio station WBAI-FM. Benny next gave concerts in Vancouver, Portland and Seattle, on April 23, 24 and 25 respectively, engagements that afford no known recordings. He and Mary Lou Williams entertained at New York's Century Club on the 27th. On May 1 a Doctorate of Music was conferred upon Benny by Union College, Schenectady, New York. Then on May 8 Benny assembled his Septet in his studio at his home in Stamford for an experimental recording session. The resultant tapes are detailed in their entireties following, save that miscellaneous rehearsals between the renditions are omitted:

BENNY GOODMAN QUINTET/SEPTET   May 8, 1976, Stamford

Benny Goodman, clt; Warren Vache, tpt; Buddy Tate, ts; Tommy Fay, p; Gene Bertoncini, g; Mike Moore, b; Connie Kay, d. Marta Heflin, voc.

QUINTET: Goodman, Fay, Bertoncini, Moore, Kay

-0-   UNISSUED - Tape
         Sweet And Lovely - QUINTET (n/c)

-0-   UNISSUED - Tape
         Somebody Loves Me - SEPTET (2 complete takes)

-0-   UNISSUED - Tape
         Sweet And Lovely - QUINTET

-0-   UNISSUED - Tape
         All Of Me - SEPTET, feat. Tate

-0-   UNISSUED - Tape
         You Must Meet My Wife - QUINTET (2 complete takes)

-0-   UNISSUED - Tape
         Send In The Clowns - QUINTET

-0-   UNISSUED - Tape
         You Must Meet My Wife - QUINTET

MIKE ABENE, p, replaces Fay.

-0-   UNISSUED - Tape
         Just In Time - voc Marta Heflin - SEPTET (n/c)

-0-   UNISSUED - Tape
         You Made Me Love You - voc Marta Heflin - SEPTET

Marta Heflin w/rhythm section - NO BG:

-0-   UNISSUED - Tape
         (What Will We Say To The Child? - voc Marta Heflin (3 complete takes)

Marta Heflin w/Vache, Tate, rhythm section - NO BG:

-0-   UNISSUED - Tape
         (When Sunny Gets Blue - voc Marta Heflin

Benny returns.

-0-   UNISSUED - Tape
         There'll Be Some Changes Made - voc Marta Heflin (3 complete takes)

The audio fidelity of Benny's home-studio tapes is quite good, reflecting his use of high-tech equipment in a room that has essentially ''flat'' acoustical properties. Although the May 8 material is not musically exceptional, perhaps two or three of those cuts merit public dissemination.

''Professor'' Goodman next appeared in the role of commentator on the campus of the University of Indiana, Bloomington, on May 11, narrating performances by the university's orchestral and choral groups. Public Broadcasting System videotaped the event, televised it on various dates in June via a program titled, ''Echoes Bright And Clear - A Discovery Of American Music.'' And all of the networks televised Benny's ''Do you know me?'' spot commercials for American Express credit cards.

There is no known recording of Benny's performance at a private party in New York's Waldorf-Astoria on May 14. His next engagement was as a guest on Merv Griffin's television program, devoted entirely to Mr. Goodman. The program's highlight was a reunion with Mel Powell who, despite many years' absence from jazz piano, played brilliantly:

''THE MERV GRIFFIN SHOW''   *May 20, 1976, Los Angeles*
  METROMEDIA Television Network

Televised on various dates in June via Metromedia and independent television stations.

Benny Goodman, clt, and Mort Lindsey's studio orchestra. Martha Tilton, Merv Griffin, voc.

SEPTET: Benny Goodman, clt; Jack Sheldon, tpt; Jimmy Cleveland, tbn; Lou Levy, p; unknown g, b; Nick Ceroli, d.
TRIO: Goodman, Mel Powell, p; Ceroli

Let's Dance (theme)
Indiana - SEPTET
Goody-Goody - voc Martha Tilton
And The Angels Sing - voc Martha Tilton
Don't Be That Way
Stompin' At The Savoy
A String Of Pearls
The Shadow Of Your Smile - voc Merv Griffin
Body And Soul - TRIO
Avalon - TRIO
Oh, Lady Be Good! - TRIO
Sing, Sing, Sing
Good-Bye (theme)

Benny remained on the West Coast, appeared with the Santa Barbara, California, Symphony on May 22; no recording of the concert is known. He then did four dates backed by Louis Bellson's big band: June 3 in Phoenix, Arizona, and June 4, 5 and 6 in the Circle Star Theater in San Carlos, California. A tape of the June 4 concert is minimally-satisfactory audio, but is listed principally because it offers new arrangements by Gordon Jenkins. Names of the sidemen whose instruments are not known are listed alphabetically:

SAN CARLOS CONCERT   *June 4, 1976, San Carlos, Calif.*

Benny Goodman, clt, and Louis Bellson's Orchestra, including: Snooky Young, tpt; Dick Nash, tbn; Buddy Tate, Bobby Shu, ts; Lou Levy, p; Eddie Duran, g; Louis Bellson, d; and Larry Covelli, Gary Foster, Jerry Hey, Dana Hughes, George Leo, Nick Maio, Don Menza, Rich Mitchell, Bob Payne, Dick Spencer, John Williams.

OCTET: Goodman, Young, Nash, Tate, Levy, Duran, unknown b, Bellson

Let's Dance (theme)
Indiana - OCTET
King Porter Stomp
Star Dust (new GJ arr)
(All Of Me - Tate w/rhythm - NO BG
South (arr GJ)
(I Got It Bad (And That Ain't Good) - Duran w/rhythm - NO BG
Medley: Don't Be That Way   )
*   Stompin' At The Savoy) (arr GJ)*
*   And The Angels Sing   )*
When Your Lover Has Gone (arr GJ)
Avalon - OCTET
Royal Garden Blues (arr GJ)

A String Of Pearls (new GJ arr)
Sing, Sing, Sing
You're Driving Me Crazy (new GJ arr)
Good-Bye - in its entirety

Benny took a small group to the Reykjavik, Iceland, Festival on June 12; no tape from there. Nor, unfortunately, has a professional recording of his next appearance, at the Mississippi River Festival in Edwardsville, Illinois, June 24, become available to Mr. Goodman or the author. Southern Illinois University officials, hosts of the festival, now cannot locate the tape or the employee who made the recording. After the concert, Benny was interviewed by Charlie Menees of radio station KWMV-FM, St. Louis. Their conversation was broadcast June 26. The day after the Edwardsville appearance, the Septet was at Meadow Brook:

MEADOW BROOK CONCERT   June 25, 1976, Rochester, Michigan

Benny Goodman, clt; Warren Vache, tpt; Peter Appleyard, vib; Tommy Fay, p; Gene Bertoncini, g; Mike Moore, b; Connie Kay, d.

QUINTET: Goodman, Fay, Bertoncini, Moore, Kay

Avalon - QUINTET
Here's That Rainy Day - QUINTET
Sweet And Lovely - QUINTET
I've Found A New Baby - QUINTET
You Took Advantage Of Me - Vache w/rhythm - BG in coda
(Polka Dots And Moonbeams - Vache w/rhythm - NO BG
You Must Meet My Wife - QUINTET
Medley: Don't Be That Way
         Stompin' At The Savoy
Dinah
Send In The Clowns - QUINTET
Indiana
Rose Room
Sweet Georgia Brown
Sing, Sing, Sing
Honeysuckle Rose
Good-Bye (theme)

Three days later, a satisfactory audience recording from Carnegie Hall, Benny's contribution to the Newport Jazz Festival-Jazz Interactions 1976 concert series. Program offers a guest appearance by Teddy Wilson, and presentation of a plaque to Benny for "outstanding contributions to jazz" by Joe Newman.

The second selection, "Dearly Beloved," was an unusual tune for Benny to program. Sadly, it was dedicated to the memories of Bobby Hackett and Johnny Mercer, both of whom had recently passed away. Little has been said critically about Benny's work through the 70's; it can be noted that he seemed to be at his best when Bobby was by his side. Bobby's death on June 7 elicited Benny's highest praise: "He was a player." He was, indeed.

CARNEGIE HALL CONCERT   June 28, 1976, New York

Benny Goodman, clt; Warren Vache, tpt; Buddy Tate, ts; Peter Appleyard, vib; Tommy Fay, p; Eddie Duran, g; Mike Moore, b; Connie Kay, d.

TRIO: Goodman, Fay, Kay
QUINTET: Trio plus Duran, Moore

Avalon
Dearly Beloved - QUINTET
All Of Me - Tate w/rhythm - BG in coda
(Polka Dots And Moonbeams - Tate w/rhythm - NO BG
That's A Plenty
(You Took Advantage Of Me - Vache w/rhythm - NO BG
You Must Meet My Wife - TRIO
Indiana
(Come Sunday - Moore w/rhythm - NO BG
(Fascinating Rhythm - Appleyard w/rhythm - NO BG

Teddy Wilson, p, replaces Fay in the Trio and full group.

Ain't Misbehavin' - TRIO
I'm Gonna Sit Right Down And Write Myself A Letter - TRIO
Body And Soul - TRIO
After You've Gone

Fay returns.

Send In The Clowns - QUINTET

I Got It Bad (And That Ain't Good) - Duran w/rhythm - BG in coda
Medley: Don't Be That Way
         Stompin' At The Savoy
Sing, Sing, Sing
Good-Bye (theme)

On the Wednesday following the Monday evening kickoff of the Jazz Festival, Benny, Vache and the rhythm section reassembled in his Stamford studio. Almost a decade later, five of the eight tunes recorded that day by various combinations will be released for the first time on a compact disc. The master tapes have not been audited, and so our listing omits take numbers for two of the performances.

BENNY GOODMAN SMALL GROUPS   **June 30, 1976, Stamford**

Benny Goodman, clt; Warren Vache, tpt; Tommy Fay, p; Eddie Duran, g; Mike Moore, b; Connie Kay, d.

-0-   **CD:** LON 820 197-2 - Track 11
       UNISSUED: 9 additional partial & complete takes
       Somebody Loves Me

BG Quintet: Omit Vache

-0-   **CD:** LON 820 179-2 - Track 6
       You Must Meet My Wife (only take registered)

-0-   **CD:** LON 820 179-2 - Track 10
       (You Forgot To) Remember (only take registered)

Trio: Goodman, Fay, Moore

-0-   **CD:** LON 820 179-2 - Track 9
       Send In The Clowns (only take registered)

Vache Quintet: Vache, rhythm section - NO BG

-0-   **CD:** LON 820 179-2 - Track 5
       UNISSUED: 1 additional take
       (Felicidade

-0-   UNISSUED
       Dearly Beloved - BG Quintet - 2 takes
       (Come Sunday - Fay, Moore duet - 2 takes
       (I Got It Bad (And That Ain't Good) - Duran featured
         with rhythm section only - 4 takes
       (Remember - Fay solo - 1 take

(London's sketchy liner notes—no dates, personnels—list "You Must Meet My Wife" as "Have You Met My Wife?".)

The recordist elected to omit some renditions, and there are some dropouts in his cassette; but generally the tape provides satisfactory listening to Benny's next engagement:

RAVINIA CONCERT   July 4, 1976, Highland Park, Ill.

Personnels as June 28, except GENE BERTONCINI, g, replaces Duran.

Dearly Beloved - QUINTET
I've Found A New Baby - QUINTET
(You Took Advantage Of Me - Vache w/rhythm - NO BG
(All Of Me - Tate w/rhythm - BG in coda
That's A Plenty
(Come Sunday - Moore w/p - NO BG
You Must Meet My Wife - QUINTET
(But Beautiful - Bertoncini solo - NO BG
Medley: Don't Be That Way
         Stompin' At The Savoy
(Fascinating Rhythm - Appleyard w/rhythm - NO BG
(After You've Gone - Appleyard w/rhythm - NO BG
Send In The Clowns - QUINTET
Makin' Whoopee
Indiana
Sing, Sing, Sing
Good-Bye (theme)

Four additional engagements in July afford no known audience recordings: a combined classical and jazz date in San Diego on the 10th, the Cohasset (Massachusetts) Music Circus on the 25th, the Interlochen (Michigan) Music Camp on the 28th, and a guest appearance with the Minnesota Symphony in Minneapolis on the 30th. Benny's first two concerts in August offer satisfactory tapes:

TEMPLE MUSIC FESTIVAL   *August 4, 1976, Ambler, Pa.*

Benny Goodman, clt; Warren Vache, tpt; Buddy Tate, ts; Tommy Fay, p; Wayne Wright, g; Major Holley, b; Connie Kay, d.

QUINTET: Goodman, Fay, Wright, Holley, Kay

China Boy - QUINTET
Here's That Rainy Day - QUINTET
Avalon - QUINTET
(The One I Love Belongs To Somebody Else - Vache w/rhythm - NO BG
All Of Me - Tate w/rhythm - BG in coda
That's A Plenty
(Ballade In Blue - Fay solo - NO BG
(Body And Soul - Tate w/rhythm - NO BG
(Samba Of The Orpheum - Vache w/rhythm - NO BG
Send In The Clowns - QUINTET
Medley: Don't Be That Way
*   Stompin' At The Savoy*
Indiana
Sing, Sing, Sing
Good-Bye - QUINTET
Makin' Whoopee (encore)

William F. Hyland, then Attorney General for the State of New Jersey and an accomplished clarinetist who had played professionally, joins Benny on our next entry. Introduced to Benny by Percival Leach, co-founder of Waterloo Village, Hyland had convinced Benny of his competence during an afternoon of clarinet duets at Stamford prior to the concert.

WATERLOO VILLAGE CONCERT   *August 7, 1976, Stanhope, N.J.*

Benny Goodman, clt; Warren Vache, tpt; Buddy Tate, ts; Tommy Fay, p; Wally Richardson, g; Mike Moore, b; Connie Kay, d.

DUET: Goodman, Fay
QUINTET: Goodman, Fay, Richardson, Moore, Kay

Hallelujah! - QUINTET
Here's That Rainy Day - QUINTET
You Took Advantage Of Me - QUINTET
China Boy - QUINTET
(The One I Love Belongs To Somebody Else - Vache w/rhythm - NO BG
(All Of Me - Tate w/rhythm - NO BG
I've Found A New Baby

Bill Hyland, clt, joins.

(Body And Soul - Hyland w/rhythm - NO BG
(Gone With The Wind - Hyland w/rhythm - NO BG
Undecided - QUINTET plus Hyland - full group in coda
The Man I Love - QUINTET plus Hyland

Hyland out.

That's A Plenty
(Just Friends - Richardson w/rhythm - NO BG
Send In The Clowns - DUET
Honeysuckle Rose
Sing, Sing, Sing
Good-Bye - QUINTET

There are no known recordings of Benny's appearances at the University of Delaware in Wilmington on August 11; at the Hyannis (Massachusetts) Music Tent on August 22; at Concord, California on August 27; and with the San Francisco Symphony on August 29. On September 2 Southern Illinois University at Edwardsville conferred a doctorate degree upon Benny. He played a private affair for the Ford Motor Company in Detroit on September 9; reputedly, the event was recorded professionally, but neither Benny nor the author has a copy of the tape. Nor has either a tape of his next engagement, in Toronto's Forum on September 11.

Ever loyal to his alma mater, at mid-month Benny played a benefit for Hull House in Chicago's Conrad Hilton Hotel. While there he auditioned veteran drummer Barrett Deems, perhaps best known to jazz fans for his work with Louis Armstrong's All-Stars. Both the benefit and the audition are on privately-recorded cassette:

HULL HOUSE BENEFIT   *September 15, 1976, Chicago*

Benny Goodman, clt; Warren Vache, tpt; Buddy Tate, ts; Tommy Fay, p; Cal Collins, g; Keter Betts, b; Connie Kay, d.

DUET: Goodman, Fay
TRIO: Goodman, Fay, Kay
QUINTET: Trio plus Collins, Betts

Avalon - QUINTET
Here's That Rainy Day - TRIO
After You've Gone - QUINTET
All Of Me - Tate w/rhythm - BG in coda
That's A Plenty
(The One I Love Belongs To Somebody Else - Vache w/rhythm - NO BG
Send In The Clowns - DUET
Medley: Don't Be That Way
*   Stompin' At The Savoy*
Medley: If I Had You
*   Poor Butterfly*
Honeysuckle Rose
Makin' Whoopee
Sing, Sing, Sing
Good-Bye (theme)

BARRETT DEEMS AUDITION   *same date*

Personnel as Hull House Benefit, except BARRETT DEEMS, d, replaces Kay.

Chicago
Medley: Don't Be That Way
*   Stompin' At The Savoy*
Makin' Whoopee

There's no tape of Benny's guest appearance with the Memphis (Tennessee) Symphony Orchestra, Arthur Fiedler conducting, on September 17. But there is a satisfactory audience recording of the Septet's concert the next day at the Fair Grounds in Baltimore, Maryland. The date was proclaimed "Benny Goodman Night" by the city's mayor. More meaningful to Benny, Baltimore was where his mother and father were married eight decades earlier. (Baltimore has a special meaning for John Bunch, too; enroute by train to the Fair Grounds, someone swiped his coat, including his wallet and his return ticket.)

BALTIMORE CONCERT   *September 18, 1976, Baltimore*

Benny Goodman, clt; Warren Vache, tpt; Frank Wess, ts; John Bunch, p; Cal Collins, g; Keter Belts, b; Connie Kay, d.

TRIO: Goodman, Bunch, Kay
QUINTET: Trio plus Collins, Betts

Avalon - QUINTET
Here's That Rainy Day - TRIO
Oh, Lady Be Good! - QUINTET
That's A Plenty
Medley: Don't Be That Way
*   Stompin' At The Savoy*
Send In The Clowns - TRIO
Indiana
(The One I Love Belongs To Somebody Else - Vache w/rhythm - NO BG
One O'Clock Jump
Sing, Sing, Sing
Good-Bye (theme)

A jazz date in Ann Arbor, Michigan on October 2 produced no known recording. Three days later, Benny was off to England and the Continent for the balance of the month. His first engagement was in London, a benefit for St. John's (church and concert hall) in Smith Square, and its resident orchestra, the Park Lane Music Players. St. John's, 250 years old and considered a foremost example of English Baroque architecture, was in process of renovation and Benny was pleased to contribute. In the presence of St. John's patron H.R.H. Princess Margaret, Benny performed the Mozart Clarinet Concerto, and then Malcolm Arnold's Clarinet Concerto, with the composer conducting. Following those performances, Benny's small group entertained the audience with three jazz selections.

The two classical pieces were recorded professionally, and were released on the Book-Of-The-Month Club's Classic Record Library label. Audience recordings supplement the LP: They provide the jazz numbers, and also two "takes" of the third movement of the Arnold Concerto. Benny wasn't satisfied with the first rendition, repeated it to provide a choice.

BENNY GOODMAN - CONCERT IN LONDON   **October 11, 1976, London**

Benny Goodman, clt, with The Park Lane Music Players, Malcolm Arnold conducting.

BOM-30-5550-A   **StLP:** CLRL 30-5550 - Side 1
Clarinet Concerto In A, K.622 (Mozart)
I. Allegro
II. Adagio

BOM-30-5550-B   same issue, except Side 2
Clarinet Concerto in A, K.622 (Mozart) - Concluded
III. Rondo: Allegro

Clarinet Concerto No. 2. Op. 115 (Arnold)
I. Allegro vivace
II. Lento
III. Allegro non troppo

Air Check: Two takes, third movement, Arnold Concerto

ST. JOHN'S SMITH SQUARE CONCERT   *same date*

Benny Goodman, clt; John McLevy, tpt; Bob Burns, as; Buddy Tate, ts; John Bunch, p; Cal Collins, g; Lennie Bush, b; Barrett Deems, d.

Oh, Lady Be Good!
Here's That Rainy Day
Honeysuckle Rose

Benny's next engagement was in Malmo, Sweden, on October 14; an audience recording is extant, is unheard by the author, but is described as being of marginal audio fidelity. The Konserthuset in Gothenburg followed; a partial tape of that concert offers satisfactory listening:

GOTHENBURG CONCERT   *October 16, 1976, Gothenburg*

Benny Goodman, clt; Warren Vache, tpt; Buddy Tate, ts; Peter Appleyard, vib; John Bunch, p; Cal Collins, g; Lennie Bush, b; Barrett Deems, d.

QUINTET: Goodman, Bunch, Collins, Bush, Deems

Oh, Lady Be Good! - QUINTET
Here's That Rainy Day - QUINTET
Hallelujah! - QUINTET
(The One I Love Belongs To Somebody Else - Vache w/rhythm - NO BG
(I Can't Get Started - Vache w/rhythm - NO BG
(All Of Me - Tate w/rhythm - NO BG
(Body And Soul - Tate w/rhythm - NO BG
That's A Plenty
Send In The Clowns - QUINTET
(Fascinating Rhythm - Appleyard w/rhythm - NO BG

(The "Don't Be That Way/Stompin' At The Savoy" medley, "Sing, Sing, Sing" and possibly other performances were not recorded.)

Another partial cassette, from the Concert Hall in Vasteras, Sweden:

VASTERAS CONCERT   *October 18, 1976, Vasteras*

Personnels as October 16.

Oh, Lady Be Good! - QUINTET
Here's That Rainy Day - QUINTET
Ain't Misbehavin' - QUINTET
After You've Gone - QUINTET
(The One I Love Belongs To Somebody Else - Vache w/rhythm - NO BG
I Can't Get Started - Vache w/rhythm - BG in coda
All Of Me - Tate w/rhythm - BG in coda
Body And Soul - Tate w/rhythm - BG obligato
That's A Plenty
(Cherry - Collins solo - NO BG
(Fascinating Rhythm - Appleyard w/rhythm - NO BG

("Send In The Clowns" and likely other performances were not recorded.)

Radio Sweden stereo-taped the next day's concert, in Stockholm's Concert Hall, and broadcast three-quarters of it on Christmas Eve. Audience cassettes flesh out the balance of the performance:

STOCKHOLM CONCERT   *October 19, 1976, Stockholm*
Swedish Radio

Broadcast December 24. Personnels as October 16.

Oh, Lady Be Good! - QUINTET
Here's That Rainy Day - QUINTET
China Boy
(All Of Me - Tate w/rhythm - NO BG
(Body And Soul - Tate w/rhythm - NO BG
(The One I Love Belongs To Somebody Else - Vache w/rhythm - NO BG
(I Can't Get Started - Vache w/rhythm - NO BG
That's A Plenty
(Cherry - Collins w/rhythm - NO BG
Send In The Clowns - QUINTET
Honeysuckle Rose

Not broadcast, extant via audience recording:

(Fascinating Rhythm - Appleyard w/rhythm - NO BG
Medley: Don't Be That Way
*   Stompin' At The Savoy*
Sing, Sing, Sing
Good-Bye (theme)

Concerts in Umea, Sweden on October 21 and 22, in Warsaw on October 24, and the final stop on this tour, Budapest on October 28, provide no recordings. But the next to last engagement, in Prague's Lucerna Concert Hall, does offer a portion of that performance, via an East German television program:

PRAGUE JAZZ FESTIVAL   *October 26, 1976, Prague*
East German TV

Telecast date unknown. Personnels as October 16.

(Tin Roof Blues - full group sans BG
(Take The "A" Train - full group sans BG
Oh, Lady Be Good! - QUINTET
Here's That Rainy Day - QUINTET
China Boy - QUINTET

We've no further Goodman performance recordings for the rest of 1976. Engagements in Detroit, November 7; Queens, New York, November 9; Gary, Indiana, November 13; Grand Rapids, November 17; Elgin, Illinois, November 21; Daverport & Rock Island, Iowa, December 3–5; a benefit in Stamford, December 10; Bakersfield, California, December 13; and Baltimore, December 18, give evidence of Benny's cross-country travels, but yield no tapes.

There is, however, one Goodman-related tape that has a special meaning for the author. On November 11 New York's century-old Lotos Club honored Benny as its "Man Of The Year," adding his name to Presidents of the United States, foreign kings and princes, and those preeminent in the arts who had been similarly honored throughout its history. Morton Gould—a funny man—and Teddy Wilson gave testimony to Mr. Goodman's accomplishments. The author, however, elected to couch his remarks in the nature of a gentle "roast," gentle enough to keep Benny laughing, but barbed enough to cause Alice Goodman to chortle gleefully. The author is rather proud of that.

There is no known cassette of Benny's initial engagement in 1977, January 19 in Little Rock, Arkansas; but two days' later he recorded the small group in his Stamford studio. Eventually, four of the six tunes recorded will surface on a compact disc. The master tapes have not been audited, and so take numbers are omitted.

BENNY GOODMAN QUARTET/SEPTET   **January 21, 1977, Stamford**

Benny Goodman, clt; Cal Collins, g; Percy Heath, b; Connie Kay, d.

-0-   **CD:** LON 820 179-2- Track 1
        UNISSUED: 5 complete, 4 partial takes
        China Boy

-0-   **CD:** LON 820 179-2 - Track 2
        UNISSUED: 1 complete take
        Please Be Kind

-0-   UNISSUED
        La Mer (Beyond The Sea) - 3 complete, 1 partial take

Add: Warren Vache, tpt; Scott Hamilton, ts; John Bunch, p

-0-   UNISSUED
        Makin' Whoopee - 2 complete takes

-0-   **CD:** LON 820 179-2 - Track 8
        UNISSUED: 1 breakdown
        Dream A Little Dream Of Me

-0-   **CD:** LON 820 179-2 - Track 3
        UNISSUED: 2 complete, 2 partial takes
        I Ain't Got Nobody

(Some of the partial takes above are noted as, "false start-engineering error." Such mistakes cannot here be blamed on Benny, for two professional engineers were engaged to record the session. They would be more understandable had Benny been at the controls; he is heavy-handed with recordings, and many times the author has shuddered as Benny slid a stylus across an LP.)

Guest appearances with symphony orchestras in Jackson, Mississippi (January 23 & 24), New Haven, Connecticut (January 29), and Kansas City (February 5) produced no known tapes; nor did a jazz date in Wabash, Indiana on February 9. The next day the Septet was in Clowes Memorial Hall, and a satisfactory cassette from the concert there is extant:

INDIANAPOLIS CONCERT   *February 10, 1977, Indianapolis*

Benny Goodman, clt; Warren Vache, tpt; Buddy Tate, ts; John Bunch, p; Cal Collins, g; Knobby Totah, b; Connie Kay, d.

QUINTET: Goodman, Bunch, Collins, Totah, Kay

Oh, Lady Be Good! - QUINTET
Send In The Clowns - QUINTET
China Boy - QUINTET
The One I Love Belongs To Somebody Else - Vache w/rhythm - BG in coda
(All Of Me - Tate w/rhythm - NO BG
Medley: Don't Be That Way
*   Stompin' At The Savoy*
Poor Butterfly - QUINTET
Makin' Whoopee
That's A Plenty
(Exactly Like You - Collins solo - NO BG
Dream A Little Dream Of Me - QUINTET
I've Found A New Baby
Body And Soul - QUINTET
Avalon
Sing, Sing, Sing
Good-Bye (theme)

A combined jazz/classical performance February 15 in Chattanooga, Tennessee's Tivoli Theater offers no known recording, but the next engagement in Chicago's Civic Opera House does:

CHICAGO CONCERT   *February 19, 1977, Chicago*

Benny Goodman, clt; Warren Vache, tpt; Buddy Tate, ts; John Bunch, p; Cal Collins, g; Percy Heath, b; Connie Kay, d.

DUET: Goodman, Bunch
TRIO: Duet plus Kay
QUINTET: Trio plus Collins, Heath

Chicago - QUINTET
Send In The Clowns - TRIO
After You've Gone - QUINTET
Medley: Don't Be That Way
*   Stompin' At The Savoy*

The One I Love Belongs To Somebody Else - Vache w/rhythm - BG in coda
(All Of Me - Tate w/rhythm - NO BG
How Long Has This Been Going On? - Collins w/rhythm - BG obligato
Oh, Lady Be Good! - feat. Heath - full group in coda
That's A Plenty
Body And Soul - DUET
(unidentified title - Bunch solo - NO BG
Sing, Sing, Sing
Makin' Whoopee
Good-Bye (theme)

March is a washout insofar as tapes of Benny's performances are concerned; none is known from Dallas (classical, 5th), Boston (jazz, 18th), New York (Century Club with Jean-Pierre Rampal, 24th) and Richmond, Virginia (classical, 26th). A jazz date in Buffalo, New York on April 1 also went unrecorded, so far as it is known.

While Benny was on tour, Herman (Hymie) Schertzer died in Mount Sinai Hospital in New York on March 22. Hymie, more than anyone responsible for the feather-light sound of Benny's best reed sections, was 67, just about two month's older than his former boss. Another of the irreplaceables is gone . . .

Next is a studio recording session whose full documentation is lacking. Its purpose, Benny recalled recently, was to master-tape some arrangements he had commissioned in the first half of the 1970s. He had performed some of them—for example, Gordon Jenkins's charts, the year before in California—but others had never been played. He assembled a big band of New York studio musicians in RCA's facility on 44th Street; but, he believes, he recorded under the aegis of Park Recording, not RCA. Recent efforts to find the fruits of the four-hour session in Benny's tape library failed. Conjecture that London Records' interest may also have prompted the session, and that it may have had access to the tapes, is unconfirmed.

BENNY GOODMAN AND HIS ORCHESTRA   **April 5, 1977, New York**

Benny Goodman, clt; Warren Vache, John Frosk, Bert Collins, John Faddis, tpt; Eddie Bert, Al Grey, Paul Faulise, Mickey Gravine, tbn; Phil Bodner, George Young, as, fl, clt; Al Klink, Hal Ashby, ts, fl, clt; Sol Schlinger, bar, clt; John Bunch, p; Cal Collins, g; Percy Heath, b; Connie Kay, d. Gordon Jenkins (GJ), Peter Knight (PK), arr.

-0-   UNISSUED
        South (arr GJ)
        For Once In My Life (arr GJ)
        Molto Benny (arr PK)
        Coquette (arr GJ)
        When Your Lover Has Gone (arr GJ)
        Star Dust (arr GJ)

(Benny's file notes indicate the order-of-performance listed above, but do not reveal how many takes of each selection were cut.)

Ten more new arrangements by Jenkins remained to be recorded: "Basin Street Blues," "Blue Prelude," "Gentle Ben," "I May Be Wrong," "Lonesome Road," "Makin' Whoopee," "Royal Garden Blues," "A String Of Pearls," "You're Driving Me Crazy" and a medley: "Don't Be That Way" / "Stompin' At The Savoy" / "And The Angels Sing." To get at least some of them on tape, Benny scheduled a follow-up session in the same RCA studio for April 13. Unluckily, for whatever reason, that date was cancelled and Benny's good intentions came to naught.

Independent British Television aired the ninth of 17 one-hour programs in a series titled, "All You Need Is Love," on April 9. This segment featured an interview with Mr. Goodman (and others), plus various film clips.

The second of two consecutive evening concerts at the Valley Forge Music Circus produces our next audience recording:

VALLEY FORGE MUSIC CIRCUS   *April 10, 1977, Devon, Pa.*

Benny Goodman, clt; Warren Vache, tpt; Scott Hamilton, ts; Peter Appleyard, vib; John Bunch, p; Cal Collins, g; Knobby Totah, b; Connie Kay, d.

DUET: Goodman, Collins
QUINTET: Goodman, Bunch, Collins, Totah, Kay

Oh, Lady Be Good! - QUINTET
Here's That Rainy Day - DUET
I Know That You Know - QUINTET
(The One I Love Belongs To Somebody Else - Vache w/rhythm - NO BG

(A Ghost Of A Chance - Hamilton w/rhythm - NO BG
That's A Plenty
(Swingin' On A Star - Totah w/rhythm - NO BG
(How Long Has This Been Going On? - Collins w/rhythm - NO BG
You Must Meet My Wife - QUINTET
I've Found A New Baby
Medley: Don't Be That Way
*   Stompin' At The Savoy*
Sing, Sing, Sing
Good-Bye (theme)

Benny's dates in St. Louis, Jacksonville, Florida and Norfolk, Virginia on April 14, 18–19, and 25–26 respectively afford no known cassettes. On May 2 Benny's big band (many of the sidemen from the April 5 session), Morton Gould and concert pianist Patricia Prattis-Jennings were in Lincoln Center's Avery Fisher Hall for a benefit titled, "Benny Goodman Swings For Planned Parenthood." An audience recording is extant, but its poor quality eliminates its detailing herein.

Concerts in Orchestra Hall in Minneapolis, May 27–28, are unrecorded, to the best of the author's knowledge. An audience recording is extant from the Place des Arts, Montreal, June 16; it is unheard, but is represented as being of marginal quality. There is a good cassette from Benny's succeeding engagement in an unusual locale, Long Island's Belmont Park race track:

BELMONT PARK CONCERT   *June 18, 1977, Bellerose, N.Y.*

Benny Goodman, clt; Warren Vache, tpt; Al Grey, tbn; Buddy Tate, ts; John Bunch, p; Knobby Totah, b; Connie Kay, d.

TRIO: Goodman, Bunch, Kay
QUARTET: Trio plus Totah

Avalon - QUARTET
Poor Butterfly - QUARTET
(Topsy - Tate w/rhythm - NO BG
(The One I Love Belongs To Somebody Else - Vache w/rhythm - NO BG
(You Are The Sunshine Of My Life - Grey w/rhythm - NO BG
Medley: Don't Be That Way
*   Stompin' At The Savoy*
Send In The Clowns - TRIO
Indiana
(Maple Leaf Rag - Bunch solo - NO BG
That's A Plenty
(All Of Me - Tate w/rhythm - NO BG
Makin' Whoopee
Sing, Sing, Sing
Honeysuckle Rose
Good-Bye (theme)

Benny's private performance June 24 for the Mead Corporation in Dayton, Ohio, went unrecorded so far as it is known. But both a rehearsal and concert at Wolf Trap Farm Park were taped in their entireties, and eventually excerpts from them were televised by the Public Broadcasting Service network:

WOLF TRAP TELECAST   *July 2, 1977, Vienna, Virginia*
* PBS Television Network*

Televised nationally December 6, 1977, and at later random dates by individual PBS stations.

Benny Goodman, clt; Warren Vache, Wayman Reed, Joe Ferrante, tpt; Mickey Gravine, Bob Alexander, George Masso, tbn; George Young, Arnie Lawrence, as; Buddy Tate, Scott Hamilton, Al Klink, ts; Sol Schlinger, bar; John Bunch, p; Cal Collins, g; Knobby Totah, b; Connie Kay, d. Susan Mellikian, voc.

QUINTET: Goodman, Bunch, Collins, Totah, Kay
OCTET: Quintet plus Vache, Gravine, Tate

When Your Lover Has Gone (arr. GJ) (excerpt, background to opening
* credits)*
Let's Dance (theme)
Bugle Call Rag (excerpts, rehearsal sequence)
King Porter Stomp (excerpts, rehearsal sequence)
When Your Lover Has Gone (arr GJ)

Add: Patricia Prattis-Jennings, p; Morton Gould, conductor

Rhapsody In Blue (Philip D. Lane, arr.)

Prattis-Jennings, Gould leave.

(All Of Me - Tate w/rhythm - NO BG (excerpt, background to dialog)
Avalon - QUINTET
Here's That Rainy Day - QUINTET
That's A Plenty - OCTET
Sing, Sing, Sing (excerpt; in main, Part 2)
Good-Bye (first note of theme)

(PBS's Paul Anthony interviewed Benny prior to the concert. The tape was broadcast via PBS's radio network on various dates in November 1977 as a promo for the telecast.)

The author missed the next concert in Philadelphia, July 11; he recalls a horrendous traffic jam prevented his attendance and a post-concert snack with Benny. He has, however, a good-quality recording of Benny's appearance at the Music Center of the Dorothy Chandler Pavilion, almost two hours' in length:

CHANDLER PAVILION CONCERT   *July 17, 1977, Los Angeles*

Benny Goodman, clt; Art DePew, Warrent Vache, John Bello tpt; Mickey Gravine, Benny Powell, Dick Nash, tbn; George Young, Willie Schwartz, as; Scott Hamilton, Don Lodice, Don Raffell, ts; Chuck Gentry, bar; John Bunch, p; Cal Collins, g; Knobby Totah, b; Connie Kay, d. Susan Mellikian, voc. (Patricia Prattis-Jennings, voc on one selection.)

QUARTET: Goodman, Bunch, Collins, Kay
QUINTET: Quartet plus Totah
OCTET: Quintet plus Vache, Gravine, Hamilton
NONET: Quintet plus DePew, Nash, Powell, Young

Let's Dance (theme)
Bugle Call Rag
For Once In My Life (arr GJ)
King Porter Stomp
(Please Don't Talk About Me When I'm Gone - Collins w/rhythm - NO BG
Gee, Baby, Ain't I Good To You? - voc Susan Mellikian - QUINTET
The Lady Is A Tramp - voc Susan Mellikian - QUINTET
Body And Soul - QUARTET
Big John Special

Add: Patricia Prattis-Jennings, p; Russell Stanford, conductor

Rhapsody In Blue

. . . Intermission

Omit Prattis-Jennings, Stanford

Oh, Lady Be Good! - QUINTET
(Time After Time - Hamilton w/rhythm - NO BG
(Them There Eyes - Vache w/rhythm - NO BG
That's A Plenty - OCTET
(Only For A Moment - voc Patricia Prattis-Jennings - NO BG
Medley: Don't Be That Way   )
*   Stompin' At The Savoy) - OCTET*
Honeysuckle Rose - NONET
Sing, Sing, Sing
Poor Butterfly - QUINTET
Makin' Whoopee - OCTET
Good-Bye (theme)

The author has a partial tape of Benny's concert in San Diego's Golden Hall, July 20, and a complete cassette of his next, in the Concord Pavilion, Concord, July 22; neither is of suitable audio quality for inclusion herein. He does not have a recording of Benny's performance at a private party (a house-warming; that's class) or at the Mondavi Vineyard, both in California's Napa Valley, on the 23rd and 24th, respectively.

Benny remained in California until August 3; a report that he appeared on the late night/early morning "Tomorrow" television talk show is unconfirmed. A passable cassette is available from his first engagement upon his return East:

WATERLOO VILLAGE CONCERT　　　August 6, 1977, Stanhope, N.J.

Benny Goodman, clt; Warren Vache, tpt; Mickey Gravine, tbn; Buddy Tate, ts; John Bunch, p; Cal Collins, acou g; Bucky Pizzarelli, elec g; Knobby Totah, b; Connie Kay, d. Susan Mellikian, voc.

DUET: Goodman, Collins
QUINTET: Goodman, Bunch, Collins, Totah, Kay
SEXTET: Quintet plus Pizzarelli

Air Mail Special - QUINTET
Here's That Rainy Day - QUINTET
. . . unannounced title - QUINTET
(The One I Love Belongs To Somebody Else - Vache w/rhythm - NO BG
Somebody Loves Me - voc Susan Mellikian
Gee, Baby, Ain't I Good To You? - voc Susan Mellikian
(All Of Me - Tate w/rhythm - NO BG
(Satin Doll - Collins, Pizzarelli w/rhythm - NO BG
(That's All - Gravine w/rhythm - NO BG
That's A Plenty
(You've Changed - Bunch solo - NO BG
Medley: Don't Be That Way
*　　　Stompin' At The Savoy*
Body And Soul - DUET

Bill Hyland, clt, replaces Benny:

(A Foggy Day - Hyland w/rhythm - NO BG
(Memories Of You - Hyland w/rhythm - NO BG

Benny returns; Hyland remains:

Makin' Whoopee

Hyland out.

Sing, Sing, Sing
Good-Bye (theme)

Nothing to report about Benny for the next seven weeks-odd; but his next known date, a benefit in the Bismarck Hotel for Hull House, is on tape, and a good one at that:

HULL HOUSE BENEFIT　　　September 25, 1977, Chicago

Benny Goodman, clt; Warren Vache, tpt; Buddy Tate, ts; John Bunch, p; Cal Collins, g; Phil Flanigan, b; Connie Kay, d.

TRIO: Goodman, Bunch, Kay
QUARTET: Trio plus Flanigan
QUINTET: Quartet plus Collins
SEXTET: Quintet plus Vache

Avalon - QUINTET
Here's That Rainy Day - QUARTET
Sweet Georgia Brown - SEXTET
(Topsy - Tate w/rhythm - NO BG
(I Got It Bad (And That Ain't Good) - Collins w/rhythm - NO BG
I Love You - Vache w/rhythm - BG in coda
Send In The Clowns - TRIO
Medley: Don't Be That Way
*　　　Stompin' At The Savoy*
Medley: Poor Butterfly - QUINTET
*　　　It Had To Be You - full group*
Just One Of Those Things
Rose Room
When The Saints Go Marching In
Oh, Lady Be Good!
Body And Soul
I Want To Be Happy
That's A Plenty
Good-Bye (theme)
Sing, Sing, Sing (encore)
Good-Bye (theme)

Next, the Fox Theater in Atlanta, and another audience recording:

ATLANTA CONCERT　　　October 8, 1977, Atlanta

Benny Goodman, clt; Warren Vache, tpt; Scott Hamilton, ts; John Bunch, p; Cal Collins, g; Mike Moore, b; Connie Kay, d. Susan Mellikian, voc.

TRIO: Goodman, Bunch, Kay
QUINTET: Trio plus Collins, Moore

Avalon - QUINTET
Here's That Rainy Day - TRIO
Oh, Lady Be Good! - QUINTET
(Time After Time - Hamilton w/rhythm - NO BG
That's A Plenty
Gee, Baby, Ain't I Good To You? - voc Susan Mellikian
Am I Blue? - voc Susan Mellikian
Love Me Or Leave Me - voc Susan Mellikian
(Come Sunday - Moore w/rhythm - NO BG
(I Thought About You - Vache w/rhythm - NO BG
The Girl Friend - QUINTET
Send In The Clowns - TRIO
Medley: Don't Be That Way
*　　　Stompin' At The Savoy*
(Have You Met Miss Jones? - Collins w/rhythm - NO BG
Makin' Whoopee
Honeysuckle Rose

Once again, Benny recorded his "touring pro's" at his studio in Stamford. And as before, two of their renditions will be issued on a compact disc, but not until eight years have elapsed. Take numbers are not shown because the master tapes have not been audited; data are from Benny's files, which are terse. Note that some of the unheard performances may be incomplete, and some may be by combinations other than the full Sextet. Listing is in order-of-performance.

BENNY GOODMAN SEXTET　　　October 11, 1977, Stamford

Benny Goodman, clt; Warren Vache, tpt; John Bunch, p; Cal Collins, g; Mike Moore, b; Connie Kay, d.

-0-	UNISSUED	
	Here's That Rainy Day - 3 takes	
	Cheerful Little Earful - 2 takes	
	I Thought About You - feat. Vache - 1 take	
-0-	**CD:** LON 820 179-2 - Track 7	
	The Girl Friend (only take indicated)	
-0-	**CD:** LON 820 179-2 - Track 4	
	UNISSUED: 3 takes	
	Have You Met Miss Jones?	
-0-	UNISSUED	
	Alone Together - 1 take	
	Runnin' Wild - 1 take	

The "Stamford Six" plus Scott Hamilton and Susan Mellikian performed in the Fine Arts Center of the University of Massachusett's Concert Hall, in Amherst, on October 15. A cassette of the concert is just below the standard set for inclusion herein. On the same day, Milt Raskin died in Sawtelle, California at age 61. Milt, a good pianist and composer and conductor for a number of motion pictures, played briefly for Benny, but is more noted for his work with Tommy Dorsey, Gene Krupa and Artie Shaw.

Earlier in the year Benny had just about decided that he'd do a 40th anniversary reprise of his celebrated 1938 Carnegie Hall concert, and on November 1 he invited the press to a conference in the Rainbow Grill for an unspecified announcement. His plans were revealed in his typical casual manner, but they made international news. WNEW-TV featured an interview with Benny on its late evening news telecast, and captured Benny and John Bunch in an impromptu duet:

NEWS TELECAST　　　November 1, 1977, New York

Benny Goodman, clt; John Bunch, p. (Stewart Klein, interviewer.)

Avalon (brief excerpt)

The television networks also carried brief Goodman endorsements of Geico, a Washington-based insurance company, in the fall and winter of 1977. Each has Benny blow a few notes of "Jersey Bounce" as introduction to his remarks.

In mid-month Benny granted a telephone interview to Miami disc jockey Jack Sohmer, as a promo for a November 27 engagement in the Dade County Auditorium. It is not known if the interview was broadcast (a tape of a portion of it is extant), but the concert was recorded from the audience in acceptable fashion:

MIAMI CONCERT   *November 27, 1977, Miami*

Benny Goodman, clt; Warren Vache, tpt; Buddy Tate, ts; John Bunch, p; Cal Collins, g; Mike Moore, b; Connie Kay, d. Susan Mellikian, voc.

QUINTET: Goodman, Bunch, Collins, Moore, Kay

Avalon - QUINTET
Body And Soul - QUINTET
Runnin' Wild - QUINTET
Send In The Clowns - QUINTET
Oh, Lady Be Good! - QUINTET
(Topsy - Tate w/rhythm - NO BG
I Thought About You - Vache w/rhythm - BG in coda
That's A Plenty
(Gee, Baby, Ain't I Good To You? - voc Susan Mellikian - NO BG
(Am I Blue? - voc Susan Mellikian - NO BG
Medley: Don't Be That Way
*   Stompin' At The Savoy*
Rose Room - QUINTET
China Boy - QUINTET
The Man I Love - QUINTET
Seven Come Eleven
(Come Sunday - Moore w/rhythm - NO BG
Sing, Sing, Sing
Makin' Whoopee
I've Found A New Baby
Good-Bye (theme)

In late November Benny was interviewed by Whitney Balliett of The New Yorker; his resultant article is in the December 26 edition of the magazine. Benny's last engagement in 1977 was a jazz date in Birmingham, Alabama, on December 6, the same day his July 2 Wolf Trap concert was televised by PBS; no recording of the Birmingham performance has come to the author's attention. On December 15 Benny flew to his St. Martin's retreat for some swimming and fishing. He remained there for almost a full month, returned to New York January 13.

In the interim, alto saxophonist Mel Rodnon, acting on Benny's instructions, assembled the 1978 Carnegie Hall orchestra. By the end of December it was determined that Harry James, Teddy Wilson, and Jess Stacy could not participate; only Benny, Lionel Hampton and Martha Tilton from the original cast would be present for the commemorative concert. A tentative inquiry to Buddy Rich drew a favorable response, but Benny eventually decided he'd stick with his regular drummer, Connie Kay. Mary Lou Williams, Jack Sheldon and Jimmy Rowles would appear as featured performers, and a new vocalist, Debi Craig, would be introduced.

Time was short and there was much to do; although Benny was familiar with all of the instrumentalists, they needed to be meshed into a cohesive orchestra, had to become familiar with old and new arrangements alike. Intensive rehearsals were scheduled for three consecutive days in New York's Wellington Hotel; a fourth would take place the afternoon of the concert in Carnegie Hall itself.

The several rehearsals were taped non-professionally by an invited guest. The cassettes offer satisfactory listening, and are detailed below. It should be understood that some of the performances may not be complete, and that miscellaneous instrumental practice occurs between the renditions:

WELLINGTON HOTEL REHEARSAL   *January 14, 1978, New York*

Orchestra as January 17 Carnegie Hall concert. Lionel Hampton joins for some selections, on vibraphone or drums, as noted. Mary Lou Williams replaces Bunch on piano for some selections, as noted. It is uncertain whether both Cal Collins and Wayne Wright are in the rhythm section for the orchestra and small group performances.

OCTET/NONET: Goodman, Sheldon, Andre, Tate, rhythm section (Bunch, Collins and/or Wright, Moore, Kay)
NONET/TENTET: "Octet/Nonet" plus Hampton, vib.

Other small groups identified following tune titles

Roll 'Em - orchestra plus Hampton (vib), ML Williams
(unidentified tune "Sharpie"? - Hampton w/rhythm - NO BG
(unidentified tune - Bunch w/rhythm - NO BG

(No other selections from this rehearsal were recorded.)

WELLINGTON HOTEL REHEARSAL   *January 15, 1978, New York*

Personnels as January 14.

Air Mail Special - orchestra plus Hampton, vib.
Flying Home - orchestra plus Hampton, vib
Moon Glow - Goodman, Hampton (vib), Moore, Kay
Sing, Sing, Sing - orchestra w/Hampton, d, replacing Kay
(Someone To Watch Over Me - p solo - NO BG
Rocky Raccoon - voc Jack Sheldon - Octet/Nonet
The Octupus's Garden - voc Jack Sheldon - Octet/Nonet
Medley: Don't Be That Way
*   Stompin' At The Savoy*
Let's Dance
I've Found A New Baby
Send In The Clowns - Goodman, Bunch, Moore, Kay
Star Dust (arr GJ)
Clarinet A La King
Clarinade
Loch Lomond - voc Martha Tilton (arr Steve Rawitz)
Goody-Goody - voc Martha Tilton (arr Steve Rawitz)
The Dixieland Band - voc Martha Tilton
(The Best Things In Life Are Free - Hampton w/rhythm - NO BG
Moon Glow - Goodman, Hampton (vib), Moore, Kay
That's A Plenty - Nonet/Tentet
'Swonderful - voc Debi Craig - Nonet/Tentet
Someone To Watch Over Me - voc Debi Craig - Nonet/Tentet
Seven Come Eleven - Nonet/Tentet
unidentified tune - Goodman, piano

WELLINGTON HOTEL REHEARSAL   *January 16, 1978, New York*

Personnels as January 14.

unidentified tune - orchestra
Whistle Blues
Good-Bye
Good-Bye
Stompin' At The Savoy
And The Angels Sing
A String Of Pearls
I've Found A New Baby
King Porter Stomp
Stompin' At The Savoy
And The Angels Sing
And The Angels Sing
A String Of Pearls

CARNEGIE HALL REHEARSAL   *January 17, 1978, New York*

Personnels as January 14.

Sing, Sing, Sing - orchestra w/ML Williams, p
Loch Lomond - voc Martha Tilton, Benny Goodman
Goody-Goody - voc Martha Tilton
The Dixieland Band - voc Martha Tilton
I Love A Piano - voc Benny Goodman - w/Rowles, Kay
Jersey Bounce - Goodman, Hampton (vib), rhythm section
('Swonderful - voc Debi Craig w/rhythm section - NO BG
Runnin' Wild - Goodman, Hampton (vib), rhythm section
Stompin' At The Savoy
And The Angels Sing
Why Don't You Do Right?
A String Of Pearls
Sing, Sing, Sing - orchestra w/ML Williams, p
Loch Lomond - voc Martha Tilton, Benny Goodman
Goody-Goody - voc Martha Tilton
The Dixieland Band - voc Martha Tilton
Rocky Raccoon - voc Jack Sheldon—Goodman, rhythm section
(The Octopus's Garden - Sheldon, rhythm section - NO BG
I Love A Piano - voc Benny Goodman - w/Rowles, Kay
Jersey Bounce - Goodman, Hampton (vib), rhythm section
('Swonderful - voc Debi Craig w/rhythm section - NO BG
Someone To Watch Over Me - voc Debi Craig - Goodman, Hampton (vib), rhythm section
Please Don't Talk About Me When I'm Gone - voc Debi Craig - Goodman, Andre, rhythm section
Runnin' Wild - Goodman, Hampton (vib), rhythm section

Now, the concert itself. Lengthily titled, "An Evening With Benny Goodman . . . In celebration of the 40th Anniversary Concert at Carnegie Hall . . . with special friends Lionel Hampton, Mary Lou Williams, Martha Tilton, Jack Shelton (sic)," the program began promptly at 8:00 p.m. on a snowy, sleety, rainy Tuesday evening in Manhattan. The author's liner notes for the London two-LP album that excerpted the concert for public release detail much of the event, but a few further explanations are in order:

London's engineers recorded the concert in its entirety, then devoted the next 36 hours to editing their tapes and selecting the renditions to be included in the album. Simultaneously the author, working at home but in constant telephonic communication with London's executive producer, wrote and rewrote copy for the album as decisions were made, were altered, and finally were confirmed. By Friday morning the contents of the album, music and liner notes, were ready for production.

The London album does not follow the order-of-performance of the concert; the listing below reflects the concert as it was performed. Each selection in the album is identified as to its Side and Track in the type style used throughout this work for authorized studio recordings. Selections not included in the commercial release are shown in the type used for air checks. Because the constituency of the various small groups shifted from one selection to another, their differing personnels are listed in parentheses below each tune title.

Pressing matrices for the London album are ZAL 15603, 15604, 15605 and 15606-RE1 for Sides 1, 2, 3 and 4 respectively. They have no real significance and are omitted from the listing. Subsidiary labels include TELDEC (Telefunken/Decca, continental Europe) and JG (Jazz Gala, another Decca label for continental Europe).

BENNY GOODMAN
Live At Carnegie Hall
40th ANNIVERSARY CONCERT   January 17, 1978, New York

Benny Goodman, clt; Victor Paz, Warren Vache, Jack Sheldon, tpt; Wayne Andre, George Masso, John Messner, tbn; George Young, Mel Rodnon, as; Buddy Tate, Frank Wess, ts & fl; Sol Schlinger, bar; John Bunch, p; Cal Collins, acou g; Wayne Wright, elec g; Mike Moore, b; Connie Kay, d. Martha Tilton, Jack Sheldon, Debi Craig, voc. Mike Abene (MA), Gordon Jenkins (GJ), Steve Rawitz (SR), arr.

StLP: LON 2PS 918/919, TELDEC 6.28451DP. **StCas:** LON 2PS5-918/19, TELDEC 4.28451CT.

Let's Dance (theme) - Side 1, Track 1; also on StLP, JG 383349

Clarinet A La King

Send In The Clowns - QUARTET - Side 1, Track 3; also on StLP, JG 383349
(Goodman, Bunch, Moore, Kay)

Loch Lomond - voc Martha Tilton, Benny Goodman - Side 1, Track 4 (arr SR)

Goody-Goody - voc Martha Tilton (arr SR)
The Dixieland Band - voc Martha Tilton (arr SR)

I've Found A New Baby - Side 1, Track 2; also on StLP, JG 383349

(I've Got It Bad (And That Ain't Good) - Collins w/Moore, Kay - NO BG

I Love A Piano - voc Benny Goodman - SEXTET - Side 1, Track 6
(Goodman, Bunch; Jimmy Rowles, p; Collins, Moore, Kay)

. . . Mary Lou Williams, p, replaces Bunch, remains until "Jersey Bounce"

Roll 'Em - Side 1, Track 7

Intermission.

King Porter Stomp - Side 2, Track 1; also on StLP, JG 383349, LON MIP-1-9311

Rocky Raccoon - voc Jack Sheldon - NONET - Side 2, Track 2
(Goodman, Sheldon, Andre, Williams, Rowles, Collins, Wright, Moore, Kay)

The Octopus's Garden - voc Jack Sheldon - OCTET - (Personnel as "Rocky Raccoon," except omit Rowles)

Yesterday - QUARTET - Side 2, Track 3; also on StLP, JG 383349
(Goodman, Collins, Moore, Kay)

That's A Plenty - OCTET - Side 2, Track 4
(Goodman, Vache, Andre, Tate, Williams, Collins, Moore, Kay)

Star Dust - Side 1, Track 5 (arr GJ)

Clarinade

How High The Moon - SEPTET - Side 2, Track 5; also on StLP, JG 383349, LON MIP-1-9311

Moon Glow - SEPTET - Side 3, Track 1

Oh, Lady Be Good! - SEPTET, orch. in coda - Side 3, Track 2; also on StLP, JG 383349

Seven Come Eleven - SEPTET - Side 3, Track 4; also on StLP, JG 383349
(Goodman; Lionel Hampton, vib; Williams, Collins, Wright, Moore, Kay)

Jersey Bounce - SEPTET - Side 3, Track 3; also on StLP, LON MIP-1-9311
(Goodman, Hampton, Bunch, Collins, Wright, Moore, Kay)

('Swonderful - voc Debi Craig, w/Williams, Collins, Moore, Kay - NO BG

(Someone To Watch Over Me - voc Debi Craig, w/Williams, Collins, Moore, Kay - Side 4, Track 1 - NO BG

Please Don't Talk About Me When I'm Gone - voc Debi Craig - SEPTET - Side 1, Track 2; also on StLP, LON MIP-1-9311
(Goodman, Andre, Hampton, Williams, Collins, Moore, Kay)

. . . Lionel Hampton, vib, joins the orchestra and Mary Lou Williams, p, remains, both for the balance of the concert.

Medley: **Don't Be That Way**   )
      Stompin' At The Savoy)
      And The Angles Sing   ) - Side 4, Track 3 (arr MA)
      Why Don't You Do Right)
      A String Of Pearls   )

(The first three tunes are also on StLP, JG 383349: "Don't Be That Way," and possibly the entire medley, is also on StLP, LON MIP-1-9311.)

Sing, Sing, Sing - Part 1 & 2 - Side 4, Track 4; also on StLP, JG 383349

Good-Bye (in its entirety) - Side 4, Track 5 (arr GJ)

In general, critical review of the concert was unfavorable; comments ranged from "ragged" and "peculiar" to "a disaster." The author's one-word description would be, "uneven," for there were some highlights as well as too many indifferent performances. He found Jack Sheldon's humor and two vocal contributions entirely out of keeping with the event, a view shared by many of the critics. Up to the intermission, the pace of the program was good, and held the audience's attention; following it there were interminable voids between selections, and the audience began to leave long before the end of the concert. The full orchestra seemed never to get fully warmed up, perhaps because it never played, say, a half-dozen instrumentals in a row, but was interrupted by small group and vocal selections. He would much have preferred more of Bunch and/or Rowles and less of Mary Lou, who seemed unfamiliar with some of the compositions she was asked to play; and would have welcomed more of Martha and less of Debi Craig. And his continuing opinion is that Connie Kay is basically a small-group drummer, uncomfortable in a big band role.

But, as ever, Benny and Lionel both played well, and on occasion Vache, Tate and a few others were effective. Too, Gordon Jenkins's new arrangement of "Star Dust" is on record, and that lovely interpretation is almost worth the price of the London album. The author's recommendation is to treat the album selectively—tape those tracks that appeal, skip those that do not, listen only to the excerpts. In that mode, the concert isn't all bad.

Various of the Nation's television networks and independent stations showed brief bits of the rehearsal and concert at Carnegie Hall, and collectors have audio tapes of some of those telecasts.

Benny was playing in Youngstown, Ohio, Saturday, February 4, when tragedy struck; suddenly, wholly unexpectedly, his wife Alice died at their home in St. Martin's. Her body was returned to the United States, and private services were held Thursday, February 9, at St. Francis Church in North Stamford, Connecticut. She was survived by Benny; her daughters from her first marriage, Gillian Hunt, Shirley Deeter, and Sophia Schacnter; their daughters, Rachel Edelson and Benjie Lasseau; her brother John Hammond, and her sisters Emily Franklin, Adele Emery and Rachel Breck; and seven grandchildren. A gracious lady, a good wife, Alice H. Goodman, dead at age 72.

Benny was booked for a jazz date in the Hyatt House, Cherry Hill, New Jersey, the day after Alice's cremation. There was every reason to cancel, but the performance was a benefit for the West Jersey Hospital. What to do? Benny decided that Alice would have preferred that he appear at the charity affair, so he kept the date. On Sunday, February 12, he was also scheduled for a benefit performance for Hymie Schertzer at the Rainbow Room in Rockefeller Center. For much the same reason, he appeared there, too.

Life goes on; Benny's next engagement was in San Diego's Golden Hall as guest soloist with the San Diego Symphony Orchestra. An audience recording is extant from the concert:

SAN DIEGO CONCERT   *February 21, 1978, San Diego*

Benny Goodman, clt, and the San Diego Symphony Orchestra, Charles Ketcham conducting. Medley arrangement, Peter Knight.

Concerto For Clarinet And Strings No. 1 (Arnold)
Medley: Let's Dance
        Here's That Rainy Day
        i've Got You Under My Skin
        Send In The Clowns
        Honeysuckle Rose
        Good-Bye
        Honeysuckle Rose (encore)

With tpt, tbn, vib, p, b and d from the orchestra:

Sweet Georgia Brown

We've no tapes from Benny's dates in Detroit, March 3–5, and St. Louis, March 11. But there are two from March 16: at noon, he appeared on the "Mitzi Gaynor Show," then at 5:00 p.m. he videotaped the "Merv Griffin Show." (While still in St. Louis, Benny was interviewed by Jack Carney on March 12; excerpts were broadcast via KMOX Radio on May 23, 1979.)

"THE MITZI GAYNOR SHOW"   *March 16, 1978, Hollywood*
   CBS Television Network

Initially televised April 6. Benny Goodman, clt; Jack Sheldon, tpt; Carl Fontana, tbn; Buddy Tate, ts; John Bunch, p; John Pisano, g; Chuck Berghofer, b; Connie Kay, d.

. . . novelty tune - "I'm Hip"? - voc Mitzi Gaynor, Benny Goodman
That's A Plenty

"THE MERV GRIFFIN SHOW"   *March 16, 1978, Hollywood*
   METROMEDIA Television Network

Televised on Metromedia and independent television stations on various dates in March. Benny Goodman, clt; Jack Sheldon, tpt; Buddy Tate, ts; John Bunch, p; Mundell Lowe, g; Monty Budwig, b; Connie Kay, d.

QUINTET: Goodman, Bunch, Lowe, Budwig, Kay

How High The Moon
Yesterday - voc Merv Griffin - QUINTET

The author knows of no audience recordings from Benny's concerts in Houston, March 25, Baltimore, April 8, or Dayton, Ohio, April 16. His next is from the Orpheum Theater in Omaha, Nebraska:

OMAHA CONCERT   *April 29, 1978, Omaha*

Benny Goodman, clt; Warren Vache, tpt; Wayne Andre, tbn; John Bunch, p; Cal Collins, g; Major Holley, b; Connie Kay, d. Debi Craig, voc.

TRIO: Goodman, Bunch, Kay
QUINTET: Trio plus Collins, Holley

Runnin' Wild - QUINTET
Yesterday - TRIO
Oh, Lady Be Good! - QUINTET
(You've Changed - Andre w/rhythm - NO BG
(Tangerine - Vache w/rhythm - NO BG
That's A Plenty
Please Don't Talk About Me When I'm Gone - voc Debi Craig
Get Out And Get Under The Moon - voc Debi Craig
Ridin' High - voc Debi Craig - QUINTET
(I Got It Bad (And That Ain't Good) - Collins w/rhythm - NO BG
Medley: Don't Be That Way
        Stompin' At The Savoy
(. . . unidentified tune - Holley w/rhythm - NO BG
Send In The Clowns - TRIO
Seven Come Eleven
Sing, Sing, Sing
Good-Bye (theme)

The author has no cassettes from Benny's engagements in Madison, Wisconsin, May 6, or Minneapolis, Minnesota, May 14. Two days' later Benny was in Philadelphia's KYW-Westinghouse studios:

"THE MIKE DOUGLAS SHOW"   *May 16, 1978, Philadelphia*
   WESTINGHOUSE Television Network

Televised via Westinghouse and independent stations on various dates in June.

Benny Goodman, clt; Mary Lou Williams, p; Cal Collins, g; Major Holley, b; Connie Kay, d.

Runnin' Wild
Ain't Misbehavin'

Benny's birthday, May 30, found him in Washington's National Art Gallery, playing a private party for the Mellon family. On June 9 he appeared with the Milwaukee Symphony; there are no known recordings of either performance. Next was a private dinner-dance to introduce the new president of the Magnavox electronics company to its franchised dealers. Given in the Hyatt House, the recital was videotaped for promotional purposes:

MAGNAVOX PROMOTION   *June 12, 1978, Chicago*

Benny Goodman, clt; Buddy Tate, ts; John Bunch, p; Cal Collins, g; Major Holley, b; Connie Kay, d.

TRIO: Goodman, Bunch, Kay
QUINTET: Trio plus Collins, Holley

Runnin' Wild - QUINTET
Send In The Clowns - TRIO
All Of Me - Tate w/rhythm - BG in coda
(I Got It Bad (And That Ain't Good) - Collins w/rhythm - NO BG
Ain't Misbehavin'
Medley: Don't Be That Way
        Stompin' At The Savoy
Sing, Sing, Sing
Air Mail Special

Off to California for a concert in the Terrace Theater in Long Beach, and a date with Johnny Carson:

LONG BEACH CONCERT   *June 18, 1978, Long Beach*

Benny Goodman, clt; Jack Sheldon, tpt; Wayne Andre, tbn; Buddy Tate, ts; John Bunch, p; Cal Collins, g; Major Holley, b; Connie Kay, d.

TRIO: Goodman, Bunch, Kay
QUINTET: Trio plus Collins, Holley

Oh, Lady Be Good! - QUINTET
You Must Meet My Wife - TRIO
Ain't Misbehavin' - QUINTET
(Star Dust - Andre w/rhythm - NO BG
(All Of Me - Tate w/rhythm - NO BG
Medley: Don't Be That Way
        Stompin' At The Savoy
(I Thought About You - Bunch p solo - NO BG
Send In The Clowns - TRIO
That's A Plenty
Sing, Sing, Sing
Good-Bye (theme)

"THE TONIGHT SHOW"   *June 22, 1978, Burbank*
   NBC Television Network

Benny Goodman, clt; John Bunch, p; Cal Collins, g; Major Holley, b; Connie Kay, d.

Oh, Lady Be Good!
Send In The Clowns

While on the West Coast, Benny made his first "direct-to-disc" recording for a new label, Century. Unfortunately, it was an uninspired performance for sale at a premium price:

BENNY GOODMAN   **June 24, 1978, Hollywood**
  "THE KING"

Benny Goodman, clt; Jack Sheldon, tpt; Wayne Andre, tbn; Buddy Tate, ts;
John Bunch, p; Cal Collins, g; Major Holley, b; Connie Kay, d.

QUINTET: Goodman, Bunch, Collins, Holley, Kay

CRDD1150-F1A **StLP:** CENTURY CRDD-1150 - Side A, PADDLE WHEEL
                (Jap) GP3606
              Lady Be Good (sic) - QUINTET
              Here's That Rainy Day - QUINTET
              Makin' Whoopee
              I've Got It Bad - QUINTET

CRDD1150-F1B **StLP:** as preceding, except Side B
              Ain't Misbehavin
              (All Of Me - Tate w/rhythm - NO BG
              (Darn That Dream - Andre w/rhythm - NO BG
              Alone Together - QUINTET
              Limehouse Blues

Benny appeared in Atlantic City, New Jersey, June 29—no known
recording from there—then at Ravinia:

RAVINIA CONCERT   *July 3, 1978, Highland Park, Ill.*

Benny Goodman, clt; Warren Vache, tpt; Wayne Andre, tbn; Buddy Tate, ts;
John Bunch, p; Cal Collins, g; Major Holley, b; Connie Kay, d.

TRIO: Goodman, Bunch, Kay
QUINTET: Trio plus Collins, Holley

Chicago - QUINTET
Send In The Clowns - TRIO
I Know That You Know - QUINTET
(Star Dust - Andre w/rhythm - NO BG
(Tangerine - Tate w/rhythm - NO BG
That's A Plenty
Medley: Don't Be That Way
        Stompin' At The Savoy
Body And Soul - QUINTET
Makin' Whoopee
Sing, Sing, Sing
Ain't Misbehavin'
Good-Bye (theme)

Benny's library includes an undated cassette simply identified as,
"Medley No. 2." Seemingly recorded professionally because of its excellent audio quality, the cassette offers Benny and an unidentified symphony
orchestra playing the Peter Knight arrangement that he had performed in San
Diego on February 21 of this year. (Benny refers to the other Knight medley
in his repertoire—see July 4, 1972, New York, and May 9, 1974, Boston—
as, "Medley No. 1.") Although there is no supporting documentation, the
author believes the cassette is from Benny's guest appearance with the
Atlanta Symphony:

"MEDLEY NO. 2"   *poss. July 13, 1978, Atlanta*

Benny Goodman, clt, and the Atlanta Symphony Orchestra.

Medley: Let's Dance
        Here's That Rainy Day
        I've Got You Under My Skin
        Send In The Clowns
        Honeysuckle Rose
        Good-Bye

Save for a poorly-recorded cassette from the Temple Music Festival on
August 1, and an October appearance on the "Merv Griffin Show," we've
no more Benny Goodman tapes for 1978. Following the Temple concert,
Benny took six weeks off, played once in September (the State University at
Potsdam, New York, the 14th), then laid off until a California trip in mid-
October: Marin College, the 16th; in San Jose, the 19th; in Claremont, the
21st; and in Tempe, Arizona, the 23rd. Governor Brown and the state senate
awarded Benny the first "California Jazz Award" in Sacramento during
the trip.

Can't let August go by without noting the passing of Joe Venuti, who
died on the 14th in Seattle, Washington, after a lengthy illness. He was one
of a kind, a jazz violinist and practical joker extraordinaire, who'd recorded
with Benny almost fifty years apart.

Another memory from the past echoed in October, when Benny's
Quintet appeared on the "Merv Griffin Show." Site of the program was the
Ed Sullivan Theater, in the 30's the location of Billy Rose's Music Hall:

"THE MERV GRIFFIN SHOW"   *October 26, 1978, New York*
  METROMEDIA Television Network

Televised November 16 and other dates in November by independent televi-
sion stations.

Benny Goodman, clt; John Bunch, p; Cal Collins, g; Major Holley, b; Connie
Kay, d.

The World Is Waiting For The Sunrise
I Love A Piano - voc Benny Goodman

Seven engagements in November have produced no known Goodman
audience recordings: New York Hilton, November 1; New York's Century
Club, the 2nd; New Orleans, the 7th; Spartanburg, South Carolina, the 8th;
Atlantic City, the 11th; Philadelphia's Academy of Music, the 19th; and
Elmira, New York, the 25th. On the 15th of November Benny received an
award from New York's Third Street Music Settlement for his efforts in
behalf of young musicians.

Benny appeared with the Bridgeport, Connecticut Symphony Orchestra
on December 2; at Palm Beach, Florida's, Hotel Poinciana on December 4;
at a private party for a drug company in Nutley, New Jersey on December 7;
and at the World Trade Center, Manhattan on the 15th. No cassettes from
these concerts are known to the author.

Nor are there any known tapes from Benny's first three performances in
1979: in Deland, Florida on January 13; at Charlotte, North Carolina on
January 27; and at Sun City, Arizona, on February 4. On various dates in
January, the Public Broadcasting System televised a videotape of Benny's
remarks about tenant-landlord relationships on its "Consumer Survival Kit"
series.

There is an audience recording of Benny's next engagement, Kennedy
Center in Washington, March 5, but its poor quality eliminates it from
detailing herein; concert was sponsored by an insurance company for which
Benny did some commercials. On March 8 Benny appeared on ABC-TV's
"Good Morning, America," conversed with host David Hartman. (Hartman
is a jazz buff and Goodman enthusiast, is regularly seen at Benny's concerts
in New York.) Three succeeding engagements with his Sextet offer no
known tapes: Vancouver, British Columbia, March 14; Seattle, Washington,
March 16; and Portland, Oregon, March 18. The unsatisfactory audio quality of an audience recording of a benefit for the Skowhegan School in Carnegie Hall on March 24 precludes its inclusion in this work. Too bad, for it
offers Benny's initial work with violinist Stephan Grappelli.

The Sextet was at New York's City Center on April 2, but we've no
recording of the concert. Nor is there one of Benny's appearance with the
Youngstown Symphony in Ohio on April 21. On April 29 he was honored at
Quinnipiac College, Hamden, Connecticut; CBS-TV videotaped a portion of
the banquet for its projected celebration of Benny's 70th birthday, but
eventually decided not to use this segment. An audience recording of Benny's remarks is extant.

CBS-TV also videotaped Benny at his New York apartment on April
30, and at his next engagement, in Greensboro, North Carolina on May 3.
Brief excerpts of both appeared on its late evening newscast on May 30.

Combined jazz-classical concerts in New Castle, Pennsylvania, May 9;
Decatur, Illinois, May 13; and Columbus, Ohio, May 19, afford no known
cassettes. Our next tape is from a private party celebrating Benny's 70th
birthday, given by his good friend John Fleming, an antique book collector
and dealer, in his spacious 57th Street apartment. Benny joined the group
while it was playing the first tune, remained for two more, then signaled Bill
Hyland to take over, for Benny wanted to dance:

BENNY GOODMAN'S 70th BIRTHDAY PARTY   *May 30, 1979, New York*

Benny Goodman, clt; Warren Vache, tpt; John Bunch, p; Gene Bertoncini, g;
Ron Davis, d.

Darn That Dream
Sweet Georgia Brown
If I Had You

Bill Hyland, clt, replaces Goodman

(Medley: Out Of Nowhere
        Here's That Rainy Day
        But Not For Me
        You Turned The Tables On Me
        Alexander's Ragtime Band

The Best Things In Life Are Free
On The Alamo
Don't Get Around Much Any More

Earlier in the year, a casual conversation the author had with PeeWee Erwin elicited PeeWee's puzzlement over Benny's failure to hire him for some of the small group performances. Apprised of PeeWee's complaint, Benny promptly engaged him, and PeeWee was in some of the concerts for which we have no tapes, including the next, in Ames, Iowa, on June 1. He is present for the "First Annual Playboy Jazz Festival" in the Hollywood Bowl. "Highlights" of the Festival were broadcast in stereo by the National Public Radio network, announced by Billy Taylor and MC'd by comedian Bill Cosby:

"FIRST ANNUAL PLAYBOY   *June 15, 1979, Hollywood*
   JAZZ FESTIVAL"

Broadcast on affiliated National Public Radio stations on various dates throughout 1979.

Benny Goodman, clt; PeeWee Erwin, tpt; Mickey Gravine, tbn; Bill Ramsay, ts; John Bunch, p; John Pisano, g; Mike Moore, b; Frank Capp, d.

DUET: Goodman, Bunch
QUARTET: Duet plus Moore, Capp
QUINTET: Quartet plus Pisano

Air Mail Special
Medley: Don't Be That Way
      Stompin' At The Savoy
Here's That Rainy Day - QUARTET
The World Is Waiting For The Sunrise - QUINTET
(Someday You'll Be Sorry - Erwin w/rhythm - NO BG
That's A Plenty
Seven Come Eleven
Send In The Clowns - DUET
Sing, Sing, Sing

Back in New York, Benny was interviewed by Bob Sherman (Nadia Reisenberg's son) on June 20; the interview, and a tape of Goodman classical material from the author's private collection, were broadcast on radio station WQXR's "Great Artists" program on June 24. On June 21, WOR Radio's Kathy Novak interviewed Benny about the upcoming Newport Jazz Festival before the music begins:

"LIVE FROM GRACIE MANSION"   *June 22, 1979, New York*
   WNYC-AM/FM Radio

Benny Goodman, clt; Roland Hanna, p; Bucky Pizzarelli, g; Mike Moore, b; Ron Davis, d.

Oh, Lady Be Good!
Memories Of You
The World Is Waiting For The Sunrise
Honeysuckle Rose
If I Had You
I've Found A New Baby
(I Got It Bad (And That Ain't Good) - Moore w/p accomp - NO BG

Benny Goodman Quintet plus Tri-State McDonald High School Jazz Ensemble

Don't Be That Way

Benny's contribution to the Festival was in Carnegie Hall, and for a change there is a satisfactory audience recording from that auditorium:

NEWPORT JAZZ FESTIVAL   *June 24, 1979, New York*

Benny Goodman, clt; Warren Vache, tpt; Wayne Andre, tbn; Buddy Tate, ts; Roland Hanna, p; Bucky Pizzarelli, g; Slam Stewart, b; Ron Davis, d.,

QUINTET: Goodman, Hanna, Pizzarelli, Stewart, Davis

I Know That You Know - QUINTET
As Long As I Live - QUINTET
The World Is Waiting For The Sunrise - QUINTET
It's Easy To Remember - QUINTET
(The One I Love Belongs To Somebody Else - Vache w/rhythm - NO BG
(More Than You Know - Hanna p solo - NO BG
That's A Plenty
(Star Dust - Andre w/rhythm - NO BG
Indiana
(Gotta Be This Or That - Stewart w/rhythm - NO BG

Body And Soul - QUINTET
(All Of Me - Tate w/rhythm - NO BG
Air Mail Special
Medley: Don't Be That Way
      Stompin' At The Savoy
Sing, Sing, Sing
Good-Bye (theme)

Our next audience recording is from a month hence; tapes of Sextet performances in Interlochen, Michigan on July 12 and Denton, Texas on July 21 have not been located. The engagement might be termed the "Candlelight Concert"—Ravinia's lighting system failed, and Benny played with the aid of candles:

RAVINIA CONCERT   *July 24, 1979, Highland Park, Ill.*

Benny Goodman, clt; Warren Vache, tpt; Jack Gail, tbn; Al Klink, ts; John Bunch, p; Gene Bertoncini, g; Slam Stewart, b; Ron Davis, d.

DUET: Goodman, Bunch
QUINTET: Duet plus Bertoncini, Stewart, Davis

Oh, Lady Be Good! - QUINTET
Chicago - QUINTET
Send In The Clowns - DUET
The World Is Waiting For The Sunrise - QUINTET
Medley: Don't Be That Way
      Stompin' At The Savoy
(My Funny Valentine - Vache w/rhythm - NO BG
That's A Plenty
(The Lady's In Love With You - Klink w/rhythm - NO BG
(I Got Rhythm - Stewart w/rhythm - NO BG
Avalon - QUINTET
Rose Room, incorporating contra-melody, In A Mellotone
Sing, Sing, Sing, (n/c)
Good-Bye (theme)

(The encore, "Undecided," was not recorded.)

MEADOW BROOK CONCERT   *July 27, 1979, Rochester, Michigan*

Personnels as July 24, plus Polly Podewell, voc.

Let's Dance (theme)

(Group sans Goodman plays until intermission; Goodman returns.)

Oh, Lady Be Good! - QUINTET
Here's That Rainy Day - DUET
Avalon - QUINTET
The World Is Waiting For The Sunrise - QUINTET
(My Funny Valentine - Vache w/rhythm - NO BG
(The Lady's In Love With You - Klink w/rhythm - NO BG
That's A Plenty
(But Beautiful - Bertoncini solo - NO BG
Between The Devil And The Deep Blue Sea - voc Polly Podewell - QUINTET
(I've Got A Crush On You - voc Polly Podewell w/rhythm - NO BG
There'll Be Some Changes Made - voc Polly Podewell - QUINTET
Send In The Clowns - DUET
Medley: Don't Be That Way
      Stompin' At The Savoy
(Play, Fiddle, Play - Stewart w/rhythm - NO BG
As Long As I Live - QUINTET
After You've Gone - QUINTET
If I Had You - QUINTET
Sing, Sing, Sing (n/c - mid-tune elision)
One O'Clock Jump
Air Mail Special
Good-Bye (theme)

Benny took some time off, played only two dates in August. Satisfactory audience recordings are available from both:

294

TEMPLE MUSIC FESTIVAL   *August 14, 1979, Ambler, Pa.*

Benny Goodman, clt; PeeWee Erwin, tpt; Wayne Andre, tbn; Al Klink, ts; John Bunch, p; Gene Bertoncini, g; Mike Moore, b; Ron Davis, d.

QUINTET: Goodman, Bunch, Bertoncini, Moore, Davis

Let's Dance (theme)
Oh, Lady Be Good! - QUINTET
It's Easy To Remember - QUINTET
Avalon - QUINTET
The World Is Waiting For The Sunrise - QUINTET
(Star Dust - Andre w/rhythm - NO BG
(The Lady's In Love With You - Klink w/rhythm - NO BG
(A Handful Of Stars - Klink w/rhythm - NO BG
That's A Plenty
(Someday, You'll Be Sorry - Erwin w/rhythm - NO BG
Medley: Don't Be That Way
*   Stompin' At The Savoy*
(I Got It Bad (And That Ain't Good) - Moore solo - NO BG
Air Mail Special
Sing, Sing, Sing
Good-Bye (theme)
Sweet Georgia Brown (encore)

WATERLOO VILLAGE CONCERT   *August 18, 1979, Stanhope, N.J.*

Benny Goodman, clt; Warren Vache, tpt; Jack Gail, tbn; Zoot Sims, ts; Jimmy Rowles, p; Gene Bertoncini, g; Mike Moore, b; Ron Davis, d.

QUINTET: Goodman, Rowles, Bertoncini, Moore, Davis
SEXTET: Quintet plus Bill Hyland, clt

Let's Dance (theme)
Undecided
Oh, Lady Be Good! - QUINTET
Lazy River - QUINTET
Avalon - QUINTET
The World Is Waiting For The Sunrise - QUINTET
(My Funny Valentine - Vache w/rhythm - NO BG
(In The Shadows - Sims w/rhythm - NO BG
That's A Plenty
Medley: Don't Be That Way
*   Stompin' At The Savoy*

Bill Hyland, clt, substitutes for Benny in the Quintet:

(Do You Know What It Means To Miss New Orleans?

Benny returns, Hyland remains

Sweet Georgia Brown - full group plus Hyland
The Man I Love - SEXTET

Hyland leaves.

Air Mail Special
Sing, Sing, Sing
Good-Bye (theme)

A hasty booking brought Benny in to spark the First Annual Chicago Jazz Festival in the Petrillo Bandshell at Grant Park, September 2. His home town got an unexpected bonus: Benny donated his $10,000 fee, half to Hull House and half to the Jazz Archives library of the University of Chicago. In addition to performing with his own Quintet, Benny led a big band comprised mainly of Chicago-local musicians. That called for a rehearsal; both it and the concert were taped satisfactorily from the audience:

CHICAGO JAZZ FESTIVAL REHEARSAL   *September 2, 1979, Chicago*

Benny Goodman, clt; John Bunch, p; Gene Bertoncini, g; Mike Moore, b; Connie Kay, d. Polly Podewell, voc.

Alone Together - QUINTET
Between The Devil And The Deep Blue Sea - voc Polly Podewell - QUINTET
(I've Got A Crush On You - voc Polly Podewell w/rhythm - NO BG
There'll Be Some Changes Made - voc Polly Podewell - QUINTET

Benny Goodman, clt; Danny Barber, Ron Friedman, Art Hoyle, Bobby Lewis, tpt; Bill Porter, Rich Mays, Harold Keen, tbn; Ed Peterson, Ed DuMensis, Len Drews, B. Keen, reeds; John Bunch, p; Gene Bertoncini, g; Kelly Sills, b; Connie Kay, d.

Let's Dance (theme)

Guest Mel Torme, d, replaces Kay.

Sing, Sing, Sing

(As with all rehearsals, some of the tunes are repeated, some are incomplete, and miscellaneous practice occurs between renditions.)

FIRST ANNUAL CHICAGO JAZZ FESTIVAL   *September 2, 1979, Chicago*

Personnels as rehearsal, same date.

DUET: Goodman, Bunch.
SEXTET: Quintet plus Lewis.

Let's Dance (theme)
Avalon - QUINTET
Send In The Clowns - DUET
Medley: Don't Be That Way   ) - QUINTET
*   Stompin' At The Savoy)*
Between The Devil And The Deep Blue Sea - voc Polly Podewell - QUINTET
(I've Got A Crush On You - voc Polly Podewell w/rhythm - NO BG
There'll Be Some Changes Made - voc Polly Podewell - QUINTET
Poor Butterfly - QUINTET
After You've Gone - SEXTET
The World Is Waiting For The Sunrise - QUINTET

Guest Mel Torme replaces Kay.

Sing, Sing, Sing

Kay returns.

Good-Bye (theme)

(Various announcements and an award to Benny precede "Sing, Sing, Sing.")

The only other known Goodman engagement in September is a concert at Vanderbilt University, from which an uneven audience recording is extant:

VANDERBILT CONCERT   *September 29, 1979, Nashville, Tenn.*

Benny Goodman, clt; Warren Vache, tpt; Wayne Andre, tbn; Al Klink, ts; John Bunch, p; Gene Bertoncini, g; Slam Stewart, b; Jimmy Cobb, d. Polly Podewell, voc.

DUET: Goodman, Bunch
QUINTET: Duet plus Bertoncini, Stewart, Cobb

Oh, Lady Be Good! - QUINTET
Send In The Clowns - DUET
Avalon - QUINTET
The World Is Waiting For The Sunrise - QUINTET
(It Had To Be You - Vache w/rhythm - NO BG
(The Lady's In Love With You - Klink w/rhythm - NO BG
(Star Dust - Andre w/rhythm - NO BG
Medley: Don't Be That Way
*   Stompin' At The Savoy*
Goody-Goody - voc Polly Podewell - QUINTET, full group in coda
(More Than You Know - voc Polly Podewell w/rhythm - NO BG
There'll Be Some Changes Made - voc Polly Podewell
(Play, Fiddle, Play - Stewart w/rhythm - NO BG
That's A Plenty
Sing, Sing, Sing (n/c - mid-tune elision)
Honeysuckle Rose
Good Bye (theme)

(The concert's initial tune in which Goodman participated, "Undecided," was not recorded.)

Benny appeared as soloist with the Springfield, Missouri Symphony Orchestra on October 14. The next day he was back in New York for a television date with Merv Griffin, whose other guest was Buddy Rich, then a resident of Manhattan. Buddy's support on three Quintet selections is outstanding:

"THE MERV GRIFFIN SHOW"   October 15, 1979, New York
  METROMEDIA Television Network

Televised on various dates in November by Metromedia and independent television stations.

Benny Goodman, clt, and a studio orchestra.

Let's Dance (theme)

Benny Goodman, clt; Jimmy Rowles, p; Bucky Pizzarelli, g; Jack Six, b; Buddy Rich, d.

Limehouse Blues
As Long As I Live
I Got Rhythm

Benny had three classical/jazz dates in California, went west by himself, engaged Hollywood studio men for the pop portions of his concerts: October 19, Oakland; October 21, Pasadena; and October 23, Redlands. A minimally satisfactory audience recording from the Pasadena performance in the Ambassador Auditorium is detailed because it presents some different sidemen:

PASADENA CONCERT   October 21, 1979, Pasadena

Benny Goodman, clt; Chuck Findley, tpt; Dick Nash, tbn; Pete Christlieb, ts; Lou Levy, p; John Pisano, g; Monty Budwig, b; Frank Capp, d.

QUINTET: Goodman, Levy, Pisano, Budwig, Capp

Let's Dance (theme)
Undecided

(Goodman leaves, balance of group plays until intermission.)

Goodman returns.

Oh, Lady Be Good! - QUINTET
Here's That Rainy Day - QUINTET
I've Found A New Baby - QUINTET
Body And Soul - QUINTET
The World Is Waiting For The Sunrise - QUINTET
(The Shadow Of Your Smile - Nash w/rhythm - NO BG
(Love For Sale - Christlieb w/rhythm - NO BG
That's A Plenty
(Levy p solo not recorded)
Medley: Don't Be That Way
      Stompin' At The Savoy
(Three Little Words - Findley w/rhythm - NO BG
Poor Butterfly - QUINTET
Air Mail Special
Sing, Sing, Sing
Good-Bye (theme)

Benny's guest appearance with the Huntsville, Alabama Symphony Orchestra on October 27 affords no known recording; our next is his early-morning date with Gene Shalit on NBC-TV's "The Today Show." It was the beginning of a long day for Benny, ending with a press party at the Rainbow Grill to introduce a handsome new pictorial book depicting his life, "Benny - King of Swing," William Morrow & Company, New York, 1979. First, the television program:

"THE TODAY SHOW"   October 30, 1979, New York
  NBC Television Network

Benny Goodman, clt; Jimmy Rowles, p; Bucky Pizzarelli, g; Mike Moore, b; Grady Tate, d.

Alone Together
Bewitched
I Know That You Know
Good-Bye (theme) - to signoff

Family, friends, representatives of the publisher and the press, possibly one hundred in all, gathered atop Rockefeller Center to help Benny introduce the cocktail table-type photo album that evening. Initially contemplated some 10 years' earlier as a biography, and first commissioned by a different publisher, the book had languished because Benny was dissatisfied with outline scripts produced by several authors. Finally Stanley Baron, a native Philadelphian who now lives most of the year in London, and who represents the Thames and Hudson, Ltd., publishing company, persuaded Benny that a photo format would have the most appeal. With the aid of Benny's secretary,

Muriel Zuckerman, the files were searched for unusual photographs, and an appeal to the public brought in many more. Assisted by the author of this work, Baron then wrote and rewrote an accompanying manuscript to the photographs.

Reviews of the book were in general unfavorable, and its sales have been disappointing. A main criticism was that it offered little new information; for the knowledgeable Goodman enthusiast, that complaint is valid. And probably inevitable: it is very difficult to unearth fresh revelations about a man who is so much in the public eye, whose every performance is detailed by the media, who is interviewed again and again on every possible occasion—and who at heart is a very private person who rarely discloses his personal thinking. Woe betide the interviewer who asks a stale or inane question; "the Ray" is as devastating as ever. Benny Goodman does not suffer incompetents gladly.

An arms-length assessment of "Benny - King Of Swing" is that the photographs are excellent, the script accurate and literate. Between them they provide a panorama of a crowded life in one volume, no mean accomplishment. Given that the book's original $25 price tag is now heavily discounted, it's a worthwhile purchase.

Benny Goodman simply cannot attend a party and not play; he's done so all his life. Thus the Quintet was present for the book's introduction, and a privately-recorded cassette offers its program:

MORROW PRESS PARTY   October 30, 1979, New York

Benny Goodman, clt; John Bunch, p; Bucky Pizzarelli, g; Mike Moore, b; Ron Davis, d. Helen Ward, Polly Podewell, voc.

QUARTET: Quintet sans d.

Alone Together
Bewitched - QUARTET
I Know That You Know
You Turned The Tables On Me - voc Helen Ward
Between The Devil And The Deep Blue Sea - voc Polly Podewell
There'll Be Some Changes Made - voc Polly Podewell
Ain't Misbehavin'

Goodman plays the first two clarinet soli on the next tune; he then leaves to dance, is replaced by Bill Hyland, clt.

Just One Of Those Things

Hyland replaces Goodman.

(Memories Of You
(Gone With The Wind

"THE DICK CAVETT SHOW"   November 1, 1979, New York
  PBS Television Network

Televised December 28 and on other dates in December on various PBS television stations.

Benny Goodman, clt; Hank Jones, p; Mike Moore, b; Frederick Waits, d.

Nice Work If You Can Get It
I Didn't Know What Time It Was
Three Little Words

Benny Goodman, clt; Harriet Wingren, p.

First Rhapsody For Clarinet (Debussy) (excerpt)

Guest solo appearances with the Northeastern Pennsylvania Philharmonic Orchestra on November 3 and 4 in Scranton and Wilkes-Barre did not produce any known tapes. On November 10 ABC-TV videotaped portions of a jazz concert in Troy, New York, and later televised very brief segments on its "20/20" program. Benny's 15-minute share of the telecast also offers film clips of "Hollywood Hotel," newsreel coverage of the 1938 Carnegie Hall concert, film clips of various big bands, a portion of a kinescope of the "Perry Como Show" of March 23, 1957, comment by Mel Powell and others, a concert appearance of Tex Beneke leading the Glenn Miller orchestra, and miscellaneous tidbits. Approximately seven minutes into the program, the Troy excerpts surface:

"20/20"   *November 10, 1979, Troy, N.Y.*
  ABC Television Network

Televised January 3, 1980.

Fascinating Rhythm - Goodman clt solo

Benny Goodman, clt; Glen Zottola, tpt; Wayne Andre, tbn; Al Klink, ts; John Bunch, p; Jack Wilkins, g; Arvell Shaw, b; Bobby Rosengarden, d.

Sing, Sing, Sing (excerpt)

Additionally for the Troy concert, there is extant a collector-held copy of the master ABC videotape, from which the brief excerpt on "20/20" was extracted. Since ABC's obvious intent was to videotape only representative samples of the concert for its purposes, few of the renditions are complete, and the tape has abrupt starts and stops. Its first 15 minutes record an interview given the afternoon of the concert. There follows 34 minutes' worth of the evening performance:

ABC VIDEOTAPE, TROY CONCERT   *November 10, 1979, Troy, N.Y.*

Octet as "20/20," preceding.

QUINTET: Goodman, Bunch, Wilkins, Shaw, Rosengarden

Afternoon: Interview, plus illustrative clarinet soli: Fascinating Rhythm; Sing, Sing, Sing

Concert:

I Know That You Know - QUINTET (n/c)
Fascinating Rhythm - QUINTET (n/c)
I Didn't Know What Time It Was - QUINTET (n/c)
Nice Work If You Can Get It - QUINTET (n/c)
Air Mail Special (n/c)
I've Found A New Baby
Sing, Sing, Sing
Good-Bye (theme)

A combined classical-jazz concert, with the National Arts Orchestra and an Octet, in Ottawa, Canada on November 17 does not afford any recording known to the author. A week later an appearance in the Macky Auditorium of the University of Colorado was taped professionally:

BOULDER CONCERT   *November 24, 1979, Boulder*

Benny Goodman, clt; Bill Barry, tpt; Herbie Harper, tbn; Pete Christlieb, ts; Lou Levy, p; John Pisano, g; Monty Budwig, b; Nick Ceroli, d.

QUINTET: Goodman, Levy, Pisano, Budwig, Ceroli

Oh, Lady Be Good! - QUINTET
Here's That Rainy Day - QUINTET
Nice Work If You Can Get It - QUINTET
The World Is Waiting For The Sunrise - QUINTET
(I Hadn't Anyone Till You - Christlieb w/rhythm - NO BG
That's A Plenty
Medley: Don't Be That Way
      Stompin' At The Savoy
(. . . unidentified tune - Pisano w/rhythm - NO BG
I Didn't Know What Time It Was - QUINTET
Avalon - QUINTET
Sing, Sing, Sing

(Closing theme, "Good-Bye," was not recorded.)

There's no known audience recording of a Goodman concert in Syracuse, New York, December 2. A cassette is extant from Benny's next engagement, in the Fox Theater in Atlanta, Georgia on December 8, but its poor quality eliminates it from detailing herein. His final appearance for 1979, as guest soloist with the New Britain, Connecticut Symphony Orchestra on December 16 was unrecorded, to the best of the author's knowledge. Benny's final professional activity was an interview conducted by WOR Radio's Arlene Francis, December 21.

Benny's produce in the 1970's is not highly esteemed by Goodman enthusiasts, and likely never will be compared favorably with his work in other decades by Goodman collectors. There seem several reasons for this attitude, and one of them may be unfamiliarity: Only nine jazz albums, and one classical LP, offer examples of his performances for that decade (two "souvenir" releases received very limited distribution). In contrast, literally thousands of tracks from earlier periods were made available on legitimate reissues and bootleg LP's, and their sheer number dilutes consideration of his contemporary releases. When the bootleggers begin to acquire and market the material shown in this work, as inevitably they will despite legal restrictions, certain of Benny's efforts in the '70's will receive the regard due them, even comparatively.

A second reason is the quality of Benny's sidemen. It has been reiterated in this work that he played best when in the company of other jazz giants, Teagarden, Berigan, Hampton, Christian, Wilson-Stacy-Powell, James, Krupa, the list goes on. Stimulated by their work, Goodman soared; without them, he had to plumb the depths of his own enthusiasm to stay on a plateau. Thus his constant experimentation throughout the 1970's with new instrumentalists, in hopes of discovering players compatible with his style who could inspire him. He found a few: certain of the British bandsmen, Cal Collins, Warren Vache. But over time the position reversed; Benny inspired them, not the other way 'round.

A third reason is time itself, possibly pinpointed to a particular few weeks in 1978, the disappointing Carnegie Hall concert in January and Alice's death shortly thereafter. In the years prior to those events, Benny played well consistently: with the English band in '70 and '71, at the Rainbow Grill, with Zoot in Europe and Australia, with the Original Quartet in '72 and '73, with Bobby Hackett in '73 and '74, and on concert and television programs up to the end of 1977. After that he played well occasionally—in the context of the Goodman definition of playing "well"—but much of the time his work was uninspired, pedestrian. He himself says that he was playing "cocktail lounge music," and found little enjoyment in it.

Did his age have anything to do with it? Certainly; none of us can do what we did 50, 40, 30, 20, even 10 years ago. Did the rigors of travel take its toll on a man in his late sixties, when earlier new cities and new countries and new continents were welcomed as adventures? Of course. Did ennui, boredom, endless repetition stale his invention? Without a doubt. But above all, a blazing Goodman chorus here and there assures us his talent persisted, only stimulation was lacking.

First of all, Benny Goodman plays for his own pleasure. Second, he plays for the enjoyment of his audiences. If he is satisfied, and they are satisfied, he is content. By those standards the 'Seventies were only partially successful. At their end he became disenchanted with his performances. His audiences did not; his engagements invariably sold out in the same locations year after year. And the great majority of those who produced his concerts, and those who paid increasing amounts to witness them, were pleased with their separate investments.

THE 1980'S—
THE FINAL CHAPTER

The first month of the first year of the new decade found Benny Goodman on network television on two consecutive evenings. He appeared on the Johnny Carson program, an embarrassment that's better forgotten; he played poorly, gave perhaps his worst-ever performance on the tube:

"THE TONIGHT SHOW"   January 17, 1980, Burbank, Calif.

   NBC Television Network

Benny Goodman, clt; Lou Levy, p; Mundell Lowe, g; Bob Dougherty, b; Frank Capp, d.

Hallelujah!
Come Rain Or Come Shine
Ridin' High

The next night ABC-TV honored Benny on its "American Music Awards" telecast. Henry Mancini, Peggy Lee, Doc Severinson, Mel Torme and Barry Manilow (!) reminisced, spoke glowingly of Benny's accomplishments. Film clips and television kinescopes and tapes, suggested by the author, were shown, and Lionel Hampton played vibes with George Weil's studio orchestra. Benny did not join in, simply acknowledged the award.

On the 19th, accompanied by Chuck Findley, Herbie Harper, Pete Christlieb (years earlier, Benny had played with Pete's dad, a bassoonist), Levy, Lowe, Monty Budwig and Capp, Benny was in concert at the Marin Center, San Rafael, California. An audience recording is extant, but its poor quality precludes its detailing herein. And that's unfortunate: Benny was playing better.

Advertised to ". . . reincarnate its famous 'Make Believe Ballroom' . . . 'Live' . . . 'Remote'," WNEW-AM Radio, New York, broadcast Benny's Octet from Roseland Ballroom on Valentine's Day. Static and technical difficulties—at one point WNEW lost its remote feed, substituted a few choruses of a Goodman recording; at another, mike feedback caused Benny to abort and begin again—mar an otherwise interesting hour:

"THE MAKE BELIEVE BALLROOM"   February 14, 1980, New York
   WNEW-AM Radio

Benny Goodman, clt; Bob Zottola, tpt; Britt Woodman, tbn; Al Klink, ts; Roland Hanna, p; Bucky Pizzarelli, g; Jack Six, b; Bobby Rosengarden, d.

DUET: Goodman, Hanna
QUINTET: Duet plus Pizzarelli, Six, Rosengarden

Let's Dance (theme)
After You've Gone - QUINTET
Here's That Rainy Day - QUINTET
That's A Plenty
(Like Someone In Love - Zottola w/rhythm - NO BG
Medley: Don't Be That Way
          Stompin' At The Savoy
Send In The Clowns - DUET (false start)
(No Greater Love - Woodman w/rhythm - NO BG
Body And Soul - QUINTET
Sing, Sing, Sing
Good-Bye (theme)

At about this time Benny taped some promotional material for old friends Andre Baruch and Bea Wain, hosts of a nationally-syndicated, re-created "Your Hit Parade" radio series. His remarks serve to introduce his Victor recording of "Roll 'Em" on the reconstituted September 27, 1937 program, among others.

Two days later, Benny fulfilled a jazz-classical obligation at the Tarrant County Convention Center in Fort Worth, Texas, his only other engagement in February. There is extant an audience recording of the jazz portion, with Don Haas, Eddie Duran, Al Obidinski and John Markham, a rhythm section he'll use much of the year. The tape is poor, and is omitted herein; there's no known cassette of his classical performance with the Fort Worth Symphony.

When in Boulder, Colorado the previous November, Benny had heard a vocal trio, Mary Lynn Gillaspie, Gail Gillaspie and Marguerite Juenemann, who billed themselves as, "Rare Silk," and sang much in the manner of "Manhattan Transfer." He invited them to join him for the inaugural concert of the Ninth Annual Boston Globe Jazz Festival, first in the nine-day, 14-group presentation. Evidently captivated by them, he featured "Rare Silk" in 10 of the 19 selections performed that Friday evening in Symphony Hall, taped and broadcast nationally by the Public Radio Broadcasting network.

Unfortunately, there'd been little time to rehearse the program, and it was disjointed, much like the second half of the 1978 Carnegie Hall concert. The reviews were critical, and even the sell-out audience seemed puzzled by the awkward silences:

"NINTH ANNUAL BOSTON GLOBE   March 7, 1980, Boston
   JAZZ FESTIVAL"
   PBS Radio Network

WGBH-FM, Boston, station of origin. Broadcast nationally on affiliated stations later in the year.

Benny Goodman, clt; Ernie Figueroa, tpt; Britt Woodman, tbn; Don Haas, p; Eddie Duran, g; Al Obidinski. b; John Markham, d. Rare Silk, voc.

QUARTET: Goodman, Haas, Obidinski, Markham
QUINTET: Quartet plus Duran

Avalon - QUINTET
Here's That Rainy Day - QUINTET
The World Is Waiting For The Sunrise - QUINTET
(How High The Moon - voc Rare Silk w/rhythm, tpt in coda, - NO BG
Sentimental Gentleman From Georgia - voc Rare Silk w/rhythm, tbn - BG
   in coda
Splanky - voc Rare Silk
Little Brown Jug - voc Rare Silk - a cappella, BG obligato, b accomp.
Fascinating Rhythm - voc Rare Silk
Tuxedo Junction - voc Rare Silk
Girl Talk - voc Rare Silk
Everybody's Boppin' - voc Rare Silk - QUINTET

Intermission.

Stompin' At The Savoy
(Almost Like Being In Love - Duran w/rhythm - NO BG
(Sweet And Lovely - Figueroa w/rhythm - NO BG
(Love Walked In - Woodman w/rhythm - NO BG
That's A Plenty
Broadway - voc Rare Silk
Sing, Sing, Sing - voc Rare Silk
Good-Bye (theme)

Audience recordings of Benny as soloist with the Allentown (Pennsylvania) Symphony on March 16, and with his small group for the Florida Atlantic University Foundation in Boca Raton, Florida on March 19 are unknown to the author. There is a satisfactory cassette from his next engagement, at the Brooklyn Academy of Music Opera House:

BROOKLYN CONCERT   March 27, 1980, Brooklyn, N.Y.

Benny Goodman, clt; Bob Zottola, tpt; Britt Woodman, tbn; Don Haas, p; Eddie Duran, g; Al Obidinski, b; John Markham, d.

DUET: Goodman, Haas
TRIO: Duet plus Markham
QUINTET: Trio plus Duran, Obidinski

Oh, Lady Be Good! - QUINTET
Here's That Rainy Day - TRIO

March 27, 1980, continued

297

March 27, 1980, continued
The World Is Waiting For The Sunrise - QUINTET
(The Boy Next Door - Duran w/rhythm - NO BG
That's A Plenty
(Soon - Haas w/rhythm - NO BG
Send In The Clowns - DUET
Medley: Don't Be That Way
          Stompin' At The Savoy

Intermission.

Hallelujah! - QUINTET
I Didn't Know What Time It Was - QUINTET
Avalon - QUINTET
(Don't Get Around Much Anymore - Obidinski w/rhythm - NO BG

Bill Hyland, clt, replaces Goodman in the Quintet:

(Body And Soul - Hyland w/rhythm - NO BG
(Gone With The Wind - Hyland w/rhythm - NO BG

Hyland leaves, Goodman returns:

I'm Old Fashioned - Zottola w/rhythm - BG in coda
Air Mail Special
Sing, Sing, Sing
Good-Bye (theme)

April is a complete loss insofar as audience recordings are concerned. An awards ceremony for Morton Gould in the Hotel Pierre, New York, on the 10th; a guest soloist stint in Houston's Jones Hall, with the Houston "Pops" Orchestra on the 26th; and a jazz date in the South Hampton Princess in Bermuda on the 30th produced no known tapes. There is a cassette from his next engagement, May 14 in San Francisco's Masonic Auditorium, but its overall poor quality excludes it from listing herein. A better tape would be welcome, for Benny played very well, especially on a scintillating "I Know That You Know." The next night the Septet and Rare Silk were in Seattle, Washington; there's no known audience recording from that performance, nor is there one from the Corning Museum of Glass, Corning, New York, on the 28th.

Benny celebrated his 71st birthday on May 30, and William B. Williams of WNEW Radio, New York, marked the day with a conversation with Benny, and some illustrative recordings. Two days later he was in Chicago's Don Maxwell Hall, and an inexplicably brief presentation—21 minutes—for the Roxbury Convention:

ROXBURY CONVENTION   June 1, 1980, Chicago

Benny Goodman, clt; Don Haas, p; Eddie Duran, g; Al Obidinski, b; John Markham, d.

DUET: Goodman, Haas

Oh, Lady Be Good!
Send In The Clowns - DUET
Avalon
Here's That Rainy Day
The World Is Waiting For The Sunrise

An audience recording of a concert in Carnegie Hall on the 5th doesn't pass muster, unfortunately; press reviews were favorable, with Rare Silk singled out for special mention. A combined jazz/classical engagement in Dallas, Texas on the 7th went unrecorded. A week later Benny was in Echternach, Luxembourg, where he performed the Mozart and Arnold clarinet concertos; no known tapes from there. There is one from the Playboy Jazz Festival in the Hollywood Bowl on the 21st, but it is so poor as to be barely audible. June ended with a concert in the Theater of Performing Arts in San Antonio, Texas on the 23rd, which failed to produce a known recording. While in Hollywood, Benny taped a segment for NBC's "The Today Show," which was not televised until August 28. Unspecified in published program listings, this telecast was missed by Goodman collectors.

Benny's July itinerary included engagements in the Marine Stadium, Miami, on the 5th; the National Music Camp at Interlochen, Michigan, the 11th; the Greater Des Moines (Iowa) Civic Center, the 12th; Douglas Park, Chicago, the 14th; Ravinia, Highland Park, Illinois, the 16th; the Flint Center for the Performing Arts, Cupertino, California, the 19th; and the Robert Mondavi Winery, Oakville, California, the 20th. None affords known recordings. On August 6 Benny sat in with Bob Wilber's group in Michael's Pub, a Manhattan bistro. Impressed by Wilber's rhythm section, Benny invited them to join him for a classical/jazz performance August 10 at the Vermont Mozart Festival in Burlington, his only engagement for the month. No known cassettes from there.

To introduce its new line of "Aurex" audio and video components, Toshiba Corporation brought Benny to Japan for three concert appearances, known collectively as the "Aurex Jazz Festival '80." Separately, Toshiba hired Teddy Wilson to perform with the Goodman group, and Don Haas remained in California.

All three concerts were recorded, and from the tapes Toshiba extracted selected performances to constitute a 12″ LP. All of Side 1 of the LP is from the initial concert in Nippon Budah-kan, Tokyo, as are two tracks on Side 2. Both the second concert—in Banpaku Memorial (Expo) Park, Suita, Csaka—and the third—in Yokahama Stadium—contribute two tracks each to complete Side 2.

The master tapes are listed below in their entireties. Selections included in the LP are shown in the type style reserved for authorized recordings; those not in the LP are in the type employed for air checks. The tapes are, of course, in true stereo, and are displayed herein in order-of-performance. Here's the first, from Tokyo:

AUREX JAZZ FESTIVAL '80 -   September 3, 1980, Tokyo
KING OF SWING

Benny Goodman, clt; Tony Terran, tpt; Dick Nash, tbn; Teddy Wilson, p; Eddie Duran, g; Al Obidinski, b; John Markham, d. Rare Silk, voc.

DUET: Goodman, Duran
QUARTET: Goodman, Wilson, Obidinski, Markham
QUINTET: Quartet plus Duran

EWJ-80187-A   **StLP: AUREX-TOSHIBA (EMI) EWJ-80187**
               Avalon - QUINTET - Side 1, Track 1
               Body And Soul - QUINTET - Side 1, Track 2
               Oh, Lady Be Good! - QUINTET - Side 1, Track 3

               Bewitched - DUET

               The World Is Waiting For the Sunrise - QUINTET - Side 1, Track 4

               (I Cover The Waterfront - Nash w/rhythm - NO BG

               That's A Plenty - Side 1, Track 5
               Broadway - voc Rare Silk - Side 1, Track 6

               Girl Talk - voc Rare Silk

               Goody-Goody - voc Rare Silk - Side 1, Track 7

               (Prelude To A Kiss - Duran w/b, d - NO BG

EWJ-80187-B   **StLP: AUREX-TOSHIBA (EMI) EWJ-80187**
               Medley: Don't Be That Way   ) - Side 2, Track 1
                        Stompin' At The Savoy)
               Memories Of You - QUARTET - Side 2, Track 3

               Sing, Sing, Sing - voc Rare Silk
               Sweet Georgia Brown
               Good-Bye (theme)

AUREX JAZZ FESTIVAL '80 -   September 6, 1980, Osaka
KING OF SWING

Personnels as September 3.

               Avalon - QUINTET
               Body And Soul - QUINTET
               Oh, Lady Be Good! - QUINTET
               The World Is Waiting For The Sunrise - QUINTET
               (I Cover The Waterfront - Nash w/rhythm - NO BG
               That's A Plenty
               Broadway - voc Rare Silk
               (Hold Tight - voc Rare Silk - a cappella - NO BG
               Tuxedo Junction - voc Rare Silk
               Goody-Goody - voc Rare Silk
               Memories Of You - QUARTET
               Medley: Don't Be That Way
                        Stompin' At The Savoy
               It's Easy To Remember - DUET

EWJ-80187-B   **StLP:** AUREX-TOSHIBA (EMI) EWJ-80187
Air Mail Special - voc Rare Silk - Side 2, Track 2

Sing, Sing, Sing - voc Rare Silk
Good-Bye (theme)

Sweet Georgia Brown - Side 2, Track 5

AUREX JAZZ FESTIVAL '80 -   September 7, 1980, Yokohama
KING OF SWING

Personnels as September 3.

Avalon - QUINTET
Memories Of You - QUARTET
Oh, Lady Be Good! - QUINTET
If I Had You - QUINTET
The World Is Waiting For The Sunrise - QUINTET
(I Cover The Waterfront - Nash w/rhythm - NO BG
That's A Plenty
Broadway - voc Rare Silk
Girl Talk - voc Rare Silk
(Little Brown Jug - voc Rare Silk - a cappella - NO BG
Goody-Goody - voc Rare Silk
(What Is This Thing Called Love? - Duran w/rhythm - NO
   BG
It's Easy To Remember - DUET
I've Found A New Baby - QUINTET
Medley: Don't Be That Way
          Stompin' At The Savoy

EWJ-80187-B   **StLP:** AUREX-TOSHIBA (EMI) EWJ-80187
Sing, Sing, Sing - voc Rare Silk - Side 2, Track 4
Good-Bye (theme) - Side 2, Track 6

Portions (at least) of all three Aurex Festival concerts were televised and/or broadcast by the Japan Broadcasting Corporation (NHK) and the Osaka Broadcasting Co., Ltd. From the delayed telecasts and FM radio broadcasts collectors have assembled near-duplicates of the Toshiba master tapes. All of them, however, seemed to have missed Benny's first appearance in Japan this time around: On September 2 he and Eddie Duran played "Stompin' At The Savoy" and "Memories Of You" on a top-of-the-morning NHK-TV program. Nor has anyone yet managed to copy a commercial Benny filmed for Toshiba while in Japan. It is believed to have been unsatisfactory, for an unknown reason, and may never have been displayed.

Before leaving for three engagements in California, Benny appeared on the "Merv Griffin Show," videotaped in Lincoln Center:

"THE MERV GRIFFIN SHOW"   September 30, 1980, New York
  METROMEDIA Television Network

Televised on various dates in October via Metromedia and other television stations.

Benny Goodman, clt; Mort Lindsey, p; Mundell Lowe, g; George Duvivier, b; Don Lamond, d.

I Cried For You
September Song
I Know That You Know

Concerts in California—Pasadena, October 8, for the Ambassador Foundation; Torrance, October 10, for El Camino College; and Claremont, October 12, Claremont College—produced no recordings known to the author. While Benny was on the West Coast, the East Coast saw him inducted into the National Broadcasters Hall of Fame—at Caesar's Boardwalk Regency Casino, Atlantic City, October 12. On the 15th Benny received the 1980 individual Communications Award from the ICD Rehabilitation and Research Center (David Rockefeller got the Corporate Award). Following his usual custom, Benny played for the guests at the Waldorf-Astoria, following the ceremony:

1980 ICD COMMUNICATIONS   October 15, 1980, New York
  AWARD DINNER

Benny Goodman, clt; Harriet Wingren, p.

Grand Duo Concertante for Clarinet and Piano, Op. 48 (von Weber)
Third Movement: Allegro

Benny Goodman, clt; John Bunch, p; Chris Flory, g; Phil Flanigan, b; Chuck Riggs, d.

DUET: Goodman, Bunch

Send In The Clowns - DUET
Oh, Lady Be Good!
Here's That Rainy Day
Honeysuckle Rose
It's Easy To Remember

Benny's scheduled solo appearances with the New Jersey Symphony Orchestra—New Brunswick, October 18; Newark, October 19; and Trenton, November 2—were cancelled when the orchestra members went on strike. Taking only Don Haas with him, Benny went to Berlin for two concerts on consecutive evenings in Philharmonie Hall. There he was joined by the balance of the rhythm section, Europeans recommended to him by a friend, Kurt Mueller. An audition-rehearsal consisting of but two tunes convinced Benny, language barrier or not, they were compatible, they could play. An audience of one, Mueller recorded both that audition and a second brief runthrough the day of the concert:

REHEARSALS, BERLIN CONCERT   November 6 & 7, 1980, Berlin

Benny Goodman, clt; Don Haas, p; Harry Pepl, g; Peter Witte, b; Charley Antolini, d.

November 6: I Cried For You
           The World Is Waiting For The Sunrise

November 7: Oh, Lady Be Good!
           Body And Soul (n/c - intro only; Goodman says no further
           rehearsal needed)

German Radio recorded and broadcast the November 7 concert. Its program begins with a brief interview over the first selection, ends with an announcement over the last tune, omits the closing theme. Zweites Deutsches Fernsehen (ZDF) videotaped part of the concert, televised an excerpt on a news telecast. The listing below is from the master tape:

BERLIN CONCERT   November 7, 1980, Berlin
  ZDF Television

Broadcast and televised in part on November 8.

Quintet as November 6 & 7 rehearsals.

DUET: Goodman, Haas
TRIO: Duet plus Antolini
QUARTET: Trio plus Witte

Oh, Lady Be Good!
Send In The Clowns - DUET
(I Should Care - Haas w/rhythm - NO BG
Avalon
Bewitched - QUARTET
Air Mail Special
You Must Meet My Wife - DUET
If I Had You
The World Is Waiting For The Sunrise
Memories Of You
Medley: Don't Be That Way
          Stompin' At The Savoy
Bei Mir Bist Du Schon
Good-Bye (theme)

The Armed Forces Television network videotaped an interview with Benny in his Berlin apartment prior to the second concert, then took its cameras to Philharmonie Hall for the first 20 minutes of the performance. The author has been unable to determine if any of this material was televised; the listing below is from a master audio tape:

BERLIN CONCERT   *November 8, 1980, Berlin*

Personnels as November 7.

Oh, Lady Be Good!
Here's That Rainy Day - TRIO
"Harry Pepl's Blues"
(All The Things You Are - Haas w/rhythm - NO BG
Send In The Clowns - DUET
Avalon
Poor Butterfly
Air Mail Special
You Must Meet My Wife - TRIO
Medley: Don't Be That Way
*   Stompin' At The Savoy*
Sing, Sing, Sing
Good-Bye (theme)

The new personnel inspired Benny to some of his best playing of the year, so good that he considered releasing selected cuts from both concerts on LP. Potential producers shied away from a contemporary release, however, because of the German broadcast and telecast, widely taped by collectors. A future issue is a possibility.

Benny appeared as soloist with the Springfield (Massachusetts) Symphony Orchestra on November 15, with his Septet in Lowell, Massachusetts on November 22; there are no known recordings from either concert. The Septet then performed in the Theresa L. Kaufmann Concert Hall of Manhattan's 92nd Street YMHA, from which an audience recording is extant:

YMHA CONCERT   *November 23, 1980, New York*

Benny Goodman, clt; Graham Young, tpt; Britt Woodman, tbn; Benny Aronov, p; Chris Flory, g; Phil Flanigan, b; Chuck Riggs, d.

DUET: Goodman, Aronov
QUINTET: Duet plus Flory, Flanigan, Riggs

Oh, Lady Be Good! - QUINTET
Here's That Rainy Day - QUINTET
The World Is Waiting For The Sunrise - QUINTET
(I Can't Get Started - Young w/rhythm - NO BG
(Love Walked In - Woodman w/rhythm - NO BG
That's A Plenty
It's Easy To Remember
Medley: Don't Be That Way
*   Stompin' At The Savoy*
This Can't Be Love - Flory w/rhythm - BG obligato
Send In The Clowns - DUET
Air Mail Special
(Sophisticated Lady - Woodman w/rhythm - NO BG
Honeysuckle Rose
Sing, Sing, Sing
Good-Bye (theme)

Ending 1980, Benny performed with the Tulsa (Oklahoma) Philharmonic on December 6, and as soloist in Pasadena, California and Torrance, California, on December 10 and 14. There are known tapes from the three concerts.

The new year began much as the old had ended for Benny, guest appearances as soloist with the Virginia Philharmonic Orchestra—Newport News, January 10; Virginia Beach, January 11; and with the Charlotte Pops Orchestra, Charlotte, North Carolina, January 26. Audience recordings of the first two engagements are unknown; but NBC-TV videotaped the third, and portions of it are extant. It came about this way:

Commentator/newsman David Brinkley is a devoted Goodman enthusiast. Meeting by chance on a flight to California in December, Brinkley suggested to Benny that he be the subject of an NBC series that Brinkley then headed. Agreed, Benny was interviewed by Brinkley in his New York apartment on January 23, and in Stamford on January 28 and 29. On the 23rd, NBC also videotaped a duet between Benny and pianist Mischa Dichter in the apartment. On the 26th, it videotaped Benny in Charlotte, performing with the Pops orchestra and a trio whose personnel is unknown. Excerpts of all of this were compressed into a quarter-hour segment, along with brief choruses from Benny's records and a 1944 Goodman feature film, "Sweet And Lowdown." Contemporary performances are listed below.

"NBC MAGAZINE"   *various dates - see below*
  NBC Television Network

Televised April 4, 1981.

DUET: Benny Goodman, clt; Mischa Dichter, p - January 23.

Benny Goodman, clt, and an unknown trio - January 26.

Benny Goodman, clt, and the Charlotte Pops Orchestra - January 26.

Oh, Lady Be Good! - Benny Goodman and a trio (n/c)
. . . unidentified classical theme - DUET (n/c)
. . . unidentified orchestral selection - Goodman, Charlotte Pops Orchestra
* (n/c)*
Poor Butterfly - Benny Goodman and a trio (n/c)
It's Easy To Remember - Benny Goodman and a trio (n/c)

Composer "Riz" Ortolani ("Volare") approached Benny in New York with an invitation to record two of his new tunes for the sound track of a film then underway in Rome, "Fantasma D'Amore," starring Marcello Mastroianni and Romy Schneider. In Technicolor, the full length motion picture was produced by Dean Film & Cam, directed by Dino Risi, with music composed, arranged and conducted by Ortolani. Was Benny interested?

Benny listened as Ortolani played the tunes in Benny's apartment, "kind of" liked them, accepted the invitation. Besides, he could first renew some personal friendships in London, then visit daughter Benjie who was studying in Italy. He flew to England February 7, went to Pisa, Italy on the 11th, got to Rome on the 14th.

The author has not seen the film and thus is unable to detail the incidence of Goodman's contributions to its sound track. However, Warner Communications Company released an LP containing Benny's efforts, and it may be assumed that its tracks are similar to the contents of the film. But not necessarily so, for the Goodman cuts are complex, seem to be splices of more than one take of a given rendition, segue from one tune to another, may even be combinations of Goodman and non-Goodman performances. As they are listed on its label, the Goodman tracks on the LP are:

Original Sound-Track   **February 16-17-18, 1981, Rome**
BENNY GOODMAN Plays Fantasma D'Amore
(Phantom Of Love)

Benny Goodman, clt, and a full orchestra, personnel unknown.

TRIO: Benny Goodman, clt; Harry Pepl, g; Peter Witte, b.
QUARTET: Trio plus unknown d.

MD 1297-A   **StLP:** WCC (WEA-It) T58308 - Side 1
                Phantom Of Love (Main Title) - Track 1
                Unforgettable Love - Track 2
                Unforgettable Love (variations on the theme) - Track 4
                Phantom Of Love - TRIO - Track 5

MD 1297-B   as above, except Side 2
                Phantom Of Love (variations on the theme) - QUARTET,
                  orchestra - Track 1
                Love's Memories - Track 4
                Phantom Of Love & Unforgettable Love - Track 6

(Also on StLP, PHIL 6313-174. Note that "Unforgettable Love" is the main theme of "Love's Memories.")

The author has copies of master tapes of what Benny considered to be preferred takes of his recordings for the sound track. Their first three cuts seem to be the same as those used for like titles on Side 1 of the LP; it is difficult to be certain, because of the LP's heavy editing. The fourth cut on the master tapes has no counterpart on the release.

"PHANTOM OF LOVE"   *February 16-17-18, 1981, Rome*
  MASTER RECORDINGS

Personnels as for the WCC StLP.

Unforgettable Love
Phantom Of Love
Phantom Of Love - TRIO
Unforgettable Love - TRIO

His work for the film completed, Benny enjoyed a visit with renowned composer Sir William Walton in Ibiza, Italy, on February 19, then returned to New York on the 23rd. His two engagements in March produced no known recordings: a jazz date in Palm Springs, March 10, and a duet with

Yehudi Menuhin in Detroit's Orchestra Hall, March 20. Indeed, we have no Goodman on tape until the end of June; April and May were vacation months for Benny.

Along with the rest of the musical world, Benny was saddened by the death of Eddie Sauter, victim of a heart attack on April 21. Although our concentration has been on his memorable work for Goodman, his inventive compositions and scores for Red Norvo, Artie Shaw, Tommy Dorsey and his own Sauter-Finegan orchestra should not be overlooked. The Brooklyn-born genius, a resident of Nyack, New York in his later years, confided to friends that he felt his contributions seemed largely to have passed by unnoticed. Not so, Edward Sauter, they will live for a long, long time.

Equally distressing to Benny, if less remarked by the media, was the death of PeeWee Erwin on Saturday, June 20. Ironically, the Thursday before, he and Benny talked about doing some dates together, despite PeeWee's long bout with cancer; and just three weeks earlier, he'd played at a jazz festival in Amsterdam. George "PeeWee" Erwin, an excellent trumpet player often mistaken for Bunny Berigan, dead at age 68 in Teaneck, New Jersey.

Benny had a triple-header in Chicago on June 28. He received its "Hall Of Fame" medal from the Illinois Institute of Technology—IIT evolved from Lewis Institute, which Benny had attended in 1924. He then performed a combined classical/jazz concert for the Chicago Neighborhood Festival in Rogers Park. Curiously, the audience recording of the classical portion is quite good, but the cassette of the jazz segment—same recordist, same equipment—barely qualifies for inclusion herein:

CHICAGO CONCERT   *June 28, 1981, Chicago*

Benny Goodman, clt, and the Chicago Symphony String Quartet: Victor Artigh, Edgar Runsor, v; Frank Miller, cel; Newton Freas, viola.

Quintet for Clarinet and Strings in A Major (Mozart)

Benny Goodman, clt; Bernie Leighton, p; Cal Collins, g; Eddie DeHaas, b; Fred Stoll, d.

DUET: Goodman, Leighton

Chicago
Poor Butterfly
Runnin' Wild
Send In The Clowns - DUET
Medley: Don't Be That Way
           Stompin' At The Savoy
Bewitched

Stu Katz, p, replaces Leighton; Eric Schneider, as (from Earl Hines's band) added:

Oh, Lady Be Good!
Bei Mir Bist Du Schon

Leighton replaces Katz; Schneider out:

The World Is Waiting For The Sunrise
12th Street Rag

Katz replaces Leighton; Schneider returns:

The Blues

A private party for the Champion Corporation in Stamford, Connecticut on July 10, and an engagement in Lynnhaven Hall, Virginia Beach, Virginia, on August 30, are Benny's only performances for the two midsummer months. We've no tapes of either. On September 1, accompanied by Jimmy Maxwell and Don Haas, Benny flew to Copenhagen for two television appearances. There he was met by violinist Svend Asmussen and the rhythm section he'd used in Philharmonie Hall the previous November. The first concert was videotaped in the Tivoli's Jazzhus Skulfeter, a small room that saw the overflow audience crowding the stage. The delayed telecast omitted " 'C' Jam Blues" and an untitled improvisation featuring Harry Pepl. The listing below is from the master tape, and includes the omitted tunes in order-of-performance:

JAZZHUS SKULFETER CONCERT   *September 4, 1981, Copenhagen*
   ZDF Television Network

Televised December 25, and again on April 20, 1982.

Benny Goodman, clt; Jimmy Maxwell, tpt; Svend Asmussen, v; Don Haas, p; Harry Pepl, g; Peter Witte, b; Charley Antolini, d.

DUET: Goodman, Haas
QUINTET: Duet plus Pepl, Witte, Antolini
SEXTET: Quintet plus Asmussen

Oh, Lady Be Good! - QUINTET
Poor Butterfly - QUINTET
The World Is Waiting For The Sunrise - QUINTET
(Confessin' - Maxwell w/rhythm - NO BG
Medley: Don't Be That Way   *) - QUINTET plus Maxwell*
       Stompin' At The Savoy)
(I Should Care - Haas p solo - NO BG
If I Had You - SEXTET
After You've Gone - SEXTET
"C" Jam Blues - SEXTET (not televised)
Send In The Clowns - QUINTET
(untitled selection feat. Pepl w/rhythm - NO BG - not televised)
It's Easy To Remember - DUET
Air Mail Special
Good-Bye (theme)

The next day's program was videotaped in the Tivoli's Grosser Konzertsaal, a larger auditorium that easily accommodated the Danish Radio orchestra that accompanied Benny. As a matter of fact, the entire concert was recorded twice, once for "color," the second time for a delayed telecast. According to some eyewitnesses, the first performance was the better of the two.

"RENE KOLLO TV SHOW"   *September 5, 1981, Copenhagen*
   ZDF Television Network

Televised December 25.

Benny Goodman, clt, and the Rundfunk-Orchestra von Danmarks-Radio, Hans Wallat conducting.

Concerto for Clarinet and Orchestra in A, K.622 (Mozart)
1st. movement: Allegro

QUINTET: as September 4

Avalon - QUINTET

Benny Goodman, clt, and full orchestra, as above:

Send In The Clowns - voc Briggitte Fassbaender (intro only)

On September 12 Benny's Septet was in Boston's Ritz-Carlton for a one-night stand; no known audience recording of that engagement. He took a fortnight off, then flew to England where he would open and close the week-long Benson and Hedges Music Festival at Snape Maltings, Aldeburgh. The British Broadcasting Company elected not to broadcast the initial concert on September 28, a program shared by Benny and pianist Sir Clifford Curzon, tenor Peter Schreier and harpsichordist George Malcolm. BBC's Edward Greenfield interviewed Benny at the Festival on the 29th, and their conversation was broadcast on October 2.

The theme of the 1981 Festival was a celebration of the chamber music of Bach and Brahms. The Festival's handsome printed program discussed in detail Brahams's Clarinet Quintet in B Minor, Op. 115, to be performed by Benny Goodman on October 1. But Benny decided there simply hadn't been enough time to rehearse, substituted the Mozart Quintet instead, to the chagrin of the Brahms devotees at the concert. BBC broadcast the Mozart "live" and in stereo:

"BENSON AND HEDGES MUSIC FESTIVAL"   *October 1, 1981,*
   BBC-4 Radio   *Snape Maltings*

Benny Goodman, clt, and the Amadeus Quartet: Norbert Brainin, Siegmund Nissel, v; Peter Schidlof, viola; Martin Lovett, cel.

Quintet for Clarinet and Strings in A Major, K.581 (Mozart)

Unscheduled, Benny appeared at the tag end of the next evening's award ceremonies, ". . . gave us a tantalisingly brief taster in what he described as the 'night club part' of the show," according to a newspaper account. The "taster" was not recorded, so far as it is known. BBC did record the Festival's finale, the "Benny Goodman and Friends Jazz Concert,'' on October 4; Benny's ''friends'' were Svend Asmussen and a rhythm section comprised of British musicians.

The listing below is derived from three sources: a ''live'' BBC stereo broadcast, a delayed BBC stereo broadcast, and a stereo tape in the possession of Benny Goodman. Together they present the performance in its entirety save for what apparently was an encore, which no one seems to have recorded. The source of each selection is shown in parentheses following the tune title.

"BENSON AND HEDGES MUSIC FESTIVAL"   October 4, 1981,
BBC-3 Radio   Snape Maltings

Broadcast October 4 (1); broadcast April 10, 1982 (2); Goodman tape (BG).

Benny Goodman, clt; Svend Asmussen, v; Brian Lemmon, p; Phil Lee, g; Lennie Bush, b; Martin Drew, d.

DUET: Goodman, Asmussen
TRIO: Goodman, Lemmon, Drew
QUINTET: Trio plus Lee, Bush

Oh, Lady Be Good! - QUINTET (1, 2, BG)
Body And Soul - TRIO (1, 2)
I Want To Be Happy - QUINTET (1, 2, BG)
(La Conquantaine/Hush-A-Bye - Asmussen w/rhythm - NO BG (1; BG - n/c)
If I Had You - DUET (1)
After You've Gone - DUET (1, 2, BG)
(This Can't Be Love - Lemmon w/rhythm - NO BG (1, 2)
It's Easy To Remember - QUINTET (1, BG)
Medley: Don't Be That Way   ) (1, 2)
*   Stompin' At The Savoy)*
Memories Of You - QUINTET (1, 2, BG)
Indiana (1, 2, BG)
Lazy River (1)
The World Is Waiting For The Sunrise (1 - to signoff; 2)
Poor Butterfly (2)
Sweet Georgia Brown (2, BG)
Rose Room (BG)
I've Found A New Baby (2, BG)
Avalon (BG)
Good-Bye (theme) (BG)

("Honeysuckle Rose," likely an encore, evidently was not recorded.)

A reception and banquet for King Hussein and Queen Noor of Jordan at the White House united Benny and Buddy Rich in another of their rare collaborations, and their only known joint performance of ''Sing, Sing, Sing.'' Privately recorded, an excellent stereo tape has Benny inviting the enthusiastic guests to dance after the venerable standard, and President Reagan speaking glowingly of Benny, Buddy and the Big Band Era:

WHITE HOUSE RECEPTION   November 2, 1981, Washington

Benny Goodman, clt; Hank Jones, p; Bucky Pizzarelli, g; Milt Hinton, b; Buddy Rich, d.

DUET: Goodman, Jones

I Want To Be Happy
Send In The Clowns - DUET
Oh, Lady Be Good!
Poor Butterfly
The World Is Waiting For The Sunrise
(Entertainer Rag - Jones solo - NO BG
It's Easy To Remember
Sing, Sing, Sing
Rose Room
Air Mail Special
Good-Bye (theme)

CBS Cable TV interviewed Benny for its ''Signature'' program on November 24; the next day, NBC's Arlene Francis taped a conversation with Benny for presentation on her ''Prime Of Your Life'' TV series, televised on December 19.

Impressed with Svend Asmussen, delighted with their duets, Benny booked a quick trip to Germany with the jazz violinist and a rhythm section of his compatriots. The author has no tape of the December 7 Berlin concert, but the next, December 9 in Hamburg's CCH (Congress Centrum Hamburg) Saal, was recorded and broadcast by North German Radio. In fact, there were two broadcasts; the second added a non-Goodman ''Sweet Georgia

Brown,'' and an encore, ''It's Easy To Remember,'' not included in the first.

HAMBURG CONCERT   December 9, 1981, Hamburg
NDR-II Radio

Broadcast December 13; and on December 26, 1982.

Benny Goodman, clt; Svend Asmussen, v; Claes Crona, p; Philipe Catherine, g; Mads Winding, b; Bjarne Rostvold, d.

QUINTET: Goodman, Crona, Catherine, Winding, Rostvold

After You've Gone
If I Had You
Avalon

(Goodman exits; Asmussen and the rhythm section play "Careless Love," "The Days Of Wine And Roses," "Hush-A-Bye" and "Sweet Georgia Brown.")

Intermission; Goodman returns.

I Want To Be Happy
Here's That Rainy Day - QUINTET
Oh, Lady Be Good! - QUINTET
(Nuages - Catherine w/rhythm - NO BG
Air Mail Special
(On The Sunny Side Of The Street - Asmussen w/rhythm - NO BG
Medley: Don't Be That Way
*   Stompin' At The Savoy*
Body And Soul - QUINTET
How High The Moon
The World Is Waiting For The Sunrise
Sing, Sing, Sing
Good-Bye (theme)
It's Easy To Remember - clt solo (encore)

Bits and pieces of the Hamburg concert appeared on the ''Nordschau-Magazin'' television program on December 11. A ''live'' telecast the day before featured Benny and a studio group.

"BIO'S BAHNHOF"   December 10, 1981, Cologne
ARD-TV

Benny Goodman, clt, and Peter Herbolzheimer's Rhythm Combination and Brass.

Let's Dance (theme)
Don't Be That Way

A German Radio broadcast of the next concert—in the Beethovensaal Des Konzerthauses, Stuttgarten Liederhalle—is rather puzzling: Its opening rendition, the ''Don't Be That Way/Stompin' At The Savoy'' medley, was transposed, was actually performed much later in the concert (following ''Three Little Words''); ''I Want To Be Happy'' is for some reason incomplete; and the broadcast appears to be in a monaural mode rather than in the usual FM-stereo format. The listing below details the broadcast as it was presented:

STUTTGART CONCERT   December 11, 1981, Stuttgart
German Radio

Broadcast on an unknown date in February 1982. Personnels as December 9.

Medley: Don't Be That Way
*   Stompin' At The Savoy*
After You've Gone
If I Had You
Oh, Lady Be Good!
Avalon

(Goodman exits; Asmussen and the rhythm section play "On The Sunny Side Of The Street," "Days Of Wine And Roses," "Hush-A-Bye" and "Sweet Georgia Brown.")

Intermission; Goodman returns.

I Want To Be Happy
Here's That Rainy Day - QUINTET
Air Mail Special
(Nuages - Catherine w/rhythm - NO BG
I've Found A New Baby
Body And Soul - QUINTET

Three Little Words
(unidentified title - ? ''Laverne Walk''? - Winding w/rhythm - NO BG
Memories Of You - QUINTET
The World Is Waiting For The Sunrise
Sing, Sing, Sing
Honeysuckle Rose
Indiana
Good-Bye (theme)

We've no recordings of any kind from December 13th's engagement in Dusseldorf's Philipshalle, nor from the final concert on the 15th in Frankfurt's Jahrhunderthalle. Benny returned to New York for a few days, then went to St. Martin's for the holiday season, as has been his custom in recent years.

The first event of the new year was an award ceremony January 12 in New York's St. Regis Hotel: Benny received Stereo Review's annual Certificate of Merit. WOR Radio's Kathy Novak interviewed Benny, broadcast their brief chat on the station's ''P.M. New York'' program that evening. The WOR-Goodman connection repeated a month later: On February 11 Jack O'Brian interviewed Benny in his New York apartment, broadcast excerpts of the tape February 15 on WOR's ''Critic's Circle.'' Then Benny began his limited concert schedule for 1982.

In California for an appearance with his Quintet at the Desert Museum in Palm Springs on February 19—for which there's no known recording—Benny visited Merv Griffin the day before:

''THE MERV GRIFFIN SHOW''   *February 18, 1982, Los Angeles*
   METROMEDIA Television Network

Televised on several dates in March by Metromedia and other television stations.

Benny Goodman, clt; Lou Levy, p; Mundell Lowe, g; Monty Budwig, b; Nick Ceroli, d.

Sweet Lorraine
Limehouse Blues

Benny remained on the West Coast to spend some time with daughter Rachel (Mrs. Edelson) and a new grandchild, prior to combined classical/jazz concerts March 6 and 7 in San Diego—no known tapes from them. Then it was back to New York for a date in the Colden Theater of Queens College on March 27. Tapes of a rehearsal for the concert and the second half of the concert itself are extant, but their quality does not merit listing herein. Next was an engagement April 16 at Southern Connecticut State College in New Haven; it affords no recording known to the author. There is an excellent tape extant of the succeeding concert, a benefit for the American Lung Association in Philadelphia's Academy of Music:

AMERICAN LUNG   *May 10, 1982, Phila.*
   ASSOCIATION BENEFIT

Benny Goodman, clt; Spanky Davis, tpt; Britt Woodman, tbn; Scott Hamilton, ts; John Bunch, p; Chris Flory, g; Phil Flanigan, b; Panama Francis, d.

DUET: Goodman, Bunch
QUINTET: Duet plus Flory, Flanigan, Francis

Oh, Lady Be Good! - QUINTET
Body And Soul - QUINTET
The World Is Waiting For The Sunrise - QUINTET
That's A Plenty
Medley: Don't Be That Way
       Stompin' At The Savoy
Undecided
Send In The Clowns - DUET
(The Duke - Bunch solo - NO BG
Air Mail Special
Seven Come Eleven
Sing, Sing, Sing
Good-Bye (theme)

(Save for ''The Duke,'' the recordist did not tape performances that did not include Goodman. The cassette does contain a brief ceremony in which Benny was presented the Philadelphia Award.)

A date in New York's Waldorf-Astoria on May 12 offers no known recordings. On May 24 Yale University conferred an honorary doctor's degree in music on Benny, one of a number he has received, the one of which he is especially proud. Next he went to Kennedy Center in Washington for a weekend engagement that inaugurated the 1982 ''Kool Jazz

Festival.'' Sponsored in part since 1975 by the makers of the mentholated cigarette, George Wein's original ''Newport Jazz Festival'' was now renamed, was presented in various locations throughout the Nation, persisted for some six months.

A half-hour rehearsal in Kennedy Center the day before the first performance was taped clandestinely. The cassette has an amusing moment: A slightly-altered small-group arrangement of ''Sing, Sing, Sing'' was written in the wrong key, had the Octet mystified for a few choruses, was aborted when they realized what was wrong. Various partial renditions and miscellaneous rehearsal include:

KENNEDY CENTER REHEARSAL   *May 28, 1982, Washington*

Benny Goodman, clt; Warren Vache, tpt; Urbie Green, tbn; Harold (Hal) Ashby, ts; John Bunch, p; Chris Flory, g; Phil Flanigan, b; Panama Francis, d.

Stompin' At The Savoy
Sing, Sing, Sing
Good-Bye
Indiana
Air Mail Special
Poor Butterfly
You've Changed
When Sunny Is Blue
Star Dust
Seven Come Eleven

There are no known recordings of the first concert, May 29; Teddy Wilson, whose group was on the same bill, sat in with the Octet for its final few selections. (ABC-TV did televise a few minutes' worth of the Octet in action, but it's uncertain which concert was videotaped for its June 1 ''Entertainment Tonight'' program.) However, the concert on the 30th, Benny's 73rd birthday, was audio-taped professionally:

KOOL JAZZ FESTIVAL   *May 30, 1982, Washington*

Personnel as May 28, except OLIVER JACKSON, d, replaces Francis.

QUINTET: Goodman, Bunch, Flory, Flanigan, Jackson.

Poor Butterfly - QUINTET
I Know That You Know - QUINTET
After You've Gone - QUINTET
(You've Changed - Green w/rhythm - NO BG
(Out Of Nowhere - Vache w/rhythm - NO BG
That's A Plenty
(I Got It Bad (And That Ain't Good) - Ashby w/rhythm - NO BG
(East Of The Sun - Flory w/rhythm - NO BG
Air Mail Special
It's Easy To Remember - QUINTET
(The Duke - Bunch w/rhythm - NO BG
Medley: Don't Be That Way
      Stompin' At The Savoy
Sing, Sing, Sing
''Happy Birthday To You'' (Benny's 73rd.)

On June 1 a delayed celebration of Benny's birthday was hosted by Jack Ellsworth, owner of radio station WLIM in Patchogue, New York. It is not known if any of the festivities were broadcast. Then Benny was off to his second appearance for Kool's jazz hegira, in the Starlight Bowl, Balboa Park, San Diego, California. Occasional planes overhead in the outdoor arena (at one point Benny repeats a phrase because of the noise), and deteriorating sound quality on its side B, mar an otherwise satisfactory cassette:

KOOL JAZZ FESTIVAL June 2, 1982, San Diego

Benny Goodman, clt; Graham Young, tpt; Dick Nash, tbn; Bill Ramsay, ts; Paul Smith, p; Chris Flory, g; Phil Flanigan, b; Mel Lewis, d.

QUINTET: Goodman, Smith, Flory, Flanigan, Lewis

Oh, Lady Be Good! - QUINTET
You Go To My Head - QUINTET
After You've Gone - QUINTET
(I Cover The Waterfront - Nash w/rhythm - NO BG
(I Can't Get Started - Young w/rhythm - NO BG
That's A Plenty
(Where Or When - Flory w/rhythm - NO BG
Air Mail Special
It's Easy To Remember - QUINTET
Seven Come Eleven
Sing, Sing, Sing
Good-Bye (theme)

Three consecutive engagements at the Paul Masson Vineyards in Saratoga, California, were next, June 4, 5, and 6. There is an audience recording of the middle concert; barely acceptable, it is listed primarily because it offers a few different tunes:

PAUL MASSON CONCERT June 5, 1982, Saratoga, Calif.

Personnels as June 2.

Undecided
In A Sentimental Mood - QUINTET
. . . few bars, In A Mellotone
This Can't Be Love - QUINTET
You Go To My Head - QUINTET
After You've Gone - QUINTET
(I Cover The Waterfront - Nash w/rhythm - NO BG
That's A Plenty
Memories Of You - QUINTET
Air Mail Special
Poor Butterfly - QUINTET
Sing, Sing, Sing
Good-Bye (theme)

Benny's participation in the "Kool Jazz Festival" continued with appearances in Heinz Hall, Pittsburgh, June 19, and in the Fox Theater, Atlanta, Georgia, June 22; no known recordings available from either concert. Then it was a return to New York and Carnegie Hall, and a reunion with Lionel and Teddy, the kick-off concert in the 10-day Festival series in Manhattan.

As in Kennedy Center, a cassette recorder captured the rehearsal in Carnegie Hall the afternoon of the concert. Lorne Schoenberg, then on Benny's staff and a schooled musician and arranger in his own right, replaced Teddy Wilson for "Moon Glow" and the beginning of "Oh, Lady Be Good!" Just why he did is now forgotten, but it may have been because of Teddy's years' long displeasure at Benny's insistence on rehearsal. Teddy felt that none was needed, they were so familiar with each other; but Benny was adamant. (On the other hand, Lionel never demurred; he likes to play anywhere, anytime, under any circumstances.) In any event, the rehearsal tape, with each of the tunes listed reasonably complete:

CARNEGIE HALL REHEARSAL June 25, 1982, New York

Benny Goodman, clt; Lionel Hampton, vib; Teddy Wilson, p; Phil Flanigan, b; Panama Francis, d.

TRIO: Goodman, Wilson, Francis

Avalon
Body And Soul - TRIO

Lorne Schoenberg, p, substitutes for Wilson:

Moon Glow

Schoenberg plays first chorus of next tune only, is replaced by Wilson for balance of rehearsal:

Oh, Lady Be Good!
Seven Come Eleven
I Know That You Know
You Go To My Head - segue to,
Body And Soul
After You've Gone

Early response to announcement of the Quintet's appearance indicated demand far in excess of Carnegie's seating capacity. Would Benny, Lionel and Teddy consider two performances in one evening? Yes, for double their original fees. Agreed; we'll schedule the first for 7:00 p.m., we'll empty the hall, begin the second at 10:30 p.m. The Stan Getz Quartet will open each concert, so you'll have plenty of free time between your stints. Thus all of Goodman's Quintet, Benny included, likely earned their biggest salary checks ever for a single night's work.

The Nation's public broadcasting network, National Public Radio, supported by volunteer subscription and subsidized by private and governmental grants, recorded the Festival extensively. To do so it first obtained permission from each artist, for which it paid them a small sum. Later in the year it broadcast excerpts of its tapes. But something went awry with Goodman's release, and the NPR broadcast of his first show (NPR did not record the second) was delayed until March of the next year.

The broadcast did not include the second selection, "Moon Glow," nor the last, "Flying Home." There's no explanation for omission of "Moon Glow," but there is for "Flying Home": NPR's master indicates it simply ran out of tape before the extended Hampton signature was completed. The listing following includes both performances, for both are extant, from the NPR master and an audience recording:

KOOL JAZZ FESTIVAL: FIRST SHOW June 25, 1982, New York
NPR Radio Network

Broadcast nationally on NPR-affiliated FM radio stations in March 1983.

Benny Goodman, clt; Lionel Hampton, vib; Teddy Wilson, p; Phil Flanigan, b; Panama Francis, d.

QUARTET: Goodman, Wilson, Flanigan, Francis

After You've Gone
Moon Glow
Air Mail Special
Body And Soul - QUARTET
I Know That You Know
You Go To My Head
Oh, Lady Be Good!
Seven Come Eleven
Stompin' At The Savoy
Poor Butterfly - QUARTET
I Got Rhythm
Flying Home

(That's Benny thumping the piano between "Seven Come Eleven" and "Stompin' At The Savoy.")

The author has a copy of an audience recording of excerpts of the second show, but its poor audio quality precludes its detailing herein. Probably there are other, complete cassettes of the later performance, and likely they are as bad as his. Brief interviews of Benny and Lionel were taped for late night news telecasts.

Dubs of the NPR broadcast are in wide circulation, and Goodman fans can make their own judgments about his playing. The author's opinion is that Benny was inconsistent, better on the slow tunes than on the uptempo renditions, better in the second set than in the first. Overall, Lionel stole the shows.

Three concerts in the midwest, none connected with the Festival, followed: Ravinia, July 7; National Music Camp at Interlochen, Michigan, July 8; and Meadow Brook, Rochester, Michigan, July 9. An audience recording of the tunes in which Benny participated is available from Ravinia; none from the other two are known to the author. The first two selections on the extant cassette reflect the recordist's poor location at the beginning of the concert; he moved after intermission, and the sound improved:

RAVINIA CONCERT July 7, 1982, Highland Park, Ill.

Benny Goodman, clt; Warren Vache, tpt; Scott Hamilton, ts; John Bunch, p; Chris Flory, g; Phil Flanigan, b; Mel Lewis, d.

QUINTET: Goodman, Bunch, Flory, Flanigan, Lewis

Chicago
That's A Plenty
I Know That You Know - QUINTET
Seven Come Eleven
Sing, Sing, Sing
Good-Bye (theme)

The Septet appeared in Point Lookout Park, near Hempstead, New York on July 11; no known tapes from there. Then, since "jazz festivals" were in season internationally this summer, it went to Europe for four of them. The first was the Pori International Jazz Festival in Pori, Finland. An excellent-quality cassette is available from there, but it, too, offers only those performances in which Benny participated:

PORI INTERNATIONAL JAZZ FESTIVAL   July 16, 1982, Pori, Finland

Benny Goodman, clt; Warren Vache, tpt: Scott Hamilton, ts; John Bunch, p; Chris Flory, g; Phil Flanigan, b; Mel Lewis, d.

DUET: Goodman, Bunch
TRIO: Goodman, Flory, Flanigan
QUARTET: Goodman, Bunch, Flanigan, Lewis
QUINTET: Quartet plus Flory

Oh, Lady Be Good! - QUINTET
Here's That Rainy Day - QUARTET
After You've Gone - QUINTET
That's A Plenty
Send In The Clowns - DUET
Air Mail Special
Poor Butterfly - QUINTET
Medley: Don't Be That Way
*   Stompin' At The Savoy*
Sing, Sing, Sing

The next stop was the North Sea festival in the Netherlands Congress Centre, The Hague. The concert was videotaped by A.V.R.O. Television, and excerpts were televised via its network in September and just over a year later. There were two performances, and it is believed that the first telecast was from the earlier one, the second from the later. In any event, note that the two renditions of "Air Mail Special" are different:

NORTH SEA JAZZ FESTIVAL   July 18, 1982,
*   A.V.R.O. Television   The Hague, Netherlands*

Personnels as July 16.

September 1982 telecast:

Air Mail Special
It's Easy To Remember - TRIO
Sing, Sing, Sing

July 31, 1983 telecast:

Air Mail Special
(I'm Old Fashioned - Vache w/rhythm - NO BG
You Go To My Head - TRIO .
I Know That You Know - TRIO
(I Can't Believe That You're In Love With Me - Hamilton w/rhythm - NO BG
Medley: Don't Be That Way
*   Stompin' At The Savoy*

A personal side trip to London, then Benny returned to the Continent for the Antibes festival in Juan-les-Pins on the lovely French Riviera. The concert there was taped by Radio France (Societe Nationale de Radiodiffusion); the listing below is from its master tape. It is believed that excerpts, at least, were broadcast, but if so the date of the broadcast is not known. (Indeed, the concert may have been videotaped and later televised; the author has not been able to determine whether the cameras were on in Antibes.) It is known that the Japanese broadcasting network, NHK-FM, obtained a partial audio tape of the concert and broadcast one selection and a medley. Those two cuts are noted in parentheses following the tunes:

ANTIBES JAZZ FESTIVAL   July 21, 1982,
*   RADIO FRANCE   Juan-les-Pins, France*

Possibly broadcast and/or televised on unknown dates in France. Personnels as July 16.

Air Mail Special (also broadcast by NHK-FM, Japan)
(When I Fall In Love - Hamilton w/rhythm - NO BG
(I'm Old Fashioned - Vache w/rhythm - NO BG
That's A Plenty
(East Of The Sun (And West Of The Moon) - Flory w/rhythm - NO BG
Send In The Clowns - DUET
This Can't Be Love - TRIO
(Ain't Misbehavin' - Bunch w/rhythm - NO BG
(I Can't Believe That You're In Love With Me - Hamilton w/rhythm - NO BG

Memories Of You - TRIO
Medley: Don't Be That Way   ) (also broadcast by
*   Stompin' At The Savoy) NHK-FM, Japan*
Sing, Sing, Sing
Good-Bye (theme)

The festival in the open-air Kalkbergtheatre, Bad Segeberg, West Germany on July 24 found Ella Fitzgerald scheduled to appear before the main attraction, Benny's Septet. Asked to let Ella perform last, Benny agreed, "only because she's a girl!" As the Septet exited, Ella joined for one tune. The next day the nationwide German network televised a brief excerpt from it, and a few bars of an earlier selection:

BAD SEGEBERG JAZZ FESTIVAL   July 24, 1982,
*   ZDF-TV   Bad Segeberg, W. Germany*

Televised July 25. Personnels as July 16, plus Ella Fitzgerald, guest.

Alexander's Ragtime Band (n/c)
I Can't Believe That You're In Love With Me - voc Ella Fitzgerald (n/c)

A portion of the concert was recorded from the audience, ending with the Fitzgerald-Goodman collaboration:

BAD SEGEBERG JAZZ FESTIVAL   July 24, 1982,
*   Bad Segeberg, W. Germany*

Personnels as July 16, plus Ella Fitzgerald, guest.

Air Mail Special
That's A Plenty (n/c - intro excised)
This Can't Be Love - QUINTET (n/c - intro excised)
It's Easy To Remember - TRIO (n/c - intro excised)
Slipped Disc
Sing, Sing, Sing
Good-Bye (theme) (n/c - intro excised)
I Can't Believe That You're In Love With Me - voc Ella Fitzgerald

Those are the only known recordings from the concert at the spa; perhaps that's as well, for the performance was treated unkindly by the German press. (An attendee says the audience was enthusiastic.) There are no known tapes from the last engagement on the tour, the "Capitol Radio Show," London, July 25. BBC recorded other groups on the program, but not the Septet.

Despite the German press reviews, the tapes available from this European tour reveal that Benny was playing rather well. (One is tempted to say that it was his final overseas concert series; at this writing he has accepted none for the future. But a quarter-century close relationship with Mr. Goodman teaches that he should never be anticipated; he may book another tomorrow.) As he did at Carnegie for the "Kool Jazz Festival," he executed better at slower tempi, improved from the first concert to the second and the third. In fact, so did the sidemen; and all seemed more comfortable when the beat was other than furious. On occasion the fast tunes went well, but generally the slower renditions seem more assured, less prone to fluff.

Criticism of Goodman's playing is subject to a constant caveat: He is invariably compared to himself, not to contemporary clarinetists. Because of records and tapes, even the casual fan "knows" the Benny Goodman of earlier years, and his performances then are the standard against which he is measured. We forget that we are listening to a man in his seventies, playing a given tune for an uncounted multi-thousandth time. If he no longer does what he once did, we should understand that whatever he does is quite remarkable. And on occasion that immense talent sparks and flashes, moments when the years dissolve and The Man overmatches his imitators and would-be successors.

Benny's itinerary for the balance of 1982 included seven engagements. The first two—the Hollywood Bowl, August 4, and the Stratford Shakespearian Festival in Ontario, August 16—offer no known recordings. The next two provide minimally-satisfactory cassettes. Because we are "winding down," they are detailed despite their audio-quality shortcomings. The first is from the Garden State Arts Center in Holmdel, New Jersey, the second from Jones Beach on Wantagh, Long Island, New York:

HOLMDEL CONCERT   August 22, 1982, Holmdel, N.J.

Benny Goodman, clt; Spanky Davis, tpt; Joel Helleny, tbn; Scott Hamilton, ts; John Bunch, p; Chris Flory, g; Phil Flanigan, b; Chuck Riggs, d.

DUET: Goodman, Bunch
QUINTET: Duet plus Flory, Flanigan, Riggs

Avalon - QUINTET
September Song - QUINTET
You Go To My Head - QUINTET
After You've Gone - QUINTET
(When I Fall In Love - Hamilton w/rhythm - NO BG
(I Can't Get Started - Davis w/rhythm - NO BG
That's A Plenty
(East Of The Sun (And West Of The Moon) - Flory w/rhythm - NO BG
Darn That Dream - feat. Helleny
Medley: Don't Be That Way
        Stompin' At The Savoy
Send In The Clowns - DUET
(Ain't Misbehavin' - Bunch w/rhythm - NO BG
Sing, Sing, Sing
Good-Bye (theme)

JONES BEACH CONCERT   August 26, 1982, Long Island, N.Y.

Personnels as August 22.

Avalon - QUINTET
Here's That Rainy Day - QUINTET
You Go To My Head - QUINTET
Oh, Lady Be Good! - QUINTET
(I Should Care - Hamilton w/rhythm - NO BG
I Can't Get Started - Davis w/rhythm - BG in coda
That's A Plenty
(Darn That Dream - Helleny w/rhythm - NO BG
More Than You Know - DUET
(East Of The Sun (And West Of The Moon) - Flory w/rhythm - NO BG
Medley: Don't Be That Way
        Stompin' At The Savoy
Sing, Sing, Sing
Good-Bye (theme)

(At both concerts preceding, Bucky Pizzarelli and his son, John Jr., were guest artists, and played prior to Benny's entrance.)

A combined classical/jazz concert in Raleigh, North Carolina's Memorial Auditorium on October 15 affords no known recording. Our final cassette for 1982, of indifferent audio quality, is from the C. W. Post (College) Concert Theater, where Benny was introduced by the screen's Arlene Dahl. Once again the Pizzarellis, father and son, were guest artists, but did not perform with the Goodman group:

C.W. POST CONCERT   November 6, 1982, Greenvale, N.Y.

Benny Goodman, clt; Spanky Davis, tpt; Joel Helleny, tbn; Mike LeDonne, p; Chris Flory, g; Todd Coolman, b; Chuck Riggs, d.

DUET: Goodman, LeDonne
QUINTET: Duet plus Flory, Coolman, Riggs

Oh, Lady Be Good! - QUINTET
It's Easy To Remember - QUINTET
After You've Gone - QUINTET
(I Can't Get Started - Davis w/rhythm - NO BG
(In A Sentimental Mood - Helleny w/rhythm - NO BG
That's A Plenty
Send In The Clowns - DUET
(East Of The Sun - Flory w/rhythm - NO BG
Medley: Don't Be That Way
        Stompin' At The Savoy
Sing, Sing, Sing
Good-Bye (theme)

On November 10 Benny was interviewed in his New York apartment by Dick Shepard of The United Stations, a transcription service that offers prepackaged programs to subscribing radio stations. Each program, four hours in length, is devoted to one artist and his (or her) recordings, plus prerecorded commercials, and are targeted to a specific weekend. The programs are distributed via cassettes and 12" LP's; the four LP's required for a single program bear "matrices" indicating the intended broadcast date.

Benny was featured on the weekend of January 28–30, 1983, so the applicable LP's are numbered TGS-1/28/83-1A, -1B, through -4B. Benny's comments between his recordings are interesting, and a tape of the broadcast is recommended to collectors. The final tune is Benny's 1952 all-string Columbia recording of "Good-Bye"; unfortunately, interviewer Shepard gratuitously adds that it includes a trumpet solo by Bunny Berigan . . .

Benny took a rhythm section to Avery Fisher Hall in Lincoln Center November 15, his 20-minute contribution to a benefit for Yank Magazine and U.S. servicemen. It was his last performance of 1982, and regrettably there is no known recording of the benefit.

In 1978 the trustees of the John F. Kennedy Center for the Performing Arts in the Nation's capital inaugurated an annual awards presentation ". . . to provide national recognition to individuals who throughout their lifetimes have made significant contributions to American culture through the performing arts." On December 5 Benny Goodman was so honored, together with George Abbott, Lillian Gish, Gene Kelly and Eugene Ormandy. A massive souvenir program of the event contains many unique photographs of the recipients, and includes a foreword about Benny Goodman by the author. Andre Previn spoke of Benny's accomplishments at the ceremony, and Lionel Hampton played in his honor. The fifth "Kennedy Center Honors" program was videotaped by the National Broadcasting Company, and was televised on Christmas night, December 25.

Home from his annual holiday season sojourn in St. Martin's, Benny performed for fellow-members of his Century Club on January 12 with cellist Nick Rosen and pianist Todd Crow. A cassette of the classical mini-concert is extant, but has not been heard by the author. The next day he was interviewed in his apartment by WNEW's Jim Lowe for the station's January 16 commemoration of the Carnegie Hall concert. The broadcast included taped reminiscences by Helen Ward and Bill Savory, Willard Alexander, and Lionel Hampton, all recorded earlier in the month; and comments by Sol Hurok, Gene Krupa and Martha Tilton, excerpted from Benny's 1968 30th Anniversary Party.

The Lehman College Center for the Performing Art's "Midwinter Jazz Festival" was Benny's first play-for-pay engagement in 1983. A minimally-satisfactory audience recording finds the group having some fun with "Jingle Bells":

LEHMAN COLLEGE CONCERT   January 30, 1983, Bronx, New York

Benny Goodman, clt; Spanky Davis, tpt; Joel Helleny, tbn; Mike LeDonne, p; Chris Flory, g; Phil Flanigan, b; Frank Bennett, d.

QUINTET: Goodman, LeDonne, Flory, Flanigan, Bennett

I Want To Be Happy - QUINTET
Body And Soul - QUINTET
Avalon - QUINTET
(I Can't Get Started - Davis w/rhythm - NO BG
Medley: Don't Be That Way
        Stompin' At the Savoy
(In A Sentimental Mood - Helleny w/rhythm - NO BG
Jingle Bells
(East Of The Sun (And West Of The Moon) - Flory w/rhythm - NO BG
(Gone With The Wind - LeDonne w/rhythm - NO BG
Memories Of You - QUINTET
Air Mail Special
Sing, Sing, Sing
Good-Bye (theme)

Accompanied by LeDonne, Flory, Flanigan and Bennett, Benny played three college dates in February: El Camino Community College, Torrance, California, February 18; Grady Gammage Center, Arizona State University, Tempe, February 20; and the University of North Carolina, Wilmington, February 26. March was an open month, but the college circuit continued in April: Iowa State University, Ames, April 16, with the full group that appeared at Lehman College; and a benefit at Yale University with the Muir String Quartet, and with LeDonne, Flory, Todd Coolman and Bennett, April 22. Rounding out the month, Benny performed at the Pierpont Morgan Library in Manhattan on April 28 with the Ridge String Quartet, and with LeDonne, Flory, Flanigan and Bennett. No tapes of any of these engagements have become available to the author. There is extant, however, a recorded interview, via telephone, between Benny and Murray Kent of radio station WMT, Cedar Rapids, Iowa. It was broadcast April 10, to promote the Iowa State University concert.

Benny's next public appearance—it would prove to be his last for some time to come—was a reunion with Andre Previn, then the conductor of the Pittsburgh Symphony Orchestra, in Heinz Hall, Pittsburgh, Pennsylvania. The engagement is especially noteworthy for two reasons: Previn induced

Benny to play the concerto that Goodman had commissioned from Paul Hindemith, a composition that Benny seldom performed. And the Westinghouse Broadcasting and Cable Company, Inc., videotaped the event; an hour-long videocassette is extant.

The videocassette begins with a charming chat between Benny and Previn. In an oft-told tale illustrative of Benny's intense preoccupation with playing, Previn reminds Benny of an October 1958 recording session in Benny's studio in Stamford. The weather was cold, the unheated studio frigid, and the sidemen nominated Previn to ask Benny to do something about it. Benny did; he put on a sweater . . . And in response to Previn's question, "Who was your favorite drummer?", Benny replies with an emphatic "Gene Krupa, without a doubt," and then takes a minute or two to explain his reasons for that choice.

Next on the videocassette are five renditions by the Quintet; it then ends with Benny as guest soloist with the symphony orchestra:

PITTSBURGH CONCERT   May 3, 1983, Pittsburgh

. . . conversation Goodman & Previn

Benny Goodman, clt; Andre Previn, p; Chris Flory, g; Todd Coolman, b; Grady Tate, d.

Avalon
Here's That Rainy Day
Air Mail Special
Poor Butterfly
After You've Gone

Benny Goodman, clt, and the Pittsburgh Symphony Orchestra, Andre Previn, conductor.

Clarinet Concerto (Hindemith)

To the best of the author's knowledge, the videotape was never televised; he suspects, however, that brief excerpts of it may have appeared on news telecasts in the Western Pennsylvania area.

No other engagements were scheduled until June 17, when Benny was to perform at Manhattanville College in Purchase, New York, with cellist Nick Rosen and pianist Irma Vallecillo. An aching shoulder caused him to cancel this date. On June 19 he was among those honored as "Father Of The Year" for the annual celebration of Father's Day.

On July 5 Harry Haag James, age 67, died in the Valley Hospital, Las Vegas, a victim of lymphatic cancer. Among the most talented of the Goodman alumni, Harry was one of a very few orchestra leaders of the Swing Era who successfully persisted with a big band through decades of shifting changes in America's musical preferences. He performed until the very end, an appearance in Los Angeles on June 26. His legacy to the world of jazz is a vast catalog of some of the most inventive and exciting trumpet soli ever recorded. In Benny's words, "Harry was the one guy I could count on to get the whole band going. He was full of ideas, and what's more, he could execute them." Look to your laurels, Gabriel, here comes Harry James.

There's little to recount of Benny's professional activities in the summer and fall of 1983. He booked a private party in Far Hills, New York on August 17, but his rhythm section appeared without him. An interview videotaped in his apartment was televised on the CBS "Morning News," September 6; mentioned is a trip to Japan, which did not eventuate. Scheduled concerts with the rhythm section for November 12, in the Strand-Capital in York, Pennsylvania, and for November 19, in Ruth Eckerd Hall, Clearwater, Florida, were cancelled. Benny's recurrent back pain had flared up, arthritis afflicted his hands and affected his fingering, and he had an aching knee. He decided he'd better see a doctor.

During the consultation, his doctor suggested that it had been a long time since Benny had had a general physical examination; would he agree to undergo some tests? Certainly; and the results were alarming, the electrocardiograph indicated a serious problem that demanded immediate attention. Rushed to a hospital on November 23, he spent 18 hours on an operating table while a team of surgeons strove to dissolve an embolism in his descending aorta. The operation was successful but entailed a lengthy recuperative period, the first part of which Benny spent in his surgeon's home. In January 1984 he had a second operation, this time to implant a pacemaker.

The precise nature of Benny's surgery was withheld from the news media; in print and on the air, it was variously ascribed to "a stomach upset," "an abdominal problem," etc. The concealment was deliberate and in the tradition of show business: even at age 74, Benny intended to resume his career when he recovered, and wanted no intimation abroad that he was in any way incapacitated. This deception extended to the author, who regularly updated the biographical portion of Benny's press kit (background

information sent to the promoters of his engagements). In 1985, when Benny was about to go back to work in earnest, the author wrote a bland paragraph to explain Benny's two-year absence from public performances, suggesting a "minor operation, long overdue," its nature undisclosed, had caused Benny to take a protracted "vacation." But Benny would have no part of it, the paragraph was simply deleted, resulting in a rather awkward gap in the chronology.

The ensuing 15 months found Benny accepting various honors, making an occasional public statement, mourning the deaths of a growing list of his former associates. On April 14, 1984, the National Academy of Popular Music gave him its "Lifetime Achievement Award" at a ceremony in the Waldorf-Astoria. After a lengthy illness, William "Count" Basie passed away in Florida on April 26; CBS-TV network news telecasts carried Benny's brief remarks the same day. Fellow-Chicagoan and composer-arranger Gordon Jenkins said his last "Good-Bye" May 1, in Malibu, California; it's worth noting that he arranged for Goodman for more years than anyone else, from the mid-'Thirties to the late 'Seventies. Harvard University conferred an honorary degree of Doctor of Music upon Benny on June 7.

Well meaning attempts to lure Benny back to work were underway. It was hoped he would appear, might even play, at a "Salute To Benny Goodman" at Waterloo Village, Stanhope, New Jersey on August 18. For the concert, Benny loaned some of his arrangements to leader-clarinetist Bob Wilber, who had assembled a big band of competent studio musicians. Benny, however, finally elected not to attend; but he was intrigued by professional tapes of the performance, especially those of the Henderson charts. They started him thinking about the future.

The necrology lengthened: Willard Alexander, the Music Corporation of America manager whose perspicacity and conviction were key factors in bringing the 1935 Goodman orchestra national acclaim, died August 28. James "Trummy" Young died of a cerebral hemorrhage September 10. Heart attacks felled Shelly Manne on September 26, and Albert "Budd" Johnson on October 20. James Caesar Petrillo, longtime leader of the American Federation of Musicians, died October 23.

Producer Jonas Sima's "The Stan Hasselgard Story," a documentary filmed for Swedish Television, includes reminiscences about the tragic clarinetist by, among others, Benny Goodman, Billy Bauer and Patti Page, who were with him at the "Click" in Philadelphia in 1948. The film was shown at the London Film Festival, National Film Theatre, on November 24. Three weeks earlier (November 2), Benny was named a Samuel Simons Sanford Fellow of the School of Music, Yale University.

The new year began sadly when Johnny Guarnieri, on a trip east from his home in Los Angeles, succumbed to a heart attack in Livingston, New Jersey, on January 7, 1985. His 1939–1941 tenure with Goodman, interrupted by Benny's back operation and enforced absence from the big band scene, proved him a thoroughly schooled musician and another in a succession of top rank Goodman pianists.

On February 15 Benny was in Chicago to help open an exhibit on the history of music in the Windy City, sponsored by the Chicago Historical Society. (He sat in with a nine-piece orchestra at a dinner-dance that evening, played "Sweet Georgia Brown," but there are no known tapes of the performance.) While there he taped a lengthy interview with Roy Leonard; it was broadcast on Leonard's program on April 16, via radio station WGN, Chicago.

Annette Hanshaw, whom Benny had accompanied more than a half-century earlier, died of cancer on March 13. The novelty vocalist, highly popular as a teenager in the late 1920s and early 1930s, retired from show business at age 24; her November 1933 recording date with Benny was one of her last professional engagements. John Haley "Zoot" Sims, who like Hanshaw had worked for Benny at a very young age, also was a victim of the dread disease 10 days later, passed away March 23. Sims, whose progressive style accommodated to many styles of jazz, played tenor for Benny at intervals over three decades, and played well, indeed. Benny attended a tribute to him at New York's "jazz church," St. Peter's Lutheran, on March 25.

March also brought some pleasant news: headed by Gil Glynn of Baton Rouge, an intensive campaign to put forward Benny Goodman as a nominee for a Presidential Medal Of Freedom accelerated into high gear. The award is presented annually to those who ". . . have made especially meritorious contributions to (1) the security or national interests of the United States, or (2) world peace, or (3) cultural or other significant public or private endeavors." Over the next 15 months Glynn's efforts would attract glowing recommendations to President Reagan from former presidents of the United States, senators, congressmen and other elected officials; from the heads of many major colleges, conservatories and universities; and from many luminaries of show business, among others. Glynn's target was the 1986 awards, which unfortunately was not realized. He looks forward confidently to 1987.

But the best news of all in March 1985 was that Benny decided it was high time he went back to work. And in the age-old tradition of musicians starting out, he played for a wedding reception! This one, however, had an ultramodern twist: it was recorded on videocassette.

Confiding in no one, Benny had been contemplating just how he might best perform once again in public. His health, his endurance, his ability to play well, all would be on trial; he needed a venue in which, above all else, he would be comfortable. It had to be nearby, to minimize the rigors of travel; ideally, his audience should be small, and hopefully uncritical; and there must be no publicity. The tentative offers coming in satisfied none of his requirements.

His attorney, Bill Hyland, had been approached by a friend, Charles Foulke: Would Benny consider playing for the wedding reception of his daughter, Michelle Maria, at the posh Ramshead Inn (a favorite hangout of Frank Sinatra's), in Absecon, New Jersey? Thinking there was no chance Benny would accept, Bill passed along the proposal. To his amazement, Benny said, "I'll do it," for it was just the milieu he'd been seeking.

The video portion of the souvenir cassette lacks definition, color isn't true, and fast dissolves during its latter segment, when the guests are dancing, merely sample the musical performances. But the audio track is quite good, and Benny is excellent. He's more than that; his playing is brilliant, effortless, faultless, inspiring. He takes blazing, extended choruses in the uptempo tunes, emotional soli in the ballads; the sidemen are visibly impressed. And to show he remembers the conventions of this kind of event, he invites the bride and her father to dance to a tune he'd likely not played in more than 60 years, the prescriptive "Daddy's Little Girl."

In the author's view, Benny had not played this well, for 45 minutes, through the late '70s and early '80s; and he considers his performance here superior to those that lie ahead.

WEDDING RECEPTION   *March 8, 1985, Absecon, N.J.*

Benny Goodman, clt; Randy Sandke, tpt; Urbie Green, tbn; Ben Aronov, p; Bucky Pizzarelli, g; Bill Crow, b; Chuck Riggs, d.

QUINTET: Goodman, Aronov, Pizzarelli, Crow, Riggs
SEXTET: Quintet plus Bill Hyland, clt

Let's Dance (theme)
Avalon
Memories Of You - QUINTET
Air Mail Special
Body And Soul - QUINTET
That's A Plenty
Daddy's Little Girl

Intermission; dancing to follow

Stompin' At The Savoy (n/c)
Undecided - SEXTET (Hyland remains for balance of performance)
. . . unidentified tune, full group (possibly reprise, "Undecided")
Rose Room (n/c)
Seven Come Eleven (n/c)

Producer Irving Mills, whose other music-related credits include those as arranger, composer, violinist and vocalist, died April 21 in Los Angeles at age 90. His varied talents are reflected in Benny's "Whoopee Makers" recordings of the late 1920s.

On May 14 Benny received Hull House's First Annual Distinguished Service Award at the Marriott Hotel in Chicago. Bud Freeman's quartet provided the entertainment at dinner that evening. He spoke fondly of Benny, then induced him to sit in. An excellent-quality recording is extent:

HULL HOUSE AWARD DINNER   *May 14, 1985, Chicago*
Benny Goodman, clt; Art Hodes, p; John Bany, b; Jerry Coleman, d.

Body And Soul

Add Bud Freeman, ts

The Blues

The University of Hartford (Connecticut) conferred an honorary degree of Doctor of Music upon Benny on May 19.

John Hammond suffered a stroke in June; although recovering, he was unable to attend the Kool Jazz Festival's tribute to him at Avery Fisher Hall in Lincoln Center. Producer George Wein, with but faint hope that Benny would perform, invited him to a rehearsal on the afternoon of June 25. Benny didn't play, left with the announcement that he didn't think he'd come to the evening concert. Twenty minutes later, he called Wein from his

apartment, said he'd changed his mind. A surprise guest greeted with a storm of applause, he sat in with pianist Dick Hyman, guitarist George Benson, bassist Cecil McBee and drummer Gus Johnson for two tunes, "Oh, Lady Be Good!" and "Body And Soul." With trumpeter Harry "Sweets" Edison and tenor saxophonist Scott Hamilton added, Benny concluded with "Indiana" and the medley, "Don't Be That Way/Stompin' At The Savoy." Apparently no professional recording of Benny's contribution to his brother-in-law's tribute was made, and no audience recording of it has come to the author's attention.

His Kool Jazz Festival appearance was Benny's first truly professional engagement in some 25 months. Although it was emotionally stressful, he was encouraged that it caused him no ill aftereffects, and it stimulated him to consider in earnest a return to performing. His opportunities were several: he could concentrate on classical music or on jazz, or do both; and if he elected to play jazz, he could have a small group or a big band. After much thought and heedless of well-meaning advice from his close friends, he decided that if he was to return, it would be full bore: He would play both classical and jazz; he would have a big band; and he would feature his prized Fletcher Henderson arrangements, which he believed to be woefully neglected. He had had that last thought in mind ever since Bob Wilber's concert at Waterloo Village the previous August.

Too, he was resolved that this time his orchestra would be well-rehearsed, there would be no repetition of the ill-prepared 1978 Carnegie Hall concert. He had had informal conversations with the management of Manhattan's PBS television station about the possibility of a major production, likely in October, so there was plenty of time. He set out to assemble a new "Benny Goodman and his Orchestra."

His thinking first turned to the studio musicians, many of whom he'd hired in the past, and who were familiar with the Henderson charts. But a former office assistant, tenor saxophonist Loren Schoenberg, suggested an alternative: For the last several years he had been leader of and booking agent for a 16-piece orchestra that had reasonably stable personnel. Their jobs had been few, but they had assembled even for the most meagre of engagements because they liked the music. More, they had been playing some of Henderson's arrangements which Loren, with Benny's permission, had Xeroxed while working in the office. Would Benny care to hear them play?

Benny listened, and liked what he heard. He was familiar with but few of the sidemen, but found them all obviously talented and manifestly enthusiastic. Oh, they needed guidance, leadership, perhaps a change here and there . . . But the nucleus was there, no question about that, and Benny was certain he could mold them into a representative Benny Goodman Orchestra, one with which he would be satisfied.

Benny then began a series of rehearsals, a regimen he'd not followed since the height of the Big Band Era. We are indebted to Lloyd Rauch, who soon would become Benny's office aide, for meticulously logging the rehearsals, and for recording them via cassette. The first half-dozen were in RCA's New York studios, beginning with:

BENNY GOODMAN AND HIS ORCHESTRA   *August 16, 1985, New York*

Benny Goodman, clt; Paul Cohen, John Eckert, Laurie Frink, Bob Livingood, tpt; Eddie Bert, Matt Finders, Matt Havilland, tbn; Chuck Wilson, Mark Lopeman, as; Ken Peplowski, Doug Lawrence, ts; Tom Olin, bar; Dick Katz, p; James Chirillo, g; Jon Goldsby, b; Mel Lewis, d.

Blue Skies
Down South Camp Meetin'
Don't Be That Way
Stealin' Apples

(This rehearsal, and all that follow, include many false starts and incidental practice that are not detailed. Audio quality is satisfactory.)

BENNY GOODMAN AND HIS ORCHESTRA   *August 22, 1985, New York*

Goodman, clt; Cohen, Eckert, DICK SUDHALTER, RANDY SANDKE, tpt; Bert, Finders, BRITT WOODMAN, tbn; Wilson, JACK STUCKEY, as; Peplowski, LOREN SCHOENBERG, ts; DANNY BANK, bar; Katz, p; Chirillo, g; ARVELL SHAW, b; ROBBIE SCOTT, d. IRENE DATSCHER, voc.

ELEVEN: Goodman, Sudhalter, Woodman, Peplowski, Schoenberg, Bank, Katz, Chirillo, Shaw, Scott

The Blues - ELEVEN
Don't Be That Way
Down South Camp Meetin'
Blue Skies

Blue Room
If I Could Be With You
Stealin' Apples
More Than You Know
Don't Be That Way
Embraceable You-voc Irene Datscher - BG, band contingent
Bye Bye Blackbird-voc Irene Datscher - BG, band contingent
King Porter Stomp
Honeysuckle Rose-voc Irene Datscher - BG, band contingent
Wrappin' It Up

BENNY GOODMAN AND HIS ORCHESTRA   August 27, 1985, New York

Goodman, clt; Cohen, Eckert, Sandke, tpt; Finders, BOBBY PRING, tbn; Stuckey, MARK LOPEMAN, as; Peplowski, Schoenberg, ts; Bank, bar; Katz, p; HOWARD ALDEN, g; Shaw, b; Scott, d.

SEPTET: Goodman, Finders, Schoenberg, Katz, Alden, Shaw, Scott

Blue Skies
Down South Camp Meetin'
If I Could Be With You
Sometimes I'm Happy
At The Darktown Strutters' Ball
Sometimes I'm Happy
You Turned The Tables On Me
King Porter Stomp
If I Could Be With You
Blue Room
Moon Glow - SEPTET
Stealin' Apples

It should be noted that not all the rehearsal tapes have been heard; the listings throughout this period are based on documentation. Those tapes that have been available correspond with the written records.

A fourth trumpeter whose identity is unknown began the next session; midway through, Laurie Frink replaced him:

BENNY GOODMAN AND HIS ORCHESTRA   September 4, 1985, New York

Goodman, clt; Cohen, Eckert, Sandke, unknown, tpt; Finders, Pring, EDDIE BERT, tbn; Stuckey, CHUCK WILSON, as: Peplowski, Schoenberg, ts; Bank, bar; Katz, p; JAMES CHIRILLO, g; Shaw, b; RICHIE PRATT, d.

Blue Skies
You Brought A New Kind Of Love To Me
Let's Dance (theme)
And The Angels Sing
Just You, Just Me

LAURIE FRINK replaces unidentified tpt

At The Darktown Strutters' Ball
More Than You Know
(I Would Do) Anything For You
When Buddha Smiles
Stealin' Apples

BENNY GOODMAN AND HIS ORCHESTRA September 12, 1985, New York

Personnel as September 4, including Frink, except RAY MOSCA, d, replaces Pratt.

TRIO: Goodman, Katz, Chirillo

Don't Be That Way
You Brought A New Kind Of Love To Me
Blue Room
Let's Dance (theme)
Down South Camp Meetin'
Body And Soul - TRIO
If I Could Be With You

Dick Hyman conducted prior to Benny's arrival at the next rehearsal, and sat in for some tunes when Benny was present - but these were not notated.

BENNY GOODMAN AND HIS ORCHESTRA   September 17, 1985, New York

Personnel as September 12, except DICK HYMAN, p, replaces Katz on some selections. BARBARA LEA, voc.

King Porter Stomp
Don't Be That Way
Let's Dance (theme)
Blue Skies
You Turned The Tables On Me-voc Barbara Lea
Blue Room
If I Could Be With You
King Porter Stomp

Alert to Benny's imminent return to the big band business, NBC-TV videotaped portions of the next rehearsal, now in Manhattan's S I R Studios. Brief excerpts of the videotape were televised via WNBC-TV, New York, on its October 1 local news programs. The studio audio tape includes:

BENNY GOODMAN AND HIS ORCHESTRA   September 26, 1985, New York

Personnel as September 4, including Laurie Frink. Barbara Lea, voc.

Let's Dance
Between The Devil And The Deep Blue Sea-voc Barbara Lea
Restless-voc Barbara Lea
Goodnight, My Love-voc Barbara Lea
Don't Be That Way
Sometimes I'm Happy
King Porter Stomp
At The Darktown Strutters' Ball
You Brought A New Kind Of Love To Me-voc Barbara Lea

Benny was privately enthusiastic about his new orchestra, felt it had improved with each rehearsal. Almost on a "don't-let-them-know" basis, he told the author, "It's really a pretty good band." He himself was mentally refreshed, felt well physically, despite the rigors of the rehearsals. He now was confident that the first public appearance at Waterloo Village on the 27th would bear out his assessment, and he looked forward to the "try-out," as he put it, eagerly. But Hurricane Gloria rained on his parade, caused the outdoor tent concert to be rescheduled for October 1. Disappointed but still driving toward perfection, he called for another rehearsal, this one in New York's Public Theater:

BENNY GOODMAN AND HIS ORCHESTRA   September 30, 1985, New York

Personnel as September 26, except: Arvell Shaw is absent the first two tunes; JOHN MARSHALL, tpt, replaces Frink at some juncture; JORDAN SANDKE replaces Randy Sandke for the final tune; and Chirillo is absent the last two selections.

Sometimes I'm Happy
Don't Be That Way
You're A Heavenly Thing-voc Barbara Lea
Good-Bye
And The Angels Sing-voc Barbara Lea
Let's Dance
Blue Skies
Restless-voc Barbara Lea
Down South Camp Meetin'
Blue Room

Before we leave September, we note with sorrow the deaths of Jonathan David Samuel "Jo" Jones (September 3) and Charles Melvin "Cootie" Williams (September 15), both in New York. Jo had only been an occasional substitute for Benny, but Cootie had been with him for a full year, and Benny remembered him fondly as ". . . really a good guy to have in the band."

At last, the delayed debut of the new Benny Goodman Orchestra, and a full tent on hand to welcome Benny back. A mismatch between microphones and Benny's portable Nagra produced piercingly shrill tapes that require heavy equalization, but a backup stereo cassette system recorded the concert excellently. Even more noteworthy, WNET-TV, New York's Channel 13 Public Service television station, videotaped the concert in full, its own rehearsal for the upcoming October 7 gala:

BENNY GOODMAN AND HIS ORCHESTRA   *October 1, 1985, Waterloo*
                                            Village, Stanhope, N.J.

Benny Goodman, clt; Laurie Frink, Randy Sandke, John Eckert, Paul Cohen, tpt; Matt Finders, Bobby Pring, Eddie Bert, tbn; Chuck Wilson, Jack Stuckey, as; Ken Peplowski, Loren Schoenberg, ts; Danny Bank, bar; Dick Katz, p; James Chirillo, g; Arvell Shaw, b; Richie Pratt, d. Barbara Lea, voc.

OCTET: Goodman, Eckert, Peplowski, Schoenberg, rhythm section

Let's Dance (theme)
Don't Be That Way
Sometimes I'm Happy
King Porter Stomp
You Turned The Tables On Me-voc Barbara Lea
Between The Devil And The Deep Blue Sea-voc Barbara Lea
Exactly Like You - OCTET
Blue Skies
. . . reprise, intro, Blue Skies
(I Would Do) Anything For You

Intermission

Down South Camp Meetin'

(Summertime-voc Rosemary Barenz, accomp. Jayson Enquist, p - NO BG
(Puccini: Aria from La Boheme-voc Barenz, accomp. Enquist - NO BG

Blue Room
Restless-voc Barbara Lea
You Brought A New Kind Of Love To Me-voc Barbara Lea

(Gone With The Wind - Bill Hyland, clt, w/rhythm section - NO BG
(Body and Soul - as "Gone With The Wind" - NO BG

Stealin' Apples
Good-Bye (in its entirety)
At The Darktown Strutters' Ball
And The Angels Sing-voc Barbara Lea
You're A Heavenly Thing-voc Barbara Lea
"That's All!"

(Benny has the band repeat the introduction to "Blue Skies" to illustrate Fletcher Henderson's explanation to Benny that the crashing intro - followed by a quiet passage - represents "The storm before the blue skies appear.")

The band rehearsed without Benny on October 5; pianist Dick Hyman conducted. The next day Benny assembled it in the Grand Ballroom of the just-opened Marriott Marquis Hotel for its final session before the WNET-PBS special. Guest performers Red Norvo, Teddy Wilson, Slam Stewart and Louis Bellson got in their licks following the orchestra's practice:

BENNY GOODMAN AND HIS ORCHESTRA   *October 6, 1985, New York*

Personnel as October 1, except: DICK HYMAN, p, replaces Katz; BOB HAGGART, b, replaces Shaw; and LOUIS BELLSON, d, alternates with Pratt.

TRIO: Benny Goodman, clt; Teddy Wilson, p; Louis Bellson, d
QUARTET: Goodman, clt; Red Norvo, vib; Haggart, b; Bellson, d
QUINTET: Quartet plus Hyman, p

Let's Dance (theme)
Don't Be That Way
You Brought A New Kind Of Love To Me
King Porter Stomp
(I Would Do) Anything For You
Down South Camp Meetin' (n/c)
Blue Room
Stealin' Apples
Let's Dance (sound check - 4 takes)
Good-Bye (theme)

Body And Soul - TRIO
(Flat Foot Floogie-voc Slam Stewart, b, w/Hyman, Bellson - NO BG
(I Surrender, Dear (n/c) - Norvo, Hyman, Haggart, Bellson - NO BG
(There Will Never Be Another You - as "I Surrender, Dear" - NO BG
Indiana - QUINTET
I Surrender, Dear - QUARTET
Indiana - QUINTET
(Summertime - Wilson p solo - NO BG
(But Not For Me - Wilson p solo - NO BG
(Medley: The Man I Love/But Not For Me - Wilson p solo - NO BG

Some 600 guests began arriving at the sumptuous Marriott Marquis even before the 6:00 p.m. cocktail hour that would open the festivities attendant WNET-PBS's "Benny Goodman - Let's Dance - A Musical Tribute." Promptly at 7:00, the band, sans Benny, warmed up the audience, then Benny entered to thunderous applause, the cameras rolled, and the program was underway.

Morton Gould, Bobby Short, Frank Sinatra and Yale University president A. Bartlett Giamatti paid tribute to Benny and recounted reminiscences about him. The live performances were interspersed with film clips, videotapes and still photographs (with recorded music over), all displayed on screen for the audience. Vocalists Carrie Smith and Rosemary Clooney performed with the band, but without Benny.

The edited videotape that would be televised some five months later — the highlight of the PBS network's solicitation drive — omits Benny's participation with Red Norvo, Dick Hyman, Slam Stewart and Louis Bellson; and fund raisers' voices-over interrupt the full rendition of "Good-Bye." But Benny did not join with Teddy Wilson during the program, so nothing is missing there.

"BENNY GOODMAN: LET'S DANCE, A   *October 7, 1985, Marriott*
MUSICAL TRIBUTE" - PBS Telecast   *Marquis Hotel, New York*

Televised nationally on the PBS network on various dates in March 1986. John Bartholomew Tucker, anncr.

Orchestra as October 6, except Bellson on d throughout. Carrie Smith, Rosemary Clooney, voc.

GOODMAN QUARTET: Goodman, Hyman, Stewart, Bellson
WILSON TRIO: Wilson, Stewart, Bellson
NORVO QUARTET: Norvo, Hyman, Stewart, Bellson

Let's Dance (theme)
Don't Be That Way
(I Would Do) Anything For You

(excerpt, "After You've Gone," from Disney's "Make Mine Music"
(Morton Gould tribute; introduces Teddy Wilson
(Wilson Trio medley: The Man I Love/But Not For Me - NO BG
(Bobby Short tribute; introduces Carrie Smith
(Gimme A Pigfoot-voc Carrie Smith, w/Sandke, rhythm section - NO BG
(Ja-Da-voc Carrie Smith, w/orchestra - NO BG
(excerpt, "Sing, Sing, Sing," from "Hollywood Hotel"

King Porter Stomp

(film excerpts from 1962 USSR tour: classical composition, "One O'Clock Jump"

The Flat Foot Floogie-voc Slam Stewart - GOODMAN QUARTET (BG trill)
Memories Of You - GOODMAN QUARTET

(Frank Sinatra tribute
(Medley: Somebody Else Is Taking My Place)
*   You Turned The Tables On Me   ) - voc Rosemary Clooney*
*   And The Angels Sing   ) - NO BG*
(There's No Business Like Show Business - voc Rosemary Clooney - NO BG
(reprise, "Let's Dance"
(excerpt, 1954 "Person To Person" TV program
(There Will Never Be Another You - NORVO QUARTET - NO BG

You Brought A New Kind Of Love To Me
The Blue Room

(A. Bartlett Giamatti tribute
(various film & still photo's, commercial records' background

Down South Camp Meetin'
Stealin' Apples
Good-Bye (n/c - voice over)

(NOTE: Under consideration in September 1986 by WNET and executors for the Goodman estate is public sale of this videotape.)

Some Marriott Marquis sidelights:
Except when he rose to perform, Red Norvo spent the entire evening in a wheel chair. He had hurt his back on the flight from his Santa Monica, California home, and was in considerable pain.

A tentative agreement between Frank Sinatra's manager and Benny's staff that Frank would sing one song with the Goodman Quartet didn't happen. On camera, Frank begged off, said he hadn't time, hadn't rehearsed; this despite the audience's clamor and Benny's invitation. His refusal and Benny's consternation were an awkward few moments that were deleted from the telecast.

Teddy Wilson, his wife and son Theodore sat with the author and his wife at dinner after the performance. Ever polite and responsive, Teddy nevertheless seemed preoccupied, joined only occasionally in the chatter about old times and future events. Midway through the meal he excused himself, said he wanted to get some cough drops at a stand in the hotel, he'd be right back. He never returned. After dinner his son, the author and his wife searched the lobby but failed to find him. Evidently fatigued and possibly unwell, he'd gone to his room and to bed.

In an open letter to the WNET producers, the bandsmen complained that although such utility participants as hair stylists, makeup artists and the like were named in the videotape's credits, no orchestra personnel were similarly recognized. Their signed letter was reproduced in the musicians' magazine "Allegro," April 1986 issue.

Concurrently with the PBS national subscription drive in March 1986, the Musical Heritage Society transcribed and released the videotape's orchestral performances on two labels. Under its own name, an album was made available as a bonus for subscribers; for retail outlets, the LP appeared on the "Musicmasters' label. Three details bear notice: Laurie Frink's "clinker" in the intro to "King Porter Stomp" is retained in the album, deleted in the telecast, but one other trumpet solo is excised from the album, kept in the videotape; the order-of-performance is altered slightly; and artist credit for Danny Bank is omitted in the LP's liner notes. In all other respects the LP is faithful to the performance, and affords the complete rendition of "Good-Bye."

BENNY GOODMAN AND HIS ORCHESTRA:
LIVE! BENNY LET'S DANCE   **October 7, 1985, New York**

Personnel as October 7 PBS telecast.

-0-	**StLP:** MHS 7412X, MM 20112Z. **CD:** MM 60112X
	Let's Dance
	Don't Be That Way
	You Brought A New Kind Of Love To Me
	King Porter Stomp
	(I Would Do Most) Anything For You
-0-	**StLP:** as above, except Side 2. **CD:** MM 60112X
	(The) Blue Room
	Down South Camp Meetin'
	Stealin' Apples
	Goodbye

(The LP's use their respective catalog numbers as "matrix" numbers.)

The author visited with Benny the week after the PBS special. Pleased with the band—and undoubtedly delighted with once again being in the limelight—Benny was full of plans for the future. Offers for concert appearances with the big band were already coming in, and he'd decided he would accept some of them. His "Private Collection" album had revived his interest in releasing some of the material in his library, and it took time to review the tapes. He wanted to go to California to visit daughter Rachel, he thought he'd go to St. Martin's, he'd been neglecting the art museums . . . there was lots to do.

"Benny, are you sure this won't be too much for you? After all . . ." "No, not at all. I'm watching my diet, I'm swimming a little bit every day, I feel fine. Don't worry." But the author did.

The first concert appearance Benny would accept was at Yale University on December 8. But before it, in mid-November, he taped an interview for Bob Sherman's WQXR (the New York Times station) "The Listening Room." Broadcast on Thanksgiving Day, November 28, the tape included selections from various Goodman jazz and classical albums, miscellaneous recordings, and good conversation. Then it was in to the Wellington Hotel, to rehearse for the Yale concert:

BENNY GOODMAN AND HIS ORCHESTRA   *December 2, 1985, New York*

Benny Goodman, clt; Randy Sandke, John Eckert, Paul Cohen, Joe Mosello, tpt; Bobby Pring, Eddie Bert, Dan Barrett, tbn; Chuck Wilson, Jack Stuckey, as; Ken Peplowski, Ted Nash, ts; Danny Bank, bar; Ben Aronov, p; James Chirillo, g; Jack Lesberg, b; Robbie Scott, d. Carrie Smith, voc.

My Honey's Lovin' Arms
(Gimme A Pigfoot-voc Carrie Smith, w/Sandke, rhythm section - NO BG
Ja-Da-voc Carrie Smith

(Nobody Knows You When You're Down And Out-voc Carrie Smith, w/Sandke, rhythm section - NO BG
Don't Be That Way
You Brought A New Kind Of Love To Me
(I Would Do) Anything For You

(Ted Nash is the nephew of the older Ted Nash who was prominent in the mid-Forties.)

BENNY GOODMAN AND HIS ORCHESTRA   *December 7, 1985, New York*

Personnel as December 2, except MURRAY WALL, b, replaces Lesberg midway through.

Let's Dance (theme)
Don't Be That Way
You Brought A New Kind Of Love To Me
(I Would Do) Anything For You
Ballad In Blue
If I Could Be With You
Down South Camp Meetin'
Sometimes I'm Happy
Wrappin' It Up
More Than You Know
King Porter Stomp
Between The Devil And The Deep Blue Sea
Memories Of You - QUARTET (BG, Aronov, Chirillo, Wall)

Louis Bellson flew in from Jacksonville, Florida, where he was on tour with his wife Pearl Bailey, to rejoin for the Yale engagement. He arrived at Woolsey Hall in time for an afternoon rehearsal, and this taped extract:

YALE CONCERT - REHEARSAL   *December 8, 1985, New Haven*

Personnel as December 7, except LOUIS BELLSON, d, replaces Scott.

SEPTET: BG, Sandke, Barrett, Peplowski, Aronov, Chirillo, Wall (no d)

Runnin' Wild - SEPTET
Stealin' Apples (intro only)
My Honey's Lovin' Arms

A tape of the first half of the Yale concert is in Benny's library. Missing from it are "Runnin' Wild" and "Poor Butterfly" by the Octet (rehearsal Septet plus Bellson), "Stealin' Apples," "Good-Bye" and possibly two or three other big band renditions not notated.

YALE CONCERT   *December 8, 1985, New Haven*

Personnel as December 8 rehearsal.

Let's Dance (theme)
Don't Be That Way
(I Would Do) Anything For You
King Porter Stomp
(Gimme A Pigfoot-voc Carrie Smith, w/Sandke, rhythm section - NO BG
Ja-Da-voc Carrie Smith
You Brought A New Kind Of Love To Me
Down South Camp Meetin'
(Stars Fell On Alabama - Barrett w/rhythm section - NO BG

The great majority of Fletcher's Victor-era arrangements were scored for three trumpets, two trombones, two alto's, two tenor's, piano, guitar, string bass and drums, plus, of course, Benny's clarinet. Parts were added— a fourth trumpet, a third trombone, baritone and/or bass sax, etc.—as the composition of Benny's bands changed in later years. But now Benny determined to play those scores as originally written to assure authenticity; from this point forward, his instrumentation reflects that decision.

Prior to his customary trip to St. Martin's for the year-end holidays, Benny rehearsed the band again in the Wellington Hotel, sometimes referred to as Studio 58:

BENNY GOODMAN AND HIS ORCHESTRA   December 13, 1985, New York

Benny Goodman, clt; Randy Sandke, John Eckert, Joe Mosello, tpt; Eddie Bert, Dan Barrett, tbn; Chuck Wilson, Jack Stuckey, as; Ken Peplowski, Ted Nash, ts; Ben Aronov, p; James Chirillo, g; Murray Wall, b; Kenny Washington, d.

Can't We Be Friends?
Am I Blue?
Between The Devil And The Deep Blue Sea
My Honey's Lovin' Arms
Ballad In Blue

Satisfied with his own playing as well as that of the sidemen, Benny agreed to a proposal from the Musical Heritage Society/Musicmasters to record the band in a studio, with intent to release selected cuts on both LP and CD. But first, of course, more rehearsals, in the Wellington:

BENNY GOODMAN AND HIS ORCHESTRA   January 7, 1986, New York

Orchestra as December 13, 1985, except LAURIE FRINK, tpt, replaces Mosello, and CY JOHNSON, p & arr, replaces Aronov.

DUET: Goodman, Chirillo
TRIO: Duet plus Wall

Mean To Me
Muskrat Ramble
Sunrise Serenade (n/c)
Rosetta
You Must Meet My Wife (arr Cy Johnson)
Smile - DUET
Memories Of You - DUET
You Must Meet My Wife - TRIO

BENNY GOODMAN AND HIS ORCHESTRA   January 14, 1986, New York

Orchestra as December 13, 1985, except MATT FINDERS, tbn, replaces Bert.

QUINTET: Goodman, Aronov, Chirillo, Wall, Washington

Muskrat Ramble
Mean To Me
Sunrise Serenade
Smile - QUINTET
Wrappin' It Up

Reminiscent of countless tours in the years gone by, it was "back on the bus" each of three days in mid-January for what would prove to be Benny's last studio recording sessions. The band assembled each morning at the Wellington Hotel for the trip to the State University of New York - SUNY - at Purchase, New York, whose facilities had been engaged by the Musical Heritage Society. When Benny was satisfied with what had been accomplished, the band returned to Manhattan each evening on board a Campus Coach.

In toto, 10 different selections were recorded over the long weekend, nine Henderson arrangements by the full orchestra, and Charlie Chaplin's "Smile" by Benny and various combinations of his rhythm section. At this writing (September 1986) the Society, which underwrote the venture, is auditing the tapes for future release; no matrices are yet assigned to the performances.

The listings below include complete renditions (designated as takes), plus aborted renditions (cited as breakdowns). They omit lengthy rehearsals between takes and breakdowns. All recordings are listed in order-of-performance.

BENNY GOODMAN AND HIS ORCHESTRA   January 17, 1986, Purchase, New York

Benny Goodman, clt; Randy Sandke, John Eckert, Joe Mosello, tpt; Dan Barrett, Matt Finders, tbn; Chuck Wilson, Jack Stuckey, as; Ken Peplowski, Ted Nash, ts; Ben Aronov, p; James Chirillo, g; Murray Wall, b; Louis Bellson, d.

- 0 -   UNISSUED - 3 takes, 2 breakdowns
               You Brought A New Kind Of Love To Me

- 0 -   UNISSUED - 4 takes, 1 breakdown
               Muskrat Ramble

- 0 -   UNISSUED - 1 take, 1 breakdown
               Sunrise Serenade

BENNY GOODMAN AND HIS ORCHESTRA   January 18, 1986, Purchase, New York

Personnel as January 17.

- 0 -   UNISSUED - 6 takes
               Blue Room

- 0 -   UNISSUED - 4 takes
               Mean To Me

- 0 -   UNISSUED - 3 takes
               Between The Devil And The Deep Blue Sea

BENNY GOODMAN SMALL GROUPS   same session

QUINTET: Goodman, Aronov, Chirillo, Wall, Bellson
QUARTET: Goodman, Aronov, Chirillo, Bellson
DUET: Goodman, Chirillo

- 0 -   UNISSUED - 1 take, 1 breakdown
               Smile - Quintet

- 0 -   UNISSUED - 1 take
               Smile - Quartet

- 0 -   UNISSUED - 1 take, 1 breakdown
               Smile - Duet

BENNY GOODMAN AND HIS ORCHESTRA   January 19, 1986, Purchase, New York

Personnel as January 17.

- 0 -   UNISSUED - 4 takes, 6 breakdowns
               Lulu's Back In Town

- 0 -   UNISSUED - 4 takes
               Star Dust

- 0 -   UNISSUED - 2 takes
               Wrappin' It Up

(NOTE: Trumpeter Dean Pratt sat in for Joe Mosello prior to Benny's participation; Mosello is on all takes listed above.)

Just four days later, Benny called for another rehearsal, the last one that will be in the Wellington. He'd dug out some additional Henderson arrangements, thinking to expand his concert repertoire. Too, he ran through a new composition written and arranged by Randy Sandke, and a new arrangement of "Runnin' Wild," also by Sandke:

BENNY GOODMAN AND HIS ORCHESTRA   January 23, 1986, New York

Benny Goodman, clt; Randy Sandke, LAURIE FRINK, TIM OUIMETTE, tpt; Dan Barrett, Matt Finders, tbn; Chuck Wilson, Jack Stuckey, as; Ken Peplowski, KEN HITCHCOCK, ts; Ben Aronov, p; RICHARD LIEBERSON, g; Murray Wall, b; KENNY WASHINGTON, d.

Oh, Lady Be Good!
Runnin' Wild (arr Randy Sandke)
When You're Away (arr Randy Sandke)
Oh, Lady Be Good!
Am I Blue?
Am I Blue? - jam version, full band
Keep Smiling At Trouble
Sometimes I'm Happy
Ballad In Blue
Chicago

Next, a rehearsal in the S I R Studios:

BENNY GOODMAN AND HIS ORCHESTRA   February 4, 1986, New York

Benny Goodman, clt; Randy Sandke, Laurie Frink, JOHN ECKERT, tpt; Dan Barrett, Matt Finders, tbn; Chuck Wilson, Jack Stuckey, as; PHIL BODNER, TED NASH, ts; Ben Aronov, p; JAMES CHIRILLO, g; JOHN BEAL, b; ERIC BOGART, d. Carrie Smith, voc.

(I Would Do) Anything For You
Mean To Me
Star Dust
(Gimme A Pigfoot-voc Carrie Smith - Sandke, rhythm section - NO BG

Ja-Da-voc Carrie Smith
Muskrat Ramble
Let's Dance
Coquette (arr FH)

Richard Harrington of the ''Washington Post'' interviewed Benny in New York in anticipation of Benny's upcoming concert in Kennedy Center; his article appeared on the 14th. Benny had scheduled a rehearsal for the 13th, but instead took the whole band to lunch. Then it was on to the Nation's capital and the first concert of 1986:

KENNEDY CENTER CONCERT   *February 15, 1986, Washington, D.C.*

Benny Goodman, clt; Randy Sandke, Laurie Frink, John Eckert, tpt; Dan Barrett, Matt Finders, tbn; Jack Stuckey, Chuck Wilson, as; KEN PEPLOWSKI, Ted Nash, ts; Ben Aronov, p; James Chirillo, g; MURRAY WALL, b; LOUIS BELLSON, d. Carrie Smith, voc.

DUET: Goodman, Chirillo
OCTET: Goodman, Sandke, Barrett, Nash, Aronov, Chirillo, Wall, Bellson

Let's Dance (theme)
Don't Be That Way
You Brought A New Kind Of Love To Me
Down South Camp Meetin'
Smile - DUET
(Stars Fell On Alabama - Barrett w/rhythm - NO BG
(I Would Do) Anything For You
Sunrise Serenade
King Porter Stomp
Poor Butterfly - OCTET
(Gimme A Pigfoot-voc Carrie Smith w/Sandke, rhythm - NO BG
Ja-Da-voc Carrie Smith
Blue Room
Star Dust
Stealin' Apples
Wrappin' It Up
Good-Bye (in its entirety)

(NOTE: Listing above is complete concert. One audience recording in Benny's library omits ''Stars Fell On Alabama'' and both Carrie Smith vocals, but includes brief bits and pieces of the afternoon rehearsal.)

NARAS, the National Academy of Recording Arts and Sciences, presented its Lifetime Achievement Award to Benny during CBS-TV's ''Grammy Awards'' telecast from the Shrine Auditorium in Los Angeles on February 25. Benny thanked the Academy, but did not perform. In absentia, the Academy also honored John Hammond with its President's Merit Award. Back in New York, Benny was interviewed by Doug Hall for the syndicated radio program, ''The Great Sounds,'' on February 28.

William B. Williams interviewed Benny in his office on March 4; portions were broadcast via WNEW-AM, New York, and via the Mutual Radio Network, as part of its ''Encore'' series. Benny flew to Los Angeles March 9, received its Presidential Award from the National Association of Recording Merchandisers the next day in Century City. The Cable News Network focused its cameras on Benny in his apartment March 14, later that day televised his comments about his upcoming concert in Radio City Music Hall with Frank Sinatra.

With the same sidemen who had performed in Kennedy Center (save that Kenny Washington substituted for Louis Bellson), Benny rehearsed in the Music Hall on March 15. No tape of that rehearsal has been located. A tape of the next afternoon's rehearsal is extant:

RADIO CITY MUSIC HALL - REHEARSAL   *March 16, 1986, New York*

Personnel as February 15 (including Bellson).

QUINTET: Goodman, Aronov, Chirillo, Wall, Bellson

You Brought A New Kind Of Love To Me
King Porter Stomp
(I Would Do) Anything For You
Sunrise Serenade
Down South Camp Meetin'
Stealin' Apples
. . . ad lib blues
Let's Dance (theme)
Don't Be That Way
Memories Of You - QUINTET (n/c)

Sinatra's staff recorded the entire performance that evening, but at this writing (September 1986) the tape of Benny's 40-minute participation has not been forthcoming. With the expectation that it will in future become available, it is detailed next, per an eyewitness account:

RADIO CITY MUSIC HALL CONCERT   *March 16, 1986, New York*

Personnels as March 16 rehearsal.

Let's Dance (theme)
Don't Be That Way
You Brought A New Kind Of Love To Me
(I Would Do) Anything For You
Memories Of You - QUINTET
Blue Room
King Porter Stomp
Stealin' Apples
Sometimes I'm Happy
Good-Bye

During the ensuing week Benny suffered with a heavy cold, dosed himself with proprietary medicines, ate little, slept fitfully. Feeling ''. . . just miserable, I can hardly breathe, let alone play,'' he considered momentarily cancelling his next concert, Saturday evening. But buoyed by the massive favorable publicity given the mid-March telecasts of his PBS ''Benny Goodman: Let's Dance, A Musical Tribute,'' he elected to keep the engagement. It proved an unwise decision.

The concert was for the University Musical Society of the University of Michigan, in Hill Auditorium, Ann Arbor. Following an introductory performance by James Dapogny's Chicago Jazz Band, Benny and his orchestra came on stage. An audience-recorded cassette reveals Benny and the band in good form through ''Stealin' Apples.'' Then there is silence, interrupted finally by a buzz from the full house. Benny can be heard to mutter, ''Good-Bye,'' and again, ''Good-Bye.'' He plays the first few bars of his closing theme, then John Eckert hurriedly picks up Benny's part. The audience seems startled.

At the conclusion of ''Stealin' Apples,'' Benny stood rigid, immobile, obviously in difficulty. Carrie Smith was the first to reach him, helped him offstage. Police and fire medics were called; Down Beat writer John McDonough's wife Diane, a nurse-practitioner, attended him. At first he seemed unaware of his surroundings, failed to recognize those assisting him. A half hour later he had apparently recovered. The medics were thanked and dismissed, Benny was accompanied to his hotel room, and the next morning he flew back to New York.

In retrospect, Benny's illness in Ann Arbor is considered to have resulted from his cold, not his coronary condition. The patent medicines, his lack of food and sleep, and possibly hyperventilation—the tape reveals his playing is frenetic, as if to compensate for his knowing he's not well, he'll rush through the concert—are likely the causative factors of this scary episode. It is a false signal, but nonetheless a dire harbinger of things to come.

UNIVERSITY OF MICHIGAN CONCERT   *March 22, 1986, Ann Arbor*

Orchestra personnel as March 16. Carrie Smith, voc.

Let's Dance (theme)
Don't Be That Way
(I Would Do) Anything For You
Down South Camp Meetin'
Blue Room
(Gimme A Pigfoot-voc Carrie Smith, w/Sandke, rhythm section - NO BG
(Ja-Da-voc Carrie Smith, w/sections of the band - NO BG
(You've Changed-voc Carrie Smith, w/rhythm section - NO BG
Big John Special
You Turned The Tables On Me
Blue Skies
Stealin' Apples
Good-Bye (theme)

Benny remarked to the author the following week that his malaise in Ann Arbor didn't worry him. But the fact that he brought the subject up— the author hadn't mentioned it—spoke silently of some concern. In any event, Benny said, he had an open schedule in April, looked forward to relaxing in St. Martin's, to which he flew on the 4th. Home and rested on April 14, he jammed in his apartment with pianist Mark Shane, bassist Bill Ellison and drummer Ed Ornowski on the 16th, ''just for kicks.'' Pulse Magazine interviewed him on April 23; its article—with revisions—was published in its July issue. That same day, composer Harold Arlen, who'd recorded with Benny for Red Nichols in the 'Thirties, died of cancer in New York.

Benny had celebrated his 70th birthday in friend John Fleming's 57th Street apartment, where he had entertained the guests by playing in its spacious ballroom. Now approaching his 77th year, he reassembled the band there for its next rehearsal. All his succeeding studio rehearsals will light up that room.

BENNY GOODMAN AND HIS ORCHESTRA   *May 2, 1986, New York*

Benny Goodman, clt; Randy Sandke, Laurie Frink, John Eckert, tpt; Dan Barrett, Matt Finders, tbn; Chuck Wilson, Jack Stuckey, as; Ken Peplowski, Mark Lopeman, ts; Ben Aronov, p; Chris Flory, g; Murray Wall, b; Chuck Riggs, d.

Lullaby In Rhythm
Big John Special
Star Dust
Dear Old Southland
Bach Goes To Town
If I Could Be With You
Lulu's Back In Town

BENNY GOODMAN AND HIS ORCHESTRA   *May 12, 1986, New York*

Personnel as May 2, except TED NASH, ts, replaces Lopeman, and KENNY WASHINGTON, d, replaces Riggs.

OCTET: Goodman, Eckert, Barrett, Nash, Aronov, Flory, Wall, Washington

Hunkadola
Bach Goes To Town
Hunkadola
I Hadn't Anyone Till You - OCTET
Oh, Lady Be Good! (head arrangement)

On May 14 Benny received an honorary degree from Columbia University; he was similarly honored by Brandeis University on the 18th, and Bard College on the 31st. The May 27 edition of the Wall Street Journal reported Benny's emphatic position on "ghost bands" (posthumous revivals of famous orchestras, such as the "Guy Lombardo Royal Canadians," fronted by Art Mooney): "I absolutely don't want it. Anything under my name should be me. I'm the product." Also on the 27th, he rehearsed in his apartment with a string quartet, in preparation for his scheduled August 18 concert in Avery Fisher Hall, as part of Lincoln Center's "Mostly Mozart" summer festival.

A rehearsal May 28 in the Fleming "57th Street Studio" was not recorded; in the afternoon, Benny attended services for John Hammond's wife Esmé, who had passed away earlier that week. On the 30th, his family helped Benny celebrate his 77th birthday in Stamford. Before we leave May, note that extensive renovations to the interior of venerable Carnegie Hall had begun, a project scheduled for completion in December 1986.

On June 2 the Chattanooga (Tennessee) Times interviewed Benny by 'phone, in anticipation of his slated June 20 Riverbend Jazz Festival concert in that city; the article was published June 12. The next day Benny presented the National Music Council's Fifth Annual Award to his good friend Morton Gould at the Palace Hotel, Manhattan. On the 5th, the final rehearsal in the Fleming apartment:

BENNY GOODMAN AND HIS ORCHESTRA   *June 5, 1986, New York*

Benny Goodman, clt; Randy Sandke, Laurie Frink, John Eckert, tpt; Dan Barrett, Matt Finders, tbn; Chuck Wilson, Jack Stuckey, as; Ken Peplowski, Ted Nash, ts; Don Coates, p; Murray Wall, b; Steve Little, d. (No guitar.) Carrie Smith, voc.

QUINTET: Goodman, Nash, Coates, Wall, Little

Rosetta (BG, brass only)
Star Dust (BG, brass only)
(Stormy Weather-voc Carrie Smith - band sans Benny - n/c
(It's Love I'm After-voc Carrie Smith - band sans Benny - n/c
After You've Gone-voc Carrie Smith
(Gimme A Pigfoot-voc Carrie Smith, w/Sandke, rhythm - NO BG
Ja-Da-voc Carrie Smith
You've Changed-voc Carrie Smith - QUINTET
St. Louis Blues-voc Carrie Smith
Don't Be That Way
You Turned The Tables On Me-voc Carrie Smith
Rosetta

Let's Dance (theme)
Don't Be That Way (n/c)
You Brought A New Kind Of Love To Me

BEN ARONOV, p, replaces Coates

(I Would Do) Anything For You
Down South Camp Meetin'
Blue Room
Clarinade (2 complete renditions)

(A written resume of this rehearsal includes "Star Dust," preceding "You Turned The Tables On Me"; it is not on the tape.)

Benny went to Wolf Trap, Vienna, Virginia on June 6, rehearsed the next afternoon there prior to that evening's concert:

WOLF TRAP CONCERT - REHEARSAL   *June 7, 1986, Vienna, Va.*

Orchestra as June 5 (including Aronov), plus CHRIS FLORY, g, and substituting ERIC BOGART, d, for Little. Carrie Smith, voc.

SEXTET: Goodman, Sandke, Aronov, Flory, Wall, Bogart

Let's Dance (theme)
Don't Be That Way
You Brought A New Kind Of Love To Me
Rosetta
(I Would Do) Anything For You
Rosetta
Gimme A Pigfoot-voc Carrie Smith - SEXTET
You've Changed-voc Carrie Smith (arr Dan Barrett)
Ja-Da-voc Carrie Smith (n/c)

And then, to a standing ovation and with couples dancing in the aisles,

WOLF TRAP - THE FINAL CONCERT   *June 7, 1986, Vienna, Va.*

Benny Goodman, clt; Randy Sandke, Laurie Frink, John Eckert, tpt; Dan Barrett, Matt Finders, tbn; Chuck Wilson, Jack Stuckey, as; Ken Peplowski, Ted Nash, ts; Ben Aronov, p; Chris Flory, g; Murray Wall, b; Eric Bogart, d. Carrie Smith, voc.

OCTET: Goodman, Sandke, Finders, Nash, Aronov, Flory, Wall, Bogart
ELEVEN: Octet plus Eckert, Barrett, Peplowski

Let's Dance (theme)
Don't Be That Way
You Brought A New Kind Of Love To Me
(I Would Do) Anything For You
(Gimme A Pigfoot-voc Carrie Smith, w/Sandke, rhythm - NO BG
(You've Changed-voc Carrie Smith, w/orchestra - NO BG
(Ja-Da-voc Carrie Smith, w/orchestra - NO BG
(St. Louis Blues-voc Carrie Smith, w/orchestra - NO BG

Intermission

Down South Camp Meetin'
Star Dust
Blue Room
Rosetta
Poor Butterfly - OCTET
Oh, Lady Be Good! - ELEVEN
You Turned The Tables On Me
King Porter Stomp
Sometimes I'm Happy
Stealin' Apples
Good-Bye (in its entirety)
"That's All"

The sidemen are unanimous that Benny was in good form at Wolf Trap; the author does not concur. His cold analysis of the concert tape, his mind disciplined to shut out the influence of events to come, tells him that the Benny Goodman who performed on June 7 was obviously fatigued and likely unwell. True, there are no striking examples (such as the incident at Ann Arbor) to illustrate his conviction; and true, some of Benny's soli are up to his contemporary standards. But half a lifetime's association with Benny, and critical audit of the recording, from "Let's Dance" to the last "Good-Bye," persuade him that something was dreadfully wrong.

These are the events of the second week in June 1986:

Sunday and Monday, June 8 and 9:

Benny returns directly to his 66th Street apartment from Wolf Trap. Saying that he feels "very tired," he is driven to his home in Stamford later on Sunday, remains there all of Monday, resting.

Tuesday, June 10:

Benny is driven by his attorney Bill Hyland to New Haven, Connecticut, there to discuss establishment of the Benny Goodman Archive at Yale University. (Late in 1985, Benny had decided that Yale would be the repository for his master tapes and other recordings, his arrangements, his memorabilia and other appurtenances of his career in music, upon his death. To that end he had donated 14 arrangements by Fletcher Henderson, 13 by Gordon Jenkins, and one each by Mary Lou Williams and Peter Knight, to the university's Music Library in December.)

Benny telephones the author Tuesday evening. He recounts in detail his meeting at Yale, says that implementation of the Benny Goodman Archive will be guided by provisions already incorporated into his last will and testament. He asks that the author cooperate with Yale "when I'm gone," questions him about the status of this manuscript and the author's intentions in regard to its publication.

Benny's speech is thick and hesitant, alarming the author. Just how is he? "Well, it's been a long day, a very long day, and I'm tired; and you know what riding in an automobile does to my back." Yes, but doesn't he think he's doing too much? "No, nothing's on until the weekend after next, I'm going to Chattanooga. You'll see, I've sent you a list of the jobs we've booked." Well, take it easy, won't you? "Look, don't worry, I'll be OK. Say 'so long' to Georgia, I'll be in touch. Come up when you can."

Wednesday, June 11:

Benny consents to a 10- or 15-minute interview, from the office via telephone, for Boston radio station WRKO's "Jerry Williams Show." Williams keeps Benny on the air for almost three-quarters of an hour, induces him to respond "live" to listeners' questions. Benny says he's never done that before, seems to enjoy it.

Author James T. Maher, his friend from the 'Fifties, 'phones Benny to chat about Lincoln Center's coming Mozart festival. In an aside, Benny admits he'd ". . . had a rough time at Wolf Trap, couldn't get his breath" for the latter part of the concert. Disturbed, Maher calls the author, who tells him about the episode at Ann Arbor. They agree Benny is doing much too much.

Thursday, June 12:

Benny is elated at news from Lincoln Center: His August 18 "Mostly Mozart" concert at Avery Fisher Hall, with the Mendelssohn String Quartet, is already sold out. He readily consents to appear there also on July 7, opening day of the Mozart series. He spends the morning shuffling through his filed arrangements, choosing additional charts for the band, including "I Can't Give You Anything But Love, Baby," "I Didn't Know What Time It Was," "Lullaby In Rhythm" and "Roll 'Em." At noon he goes to his apartment for lunch, returns to the office to continue the file search, considers buying the sidemen white band jackets for the summer bookings. (Benny's office is in the "E" wing of the Manhattan House, the Second Avenue side of 66th Street; his penthouse apartment is atop the "B" wing, off Third Avenue.)

In the evening Benny visits "Mr. Sam's," a new Manhattan night club, there to listen to vocalist Marlene VerPlanck. (Carrie Smith is unavailable for Benny's next concert, and he's seeking a replacement.) He's immediately recognized, responds graciously to friends and fans who stop by his table.

In Thursday morning's mail, the author receives Benny's itinerary:

June 20:   Riverbend Jazz Festival, Chattanooga, Tenn.
June 28:   Melody Tent, Hyannis, Mass.
July 7:   Avery Fisher Hall, Lincoln Center, N.Y. (classical)
July 10:   Riverbend Music Center, Cincinnati, Ohio
Aug. 2:   CIGNA Insurance Company, Bloomfield, Conn.
Aug. 18:   Avery Fisher Hall, Lincoln Center, N.Y. (classical)
Sept. 5:   Southshore Music Circus, Cohasset, Mass.
Oct. 11:   Princeton, New Jersey
Oct. 19:   Avery Fisher Hall, Lincoln Center, N.Y.
Nov. 8:   Pasadena Civic Auditorium, Pasadena, Calif.
Nov. 13:   Davies Hall, San Francisco, Calif.

April 24, 1987: Kennedy Center, Washington, D.C. (rescheduled from October 10, 1986)

The itinerary lists only those engagements for which commitments have been made; others are under consideration. The author feels the schedule is too demanding, given Benny's medical problems.

Friday the Thirteenth of June:

An early riser, Benny breakfasts in his pajamas, waits impatiently for delivery of the New York Times and its crossword puzzle. He reads, practices the Brahms Sonata, leaves it on his music stand. He dresses, goes to his office at 11:00 a.m., picking up his mail at the first floor reception desk on his way. He consults with Lloyd Rauch: John Fleming's apartment is unavailable for the next rehearsal, another site must be found. He returns to his apartment at noon for lunch prepared by his Finnish housekeeper, Anna Lekander.

After a leisurely meal, Benny retires to a small room at the east end of the apartment, there to nap on a daybed. Prior to leaving for her home, Mrs. Lekander "looks in" on Benny. He doesn't respond to her approach. A friend is called, the house physician is summoned, to no avail. At approximately 2:35 p.m., Benny has succumbed to "cardiac failure." There will be no autopsy.

The King Is Dead. But there is no line of succession, there is no one to replace him. Long Live His Music.

*

News of Benny's demise was withheld until his older daughter, Rachel Edelson, could be notified. A telephone call to her home in California disclosed that she was on a short trip in her automobile, and it was unthinkable that she should first learn of her father's death via its radio. His younger daughter, Benjie Lasseau; his brothers Freddy, Gene, Harry and Irving; his sisters Ethel and Ida Winsberg; his stepdaughters Gilly, Shirley and Sophia, and his other relatives, were all apprised quickly. His body was transported to a funeral home in Manhattan, and rumors of Benny's death reached the media soon thereafter. By four o'clock the reports were confirmed, and by five o'clock the sad news was on radio and television throughout the Nation and the world.

His family agreed that Benny's burial would be private; even such associates as Lionel Hampton, who lives nearby in New York, were asked not to attend. Benny's remains were interred in a plain wooden casket next to his wife Alice in the Long Ridge Union Cemetery in Stamford on Sunday June 15. His two daughters and three stepdaughters each read a short passage from the Bible at graveside. His attorney, Bill Hyland, delivered a brief eulogy, saying in part that although the distance between Chicago and Stamford is not far, that it represented ". . . a long and fascinating journey that took (Benny) to virtually every part of the world, and established him as a man . . . whom the grave will never silence." Amen.

His family also decided against a commemorative service such as those customarily held for musicians in St. Peter's Lutheran Church in Manhattan. Under early discussion was a musical tribute in Carnegie Hall in December, when renovations were to be completed, but that too was ruled out. Instead, his family, friends and close associates will gather November 8 in New York's Century Club, of which Benny was a member, to honor his memory. Scheduled speakers, among them Morton Gould, Herb Caen and the author, have been cautioned that there are to be no maudlin accolades, but rather upbeat recollections of their personal relationships. The evening is to be a party, something Benny always enjoyed.

An exchange of correspondence with the Smithsonian Institution is exploring the feasibility of establishing there a display that would include a clarinet (one of eight among Benny's effects on June 13); his music stand and the Brahms Sonata he was practicing that last day; his favorite chair; and a Vlaminck painting from his apartment. Space at the Smithsonian is at a premium, but apparently its directors are interested in the proposed exhibit.

Over a six-year period beginning in 1979, more than 200 of Benny's arrangements, including some of his biggest hits, were donated to the Lincoln Center division of the New York Public Library. They are available for examination and study. The bulk of Benny's musical memorabilia, however, is in the developing Benny Goodman Archive at Yale University. Now in process of collation and cataloging there are the remainder of his arrangements, possibly totaling more than a thousand; his tapes and other recordings; several thousand photographs; books and other documents, his files, plaques, citations and miscellany. It may take years to sort them all out.

The bequest to Yale University in itself practically guarantees the future availability of "new" Goodman recordings: Benny's will provides that, in order to fund the continuing operations of the Archive, Yale is to receive all royalties accruing from releases of previously-unissued performances transferred from Benny's tapes in its possession. The author is familiar with the contents of some of those tapes; their public release will be welcome.

Too, those companies for which Benny recorded under contract can be expected to release the recordings they own in the years ahead. Their initial intentions center on issues of compact discs, in main re-releases of earlier 78s and LPs, via this superior medium. Hopefully in future they will expand their horizons to include the alternate takes and other unissued tracks in their inventories.

Sight-and-sound Goodman performances, via videocassette and videodisc, are making their entry into the retail stream, and more likely lie ahead. One feature film, ''Stage Door Canteen,'' has been released commercially on videotape; it seems inevitable that others will follow. Benny's television appearances are also candidates for public sale; the October 1972 Timex ''All Star Festival'' is available via these media. As noted, the October 1985 PBS telecast is under active consideration for commercial release, no matter that thousands of home video recorders captured its March 1986 presentation. Additionally, a few Goodman devotees with access to the libraries of the television networks are known to possess videocassette copies of such memorable Goodman TV programs as the Texaco ''Swing Into Spring'' specials. In sum, video recordings likely will supplant film as the visual medium for the Goodman collector, tomorrow and beyond.

Of especial interest to the jazz collector are Goodman recordings neither at Yale nor in the vaults of the commercial audio, video and film producers. These are the transcriptions of his 1930s' and early 1940s' radio broadcasts, recorded professionally and in excellent condition. Some are in public institutions, some are held by sponsors, some are in private hands. One private stockpile, in particular, includes such intriguing performances as some from the Hotel Roosevelt, New York, in 1935, the disastrous engagement that saw Benny's band put on notice its opening night, because it ''played too loud.'' The author considers this treasure trove to be the major source of future releases of Goodman air checks from his most desirable years.

What we are unlikely to see in future are recordings purporting to be ''re-creations'' of the Benny Goodman Orchestra. Publicly, Benny made it clear that there should be no ''ghost'' bands appropriating his name. Privately, Benny instructed his attorney to deny permission to all and sundry who sought to perform in his name. To the extent possible, the executors of his estate intend that his wishes shall be carried out.

Benny Goodman has left behind him, already in the hands of his public, a vast number of recordings, as this volume testifies. There is every reason to believe that his heritage to us will expand even beyond its present dimensions, in the years ahead.

ADDENDA

Data in this section became available to the author after submission of his manuscript for the body of this work. The listings herein are chronological, enhance recording sessions in the text, add air checks, and offer other information of general interest.

Not detailed in the Addenda are such latterday authorized LP, CD and cassette releases as: Columbia's "Collectors Edition" (classical), and the 1938 Carnegie Hall concert; Reader's Digest's "King of Swing" boxed set (Victor sides); RcaBluebird's 16-LP boxed set 5704-1RB, "The Rca-Victor Years"; CBSAustralia's 2CP24 "Memorial" album; an array of CBS-, Rca- and Vogue-France LP singles and multiple-LP albums; Japan's "Doctor Jazz" K32Y-6130 CD and K26P-6447 LP (air checks), Eastworld CP35-5010 CD (Aurex), MCA 35XD-512/3 and 35XD-508 CD's, Rca RJL 2027-2042 16-LP boxed set, SONY 32DP-482 CD ("Lady Day"), et cetera; London's 1978 Carnegie Hall concert CD; and so on.

Some of the authorized releases have been digitally re-mastered, afford excellent reproduction, especially those available on CD's. None, however, contains performances not in the text. Overall, their liner notes are accurate. Ascriptions of the contents of these releases to listings in the text can be made readily by tune title.

Also omitted are unauthorized releases on such labels as Affinity, Ajax, Artistry, BBC, Blu-Disc, Magic, Radio Yesteryear, Tax, et al. All contain performances listed in the text. Care need be exercised in cross-referencing their contents; some liner notes are vague or erroneous.

*

Some expert Goodman collectors continue to believe Benny is present on Sam Lanin's "When Kentucky Bids The World Good Morning," Supertone 2576-A and Champion 16177-B, possibly recorded January 9, 1931. The author played a tape of this rare record for Mr. Goodman, who said its clarinet solo was not his. The author agrees with Benny's judgment, but suggests that the compleat collector should obtain a tape copy, just in case . . .

A 96-second recording of "Bugle Call Rag," transcribed from a 1931 radio broadcast sponsored by "Sonatone," contains a clarinet solo thought by some to be Goodman's. The author leans toward Jimmy Dorsey. Again, a tape copy seems a provident acquisition.

Ben Selvin Columbia matrices W 151850-3, "Little Mary Brown," and W 151892-2, "Potatoes Are Cheaper . . . ," were dubbed onto a "Skinner's Romancers" radio transcription, pressing matrix 305129-1.

Transcriptions of radio broadcasts sponsored by the Bulova Watch Company in spring and summer of 1931 feature the orchestra of, "General Time and his 15 Minute Men." Selections audited by the author include various instrumental soli, but none by Benny Goodman.

*

There is a credible report of extant acetates of a portion of a 1934 Goodman broadcast from Billy Rose's Music Hall, and of others that may provide now-unlisted performances from the "Let's Dance" series. Their owner is exploring various methods of transferring the fragile discs safely to tape.

*

Absent a catalog number, a 10″ Electro-Vox pressing, crediting "The California Collegians Orchestra under the direction of Lou Wood," has a clarinet solo on one side, "Philadelphia." Inscribed matrix for this side is 5136. The flip side, matrix 5126, is "Here's Love In Your Eyes."

Decision here, buttressed by the judgments of other Goodman specialists, is that the clarinet solo on "Philadelphia" is not Benny Goodman's. "Here's Love In Your Eyes" offers nothing to suggest Goodman's participation other than the tune itself, a tenuous link to Benny's 1936 film, "The Big Broadcast Of 1937."

*

V-Disc 731 B, "Bolero," may be from the CBS broadcast of October 13, 1939, and not from the earlier Columbia studio recording session of August 11, 1939. Factors suggesting this reassignment are: The V-Disc version of "Bolero" is on one side of a Columbia safety recording whose flip side contains the extant performances from the "Young Man With A Band" broadcast. A program log names "Bolero" as the final tune on the broadcast. Because safeties of the entire studio session have been unavailable, cross-matching of the V-Disc with all potential takes has not been possible.

Those factors are persuasive, but not conclusive. For example, some other Columbia safeties mix studio recordings and air checks. Nonetheless, the provenance of the V-Disc "Bolero" must now be considered an open question.

*

Startling information provided by letters of transmittal from the World Broadcasting System, Inc., in Hollywood to the Columbia Recording Corp. in New York, reveals that the dates assigned by Columbia to five Goodman recording sessions in 1940 are wrong. The letters accompanied express shipments of 16″ vertical-cut acetates of the sessions, which World had recorded for Columbia under contract. Unequivocally, the letters specify recording dates earlier than those assigned by Columbia, and so listed in the text. The correspondence also supplies additional details for four of the five recording sessions.

Listed below are the Columbia-assigned dates in quotations, followed by World's dates, all in 1940.

"April 10" should be April 3. No additional information.

"April 16" should be April 10. "I Can't Love You Any More," takes 6, 7 and 8 (possibly takes 1 through 5 were recorded April 3). "The Hour Of Parting," three takes. "Ev'ry Sunday Afternoon," two takes. "Crazy Rhythm," four takes. "I Surrender, Dear," five takes. "Boy Meets Goy," four takes.

"May 9" should be April 30. "Who Cares," five takes. "The Moon Won't Talk," three takes. "Just Like Taking Candy From A Baby," three takes. "Mister Meadowlark," two takes. "I Can't Love You Any More," one take.

"June 20" should be June 11. "Six Appeal," "These Foolish Things" and "Good Enough To Keep," three takes each. World's assigned matrices indicate "Good Enough To Keep" was the first tune recorded, not the last.

"July 3" should be June 25. "I Can't Resist You," three takes. "Dreaming Out Loud" and "Li'l Boy Love," four takes each. "Nostalgia," five takes.

For each recording, the letters specify the "preferred" take, as selected by ". . . the Columbia representative, Mr. John Hammond (and/or) Mr. Bill Richards." In most instances, their second choices are noted; in a few cases, their firm rejections of some takes are stated. Handwritten inscriptions on the letters, by Columbia personnel, indicate that the second choice of "The Moon Won't Talk" and "Nostalgia" was used for initial release.

The only other Goodman recording session on the West Coast in 1940 was that of "May 13," Bartok's "Contrasts." It seems likely that World also recorded that session, but no letter of transmittal covering it has been found.

The author has no explanation for Columbia's evident mis-dating, other than the obvious one that Columbia used those dates on which it assigned its matrices to its preferential releases.

*

On an undetermined date in spring 1941, Benny Goodman and his Sextet participated in the 40th program of the Municipal Broadcasting System's "Second American Music Festival" radio series. Drummer Vic Berton's son Ralph was MC, and he preserved Benny's contribution on acetate:

"AMERICA IN SWINGTIME"   Spring 1941, New York
  WNYC Radio

*Benny Goodman, clt; Cootie Williams, tpt; George Auld, ts; Johnny Guarnieri,
p; Charlie Christian, g; Art Bernstein, b; Dave Tough, d.*

The Blues
The Sheik Of Araby
Gone With "What" Wind
Stompin' At The Savoy - theme - to signoff

*

Trumpeter Conrad Gozzo and trombonist Earl LeFave both had left Benny by the end of November 1942 to join Artie Shaw's U.S. Navy band, then forming in San Francisco. The text erroneously extends their tenure. Jack Jenney supplanted LeFave in December, but Gozzo's immediate replacement is not known.

*

Content of the Columbia Reference Recording transcription of the CBS broadcast of October 16, 1943, from the Hotel New Yorker, is now circulating among collectors. In addition to the listing in the text, tapes of the broadcast include "Paducah" (following the mid-theme), which Benny both announces and sings. Broadcast is also on an unauthorized cassette, RADY 20336.

*

Eddie Sauter arranged "Dance With A Dolly" and "My Ideal" for the October 23, 1944 Chesterfield audition. Advice of an alternate transcription to that shown in the text is under investigation; purportedly, a full studio audience is present on this ET. If so, a second rehearsal took place, and was recorded.

*

Extending into 1945, "The Permanent Goodman," Phontastic's 3-LP boxed set 7659-61, samples Goodman recordings beginning in 1926, and air checks from 1935 and 1938. Special mention is made of this album, released in December 1986, because it includes first issues of rare test pressings and studio reference recordings available only from this source. The set erroneously includes a non-Goodman item, "Coffee In The Morning." Its liner notes also err in two instances: "That's A Plenty" was recorded June 13, 1928, and the correct matrix for "If I Had You" is CO 31609-2. Otherwise, the discography is accurate and detailed, permitting easy assignment to entries in the text or in this Addenda.

*

Newly-discovered Columbia safety recordings augment ten studio sessions in 1945 and two in 1946. For each of these dates, the listings below should be ADDED TO the entries in the text. As heretofore, the unissued complete renditions and aborted takes marked "Tape" are in the author's library. He has no copies of those not so notated, and believes them to be solely in Columbia's possession at this time.

BENNY GOODMAN SEXTET   February 4, 1945, New York

See text this date for personnel.

CO 34263   UNISSUED - 5 complete takes, 2 breakdowns - Tape
           Slipped Disc

CO 34264   UNISSUED - 1 complete take - Tape
           Oomph Fah Fah

CO 34265   UNISSUED - 1 complete take, 1 breakdown - Tape
           She's Funny That Way-voc Jane Harvey

(NOTE: It is unascertainable in what order-of-performance the takes above should be integrated into their counterparts in the text. A best guess is that they were recorded prior to those in the text; some of them seem to be rehearsals, and they evidence a progression toward an acceptable rendition and eventual release. This general statement applies equally to most of the 12 sessions.)

BENNY GOODMAN AND HIS ORCHESTRA   March 17, 1945, New York

See text this date for personnel.

CO 34474   UNISSUED - 6 complete takes, 1 breakdown
           Two Little Fishes And Five Loaves Of Bread-voc Jane Harvey

CO 34475   UNISSUED - 4 complete takes, 1 breakdown
           Clarinade

CO 34477   UNISSUED - 5 complete takes, 4 breakdowns
           Love Walked In

(NOTE: Unavailability of the above to the author prevents direct comparison with takes in his possession, and may result in some duplication. Also, one of the safeties from this session includes an unidentified tune.)

BENNY GOODMAN SEXTET   May 7, 1945, New York

See text this date for personnel.

CO 34673   UNISSUED - 3 complete takes, 3 breakdowns - Tape
           Just One Of Those Things

(NOTE: All of the takes above precede issued takes 1 and 2.)

A vague intimation that there may exist an additional take of Columbia matrix CO 34713, "Ain't Misbehavin'," from the May 16 studio session is unconfirmed.

BENNY GOODMAN AND HIS ORCHESTRA   June 18, 1945, New York

See text this date for personnel.

CO 35010   UNISSUED - 6 complete takes, 1 breakdown
           It's Only A Paper Moon-voc Dottie Reid

(NOTE: Again, the author's inability to make direct comparisons may result in overstatement above.)

BENNY GOODMAN AND HIS ORCHESTRA   August 29, 1945, New York

See text this date for personnel.

CO 35142   UNISSUED - 4 complete takes, 1 breakdown
           Baby, Won't You Please Come Home

BENNY GOODMAN SEXTET   same session

See text this date for personnel.

CO 35143   UNISSUED - 2 complete takes, 4 breakdowns
           Tiger Rag

CO 35144   UNISSUED - 3 complete takes, 2 breakdowns
           Shine

(NOTE: 1 breakdown intervenes between takes 2 and 1 of both "Tiger Rag" and "Shine." All complete takes and the other breakdowns were recorded prior to the issued takes for both tunes.)

BENNY GOODMAN AND HIS ORCHESTRA   September 12, 1945, New York

See text this date for personnel.

CO 35190   UNISSUED - 1 breakdown - Tape
           My Guy's Come Back-voc Liza Morrow

CO 35191   UNISSUED - 1 complete take, 2 breakdowns - Tape
           That's All That Matters To Me-voc Liza Morrow

BENNY GOODMAN AND HIS ORCHESTRA   September 19, 1945, New York

See text this date for personnel.

CO 35209   UNISSUED - 3 complete takes - Tape
           Fishin' For The Moon-voc Liza Morrow

CO 35210   UNISSUED - 3 complete takes, 2 breakdowns - Tape
           Give Me The Simple Life-voc Liza Morrow

BENNY GOODMAN AND HIS ORCHESTRA   September 24, 1945, New York

See text this date for personnel.

- 0 -   UNISSUED - 1 breakdown - Tape
           King Porter Stomp

CO 35237   UNISSUED - 3 complete takes, 1 breakdown - Tape
           Lucky

Via a highly unusual track on a Columbia safety, Jack Green interviews Benny on November 7; Benny comments on his recent Columbia releases,

Green mentions that Benny is appearing in Atlanta on November 10. It may be that Columbia intended to use the interview for promotional purposes, but the author knows of no other recording of their conversation.

BENNY GOODMAN AND HIS ORCHESTRA   November 20, 1945, New York

See text this date for personnel.

| CO 35210 | UNISSUED - 5 complete takes, 3 breakdowns - Tape |
| | **Give Me The Simple Life**-voc Liza Morrow |

BENNY GOODMAN AND HIS ORCHESTRA   December 19, 1945, New York .

See text this date for personnel.

| CO 35237 | UNISSUED - 3 complete takes - Tape |
| | **Lucky** |

| CO 35523 | UNISSUED - 2 complete takes, 1 breakdown - Tape |
| | **Rattle And Roll** |

BENNY GOODMAN AND HIS ORCHESTRA   May 14, 1946, New York

See text this date for personnel.

| CO 36288 | UNISSUED - 3 complete takes, 1 breakdown |
| | **Blue Skies**-voc Art Lund |

| CO 36289 | UNISSUED - 3 complete takes, 3 breakdowns |
| | **I Ain't Mad At Nobody**-voc Johnny White |

(NOTE: All takes above precede issued takes 1 for both tunes.)

BENNY GOODMAN AND HIS ORCHESTRA   August 7, 1946, New York

See text this date for personnel.

| CO 36736 | UNISSUED - 2 complete takes, 2 breakdowns |
| | **A Kiss In The Night**-voc Art Lund |

*

Speculation in the text that two tracks on SB LP 144 may be from a V-Disc studio session, rather than from a broadcast of July 1948, is now substantiated as fact: A 16″ acetate marked ''V-Disc Session'' has been discovered that includes one of the LP cuts, an alternate take of the other, and a hitherto undocumented recording of a third tune. Undated, the disc does not offer a positive link to the session(s) that produced V-Disc 880 A, ''Benny's Bop,'' and V-Disc 890 B, ''There's A Small Hotel.'' Its clarity, however, permits certain identification of the personnel.

The text entry headed, ''Possibly, 'The Benny Goodman Show, July 1948','' should be deleted, and the following SUBSTITUTED:

BENNY GOODMAN SEXTET   prob. July 1948, New York

See text, July 3, 1948, for personnel.

| - 0 - | **LP: SB 144** |
| | **I Can't Give You Anything But Love, Baby**-voc Jackie Searle |

| - 0 - | UNISSUED - Tape |
| | **Blue Views** |

- 0 -	**LP: SB 144**
- 0 - alt take	UNISSUED - Tape
	Bye Bye Blues

(''Just An Idea'' may also have been recorded at this, or a contemporary, session. If so, a transcription of it has eluded search.)

*

Claes Dahlgren of Radio Sweden interviewed Benny in his New York apartment on April 12, 1950. A tape of their conversation about Benny's imminent initial visit to Scandinavia is extant.

*

At least one reel at Yale has been identified as an additional ''Magnecord'' tape, from the Blue Note engagement of August 28, 1952. Its contents have not been documented in detail, but it is known to include performances not listed in the text. These are believed to have been recorded immediately prior to the incomplete ''Tea For Two.'' The author has strongly recom-

mended that selections from the Magnecord tapes be released to the public; many are excellent.

*

Portions of the ''mood'' music (not the ''jazz'' passages at the end of the film) from the winter 1953–54 documentary, ''The Lonely Night,'' are on LP, VAN 101-A. The LP is dedicated to, ''Original Scores by Melvin Powell.''

*

Still more out-takes from ''The Benny Goodman Story'' have been found among the tracks on two non-public LPs and seven acetates. The NET ADDITIONS to the recordings cited in the text are listed next, beginning with those on the LPs, which apparently were distributed for promotional purposes:

THE BENNY GOODMAN STORY   August 1955, Hollywood

Benny Goodman, clt, and a symphony orchestra, personnel unknown.

| DCLA 1106 | **LP:** U-I ''Benny Goodman Story'' - Side 1, Track 1 |
| | **Clarinet Concerto (Mozart Concerto for Clarinet and Orchestra in A, K.622) First Movement: Allegro** |

Benny Goodman and his Orchestra - see text for personnel.

| DCLA 1106 | **LP:** U-I ''Benny Goodman Story'' - Side 1, Track 2 |
| | **Stompin' At The Savoy** |

(This cut of ''Stompin' At The Savoy'' includes a second tenor sax solo, and a trombone solo, not in the commercial release.)

Benny Goodman, clt; Kid Ory, tbn; plus studio musicians.

| DCLA 1107 | **LP:** U-I ''Benny Goodman Story'' - Side 2, Track 3 |
| | **(Original) Dixieland One-Step** |

(The LPs also include the DJ version of ''Sing, Sing, Sing,'' and the orchestral version of ''Memories Of You,'' both listed in the text.)

The seven acetates, all recorded at 33-1/3 rpm, together contain 23 full renditions, plus two partial cuts that are the intro's of two of the complete tracks. The great majority of these tracks are identical to those on the commercial releases, or the LPs displayed above. Among the latter are ''Stompin' At The Savoy,'' ''(Original) Dixieland One-Step,'' ''Sing, Sing, Sing'' and the orchestral version of ''Memories Of You.'' Unique to the acetates are:

THE BENNY GOODMAN STORY   August 1955, Hollywood

Benny Goodman Quartet - see text for personnel.

| - 0 - | Universal-International Studio Reference Recording |
| | **No Name Blues** |

Benny Goodman and his Orchestra - see text for personnel.

| - 0 - | Universal-International Studio Reference Recording |
| | **''Main Title Music'' (Don't Be That Way)** |

(This cut of ''Don't Be That Way'' appears to be an extended introduction to the commercial release.)

*

Review of tapes of the Septet session of September 8, 1955 now at Yale reveals that at least one rendition of ''Soft Lights'' has no vocal chorus. (One tape is in poor condition; its contents are uncertain.) And the other three tunes might as well be instrumentals also, for vocals by Art Lund, Nancy Reed and Benny are off-mike and barely audible. Extant are (at least) one take each of ''Soft Lights'' and ''It's Bad For Me,'' three takes of ''Easy To Love'' plus two breakdowns, and three takes of ''Oh, By Jingo!''. Al Cohn wrote all four arrangements.

*

A sampling from several cans of 35mm sound film discloses that the Sextet session of December 6, 1955 was also recorded visually as well as via audio tape, possibly by Irving Jacoby, one of the producers of ''The Lonely Night.'' Full extent of this unique film chronicle of a studio recording date— there may be as much as two hours' worth—is unknown and under investigation.

*

Contrary to its liner notes, Blu-Disc T-1015's "King Porter Stomp" was recorded December 8, 1955, and its "Don't Be That Way" is the issued take, recorded December 12.

*

The "Unissued" portion ONLY of the text listing for the Park Recording session of May 17, 1956, should be REVISED as follows:

BENNY GOODMAN AND HIS ORCHESTRA   **May 17, 1956, New York**

See text this date for personnel.

     UNISSUED - Tape
- 0 -   **Delia's Gone**-voc Mitzi Cottle - false start
- 0 -   **Delia's Gone**-voc Mitzi Cottle, Benny Goodman, band

     UNISSUED - Tape
- 0 -   **The Earl**
- 0 -   **The Earl**
- 0 -   **The Earl**

     UNISSUED - Tape
- 0 -   **Fascinating Rhythm** - false start

     UNISSUED - Tape
- 0 -   **Stealin' Apples** - false start
- 0 -   **Stealin' Apples**
- 0 -   **Stealin' Apples** - false start
- 0 -   **Stealin' Apples**
- 0 -   **Stealin' Apples**

     UNISSUED
- 0 -   **More Than You Know**-voc Mitzi Cottle

(Although the issued take of "Fascinating Rhythm" is represented as in "stereo" on several releases, the source master tapes for this session appear to have been recorded monaurally.)

*

Not fully satisfied with the playbacks of the complete medleys recorded by his Trio on May 16, 1957, Benny also taped brief passages of several of the tunes separately. These remain apart on their own reel, were not spliced into the performances displayed in the text.

*

Partial audit of the tapes from the July 7, 1958 session in the Metropolitan Studios divulges that multiple takes of three of the four tunes are extant: "Nobody's Heart," four takes and one breakdown; "You Couldn't Be Cuter," eight takes and two breakdowns; and "Oh! Gee, Oh! Joy," five takes and one breakdown. The hunt goes on for one or more additional reels, necessarily to include "My Lover."

*

Eddie Bert's date book adds some information to a reel of tape at Yale that is labeled only, "8-5-58, ABC." Hitherto undisclosed, Benny conducted a big band rehearsal in Engineers' Hall, New York, on that date, and recorded it. Unfortunately, Bert did not list the personnel in his diary, and only a few of the sidemen are identifiable. It seems likely that this complement was similar to that of the July 14, 1958 studio session.

BENNY GOODMAN REHEARSAL   **August 5, 1958, New York**

Benny Goodman and his Orchestra; including Benny Goodman, clt; probably Taft Jordan, tpt; Eddie Bert, tbn; Buddy Tate, ts; probably Gene Allen, bar; Roland Hanna, p; plus unknown brass, reeds, rhythm.

     UNISSUED
- 0 -   **Too Marvelous For Words** - n/c

Benny Goodman Nonet: Goodman, Jordan, Bert, Tate, Allen, Hanna, g, b, d.

     UNISSUED
- 0 -   **Too Marvelous For Words**

Add: 2nd trombone to Nonet

     UNISSUED
- 0 -   **Ain't Misbehavin'**

Benny Goodman and his Orchestra

     UNISSUED
- 0 -   **Too Marvelous For Words** - n/c
- 0 -   **The One I Love Belongs To Somebody Else** - 2
        complete takes

(Following "Ain't Misbehavin'," Benny begins "Great Day," but the men seem unfamiliar with this tune and he soon segue's into "I Know That You Know." This is cut off abruptly during his clarinet solo.)

*

An alternate take of each of two recordings by the Benny Goodman Quintet, session of September 4, 1958, should be ADDED to the entry in the text:

BENNY GOODMAN QUINTET   **September 4, 1958, Hollywood**

See text this date for personnel.

     UNISSUED - Tape
- 0 -alt take   **You'd Be So Nice To Come Home To**

     UNISSUED - Tape
- 0 -alt take   **Stereo Stomp**

*

What's left of a master transcription of the 1959 Stockholm concert doubles the performances broadcast by Radio Sweden. The tapes are flawed: there is a certain omission following the Norvo Sextet, and a likely one after "Sing, Sing, Sing." Another rendition is truncated, but "Sing, Sing, Sing" is now complete, almost nine minutes' worth.

The new material reinforces the author's opinion that Benny never played better, consistently, after World War II than he did during this European tour. Each of the five concerts extant offers multiple choices of its highlight. Stockholm's might be, "When You're Smiling," wherein Benny seems to reach for an impossible note, ala Kirk Douglas in the 1950 Warner Brothers' production of Dorothy Baker's, "Young Man With A Horn." It eludes him; but he gets his second wind, explores a different approach to the unattainable, and almost casually knocks it off. As if to prove that was no fluke, he then races through a cascade of intimidating soli in, "After You've Gone." This is marvelous stuff.

The listing below incorporates, in correct sequence, the Swedish radio broadcast in the text.

STOCKHOLM CONCERT   *October 18, 1959, Konserthuset, Stockholm*

See text this date for personnels.

Let's Dance (theme)
Air Mail Special
Rachel's Dream - SEXTET
Memories Of You - SEXTET
Slipped Disc - SEXTET
Get Happy - SEPTET
(Everything I've Got Belongs To You - NORVO SEXTET
(Don't Get Around Much Anymore - NORVO SEXTET
(Tenbone - feat. Harris, Phillips - NO BG
Raising The Riff (n/c)
Honeysuckle Rose-voc Anita O'Day
. . . one chorus, "Happy Birthday"
Come Rain Or Come Shine-voc Anita O'Day
Medley: Ooh, Hot Dog-voc Anita O'Day
     Let Me Off Uptown-voc Anita O'Day, Jack Sheldon
You Turned The Tables On Me-voc Anita O'Day
Tea For Two-voc Anita O'Day

Intermission.

A Smo-o-o-oth One
Breakfast Feud
When You're Smiling - SEXTET
After You've Gone - SEXTET
Medley: Don't Be That Way
     Stompin' At The Savoy
     On The Sunny Side Of The Street
     Rose Room - contra melody, In A Mellotone
     Moon Glow
Sing, Sing, Sing
Four Brothers-voc Anita O'Day
I Want To Be Happy

Jammin' On The Breaks
Marching And Swinging
Good-Bye (theme)

(Despite an eyewitness's recollection, Zoot Sims does not join for "Four Brothers." Anita dedicates the tune to him, and Zoot acknowledges the compliment from the audience.)

*

Access to (at least the majority of) master tapes of the studio session of July 6, 1960, revises the text entry materially: Additional takes are extant, Columbia matrices are appended, and it is confirmed that no performances from this session are released on Columbia LP CL 1579 et al.

Except for personnel, SUBSTITUTE this listing for that in the text in toto:

BENNY GOODMAN AND HIS ORCHESTRA   **July 6, 1960, New York**

See text this date for personnel.

CO 54737   UNISSUED - 4 complete takes, 2 breakdowns - Tape
           I Want To Be Happy (arr AC or BS)

CO 54738   UNISSUED - 4 complete takes, 3 breakdowns - Tape
           I Can't Believe That You're In Love With Me-voc Maria
           Marshall (arr PM)

CO 54739   UNISSUED - 2 complete takes, 1 breakdown - Tape
           St. James Infirmary (arr BS)

CO 54740   UNISSUED - 3 complete takes, 2 breakdowns - Tape
           Too Many Tears (arr BS)

CO 54741   UNISSUED - 4 complete takes, 2 breakdowns - Tape
           Air Mail Special (arr BS)

CO 54742   UNISSUED - 3 complete takes, 2 breakdowns, - Tape
           My Baby Done Tol' Me-voc Jack Sheldon

CO 54743   UNISSUED - 2 complete takes, 1 breakdown - Tape
           Between The Devil And The Deep Blue Sea (arr RW)

(Preceding the first take of "My Baby Done Tol' Me," Benny says, "Let's play the blues." For that reason, "The Blues" is given as the title of this selection on Columbia's recording sheets.)

*

Benny occasionally added a grace note to his solo classical performances by playing a few jazz tunes with members of the symphony orchestra with which he was appearing. He did so following a concert in Tucson, Arizona, and the encore was taped. He introduces, "My friend Jimmy Glasgow, clarinetist in the orchestra, who'd like to play a little jazz," but the other instrumentalists are unidentified. Nor can the date be specified, but there is some indication that the engagement was in October 1960:

TUCSON CONCERT   *? October 1960, Tucson*

Benny Goodman, clt; unknown tbn, ts, p, b, d.

Blue Skies
Memories Of You
After You've Gone

Add Jimmy Glasgow, clt:

Moon Glow - BG in coda

Glasgow out.

Sweet Georgia Brown

*

These multiple takes from the "Hawaiian" sessions of January 1961 are now known to be extant:

January 12: "The Moon Of Manakoora," two takes; "On The Beach At Waikiki," three takes, two breakdowns.
January 16: "My Little Grass Shack," two takes; "Song Of The Islands," five takes, two breakdowns; "Sweet Leilani," five takes, three breakdowns. There is no audible tenor saxophone on the takes that have been heard.
January 24: "Too Many Tears," three takes; "Willow Weep For Me,"

three takes, two breakdowns; "Blue Hawaii," two takes; "Song Of The Islands" and "My Little Grass Shack," one take each only; "The Moon Of Manakoora," two takes; "Sweet Leilani," one take, one breakdown; "On The Beach At Waikiki," three takes.

*

Two days before the October 27, 1961 "Bell Telephone Hour" telecast, the Trio's rehearsal was taped. The intro of the first tune is excised on the author's copy of the medley:

"BELL TELEPHONE HOUR" REHEARSAL   *October 25, 1961, New York*

Benny Goodman, clt; Teddy Wilson, p; Gene Krupa, d.

Avalon (n/c)
Body And Soul
China Boy
Poor Butterfly
I Can't Give You Anything But Love, Baby
The Sheik Of Araby

*

In mid-April 1964, in preparation for his May 2 recital for the Lily Boulanger Memorial Fund benefit, Benny taped a rehearsal with pianist Guillaume Desavouret at his studio in Stamford. He also recorded a duet with engineer Bill Savory on piano, an extended version of "Yesterdays." The tape is now presumably at Yale.

*

Drummer Eric Bogart, who played the "Final Concert" with Benny, provides a tape of the Schaefer Music Festival, Central Park, 12 years earlier:

SCHAEFER MUSIC FESTIVAL   *June 12, 1974, New York*

Benny Goodman, clt; Chris Griffin, tpt; Urbie Green, tbn; Al Klink, ts; Peter Appleyard, vib; Hank Jones, p; Bucky Pizzarelli, g; Slam Stewart, b; Ronnie Bedford, d.

QUINTET: Goodman, Jones, Pizzarelli, Stewart, Bedford

I Know That You Know - QUINTET
You Must Meet My Wife - QUINTET
(Oh, Lady Be Good! - Stewart w/rhythm - NO BG
(Fascinating Rhythm - Appleyard w/rhythm - NO BG
(Star Dust - Green w/rhythm - NO BG
Slipped Disc (n/c - elision)
(I Can't Get Started - Griffin w/rhythm - NO BG
Entertainer Rag
(Love Song - Pizzarelli solo - NO BG
(Maple Leaf Rag - Jones solo- NO BG
Avalon
Memories Of You - QUINTET
(The Girl From Ipanema - Klink w/rhythm - NO BG
That's A Plenty
Medley: Don't Be That Way
*   Stompin' At The Savoy*
Sweet Georgia Brown
Good-Bye (theme)

*

An undated tape in Benny's library is assigned with some degree of confidence to mid-1977, because of audibly identifiable personnel. It may be a recording of his June 24 engagement for the Mead Corporation, but that assumption is now unprovable.

BENNY GOODMAN NONET   *c. mid-1977, unknown location*

Benny Goodman, clt; Mickey Gravine, tbn; George Young, as; Buddy Tate, ts; Cal Collins, g. Susan Mellikian, voc. (Others may be Warren Vache, tpt; John Bunch, p; Knobby Totah, b; Connie Kay, d.)

QUINTET: Goodman, rhythm section

Avalon - QUINTET
Here's That Rainy Day - QUINTET
(All Of Me - Tate w/rhythm - NO BG
That's A Plenty - full group sans Young
(Cherry - Collins w/rhythm - NO BG
Somebody Loves Me-voc Susan Mellikian - full group sans Young
The Lady Is A Tramp-voc Susan Mellikian - as preceding
Gee, Baby, Ain't I Good To You-voc Susan Mellikian - as preceding
Makin' Whoopee
Sing, Sing, Sing

*

The February 1981 film "Fantasma D'Amore" was retitled "Fantome D'Amour" for French language audiences, and was televised via the CBC-TV station in Vancouver, Canada, in 1985. To the best of the author's knowledge, it has not appeared in the United States.

*

Discovery of a good-quality cassette of Benny's recital at his Century Club on January 12, 1982, reveals that he entertained the membership with unaccompanied jazz soli following the classical performances:

BENNY GOODMAN AT THE CENTURY CLUB   *January 12, 1982, New York*

Benny Goodman, clt; Nathaniel (Nick) Rosen, cel; Todd Crow, p.

Trio in A Minor for Clarinet, Cello and Piano, Op. 114 (Brahms)
. . . excerpt: Habanera (Ravel)

Benny Goodman, clt soli:

The Man I Love
Oh, Lady Be Good!
I Got Rhythm

*

National Public Radio's master tapes of the June 25, 1982 Kool Jazz

Festival include the entire performance of the final selection, "Flying Home." The rendition on its broadcast tape was incomplete.

*

An audience recording of the concert of December 8, 1985, adds these performances to those on Benny's tape: Poor Butterfly - Octet; Runnin' Wild - Octet; Sometimes I'm Happy; Wrappin' It Up; Memories Of You - BG, rhythm section; Stealin' Apples; Good-Bye.
The cassette's audio quality is marginal.

*

Benny's unfailing dedication of each of his 1985–1986 concerts to Fletcher Henderson's arrangements was explained this way to Hal Davis, his longtime publicist and companion on overseas tours: "They were the best, and they've been neglected." And, "I always intended my music for dancing; that's why we played so many insipid (not Benny's word) pop tunes. Now, you take Eddie Sauter. He wrote some great things, but you couldn't possibly dance to them. Fletcher's, you could."

*

Teddy Wilson's death on July 31, 1986, was given sparse media coverage in the U.S., much less than it was accorded elsewhere. He deserved better; he had few peers as a jazz pianist for the more than half century of his active career.

*

Evaluation of the master tapes Benny bequeathed to his Archive at Yale University is ongoing, will take time to complete. As of early 1987, selections from a half-dozen studio sessions and live performances have been earmarked as worthy of eventual release.

*

Throughout this work, many references to Mr. Goodman are written in the present tense. Following his death on June 13, 1986, due consideration was given to recasting those references into the past tense. It was the author's decision not to do so. For him, the music lives, and so does his memory of the man who made it.

*

Additional contributions are acknowledged from Ed Burke, Fred Cohen, Harold Kaye, Lou Loewenstein, MusicMaster's Jeff Nissim, and Bob Ripps.

THE GOODMAN ARRANGERS

Some measure of Benny Goodman's success is rightfully attributable to the talent, and even genius, of the men and women who wrote the arrangements performed by his various orchestras and small groups. Those responsible for the great majority of Goodman's manuscripts are listed below.

Arranger credit, where known, is specified in the text. Generally, the arranger's name appears in the personnel listing for that performance that is his or her initial contribution to the Goodman repertoire. The credit follows the tune title, usually by means of a derivative code: e.g., Fletcher Henderson (FH). The code persists throughout the text.

A credit first noted in the listing of an authorized recording session is not repeated for succeeding performances. A credit first noted in an air check listing is repeated in the following proximate listing for an authorized record-ing session. Exceptions to this format may be made for an arrangement whose performances are separated by a span of years.

Not all of the arrangers named below are represented in the text; there are no known recordings, or extant performances, of their works. Their manuscripts, commissioned by Goodman, are now in the New York Public Library and/or the Goodman Archive at Yale University, if still existent.

Copyists who fleshed out the scores written by the arrangers are not named below. The more prominent of them are Charles Harrison Cooper, Leora Henderson (Fletcher's wife), and Kay Lois Parker.

A few arrangers, among them Bob Haring, Elliott Jacoby, Irving Mills, Jack Pettis and Fred Van Eps, Jr., are credited in the text for recordings in which Goodman participated as a sideman, not as a leader. Their names are omitted in the listing.

Abene, Mike	Guiffre, Tommy	Mancini, Henry	Sampson, Edgar
Albam, Mannie	Gutesha, Bobby	Manning, Irv	Sampson, Kenny
Aless, Tony	Hallenbeck, Ralph	Martin, Roy	Sandke, Randy
Alexander, Jeff	Harding, Buster	Martin, Skippy	Sauter, Eddie
Basie, Count	Harney, E. T.	Masso, George	Schutt, Arthur
Bassman, George	Haskell, Jimmy	Matz, Peter	Shavers, Charlie
Bee, David	Hefti, Neal	Maxwell, Jimmy	Shuller, Gunther
Beittel, Will	Henderson, Fletcher	May, Billy	Siravo, George
Belford, Joe	Henderson, Horace	McFarland, Greg	Skylar, Sonny
Bernardi, Noni	Henderson, Luther, Jr.	McGuffie, Bill	South, Harry
Brandt, Henry	Hensel, Wes	Miller, Glenn	Stegmeyer, Bill
Brennan, Ted	Hite, Les	Miller, William	Steinert, Alexander L.
Brooks, Dudley	Holman, Bill	Mundy, Jimmy	Still, William G.
Bunch, John	Hudson, Will	Murphy, Spud	Stott, Wally
Burke, Sonny	Hunter, Frank	Nelson, Oliver	Thompson, Johnny
Burns, Ralph	Huxley, C.	New, Paul	Thornhill, Claude
Bushkin, Joe	Jackson, James B.	Newman, Joe	Todd, Tommy
Camarata, Tutti	James, Harry	Newsom(e), Tommy	Tunick, Jonathan
Carisi, Johnny	Jenkins, Cliff	Noble, Jiggs	Van Lake, Turk
Carter, Benny	Jenkins, Gordon	Norman, Fred	Villepigue, Paul
Cavanaugh, Dave	Johnson, Budd	O'Farrell, Chico	White, Johnny
Childers, Buddy	Jones, Hoyt	Ogerman, Claus	Wilber, Bob
Clayton, Buck	Karlin, Fred	Pierce, Nat	Wilcox, Larry
Cohn, Al	Kincaide, Dean	Potts, Bill	Wilder, Alec
Conniff, Ray	Kirkpatrick, Don	Powell, Mel	Wilkins, Ernie
Dameron, Tadd	Knepper, Kenny	Previn, Andre	Wilkinson, Don
DiNovi, Gene	Knight, Peter	Prince, Bob	Wilkinson, Ralph
Edwards, Teddy	Lang, Philip D.	Rains, Grey	Williams, George
Evans, Gil	Larkins, Ellis	Ramin, Sid	Williams, Ken
Feller, Sid	Leemans, P.	Rawitz, Steve	Williams, Mary Lou
Fontaine, Bill	Levant, Oscar	Reidy, Frank	Wilson, Augustus
Foster, Frank	Levinsky, Walt	Ripaso, Joe	Wilson, George
Geller, Harry	Lieb, Dick	Riskin, Irving	Wilson, Gerald
Gibson, Margie	Lippman, Joe	Rose, David	Winterhalter, Hugo
Goodman, Thomas	Livingston, Fud	Ross, Bert	Woode, Henri
Gould, Morton	Lowe, Sammy	Roumanis, George	Wootten, Red
Grove, Dick	Maltby, Richard	Salim, A. K.	Zimmerman, Harry

THE GOODMAN FILMS

NOTE: Other possible Goodman film participations are discussed in the text.

U. S. GOVERNMENT & CHARITABLE ELECTRICAL TRANSCRIPTIONS: ORIGINAL RELEASES

NOTE: Cross-dubbed and other subsidiary U.S. Government electrical transcriptions are displayed in apposition to the original releases cited above, in the text.

STUDIO AND LOCATION RECORDING UNITS: ARTIST CREDIT ON AUTHORIZED RELEASES

NOTE: This index reflects artists' credits as they appear on the labels of authorized original releases of studio and location recording sessions in which Benny Goodman participated. Appropriate credit is extended to unissued performances from such studio and location recording sessions. The several complements of his recording units that may appear on composite releases — those that include various combinations of small groups and orchestras — are also listed.

With but few exceptions, Benny Goodman's various groups are not named on the labels of U.S. Government electrical transcriptions. Those exceptions are listed herein. For all others, see the Index of "Government & Charitable Electrical Transcriptions: Original Releases".

Components of Benny Goodman's orchestras and small groups displayed as "air checks" in the text — i.e., radio broadcasts, telecasts, concerts and motion pictures — for which there are no known authorized releases, may be found in the Personnel Listing preceding each such performance.

(See U.S. Government electrical transcription index for AFRS ETs crediting Mildred Bailey, Jack Benny, Nelson Eddy, James Melton, Vaughn Monroe and Frank Sinatra.)

INDEX OF PERFORMING ARTISTS

Lane, Lillian (voc), 184–186
Lane, Rosemary (voc), 70
Lang, Eddie (g), 3, 10, 13–15, 17–28, 30, 32–34, 36
Langford, Frances (voc), 69, 70, 185, 200, 201
Lanin, S. C. (Sam) (dir), 5
LaPerche, Sol (tpt), 141
LaPolla, Ralph (reeds), 169–172
Larsson, Rolf (p), 266
LaRue, Charles (tbn), 175
Lavalle, Paul (dir), 148
Lawman, Charles (voc), 24
Lawrence, Arnie (as), 287
Lawrence, Doug (ts), 308
Lawson, Yank (tpt), 141, 152, 153, 249
Lazan, Albert (v), 210, 219
Lea, Barbara (voc), 309, 310
LeDonne, Mike (p), 306
Lee, Peggy (voc), 124–142, 174, 188, 190, 202, 203, 228
Lee, Phil (g), 302
Lee, Sonny (tbn), 42
LeFave, Earl (Dick) (tbn), 139, 140, 163–165, 168, 319
Leggio, Carmen (ts), 277
Leibrook, Min (b-sax, b), 15, 18
Leightner, F. (p), 37
Leighton, Bernie (p), 114–116, 204, 205, 207, 244, 250, 252–254, 301
Lemmon, Brian (p), 302
Leo, George (instr unknown), 282, 283
LePinto, Frank (tpt), 159–162, 318
LeSage, Bill (vib), 248
Lesberg, Jack (b), 172, 173, 205, 228, 238, 253, 255, 311
Levant, Oscar (p), 141, 154
Levey, Stan (d), 237
Levinsky, Walt (as), 215, 220, 221, 256, 273, 320
Levy, Lou (p), 248, 249, 282, 283, 295–297, 303
Lewis, Bobby (tpt), 294
Lewis, Cappy (tpt), 237
Lewis, Meade Lux (p), 94, 98
Lewis, Mel (d), 239–242, 304, 305, 308
Lewis, S. (tbn), 32
Lewis, Ted (clt, as, voc), 20, 21, 24–26, 29, 33, 35, 36
Ley, Ward (b), 13, 14, 32–34, 37
Lieberman, Harold (tpt), 241
Lieberson, Richard (g), 312
Lillie, Bea (voc), 80, 82
Lindsey, Mort (p, dir), 254, 282, 299
Linn, Ray (tpt), 142, 143, 179, 190, 211–213, 319
Little, Steve (d), 314
Livingood, Bob (tpt), 308
Livingston, Fud (ts, as, clt, foot org), 1–3, 8
Lodice, Don (ts), 287
Lodwig, Ray (tpt), 2, 15, 18
Lofaro, Scotty (b), 228
Loft, Abraham (v), 236
Logan, Ella (voc), 45
Lombardi, Clyde (b), 157–163, 193–197, 318, 319
London (Lund), Art (voc), see under Art Lund
Long, Emily (voc), 198
Lopeman, Marck (as), 308, 309, 314
Lopez, Perry (g), 210
Los Angeles Symphony Orchestra (instr grp), 281
Lott, Sinclair (Fr-h), 190
Lovett, Martin (cel), 301
Lowe, Mundell (g), 193, 205, 291, 297, 299, 303
Lube, Dan (v), 176
Lucas, John (d), 20, 21, 24–26, 29, 33, 35, 36
Lund (London), Art (voc), 129–136, 164–176, 180, 213, 319
(The) Lynn Murray Chorus (voc grp), 105
Lyons, Jimmy (p), 206
Maag, Fritz (cel), 210, 211, 219
Maag, Peter (cel), 210, 211
McAfee, Johnny (bar), 137
McAfree, E'Lane (voc), 143
McConnell, Bob (tbn), 266, 267, 271, 272
McConville, Leo (tpt), 3, 9
McCrae, Margaret (voc), 64

McDonough, Dick (g, bjo), 8, 14, 17, 21, 23, 37–43
McEachern, Murray (tbn), 58–75, 77, 211–213, 226, 235, 319
McGarity, Lou (tbn, voc), 114–139, 168–173, 179–186, 189, 202–205, 207, 214, 220, 221, 233, 236, 237, 253, 256, 319
McGrath, Fulton (p), 26, 36, 38–42, 45
McGuffie, Bill (p), 257–262, 264–266
McGuire Sisters (voc grp), 220, 221
McKenna, Dave (p), 213
McKenzie, Red (comb, kazoo, voc), 19, 43
McKeon, Jeannie (voc), 180, 182, 183
McKinley, Barry (voc), 47
McKinley, Ray (d, voc), 43, 120, 144
McLarand, Paul (as), 190
McLe(a)vy, John (tpt, Fluegelhorn), 258–262, 272, 273, 275, 285
McManus, L. (instr unknown), 31
McMickle, Mickey (tpt), 151–153, 173–175, 205, 319
McPartland, Dick (g), 6
McPartland, Jimmy (cnt, tpt), 2–10
McPartland, Marian (p), 245
McQuary, Jim (tbn), 249
McQuator, Tommy (tpt), 257, 262
Magnante, Charles (acc), 20, 25, 32
Mains, Dick (tpt), 169–179, 319
Maio, Nick (instr unknown), 282, 283
Maiorca, Al (tpt), 215, 320
Majewski, Virginia (viola), 190, 202, 204, 205
Maliwheny, Les (viola), 248
Malneck, Matty (v), 3, 5, 9, 15
Mangano, Mickey (tpt), 150, 151, 175
Mann, Belle (voc), 4
Mann, Peggy (voc), 154
Manne, Shelly (d), 226–228
Manning, Irv (b), 215, 218, 320
Mannone, Wingy (tpt, voc), 10, 11, 19, 20
Margulis, Charlie (tpt), 34, 38, 42
Markham, John (d), 229–231, 233–236, 297–299, 320, 321
Markowitz, Irving (tpt), 244
Marowitz, Sam (ts), 207
Marsh, Audrey (voc), 40
Marshall, Joe (d), 233, 238, 252, 253
Marshall, John (tpt), 309
Marshall, Johnny (tbn), 257
Marshall, Maria (voc), 233–236, 239, 321
Marshall, Neil (d), 33, 37
Martel, Benny (g), 43
Martel, Johnny (tpt), 104–109
Martin, Louis (as), 30, 32–34
Martin, Skip(py) (as, bar), 119–128
Martinez, Louis (bo), 195, 196
Martinon, Jean (dir), 252, 255
Marvin, Johnny (voc), 3
Masso, George (tbn), 270–273, 281, 287, 289, 290
Mastin, Will (tap dancing), 219
Mastren, Al (tbn), 144–146, 150, 151, 157
Mastren, Carmen (g), 95
Matthew, Don (tbn), 157
Matthews, Dave (as), 83–95
Mauro, Ernie (as), 221–225
Maxwell, Jimmy (tpt), 103–112, 114–140, 202, 203, 207, 214, 215, 218, 239–242, 301, 320
Mayes, Samuel (cel), 215
Mayhew, Jack (as), 37
Mays, Rich (tbn), 294
Melchior, Lauritz (voc), 180
Mellikian, Susan (voc), 287–289, 322
Melton, James (voc), 11
Mensch, Homer (b), 244
Menuhin, Yehudi (v), 205
Menza, Don (instr unknown), 282, 283
Mercer, Johnny (voc), 94–100, 172, 181, 188, 190, 191
Merrill, Reggie (as), 152, 153
Mertz, Paul (p), 2
Messner, John (tbn), 289, 290
Mettome, Doug (tpt), 194–198
Meyers, Bumps (ts), 189, 190

INDEX OF TUNE TITLES

Guide to use:

To assist the collector,

Boldface type is employed to denote page numbers of **authorized releases** of tunes performed in recording studios, and to denote page numbers of unissued performances from those studio sessions.

Boldface type is also employed to denote page numbers of authorized releases of tunes transcribed during motion picture, radio, television and concert performances. Such authorized releases include producer, governmental and charitable electrical transcriptions.

Regular type face is employed to list page numbers of all other ''air check'' tunes in whose performances Benny Goodman is certain to have participated. Such performances may be available to the collector via releases not authorized by Mr. Goodman, or via acetate, audio- or video-tape.

(Note that recent examination of Mr. Goodman's contractual commitments reveals that he authorized the release of the Doctor Jazz album, W2X 40350 (1936–1938 air checks), and follow-on issues; and the Mark '56 Lp, 736 (1946 air checks). This information was obtained too late to cast these issues in the text as authorized releases. Prior to these releases, their contents were available via audio tape.)

Tunes in whose performances Benny Goodman did not participate during motion pictures and transcriptions of radio broadcasts, telecasts and concerts are displayed in the text but are not indexed herein. Generally, listings in the text for such tune titles are preceded by a parenthesis, and are followed by the notation, ''NO BG''. In some cases, other specific mention of Goodman's non-participation is noted in the text.

Because of multiple takes, cross-dubbing in certain AFRS releases, and the similarity of program content of proximate air check performances, a tune title may appear two or more times on a single page in the text. To limit redundancy, that tune title-page is indexed once. EXCEPTION: When a tune title appears on a single page as an authorized release, and separately as an air check, that page is numbered twice herein, both in boldface and in regular type face.

The theme songs, ''Let's Dance'' and ''Good-Bye,'' because of their frequency, are indexed in this fashion: When either appears in the text as an authorized release; when either is performed in its entirety; and when either is performed in a motion picture, as part of a medley, or during certain rehearsals, it is indexed herein. To highlight such performances, all other performances are not indexed, but are displayed in the text.

Beginning in the middle 1960s, Benny Goodman regularly combined ''Don't Be That Way'' and ''Stompin' At The Savoy'' as a two-tune medley. To distinguish such performances from individual renditions of these tunes, the medley is indexed separately.

*